Popular Writing in America

POPULAR WRITING IN AMERICA

THE INTERACTION OF STYLE AND AUDIENCE

THIRD EDITION

Donald McQuade
Queens College
of the City of New York

Robert Atwan

New York Oxford
OXFORD UNIVERSITY PRESS
1985

OXFORD UNIVERSITY PRESS
Oxford London New York Toronto
Delhi Bombay Calcutta Madras Karachi
Kuala Lumpur Singapore Hong Kong Tokyo
Nairobi Dar es Salaam Cape Town
Melbourne Auckland

and associated companies in
Beirut Berlin Ibadan Mexico City Nicosia

Published by Oxford University Press, 200 Madison Avenue, New York, New York 10016

Library of Congress Cataloging in Publication Data
Main entry under title:

Popular writing in America.

1. American literature. 2. Popular literature—United States. I. McQuade, Donald. II. Atwan, Robert.
PS507.P646 1985 810'.8 84-29443
ISBN 0-19-503589-5 (pbk.)

Printing (last digit): 9 8 7 6 5 4 3 2 1

Printed in the United States of America

Allen Ginsberg: Copyright © 1956, 1959 by Allen Ginsberg. Reprinted by permission of City Lights Books.

John Goldman: "Beatle John Lennon Slain..." by John Goldman. Copyright © 1980, Los Angeles Times. Reprinted by permission.

Ellen Goodman: Copyright © 1977, The Boston Globe Newspaper Company/Washington Post Writers Group. Reprinted with permission.

Vivian Gomick: *The Village Voice*, November 27, 1969. Copyright © 1969 by The Village Voice, Inc. Reprinted by permission of The Village Voice.

Bob Greene: Reprinted by permission of the Sterling Lord Agency, Inc. Originally appeared in *Esquire* magazine, August, 1982. Copyright © 1982 by John Deadline Enterprises.

Alex Haley: Extracts from *Roots* by Alex Haley. Copyright © 1976 by Alex Haley. Reprinted by permission of Doubleday & Company, Inc.

Barry Hannah: Copyright by Southern Living, Inc., October 1982. Reprinted with permission.

Sally Helgeson: Reprinted with permission of *TWA Ambassador*. Originally appeared July 1980 in *TWA Ambassador*. Copyright © 1980 by Sally Helgeson.

Ernest Hemingway: "Soldier's Home" from *In Our Time* by Ernest Hemingway. Copyright 1925, 1930 by Charles Scribner's Sons; copyright renewed 1953, 1958 by Ernest Hemingway. Reprinted by permission of the Executors of the Ernest Hemingway Estate and Charles Scribner's Sons.

Nat Hentoff: Copyright © 1983, The Progressive, Inc. Reprinted by permission from *The Progressive*, 409 East Main Street, Madison, Wisconsin 53703.

Hill Street Blues: Script of "Grace under Pressure" segment of *Hill Street Blues* is used by permission of MTM Enterprises, Inc.

Manuella Hoelterhoff: Reprinted by permission of The Wall Street Journal, © by Dow Jones & Company, Inc., 1982. All rights reserved.

Peter Homans: "The Western; The Legend and the Cardboard Hero," *Look* magazine, March 13, 1962. Reprinted by permission.

Susan Jacoby: "Too Many Women Are Misconstruing Feminism's Nature," originally appeared in *The New York Times*, April 14, 1983. Copyright © 1983 by Susan Jacoby. Reprinted by permission of the author.

Robinson Jeffers. Copyright 1954 by Robinson Jeffers. Reprinted from SELECTED POEMS, by Robinson Jeffers, by permission of Random House, Inc.

The Jeffersons: "The Black Out" segment of *The Jeffersons*, written by Richard Eckhaus, is reprinted by permission of Embassy TV.

Martin Luther King, Jr.: Reprinted by permission of Joan Daves. Copyright © 1963 by Martin Luther King, Jr.

Stephen King: "Now You Take 'Bambi' and 'Snow White'—*That's* Scary," reprinted with permission from TV GUIDE® Magazine. Copyright © 1981 by Triangle Publications, Inc., Radnor, Pennsylvania. "Trucks," from *Night Shift: Excursions into Horror*. Copyright © 1973. 1978 by Stephen King. Reprinted by permission of Doubleday & Company.

Jack Lait: International News Service, July 23, 1934. Copyright © 1934. by King Features Syndicate. Reprinted by permission of King Features Syndicate.

Louis L'Amour: From *Bowdrie*. Copyright © 1983 by Louis L'Amour. Reprinted by permission of Bantam Books Inc.

Ann Landers: "Love or Infatuation," copyright © 1983 by Ann Landers. Reprinted by permission.

Fran Lebowitz: From *Social Studies*, by Fran Lebowitz. Copyright © 1981 by Fran Lebowitz. Reprinted by permission of Random House, Inc.

Robert Jay Lifton: Copyright © 1981 by Robert Jay Lifton. First published in The Dial, national magazine for public broadcasting. Reprinted by permission.

John McPhee: Excerpts from *Coming into the Country*, by John McPhee. Copyright © 1976, 1977, by John McPhee. This material first appeared in *The New Yorker*. Reprinted by permission of Farrar, Straus & Giroux, Inc.

George Mahawinney: The *Philadelphia Inquirer*, November 1, 1938. Reprinted by permission of the publisher.

Norman Mailer: *Of a Fire on the Moon*. Copyright © 1969, 1970 by Norman Mailer. Reprinted by permission of Little, Brown and Company.

H.L. Mencken: Copyright 1927 by Alfred A. Knopf, Inc. and renewed 1955 by H.L. Mencken. Reprinted from *A Mencken Chrestomathy*, edited and annotated by H.L. Mencken, by permission of the publisher.

Grace Metalious: *Peyton Place*. Copyright © 1965 by Grace Metalious. Reprinted by permission of Simon & Schuster, Inc.

Eugene H. Methvin: Reprinted with permission from the January 1983 Reader's Digest. Copyright © 1982 by The Reader's Digest Assn., Inc.

James A. Michener: From *Space*, by James A. Michener. Copyright © 1982 by James A. Michener. Reprinted by permission of Random House, Inc.

N. Scott Momaday: *National Geographic*, June 1976. Copyright 1976 by the National Geographic Society. Reprinted by the permission of the author.

William Least Heat Moon: From *Blue Highways: A Journey into America* by William Least Heat Moon. Copyright © 1982 by William Least Heat Moon. Reprinted by permission of Little, Brown and Company in association with the Atlantic Monthly Press.

Marianne Moore: "Correspondence with the Ford Motor Company" from *A Marianne Moore Reader:* originally appeared in *The New Yorker*. Copyright © 1957 by The New Yorker Magazine, Inc. Reprinted by permission of the Ford Motor Company.

Toni Morrison: "Cinerella's Stepsisters," *MS.* magazine, September 1979. Copyright © 1979 by Toni Morrison. Reprinted by permission.

Ogden Nash: From *Verses from 1929 On* by Ogden Nash, by permission of Little, Brown and Co. Copyright 1935 by Ogden Nash.

National Enquirer: "Type of Vehicle You Drive Reveals Your Personality," May 24, 1983; "Puzzles You Enjoy Most Reveal Your Personality," May 31, 1983. Reprinted by permission of the publisher.

Newsweek: Copyright © 1982 by Newsweek, Inc. All rights reserved. Reprinted by permission.

The New York Times: "One Small Life" by Joseph Farkas, September 29, 1972; © 1972 by The New York Times Company; "And What Would Henry Thoreau..." September 1974; Letters to the Editor, © 1972 by The New York Times Company. "Atomic Bombing of Nagasaki Told by Flight Member" by William L. Laurence, Septempber 9, 1945; © 1945 by The New York Times Company; "Kennedy is Killed by Sniper as He Rides in Car in Dallas" by Tom Wicker, November 23, 1963; © 1963 by The New York Times Company; "The Assassination" by Tom Wicker, December 1963 (*Times Talk*). All articles reprinted by permission.

Flannery O'Connor: *A Good Man Is Hard to Find and Other Stories*. Copyright 1953 by Flannery O'Connor. Reprinted by permission of Harcourt Brace Jovanovich, Inc.

David Ogilvy: *Confessions of an Advertising Man*. Copyright © 1963 by David Ogilvy Trustee. Reprinted by permission of Atheneum Publishers.

Tillie Olsen: "I Stand Here Ironing" excerpted from the book *Tell Me a Riddle* by Tillie Olsen. Copyright © 1956 by Tillie Olsen. Reprinted by permission of Delacorte Press/Seymour Lawrence.

Dick Orkin and Bert Berdis: "Puffy Sleeves"—a TIME magazine commercial; reprinted by permission of DICK & BERT, a division of the DOCSI Corporation.

Thomas O'Toole: The *Washington Post,* July 21, 1969. Reprinted by permission of the publisher.

Vance Packard: *The Hidden Persuaders.* Copyright © 1957 by Vance Packard. Reprinted by permission of David McKay Company.

Darryl Pinckney: Copyright © 1983 by the Condé Nast Publications Inc. Reprinted by permission of the author.

Sylvia Plath: "America, America" from *Johnny Panic and the Bible of Dreams* by Sylvia Plath. Copyright © 1979 by Ted Hughes. Reprinted by permission of Harper & Row, Publishers, Inc.

Elizabeth L. Post: "Preface" to *The New Emily Post's Etiquette* by Elizabeth L. Post. (Funk & Wagnalls). Copyright © 1975 by the Emily Post Institute, Inc. Reprinted by permission of Harper & Row, Publishers, Inc.

Mario Puzo: *The Godfather.* Copyright © 1969 by Mario Puzo. Reprinted by permission of G. P. Putnam's Sons.

"Ring around the Collar": Reprinted by permission of Lever Brothers Co.

Andrew A. Rooney: "Advertising" and "Good News," from *A Few Minutes with Andy Rooney.* Copyright © 1981 by Essay Productions, Inc. Reprinted with permission of Atheneum Publishers.

Mike Royko: "How to Kick a Machine" by Mike Royko from *The Chicago Daily News,* November 15, 1971. Reprinted with permission from Field Enterprises, Inc.

Jonathan Schell: From *The Fate of the Earth,* by Jonathan Schell. Copyright © 1982 by Jonathan Schell. Reprinted by permission of Alfred A. Knopf, Inc. Originally appeared in *The New Yorker.*

Marshall Schuon: Copyright © 1983 by The New York Times Company. Reprinted by permission.

Mickey Spillane: *I, the Jury.* Copyright 1947 by E. P. Dutton & Co.: renewed © 1975 by Mickey Spillane. Reprinted by permission of the publisher. E. P. Dutton & Co., Inc.

Benjamin Spock: From *Baby and Child Care.* Copyright © 1945, 1946, 1957, 1968, 1976 by Benjamin Spock, M.D. Reprinted by permission of Pocket Books, a division of Simon & Schuster, Inc.

Gay Talese: *Esquire,* December 1964. Reprinted by permission of the author.

Studs Terkel: From AMERICAN DREAMS: LOST AND FOUND, by Studs Terkel. Copyright © 1980 by Studs Terkel. Reprinted by permission of Pantheon Books, a division of Random House, Inc.

Lewis Thomas: From *Lives of a Cell* by Lewis Thomas. Copyright © 1972 by the Massachusetts Medical Society. Originally published in the New England Journal of Medicine. Reprinted by permission of Viking Penguin Inc.

James Thurber: Copyright © 1942 by James Thurber. Copyright © 1970 by Helen W. Thurber and Rosemary T. Sauers. From *My World—and Welcome to It,* published by Harcourt Brace Jovanovich.

Time: "Death of a Maverick Mafioso," April 1972. Copyright Time Inc. Reprinted by permission of *Time,* The Weekly Newsmagazine.

John Updike: Copyright © 1962 by John Updike. Reprinted from *Pigeon Feathers and Other Stories,* by John Updike, by permission of Alfred A. Knopf, Inc.

Gore Vidal: "Tarzan Revisited," *Esquire,* December 1963. Copyright © 1963 by Gore Vidal. Reprinted by permission.

Judith Viorst: Copyright © 1977 by Judith Viorst. Originally appeared in *Redbook.*

Kurt Vonnegut, Jr.: "Epicac" excerpted from the book *Welcome to the Monkey House* by Kurt Vonnegut Jr. Copyright © 1950 by Kurt Vonnegut Jr. Originally published in *Collier's.* Reprinted by permission of Delacorte Press/Seymour Lawrence.

David Wagoner: From *New and Selected Poems* by David Wagoner. Reprinted by permission of Indiana University Press.

Eudora Welty: Copyright © 1975 by Eudora Welty. Reprinted from *The Eye of the Story: Selected Essays and Reviews,* by Eudora Welty, by permission of Random House, Inc.

E.B. White: "The Ring of Time" from *Essays of E.B. White.* Originally appeared in *The New Yorker.* Copyright © 1956 by E.B. White. Reprinted by permission of Harper & Row, Publishers, Inc.

William Carlos Williams: "The Use of Force" from William Carlos Williams, *The Farmer's Daughters.* Copyright 1938 by William Carlos Williams. Reprinted by permission of New Directions.

Ellen Willis: *Ramparts,* June 1970. Copyright 1970 by Noah's Ark Inc. (for *Ramparts* Magazine). Reprinted by permission of the editors.

Tom Wolfe: Excerpt from *The Right Stuff,* by Tom Wolfe. Copyright © 1979 by Tom Wolfe. Reprinted by permission of Farrar, Straus & Giroux, Inc.

Richard Wright: *Black Boy.* Copyright 1937, 1944, 1945 by Richard Wright. Reprinted by permission of Harper & Row, Publishers, Inc.

For Our Parents

PREFACE

For the third edition of *Popular Writing in America,* we have retained the organization and principles of earlier editions and have made a number of changes that we trust will once again enhance the book's overall flexibility and usefulness. We have revised—and expanded—the table of contents considerably. We have included a wealth of new material for reading, writing, and class discussion in each of the original five sections—Advertising, Press, Magazines, Best Sellers, and Classics. We have also added a new section, "Scripts." Reprinted here are the entire script for the television rendition of Ernest Hemingway's " Soldier's Home," as well as a full-length script from each of the celebrated and controversial television series *Hill Street Blues* and *The Jeffersons,* along with television commercials and such classic radio scripts as Abbott and Costello's "Who's on First" and Orson Wells' *The War of the Worlds.*

We have chosen new reading material—as we did in the previous editions—that represents a variety of cultural, professional, and commercial interests. Yet we have also aimed to reprint selections whose length would be manageable for individual class sessions and assignments. Our choices were also guided by the principle of interconnectedness that we believe is one of the most important features of the book: virtually every selection in *Popular Writing in America* is connected either stylistically or thematically with one or more of the other selections. A chart mapping these interconnections is conveniently placed after the tables of contents to encourage students to discover the different ways the same subject (the image of women in popular media and the threat of nuclear war,for example) can be treated in various forms of writing to emphasize different writer-reader relationships. In a similar vein, we have reprinted the work of some authors (Stephen King, Ernest Hemingway, and Stephen Crane, for example) in more than one selection to highlight the stylistic changes made by writers to meet different audience expectations.

In choosing new reading materials, we sought to locate effective representations of each form of popular writing, moving from writing intended for vast numbers of people (Advertising, Press) to writing of more specialized appeal (Magazines, Best Sellers), and to writing usually regarded as addressed to fewer readers (Classics). However, scripts, perhaps currently the most popular writing in America, are meant to be *heard,* not read. Yet, when we watch a situation comedy on television, or go to a movie, or tune in to a radio news program, we easily forget that the language we are listening to was originally written. Even with today's electronic media, the written word still precedes the performance: the most visually impressive movie probably started out as an idea in a scriptwriter's head. And much of what we hear on radio and television came out of a typewriter before it went over the air. Reading a script, then, is like going behind the scenes; we see what was not intended to be seen. As the audience of an advertisement, a news item, essay, or story, we are doing exactly what the writer intended—reading it. Scripts, however, require that we put ourselves in the role of two different audiences: the individual reader of the actual script and the larger, intended audience of the imagined performance.

We want to remind readers that our selections are not meant to serve only as models for student compositions. The selections are intended in part to generate lively and productive discussions about writing and to help students become more analytically familiar with the diversity of styles and strategies that develop within a contemporary system of communications increasingly dependent upon corporate enterprise, mass audiences, interlocking media industries, and vast outlays of money. Few acts of writing—and surely student compositions are no exception—exist completely outside of competitive, socio-economic considerations. We assume that the more conscious students are of the public and commercial pressures behind a piece of writing (pressures that can be felt *in* the writing, whether an advertisement, news item, magazine article, best seller, or script), the more sensitive they will become to whatever particular commercial or institutional styles or "voices" they may inadvertently be endorsing in their own writing. In order to make this particular interaction of style and audience dramatically visible to students, we have added a considerable number of selections dealing with the ways in which mass-media artists and artifacts determine the shape of our consumer culture.

An awareness of how one sounds is crucial for all effective writing. "Whom or what does the writer sound like here?" and "What sort of reader does the writer imagine here?" are questions worth asking of any kind of writing, be it the work of a professional or a student, be it inspired or required. Many contemporary writers (see for example the selections from Norman Mailer, Joan Didion, and Tom Wolfe) depend upon an audience critically alert to the ways in which their sentences assimilate, parody, and challenge the highly competitive languages of the mass communication industries. The work of such writers reminds us that practical matters of style and audience remain vital topics in any writing curriculum.

In general, most of the changes we have made for this new edition—the inclusion of more recent advertisements and articles about advertising; more newspaper columns and feature articles; a greater range of recent magazine articles; more attention to genre in the Best Sellers section, and especially in nonfiction; and more accessible modern classics—represent our considered responses to the many instructors throughout the country who have used *Popular Writing in America* and have generously suggested specific ways they thought the book could be improved. We hope that our decisions have resulted in a stronger, more practical book—one that will be welcomed by those who have worked with the book before as well as by those who will try it for the first time.

Acknowledgments

The continued success of *Popular Writing in America,* like any book in its third edition, depends on the generous advice of the colleagues across the country who work with it in class each year. We are grateful for the many helpful suggestions instructors have sent to us over the past decade. We have included as many of their recommendations as possible. In particular, we would like to thank: Charles Bazerman, Richard Bonomo, Gail Bounds, Addison Bross, Douglas Butturff, John Clifford, Edward P.J. Corbett, Mary Corboy, Frank D'Angelo, Kenneth O. Danz, Wheeler Dixon, Kent Ekberg, Lyman Fink, Jr., Christine Freeman, David Gaines, Kate Hirsh, R.S. Hootman, Lee A. Jacobus, Ed Joyce, D.G. Kehl, Helene Keyssar, Kay Kier, Henry Knepler, Roberta Kramer, Andrea Lundsford, William Lutz, William Miller, Helen Naugle, Matthew O'Brien, Paul O'Connell, Ed Quinn, Lori Rath, Harold Schechter, Michael Schudson, Sharon Shaloo, Phillip Shew, Nancy

Sommers, Charles Taylor, Victor H. Thompson, Barbara H. Traister, Patrick van den Bossche, Ruth Vande Kieft, Maureen Waters, and Harvey Wiener. Special thanks to William Vesterman, a long-time friend of the book who helps keep us alert to the classroom possibilities of new material. In addition, we would like to recognize the special assistance of Trudy Baltz, Richard Mikita, and Christopher Motley. Their intelligence, critical judgment, and generous encouragement continue to be felt in this third edition and in the Teacher's Manual that accompanies it.

We would like to acknowledge once again all those who helped us structure the original text and whose influence is still very much evident in each new edition: Paul Bertram, Anthony Cardoza, Thomas R. Edwards, Christopher Gray, the late Mark Gibbons, Ron Holland, Daniel F. Howard, Betsy B. Kaufman, Robert E. Lynch, Robert Lyons, C.F. Main, George Mandelbaum, Barbara Maxwell, Max Maxwell, John McDermott, Kevin McQuade, Charles Molesworth, Frank Moorman, Richard Poirier, Marie Ponsot, Douglas Roehm, Sandra Schor, Louisa Spencer, Gary Tate, Thomas Van Laan, Ridley Whitaker, and Elissa Weaver. John Wright, Gerald Mentor, and Jean Shapiro played important roles in the success of earlier editions, and we continue to value that thoughtful assistance.

We are grateful for the cooperation of the library staffs at Columbia, Princeton, and Rutgers Universities, at Queens College, as well as at the New York Public Library and the St. Louis Public Library. John Leypoldt of the Princeton University Library was extremely helpful in producing many of the illustrations. We would like to thank Errol Somay and David Wheeler of the Columbia University Library for extraordinary research assistance. Bruce Forer, as usual, gave generously of his time and intelligence, and his efforts helped make the "Scripts" section possible. Thanks also to Christine Pellicano for her work on the manuscript and for her help in keeping so many moving parts intact. We are especially grateful to James Barszcz, whose first-rate revision has made the Teacher's Manual an even more useful teaching resource.

We are indebted to the kind people at Oxford University Press who made working on this third edition so pleasant and productive. In particular, we would like to thank: Ed Barry, Harriet Emanuel, Ellie Fuchs, Fred Schneider, Bill Sisler, and Natalie Tutt. Our editor, Curtis Church, has been a paragon of tireless encouragement and wise counsel. We recognize his intelligence in the best of what we think we have done. As always, Helene Atwan and Susanne McQuade have helped in innumerable ways. And finally, we are ever grateful to Christine and Marc McQuade,and to the newly born Gregory Atwan, who are quickly growing to understand—and respect—the curious working hours and reading habits of their fathers.

CONTENTS

SCRIPTS 601

RHETORICAL TABLE OF CONTENTS

DESCRIPTION

PEOPLE

PLACES

OBJECTS

Advertisements:

NARRATION

FACTUAL AND HISTORICAL

FICTIONAL

EXPOSITION

DEFINITION

CLASSIFICATION

ANALOGY

PROCESS ANALYSIS

CAUSE AND EFFECT

ARGUMENT

PERSUASION

TABLE OF LINKED SELECTIONS

A Woman's Identity

The Power of Books

INTRODUCTION

This book grew out of our commitment to the notion—one that still might seem peculiar to many people—that *any* form of writing can be made the subject of rewarding critical attention. And because we are most interested in the written products of American culture that are continually shaping the ways we think, talk, and feel, our editorial effort has been to include as great a variety of American themes and prose styles as could be managed within a single text. Along with some traditional selections from such classic American writers as Thoreau, Twain, Crane, and Faulkner, we have brought together an assortment of material from scripts, best sellers, popular magazines, newspapers, and advertisements. One critical principle informs our selections: we want to illustrate through historical sequences, thematic cross references, and divergent creative intentions precisely how the most widely read forms of American writing interact with each other and with their audiences to produce that intricate network of artistic and commercial collaboration known as "popular culture."

Popular Writing in America is divided into six parts. The opening section consists of some of the most successful copywriting in the history of American advertising. We have arranged the ads in clusters dealing with similar products (automobiles, cosmetics, clothing, etc.) over a number of decades both to provide a brief historical perspective on the language and rhetorical strategies of advertising and to invite speculation on changes in American culture as they are reflected in the ways our society is talked to in its advertisements. In addition, to demonstrate some of the ways advertising is thought about both inside and outside the industry, we have also included essays on the art of copywriting, several critiques of advertising, and a series of delightful letters showing a prominent American poet exercising her imagination and vocabulary in an attempt to invent a suitable name for a new automobile.

The examples of newspaper writing we include in the next chapter (Press) range from different styles of headlines through the compressed prose of teletype releases to extended forms of news coverage. Events of such historical magnitude as the Lincoln and Kennedy assassinations and the use of the atom bomb on Japan are interspersed among some of the usual kinds of news stories, feature articles, interviews, and editorials that comprise the substance of the daily American newspaper. Since we want to emphasize in this chapter the stylistic and structural consequences of writing performed under emergency conditions and against competitive deadlines—"Journalism is literature in a hurry," according to Matthew Arnold—we have weighted our selections in favor of the kinds of violence and tragedies that have inspired reporters, made history, and sold newspapers.

Magazines are eclectic by necessity. Represented are a variety of topics from some of the most popular "big" and "little" magazines published in America. With very few exceptions, an article from a particular magazine is intended to be at least fairly typical of the kind of material and tonal quality found in that magazine around the time the article appeared. Our selections in this chapter are limited to nonfiction because a good deal of the fiction in Best Sellers and Classics was originally published in magazines. Consequently, an important periodical like *Scribner's* is not represented by an article in this section but by Stephen Crane's short story that appears in Classics.

The material reprinted in "Best Sellers" affords the reader the opportunity to examine some of the most commercially successful prose in American publishing history. It is, for the most part, writing that the academic community has seldom paid serious attention to—selections from best sellers are rarely made available in textbooks or anthologies. Yet, because of their massive audiences and their frequent interactions with other forms of media, best sellers deserve to be attended to by readers interested in examining the relationship between their own verbal experiences and those of a literate public. Passages such as Tarzan's rescue of Jane in *Tarzan of the Apes* or the shooting of Don Corleone from *The Godfather* were selected not as specimens of mediocre writing—mediocre, that is, *because* they are from best sellers—but as examples of writing that has had enormous impact on the American reading public.

The success of many of the best selling books represented in this section depended, to a great extent, on their public's previous acceptance of similar subjects and verbal strategies in advertisements, newspapers, and magazine articles. To cite but one example, the phenomenal attention Mario Puzo's *The Godfather* received was due, in large measure, to the extensive news coverage given to the felonies and frolics of underworld characters. Popular fiction, in turn, affects other forms of media, as can be seen from the account of the murder of Joey Gallo in *Time* magazine, where the report of a ritualist gangland shooting self-consciously trades on the rendition of a similar event in *The Godfather.* Throughout the book, connections such as this one are signaled in headnotes and discussion questions in order to map out a network of thematic and stylistic interrelations.

Though our emphasis in Classics is on short fiction and poetry, we also include essays, excerpts from autobiographies, and other selected nonfiction from some of America's major authors. We have taken the liberty of designating the work of such contemporary writers as John Updike, Norman Mailer, Flannery O'Connor, and Joan Didion as "classic" because we feel that the quality of their performances and their critical alertness to the present condition of our language entitle them to be viewed in the same historical perspective as Thoreau, Twain, Crane, and Faulkner. *Classic* is a term we adopt for the sake of convenience; it is not intended to suggest writing that is antiquated, writing that is easily dissociated from popular culture because it sounds serious and elevated, but writing that has, so far, stayed around because it has stayed alive. We want to show from our selections that "classic" authors have not remained socially and intellectually superior to the various ordinary languages of popular culture but have tried to come to terms with those languages by appropriating them, occasionally discarding them, often shaping or extending them so that their writing can reflect the complex interplay between what we call literature and what we recognize as the accents of the life around us.

In "Scripts" we introduce popular language that is heard rather than read. Though surely the most widely responded to form of writing, radio and television scripts are seldom ever seen and examined by anyone other than professionals. People tend to forget that much of what they *see* in the movies or on television started first with the written word. In some cases, as in the film version of Ernest Hemingway's "Soldier's Home," what is being seen is a transcription of classic literature. Hemingway's "Soldier's Home" is included in "Classics" so that readers can examine how such adaptations are accomplished and also learn how the shaping of a text for a film audience affects the way the original material is interpreted. Episodes from such popular television series as "The Jeffersons" and "Hill Street Blues" will show how writers work to create an interplay of authentic dialogue and believable characters.

It might be argued that this type of book is unnecessary since the abundance of ads, newspapers, magazines, and best sellers makes them so available as "texts" that there is really no need to collect samples of them in a separate volume. If our "texts" had been chosen indiscriminately, simply to document different types of writing, that might be the case. But, quite clearly, one way the book can be used is to illustrate a verbal progression from the readily accessible language and strategies of advertising to the more obviously complicated styles of expression that characterize outstanding prose. The risk of this procedure, however, is that it may prove too schematic, may even encourage readers to regard the ads, some of the journalism and magazine articles, and most of the best sellers as blatantly inferior forms of writing, "straw men" set up to be discarded all too easily in favor of the durable excellence of the "great works." It should be noted, therefore, that our categories and sequence were not specially designed to endorse already entrenched hierarchies by setting up fairly obvious gradations in the quality of several particular types of prose and poetry, but were intended to illustrate how various kinds of writing shaped by quite different commercial purposes and intended audiences interact with and modify each other to produce what we can reasonably call a common culture.

It might also be argued that Classics have no place in an anthology devoted to popular writing. Classics are among the finest holdings of an educated minority; popular writing belongs to something as repugnant as "mass culture." That is one way to look at it. Another, and one that this book is premised on, is that Classics are among the best things we have to share with each other, and they ought to be encountered in all their challenging complexity as opportunities to enliven and, if need be,toughen the questions we ask of all the other modes of expression we participate in daily. That is why we have included an excerpt from Norman Mailer's *Of a Fire on the Moon* in Classics. Throughout his comprehensive report on the Apollo expedition, Mailer is critically aware of the ways his own prose interrelates with a variety of other, mainly competing verbal efforts. Mailer's original contract to write about the Apollo XI astronauts was with *Life,* a popular magazine. But Mailer is no ordinary reporter, and for him the moonshot was no ordinary assignment. As a writer, Mailer is so attuned to his own participation in any form of media that it was only natural his coverage of the moon landing would inform us as much about the special tasks of modern journalism as it would tell us about one of the great episodes in American history. As it stands, *Of a Fire on the Moon* is a fascinating social document incorporating the many voices of technology, science, and broadcasting that converged at that particular moment in our culture to produce the moon spectacle. Such responsiveness to the shaping influences of our verbal environment is what we want the word "classic" to suggest.

A word about the introduction to each section. A full survey outlining the history of the various forms of printed media that make up our categories would not have been practical. Also, we wanted to avoid introducing such essentially futile, if not paralyzing, questions as "Is the news truly objective?" and "Is advertising an abuse of language?" Instead, we have tried in each introduction to strike an agreeable balance between saying something general about the type of material in that section and something specific about the verbal qualities of a particular passage. Of course, no single excerpt can typify all the writing in a chapter. Yet, we have chosen to examine closely, though not at great length, those passages that we feel will conveniently clarify the relations between the distinctive features of an individual style and the kind of reader that style seems directed to. We thought that by providing models of the analytic procedure we want to encourage we would, in fact, be offering something of a consistent critical approach to what might seem a bewildering assortment of material.

Any act of composition presupposes an audience. To read a "text" attentively is to discover something specific about the characteristics of the people it is intended to appear to—their interests and the ways of talking they can respond to most readily. Once we ask the question "Whom is this ad or magazine article addressed to?" we invite statements about the traits of large groups of people. Questions like this one can be best approached not from a reader's preconceived idea of what certain groups of people in America are supposed to be like but from his responsiveness to the specific ways in which a society is talked to in print. Our responses to popular writing will be the more attuned to the culture we live in the more our terms can encompass the aesthetic significance of a particular work and the bearings that significance has on our shared social experiences. In the model analysis we provide in each of our introductions, especially in the one to "Best Sellers," we try to show that it is only when we make an effort to measure the responses of the audience implicit in a specific passage—an audience, it should be noted, that very often *literally* appears in the work as spectators, witnesses, advertising models, etc.—against the quality of our own participation that we can assess more comprehensively the interactions between the various styles and audiences within a single society.

Popular forms of writing pose special challenges to traditional analytical methods. Popular writing is often, or so it would seem, so opaquely simple and ordinary that a standard critical vocabulary might come across as too labored or too imposing for the occasion. Yet, finding an appropriate tone has always been a problem even for traditional literary criticism. It would *sound* wrong to talk about Ernest Hemingway in the highly idiosyncratic critical language of Henry James' "Prefaces" or to take the same psychological approach in a discussion of Allen Ginsberg that we would take for Emily Dickinson. Writers exist for us, unless we know them in other, more personal ways, essentially in the specific qualities of their tone and idiom. This should always be our starting point. If, for example, we try to adopt a standard analytical procedure (e.g., searching for symbols) to discuss *Tarzan of the Apes,* and our method becomes too irritatingly cumbersome, that can be an occasion for testing the critical language we are working with and for re-examining the quality of our literary responses rather than concluding that Tarzan was not worth talking about in the first place.

It should be apparent from our model of analysis in each introduction that we have made an effort to avoid using a language that relies too heavily on the terminology of traditional literary criticism, a terminology that has, for the most part, evolved from allegiances and inveterate responses to only the most highly regarded forms of literature. We certainly do not mean to disqualify any of the standard critical approaches, as we trust our Rhetorical Table of Contents will amply indicate, but we want instead to encourage a lively reciprocity between the academically certified terms of serious literary criticism and the ordinary languages of our popular culture. What we hope will come out of such transactions is a resilient critical language applicable to all forms of public discourse. If we cannot adjust our critical vocabularies and find interesting ways to talk about Tarzan, or advertising, or a newspaper item, then it is doubtful we have found the most spirited ways to approach even the best things in our culture.

Popular Writing in America

ADVERTISING

Advertising is a business of words.

DAVID OGILVY

WE are so accustomed to signs, posters, billboards, songs, jingles, graffiti, circulars, placards, announcements, brochures, packages, commercials, and ads in newspapers and magazines that it is difficult for any of us to imagine a world without public and personal advertisements. Ads are practically inescapable; they literally surround us. Few places are remote enough to be completely free from the appeals of advertising. Suppose we picture ourselves on a secluded tropical beach experiencing a dazzling sunset. Even if we have not noticed any discarded packaging or unobtrusively placed signs, we must still recognize the alluring tropical scene itself as one continually promoted by airlines and travel agencies in newspapers, in magazines, and especially on decorative posters. Efforts to escape advertising, to "discover" landscapes removed from the intrusions of advertisements may be merely another way of participating in the kind of world advertisements typically endorse. No place, no object, no life style, and certainly no way of talking can be totally exempt from commercialized public notice. The world we live in is an advertised world.

The business of advertising is to invent methods of addressing massive audiences in a language designed to be easily accessible and immediately persuasive. No advertising agency wants to put out an ad that is not clear and convincing to millions of people. But the agencies, though they would agree that ads should be written to sell products, disagree when it comes down to the most effective methods of doing so. Over the years, advertising firms have developed among themselves a variety of distinctive styles based on their understanding of the different kinds of audiences they want to reach. No two agencies would handle the same product identically. To people for whom advertising is an exacting discipline and a highly competitive profession, an ad is much more than a sophisticated sales pitch, an attractive verbal and visual device to serve manufacturers. In fact, for those who examine ads critically or professionally, products may very well be no more than merely points of departure. Ads often outlive their products, and in the case of early advertisements for products that are no longer available, we cannot help but consider the advertisement independently of our responses to those products. The point of examining ads apart from their announced subjects is not that we ignore the product completely, but that we try to see the product only as it is talked about and portrayed in the full context of the ad. Certainly, it is not necessary to have tried a particular product to be able to appreciate the technique and design used in its advertisement.

The emphasis of the following section is on the advertisements themselves, not the commodities they promote. To illustrate a variety of American advertising strategies and styles, we have included advertisements from the late nineteenth century to the present. Some ads have been grouped according to their products, that is, there are a number of ads regarding smoking, transportation, cosmetics, and fashions. This arrangement will allow you to observe some of the ways both advertisements and audiences have changed over the past one hundred years. Many of these ads have been selected because they represent important developments in advertising methodology. But our intentions are not exclusively historical. Other ads were chosen to display significant aspects of standard advertising procedures. We wanted to introduce advertisements that were both interesting and typical. Nearly all the ads we reprint have achieved a good deal of professional recognition. Many have been frequently singled out as examples of some of the finest copy in the history of American advertising.

A few of the early ads may strike you as unimaginative and typographically crude. They appeared in newspapers and magazines before printing innovations and marketing research radically altered advertising techniques. Yet, given their frequent inelegance, naïveté, and commandeering tones, many early ads remind us how advertisers have persistently played on certain themes despite noticeable changes in decorum, style, and methods of persuasion. Perhaps the early ads only put very bluntly the promises and claims that later on would be more politely disguised. Consider the advertisement for Madame Rowley's Toilet Mask that first appeared in 1887. This ad makes no attempt to introduce its product in a pleasing manner. The advantages of using the toilet mask are delivered in a decisively impersonal and mechanically repetitive fashion. No effort was spent on setting up an attractive backdrop or atmosphere. The only graphic detail we are allowed is the sketch of the curious toilet device in operation, appearing ingenuously at the center of an imposingly designed typographical layout.

If the advertisement for Madame Rowley's Toilet Mask makes little attempt to attract visually, neither does it try very hard to gratify its audience verbally. Even the name of the product is deliberately and unappealingly direct—no charming or engaging brand name suggests that the mask is anything more than what it announces itself to be. The copywriter uses none of the enticing and intimately sensuous language that advertisers so often turned to later when addressing women on matters of personal hygiene and beauty. Realizing that Madame Rowley's beauty apparatus was almost embarrassingly unstylish, the writer must have decided he could promote his client's product best by sounding unadornedly legalistic and scientific. While the copywriter assumes that facial beauty is desirable, he restricts his copy to "claims," "grounds," and "proofs" of the toilet mask's effectiveness, instead of extolling the advantages of a blemish free, "cover girl" complexion. Flattering metaphors that would describe the product or its results more sensitively are avoided, apparently so as not to call into question the speaker's assertions. Only once does the idiom anticipate the language of modern cosmetic advertisements. Facial blemishes are said to "vanish from the skin, leaving it soft, clear, brilliant, and beautiful." Future copywriters would capitalize on words, like "vanish," that suggest magical and instantaneous remedies. Later ads for skin care would also focus more directly on the personal and social advantages of having a "soft, clear, brilliant, and beautiful" complexion. But in Madame Rowley's day, beauty in itself had not yet become an advertising commodity.

Apparently, Madame Rowley's Toilet Mask did not put the cosmetic industry out of business. As early as 1912, we find an advertisement for make-up using what has since become a familiar merchandising tactic. The claims made by Madame Rowley's copywriter stopped at a "brilliant" complexion. The ad promised women nothing more than that. But for the writer of the Pompeian Massage Cream copy, a blemish-free countenance was not all his product could supply. The Pompeian ad is one of the first ads for women to promise along with its product's "beautifying" benefits, the additional advantages of marital love and social acceptance. A beautiful complexion, the ad writer suggests, means little by itself. At the heart of the Pompeian ad lies one of the most important developments in the history of advertising technique—the realization that "grounds" and "claims" restricted to the product alone will not always sell the goods. Since the Pompeian ad, copywriters have concentrated more and more on an audience's psychological needs, its attitudes, and anxieties. In the Pompeian ad, the writer promotes not only an effective way to check the wrinkles and blemishes he poetically calls "Time's ravages" but also adopts an attitude toward the nature and effects of feminine appeal: "a beautiful complexion—that greatest aid to woman's power and influence." This comment, obviously made by a male copywriter, is offered after we have been told that a "Pompeian complexion" will win over any man's mother, "as it does in every other instance in social or business life." The ad inadver-

MADAME ROWLEY'S TOILET MASK.

TOILET MASK
OR
FACE GLOVE.

The following are the claims made for Madame Rowley's Toilet Mask, and the grounds on which it is recommended to ladies for Beautifying, Bleaching, and Preserving the Complexion:

TOILET MASK
OR
FACE GLOVE.

First—The **Mask** is **Soft** and **Flexible** in form, and can be **Easily Applied** and **Worn** without **Discomfort** or **Inconvenience.**

Second—It is durable, and does not dissolve or come asunder, but holds its original mask shape.

Third—It has been **Analyzed** by **Eminent Scientists** and **Chemical Experts,** and pronounced **Perfectly Pure** and **Harmless.**

Fourth—With ordinary care the **Mask** will **last for years,** and its VALUABLE PROPERTIES **Never Become Impaired.**

Fifth—The **Mask** is protected by letters patent, and is the **only Genuine** article of the kind.

Sixth—It is **Recommended** by **Eminent Physicians** and **Scientific Men** as a SUBSTITUTE FOR INJURIOUS COSMETICS.

Seventh—The **Mask** is a **Natural Beautifier,** for **Bleaching** and **Preserving** the **Skin** and **Removing Complexional Imperfections.**

Eighth—Its use cannot be detected by the closest scrutiny, and it may be worn with **perfect privacy,** if desired.

Ninth—The **Mask** is sold at a moderate price, and is to be PURCHASED BUT ONCE.

Tenth—Hundreds of dollars uselessly expended for cosmetics, lotions, and like preparations, may be saved its possessor.

Eleventh—**Ladies** in every section of the country are using the **Mask** with gratifying results.

Twelfth—It is safe, simple, cleanly, and effective for beautifying purposes, and never injures the most delicate skin.

Thirteenth—While it is intended that the **Mask** should be **Worn During Sleep,** it may be applied WITH EQUALLY GOOD RESULTS **at any time** to suit the convenience of the wearer.

Fourteenth—The **Mask** has received the testimony of well-known society and professional ladies, who proclaim it to be the greatest discovery for beautifying purposes ever vouchsafed to womankind.

The Toilet Mask (or Face Glove) in position to the face.
TO BE WORN THREE TIMES IN THE WEEK

COMPLEXION BLEMISHES

May be hidden imperfectly by cosmetics and powders, but can only be removed permanently by the Toilet Mask. By its use every kind of spots, impurities, roughness, etc., vanish from the skin, leaving it soft, clear, brilliant, and beautiful. It is harmless, costs little, and saves its user money. It prevents and removes wrinkles, and is both a complexion preserver and beautifier. Famous Society Ladies, actresses, belles, etc., use it.

VALUABLE ILLUSTRATED TREATISE, WITH PROOFS AND PARTICULARS.

—MAILED FREE BY—

TOILET MASK
OR
FACE GLOVE.

THE TOILET MASK COMPANY,

Send for Descriptive Treatise. 1164 BROADWAY, **Send for Descriptive Treatise.**

NEW YORK.

☞ **Mention this paper when you Write.**

TOILET MASK
OR
FACE GLOVE.

[1887]

OF all moments the most trying—when the son brings *her* to his mother, of all critics the most exacting. Mother-love causes her to look with penetrating glance, almost *trying* to find flaws. No quality of beauty so serves to win an older woman as a skin smooth, fresh and healthy *in a natural way*, as easily provided by

POMPEIAN MASSAGE CREAM

Where artificial beautifiers—cosmetics and rouges—would only antagonize; and an uncared-for, pallid, wrinkled skin prove a negative influence—the Pompeian complexion immediately wins the mother, as it does in every other instance in social or business life.

You can have a beautiful complexion—that greatest aid to woman's power and influence. A short use of Pompeian will surprise you and your friends. It will improve even the best complexion, and retain beauty and youthful appearance against Time's ravages.

"Don't *envy* a good complexion; use Pompeian and *have* one."

Pompeian is not a "cold" or "grease" cream, nor a rouge or cosmetic, and positively can not grow hair on the face. Pompeian simply affords a natural means toward a complete cleanliness of the facial pores. And in pores that are "Pompeian clean" lies skin health.

TRIAL JAR

sent for 6c (stamps or coin). Find out for yourself, now, why Pompeian is used and prized in a million homes where the value of a clear, fresh, youthful skin is appreciated. Clip coupon now.

All dealers 50c, 75c, $1

Cut along this line, fill in and mail today

The Pompeian Mfg. Co. 36 Prospect St., Cleveland, Ohio

Gentlemen:—Enclosed find 6c (stamps or coin) for a trial jar of Pompeian Massage Cream.

Name..

Address...

City...................................State...................

[1912]

tently acknowledges that beauty is only skin deep, after all. Deeper than a woman's worry about facial blemishes, the copywriter intimates, is her terror of not being loved and approved.

Unlike Madame Rowley's mask, the Pompeian Massage Cream does not appear at the center of its advertisement. To be sure, the brand name (chosen to suggest the shade of red found on the walls of the "preserved" ancient city of Pompeii) has been allowed central prominence, and the illustration of the product is barely squeezed into the bottom left corner of the ad. More important than the actual cream is the rendition of the familiar dramatic situation in which a young lady is first introduced to the wary scrutiny of her suitor's mother: "Of all the moments the most trying—the son brings *her* to his mother, of all critics the most exacting." With a tone and diction borrowed from the melodramatic superlatives of soap opera and best-selling fiction, the copywriter maintains that with so much at stake a young woman cannot risk using a cosmetic that would make her look vulgar and unacceptable to such an "exacting" critic as a potential mother-in-law. The writer offers, in addition, the ultimate emotional reassurance that the massage cream "positively can not grow hair on the face." The ad leaves little doubt, then, that the "beautiful complexion" its product guarantees is not what is finally being promoted. The clear complexion, in this case, ultimately stands for something else, as it did not in the ad for Madame Rowley's Toilet Mask. Pompeian Massage Cream, not of much consequence in itself, merely personifies the real "product" of the ad—a natural, artless appearance that will ensure unqualified social approval.

Cosmetic advertisements, for the most part, avoid the slightest allusion to artificiality. Madame Rowley's Toilet Mask, which must have looked like an odd contrivance even in its own time, was nevertheless introduced as a "natural beautifier." To bring home a girl whose make-up looked artificial was, to the copy writer for Pompeian Massage Cream at least, an undeserving affront to American motherhood. In our final example of cosmetic advertising, the ad for Yardley's Next to Nature, the entire copy depends on the single notion that make-up must allow a woman to appear *natural,* to look, that is, as if she were not wearing any cosmetic at all. Though the ad does not associate its product with a comforting aura of love and matrimony, like the Pompeian ad, it still assumes that a fine complexion is not an end in itself but a means of possessing a particular kind of "look." Throughout the Next to Nature ad, the copywriter insists on the product's naturalness. The brand itself bears, as Pompeian did not, more than a loose metaphorical relationship to the product: the name suggests not only that the cosmetic formula is literally close to Nature but also that the product's use will engender an appearance that will be the next best thing to natural beauty. Since Madame Rowley's time, advertisers have discovered that probably no word of copy works so effectively as "natural." The copywriter for Next to Nature appropriately avoids gimmicks and artificiality by adopting a casual manner of speaking and by offering a photograph of a demure and innocent looking woman as evidence of his product's "transparent" purity. Apparently, he does not feel that he need convince us of his honesty by citing indisputable "claims" and "grounds" nor does he bank on his audience's fear of social or parental disapproval. He is confident that his readers will need no more than his own sincere tone to be persuaded that by using Next to Nature they can have "the fresh, wholesome look" of natural beauty.

These three cosmetic advertisements furnish a brief record of some of the major developments of American advertising. A glance at the ads demonstrates vividly the changes in the layout of advertisements brought about by advances in photography and graphic design. The space apportioned for illustration increases sub-

Of all the make-ups on earth,
only one is called Next to Nature.™
One of the freshest things that's happened to girls' faces since sunshine and country air: Yardley's Next to Nature Liquid Make-up.
It's made with vitamin A to moisturize, the purest of waters, and all natural colorings. They're blended into a formula so sheer, you can use it generously and still look like a natural beauty.
Try Next to Nature blushers and new Transparent Pressed Powder too.
Because when it comes to giving you the fresh, wholesome look—there's nobody on earth like Yardley.
Yardley
How to make the most
of what you have.
©1973, Yardley of London, Inc.
Yardley
Next to Nature
Next to Nature
Next to Nature
Next to Nature

[1973]

stantially. We move from the cameo-like sketch of the figure in the toilet mask to the poster-like photograph of an attractive woman which dominates the Next to Nature advertisement and also conveniently eliminates the copywriter's need to write a lengthy description of what the product can do. The size of the headlines increases; the style becomes more informal. The headline for Madame Rowley's Toilet Mask is intended to do no more than name the product explicitly. In the Pompeian ad, however, there are actually two headlines. One simply mentions the product by name, while the other invites a reader's response to a fictional scene. In the Next to Nature ad, after the reader is introduced directly to the brand name and the special quality of the product, she is then talked to marginally in a perky and congenial voice. Few ads in Madame Rowley's day would have taken the liberty of speaking to their readers in such a casual and ingratiating fashion. Neither would a nineteenth-century copywriter have violated grammatical decorum by writing the kind of breezy and fragmented sentences that characterize the brisk style of the Next to Nature copy. Quite clearly, the writing in the Next to Nature ad is meant to sound as natural, relaxed, and sincere as the copywriter imagines his audience would like to talk and behave. By examining these advertisements, then, we are introduced not only to three markedly different styles of

Even though advertisements represent some of the most expensive and calculated acts of composition in America, the audiences they are directed to seldom attend to them analytically. No one would deny that ads exert tremendous economic and social pressures. (See, for example, the essays by Carol Caldwell in Advertising and Vance Packard in Best Sellers.) Yet, few people, aside from those in the advertising profession, seldom bother to ask how or why a particular advertisement happened to be written and designed in a certain way. The public generally reacts to advertisements exactly the way advertising agencies would like them to—as consumers, not critics. Assuming, however, that "advertising is a business of *words*," not necessarily of products, we have included examples of successful copy to invite you to consider more carefully *how* the language and strategies of advertisements affect the ways we talk and think. Advertisements constitute a lively repository of American vocabulary, idiom, metaphor, and style, in short a fairly reliable index of the state of public discourse. They create the one verbal environment in which we all participate, willingly or unwillingly.

Often a bridesmaid but never a bride
EDNA'S case was really a pathetic one. Like every woman, her primary ambition was to marry. Most of the girls of her set were married—or about to be. Yet not one possessed more grace or charm or loveliness than she.
And as her birthdays crept gradually toward that tragic thirty-mark, marriage seemed farther from her life than ever. She was often a bridesmaid but never a bride.
* * *
That's the insidious thing about halitosis (unpleasant breath). You, yourself, rarely know when you have it. And even your closest friends won't tell you.
Sometimes, of course, halitosis comes from some deep-seated organic disorder that requires professional advice. But usually—and fortunately—halitosis is only a local condition that yields to the regular use of Listerine as a mouth wash and gargle. It is an interesting thing that this well-known antiseptic that has been in use for years for surgical dressings, possesses these unusual properties as a breath deodorant.
It halts food fermentation in the mouth and leaves the breath sweet, fresh and clean. *Not* by substituting some other odor but by really removing the old one. The Listerine odor itself quickly disappears. So the systematic use of Listerine puts you on the safe and polite side.
Your druggist will supply you with Listerine. He sells lots of it. It has dozens of different uses as a safe antiseptic and has been trusted as such for a half a century. Read the interesting little booklet that comes with every bottle.
—*Lambert Pharmacal Company, Saint Louis, U. S. A.*
HALITOSIS
LISTERINE

[1923] WOMEN

Should a gentleman offer a Tiparillo to a lab technician?

Behind that pocket of pencils beats the heart of a digital computer. This girl has already cross-indexed Tiparillo® as a cigar with a slim, elegant shape and neat, white tip.

She knows that there are two kinds. Regular Tiparillo, for a mild smoke. Or new Tiparillo M with menthol, for a cold smoke.

She knows. She's programmed.

And she's ready.

But how about you? Which Tiparillo are you going to offer? Or are you just going to stand there and stare at her pencils?

[1968]

*"Equal pay, equal recognition
and the first woman admitted
to The Club...
What more could you ask for?"*

"Old Grand-Dad!"

Head of the Bourbon Family.

Old Grand-Dad

When you ask a lot more from life.

Kentucky Straight Bourbon Whiskeys. 86 proof and 100 proof. Bottled in Bond. Old Grand-Dad Distillery Co., Frankfort, Ky. 40601.

[1976]

ALASKAN TOWN ALLOWS WOMAN TO SMOKE!

BROKEN NECK, ALASKA, NOV. 5—By unanimous decision the citizens of Broken Neck voted to allow female smoking within city limits. Mayor Robert Sherman explained the vote by saying, "When you gots only one woman in town you lets her smoke."

You've come a long way, baby.

VIRGINIA SLIMS

Slimmer than the fat cigarettes men smoke.

Fashions: Bill Blass

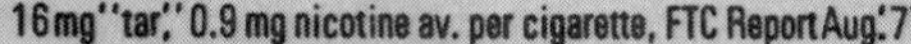

16 mg "tar," 0.9 mg nicotine av. per cigarette, FTC Report Aug.'77

Warning: The Surgeon General Has Determined That Cigarette Smoking Is Dangerous to Your Health.

[1978]

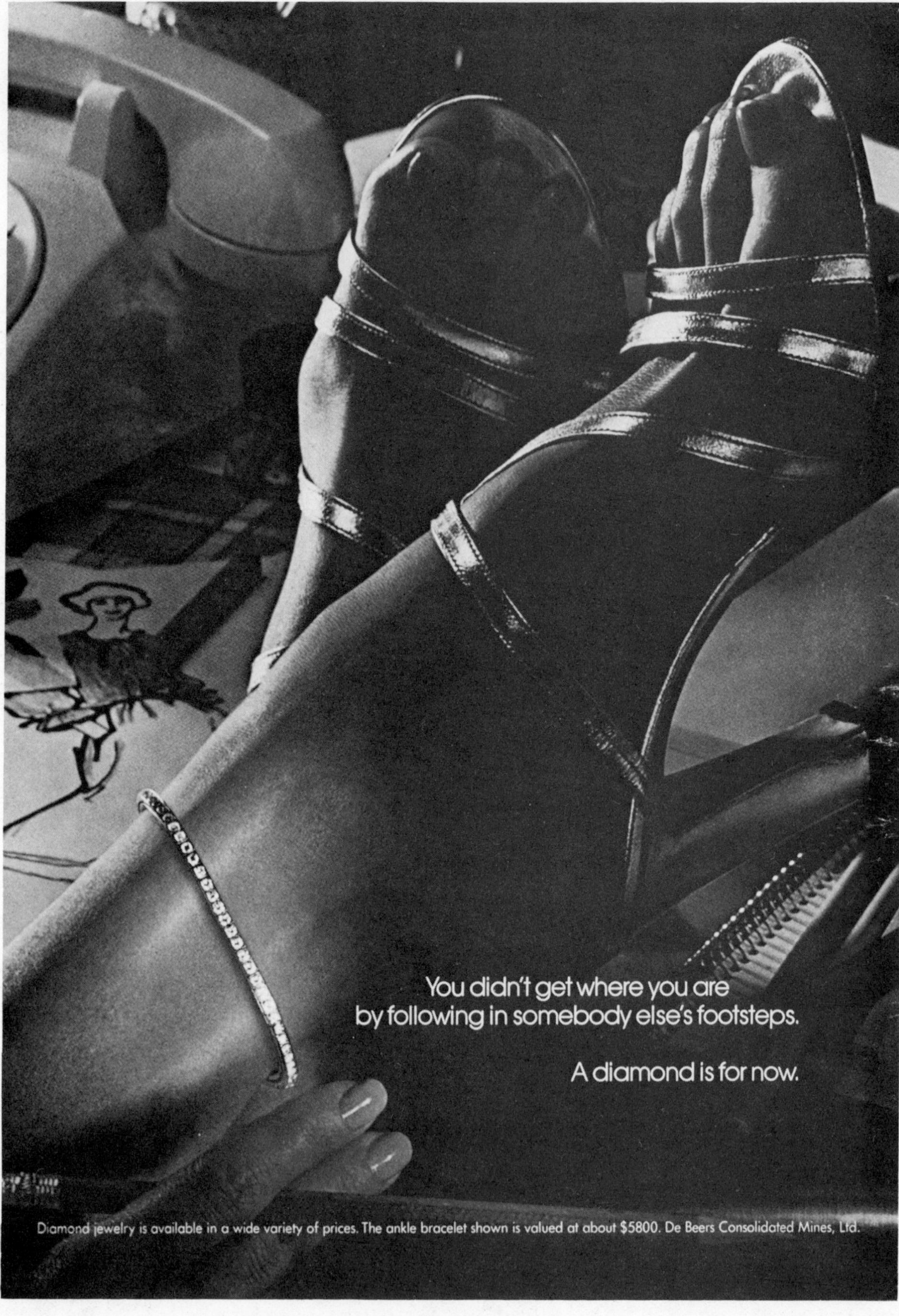
You didn't get where you are
by following in somebody else's footsteps.
A diamond is for now.
Diamond jewelry is available in a wide variety of prices. The ankle bracelet shown is valued at about $5800. De Beers Consolidated Mines, Ltd.

[1978]

"...Guess who's the new Marketing V.P.?"

Peggy Ross. It's time.

Time for the Chase Advantage. Chase has helped a lot of successful people. And Chase knows you need more than just ordinary checking or savings to truly maximize your assets.

So how can Chase really help? To begin with, no bank can give you more imaginative and comprehensive banking than Chase can. With 4 different checking plans. And with a full range of credit and loan services. With 12 different savings plans—including plans that pay extra high interest without tying up your money for years, like our 6 month certificate of deposit, or our 90 day Nest Egg Account.

But most importantly, it's time for the professional and expert guidance you'll get from the world's most knowledgeable bank.

The Chase Advantage means all this and more. That's why, now it's time to put the Chase Advantage to work for you.

The Chase Advantage

Member F.D.I.C

[1979]

Your chances of making it into public office are very slim.
Only 23 of 657 FEDERAL JUDGES are women.
Only 2 of 100 SENATORS are women.
No woman has ever been PRESIDENT.
But you do have a 99% chance to be a NURSE.
(You'll earn less than a tree-trimmer.)
Or a 97% chance to be a TYPIST.
(You'll earn less than the janitor.)
Or a 60% chance to be a SCHOOL TEACHER.
(You'll earn less than a zoo-keeper.)

Concerned mamas and daddies are asking how they can help their female children to get an equal crack at vocational training —training that opens doors to non-stereotypical, better paying jobs. Parents want their female children to get the same kind of coaching in sports and physical education as boys do.

Parents want the kind of counseling that will encourage wider career options for girls. (Most young women graduate without the science and math credits they need to exercise full options for higher education.) If your female children attend a federally supported public school in this country you can and should help them get a more equal education.

YOU CAN HELP TO CREATE A BETTER FUTURE.
Write NOW Legal Defense & Education Fund (H) 132 W. 43rd Street, N.Y., N.Y. 10036

Space for this message contributed as a public service by Newsweek Inc.

[1980]

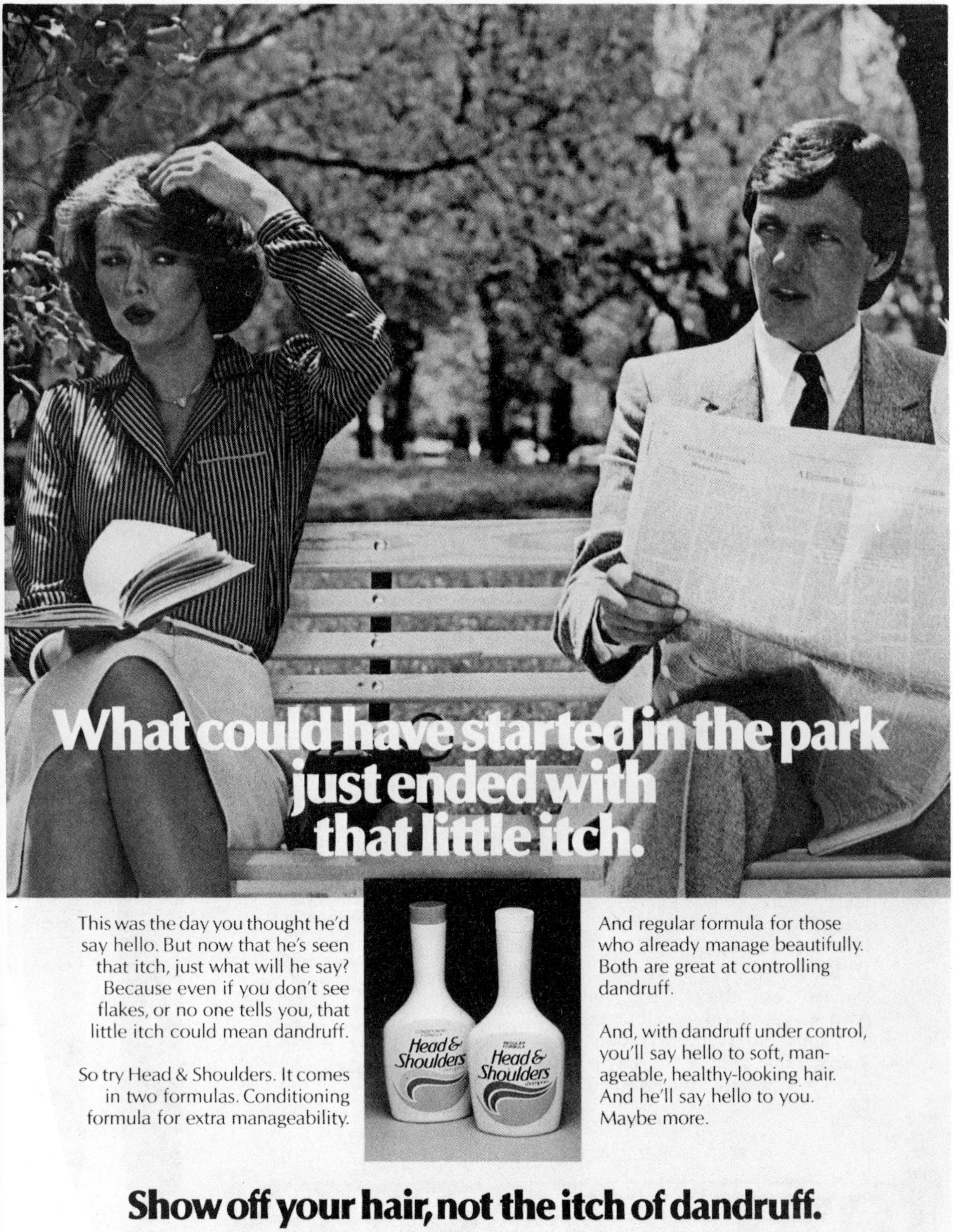

What could have started in the park just ended with that little itch.

This was the day you thought he'd say hello. But now that he's seen that itch, just what will he say? Because even if you don't see flakes, or no one tells you, that little itch could mean dandruff.

So try Head & Shoulders. It comes in two formulas. Conditioning formula for extra manageability.

And regular formula for those who already manage beautifully. Both are great at controlling dandruff.

And, with dandruff under control, you'll say hello to soft, manageable, healthy-looking hair. And he'll say hello to you. Maybe more.

Show off your hair, not the itch of dandruff.

[1983]

THE SATURDAY EVENING POST

"We smash 'em HARD"

One of the Yank Veterans

"Did I bayonet my first Hun? Sure! How did it feel? It *doesn't* feel! There *he* is. There *you* are. One of you has got to go. I preferred to stay.

"So when sergeant says, 'Smash 'em, boys'—we do. And we go them one better like good old Yankee Doodle Yanks. For bullets and bayonets are the only kind of lingo that a Hun can *understand!*"

* * * *

The *dependable* Yank, whose photograph appears above, first met the *dependable* Owl Cigar while boosting that *dependable* investment—the Liberty Loan.

We didn't tell him about the $2,000,000 stock of leaf that is always aging for Owl and White Owl. Nor the over 100,000,000 Owls and White Owls sold last year. We just swapped him a White Owl for a smile. And it doesn't look like the smile came hard, does it?

Why don't you, too, try an Owl or White Owl—*today?*

DEALERS:
If your distributor does not sell these dependable cigars, write us.
GENERAL CIGAR CO., INC., 119 West 40th Street, New York City

TWO DEPENDABLE CIGARS

OWL 6c white OWL 7c

OWL
Square-end
6c

WHITE OWL
Invincible Shape
7c

Branded for your  Banded protection

[1918]

HOW JOE'S BODY BROUGHT HIM FAME INSTEAD OF SHAME

Charles Atlas

—actual photo of the man who holds the title, "The World's Most Perfectly Developed Man."

I Can Make YOU A New Man, Too, in Only 15 Minutes A Day!

If YOU, like Joe, have a body that others can "push around"—if you're ashamed to strip for sports or a swim—then give me just 15 minutes a day! I'll PROVE you can have a body you'll be proud of, packed with red-blooded vitality! "*Dynamic Tension.*" That's the secret! That's how I changed myself from a spindle-shanked, scrawny weakling to winner of the title, "World's Most Perfectly Developed Man."

Do you want big, broad shoulders—a fine, powerful chest—biceps like steel—arms and legs rippling with muscular strength—a stomach ridged with bands of sinewy muscle—and a build you can be proud of? Then just give me the opportunity to prove that "*Dynamic Tension*" is what you need.

"Dynamic Tension" Does It!

Using "*Dynamic Tension*" only 15 minutes a day, in the privacy of your own room, you quickly begin to put on muscle, increase your chest measurements, broaden your back, fill out your arms and legs. Before you know it, this easy, NATURAL method will make you a finer specimen of REAL MANHOOD than you ever dreamed you could be! You'll be a New Man!

FREE BOOK

Send NOW for my FREE book. It tells about "*Dynamic Tension,*" shows photos of men I've turned from weaklings into Atlas Champions, tells how I can do it for YOU. Don't put it off! Address me personally: Charles Atlas, Dept. 217B, 115 E. 23 St., New York 10, N. Y.

CHARLES ATLAS, Dept. 217B,
115 East 23rd St., New York 10, N. Y.

I want the proof that your system of "*Dynamic Tension*" will help make a New Man of me—give me a healthy, husky body and big muscular development. Send me your free book, "Everlasting Health and Strength."

Name..
(Please print or write plainly)

Address..

City..............................State..........

☐ Check here if under 16 for Booklet A

[1944]

A NEW JOE WEIDER SCIENTIFIC WEIGHT-GAINING BREAKTHROUGH

The end of the SKINNY BODY!

He's "Drinking-On" A-POUND-A-DAY Our New Delicious Fun-Way!

Thousands are doing it—Monthly... WHY NOT YOU? Here's a totally new breed of nutritional "wildcat" that's guaranteed to put an end to your muscle-starved, hungry-looking skinny body—through a new, scientifically blended, delicious milkshake-flavored drink. It fills out your body and face—for a fresher, more exciting, fun-going you!

From near death by tuberculosis, emphysema, chronic bronchial asthma, collapsed lungs, alcoholism and drug addiction, this sickly 5'10" skinny 110-lb. weakling gained 65 pounds of solid muscle—added 12 inches of boulder-sized bulges to his chest, 9½ inches to each arm, 8 inches to each leg, and reduced his waist to 28 inches—to become a body building champion... all through the use of Joe Weider's Trainer of the Champions CRASH-WEIGHT GAIN FORMULA #7 Plan!—That's the **true** story of Charlie Kemp!

A Long History of Physical Weakness Problems

Charlie's trouble started early. All his life he had been frail and sick—by the time he was 10 he had developed asthma, and at 16 his left lung had collapsed. Yet these were only hints of problems that would follow, for during the next three years his left lung collapsed five more times and his right lung collapsed twice—he had cystic emphysema complicated by tuberculosis. This, combined with his sickly appearance, was too much for Charlie's battered ego, and by the time he was 25 he was a bona-fide alcoholic with severe cirrhosis of the liver.

Just when things looked darkest, they got darker. His dismal health brought on narcolepsy, and in order to combat this disease he had to take powerful doses of amphetamines—pep pills. They, in turn, brought on more pernicious complications—loss of appetite and, ironically, insomnia, which required drug depressants. The combination of alcohol and drugs destroyed not only Charlie's physical health but also his mental health, and before long he entered the Seton Psychiatric Institute.

For a full year, psychiatrists bolstered Charlie's psyche, but when he was released, emphysema hit again and his right lung collapsed once more. Was his life really doomed?

Into the hospital again. Surgery curtailed the collapsing of his lungs and removed the diseased portions, and when he was released he found new determination to rebuild his body. But that meant gaining weight—and Charlie, who had to continue taking amphetamines which killed his appetite, began to rely almost entirely on food supplements.

Weider Formula/Method Creates a New Life!

Charlie devoured Joe Weider's CRASH-WEIGHT GAIN FORMULA #7 by the case, altered his eating habits as prescribed for him by Joe Weider, and followed a few simple daily exercises, which helped to turn the weight gains he made into a firmer, more muscular and handsomer body.

His progress was astounding—you see here the gains he made—absolutely phenomenal, especially for a man entering his 40's and a truly great testimonial for the Weider System and Crash Weight Gain Formula #7.

His life changed with him—from a pathetic, undesired, unloved loser whose only companions were dogs—to a prize-winning "Mr. America Physical Achievement Award" body surrounded by the world's most beautiful girls.—This is the miracle of courageous Charlie Kemp!

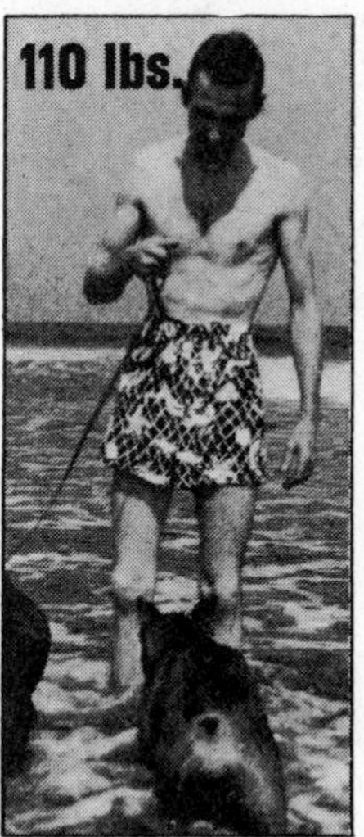

"Tuberculosis, emphysema, chronic bronchial asthma, collapsed lungs, two lung operations, cirrhosis of the liver, narcolepsy, alcoholic, drug addict, a life in and out of the hospital, psychiatric patient, three packs of cigarettes a day, no SEX desire, unloved—only dogs as companions."

175 lbs. PHOTOS UNRETOUCHED

"After years of struggling to stay alive he decided to follow Joe Weider's miraculous Weight-Gaining Plan. The result today is a muscular man of vitality—athletic, handsome, earning $40,000 a year, cured of the sicknesses that used to plague him, and now—surrounded by beautiful girls!"

You Can "Build-Up" Too!

Now, that miracle can be yours. If Charlie Kemp, who was a hopelessly sick underweight weakling struggling daily to live, could achieve so much, just think what you—underweight but medically fit—can accomplish by using the same milkshake flavored drink plan that Charlie used.

Start today to put an end to your skinny body by following the exact same successful weight-Gaining Formula that Charlie Kemp and thousands of others are using—Monthly! Just drink 4 zestful glasses of delicious CRASH-WEIGHT GAIN FORMULA #7 daily. It's full of calories, vitamins, minerals, carbohydrates and tastes delicious with your regular meals. It's safe and healthy, made from all-natural nutrients—NO DRUGS—and does all its work in a relaxed manner, piling on pound after pound of handsome weight to flesh out your bones. Combine CRASH-WEIGHT GAIN FORMULA #7 with five simple daily exercises, and watch how you fill our your narrow chest, your skinny arms and spindly legs. Put an end to your skinny body once, for all—in **JUST 14 TO 30 DAYS**! And, oh yes—it also fills out your face for a healthier, more exciting, fun-loving you, and that's a lot!

BEFORE AND AFTER MEASUREMENTS

	BEFORE	AFTER	GAINS
Weight	110	175	65 lbs.
Chest	33	45	12 in.
Arms	7½	17	9½ in.
Thighs	16	24	8 in.
Calves	10	16	6 in.
Waist	29	28	Lost 1 in.

THE DO-IT-YOURSELF GAIN-A-POUND-A-DAY-KIT

It's a one-day supply of CRASH-WEIGHT, chock full of weight-gaining nutrients that can smash the weight-gaining barrier! You want to gain a pound a day? Half a pound a day? Maybe you just want to add a few pounds here and there. You want it easily—enjoyably—without stuffing yourself with heavy-as-lead foods? Now you can do it! It's as simple as drinking a delicious milkshake.

FREE:

"Valuable Weight-Gaining and Muscle-Building Course." This Illustrated Guide sent FREE with each CRASH-WEIGHT FORMULA #7 Kit. Crammed with step-by-step instructions in muscle-building and weight-gaining basics. Filled with all the latest ideas and how to adapt them for your own personal, fun-going weight gains!

PUT AN END TO YOUR SKINNY BODY!

JOE WEIDER DEPT. P-5
TRAINER OF CHAMPIONS SINCE 1936
21100 ERWIN STREET
WOODLAND HILLS, CALIF. 91364

Dear Joe: I want to put an end to my skinny body and have everyone compliment me on my athletic appearance and muscular gains. Rush me the "Pound-A-Day" CRASH-WEIGHT FORMULA #7 package I have checked below.

Check Plan & Flavor Desired:

☐ 7-Day Supply...... $ 8.00) ☐ Chocolate
☐ 14-Day Supply...... $14.95) ☐ Vanilla
☐ 21-Day Supply...... $20.00) ☐ Strawberry
☐ 30-Day Supply...... $25.00) ☐ Butterscotch

Pick any group of flavors desired with 2, 3 or 4-week order.
California residents add 5% sales tax. We pay postage.

Name ____________ Age ____

Address ____________

City ________ State ______ Zip ______

(please print clearly)

In Canada: CRASH-WEIGHT, 2875 Bates Rd., Montreal, Quebec

[1973]

CITY BOY. Paul spotted him first, just a bouncin' along, an' a grinnin' away like he know'd somethin' everybody else didn't. When he finally got to where we were a settin', Paul winked at me an' ask him real straight-faced, "You lost, city boy?"

"Not necessarily," he smiled.

Bobby ask him what it was that he was ridin', an' city boy said it was a Kawasaki. "A whut?" Bobby said. "A Kawasaki, KE175," city boy told him, real proud. Said it had some kinda new-fangled engine, an' a five-speed transmission, an' all kinds'a other fancy stuff. Said he could ride it just about anywhere he pleased, too...on the road or off—didn't make no difference. Bobby said, "I'll take my palomino any day, he don't get lost." "That's right," Paul said, "horses got brains. Know where they're goin', even if you don't."

City boy just grinned an' said, "Which way's town?"

Well, right away Paul starts ta' pointin' up the road, toward the bunkhouse. An' no sooner'n he had his finger stuck out, an' Bobby was a pointin' up t'other way.

City boy just eyed 'em both for a minute, an' then, with that same grin on his face, he started up his motor-sickle. First kick. Then he pulled out a map an' handed it over ta' Bobby an' said straight-out, "Stick it where your brains are, cowboy...and maybe you'll end up smart as your horse," An' off he rode.

Thought Paul and Bobby's faces were gonna turn redder'n their necks. Good thing that machine didn't stall.

Kawasaki
lets the good times roll.

[1976]

"Life hasn't been the same since I bought my California Cooperage Hot Tub."

"Just take a look at my neighbors, Susan and Donna . . . they've never been so . . . well, neighborly before!

"You see, it all started about a year ago when I was visiting friends on the West Coast. There I was, a normal guy from Cleveland when my date casually asked me to go hot tubbing. I wasn't even sure what a hot tub was, but I decided to go for it . . .

"Next thing I knew, I was sitting in this huge redwood tub, submerged in bubbling hot water and loving it! An old California custom, she told me, and I thought . . . 'Why not Cleveland?'

"So I called my local California Cooperage dealer and they had all the answers. I received their brochure and book describing several do-it-yourself packages, complete with hot tub, heater, filter, plumbing, the works — all for well under $2000. I did it!

"When the boxes arrived, I tried to explain the physical, spiritual and social benefits to Susan and Donna. But they just stood there, amused. Well, an office buddy helped me put it together over a weekend and the system worked fine, right from the start.

"That was a year ago. As you can see, Susan, Donna and I have added a new dimension to our lives. Regardless of sun, rain or snow, my back yard simply has never been so healthy, fun or sexy — and the same goes for me too!"

Find out what a hot tub can do for your life. Check the Yellow Pages for your local dealer, or call California Cooperage at (805) 544-9300, or write P.O. Box E, San Luis Obispo, CA 93406.

Dealer Inquiries Invited

☐ Rush me your 20-page color brochure on hot tubs, and your 64-page book on hot tubbing, via First Class Priority mail. I've enclosed $2 for postage and handling.

☐ Just send me your free brochure, via Third Class mail.

Name

Address

City State

Zip Phone

P.O. Box E, San Luis Obispo, CA 93406 (805) 544-9300 W-4

CALIFORNIA COOPERAGE

[1980]

Some people work to live.
Others live to work.

ModernMode
Manufacturers of fine wood office furniture.

P.O. Box 6667, 6425 San Leandro Street, Oakland, CA 94603, (415) 568-6650.
Showrooms in: New York, Chicago, Miami, San Francisco, Los Angeles, Dallas, Houston, Seattle.

S-3 Double pedestal desk and credenza in select cherry woods
Seating: 6 series guest chairs, 15 series executive chair

[1981]

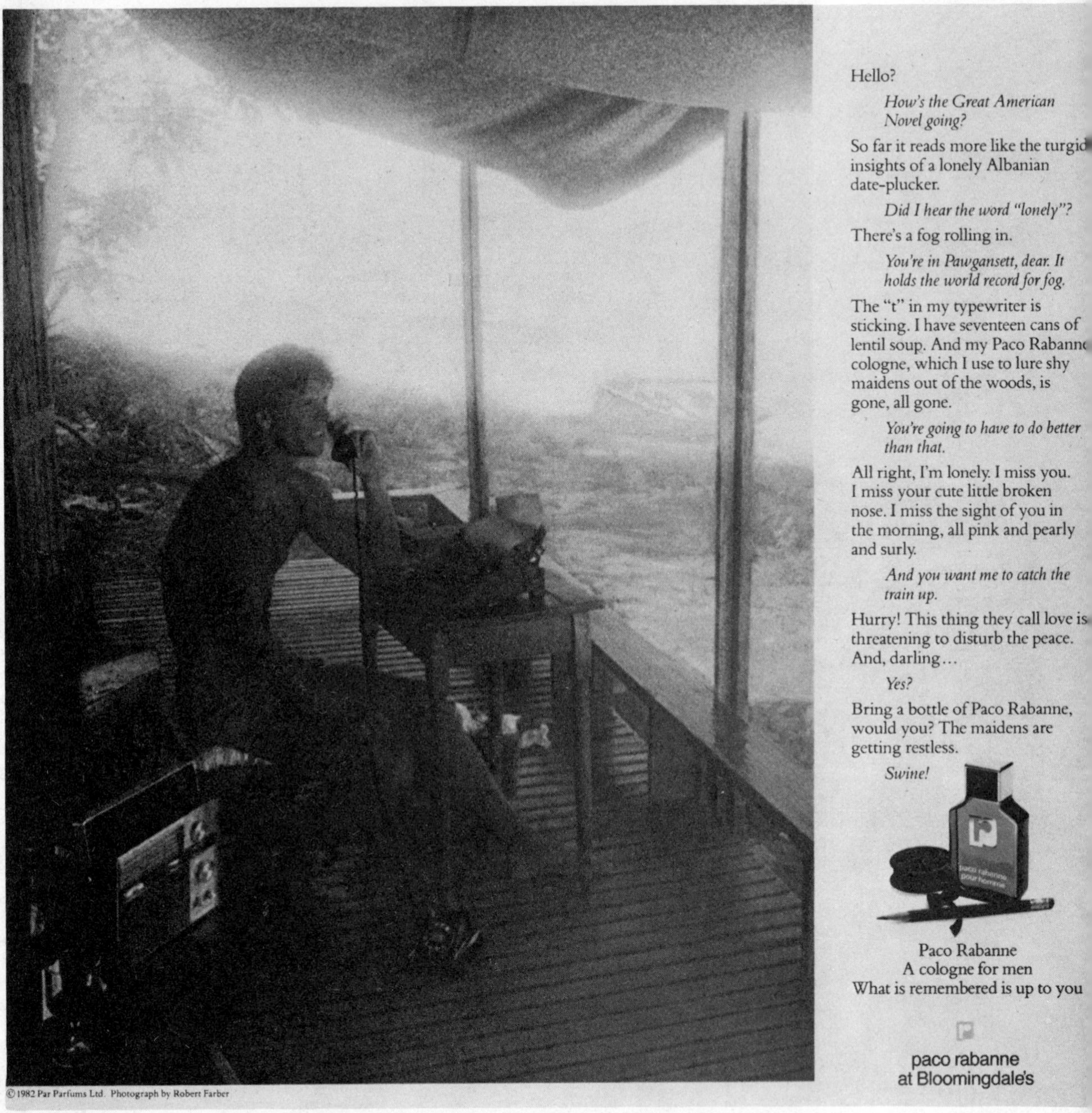

Hello?

How's the Great American Novel going?

So far it reads more like the turgid insights of a lonely Albanian date-plucker.

Did I hear the word "lonely"?

There's a fog rolling in.

You're in Pawgansett, dear. It holds the world record for fog.

The "t" in my typewriter is sticking. I have seventeen cans of lentil soup. And my Paco Rabanne cologne, which I use to lure shy maidens out of the woods, is gone, all gone.

You're going to have to do better than that.

All right, I'm lonely. I miss you. I miss your cute little broken nose. I miss the sight of you in the morning, all pink and pearly and surly.

And you want me to catch the train up.

Hurry! This thing they call love is threatening to disturb the peace. And, darling…

Yes?

Bring a bottle of Paco Rabanne, would you? The maidens are getting restless.

Swine!

Paco Rabanne
A cologne for men
What is remembered is up to you

paco rabanne
at Bloomingdale's

[1982]

Again She Orders—
"A Chicken Salad, Please"

FOR him she is wearing her new frock. For him she is trying to look her prettiest. If only she can impress him—make him like her—just a little.

Across the table he smiles at her, proud of her prettiness, glad to notice that others admire. And she smiles back, a bit timidly, a bit self-consciously.

What wonderful poise he has! What complete self-possession! If only *she* could be so thoroughly at ease.

She pats the folds of her new frock nervously, hoping that he will not notice how embarrassed she is, how uncomfortable. He doesn't—until the waiter comes to their table and stands, with pencil poised, to take the order.

"A chicken salad, please." She hears herself give the order as in a daze. She hears him repeat the order to the waiter, in a rather surprised tone. Why *had* she ordered that again! This was the third time she had ordered chicken salad while dining with him.

He would think she didn't know how to order a dinner. Well, did she? No. She didn't know how to pronounce those French words on the menu. And she didn't know how to use the table appointment as gracefully as she would have liked; found that she couldn't create conversation—and was actually tongue-tied; was conscious of little crudities which she just knew he must be noticing. She wasn't sure of herself, she didn't *know*. And she discovered, as we all do, that there is only one way to have complete poise and ease of manner, and that is to know definitely what to do and say on every occasion.

Are You Conscious of Your Crudities?

It is not, perhaps, so serious a fault to be unable to order a correct dinner. But it is just such little things as these that betray us—that reveal our crudities to others.

Are you sure of yourself? Do you know precisely what to do and say wherever you happen to be? Or are you always hesitant and ill at ease, never quite sure that you haven't blundered?

Every day in our contact with men and women we meet little unexpected problems of conduct. Unless we are prepared to meet them, it is inevitable that we suffer embarrassment and keen humiliation.

Etiquette is the armor that protects us from these embarrassments. It makes us aware instantly of the little crudities that are robbing us of our poise and ease. It tells us how to smooth away these crudities and achieve a manner of confidence and self-possession. It eliminates doubt and uncertainty, tells us exactly what we want to know.

There is an old proverb which says "Good manners make good mixers." We all know how true this is. No one likes to associate with a person who is self-conscious and embarrassed; whose crudities are obvious to all.

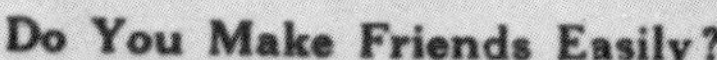

Do You Make Friends Easily?

By telling you exactly what is expected of you on all occasions, by giving you a wonderful new ease and dignity of manner, the Book of Etiquette will help make you more popular—a "better mixer." This famous two-volume set of books is the recognized social authority—is a silent social secretary in half a million homes.

Let us pretend that you have received an invitation. Would you know exactly how to acknowledge it? Would you know what sort of gift to send, what to write on the card that accompanies it? Perhaps it is an invitation to a formal wedding. Would you know what to wear? Would you know what to say to the host and hostess upon arrival?

If a Dinner Follows the Wedding—

Would you know exactly how to proceed to the dining room, when to seat yourself, how to create conversation, how to conduct yourself with ease and dignity?

Would you use a fork for your fruit salad, or a spoon? Would you cut your roll with a knife, or break it with your fingers? Would you take olives with a fork? How would you take celery—asparagus—radishes? Unless you are absolutely sure of yourself, you will be embarrassed. And embarrassment *cannot be concealed*.

Book of Etiquette Gives Lifelong Advice

Hundreds of thousands of men and women know and use the Book of Etiquette and find it increasingly helpful. Every time an occasion of importance arises—every time expert help, advice and suggestion is required—they find what they seek in the Book of Etiquette. It solves all problems, answers all questions, tells you exactly what to do, say, write and wear on every occasion.

If you want always to be sure of yourself, to have ease and poise, to avoid embarrassment and humiliation, send for the Book of Etiquette at once. Take advantage of the special bargain offer explained in the panel. Let the Book of Etiquette give you complete self-possession; let it banish the crudities that are perhaps making you self-conscious and uncomfortable when you should be thoroughly at ease.

Mail this coupon *now* while you are thinking of it. The Book of Etiquette will be sent to you in a plain carton with no identifying marks. Be among those who will take advantage of the special offer. Nelson Doubleday, Inc., Dept. 3911, Garden City, New York.

A Social Secretary for Life!

The Famous Book of Etiquette Nearly 500,000 Sold for $3.50

NOW ONLY $1.98

We have on our shelves at the present time several thousand sets of the Book of Etiquette in the regular $3.50 edition. To clear the shelves quickly and make room for new editions now being printed, Nelson Doubleday, Inc., makes this unusual offer. To the next few thousand people who order the Book of Etiquette, the special bargain price of $1.98 will be extended. In other words, if you act without delay you can secure the complete, two-volume set of the Book of Etiquette at practically *half* the usual cost.

Use the special coupon. It will bring the Book of Etiquette to you promptly, at the special bargain price.

Nelson Doubleday, Inc., Dept. 3911
Garden City, New York

I accept your special bargain offer. You may send me the famous two-volume Book of Etiquette, in a plain carton, for which I will give the postman only $1.98 (plus delivery charges) on arrival—instead of the regular price of $3.50. I am to have the privilege of returning the books within 5 days and having my money refunded if I am not delighted with them.

Name ....

Address ....

☐ Check this square if you want these books with the **beautiful full-leather binding** at $2.98 with same return privilege.

(Orders from outside the U. S. are payable $2.44 cash with order. Leather binding, outside U. S., $3.44 cash with order.)

ANXIETIES

[1921]

Don't walk when you can ride.

Presenting Another Lesson in How To Kill Yourself.

In an earlier lesson, we told you to eat, drink, be merry, and most important, to overdo it.

Now we are going to suggest that, once you've taken in all those calories, do nothing–absolutely nothing–to burn any of them off.

No matter how short the trip, don't walk when you can ride.

And if walking is out, jogging is unthinkable. Even though your doctor told you you're one of those people who could well invest in some exercise–to get your heart muscle pumping and your blood circulating.

True, you have heard it said that most children in America learn to walk by 16 months and stop walking by 16 years. But then, *you're* no child.

And, anyway, exercise is a big, fat bore.

Why Are America's Doctors Telling You This?

Well, for a long time we've been telling you how to stay alive and healthy. (In fact, about 70% of the annual budget of the American Medical Association goes to health education.) But many of you go do the opposite.

Now we figure we'll tell you how to kill yourselves. In the fervent hope that once again you'll do the exact opposite. If you do, there's every chance we'll be seeing less of you. Just for check-ups. And that's it.

Doing your bit to take care of yourself (such as exercising, but only if your doctor says it's OK) means your doctor can give everyone the best care possible. When *only* his care will do.

For a free booklet on the right kind and right amount of exercise for you, write: Box X, American Medical Association, 535 North Dearborn Street, Chicago, Illinois 60610.

America's Doctors of Medicine

(Our Best Patients Take Care of Themselves)

[1972]

How do you explain to a .400 hitter that his Dad's been transferred to a different city? What can you say that will ease the pain of leaving his teammates behind?

Sure, there'll be another team—maybe even better—in the city he's moving to. But for awhile at least, it won't be the same.

These are the heart-tugging moments that are so often a part of moving. And United Van Lines knows how important they are to you and your family.

That's why we do our very best to take the load off your mind . . . as well as your hands. We think you should have the time you need to spend with the people you care about most.

Your nearby United agent is waiting to help. Why not give him a call today? He's listed in the Yellow Pages.

SERVING 150 COUNTRIES WORLD-WIDE

United Van Lines I.C.C. No. MC 67234

[1980]

How to spell

By John Irving

International Paper asked John Irving, author of "The World According to Garp," "The Hotel New Hampshire," and "Setting Free the Bears," among other novels—and once a hopelessly bad speller himself—to teach you how to improve your spelling.

Let's begin with the bad news.

If you're a bad speller, you probably think you always will be. There are exceptions to every spelling rule, and the rules themselves are easy to forget. George Bernard Shaw demonstrated how ridiculous some spelling rules are. By following the rules, he said, we could spell fish this way: ghoti. The "f" as it sounds in enough, the "i" as it sounds in women, and the "sh" as it sounds in fiction.

With such rules to follow, no one should feel stupid for being a bad speller. But there are ways to improve. Start by acknowledging the mess that English spelling is in—but have sympathy: English spelling changed with foreign influences. Chaucer wrote "gesse," but "guess," imported earlier by the Norman invaders, finally replaced it. Most early printers in England came from Holland; they brought "ghost" and "gherkin" with them.

If you'd like to intimidate yourself—and remain a bad speller forever—just try to remember the 13 different ways the sound "sh" can be written:

shoe	suspicion
sugar	nauseous
ocean	conscious
issue	chaperone
nation	mansion
schist	fuchsia
pshaw	

Now the good news

The good news is that 90 percent of all writing consists of 1,000 basic words. There is, also, a method to most English spelling and a great number of how-to-spell books. Remarkably, all these books propose learning the same rules! Not surprisingly, most of these books are humorless.

Just keep this in mind: If you're familiar with the words you use, you'll probably spell them correctly—and you shouldn't be writing words you're unfamiliar with anyway. USE a word—out loud, and more than once—before you try writing it, and make sure (with a new word) that you know what it means before you use it. This means you'll have to look it up in a dictionary, where you'll not only learn what it means, but you'll see how it's spelled. Choose a dictionary you enjoy browsing in, and guard it as you would a diary. You wouldn't lend a diary, would you?

A tip on looking it up

Beside every word I look up in my dictionary, I make a mark.

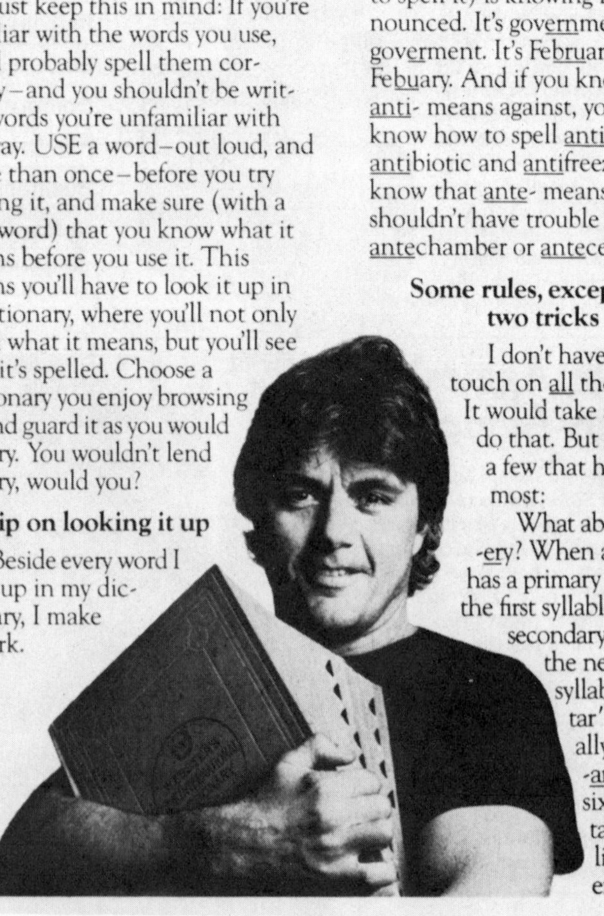

"Love your dictionary."

Beside every word I look up mor than once, I write a note to mys —about WHY I looked it up. I h looked up "strictly" 14 times sinc 1964. I prefer to spell it with a k as in "stricktly." I have looked u "ubiquitous" a dozen times. I car remember what it means.

Another good way to use yo dictionary: When you have to lo up a word, for any reason, learn— and learn to *spell*—a *new* word at the same time. It can be any use word on the same page as the w you looked up. Put the date besi this new word and see how quic or in what way, you forget it. Eve tually, you'll learn it.

Almost as important as kno ing what a word means (in orde to spell it) is knowing how it's p nounced. It's government, not goverment. It's February, not Febuary. And if you know that anti- means against, you should know how to spell antidote and antibiotic and antifreeze. If you know that ante- means before, y shouldn't have trouble spelling antechamber or antecedent.

Some rules, exceptions, a two tricks

I don't have room to touch on all the rules he It would take a book to do that. But I can sha a few that help me most:

What about -ary o -ery? When a word has a primary accent o the first syllable and a secondary accent o the next-to-last syllable (sec're tar'y), it usually ends in -ary. Only six important words like this end in -ery

cemetery monastery
millinery confectionery
distillery stationery
(as in paper)

Here's another easy rule. Only
ur words end in -efy. Most people
isspell them—with -ify, which is
ually correct. Just memorize these,
), and use -ify for all the rest.

stupefy putrefy
liquefy rarefy

As a former bad speller, I have
arned a few valuable tricks. Any
od how-to-spell book will teach
u more than these two, but these
o are my favorites. Of the
0,000 words in the English lan-
age, the most frequently mis-
elled is alright; just remember
at alright is all wrong. You
uldn't write alwrong, would you?
at's how you know you should
ite all right.

The other
ck is for the
ly *worst*
ellers. I mean
ose of you who
ell so badly that you
n't get close enough to
e right way to spell a word in
der to even FIND it in the dic-
nary. The word you're looking
r is there, of course, but you
n't find it the way you're trying
spell it. What to do is look up
synonym—another word that
eans the same thing. Chances
e good that you'll find the word
u're looking for under the defini-
n of the synonym.

Demon words and bugbears

Everyone has a few demon
rds—they never look right, even
en they're spelled correctly.
ree of my demons are medieval,
stasy, and rhythm. I have learned
hate these words, but I have not
arned to spell them; I have to
k them up every time.

And everyone has a spelling
le that's a bugbear—it's either too
fficult to learn or it's impossible
remember. My personal bugbear
nong the rules is the one govern-
g whether you add -able or -ible.
can teach it to you, but I can't
remember it myself.

You add -able to a full word: adapt, adaptable; work, workable. You add -able to words that end in e—just remember to drop the final e: love, lovable. But if the word ends in two e's, like agree, you keep them both: agreeable.

You add -ible if the base is not a full word that can stand on its own: credible, tangible, horrible, terrible. You add -ible if the root word ends in -ns: responsible. You add -ible if the root word ends in -miss: permissible. You add -ible if the root word ends in a soft c

"This is one of the longest English words in common use. But don't let the length of a word frighten you. There's a rule for how to spell this one, and you can learn it."

(but remember to drop the final e!): force, forcible.

Got that? I don't have it, and I was introduced to that rule in prep school; with that rule, I still learn one word at a time.

Poor President Jackson

You must remember that it is permissible for spelling to drive you crazy. Spelling had this effect on Andrew Jackson, who once blew his stack while trying to write a Presidential paper. "It's a damn poor mind that can think of only one way to spell a word!" the President cried.

When you have trouble, think of poor Andrew Jackson and know that you're not alone.

What's really important

And remember what's really important about good writing is not good spelling. If you spell badly but write well, you should hold your head up. As the poet T.S. Eliot recommended, "Write for as large and miscellaneous an audience as possible"—and don't be overly concerned if you can't spell "miscellaneous." Also remember that you can spell correctly and write well and still be misunderstood. Hold your head up about that, too.

As good old G.C. Lichtenberg said, "A book is a mirror: if an ass peers into it, you can't expect an apostle to look out"—whether you spell "apostle" correctly or not.

John Irving

Today, the printed word is more vital than ever. Now there is more need than ever for all of us to *read* better, *write* better, and *communicate* better.

International Paper offers this series in the hope that, even in a small way, we can help.

If you'd like to share this article with others—students, friends, employees, family—we'll gladly send you reprints. So far we've sent out over 9,000,000 in response to requests from people everywhere.

Please write: "Power of the Printed Word," International Paper Company, Dept. 12B, P.O. Box 954, Madison Square Station, New York, NY 10010. ©1982, INTERNATIONAL PAPER COMPANY

INTERNATIONAL PAPER COMPANY
We believe in the power of the printed word.

[1982]

When the moment becomes more...be sure.
You don't plan it. It just happens. And when it does, be sure you have Encare® with you. It's discreet, convenient, and easy to use.
Doctors recommend Encare more than any other contraceptive suppository. Pharmacists recommend it 3 times more often than any other contraceptive suppository. But, more importantly, women trust Encare so much, it's America's leading contraceptive suppository.
Encare contains a potent, yet safe, spermicide. And, once inserted, it gently foams and forms a powerful barrier against pregnancy.
So be sure to carry Encare. Because you never know what one wonderful moment will lead to.
© 1982 Eaton-Merz Laboratories, Inc.
If your doctor has advised you against pregnancy, discuss Encare with him or her before using it. Encare is approximately as effective as vaginal foam contraceptives in actual use, without the inconvenience of an applicator.
It is essential that you insert Encare at least ten minutes before intercourse. Some Encare users experience irritation in using the product.
For best protection, follow the package instructions carefully.
The information supplied in this advertisement is based on data available as of November 1981.
Encare
Encare®

[1982]

Sexual Confidence

You can tell when someone's got it the moment they enter a room—the ability to turn people on with just the look in their eyes. And, NOW you can have it too, with the amazing bestseller, SEXUAL CONFIDENCE.

You'll learn: **How to project Sexual Charisma** • Ways to attract new mates • **How to create laughter in the bedroom, and why this will *instantly* triple your capacity for sexual enjoyment** • Touching techniques that help you get intimate right away • **Why "letting-go" during lovemaking will make you a *better* lover** • How to take a "Sexual Holiday" • **Ten techniques for ending sexual anxiety** • How to change your "sexual image" (and why people will suddenly find you far more attractive than ever before) • **Stimulating your lovemate with sensual, new kissing techniques** • A Great Lover's Vocabulary • **And so much more!**

Yes, this revolutionary, 230 page, hardcover bestseller is *fully* guaranteed to make you a better lover. In fact, within just one hour it'll have you radiating Total Sexual Confidence...because from now on you'll know exactly what your lovers want *even before they ask!* Remember, SEXUAL CONFIDENCE has been acclaimed by doctors and therapists as a breakthrough in increasing sexual pleasure. So order today. SEXUAL CONFIDENCE costs far less than a new shirt or blouse, yet it'll bring so many more wonderful people into your love life!

(To order, see coupon at right)

Shy Person's Guide To A Successful Love Life!

A brilliant psychological writer explains how you can conquer shyness literally overnight.

by P. Woodland-Smith

I am a shy person myself.

Yet I could walk into a party tonight and within five minutes be talking, laughing, dancing . . . even making dates with the most attractive people in the room.

I could walk into a restaurant or pub and walk out an hour later with a new acquaintance, a new friend, even a new lover.

Yet the extraordinary thing about all this is that up until recently I was so pathetically shy I often didn't go out for months at a time.

At work I did fine. Socially I was a bust. My lack of dates even became sort of a joke among my friends. Some joke.

Then about six months ago a kindly relative lent me a copy of a book called THE SHY PERSON'S GUIDE TO A HAPPIER LOVE LIFE. The rest is history. In slightly more than two weeks I was dating several new people. And today . . . just six months later . . . I have so many friends and lovers I hardly ever spend an evening home alone. My social life has blossomed to the point that it's started interfering with my work life. Sometimes I actually have to take the phone off the hook to get some of my writing done.

If only I'd known that in two short weeks I'd be able to cure myself of something that had been making me miserable every day of my life. Why, lately I've been having a ball. And I'm absolutely convinced that anyone . . . no matter how incurably shy they *think* they are . . . can do the same.

What THE SHY PERSON'S GUIDE taught me is that there are more people ready to love you than you ever dreamed possible. At work, at school, on the street, in parks, museums, restaurants, *everywhere!* All you have to do is ask. And that's precisely why THE SHY PERSON'S GUIDE can be such a help.

THE SHY PERSON'S GUIDE will show you exactly how to unleash your natural, inborn talent for charming and attracting new people. Imagine how successful you'd be with others if you weren't afraid to speak what was in your heart. . to be as free and as open as you'd like.

Well, THE SHY PERSON'S GUIDE will show you scores of techniques for doing just that: For example, you will discover: **A simple, upfront way of letting someone know you're attracted to them without appearing weak or desperate . . .** a brilliant technique for making someone feel "special" when they're in your company . . . A completely reliable way of telling if someone likes you (you'll be amazed at how many potential lovemates you've been overlooking)...**A simple way to "trick" yourself into being looser and friendlier at parties . . .** How to get invited to more parties and what to do once you get there (not the same old things that make you angry and frustrated with yourself the moment you get home) . . . AND MUCH, MUCH MORE!

The Sooner You Attack Your Shyness, The Easier It Is To Cure

Don't kid yourself into thinking that *next time* you go to a party you'll be braver, more outgoing, That's the classic shy person's trick for *staying* shy. No, if you really want to get better, really want to know the joy of laughing, dancing, meeting people who want to be with you . . . then send for this mind-opening bestseller today.

Alright, maybe you're thinking, *but what if THE SHY PERSON'S GUIDE doesn't work for me.* No problem. Simply return the book and the publisher will send you a complete and immediate refund. No questions asked. Even if you secretly feel the book has done you some good.

But I'm so thoroughly convinced THE SHY PERSON'S GUIDE will change your life, so incredibly *bullish* about its shyness-conquering techniques, I hate to even bring up the guarantee. That's how sure I am this amazing book will work for you.

So send for THE SHY PERSON'S GUIDE TO A HAPPIER LOVE LIFE today. And start enjoying all the love and romance you've been dreaming about. It's out there alright. And it's so darn easy to find, it'd be a crying shame not to get your share.

Free Book

If you order our two bestsellers above we'll send you 100 BEST OPENING LINES, a $6.95 value, absolutely **FREE!** It's filled with 100 humorous, interesting and clever conversation openers, just right for capturing the attention of people you're attracted to. A perfect line for *every* situation—and best of all, it's **FREE!**

100 BEST OPENING LINES

FREE BOOK OFFER!

____ Please send me SEXUAL CONFIDENCE right away. I've enclosed $10.95 plus $2.00 shipping.

____ Please send me the SHY PERSON'S GUIDE TO A HAPPIER LOVE LIFE right away. I've enclosed $11.95 plus $2.00 shipping.

____ Please send me BOTH BOOKS for the low, low price of $22.90 plus $2.00 shipping. I understand I will receive as a bonus, 100 BEST OPENING LINES, a $6.95 value, absolutely FREE!

MasterCard and Visa accepted. Cardholders send card # and exp. date or call toll free anytime: **800-631-2560.** (In NJ call **201-569-8555**). Allow 1-3 weeks.

Name ______________________

Street ______________________

City, State, Zip ______________________

Mail check or money order to:
SYMPHONY PRESS, INC.
DEPT. NY
P.O. BOX 515
TENAFLY, N.J.
07670

All books fully guaranteed for 30 days.

[1983]

[1921]

AUTOMOBILES

Lemon.

This Volkswagen missed the boat.

The chrome strip on the glove compartment is blemished and must be replaced. Chances are you wouldn't have noticed it; Inspector Kurt Kroner did.

There are 3,389 men at our Wolfsburg factory with only one job: to inspect Volkswagens at each stage of production. (3000 Volkswagens are produced daily; there are more inspectors than cars.)

Every shock absorber is tested (spot checking won't do), every windshield is scanned. VWs have been rejected for surface scratches barely visible to the eye.

Final inspection is really something! VW inspectors run each car off the line onto the Funktionsprüfstand (car test stand), tote up 189 check points, gun ahead to the automatic brake stand, and say "no" to one VW out of fifty.

This preoccupation with detail means the VW lasts longer and requires less maintenance, by and large, than other cars. (It also means a used VW depreciates less than any other car.)

We pluck the lemons; you get the plums.

[1960]

Separates the men from the boys.

There are boy-type cars. And there are man-type cars. And Toronado is all man, all the way. Its styling is bold, brawny and massively male. Its handling is authoritative —thanks to the pulling power of front-wheel drive. Its ride is revolutionary, sure, unique—different from any other car.

Its engine is the strongest Rocket ever built: a bigger-than-ever, 455-cubic-inch V-8. Frankly, not everybody is cut out for a Toronado. But, then, who wants to be everybody?

Toronado.
Test drive the front-wheel-drive "youngmobile" from Oldsmobile.

GM
MARK OF EXCELLENCE

See special Toronado and 4-4-2 models! On display at the New York International Auto Show—now through April 7.

[1969]

Which man would you vote for?

Ah yes, what could be more dazzling than watching the candidates parade about, kissing babies and flashing winning smiles.

Consider the man in the top picture.

He promises to spend your tax dollars wisely.

But see how he spends his campaign dollars.

On a very fancy convertible.

Resplendent with genuine leather seats. A big 425-horsepower engine.

And a price tag that makes it one of the most expensive convertibles you can buy.

Now consider his opponent.

He promises to spend your tax dollars wisely.

But see how he spends his campaign dollars.

On a Volkswagen Convertible.

Resplendent with a hand-fitted top. A warranty and four free diagnostic check-ups that cover you for 24 months or 24,000 miles.*

And a price tag that makes it one of the least expensive convertibles you can buy.

So maybe this year you'll find a politician who'll do what few politicians ever do:

Keep his promises before he's elected.

*If an owner maintains and services his vehicle in accordance with the Volkswagen maintenance schedule any factory part found to be defective in material or workmanship within 24 months or 24,000 miles, whichever comes first (except normal wear and tear and service items), will be repaired or replaced by any U.S. or Canadian Volkswagen Dealer. And this will be done free of charge. See your Volkswagen dealer for details.

[1972]

Are you ready for an Alfa Romeo?

Sheila C.

"When I was 25 I was really the perfect wife, the perfect mother and the perfect homemaker.

"I drove a great big stationwagon.

"Well, I'm no longer 25 and I'm no longer anyone's wife—my kids are grown and have kids of their own and I have a career.

"And that stationwagon is just a rusted memory.

"You know what I did? I went out and bought myself an Alfa Romeo Spider.

"It's red and it's got a convertible top and sometimes when I pass those ladies in their huge stationwagons full of kids, and dogs, and groceries I wave—and say to myself, there but for the grace of my Alfa go I."

"When I was a young man I dreamed that one day I would own an Alfa Romeo.

Bill B.

"But then I got married and Jennifer arrived a year later; two years after that, Robert.

"My dream of owning an Alfa gave way to the reality of a mortgage, dentist's bills, and college tuition.

"But now Jennifer is married and has a Jennifer of her own, Robert Junior is through law school.

"And this 50 year old kid went out and bought himself an Alfa Romeo Spider.

"Do I love my Alfa as much as I thought I would? Well, It's a dream come true."

Ray R.

"I limped through college and graduate school with one crummy used car after another.

"But now that I've got a grown up job with grown up responsibility, I thought I'd treat myself to a brand new car.

"Well, at first, I thought the world had passed me by—all those cars were so boring!

"Then I discovered the Alfa Spider. First of all, it's a convertible! And most of all it's an Alfa Romeo.

"What a machine!

"Today when I leave the office after all those meetings, my hair cut short, necktie in place, I'll jump into my very own Alfa Romeo Spider.

"You know, all that college was worth it."

The Alfa Romeo Spider Veloce: $13,995 1980 manufacturer's suggested retail price POE. Inland transportation, dealer preparation, local taxes, and optional equipment not included. For the name of your nearest Alfa Romeo Dealer, call us anytime, toll free at 800-447-4700; in Illinois call 800-322-4400.

Alfa Romeo

[1980]

A CAR FOR THE LEFT SIDE OF YOUR BRAIN.

A CAR FOR THE RIGHT SIDE OF YOUR BRAIN.

The left side of your brain, recent investigations tell us, is the logical side.

It figures out that 1+1=2. And, in a few cases, that $E=mc^2$

On a more mundane level, it chooses the socks you wear, the cereal you eat, and the car you drive. All by means of rigorous Aristotelian logic.

However, and a big however it is, for real satisfaction, you must achieve harmony with the other side of your brain.

The right side, the poetic side, that says, "Yeah, Car X has a reputation for lasting a long time but it's so dull, who'd want to drive it that long anyway?"

The Saab Turbo looked at from all sides.

To the left side of your brain, Saab turbocharging is a technological feat that retains good gas mileage while also increasing performance.

To the right side of your brain, Saab turbocharging is what makes a Saab go like a bat out of hell.

The left side sees the safety in high performance. (Passing on a two-lane highway. Entering a freeway in the midst of high-speed traffic.)

The right side lives only for the thrills.

The left side considers that *Road & Track* magazine just named Saab "The Sports Sedan for the Eighties." By unanimous choice of its editors.

The right side eschews informed endorsements by editors who have spent a lifetime comparing cars. The right side doesn't know much about cars, but knows what it likes.

The left side scans this chart.

Wheelbase	*99.1 inches*
Length	*187.6 inches*
Width	*66.5 inches*
Height	*55.9 inches*
Fuel-tank capacity	*16.6 gallons*
EPA City	*19 mpg**
EPA Highway	*31 mpg**

The right side looks at the picture on the right.

The left side compares a Saab's comfort with that of a Mercedes. Its performance with that of a BMW. Its braking with that of an Audi.

The right side looks at the picture.

The left side looks ahead to the winter when a Saab's front-wheel drive will keep a Saab in front of traffic.

The right side looks at the picture.

The left side also considers the other seasons of the year when a Saab's front-wheel drive gives it the cornering ability of a sports car.

The right side looks again at the picture.

Getting what you need vs. getting what you want.

Needs are boring; desires are what make life worth living.

The left side of your brain is your mother telling you that a Saab is good for you. "Eat your vegetables." (In today's world, you need a car engineered like a Saab.) "Put on your raincoat." (The Saab is economical. Look at the price-value relationship.) "Do your homework." (The passive safety of the construction. The active safety of the handling.)

*1982 SAAB PRICE** LIST*

900 3-Door	*5-Speed*	*$10,400*
	Automatic	*10,750*
900 4-Door	*5-Speed*	*$10,700*
	Automatic	*11,050*
900S 3-Door	*5-Speed*	*$12,100*
	Automatic	*12,450*
900S 4-Door	*5-Speed*	*$12,700*
	Automatic	*13,050*
900 Turbo 3-Door	*5-Speed*	*$15,600*
	Automatic	*15,950*
900 Turbo 4-Door	*5-Speed*	*$16,260*
	Automatic	*16,610*

All turbo models include a Sony XR70, 4-Speaker Stereo Sound System as standard equipment. The stereo can be, of course, perfectly balanced: left and right.

The right side of your brain guides your foot to the clutch, your hand to the gears, and listens for the "zzzooommm."

Together, they see the 1982 Saab Turbo as the responsible car the times demand you get. And the performance car you've always, deep down, wanted with half your mind.

**Saab 900 Turbo. Remember, use estimated mpg for comparison only. Mileage varies with speed, trip length, and weather. Actual highway mileage will probably be less. **Manufacturer's suggested retail price. Not including taxes, license, freight, dealer charges or options desired by either side of your brain.*

THE NEW YORK TIMES MAGAZINE / JANUARY 24, 1982

[1982]

ERNEST HEMINGWAY, who has been called the greatest living American writer, is also internationally famous as a deep-sea fisherman. Since publication of *The Sun Also Rises* in 1926, his novels and short stories have enriched the literature of the English language consistently, year after year. His newest book is *The Old Man and the Sea.*

EATING AND DRINKING

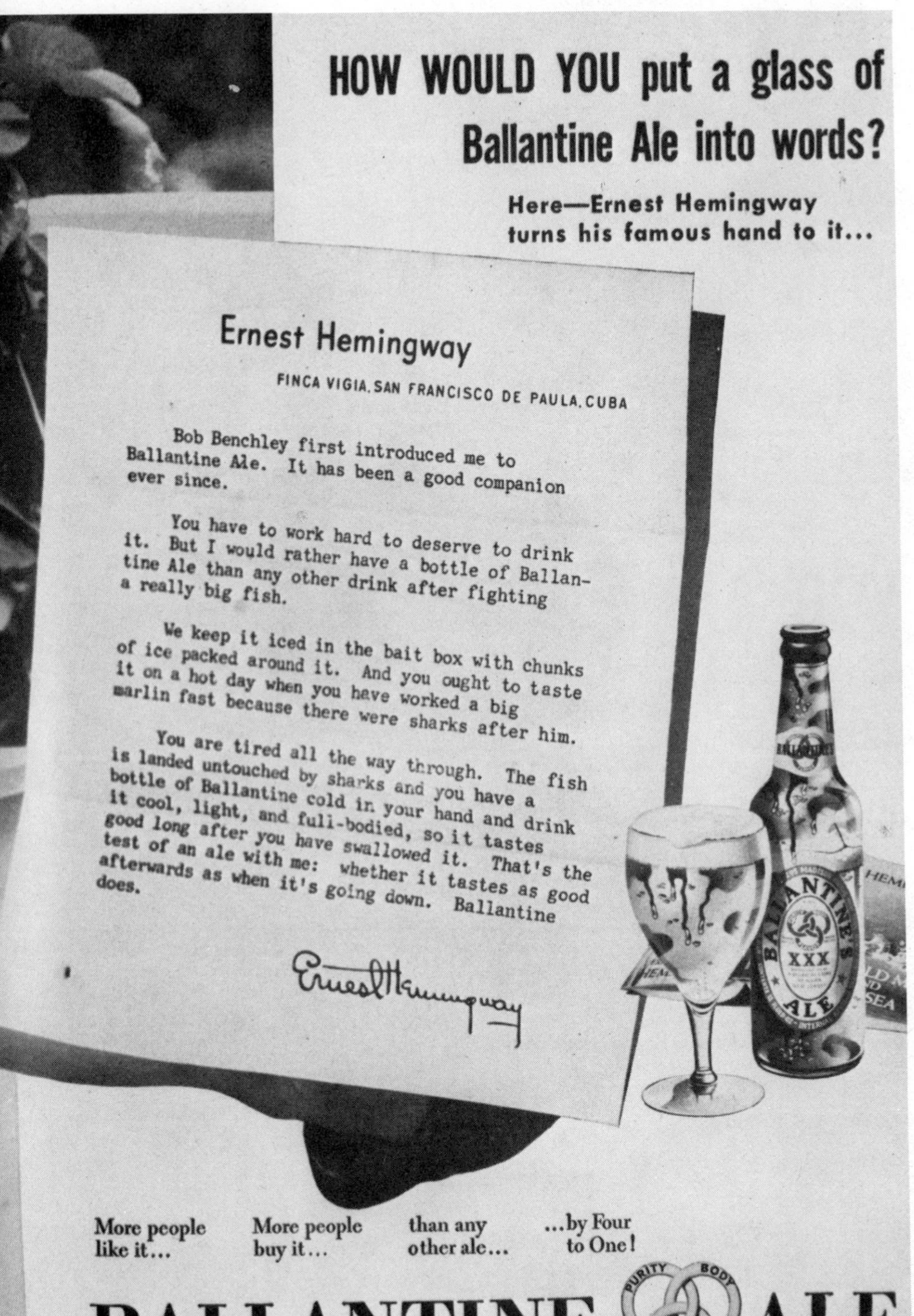
HOW WOULD YOU put a glass of Ballantine Ale into words?
Here—Ernest Hemingway turns his famous hand to it...
Ernest Hemingway
FINCA VIGIA, SAN FRANCISCO DE PAULA, CUBA
Bob Benchley first introduced me to Ballantine Ale. It has been a good companion ever since.
You have to work hard to deserve to drink it. But I would rather have a bottle of Ballantine Ale than any other drink after fighting a really big fish.
We keep it iced in the bait box with chunks of ice packed around it. And you ought to taste it on a hot day when you have worked a big marlin fast because there were sharks after him.
You are tired all the way through. The fish is landed untouched by sharks and you have a bottle of Ballantine cold in your hand and drink it cool, light, and full-bodied, so it tastes good long after you have swallowed it. That's the test of an ale with me: whether it tastes as good afterwards as when it's going down. Ballantine does.
Ernest Hemingway
More people like it...
More people buy it...
than any other ale...
...by Four to One!
BALLANTINE ALE
PURITY BODY FLAVOR
Since 1840
P. Ballantine & Sons, Newar

[1952]

"You're some tomato. California's written all over you.
We could make beautiful Bloody Marys together.
I'm different from those other fellows."

"I like you, Wolfschmidt.
You've got taste."

Wolfschmidt in a Bloody Mary is a tomato in triumph. Wolfschmidt has the touch of taste that marks genuine old world vodka. It heightens, accents, brings out the best in every drink.

"You sweet California doll. I appreciate you. I've got taste.
I'll bring out your inner orange. I'll make you famous. Roll over here and kiss me."

"Who was that tomato
I saw you with last week?"

Wolfschmidt in a Screwdriver is an orange in ecstasy. Wolfschmidt has the touch of taste that marks genuine old world vodka. It heightens, accents, brings out the best in every drink.

[1961]

Why husbands leave home:

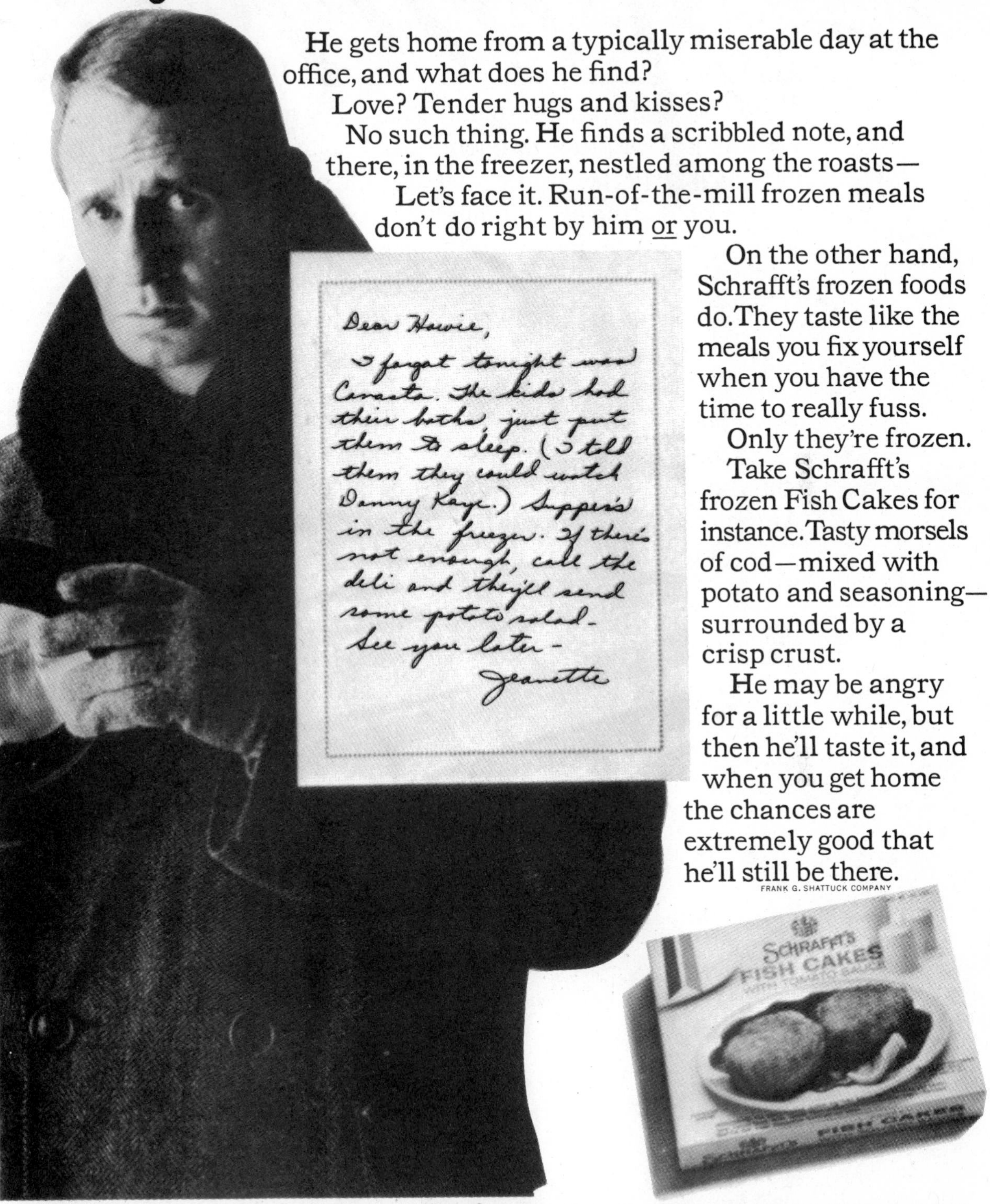

He gets home from a typically miserable day at the office, and what does he find?

Love? Tender hugs and kisses?

No such thing. He finds a scribbled note, and there, in the freezer, nestled among the roasts—

Let's face it. Run-of-the-mill frozen meals don't do right by him or you.

On the other hand, Schrafft's frozen foods do. They taste like the meals you fix yourself when you have the time to really fuss.

Only they're frozen.

Take Schrafft's frozen Fish Cakes for instance. Tasty morsels of cod—mixed with potato and seasoning—surrounded by a crisp crust.

He may be angry for a little while, but then he'll taste it, and when you get home the chances are extremely good that he'll still be there.

FRANK G. SHATTUCK COMPANY

HURRY-UP MEALS YOU DON'T HAVE TO MAKE EXCUSES FOR.

SCHRAFFT'S

[1966]

America

If you'll stop and think for just a moment, you'll find we have more of the good things in this country than anywhere else in the world.

Think of this land. From the surf at Big Sur to a Florida sunrise. And all the places in between.

The Grand Canyon... the wheat fields of Kansas... Autumn in New Hampshire...

You could go on forever. But America is more than a place of much beauty. It's a place for good times.

It's Saturday night.

It's a trip down a dirt road in a beat up old jalopy.

It's your team winning. It's a late night movie you could enjoy a thousand times.

And, yes, when you're thirsty, it's the taste of ice- cold Coca-Cola. It's the real thing.

In fact, all of the good things in this country are real. They're all around you, plainly visible. We point to many of them in our advertising. But you can discover many, many more without ever seeing a single commercial for Coke.

So have a bottle of Coke... and start looking up.

The Coca-Cola Company

Coca-Cola and Coke are registered trade-marks which identify the same product of The Coca-Cola Company

[1975]

With my cooking, the army that travels on its stomach is facing a pretty bumpy road.

As far as being a rookie cook goes, I was as green as the guys who ate what I cooked.

They said my hamburgers tasted like hockey pucks.

They said my chipped beef stuck to their ribs, permanently.

And what they said about my sloppy joes could have gotten them all arrested.

I finally had to face up to it. No one could stomach my cooking. And my brilliant military career would have gone down the drain then and there if it wasn't for McCormick/Schilling.

They're the experts on spice and flavor. And they make all kinds of sauces, seasonings and gravies that can really make things taste good. Even the stuff I cook.

So, I tried their sloppy joes mix. All I had to do was brown 1,000 pounds of ground beef, mix in the McCormick/Schilling seasoning; add tomato paste and 150 gallons of water.

And in no time, I had enough to feed an army.

It was easy. And more important, it was good.

Guys were standing in line for seconds. (Before, they never stuck around for firsts).

Matter of fact, they stopped griping about my cooking long enough for me to finally get my stripes.

And I owe it all to McCormick/Schilling.

I guess you could say that when it comes to cooking, they turned me into a seasoned veteran.

My sloppy joes recipe for 6,000:

Brown 1,000 lbs. of ground beef. Mix in 1,000 packages of McCormick/Schilling Sloppy Joes Mix and blend thoroughly. Stir in 1,000 6-ounce cans of tomato paste and 1,250 cups of water. Bring to a boil. Then reduce heat and simmer 10 minutes, stirring occasionally. Spoon over hamburger buns. Makes 6,000 ½-cup servings. (To get 6 servings, divide by 1,000).

McCormick/Schilling flavor makes all the difference in the world.

McCormick/Schilling

[1976]

McDonald's®

DO YOUR DINNERTIMIN'™ AT McDONALD'S.

When you're looking for a different place to have dinner, check out McDonald's. You don't have to get dressed up, there's no tipping and the kids love it.

You can relax and get down with good food that won't keep you waitin'.

Dinnertimin' or anytimin', going out is easy at McDonald's.

WE DO IT ALL FOR YOU ™

[1976]

Geraldine Chaplin talks about her 'first time.'

CHAPLIN: To be perfectly blunt, it was a bit disappointing. Oh, it was good... but not at all what I had expected. In fact, I couldn't for the life of me understand why all my friends thought it was such a big deal.

INTERVIEWER: Miss Chaplin, you'd be surprised how many people feel that way. So, don't be embarrassed ... just tell me what happened.

CHAPLIN: It all started at a party in Madrid. I felt a tap on my shoulder and when I turned around there stood this wonderfully attractive young man.

"Campari?" he asked.

"No," I said, "Geraldine."

He laughed and ordered a Campari and soda for me and a Campari and orange juice for himself.

INTERVIEWER: He certainly was a very assertive young man.

CHAPLIN: Yes. You see he turned out to be a cinematographer from Chile and they're like that, you know.

INTERVIEWER: Well? What was it like?

CHAPLIN: A truly bittersweet experience.

INTERVIEWER: Could you be more specific?

CHAPLIN: Yes...it was like eating a mango.

INTERVIEWER: I beg your pardon???

CHAPLIN: Well, I wasn't crazy about them the first time, either. Yet I was so intrigued by their uniqueness, I tried again ... then I was a believer.

INTERVIEWER: So now you like it?

CHAPLIN: Love it. There are so many different ways to enjoy it. Once I even tried it on the rocks. But I wouldn't recommend that for beginners.

INTERVIEWER: That's great. Tell me, whatever happened to that handsome young Chilean?

CHAPLIN: We're still very close. But I'll let you in on a secret. That was his first time, too. And to this day, he still hasn't acquired a taste for it.

INTERVIEWER: That's a shame.

CHAPLIN: Yes, it is ... I guess it's because he's never had it a second time.

CAMPARI. THE FIRST TIME IS NEVER THE BEST.

[1981]

You told her you have
your own place.
Now you have to tell your roommates.
LÖWENBRÄU
You've been trying to get to know her better since the beginning of the term. And when she mentioned how hard it is to study in the dorm, you said, "My place is nice and quiet. Come on over and study with me."
Your roommates weren't very happy about it. But after a little persuading they decided the double feature at the Bijou might be worth seeing.
They're pretty special friends. And they deserve a special "Thanks." So, tonight, let it be Löwenbräu.
Löwenbräu. Here's to good friends.
© 1981 Beer brewed in U.S.A. by Miller Brewing Company, Milwaukee, Wisconsin

[1981]

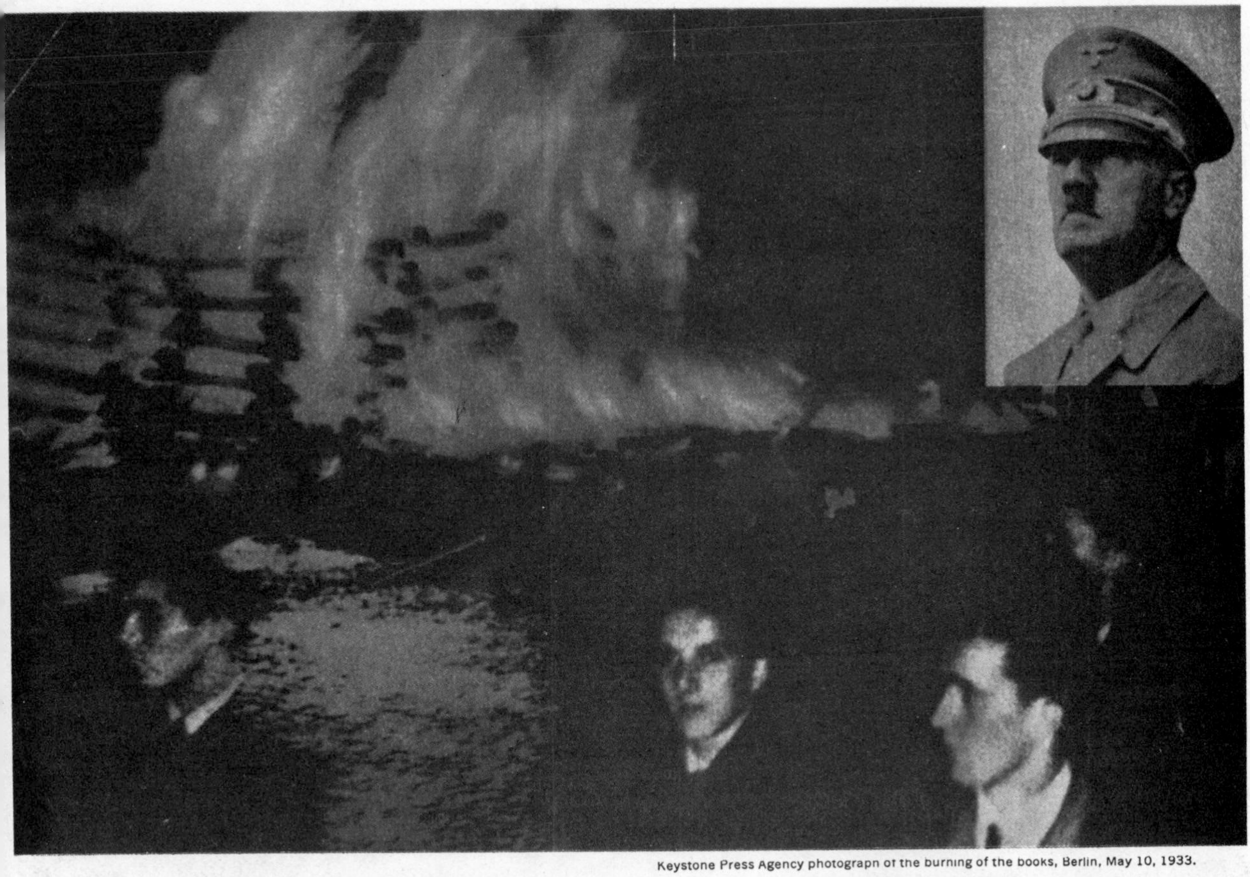

Keystone Press Agency photograph of the burning of the books, Berlin, May 10, 1933.

These are the books that Hitler burned

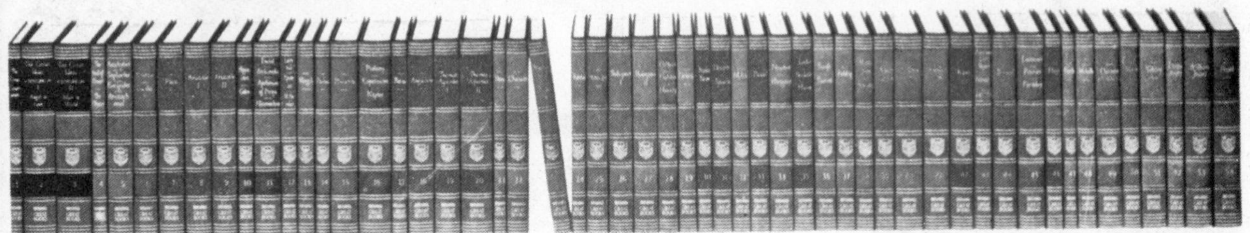

He had to.

These books riddle superstition and viciousness with *truth.*

These thoughts and theories built our democracies and broke the chains of bondage.

These words are more powerful than any Gestapo or thought police.

Here, in 54 superbly bound volumes, you'll find the wisdom of Shakespeare, Plato, Thomas Aquinas, Adam Smith, Tolstoy, Darwin and Freud. The truths of Homer, Augustine and many, many more.

No power-hungry madman could stand for long against these books. That's why Hitler burned them.

Now these Great Books can all be yours, 443 works by 74 immortal authors. Yours, in your own home. To enlighten you, console you, to help you guide your children.

The amazing Syntopicon

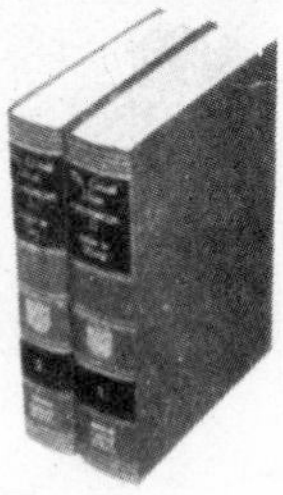

With Great Books you receive the two-volume Syntopicon, an *idea* index that took 8 years and over a million dollars to build. With the Syntopicon, you can trace every thought in the Great Books as easily as you look up words in your dictionary.

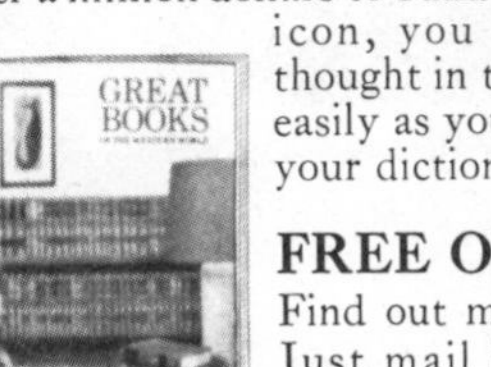

FREE OFFER...act now

Find out more about Great Books. It's free. Just mail in the attached post card for a profusely illustrated 16-page booklet—*free.* Do it today, no postage required. GREAT BOOKS, Dept. 142-J, 425 No. Michigan, Chicago, Illinois 60611.

GREAT BOOKS

54 superb volumes • 74 immortal authors • 443 works

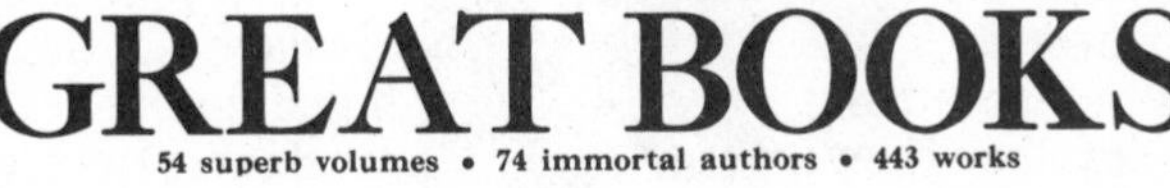

[1966]

MEDIA

"The soaps are like Big Macs...a lot of people who won't admit it eat them up."

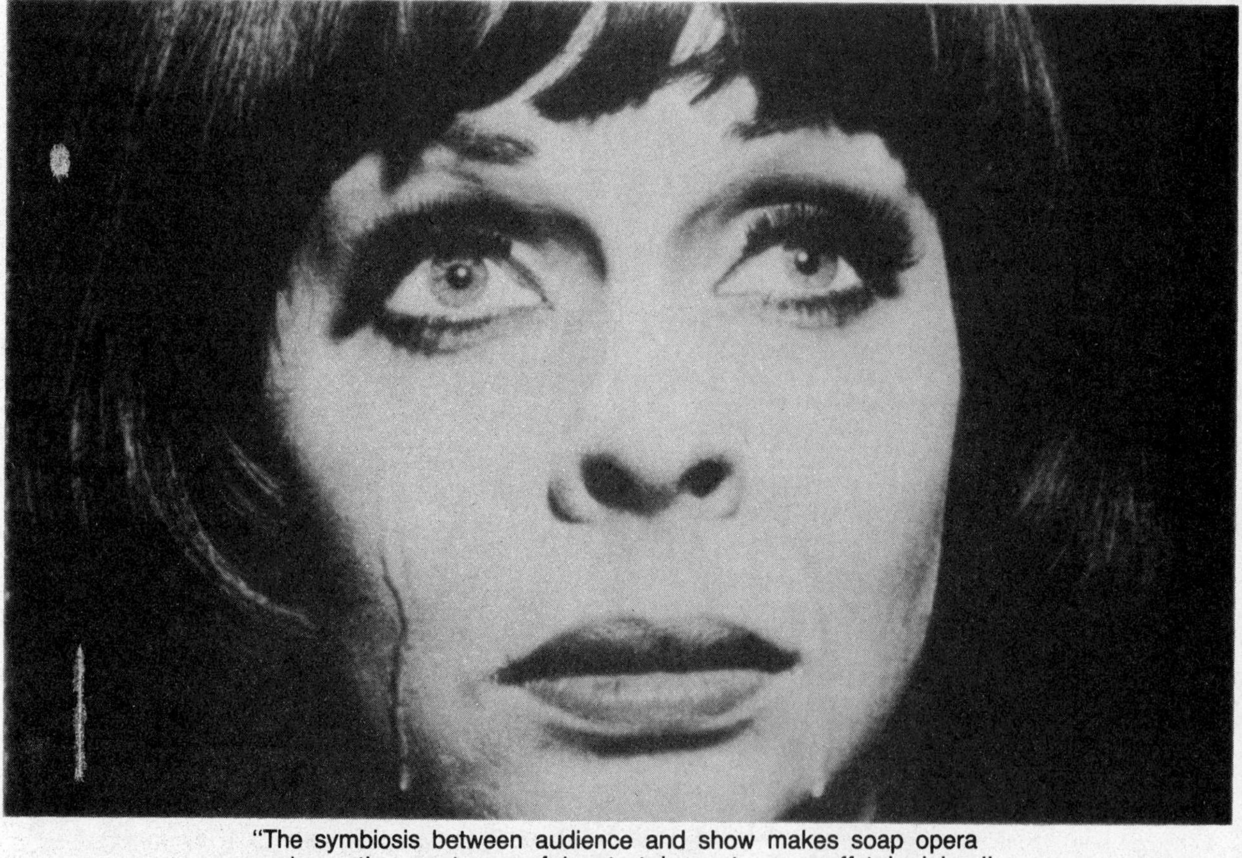

"The symbiosis between audience and show makes soap opera unique, the most powerful entertainment on or off television."

Academic amnesia, vicarious VD, hypothetical hysterectomies: the world of TV soap opera. But TIME readers are among the least avid watchers of daytime television. Why was TIME inspired to devote a cover story to TV soap opera?

Because TIME readers are also insatiably curious. TIME probed the hypnotic appeal

of the soaps, found a whole subculture, discovered the iron hand behind the wet handkerchief. And in so doing, TIME demonstrates once again the rewards of analyzing seriously what seems on the surface to be egregious frivolity.

You know what TIME does. And reading it every week reminds you how well.

The Weekly Newsmagazine

[1976]

Scoop McClain?
He doesn't work here anymore.

You remember Scoop McClain—sarcastic and swaggering, a tough guy with a press card in his hat who liked pretty girls and whiskey and telling the world to go to hell. He was something else, Scoop was: a star reporter, streetwise and cynical, but with a heart of gold. He never let the facts get in the way of a good story.

Scoop graduated from the school of hard knocks. He typed with one finger, got news tips from bookies and barmaids and yelled "STOP THE PRESS!" with every fresh exposé. Murder was his specialty, but he fought City Hall, too, and saved widows from eviction. He never forgot a friend and he never told a lie—except to get a story. So here's to Scoop McClain; they don't make 'em like that anymore.

And, of course, they never did. That movie stereotype of American newspaper reporters is part of our folklore; it never had much to do with reality. But there's no question that journalism and the people who practice it have changed over the years.

Today, our reporters and editors come from universities with degrees in economics and sociology, law and public administration, literature and even medicine. Nobody specializes in murder anymore; it's labor and international affairs, politics and education, science and religion. Our exposés take more than a couple of phone calls: months of work by teams of investigators who are more likely to ask help from a computer than a bookie. Our star reporters are streetwise still—but lots smarter than Scoop ever was. They have to be.

Some of the best reporters in the country work for Knight-Ridder newspapers. We're proud of them.

Philadelphia Inquirer • Philadelphia Daily News
Detroit Free Press • Miami Herald
St. Paul Dispatch • St. Paul Pioneer Press
Charlotte Observer • Charlotte News
San Jose Mercury • San Jose News • Wichita Eagle
Wichita Beacon • Akron Beacon Journal
Long Beach Press-Telegram • Long Beach Independent
Lexington Herald • Lexington Leader
Gary Post-Tribune • Duluth News-Tribune
Duluth Herald • Macon Telegraph • Macon News
Columbus Enquirer • Columbus Ledger
Pasadena Star-News • Tallahassee Democrat
Grand Forks Herald • Journal of Commerce
Bradenton Herald • Boulder Daily Camera
Aberdeen American News • Boca Raton News

Knight-Ridder Newspapers

[1977]

Why teenage girls stick with their mouthwash longer than their boyfriends.

Love is different from mouthwash.

Consider: Not too many women aged 20-34 are still going steady with their first boyfriends.

Yet more than one out of every three of them still use the same mouthwash they decided to use as a teenager.

That was one of the findings of a recent major Yankelovich study. Which showed that, besides

mouthwash, girls are about equally loyal to their mascara, packaged goods, and even panty hose.

All this isn't to disparage boyfriends. But it does tend to prove what common sense and we have been saying for some time:

Long before a teenage girl is ready to settle down with the right boy, she is ready to settle down with the right product.

And the place where she does her settling down is Seventeen magazine. Where, each month, over 6,400,000 teenage girls begin lasting relationships.

If you'd like to know more about this new research, please call our Advertising Director, Bob Bunge, at (212) 759-8100.

He'll show you that, when the right one comes along, a girl knows it.

Come to think of it, maybe love isn't very different from mouthwash at all.

®seventeen

Today, she's really 18-34.

[1980]

While you're racing after success, retirement's the last thing on your mind.

You're having too much fun to think about quitting.

But someday maybe you'll be ready to kick your feet up and relax on a couple hundred sweet green acres.

You want to be able to take your pick of pastures or castles or tropical isles. And that takes drive.

The nice thing is, you don't have to hide your ambition anymore.

"If you've got it, go get it." That's what society is telling you these days.

If *you're* out there on the fast track, your business reading starts with FORTUNE.

It's the horse's mouth. The authority. The one you rely on when you've just *got* to be right.

It's where you get a vital couple of steps on the competition. In management, technology, the economy, *everything*.

FORTUNE's how to make it. And keep it.

And it's where to put your advertising if you want to succeed with the fast-track people.

FORTUNE
How to succeed.

[1982]

SOME PEOPLE ARE SO OPPOSED TO MURDER THEY'LL KILL ANYONE WHO COMMITS IT.

"DO YOU WANT THEM DEAD?"

There are now thirty-seven states that stand united behind the death sentence. And a total of five methods by which it's carried out. The electric chair, cyanide gas, hanging, lethal injection and firing squad.

But no matter which method is used, the result is the same. The taking of a human life.

This week, in an Eyewitness News Special Report, Roger Grimsby takes a good hard look at capital punishment.

You'll meet murderers on death row who are waiting to die. And families of their victims. Who can't wait to see them dead.

Watch "Do You Want Them Dead?" Then decide for yourself if the death penalty should become a way of life.

EYEWITNESS NEWS 6PM 7

[1982]

Can a girl be too busy? I'm taking seventeen units at Princeton, pushing on with my career during vacations and school breaks, study singing and dancing when I can, try never to lose track of my five closest chums, steal the time for Michael Jackson and Thomas Hardy, work for an anti-drug program for kids and, oh yes, I hang out with three horses, three cats, two birds and my dog Jack. My favorite magazine says "too busy" just means you don't want to miss anything...don't stop 'til you're gasping. I love that magazine. I guess you could say I'm That COSMOPOLITAN Girl.
© 1984, The Hearst Corporation.
Photographed by Francesco Scavullo
One of my most satisfying relationships is with a magazine.
COSMOPOLITAN®
A PUBLICATION OF THE HEARST CORPORATION

[1984]

Is this how you see our readers?

Well, look again. Our readers have evolved and so have we.

Sure our readers still wear blue collar shirts, only now they have alligators on them. They also eat more mousse than they hunt and drink as many screwdrivers as they use.

They look to MI for detailed information on how to manage their two greatest investments—their home and their car.

MI is the only magazine devoted exclusively to this market.

You won't find stories about fantasy technology or military hardware between our covers.

Last year 95% of our readers did a home improvement project. Almost 90% do their own auto maintenance. In fact, they're so involved with their home and car, they insist on being involved in every buying decision.

From power tools and tires to wall coverings and microwave ovens.

So now that you see our readers in a new light, put Mechanix Illustrated on your ad schedule. When your clients see the results they'll think you've reinvented the wheel.

For more information call Ernie Renzulli, Ad Director (212) 719-6570.

5 million home and car fanatics swear by MI

[1984]

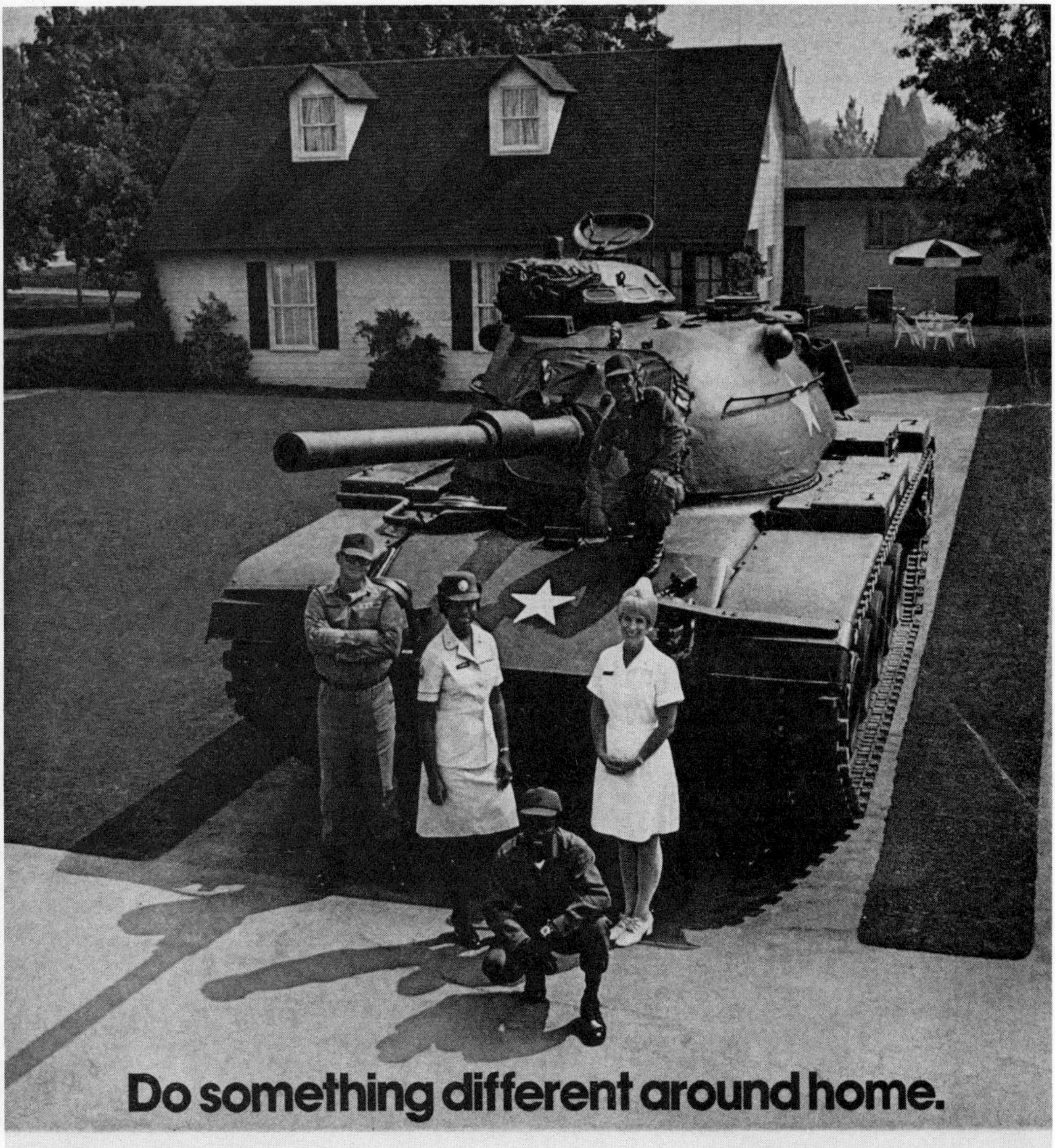

Do something different around home.

You won't have 50 tons of steel parked in your driveway. But it won't be farther away than your local Army National Guard Armory. And that's important. Because you never know when you're going to need it in a hurry.

Last year, for instance, Guard tanks were called out to make war on winter. Hauling 18-wheelers out of snow drifts. Keeping roads open during the blizzards.

And like your tank crews, Guardsmen everywhere use the skills they learn in the Guard to help people in trouble.

What about you? There are a lot of ways you can help your friends and neighbors. And help yourself while you're at it. The National Guard can teach you valuable career skills. Anything from communications to paramedicine to handling heavy equipment.

Skills that could very well make the difference should disaster strike your town.

It's good work. And the pay's good, too.

So do something that'll make a difference. See your nearest Army Guard recruiter. Or call us, toll free, 800-638-7600. (In Alaska, Hawaii, Puerto Rico or the Virgin Islands, consult your white pages). In Maryland call 301-728-3388.

Help Somebody. Including Yourself.

[1978]

INSTITUTIONAL AND CORPORATE ADVERTISING

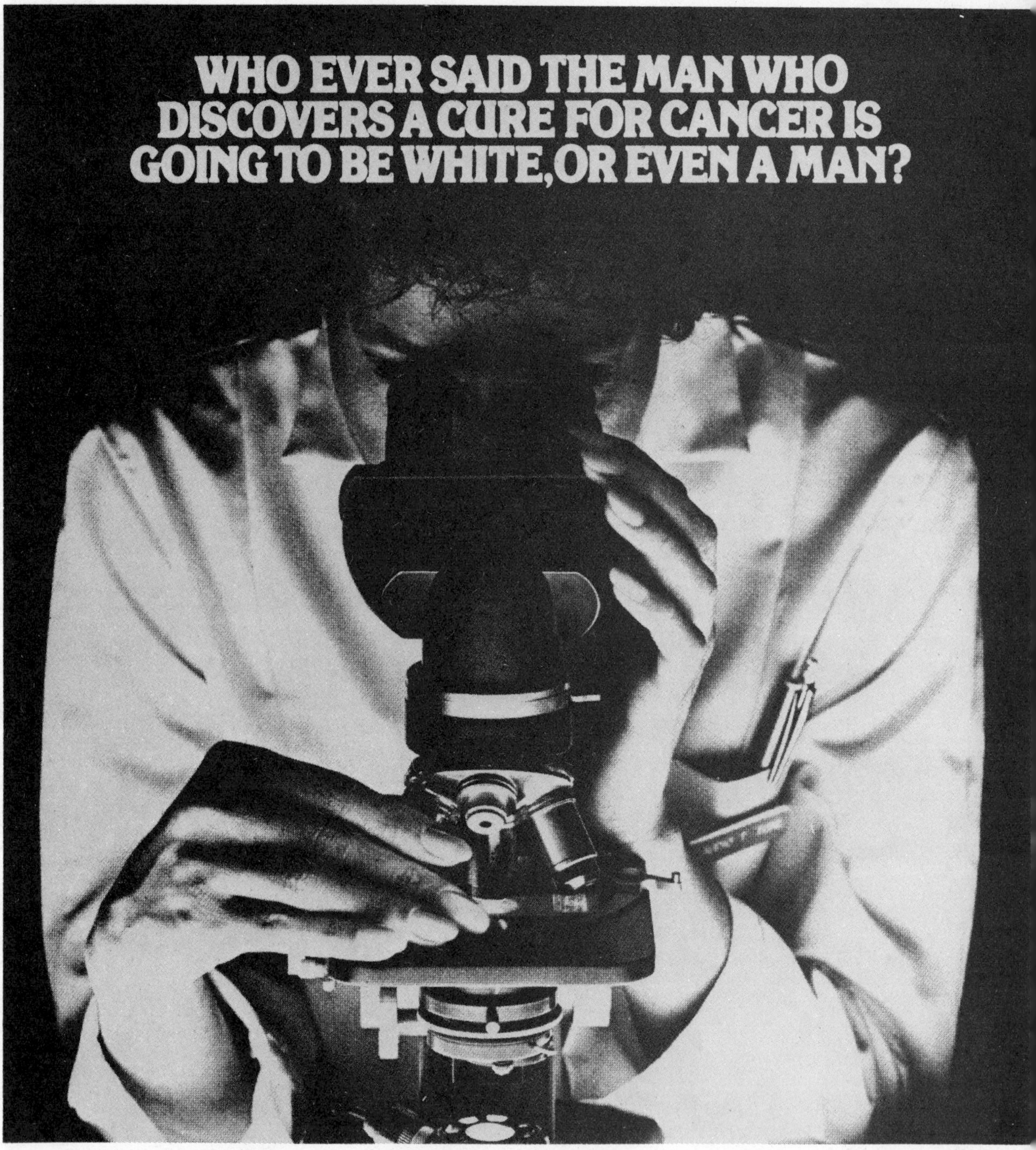

WHO EVER SAID THE MAN WHO DISCOVERS A CURE FOR CANCER IS GOING TO BE WHITE, OR EVEN A MAN?

This black woman could be America's hope...she's a United Negro College Fund graduate who could dedicate her life to finding a cure for cancer. A cure that could save thousands of lives each year. And fill every black person's heart with pride. That's why it's so important that blacks support the United Negro College Fund, 100 percent.

If she discovered the cure, in a sense, it would also be your discovery because the world would recognize it as a major black contribution.

When you give to the United Negro College Fund, you help support 41 private, predominantly black, four-year colleges and universities. Colleges that give us thousands of black graduates each year, who go on to become doctors, lawyers, accountants, engineers and scientists.

So support black education. Because black contributions help make black contributions. Send your check to the United Negro College Fund, Box Q, 500 East 62nd St., New York, N.Y. 10021. We're not asking for a handout, just a hand.

GIVE TO THE UNITED NEGRO COLLEGE FUND.

A mind is a terrible thing to waste.

PHOTOGRAPHER: PACCIONE

A Public Service of This Magazine & The Advertising Council

[1979]

A Fable For Now:

Why Elephants Can't Live on Peanuts

The Elephant is a remarkable animal...huge, yet able to move quickly...stronger than any person, yet willing to work hard if properly treated.

One day, an Elephant was ambling through the forest. To her surprise, she found her path to the water hole blocked by a huge pile of sticks, vines, and brambles.

"Hello?" she called out over the barricade. "What gives?"

From behind the pile popped the Monkey. "Buzz off, snake-snoot," the Monkey shouted. "It's an outrage to little folk how much you take in, so the rest of us animals have seized the water hole and the food supply. You're gross, and we're revolting!"

"You certainly give that appearance," the Elephant noted quietly. "What's eating you?"

"It's *you* that's doing too much eating," the Monkey replied, "but we're going to change all that. Strict rations for you, fat friend. No more of your obscene profiteering at the feed trough." Overhead, a Parrot screamed: "From each according to your ability. To each according to our need. Gimme your crackers, gimme *all* your crackers!"

The Elephant was upset at this enormous misunderstanding. Yet, though her heart pounded, between the ears she was quite unflappable. "A moment, please," she said. "Though it may seem that I consume a great deal, it's no more than my share. Because I am large—not fat—it just takes more to keep me going. How can I work hard if you won't let me have the proper nourishment?"

The Monkey sneered. "Knock off that mumbo-jumbo, Dumbo," he said. "You already net more than a million Spiders. You take in more than a thousand Pack Rats. You profit more from the jungle's abundance than a hundred Monkeys!"

"But I also can haul tree trunks too heavy for any other creature," the Elephant said. "I can explore for new food supplies and water holes, and clear paths through the jungle with my strong legs. My feet can crush, my shoulders can pull, my trunk can lift. I am full of energy. I even give rides to the little ones. But I can't survive on peanuts."

Hours passed. The Elephant, denied access to her eating and drinking grounds, felt hungrier and hungrier, thirstier and thirstier. But soon, so did the other animals. For the sticks and vines that the animals had dragged together and woven into a barricade had become a solid dam, diverting the stream that fed the watering hole. "Help, help," the animals shouted, "crisis, crisis!"

The Elephant surveyed the scene. "Friends," she said, "see what a fix we're all in. Thank goodness I still have the energy to help. And, with your permission, I will." They quickly consented, and she set to work on the dam, pushing earth and pulling plants until the water hole again began to fill. "That's nice," the animals cried, greeting her undamming with faint praise.

"You see," the Elephant said, "you need a big beast for a big job, and a big beast has big needs. Not just to stay alive and growing, but to put a bit aside for tomorrow. And to have a bit extra for working especially hard, or for sharing with have-not animals."

She noticed that everybody had resumed drinking thirstily. Well, that tickled her old ivories, for all she really wanted was to be allowed to go on doing her customary work without any new wrinkles. No need for hurt feelings. After all, who ever heard of a thin-skinned Elephant?

Moral: Meeting America's energy needs is a big job and it takes big companies. If an energy company doesn't earn a profit proportionate to its size, it won't be able to seek and produce more energy. And that's no fable.

Mobil

A word to smokers
(about people who build walls)

It's no secret that there are some folks these days who are trying to build walls between smokers and nonsmokers.

The theory behind all this is that some smokers annoy nonsmokers and, of course, that can happen.

But if you want to get an idea of the ridiculous lengths that some of the wall-builders would like to go to, you have only to consider this:

In one state alone, it was estimated that the first year's cost of administering and enforcing a proposed anti-smoking law and building the physical walls required was nearly $250,000,000.

The proposal was, of course, defeated—for the plain fact is the one you have observed in your own daily life, that the overwhelming majority of smokers and nonsmokers get along very well and don't need or want to be separated.

This infuriates the wall-builders. Since they cannot have their own way in a world of free choice, they would like to eliminate that world by government fiat, by rules and regulations that would tell you where, and with whom, you may work, eat, play and shop. And the enormous burden that would place on all of us, in higher taxes and costs, does not bother them.

Certainly no one, including smokers, can properly object to the common sense rules of, for instance, banning smoking in crowded elevators, poorly ventilated spaces or, indeed, in any place where it is clearly inappropriate. And individual managers in their own interest should see to the mutual comfort of their smoking and nonsmoking patrons. It is only when the long arm, and notoriously insensitive hands, of government regulators start making these private arrangements for us that we all, smoker and nonsmoker alike, begin to lose our freedom of choice.

In the long run, the wall-builders must fail, and the walls will come tumbling down—if not to the sound of a trumpet, then at least to the slower but surer music of common decency and courtesy practiced on both sides of them.

THE TOBACCO INSTITUTE
1776 K St. N.W., Washington, D.C. 20006
Freedom of choice
is the best choice.

A word to nonsmokers
(about people who build walls)

The chances are that you made up your mind about smoking a long time ago — and decided it's not for you.

The chances are equally good that you know a lot of smokers — there are, after all about 60 million of them — and that you may be related to some of them, work with them, play with them, and get along with them very well.

And finally it's a pretty safe bet that you're open-minded and interested in all the various issues about smokers and nonsmokers — or you wouldn't be reading this.

And those three things make you incredibly important today.

Because they mean that yours is the voice — not the smoker's and not the anti-smoker's — that will determine how much of society's efforts should go into building walls that separate us and how much into the search for solutions that bring us together.

For one tragic result of the emphasis on building walls is the diversion of millions of dollars from scientific research on the causes and cures of diseases which, when all is said and done, still strike the nonsmoker as well as the smoker. One prominent health organization, to cite but a single instance, now spends 28¢ of every publicly-contributed dollar on "education" (much of it in anti-smoking propaganda) and only 2¢ on research.

There will always be some who want to build walls, who want to separate people from people, and up to a point, even these may serve society. The anti-smoking wall-builders have, to give them their due, helped to make us all more keenly aware of the value of courtesy and of individual freedom of choice.

But our guess, and certainly our hope, is that you are among the far greater number who know that walls are only temporary at best, and that over the long run, we can serve society's interests better by working together in mutual accommodation.

Whatever virtue walls may have, they can never move our society toward fundamental solutions. People who work together on common problems, common solutions, can.

THE TOBACCO INSTITUTE
1776 K St. N.W., Washington, D.C. 20006
Freedom of choice
is the best choice.

Warning: The Surgeon General Has Determined That Cigarette Smoking Is Dangerous to Your Health.

[1979]

Without chemicals, life itself would be impossible.

Some people think anything "chemical" is bad and anything "natural" is good. Yet nature is chemical.

Plant life generates the oxygen we need through a chemical process called photosynthesis. When you breathe, your body absorbs that oxygen through a chemical reaction with your blood.

Life is chemical. And with chemicals, companies like Monsanto are working to help improve the quality of life.

Chemicals help you live longer. Rickets was a common childhood disease until a chemical called Vitamin D was added to milk and other foods.

Chemicals help you eat better. Chemical weed-killers have dramatically increased the supply and availability of our food. But no chemical is totally safe, all the time, everywhere. In nature or the laboratory. The real challenge is to use chemicals properly. To help make life a lot more livable.

For a new edition of our free booklet on chemical benefits and risks, mail to:
Monsanto, 800 N. Lindbergh Blvd., St. Louis, Mo. 63166. Dept. A3NA-H1

Name ____________________

Address ____________________

City & state ____________________ Zip ________

Monsanto

Without chemicals,
life itself would be impossible.

[1979]

Really tying one on.

Getting s___ faced.

Having one more for the road.

Becoming polluted.

Drinking someone under the table.

Being plastered.

Bragging about the size of your hangover.

Going out and getting looped.

IF YOUR IDEA OF A GOOD TIME IS LISTED ON THIS PAGE, YOU OUGHT TO HAVE YOUR HEAD EXAMINED.

With the possible exception of sex, no single subject generates as many foolish tales of prowess as the consumption of alcoholic beverages.

But there is a basic difference between the two subjects. Excelling at the former can be highly productive. Excelling at the latter, very destructive.

We, the people who make and sell distilled spirits, urge you to use our products with common sense. If you choose to drink, drink responsibly.

Then the next time someone tells you how lousy he feels because he had "one too many," you can tell him how great you feel because you had "one too few."

That's having a good time.

IT'S PEOPLE WHO GIVE DRINKING A BAD NAME.

Distilled Spirits Council of the U.S. (DISCUS)
1300 Pennsylvania Building, Washington, D.C. 20004

[1979]

It starts out innocently enough.

A man tunes in a football game and tunes out his wife's attempts to be heard.

A woman gets so wrapped up in her problems she barely listens as her husband talks about his own.

And before long, without even realizing how it came about, a deadly silence starts to grow between them.

The fact is, listening, like marriage, is a partnership; a shared responsibility between the person speaking and the person listening. And if the listener doesn't show genuine interest and sensitivity to what's being said, the speaker will stop talking. And the communication will fail.

Which is why we at Sperry feel it's so critical that we all become better listeners. In our homes. And in our businesses.

We've recently set up special listening programs that Sperry personnel worldwide can attend. And what we're discovering is that when people really know how to listen (and believe us, there's a lot to know) they can actually encourage

HE POINT OF TALKING,
LISTEN TO ME, ANYWAY."

the speakers to share more of their thoughts and feelings, bringing everyone closer together.

Which is of great value to us when we do business.
And perhaps even greater value when we go home.

We understand how important it is to listen.

Sperry is Sperry Univac computers, Sperry New Holland farm equipment, Sperry Vickers fluid power systems, and guidance and control equipment from Sperry division and Sperry Flight Systems.

[1982]

Funny stage they're at: George is older, but somehow he doesn't quite measure up to kid sister Shirley. "It's a stage," Dad consoles his son. "You'll outgrow it." The kids are growing up. Almost too fast. So, be sure to share those little moments, as well as the big, with faraway friends and family. Just reach out with a phone call, and they're sharing your day.
Bell System
Reach out and touch someone.

[1980]

THE
BEST REASON
TO RAISE THE AGE
FOR BUYING ALCOHOL
OFTEN GETS BURIED.
The question of raising the alcohol-purchase age to 21 has stirred emotional arguments, economic arguments, freedom-of-choice arguments.
But at Metropolitan Life, we fear the debate may have obscured the most basic argument of all. Simply stated, the lower the legal-purchase age, the more young people will die on the highways.
How do we know for sure? In states that have already increased the purchase age to 21, alcohol-related fatalities among drivers 18 to 20 have dropped as much as 21%.
If all states adopted the 21-year-old limit, it is estimated that at least 700 lives would be saved each year.
You can help save those lives. Wire or call your Senators to urge their support of the Uniform Minimum Drinking Age Act (S2719) when it is offered in the Senate. Wire or call President Reagan and let him know you want to see this bill passed.
Because if this bill gets buried, so will 700 people. One of them could be you or your child.
Metropolitan
Insurance Companies

[1984]

Marianne Moore / Correspondence with the Ford Motor Company 1955

In the following exchange of letters, the distinguished American poet, Marianne Moore (1887–1972), a professed "amateur" at the art of copywriting, tries to come up with the best name for a product that the Ford Motor Company thought would revolutionize the automobile industry.

According to Printer's Ink, *the one-time leading advertising trade publication, Ford spent over $350 million "to create and promote the biggest and most expensive new product ever born."*

October 19, 1955

Miss Marianne Moore,
Cumberland Street,
Brooklyn 5, New York

Dear Miss Moore:

This is a morning we find ourselves with a problem which, strangely enough, is more in the field of words and the fragile meaning of words than in car-making. And we just wonder whether you might be intrigued with it sufficiently to lend us a hand.

Our dilemma is a name for a rather important new series of cars.

We should like this name to be more than a label. Specifically, we should like it to have a compelling quality in itself and by itself. To convey, through association or other conjuration, some visceral feeling of elegance, fleetness, advanced features and design. A name, in short, that flashes a dramatically desirable picture in people's minds. (Another "Thunderbird" would be fine.)

Over the past few weeks this office has confected a list of three hundred-odd candidates which, it pains me to relate, are characterized by an embarrassing pedestrianism. We are miles short of our ambition. And so we are seeking the help of one who knows more about this sort of magic than we.

As to how we might go about this matter, I have no idea. But, in any event, all would depend on whether you find this overture of some challenge and interest.

Should we be so fortunate as to have piqued your fancy, we will be pleased to write more fully. And, of course, it is expected that our relations will be on a fee basis of an impeccably dignified kind.

Respectfully,
David Wallace
Special Products Division

October 21, 1955

Let me take it under advisement, Mr. Wallace. I am complimented to be recruited in this high matter.

I have seen and admired "Thunderbird" as a Ford designation. It would be hard to match; but let me, the coming week, talk with my brother, who would bring ardor and imagination to bear on the quest.

Sincerely yours,
Marianne Moore

October 27, 1955

Dear Mr. Wallace:

My brother thought most of the names I had considered suggesting to you for your new series too learned or too labored, but thinks I might ask if any of the following approximate the requirements:

THE FORD SILVER SWORD

This plant, of which the flower is a silver sword, I believe grows only on the Hawaiian Island Maui, on Mount Haleakala (House of the Sun); found at an altitude of from 9,500 to 10,000 feet. (The leaves—silver-white—surrounding the individual blossoms—have a pebbled texture that feels like Italian-twist backstitch allover embroidery.)

My first thought was of a bird series—the swallow species—Hirundo, or, phonetically, Aerundo. Malvina Hoffman is designing a device for the radiator of a made-to-order Cadillac, and said in her opinion the only term surpassing Thunderbird would be hurricane; and I then thought Hurricane Hirundo might be the first of a series such as Hurricane Aquila (eagle), Hurricane Accipiter (hawk), and so on. A species that takes its dinner on the wing ("swifts").

If these suggestions are not in character with the car, perhaps you could give me a sketch of its general appearance, or hint as to some of its exciting potentialities—though my brother reminds me that such information is highly confidential.

Sincerely yours,
MARIANNE MOORE

NOVEMBER 4, 1955

DEAR MISS MOORE:

I'm delighted that your note implies that you are interested in helping us in our naming problem.

This being so, procedures in this rigorous business world dictate that we on this end at least document a formal arrangement with provision for a suitable fee or honorarium before pursuing the problem further.

One way might be for you to suggest a figure which could be considered for mutual acceptance. Once this is squared away, we will look forward to having you join us in the continuation of our fascinating search.

Sincerely,
DAVID WALLACE
Special Products Division

NOVEMBER 7, 1955

DEAR MR. WALLACE:

It is handsome of you to consider remuneration for service merely enlisted. My fancy would be inhibited, however, by acknowledgment in advance of performance. If I could be of specific assistance, we could no doubt agree on some kind of honorarium for the service rendered.

I seem to exact participation; but if you could tell me how the suggestions submitted strayed—if obviously—from the ideal, I could then perhaps proceed more nearly in keeping with the Company's objective.

Sincerely yours,
MARIANNE MOORE

NOVEMBER 11, 1955

DEAR MISS MOORE:

Our office philodendron has just benefitted from an extra measure of water as, pacing about, I have sought words to respond to your recent generous note. Let me state my quandary thus. It is unspeakably contrary to procedure to accept counsel—

They'll know you've *arrived* when you drive up in an Edsel

Step into an Edsel and you'll learn where the excitement is this year.

Other drivers spot that classic vertical grille a block away—and never fail to take a long look at this year's most exciting car.

On the open road, your Edsel is watched eagerly for its already-famous performance.

And parked in front of your home, your Edsel always gets even more attention—because it always says a lot about you. It says you chose elegant styling, luxurious comfort and such exclusive features as Edsel's famous Teletouch Drive—only shift that puts the buttons where they belong, on the steering-wheel hub.

Your Edsel also means you made a wonderful buy. For of all medium-priced cars, this one really new car is actually priced the lowest.* See your Edsel Dealer this week.

**Based on comparison of suggested retail delivered prices of the Edsel Ranger and similarly equipped cars in the medium-price field.*

Above: Edsel Citation 2-door Hardtop. Engine: the E-475, with 10.5 to one compression ratio, 345 hp, 475 ft.-lb. torque. Transmission: Automatic with Teletouch Drive. Suspension: Ball-joint with optional air suspension. Brakes: self-adjusting.

EDSEL DIVISION · FORD MOTOR COMPANY

1958 EDSEL

Of all medium-priced cars, the one that's really new is the lowest-priced, too!

[1958]

even needed counsel—without a firm prior agreement of conditions (and, indeed, to follow the letter of things, without a Purchase Notice in quadruplicate and three Competitive Bids). But then, seldom has the auto business had occasion to indulge in so ethereal a matter as this. So, if you will risk a mutually satisfactory outcome with us, we should like to honor your wish for a fancy unencumbered.

As to wherein your earlier suggestions may have "strayed," as you put it—they did not at all. Shipment No. 1 was fine, and we would like to luxuriate in more of same—even those your brother regarded as overlearned or labored. For us to impose an ideal on your efforts would, I fear, merely defeat our purpose. We have sought your help to get an approach quite different from our own. In short, we should like suggestions that we ourselves would not have arrived at. And, in sober fact, have not.

Now we on this end must help you by sending some tangible representation of what we are talking about. Perhaps the enclosed sketches will serve the purpose. They are not IT, but they convey the feeling. At the very least, they may give you a sense of participation should your friend Malvina Hoffman break into brisk conversation on radiator caps.

Sincerely yours,
DAVID WALLACE
Special Products Division

NOVEMBER 13, 1955

DEAR MR. WALLACE:

The sketches. They are indeed exciting; they have quality, and the toucan tones lend tremendous allure—confirmed by the wheels. Half the magic—sustaining effects of this kind. Looked at upside down, furthermore, there is a sense of fish buoyancy. Immediately your word "impeccable" sprang to mind. Might it be a possibility? The Impeccable. In any case, the baguette lapidary glamour you have achieved certainly spurs the imagination. Car-innovation is like launching a ship—"drama."

I am by no means sure that I can help you to the right thing, but performance with elegance casts a spell. Let me do some thinking in the direction of impeccable, symmechromatic, thunderblender. . . . (The exotics, if I can shape them a little.) Dearborn might come into one.

If the sketches should be returned at once, let me know. Otherwise, let me dwell on them for a time. I am, may I say, a trusty confidante.

I thank you for realizing that under contract esprit could not flower. You owe me nothing, specific or moral.

Sincerely,
MARIANNE MOORE

NOVEMBER 19, 1955

Some other suggestions, Mr. Wallace, for the phenomenon:

THE RESILIENT BULLET
or Intelligent Bullet
or Bullet Cloisonné or Bullet Lavolta

(I have always had a fancy for THE INTELLIGENT WHALE—the little first Navy submarine, shaped like a sweet potato; on view in our Brooklyn Yard.)

THE FORD FABERGE

(That there is also a perfume Fabergé seems to me to do no harm, for here allusion is to the original silversmith.)

THE ARC-en-CIEL (the rainbow) ARCENCIEL?

Please do not feel that memoranda from me need acknowledgment. I am not working day and night for you; I feel that etymological hits are partially accidental.

The bullet idea has possibilities, it seems to me, in connection with Mercury (with Hermes and Hermes Trismegistus) and magic (white magic).

Sincerely,
MARIANNE MOORE

NOVEMBER 28, 1955

DEAR MR. WALLACE:

MONGOOSE CIVIQUE

ANTICIPATOR

REGNA RACER (couronne à couronne) sovereign to sovereign

AEROTERRE

Fée Rapide (Aérofée, Aéro Faire, Fée Aiglette, Magi-faire) Comme Il Faire

Tonnerre Alifère (winged thunder)

Aliforme Alifère (wing-slender, a-wing)

TURBOTORC (used as an adjective by Plymouth)

THUNDERBIRD Allié (Cousin Thunderbird)

THUNDER CRESTER

DEARBORN Diamante

MAGIGRAVURE

PASTELOGRAM

I shall be returning the sketches very soon.

M.M.

DECEMBER 6, 1955

DEAR MR. WALLACE:

Regina-rex
Taper Racer Taper Acer
Varsity Stroke

Angelastro
Astranaut

Chaparral

Tir à l'arc (bull's eye)
Cresta Lark
Triskelion (three legs running)

Pluma Piluma (hairfine, feather-foot)

Andante con Moto (description of a good motor?)

My findings thin, so I terminate them and am returning the sketches. Two principles I have not been able to capture: 1, the topknot of the peacock and topnotcher of speed. 2, the swivel-axis (emphasized elsewhere), like the Captain's bed on the whaleship, Charles Morgan—balanced so that it levelled whatever the slant of the ship.

If I stumble on a hit, you shall have it. Anything so far has been pastime. Do not ponder appreciation, Mr. Wallace. That was embodied in the sketches.

M.M.

I cannot resist the temptation to disobey my brother and submit

TURCOTINGA (turquoise cotinga—the cotinga being a South-American finch or sparrow) solid indigo.

(I have a three-volume treatise on flowers that might produce something but the impression given should certainly be unlabored.)

DECEMBER 8, 1955

MR. WALLACE:

May I submit UTOPIAN TURTLE-TOP? Do not trouble to answer unless you like it.

MARIANNE MOORE

DECEMBER 23, 1955

MERRY CHRISTMAS TO OUR FAVORITE TURTLETOPPER.

DAVID WALLACE

DECEMBER 26, 1955

DEAR MR. WALLACE:

An aspiring turtle is certain to glory in spiral eucalyptus, white pine straight from the forest, and innumerable scarlet roses almost too tall for close inspection. Of a temperament susceptible to shock though one may be, to be treated like royalty could not but induce sensations unprecedented august.

Please know that a carfancyer's allegiance to the Ford automotive turtle—extending from the Model T Dynasty to the Wallace Utopian Dynasty—can never waver; impersonal gratitude surely becoming infinite when made personal. Gratitude to unmiserly Mr. Wallace and his idealistic associates.

MARIANNE MOORE

NOVEMBER 8, 1956

DEAR MISS MOORE:

Because you were so kind to us in our early days of looking for a suitable name, I feel a deep obligation to report on events that have ensued.

And I feel I must do so before the public announcement of same come Monday, November 19.

We have chosen a name out of the more than six thousand-odd candidates that we gathered. It fails somewhat of the resonance, gaiety, and zest we were seeking. But it has a personal dignity and meaning to many of us here. Our name, dear Miss Moore, is—Edsel.

I hope you will understand.

Cordially,

DAVID WALLACE

Special Products Division

David Ogilvy / How To Write Potent Copy 1963

David Ogilvy was born in England in 1911 and received his education at Christ Church College, Oxford. His professional experiences have been varied: At one time he served as an apprentice chef in the kitchens of the Hotel Majestic in Paris and at another time as a salesman for kitchen stoves. With the founding of Ogilvy, Benson and Mather in 1948, Ogilvy went on to become one of the leading figures of and voices of American advertising. His best known ads—those for Hathaway shirts, Schweppes tonic, and Rolls Royce—have focused on distinctive images of Anglo-American sophistication. His most recent book, Ogilvy on Advertising, *was published in 1983.*

"How to Write Potent Copy" appeared as a chapter in Ogilvy's best seller, Confessions of an Advertising Man.

I. HEADLINES

The headline is the most important element in most advertisements. It is the telegram which decides the reader whether to read the copy.

On the average, five times as many people read the headline as read the body copy. When you have written your headline, you have spent eighty cents out of your dollar.

If you haven't done some selling in your headline, you have wasted 80 per cent of your client's money. The wickedest of all sins is to run an advertisement *without* a headline. Such headless wonders are still to be found; I don't envy the copywriter who submits one to me.

A change of headline can make a difference of ten to one in sales. I never write fewer than sixteen headlines for a single advertisement, and I observe certain guides in writing them:

(1) The headline is the "ticket on the meat." Use it to flag down the readers who are prospects for the kind of product you are advertising. If you are selling a remedy for bladder weakness, display the words BLADDER WEAKNESS in your headline; they catch the eye of everyone who suffers from this inconvenience. If you want *mothers* to read your advertisement, display MOTHERS in your headline. And so on.

Conversely, do not say anything in your headline which is likely to *exclude* any readers who might be prospects for your product. Thus, if you are advertising a product which can be used equally well by men and women, don't slant your headline at women alone; it would frighten men away.

(2) Every headline should appeal to the reader's *self-interest*. It should promise her a benefit, as in my headline for Helena Rubinstein's Hormone Cream: HOW WOMEN OVER 35 CAN LOOK YOUNGER.

(3) Always try to inject *news* into your headlines, because the consumer is always on the lookout for new products, or new ways to use an old product, or new improvements in an old product.

The two most powerful words you can use in a headline are FREE and NEW. You can seldom use FREE, but you can almost always use NEW—if you try hard enough.

(4) Other words and phrases which work wonders are HOW TO, SUDDENLY, NOW, ANNOUNCING, INTRODUCING, IT'S HERE, JUST ARRIVED, IMPORTANT DEVELOPMENT, IMPROVEMENT, AMAZING, SENSATIONAL, REMARKABLE, REVOLUTIONARY, STARTLING, MIRACLE, MAGIC, OFFER, QUICK, EASY, WANTED, CHALLENGE, ADVICE TO, THE TRUTH ABOUT, COMPARE, BARGAIN, HURRY, LAST CHANCE.

Don't turn up your nose at these clichés. They may be shopworn, but they work.

That is why you see them turn up so often in the headlines of mail-order advertisers and others who can measure the results of their advertisements.

Headlines can be strengthened by the inclusion of *emotional* words, like DARLING, LOVE, FEAR, PROUD, FRIEND, and BABY. One of the most provocative advertisements which has come out of our agency showed a girl in a bathtub, talking to her lover on the telephone. The headline: *Darling, I'm having the most extraordinary experience . . . I'm head over heels in* DOVE.

(5) Five times as many people read the headline as read the body copy, so it is important that these glancers should at least be told what brand is being advertised. That is why you should always include the brand name in your headlines.

(6) Include your selling promise in your headline. This requires long headlines. When the New York University School of Retailing ran headline tests with the cooperation of a big department store, they found that headlines of ten words or longer, containing news and information, consistently sold more merchandise than short headlines.

Headlines containing six to twelve words pull more coupon returns than short headlines, and there is no significant difference between the readership of twelve-word headlines and the readership of three-word headlines. The best headline I ever wrote contained *eighteen* words: *At Sixty Miles an Hour the Loudest Noise in the New Rolls-Royce comes from the electric clock.*[1]

(7) People are more likely to read your body copy if your headline arouses their curiosity; so you should end your headline with a lure to read on.

(8) Some copywriters write *tricky* headlines—puns, literary allusions, and other obscurities. This is a sin.

In the average newspaper your headline has to compete for attention with 350 others. Research has shown that readers travel so fast through this jungle that they don't stop to decipher the meaning of obscure headlines. Your headline must *telegraph* what you want to say, and it must telegraph it in plain language. Don't play games with the reader.

In 1960 the *Times Literary Supplement* attacked the whimsical tradition in British advertising, calling it "self-indulgent—a kind of middle-class private joke, apparently designed to amuse the advertiser and his client." Amen.

(9) Research shows that it is dangerous to use *negatives* in headlines. If, for example, you write OUR SALT CONTAINS NO ARSENIC, many readers will miss the negative and go away with the impression that you wrote OUR SALT CONTAINS ARSENIC.

(10) Avoid *blind* headlines—the kind which mean nothing unless you read the body copy underneath them; most people *don't*.

II. BODY COPY

When you sit down to write your body copy, pretend that you are talking to the woman on your right at a dinner party. She has asked you, "I am thinking of buying a new car. Which would you recommend?" Write your copy as if you were answering that question.

(1) Don't beat about the bush—go straight to the point. Avoid analogies of the "just as, so too" variety. Dr. Gallup has demonstrated that these two-stage arguments are generally misunderstood.

(2) Avoid superlatives, generalizations, and platitudes. Be specific and factual. Be enthusiastic, friendly, and memorable. Don't be a bore. Tell the truth, but make the truth fascinating.

How long should your copy be? It depends on the product. If you are advertising chewing gum, there isn't much to tell, so make your copy short. If, on the other

1. When the chief engineer at the Rolls-Royce factory read this, he shook his head sadly and said, "It is time we did something about that damned clock."

The Rolls-Royce Silver Cloud—$13,550

"At 60 miles an hour the loudest noise in this new Rolls-Royce comes from the electric clock"

What makes Rolls-Royce the best car in the world? "There is really no magic about it—it is merely patient attention to detail," says an eminent Rolls-Royce engineer.

1. "At 60 miles an hour the loudest noise comes from the electric clock," reports the Technical Editor of THE MOTOR. The silence of the engine is uncanny. Three mufflers tune out sound frequencies—acoustically.

2. Every Rolls-Royce engine is run for seven hours at full throttle before installation, and each car is test-driven for hundreds of miles over varying road surfaces.

3. The Rolls-Royce is designed as an *owner-driven* car. It is eighteen inches shorter than the largest domestic cars.

4. The car has power steering, power brakes and automatic gear-shift. It is very easy to drive and to park. No chauffeur required.

5. There is no metal-to-metal contact between the body of the car and the chassis frame—except for the speedometer drive. The entire body is insulated and under-sealed.

6. The finished car spends a week in the final test-shop, being fine-tuned. Here it is subjected to ninety-eight separate ordeals. For example, the engineers use a *stethoscope* to listen for axle-whine.

7. The Rolls-Royce is guaranteed for *three years.* With a new network of dealers and parts-depots from Coast to Coast, service is no longer any problem

8. The famous Rolls-Royce radiator has never been changed, except that when Sir Henry Royce died in 1933 the monogram RR was changed from red to black.

9. The coachwork is given five coats of primer paint, and hand rubbed between each coat, before *fourteen* coats of finishing paint go on.

10. By moving a switch on the steering column, you can adjust the shock-absorbers to suit road conditions. (The lack of fatigue in driving this car is remarkable.)

11. Another switch defrosts the rear window, by heating a network of 1360 invisible wires in the glass. There are two separate ventilating systems, so that you can ride in comfort with all the windows closed. Air conditioning is optional.

12. The seats are upholstered with eight hides of English leather—enough to make 128 pairs of soft shoes.

13. A picnic table, veneered in French walnut, slides out from under the dash. Two more swing out behind the front seats.

14. You can get such optional extras as an Espresso coffee-making machine, a dictating machine, a bed, hot and cold water for washing, an electric razor.

15. You can lubricate the entire chassis by simply pushing a pedal from the driver's seat. A gauge on the dash shows the level of oil in the crankcase.

16. Gasoline consumption is remarkably low and there is no need to use premium gas; a happy economy.

17. There are two separate systems of power brakes, hydraulic and mechanical. The Rolls-Royce is a very *safe* car—and also a very *lively* car. It cruises serenely at eighty-five. Top speed is in excess of 100 m.p.h.

18. Rolls-Royce engineers make periodic visits to inspect owners' motor cars and advise on service.

ROLLS-ROYCE AND BENTLEY

19. The Bentley is made by Rolls-Royce. Except for the radiators, they are identical motor cars, manufactured by the same engineers in the same works. The Bentley costs $300 less, because its radiator is simpler to make. People who feel diffident about driving a Rolls-Royce can buy a Bentley.

PRICE. The car illustrated in this advertisement—f.o.b. principal port of entry—costs **$13,550.**

If you would like the rewarding experience of driving a Rolls-Royce or Bentley, get in touch with our dealer. His name is on the bottom of this page. Rolls-Royce Inc., 10 Rockefeller Plaza, New York, N.Y.

JET ENGINES AND THE FUTURE

Certain airlines have chosen Rolls-Royce turbo-jets for their Boeing 707's and Douglas DC8's. Rolls-Royce prop-jets are in the Vickers Viscount, the Fairchild F.27 and the Grumman Gulfstream.

Rolls-Royce engines power more than half the turbo-jet and prop-jet airliners supplied to or on order for world airlines.

Rolls-Royce now employ 42,000 people and the company's engineering experience does not stop at motor cars and jet engines. There are Rolls-Royce diesel and gasoline engines for many other applications.

The huge research and development resources of the company are now at work on many projects for the future, including nuclear and rocket propulsion.

Special showing of the Rolls-Royce and Bentley at Salter Automotive Imports, Inc., 9009 Carnegie Ave., tomorrow through April 26.

[1958]

hand, you are advertising a product which has a great many different qualities to recommend it, write long copy: the more you tell, the more you sell.

There is a universal belief in lay circles that people won't read long copy. Nothing could be farther from the truth. Claude Hopkins once wrote five pages of solid text for Schlitz beer. In a few months, Schlitz moved up from fifth place to first. I once wrote a page of solid text for Good Luck Margarine, with most gratifying results.

Research shows that readership falls off rapidly up to fifty words of copy, but drops very little between fifty and 500 words. In my first Rolls-Royce advertisement I used 719 words—piling one fascinating fact on another. In the last paragraph I wrote, "People who feel diffident about driving a Rolls-Royce can buy a Bentley." Judging from the number of motorists who picked up the word "diffident" and bandied it about, I concluded that the advertisement was thoroughly read. In the next one I used 1400 words.

Every advertisement should be a *complete* sales pitch for your product. It is unrealistic to assume that consumers will read a *series* of advertisements for the same product. You should shoot the works in every advertisement, on the assumption that it is the only chance you will ever have to sell your product to the reader—*now or never.*

Says Dr. Charles Edwards of the graduate School of Retailing at New York University, "The more facts you tell, the more you sell. An advertisement's chance for success invariably increases as the number of pertinent merchandise facts included in the advertisement increases."

In my first advertisement for Puerto Rico's Operation Bootstrap, I used 961 words, and persuaded Beardsley Ruml to sign them. Fourteen thousand readers clipped the coupon from this advertisement, and scores of them later established factories in Puerto Rico. The greatest professional satisfaction I have yet had is to see the prosperity in Puerto Rican communities which had lived on the edge of starvation for four hundred years before I wrote my advertisement. If I had confined myself to a few vacuous generalities, nothing would have happened.

We have even been able to get people to read long copy about gasoline. One of our Shell advertisements contained 617 words, and 22 per cent of male readers read more than half of them.

Vic Schwab tells the story of Max Hart (of Hart, Schaffner & Marx) and his advertising manager, George L. Dyer, arguing about long copy. Dyer said, "I'll bet you ten dollars I can write a newspaper page of solid type and you'd read every word of it."

Hart scoffed at the idea. "I don't have to write a line of it to prove my point," Dyer replied. "I'll only tell you the headline: THIS PAGE IS ALL ABOUT MAX HART."

Advertisers who put coupons in their advertisements *know* that short copy doesn't sell. In split-run tests, long copy invariably outsells short copy.

Do I hear someone say that no copywriter can write long advertisements unless his media department gives him big spaces to work with? This question should not arise, because the copywriter should be consulted before planning the media schedule.

(3) You should always include testimonials in your copy. The reader finds it easier to believe the endorsement of a fellow consumer than the puffery of an anonymous copywriter. Says Jim Young, one of the best copywriters alive today, "Every type of advertiser has the same problem; namely to be believed. The mail-order man knows nothing so potent for this purpose as the testimonial, yet the general advertiser seldom uses it."

Testimonials from celebrities get remarkably high readership, and if they are honestly written they still do not seem to provoke incredulity. The better known the celebrity, the more readers you will attract. We have featured Queen Elizabeth and Winston Churchill in "Come to Britain" advertisements, and we were able to persuade Mrs. Roosevelt to make television commercials for Good Luck Margarine. When we advertised charge accounts for Sears, Roebuck, we reproduced the credit card of Ted Williams, "recently traded by Boston to Sears."

Sometimes you can cast your entire copy in the form of a testimonial. My first advertisement for Austin cars took the form of a letter from an "anonymous diplomat" who was sending his son to Groton with money he had saved driving an Austin—a well-aimed combination of snobbery and economy. Alas, a perspicacious *Time* editor guessed that I was the anonymous diplomat, and asked the headmaster of Groton to comment. Dr. Crocker was so cross that I decided to send my son to Hotchkiss.

(4) Another profitable gambit is to give the reader helpful advice, or service. It hooks about 75 per cent more readers than copy which deals entirely with the product.

One of our Rinso advertisements told housewives how to remove stains. It was better read (Starch) and better remembered (Gallup) than any detergent advertisement in history. Unfortunately, however, it forgot to feature Rinso's main selling promise—that Rinso washes whiter; for this reason it should never have run.[2]

(5) I have never admired the *belles lettres* school of advertising, which reached its pompous peak in Theodore F. MacManus' famous advertisement for Cadillac, "The Penalty of Leadership," and Ned Jordan's classic, "Somewhere West of Laramie." Forty years ago the business community seems to have been impressed by these pieces of purple prose, but I have always thought them absurd; they did not give the reader a single *fact*. I share Claude Hopkins' view that "fine writing is a distinct disadvantage. So is unique literary style. They take attention away from the subject."

(6) Avoid bombast. Raymond Rubicam's famous slogan for Squibb, "The priceless ingredient of every product is the honor and integrity of its maker," reminds me of my father's advice: when a company boasts about its integrity, or a woman about her virtue, avoid the former and cultivate the latter.

(7) Unless you have some special reason to be solemn and pretentious, write your copy in the colloquial language which your customers use in everyday conversation. I have never acquired a sufficiently good ear for vernacular American to write it, but I admire copywriters who can pull it off, as in this unpublished pearl from a dairy farmer:

Carnation Milk is the best in the land,
Here I sit with a can in my hand.
No tits to pull, no hay to pitch,
Just punch a hole in the son-of-a-bitch.

It is a mistake to use highfalutin language when you advertise to uneducated people. I once used the word OBSOLETE in a headline, only to discover that 43 per cent of housewives had no idea what it meant. In another headline, I used the word INEFFABLE, only to discover that I didn't know what it meant myself.

However, many copywriters of my vintage err on the side of underestimating the educational level of the population. Philip Hauser, head of the Sociology Department at the University of Chicago, draws attention to the changes which are taking place:

> The increasing exposure of the population to formal schooling . . . can be expected to effect important changes in . . . the style of advertis-

2. The photograph showed several different kinds of stain—lipstick, coffee, shoe-polish, blood and so forth. The blood was my own; I am the only copywriter who has ever *bled* for his client.

> ing. . . . Messages aimed at the "average" American on the assumption that he has had less than a grade school education are likely to find themselves with a declining or disappearing clientele.[3]

Meanwhile, all copywriters should read Dr. Rudolph Flesch's *Art of Plain Talk*. It will persuade them to use short words, short sentences, short paragraphs, and highly *personal* copy.

Aldous Huxley, who once tried his hand at writing advertisements, concluded that "any trace of literariness in an advertisement is fatal to its success. Advertisement writers may not be lyrical, or obscure, or in any way esoteric. They must be universally intelligible. A good advertisement has this in common with drama and oratory, that it must be immediately comprehensible and directly moving." [4]

(8) Resist the temptation to write the kind of copy which wins awards. I am always gratified when I win an award, but most of the campaigns which produce *results* never win awards, because they don't draw attention to themselves.

The juries that bestow awards are never given enough information about the *results* of the advertisements they are called upon to judge. In the absence of such information, they rely on their opinions, which are always warped toward the highbrow.

(9) Good copywriters have always resisted the temptation to *entertain*. Their achievement lies in the number of new products they get off to a flying start. In a class by himself stands Claude Hopkins, who is to advertising what Escoffier is to cooking. By today's standards, Hopkins was an unscrupulous barbarian, but technically he was the supreme master. Next I would place Raymond Rubicam, George Cecil, and James Webb Young, all of whom lacked Hopkins' ruthless salesmanship, but made up for it by their honesty, by the broader range of their work, and by their ability to write civilized copy when the occasion required it. Next I would place John Caples, the mail-order specialist from whom I have learned much.

These giants wrote their advertisements for newspapers and magazines. It is still too early to identify the best writers for television.

Daniel J. Boorstin / The Rhetoric of Democracy 1974

"We are perhaps the first people in history to have a centrally organized mass-produced folk culture," writes Daniel J. Boorstin in "The Rhetoric of Democracy," and "advertising has become the heart of the folk culture and even its very prototype." In the following essay, which first appeared in Democracy and Its Discontents *(1974) and in 1976 was featured in the advertising trade magazine called* Advertising Age, *Boorstin constructs a historical context for the complex role advertising now plays in contemporary American culture.*

One of America's leading historians, Daniel J. Boorstin is the author of the critically acclaimed three-volume study, The Americans. *He has served as director of the National Museum of History and Technology, as senior historian of the Smithsonian Institution, and is currently director of the Library of Congress. His most recent book is* The Discoverers *(1984).*

3. *Scientific American* (October 1962).

4. *Essays Old And New* (Harper & Brothers, 1927). Charles Lamb and Byron also wrote advertisements. So did Bernard Shaw, Hemingway, Marquand, Sherwood Anderson, and Faulkner—none of them with any degree of success.

Advertising, of course, has been part of the mainstream of American civilization, although you might not know it if you read the most respectable surveys of American history. It has been one of the enticements to the settlement of this New World, it has been a producer of the peopling of the United States, and in its modern form, in its world-wide reach, it has been one of our most characteristic products.

Never was there a more outrageous or more unscrupulous or more ill-informed advertising campaign than that by which the promoters for the American colonies brought settlers here. Brochures published in England in the seventeenth century, some even earlier, were full of hopeful overstatements, half-truths, and downright lies, along with some facts which nowadays surely would be the basis for a restraining order from the Federal Trade Commission. Gold and silver, fountains of youth, plenty of fish, venison without limit, all these were promised, and of course some of them were found. It would be interesting to speculate on how long it might have taken to settle this continent if there had not been such promotion by enterprising advertisers. How has American civilization been shaped by the fact that there was a kind of natural selection here of those people who were willing to believe advertising?

Advertising has taken the lead in promising and exploiting the new. This was a new world, and one of the advertisements for it appears on the dollar bill on the Great Seal of the United States, which reads *novus ordo seclorum,* one of the most effective advertising slogans to come out of this country. "A new order of the centuries"—belief in novelty and in the desirability of opening novelty to everybody has been important in our lives throughout our history and especially in this century. Again and again advertising has been an agency for inducing Americans to try anything and everything—from the continent itself to a new brand of soap. As one of the more literate and poetic of the advertising copywriters, James Kenneth Frazier, a Cornell graduate, wrote in 1900 in "The Doctor's Lament":

> This lean M.D. is Dr. Brown
> Who fares but ill in Spotless Town.
> The town is so confounded clean,
> It is no wonder he is lean,
> He's lost all patients now, you know,
> Because they use *Sapolio*.

The same literary talent that once was used to retail Sapolio was later used to induce people to try the Edsel or the Mustang, to experiment with Lifebuoy or Body-All, to drink Pepsi-Cola or Royal Crown Cola, or to shave with a Trac II razor.

And as expansion and novelty have become essential to our economy, advertising has played an ever-larger role: in the settling of the continent, in the expansion of the economy, and in the building of an American standard of living. Advertising has expressed the optimism, the hyperbole, and the sense of community, the sense of reaching which has been so important a feature of our civilization.

Here I wish to explore the significance of advertising, not as a force in the economy or in shaping an American standard of living, but rather as a touchstone of the ways in which we Americans have learned about all sorts of things.

The problems of advertising are of course not peculiar to advertising, for they are just one aspect of the problems of democracy. They reflect the rise of what I have called Consumption Communities and Statistical Communities, and many of the special problems of advertising have arisen from our continuously energetic effort to give everybody everything.

If we consider democracy not just as a political system, but as a set of institutions which do aim to make everything available to everybody, it would not be an overstatement to describe advertising as the characteristic rhetoric of democracy. One of the tendencies of democracy, which Plato and other antidemocrats warned against a long time ago, was the danger that rhetoric would displace or at least overshadow epistemology; that is, *the temptation to allow the problem of persuasion to overshadow the problem of knowledge.* Democratic societies tend to become more concerned with what people believe than with what is true, to become more concerned with credibility than with truth. All these problems become accentuated in a large-scale democracy like ours, which possesses all the apparatus of modern industry. And the problems are accentuated still further by universal literacy, by instantaneous communication, and by the daily plague of words and images.

In the early days it was common for advertising men to define advertisements as a kind of news. The best admen, like the best journalists, were suppose to be those who were able to make their news the most interesting and readable. This was natural enough, since the verb to "advertise" originally meant, intransitively, to take note or to consider. For a person to "advertise" meant originally, in the fourteenth and fifteenth centuries, to reflect on something, to think about something. Then it came to mean, transitively, to call the attention of another to something, to give him notice, to notify, admonish, warn or inform in a formal or impressive manner. And then, by the sixteenth century, it came to mean: to give notice of anything, to make generally known. It was not until the late eighteenth century that the word "advertising" in English came to have a specifically "advertising" connotation as we might say today, and not until the late nineteenth century that it began to have a specifically commercial connotation. By 1879 someone was saying, "Don't advertise unless you have something worth advertising." But even into the present century, newspapers continue to call themselves by the title "Advertiser"—for example, the Boston *Daily Advertiser,* which was a newspaper of long tradition and one of the most dignified papers in Boston until William Randolph Hearst took it over in 1917. Newspapers carried "Advertiser" on their mastheads, not because they sold advertisements but because they brought news.

Now, the main role of advertising in American civilization came increasingly to be that of persuading and appealing rather than that of educating and informing. By 1921, for instance, one of the more popular textbooks, Blanchard's *Essentials of Advertising,* began: "Anything employed to influence people favorably is advertising. The mission of advertising is to persuade men and women to act in a way that will be of advantage to the advertiser." This development—in a country where a shared, a rising, and a democratized standard of living was the national pride and the national hallmark—meant that advertising had become the rhetoric of democracy.

What, then, were some of the main features of modern American advertising—if we consider it as a form of rhetoric? First, and perhaps most obvious, is *repetition.* It is hard for us to realize that the use of repetition in advertising is not an ancient device but a modern one, which actually did not come into common use in American journalism until just past the middle of the nineteenth century.

The development of what came to be called "iteration copy" was a result of a struggle by a courageous man of letters and advertising pioneer, Robert Bonner, who bought the old New York *Merchant's Ledger* in 1851 and turned it into a popular journal. He then had the temerity to try to change the ways of James Gordon Bennett, who of course was one of the most successful of the American newspaper pioneers, and who was both a sensationalist and at the same time an extremely stuffy man when it came to things that he did not consider to be news. Bonner was determined to use advertisements in Bennett's wide-circulating New York *Herald* to sell his own literary product, but he found it difficult to persuade

Bennett to allow him to use any but agate type in his advertising. (Agate was the smallest type used by newspapers in that day, only barely legible to the naked eye.) Bennett would not allow advertisers to use larger type, nor would he allow them to use illustrations except stock cuts, because he thought it was undignified. He said, too, that to allow a variation in the format of ads would be undemocratic. He insisted that all advertisers use the same size type so that no one would be allowed to prevail over another simply by presenting his message in a larger, more clever, or more attention-getting form.

Finally Bonner managed to overcome Bennett's rigidity by leasing whole pages of the paper and using the tiny agate type to form larger letters across the top of the page. In this way he produced a message such as "Bring home the New York Ledger tonight." His were unimaginative messages, and when repeated all across the page they technically did not violate Bennett's agate rule. But they opened a new era and presaged a new freedom for advertisers in their use of the newspaper page. Iteration copy—the practice of presenting prosaic content in ingenious, repetitive form—became common, and nowadays of course is commonplace.

A second characteristic of American advertising which is not unrelated to this is the development of *an advertising style*. We have histories of most other kinds of style—including the style of many unread writers who are remembered today only because they have been forgotten—but we have very few accounts of the history of advertising style, which of course is one of the most important forms of our language and one of the most widely influential.

The development of advertising style was the convergence of several very respectable American traditions. One of these was the tradition of the "plain style," which the Puritans made so much of and which accounts for so much of the strength of the Puritan literature. The "plain style" was of course much influenced by the Bible and found its way into the rhetoric of American writers and speakers of great power like Abraham Lincoln. When advertising began to be self-conscious in the eary years of this century, the pioneers urged copywriters not to be too clever, and especially not to be fancy. One of the pioneers of the advertising copywriters, John Powers, said, for example, "The commonplace is the proper level for writing in business; where the first virtue is plainness, 'fine writing' is not only intellectual, it is offensive." George P. Rowell, another advertising pioneer, said, "You must write your advertisement to catch damned fools—not college professors." He was a very tactful person. And he added, "And you'll catch just as many college professors as you will of any other sort." In the 1920's, when advertising was beginning to come into its own, Claude Hopkins, whose name is known to all in the trade, said, "Brilliant writing has no place in advertising. A unique style takes attention from the subject. Any apparent effort to sell creates corresponding resistance. . . . One should be natural and simple. His language should not be conspicuous. In fishing for buyers, as in fishing for bass, one should not reveal the hook." So there developed a characteristic advertising style in which plainness, the phrase that anyone could understand, was a distinguishing mark.

At the same time, the American advertising style drew on another, and what might seem an antithetic, tradition—the tradition of hyperbole in tall talk, the language of Davy Crockett and Mike Fink. While advertising could think of itself as 99.44 percent pure, it used the language of "Toronado" and "Cutlass." As I listen to the radio in Washington, I hear a celebration of heroic qualities which would make the characteristics of Mike Fink and Davy Crockett pale, only to discover at the end of the paean that what I have been hearing is a description of the Ford dealers in the District of Columbia neighborhood. And along with the folk tradition of hyperbole and tall talk comes the rhythm of folk music. We hear that Pepsi-Cola hits the spot, that it's for the young generation—and we hear other products celebrated in music which we cannot forget and sometimes don't want to remember.

There grew somehow out of all these contradictory tendencies—combining the commonsense language of the "plain style," and the fantasy language of "tall talk"—an advertising style. This characteristic way of talking about things was especially designed to reach and catch the millions. It created a whole new world of myth. A myth, the dictionary tells us, is a notion based more on tradition or convenience than on facts; it is a received idea. Myth is not just fantasy and not just fact but exists in a limbo, in the world of the "Will to Believe," which William James has written about so eloquently and so perceptively. This is the world of the neither true nor false—of the statement that 60 percent of the physicians who expressed a choice said that our brand of aspirin would be more effective in curing a simple headache than any other leading brand.

That kind of statement exists in a penumbra. I would call this the "advertising penumbra." It is not untrue, and yet, in its connotation it is not exactly true.

Now, there is still another characteristic of advertising so obvious that we are inclined perhaps to overlook it. I call that *ubiquity*. Advertising abhors a vacuum and we discover new vacuums every day. The parable, of course, is the story of the man who thought of putting the advertisement on the other side of the cigarette package. Until then, that was wasted space and a society which aims at a democratic standard of living, at extending the benefits of consumption and all sorts of things and services to everybody, must miss no chances to reach people. The highway billboard and other outdoor advertising, bus and streetcar and subway advertising, and skywriting, radio and TV commercials—all these are of course obvious evidence that advertising abhors a vacuum.

We might reverse the old mousetrap slogan and say that anyone who can devise another place to put another mousetrap to catch a consumer will find people beating a path to his door. "Avoiding advertising will become a little harder next January," the *Wall Street Journal* reported on May 17, 1973, "when a Studio City, California, company launches a venture called StoreVision. Its product is a system of billboards that move on a track across supermarket ceilings. Some 650 supermarkets so far are set to have the system." All of which helps us understand the observation attributed to a French man of letters during his recent visit to Times Square. "What a beautiful place, if only one could not read!" Everywhere is a place to be filled, as we discover in a recent *Publishers Weekly* description of one advertising program: "The $1.95 paperback edition of Dr. Thomas A. Harris' million-copy best seller 'I'm O.K., You're O.K.' is in for full-scale promotion in July by its publisher, Avon Books. Plans range from bumper stickers to airplane streamers, from planes flying above Fire Island, the Hamptons and Malibu. In addition, the $100,000 promotion budget calls for 200,000 bookmarks, plus brochures, buttons, lipcards, floor and counter displays, and advertising in magazines and TV."

The ubiquity of advertising is of course just another effect of our uninhibited efforts to use all the media to get all sorts of information to everybody everywhere. Since the places to be filled are everywhere, the amount of advertising is not determined by the *needs* of advertising, but by the *opportunities* for advertising which become unlimited.

But the most effective advertising, in an energetic, novelty-ridden society like ours, tends to be "self-liquidating." To create a cliché you must offer something which everybody accepts. The most successful advertising therefore self-destructs because it becomes cliché. Examples of this are found in the tendency for copyrighted names of trademarks to enter the vernacular—for the proper names of products which have been made familiar by costly advertising to become common nouns, and so to apply to anybody's products. Kodak becomes a synonym for camera, Kleenex a synonym for facial tissue, when both begin with a small *k*, and Xerox (now, too, with a small *x*) is used to describe all processes of copying, and so on. These are prototypes of the problem. If you are successful enough, then you will defeat your purpose in the long run—by making the name and the message so familiar that people won't notice them, and then people will cease to distinguish your product from everybody else's.

In a sense, of course, as we will see, the whole of American civilization is an example. When this was a "new" world, if people succeeded in building a civilization here, the New World would survive and would reach the time—in our age—when it would cease to be new. And now we have the oldest written Constitution in use in the world. This is only a parable of which there are many more examples.

The advertising man who is successful in marketing any particular product, then—in our high-technology, well-to-do democratic society, which aims to get everything to everybody—is apt to be diluting the demand for his particular product in the very act of satisfying it. But luckily for him, he is at the very same time creating a fresh demand for his services as advertiser.

And as a consequence, there is yet another role which is assigned to American advertising. This is what I call "erasure." Insofar as advertising is competitive or innovation is widespread, erasure is required in order to persuade consumers that this year's model is superior to last year's. In fact, we consumers learn that we might be risking our lives if we go out on the highway with those very devices that were last year's lifesavers but without whatever special kind of brakes or wipers or seat belt is on this year's model. This is what I mean by "erasure"—and we see it on our advertising pages or our television screen every day. We read in the *New York Times* (May 20, 1973), for example, that "For the price of something small and ugly, you can drive something small and beautiful"—an advertisement for the Fiat 250 Spider. Or another, perhaps more subtle example is the advertisement for shirts under a picture of Oliver Drab: "Oliver Drab. A name to remember in fine designer shirts? No kidding. . . . Because you pay extra money for Oliver Drab. And for all the other superstars of the fashion world. Golden Vee [the name of the brand that is advertised] does not have a designer's label. But we do have designers. . . . By keeping their names *off* our label and simply saying Golden Vee, we can afford to sell our $7 to $12 shirts for just $7 to $12, which should make Golden Vee a name to remember. Golden Vee, you only pay for the shirt."

Having mentioned two special characteristics—the self-liquidating tendency and the need for erasure—which arise from the dynamism of the American economy, I would like to try to place advertising in a larger perspective. The special role of advertising in our life gives a clue to a pervasive oddity in American civilization. A leading feature of past cultures, as anthropologists have explained, is the tendency to distinguish between "high" culture and "low" culture—between the culture of the literate and the learned on the one hand and that of the populace on the other. In other words, between the language of literature and the language of the vernacular. Some of the most useful statements of this distinction have been made by social scientists at the University of Chicago—first by the late Robert Redfield in his several pioneering books on peasant society, and then by Milton Singer in his remarkable study of Indian civilization. *When a Great Tradition Modernizes* (1972). This distinction between the great tradition and the little tradition, between the high culture and the folk culture, has begun to become a commonplace of modern anthropology.

Some of the obvious features of advertising in modern America offer us an opportunity to note the significance or insignificance of that distinction for us. Elsewhere I have tried to point out some of the peculiarities of the American attitude toward the *high* culture. There is something distinctive about the place of thought in American life, which I think is not quite what it has been in certain Old World cultures.

But what about distinctive American attitudes to *popular* culture? What is our analogue to the folk culture of other peoples? Advertising gives us some clues—to a characteristically American democratic folk culture. Folk culture is a name for the culture which ordinary people everywhere lean on. It is not the writings of Dante and Chaucer and Shakespeare and Milton, the teachings of Machiavelli and Descartes, Locke or Marx. It is, rather, the pattern of slogans, local traditions, tales, songs, dances, and ditties. And of course holiday observances. Popular culture in other civilizations has been for the most part both an area of continuity with the past, a way in which people reach back into the past and out to their community, and at the same time an area of local variations. An area of individual and amateur expression in which a person has his own way of saying, or notes his mother's way of saying or singing, or his own way of dancing, his own view of folk wisdom and the cliché.

And here is an interesting point of contrast. In other societies outside the United States, it is the *high* culture that has generally been an area of centralized, organized control. In Western Europe, for example, universities and churches have tended to be closely allied to the government. The institutions of higher learning have had a relatively limited access to the people as a whole. This was inevitable, of course, in most parts of the world, because there were so few universities. In England, for example, there were only two universities until the early nineteenth century. And there was central control over the printed matter that was used in universities or in the liturgy. The government tended to be close to the high culture, and that was easy because the high culture itself was so centralized and because literacy was relatively limited.

In our society, however, we seem to have turned all of this around. Our high culture is one of the least centralized areas of our culture. And our universities express the atomistic, diffused, chaotic, and individualistic aspect of our life. We have in this country more than twenty-five hundred colleges and universities, institutions of so-called higher learning. We have a vast population in these institutions, somewhere over seven million students.

But when we turn to our popular culture, what do we find? We find that in our nation of Consumption Communities and emphasis on Gross National Product (GNP) and growth rates, advertising has become the heart of the folk culture and even its very prototype. And as we have seen, American advertising shows many characteristics of the folk culture of other societies: repetition, a plain style, hyperbole and tall talk, folk verse, and folk music. Folk culture, wherever it has flourished, has tended to thrive in a limbo between fact and fantasy, and of course, depending on the spoken word and the oral tradition, it spreads easily and tends to be ubiquitous. These are all familiar characteristics of folk culture and they are ways of describing our folk culture, but how do the expressions of our peculiar folk culture come to *us?*

They no longer sprout from the earth, from the village, from the farm, or even from the neighborhood or the city. They come to us primarily from enormous centralized self-consciously *creative* (an overused word, for the overuse of which advertising agencies are in no small part responsible) organizations. They come from advertising agencies, from networks of newspapers, radio, and television, from outdoor-advertising agencies, from the copywriters for ads in the largest-circulation magazines, and so on. These "creators" of folk culture—or pseudo-folk culture—aim at the widest intelligibility and charm and appeal.

But in the United States, we must recall, the advertising folk culture (like all advertising) is also confronted with the problems of self-liquidation and erasure.

These are by-products of the expansive, energetic character of our economy. And they, too, distinguish American folk culture from folk cultures elsewhere.

Our folk culture is distinguished from others by being discontinuous, ephemeral, and self-destructive. Where does this leave the common citizen? All of us are qualified to answer.

In our society, then, those who cannot lean on the world of learning, on the high culture of the classics, on the elaborated wisdom of the books, have a new problem. The University of Chicago, for example, in the 1930's and 1940's was the center of a quest for a "common discourse." The champions of that quest, which became a kind of crusade, believed that such a discourse could be found through familiarity with the classics of great literature—and especially of Western European literature. I think they were misled; such works were not, nor are they apt to become, the common discourse of our society. Most people, even in a democracy, and a rich democracy like ours, live in a world of popular culture, our special kind of popular culture.

The characteristic folk culture of our society is a creature of advertising, and in a sense it *is* advertising. But advertising, our own popular culture, is harder to make into a source of continuity than the received wisdom and commonsense slogans and catchy songs of the vivid vernacular. The popular culture of advertising attenuates and is always dissolving before our very eyes. Among the charms, challenges, and tribulations of modern life, we must count this peculiar fluidity, this ephemeral character of that very kind of culture on which other peoples have been able to lean, the kind of culture to which they have looked for the continuity of their traditions, for their ties with the past and with the future.

We are perhaps the first people in history to have a centrally organized mass-produced folk culture. Our kind of popular culture is here today and gone tomorrow—or the day after tomorrow. Or whenever the next semiannual model appears. And insofar as folk culture becomes advertising, and advertising becomes centralized, it becomes a way of depriving people of their opportunities for individual and small-community expression. Our technology and our economy and our democratic ideals have all helped make that possible. Here we have a new test of the problem that is at least as old as Heraclitus—an everyday test of man's ability to find continuity in his experience. And here democratic man has a new opportunity to accommodate himself, if he can, to the unknown.

Carol Caldwell / You Haven't Come a Long Way, Baby: Women in Television Commercials

1977

Despite the continual efforts of feminist groups to combat sexism in the mass media, unflattering stereotypes of women still persist in advertising, especially in tv commercials targeted to housewives. Though advertisers often try to cash in on social issues (see the ad for Virginia Slims or the many ads depicting high-energy and high-heeled professional women), their message frequently contains the same old sell: more so than men, women are likely to be pictured as ideal consumers first, real people second.

In the following essay, Carol Caldwell, a former copywriter, explains why there has been so little progress in advertising's depiction of women. The article originally appeared in New Times *for June 10, 1977. "From the beginning," wrote editor Jonathan Z. Larsen in the final issue of* New Times *(January 8,*

> *1979), "it was our hope that there was a place out there for a medium-sized magazine that did not have to be sold on the basis of celebrities, sex, or 'service journalism,' but rather on the strength of solid reporting by the best writers we would find. . . . We were determined to make the magazine a place where journalists could practice their craft at its best. And on that score we think we were successful." But as advertisers continued to move to more readily defined markets,* New Times *failed in the marketplace.*

It's the beginning of the age of television, and all around it's black and white. Millions of minuscule scan dots collide in electronic explosion to create Woman in her Immaculate Kitchen. She is Alpha, Omega, eternal and everlasting Mother Video, toasting and frying, cleansing and purifying, perfectly formed of fire and ice. Permanent-waved, magenta-lipped, demurely collared and cuffed, cone-shaped from her tightly cinched waist down through yards and yards of material that brush coquettishly mid-calf, she is Betty Furness for Westinghouse, and you can be *sure* if it's Westinghouse.

The year is 1951. On the set of CBS-TV's *Studio One,* Furness has just captured the part to become America's first full-time product spokeswoman on television. Advertising execs at Westinghouse are taking a stab at having someone other than the host sell their product; they reason (and quite correctly) that Furness, with her Brearley School cool and her Broadway glamor, is a figure thousands of women will admire and listen to. During the audition Betty alters the script supplied by the casting director. Later, she tells *Time* magazine that she adlibbed the refrigerator routine because "it was written like men think women talk!"

1952. While John Daly, Bill Henry, and Walter Cronkite monitor Ike and Adlai at the conventions, Betty Furness opens and shuts forty-nine refrigerators, demonstrates the finer points of forty-two television sets, twenty-three dishwashers and twelve ovens for a total of four-and-a-half hours of air time. General Eisenhower is on the air approximately an hour and twenty minutes; Mr. Stevenson, fifty minutes.

1956. Bright and blondeened, twenty-eight-year-old Julia Meade is the commercial spokeswoman for Lincoln on the *Ed Sullivan Show,* for Richard Hudnut hair products on *Your Hit Parade,* for *Life* magazine on John Daly's news show. She is pulling down a hundred thousand dollars a year, which moves *Time* to comment, "Julia (34–20–34) is one of a dozen or so young women on TV who find self-effacement enormously profitable." Howard Wilson, a vice-president of Kenyon & Eckhardt, Lincoln's ad agency, hired Julia for the spots with trepidation: a woman just couldn't be convincing about such things as high torque, turbo drive, and ball-joint suspensions. His fears, it turns out, were unfounded, and Meade becomes the perky prototype for a whole slew of carefully coiffed women selling cars—selling *anything*—by means other than their technical knowledge. And so Julia Meade begat Bess Myerson, who begat Anita Bryant, who begat Carmelita Pope, who begat Florence Henderson, each wholesome, flawless, clear of eye and enunciation, in short, sixty-second reminders of everything the American woman ought to be.

Times change, however, and eventually infant TV's ideal, untouchable dozen spokeswomen were replaced by hundreds of nameless actresses who portray "the little woman" in scenarios believed, by the agencies who create them, to be honest-to-God, middle-American, slice-of-life situations. As early as 1955, this new wave of commercial realism got a pat on the back by the industry's weekly trade paper, *Advertising Age.* Procter & Gamble had just come out with a revolutionary new way to sell soap on TV: "It is very difficult for a soap commercial to emerge from the mass of suds, with every known variant on the familiar theme of the woman holding up a box of 'X' soap powder with a grisly smile pointing to a pile of clothes she has just washed. Cheer has come up with the unique approach of dramatizing an everyday washing problem from the poor woman's point of view with a sound-over technique of stream of consciousness.''

That stream of consciousness flowed unchecked until Bill Free's famous National Airlines ''Fly Me'' faux pas in 1971. Women activists carried signs, stormed Free's and National's offices, read proclamations, and permeated the media with protest. Free talks of this trying and critical time with a humor and stoicism that comes from a six-year perspective, and from no longer handling the account. ''The women's movement was identifying itself—and our 'Fly Me' campaign was an opportunity for a public platform. We were deluged with letters and calls. I even got an absurd letter from one of the leaders of the movement (who must go unnamed) demanding that I surely planned the sexual innuendo in the word 'fly'—she meant as in men's trouser pants.'' He paused. ''The ad community continues to demean women, far more subtly than in our campaign.''

There are some easy hints at why this is so: Of the seventy-five thousand people currently employed in advertising, only 16.7 percent are women in other than clerical positions—not exactly an overwhelming voice. And, while advertising executives often live in the suburbs of large cities, they just as often tend to have a low regard for anyone who isn't an urbanite. As one New York agency executive quipped, ''All I really know about the Middle America I sell to everyday is that it's the place I fly over to get to L.A.''

But these notations still don't answer the question: Why have advertisers, who make their living keeping up with trends, been so slow to get on board with the women's revolution? Where was everybody the recent night David Brinkley closed the book on America's traditional homelife structure, citing the fact that a mere seven percent of our nation's homes still maintained the time-honored tradition of the everyday housewife. Mom has officially flown the coop just about everywhere, except on TV in the commercials.

At a roundtable on women's advertising sponsored by the agency trade publication *Madison Avenue,* Harriet Rex, a vice-president at J. Walter Thompson, had this comment to make: ''There's always been a lag between what is and what the ad business has codified as what 'is.' '' And Rena Bartos, a senior VP at the same agency, said, ''Advertising may be a mirror of society but somehow the image in that mirror is a little out of focus. It plays back a 1950s reflection in a 1970s world.''

Madison Avenue's ''little woman'' is hardly new, and only partially improved. When feminists cite advertising that is ''acceptable,'' it's invariably print ads. This isn't surprising, since magazine ads are prepared for specific subscribers whose personal backgrounds and attitudes have been carefully documented by the publication and noted by the agency. Television, on the other hand, commands a much larger and subsequently less definable audience.

So it is left to the advertisers and their agencies to define who television's consuming woman might be and what type of commercial she might like. The reward is compelling: Americans heap a total $9.2 billion every year into the coffers of the nation's top three TV advertisers—Procter & Gamble, Bristol-Myers, and General Foods. Still, the women portrayed aren't always to the customers' liking, and last year agitated viewers marched en masse outside P&G headquarters in Cincinnati, suggesting in rather unladylike terms what to do with Mr. Whipple and his grocery store groupies. Inside, P&G stockholders took little heed, voting down a suggestion that their commercial portrayal of women be reconsidered.

Others in the business did listen. When the National Organization for Women sent all major advertising agencies a position paper on the role of women in commercials, no one was surprised that most of the commercials on the air didn't jibe with the NOW requirements. Several agencies, fearing intervention by the Federal

Trade Commission, prodded their own regulatory outfit to consider the matter. The National Advertising Review Board formed a panel, including Patricia Carbine, publisher of *Ms.;* Joyce Snyder, coordinator of the task force on the image of women for NOW; the vice-presidents of broadcast standards for ABC and NBC; and a number of officers of sponsoring companies. A twenty-one page directive came out in 1975, in which the panel made a number of suggestions concerning ways in which advertisers could improve their portrayal of women. Here's what came out in the wash: "Advertising must be regarded as one of the forces molding society," the study asserted. "Those who protest that advertising merely reflects society must reckon with the criticism that much of the current reflection of women in advertising is out of date." Before airing a commercial, the panel urged advertisers to run down the NARB checklist, which included the following points:

• Are sexual stereotypes perpetuated in my ads? Do they portray women as weak, silly and over-emotional?

• Are the women portrayed in my ads stupid?

• Do my ads portray women as ecstatically happy over household cleanliness or deeply depressed because of their failure to achieve near-perfection in household tasks?

• Do my ads show women as fearful of not being attractive, of not being able to keep their husbands or lovers, fearful of in-law disapproval?

• Does my copy promise unrealistic psychological rewards for using the product?

Well now, does it? With these self-regulatory commandments in mind, I spent four weeks in front of daytime TV, logging current household product commercials and trying to determine just where women stand in the advertising scheme of things. During that time, Iris dickered with Rachel and Mac's teetering marriage, Beth died, Stacy miscarried, and Jennifer killed John's wife so they could finally be together.

Now a word from our sponsors.

Ring around the collar lives. After eight long years, the little woman is still exposing hubby and the kids to this awful embarrassment. It can strike virtually anywhere—in taxis, at ballgames, even on vacation doing the limbo. Our lady of the laundry is always guilty, always lucky to have a next-door neighbor who knows about Wisk, the washday miracle, and always back in hubby's good, but wary, graces by the happy ending. The Wisk woman faces the same unspoken commercial threat that the Geritol woman faces: "My wife, I think I'll keep her . . . " *if* she keeps in line.

Jim Jordan is president of Batten, Barton, Durstine and Osborn Advertising. Eight years ago, in a fit of cosmic inspiration, he came up with "ring around the collar" for his agency's client, Lever Bros. Since then, Jordan has run check-out-counter surveys on his commercials, asking shoppers who were purchasing Wisk, "You must be buying this product because you like the commercials." The reply he got was always the same: "Why no! I hate those commercials; but why should I hold that against the product?"

Jim Jordan echoes advertising's premier axiom: "The purpose of the commercial is not the aesthetic pleasure of the viewer—it's to sell the product." And Wisk is selling like gangbusters. He doesn't believe "ring around the collar" commercials show women in an embarrassing light; and to assume that, he says, "would be giving commercials more credit than they deserve."

Perhaps. And perhaps his "ring around the collar" campaign is getting more credit than it deserves for selling Wisk. Take any commercial with a simple message, repeat it again and again, and the product, if it's good, will sell, even if the spot is mindless and annoying. It's fixing the name of the product in the consumer's mind with a quick, catchy phrase that's important.

The household slice-of-life commercial is one of the classic offenders of the

NARB checklist. (Are sexual stereotypes perpetuated? You'd best believe it. Are the women portrayed stupid? And how.) Crisco's current campaign is a flawless example of this much-imitated genre, which has been developed and designed by Procter & Gamble. In it various long-suffering husbands and condescending neighbors are put through the heartache of greasy, gobby chicken and fries, all because some unthinking corner cutter spent "a few pennies less" on that mainstay of American cookery, lard. These pound-foolish little women cause their loved ones to live through "disasters" and "catastrophes." At the cue word "catastrophe," our video crumples into wavy electronic spasms and thrusts us back to the scene of the crime: to that excruciating point in the Bicentennial picnic or the backyard cookout when Dad has to wrinkle his upper lip and take Mom aside for a little set-to about her greasy chicken. The moral, delivered by some unseen pedantic male announcer, is plain: "Ladies who've learned—buy Crisco."

These examples are, sad to say, still very much the rule for women's portrayals in thirty- and sixty-second spots. They occur with alarming regularity during the daytime hours, when stations may sell up to sixteen commercial minutes an hour. (The nighttime rate is a mere eight minutes, forty seconds per hour.) Now, you are probably not the average American who spends some six hours a day in front of the old boob tube (which, when the maximum number of commercials per hour is computed, means over an hour and a half of product propaganda). And you probably are quite sure that commercials have absolutely no effect on you. Maybe they don't. But a shaken agency copywriter told me the first word his child spoke was "McDonald's," and I've stood in a grocery line and watched while a mother, tired of her child's tears, lets him wander off and return—not with a candy bar, but with a roll of Charmin. Make no mistake about it: the cumulative effects of commercials are awesome. As the NARB study argues: "An endless procession of commercials on the same theme, all showing women using household products in the home, raises very strong implications that women have no other interests except laundry, dishes, waxing floors, and fighting dirt in any form. . . . Seeing a great many such advertisements in succession reinforces the traditional stereotype that a 'woman's place is *only* in the home.' "

There have, in the past few years, been commercials that break the homebody mold. The Fantastik spray commercial, "I'm married to a man, not a house" (which, incidentally, was written and produced by men), has reaped much praise, as has L'Oreal's "I'm worth it" campaign. "Ten years ago, it would have been, 'John thinks I'm worth it,' " says Lenore Hershey, editor of *Ladies' Home Journal. Ms.'* Pat Carbine thinks United Airlines is flying right when they address women executives, "You're the boss." She also likes the Campbell's soup "working wife" commercial, in which a man scurries around the kitchen, preparing soup for his woman, but adds, "I'm afraid they took the easy route and resorted to total role reversal—making her look good at the expense of the man."

Indeed, Lois Wyse of Wyse Advertising fears that advertisers are not only failing to talk to today's women, but they're missing men as well. The reason for this, as she sees it, is research—the extensive demographic studies done on who buys what product. Last winter Wyse told *Madison Avenue,* "About twenty years ago we were all little Ozzies and Harriets to all the people who do research, and now their idea of contemporizing is to make the Ozzies into Harriets and the Harriets into Ozzies."

Marketing research, with its charts and graphs and scientific jargon, has increased in importance over the last ten years or so, while creativity, the keystone to the Alka-Seltzer, Volkswagen, and Benson & Hedges campaigns of the sixties, has taken the backseat. Ask anybody in advertising why commercials still show the little woman bumbling around in a fearful daze, and you'll find the answer is always the same: "Because our research tells us it is so." Agencies devote hundreds of thousands of dollars to find out who's buying their client's stuff and why. And it's not just Mom up there on the charts and graphs. Marketing researchers dissect and analyze the buying habits, educational and income levels of every member of the family. They even know what we do with our leisure time, and how much God we've got.

This subjective form of research is amorphously titled life-style research, explained by the respected *Journal of Marketing* in the following brave-new-world lingo: "Life-style data—activities, interests, opinions—have proved their importance as a means of *duplicating* the consumer for the marketing researcher. . . ."And more: "Life-style attempts to answer questions like: What do women think about the job of housekeeping? Do they see themselves as homebodies or swingers? Life-style provides definitions like 'housewife role haters,' 'old fashioned homebodies' and 'active affluent urbanites.' "

But life-style research is still in its infancy and very, very expensive. The trendiest and most attainable form of research going is called focus-group research, the grassroots movement of advertising research. From lairs of hidden cameras and tape-recording devices, agency and client-types, despite the experts' warnings that focus-group samples are far too small to be projected on a national scale, eke out a vision of their consumer that almost invariably fits just the stereotype they had in mind in the first place, and proceed to advertise accordingly.

The theory, quite simply, is to get inside women's heads in order to get inside their pocketbooks. From Satellite Beach to Spokane, fact-finding specialists are retained at grand sums to commune with the natives and document their particular buying habits. For instance:

The canned-meat industry's advertising wasn't paying off in the Southeast. Focus-group researchers were called in and groups of eight women were randomly selected from Memphis neighborhoods. The women fit the product's buyer profile—in this case, all came from families with middle to lower-middle incomes. Each woman was paid ten dollars. On an assigned day each focus group would meet for a two-hour session at the suburban home of the researcher's field representative—a woman who was a veteran of several similar exercises. As the women took their seats around the dining room table, loosening up with coffee and home-made cake, the client and agency folk sat, out of sight, in the rumpus room, carefully scanning the meeting on closed-circuit monitors. This is what they heard.

MODERATOR: Do any of you ever buy canned meats?

VOICES: Oh yes. Yeah. Uh, huh.

MODERATOR: When do you buy them?

ANN: Well, my husband went to New Orleans, so I bought a lot of canned goods. The children enjoy them.

LOU: Well, I bought Vienna sausage the other day 'cause the Giant had a special on it—seventy-nine cents a can—it's usually a dollar nine, a dollar nineteen. You could only get four at a time, so I went back twice that week.

MODERATOR: Do you buy these for particular members of the family?

NORMA: If they didn't like it, I wouldn't buy it.

DELORES: Melvin loves the hot dog chili. And the baby—you can just stick a Vienna sausage in her hand and she'll go 'round happy all day.

MODERATOR: Do you read the labels on canned meats?

VOICES: Oh sure. Yes.

NORMA: The children read the labels first and called my attention to it. When I saw it had things like intestines and things like that, I didn't want to buy potted meat any more.

LOU: Fats, tissues, organs. If you read the labels on this stuff—when they say hearts . . . I don't know. I don't like hearts.

VIRGINIA: Well, psychologically you're not geared to it.

ALMA: They could lie on the label a little bit. Just don't tell us so much. (Laugh.) It would taste pretty good, but . . . yeah. I'd rather not know.

MODERATOR: What do you think ought to be on the labels?

ANNE: I think you ought to know about the chemicals.

NORMA: I love to read calories on the side of a can.

DELORES: I wonder what all's in those preservatives?

IDA: The side of this Hormel can here says that this meat is made by the same company that makes Dial soap. Says Armour-Dial.

NORMA: At least you think it's clean.

DELORES: Some preservatives do taste like soap. . . .

IDA: I wouldn't be eating that stuff with them chemicals.

ANN: Well, if you worry about that, you're going to starve to death.

VIRGINIA: You'd never eat in a restaurant if you ever got back in the kitchen.

MODERATOR: Would you buy a product because of the advertising?

VOICES: No. No. Maybe.

IDA: My children love that Libby's—the one, "Libby's, Libby's, Libby's. . . ."

NORMA: Now, if there's young kids that go to the grocery store with you, everytime they'll pick up something . . . "Libby's, Libby's, Libby's."

DELORES: Every time I see Hormel chili . . . I think about them people out at a fireside by the beach eating that chili. One of them is playing a guitar and they start singing.

VIRGINIA: Armour has a cute hot dog commercial, that's where they're all marching around, weenies, ketchup and mustard. . . .

IDA: Yeah. That's cute.

MODERATOR: Do any of you ever buy Spam?

IDA: What's Spam?

ANNE: It's chopped something. Or pressed.

LOU: It's beaver board.

MODERATOR: Beaver what?

Most researchers claim that their studies are only as good as the people who interpret them. The interpreters are usually the agency and clients who—many advertising executives will admit, but only off the record—read their own product concerns into the comments of the panelists. Quite often, complaints about daytime commercials ("They're awful!" "Ridiculous!" "Laughable!") are brushed aside. "You can formulate breakthrough approaches in order to reach this new woman," Joan Rothberg, a senior VP at Ted Bates, told *Madison Avenue,* "and yet the traditional 'Ring Around the Collar' approach wins out in terms of creating awareness and motivating people to buy the product."

One of the final research tests a commercial can go through after it's been created and storyboarded is the Burke test. One day up at my old agency, the creative director, a writer, and an art director came blazing through the halls with hats and horns, announcing at 120 decibels, "We Burked twenty-nine! We Burked twenty-nine!" Now this may sound to you as it did to me that day, as if these people were talking in tongues. What having "Burked twenty-nine" actually means is the percentage the commercial scored in recall after one viewing by a large audience. The average number on the Burke scale for the particular product my friends were testing was twenty-five—so you can understand the celebration.

Because the agencies and their clients accept Burke scores as valid, the scores become a powerful factor in what types of commercials will run. It's no accident that the Burke company is located in Cincinnati, since Cincinnati is the birthplace of Crest, Crisco, Comet, Charmin, Cheer, Bonus, Bounce, Bounty, Bold, Lava,

Lilt, Pampers, Prell, Downy, Dash, and Duz—in other words, Cincinnati is the home of the King Kong of Household Cleanliness, Procter & Gamble. From high atop magnificent offices, P&G executives control daytime television and a goodly portion of prime time, too. They are the top-dollar spender on TV, having put out $260 million last year alone in commercial time bought. They produce and have editorial control over five of the biggest soap operas on TV: *As the World Turns, Another World, Edge of Night, Guiding Light,* and *Search for Tomorrow,* which reach some forty million women every day.

Procter & Gamble is the most blatant offender in perpetuating "the little woman" commercial stereotype. Because of its monopoly on both media and marketplace (it pulls in $3.6 billion every year) and because its research is the most expensive and extensive, P&G is the recognized leader and arbiter of format and content in household product commercials—where P&G goes, others will follow.

This does not spur innovation. In one P&G agency, the creative people have two formulae they use for "concepting" a commercial: regular slice-of-life (problem in the home, solution with the wonderful product) or what the agency guys call "two C's in a K." The "K" stands for kitchen; the "C" is a four-letter word.

Once a commercial is written, tested, and approved by the client, it's got to be cast and shot. I asked Barbara Claman to talk about what agency people and their clients ask for when they're casting housewife roles. She should know: Barbara's built up one of the largest commercial casting agencies in the country. The day we talked all hell was breaking loose outside her office door. Scores of women and children had come to try out for a McDonald's commercial.

I wondered if agencies ever called for a P&G-type housewife for their commercials.

"Absolutely. She should be blond—or, if brunette, not too brunette. Pretty, but not too pretty. Midwestern in speech, middle-class looking, gentile. If they want to use blacks, they want *waspy* blacks."

"What about P&G-type husbands?"

"Same thing," Claman said. "But you'll find that the husband is getting to play the asshole more and more in American commercials."

"But do you see a change occurring? A trend in women's portrayals away from the traditional P&G type?"

"A little. I think they'd like to be a little more real. They're realizing, very slowly, that the working woman has a lot of money."

"What if they want a Rosie, a Madge or a Cora—one of the Eric Hoffer working-class philosopher-queens?"

Barbara laughed. "They'll say, 'Let's cast a ballsy one.' "

"Are you offended by the roles they want to put women in? Do you try to change their thinking on this?"

"I'm totally offended. I'm tired of seeing women hysterical over dirt spots on their glasses. I get lady producers in here all the time. We've tried to change their minds about the roles. You see how successful we've been."

Jane Green is another casting director in New York. She tells of a friend who was auditioning for a P&G spot in which the agency's creative people were trying to break out of the housewife mold. They'd called interesting faces—real people who wore real clothes. A couple of hours passed and the P&G client was obviously agitated. He turned to the agency producer: "What are you people trying to pull over on me? The woman in this commercial needs to be *my* wife, in *my* bathroom in Cincinnati—not some hip little chickie. Whom do you think we're selling to?"

One wonders. Recently an agency producer asked me and my cat Rayette to be in a kitty litter commercial. I arrived wearing blue jeans and a shirt, my usual at-home ensemble. The art director, who was wearing jeans himself, wasn't pleased:

"Where is your shirtwaist? I told the producer I wanted a *housewife* look in this commercial." I tried to explain that most women—housewives and otherwise—had left those McMullans and Villagers back at the Tri Delt house in '66. The shoot was postponed until we found something that looked more housewifey.

Some commercial trends have passed: The damsel in distress has, for the time being, retreated to her tower. (Remember the thundering White Knight? The mystical, spotless Man from Glad? Virile, barrel-chested Mr. Clean?) But others remain, the most blatantly offensive, perhaps, being those commercials using women as sex objects to entice the consumer into buying the product. Most agency people aren't allowed to comment on the scheme of things in such commercials (one slip of the tongue and that multimillion-dollar account might choose another, more circumspect agency). But Dwight Davis, VP and creative director on the Ford dealers' account with J. Walter Thompson in Detroit, says it's no secret Detroit is still the national stronghold of selling with sex. Why? The male is still the decision maker in car buying ("Our research tells us it is so"); and the auto is still an extension of the American male libido. So we've got Catherine Deneuve hawking Lincoln-Mercurys. She circles the car in her long, slinky gown and slips inside to fondle the plush interior. Catherine signs off, sprawled across the hood of the car, with a seductive grrrrr. She is, as Davis describes the phenomenon, the car advertisers' "garnish on the salad."

Commercials like this, and the little woman slice-of-life, are caricatures of themselves. That's precisely why Carol Burnett and the people at *Saturday Night Live* have so much fun with them. Even the new wave of women's commercials isn't spared. In a spoof Anne Beatts wrote for *Saturday Night,* a middle-class Mom, dressed not in a shirt-waist but a polyester pantsuit, rushes into the kitchen, crashing through a café-curtained dutch door. She starts to have a heart-to-heart with the camera: "I'm a nuclear physicist and Commissioner of Consumer Affairs." She starts to put her groceries away.

"In my spare time, I do needlepoint, read, sculpt, take riding lessons, and brush up on my knowledge of current events. Thursday's my day at the day-care center, and then there's my work with the deaf; but I still have time left over to do all my own baking and practice my backhand, even though I'm on call twenty-four hours a day as a legal aid lawyer in Family Court. . . . " Our New-Wave Mom is still running on, all the time very carefully folding the grocery bags and stuffing them into a cabinet where literally hundreds of other carefully folded bags are stacked incredibly neatly, when the omniscient announcer comes in:

"How does Ellen Sherman, Cleveland housewife, do it all? She's smart! She takes Speed. Yes, Speed—the tiny blue diet pill you don't have to be overweight to need."

If the "average" woman is true to her portrayal in commercials, we've got a pretty bitter pill to swallow. But you know, we all know, commercials don't portray real life. Nice Movies' Dick Clark, who's done spots for Coca-Cola, Toyota, and Glade, points out, most commercials are "formula answers to advertising questions—bad rip-offs of someone else's bad commercials." They are bad rip-offs of their viewers too. But, someday, some bright young advertising prodigy will begin a whole new trend of commercials that don't talk down, don't demean or debase, and still sell soap or toothpaste or cars like crazy. And then everyone will be doing it. Double your money back, guaranteed.

Why am I so sure? Because, as Brinkley so neatly points out, only seven percent of our homes have the traditional resident Mom. Because there are more women doctors, engineers, copywriters, jockeys, linesmen, you name it, than ever before. Because women are becoming more selective in their buying habits. Because, quite simply, research tells me it is so.

DISCUSSION QUESTIONS

1. Do you think Caldwell's argument about sexism in advertising is still accurate? Choose one or two recent television commercials to support your point of view.

2. Look at the ads reprinted in this section from the prespective of Caldwell's argument. Which ads conform to her contention about the role of women in advertising; which do not? How might she respond to ads you think show women in a positive manner?

Ralph Nader / Challenging the Corporate Ad

1983

America's foremost consumer watchdog, Ralph Nader is generally regarded as the prime motivator behind the current nationwide concern over product safety and value. His first book, Unsafe at Any Speed *(1965), sparked enormous controversy and led to the passage of government-enforced auto-safety standards. Since then, he and his associates (known as ''Nader's Raiders'') have made pioneering contributions in the areas of mental health, water and air pollution, and nuclear power.*

While still actively involved in immediate consumer matters, Nader remains most concerned with raising public response to the broader issues suggested by the use and misuse of corporate power.

With a weekly circulation of 80,000, Ad Age *is the leading trade journal of marketing information for the advertising industry. (See pp. 000-000 for examples of ads discussed by Nader.)*

What comes to mind whenever I read about image/issue advertising are the Mobil advocacy ads and the Sperry Rand learning to listen messages. These recollections are followed by others: ''When E.F. Hutton talks, people listen'' (possibly the deepest mental imprint image ad ever developed); the misapplied $7 million campaign of Monsanto telling the audience that ''without chemicals, life itself would be impossible,'' and the now legendary blunder by Potlatch Industries, which, in promoting its alleged pollution control sensitivity, showed a clean, flowing Clearwater River.

Later disclosure pointed out that the picture of the river was at a point upstream from the plant.

None of these ads sells products; all of them sell impressions or ideas. As such, billions of dollars of similar advertisements over the past decades have generated many questions. Are corporations spending their shareholders' money prudently? Should shareholders approve such campaigns, especially since their costs increase the price of products or services the companies are selling? Should these ads be regulated by the Federal Trade Commission for factual deceptions just as commercial product ads are supposed to be? Should ads dealing with issues of public controversy be shown on tv or broadcast on radio? If so, should the Fairness Doctrine be made available routinely to critics for reply? How far should the First Amendment embrace commercial speech, and what protections should consumers be accorded?

Basic to these questions is an uneasiness about allowing corporate money machines to dominate the communication highways to the public about important political, economic and safety matters.

As Alfred Schneider, a vp with ABC Inc., said: "You cannot let those with the financial funds, the money to be able to buy the time, dictate the agenda of public debate."

In a similar vein, Michael Gerrard, writing about Mobil's purchase of op-ed advertorials on the editorial pages of leading newspapers, observed: "With sheer cash, Mobil has become a *New York Times* columnist." With sheer gall, the same oil company has purchased time from local tv stations just before their evening news for the "Mobil Information Center," designed to appear as if it was a real news spot instead of pure company propaganda complete with actors and actresses playing anchorman and reporter.

Most critics of image/idea/issue advertisements challenge their legitimacy, deductibility and accuracy. From the public relations side, there have also been doubts expressed. Loet Velmans, president of Hill & Knowlton, said of the Mobil ads in 1979: "What's the audience? Is Mobil speaking to the converted? I don't know who they're talking to." And Craig Lewis of Earl Newsom & Co. noted that Mobil's advocacy campaign "has gotten attention for the company but has not advanced the cause of the oil industry significantly. The tone of the ads has gotten too peevish."

Certainly, Mobil incurred greater ill will, if not antagonism, by the Carter Administration. President Carter called Mobil irresponsible. Members of Congress used stronger language in private. Mobil has succeeded in alienating more media barons than any consumer group could have ever anticipated possible. But then, why should Mobil care? With more than $60 billion in annual sales, the company may think it is in the position of the 800 lb. gorilla—able to sleep anywhere it wants.

Many companies watched Mobil's bold foray into fast-track nonproduct, advocacy advertisements, often replying quickly to charges or news stories, to see whether it was worth emulating.

The rest of the oil majors demurred. But others, like Dresser Industries, United Technologies and St. Paul Property and Liability Co., took the plunge with some pretty strong advertorials. Still, most corporations prefer to work through their trade associations on specific controversial issues before legislatures and agencies, and maintain a lower public profile for their own actions. Too much public attention and spotlight could lead to additional stoking of corporate coals hitherto undisturbed.

There is little doubt, however, that institutional advertising is absorbing more and more of the corporations' dollars. Big money is going into campaigns by military contractors touting their latest jet aircraft or other weapons systems.

General Motors Corp. is currently demonstrating to tv viewers its supposed commitment to crash safety engineering by showing life-size dummies in stress and crash situations.

Obviously these campaigns were launched in the belief that the selected audiences would be favorably impressed. While this may be true for noninvolved readers and viewers at a rather superficial impact level, there is a greater likelihood of generating deeper adverse involvement by people who read and see these ads and become outraged. There are taxpayers and citizen groups who will be moved to questioning why tax dollars directly or indirectly are being used to promote weapons already produced and sold to their only customer—the U.S. government. And there are auto safety advocates inside and outside the insurance industry who are indignant at GMC's crashworthiness ad.

They remember the company dismantling in April, 1981, its technical unit working on automatic crash protection systems and opposing a government safety standard that previous GMC executives supported in the early 1970s.

In their book "The Mass Image of Big Business" (1955), Gardner and Rainwater made this enduring point: "Unless management understands the public's underlying feeling, it can unwittingly pave the way for hostile reactions and a lowering of the prestige of big business." That was Potlatch Industries' error.

By contrast Sperry Rand's listening ads evoke an image, whether accurate or not, of a willingness to learn, to have a give and take and to eschew arrogance. Sperry's listening advice also can be helpful to the reader's self-development. All in all, a winner in the institutional ad sweepstakes!

In the main, though, the thousands of corporate image/idea ads are pushing corporate values, corporate programs and corporate priorities. Consumers should seize these provocations and turn them into opportunities. Demanding FTC regulation of factual errors or Treasury Department scrutiny of which ad budgets cannot be deducted may produce some media copy but little else. What is needed is to transform the growing sense of unfairness and imbalance that these well financed campaigns induce among the public—whose voice is not being heard—into durable reforms or customs.

First, consumers should turn these corporate issue ads into public controversies via letters to the editor, op-ed articles and by alerting both electronic and print media to the value of reporting or featuring the underlying story. In short, the ad can buy itself inadvertently one or a series of articles and editorials.

Second, as the media make increasing profits off these institutional ads, the argument of institutionalizing citizen access to pages and air time becomes more persuasive. When the *New York Times* places full page ads in its newspaper soliciting image/issue corporate ads by indicating that the *Times'* integrity is wrapped around the message, it is time to ask its editors whether such integrity extends to expansion of space for reader opinion. Some newspapers place reader letters replying to corporate ads in a second-class category and rarely print them.

Similarly, more public airwave time should be given to viewer and listener commentary—at the least a weekly electronic letters-to-the-editor slot—if not a more ambitious opening of the airwaves to the public's enjoyment of *its* First Amendment rights.

In an electronic and mass communication society, the First Amendment can be deployed by the favored few against the excluded many. If free speech over the mass media is largely a function of licenses, monopolies and those wealthy enough to buy space or time, instead of being a function of diversity of ideas, our country will continue to deprive itself of the rewarding fruits of free speech.

The flood of corporate image/issue advertisements, ever more penetrating, timely and controversial, keeps the critical issues of corporate power and limited citizen access in the minds of more people. If these issues are not yet on your agenda, rest assured that the *Fortune* 500 will be provoking you to do something about them almost daily. If perceived injustice is the seed for change, call for a blunt Mobil rather than a bland Exxon.

Marshall Schuon / Cars and Self-Image

1983

As members of a nation on wheels, American men have traditionally used the automobile to project themselves and advertise their individual personalities. In "Cars and Self-Image," Marshall Schuon notes how our private whims, the attitudes of our era, and the interests of the corporate auto-makers change the ways in which we view—and embrace—these emblems of self-importance.

Marshall Schuon, deputy editor of The New York Times *national edition, writes the consumer-oriented column, "About Cars."*

I once had a fistfight with a kid named Alan. I think I won, although both Alan and my nose may dispute it. What we were fighting about was electric trains, specifically my insistence on the superior realism of American Flyer when compared to those clunky, three-rail Lionels. We were always arguing about something like that. We identified with *stuff,* and if it wasn't trains, it was comic strips, or the contention that the P-38 was a better fighter plane than the P-47. Later, in the early 1950's, it was cars, and the argument extended to all of our friends.

Back then, a sports car was an MG-TC with spindly wheels, wooden floorboards and a body made of old chewing-gum wrappers, nothing a real 17-year-old man would own. You were either a Ford guy or a Chevy guy. Plymouths didn't count, and we didn't *talk* to the guy who bought a '41 Packard. Shows how much we knew. It also shows how tightly rapt we were by the idea of a package to suit our image.

Ford had a V-8 engine. You could put dual exhausts on it. You could top it off with a whole gaggle of carburetors. You could throw in a hot cam and have something that was truly the terror of the streets. Or you could take a Jimmy truck engine, stuff it into a Chevy sedan and make a mohair monster that ate Fords for lunch. It all depended.

It still does, of course. A car says a lot about a man, and that is the real reason that dealers don't have generic automobiles on their shelves. No sensibly priced, plain-white, three-sizes-fit-all vehicles for us. What we want, whether we admit it or not, are rolling advertisements for ourselves, and the chief difficulty is in choosing the right billboard.

For myself, and for a long time after I gave up the hot-rod Fords, it was a successive line of vans and funny cars like Corvairs. And, finally, it was a Cadillac. I was wearing a cowboy hat then and, night after night, I would arrive at the newspaper I worked for, Stetson on my head, blonde on my arm and goblet of brandy in my hand. The guards in the lobby thought I was a real character. I know that because one of them told me about this bozo who was a real character. We were in the men's room and he didn't recognize me without my hat and blonde and brandy, which is what happens when you shuck the trappings.

The problem with the Cadillac, of course, was that it had to stay outside. It was just right for a man in a cowboy hat—powerful, lush and big to the point of being a crime against nature. But it wasn't any good out there in the parking lot with me in the office. I solved that by carrying the owner's manual and leaving it discreetly on the desk.

Since then, I've worked a bit on my profile, and these days I've got it down to a small Buick. I tell myself I'm more mature, less flamboyant. And I like to think it says something about increasing self-confidence. Those are nice things to think, even though I know it's only the recession.

Subtlety does have its place, however, and Mercedes-Benz has capitalized nicely on a slice of the market that demands quiet flare. "What it is," a smugly happy owner once told me, "is quality and engineering. You drive that car and it says something about you, about being smart enough to know it—and, second, being rich enough to afford it."

If money is no object, naturally, you can suit your image in the same disgusting way you can do anything when money is no object. I have a friend in the automobile business whose name is Fred. He did it by going on a diet and then buying a white Jaguar for days and a blue Ferrari for nights. He had to go on the diet because a Ferrari is a *thin* car. When you drive a Ferrari, you don't have room for an extra pack of king-size cigarettes, let alone your very own spare tire.

"The Jag is an open car, that's why it's for days," Fred says. "The Ferrari's a coupe and that's why it's for nights. But you talk about this image thing—you can pretty much typecast who will own what kind of car. If you're a pilot, for instance, you buy a Saab. Guys who are into mechanical weirdness always buy Saabs."

You can look at a guy, says Fred, and know he's an old Fiat or he's American Motors. "Take a Porsche guy," he says. "A Porsche owner is very image-conscious. He wants to be daring on the outside, but he'd never own a Ferrari because a Porsche is more practical. With a Ferrari, if you run into a repair problem, you can be in for as much as $2,000 or $3,000."

Another thing, says Fred, is the kind of man who owns a Corvette or a Pontiac Trans Am. "Those are cars people move out of," he says. "You'll see an ad that says 'Must sell my Corvette—getting married,' but you don't see it the other way, you don't see that ad for a Ferrari or a Mercedes 450 SL."

It is not just drivers who think about image though; the men who make the cars think about it too, and there have been some spectacular changes over the years in what a car is meant to say. When I was a kid, the Dodge was gray and grandfatherly. Stodgy. Nothing at all like the Dodges that were the hot ticket on the racing circuits of the late 1960's and early 1970's. And John Z. DeLorean, before garnering all his other celebrity, made a name for himself at General Motors by changing Pontiac from a dull and middle-aged widget into a wide-track screamer that was panted over by a nation's entire zit-set.

It must be admitted, however, that power and pizazz are not all things to all men. There are those, a relative few in the scheme of things, who see the positive advantage in projecting a negative image. They delight in their perversity. They don't want flashy performance or Italian good looks or a car that drips gold instead of brake fluid. They are the people who made the Volkswagen Beetle a hit, and today they are the people who joyfully fling their arms and leap into the air when they see a Toyota Tercel.

Rolls-Royce is the ultimate image car, of course, but the company has only recently tried to find out who buys its product. "You know, we've always been a sort of cottage industry," says Reginald Abbiss, a former BBC reporter who now employs his dulcet British tones as the Rolls spokesman in the colonies. "We only make 60 cars a week, but we have to look ahead, and we are adopting a more aggressive approach in promotion and advertising."

What the company is finding, he said, is that—particularly in America—a Rolls customer is saying "I've worked damned hard for my money, and this is a tangible result."

Image, too, is the real reason the company continues to make the Bentley, which differs from the Rolls only in its radiator shell and costs $530 less than the $93,000 bottom-of-the-line Rolls. "With that sort of tariff," says Reg Abbiss, "the $530 obviously doesn't make any difference. What we like to believe is that the Bentley is for the man who has won the race but declines to wear the laurel."

DISCUSSION QUESTIONS

1. Look over the automobile ads in this section. Select one ad that you believe supports Schuon's analysis. Explain why.

2. Do the advertisers themselves see a connection between an individual's car and his personality? How does the ad for Alpha Romeo (see p. 000) portray such connections?

3. What about women? Have their self-images no connection to automobiles? Explain your answer.

PRESS

Journalism is literature in a hurry.

MATTHEW ARNOLD

NEWS may be America's best-selling product. Despite the intense competition from radio and television broadcasts, where news is delivered instantaneously and free of charge, well over fifty-eight million Americans are still willing to pay for their daily newspaper. Serving this immense market is an industry built around twenty-three thousand daily and weekly newspapers. The industry ranges from the picturesque one room office of a country paper, where the news is gathered, written, edited, and printed by a handful of people, to multilevel, worldwide corporate enterprises employing thousands in the strenuous business of compiling, disseminating, and even occasionally making the news. A news item, whether in a two page rural paper or in that monstrous, practically unfinishable, several hundred page Sunday edition of the *New York Times*, needs to be seen, then, as something more than simply a report of current events. To be comprehended fully, the news should be considered in its largest corporate context—as the result of individual and group writing performed under the pressures of advertising revenue, available space, deadlines, audience surveys, ownership policy, editorial selection, and professional competition. The "news" is not only transmitted information, it is the commodity of newspapers.

The pledge "All the News That's Fit To Print" on the front page of every copy of the *New York Times* reminds us that only news deemed suitable to print has been *selected* for us by editors apparently fastidious in their taste and conscience. The *Times'* motto, however, once prompted the following slightly cynical parody: "All the News That Fits We Print." The joke here works not only at the expense of the *New York Times;* it could easily apply to any large newspaper. A simple experiment shows how relatively small is the percentage of space allotted for what is supposedly a newspaper's main product, news. If you cut out from any newspaper with a fairly large circulation all the commercial and classified advertisements, the theater, movie, radio, and television listings, the national and local gossip, the personal advice columns, the horoscope, the puzzles and games, the cartoons, the letters to the editor, the "human interest" tid-bits, and the fillers, you are left with very few of what are, strictly speaking, genuine news items. In short, little of the shape and essence of a modern newspaper remains. The parody of the *Times'* pledge is right on target. It does seem that readers of most newspapers are given only the news that "fits" between the spaces reserved for more profitable or entertaining pieces.

To make sure that all the news will "fit"—in the sense of meeting editorial standards and conforming to the physical confines of the paper—newspapers impose a strictly regulated system of reportorial procedures and conventions. A person who writes for a newspaper must not only contend with tight deadlines but must also satisfy an experienced copy editor whose job is to see to it that the report will conform to the paper's public image and fit easily into its style. The writer must also be aware that the report will compete with all other news and non-news for prominent display in the layout of each edition. The exigencies of the newspaper business demand that the writer develop a comformable, transferable, and conveniently alterable prose.

Any respected editor will say that clear and concise writing is encouraged. This usually means prose whittled down to short, simple sentences, the sparing use of adjectives and adverbs, a minimal reliance on synonyms, an avoidance of cumbersome syntactical relations, and brief paragraphs with few transitions. Most of the journalism reprinted in this section illustrates writing that conforms to these editorial strictures. Such standards are double-edged: they ensure the kind of writing generally considered to be most appropriate to rendering factual information quickly and precisely, and they guarantee sentences that are uniform and formulaic enough so as to be easily maneuvered into each newspaper's particular editorial requirements and emphases.

A stylistic uniformity for reporting important news stories (feature articles, editorials, and so on, are not so restricted) is enforced even further by a standardized narrative procedure newspapermen call the "inverted pyramid." The opening of a news story conventionally contains all the significant facts—the who, what, when, where, and occasionally the why—and the story tapers off gradually (picture a pyramid upside down), delivering additional facts and embellishments in a diminishing order of importance. Editors assume that their readers will want all the major details of a story right away, and that they should have the opportunity to move on to another story as soon as they feel they have absorbed enough information. Consequently, the emphasis in news writing is placed on the "lead," the opening sentences or paragraphs. In writing about a major news event, the reporter is obligated to pack in the principal facts in the first few lines. Since each succeeding sentence becomes less significant and, from an editor's point of view, increasingly dispensable, it is not unusual for reporters to let their prose slacken as their story moves further away from the top.

By opening the story with its climax, the writer gives up the possibility of sequential development and narrative suspense so that his readers can focus on the most important details immediately and his editor can lop off, should he need space for something else, the tapered strands of the report without losing any essential points. Therefore, paragraphs in most news stories are not connected to each other within a coherent expository framework. Instead, they can be thought of as self-contained, transferable, and, occasionally, disposable units. As a result, the reporter continually faces a rather disconcerting problem: he must write in such a manner that enables, even encourages, his audience to stop reading after the main points have been made, and, at the same time, he must make his writing compelling enough so that his readers will want to read on.

Yet reporters contend with more than the difficulties of composition. News stories need to be covered before they can be written. Reporters are men and women often entangled in the intricacies and drawn into the pace of the events they are trying to write about. They compose stories under pressure and in a hurry. To be "on the spot" during an event of some magnitude means most often to get caught up in the uncertain movements of participants and in the prevailing mood of the occasion. The inconveniences are many and unpredictable. One famous reporter, Stephen Crane, accompanying a crew of gun runners headed for Cuba during the insurrection at the close of the last century, was shipwrecked off the coast of Florida (see "Stephen Crane's Own Story"), and wound up with a tale far different from the one he had intended to write (see "The Open Boat" in Classics). To illustrate most dramatically the kind of difficulties encountered during a strenuous and emotionally trying reportorial assignment, we have included Tom Wicker's recollections of his efforts to cover the assassination of President Kennedy (see "The Assassination").

November 22, 1963, was for Wicker a day of great confusion and physical exhaustion. Though he was on the spot, Wicker was not close enough to the President's car to witness the shooting directly, nor did he even have the opportunity to view the principal characters afterward for more than a few moments. Covering the story of Kennedy's assassination was mainly an ordeal of getting quickly from one good news position to another and of assimilating the disparate and occasionally contradictory details of the event as rapidly as possible. The information came, as Wicker says, "in bits and pieces," and most of the time he had no way of verifying the data. The news story of the assassination was not "out there" to be copied down leisurely, without risks of inaccuracy. It was a matter of acting on hunches, recovering quickly from wrong turns, finding reliable contacts, getting around physical and bureaucratic obstacles, and all the while trying to put as many details into as coherent a shape as conditions allowed so the story could get to press on time.

Yet the by-line report printed in the *New York Times* the next day (see "Kennedy Is Killed by Sniper") conveys nothing at all of the frantic pace and exasperating confusions Wicker tells us obstructed his coverage. What Wicker went through that day—whatever public and private significances the event had for him—was not news. The conventions of newspaper reporting are exacting on one point: the reporter must not figure as a main character in his own story. If indeed, as Thoreau says, "It is, after all, always the first person that is speaking," we nevertheless need to work quite hard to imagine the "I" who is the eyewitness behind Wicker's writing. Not even an effort to read "between the lines" could help us reconstruct from his prose alone the tensions of Wicker's day as he hustled around Dallas for the news.

Wicker's report provides us with a fine instance of journalistic workmanship. The assassination was far too important an event for Wicker to take stylistic chances. The *Times* got what it wanted: the straightforward, informative account that is the marrow of news reporting. It saved the expressions of personal grief and the emotional record of the public sentiment appropriate to such occasions for its features and editorials. Part of Wicker's accomplishment in this by-line report is his cool, professional manner—he resists the impulse to attract attention to himself as a writer privileged to have been an eyewitness to one of the most sensational news events of the twentieth century. As a narrator, Wicker is never anxious to assure his readers of his presence at the scene. He never pauses in the account to remind us that his perspectives depend on his following the day's developments through several different locations in Dallas. Wicker deliberately avoids commenting on his own emotional connection to an event that we know from his own recollection shocked and grieved him. Nor, as he writes, does he allow himself the liberty of sounding like a worried citizen reflecting on the political and social significance of Kennedy's murder. It is clear that we cannot properly read Wicker's piece as a *personal* account of the assassination. In other words, we can not respond to his writing as if it were—what most of us usually expect writing to be—the disclosure of a particular personality. If Wicker tells us anything at all about himself, it is that he has mastered the discipline of news reporting.

Wicker's prose conforms to all the rules of journalistic style outlined earlier. The writing consists, for the most part, of syntactically simple, declarative sentences. The paragraphs are brief; only one contains as many as five sentences. The first few paragraphs provide the reader with all the crucial information, and the narrative proceeds to register details in what Wicker and his editors presumably considered to be a scale of decreasing importance. Though the narrative procedure would seem to recall the "inverted pyramid" mentioned previously, a closer look at Wicker's prose reveals a movement less narrowing than it would have been had Wicker adhered strictly to that often tyrannizing model. Instead, the narrative proceeds with a spiraling effect, moving from the center outward, moving, that is, away from its "lead" only to return to it repeatedly, though each time with a new angle and a diminishing emphasis.

Wicker, however, is not fully responsible for the narrative shape the story eventually took. He mentions in his retrospective analysis that he sent off to the *Times* information in "a straight narrative" he knew would be cut up by his editors as they decided on the best sequence and appropriate emphases. Although the by-line officially recognizes Wicker as the "author" of the news release, the final report the *Times* printed was, as is usually the case in news writing, the result of a collective activity that included Wicker and several other reporters who assisted him in Dallas, along with a New York staff of rewrite, copy, and managing editors.

While he was writing his report, Wicker must have been acutely conscious of the extensive television coverage given to the assassination. In fact, Wicker tells us that he filled in a few of the gaps in his own report by drawing on some of the information provided by television. Yet, as an antidote to the bewildering discontinuities and the numbing replays of the television reports, Wicker articulated a full, dispassionate recapitulation of the Kennedy assassination, accentuating the official interconnections between people and events rather than the panorama of personalities on location. To illustrate how a journalist responded to a similar incident almost a hundred years earlier, we have included the *New York Herald's* coverage of President Lincoln's assassination. The April 15, 1865, issue of the *New York Herald* furnishes us with reportorial styles that were beginning to be conditioned by the invention of the telegraph but were not yet forced into competition with radio and television networks.

Tom Wicker's task as a reporter competing with the "live" transmission of news was not nearly so problematic as was Thomas O'Toole's assignment for the *Washington Post* to watch and write about the first landing on the moon in July 1969 (see " 'The Eagle Has Landed': Two Men Walk on the Moon"). Given the hermetic nature of such an electronically engineered event as *Apollo XI*'s flight to the moon, O'Toole could not claim a better vantage point for viewing the episode than could anyone else in the world with access to a television set. If the event O'Toole reported were, as he says in his lead, "a show that will long be remembered by the worldwide television audience," then he must have seen his function as that of a television reviewer rather than a privileged eyewitness commentator. In fact, his report makes it clear that the astronauts spent a good deal of their time transforming the moon into a television studio in which they then performed and improvised before the camera. Overshadowed by television, O'Toole's report could be little more than a public transcript of conversations everyone heard and descriptions of what everyone witnessed, punctuated by hyperbolic remarks that could express only the exclamatory mood of millions. Whether viewed as a technological triumph or as a television spectacular, the moon landing came as no special blessing to the newspaper industry. Upstaged by the extensive, unprecedented television coverage, reporters like O'Toole were left with relatively little to do but gather feature stories, collate information from television broadcasts, and turn NASA press releases into intelligible prose.

Each new day does not supply newspapers with a calamity or a triumph—most days newspapers need to find their news in the ordinary occurrences of life. Though a new headline appears daily, it may be merely perfunctory. Given standard newspaper format, one event must always be given more prominence than others. In our selections, we have tried to represent a good portion of the kind of news material you would normally find in American newspapers. We have included many of the standard forms and predominant styles of journalism: headlines, the "inverted pyramid" of major news stories, the fictional structures of feature stories, the polemical mode of editorials, along with by-lines, personal commentaries and columns, interviews, and humorous and whimsical anecdotes. Still, if the subjects for a good deal of the writing that follows strike you as disproportionately unpleasant, that is because the newspaper business generally thrives on the purveyance of "bad news." Pick up any newspaper, and you will be likely to find some account of individual or public violence, organized crime, political scandal, skirmishes with minorities and subcultures, domestic and international conflicts, the catastrophes of floods, earthquakes, and fires, and the routine disasters of modern transportation.

The material in this section is not intended as an introduction to the profession of journalism. The "texts" are meant to be read as examples of the often special language of the "reported" world. Our purpose is to invite you to consider the compositional procedures and prose styles of various kinds of reporting in order to observe how the reporter's method of writing appropriates public events in a way that makes it especially difficult for any of us to talk or to write about those events independently of the language provided by newspapers.

Staff Correspondent / Important. Assassination of President Lincoln

New York Herald, April 15, 1865

The following series of telegraphic dispatches and reports appeared in the New York Herald *the morning after President Lincoln's assassination.*

IMPORTANT.

•

ASSASSINATION
OF
PRESIDENT LINCOLN.

•

The President Shot at the
Theatre Last Evening.

•

SECRETARY SEWARD
DAGGERED IN HIS BED,
BUT
NOT MORTALLY WOUNDED.

•

Clarence and Frederick Seward Badly Hurt.

•

ESCAPE OF THE ASSASSINS.

•

Intense Excitement in
Washington.

•

Scene at the Deathbed of
Mr. Lincoln.

•

FIRST DISPATCH

Washington, April 14, 1865.

Assassination has been inaugurated in Washington. The bowie knife and pistol have been applied to President Lincoln and Secretary Seward. The former was shot in the throat, while at Ford's theatre to-night. Mr. Seward was badly cut about the neck, while in his bed at his residence.

SECOND DISPATCH

Washington, April 14, 1865.

An attempt was made about ten o'clock this evening to assassinate the President and Secretary Seward. The President was shot at Ford's Theatre. Result not yet known. Mr. Seward's throat was cut, and his son badly wounded.

There is intense excitement here.

DETAILS OF THE ASSASSINATION

Washington, April 14, 1865.

Washington was thrown into an intense excitement a few minutes before eleven o'clock this evening, by the announcement that the President and Secretary Seward had been assassinated and were dead.

The wildest excitement prevailed in all parts of the city. Men, women and children, old and young, rushed to and fro, and the rumors were magnified until we had nearly every member of the Cabinet killed. Some time elapsed before authentic data could be ascertained in regard to the affair.

The President and Mrs. Lincoln were at Ford's theatre, listening to the performance of *The American Cousin,* occupying a box in the second tier. At the close of the third act a person entered the box occupied by the President, and shot Mr. Lincoln in the head. The shot entered the back of his head, and came out above the temple.

The assassin then jumped from the box upon the stage and ran across to the other side, exhibiting a dagger in his hand, flourishing it in a tragical manner, shouting the same words repeated by the desperado at Mr. Seward's house, adding to it, "The South is avenged," and then escaped from the back entrance to the stage, but in his passage dropped his pistol and his hat.

Mr. Lincoln fell forward from his seat, and Mrs. Lincoln fainted.

The moment the astonished audience could realize what had happened, the President was taken and carried to Mr. Peterson's house, in Tenth Street, opposite to the theatre. Medical aid was immediately sent for, and the wound was at first supposed to be fatal, and it was announced that he could not live, but at half-past twelve he is still alive, though in a precarious condition.

As the assassin ran across the stage, Colonel J.B. Stewart, of this city, who was occupying one of the front seats in the orchestra, on the same side of the house as the box occupied by Mr. Lincoln, sprang to the stage and followed him; but he was obstructed in his passage across the stage by the fright of the actors, and reached the back door about three seconds after the assassin had passed out. Colonel Stewart got to the street just in time to see him mount his horse and ride away.

The operation shows that the whole thing was a preconcerted plan. The person who fired the pistol was a man about thirty years of age, about five feet nine, spare built, fair skin, dark hair, apparently bushy, with a large moustache. Laura Keene and the leader of the orchestra declare that they recognized him as J. Wilkes Booth the actor, and a rabid secessionist. Whoever he was, it is plainly evident that he thoroughly understood the theatre and all the approaches and modes of escape to the stage. A person not familiar with the theatre could not have possibly made his escape so well and quickly.

The alarm was sounded in every quarter. Mr. Stanton was notified, and immediately left his house.

All the other members of the Cabinet escaped attack.

Cavalrymen were sent out in all directions, and dispatches sent out to all the fortifications, and it is thought they will be captured.

About half-past ten o'clock this evening a tall, well dressed man made his appearance at Secretary Seward's residence, and applied for admission. He was refused admission by the servant, when the desperado stated that he had a prescription from the Surgeon General, and that he was ordered to deliver it in person. He was still refused, except upon the written order of the physician. This he pretended to show, and pushed by the servant and rushed up stairs to Mr. Seward's room. He was met at the door by Mr. Fred Seward, who notified him that he was master of the house, and would take charge of the medicine. After a few words had passed between them he dodged by Fred Seward and rushed to the Secretary's bed and struck him in the neck with a dagger, and also in the breast.

It was supposed at first that Mr. Seward was killed instantly, but it was found afterwards that the wound was not mortal.

Major Wm. H. Seward, Jr., paymaster, was in the room, and rushed to the defense of his father, and was badly cut in the *melee* with the assassin, but not fatally.

The desperado managed to escape from the house, and was prepared for escape by having a horse at the door. He immediately mounted his horse, and sung out the motto of the State of Virginia, "*Sic Semper Tyrannis!*" and rode cff.

Surgeon General Barnes was immediately sent for, and he examined Mr. Seward and pronounced him safe. His wounds were not fatal. The jugular vein was not cut, nor the wound in the breast deep enough to be fatal.

Washington, April 15—1 A.M.

The streets in the vicinity of Ford's Theatre are densely crowded by an anxious and excited crowd. A guard has been placed across Tenth Street and F and K Streets, and only official persons and particular friends of the President are allowed to pass.

The popular heart is deeply stirred, and the deepest indignation against leading rebels is freely expressed.

The scene at the house where the President lies in *extremis* is very affecting. Even Secretary Stanton is affected to tears.

When the news spread through the city that the President had been shot, the people, with pale faces and compressed lips, crowded every place where there was the slightest chance of obtaining information in regard to the affair.

After the President was shot, Lieutenant Rathbun, caught the assassin by the arm, who immediately struck him with a knife, and jumped from the box, as before stated.

The popular affection for Mr. Lincoln has been shown by this diabolical assassination, which will bring eternal infamy, not only upon its authors, but upon the hellish cause which they desire to avenge.

Vice President Johnson arrived at the White House, where the President lies, about one o'clock, and will remain with him to the last.

The President's family are in attendance upon him also.

As soon as intelligence could be got to the War Department, the electric telegraph and the Signal corps were put in requisition to endeavor to prevent the escape of the assassins, and all the troops around Washington are under arms.

Popular report points to a somewhat celebrated actor of known secession proclivities as the assassin; but it would be unjust to name him until some further evidence of his guilt is obtained. It is rumored that the person alluded to is in custody.

The latest advices from Secretary Seward reveals more desperate work there than at first supposed. Seward's wounds are not in themselves fatal, but, in connection with his recent injuries, and the great loss of blood he has sustained, his recovery is questionable.

It was Clarence A. Seward, instead of William H. Seward, Jr., who was wounded. Fred Seward was also badly cut, as were also three nurses, who were in attendance upon the Secretary, showing that a desperate struggle took place there. The wounds of the whole party were dressed.

One o'clock A.M.

The President is perfectly senseless, and there is not the slightest hope of his surviving. Physicians believe that he will die before morning. All of his Cabinet, except Secretary Seward, are with him. Speaker Colfax, Senator Farwell, of Maine, and many other gentlemen, are also at the house awaiting the termination.

The scene at the President's bedside is described by one who witnessed it as most affecting. He was surrounded by his Cabinet ministers, all of whom were bathed in tears, not even excepting Mr. Stanton, who, when informed by Surgeon General Barnes, that the President could not live until morning, exclaimed, "Oh, no, General; no—no;" and with an impulse, natural as it was unaffected, immediately sat down on a chair near his bedside and wept like a child.

Senator Sumner was seated on the right of the President's couch, near the head, holding the right hand of the President in his own. He was sobbing like a woman, with his head bowed down almost on the pillow of the bed on which the President was lying.

Two o'clock A.M.

The President is still alive, but there is no improvement in his condition.

DISCUSSION QUESTION

1. How does the *Herald* account differ from Wicker's report of President Kennedy's assassination? How is the President described in each? Which account do you think describes the assassination most vividly? Most informatively? With the most feeling?

Francis Pharcellus Church / Is There a Santa Claus?

New York Sun, December 31, 1897

Francis Pharcellus Church (1839–1906) was not eager to reply to the letter asking for his newspaper's official stance on the existence of Santa Claus, but papers around the world have not been at all reluctant to reprint the editorial Church finally did write. The New York Sun, *which first printed the piece, was noted at the time for its clear, colorful writing—a reputation it owed in large part to Church's prose.*

Thirty-seven years after Church wrote "Yes, Virginia, there is a Santa Claus," Heywood Broun countered with "There isn't any Santa Claus" in the New York World-Telegram. *Broun's editorial* *(see p. 000)* *responds to Church's famous letter and should be contrasted to it.*

We take pleasure in answering at once and thus prominently the communication below, expressing at the same time our great gratification that its faithful author is numbered among the friends of The Sun.

Dear Editor:

I am 8 years old.

Some of my little friends say there is no Santa Claus.

Papa says "If you see it in *The Sun* it's so."

Please tell me the truth, is there a Santa Claus?

Virginia O'Hanlon,
115 West 95th Street

Virginia, your little friends are wrong. They have been affected by the skepticism of a skeptical age. They do not believe except they see. They think that nothing can be which is not comprehensible by their little minds. All minds Virginia, whether they be men's or children's, are little. In this great universe of ours man is a mere insect, an ant, in his intellect, as compared with the boundless world about him, as measured by the intelligence capable of grasping the whole of truth and knowledge.

Yes, Virginia, there is a Santa Claus. He exists as certainly as love and generosity and devotion exist, and you know that they abound and give to your life its highest beauty and joy. Alas! How dreary would be the world if there were no Santa Claus! It would be as dreary as if there were no Virginias. There would be no childlike faith then, no poetry, no romance to make tolerable this existence. We should have no enjoyment, except in sense and sight. The eternal light with which childhood fills the world would be extinguished.

Not believe in Santa Claus! You might as well not believe in fairies! You might get your papa to hire men to watch in all the chimneys on Christmas Eve to catch Santa Claus, but even if they did not see Santa Claus coming down, what would that prove? Nobody sees Santa Claus, but that is no sign that there is no Santa Claus. The most real things in the world are those that neither children nor men can see. Did you ever see fairies dancing on the lawn? Of course not, but that's no proof that they are not there. Nobody can conceive or imagine all the wonders there are unseen and unseeable in the world.

You tear apart the baby's rattle and see what makes the noise inside but there is a veil covering the unseen world which not the strongest man, nor even the united strength of all the strongest men that ever lived, could tear apart. Only faith, fancy, poetry, love, romance, can push aside that curtain and view and picture the supernal beauty and glory beyond. Is it all real? Ah, Virginia, in all this world there is nothing else real and abiding.

No Santa Claus! Thank God he lives and he lives forever. A thousand years from now, Virginia, nay ten times ten thousand years from now, he will continue to make glad the heart of childhood.

Heywood Broun / There Isn't a Santa Claus

New York World-Telegram, December 20, 1934

"After we have shot Santa Claus what can we put in his place?" Heywood Broun asks at the end of his rebuttal to Francis Pharcellus Church's famous editorial, "Is there a Santa Claus?" *(see p. 000).* *Though seriously opposed to Church's position, Broun was not the Scrooge his question implies. Writing during the Depression, Broun was as considerate of the disappointment of the poor as Church was of the disillusionment of the innocent.*

Heywood Broun (1888–1939) was the first president of the American Newspaper Guild and a one-time candidate for Congress on the Socialist Party ticket. He was an important and influential journalist in New York throughout his distinguished career.

Almost any day now *The Sun* will reprint the letter from a little girl about Santa Claus and what the editor said in reply. I am sorry I can't remember the names.

This annual tribute to Santa Claus has always left me cold, and I grow more chilly to the piece as the years roll on.

In the first place, the little girl showed a reasonable degree of skepticism. She was just about ready to throw off the shackles of an old myth.

The editor clamped them on again. He didn't tell her the truth. Possibly this bad precedent may account for many editorials on other subjects which have appeared from time to time in various papers.

I am all for legends and fairy stories and ancient customs. A folk story is generally true in spirit no matter how fantastic its details. It is a sort of parable built upon the accumulated wisdom of the ages.

But I have a grievance against the figure called Santa Claus. Unlike most myths, the tale of the old gentleman and his reindeer glorifies an untruth. It warps the minds of the very young with a most pernicious notion. To be sure, the average girl or boy finds out the fake about the age of 3 or 4. The child of 6 who still believes in Santa Claus I would set down as definitely backward.

But even after the literal belief is gone there lingers in the mind a yearning for some other sort of Santa Claus. Oppressed people of various kinds sometimes go from the cradle to the grave without registering any adequate protest against their lot. They are waiting for the sound of the sleigh bells. Santa Claus will come down the chimney and bestow those rights and necessities which they lack. He may be the inspired leader, or he is sent in the guise of some governmental agency or act of legislation.

Naturally, it would be folly to deny that leadership and legislation may nick deeply into many problems, and for my own part I do believe in a paternalistic government. Even so complete reliance should not be placed on any of these three factors or even on them all in combination. There isn't any Santa Claus. Groups of men and woman can obtain their hopes and desires only by massing together and going out to fight and agitate for their objectives. It is far more satisfactory to pick an orange directly from the tree than to find it in the toe of your stocking.

Harsh names are hurled at those who go out telling little children that Santa Claus is a fake. These disciples of the whole truth are called cynical and crabbed and spoilsports. But man must find out sooner or later that he stands on his own feet and this information might as well come early rather than late.

If anybody intrusted a baby to my tender care I would spring the truth about Santa Claus the instant the child could walk. I'd say, "And now, fine fellow, you have achieved the art of locomotion. You can go just as far and as fast as your feet will carry you. Forget about the reindeer. They make indifferent draft animals and singularly tough steak. Let me hear no nonsense out of you about Santa Claus. You and I are rational human beings up to the extent of our ability, I hope."

I even wonder whether children do get a great deal of fun out of the old gentleman in the sleigh. No very warm memories linger in my mind. He gave me a wakeful night once a year. Always I waited with rather more fear than anticipation for the sound of his fat belly scraping down the chimney. It gave me a sense of insecurity. If Santa Claus could sneak up on me in that way so might the bogey man, or any evil witch of whom I had read in the fairy books.

As a matter of fact, it was my annual inclination to sell Santa Claus short. My invariable bet was that his gifts would be disappointing. You see, I took the story very literally. It was said that Santa Claus would be lavish and generous with only those children who were very good and had a year's record of complete compliance to all the orders of their elders. No wonder I was bearish on the entire proposition!

In childhood, as in later life, everybody hopes for more than he is likely to get—particularly if the gifts are to be dropped in his lap. The Santa Claus myth has made for more disappointment than joy, if you look over the statistics very carefully. I know of many districts in the large and crowded cities where the old gentlemen couldn't muster as much as a single vote. Of course, from my point of view, it would be better to hold the election the day after Christmas rather than the night before.

The question may be asked, "After we have shot Santa Claus what can be put in his place?" I think we don't need a single figure. How about just centering the spirit of the day around the factor of universal fellowship? Not one Santa Claus but a hundred million!

Stephen Crane / Stephen Crane's Own Story

[He Tells How the Commodore *Was Wrecked and How He Escaped]*

New York Press, January 7, 1897

Though Stephen Crane had not witnessed a single battle before he wrote The Red Badge of Courage *in 1895, the immense popularity of the novel helped to establish a career for him as a leading war correspondent. Crane spent most of his remaining years traveling, despite ill-health, to cover the Greco-Turkish, the Boer, and the Spanish American wars.*

"Stephen Crane's Own Story" details his experiences during the wreck of the Commodore, *a cargo ship carrying guns and ammunition to Cuban insurgents. This account served as the basis for Crane's well-known short story, "The Open Boat" (see Classics).*

JACKSONVILLE, FLA., Jan. 6.—It was the afternoon of New Year's. The Commodore lay at her dock in Jacksonville and negro stevedores processioned steadily toward her with box after box of ammunition and bundle after bundle of rifles. Her hatch, like the mouth of a monster, engulfed them. It might have been the feeding time of some legendary creature of the sea. It was in broad daylight and the crowd of gleeful Cubans on the pier did not forbear to sing the strange patriotic ballads of their island.

Everything was perfectly open. The Commodore was cleared with a cargo of arms and munition for Cuba. There was none of that extreme modesty about the proceeding which had marked previous departures of the famous tug. She loaded up as placidly as if she were going to carry oranges to New York, instead of Remingtons to Cuba. Down the river, furthermore, the revenue cutter Boutwell, the old isosceles triangle that protects United States interests in the St. John's, lay at anchor, with no sign of excitement aboard her.

EXCHANGING FAREWELLS

On the decks of the Commodore there were exchanges of farewells in two languages. Many of the men who were to sail upon her had many intimates in the old Southern town, and we who had left our friends in the remote North received our first touch of melancholy on witnessing these strenuous and earnest goodbys.

It seems, however, that there was more difficulty at the custom house. The officers of the ship and the Cuban leaders were detained there until a mournful twilight settled upon the St. John's, and through a heavy fog the lights of Jacksonville blinked dimly. Then at last the Commodore swung clear of the dock, amid a tumult of goodbys. As she turned her bow toward the distant sea the Cubans ashore cheered and cheered. In response the Commodore gave three long blasts of her whistle, which even to this time impressed me with their sadness. Somehow, they sounded as wails.

Then at last we began to feel like filibusters. I don't suppose that the most stolid brain could contrive to believe that there is not a mere trifle of danger in filibustering, and so as we watched the lights of Jacksonville swing past us and heard the regular thump, thump, thump of the engines we did considerable reflecting.

But I am sure that there were no hifalutin emotions visible upon any of the faces which fronted the speeding shore. In fact, from cook's boy to captain, we were all enveloped in a gentle satisfaction and cheerfulness. But less than two miles from Jacksonville, this atrocious fog caused the pilot to ram the bow of the Commodore hard upon the mud and in this ignominious position we were compelled to stay until daybreak.

HELP FROM THE BOUTWELL

It was to all of us more than a physical calamity. We were now no longer filibusters. We were men on a ship stuck in the mud. A certain mental somersault was made once more necessary.

But word had been sent to Jacksonville to the captain of the revenue cutter Boutwell, and Captain Kilgore turned out promptly and generously fired up his old triangle, and came at full speed to our assistance. She dragged us out of the mud, and again we headed for the mouth of the river. The revenue cutter pounded along a half mile astern of us, to make sure that we did not take on board at some place along the river men for the Cuban army.

This was the early morning of New Year's Day, and the fine golden southern sunlight fell full upon the river. It flashed over the ancient Boutwell, until her white sides gleamed like pearl, and her rigging was spun into little threads of gold.

Cheers greeted the old Commodore from passing ship and from the shore. It was a cheerful, almost merry, beginning to our voyage. At Mayport, however, we changed our river pilot for a man who could take her to open sea, and again the Commodore was beached. The Boutwell was fussing around us in her venerable way, and, upon seeing our predicament, she came again to assist us, but this time, with engines reversed, the Commodore dragged herself away from the grip of the sand and again headed for the open sea.

The captain of the revenue cutter grew curious. He hailed the Commodore: "Are you fellows going to sea to-day?"

Captain Murphy of the Commodore called back: "Yes, sir."

And then as the whistle of the Commodore saluted him, Captain Kilgore doffed his cap and said: "Well, gentlemen, I hope you have a pleasant cruise," and this was our last word from shore.

When the Commodore came to enormous rollers that flee over the bar a certain light-heartedness departed from the ship's company.

SLEEP IMPOSSIBLE

As darkness came upon the waters, the Commodore was a broad, flaming path of blue and silver phosphorescence, and as her stout bow lunged at the great black waves she threw flashing, roaring cascades to either side. And all that was to be heard was the rhythmical and mighty pounding of the engines. Being an inexperienced filibuster, the writer had undergone considerable mental excitement since the starting of the ship, and in consequence he had not yet been to sleep and so I went to the first mate's bunk to indulge myself in all the physical delights of holding one's-self in bed. Every time the ship lurched I expected to be fired through a bulkhead, and it was neither amusing nor instructive to see in the dim light a certain accursed valise aiming itself at the top of my stomach with every lurch of the vessel.

THE COOK IS HOPEFUL

The cook was asleep on a bench in the galley. He is of a portly and noble exterior, and by means of a checker board he had himself wedged on this bench in such a manner the motion of the ship would be unable to dislodge him. He woke as I entered the galley and delivered himself of some dolorous sentiments: "God," he said in the course of his observations, "I don't feel right about this ship, somehow. It strikes me that something is going to happen to us. I don't know what it is, but the old ship is going to get it in the neck, I think."

"Well, how about the men on board of her?" said I. "Are any of us going to get out, prophet?"

"Yes," said the cook. "Sometimes I have these damned feelings come over me, and they are always right, and it seems to me, somehow, that you and I will both get out and meet again somewhere, down at Coney Island, perhaps, or some place like that."

ONE MAN HAS ENOUGH

Finding it impossible to sleep, I went back to the pilot house. An old seaman, Tom Smith, from Charleston, was then at the wheel. In the darkness I could not see Tom's face, except at those times when he leaned forward to scan the compass and the dim light from the box came upon his weatherbeaten features.

"Well, Tom," said I, "how do you like filibustering?"

He said "I think I am about through with it. I've been in a number of these expeditions and the pay is good, but I think if I ever get back safe this time I will cut it."

I sat down in the corner of the pilot house and almost went to sleep. In the meantime the captain came on duty and he was standing near me when the chief engineer rushed up the stairs and cried hurriedly to the captain that there was something wrong in the engine room. He and the captain departed swiftly.

I was drowsing there in my corner when the captain returned, and, going to the door of the little room directly back of the pilot house, he cried to the Cuban leader:

"Say, can't you get those fellows to work. I can't talk their language and I can't get them started. Come on and get them going."

HELPS IN THE FIREROOM

The Cuban leader turned to me and said: "Go help in the fireroom. They are going to bail with buckets."

The engine room, by the way, represented a scene at this time taken from the middle kitchen of hades. In the first place, it was insufferably warm, and the lights burned faintly in a way to cause mystic and grewsome shadows. There was a quantity of soapish sea water swirling and sweeping and swishing among machinery that roared and banged and clattered and steamed, and, in the second place, it was a devil of a ways down below.

Here I first came to know a certain young oiler named Billy Higgins. He was sloshing around this inferno filling buckets with water and passing them to a chain of men that extended up the ship's side. Afterward we got orders to change our point of attack on water and to operate through a little door on the windward side of the ship that led into the engine room.

NO PANIC ON BOARD

During this time there was much talk of pumps out of order and many other statements of a mechanical kind, which I did not altogether comprehend but understood to mean that there was a general and sudden ruin in the engine room.

There was no particular agitation at this time, and even later there was never a panic on board the Commodore. The party of men who worked with Higgins and me at this time were all Cubans, and we were under the direction of the Cuban leaders. Presently we were ordered again to the afterhold, and there was some hesitation about going into the abominable fireroom again, but Higgins dashed down the companion way with a bucket.

LOWERING BOATS

The heat and hard work in the fireroom affected me and I was obliged to come on deck again. Going forward, I heard as I went talk of lowering the boats. Near the corner of the galley the mate was talking with a man.

"Why don't you send up a rocket?" said this unknown man. And the mate replied: "What the hell do we want to send up a rocket for? The ship is all right."

Returning with a little rubber and cloth overcoat, I saw the first boat about to be lowered. A certain man was the first person in this first boat, and they were handing him in a valise about as large as a hotel. I had not entirely recovered from astonishment and pleasure in witnessing this noble deed when I saw another valise go to him.

HUMAN HOG APPEARS

This valise was not perhaps so large as a hotel, but it was a big valise anyhow. Afterward there went to him something which looked to me like an overcoat.

Seeing the chief engineer leaning out of his little window, I remarked to him:

"What do you think of that blank, blank, blank?"

"Oh, he's a bird," said the old chief.

It was now that was heard the order to get away the lifeboat, which was stowed on top of the deckhouse. The deckhouse was a mighty slippery place, and with each roll of the ship, the men there thought themselves likely to take headers into the deadly black sea.

Higgins was on top of the deckhouse, and, with the first mate and two colored stokers, we wrestled with that boat, which, I am willing to swear, weighed as much as a Broadway cable car. She might have been spiked to the deck. We could have pushed a little brick schoolhouse along a corduroy road as easily as we could have moved this boat. But the first mate got a tackle to her from a leeward davit, and on the deck below the captain corralled enough men to make an impression upon the boat.

We were ordered to cease hauling then, and in this lull the cook of the ship came to me and said: "What are you going to do?"

I told him of my plans, and he said:

"Well, my God, that's what I am going to do."

A WHISTLE OF DESPAIR

Now the whistle of the Commodore had been turned loose, and if there ever was a voice of despair and death, it was in the voice of this whistle. It had gained a new tone. It was as if its throat was already choked by the water, and this cry on the sea at night, with a wind blowing the spray over the ship, and the waves roaring over the bow, and swirling white along the decks, was to each of us probably a song of man's end.

It was now that the first mate showed a sign of losing his grip. To us who were trying in all stages of competence and experience to launch the lifeboat he raged in all terms of fiery satire and hammerlike abuse. But the boat moved at last and swung down toward the water.

Afterward, when I went aft, I saw the captain standing, with his arm in a sling, holding on to a stay with his one good hand and directing the launching of the boat. He gave me a five-gallon jug of water to hold, and asked me what I was going to do. I told him what I thought was about the proper thing, and he told me then that the cook had the same idea, and ordered me to go forward and be ready to launch the ten-foot dingy.

IN THE TEN-FOOT DINGY

I remember well that he turned then to swear at a colored stoker who was prowling around, done up in life preservers until he looked like a feather bed. I went forward with my five-gallon jug of water, and when the captain came we launched the dingy, and they put me over the side to fend her off from the ship with an oar.

They handed me down the water jug, and then the cook came into the boat, and we sat there in the darkness, wondering why, by all our hopes of future happiness, the captain was so long in coming over to the side and ordering us away from the doomed ship.

The captain was waiting for the other boat to go. Finally he hailed in the darkness: "Are you all right, Mr. Graines?"

The first mate answered: "All right, sir."

"Shove off, then," cried the captain.

The captain was just about to swing over the rail when a dark form came forward and a voice said: "Captain, I go with you."

The captain answered: "Yes, Billy; get in."

HIGGINS LAST TO LEAVE SHIP

It was Billy Higgins, the oiler. Billy dropped into the boat and a moment later the captain followed, bringing with him an end of about forty yards of lead line. The other end was attached to the rail of the ship.

As we swung back to leeward the captain said: "Boys, we will stay right near the ship till she goes down."

This cheerful information, of course, filled us all with glee. The line kept us headed properly into the wind, and as we rode over the monstrous waves we saw upon each rise the swaying lights of the dying Commodore.

When came the gray shade of dawn, the form of the Commodore grew slowly clear to us as our little ten-foot boat rose over each swell. She was floating with such an air of buoyancy that we laughed when we had time, and said "What a gag it would be on those other fellows if she didn't sink at all."

But later we saw men aboard of her, and later still they began to hail us.

HELPING THEIR MATES

I had forgot to mention that previously we had loosened the end of the lead line and dropped much further to leeward. The men on board were a mystery to us, of course, as we had seen all the boats leave the ship. We rowed back to the ship, but did not approach too near, because we were four men in a ten-foot boat, and we knew that the touch of a hand on our gunwale would assuredly swamp us.

The first mate cried out from the ship that the third boat had foundered alongside. He cried that they had made rafts, and wished us to tow them.

The captain said, "All right."

Their rafts were floating astern. "Jump in!" cried the captain, but there was a singular and most harrowing hesitation. There were five white men and two negroes. This scene in the gray light of morning impressed one as would a view into some place where ghosts move slowly. These seven men on the stern of the sinking Commodore were silent. Save the words of the mate to the captain there was no talk. Here was death, but here also was a most singular and indefinable kind of fortitude.

Four men, I remember, clambered over the railing and stood there watching the cold, steely sheen of the sweeping waves.

"Jump," cried the captain again.

The old chief engineer first obeyed the order. He landed on the outside raft and the captain told him how to grip the raft and he obeyed as promptly and as docilely as a scholar in riding school.

THE MATE'S MAD PLUNGE

A stoker followed him, and then the first mate threw his hands over his head and plunged into the sea. He had no life belt and for my part, even when he did this horrible thing, I somehow felt that I could see in the expression of his hands, and in the very toss of his head, as he leaped thus to death, that it was rage, rage, rage unspeakable that was in his heart at the time.

And then I saw Tom Smith, the man who was going to quit filibustering after this expedition, jump to a raft and turn his face toward us. On board the Commodore three men strode, still in silence and with their faces turned toward us. One man had his arms folded and was leaning against the deckhouse. His feet were crossed, so that the toe of his left foot pointed downward. There they stood gazing at us, and neither from the deck nor from the rafts was a voice raised. Still was there this silence.

TRIED TO TOW THE RAFTS

The colored stoker on the first raft threw us a line and we began to tow. Of course, we perfectly understood the absolute impossibility of any such thing; our dingy was within six inches of the water's edge, there was an enormous sea running, and I knew that under the circumstances a tugboat would have no light task in moving these rafts.

But we tried it, and would have continued to try it indefinitely, but that something critical came to pass. I was at an oar and so faced the rafts. The cook controlled the line. Suddenly the boat began to go backward and then we saw this negro on the first raft pulling on the line hand over hand and drawing us to him.

He had turned into a demon. He was wild—wild as a tiger. He was crouched on this raft and ready to spring. Every muscle of him seemed to be turned into an elastic spring. His eyes were almost white. His face was the face of a lost man reaching upward, and we knew that the weight of his hand on our gunwale doomed us.

THE COMMODORE SINKS

The cook let go of the line. We rowed around to see if we could not get a line from the chief engineer, and all this time, mind you, there were no shrieks, no groans, but silence, silence and silence, and then the Commodore sank.

She lurched to windward, then swung afar back, righted and dove into the sea, and the rafts were suddenly swallowed by this frightful maw of the ocean. And then by the men on the ten-foot dingy were words said that were still not words—something far beyond words.

The lighthouse of Mosquito Inlet stuck up above the horizon like the point of a pin. We turned our dingy toward the shore.

The history of life in an open boat for thirty hours would no doubt be instructive for the young, but none is to be told here and now. For my part I would prefer to tell the story at once, because from it would shine the splendid manhood of Captain Edward Murphy and of William Higgins, the oiler, but let it suffice at this time to say that when we were swamped in the surf and making the best of our way toward the shore the captain gave orders amid the wildness of the breakers as clearly as if he had been on the quarter deck of a battleship.

John Kitchell of Daytona came running down the beach, and as he ran the air was filled with clothes. If he had pulled a single lever and undressed, even as the fire horses harness, he could not seem to me to have stripped with more speed. He dashed into the water and dragged the cook. Then he went after the captain, but the captain sent him to me, and then it was that he saw Billy Higgins lying with his forehead on sand that was clear of the water, and he was dead.

Staff Correspondent / Flying Machine Soars 3 Miles in Teeth of High Wind

[*First Account of the Wright Brothers' Success*]

Norfolk *Virginian Pilot,* December 18, 1903

Wilbur and Orville Wright, the owners of a bicycle shop in Dayton, Ohio, where they also at one time edited a weekly newspaper, had been experimenting since their youth on designs for a workable "flying machine." Venturing to the wind-swept coast near Kittyhawk, North Carolina, the Wright brothers set up a primitive monorail-like skid from which to launch their craft. Powered by a twelve horse-power gasoline engine, the "monster bird hovered above the breakers" for almost a minute, traveling a distance of nearly a quarter of a mile. Surrounded by several highly publicized failures, this event, one of the major advances in twentieth century science, went practically unnoticed. Only the Norfolk Virginian-Pilot *printed a full story of the world's first successful flight.*

FLYING MACHINE SOARS 3 MILES
IN TEETH OF HIGH WIND OVER SAND HILLS AND WAVES AT KITTY-HAWK ON CAROLINA COAST.

•

NO BALLOON ATTACHED TO AID IT.

•

The problem of aerial navigation without the use of a balloon has been solved at last.

Over the sand hills of the North Carolina coast yesterday, near Kittyhawk, two Ohio men proved that they could soar through the air in a flying machine of their own construction, with the power to steer and speed it at will.

This, too, in the face of a wind blowing at the registered velocity of twenty-one miles an hour.

Like a monster bird, the invention hovered above the breakers and circled over the rolling sand hills at the command of its navigator and, after soaring for three miles, it gracefully descended to earth again, and rested lightly upon the spot selected by the man in the car as a suitable landing place.

While the United States government has been spending thousands of dollars in an effort to make practicable the ideas of Professor Langley, of the Smithsonian Institute, Wilbur and Orville Wright, two brothers, natives of Dayton, Ohio, have, quietly, even secretly, perfected their invention and put it to a successful test.

They are not yet ready that the world should know the methods they have adopted in conquering the air, but the *Virginian-Pilot* is able to state authentically the nature of their invention, its principles and its chief dimensions.

The idea of the box kite has been adhered to strictly in the basic formation of the flying machine.

A huge framework of light timbers, thirty-three feet wide, five feet deep, and five feet across the top, forms the machine proper.

This is covered with a tough, but light canvas.

In the center, and suspended just below the bottom plane, is the small gasoline engine which furnished the motive power for the propelling and elevating wheels.

There are two six-bladed propellers, one arranged just below the center of the frame, so gauged as to exert an upward force when in motion, and the other extends horizontally to the rear from the center of the car, furnishing the forward impetus.

Protruding from the center of the car is a huge, fan-shaped rudder of canvas, stretched upon a frame of wood. This rudder is controlled by the navigator and may be moved to each side, raised, or lowered.

Wilbur Wright, the chief inventor of the machine, sat in the operator's car, and when all was ready his brother unfastened the catch which held the invention at the top of the slope.

The big box began to move slowly at first, acquiring velocity as it went, and when halfway down the hundred feet the engine was started.

The propeller in the rear immediately began to revolve at a high rate of speed, and when the end of the incline was reached the machine shot out into space without a perceptible fall.

By this time the elevating propeller was also in motion, and keeping its altitude, the machine slowly began to go higher and higher until it finally soared sixty feet above the ground.

Maintaining this height by the action of the under wheel, the navigator increased the revolutions of the rear propeller, and the forward speed of the huge affair increased until a velocity of eight miles was attained.

All this time the machine headed into a twenty-one-mile wind.

The little crowd of fisherfolk and coast guards, who have been watching the construction of the machine with unconcealed curiosity since September, were amazed.

They endeavored to race over the sand and keep up with the thing in the air, but it soon distanced them and continued its flight alone, save the man in the car.

Steadily it pursued its way, first tacking to port, then to starboard, and then driving straight ahead.

''It is a success,'' declared Orville Wright to the crowd on the beach after the first mile had been covered.

But the inventor waited. Not until he had accomplished three miles, putting the machine through all sorts of maneuvers en route, was he satisfied.

Then he selected a suitable place to land and, gracefully circling, drew his invention slowly to the earth, where it settled, like some big bird, in the chosen spot.

"Eureka!" he cried, as did the alchemists of old.

The success of the Wright brothers in their invention is the result of three years of hard work. Experiment after experiment has been made and failure resulted, but each experiment had its lesson, and finally, when the two reappeared at Kittyhawk last fall, they felt more confident than ever.

The spot selected for the building and perfecting of the machine is one of the most desolate upon the Atlantic seaboard. Just on the southern extremity of that coast stretch known as the graveyard of American shipping, cut off from civilization by a wide expanse of sound water and seldom in touch with the outer world save when a steamer once or twice a week touches at the little wharf to take and leave government mail, no better place could scarcely have been selected to maintain secrecy.

And this is where the failures have grown into success.

The machine which made yesterday's flight easily carried the weight of a man of 150 pounds, and is nothing like so large as the ill-fated *Buzzard* of Potomac River fame.

It is said the Wright brothers intend constructing a much larger machine, but before this they will go back to their homes for the holidays.

Wilbur Wright, the inventor, is a well-groomed man of prepossessing appearance. He is about five feet, six inches tall, weighs about 150 pounds, and is of swarthy complexion. His hair is raven-hued and straight, but a piercing pair of deep-blue eyes peer at you over a nose of extreme length and sharpness.

His brother, Orville, on the other hand, is a blond, with sandy hair and fair complexion, even features, and sparkling black eyes. He is not quite as large as Wilbur, but is of magnificent physique.

The pair have spent almost the entire fall and winter and early spring months of the past three years at Kittyhawk, working upon their invention, leaving when the weather began to grow warm and returning in the early fall to work.

Their last appearance was on September 1, and since then they have been actively engaged upon the construction of the machine which made yesterday's successful flight.

H. L. Mencken / Under the Elms

Trenton *Sunday Times,* April 3, 1927

An editor, reporter, and essayist, H. L. Mencken (1880–1956) spent nearly his entire life in Baltimore, where he worked tirelessly as a staff writer for the Baltimore Sun. *His pungent and highly controversial social, cultural, political, and literary criticism made him one of the outstanding figures of American letters in the years between the two world wars. An irreverent debunker of many cherished notions—he once called the American people "the most timorous, sniveling, poltroonish, ignominious mob of serfs and goose-steppers ever gathered under one flag in Christendom since the end of the Middle Ages"—Mencken loved to satirize* both *the common people and the intellectuals, political leaders and the electorate. In 1919, Mencken, who never presumed to be a scholar, published the first edition of what eventually came to be considered a classic work of linguistics and semantics,* The American Language.

Mencken's series of autobiographies, Happy Days *(1940),* Newspaper Days *(1941), and* Heathen Days *(1943), makes it clear that he always regarded him-*

self as a reporter and journalist. The following item responding to a rash of student suicides appeared in the Trenton, New Jersey, Sunday Times *for April 3, 1927.*

I see nothing mysterious about these suicides. The impulse to self-destruction is a natural accompaniment of the educational process. Every intelligent student, at some time or other during his college career, decides gloomily that it would be more sensible to die than to go on living. I was myself spared the intellectual humiliations of a college education, but during my late teens, with enlightening gradually dawning within me, I more than once concluded that death was preferable to life. At that age the sense of humor is in a low state. Later on, by the mysterious working of God's providence, it usually recovers.

What keeps a reflective and skeptical man alive? In large part, I suspect, it is this sense of humor. But in addition there is curiosity. Human existence is always irrational and often painful, but in the last analysis it remains interesting. One wants to know what is going to happen tomorrow. Will the lady in the mauve frock be more amiable than she is today? Such questions keep human beings alive. If the future were known, every intelligent man would kill himself at once, and the Republic would be peopled wholly by morons. Perhaps we are really moving toward that consummation now.

I hope no one will be upset and alarmed by the fact that various bishops, college presidents, Rotary lecturers and other such professional damned fools are breaking into print with highfalutin discussions of the alleged wave of student suicides. Such men, it must be manifest, seldom deal with realities. Their whole lives are devoted to inventing bugaboos, and then laying them. Like the news editors, they will tire of this bogus wave after a while, and go yelling after some other phantasm. Meanwhile, the world will go staggering on. Their notions are never to be taken seriously. Their one visible function on earth is to stand as living proofs that education is by no means synonymous with intelligence.

What I'd like to see, if it could be arranged, would be a wave of suicides among college presidents. I'd be delighted to supply the pistols, knives, ropes, poisons and other necessary tools. Going further, I'd be delighted to load the pistols, hone the knives, and tie the hangman's knots. A college student, leaping uninvited into the arms of God, pleases only himself. But a college president, doing the same thing, would give keen and permanent joy to great multitudes of persons. I drop the idea, and pass on.

Jack Lait / Dillinger "Gets His"

International News Service, July 23, 1934

On a steamy July evening in 1934, after having seen Clark Gable and William Powell star in a popular gangster film, Manhattan Melodrama, *John Dillinger, "Public Enemy No. 1," left a run-down movie house on Chicago's East Side and walked into the waiting bullets of federal police forces. By all accounts one of the most notorious criminals of modern times, Dillinger had blazed out a legendary "career" for himself that had all the earmarks of best-selling detective fiction: daring bank robberies, raids on police arsenals, bloody shoot-outs, bold escapes from prison, along with disguises, blurred fingerprints, and plastic surgery to help him defy what was then described as "the greatest manhunt in contemporary criminal annals." Yet, like Joey Gallo (see "Death of a Maverick Mafioso," in Magazines), Dillinger eventually found the heat of the limelight deadly. Betrayed by one of the many women he supported, Dillinger finally fell victim to the facts that fed the fictions he provoked.*

Jack Lait, a hard-nosed reporter who later took over as editor of the New York Daily Mirror, turned out this "scoop" for the International News Service, an agency set up by William Randolph Hearst in 1909 to offer news items to a network of morning newspapers.

"Dillinger 'Gets His' " should be compared to David Wagoner's poem on the same subject in Classics.

John Dillinger, ace bad man of the world, got his last night—two slugs through his heart and one through his head. He was tough and he was shrewd, but wasn't as tough and shrewd as the Federals, who never close a case until the end. It took twenty-seven of them to end Dillinger's career, and their strength came out of his weakness—a woman.

Dillinger was put on the spot by a tip-off to the local bureau of the Department of Justice. It was a feminine voice that Melvin H. Purvis, head of the Chicago office, heard. He had waited long for it.

It was Sunday, but Uncle Sam doesn't observe any NRA* and works seven days a week.

The voice told him that Dillinger would be at a little third-run movie house, the Biograph, last night—that he went there every night and usually got there about 7:30. It was almost 7:30 then. Purvis sent out a call for all men within reach and hustled all men on hand with him. They waited more than an hour. They knew from the informer that he must come out, turn left, turn again into a dark alley where he parked his Ford-8 coupé.

Purvis himself stood at the main exit. He had men on foot and in parked inconspicuous cars strung on both sides of the alley. He was to give the signal. He had ascertained about when the feature film, *Manhattan Melodrama,* would end. Tensely eying his wrist watch he stood. Then the crowd that always streams out when the main picture finishes came. Purvis had seen Dillinger when he was brought through from Arizona to Crown Point, Indiana, and his heart pounded as he saw again the face that has been studied by countless millions on the front pages of the world.

Purvis gave the signal. Dillinger did not see him. Public Enemy No. 1 lit a cigarette, strolled a few feet to the alley with the mass of middle-class citizens going in that direction, then wheeled left.

A Federal man, revolver in hand, stepped from behind a telegraph pole at the mouth of the passage. "Hello, John," he said, almost whispered, his voice husky with the intensity of the classic melodrama. Dillinger went with lightning right hand for his gun, a .38 Colt automatic. He drew it from his trousers pocket.

But, from behind, another government agent pressed the muzzle of his service revolver against Dillinger's back and fired twice. Both bullets went through the bandit's heart.

He staggered, his weapon clattered to the asphalt paving, and as he went three more shots flashed. One bullet hit the back of his head, downward, as he was falling, and came out under his eye.

Police cleared the way for the police car which was there in a few minutes. The

* National Recovery Administration, a New Deal Agency that, among other functions, regulated hours of work in industry.

police were there not because they were in on the capture, but because the sight of so many mysterious men around the theater had scared the manager into thinking he was about to be stuck up and he had called the nearest station.

When the detectives came on the run, Purvis intercepted them and told them what was up. They called headquarters and more police came, but with instructions to stand by and take orders from Purvis.

Dillinger's body was rushed to Alexian Brothers' hospital in a patrol wagon. There were no surgeons in it. But the policeman knew he was dead, and at the entrance of the hospital, where a kindly priest in a long cassock had come to the door to see who might be in need of help, the driver was ordered to the morgue.

I was in a taxi that caught up with the police car at the hospital, and we followed across town to the old morgue. No one bothered us, though we went fifty miles an hour.

There was no crowd then. We pulled in. Strong arms carried the limp, light form of the man who had been feared by a great government through that grim door of many minor tragedies. It lay on a rubber stretcher.

In the basement, the receiving ward of the last public hospice of the doomed, they stripped the fearsome remains.

What showed up, nude and pink, still warm, was the body of what seemed a boy, the features as though at rest and only an ugly, bleeding hole under the left eye, such as a boy might have gotten in a street fight. His arms were bruised from the fall and the bumping in the wagon.

But under the heart were two little black, bleeding holes, clean and fresh. These could not have been anything but what they were. That part of John Dillinger did not look as though it was a boy's hurt—it was the fatal finish of a cold-blooded killer and not half of what he had given Officer O'Malley in East Chicago, Indiana, in the bank robbery when he cut the policeman almost in half with a machine gun.

The marks of the garters were still on the skin of his sturdy calves, the only part of him that looked like any part of a strong man. His arms were slender, even emaciated. But his legs were powerful-looking. His feet were neat and almost womanish, after the white socks and dudish white shoes had been taken from them.

His clothes were shabby with still an attempt at smartness. The white shirt was cheap, the gray flannel trousers, and the uninitialed belt buckle were basement-counter merchandise, his maroon-and-white print tie might have cost half a dollar.

In his pockets were $7.70 and a few keys and a watch in which was the picture of a pretty female.

Two women bystanders were caught in the line of fire and wounded slightly as the Federal men blazed away. They were Miss Etta Natalsky, forty-five, and Miss Theresa Paulus, twenty-nine, both residents of the neighborhood.

Miss Natalsky was taken to the Columbus Memorial Hospital with a wound in the leg and Miss Paulus to the Grant Hospital, but her wound, also in the leg, was found to be only superficial.

The notorious desperado had resorted to facial surgery to disguise himself, and it was only by his piercing eyes—described by crime experts as "the eyes of a born killer"—that he was recognized.

In addition to the facial alterations, he had dyed his hair a jet black from its natural sandy shade, and he wore gold-rimmed glasses. Identification of the fallen man was confirmed by Purvis on the spot. Later, at the morgue, an attempt was made to identify the body from fingerprints, but the tips of the fingers had been scarred, as if with acid.

A recent wound in the chest, which had just healed, was revealed in the morgue examination. It was believed this was a memento of a recent bank robbery.

Dr. Charles D. Parker, coroner's physician, remarked on the alteration in the slain man's features. Scars which he carried on each cheek Dillinger had had smoothed out by facial surgery. Purvis, after closely examining the changed features, said:

"His nose, that originally was pronounced 'pug,' had been made nearly straight. His hair had been dyed recently."

Souvenir hunters among the excited crowds that swarmed to the scene of the shooting frantically dipped newspapers and handkerchiefs in the patch of blood left on the pavement.

Traffic became so jammed that streetcars were rerouted, police lines established, and all traffic finally blocked out of the area.

Unsatiated by their morbid milling around the death spot, the crowds a little later rushed to the morgue to view the body. Denied admittance, they battled police and shouted and yelled to get inside. More than two thousand at one time were struggling to force the doors.

I have indisputable proof that the bureau had information that Dillinger had been here for at least three days. It was the first definite location of the hunted murderer since the affray in the Little Bohemia (Wisconsin) lodge.

"We didn't have time to get him then, but we had time enough this time," Purvis said.

Evidently Purvis not only had enough time, but used it with the traditional efficiency of his department. There has always been open rancor between the Chicago police and the Federals, who have several times done them out of rewards. The Federals are not permitted to accept rewards.

But the East Chicago force—Dillinger had slaughtered three of their outfit in two raids, and the "coincidence" of their presence "when the tip came in" is obvious.

That Dillinger suspected nothing is proven by nothing as much as that the safety catch on his magazine gun was set. It was a new, high-type weapon, so powerful that its slugs would penetrate the bulletproof vests of the sort that Dillinger himself had worn in other spots. The number had been filed off. Close examination indicated it had never been fired. It was fully loaded, and a clip of extra cartridges was in a pocket.

He had no other possible instrument of offense or defense, this desperado, except a slender penknife on the other end of a thin chain that held his watch.

All his possessions lay on the marble slab beside the rubber stretcher in the basement of the morgue as the internes pawed his still warm face and body as they threw his head to this side and that, slung him over on his face, and dabbed the still-wet blood from where the bullets had bitten into him.

I wondered whether, a few brief minutes earlier, they would have had the temerity to treat John Dillinger's flesh so cavalierly.

They pointed to the scar on his shinbone, the one which had been so heavily broadcast as maiming and even killing Dillinger. It was a little bit of a thing and looked more like the result of a stone bruise than a volley from the muzzle of outraged society.

They flopped him over on the slab, quite by a clumsy accident, because the body didn't turn easily within the stretcher, what with its gangly, rubbery legs, and its thin, boneless arms. And as what was left of Dillinger clamped like a clod, face down, upon the slab which had held the clay of hoboes and who knows, a still warm but spent hand knocked off the straw hat which had fallen off his head in the alley and been trampled upon. And a good ten-cent cigar. Strangely intact.

The man who had killed him stood two feet away, smoking a cigar of the same brand. I must not mention his name. Purvis says "keep that a trade secret." With John ("Happy Jack") Hamilton and George ("Baby Face") Nelson, Dillinger's lieutenants, still at large, perhaps that is a fair enough precaution.

The Bureau of Identification men were on the job in a jiffy. They proved up the fingerprints, though they had been treated with a biting acid in an effort to obliterate the telltale. But the deltas and cores were unmistakable.

Behind the ears were well-done scars of a face-lifting job by a skillful plastic specialist. A mole on the forehead had been trimmed off rather well. His hair, by rights sandy, had been painted a muddy black with a poor grade of dye.

So had his mustache. The one identifying mark known around the globe as the Dillinger characteristic was there. And even in death he looked just like the Dillinger we all knew from the photographs. Probably the last breath of his ego.

Dillinger was a ladies' man. He didn't want to be picked up and identified by a rube sheriff. But, still, he wanted to whisper to a new sweetie in the confidences of the night:

"Baby, I can trust you—I'm John Dillinger!"

And she would look, and—he was! That mustache!

Having gone to astonishing lengths to change his inconspicuous identifying marks, with the necessary aid and advice of expert medical men, he had still refused to shave off that familiar trade-mark that every newspaper reader could see with eyes shut.

A scar on his chin had been reopened and smoothed up some, but not very convincingly. The droop at the left corner of his mouth was unmistakably intact. But the most striking facial change was in the tightening of the skin on his chin, almost completely killing his dimple, which was almost as widely known as his mustache.

Gold-rimmed eyeglasses fell off his face as he toppled over. These, one of the most amateurish of elements in disguise, did change his appearance decisively, the officers tell me.

The Federal office, as usual, issued contradictory statements and frankly admitted that certain information would not be given out.

Of the twenty-seven men who worked with Purvis, one was Captain Tim O'Neill of East Chicago, and four others were O'Neill's men. Purvis said they were there quite by chance and he had taken them in on the big adventure. A second statement also gave forth that Purvis had seen Dillinger enter as well as leave the theater.

As Dillinger emerged, walking near him were two youngish women, one of them wearing a red dress. Hundreds were leaving the house at the time, and almost any number of women would naturally have been near him. But the one with the red dress hurried up the alley, and four Federals made a formation between her and Dillinger before the first shot was fired. It is my theory that she was with Dillinger and that she was the tip-off party or in league with Purvis.

DISCUSSION QUESTIONS

1. Compare Lait's report of Dillinger's death with that of David Wagoner in his poem, "The Shooting of John Dillinger Outside the Biograph Theater, July 22, 1934" (see Classics). What do the titles of the two pieces suggest about their differences? How do the details of the shooting differ from news item to poem? What are the effects of those differences?

2. What can you tell about Lait's opinion of Dillinger? From what facts are you able to infer his opinion? What can you tell about Wagoner's opinion of Dillinger? How do they compare? From the style of Lait's news report and Wagoner's poem, how do they expect their respective audiences to feel about Dillinger?

George M. Mahawinney / An Invasion from the Planet Mars

Philadelphia Inquirer, November 1, 1938

George M. Mahawinney, a rewrite man on duty at the Philadelphia Inquirer *the evening of the famous Orson Welles broadcast of "The War of the Worlds," was besieged by frantic telephone calls seeking information about the invasion from Mars. The* Inquirer, *close to the reputed scene of the Martian landing at Grovers Mill, near Princeton, New Jersey, became the focal point for the nation's coverage of the bizarre results of Welles' broadcast. With America's news services clamoring for reports, Mahawinney wrote the following account in less than an hour. (For an excerpt from the radio broadcast of "The War of the Worlds," see* Scripts.)

Terror struck at the hearts of hundreds of thousands of persons in the length and breadth of the United States last night as crisp words of what they believed to be a news broadcast leaped from their radio sets—telling of catastrophe from the skies visited on this country.

Out of the heavens, they learned, objects at first believed to be meteors crashed down near Trenton, killing many.

Then out of the "meteors" came monsters, spreading destruction with torch and poison gas.

It was all just a radio dramatization, but the result, in all actuality, was nationwide hysteria.

In Philadelphia, women and children ran from their homes, screaming. In Newark, New Jersey, ambulances rushed to one neighborhood to protect residents against a gas attack. In the deep South men and women knelt in groups in the streets and prayed for deliverance.

In reality there was no danger. The broadcast was merely a Halloween program in which Orson Welles, actor-director of the Mercury Theater on the Air, related, as though he were one of the few human survivors of the catastrophe, an adaptation of H. G. Wells' *The War of the Worlds.*

In that piece of fiction men from Mars, in meteorlike space ships, come to make conquest of earth. The circumstances of the story were unbelievable enough, but the manner of its presentation was apparently convincing to hundreds of thousands of persons—despite the fact that the program was interrupted thrice for an announcement that it was fiction, and fiction only.

For the fanciful tale was broadcast casually, for all the world like a news broadcast, opening up serenely enough with a weather report.

The realism of the broadcast, especially for those who had tuned in after it had started, brought effects which none—not the directors of the Federal Radio Theater Project, which sponsored it, nor the Columbia Broadcasting Company, which carried it over a coast-to-coast chain of 151 stations, nor Station WCAU, which broadcast it locally—could foresee.

Within a few minutes newspaper offices, radio stations, and police departments everywhere were flooded with anxious telephone calls. Sobbing women sought advice on what to do; broken-voiced men wished to know where to take their families.

Station WCAU received more than four thousand calls and eventually interrupted a later program to make an elaborate explanation that death had not actually descended on New Jersey, and that monsters were not actually invading the world.

But calm did not come readily to the frightened radio listeners of the country.

The hysteria reached such proportions that the New York City Department of Health called up a newspaper and wanted advice on offering its facilities for the protection of the populace. Nurses and physicians were among the telephone callers everywhere. They were ready to offer their assistance to the injured or maimed.

Hundreds of motorists touring through New Jersey heard the broadcast over their radios and detoured to avoid the area upon which the holocaust was focused—the area in the vicinity of Trenton and Princeton.

In scores of New Jersey towns women in their homes fainted as the horror of the broadcast fell on their ears. In Palmyra some residents packed up their worldly goods and prepared to move across the river into Philadelphia.

A white-faced man raced into the Hillside, New Jersey, police station and asked for a gas mask. Police said he panted out a tale of "terrible people spraying liquid gas all over Jersey meadows."

A weeping lady stopped Motorcycle Patrolman Lawrence Treger and asked where she should go to escape the "attack."

A terrified motorist asked the patrolman the way to Route 24. "All creation's busted loose. I'm getting out of Jersey," he screamed.

"Grovers Mill, New Jersey," was mentioned as a scene of destruction. In Stockton more than a half-hundred persons abandoned Colligan's Inn after hearing the broadcast and journeyed to Groveville to view the incredible "damage." They had misheard the name of the hypothetical town of "Grovers Mill," and believed it to be Groveville.

At Princeton University, women members of the geology faculty, equipped with flashlights and hammers, started for Grovers Corners. Dozens of cars were driven to the hamlet by curious motorists. A score of university students were phoned by their parents and told to come home.

An anonymous and somewhat hysterical girl phoned the Princeton Press Club from Grovers Corners and said:

"You can't imagine the horror of it! It's hell!"

A man came into the club and said he saw the meteor strike the earth and witnessed animals jumping from the alien body.

The Trenton police and fire telephone board bore the brunt of the nation's calls, because of its geographical location close to the presumed scene of catastrophe. On that board were received calls from Wilmington, Washington, Philadelphia, Jersey City, and Newark.

North of Trenton most of New Jersey was in the midst of a bad scare.

A report spread through Newark that the city was to be the target of a "gas-bomb attack." Police headquarters were notified there was a serious gas accident in the Clinton Hills section of that city. They sent squad cars and ambulances.

They found only householders, with possessions hastily bundled, leaving their homes. The householders returned to their homes only after emphatic explanations by the police.

Fifteen persons were treated for shock in one Newark hospital.

In Jersey City one resident demanded a gas mask of police. Another telephoned to ask whether he ought to flee the area or merely keep his windows closed and hope for the best.

Many New Yorkers seized personal effects and raced out of their apartments, some jumping into their automobiles and heading for the wide-open spaces.

Samuel Tishman, a Riverside Drive resident, declared he and hundreds of others evacuated their homes, fearing "the city was being bombed."

He told of going home and receiving a frantic telephone call from a nephew.

Tishman denounced the program as "the most asinine stunt I ever heard of" and as "a pretty crumby thing to do."

The panic it caused gripped impressionable Harlemites, and one man ran into the street declaring it was the President's voice they heard, advising: "Pack up and go North, the machines are coming from Mars."

Police in the vicinity at first regarded the excitement as a joke, but they were soon hard pressed in controlling the swarms in the streets.

A man entered the Wadsworth Avenue station uptown and said he heard "planes had bombed Jersey and were headed for Times Square."

A rumor spread over Washington Heights that a war was on.

At Caldwell, New Jersey, an excited parishioner rushed into the First Baptist Church during evening services and shouted that a tremendous meteor had fallen, causing widespread death, and that north Jersey was threatened with a shower of meteors. The congregation joined in prayer for deliverance.

Reactions as strange, or stranger, occurred in other parts of the country. In San Francisco, a citizen called police, crying:

"My God, where can I volunteer my services? We've got to stop this awful thing."

In Indianapolis, Indiana, a woman ran screaming into a church.

"New York is destroyed; it's the end of the world," she cried. "You might as well go home to die."

At Brevard College, North Carolina, five boys in dormitories fainted on hearing the broadcast. In Birmingham, Alabama, men and women gathered in groups and prayed. Women wept and prayed in Memphis, Tennessee.

Throughout Atlanta was a wide-spread belief that a "planet" had struck New Jersey, killing from forty to seven thousand persons.

At Pittsburgh one man telephoned a newspaper that he had returned to his home in the middle of the broadcast and found his wife in the bathroom, clutching a bottle of poison.

"I'd rather die this way than like that," she screamed before he was able to calm her.

Another citizen telephoned a newspaper in Washington, Pennsylvania, that a group of guests in his home playing cards "fell down on their knees and prayed," and then hurried home.

At Rivesville, West Virginia, a woman interrupted the pastor's sermon at a church meeting with loud outcries that there had been "an invasion." The meeting broke up in confusion.

Two heart attacks were reported by Kansas City hospitals, and the Associated Press Bureau there received calls of inquiry from Los Angeles, Salt Lake City, Beaumont, Texas, and St. Joseph, Missouri.

Minneapolis and St. Paul police switchboards were deluged with calls from frightened people.

Weeping and hysterical women in Providence, Rhode Island, cried out for officials of the electric company there to "turn off the lights so that the city will be safe from the enemy."

In some places mass hysteria grew so great that witnesses to the "invasion" could be found.

A Boston woman telephoned a newspaper to say she could "see the fire" from her window, and that she and her neighbors were "getting out of here."

The broadcast began at eight P.M. Within a few minutes after that time it had brought such a serious reaction that New Jersey state police sent out a teletype message to its various stations and barracks, containing explanations and instructions to police officers on how to handle the hysteria.

These and other police everywhere had problems on their hands as the broadcast moved on, telling of a "bulletin from the Intercontinental Radio News Bureau" saying there had been a gas explosion in New Jersey.

"Bulletins" that came in rapidly after that told of "meteors," then corrected that statement and described the Mars monsters.

The march of the Martians was disastrous. For a while they swept everything before them, according to the pseudo-bulletins. Mere armies and navies were being wiped out in a trice.

Actually, outside the radio stations, the Martians were doing a pretty good job on the Halloween imaginations of the citizenry. The radio stations and the Columbia Broadcasting Company spent much of the remainder of the evening clearing up the situation. Again and again they explained the whole thing was nothing more than a dramatization.

In the long run, however, calm was restored in the myriad American homes which had been momentarily threatened by interplanetary invasion. Fear of the monsters from Mars eventually subsided.

There was no reason for being afraid of them, anyway. Even the bulletins of the radio broadcast explained they all soon died. They couldn't stand the earth's atmosphere and perished of pneumonia.

Dorothy Thompson / Mr. Welles and Mass Delusion

New York Herald Tribune, November 2, 1938

Dorothy Thompson (1894–1961) remained one of America's most distinguished columnists for more than a generation. Her syndicated reports, "On the Record," appeared three times a week and discussed such contemporary issues as President Roosevelt's "New Deal" and the emerging Nazi regime—each column marked by her commitment to journalistic candor. In "Mr. Welles and Mass Delusion," Dorothy Thompson, two days after the Welles broadcast, poignantly depicts the malleability of the national psychology on the eve of another world war and reminds us of the terrifying power of mass media. (For an excerpt from the radio broadcast of "The War of the Worlds," see Scripts.)

All unwittingly Mr. Orson Welles and the Mercury Theater on the Air have made one of the most fascinating and important demonstrations of all time. They have proved that a few effective voices, accompanied by sound effects, can so convince masses of people of a totally unreasonable, completely fantastic proposition as to create nation-wide panic.

They have demonstrated more potently than any argument, demonstrated beyond question of a doubt, the appalling dangers and enormous effectiveness of popular and theatrical demagoguery.

They have cast a brilliant and cruel light upon the failure of popular education.

They have shown up the incredible stupidity, lack of nerve and ignorance of thousands.

They have proved how easy it is to start a mass delusion.

They have uncovered the primeval fears lying under the thinnest surface of the so-called civilized man.

They have shown that man, when the victim of his own gullibility, turns to the government to protect him against his own errors of judgment.

The newspapers are correct in playing up this story over every other news event in the world. It is the story of the century.

And far from blaming Mr. Orson Welles, he ought to be given a Congressional medal and a national prize for having made the most amazing and important contribution to the social sciences. For Mr. Orson Welles and his theater have made a greater contribution to an understanding of Hitlerism, Mussolinism, Stalinism, anti-Semitism and all the other terrorisms of our times than all the words about them that have been written by reasonable men. They have made the reductio ad absurdum of mass manias. They have thrown more light on recent events in Europe leading to the Munich pact than everything that has been said on the subject by all the journalists and commentators.

Hitler managed to scare all Europe to its knees a month ago, but he at least had an army and an air force to back up his shrieking words.

But Mr. Welles scared thousands into demoralization with nothing at all.

That historic hour on the air was an act of unconscious genius, performed by the very innocence of intelligence.

Nothing whatever about the dramatization of the "War of the Worlds" was in the least credible, no matter at what point the hearer might have tuned in. The entire verisimilitude was in the names of a few specific places. Monsters were depicted of a type that nobody has ever seen, equipped with "rays" entirely fantastic; they were described as "straddling the Pulaski Skyway" and throughout the broadcast they were referred to as Martians, men from another planet.

A twist of the dial would have established for anybody that the national catastrophe was not being noted on any other station. A second of logic would have dispelled any terror. A notice that the broadcast came from a non-existent agency would have awakened skepticism.

A reference to the radio program would have established that the "War of the Worlds" was announced in advance.

The time element was obviously lunatic.

Listeners were told that "within two hours three million people have moved out of New York"—an obvious impossibility for the most disciplined army moving exactly as planned, and a double fallacy because only a few minutes before, the news of the arrival of the monster had been announced.

And of course it was not even a planned hoax. Nobody was more surprised at the result than Mr. Welles. The public was told at the beginning, at the end and during the course of the drama that it *was* a drama.

But eyewitnesses presented themselves; the report became second hand, third hand, fourth hand, and became more and more credible, so that nurses and doctors and National Guardsmen rushed to defense.

When the truth became known the reaction was also significant. The deceived were furious and of course demanded that the state protect them, demonstrating that they were incapable of relying on their own judgment.

Again there was a complete failure of logic. For if the deceived had thought about it they would realize that the greatest organizers of mass hysterias and mass delusions today are states using the radio to excite terrors, incite hatreds, inflame masses, win mass support for policies, create idolatries, abolish reason and maintain themselves in power.

The immediate moral is apparent if the whole incident is viewed in reason: no political body must ever, under any circumstances, obtain a monopoly of radio.

The second moral is that our popular and universal education is failing to train reason and logic, even in the educated.

The third is that the popularization of science has led to gullibility and new superstitions, rather than to skepticism and the really scientific attitude of mind.

The fourth is that the power of mass suggestion is the most potent force today and that the political demagogue is more powerful than all the economic forces.

For, mind you, Mr. Welles was managing an obscure program, competing with one of the most popular entertainments on the air!

The conclusion is that the radio must not be used to create mass prejudices and mass divisions and schisms, either by private individuals or by government or its agencies, or its officials, or its opponents.

If people can be frightened out of their wits by mythical men from Mars, they can be frightened into fanaticism by the fear of Reds, or convinced that America is in the hands of sixty families, or aroused to revenge against any minority, or terrorized into subservience to leadership because of any imaginable menace.

The technique of modern mass politics calling itself democracy is to create a fear—a fear of economic royalists, or of Reds, or of Jews, or of starvation, or of an outside enemy—and exploit that fear into obtaining subservience in return for protection.

I wrote in this column a short time ago that the new warfare was waged by propaganda, the outcome depending on which side could first frighten the other to death.

The British people were frightened into obedience to a policy a few weeks ago by a radio speech and by digging a few trenches in Hyde Park, and afterward led to hysterical jubilation over a catastrophic defeat for their democracy.

But Mr. Welles went all the politicians one better. He made the scare to end scares, the menace to end menaces, the unreason to end unreason, the perfect demonstration that the danger is not from Mars but from the theatrical demagogue.

Langston Hughes / Family Tree

Chicago Defender, ca. 1942

The author of more than sixty volumes of fiction, poetry, drama, gospel song-plays, opera lyrics, translations, and children's books, Langston Hughes has also written scores of essays and news reports. Born in Joplin, Missouri in 1902, Hughes studied at Columbia University and later signed on as a cook's helper aboard a tramp freighter bound for Africa. He also worked as a cook in a Paris night club, as a busboy in a Washington hotel, and, after his writing had been "discovered" during the Harlem Renaissance of the late 1920s, served as a correspondent for the Baltimore Afro-American *reporting on the Spanish Civil War.*

Hughes' most popular writing features the exploits, opinions, and musings of Jesse B. Semple ("Simple"), a masterful rendition of a battered but resilient character Hughes had met in a Harlem bar in 1942. "Simple" tells a story (see Mark Twain's "How To Tell a Story" in Classics) with an engaging combination of humor and irony, penetrating wit and realistic observation.

Hughes' conversations with "Simple" were recorded for over two decades in the Chicago Defender, *a newspaper addressed to that city's black community, and were subsequently collected in four volumes.*

"Anybody can look at me and tell I am part Indian," said Simple.

"I see you almost every day," I said, "and I did not know it until now."

"I have Indian blood but I do not show it much," said Simple. "My uncle's cousin's great-grandma were a Cherokee. I only shows mine when I lose my temper—then my Indian blood boils. I am quick-tempered just like a Indian. If somebody does something to me, I always fights back. In fact, when I get mad, I am the toughest Negro God's got. It's my Indian blood. When I were a young man, I used to play baseball and steal bases just like Jackie. If the empire would rule me out, I would get mad and hit the empire. I had to stop playing. That Indian temper. Nowadays, though, it's mostly womens that riles me up, especially landladies, waitresses, and girl friends. To tell the truth, I believe in a woman keeping her place. Womens is beside themselves these days. They want to rule the roost."

"You have old-fashioned ideas about sex," I said. "In fact, your line of thought is based on outmoded economics."

"What?"

"In the days when women were dependent upon men for a living, you could be the boss. But now women make their own living. Some of them make more money than you do."

"True," said Simple. "During the war they got into that habit. But boss I am still due to be."

"So you think. But you can't always put your authority into effect."

"I can try," said Simple. "I can say, 'Do this!' And if she does something else, I can raise my voice, if not my hand."

"You can be sued for raising your voice," I stated, "and arrested for raising your hand."

"And she can be annihilated when I return from being arrested," said Simple. "That's my Indian blood!"

"You must believe in a woman being a squaw."

"She better not look like no squaw," said Simple. "I want a woman to look sharp when she goes out with me. No moccasins. I wants high-heel shoes and nylons, cute legs—and short dresses. But I also do not want her to talk back to me. As I said, I am the man. *Mine* is the word, and she is due to hush."

"Indians customarily expect their women to be quiet," I said.

"I do not expect mine to be *too* quiet," said Simple. "I want 'em to sweet-talk me—'Sweet baby, this,' and 'Baby, that,' and 'Baby, you's right, darling,' when they talk to me."

"In other words, you want them both old-fashioned and modern at the same time," I said. "The convolutions of your hypothesis are sometimes beyond cognizance."

"Cog hell!" said Simple. "I just do not like no old loud back-talking chick. That's the Indian in me. My grandpa on my father's side were like that, too, an Indian. He was married five times and he really ruled his roost."

"There are a mighty lot of Indians up your family tree," I said. "Did your granddad look like one?"

"Only his nose. He was dark brownskin otherwise. In fact, he were black. And the womens! Man! They was crazy about Grandpa. Every time he walked down the street, they stuck their heads out the windows and kept 'em turned South—which was where the beer parlor was."

"So your grandpa was a drinking man, too. That must be whom you take after."

"I also am named after him," said Simple. "Grandpa's name was Jess, too. So I am Jesse B. Semple."

"What does the *B* stand for?"

"Nothing. I just put it there myself since they didn't give me no initial when I was born. I am really Jess Semple—which the kids changed around into a nickname when I were in school. In fact, they used to tease me when I were small, calling me 'Simple Simon.' But I was right handy with my fists, and after I beat the 'Simon' out of a few of them, they let me alone. But my friends still call me 'Simple.' "

"In reality, you are Jesse Semple," I said, "colored."

"Part Indian," insisted Simple, reaching for his beer.

"Jess is certainly not an Indian name."

"No, it ain't," said Simple, "but we did have a Hiawatha in our family. She died."

"She?" I said. "Hiawatha was no *she.*"

"She was a *she* in our family. And she had long coal-black hair just like a Creole. You know, I started to marry a Creole one time when I was coach-boy on the L. & N. down to New Orleans. Them Louisiana girls are bee-oou-te-ful! Man, I mean!"

"Why didn't you marry her, fellow?"

"They are more dangerous than a Indian," said Simple, "also I do not want no pretty woman. First thing you know, you fall in love with her—then you got to kill somebody about her. She'll make you so jealous, you'll bust! A pretty woman will get a man in trouble. Me and my Indian blood, quick-tempered as I is. No! I do not crave a pretty woman."

"Joyce is certainly not bad-looking," I said. "You hang around her all the time."

"She is far from a Creole. Besides, she appreciates me," said Simple. "Joyce knows I got Indian blood which makes my temper bad. But we take each other as we is. I respect her and she respects me."

"That's the way it should be with the whole world," I said. "Therefore, you and Joyce are setting a fine example in these days of trials and tribulations. Everybody should take each other as they are, white, black, Indians, Creole. Then there would be no prejudice, nations would get along."

"Some folks do not see it like that," said Simple. "For instant, my landlady—and my wife. Isabel could never get along with me. That is why we are not together today."

"I'm not talking personally," I said, "so why bring in your wife?"

"Getting along *starts* with persons, don't it?" asked Simple. "You *must* include my wife. That woman got my Indian blood so riled up one day I thought I would explode."

"I still say, I'm not talking personally."

"Then stop talking," exploded Simple, "because with me it is personal. Facts, I cannot even talk about my wife if I don't get personal. That's how it is if you're part Indian—everything is personal. *Heap much personal.*"

William L. Laurence / Atomic Bombing of Nagasaki Told by Flight Member

The New York Times, September 9, 1945

Science dominated the life of William L. Laurence from his early youth. When he was growing up in Lithuania, according to a biographical profile in the New Yorker, *Laurence received as a gift a book "that speculated on the possibility of a civilization on Mars, and young [Laurence] was so impressed that he decided to go to the United States when he was old enough, because from there . . . he might most easily be able to establish contact with that planet."*

He arrived in Hoboken, New Jersey, in 1905, and proceeded to study at Harvard and the Boston University Law School. After five years of reporting for the New York World, *Laurence went to work for the* New York Times *where he covered some of the most momentous events in the history of twentieth century science. The only reporter with access to the "top secret" testing and development of the atomic bomb, Laurence also prepared the War Department's press releases on the weapon.*

On August 9, 1945, Laurence flew with the mission to bomb Nagasaki, barely three days after one hundred thousand people had been killed at Hiroshima in what Time *magazine called "The Birth of an Era." Laurence's Pulitzer Prize eyewitness account is underlined by a curious aesthetic sense—one that watches this "thing of beauty" destroy a major Japanese city.*

With the atomic-bomb mission to Japan, August 9 (Delayed)—We are on our way to bomb the mainland of Japan. Our flying contingent consists of three specially designed B-29 Superforts, and two of these carry no bombs. But our lead plane is on its way with another atomic bomb, the second in three days, concentrating in its active substance an explosive energy equivalent to twenty thousand and, under favorable conditions, forty thousand tons of TNT.

We have several chosen targets. One of these is the great industrial and shipping center of Nagasaki, on the western shore of Kyushu, one of the main islands of the Japanese homeland.

I watched the assembly of this man-made meteor during the past two days and was among the small group of scientists and Army and Navy representatives privileged to be present at the ritual of its loading in the Superfort last night, against a background of threatening black skies torn open at intervals by great lightning flashes.

It is a thing of beauty to behold, this "gadget." Into its design went millions of man-hours of what is without doubt the most concentrated intellectual effort in history. Never before had so much brain power been focused on a single problem.

This atomic bomb is different from the bomb used three days ago with such devastating results on Hiroshima.

I saw the atomic substance before it was placed inside the bomb. By itself it is not at all dangerous to handle. It is only under certain conditions, produced in the bomb assembly, that it can be made to yield up its energy, and even then it gives only a small fraction of its total contents—a fraction, however, large enough to produce the greatest explosion on earth.

The briefing at midnight revealed the extreme care and the tremendous amount of preparation that had been made to take care of every detail of the mission, to make certain that the atomic bomb fully served the purpose for which it was intended. Each target in turn was shown in detailed maps and in aerial photographs. Every detail of the course was rehearsed—navigation, altitude, weather, where to land in emergencies. It came out that the Navy had submarines and rescue craft, known as Dumbos and Superdumbos, stationed at various strategic points in the vicinity of the targets, ready to rescue the fliers in case they were forced to bail out.

The briefing period ended with a moving prayer by the chaplain. [1] We then proceeded to the mess hall for the traditional early-morning breakfast before departure on a bombing mission.

[1] "Almighty God, Father of all mercies, we pray Thee to be gracious with those who fly this night. Guard and protect those of us who venture out into the darkness of Thy heaven. Uphold them on Thy wings. Keep them safe both in body and soul and bring them back to us. Give to us all the courage and strength for the hours that are ahead; give to them rewards according to their efforts. Above all else, our Father, bring peace to Thy world. May we go forward trusting in Thee and knowing we are in Thy presence now and forever. Amen." Prayer by Chaplain Downey, ending the briefing session preliminary to the bombing of Nagasaki *[edd.]*.

A convoy of trucks took us to the supply building for the special equipment carried on combat missions. This included the Mae West, a parachute, a lifeboat, an oxygen mask, a flak suit, and a survival vest. We still had a few hours before take-off time, but we all went to the flying field and stood around in little groups or sat in jeeps talking rather casually about our mission to the Empire, as the Japanese home islands are known hereabouts.

In command of our mission is Major Charles W. Sweeney, twenty-five, of 124 Hamilton Avenue, North Quincy, Massachusetts. His flagship, carrying the atomic bomb, is named *The Great Artiste,* but the name does not appear on the body of the great silver ship, with its unusually long, four-bladed, orange-tipped propellers. Instead, it carries the number 77, and someone remarks that it was "Red" Grange's winning number on the gridiron.

We took off at 3:50 this morning and headed northwest on a straight line for the Empire. The night was cloudy and threatening, with only a few stars here and there breaking through the overcast. The weather report had predicted storms ahead part of the way but clear sailing for the final and climactic stages of our odyssey.

We were about an hour away from our base when the storm broke. Our great ship took some heavy dips through the abysmal darkness around us, but it took these dips much more gracefully than a large commercial air liner, producing a sensation more in the nature of a glide than a "bump," like a great ocean liner riding the waves except that in this case the air waves were much higher and the rhythmic tempo of the glide was much faster.

I noticed a strange eerie light coming through the window high above the navigator's cabin, and as I peered through the dark all around us I saw a startling phenomenon. The whirling giant propellers had somehow become great luminous disks of blue flame. The same luminous blue flame appeared on the plexiglas windows in the nose of the ship, and on the tips of the giant wings. It looked as though we were riding the whirlwind through space on a chariot of blue fire.

It was, I surmised, a surcharge of static electricity that had accumulated on the tips of the propellers and on the di-electric material of the plastic windows. One's thoughts dwelt anxiously on the precious cargo in the invisible ship ahead of us. Was there any likelihood of danger that this heavy electric tension in the atmosphere all about us might set it off?

I expressed my fears to Captain Bock, who seems nonchalant and unperturbed at the controls. He quickly reassured me.

"It is a familiar phenomenon seen often on ships. I have seen it many times on bombing missions. It is known as St. Elmo's fire."

On we went through the night. We soon rode out the storm and our ship was once again sailing on a smooth course straight ahead, on a direct line to the Empire.

Our altimeter showed that we were traveling through space at a height of seventeen thousand feet. The thermometer registered an outside temperature of thirty-three degrees below zero Centigrade, about thirty below Fahrenheit. Inside our pressurized cabin the temperature was that of a comfortable air-conditioned room and a pressure corresponding to an altitude of eight thousand feet. Captain Bock cautioned me, however, to keep my oxygen mask handy in case of emergency. This, he explained, might mean either something going wrong with the pressure equipment inside the ship or a hole through the cabin by flak.

The first signs of dawn came shortly after five o'clock. Sergeant Curry, of Hoopeston, Illinois, who had been listening steadily on his earphones for radio reports, while maintaining a strict radio silence himself, greeted it by rising to his feet and gazing out the window.

"It's good to see the day," he told me. "I get a feeling of claustrophobia hemmed in in this cabin at night."

He is a typical American youth, looking even younger than his twenty years. It takes no mind reader to read his thoughts.

"It's a long way from Hoopeston," I find myself remarking.

"Yep," he replies, as he busies himself decoding a message from outer space.

"Think this atomic bomb will end the war?" he asks hopefully.

"There is a very good chance that this one may do the trick," I assured him, "but if not, then the next one or two surely will. Its power is such that no nation can stand up against it very long." This was not my own view. I had heard it expressed all around a few hours earlier, before we took off. To anyone who had seen this man-made fireball in action, as I had less than a month ago in the desert of New Mexico, this view did not sound overoptimistic.

By 5:50 it was really light outside. We had lost our lead ship, but Lieutenant Godfrey, our navigator, informs me that we had arranged for that contingency. We have an assembly point in the sky above the little island of Yakushima, southeast of Kyushu, at 9:10. We are to circle there and wait for the rest of our formation.

Our genial bombardier, Lieutenant Levy, comes over to invite me to take his front-row seat in the transparent nose of the ship, and I accept eagerly. From that vantage point in space, seventeen thousand feet above the Pacific, one gets a view of hundreds of miles on all sides, horizontally and vertically. At that height the vast ocean below and the sky above seem to merge into one great sphere.

I was on the inside of that firmament, riding above the giant mountains of white cumulus clouds, letting myself be suspended in infinite space. One hears the whirl of the motors behind one, but it soon becomes insignificant against the immensity all around and is before long swallowed by it. There comes a point where space also swallows time and one lives through eternal moments filled with an oppressive loneliness, as though all life had suddenly vanished from the earth and you are the only one left, a lone survivor traveling endlessly through interplanetary space.

My mind soon returns to the mission I am on. Somewhere beyond these vast mountains of white clouds ahead of me there lies Japan, the land of our enemy. In about four hours from now one of its cities, making weapons of war for use against us, will be wiped off the map by the greatest weapon ever made by man: In one tenth of a millionth of a second, a fraction of time immeasurable by any clock, a whirlwind from the skies will pulverize thousands of its buildings and tens of thousands of its inhabitants.

But at this moment no one yet knows which one of the several cities chosen as targets is to be annihilated. The final choice lies with destiny. The winds over Japan will make the decision. If they carry heavy clouds over our primary target, that city will be saved, at least for the time being. None of its inhabitants will ever know that the wind of a benevolent destiny had passed over their heads. But that same wind will doom another city.

Our weather planes ahead of us are on their way to find out where the wind blows. Half an hour before target time we will know what the winds have decided.

Does one feel any pity or compassion for the poor devils about to die? Not when one thinks of Pearl Harbor and of the Death March on Bataan.

Captain Bock informs me that we are about to start our climb to bombing altitude.

He manipulates a few knobs on his control panel to the right of him, and I alternately watch the white clouds and ocean below me and the altimeter on the bombardier's panel. We reached our altitude at nine o'clock. We were then over Japanese waters, close to their mainland. Lieutenant Godfrey motioned to me to look through his radar scope. Before me was the outline of our assembly point. We shall soon meet our lead ship and proceed to the final stage of our journey.

We reached Yakushima at 9:12 and there, about four thousand feet ahead of us, was *The Great Artiste* with its precious load. I saw Lieutenant Godfrey and Sergeant Curry strap on their parachutes and I decided to do likewise.

We started circling. We saw little towns on the coastline, heedless of our presence. We kept on circling, waiting for the third ship in our formation.

It was 9:56 when we began heading for the coastline. Our weather scouts had sent us code messages, deciphered by Sergeant Curry, informing us that both the primary target as well as the secondary were clearly visible.

The winds of destiny seemed to favor certain Japanese cities that must remain nameless. We circled about them again and again and found no opening in the thick umbrella of clouds that covered them. Destiny chose Nagasaki as the ultimate target.

We had been circling for some time when we noticed black puffs of smoke coming through the white clouds directly at us. There were fifteen bursts of flak in rapid succession, all too low. Captain Bock changed his course. There soon followed eight more bursts of flak, right up to our altitude, but by this time were too far to the left.

We flew southward down the channel and at 11:33 crossed the coastline and headed straight for Nagasaki, about one hundred miles to the west. Here again we circled until we found an opening in the clouds. It was 12:01 and the goal of our mission had arrived.

We heard the prearranged signal on our radio, put on our arc welder's glasses, and watched tensely the maneuverings of the strike ship about half a mile in front of us.

"There she goes!" someone said.

Out of the belly of *The Great Artiste* what looked like a black object went downward.

Captain Bock swung around to get out of range; but even though we were turning away in the opposite direction, and despite the fact that it was broad daylight in our cabin, all of us became aware of a giant flash that broke through the dark barrier of our arc welder's lenses and flooded our cabin with intense light.

We removed our glasses after the first flash, but the light still lingered on, a bluish-green light that illuminated the entire sky all around. A tremendous blast wave struck our ship and made it tremble from nose to tail. This was followed by four more blasts in rapid succession, each resounding like the boom of cannon fire hitting our plane from all directions.

Observers in the tail of our ship saw a giant ball of fire rise as though from the bowels of the earth, belching forth enormous white smoke rings. Next they saw a giant pillar of purple fire, ten thousand feet high, shooting skyward with enormous speed.

By the time our ship had made another turn in the direction of the atomic explosion the pillar of purple fire had reached the level of our altitude. Only about forty-five seconds had passed. Awe-struck, we watched it shoot upward like a meteor coming from the earth instead of from outer space, becoming ever more alive as it climbed skyward through the white clouds. It was no longer smoke, or dust, or even a cloud of fire. It was a living thing, a new species of being, born right before our incredulous eyes.

At one stage of its evolution, covering millions of years in terms of seconds, the entity assumed the form of a giant square totem pole, with its base about three miles long, tapering off to about a mile at the top. Its bottom was brown, its center was amber, its top white. But it was a living totem pole, carved with many grotesque masks grimacing at the earth.

Then, just when it appeared as though the thing had settled down into a state of permanence, there came shooting out of the top a giant mushroom that increased the height of the pillar to a total of forty-five thousand feet. The mushroom top was even more alive than the pillar, seething and boiling in a white fury of creamy foam, sizzling upward and then descending earthward, a thousand Old Faithful geysers rolled into one.

It kept struggling in an elemental fury, like a creature in the act of breaking the bonds that held it down. In a few seconds it had freed itself from its gigantic stem and floated upward with tremendous speed, its momentum carrying it into the stratosphere to a height of about sixty thousand feet.

But no sooner did this happen when another mushroom, smaller in size than the first one, began emerging out of the pillar. It was as though the decapitated monster was growing a new head.

As the first mushroom floated off into the blue it changed its shape into a flower-like form, its giant petals curving downward, creamy white outside, rose-colored inside. It still retained that shape when we last gazed at it from a distance of about two hundred miles. The boiling pillar of many colors could also be seen at that distance, a giant mountain of jumbled rainbows, in travail. Much living substance had gone into those rainbows. The quivering top of the pillar was protruding to a great height through the white clouds, giving the appearance of a monstrous prehistoric creature with a ruff around its neck, a fleecy ruff extending in all directions, as far as the eye could see.

DISCUSSION QUESTIONS

1. How does William Laurence respond to the disastrous event he is covering? Does he include in his report his own feelings about what he is witnessing? What rhetorical devices characterize his account? What effects do these devices have on your response to his report?

2. Laurence calls the atomic bomb ''a thing of beauty.'' Does he find any other examples of ''beauty'' on the mission? Explain. How does his use of detail contribute to (detract from) the aesthetic effects he wants to convey?

3. Does Laurence have any political or moral attitudes toward the bombing? Explain. Point to specific words and phrases to verify your contention. What is the effect of the final image in Laurence's report?

Tom Wicker / Kennedy Is Killed by Sniper as He Rides in Car in Dallas

The New York Times, November 23, 1963

Tom Wicker had a great deal of experience in journalism before he joined the Washington office of the New York Times *in 1960. Born and educated in North Carolina, Wicker worked in his home state as editor of the* Sanhill Citizen *and as managing editor of the* Robesonian. *After serving as copy editor, sports editor, and Washington correspondent for the* Winston-Salem Journal, *Wicker took on the responsibilities of the associate editorship of the* Nashville Tennessean. *Since his report on the assassination of President Kennedy, Wicker has moved from a featured reporter to columnist and associate editor of the* New York Times. *He has also written serval novels. His most recent books include* On Press *(1978) and* Unto This Hour *(1984).*

Tom Wicker's recollections of his coverage of the tumultuous events of November 22, 1963, follow the report below. They are reprinted from Times Talk, *the monthly report circulated to members of the Times organization.*

KENNEDY IS KILLED BY SNIPER AS HE RIDES IN CAR IN DALLAS; JOHNSON SWORN IN ON PLANE.

Gov. Connally Shot;
Mrs. Kennedy Safe.

•

President Is Struck Down by a Rifle Shot
From Building on Motorcade Route—
Johnson, Riding Behind, Is Unhurt.

•

DALLAS, Nov. 22—President John Fitzgerald Kennedy was shot and killed by an assassin today.

He died of a wound in the brain caused by a rifle bullet that was fired at him as he was riding through downtown Dallas in a motorcade.

Vice President Lyndon Baines Johnson, who was riding in the third car behind Mr. Kennedy's, was sworn in as the 36th President of the United States 99 minutes after Mr. Kennedy's death.

Mr. Johnson is 55 years old; Mr. Kennedy was 46.

Shortly after the assassination, Lee H. Oswald, who once defected to the Soviet Union and who has been active in the Fair Play for Cuba Committee, was arrested by the Dallas police. Tonight he was accused of the killing.

SUSPECT CAPTURED AFTER SCUFFLE

Oswald, 24 years old, was also accused of slaying a policeman who had approached him in the street. Oswald was subdued after a scuffle with a second policeman in a nearby theater.

President Kennedy was shot at 12:30 P.M., Central Standard Time (1:30 P.M., New York time). He was pronounced dead at 1 P.M. and Mr. Johnson was sworn in at 2:39 P.M.

Mr. Johnson, who was uninjured in the shooting, took his oath in the Presidential jet plane as it stood on the runway at Love Field. The body of Mr. Kennedy was aboard. Immediately after the oath-taking, the plane took off for Washington.

Standing beside the new President as Mr. Johnson took the oath of office was Mrs. John F. Kennedy. Her stockings were spattered with her husband's blood.

Gov. John B. Connally, Jr., of Texas, who was riding in the same car with Mr. Kennedy, was severely wounded in the chest, ribs and arm. His condition was serious, but not critical.

The killer fired the rifle from a building just off the motorcade route. Mr. Kennedy, Governor Connally and Mr. Johnson had just received an enthusiastic welcome from a large crowd in downtown Dallas.

Mr. Kennedy apparently was hit by the first of what witnesses believed were three shots. He was driven at high speed to Dallas Parkland Hospital. There, in an emergency operating room, with only physicians and nurses in attendance, he died without regaining consciousness.

Mrs. Kennedy, Mrs. Connally and a Secret Service agent were in the car with Mr. Kennedy and Governor Connally. Two Secret Service agents flanked the car. Other than Mr. Connally, none of this group was injured in the shooting. Mrs. Kennedy cried, "Oh no!" immediately after her husband was struck.

Mrs. Kennedy was in the hospital near her husband when he died, but not in the operating room. When the body was taken from the hospital in a bronze coffin about 2 P.M., Mrs. Kennedy walked beside it.

Her face was sorrowful. She looked steadily at the floor. She still wore the raspberry-colored suit in which she had greeted welcoming crowds in Fort Worth and Dallas. But she had taken off the matching pillbox hat she wore earlier in the day, and her dark hair was windblown and tangled. Her hand rested lightly on her husband's coffin as it was taken to a waiting hearse.

Mrs. Kennedy climbed in beside the coffin. Then the ambulance drove to Love Field, and Mr. Kennedy's body was placed aboard the Presidential jet. Mrs. Kennedy then attended the swearing-in ceremony for Mr. Johnson.

As Mr. Kennedy's body left Parkland Hospital, a few stunned persons stood outside. Nurses and doctors, whispering among themselves, looked from the window. A larger crowd that had gathered earlier, before it was known that the President was dead, had been dispersed by Secret Service men and policemen.

PRIESTS ADMINISTER LAST RITES

Two priests administered last rites to Mr. Kennedy, a Roman Catholic. They were the Very Rev. Oscar Huber, the pastor of Holy Trinity Church in Dallas, and the Rev. James Thompson.

Mr. Johnson was sworn in as President by Federal Judge Sarah T. Hughes of the Northern District of Texas. She was appointed to the judgeship by Mr. Kennedy in October, 1961.

The ceremony, delayed about five minutes for Mrs. Kennedy's arrival, took place in the private Presidential cabin in the rear of the plane.

About 25 to 30 persons—members of the late President's staff, members of Congress who had been accompanying the President on a two-day tour of Texas cities and a few reporters—crowded into the little room.

No accurate listing of those present could be obtained. Mrs. Kennedy stood at the left of Mr. Johnson, her eyes and face showing the signs of weeping that had apparently shaken her since she left the hospital not long before.

Mrs. Johnson, wearing a beige dress, stood at her husband's right.

As Judge Hughes read the brief oath of office, her eyes, too, were red from weeping. Mr. Johnson's hands rested on a black, leatherbound Bible as Judge Hughes read and he repeated:

"I do solemnly swear that I will perform the duties of the President of the United States to the best of my ability and defend, protect and preserve the Constitution of the United States."

Those 34 words made Lyndon Baines Johnson, one-time farmboy and schoolteacher of Johnson City, the President.

JOHNSON EMBRACES MRS. KENNEDY

Mr. Johnson made no statement. He embraced Mrs. Kennedy and she held his hand for a long moment. He also embraced Mrs. Johnson and Mrs. Evelyn Lincoln, Mr. Kennedy's private secretary.

"O.K.," Mr. Johnson said. "Let's get this plane back to Washington."

At 2:46 P.M., seven minutes after he had become President, 106 minutes after Mr. Kennedy had become the fourth American President to succumb to an assassin's wounds, the white and red jet took off for Washington.

In the cabin when Mr. Johnson took the oath was Cecil Stoughton, an armed forces photographer assigned to the White House.

Mr. Kennedy's staff members appeared stunned and bewildered. Lawrence F. O'Brien, the Congressional liaison officer, and P. Kenneth O'Donnell, the appointment secretary, both long associates of Mr. Kennedy, showed evidences of weeping. None had anything to say.

Other staff members believed to be in the cabin for the swearing-in included David F. Powers, the White House receptionist; Miss Pamela Turnure, Mrs. Kennedy's press secretary; and Malcolm Kilduff, the assistant White House press secretary.

Mr. Kilduff announced the President's death, with choked voice and red-rimmed eyes, at about 1:36 P.M.

"President John F. Kennedy died at approximately 1 o'clock Central Standard Time today here in Dallas," Mr. Kilduff said at the hospital. "He died of a gunshot wound in the brain. I have no other details regarding the assassination of the President."

Mr. Kilduff also announced that Governor Connally had been hit by a bullet or bullets and that Mr. Johnson, who had not yet been sworn in, was safe in the protective custody of the Secret Service at an unannounced place, presumably the airplane at Love Field.

Mr. Kilduff indicated that the President had been shot once. Later medical reports raised the possibility that there had been two wounds. But the death was caused, as far as could be learned, by a massive wound in the brain.

Later in the afternoon, Dr. Malcolm Perry, an attending surgeon, and Dr. Kemp Clark, chief of neurosurgery at Parkland Hospital, gave more details.

Mr. Kennedy was hit by a bullet in the throat, just below the Adam's apple, they said. This wound had the appearance of a bullet's entry.

Mr. Kennedy also had a massive, gaping wound in the back and one on the right side of the head. However, the doctors said it was impossible to determine immediately whether the wounds had been caused by one bullet or two.

RESUSCITATION ATTEMPTED

Dr. Perry, the first physician to treat the President, said a number of resuscitative measures had been attempted, including oxygen, anesthesia, an indotracheal tube, a tracheotomy, blood and fluids. An electrocardiogram monitor was attached to measure Mr. Kennedy's heart beats.

Dr. Clark was summoned and arrived in a minute or two. By then, Dr. Perry said, Mr. Kennedy was "critically ill and moribund," or near death.

Dr. Clark said that on his first sight of the President, he had concluded immediately that Mr. Kennedy could not live.

"It was apparent that the President had sustained a lethal wound," he said. "A missile had gone in and out of the back of his head causing external lacerations and loss of brain tissue."

Shortly after he arrived, Dr. Clark said, "the President lost his heart action by the electrocardiogram." A closed-chest cardiograph massage was attempted, as were other emergency resuscitation measures.

Dr. Clark said these had produced "palpable pulses" for a short time, but all were "to no avail."

IN OPERATING ROOM 40 MINUTES

The President was on the emergency table at the hospital for about 40 minutes, the doctors said. At the end, perhaps eight physicians were in Operating Room No. 1, where Mr. Kennedy remained until his death. Dr. Clark said it was difficult to determine the exact moment of death, but the doctors said officially that it occurred at 1 P.M.

Later, there were unofficial reports that Mr. Kennedy had been killed instantly. The source of these reports, Dr. Tom Shires, chief surgeon at the hospital and professor of surgery at the University of Texas Southwest Medical School, issued this statement tonight:

"Medically, it was apparent the President was not alive when he was brought in. There was no spontaneous respiration. He had dilated, fixed pupils. It was obvious he had a lethal head wound.

"Technically, however, by using vigorous resuscitation, intravenous tubes and all the usual supportive measures, we were able to raise a semblance of a heartbeat."

Dr. Shires was not present when Mr. Kennedy was being treated at Parkland Hospital. He issued his statement, however, after lengthy conferences with the doctors who had attended the President.

Mr. Johnson remained in the hospital about 30 minutes after Mr. Kennedy died.

The details of what happened when shots first rang out, as the President's car moved along at about 25 miles an hour, were sketchy. Secret Service agents, who might have given more details, were unavailable to the press at first, and then returned to Washington with President Johnson.

KENNEDYS HAILED AT BREAKFAST

Mr. Kennedy had opened his day in Fort Worth, first with a speech in a parking lot and then at a Chamber of Commerce breakfast. The breakfast appearance was a particular triumph for Mrs. Kennedy, who entered late and was given an ovation.

Then the Presidential party, including Governor and Mrs. Connally, flew on to Dallas, an eight-minute flight. Mr. Johnson, as is customary, flew in a separate plane. The President and the Vice President do not travel together, out of fear of a double tragedy.

At Love Field, Mr. and Mrs. Kennedy lingered for 10 minutes, shaking hands with an enthusiastic group lining the fence. The group called itself "Grassroots Democrats."

Mr. Kennedy then entered his open Lincoln convertible at the head of the motorcade. He sat in the rear seat on the right-hand side. Mrs. Kennedy, who appeared to be enjoying one of the first political outings she had ever made with her husband, sat at his left.

In the "jump" seat, directly ahead of Mr. Kennedy, sat Governor Connally, with Mrs. Connally at his left in another "jump" seat. A Secret Service agent was driving and the two others ran alongside.

Behind the President's limousine was an open sedan carrying a number of Secret Service agents. Behind them, in an open convertible, rode Mr. and Mrs. Johnson and Texas's senior Senator, Ralph W. Yarborough, a Democrat.

The motorcade proceeded uneventfully along a 10-mile route through downtown Dallas, aiming for the Merchandise Mart. Mr. Kennedy was to address a group of the city's leading citizens at a luncheon in his honor.

In downtown Dallas, crowds were thick, enthusiastic and cheering. The turnout was somewhat unusual for this center of conservatism, where only a month ago Adlai E. Stevenson was attacked by a rightist crowd. It was also in Dallas, during the 1960 campaign, that Senator Lyndon B. Johnson and his wife were nearly mobbed in the lobby of the Baker Hotel.

As the motorcade neared its end and the President's car moved out of the thick crowds onto Stennonds Freeway near the Merchandise Mart, Mrs. Connally recalled later, "we were all very pleased with the reception in downtown Dallas."

APPROACHING 3-STREET UNDERPASS

Behind the three leading cars were a string of others carrying Texas and Dallas dignitaries, two buses of reporters, several open cars carrying photographers and other reporters, and a bus for White House staff members.

As Mrs. Connally recalled later, the President's car was almost ready to go underneath a "triple underpass" beneath three streets—Elm, Commerce and Main—when the first shot was fired.

That shot apparently struck Mr. Kennedy. Governor Connally turned in his seat at the sound and appeared immediately to be hit in the chest.

Mrs. Mary Norman of Dallas was standing at the curb and at that moment was aiming her camera at the President. She saw him slump forward, then slide down in the seat.

"My God," Mrs. Norman screamed, as she recalled it later, "he's shot!"

Mrs. Connally said that Mrs. Kennedy had reached and "grabbed" her husband. Mrs. Connally put her arms around the Governor. Mrs. Connally said that she and Mrs. Kennedy had then ducked low in the car as it sped off.

Mrs. Connally's recollections were reported by Julian Reade, an aide to the Governor.

Most reporters in the press buses were too far back to see the shootings, but they observed some quick scurrying by motor policemen accompanying the motorcade. It was noted that the President's car had picked up speed and raced away, but reporters were not aware that anything serious had occurred until they reached the Merchandise Mart two or three minutes later.

RUMORS SPREAD AT TRADE MART

Rumors of the shooting already were spreading through the luncheon crowd of hundreds, which was having the first course. No White House officials or Secret Service agents were present, but the reporters were taken quickly to Parkland Hospital on the strength of the rumors.

There they encountered Senator Yarborough, white, shaken and horrified.

The shots, he said, seemed to have come from the right and the rear of the car in which he was riding, the third in the motorcade. Another eyewitness, Mel Crouch, a Dallas television reporter, reported that as the shots rang out he saw a rifle extended and then withdrawn from a window on the "fifth or sixth floor" of the Texas Public School Book Depository. This is a leased state building on Elm Street, to the right of the motorcade route.

Senator Yarborough said there had been a slight pause between the first two shots and a longer pause between the second and third. A Secret Service man riding in the Senator's car, the Senator said, immediately ordered Mr. and Mrs. Johnson to get down below the level of the doors. They did so, and Senator Yarborough also got down.

The leading cars of the motorcade then pulled away at high speed toward Parkland Hospital, which was not far away, by the fast highway.

"We knew by the speed that something was terribly wrong," Senator Yarborough reported. When he put his head up, he said, he saw a Secret Service man in the car ahead beating his fists against the trunk deck of the car in which he was riding, apparently in frustration and anguish.

MRS. KENNEDY'S REACTION

Only White House staff members spoke with Mrs. Kennedy. A Dallas medical student, David Edwards, saw her in Parkland Hospital while she was waiting for news of her husband. He gave this description:

"The look in her eyes was like an animal that had been trapped, like a little rabbit—brave, but fear was in the eyes."

Dr. Clark was reported to have informed Mrs. Kennedy of her husband's death.

No witnesses reported seeing or hearing any of the Secret Service agents or policemen fire back. One agent was seen to brandish a machine gun as the cars sped away. Mr. Crouch observed a policeman falling to the ground and pulling a weapon. But the events had occurred so quickly that there was apparently nothing for the men to shoot at.

Mr. Crouch said he saw two women, standing at a curb to watch the motorcade pass, fall to the ground when the shots rang out. He also saw a man snatch up his little girl and run along the road. Policemen, he said, immediately chased this man under the impression he had been involved in the shooting, but Mr. Crouch said he had been a fleeing spectator.

Mr. Kennedy's limousine—license No. GG300 under District of Columbia registry—pulled up at the emergency entrance of Parkland Hospital. Senator Yarborough said the President had been carried inside on a stretcher.

By the time reporters arrived at the hospital, the police were guarding the Presidential car closely. They would allow no one to approach it. A bucket of water stood by the car, suggesting that the back seat had been scrubbed out.

Robert Clark of the American Broadcasting Company, who had been riding near the front of the motorcade, said Mr. Kennedy was motionless when he was carried inside. There was a great amount of blood on Mr. Kennedy's suit and shirtfront and the front of his body, Mr. Clark said.

Mrs. Kennedy was leaning over her husband when the car stopped, Mr. Clark said, and walked beside the wheeled stretcher into the hospital. Mr. Connally sat with his hands holding his stomach, his head bent over. He, too, was moved into the hospital in a stretcher, with Mrs. Connally at his side.

Robert McNeill of the National Broadcasting Company, who also was in the reporters' pool car, jumped out at the scene of the shooting. He said the police had taken two eyewitnesses into custody—an 8-year-old Negro boy and a white man—for informational purposes.

Many of these reports could not be verified immediately.

EYEWITNESS DESCRIBES SHOOTING

An unidentified Dallas man, interviewed on television here, said he had been waving at the President when the shots were fired. His belief was that Mr. Kennedy had been struck twice—once, as Mrs. Norman recalled, when he slumped in his seat; again when he slid down in it.

"It seemed to just knock him down," the man said.

Governor Connally's condition was reported as "satisfactory" tonight after four hours in surgery at Parkland Hospital.

Dr. Robert R. Shaw, a thoracic surgeon, operated on the Governor to repair damage to his left chest.

Later, Dr. Shaw said Governor Connally had been hit in the back just below the shoulder blade, and that the bullet had gone completely through the Governor's chest, taking out part of the fifth rib.

After leaving the body, he said, the bullet struck the Governor's right wrist, causing a compound fracture. It then lodged in the left thigh.

The thigh wound, Dr. Shaw said, was trivial. He said the compound fracture would heal.

Dr. Shaw said it would be unwise for Governor Connally to be moved in the next 10 to 14 days. Mrs. Connally was remaining at his side tonight.

TOUR BY MRS. KENNEDY UNUSUAL

Mrs. Kennedy's presence near her husband's bedside at his death resulted from somewhat unusual circumstances. She had rarely accompanied him on his trips about the country and had almost never made political trips with him.

The tour on which Mr. Kennedy was engaged yesterday and today was only quasi-political; the only open political activity was to have been a speech tonight to a fund-raising dinner at the state capitol in Austin.

In visiting Texas, Mr. Kennedy was seeking to improve his political fortunes in a pivotal state that he barely won in 1960. He was also hoping to patch a bitter internal dispute among Texas's Democrats.

At 8:45 A.M., when Mr. Kennedy left the Texas hotel in Fort Worth, where he spent his last night, to address the parking lot crowd across the street, Mrs. Kennedy was not with him. There appeared to be some disappointment.

''Mrs. Kennedy is organizing herself,'' the President said good-naturedly. ''It takes longer, but, of course, she looks better than we do when she does it.''

Later, Mrs. Kennedy appeared late at the Chamber of Commerce breakfast in Fort Worth.

Again, Mr. Kennedy took note of her presence. ''Two years ago,'' he said, ''I introduced myself in Paris by saying that I was the man who had accompanied Mrs. Kennedy to Paris. I am getting somewhat that same sensation as I travel around Texas. Nobody wonders what Lyndon and I wear.''

The speech Mr. Kennedy never delivered at the Merchandise Mart luncheon contained a passage commenting on a recent preoccupation of his, and a subject of much interest in this city, where right-wing conservatism is the rule rather than the exception.

''Voices are being heard in the land,'' he said, ''voices preaching doctrines wholly unrelated to reality, wholly unsuited to the sixties, doctrines which apparently assume that words will suffice without weapons, that vituperation is as good as victory and that peace is a sign of weakness.''

The speech went on: ''At a time when the national debt is steadily being reduced in terms of its burden on our economy, they see that debt as the greatest threat to our security. At a time when we are steadily reducing the number of Federal employees serving every thousand citizens, they fear those supposed hordes of civil servants far more than the actual hordes of opposing armies.

''We cannot expect that everyone, to use the phrase of a decade ago, will 'talk sense to the American people.' But we can hope that fewer people will listen to nonsense. And the notion that this nation is headed for defeat through deficit, or that strength is but a matter of slogans, is nothing but just plain nonsense.''

DISCUSSION QUESTIONS

1. What is the verb tense at the beginning of the headline for Wicker's story? What effect is created by the use of this particular verb form? Does the tense remain consistent with the verb form used in the remainder of the headline? In the text of the story?

2. Compare the headline to this story with that of the *New York Herald* on the assassination of President Lincoln. What can these examples tell you about the language of headlines in general?

3. How is the first paragraph of each story partly determined by the information presented in the headline? Contrast the leads of each news story. Which do you find most successful? Why? Does each story adhere to the format of the ''inverted pyramid'' as described in the introduction to Press?

Tom Wicker / The Assassination

Times Talk, December 1963

WASHINGTON

I think I was in the first press bus. But I can't be sure. Pete Lisagor of The Chicago Daily News says he *knows* he was in the first press bus and he describes things that went on aboard it that didn't happen on the bus I was in. But I still *think* I was in the first press bus.

I cite that minor confusion as an example of the way it was in Dallas in the early afternoon of Nov. 22. At first no one knew what happened, or how, or where, much less why. Gradually, bits and pieces began to fall together and within two hours a reasonably coherent version of the story began to be possible. Even now, however, I know no reporter who was there who has a clear and orderly picture of that surrealistic afternoon; it is still a matter of bits and pieces thrown hastily into something like a whole.

It began, for most reporters, when the central fact of it was over. As our press bus eased at motorcade speed down an incline toward an underpass, there was a little confusion in the sparse crowds that at that point had been standing at the curb to see the President of the United States pass. As we came out of the underpass, I saw a motorcycle policeman drive over the curb, across an open area, a few feet up a railroad bank, dismount and start scrambling up the bank.

Jim Mathis of The Advance (Newhouse) Syndicate went to the front of our bus and looked ahead to where the President's car was supposed to be, perhaps ten cars ahead of us. He hurried back to his seat.

"The President's car just sped off," he said. "Really gunned away." (How could Mathis have seen that if there had been another bus in front of us?)

But that could have happened if someone had thrown a tomato at the President. The press bus in its stately pace rolled on to the Trade Mart, where the President was to speak. Fortunately, it was only a few minutes away.

At the Trade Mart, rumor was sweeping the hundreds of Texans already eating their lunch. It was the only rumor that I had ever *seen;* it was moving across that crowd like a wind over a wheatfield. A man eating a grapefruit seized my arm as I passed.

"Has the President been shot?" he asked.

"I don't think so," I said. "But something happened."

With the other reporters—I suppose 35 of them—I went on through the huge hall to the upstairs press room. We were hardly there when Marianne Means of Hearst Headline Service hung up a telephone, ran to a group of us and said, "The President's been shot. He's at Parkland Hospital."

One thing I learned that day; I suppose I already knew it, but that day made it plain. A reporter must trust his instinct. When Miss Means said those eight words—I never learned who told her—I knew absolutely they were true. Everyone did. We ran for the press buses.

Again, a man seized my arm—an official-looking man.

"No running in here," he said sternly. I pulled free and ran on. Doug Kiker of The Herald Tribune barreled head-on into a waiter carrying a plate of potatoes. Waiter and potatoes flew about the room. Kiker ran on. He was in his first week with The Trib, and his first Presidential trip.

I barely got aboard a moving press bus. Bob Pierrepoint of C.B.S. was aboard and he said that he now recalled having heard something that could have been shots—or firecrackers, or motorcycle backfire. We talked anxiously, unbelieving, afraid.

Fortunately again, it was only a few minutes to Parkland Hospital. There at its emergency entrance, stood the President's car, the top up, a bucket of bloody water beside it. Automatically, I took down its license number—GG300 District of Columbia.

The first eyewitness description came from Senator Ralph Yarborough, who had been riding in the third car of the motorcade with Vice President and Mrs. Johnson. Senator Yarborough is an East Texan, which is to say a Southerner, a man of quick emotion, old-fashioned rhetoric.

"Gentlemen," he said, pale, shaken, near tears. "It is a deed of horror."

The details he gave us were good and mostly—as it later proved—accurate. But he would not describe to us the appearance of the President as he was wheeled into the hospital, except to say that he was "gravely wounded." We could not doubt, then, that it was serious.

I had chosen that day to be without a notebook. I took notes on the back of my mimeographed schedule of the two-day tour of Texas we had been so near to concluding. Today, I cannot read many of the notes; on Nov. 22, they were as clear as 60-point type.

A local television reporter, Mel Crouch, told us he had seen a rifle being withdrawn from the corner fifth or sixth floor window of the Texas School Book Depository. Instinct again—Crouch sounded right, positive, though none of us knew him. We believed it and it was right.

Mac Kilduff, an assistant White House press secretary in charge of the press on that trip, and who was to acquit himself well that day, came out of the hospital. We gathered round and he told us the President was alive. It wasn't true, we later learned; but Mac thought it was true at that time, and he didn't mislead us about a possible recovery. His whole demeanor made plain what was likely to happen. He also told us—as Senator Yarborough had—that Gov. John Connally of Texas was shot, too.

Kilduff promised more details in five minutes and went back into the hospital. We were barred. Word came to us secondhand—I don't remember exactly how—from Bob Clark of A.B.C., one of the men who had been riding in the press "pool" car near the President's, that he had been lying face down in Mrs. Kennedy's lap when the car arrived at Parkland. No signs of life.

That is what I mean by instinct. That day, a reporter had none of the ordinary means or time to check and double-check matters given as fact. He had to go on what he knew of people he talked to, what he knew of human reaction, what two isolated "facts" added to in sum—above all on what he felt in his bones. I knew Clark and respected him. I took his report at face value, even at second hand. It turned out to be true. In a crisis, if a reporter can't trust his instinct for truth, he can't trust anything.

When Wayne Hawks of the White House staff appeared to say that a press room had been set up in a hospital classroom at the left rear of the building, the group of reporters began struggling across the lawn in that direction. I lingered to ask a motorcycle policeman if he had heard on his radio anything about the pursuit or capture of the assassin. He hadn't, and I followed the other reporters.

As I was passing the open convertible in which Vice President and Mrs. Johnson and Senator Yarborough had been riding in the motorcade, a voice boomed from its radio:

"The President of the United States is dead. I repeat—it has just been announced that the President of the United States is dead."

There was no authority, no word of who had announced it. But—instinct again—

I believed it instantly. It sounded true. I knew it was true. I stood still a moment, then began running.

Ordinarily, I couldn't jump a tennis net if I'd just beaten Gonzales. That day, carrying a briefcase and a typewriter, I jumped a chain fence looping around the drive, not even breaking stride. Hugh Sidey of Time, a close friend of the President, was walking slowly ahead of me.

"Hugh," I said, "the President's dead. Just announced on the radio. I don't know who announced it but it sounded official to me."

Sidey stopped, looked at me, looked at the ground. I couldn't talk about it. I couldn't think about it. I couldn't do anything but run on to the press room. Then I told others what I had heard.

Sidey, I learned a few minutes later, stood where he was a minute. Then he saw two Catholic priests. He spoke to them. Yes, they told him, the President was dead. They had administered the last rites. Sidey went on to the press room and spread that word, too.

Throughout the day, every reporter on the scene seemed to me to do his best to help everyone else. Information came only in bits and pieces. Each man who picked up a bit or a piece passed it on. I know no one who held anything out. Nobody thought about an exclusive; it didn't seem important.

After perhaps 10 minutes when we milled around in the press room—my instinct was to find the new President, but no one knew where he was—Kilduff appeared red-eyed, barely in control of himself. In that hushed classroom, he made the official, the unbelievable announcement. The President was dead of a gunshot wound in the brain. Lyndon Johnson was safe, in the protective custody of the Secret Service. He would be sworn in as soon as possible.

Kilduff, composed as a man could be in those circumstances, promised more details when he could get them, then left. The search for phones began. Jack Gertz, traveling with us for A.T. & T., was frantically moving them by the dozen into the hospital, but few were ready yet.

I wandered down the hall, found a doctor's office, walked in and told him I had to use his phone. He got up without a word and left. I battled the hospital switchboard for five minutes and finally got a line to New York—Hal Faber on the other end, with Harrison Salisbury on an extension.

They knew what had happened, I said. The death had been confirmed. I proposed to write one long story, as quickly as I could, throwing in everything I could learn. On the desk, they could cut it up as they needed—throwing part into other stories, putting other facts into mine. But I would file a straight narrative without worrying about their editing needs.

Reporters always fuss at editors and always will. But Salisbury and Faber are good men to talk to in a crisis. They knew what they were doing and realized my problems. I may fuss at them again sometime, but after that day my heart won't be in it. Quickly, clearly, they told me to go ahead, gave me the moved-up deadlines, told me of plans already made to get other reporters into Dallas, but made it plain they would be hours in arriving.

Salisbury told me to use the phone and take no chances on a wire circuit being jammed or going wrong. Stop reporting and start writing in time to meet the deadline, he said. Pay anyone $50 if necessary to dictate for you.

The whole conversation probably took three minutes. Then I hung up, thinking of all there was to know, all there was I didn't know. I wandered down a corridor and ran into Sidey and Chuck Roberts of Newsweek. They'd seen a hearse pulling up at the emergency entrance and we figured they were about to move the body.

We made our way to the hearse—a Secret Service agent who knew us helped us through suspicious Dallas police lines—and the driver said his instructions were to take the body to the airport. That confirmed our hunch, but gave me, at least, another wrong one. Mr. Johnson, I declared, would fly to Washington with the body and be sworn in there.

We posted ourselves inconspicuously near the emergency entrance. Within minutes, they brought the body out in a bronze coffin.

A number of White House staff people—stunned, silent, stumbling along as if dazed—walked with it. Mrs. Kennedy walked by the coffin, her hand on it, her head down, her hat gone, her dress and stockings spattered. She got into the hearse with the coffin. The staff men crowded into cars and followed.

That was just about the only eyewitness matter that I got with my own eyes that entire afternoon.

Roberts commandeered a seat in a police car and followed, promising to "fill" Sidey and me as necessary. We made the same promise to him and went back to the press room.

There, we received an account from Julian Reade, a staff assistant, of Mrs. John Connally's recollection of the shooting. Most of his recital was helpful and it established the important fact of who was sitting in which seat in the President's car at the time of the shooting.

The doctors who had treated the President came in after Mr. Reade. They gave us copious detail, particularly as to the efforts they had made to resuscitate the President. They were less explicit about the wounds, explaining that the body had been in their hands only a short time and they had little time to examine it closely. They conceded they were unsure as to the time of death and had arbitrarily put it at 1 P.M., C.S.T.

Much of their information, as it developed later, was erroneous. Subsequent reports made it pretty clear that Mr. Kennedy probably was killed instantly. His body, as a physical mechanism, however, continued to flicker an occasional pulse and heartbeat. No doubt this justified the doctors' first account. There also was the question of national security and Mr. Johnson's swearing-in. Perhaps, too, there was a question about the Roman Catholic rites. In any case, until a later doctors' statement about 9 P.M. that night, the account we got at the hospital was official.

The doctors hardly had left before Hawks came in and told us Mr. Johnson would be sworn in immediately at the airport. We dashed for the press buses, still parked outside. Many a campaign had taught me something about press buses and I ran a little harder, got there first, and went to the wide rear seat. That is the best place on a bus to open up a typewriter and get some work done.

On the short trip to the airport, I got about 500 words on paper—leaving a blank space for the hour of Mr. Johnson's swearing-in, and putting down the mistaken assumption that the scene would be somewhere in the terminal. As we arrived at a back gate along the airstrip, we could see Air Force One, the Presidential jet, screaming down the runway and into the air.

Left behind had been Sid Davis of Westinghouse Broadcasting, one of the few reporters who had been present for the swearing-in. Roberts, who had guessed right in going to the airport when he did, had been there too and was aboard the plane on the way to Washington.

Davis climbed on the back of a shiny new car that was parked near where our bus halted. I hate to think what happened to its trunk deck. He and Roberts—true to his promise—had put together a magnificent "pool" report on the swearing-in. Davis read it off, answered questions, and gave a picture that so far as I know was complete, accurate and has not yet been added to.

I said to Kiker of The Trib: "We better go write. There'll be phones in the terminal." He agreed. Bob Manning, an ice-cool member of the White House transportation staff, agreed to get our bags off the press plane, which would return to Washington as soon as possible, and put them in a nearby telephone booth.

Kiker and I ran a half-mile to the terminal, cutting through a baggage-handling room to get there. I went immediately to a phone booth and dictated my 500-word lead, correcting it as I read, embellishing it too. Before I hung up, I got Salisbury and asked him to cut into my story whatever the wires were filing on the assassin. There was no time left to chase down the Dallas police and find out those details on my own.

Dallas Love Field has a mezzanine running around its main waiting room; it is equipped with writing desks for travelers. I took one and went to work. My recollection is that it was then about 5 P.M. New York time.

I would write two pages, run down the stairs, across the waiting room, grab a phone and dictate. Miraculously, I never had to wait for a phone booth or to get a line through. Dictating each take, I would throw in items I hadn't written, sometimes whole paragraphs. It must have been tough on the dictating room crew.

Once, while in the booth dictating, I looked up and found twitching above me the imposing mustache of Gladwin Hill. He was the first Times man in and had found me right off; I was seldom more glad to see anyone. We conferred quickly and he took off for the police station; it was a tremendous load off my mind to have that angle covered and out of my hands.

I was half through, maybe more, when I heard myself paged. It turned out to be Kiker, who had been separated from me and was working in the El Dorado room, a bottle club in the terminal. My mezzanine was quieter and a better place to work, but he had a TV going for him, so I moved in too.

The TV helped in one important respect. I took down from it an eyewitness account of one Charles Drehm, who had been waving at the President when he was shot. Instinct again: Drehm sounded positive, right, sure of what he said. And his report was the first real indication that the President probably was shot twice.

Shortly after 7 P.M., New York time, I finished. So did Kiker. Simultaneously we thought of our bags out in that remote phone booth. We ran for a taxi and urged an unwilling driver out along the dark airstrip. As we found the place, with some difficulty, an American Airlines man was walking off with the bags. He was going to ship them off to the White House, having seen the tags on them. A minute later and we'd have been stuck in Dallas without even a toothbrush.

Kiker and I went to The Dallas News. The work wasn't done—I filed a number of inserts later that night, wrote a separate story on the building from which the assassin had fired, tried to get John Herbers, Don Janson, Joe Loftus on useful angles as they drifted in. But when I left the airport, I knew the worst of it was over. The story was filed on time, good or bad, complete or incomplete, and any reporter knows how that feels. They couldn't say I missed the deadline.

It was a long taxi ride to The Dallas News. We were hungry, not having eaten since an early breakfast. It was then that I remembered John F. Kennedy's obituary. Last June, Hal Faber had sent it to me for updating. On Nov. 22, it was still lying on my desk in Washington, not updated, not rewritten, a monument to the incredibility of that afternoon in Dallas.

Thomas O'Toole / "The Eagle Has Landed": Two Men Walk on the Moon

Washington Post, July 24, 1969

On July 20, 1969, Thomas O'Toole, staff writer for the Washington Post, *covered his story by watching Neil Armstrong and Buzz Aldrin participate in what President Richard Nixon called "the greatest moment in history since the Creation."*

HOUSTON, July 20—Man stepped out onto the moon tonight for the first time in his two-million-year history.

"That's one small step for man," declared pioneer astronaut Neil Armstrong at 10:56 P.M. EDT, "one giant leap for mankind."

Just after that historic moment in man's quest for his origins, Armstrong walked on the dead satellite and found the surface very powdery, littered with fine grains of black dust.

A few minutes later, Edwin (Buzz) Aldrin joined Armstrong on the lunar surface and in less than an hour they put on a show that will long be remembered by the worldwide television audience.

AMERICAN FLAG PLANTED

The two men walked easily, talked easily, even ran and jumped happily so it seemed. They picked up rocks, talked at length of what they saw, planted an American flag, saluted it, and talked by radiophone with the President in the White House, and then faced the camera and saluted Mr. Nixon.

"For every American, this has to be the proudest day of our lives," the President told the astronauts. "For one priceless moment in the whole history of man, all the people on this earth are truly one."

Seven hours earlier, at 4:17 P.M., the Eagle and its two pilots thrilled the world as they zoomed in over a rock-covered field, hovered and then slowly let down on the moon. "Houston, Tranquillity base here," Armstrong radioed. "The Eagle has landed."

At 1:10 A.M. Monday—2 hours and 14 minutes after Armstrong first stepped upon the lunar surface—the astronauts were back in their moon craft and the hatch was closed.

In describing the moon, Armstrong told Houston that it was "fine and powdery. I can kick it up loosely with my toe.

"It adheres like powdered charcoal to the boot," he went on, "but I only go in a small fraction of an inch. I can see my footprint in the moon like fine grainy particles."

Armstrong found he had such little trouble walking on the moon that he began talking almost as if he didn't want to leave it.

"It has a stark beauty all its own," Armstrong said. "It's like the desert in the Southwestern United States. It's very pretty out here."

AMAZINGLY CLEAR PICTURE

Armstrong shared his first incredible moments on the moon with the whole world, as a television camera on the outside of the wingless Eagle landing craft sent back an amazingly clear picture of his first steps on the moon.

Armstrong seemed like he was swimming along, taking big and easy steps on the airless moon despite the cumbersome white pressure-suit he wore.

"There seems to be no difficulty walking around," he said. "As we suspected, it's even easier than the one-sixth G that we did in simulations on the ground."

One of the first things he did was to scoop up a small sample of the moon with a long-handled spoon with a bag on its end like a small butterfly net.

"Looks like it's easy," Aldrin said, looking down from the Lem.

"It is," Armstrong told him. "I'm sure I could push it in farther but I can't bend down that far."

GUIDES ALDRIN DOWN LADDER

At 11:11 P.M., Aldrin started down the landing craft's ten-foot ladder to join Armstrong.

Backing down the nine-step ladder, Aldrin was guided the entire way by Armstrong, who stood at the foot of the ladder looking up at him.

"Okay," Armstrong said, "watch your 'pliss' (PLSS, for portable life support system) from underneath. Drop your pliss down. You're clear. About an inch clear on your pliss."

"Okay," Aldrin said. "You need a little arching of the back to come down."

After he stepped onto the first rung of the ladder, Aldrin went back up to the Lem's "front porch" to partially close the Lem's hatch.

"Making sure not to lock it on my way out," he said in comic fashion. "That's our home for the next couple of hours and I want to make sure we can get back in."

"Beautiful," said Aldrin when he met Armstrong on the lunar surface.

"Isn't that something," said Armstrong. "It's a magnificent sight out here."

While Armstrong watched, Aldrin went through some cautious walking experiments to see how difficult it was in his pressure suit.

"Reaching down is fairly easy," he said. "The mass of the backpack does have some effect on inertia. There's a slight tendency, I can see now, to tip backwards."

Aldrin and Armstrong then both walked around the Lem's 31-foot base, inspecting its four legs and undercarriage at the same time that they began looking over the moon's surface.

"These rocks are rather slippery," Armstrong said. "The powdery surface fills up the fine pores on the rocks, and we tend to slide over it rather easily."

While Armstrong got ready to move the television camera out about 30 feet from the Lem, Aldrin did some more experimental walking.

"If I'm about to lose my balance in one direction," said Aldrin, "recovery is quite natural and easy. You've just got to be careful leaning in the direction you want to go in."

At that, Aldrin apparently spotted an interesting rock.

"Hey, Neil," he said. "Didn't I say we'd find a purple rock?"

"Did you find a purple rock?" Armstrong asked him.

"Yep," replied Aldrin.

The next thing Armstrong did was to change lenses on the television camera, putting a telephoto lens on it for a closeup view of what was happening.

"Now we'll read the plaque for those who haven't read it before," Armstrong said, referring to a small stainless steel plaque that had been placed on one of the landing craft's legs.

"It says," Armstrong said, "Here men from the planet Earth first set foot on the moon. July 1969, A.D. We came in peace for all mankind."

"It has the crew members' signatures," Armstrong said, "and the signature of the President of the United States."

BLEAK BUT BEAUTIFUL

Armstrong next took the television camera out to a spot about 40 feet from the Lem, and placed it on a small tripod.

Incredibly clear, the picture showed a distant Lem, squatting on the bleak but beautiful lunar surface like some giant mechanical toy. It appeared to be perfectly level, not at all tilted on the rough lunar terrain.

When he got the camera mounted correctly, he walked back toward the Lem, with the camera view following him all the way.

Just after 11:30, both men removed a pole, flagstaff and a plastic American flag from one of the Lem's legs. They gently pressed the flag into the lunar surface.

After they saluted the flag, astronaut Bruce McCandless commented on the little ceremony from his perch in the Manned Spacecraft center's mission control room.

"The flag is up now," he said. "You can see the stars and stripes on the lunar surface."

At 11:48 McCandless asked both men to stand together near the flag. "The President of the United States would like to talk to you," McCandless said.

Mr. Nixon spoke to the astronauts for almost two minutes, and when he finished, the two astronauts stood erect and saluted directly at the television camera.

During most of their early time on the moon, astronaut Michael Collins not only didn't see them walking on the moon, but was behind the moon and out of radio touch in his orbiting command craft.

When he finally swung around in front of the moon again, Armstrong and Aldrin had been out almost 30 minutes.

"How's it going?" Collins asked plaintively.

"Just great," McCandless told him.

"How's the television?" he asked.

"Just beautiful," he was told.

Armstrong and Aldrin stayed out on the moon for almost two hours, with Aldrin first back into the Lem just before 1 A.M. Monday.

"Adios, Amigos," he said as he pulled himself easily back up the ladder.

Armstrong started back up the ladder a few minutes after 1 A.M. Monday. He took what seemed like the first four rungs with one huge leap upward. At 1:10 A.M., Armstrong had joined Aldrin inside the cabin. "Okay, the hatch is closed and latched," said Aldrin seconds later.

When both men had repressurized their cabin and taken off their helmets and gloves, Collins reappeared over the lunar horizon in his command craft. At once, he asked how everything had gone.

SLEEP, THEN RENDEZVOUS

"Hallelujah," he said when he was told what had happened.

All three astronauts were due to get their first sleep in almost 24 hours, a sleep that was never more richly deserved.

If nothing went wrong—and nobody was expecting anything would—Armstrong and Aldrin were due to lift back off the surface of the moon at 1:55 P.M. EDT Monday.

Burning their ascent engine full-blast for just over seven minutes, they will start a four-hour flight to rejoin Collins and the command craft 70 miles above the lunar surface.

The majestic moment of man's first steps on the moon came about six hours after Armstrong and Aldrin set their four-legged, wingless landing craft down in the moon's Sea of Tranquillity—precisely at 4:17 P.M. EDT.

"Houston, Tranquillity Base here," Armstrong announced to a breathless world. "The Eagle has landed."

"You did a beautiful job," astronaut Charles Duke said from Houston's Manned Spacecraft Center. "Be advised there's lots of smiling faces down here."

"There's two of them down here," Armstrong replied.

The landing apparently was not an easy one. It was about four miles from the target point in the southwestern edge of the Sea of Tranquillity, almost right on the lunar equator.

"We were coming down in a crater the size of a football field with lots of big rocks around and in it," Armstrong said about five minutes after landing. "We had to fly it manually over the rock field to find a place to land."

"EVERY VARIETY OF SHAPES"

A few minutes later, Aldrin gave a waiting world its first eyewitness description on the moon's surface.

"It looks like a collection of just about every variety of shapes and angularity, every variety of rock you could find," Aldrin said.

"There doesn't appear to be too much color," he went on, "except that it looks as though some of the boulders are going to have some interesting color."

Armstrong then described their landing site in a little detail.

"It's a relatively flat plain," he said, "with a lot of craters of the five- to 50-foot variety. Some small ridges 20 to 30 feet high. Thousands of little one- and two-foot craters. Some angular levees in front of us two feet in size. There is a hill in view ahead of us. It might be a half-mile or a mile away."

Armstrong then described what he said were rocks fractured by the exhaust of Eagle's rocket plume.

"Some of the surface rocks in close look like they might have a coating on them," he said. "Where they're broken, they display a very dark gray interior. It looks like it could be country basalt."

"LIKE BEING IN AN AIRPLANE"

Both men seemed to actually enjoy being in the moon's gravity, which is one-sixth that of earth's.

"It's like being in an airplane," Armstrong said. "It seems immediately natural to move around in this environment."

Armstrong and Aldrin apparently felt fine. Armstrong's heart rate went as high as 156 beats per minute at the time of landing, but dropped down into the nineties 15 minutes later.

The time leading up to the landing is difficult to describe, except to say that it was as dramatic a time as any in memory.

It all began at 3:08 P.M. EDT when Armstrong and Aldrin—flying feet first and face down—fired up their landing craft's descent engine for the first time.

Burning the engine for 27 seconds in what amounted to a braking maneuver to slow it down and start it falling, the two men were behind the moon at the time and out of radio touch with earth.

It was not until 3:47 P.M. that the men at the Manned Spacecraft Center heard that Armstrong and Aldrin were on their way down—and they heard it first from Collins, who flew from behind the moon in the command craft above and in front of the landing craft.

"Columbia, Houston," said Duke from the Center. "How did it go?"

"Listen, Babe," replied an excited Collins. "Everything's going just swimmingly. Beautiful."

Two minutes later, Duke made radio contact with Armstrong and Aldrin.

"We're standing by for your burn report," Duke said.

"The burn was on time," Aldrin told him.

"Rog, copy," Duke said. "Looks great."

At this point, the men in Mission Control bent their backs to the toughest jobs they'd ever have—following the two spacecraft at all times, to give them the guidance they would need for the Eagle's descent to the moon.

"JUST PLAY IT COOL"

Looking around the very quiet Mission Control room, flight director Gene Kranz simply said, "We're off to a good start. Just play it cool."

Flying down and westward across the moon's surface, the Eagle suddenly dropped out of radio contact with earth, but in moments was back in touch again.

"I don't know what the problem was," a totally composed Buzz Aldrin said when he came back on. "We started yawing and we're picking up a little oscillation rate now."

Still falling, the Eagle was coming up over the eastern region of the Sea of Tranquillity at an altitude of 53,000 feet and only minutes away from its second critical maneuver—the powered descent to the lunar surface.

"Five minutes to ignition," Duke radioed up. "You are go for a powered descent."

"Roger," Armstrong replied softly. "Understand."

At 4:05, Armstrong began throttling up the engine to slow the Eagle again, to drop it down toward the lunar surface.

"Light's on," he said. "Descent looks good."

Two minutes later, it was plain to everybody listening that they were indeed on their way down to the moon.

"Show an altitude of 47,000 feet," Armstrong said. "Everything looking good."

Still calm, Aldrin said he noticed a few warning lights coming on inside the spacecraft. "I'm getting some AC voltage fluctuations," he said, "and our position checks downrange show us to be a little long."

"You're looking good to us, Eagle," Duke answered. "You are go to continue powered descent. Repeat. You are go to continue powered descent."

FALLING, SLOWING APPROACH

"Altitude 27,000 feet," Aldrin read off. "This throttle down is better than the simulator."

Down they came, still falling but slowing down at the same time. At 21,000 feet, their speed had fallen to 800 miles an hour.

"You're looking great to us, Eagle," Duke said.

A minute later, it was 500 miles an hour, then it was suddenly down to less than 90 miles an hour.

"You're looking great at eight minutes. . . . You're looking great at nine minutes," Duke told them.

At this point, the two explorers began their final approach to the moon surface, coming in sideways and downwardly only 5200 feet above the moon.

When the Eagle dropped to 4200 feet Duke broke in on the radio, his voice tense and excited.

"Eagle, you are go for landing," he said.

"Roger, understand," a calm Armstrong replied. "Go for landing."

"Eagle, you're looking great," Duke said. "You're go at 1600 feet."

At that, Armstrong began to read off rapidly his altitudes and pitch angles—the angle at which the spacecraft was falling toward the lunar surface.

"Three-hundred feet," he said. "Down three and a half. A hundred feet. Three and a half down. Okay. Seventy-five feet. Looking good. Down a half."

"Sixty seconds," Duke said.

"Lights on," Armstrong replied. "Forty feet. Kicking up some dust. Great shadows.

"Four forward. Drifting to the right a little."

His voice then rose a little, as he turned off the engine for the first time and started free-falling to the moon.

"Okay, engine stop," he said. "Overdrive off. Engine arm off."

There was a pause—then the first voice came from the surface of the moon.

"Houston. Tranquillity Base here," Armstrong announced. "The Eagle has landed."

"You've got a bunch of guys about to turn blue," Duke told him. "Now we're breathing again."

"Okay, standby," Armstrong replied. "We're going to be busy for a minute."

Just then, Collins broke in from his lonesome spot 70 miles above the moon, desperately wanting in on the historic conversation.

"He has landed," Duke informed him. "Eagle has landed at Tranquillity."

"Good show," Collins said. "Fantastic."

Five minutes after touchdown, Duke told them things looked good enough for them to stay there a while.

"We thank you," Armstrong answered.

It was then that Armstrong told Houston he had to fly the spacecraft in manually to avoid a football-sized crater and a large rock field.

COULDN'T PINPOINT LOCATION

"It really was rough over the target area," he said. "It was heavily cratered and some of the large rocks may have been bigger than 10 feet around."

He then said he was not sure of his location on the moon either. "Well," he said, "the guys who said we wouldn't be able to tell exactly where we are are the winners today."

Armstrong reported that the four-legged spacecraft had landed on a level plain and appeared to be tilted at an angle no greater than 4.5 degrees.

Their first moments on the moon were truly incredible, but the entire day seemed incredible, as if the scenario for it all had been written by some bizarre science fiction writer.

"We've done everything humanly possible," Manned Spacecraft Center Director Robert C. Gilruth told one newsman, "but boy is this a tense and unreal time for me."

Preparing for the busiest and most historic day of their lives, the three crewmen hadn't even gotten to sleep until after 1 A.M.—and it was the ground that suggested they all go to bed.

"That really winds things up as far as we're concerned," astronaut Owen Garriott said in Houston. "We're ready to go to bed and get a little sleep."

COLLINS WAKES UP FIRST

"Yeah, we're about to join you," Armstrong replied.

Armstrong and Aldrin were the first to go to sleep, and then Collins finally went to sleep two hours later, at just after 3 A.M.

Four hours later, astronaut Ron Evans was manning the radio in Houston and he put in the first wake-up call.

"Apollo 11, Apollo 11," he said. "Good morning from the black team."

It was Collins who answered first, even though he'd had the least sleep. "Oh my, you guys wake up early," he said.

"You're about two minutes early on the wakeup," Evans conceded. "Looks like you were really sawing them away."

"You're right," said Collins.

Everybody got right down to business then. "Looks like the command module's in good shape," Evans told Collins. "Black team's been watching it real closely for you."

"We sure appreciate that," Collins said, "because I sure haven't."

ACTIVATES LANDING CRAFT

Just after 9:30 A.M., as the three men began their 11th orbit of the moon, Aldrin got into the Eagle for the first time—to power it up, start the oxygen flowing into the spacecraft and make sure everything was in working order. Forty-five minutes later, Armstrong joined him.

On the 13th orbit, Eagle undocked from Columbia, moving off about 40 or 50 feet from the command craft, which Collins was piloting alone.

Like most of the maneuvers they've made, this one was done behind the moon and out of contact with earth—so nobody in Houston knew for almost 45 minutes if the separation had been successful.

At 1:50 P.M., the two spacecraft came over the moon's rim.

"Eagle, we see you on the steerable," said Duke, who had just replaced Evans. "How does it look?"

"Eagle has wings," was Armstrong's simple reply.

For a while, all the astronauts did was look each other over, to make sure the two spacecraft were shipshape.

"Check that tracking light, Mike," Armstrong told Collins.

"Okay," Armstrong said next, "I'm ready to start my yaw manuever if it suits you, Mike."

ELABORATE INSTRUMENT CHECK

Aldrin got on next, reading off what seemed like endless instrument checklists. For 15 minutes, he talked on, never once missing a word, sounding totally composed.

At 2:12 P.M., Collins fired his tiny thruster jets to increase distance between the craft.

"Thrusting," Collins said. "Everything's looking real good."

The two spacecraft were 1000 feet away from each other within moments. Collins took a radar check on the distance.

"I got a solid lock on it," he said. "It looks like point 27 miles"—about 1400 feet.

"Hey," Collins said to Armstrong when he'd looked out his window, "you're upside down."

"Somebody's upside down," Armstrong replied.

Just then, Collins asked Armstrong: "Put your tracking light on, please."

"It's on, Mike," answered Aldrin.

"Give us a mark when you're at seven-tenths of a mile," Duke said to Collins from the ground.

Moments later, Duke told Collins the big radars on the ground showed the two spacecraft seven-tenths of a mile apart.

"Rog," Collins said. "I'm oscillating between point 69 and seven-tenths."

At 2:50 P.M. Houston gave the go signal for the first maneuver, the so-called descent orbit insertion burn.

"Eagle," Duke said, "you are go for DOI."

"Roger," replied Aldrin matter-of-factly. "Go for DOI."

And while the whole world listened one of the most majestic dramas in mankind's history began to unfold.

DISCUSSION QUESTION

1. Compare Thomas O'Toole's report of the moon landing with Norman Mailer's account in Classics. How does O'Toole's use of transcripts differ from Mailer's? Why doesn't O'Toole talk about the way the astronauts talk? Why does Mailer do this? What effect does O'Toole want the transcripts to have in his report? What role does television play in his report?

William F. Buckley, Jr. / Moonstruck

Washington *Star,* July 24, 1969

William F. Buckley, Jr. taught Spanish at Yale and was associate editor of American Mercury *magazine before founding* National Review, *currently a leading journal of political conservatism. The principal combatant in a weekly series of televised debates ("Firing Line") and one-time candidate for mayor of New York City, Buckley has also written several popular novels and many books on political and historical topics and numerous articles for such magazines as* Esquire, Atlantic, *and* Commonweal. *His nationally syndicated newspaper column reaches an aggregate readership of well over seven million. In his column on the Apollo XI mission, "Moonstruck," Buckley, despite his public image as a rhetorical wizard and spokesman for political restraint, allows himself an aristocratic "yip-hurroo" at the "glorious" landing of two Americans on the moon.*

As a freshman at college seeking grist for the undergraduate newspaper, I approached a famous astrophysicist, Lyman Spitzer, and asked if it was true that he intended to fly to the moon. He replied frostily, "I shouldn't know what to do if I got there."

And indeed the scientific community went back to somnambulism, leaving the moon to science fiction, until the great pressures of our competition with the Soviet Union worked their way through to the White House and John F. Kennedy wrote a memorandum to Lyndon Baines Johnson: "Do we have a chance of beating the Soviets by putting a laboratory into space, or by a trip around the moon, or by a rocket to land on the moon, or by a rocket to go to the moon and back with a man? Is there any other space program which promises dramatic results in which we could win?"

Here in London the Sunday *Times* is quite explicit about it all. The editors regret the choice of the American flag over against the choice of, say, the flag of the United Nations to plant down on the moon but concede that "without Old Glory standing there alone the objectives set by President Kennedy when he sent America to the moon in 1961 would have been betrayed in the last stride." The gentleman is saying that America suffers from *amour propre,* which is true; which should be true. Lord Ritchie-Calder is a professor of international relations at the University of Edinburgh and a past chairman of the Association of British Science

Writers. He is quite forlorn about Apollo 11. "Dare one utter the heresy 'fugitives into space' and confess that it is an evasion and an exasperation of the problems of our planet?" His lordship observes that "If Sputnik had not got into orbit first, if American prestige had not been affronted, if it had not been made the excuse for the 'missile gap' furor, we would not have had the technologically bombastic competition between the superpowers and the yip-hurroo of man on the moon by 1970. . . .' " And, he concludes, ". . . the world is crying out for bread and is being offered moondust."

The American press has diligently plied the line that the discovery of a means of reaching the moon is going to have great material benefactions for the earth. My absolute favorite, I mean my all-time favorite, was *Time* magazine's exclaiming that in the years to come it might prove economical to manufacture certain kinds of vacuum tubes on the moon, since there are vacuum-type conditions already there, suggesting that we have all these years overlooked the possibility of manufacturing ice on the North Pole, since it is already cold up there.

We cannot doubt that much will be accomplished of a material meaning by the space program—indeed much already has been, and the great achievement will be the mastery of weather, which will give Lord Ritchie-Calder the bread he wants so badly. But that isn't, let's face it, what the moonshot was all about it. It was also an Englishman—Mr. Peregrine Worsthorne of the *Telegraph*—who said it best about the whole lunatic venture: "Western man is desperate for a new horizon. Let there by no hypocrisy here. Space is not a philanthropic exercise. It will not help to feed the hungry or clothe the naked. It is, in a sense, highly irresponsible and selfish, almost an aristocratic gesture of contempt by the privileged nations for the bread-and-butter concerns of the less fortunate people and classes. But it is difficult to believe that this is wrong. The advanced nations and classes cannot limit their aspirations to the goal of material philanthropy for the backward. To be policemen or guardians to the world—perhaps. But the role of nanny is not inspiring, at least as a full-time job. Unless Western man was to atrophy in boredom, he needed some more forceful dynamic than guilt and some inspiration more magnetic than charity."

It was indeed that—an aristocratic venture. All the more so as one emphasizes, rather than deemphasizes, the commercial inutility of it all, so perfectly expressed years ago by a professor who had no idea what he would do on the moon if suddenly he were plopped there. But how unmitigatedly glorious it was, and how universal the elation! At Canaveral, surrounded by the mighty and the calloused, the blast-off swept us all off our feet, and at London for the touchdown, the crowds at Trafalgar Square were no more excited, I would wager, than the royal family huddled about their telly in Buckingham Palace.

As so often is the case, the world was given a complementary symbol, as when briefly Robert Manry, arriving alone on his 13-foot *Tinkerbelle,* competed with Apollo 3's eight swings around the earth in 1965. Now the Englishman John Fairfax comes into Fort Lauderdale after rowing *Britannia* 180 days across the Atlantic. As the lady said years ago, bringing a quick end to a donnish conversation exploring the motives of space travel. "Don't you see, boys will be boys?" To which one adds, once again, "Yes, and men will be heroes."

Vivian Gornick / The Next Great Moment in History Is Theirs

[*An Introduction to the Women's Liberation Movement*]

Village Voice, November 27, 1969

A persuasive introduction to the women's liberation movement, Vivian Gornick's "The Next Great Moment in History Is Theirs" is a closely reasoned, insightful commentary on the acculturated inequities that have entrapped the public and private lives of American women and a record of their continuing struggle for freedom and self-definition.

Founded in New York in 1955 by freelance journalist Daniel Wolf, psychologist Edward Fancher, and novelist Norman Mailer, the Village Voice *was the first successful avant-garde, antiestablishment newspaper in what has come to be known as "the underground press." Less expensively designed and printed than mass circulation daily newspapers and with few of their inhibitions or restraints, the* Village Voice *of the late sixties, published weekly with a circulation well over one hundred thousand, could afford to be eclectic and extensive in its selection and coverage of contemporary events.*

A staff writer for the Voice *for several years, Vivian Gornick has also taught English at Hunter College and at the Stony Brook campus of the State University of New York. She co-edited* Woman in Sexist Society *(1971), an impressive collection of feminist writings, and most recently has written* Women in Science: Recovering the Life Within *(1983).*

One evening not too long ago, at the home of a well-educated and extremely intelligent couple I know, I mentioned the women's liberation movement and was mildly astonished by the response the subject received. The man said: "Jesus, what *is* all that crap about?" The woman, a scientist who had given up 10 working years to raise her children, said: "I can understand if these women want to work and are demanding equal pay. But why on earth do they want to have children too?" To which the man rejoined: "Ah, they don't want kids. They're mostly a bunch of dykes, anyway."

Again: Having lunch with an erudite, liberal editor, trained in the humanist tradition, I was struck dumb by his reply to my mention of the women's liberation movement: "Ah shit, who the hell is oppressing them?"

And yet again: A college-educated housewife, fat and neurotic, announced with arch sweetness, "I'm sorry, I just don't *feel* oppressed."

Over and over again, in educated, thinking circles, one meets with a bizarre, almost determined, ignorance of the unrest that is growing daily and exists in formally organized bodies in nearly every major city and on dozens of campuses across America. The women of this country are gathering themselves into a sweat of civil revolt, and the general population seems totally unaware of what is happening—if, indeed, they realize *anything* is happening—or that there is a legitimate need behind what is going on. How is this possible? Why is it true? What relation is there between the peculiarly unalarmed, amused dismissal of the women's-rights movement and the movement itself? Is this relation only coincidental, only the apathetic response of a society already benumbed by civil rights and student anarchy and unable to rise to yet one more protest movement? Or is it not, in fact, precisely the key to the entire issue?

Almost invariably, when people set out to tell you there is no such thing as discrimination against women in this country, the first thing they hastily admit to is a *minor* degree of economic favoritism shown toward men. In fact, they will eagerly, almost gratefully, support the claim of economic inequity, as though that will keep the discussion within manageable bounds. Curious. But even on economic grounds or grounds of legal discrimination most people are dismally ignorant of the true proportions of the issue. They will grant that often a man will make as much as $100 more than a woman at the same job, and yes, it *is* often difficult for a woman to be hired when a man can be hired instead, but after all, that's really not so terrible.

This is closer to the facts:

Women in this country make 60 cents for every $1 a man makes.

Women do not share in the benefits of the fair employment practices laws because those laws do not specify "no discrimination on the basis of sex."

Women often rise in salary only to the point at which a man starts.

Women occupy, in great masses, the "household tasks" of industry. They are nurses but not doctors, secretaries but not executives, researchers but not writers, workers but not managers, bookkeepers but not promoters.

Women almost never occupy decision—or policy-making positions.

Women are almost non-existent in government.

Women are subject to a set of "protective" laws that restrict their working hours, do not allow them to occupy many jobs in which the carrying of weights is involved, do not allow them to enter innumerable bars, restaurants, hotels, and other public places unescorted.

Women, despite 100 years of reform, exist in the domestic and marriage laws of our country almost literally as appendages of their husbands. Did you know that rape by a husband is legal but that if a woman refuses to sleep with her husband she is subject to legal suit? Did you know that the word domicile in the law refers to the husband's domicile and that if a woman refuses to follow her husband to wherever he makes his home, legal suit can be brought against her to force her to do so? Did you know that in most states the law imposes severe legal disabilities on married women with regard to their personal and property rights? (As a feminist said to me: "The United Nations has defined servitude as necessarily involuntary, but women, ignorant of the law, put themselves into *voluntary* servitude.")

Perhaps, you will say, these observations are not so shocking. After all, women *are* weaker than men, they do need protection, what on earth is so terrible about being protected, for God's sake! And as for those laws, they're never invoked, no woman is dragged anywhere against her will, on the contrary, women's desires rule the middle-class household, and women can work at hundreds of jobs, in fact, a great deal of the wealth of the country is in their hands, and no woman ever goes hungry.

I agree. These observed facts of our national life are not so shocking. The laws and what accrues from them are not so terrible. It is what's behind the laws that is so terrible. It is not the letter of the law but the spirit determining the law that is terrible. It is not what is explicit but what is implicit in the law that is terrible. It is not the apparent condition but the actual condition of woman that is terrible.

"The woman's issue is the true barometer of social change," said a famous political theoretician. This was true 100 years ago; it is no less true today. Women and blacks were and are, traditionally and perpetually, the great "outsiders" in Western culture, and their erratic swellings of outrage parallel each other in a number of ways that are both understandable and also extraordinary. A hundred years ago a great abolitionist force wrenched this country apart and changed its history forever; many, many radical men devoted a fever of life to wrecking a system in which men were bought and sold; many radical women worked toward the same end; the abolitionist movement contained women who came out of educated and liberal 19th century families, women who considered themselves independent thinking beings. It was only when Elizabeth Cady Stanton and Lucretia Mott were not allowed to be seated at a World Anti-Slavery Conference held in the 1840s that the intellectual abolitionist women suddenly perceived that their own political existence resembled that of the blacks. They raised the issue with their radical men and were denounced furiously for introducing an insignificant and divisive issue, one which was sure to weaken the movement. Let's win this war first, they said, and then we'll see about women's rights. But the women had seen, in one swift visionary moment, to the very center of the truth about their own lives, and they knew that first was *now*, that there would never be a time when men would willingly address themselves to the question of female rights, that to strike out now for women's rights could do nothing but strengthen the issue of black civil rights because it called attention to all instances or rights denied in a nation that prided itself on rights for all.

Thus was born the original Women's Rights Movement, which became known as the Women's Suffrage Movement because the single great issue, of course, was legal political recognition. But it was never meant to begin and end with the vote, just as the abolitionist movement was never meant to begin and end with the vote. Somehow, though, that awful and passionate struggle for suffrage seemed to exhaust both the blacks and the women, especially the women, for when the vote finally came at the end of the Civil War, it was handed to black males—but not to women; the women had to go on fighting for 60 bitterly long years for suffrage. And then both blacks and women lay back panting, unable to catch their breath for generation upon generation.

The great civil rights movement for blacks in the 1950s and '60s is the second wind of that monumental first effort, necessary because the legislated political equality of the 1860s was never translated into actual equality. The reforms promised by law had never happened. The piece of paper meant nothing. Racism had never been legislated out of existence; in fact, its original virulence had remained virtually untouched, and, more important, the black in this country had never been able to shake off the slave mentality. He was born scared, he ran scared, he died scared; for 100 years after legal emancipation, he lived as though it had never happened. Blacks and whites did not regard either themselves or each other differently, and so they in no way lived differently. In the 1950s and '60s the surging force behind the renewed civil rights effort has been the desire to eradicate this condition more than any other, to enable the American black to believe in himself as a whole, independent, expressive human being capable of fulfilling and protecting himself in the very best way he knows how. Today, after more than 15 years of unremitting struggle, after a formidable array of reform laws legislated at the federal, state, and local level, after a concentration on black rights and black existence that has traumatized the nation, it is still not unfair to say that the psychology of defeat has not been lifted from black life. Still (aside from the continuance of crime, drugs, broken homes, and all the wretched rest of it), employers are able to say: "Sure, I'd love to hire one if I could find one who qualified," and while true, half the time it *is*, because black life is still marked by the "nigger mentality," the terrible inertia of spirit that accompanies the perhaps irrational but deeply felt conviction that no matter what one does, one is going to wind up a 35-year-old busboy. This "nigger mentality" characterizes black lives. It also characterizes women's lives. And it is this, and this alone, that is behind the second wave of feminism now sweeping the country and paralleling precisely, exactly as it does 100 years ago, the black rights movement. The fight for reform laws is just the beginning. What women are really after this time around is the utter eradication of the "nigger" in themselves.

Most women who feel "niggerized" have tales of overt oppression to tell. They feel they've been put down by their fathers, their brothers, their lovers, their bosses. They feel that in their families, in their sex lives, and in their jobs they have counted as nothing, they have been treated as second-class citizens, their minds have been deliberately stunted and their emotions warped. My own experience with the condition is a bit more subtle, and, without bragging, I do believe a bit closer to the true feminist point.

To begin with, let me tell a little story. Recently, I had lunch with a man I had known at school. He and his wife and I had all been friends at college; they had courted while we were in school and immediately upon graduation they got married. They were both talented art students, and it was assumed both would work in commercial art. But shortly after their marriage she became pregnant, and never did go to work. Within five years they had two children. At first I visited them often; their home was lovely, full of their mutual talent for atmosphere; the wife sparkled, the children flourished; he rose in the field of commercial art; I envied them both their self-containment, and she especially her apparently contented, settled state. But as I had remained single and life took me off in various other directions we soon began to drift apart, and when I again met the husband we had not seen each other in many years. We spoke animatedly of what we had both been doing for quite a while. Then I asked about his wife. His face rearranged itself suddenly, but I couldn't quite tell how at first. He said she was fine, but didn't sound right.

"What's wrong?" I asked. "Is she doing something you don't want her to do? Or the other way around?"

"No, no," he said hastily. "I want her to do whatever she wants to do. Anything. Anything that will make her happy. And get her off my back," he ended bluntly. I asked what he meant and he told me of his wife's restlessness of the last few years, of how sick she was of being a housewife, how useless she felt, and how she longed to go back to work.

"Well?" I asked, "did you object?"

"Of course not!" he replied vigorously. "Why the hell would I do that? She's a very talented woman, her children are half grown, she's got every right in the world to go to work."

"So?" I said.

"It's *her,*" he said bewilderedly. "She doesn't seem able to just go out and get a job."

"What do you mean?" I asked. But beneath the surface of my own puzzled response I more than half knew what was coming.

"Well, she's scared, I think. She's more talented than half the people who walk into my office asking for work, but do what I will she won't get a portfolio together and make the rounds. Also, she cries a lot lately. For no reason, if you know what I mean. And then, she can't seem to get up in the morning in time to get a babysitter and get out of the house. This is a woman who was always up at 7 A.M. to feed everybody, get things going; busy, capable, doing 10 things at once." He shook his head as though in a true quandary. "Oh well," he ended up "I guess it doesn't really matter any more."

"Why not?" I asked.

His eyes came up and he looked levelly at me. "She's just become pregnant again."

I listened silently, but with what internal churning! Even though the external events of our lives were quite different, I felt as though this woman had been living inside my skin all these years, so close was I to the essential nature of her experience as I perceived it listening to her husband's woebegone tale. I had wandered about the world, I had gained another degree, I had married twice, I had written, taught, edited, I had no children. And yet I knew that in some fundamental sense we were the same woman. I understood exactly—but exactly—the kind of neurotic anxiety that just beset her, and that had ultimately defeated her; it was a neurosis I shared and had recognized in almost every woman I had ever known—including

Monica Vitti, having her Schiaparellied nervous breakdown, stuffing her hand into her mouth, rolling her eyes wildly, surrounded by helplessly sympathetic men who kept saying: "Just tell me what's *wrong.*"

I was raised in an immigrant home where education was worshiped. As the entire American culture was somewhat mysterious to my parents, the educational possibilities of that world were equally unknown for both the boy and the girl in our family. Therefore, I grew up in the certainty that if my brother went to college, I too could go to college; and, indeed, he did, and I in my turn did too. We both read voraciously from early childhood on, and we were both encouraged to do so. We both had precocious and outspoken opinions and neither of us was ever discouraged from uttering them. We both were exposed early to unionist radicalism and neither of us met with opposition when, separately, we experimented with youthful political organizations. And yet somewhere along the line my brother and I managed to receive an utterly different education regarding ourselves and our own expectations from life. He was taught many things but what he learned was the need to develop a kind of inner necessity. I was taught many things, but what I learned, ultimately, was that it was the prime vocation of my life to prepare myself for the love of a good man and the responsibilities of homemaking and motherhood. All the rest, the education, the books, the jobs, that was all very nice and of course, why not? I was an intelligent girl, shouldn't I learn? *make* something of myself! but oh dolly, you'll see, in the end no woman could possibly be happy without a man to love and children to raise. What's more, came the heavy implication, if I *didn't* marry I would be considered an irredeemable failure.

How did I learn this? How? I have pondered this question 1000 times. Was it really that explicit? Was it laid out in lessons strategically planned and carefully executed? Was it spooned down my throat at regular intervals? No. It wasn't. I have come finally to understand that the lessons were implicit and they took place in 100 different ways, in a continuous day-to-day exposure to an *attitude,* shared by all, about women, about what kind of creatures they were and what kind of lives they were meant to live; the lessons were administered not only by my parents but by the men and women, the boys and girls, all around me who, of course, had been made in the image of this attitude.

My mother would say to me when I was very young, as I studied at the kitchen table and she cooked: "How lucky you are to go to school! I wasn't so lucky. I had to go to work in the factory. I wanted so to be a nurse! But go be a nurse in Williamsburg in 1920! Maybe you'll be a nurse. . . ." I listened, I nodded, but somehow the message I got was that I was like her and I would one day be doing what she was now doing.

My brother was the "serious and steady" student, I the "erratic and undisciplined" one. When he studied the house was silenced; when I studied, business as usual.

When I was 14 and I came in flushed and disarrayed my mother knew I'd been with a boy. Her fingers gripped my upper arm; her face, white and intent, bent over me: What did he do to you? *Where* did he do it? I was frightened to death. What was she so upset about? What could he do to me? I learned that I was the keeper of an incomparable treasure and it had to be guarded: it was meant to be a gift for my husband. (Later that year when I read "A Rage to Live" I knew without any instruction exactly what all those elliptical sentences were about.)

When I threw some hideous temper tantrum my mother would say: "What a little female you are!" (I have since seen many little boys throw the same tantrums and have noted with interest that they are not told they are little females.)

The girls on the street would talk forever about boys, clothes, movies, fights with their mothers. The 1000 thoughts racing around in my head from the books I was reading remained secret, no one to share them with.

The boys would be gentler with the girls than with each other when we all played roughly; and our opinions were never considered seriously.

I grew up, I went to school, I came out, wandered around, went to Europe, went back to school, wandered again, taught in a desultory fashion, and at last! got married!

It was during my first marriage that I began to realize something was terribly wrong inside me, but it took me 10 years to understand that I was suffering the classic female pathology. My husband, like all the men I have known, was a good man, a man who wanted my independence for me more than I wanted it for myself. He urged me to work, to do something, anything, that would make me happy; he knew that our pleasure in each other could be heightened only if I was a functioning human being too. Yes, yes! I said, and leaned back in the rocking chair with yet another novel. Somehow, I couldn't do anything. I didn't really know where to start, what I wanted to do. Oh, I had always had a number of interests but they, through an inability on my part to stick with anything, had always been superficial; when I arrived at a difficult point in a subject, a job, an interest, I would simply drop it. Of course, what I really wanted to do was write; but that was an altogether ghastly agony and one I could never come to grips with. There seemed to be some terrible aimlessness at the very center of me, some paralyzing lack of will. My energy, which was abundant, was held in a trap of some sort; occasionally that useless energy would wake up roaring, demanding to be let out of its cage, and then I became "emotional"; I would have hysterical depressions, rage on and on about the meaninglessness of my life, force my husband into long psychoanalytic discussions about the source of my (our) trouble, end in a purging storm of tears, a determination to do "something," and six months later I was right back where I started. If my marriage had not dissolved, I am sure that I would still be in exactly that same peculiarly nightmarish position. But as it happened, the events of life forced me out into the world, and repeatedly I had to come up against myself. I found this pattern of behavior manifesting itself in 100 different circumstances; regardless of how things began, they always seemed to end in the same place. Oh, I worked, I advanced, in a sense, but only erratically and with superhuman effort. Always the battle was internal, and it was with a kind of paralyzing anxiety at the center of me that drained off my energy and retarded my capacity for intellectual concentration. It took me a long time to perceive that nearly every woman I knew exhibited the same symptoms, and when I did perceive it, became frightened. I thought, at first, that perhaps, indeed, we were all victims of some biological deficiency, that some vital ingredient had been deleted in the female of the species, that we were a physiological metaphor for human neurosis. It took me a long time to understand, with an understanding that is irrevocable, that we are the victims of culture, not biology.

Recently, I read a marvelous biography of Beatrice Webb, the English socialist. The book is full of vivid portraits, but the one that is fixed forever in my mind is that of Mrs. Webb's mother, Laurencina Potter. Laurencina Potter was a beautiful, intelligent, intellectually energetic woman of the middle 19th century. She knew 12 languages, spoke Latin and Greek better than half the classics-trained men who came to her home, and was interested in everything. Her marriage to wealthy and powerful Richard Potter was a love match, and she looked forward to a life of intellectual companionship, stimulating activity, lively participation. No sooner were they married than Richard installed her in a Victorian fortress in the country, surrounded her with servants and physical comfort, and started her off with the first of the 11 children she eventually bore. He went out into the world, bought and sold railroads, made important political connections, mingled in London society, increased his powers, and relished his life. She, meanwhile, languished. She sat in the country, staring at the four brocaded walls; her energy remained bottled up, her mind became useless, her will evaporated. The children became symbols of her enslavement and, in consequence, she was a lousy mother: neurotic, self-absorbed, increasingly colder and more withdrawn, increasingly more involved in taking her emotional temperature. She became, in short, the Victorian lady afflicted with indefinable maladies.

When I read of Laurencina's life I felt as though I was reading about the lives of most of the women I know, and it struck me that 100 years ago sexual submission was all for a woman, and today sexual fulfillment is all for a woman, and the two are one and the same.

Most of the women I know are people of superior intelligence, developed emotions, and higher education. And yet our friendships, our conversations, our lives, are not marked by intellectual substance or emotional distance or objective concern. It is only briefly and insubstantially that I ever discuss books or politics or philosophical issues or abstractions of any kind with the women I know. Mainly, we discuss and are intimate about our Emotional Lives. Endlessly, endlessly, we go on and on about our emotional "problems" and "needs" and "relationships." And, of course, because we are all bright and well-educated, we bring to bear on these sessions a formidable amount of sociology and psychology, literature and history, all hoked out so that it sounds as though these are serious conversations on serious subjects, when in fact they are caricatures of seriousness right out of Jonathan Swift. Caricatures, because they have no beginning, middle, end, or point. They go nowhere, they conclude nothing, they change nothing. They are elaborate descriptions in the ongoing soap opera that is our lives. It took me a long time to understand that we were talking about nothing, and it took me an even longer and harder time, traveling down that dark, narrow road in the mind, back back to the time when I was a little girl sitting in the kitchen with my mother, to understand, at last, that the affliction was cultural not biological, that it was because we had never been taught to take ourselves seriously that I and all the women I knew had become parodies of "taking ourselves seriously."

The rallying cry of the black civil rights movement has always been: "Give us back our manhood!" What exactly does that mean? Where is black manhood? How has it been taken from blacks? And how can it be retrieved? The answer lies in one word: responsibility; therefore, they have been deprived of self-respect; therefore, they have been deprived of manhood. Women have been deprived of exactly the same thing and in every real sense have thus been deprived of womanhood. We have never been prepared to assume responsibility; we have never been prepared to make demands upon ourselves; we have never been taught to expect the development of what is best in ourselves because no one has ever expected *anything* of us—or for us. Because no one has ever had any intention of turning over any serious work to us. Both we and the blacks lost the ballgame before we ever got up to play. In order to live you've got to have nerve; and we were stripped of our nerve before we began. Black is ugly and female is inferior. These are the primary lessons of our experience, and in these ways both blacks and women have been kept, not as functioning nationals, but rather as operating objects. But a human being who remains as a child throughout his adult life is an object, not a mature specimen, and the definition of a child is: one without reponsibility.

At the very center of all human life is energy, psychic energy. It is the force of that energy that drives us, that surges continually up in us, that must repeatedly spend and renew itself in us, that must perpetually be reaching for something beyond itself in order to satisfy its own insatiable appetite. It is the imperative of that energy that has determined man's characteristic interest, problem-solving. The modern ecologist attests to that driving need by demonstrating that in a time when all the real problems are solved, man makes up new ones in order to go on solving. He must have work, work that he considers real and serious, or he will die, he will simply shrivel up and die. That is the one certain characteristic of human beings.

And it is the one characteristic, above all others, that the accidentally dominant white male asserts is not necessary to more than half the members of the race, i.e., the female of the species. This assertion is, quite simply, a lie. Nothing more, nothing less. A lie. That energy is alive in every woman in the world. It lies trapped and dormant like a growing tumor, and at its center there is despair, hot, deep, wordless.

It is amazing to me that I have just written these words. To think that 100 years after Nora slammed the door, and in a civilization and a century utterly converted to the fundamental insights of that exasperating genius, Sigmund Freud, women could still be raised to believe that their basic makeup is determined not by the needs of their egos but by their peculiar child-bearing properties and their so-called unique capacity for loving. No man worth his salt does not wish to be a husband and father; yet no man is raised to be a husband and father and no man would ever conceive of those relationships as instruments of his prime function in life. Yet every woman is raised, still, to believe that the fulfillment of these relationships is her prime function in life and, what's more, her instinctive choice.

The fact is that women have no special capacities for love, and, when a culture reaches a level where its women have nothing to do but "love" (as occurred in the Victorian upper classes and as is occurring now in the American middle classes), they prove to be very bad at it. The modern American wife is not noted for her love of her husband or of her children; she is noted for her driving (or should I say driven?) domination of them. She displays an aberrated, aggressive ambition for her mate and for her offspring which can be explained only by the most vicious feelings toward the self. The reasons are obvious. The woman who must love for a living, the woman who has no self, no objective external reality to take her own measure by, no work to discipline her, no goal to provide the illusion of progress, no internal resources, no separate mental existence, is constitutionally incapable of the emotional distance that is one of the real requirements of love. She cannot separate herself from her husband and children because all the passionate and multiple needs of her being are centered on them. That's why women "take everything personally." It's all they've got to take. "Loving" must substitute for an entire range of feeling and interest. The man, who is not raised to be a husband and father specifically, and who simply loves as a single function of his existence, cannot understand her abnormal "emotionality" and concludes that this is the female nature. (Why shouldn't he? She does too.) But this is not so. It is a result of a psychology achieved by cultural attitudes that run so deep and have gone on for so long that they are mistaken for "nature" or "instinct."

A good example of what I mean are the multiple legends of our culture regarding motherhood. Let's use our heads for a moment. What on earth is holy about motherhood? I mean, why motherhood rather than fatherhood? If anything is holy, it is the consecration of sexual union. A man plants a seed in a woman; the seed matures and eventually is expelled by the woman; a child is born to both of them; each contributed the necessary parts to bring about procreation; each is responsible to and necessary to the child; to claim that the woman is more so than the man is simply not true; certainly it cannot be proven biologically or psychologically (please, no comparisons with baboons and penguins just now—I am sure I can supply 50 examples from nature to counter any assertion made on the subject); all that can be proven is that some*one* is necessary to the newborn baby; to have instilled in women the belief that their child-bearing and housewifely obligations supersedes all other needs, that indeed what they fundamentally *want* and need is to be wives and mothers as distinguished from being anything else, is to have accomplished an act of trickery, an act which has deprived women of the proper forms of expression necessary to that force of energy alive in every talking creature, an act which has indeed mutilated their natural selves and deprived them of their womanhood, what*ever* that may be, deprived them of the right to say "I" and have it mean something. This understanding, grasped whole, is what underlies the current wave of feminism. It is felt by thousands of women today, it will be felt by millions tomorrow. You have only to examine briefly a fraction of the women's rights organizations already in existence to realize instantly that they form the nucleus of a genuine movement, complete with theoreticians, tacticians, agitators, manifestos, journals, and thesis papers, running the entire political spectrum from conservative reform to visionary radicalism, and powered by an emotional conviction rooted in undeniable experience, and fed by a determination that is irreversible.

One of the oldest and stablest of the feminist organizations is NOW, the National Organization for Women. It was started in 1966 by a group of professional women headed by Mrs. Betty Friedan, author of *The Feminine Mystique,* the book that was the bringer of the word in 1963 to the new feminists. NOW has more than 3000 members, chapters in major cities and on many campuses all over the country, and was read, at its inception, into the Congressional Record. It has many men in its ranks and it works, avowedly within the system, to bring about the kind of reforms that will result in what it calls a "truly equal partnership between men and women" in this country. It is a true reform organization filled with intelligent, liberal, hard-working women devoted to the idea that America is a reformist democracy and ultimately will respond to the justice of their cause. They are currently hard at work on two major issues: repeal of the abortion laws and passage of the Equal Rights Amendment (for which feminists have been fighting since 1923) which would amend the constitution to provide that "equality of rights under the law shall not be denied or abridged by the United States or by any state on account of sex." When this amendment is passed, the employment and marriage laws of more than 40 states will be affected. Also, in direct conjunction with the fight to have this amendment passed, NOW demands increased child-care facilities to be established by law on the same basis as parks, libraries, and public schools.

NOW's influence is growing by leaps and bounds. It is responsible for the passage of many pieces of legislation meant to wipe out discrimination against women, and certainly the size and number of Women's Bureaus, Women's units, Women's Commissions springing up in government agencies and legislative bodies all over the country reflects its presence. Suddenly, there are Presidential reports and gubernatorial conferences and congressional meetings—all leaping all over each other to discuss the status of women. NOW, without a doubt, is the best established feminist group.

From NOW we move, at a shocking rate of speed, to the left. In fact, it would appear that NOW is one of the few reformist groups, that mainly the feminist groups are radical, both in structure and in aim. Some, truth to tell, strike a bizarre and puzzling note. For instance, there is WITCH (Women's International Terrorists Conspiracy From Hell), an offshoot of SDS, where members burned their bras and organized against the Miss America Pageant in a stirring demand that the commercially useful image of female beauty be wiped out. There is Valerie Solanas and her SCUM Manifesto, which Solanas's penetrating observation on our national life was: "If the atom bomb isn't dropped, this society will hump itself to death." There is Cell 55. God knows what they do.

There are the Redstockings, an interesting group that seems to have evolved from direct action into what they call "consciousness-raising." That means, essentially, that they get together in a kind of group therapy session and the women reveal their experiences and feelings to each other in an attempt to analyze the femaleness of their psychology and their circumstances, thereby increasing the invaluable weapon of self-understanding.

And finally, there are the Feminists, without a doubt the most fiercely radical and intellectually impressive of all the groups. This organization was begun a year ago by a group of defectors from NOW and various other feminist groups, in rebellion against the repetition of the hierarchical structure of power in these other groups. Their contention was: women have always been "led"; if they join the rank and file of a feminist organization they are simply being led again. It will still be someone else, even if only the officers of their own interesting group, making the decisions, doing the planning, the executing, and so on. They determined to develop a leaderless society whose guiding principle was participation by lot. And this is precisely what they have done. The organization has no officers, every woman sooner or later performs every single task necessary to the life and aims of the organization, and the organization is willing to temporarily sacrifice efficiency in order that each woman may fully develop all the skills necessary to autonomous functioning. This working individualism is guarded fiercely by a set of rigid rules regarding attendance, behavior, duties, and loyalties.

The Feminists encourage extensive theorizing on the nature and function of a leaderless society, and this has led the organization to a bold and radical view of the future they wish to work for. The group never loses sight of the fact that its primary enemy is the male-female role system which has ended in women being the oppressed and men being the oppressors. It looks forward to a time when this system will be completely eradicated. To prepare for this coming, it now denounces all the institutions which encourage the system, i.e., love, sex, and marriage. It has a quota on married women (only one-third of their number are permitted to be either married or living in a marriage-like situation). It flatly names all men as the enemy. It looks forward to a future in which the family as we know it will disappear, all births will be extra-uterine, children will be raised by communal efforts, and women once and for all will cease to be the persecuted members of the race.

Although a lot of this is hard to take in raw doses, you realize that many of these ideas represent interesting and important turns of thought. First of all, these experiments with a leaderless society are being echoed everywhere: in student radicalism, in black civil rights, in hippie communes. They are part of a great radical lusting after self-determination that is beginning to overtake this country. This is true social revolution, and I believe that feminism, in order to accomplish its aims now, does need revolution, does need a complete overthrow of an old kind of thought and the introduction of a new kind of thought. Secondly, the Feminists are right: most of what men and women now are is determined by the "roles" they play, and love *is* an institution, full of ritualized gestures and positions, and often void of any recognizable naturalness. How, under the present iron-bound social laws, can one know what is female nature and what is female role? (And that question speaks to the source of the whole female pain and confusion.) It *is* thrilling to contemplate a new world, brave or otherwise, in which men and women may free themselves of some of the crippling sexual poses that now circumscribe their lives, thus allowing them some open and equitable exchange of emotion, some release of the natural self which will be greeted with resentment from no one.

But the Feminists strike a wrong and rather hysterical note when they indicate that they don't believe there is a male or female nature, that all is role. I believe that is an utterly wrong headed notion. Not only do I believe there is a genuine male or female nature in each of us, but I believe that what is most exciting about the new world that may be coming is the promise of stripping down to that nature, of the complementary elements in those natures meeting without anxiety, of our different biological tasks being performed without profit for one at the expense of the other.

The Feminists' position is extreme and many of these pronouncements are chilling at first touch. But you quickly realize that this is the harsh, stripped-down language of revolution that is, the language of icy "honesty," of narrow but penetrating vision. (As one Feminist said sweetly, quoting her favorite author: "In order to have a revolution you must have a revolutionary theory.") And besides, you sue for thousands and hope to collect hundreds.

Many Feminists, though, are appalled by the Feminists (the in-fighting in the movement is fierce), feel they are fascists, ''superweak,'' annihilatingly single-minded, and involved in a power play no matter what they say; but then again you can find feminists who will carefully and at great length put down every single feminist group going. But there's one great thing about these chicks: if five feminists fall out with six groups, within half an hour they'll all find each other (probably somewhere on Bleecker Street), within 48 hours a new splinter faction will have announced its existence, and within two weeks the manifesto is being mailed out. It's the mark of a true movement.

Two extremely intelligent and winning feminists who are about to ''emerge'' as part of a new group are Shulamith Firestone, an ex-Redstocking, and Anne Koedt, an ex-Feminist, and both members of the original radical group, New York Radical Women. They feel that none of the groups now going has the capacity to build a broad mass movement among the women of this country and they intend to start one that will. Both are dedicated to social revolution and agree with many of the ideas of many of the other radical groups. Each one, in her own words, comes equipped with ''impeccable revolutionary credentials.'' They come out of the Chicago SDS and the New York civil rights movement. Interestingly enough, like many of the radical women in this movement, they were converted to feminism because in their participation in the New Left they met with intolerable female discrimination. (''Yeah, baby, comes the revolution . . . baby, comes the revolution. . . . Meanwhile, you make the coffee and later I'll tell you where to hand out the leaflets.'' And when they raised the issue of women's rights with their radical young men, they were greeted with furious denunciations of introducing divisive issues! Excuse me, but haven't we been here before?)

The intention of Miss Firestone and Miss Koedt is to start a group that will be radical in aim but much looser in structure than anything they've been involved with; it will be an action group, but everyone will also be encouraged to theorize, analyze, create; it will appeal to the broad base of educated women; on the other hand, it will not sound ferocious to the timid non-militant woman. In other words . . .

I mention these two in particular, but at this moment in New York, in Cambridge, in Chicago, in New Haven, in Washington, in San Francisco, in East Podunk—yes! believe it!—there are dozens like them preparing to do the same thing. They are gathering fire and I do believe the next great moment in history is theirs. God knows, for my unborn daughter's sake, I hope so.

DISCUSSION QUESTIONS

1. Which of the advertisements reprinted in the Advertising section could be used to document the feminist issues discussed in Vivian Gornick's essay?

2. In what ways can Gornick's essay be used to establish an ideological context for the situations dramatized in Kate Chopin's ''The Dream of an Hour'' and Tillie Olsen's ''I Stand Here Ironing'' (see Classics)? What attitudes towards the experiences of women do they share? In what ways do they differ?

Mike Royko / How To Kick a Machine

Chicago *Daily News,* November 15, 1971

Mike Royko writes a 750-word column for the Chicago Sun-Times *five times every week. He did the same for the Chicago* Daily News *for fourteen years. He has been awarded about every major journalism prize in the business. Author of four books, one a long-time resident of the best-seller list, Royko grew up in the tough North Side of Chicago, and his columns have a street-wise slant on the social and political events of that city.*

In "How To Kick a Machine" Royko gives the "fixers, grafters, schemers, hustlers, loaders and shills" he so often writes about a breather in order to thump the malevolent inanimate objects that afflict us all.

The guy in front of me put his dime in the coffee machine. The cup dropped, the machine whirred, but nothing came out.

He muttered, then started to walk away looking dejected and embarrassed. That's the way many people react when a machine doesn't come through: as if they have been outwitted. They feel foolish.

"Aren't you going to do anything about it?" I asked.

"What's there to do?"

What a question. If he had gone in a bar and ordered a beer, and if the bartender had taken his money but not given him a beer, he'd do something. He'd yell or fight or call the police.

But he let a machine cow him.

"Kick it," I said.

"What good will that do?" he said.

"You'll feel better," I said.

He came back and got in position to kick it, but I stopped him.

"Not like that. You are going to kick it with your toe, but you can hurt yourself that way. Do it this way."

I stepped back and showed him the best way. You use the bottom of your foot, as if you're kicking in a bedroom door.

I stepped aside, and he tried it. The first time he used the ball of his foot. It was a weak effort.

"Use more of the heel," I suggested.

That did it. He gave it two good ones and the machine bounced. He has big feet.

"With feet like that," I told him, "you could knock over a sandwich machine."

He stepped back looking much more self-confident.

Somebody else who had been in line said: "I prefer pounding on it. I'll show you."

Leaning on it with his left hand, he put his forehead close to the machine, as if in deep despair. Then he pounded with his clenched fist.

"Never use the knuckles," he said, "because that hurts. Use the bottom of the fist, the way you'd pound on the table."

"Why just one fist?" someone else said. "I always use two."

He demonstrated, standing close to the machine, baring his teeth, and pounding with both fists, as if trying to break down a bedroom door with his hands.

Just then, another guy with a dime stepped up. Seeing us pounding on the machine, he asked: "Is it out of coffee?"

We told him it had shorted on a cup.

He hesitated, then said: "Sometimes it only skips one, then it works OK."

"It's your money," I told him.

He put in his dime, the cup dropped, the machine whirred, and nothing came out.

All he said was "Hmm," and started to walk away.

"Why don't you kick it?" I said.

He grimaced. "It's only a dime."

Only a dime? I don't know anyone who hasn't been cheated by a machine at least once—usually a lot more than once.

First it was the gumball machine, taking your last penny. Then it was the gum machine on the L platform. Then the peanut machine.

And now they all do it. Coffee machines, soft-drink machines, candy machines, sweet-roll machines, sandwich machines.

Only a dime? There are 200 million Americans. If each of us is taken for a dime, that adds up to $20 million.

And it has to be more, now that machines have appeared in every factory and office, depot and terminal.

I once lost an entire dollar to a dollar-changing machine. I gave it five kicks, and even that wasn't enough. For a dollar, I should have broken a chair over its intake slot.

If everyone in the country is taken for a dollar, as I suspect we all will be eventually, that's $200 million. The empty cup is a giant industry.

Putting up a note, as many people do, saying, "This machine owes me a dime," does little good. The men who service them always arrive before you get to work, or after you leave. They are ashamed to face the people they cheat.

You can put up a note saying, "Out of Coffee," which saves others from losing their dimes. But that doesn't get your dime back.

The answer is to kick and punch them. If you are old, lame, or female, bring a hammer to work with you, or an ax.

I feel better, having got this off my chest. But my foot still hurts.

WOODCHUCKS IN DEATH AND LIFE

Joseph Farkas / One Small Life

The New York Times, September 16, 1972

From its beginning in 1851, The New York Times *has been noted for its well balanced, well edited local, national, and world news coverage. Modeled on the London* Times *rather than on the American papers of the period,* The New York Times *took strong editorial positions and did not shy away from controversy.*

The following article by Joseph Farkas, chief historian for the U.S. Army Munitions Command, caused something of a stir; not the kind of controversy that results in litigation, legislation, or lots of front-page news, but the kind that occurs when a number of readers have a deep emotional response to what they find in their morning paper.

We have inserted after Farkas' essay the selection from Thoreau's Journals *that serves as the background to this op-ed piece. Letters to the editor of* The New York Times *in response to Farkas begin on page 187. Following the letters from readers are a letter from Farkas and an excerpt from Thoreau. Both are on the subject of "Woodchucks in Death and Life," which* The New York Times *published as a conclusion to the controversy.*

MAPLEWOOD, N. J.—After a period of sweltering weather, a bright cool August day dawned over Concord, Mass., in 1853, and Henry Thoreau, who had planned to sit and write in the house all day, decided that it was wiser to spend such a day outdoors. He went for a sail on the Sudbury River with his friend, William Ellery Channing. He later memorialized this glorious day in his journal.

After the recent extended hot spell, Aug. 10 similarly arrived in New Jersey as the first bright day of fall. When I left my desk for a brief outdoor walk I noticed a woodchuck scuttling across the broad lawn in front of my building. When he stopped, with his back toward me, I decided on impulse to see how close I could get to him before he became aware of me and scurried away. I walked quickly toward him until I was about six feet away and stopped. I was surprised that he hadn't detected me, but I soon saw why. He lay there with his head stretched out on the lawn and his eyes closed. He had obviously settled down for a snooze on the sun-warmed grass.

I stood there for about a minute before he suddenly raised his head and looked around at me. After contemplating me over his shoulder awhile, he turned around to face me. Then he sat up on his haunches, as though to get a better view of me.

After we had faced each other for a while, I swayed to left and right to see what effect such movement would have on him. He dropped to all fours, lowered his head, and hissed. His defensive posture indicated a readiness to fight rather than run. I moved back a few paces and then circled in back of him. He turned his head to keep me in view but did not move his body.

As I went back to the sidewalk from which I had started my confrontation I saw a small open truck in the cab of which were three workmen who had been watching the woodchuck and me. When I got alongside the truck one of the men offered to give me a club to attack the woodchuck. When I asked why I should do that, he said woodchucks were becoming too numerous and causing too much damage. They dug up lawns and ate shrubbery.

I said it would nevertheless be nice to leave the woodchuck alone, and walked away. But then I looked back and saw the man who had offered me the club walking toward the woodchuck with a four-foot metal pipe in his hand. Sensing what was coming, my first impulse was to turn my back on the scene and continue walking. But I couldn't. I watched the man get to about ten or twelve feet from the victim and stop. He waved the pipe but the woodchuck didn't move. Then the man inexplicably turned around, walked back, and got into the truck, which drove away.

I walked on, but before returning to my office I decided to have another look at my friend the woodchuck. He was still on the lawn. While I was about 200 feet away from him I saw a figure approaching him. It was the man from the truck, this time carrying a long-handled pitchfork. The truck was at the curb.

The man walked slowly toward the woodchuck. When he was about ten feet away, the woodchuck started running. The man pursued him. The woodchuck reached a small pine whose branches grew down to the ground and he ducked into it.

The man stalked around the pine, his pitchfork at the ready. Several times he lunged forward but apparently missed his prey. But then he was suddenly pushing hard on the pitchfork, his body bent forward.

After holding this position for perhaps half a minute, he let up. But the job was not yet done. He ran around to the other side of the tree and began jabbing again. Then once more he leaned hard on the pitchfork and held his position. When he straightened up I caught a glimpse of a bloody mass writhing at the end of the pine.

The man called to the truck for a shovel. The man from the truck came, not with a shovel but holding a metal pipe. He whacked the woodchuck several times, delivering the *coup de grace*. Then the man with the pitchfork impaled the woodchuck on its tines, held it aloft as he walked back to the truck, and threw it into the back of the truck. The truck drove slowly off.

After dinner I went out to my tree-encircled back yard to savor what was left of this sparkling day. I sat there watching the sunlight playing through the top of the big maple. The sky was cloudless. A helicopter chugged through in one direction and a high-flying airliner passed in another.

After sitting awhile, I reread a section of Thoreau's journal describing his encounter with a woodchuck in the spring of 1852. Although I hadn't realized it at the moment I began the episode with my woodchuck, it was residual memory of Thoreau's woodchuck account that had obviously triggered my own adventure.

Thoreau describes how he came across the woodchuck in the middle of a field, pursued it, and then sat down three feet from it when it stopped. It trembled and gritted its teeth. He touched its snout with a twig and it bit the stick. They sat looking at each other for half an hour. Thoreau talked to it in what he called forest baby talk and soothed it enough to enable him to turn it over on its back and even put his hand on it briefly. He thought that if he had had the right food to offer it he could have tamed it completely. Thoreau said that he respected the woodchuck as one of the natives and thought he might learn some wisdom from him.

I also read the journal entry on the beautiful August day of 1853, a day affecting the spirits of men and worthy of a hymn. Thoreau regretted that so few enjoyed such a day. "What do the laborer ox and the laborer man care for the beautiful days? Will the haymaker when he comes home tonight know that this has been such a beautiful day?" Did the woodchuck executioners know when they got home that afternoon that it had been such a beautiful day?

Henry David Thoreau / From *The Journals of Henry David Thoreau*

1852

April 16 . . . As I turned round the corner of Hubbard's Grove, saw a woodchuck, the first of the season, in the middle of the field, six or seven rods from the fence which bounds the wood, and twenty rods distant. I ran along the fence and cut him off, or rather overtook him, though he started at the same time. When I was only a rod and a half off, he stopped, and I did the same; then he ran again, and I ran up within three feet of him, when he stopped again, the fence being between us. I squatted down and surveyed him at my leisure. His eyes were dull black and rather inobvious, with a faint chestnut iris, with but little expression and that more resignation than of anger. The general aspect was a coarse grayish brown, a sort of grisel. A lighter brown next the skin, then black or very dark brown and tipped with whitish rather loosely. The head between a squirrel and a bear, flat on the top and dark brown, and darker still or black on the tip of the nose. The whiskers black, two inches long. The ears very small and roundish, set far back and nearly buried in the fur. Black feet, with long and slender claws for digging. It appeared to tremble, or perchance shivered with cold. When I moved, it gritted its teeth quite loud, sometimes striking the under jaw against the other chatteringly, sometimes grinding one jaw on the other, yet as if more from instinct than anger. Whichever way I turned, that way it headed. I took a twig a foot long and touched its snout, at which it started forward and bit the stick, lessening the distance between us to two feet, and still held all the ground it gained. I played with it tenderly awhile with the stick, trying to open its gritting jaw. Ever its long incisors, two above and two below, were presented. But I thought it would go to sleep if I stayed long enough. It did not sit upright as sometimes, but *standing* on its fore feet with its head down, i.e. half sitting, half standing. We sat looking at one another about half an hour, till we began to feel mesmeric influences. When I was tired, I moved away, wishing to see him run, but I could not start him. He would not stir as long as I was looking at him or could see him. I walked round him; he turned as fast and fronted me still. I sat down by his side within a foot. I talked to him *quasi* forest lingo, baby-talk, at any rate in a conciliatory tone, and thought that I had some influence on him. He gritted his teeth less. I chewed checkerberry leaves and presented them to his nose at last without a grit; though I saw that by so much gritting of the teeth he had worn them rapidly and they were covered with fine white powder, which, if you measured it thus, would have made his anger terrible. He did not mind any noise I might make. With a little stick I lifted one of his paws to examine it, and held it up at pleasure. I turned him over to see what color he was beneath (darker or more purely brown), though he turned himself back again sooner than I could have wished. His tail was also all brown, though not very dark, rat-tail like, with loose hairs standing out on all sides like a caterpillar brush. He had a rather mild look. I spoke kindly to him. I reached checkerberry leaves to his mouth. I stretched my hands over him, though he turned up his head and still gritted a little. I laid my hand on him, but immediately took it off again, instinct not being wholly overcome. If I had had a few fresh bean leaves, thus in advance of the season, I am sure I should have tamed him completely. It was a frizzly tail. His is a humble, terrestrial color like a partridge's, well concealed where dead wiry grass rises above darker brown or chestnut dead leaves—a modest color. If I had had some food, I should have ended with stroking him at my leisure. Could easily have wrapped him in my handkerchief. He was not fat nor particularly lean. I finally had to leave him without seeing him move from the place. A large, clumsy burrowing squirrel. *Arctomys*, bearmouse. I respect him as one of the natives. He lies there, by his color and habits so naturalized amid the dry leaves, the withered grass, and the bushes. A sound nap, too, he has enjoyed in his native fields, the past winter. I think I might learn some wisdom of him. His ancestors have lived here longer than mine. He is more thoroughly acclimated and naturalized than I. Bean leaves the red man raised for him, but he can do without them.

Letters / And What Would Henry Thoreau Have Thought?

The New York Times, September 1972

To the Editor:

It struck me while reading Joseph Farkas' "One Small Life" [Op-Ed, Aug. 29] that Thoreau would never have stood around and allowed another man to kill a wood chuck 200 feet away from him.

Linda Clarke
New York City

•

To the Editor:

The account of the killing of the woodchuck and the earlier account of the poodle standing guard over his collie friend killed on the highway [Op-Ed, July 11] are sad commentaries on man's destructiveness. But implicit in both stories is an increasingly frequent, linked observation: the passivity in the face of violence of men of better instincts. Could not Mr. Farkas have done more than just watch the pitchforking of the woodchuck?

Jo Coudert
New York City

•

To the Editor:

It is quite apparent Mr. Farkas was not brought up on a farm else he would know that the woodchuck is a rodent capable of much damage to crops.

In my vegetable garden a woodchuck has just destroyed seven out of twelve large cabbage plants and has ruined two rows of Swiss Chard.

I am glad to report the villain has been trapped and his remains put to rest without benefit of clergy.

V. R. Blair
White Plains, N.Y.

•

To the Editor:

Little moments, at times, are beyond themselves, and can be lifetimes in miniature. Joseph Farkas called the woodchuck his friend and yet watched the man destroy him. How could he?

Morton Mecklosky
Stony Brook, N.Y.

•

To the Editor:

I would certainly distinguish between woodchucks and human beings, yet I wonder why Mr. Farkas when in no real danger himself would not act to save the woodchuck. I doubt we could count on him when there might be real danger to his own life to resist a wrong to another human being. The point is not whether woodchucks are good or bad animals, nor that those men chose to kill the animal. The point is that Mr. Farkas chose not to act but to watch, record what he saw, and no doubt receive a fat fee from The New York Times for his trouble.

The Mylai massacre mentality is not confined to a distant tiny war-torn land; it lives among us. Does the chief historian of the U.S. Army Munitions Command record the despicable results of our munitions in Vietnam with equal lack of involvement?

And he dare speak the name Thoreau in the same breath.

Richard Steinberger
Princeton, N.J.

•

To the Editor:

At the end of the article, Mr. Farkas wonders if the woodchuck's murderers truly appreciated the beauty of the day. I would wonder if Farkas ever questioned his moral responsibility in this matter. Surely Thoreau, whom the author apparently admires, would have acted differently. Assuming that he wanted to avoid a physical confrontation, could not Farkas have been more forceful in his verbal exchange with the workmen? At the very least, he could have chased the animal while the men were choosing their respective weapons.

One cannot help feeling that the author had decided early on to abandon the woodchuck to its fate and to record this event for posterity. To what end?

Judith Zinn
Hempstead, N.Y.

•

To the Editor:

What man would not at least have frightened the animal away with a sound—a stone—something that would have given the animal a chance against the executioner?

Mary F. Peo
Short Hills, N.J.

•

To the Editor:

I sat for a long time mulling over this story of brutality to a small creature and wondering what prompted Mr. Farkas to write it.

Was it, perhaps, an attempt to expiate his sin of omission in not intervening in the woodchuck's behalf, or was he merely recording an event while accepting the right of men to destroy creatures whose habits they do not understand or whose existence inconveniences them slightly?

I noticed that Mr. Farkas is connected with the U.S. Army, which turned my thoughts to Vietnam. I think about Vietnam quite a lot during this period of intensive bombing, and I wondered if he might have intended to produce a parable of our involvement there, in order to make more real the cruelty of a few men destroying living beings while our nation stands by and quietly observes.

If that was his intent I wish him success and a wide audience.

Mary Specht
Huntingdon Valley, Pa.

•

I plead guilty to having stood idly by while a woodchuck was being pitchforked to death. I plead guilty to having done nothing to prevent the killing of over a million people in Vietnam. I plead guilty to countless sins of omission in failing to do anything to correct the injustices, the ugliness, the horrors of the life around us. I respect all those who have actively taken arms against a sea of troubles and attempted, by opposing, to end them. But to the millions who—like me—have out of inertia, cowardice, selfishness, or ignorance given silent assent (or even active support) to the perpetration of evil, I say: Let him who is without sin cast the first stone.

Joseph Farkas
Maplewood, N.J., 1972

As I came home through the woods with my string of fish, trailing my pole, it being now quite dark, I caught a glimpse of a woodchuck stealing across my path, and felt a strange thrill of savage delight, and was strongly tempted to seize and devour him raw; not that I was hungry then, except for that wildness which he represented. Once or twice, however, while I lived at the pond, I found myself ranging the woods, like a half-starved hound, with a strange abandonment, seeking some kind of venison which I might devour, and no morsel could have been too savage for me. The wildest scenes had become unaccountably familiar. I found in myself, and still find, an instinct toward a higher, or, as it is named, spiritual life, as do most men, and another toward a primitive rank and savage one, and I reverence them both.

Henry David Thoreau
Walden, Concord, Mass., 1854

Art Buchwald / Unreality of TV

Ca. 1977

In college, Art Buchwald was the managing editor of Wampus, *the University of Southern California's humor magazine. He also wrote a regular column for that school's paper before leaving for Paris and parts unknown. When his money ran out, Buchwald began writing for the Paris edition of the* New York Herald-Tribune *and became a correspondent for* Variety *magazine. He observed the European scene for fourteen years before moving to Washington, D.C., in 1962 to write a syndicated newspaper column. Buchwald's incisive observations of contemporary politics and culture have earned him the reputation as the most influential wit in American journalism. Two of his recent books are* Laid Back in Washington *(1981) and* While Reagan Slept *(1983).*

Dr. Heinrich Applebaum recently completed a study on the effects of television on children. In his case, though, he wasn't concerned with violence, but how television gives children a false sense of reality.

Dr. Applebaum told me, "The greatest danger of television is that it presents a world to children that doesn't exist, and raises expectations that can never be fulfilled."

"I don't understand, Doctor," I said.

"Well, let me cite one example. Have you ever seen a television show where a person in an automobile doesn't immediately find a parking place on the very first try?"

"Come to think of it," I said, "I haven't."

"Not only is there always a parking spot available but the driver doesn't even have to back into it. There are *two* parking spaces available whenever someone in a TV show needs one. Children are being led to believe that when they grow up they will always be able to find a parking place when and where they want it. Can you imagine the trauma when they discover that in real life you can drive around a block for three hours and still not find a place to put your car?"

"I never thought of it but it's true. What else do they show on television which gives a distorted picture of the real world?"

"Have you noticed that whenever a character walks out of a restaurant or office building or apartment and says to the doorman, 'Get me a taxi,' the taxi immediately arrives? Millions of children are under the impression that all a doorman has to do is blow his whistle and a taxi will be there. I have never seen a show where the doorman has said, 'I'm sorry. I can't get you a taxi. You better take the bus.' "

"Of course," I said. "I never knew before what bothered me about those TV action programs, but now I do. There is always a yellow taxi waiting offscreen."

"Now," said Applebaum, "have you ever said to a taxi driver, 'Follow that car and don't lose him'?"

"Not really."

"Well, if you had, the driver would have told you to blow it out your ear. No taxi driver is in a mood to follow another car because that means he's going to get involved. But on TV every cabdriver looks as if he'd like nothing better to do than to drive 90 miles an hour through a rain-swept street trying to keep up with a carful of hoods. And the worst thing is that the kids believe it."

"What else have you discovered?"

"Kids have a perverted sense of what emergency wards of hospitals are really like. On TV shows they take a kid to an emergency ward and four doctors come rushing down to bandage his leg. In a real life situation the kid would be sitting on the bench for two hours before he even saw an intern. On TV there always happens to be a hospital bed available when a kid needs it. What the kids in this country don't know is that sometimes you have to wait three days to get a hospital bed and then you have to put a cash deposit of $500 down before they give it to you."

Applebaum said the cruelest hoax of all is when TV shows a lawyer defending someone innocent of a crime.

"On the screen the lawyer spends day and night digging up the evidence to clear his client. In real life the lawyer says to the defendant, 'Look, I've got 20 minutes. Tell me your story and then I'll plead you guilty and make a deal with the DA.' In real life the defendant might say, 'But I'm innocent.' The lawyer would say, 'So what? I can't afford to find that out. I'm not Perry Mason.' "

"Then what you're saying, Dr. Applebaum, is that it isn't the violence on TV but the fantasy that is doing harm to children."

"Exactly. Even the commercials are taking their toll. Children are led to believe that when they grow up if they use a certain mouthwash they'll find the mate of their dreams. When they don't find him or her after gargling all night, they go into a tailspin and many of them never come out of it."

"What do you think is the biggest fear little girls have?"

"I have no idea."

"That someday when they get married their husbands will have ring around the collar."

"What about boys?"

"Boys worry that they'll only go around once in life and they won't have all the gusto out of their beer that they deserve."

Ellen Goodman / Protection from the Prying Camera

Washington Post, January 4, 1977

A widely syndicated columnist for the Boston Globe, *Ellen Goodman graduated from Radcliffe College in 1963. A 1980 recipient of the Pulitzer Prize for commentary, she has published a study on human change,* Turning Points *(1979), and two collections of her columns,* Close to Home *(1979) and* At Large *(1981). Ellen Goodman's writing, as illustrated by the article below, is especially attuned to the daily clash of public issues and private values, trends and traditions.*

Maybe it was the year-end picture roundup that finally did it. Maybe it was the double exposure to the same vivid photographs. Or perhaps it was the memory of three amateur photographers carefully standing in the cold last fall, calculating their f-stops and exposures with light meters, trying to find the best angle, pointing their cameras at a drunk in a doorway. Or maybe it was simply my nine-year-old cousin playing Candid Camera at the family gathering.

But whatever the reason, it has finally hit me. We have become a nation of Kodachrome, Nikon, Instamatic addicts. But we haven't yet developed a clear idea of the ethics of picture-taking. We haven't yet determined the parameters of privacy in a world of flash cubes and telescopic lenses.

We "take" pictures. As psychologist Stanley Milgram puts it, "A photographer takes a picture, he does not create it or borrow it." But who has given us the right to "take" those pictures and under what circumstances?

Since the camera first became portable, we have easily and repeatedly aimed it at public people. It has always been open shooting season on them. With new technology, however, those intrusions have intensified. This year, someone with a camera committed the gross indecency of shooting an unaware Greta Garbo in the nude—and *People* printed it.

This year, again, Ron Galella "took" the image of Jacqueline Onassis and sold it as if it belonged to him. This year, we have pictures of a crumpled Wayne Hays, an indiscreet Nelson Rockefeller, and two presidential candidates in every imaginable pose from the absurd to the embarrassing.

We have accepted the idea that public people are always free targets for the camera—without even a statute of limitations for Jackie or Garbo. We have also accepted the idea that a private person becomes public by being involved in a public event. The earthquake victims of Guatemala, the lynched leftists of Thailand, the terror-stricken of Ireland—their emotions and their bodies become frozen images.

The right of the public to know, to see and to be affected is considered more important than the right of the individual to mourn, or even die, in privacy.

What happens now, however, when cameras proliferate until they are as common as television sets? What happens when the image being "taken" is that of a butcher, a baker, or a derelict, rather than a public figure? Do we all lose our right to privacy simply by stepping into view?

Should we be allowed to point cameras at each other? To regard each other as objects of art? Does the photographer or the photographed own the image?

Several years ago, *Time* photographer Steve Northup, who had covered Vietnam, and Watergate, took a group of students around Cambridge shooting pictures. He quietly insisted that they ask every pizza-maker, truck driver and beautician for permission. His attitude toward private citizens was one of careful respect for the power of "exposure." In contrast to this, the average camera bug—like the average tourist—too often goes about snapping "quaint" people, along with "quaint" scenes: See the natives smile, see the natives carrying baskets of fruit, see the native children begging, see the drunk in the doorway. As Milgram wrote, "I find it hard to understand wherein the photographer has derived the right to keep for his own purposes the image of the peasant's face."

Where do we get the right to bring other people home in a canister? Where did we lose the right to control our image?

In a study that Milgram conducted last year, a full 65 percent of the people to whom his students talked in midtown Manhattan refused to have their pictures taken, refused to be photographed. I don't think they were camera shy, in the sense of being vain. Rather they were reluctant to have their pictures "taken."

The Navahos long believed that the photographer took a piece of them away in his film. Like them, we are coming to understand the power of these frozen images. Photographs can help us to hold onto the truth of our past, to make our history and identity more real. Or they can rip something away from us as precious as the privacy which once clothed Greta Garbo.

DISCUSSION QUESTIONS

1. Compare Ellen Goodman's essay to Nora Ephron's article on a similar theme, "The Boston Photographs" in "Magazines." Which writer do you think makes a stronger case? Why?

2. Do you think that being a practicing journalist influenced Goodman's point of view? Would her response to privacy be the same if she were not a newspaperwoman? Explain how her role as a journalist affects her response to the situation she is writing about.

John J. Goldman / Beatle John Lennon Slain

Los Angeles *Times*, December 9, 1980

Over the past twenty years, John Goldman has covered hundreds of major-breaking news stories for the L.A. Times, *including the first moon landing, the Howard Hughes/Clifford Irving hoax—and the death of John Lennon. Goldman is currently New York Bureau Chief of the Los Angeles* Times.

With a circulation of over one million, the Los Angles Times *is the third largest daily newspaper in the United States (behind* The Wall Street Journal *and the New York* Daily News*). Labelled for many years as an extremely conservative paper, the Los Angeles* Times *was infamous for its biased news coverage. In 1937, it was voted by Washington correspondents as one of America's "least fair and reliable" newspapers. But when Otis Chandler succeeded his father as publisher of the* Times *in 1960, he modernized the paper and changed its character. Now one of the west coast's most prominent and judicious newspapers, the* Times *has dedicated itself to presenting "both sides of the political spectrum and different shades within the spectrum." Many of its writers have won Pulitzer prizes, as did the* Times *itself in 1969 for public service.*

BEATLE JOHN LENNON SLAIN

SHOT DOWN OUTSIDE NEW YORK APARTMENT

Man Termed "Screwball" Held in Death of Singer

NEW YORK—Former Beatle John Lennon, 40, who led a revolution in popular music that captured the imagination of an entire generation, was shot to death Monday night outside his exclusive Manhattan apartment house.

He was rushed to Roosevelt Hospital, less than a mile from the Dakota, the famous apartment building where he lived with his wife, Yoko Ono. Doctors pronounced him dead at the hospital.

Police announced early today that Mark David Chapman, 25, of Hawaii had been charged with murder. Chief of Detectives James Sullivan said Chapman had arrived in New York about a week ago and had been seen near the apartment building at least three times in recent days.

Sullivan said Chapman had gotten Lennon's autograph when the Lennons left the Dakota about 5 p.m. and had waited outside until they returned six hours later.

Sullivan declined to speculate on a motive for the shooting. Earlier, police had described the suspect as "a local screwball" and "a wacko."

HAD HANDGUN

Police said Lennon and his wife arrived at 10:50 p.m. in a limousine from a recording studio and had just stepped out of the car when the gunman approached them.

"Mr. Lennon?" the man said, drawing a .38-caliber handgun from under his coat.

He opened fire without waiting for an answer.

Lennon, struck in the chest, back and shoulder, staggered from the sidewalk into a small vestibule of the apartment used by the doorman.

The aghast doorman looked at the gunman.

"Do you know what you just did?" he shouted.

"I just shot John Lennon," the gunman responded, throwing down the handgun.

Lennon's wife was not injured.

Police Officer Anthony Palmer was one of the first to arrive at the Dakota. He said it was quickly apparent to him that Lennon had to be rushed to the hospital without waiting for an ambulance.

"I made the decision," Palmer said. "We had to get him out of there. . . ."

Police Officer James Moran, who was in the patrol car that took Lennon to Roosevelt Hospital, said the singer was semiconscious during the ride.

He said he asked the former Beatle if he were John Lennon and Lennon nodded, moaning.

At the hospital, a physician said Lennon was dead by the time he arrived, and efforts to resuscitate him were unsuccessful. He said there had been "a significant" loss of blood from the bullet wounds.

Palmer rode to the hospital in a squad car with Yoko Ono.

He said she was distraught and kept asking, "Tell me he's all right. . . ."

As the news spread, more than 1,000 Beatles fans gathered outside the Dakota, some of them listening to Beatles music on tape recorders.

One man walked up to the tall black iron gate that guards the impressive old building's front entrance. He placed a small bouquet of flowers between the bars and then stepped back into the crowd.

Some of the Beatles fans wept, others stood in disbelief asking each other if Lennon really was dead.

Lennon suffered seven gunshot wounds in his chest, left arm and back, "causing significant injury to major blood vessels in his chest (and) causing massive blood loss," according to Dr. Stephan Lynn, director of emergency room services at Roosevelt Hospital.

Musician, actor, songwriter, singer, author and businessman—John Lennon's 40 years of life were spent in what seemed to many a headlong revolt against and assault on the society and mores of the western world.

Yet he never accepted the role.

"I'M A HUMAN BEIN', MATE"

"I'm a human bein', mate," he said in an interview shortly after the much-publicized breakup of his first and most-successful creation—The Beatles—in 1970. "A human bein', don't never forget that. Anything else you say about me—well—it's beside the point, innit!"

The statement was accepted, studied, analyzed and finally filed with the several tons of other cryptic Lennonisms that, in their way, contributed to the mystique that surrounded the young Merseyside performer during all his adult years.

Lennon never explained. He said he had given up trying to do anything like that long before his Liverpool musical phenomenon achieved its first flash of recognition in the late 1950s.

"Make what you want of it," he said. "Anything. You will anyway, won't you. . . ."

MOP-HEADED SINGERS

Beatlemania—the near-craze that centered for more than a decade around the four mop-headed singers and instrumentalists—was a phenomenon transcending social class, age group, intellectual level or geographical location.

As acknowledged organizer-leader of the Beatles, Lennon had had a hand in writing most of the group's early musical efforts, was the author of two best-selling books of humorous verse and prose, was a prime mover in organizing their early films, such as "Hard Day's Night" and "Help!" and was credited with much of the story and dialogue for the cartoon hit, "Yellow Submarine."

But he was always ready to acknowledge that the specific style and impact of the group was a thing apart, something more than the sum of its parts or of any individual's input.

POSITIVE PHENOMENON

And in the end, even the Establishment it had caricatured and criticized came to regard the Beatles as a positive phenomenon. In 1965, all four Beatles were designated members of the Most Excellent Order of the British Empire.

"Right, mate," Lennon said. "Now to think up some real insults and we'll all be Graceful Dukes!"

John Lennon was born Oct. 9, 1940, in Liverpool, and his father, Alfred Lennon, deserted the family to seek the seafaring life when John was 3 years old.

The boy's mother, Julia Lennon (whose name later became the inspiration for one of the Beatles' most successful songs), died in an automobile accident before he was 14. However, before that, he had gone—by choice—to live with a favorite aunt, Mrs. Mary Smith.

Having shown some talent for painting while in secondary school, Lennon attended the Liverpool College of Art for two years.

But art never stood a chance compared to music, and in 1958, when he met Paul McCartney, the two young men helped each other in mastering the guitar and in developing personal musical techniques.

Billed as the Nurk Twins (a title borrowed from RAF slang), they began to offer occasional performances and, in the next year, were joined by another guitarist, George Harrison, and by drummer Pete Best. They called themselves first the Quarrymen Skiffle Group (name derived from John's old private school) and then as the Moondogs, later the Moonshiners.

Then, later, they became the Silver Beatles ("Never mind where that comes from; if you don't know, you don't want to know") and finally—perhaps, as manager Brian Epstein liked to explain, because of their four-four beat insistence—as The Beatles.

That name stuck, through experiments with washboard and banjo sounds, through cellar clubs in Liverpool and in Hamburg, Germany, where they briefly became a quintet, having been joined by bass guitarist Stuart Sutliffe (who later died of a brain ailment brought on by an injury during a mugging).

It was in Hamburg, where they frequently performed for as much as seven hours at a stretch, that they began to develop their style of easy clowning and ad-libbing —a public form they retained when they returned to Liverpool.

In October, 1961, Epstein, who ran a family record business not far from the club, received a request for a record called "My Bonnie," made by The Beatles as accompaniment for Tony Sheridan, a popular singer.

Epstein ordered 200 copies of the record, promptly sold them out and went looking for the group that had made it.

"Dead scruffy and untidy they were in those days," Epstein said. "But you could feel it, something happening when they worked, something exciting—this amazing communication with the audience, and this absolutely marvelous humor. Well, I knew they could be one of the biggest theater attractions in the world, didn't I? So what was I to do—let it pass by. . . ?"

Epstein became the Beatles' manager in January, 1962, and immediately made them shed their leather "Teddy Boy" gear and begin to dress in near-Edwardian style designed by Pierre Cardin; he had their long and shaggy hair trimmed into what was later described as "a kind of male pageboy" or "dishmop" and teamed them publicly with such name singers as Cliff Richards.

He got them bookings in nightclubs, cabarets, church halls, youth centers, ballrooms, theaters and, on Oct. 17, 1962, their first television appearance, on the British Granada network.

He got them also a contract with Electrical and Musical Industries Ltd. (EMI), and their first hit, "Love Me Do" (written by Lennon and McCartney in an idle hour) sold 100,000 copies.

Meanwhile, the composition of the group had changed.

Pete Best had departed to be succeeded by Richard Starkey (also known as Ringo Starr).

"The rest," Epstein was fond of saying, "is musical history . . ."

Their appearance at the London Palladium in October, 1963, established the Beatles' status as a British musical institution.

DIVORCED WIFE

"Part luck," Lennon said. "You know, there were no wars, no invasions, no state secrets opened up that particular day. The Beatles were the only good story the London comics had—so they played it up well. Luck. . . ."

Along the way, Lennon had a bobble: In 1962 he had married Cynthia Powell; they had one son, Julian. In 1968, they were divorced, and Lennon married Ono, by whom he had a son, Sean.

There were rumors of dissension within the group; stories of ego trips and business squabbles centering on the profits of the Beatles' own music-publishing firm, Apple Enterprises.

Epstein pooh-poohed the stories, managed to hold the four together for a few more successful and profitable years. And then Epstein—the Fifth Beatle—died.

And in 1970, it was all over.

The Beatles had played together for the last time.

Lennon, on his own now, wrote and recorded "The Dream Is Over" and said publicly he wanted the memory of the Beatles "off my back."

However, in an interview with Times writer Robert Hilburn two months ago, he admitted:

"I had made the physical break from The Beatles, but mentally there was still this big thing on my back about what people expected of me. It was like this invisible ghost. . . ."

Another song, "Woman Is Nigger of the World," in 1972 (which many radio stations refused to play because of its title) also was treated ironically by Lennon in the latest interview.

"I accepted intellectually what we were saying in the song," he said, "but I hadn't really accepted it in my heart."

And so, five years ago, the Lennons suddenly became, in Ono's words, "permanently unavailable" for press interviews.

Lennon learned to cook and care for his young son, and became, he said, "a house-husband in every sense."

This change, however, only gave added intensity to the rumors that it had been Ono who had been somehow responsible for the 1970 breakup of the group; for the suspicions that she interfered rather than helped in the recording studio.

Lennon also gave the lie to that in talking to Hilburn.

She had been, he said, an artistic catalyst for him—questioning, discussing and challenging. When they split up for 18 months during the early 70s (and Lennon reacted with a drunken "long weekend" in Los Angeles) he said one of his discoveries was that he needed her as much as he needed his music.

Despite their press-avoidance, the Lennons had not lived a reclusive life in their seventh-floor apartment at The Dakota for the five years since 1975.

He and the family had traveled to Japan and elsewhere; he went out regularly in New York. But he stayed away from music business and the communications media.

Then, abruptly, he began writing music again. Last summer, during a vacation with son Sean in Bermuda, he called Yoko and played her a tape he had made; she responded by writing reply songs of her own—to play them back to him a few days later.

In the end, the songs formed a man-woman dialogue and the Lennons went into a recording studio in August to record the album which they titled, "Double Fantasy," a 14-song LP released last month by Geffen Records.

The first song, released earlier, was titled "Starting Over."

The final note—the last ever—from John Lennon, came this month in an interview with Playboy Magazine writer David Sheff.

"The unknown," the interview concluded. "The unknown is what it is. And to be frightened of it is what sends everybody scurrying around chasing dreams, illusions, wars, peace, love, hate, all that—it's all illusion.

"Unknown is what it is.

"Accept that it's unknown and it's plain sailing. Everything is unknown—then you're ahead of the game. That's what it is.

"Right . . ."

Howie Evans / Joe Louis: American Folk Hero

Amsterdam News, April 18, 1981

One of the first black sportscasters to have a network radio sports show, Howie Evans was born in New York City where he now serves as sports editor of the Amsterdam News. *A four-time varsity athlete at Maryland State, Evans coaches basketball at Fordham University and contributes regularly to numerous sports periodicals. He is currently writing a book about black athletes in America.*

The Amsterdam News, *with a circulation of over 100,000, is a weekly newspaper directed to the black community of New York City.*

There was Daniel Boone, Davey Crockett, and Joe Louis. There was Jack Dempsey, Babe Ruth, and yes! Joe Louis. All American folk heroes. But no man has ever captured the imagination, adulation, and love of a nation, as did Joe Louis.

And now he's gone. But only in body. The spirit of Joe Louis will live forever. In his lifetime, the glory of his deeds refused to turn into ashes.

Instead they became a smouldering ember that refused to be extinguished. In the beginning, he was everything to a people that had almost forgotten how to hope.

And in the brightest moments of his being, he gave a race of people something to cherish . . . something that made him a son of every Black family in the world.

Towards the twilight years of his life, his star only grew brighter as the legend grew stronger. His was a name that didn't die as the war years of the 40's tore families apart around the world. For the record, Louis never attempted to duck his responsibilities as a citizen of this nation. The records do reveal that a very famous champ, prior to Louis, did just that in the first World War.

The 50's rushed by with a startling quickness. Almost as quick as Joe's famed, left jab. And still the man who knew no other trade than that of a pugilist, continued to expose his aging body to the fists of the "Young Turks" of his day. Joe needed money and he knew of no other way to earn it.

The 60's were a period of social turmoil, and through it all, the calm wisdom of Joe Louis acted as a buffer for the more aggressive social and political-minded reformers. A young man out of Louisville, Kentucky, took the world by storm, but never completely winning over the loyal segment of Joe Louis fans.

Joe was an American folk hero and sportswriters, fans, and other fighters constantly reminded the young man that there would always be only one Joe Louis.

With the coming of the 70's the once magnificent body that destroyed opponents with a flick of his left wrist, or a jaw-shattering right that traveled a mere six inches, began to come apart.

His life became a revolving series of traumatic episodes. But still he refused to surrender to the many ailments that ravaged his body. In his final years, Joe Louis married a wheelchair.

It was not a sight for the soft at heart. The once proud and powerful Joe Louis was confined to his second wife—an old rolling chair that he disliked so much.

Where once his mighty legs would carry him to and fro, he became dependent upon a woman who was an extension of his own life. Her strength and her faith transcended miraculously into his blood. And it was because of Martha Louis that Joe Louis was able to buy some extra time.

But life is like a clock. And in time, all clocks wind down to a final tick. Joe Louis lived every tick of his life. There were no regrets, no bitterness. And other than the countless dollars he advanced to friends and families, the monies he gave away to total strangers, Joe only wished he could have been counted out on his feet.

Around this nation, thousands upon thousands of Black children bear his name. There is a first cousin by blood of a sportswriter who bears the name . . . Joe Louis McLucas.

Certainly he must feel as if a small part of him has left his own body. His feelings are shared by all the others. There are not many man-made structures in this world that would seat all Joe Louis' in this world.

It was like that with another American folk hero. They called him Martin Luther King, Jr. There are schools, recreation centers, and for sure, thousands of Black children bearing Martin's name.

In Detroit, there is the Joe Louis Arena, once known as Cobo Arena. Who was Cobo is a question that millions of Black children around the world will never know. But as they burp their way into adulthood, the name of Joe Louis will live forever on their lips. It's that way when you become an American folk hero. Rest in peace champ.

Manuela Hoelterhoff / Walt's Wonderful World Turns Out To Be Flat

Wall Street Journal, July 2, 1982

Born in Hamburg, West Germany, in 1948, Manuela Hoelterhoff served as editor in chief of Art & Auction *magazine and is currently the Arts Editor for the* Wall Street Journal. *She has published articles and essays for* Art Forum, Art News, Dial, *and* Horizon *and was awarded the 1982 Pulitzer Prize for criticism. Employing a lively and provocative style, Hoelterhoff writes on a broad range of subjects, including opera, architecture, television, and travel. "Walt's Wonderful World Turns Out To Be Flat," which appeared in the Leisure and the Arts section of the* Wall Street Journal, *reveals one critic's less than enchanted musings on the Magic Kingdom.*

The Wall Street Journal, *the most prestigious business and financial newspaper in the world, was started by an enterprising young stock-market reporter, Charles H. Dow, in 1889. Over the years, the paper has enlarged its concept of business news to include a daily quotient of social and cultural phenomena sometimes only peripherally related to the American economy.*

DISNEY WORLD, FLA.—Another happy, sunny day. I am having breakfast on Main Street, USA, the long shoplined street that leads to Cinderella's Castle—the heart of Walt Disney World's Magic Kingdom. Music fills the air. Friendly birds pick crumbs off the restaurant's balustrade. And here's a gaily decked out pony pulling smiling visitors in a festooned wagon.

By day's end, about 35,000 adults and children (adults outnumber kids four to one) will have strolled up Main Street. By year's end, the admirers of Donald, Dumbo, Mickey and Pluto are expected to reach 13.2 million, making Disney World even more popular than the older Disneyland in Anaheim, Calif. Since Disney World opened ten-and-a-half years ago, it has clocked over 131 million visitors. In fact, my travel guide says this is the most popular vacation spot on this planet. That is why I came here and why I am wearing this attractive hat. As the large 36-year-old child who accompanied me said: "Opera isn't everything, kid. You got to learn about America and talk to the people."

Over there at an adjacent table is a middle-aged couple forking in pancakes. His shortsleeved shirt reveals a tattoo; her print slack ensemble is as happily colored as a flower bed. We chat about their trip and she tells me that he is a construction worker and she a bookkeeper. They are celebrating their 25th anniversary here in Disney. Good choice? I ask. "Oh, God, yes," she says. "We're so amazed. It's better, it's more than we imagined. Everything is so clean." They were hoping to spend their next vacation here.

Their satisfaction was echoed in varying decible levels by virtually everyone I spoke to during my four-day stay. "We wouldn't change anything," said a retired couple from Mississippi. "I've been here 11 times; it's an uplifting place," said a young lawyer from Ohio. And a Vermont-based doctor and his wife sang a duet of praise of which one stanza focused on the place's cheerfulness and another on its efficiency.

This joyous ensemble of voices is offered for reasons of balance. I did not have a great time, I ate food no self-respecting mouse would eat, stayed in a hotel that could have been designed by the Moscow corps of engineers and suffered through entertainment by smiling, uniformed young people who looked like they had their hair arranged at a lobotomy clinic. Somehow the plastic heart of Disney didn't beat for me.

Still, I have to give Walt credit for standing in the swamplands surrounding Orlando and envisioning a drained, jillion-dollar amusement/vacation spot presided over by a castle and courtly mouse. Walt's world is simply immense. You need to be Peter Pan to cover its 27,400 acres. As our guide kept telling us: Disney World is much, much more than just the Magic Kingdom with its rides, attractions and restaurants. It's hotels, golf courses, a heap of shops and such other components of the perfect vacation as horsebackriding, boating and swimming. The entire fiefdom is laced together by a battalion of buses and a monorail that zooms above your head and right through the Contemporary Resort Hotel (my happy home).

Anyway, you're thinking, this all sounds neat enough, nobody promised you Paris, poisonous food is at every streetcorner, so what if people smile a lot and what really is your problem, you Fair Isle-sweater-wearing snob? Well, let me offer some highlights of Disney and its parameters, and if it seems really good and you act quickly, you can probably still book a room in the Contemporary sometime next year. The waiting list here is longer than at the George V in Paris.

The Magic Kingdom is divided into various areas bearing such names as Tomorrowland, Adventureland and Frontierland. In Adventureland we stop at an attraction called the Enchanted Tiki Birds, which has a long line of mostly adults waiting to get into "the sunshine pavilion." While we wait, two robot (or, in Disney jargon, AudioAnimatronic) parrots entertain us with a story that starts "many birdbaths ago." One of the many sunny young folks who keep things running smoothly in the kingdom pops out dressed in a disgusting orange outfit. "Aloha! he shouts. The people stare at him. "I said, 'Aloha,' " he yells smiling madly. "Aloha!" the audience shouts back, making up in volume what it had lacked in spontaneity. "Everyone raise his arm and wave goodbye!" he commands. And everyone raises his arm and waves goodbye.

Any minute, we figured, he's going to have them saluting and clicking their sandals.

We decided to break ranks and headed for Tomorrowland, where we bobbed about in the air sitting in something called sky jets and had some lunch at the Space Port shop. So many choices. We picked Splashdown Peach Punch over a Cosmic Cooler and settled for a Satellite sandwich. In Disney, language lovers will quickly note, Mickey Mouse and Donald Duck worked wonders with alliteration and little rhymes, though it must be said that Walt was no Whitman.

Fortified, we took in a short movie introducing EPCOT (the acronym for Experimental Prototype Community of Tomorrow), a new 600-acre attraction scheduled to open this fall. "Relax and enjoy," says the smooth-voiced narrator as a tenorino begins to croon: "Dreams of the future, lalala, the world belongs to the dreamer, the dreamer inside you." The future apparently includes homes that look like aquariums and people cavorting with dolphins dressed up in pretty outfits. The level of the narration is such that it could be understood by an Audio-Animatronic audience.

In contrast, there is nothing futuristic or fantastical about the next stop, our hotel, except for that monorail speeding through its innards. That was a terrific design idea. And when the hotel opened, the decor had other 21st century touches. But visitors apparently felt uncomfortable with the unfamiliar and the rooms were redecorated. As I dial to a religious program on the TV, I sit on a purple-green bedspread surrounded by swimming-pool-blue plastic furniture, enormous lamps with tumor-like bases and textured green and beige walls. I look out over a parking lot and carefully planted vegetation that is pure Middle America—boring trees and dinky little flowers. I may be in tropical Florida, but there isn't a palm tree in sight. The beach behind the parking lot is as dully laid out as the golf course.

Once outside the fun and games of the Magic Kingdom, the rest of Disney World looks like a condo village. Which is a large part, I would argue, of its attraction. Many Americans spend most of their life preparing for a retirement community and Disney provides a good prelude with its own security force and hassle-free, clean living. Unlike in Europe, you don't have to deal with funny languages, funny-colored money or funny food. And there's no garbage. Never. The smallest scrap of litter is instantly sucked underground, and rushed via pipes to the most fabulous compactor in the universe. The place is obsessively antiseptic. When the Disney characters dance and ride up Main Street in the parade scheduled for every afternoon, a special squad equipped with scoopers follows the ponies.

There's nothing left to chance here, nothing at all. The instant you arrive, you are watched over and taken care of. This place has crowd control down to a science. Mazes set up in front of the popular attractions like "20,000 Leagues Under the Sea," which features plastic-looking, half-submerged submarines paddling past plastic monsters, keep the people-flow smooth and constant. Even though it took us 30 minutes to meet the mermaid, we had the impression our sub was just around the corner. The only time I saw the system break down was in front of the Haunted Mansion. "Disney World is your land" as the song frequently heard hereabouts goes. But not if you're fat. One unhappy girl got stuck in the turnstyle and had to be pushed back out. Like Cinderella's step-sisters, no matter how hard she tried, she just wouldn't fit.

Evenings, too, were crammed with events. One night we dined at the Papeete Bay Verandah restaurant in the Polynesian Village hotel, *the* place if you aren't at the Contemporary. An overamplified and oversimplified combo entertained us as we sipped a Chi-Chi, particularly popular, the menu points out, in Pago Pago, and stared at prawns blown up with breading to look like chicken legs.

But the unquestioned highlight was the Hoop-Dee-Doo Revue at Pioneer Hall in the camping area. "Enthusiastic performers sing, dance and joke up a storm until your mouth is as sore from laughing as your stomach is from ingesting all the food," promises my guide book. I couldn't have said it better. As we sat down, the hearty sextet appeared singing "Hoop-dee-doo, hoop-dee-doo." Then they beat pans and washboards and established friendly rapport with the eating audience. With Robert, for instance, of Virile Beach (could have been Floral Beach, those washboards get noisy). And Chris. Lets hear it for Chris from Daytona Beach! He's 29 today! Let's hear it for Chris! People waved their napkins in Chris's direction. "Hoop-dee-doo" sang the ensemble, jumping up and down.

Our meal—greasy ribs and chicken—arrived in little buckets. When we were done staring again, the hearty sextet reappeared and rubbed their bellies as they sang: "Mom's in the kitchen fixing up a special dessert just for *you.*" Out came globs of possibly strawberry shortcake and then more jokes like "You got a wooden head; that's better than a cedar chest. Think about that for a while." Everybody did and whooped and hollered.

Was nothing nice in Disney? Oh, all right. We had a scary time on the roller coaster ride through darkness on Space Mountain; I always enjoy carousels and Disney has one with handsome horses. And I had a fine meal at the Empress Room aboard a riverboat anchored by the shopping complex, probably the only restaurant on the premises that doesn't microwave toast.

The next day, we left Disney World for Cypress Gardens, one of the many attractions beckoning in the Orlando area and bearing names like Sea World, Wet 'n Wild, Gatorland, Circus World, Monkey Jungle. And so on. The landscape is flat and straggled-out. The big thing seems to be gas stations with restaurants attached, chicken salad bars and shacks selling hot boiled peanuts. "Yahoo," says my pal. "Wouldn't mind trying a bag of them hot boiled peanuts." We buy a bag. They are soggy and awful. Our proximity to Cypress Gardens is periodically announced by signs for 12 million flowers and the chief attraction, dramatic ducks. (You're in Luck; A Banjo-Playing Duck.)

The gardens are much, much more than just a botanical garden. A water ski show is going on in the stadium. "He hit a wet spot!" exclaims the announcer as a performer disappears into the water. The audience jeers. A child in a carriage leans over and dribbles on my foot. "I wish you'd stop calling America a land of morons," says my friend. "It's not fitting for a foreigner." We pass 12 million flowers and don't miss a one, thanks to helpful signs like: "Look up! Don't miss the orchid." Look has little eyes painted into the o's. "Don't miss the scenic waterfall coming up on your right," warns another sign. "Have you forgotten to load your camera?" wonders a third. "Is America turning into a land of morons?" wonders my companion.

We are too early for the gator show (watch them make pocketbooks right in front of your eyes?). But Bill the Wackie-Quackie man is setting up the duck follies and we sit down just in time to see a duck waddle out onto a tiny stage, and peck at a tiny piano with its beak. "Waddaya call a rich duck?" asks Bill the Wackie-Quackie man of the audience. "A Ritzy Quacker!" he shouts. "Argh, argh" laughs the man in front of us, tugging at his visor cap. Liberace Duck leaves, followed by Kentucky Ducky playing "The Ballad of the Mallard." The Valeducktorian is introduced to a pleased audience as we fly to our car.

We press on to Circus World, which seems to have suffered an unexplained evacuation prior to our arrival. It doesn't seem to affect the place, which looks designed and run by a computer. A sound system keeps churning out electronic organ grinder music, the rides dip and turn even though there is no one waiting to get on. Holding pre-wrapped cotton candy we stand for a few horrible minutes on the deserted Avenue of Spins and Grins before peering into the concrete Big Top. An announcer is introducing what he calls "our ponderous pachyderms." The beasts do headstands in a ring without sawdust in front of a listless little crowd. The memories of my childhood circuses are stronger than any scent in the wind.

What's it all add up to? The only message I can offer after a few days down here in Central Florida is that America is getting cutified at a far more rapid rate than many of us may be aware of. In gritty New York this mania for babble, alliteration, dumb rhymes—and understandably, sanitation—had largely escaped me. Very few of the places I visited in Disney or its environs seemed to be expecting any functioning adults or intelligent children. They were expecting cartoon characters. And the visitors behave accordingly. At Cypress Gardens, a number of able oldsters very happily tucked themselves into wheel-barrow-shaped wheelchairs. At Sea World, a theme park offering large fish in large tanks, adults obligingly stuffed kids into dolphin-shaped carriages.

In fact, it was at Sea World that I had a brief encounter with insanity. There I was holding a snack bought at Snacks 'n Suds, wandering past Fountain Fantasy on my way to Hawaiian Punch Village. Shamu, I thought. Got to find Shamu, the much-praised killer whale. So I fluttered about, finally coming to this big pool with a dark half-submerged hulk at one end. It was very still, not showing an inch of killer tail. Then it moved and I thought, this can't be real, it's a plastic submarine. Shamu? Submarine? I just couldn't tell anymore. It was time to go.

And quicker than you could say Mickey Mouse, we were in the friendly skies having another indescribable meal. Hoop-do-doo, we sang. Hoop-de-doo.

Issac Asimov / A Tourist's Guide to the Moon

The New York Times, January 10, 1982

"Writing is my only interest," claims Isaac Asimov, whose voluminous output easily turns what sounds like an exaggeration into an understatement. The author of well over 200 books, Asimov was born in Russia in 1920. He received a doctorate in biochemistry from Columbia University in 1948 and soon afterwards decided to devote his life to writing.

Most of Asimov's books deal either with science fiction or scientific fact. The Foundation Triology *(1974) is considered a classic of science fiction, while such volumes as* The Chemicals of Life *(1954),* Inside the Atom *(1956),* The Realm of Numbers *(1959), and* The Wellsprings of Life *(1960) have established Asimov as one of the twentieth-century's leading writers on scientific subjects for a general audience.*

It is the year 2082 and the Moon is a settled world. There are 50,000 people who consider themselves Lunarians and who accept the Moon as their home, and of these over 5,000 have been born here and have never visited Earth. Almost all of them live in Luna City, the chief town. When tourism is at its height the total population is well in excess of 100,000.

Lunarians view tourists with mixed emotions. On the one hand, tourists crowd the space lanes and, at times, overload the Moon's living facilities—and the Moon, despite all the advances of the last century, is still not an open world. Its available air and water must be carefully recycled and every drop of water replacement (hundreds of thousands of gallons a year) must be imported.

On the other hand, the Lunarians are proud of their world, have an almost feverish desire to counter the stereotype of the Moon as a bleak and desolate place, and (let us admit) can make use of the money that tourists bring. Most are happy to answer questions and will go out of their way to make visitors feel welcome and comfortable.

Most tourists who arrive are First-Timers, people who have never before left Earth. Many book a popular two-week package that allows them eight days on the Moon. They arrive after a three-day journey in which they have experienced the thrills and inconveniences of weightlessness, and look forward with relief to reaching the surface of a world where up is up and down is down. Despite all indoctrination, however, they seem to expect only one kind of world: one with Earth's surface gravity.

This misconception is heightened by the fact that every effort is made to give the Moon an Earth-like appearance. The ship does not land on the surface, which is undeniably *bleak* (though Lunarians never use the word and would prefer to banish it from the dictionaries). The ship sinks into a huge airlock, and the passengers eventually step into a large visitor's entrance port, in which atmosphere, temperature and décor are completely Earthlike. What cannot be camouflaged, however, is the Moon's surface gravity, which is one-sixth that of Earth.

Nothing, apparently, can prevent that from being a surprise to First-Timers. After the initial shock, the reaction is inevitably amusement, and a tendency to try walking, hopping or jumping, despite the large signs that ring every possible change on the message: "Please do not run or jump, but wait quietly for processing." Falls are frequent, but the low gravity usually prevents serious damage.

The first day is usually a tedious one, for every visitor to the Moon must be thoroughly examined biologically and medically, despite the initial screening on Earth. No undesirable life forms of any sort—seeds, parasites, germs—are permitted on a world in which the ecological balance is carefully controlled.

And the first night is invariably a restless one as natural night movements tend to heave one upward unexpectedly. First-Timers quickly understand the reason for the padded barriers running along every edge of a Lunarian bed. Lunarian hotels are generally very comfortable and are otherwise closely modeled upon their Earth counterparts.

By the second day, most tourists are acclimated to the low gravity and are willing to venture out and begin exploring the Moon. For that purpose there are the Lunar vehicles which are so characteristic of the Moon that their stylized representation serves as the universally recognized symbol of our satellite as an inhabited world. In these sturdy and maneuverable rocket-powered vehicles, passengers would remain perfectly safe if they wore ordinary clothing, although regulations require them to wear spacesuits.

To be sure, these spacesuits are not the bulky and cumbersome affairs of the early astronauts (which are what the word spacesuit seems to imply to Earth people even today) but are remarkably little different from ordinary winter clothing, except for their impermeability, the oxygen cylinders discreetly attached and the arrangement whereby a helmet can be clicked tightly into place in one movement. Under ordinary conditions, the helmet is suspended from the chest—clumsy, but necessary under the rules.

There are two major areas on the Moon's surface that are musts for First-Timers and these do not include any of the natural formations. There is a certain austere interest in the mountains and craters of the Moon, but there is no denying that old bromide: "See one Lunar crater, and you've seen them all." Tycho on this side of the Moon, and Tsiolkovsky on the far side, get their share of tourist attention, but there is frequently expressed disappointment. The fact is that Earth's mountains are more rugged, and the icecaps on land and the complex life patterns undersea lend them a grandeur and interest the Moon cannot duplicate.

Not so the two major human additions to the Lunar landscape. First is the great Lunar mining complex at the Neil Armstrong rift. Almost every step in the mining process is automated and is operated by robots. Tourists view the complex at night, since it is not really practical to remain bathed in the heat and hard radiation of the Sun for any length of time, considering that there is no natural atmosphere to serve as protection.

Solar energy on the Moon is cheap, however, and the mining complex is well-lit. The ship lands on the lip of the rift and the tourists affix their helmets (each one of which is carefully examined by the stewards on board) and emerge to look down at the panorama. There is the vast pit which has been dug out through all the activity of seven decades, but within which there remains an almost unimaginable further supply of metal-rich ore. A never-ending chain of buckets moves along rails to the mass driver, where an electromagnetic field accelerates them and flings them out into space like the world's largest slingshot.

The second sight, smaller but more intensely human, is the great Karl Jansky radio telescope on the far side of the Moon. This is also best viewed at night, and considering that day and night each last two weeks on the Moon, a tourist cannot see both the mining complex and the radio telescope without usually having to wait anywhere from two to ten days in between.

The radio telescope dwarfs anything of the sort on Earth or in space. It is a kilometer in diameter and, with its auxiliary equipment placed elsewhere on the far side, its effective diameter is virtually that of the Moon itself. This radio telescope has the full width of the Moon between itself and the Earth and is free of all but minor stray radio interference from space establishments. It has, in recent decades, detected several radio-wave patterns from nearby stars which may indicate the presence of extraterrestrial intelligence. (Astronomers are still arguing.) Tourists, led through the underground laboratories, watch with rapt attention as the needles mark out the delicate rise and fall of those microwave intensities that may indicate nonhuman intelligence.

Touring the underground microlife vats on the Moon interests many since nutrients are produced in great quantities here. It must be admitted, however, that the odors encountered in the gloomy chambers are not to the ordinary taste.

Nor, it must be said, is Lunarian food. Those Lunar restaurants that cater to the tourist trade advertise "Earth-cooking" as a matter of course, but that means, at best, a rather mediocre and very expensive hamburger. Authentically Lunarian restaurants are more interesting, since they feature microorganismic seasonings, but these are not for everyone. The tourist who acclimates quickly and can eat the largely vegetarian Lunarian specialties with some semblance of pleasure will find himself instantly popular—the Lunarians will consider him almost one of themselves. (Those traveling with children will probably find themselves limited to "Earth-cooking," however—almost no Earth-born child will accept Lunarian food without considerable trouble.)

Lunarian shows are famous and they are not for export since the low surface gravity is of the essence. Expert Lunarian gymnasts can perform "gravity-defying" feats that are simply impossible on Earth, even for gibbons. Tourists cannot fail to be enthralled.

Skiing is the chief Lunar sport. Snow is not needed—under the low gravity, the body presses down against the gritty Lunar surface only lightly, and this reduces the friction to a large extent, making that surface surprisingly slippery. Add to this the manner in which professionals attach small cylinders of argon gas to their shins to produce a layer of gas under the boots which further decreases friction. Down the gentle slope of a Lunar crater and across the lunar surface (which invariably supplies sufficient unevenness to make an excellent obstacle course) the skiers race with incredible grace.

Invariably the more athletically-inclined of the tourists try their hand at it themselves, and though they are helped along, given easy equipment and gentle slopes, they just as invariably find that it is not as easy as it looks. Again, fortunately, the inevitable falls are not as hurtful as they would be on the Earth.

There is no question, though, that of all the tourist attractions on the Moon, that which is the most absorbing is the sky. Since the Moon has no atmosphere, there are no fogs, mists, smoke, or clouds to interfere with an always perfect view. From behind the high-transparency glass of an observatory, every star (non-twinkling) is about 25 percent brighter than it would seem on Earth. The planets, too, are brighter than we are accustomed to, and Venus, at its brightest, is almost mesmerizing in its brilliance.

Because of the Moon's slow rate of rotation, the sky moves at only one-thirtieth the apparent speed of Earth's sky. In a way, this is a disadvantage for one can get tired of an almost-unchanging view. On the other hand it allows a 14-day period of night before the Sun appears on the eastern horizon. The Earth itself is always visible. It goes through all the phases of the Moon in the same order and the same time. It is, however, about 13 times larger in surface area and, when full, 70 times as bright as the full Moon is in our sky. Furthermore, it is covered with a swirling cloud pattern that is always changing and is endlessly fascinating to watch.

Eventually, the Sun appears in the east and direct viewing becomes impossible. Visitors must then watch the sky indirectly by means of a computerized-television set-up in which the Sun is selectively screened out. On television one can see the Sun cross the sky, in a two-week journey, and pass the Earth either above or below. As the Sun nears, the Earth becomes a thinner and thinner crescent and then, after the Sun has passed, the crescent widens again.

Every once in a while, the Sun passes behind the Earth so that its rays are blocked and do not reach the Moon. On the Moon, this eclipse is the supreme sight. The television is turned off and direct viewing is possible again. The Earth becomes a black circle in the sky, within which no star can be seen; a circle that is rimmed by a thin edge of brilliant red-orange light. The circle is nearly four times as wide as the full Moon appears to be in Earth's sky. When the Sun is centered behind the Earth, the circle is equally bright all around. There are bound to be clouds along the rim of the Earth so that the circle may be broken here and there and, at particularly unlucky times, hardly any of it may be visible. At lucky times, all of it may be visible.

In any case, an eclipse of the Sun, as seen from the Moon, produces a vision of a kind that can never be seen from the Earth. The beauty of it must be experienced for descriptions are never adequate. It is not surprising, then, that tourism is always heavy at times when an eclipse is scheduled. Astronomers can predict, far in advance, when these times will come but there is not much use in urging my readers to make their reservations now. All shipping space to the Moon at eclipse time is booked 20 years in advance.

A final word of caution: Although most Lunarians are as honest as their day is long, beware the souvenir-mongers. Almost no souvenir you are offered is worth the money charged. Beware particularly the sidewalk vendors of "moon-rocks." The implication is that something is being offered for sale that is export-forbidden, or that is very rare. This is almost invariably untrue and you will find that you have paid a lot of money for something you could pick up anywhere on the surface—and for which you will have to pay an additional fee for space transportation home. If you must take something back, take photographs—using your own camera.

Susan Jacoby / Too Many Women Are Misconstruing Feminism's Nature

The New York Times, April 14, 1983

A free-lance journalist, Susan Jacoby is the author of three books on life in the Soviet Union and has written extensively on issues of women's rights. In this piece, from the weekly column, "Hers," in The New York Times, *Jacoby discusses the misconceptions and often perjorative definitions attached to the word "feminism."*

fem-i-nism. *n.* 1. the doctrine advocating social and political rights of women equal to those of men; 2. *(sometimes cap.) an organized movement for the attainment of such rights for women.*

The Random House Dictionary
of the English Language

For many young women today, "feminism" is a word with a shady reputation. I first became aware of this depressing fact when I was teaching a magazine writing course at New York University and one of my brighter female students said: "I know from your lectures in class that you consider yourself a feminist. But that surprises me, because you look so feminine."

By "feminine" she meant what both the dictionary and ordinary people mean: that I looked the way women are usually expected to look: I wear lipstick, comb my hair (streak it, too!) and am as likely to be found in a skirt as in blue jeans. I don't wear combat boots or have bulging biceps. My student was really saying she didn't understand how someone who was committed to equal rights for women could also display conventional feminine attributes.

This point of view is held by a surprising number of well-educated young women in their early 20's, those who have benefited the most from the professional opportunities now open to them as a result of battles waged by the feminist movement over the past 15 years.

To a woman who is proud to call herself a feminist, the most disturbing aspect of this phenomenon is not its naïveté but its adoption of the age-old patriarchal assumption that a woman who wants the same intellectual, economic and professional opportunities as a man is rejecting her sex rather than the disabilities imposed on her because of her sex.

Among organized feminists of the older generation, a common response is to insist that young women are reacting not against feminism but only against the word and its "unfair" association with strident anger. This was typified by Eleanor Smeal, outgoing president of the National Organization for Women, in an interview with Susan Bolotin that appeared last fall in The New York Times Magazine.

"People don't even like the word 'discrimination,' " Mrs. Smeal said. "One of the reasons is that they don't want you to think they have a bellyache, that they are not O.K. And the word 'feminist' is still considered a militant word. The best way of dealing with all these things is not to use catch-words. Talk about actual situations."

This approach, which suggests that resistance to feminism is largely a question of semantics, evades the concrete issues raised by that resistance. The meanings people attach to words are of the utmost importance. When a political term becomes unpopular—whether the word is feminist, liberal, conservative, socialist or capitalist—the unpopularity arises not only from a misunderstanding of what the word actually means but from genuine distrust of the ideas it represents.

My students told me they objected to feminism because it made women bitter, angry and unattractive to men. They said they felt that feminists had placed too much emphasis on careers at the expense of both romance and family life. All of them planned to take 5 to 10 years off from work to raise their children and then return to rewarding, well-paid jobs.

Most significant, my students told me that any form of sex discrimination could be overcome by individual effort and that older feminists tended to blame personal inadequacies on "the system."

Many of these beliefs can, of course, be attributed entirely to insufficient life experience. Recent college graduates do not know any more about what it takes to build a career than they know about bringing up children. The idea that one can take 10 years off from work without incurring adverse professional consequences is as phantasmagorial as the notion that one will give birth to a child who never gives its mother a moment's cause for worry.

Furthermore, these women have not experienced the entry-level discrimination that was taken for granted in the 1950's and 60's. They do not realize that their individual abilities would have counted for very little in a system in which women made up fewer than 5 percent of first-year law and medical school classes. The feminist movement has opened those doors; women in their early 20's have not had occasion to knock on doors still closed.

But it is no comfort for a feminist in her 30's to sit back, secure in the knowledge that life will change the minds of young women who do not now wish to identify themselves with feminism. The whole point of movements for social change is to make it unnecessary for each new generation to learn the same lessons over again. The older generation of feminists is in roughly the same position as scientists who have been pressured to teach creationism as a respectable alternative to the theory of evolution.

The question is: What can be done to rectify the situation?

One common response is to pretend not to be angry at all. The dishonesty of this posture is quickly, and correctly, perceived by the young. Feminism is concerned with justice, and anyone who cares about justice is bound to be angry at some of the people some of the time. There is nothing wrong with anger—and we should say so with no apologies—as long as it is directed at those who are responsible for special injustices, not at the whole world.

Is it also unrealistic to adopt the position that the most obvious goals of the feminist movement, like equal pay for equal work, have already been achieved and we must now concentrate on achieving the nirvana of a more "human" workplace, in which both men and women will be able to enjoy the rewards of equal rights and responsibilities. A workplace that takes family and child-rearing needs into account is a laudable goal, but, as the defeat of the proposed Federal equal rights amendment clearly demonstrated, we are far from a consensus on the desirability of most basic forms of equality between the sexes.

I do not believe that the amendment was turned down solely because some people identified it with lesbian rights and unisex toilets or because the right wing spent enormous amounts of money to oppose it (although these elements certainly played a role in its defeat). The amendment was rejected because a great many people still do not believe in equal rights for women.

That is why I believe Eleanor Smeal is wrong in suggesting that opposition to feminism can be neutralized by avoiding the word. Feminism is considered "militant" by many members of both sexes because equal rights for women is in fact a radical idea. By "radical" I mean not the commonly used political pejorative but the original definition, derived from the Latin word for root. Feminists should not be reluctant to identy themselves with an honorable tradition rooted in issues that every woman—regardless of how much she might prefer to be seen solely as an individual rather than as a member of the sex—must eventually face.

Ann Landers / Love or Infatuation?

San Diego *Union Tribune*, May 25, 1983

Esther Pauline Lederer was born on July 4, 1918, in Sioux City, Iowa. In 1955, the Chicago Sun-Times *was looking for a replacement for Ruth Crowley, who had written popular articles under the name of Ann Landers until her death earlier that year. Esther Lederer was chosen to fill this position and has gone on to make Ann Landers a household word.*

"Ann Landers" is one of the most widely read advice columns today, and appears in more than nine hundred newspapers across the country. Ann receives almost one thousand letters daily asking for advice on every imaginable topic. In addition to her frank, down-to-earth, and sometimes wisecracking advice, Lander's column also provides a kind of open forum where people can speak to each other through their letters.

DEAR ANN LANDERS: When I was in high school, I clipped your column that described the difference between love and infatuation. I looked at it often, and it saved me from making some foolish mistakes.

I'm a graduate student now and find myself in need of some solid emotional grounding. I wish I had that column. Will you hunt it up and run it again?

STARRY-EYED IN KANSAS

DEAR STARRY: It's one of the most requested columns of all. Thanks for asking.

LOVE OR INFATUATION?

Infatuation is instant desire. It is one set of glands calling to another. Love is friendship that has caught fire. It takes root and grows—one day at a time.

Infatuation is marked by a feeling of insecurity. You are excited and eager, but not genuinely happy. There are nagging doubts, unanswered questions, little bits and pieces about your beloved that you would just as soon not examine too closely. They might spoil the dream.

Love is quiet understanding and the mature acceptance of imperfection. It is real. It gives you strength and grows beyond you—to bolster your beloved. You are warmed by his presence, even when he is away. Miles do not separate you. You want him nearer. But near or far, you know he is yours and you can wait.

Infatuation says, "We must get married right away. I can't risk losing him."

Love says, "Be patient. Don't panic. He is yours. Plan your future with confidence."

Infatuation has an element of sexual excitement. If you are honest, you will admit it is difficult to be in one another's company unless you are sure it will end in intimacy. Love is the maturation of friendship. You must be friends before you can be lovers.

Infatuation lacks confidence. When he's away, you wonder if he's cheating. Sometimes you even check.

Love means trust. You are calm, secure and unthreatened. He feels that trust, and it makes him even more trustworthy.

Infatuation might lead you to do things you'll regret later, but love never will.

Love is an upper. It makes you look up. It makes you think up. It makes you a better person than you were before.

DEAR ANN LANDERS: Tonight I came across a shocking figure. Are you aware, Ann, that one in five Americans can't read?

When I receive thank-you notes from my teenage nieces and nephews, I am appalled at their poor grammar, spelling and penmanship. How do they get into high school when their literary skills are clearly inadequate? What can be done about this?

—MORRISTOWN, N.J.

DEAR N.J.: Many high school graduates can't read or spell or put together a grammatically correct sentence because too many teachers promote poor students to get rid of them. Shocking, isn't it?

We need higher standards, better pay for teachers, remedial classes and tutors for those who have fallen behind. If we don't get serious about this problem soon, this country will find itself in big trouble.

DEAR ANN: I cheered when I read the letter from the clergyman who was displeased with parents who let their kids cry and talk and disrupt the congregation while he was trying to deliver a sermon he had worked on all week. I hope our pastor read it and changes his tune.

Our church has an average attendance of 225. We have two nurseries—one for babies and one for toddlers and older. A couple behind us chose to bring their 2-month-old infant into the church. The child cried *loud* throughout the service. Several people gave the parents long, hard looks. We even turned around and stared a couple of times. They ignored all signs of displeasure.

Two weeks later the pastor said he had something on his mind and proceeded to give us a scorching lecture on "tolerance." He said he had worked hard and long to get a certain couple to join the congregation and because we had the audacity to give them dirty looks when their baby cried they resigned their membership. He ended by saying, "I can talk louder than any baby can cry! Don't ever let this happen again!"

The tone of his voice was like that of a parent reprimanding a child. We felt insulted. May we have your opinion?

—JUST PEW

DEAR PEW: I don't wish to speak unkindly of a servant of the Lord, but I think your pastor has cornflakes where his brains belong. To chew out his congregation because they resented having their Sunday sermon ruined by a crying baby (whose parents could easily have taken him to the nursery) was childish. I hope someone will send him a clipping of the next letter.

DEAR ANN LANDERS: Recently my husband and I attended a church play. Before the performance began, the minister appeared on the stage and said, "Crying babies and disruptive children, like good intentions, should be carried out immediately. Thank you for your cooperation."

He received a big round of applause. Please print this so other clergymen can take a page from his book.

—STILL SMILING IN OKLAHOMA CITY

DEAR OKLAHOMA: So am I. Thanks for sharing.

DEAR ANN LANDERS: This letter is for the millions of women who are being beaten by their husbands and boyfriends. You are not alone. Professionals estimate that 70 percent of all emergency room assault cases are battered wives. We, the battered women, come from every economic and intellectual segment of society. Some folks believe we enjoy getting knocked around and that we provoke the attacks. What an absurd notion! No one needs to provoke a wife-beater.

Why does she stay? Because she doesn't realize that there is a place she can go. Battered women, hear me! You have a right to live in peace! You have the right to share your feelings and not be isolated and terrified. There are shelters all over the United States for you and your children. They will take you in with no money. Write to the National Coalition Against Domestic Violence, P.O. Box 31015, Santa Barbara, Calif. 93105 for more information and make plans now to change your life.

—ALIVE AND WELL IN AUSTIN, TEXAS

DEAR TEX: Bless you for all the women you helped today.

Byron Lutz / Type of Vehicle You Drive Reveals Your Personality

National Enquirer, May 24, 1983

The National Enquirer, *with a circulation of over three million, is a weekly tabloid sold principally at supermarkets and newsstands. Specializing in what it calls "attention-grabbing" articles and photos, the paper often features celebrity profiles, scandals, the occult, medical "breakthroughs," curiosities, adventure tales, and items offering some special angle on whatever happens to be in the news.*

The following two brief articles, by Byron Lutz and Arline Brecker respectively, represent a popular approach to individual psychology, one that frequently finds its way into the mass media. (See Marshall Schuon's "Cars and Self-Image" in Advertising for a more sophisticated version of Byron Lutz's article.)

The kind of vehicle you drive reveals your personality, say behavior experts.

"Surveys have shown a direct relationship between automobiles and personality," said California psychologist Dr. Stephen Brown.

Here are the personality traits revealed by different kinds of "wheels," according to Dr. Brown and New York psychiatrist Dr. Emory Breitner.

Subcompact: These drivers like to be in control, and it's easy to be in control of a tiny subcompact. They're frugal, pragmatic people who are in a hurry. Subcompact owners don't want to be bogged down by a big car—with payments to match.

Mid-size or Compact: Reserved and conservative, these drivers rarely make moves without considerable thought. They're sensitive and emotional—but never foolish. They don't gamble, they check things out, work hard and are honest to a fault. These drivers like to blend in, not make waves.

Full-size: The drivers of these giants like to do everything in a big way. They're ambitious, desire money and material goods—and are literally driven to success.

They like big homes—and if they throw a party, they want it to be an all-out affair with people singing, eating and having a ball. They aim for important jobs, and can't stand a cramped office or a tiny car that cramps their style.

Station Wagon: Family comes first for these people. They're good neighbors, very friendly, enjoy children and animals, and will always try to help you out if you have a problem. Image isn't important. They just want to use their station wagon to enjoy life.

Jeep: These drivers are trailblazers who love adventure. They enjoy striking out on their own, and don't mind questioning authority. They're practical, energetic survivors who like to win under tough conditions, and work best when they can make their own rules.

Convertible: The top's up one day, and down the next. These drivers are exactly like their car—changing from day to day. Convertible owners are impulsive, quick-witted and restless. But they're excellent at communicating ideas and love to shine on short-term projects—jobs where they can see instant results. They love art, music and creative activities.

Pickup Truck: These people are ready to tackle any job. They have a determined, fighting spirit, and a do-it-yourself attitude that makes them self-sufficient. They're forceful, opinionated, and like to pitch right in and get a job done.

Sportscar Hardtop: The cars are fast and fashionable—so are the drivers. They're impatient, quick-paced and flashy. They like to have a lot of irons in the fire, and if a job falls through, they have another lined up and are ready to move quickly.

Hatchback: This car is a cross between a station wagon, economy car and sports car—and the people who drive them are practical, but dreamers at the same time. They're neat, discriminating and good organizers, as the practical, smart hatchback layout suggests.

Van: These drivers love to be comfortable and feel at home no matter where they are. They're romantic and idealistic, and can't stand quarreling and friction. Van drivers love peace. And as their vehicles are big enough to haul things they enjoy collecting.

Arline Brecker / Puzzles You Enjoy Most Reveal Your Personality

National Enquirer, May 31, 1983

The type of puzzle you enjoy reveals your personality, says a psychologist.

Here's what you're really like if you take pleasure in solving the following kinds of puzzles, according to Dr. Herbert Hoffman, director of the Hillside Psychological Guidance Center, Queens Village, N.Y.

Crossword: "You are well-read, work hard at keeping informed and have an excellent memory," said Dr. Hoffman, a former associate professor of education and psychology at City University of New York. "If someone asks you a question that you can't answer, you will look it up."

Rubik's Cube: You have the enviable ability to put thoughts into action. You have a high tolerance for frustration, so you stick with a task no matter how unpleasant or monotonous it is.

Anagram: "If you enjoy these puzzles, which consist of scrambled words, you frequently plunge headlong into knotty situations," said Dr. Hoffman. "But you can be depended on to get at the truth and straighten things out."

Word Find: You're well-organized, hard-driving and ambitious. When you make an important decision, you stand by it. And you can't be talked into doing anything against your better judgment.

Take-Aparts or Put-Togethers: If you like Chinese rings, intertwined nails or locking blocks, you're a person who responds best to touch. You're a "hugger" and "kisser" who prefers expressing affection physically. And you take a "hands on" approach to problems.

Jigsaw Puzzles: When it comes to problem-solving, you're not afraid to try something new. "For example," said Dr. Hoffman, "when faced with the problem of taking a group of visiting relatives sight-seeing, you'd rent a van rather than arrange for cars to transport them."

Cryptograms: You're a private person, not likely to divulge personal affairs. You don't like to borrow, and prefer to think your own way out of a problem.

Connect-the-Dots: You're a disciplined, highly responsible individual. Said Dr. Hoffman: "When faced with problems, you adopt a logical, step-by-step approach."

MAGAZINES

I'm obsessed by Time Magazine.
I read it every week.
Its cover stares at me every time I slink past the corner candystore.

ALLEN GINSBERG, "AMERICA"

From an early exposé of child labor violations to an analysis of television violence, the following selection of American magazine writing illustrates a variety of prose styles and compositional procedures adopted by writers to address many different levels of reading interest and aptitude.

No magazine is addressed to everyone. Though all magazines are eager to increase their circulation, they nevertheless operate with a fairly limited market in mind. A magazine's "image" is often as firmly established as the "brand image" devised by advertisers to ensure a commercially reliable consumer identification with a product. "What Sort of Man Reads *Playboy?*" is, according to that magazine's advertisement, a question easily answered, if not by the details of the photograph in the ad, then certainly by the language describing what the "typical" *Playboy* reader is like (see Advertising). Depending on the issue you look at, he may be "urbane," "stylish," "his own man," "literate," "free-wheeling," "an individualist." "Can a Girl Be Too Busy" and "Is This How You See Our Readers?" (see Advertising) offer further instances, though playfully exaggerated, of a magazine's personification of its public image through characters and voices that supposedly convey the life style, or desired life style, of its readers.

Regardless of the ways a magazine goes about promoting its public identity, the type of audience it wants to attract can be seen in the total environment created by such material as the magazine's fiction and nonfiction, its advertisements, editorial commentary, paper quality, and overall physical design. An article in *The New Yorker,* for example, is forced to compete for its readers' attention with glossy scenes of high fashion, mixed drinks, and the allure of exotic places. Yet not all magazines imagine or address their readers in quite such fashionable terms. An article appearing in either *Good Housekeeping, Harper's, Psychology Today,* or *Scientific American* does not usually take its tone from the modish world that forms the context of magazines like *The New Yorker, Playboy, Cosmopolitan, Vogue* and *Esquire*. For example, advertisements for precision instruments, various types of machinery, automobiles, and corporate accountability, along with mathematical games, puzzles, and instructions for home experiments, surround the technical articles published in *Scientific American.* The readers of a magazine like *Good Housekeeping* are expected to be particularly attentive to products, services, and expertise that promise to improve a family's immediate domestic environment.

The "ideal reader" for a given magazine—the reader as "housewife," "playboy," "academic," "outdoorsman"—is a vague entity, invented by the magazine more for simple identification than realistic description. No one is *just* a "housewife" or an "academic," even assuming that we know exactly who or what these categories stand for in the first place. Naturally, labels like these suggest different associations to different people. For example, the audiences imagined by Hugh Hefner for *Playboy* and by Lew Dietz in "The Myth of the Boss Bear" for *True* may both be adventurous males, but they certainly are men who find their sport in different environments. The risks and failure detailed by Dietz in his personal adventure in the outdoors would not be nearly as alluring to the self-described "urban male" readers of *Playboy* who, as one recent ad put it, "enjoy mixing up cocktails and an *hors d'oeuvre* or two, putting a little mood on the phonograph and inviting in a female acquaintance for a quiet discussion on Picasso, Nietzsche, jazz, or sex." To contend, then, that the audience for Hefner's and Dietz's articles are both male and to let it go at that, is like arguing that the reader of an article in an issue of *TV Guide* can be described solely as someone who has the capacity to watch television.

Some affinity surely exists between the readership a magazine commercially promotes and the individual reader a particular article within that magazine assumes. But to characterize more accurately the audience addressed by a particular article, we need to go beyond the conveniently stereotyped reader presupposed by the magazine's title or its public image. For instance, *Everybody's*, a popular magazine first published nationwide in 1903, certainly could not appeal to everyone in America. Like any other magazine, it selected articles that approximated most closely the style of talk and the strategies of persuasion it felt its readers were most accustomed to. For a number of years, *Everybody's* played a prominent role in helping to develop the mode of American journalism that Theodore Roosevelt scornfully christened "muckraking." Along with other leading newspapers and periodicals, *Everybody's* featured a number of successful articles devoted to exposing public scandals and attacking vice and corruption in business and politics. Its readers were assumed to be civic-minded, generally well informed people concerned with what they felt was a growing network of moral irresponsibility on the part of public administrators and industrial leaders.

William Hard's article "De Kid Wot Works at Night," which appeared in the January 1908 issue of *Everybody's*, was directed to readers already aware of the abuses of child labor and the insidious corruption of urban life through their reading of some of the very newspapers that Hard's young subjects worked so energetically to sell. The boys Hard investigated earned their living out on the streets at night, where they were sadly vulnerable to the sundry temptations of a big city after dark. Hard argued seriously for legislative reform:

> Mr. J. J. Sloan, when he was superintendent of the John Worthy School (which is the local municipal juvenile reformatory), reported that the newsboys committed to his care were, on the average, one-third below the stature and one-third below the strength of average ordinary boys of the same age. In the face of testimony of this kind, which could be duplicated from every city in the United States, it seems absurd to talk about the educative influence of the street. That it has a certain educative influence in undeniable, but it is equally undeniable that the boys who are exposed to this influence should be prevented, by proper legislation, from exposing themselves to it for too many hours a day and should especially be prevented from exposing themselves to it for even a single hour after seven o'clock in the evening.

The facts are certainly unpleasant, and Hard is confident that his readers will be persuaded by the weight of professional testimony and their own natural sympathy for the plight of such unfortunate children.

Yet Hard himself seems not always convinced that his newsboys and messengers are the hopeless victims of a ruthless economic system. It is precisely "after seven o'clock in the evening" that the children he is writing about come to life. The following description portrays "Jelly," the newsboy Hard chooses as his representative "case," and his little sister in ways not nearly so pathetic as engaging:

> At half past ten he went to an elevated railway station to meet his little sister. She was ten years old. She had dressed herself for the part. From her ragged and scanty wardrobe she had chosen her most ragged and her scantiest clothes.
>
> Accompanied by his sister, "Jelly" then went to a flower shop and bought a bundle of carnations at closing prices. With these carnations he took his sister to the entrance of the Grand Opera House. There she sold the whole bundle to the people coming out from the performance. Her appearance was picturesque and pitiful. Her net profit from the sale of her flowers was usually about thirty-five cents.

Life on the street surely has its "undeniable educative influence." If roaming the streets at night stunted "Jelly's" growth, it certainly did not cripple his resourcefulness and imagination.

Hard's attitude toward the life style of "Jelly" and his associates is ambivalent. The reader of the article is asked to acknowledge the seriousness of the terrible conditions surrounding the lives of impoverished children in the city and, at the same time, to recognize that such circumstances do not always culminate in the melodramatic ruination of their victims. Hard transforms "Jelly" into an entrepreneur responsive to the fluctuations in the flower market—he buys carnations at "closing prices." "Jelly" also knows how to profit from the "ragged and scanty wardrobe" of his little sister. She, too, willingly participates in the act, choosing only those clothes that will show her poverty to best advantage. Hard's diction ("dressed . . . for the part," "most ragged," "scantiest," "picturesque") alerts the reader to the theatricality implicit in the attempts of these children to earn a living.

It should be clear from the language of the passage that Hard does not think of "Jelly" and his sister simply as "pitiful" figures. In fact, the word "pitiful" works not so much to move his readers to compassion for the abject condition of the children as much as it does to describe the self-conscious ways the children display themselves before a fashionable urban audience. From a sociological standpoint, "Jelly" and his sister may very well be "pitiful," but they are also *acting* "pitiful," and the awareness of that distinction is what makes it so difficult for Hard to write a disinterested report wholly committed to immediate legislative reform. Hard's predicament in this article is that the corruption he is striving to eliminate as a reformer sustains the very set of characters he finds, as a writer, so appealing in their verbal energy and playful perseverance.

The attractiveness of the kids that work at night and Hard's reluctance to render them merely in sociological terms prompt him to fictionalize their lives, treating them more like characters in a short story than as subjects to be documented. He takes us beyond the limits of factual observation by vividly imagining many details of the newsboys' behavior in situations that must have been annoyingly inaccessible to him. Whatever *Everybody's* public image and vested interests, Hard's article presupposes a reader attuned to both the need for legislative action and the nuances of parody. Like Gay Talese's example of "new journalism" that also appears in this section, Hard's piece exists in a territory somewhere between the reportorial prose of newspapers and the inventions of fiction.

With the exception of highly specialized journals and periodicals, most magazines, despite their commercial or artistic differences, want their articles to be both informative and entertaining, responding to those timely topics the renowned American novelist and magazine editor, William Dean Howells, once termed "contemporarnics." Pick up any popular magazine and you will be sure to come across essays offering information about some subject that is a topic of current public interest. Sex, celebrities, success, catastrophes, scandals, the bizarre—it would be difficult to find a magazine that does not contain a single article with a contemporary slant on one of these perennial subjects. Precisely how these subjects will be rendered in prose most often depends on the vigorous interplay between an author's style and purpose and whatever specific compositional standards or general "tone" the magazine encourages or requires.

Jack London / The Story of an Eyewitness

[*An Account of the San Francisco Earthquake*]

Collier's Weekly, May 1906

Jack London (1876–1916), a native of San Francisco, happened to be working near the city when the earthquake struck on the evening of April 16, 1906. An internationally prominent novelist, reporter, and social critic, London telegraphed the following vivid eyewitness account of the disaster to Collier's Weekly *for which he was paid twenty-five cents a word. London's dramatic report, which appeared in an issue devoted entirely to photographs and articles on the earthquake, was perfectly suited to* Collier's *characteristically hard-hitting journalism. With a weekly circulation of well over one million,* Collier's *was the country's leading public affairs magazine and an important precursor of modern photojournalism.*

The earthquake shook down in San Francisco hundreds of thousands of dollars' worth of walls and chimneys. But the conflagration that followed burned up hundreds of millions of dollars' worth of property. There is no estimating within hundreds of millions the actual damage wrought. Not in history has a modern imperial city been so completely destroyed. San Francisco is gone! Nothing remains of it but memories and a fringe of dwelling houses on its outskirts. Its industrial section is wiped out. Its social and residential section is wiped out. The factories and warehouses, the great stores and newspaper buildings, the hotels and the palaces of the nabobs, are all gone. Remains only the fringe of dwelling houses on the outskirts of what was once San Francisco.

Within an hour after the earthquake shock the smoke of San Francisco's burning was a lurid tower visible a hundred miles away. And for three days and nights this lurid tower swayed in the sky, reddening the sun, darkening the day, and filling the land with smoke.

On Wednesday morning at a quarter past five came the earthquake. A minute later the flames were leaping upward. In a dozen different quarters south of Market Street, in the working-class ghetto, and in the factories, fires started. There was no opposing the flames. There was no organization, no communication. All the cunning adjustments of a twentieth-century city had been smashed by the earthquake. The streets were humped into ridges and depressions and piled with debris of fallen walls. The steel rails were twisted into perpendicular and horizontal angles. The telephone and telegraph systems were disrupted. And the great water mains had burst. All the shrewd contrivances and safeguards of man had been thrown out of gear by thirty seconds' twitching of the earth crust.

By Wednesday afternoon, inside of twelve hours, half the heart of the city was gone. At that time I watched the vast conflagration from out on the bay. It was dead calm. Not a flicker of wind stirred. Yet from every side wind was pouring in upon the city. East, west, north, and south, strong winds were blowing upon the doomed city. The heated air rising made an enormous suck. Thus did the fire of itself build its own colossal chimney through the atmosphere. Day and night, this dead calm continued, and yet, near to the flames, the wind was often half a gale, so mighty was the suck.

The edict which prevented chaos was the following proclamation by Mayor E. E. Schmitz:

"The Federal Troops, the members of the Regular Police Force, and all Special Police Officers have been authorized to KILL any and all persons found engaged in looting or in the commission of any other crime.

"I have directed all the Gas and Electric Lighting Companies not to turn on gas or electricity until I order them to do so; you may therefore expect the city to remain in darkness for an indefinite time.

"I request all citizens to remain at home from darkness until daylight of every night until order is restored.

"I warn all citizens of the danger of fire from damaged or destroyed chimneys, broken or leaking gas pipes or fixtures, or any like cause."

Wednesday night saw the destruction of the very heart of the city. Dynamite was lavishly used, and many of San Francisco's proudest structures were crumbled by man himself into ruins, but there was no withstanding the onrush of the flames. Time and again successful stands were made by the fire fighters, and every time the flames flanked around on either side, or came up from the rear, and turned to defeat the hard-won victory.

An enumeration of the buildings destroyed would be a directory of San Francisco. An enumeration of the buildings undestroyed would be a line and several addresses. An enumeration of the deeds of heroism would stock a library and bankrupt the Carnegie medal fund. An enumeration of the dead—will never be made. All vestiges of them were destroyed by the flames. The number of the victims of the earthquake will never be known. South of Market Street, where the loss of life was particularly heavy, was the first to catch fire.

Remarkable as it may seem, Wednesday night, while the whole city crashed and roared into ruin, was a quiet night. There were no crowds. There was no shouting and yelling. There was no hysteria, no disorder. I passed Wednesday night in the part of the advancing flames, and in all those terrible hours I saw not one woman who wept, not one man who was excited, not one person who was in the slightest degree panic-stricken.

Before the flames, throughout the night, fled tens of thousands of homeless ones. Some were wrapped in blankets. Others carried bundles of bedding and dear household treasures. Sometimes a whole family was harnessed to a carriage or delivery wagon that was weighted down with their possessions. Baby buggies, toy wagons, and gocarts were used as trucks, while every other person was dragging a trunk. Yet everybody was gracious. The most perfect courtesy obtained. Never in all San Francisco's history were her people so kind and courteous as on this night of terror.

All the night these tens of thousands fled before the flames. Many of them, the poor people from the labor ghetto, had fled all day as well. They had left their homes burdened with possessions. Now and again they lightened up, flinging out upon the street clothing and treasures they had dragged for miles.

They held on longest to their trunks, and over these trunks many a strong man broke his heart that night. The hills of San Francisco are steep, and up these hills, mile after mile, were the trunks dragged. Everywhere were trunks, with across them lying their exhausted owners, men and women. Before the march of the flames were flung picket lines of soldiers. And a block at a time, as the flames advanced, these pickets retreated. One of their tasks was to keep the trunk pullers moving. The exhausted creatures, stirred on by the menace of bayonets, would arise and struggle up the steep pavements, pausing from weakness every five or ten feet.

Often after surmounting a heart-breaking hill, they would find another wall of flame advancing upon them at right angles and be compelled to change anew the line of their retreat. In the end, completely played out, after toiling for a dozen hours like giants, thousands of them were compelled to abandon their trunks. Here the shopkeepers and soft members of the middle class were at a disadvantage. But the workingmen dug holes in vacant lots and back yards and buried their trunks.

At nine o'clock Wednesday evening I walked down through miles and miles of magnificent buildings and towering skyscrapers. Here was no fire. All was in perfect order. The police patrolled the streets. Every building had its watchman at the door. And yet it was doomed, all of it. There was no water. The dynamite was giving out. And at right angles two different conflagrations were sweeping down upon it.

At one o'clock in the morning I walked down through the same section. Everything still stood intact. There was no fire. And yet there was a change. A rain of ashes was falling. The watchmen at the doors were gone. The police had been withdrawn. There were no firemen, no fire engines, no men fighting with dynamite. The district had been absolutely abandoned. I stood at the corner of Kearney and Market, in the very innermost heart of San Francisco. Kearney Street was deserted. Half a dozen blocks away it was burning on both sides. The street was a wall of flame. And against this wall of flame, silhouetted sharply, were two United States cavalrymen sitting on their horses, calmly watching. That was all. Not another person was in sight. In the intact heart of the city two troopers sat on their horses and watched.

Surrender was complete. There was no water. The sewers had long since been pumped dry. There was no dynamite. Another fire had broken out further uptown, and now from three sides conflagrations were sweeping down. The fourth side had been burned earlier in the day. In that direction stood the tottering walls of the Examiner Building, the burned-out Call Building, the smoldering ruins of the Grand Hotel, and the gutted, devastated, dynamited Palace Hotel.

The following will illustrate the sweep of the flames and the inability of men to calculate their spread. At eight o'clock Wednesday evening I passed through Union Square. It was packed with refugees. Thousands of them had gone to bed on the grass. Government tents had been set up, supper was being cooked, and the refugees were lining up for free meals.

At half-past one in the morning three sides of Union Square were in flames. The fourth side, where stood the great St. Francis Hotel, was still holding out. An hour later, ignited from top and sides, the St. Francis was flaming heavenward. Union Square, heaped high with mountains of trunks, was deserted. Troops, refugees, and all had retreated.

It was at Union Square that I saw a man offering a thousand dollars for a team of horses. He was in charge of a truck piled high with trunks from some hotel. It had been hauled here into what was considered safety, and the horses had been taken out. The flames were on three sides of the square, and there were no horses.

Also, at this time, standing beside the truck, I urged a man to seek safety in flight. He was all but hemmed in by several conflagrations. He was an old man and he was on crutches. Said he: "Today is my birthday. Last night I was worth thirty thousand dollars. I bought five bottles of wine, some delicate fish, and other things for my birthday dinner. I have had no dinner, and all I own are these crutches."

I convinced him of his danger and started him limping on his way. An hour later, from a distance, I saw the truckload of trunks burning merrily in the middle of the street.

On Thursday morning, at a quarter past five, just twenty-four hours after the earthquake, I sat on the steps of a small residence of Nob Hill. With me sat Japanese, Italians, Chinese, and Negroes—a bit of the cosmopolitan flotsam of the wreck of the city. All about were the palaces of the nabob pioneers of Forty-nine. To the east and south, at right angles, were advancing two mighty walls of flame.

I went inside with the owner of the house on the steps of which I sat. He was cool and cheerful and hospitable. "Yesterday morning," he said, "I was worth six hundred thousand dollars. This morning this house is all I have left. It will go in fifteen minutes." He pointed to a large cabinet. "That is my wife's collection of china. This rug upon which we stand is a present. It cost fifteen hundred dollars. Try that piano. Listen to its tone. There are few like it. There are no horses. The flames will be here in fifteen minutes."

Outside, the old Mark Hopkins residence, a palace, was just catching fire. The troops were falling back and driving refugees before them. From every side came the roaring of flames, the crashing of walls, and the detonations of dynamite.

I passed out of the house. Day was trying to dawn through the smoke pall. A sickly light was creeping over the face of things. Once only the sun broke through the smoke pall, blood-red, and showing quarter its usual size. The smoke pall itself, viewed from beneath, was a rose color that pulsed and fluttered with lavender shades. Then it turned to mauve and yellow and dun. There was no sun. And so dawned the second day on stricken San Francisco.

An hour later I was creeping past the shattered dome of the City Hall. Than it there was no better exhibit of the destructive force of the earthquake. Most of the stones had been shaken from the great dome, leaving standing the naked framework of steel. Market Street was piled high with the wreckage, and across the wreckage lay the overthrown pillars of the City Hall shattered into short crosswise sections.

This section of the city, with the exception of the Mint and the Post Office, was already a waste of smoking ruins. Here and there through the smoke, creeping warily under the shadows of tottering walls, emerged occasional men and women. It was like the meeting of the handful of survivors after the day of the end of the world.

On Mission Street lay a dozen steers, in a neat row stretching across the street, just as they had been struck down by the flying ruins of the earthquake. The fire had passed through afterward and roasted them. The human dead had been carried away before the fire came. At another place on Mission Street I saw a milk wagon. A steel telegraph pole had smashed down sheer through the driver's seat and crushed the front wheels. The milk cans lay scattered around.

All day Thursday and all Thursday night, all day Friday and Friday night, the flames still raged.

Friday night saw the flames finally conquered, though not until Russian Hill and Telegraph Hill had been swept and three quarters of a mile of wharves and docks had been licked up.

The great stand of the fire fighters was made Thursday night on Van Ness Avenue. Had they failed here, the comparatively few remaining houses of the city would have been swept.

Here were the magnificent residences of the second generation of San Francisco nabobs, and these, in a solid zone, were dynamited down across the path of the fire. Here and there the flames leaped the zone, but these fires were beaten out, principally by the use of wet blankets and rugs.

San Francisco, at the present time, is like the crater of a volcano, around which are camped tens of thousands of refugees. At the Presidio alone are at least twenty thousand. All the surrounding cities and towns are jammed with the homeless ones, where they are being cared for by the relief committees. The refugees were carried free by the railroads to any point they wished to go, and it is estimated that over one hundred thousand people have left the peninsula on which San Francisco stood. The government has the situation in hand, and thanks to the immediate relief given by the whole United States, there is not the slightest possibility of a famine. The bankers and businessmen have already set about making preparations to rebuild San Francisco.

DISCUSSION QUESTIONS

1. Having read Jack London's essay carefully, work back over it once more and note the significant words and phrases that you find are repeated. What is the

purpose of such repetition? Examine the development of London's sentences. Do they work primarily through logic? Emotion? Accumulation of detail? How does this strategy seem best suited to London's occasion and audience?

2. What terms does London use to measure the disastrous effects of the San Francisco earthquake? Does he see the event from a personal or an objective point of view? Does he use, for example, aesthetic, economic, sociological, or psychological language to define his response?

3. Contrast London's point of view and the effects that perspective elicits from his audience with the eyewitness report of another disaster written by William L. Laurence (see Press).

William Hard / De Kid Wot Works at Night

Everybody's Magazine, January 1908

Everybody's Magazine *(1899–1929) was a leading advocate of social, economic, and political reform in the early years of the twentieth century. When William Hard's article appeared, the magazine had well over one-half million readers. Although the self-consciously melodramatic and playful tone of Hard's prose may have surprised an audience accustomed to a more earnest style of social crusading, Hard's article nevertheless accomplished its goal by helping to instigate child labor reform legislation in Illinois.*

When the shades of night look as if they were about to fall; when the atmosphere of Chicago begins to change from the dull gray of unaided local nature to the brilliant white of artificial illumination; when the Loop District, the central crater of the volcano, is filling up rapidly with large numbers of straps [trolley cars] which have been brought downtown from outlying carbarns for the convenience of those who have had enough and who now wish to withdraw; when the sound of the time clock being gladly and brutally punched is heard through every door and window—

When all these things are happening, and, besides—

When all the fat men in the city get to the streetcars first, and all the lean and energetic and profane men have to climb over them to the inner seats; when the salesladies in the department stores throw the night-covers over bargain ormolu clocks just as you pant up to the counter; when the man who has just bought a suburban house stops at the wholesale meat market and carries home a left-over steak in order to have the laugh on the high-priced suburban butcher; when you are sorry your office is on the fifth floor because there are so many people on the eleventh floor and the elevator goes by you without stopping, while you scowl through the glass partition—

When all these things are happening, and, besides—

When the clocks in the towers of the railway stations are turned three minutes ahead so that you will be sure to be on time and so that you will also be sure to drop into your seat with fractured lungs; when the policeman blows his whistle to make the streetcar stop, and the motorman sounds his gong to make the pedestrian stop, and both the motorman and the pedestrian look timorously but longingly at the area of death just in front of the fender; when the streets are full and the straps are full, and the shoes of the motor-cars of the elevated trains are throwing yellow sparks on the shoulders of innocent bystanders; when the reporters, coming back to their offices from their afternoon assignments, are turning about in their doorways to watch the concentrated agony of an American home-going and are thanking God that they go home at the more convenient hour of 1 A.M.—

When all these things are happening, and when, in short, it is between five and six o'clock in the afternoon, the night newsboy and the night messenger boy turn another page in the book of experience and begin to devote themselves once more to the thronging, picturesque, incoherent characters of the night life of a big American city.

Then it is, at just about five o'clock, that the night messenger boy opens the door of his office by pushing against it with his back, turns around and walks sidewise across the floor, throws himself down obliquely on his long, smooth bench, slides a foot or two on the polished surface, comes to a stop against the body of the next boy, and begins to wait for the telegrams, letters and parcels that will keep him engaged till one o'clock the next morning and that may lead his footsteps either to the heavily curtained drawing rooms of disorderly houses in the Red Light district or to the wet planks of the wharves on the Calumet River twelve miles away, where he will curl up under the stars and sleep till the delayed boat arrives from Duluth.

Then it is that the night messenger boy's friend and ally, the night newsboy, gets downtown from school, after having said good-by to his usually mythical "widowed mother," and after having assumed the usually imaginary burden of the support of a "bereaved family." Then it is, at about five o'clock, that he approaches his favorite corner, grins at the man who owns the corner news stand, receives "ten *Choinals*, ten *Murrikins*, ten *Snoozes*, and five *Posts*"; goes away twenty feet, turns around, watches the corner-man to see if he has marked the papers down in his notebook, hopes that he hasn't marked them down, thinks that perhaps he has forgotten just how many there were, wonders if he couldn't persuade him that he didn't give him any "*Murrikins*," calculates the amount of his profit if he should be able to sell the "*Murrikins*" without having to pay the corner-man for them, turns to the street, dodges a frenzied automobile, worms his way into a hand-packed street-car (which is the only receptacle never convicted by the city government of containing short measure), disappears at the car door, comes to the surface in the middle of the aisle, and hands a *News* to a regular customer.

From the time when the arc lamps sputter out bravely against the evening darkness to the time when they chatter and flicker themselves into extinction before the cold, reproving rays of the early morning sun, what does the street-boy do? What does he see? What films in the moving picture of a big American city are unrolled before his eyes? These are questions that are important to every American city, to every mission superintendent, to every desk sergeant, to every penitentiary warden, to every father, to every mother.

Night, in these modern times, is like the United States Constitution. It is an admirable institution, but it doesn't know what is happening beneath it. Night comes down on Chicago and spreads its wings as largely and as comfortably now as when the *Tribune* building was a sand dune. You stand on Madison Street and look upward, through the glare of the arc lamps, and you see old Mother Night still brooding about you, calmly, imperturbably, quite unconscious of the fact that her mischievous children have lined her feathers with electricity, kerosene, acetylene, coal gas, water gas, and every other species of unlawful, unnatural illuminating substance. She still spreads her wings, simply, grandly, with the cosmic unconcern of a hen that doesn't know she is hatching out ducks instead of chickens; and in the morning she rises from her nest and flutters away westward, feeling quite sure that she has fulfilled her duty in an ancient, regular and irreproachable manner.

She would be quite maternally surprised if she could know what her newsboys and messenger boys are doing while she (good, proper mother!) is nodding her head beautifully among the stars.

I do not mean by this remark to disparage the newsboy. He occupies in Chicago a legal position superior to that of the president of a railway company. The president of a railway company is only an employee. He receives a weekly, a monthly, or at least a yearly salary. The newsboy does not receive a salary. He is not an employee. He is a merchant. He buys his papers and then resells them. He occupies the same legal position as Marshall Field & Co. Therefore he does not fall within the scope of the child-labor law. Therefore no rascally paternalistic factory inspector may vex him in his pursuit of an independent commercial career.

At about five o'clock he strikes his bargain with the corner-man. The corner-man owns the corner. It is a strange and interesting system, lying totally without the pale of recognized law. Theoretically, Dick Kelly, having read the Fourteenth Amendment to the Constitution of the United States, and having become conscious of his rights, might try to set up a news stand at the southwest corner of Wabash and Madison. Practically, the Constitution does not follow the flag as far as that corner. Mr. Kelly's news stand would last a wonderfully short time. The only person who can have a news stand at the corner of Wabash and Madison is Mr. Heffner.

Mr. Heffner is the recognized owner, holder, occupant, possessor, etc., of some eighty square feet of sidewalk at that point, and his sovereignty extends halfway down the block to the next corner southward, and halfway down the other block to the next corner westward. When Mr. Heffner has been in business long enough he will deed, convey and transfer his rights to some other man for anywhere between $5 and $1,500.

These rights consist exclusively of the fact that the newspapers recognize the corner-man as their only agent at that particular spot. When the corner-man wishes to transfer his corner to somebody else, he must see that the newspapers are satisfied with his choice of a successor.

The newsboy deals, generally speaking, with the corner-man. The corner-man pays the *Daily News* sixty cents for every hundred copies. He then hands out these hundred copies in "bunches" of, say, ten or fifteen or twenty to the newsboys who come to him for supplies. Each newsboy receives, as a commission, a certain number of cents for every hundred copies that he can manage to sell. This commission varies from five to twenty cents. The profit of the corner-man varies therefore with the commission that he pays the newsboy. The public pays one hundred cents for one hundred copies of the *News*. The *News* itself gets sixty cents; the newsboy gets from five to twenty cents, the corner-man gets what is left, namely, from thirty-five down to twenty cents in net profit.

On the basis of this net profit, plus the gross profit on his own sales made directly by himself to his customers, there is more than one corner-man in Chicago who owns suburban property and who could live on the income from his real-estate investments.

From five o'clock, therefore, on to about half past six, the newsboy flips streetcars and yells "turrible murdur" on commission. But pretty soon the corner-man wants to go home. He then sells outright all the papers left on the stand. . . .

The best specimen of the finished type of newsboy, within my knowledge, is an Italian boy named "Jelly." His father's surname is Cella, but his own name has been "Jelly" ever since he can remember.

"Jelly" was born on the great, sprawly West Side. His father worked during the summer, digging excavations for sewers and gas mains. His mother worked during the winter, making buttonholes in coats, vests, and pants. Neither parent worked during the whole year.

This domestic situation was overlooked by the Hull House investigators. In their report on newsboys they found that the number of paper-selling orphans had been grossly overestimated by popular imagination. Out of 1,000 newsboys in their final tabulation, there were 803 who had both parents living. There were 74 who had only a father living. There were 97 who had only a mother living. There were only 26, out of the whole 1,000, who had neither a father nor a mother to care for them.

But "Jelly" occupied a peculiar position. He had both parents living and yet, from the standpoint of economics, he was a half-orphan, since neither parent worked all the year.

At the age of ten, therefore, "Jelly" began selling papers. His uncle had a news stand on a big important corner not far from "Jelly's" house on the West Side. At the age of ten "Jelly" was selling papers from five to eight in the morning and from five to eight in the evening. He was therefore inclined to go to sleep at his desk when he was receiving his lesson in mental arithmetic in the public school where he was an unwilling attendant. Nevertheless, he showed an extraordinary aptitude for mental arithmetic a few hours later when he was handing out change to customers on his uncle's corner.

"Jelly" was a pretty good truant in those days. There was no money to be made by going to school and it looked like a waste of time. His acquaintance among truant officers came to be broad and thorough. He was dragged back to school an indefinite number of times. Yet, with the curious limitations of a newsboy's superficially profound knowledge of human nature, he has confided to me the fact that every truant officer gets $1 for every boy that he returns to the principal of his school.

Besides being a pretty good truant, "Jelly" became also a pretty good fighter.

His very first fight won him the undying gratitude of his uncle.

It happened that at that time the struggle between the circulation departments of the evening newspapers was particularly keen. "Jelly's" uncle allowed himself, unwisely, to be drawn into it. The local circulation experts of the *News* and the *American* noticed that on the news stand kept by "Jelly's" uncle the *Journal* was displayed with excessive prominence and the *News* and the *American* were concealed down below. It was currently reported in the neighborhood that "Jelly's" uncle was receiving $10 a week from the *Journal* for behaving in the manner aforesaid.

In about twenty-four hours the corner owned by "Jelly's" uncle bore a tumultuous aspect. The *News* and the *American* had established a rival stand on the other side of the street. This stand was in charge of a man named Gazzolo. Incidentally, it happened that a man named Gazzolo had beaten and killed a man named Cella in the vicinity of Naples some five years before.

Gazzolo's news stand had confronted Cella's, frowning at it from across the street, for about a week, when it began to be guarded by some six or seven broad-chested persons in sweaters. Meanwhile Cella's news stand had also acquired a few sweaters inhabited by capable young men of a combative disposition.

On the afternoon of the eighth day the sweatered agents of the *News* and the *American* advanced across the street and engaged the willing agents of the *Journal* in a face-to-face and then hand-to-hand combat.

At least three murders have happened in Chicago since that time in similar encounters. "Nigger" Clark, an agent of the *News*, was killed on the South Side, and the Higgins brothers were killed on the Ashland Block corner in the downtown district itself, within view of the worldwide commerce transacted in the heart of Chicago. And a Chicago publisher has told me that these three open murders, recognized by everybody as circulation-department murders, must be supplemented by at least six or seven other clandestine murders before the full story of the homicidal rivalry between the agents of Chicago afternoon newspapers is told.

It was amateur murder before the *American* arrived. Then circulation agents began to be enlisted from the ranks of the pupils in the boxing schools, and since that time the circulation situation has become increasingly pugnacious, until today it has reached the State Attorney's office and has come back to the street in the form of indictments and prosecutions.

Typical of this warfare was the fray that followed when the sweatered agents of the *News* and the *American* came across the street and fell rudely upon the news stand of "Jelly's" uncle.

"Jelly's" uncle had his shoulder-blade broken, but "Jelly" himself, being young and agile, escaped from his pursuers and was instantly and miraculously filled with a beautiful idea.

The agents of the *News* and the *American,* coming across the street to attack "Jelly's" uncle, had left Gazzolo's corner unprotected. "Jelly" traversed the cedar blocks of the street and reached Gazzolo in an ecstatic moment when he was surveying the assault on Cella's shoulder-blade with absorbing glee. Just about one-tenth of a second later Mr. Gazzolo was pierced in the region of the abdomen by the largest blade of a small and blunt pocket-knife in the unhesitating right hand of Mr. Cella's nephew, "Jelly."

It was a slight wound, but in consideration of his thoughtfulness in promptly perceiving Mr. Gazzolo's unprotected situation and in immediately running across the street in order to take advantage of it, "Jelly" was transferred by his uncle to a position of independent responsibility. He was put in charge of a news stand just outside an elevated railway station on the South Side.

Nevertheless, even after this honorable promotion, "Jelly's" father continued to take all his money away from him when he came home at night. And the elder Cella did not desist from this practice till his son had been advanced to the supereminent honor of selling papers in the downtown district.

This final transfer happened to "Jelly" when he was fifteen. He still retained his stand on the South Side, selling papers there from five to ten in the morning, but he also came downtown and sold papers at a stand within the Loop from five to nine at night. His uncle had prospered and had been able to invest $1,000 in a downtown corner, which was on the point of being abandoned by a fellow Italian who desired to return to the hills just south of Naples.

Thereafter, till he was sixteen years old, "Jelly" led a full and earnest life. He rose at four; he reached his South Side stand by five; he sold papers there till ten; he reached the downtown district by eleven; he inspected the five-cent theaters and the penny arcades and the alley restaurants till five in the afternoon; he sold papers for his uncle on commission till half past six; he bought his uncle's left-over papers at half past six and sold them on his own account till nine; and then, before going home at ten in order to get his five hours of sleep, he spent a happy sixty minutes reinspecting the five-cent theaters and the penny arcades and dodging Mr. Julius F. Wengierski.

Mr. Wengierski is a probation officer of the Juvenile Court. At that time he was making nightly tours through the downtown district talking to the children on the streets and trying to induce them to go home. He made a special study of some fifty cases, looking into the home circumstances of each child and gathering notes on the reasons why the child was at work. He was assisted by the agents of a reputable and conscientious charitable society.

In only two instances, out of the whole fifty, was the boy's family in need of the actual necessaries of life. In one instance the boy's father was the owner of his house and lot and was earning $5 a day. He also had several hundred dollars in the bank. In only a few instances did the family, as a family, make any considerable gain, for the purposes of household expenses, from the child's labor.

Some fathers, it is true (notably the one who owned his house and lot), used the child selfishly and cruelly as a worker who required no wages and whose total earnings could be appropriated as soon as he came home. It was the same system as that to which "Jelly" had been subjected from ten to fifteen. But these cases were exceptional.

One of the boys was working in order to get the money for the installment payments on a violin, and another was working in order to pay for lessons on a violin of which he was already the complete and enthusiastic owner.

One little girl was selling late editions in the saloons on Van Buren Street in order to have white shoes for her first communion. Another little girl needed shoes of the same color for Easter. Still a third was working in order that after a while she might have clothes just as good as those of the girl who lived next door.

In at least ten of Mr. Wengierski's cases, the reason for earning money on the street at night was the penny arcade and the five-cent theater. The passion for these amusements among children is intense. They will, some of them, work until they have a nickel, expend it on a moving-picture performance, and then start in and work again until they have another nickel to be spent for the same purpose at another "theatorium."

The earnings of these children, according to the Hull House investigation, which is the only authoritative investigation on record, vary from ten cents a day when the children are five years old up to ninety cents a day when they are sixteen. This is the average, but of course there are many children who make less and many who, because of superior skill, make more. Among these latter is "Jelly."

"Jelly's" high average, which used to reach almost $2 a day, was due partly to his own personal power and partly to the fact that on Saturday night he employed the services of his little sister.

Saturday night was "Jelly's" big time. On other nights he went home by ten o'clock. He had to get up by four and it was necessary for even him to take some sleep. But on Saturday night he gave himself up with almost complete abandon to the opportunities of the street.

On that night he used to close up his stand by eight o'clock and then go down to the river and sell his few remaining papers to the passengers on the lake boats. "Last chanst ter git yer *Murrikin*!" "Only one *Choinal* left! De only *Choinal* on de dock!" "Buy a *Post,* mister! Youse won't be able ter sleep ter-night on de boat! De only paper fer only two cents!" "Here's yer *Noose*! Only one cent! No more *Nooses* till youse comes back! Last chanst! Dey will cost yer ten cents apiece on de boat!" "Git yer *Murrikin*. No papers sold on de boat!" "Git yer *Post*. Dey charges yer five cents w'en youse gits 'em on de boat!"

Slightly contradictory those statements of his used to be, but they attained their object. They sold the papers. And as soon as the boats had swung away from their moorings "Jelly" would come back to the region of the five-cent theaters and the penny arcades and resume his nocturnal inquiries into the state of cheap art.

At half past ten he went to an elevated railway station to meet his little sister. She was ten years old. She had dressed herself for the part. From her ragged and scanty wardrobe she had chosen her most ragged and her scantiest clothes.

Accompanied by his sister, "Jelly" then went to a flower shop and bought a bundle of carnations at closing prices. With these carnations he took his sister to the entrance of the Grand Opera House. There she sold the whole bundle to the people coming out from the performance. Her appearance was picturesque and pitiful. Her net profit from the sale of her flowers was usually about thirty-five cents.

As soon as the flowers were sold and the people had gone away, "Jelly" took his sister back to the elevated station. There he counted the money she had made and put it in his pocket. He then handed her out a nickel for carfare and, in addition, a supplementary nickel for herself. "Jelly" was being rapidly Americanized. If he had remained exactly like his father, he would have surrendered only the nickel for carfare.

It was time now to go to the office of the *American* and get the early morning Sunday editions. "Jelly" began selling these editions at about twelve o'clock. He sold them to stragglers in the downtown streets till two. It was then exactly twenty-two hours since he had left his bed. He began to feel a little bit sleepy. He therefore went down to the river and slept on a dock, next to an old berry crate, till four. At four he rose and took the elevated train to the South Side. There he reached his own news stand and opened it up at about five o'clock. This was his Saturday, Saturday-night, and Sunday-morning routine for a long time. On the other nights ''Jelly'' slept five hours. On Saturday nights he found that two hours was quite enough. And his ability to get along without sleep is characteristic of newsboys and messenger boys rather than exceptional among them.

The reason why ''Jelly'' used to dodge Mr. Wengierski is now explainable. To begin with, his opinion of all probation officers is unfavorable. He classes them with truant officers. They are not ''on the level.'' They discriminate between different classes of boys. ''Jelly'' was once accosted by a probation officer at about ten o'clock at night on Clark Street. He gave this probation officer a good tip about a lot of boys who were staying out nights attending services in the old First Methodist Church. These boys had been seen by ''Jelly'' going home as late as half past ten. The probation officer took no action in their case while at the same time he advised ''Jelly'' to stop selling papers at an early hour.

Incidents like this had convinced ''Jelly'' that probation officers were certainly not on the level and were possibly ''on the make.'' But in Mr. Wengierski's case he had an additional reason. Mr. Wengierski was looking for boys of fourteen and under, and, while ''Jelly'' was entitled by age to escape Mr. Wengierski's notice, he was not so entitled by size. He was sixteen, but he looked not more than thirteen. The street had given him a certain superficial knowledge, but it had dwarfed his body just as surely as it had dwarfed his mind.

Mr. J. J. Sloan, when he was superintendent of the John Worthy School (which is the local municipal juvenile reformatory), reported that the newsboys committed to his care were, on the average, one-third below the stature and one-third below the strength of average ordinary boys of the same age. In the face of testimony of this kind, which could be duplicated from every city in the United States, it seems absurd to talk about the educative influence of the street. That it has a certain educative influence is undeniable, but it is equally undeniable that the boys who are exposed to this influence should be prevented, by proper legislation, from exposing themselves to it too many hours a day and should especially be prevented from exposing themselves to it for even a single hour after seven o'clock in the evening.

''Jelly'' has now become a messenger boy and has been given a new name by his new associates. He will some day go back to the newspaper business because there is more money in it, and ''Jelly'' is fundamentally commercial. But there seems to be, after all, a certain struggling, unruly bubble of romanticism in his nature and it had to rise to the surface and explode.

''Jelly'' first thought of the messenger service when he was attending a five-cent theater. ''Jelly'' went in. The fleeting pictures on the screen at the farther end of the room were telling a story that filled him with swelling interest. A messenger boy is run over by an automobile. He is taken to the hospital. He regains consciousness in his bed. He remembers his message. He calls for a portable telephone. He phones the message to the young man to whom it was addressed. The young man comes at once to the hospital. The young woman who had sent the message also comes. She wants to find out what has happened to the message. The young man and the young woman meet at the bedside of the messenger boy. They fall into each other's arms and the messenger boy sinks back on his pillow and dies. And it is a mighty good story even if the rough points are not rubbed off.

''Jelly'' determined at once to be a messenger boy, without delay. [. . .]

Peter Homans / The Western: The Legend and the Cardboard Hero

Look, March 13, 1962

One way to look at the heroes and heroines of popular culture is to see them as reflections of age-old myths. This is the perspective Peter Homans adopts in the following essay, which originally appeared in Look *magazine on March 13, 1962. By analyzing all of the characteristic elements of the typical Western, Homans demonstrates what all Westerns have in common.*

Peter Homans was born in New York in 1930, and has earned degrees at Princeton and the University of Chicago. He is the author of Theology after Freud: An Interpretive Inquiry *(1970) and has written on popular culture, psychology, and theology.*

Along with Life *and the* Saturday Evening Post, Look *was one of the giant circulation, general magazines that died as a weekly in the 1970's. "The power of* Look,*" the magazine's publisher once said, "is that it spans the whole universe of interests. It is a platform of all Americans to turn to, to learn about the basic issues, the real gut issues of the day. . . . It is information and entertainment for the whole family."*

He is the Law West of Tombstone, he is The Virginian at High Noon. He is Frontier Marshal, Knight of the Range, Rider of the Purple Sage. He Has Gun, Will Travel, and his name is Matt Dillon, Destry, Shane.

He is the hero of every Western that ever thundered out of the movies or TV screen, this Galahad with a Colt .45 who stalks injustice on the dusty streets of Dodge. Or Carson City. Or Virginia City.

Once he accomplishes his mission, he vanishes into the mists, as do all true heroes of all true legends. But where Hercules goes to Olympus and King Arthur to Avalon, this galoot rides Old Paint into the sunset.

With few variations, the movies have been telling this story for more than half a century. There have, in fact, been Western movies as long as there have been movies; the first American narrative film was a Western, *The Great Train Robbery,* made in 1903. Without the Westerns, it would be hard to imagine television today. Far outstripping the rowdy little boys who were its first enraptured audience, the Western has gone round the globe to become the youngest of the world's mythologies.

For each of us, even the word "Western" brings to mind an ordered sequence of character, event and detail. There may, of course, be variations within the pattern—but the basic outline remains constant. Details often vary, especially between movie and television Westerns, because the latter are essentially continued stories. Nonetheless, from the endless number of Westerns we have all seen, a basic concept emerges:

The Western takes place in a desolate, abandoned land. The desert, as a place without life, is indispensable. The story would not be credible were it set in a jungle, a fertile lowland or an arctic wasteland. We are dealing with a form of existence deprived of vitality.

This desert effect is contradicted by the presence of a town. Among the slapped-together buildings with false fronts, lined awkwardly along a road forever thick with dust, only three stand out—the saloon, the bank and the marshal's office (the hero's dwelling).

The saloon is the most important building in the Western. It is the only place in the story where people can be seen together time after time. It thereby functions as a meetinghouse, social center, church. More important, it is the setting for the climax of the story, the gunfight. No matter where the fight ends, it starts in the saloon.

The bank is a hastily constructed, fragile affair. Its only protection consists of a sniveling, timid clerk, with a mustache and a green eyeshade, who is only too glad to hand over the loot. Has there ever been a Western in which a robber wondered whether he could pull off his robbery?

The marshal's office appears less regularly. Most noticeable is the absence of any evidence of domesticity. We rarely see a bed, a place for clothes or any indication that a person actually makes his home here. There is not even a mirror. The overall atmosphere is that of austerity, which, we are led to suspect, is in some way related to our hero's virtue, and not to his finances.

The town as a whole has no business or industry. People have money, but we rarely see them make it. Homelife is conspicuous by its absence. There are no families, children, dogs. The closest thing to a home is a hotel, and this is rarely separated from the saloon.

One of the most interesting people in the town is the "derelict professional." He was originally trained in one of the usual Eastern professions (law, medicine, letters, ministry), but since his arrival in the West, he has become corrupted by drink, gambling, sex or violence. The point is that the traditional mentors of society (counselor, healer, teacher, shepherd) cannot exist in an uncorrupted state under the pressure of Western life. Somewhat similar is the "nonviolent Easterner." He often appears as a well-dressed business man, or as a very recent graduate of Harvard. In the course of the plot's development, this character is either humiliated or killed. The East, we soon note, is incapable of action when action is most needed.

The "good girl" is another supporting type in the cast of characters. Pale and without appetite, she, too, is from the East and is classically represented as the new schoolmarm. The "bad girl" is alone in the world and usually works for her living in the saloon as a waitress or dancer. Both girls have their eye on the hero.

The bartender observes the action, but rarely becomes involved in it. "The boys," those bearded, grimy people who are always "just there" drinking and gambling in the saloon, function as an audience. No hero ever shot it out with his adversary without these people watching.

Then we come to the principals. We meet the hero in the opening phase of the action. He is, above all, a transcendent figure, originating beyond the town. He rides into the town from nowhere; even if he is the marshal, his identity is disassociated from the people he must save. We know nothing of any past activities, relationships, future plans or ambitions. There are no friends, relatives, family, mistresses—not even a dog or cat—and even with his horse, he has a strangely formal relationship.

At first, the hero is lax to the point of laziness. Take his hat, for example. It sits exactly where it was placed—no effort has been made to align it. With feet propped up on the porch rail, frame balanced on a chair or stool tilted back on its rear legs, hat pushed slightly over the eyes, hands clasped over the buckle of his gun belt, he is a study in contrived indolence. Now he has time on his hands, but he knows his time is coming, and so do we.

The hero indicates no desire for women. He appears somewhat bored with the whole business. He never blushes, or betrays any enthusiasm. His monosyllabic stammer and brevity of speech clearly indicate an intended indifference.

In the drinking scenes, we are likely to see the hero equipped with the traditional shot glass and bottle. We seldom see him pay for more than one drink. He gulps his drink, rarely enjoys it and is impatient to be off. In the gambling scenes, his poker face veils any inner feelings of greed, enthusiasm or apprehension. We note, however, that he always wins or refuses to play. Similarly, he is utterly unimpressed by and indifferent to money.

There are hundreds of variations of the villain, but each is unshaven, darkly clothed and from the West. Like the hero, he is from beyond the town. He is inclined to cheat at cards, get drunk, lust after women who do not return the compliment, rob banks and, finally, shoot people he does not care for, especially heroes.

The impact of this evil one on the town is electric, suddenly animating it with vitality and purpose. Indeed, it is evil, rather than good, that actually gives meaning to the lives of these people. Nevertheless, they all know (as we do) that they are of themselves ultimately powerless to meet this evil. What is required is the hero—a transcendent power originating from beyond the town.

Notice what has happened to this power. Gone are the hero's indolence and lack of intention. Now, he is infused with vitality, direction and seriousness, in order to confront this ultimate threat. Once the radical shift has been accomplished, the hero (like the audience) is ready for the final conflict.

While the fight can take many forms (fistfight, fight with knives or whips, even a scowling match in which the hero successfully glares down the evil one), the classic and most popular form is the encounter with six-guns. It is a built-up and drawn-out affair, always allowing enough time for an audience to gather. The two men must adhere to an elaborate and well-defined casuistry as to who draws first, when it is proper to draw, etc. Although the hero's presence makes the fight possible—i.e., he insists on obstructing the evil one in some way; it is the latter who invariably attacks first. Were the hero ever to draw first, the story would no longer be a Western. With the destruction of the evil one, the action phase is completed.

In the closing phase, the town and its hero return to their preaction ways. One more event must take place, however, before the story can conclude. The hero must renounce any further involvement with the town. Traditionally, the hero marries the heroine and settles down. The Western hero always refuses—at least on television. He cannot identify himself with the situation he has influenced. When this has been made clear, the story is over.

The Western is, as most people by this time are willing to acknowledge, a popular myth that sets forth certain meanings about what is good and bad, right and wrong. Evil, according to the myth, is the failure to resist temptation. Temptation consists of five activities: drinking, gambling, moneymaking, sex and violence. In the drinking scenes, the hero is offered not one drink, but a whole bottle. He has at his disposal the opportunity for unlimited indulgence and its consequent loss of self-control. Gambling is a situation over which one has rather limited control—one loses, but the hero does not lose. He wins, thereby remaining in control. Wealth is not seized, although it is available to him through the unguarded bank. And both good girl and bad girl seek out the hero, to no avail—he remains a hero.

We perceive in the evil one a terrible power, which he has acquired at a great price; he has forfeited the control and resistance that sustain and make the hero what he is. The villain is the embodiment of the failure to resist temptation; he is the failure of denial. This is the real meaning of evil in the myth of the Western, and it is this that makes the evil one truly evil. He threatens the hero's resistance; each taunt and baiting gesture is a lure to the forfeiture of control and leads to the one temptation that the hero cannot afford to resist: the temptation to destroy temptation.

But why must the hero wait to be attacked? Why must he refrain from drawing first? The circumstances are contrived in order to make the violent destruction of the evil one appear just and virtuous. This process whereby desire is at once indulged and veiled is the "inner dynamic." It is the key to the Western, explaining not only the climax of the story, but everything else uniquely characteristic of it. What is required is that temptation be indulged while providing the appearance of having been resisted. Each of the minor-temptation episodes—drink, cards, moneymaking and sex—takes its unique shape from this need and is a climaxless Western in itself.

The derelict professional is derelict, and the nonviolent Easterner is weak, precisely because they have failed to resist temptation in the manner characteristic of the hero. Because these two types originate in the East, they have something in common with the good girl. Everything Eastern in the Western is weak, emotional, feminine. This covers family life, intellectual life, professional life. Only by becoming Westernized can the East be redeemed. The Western therefore is more a myth about the East than it is about the West; it is a secret and bitter parody of Eastern ways.

In summary, then, the Western is a myth in which evil appears as a series of temptations to be resisted by the hero. When faced with the embodiment of these temptations, he destroys the threat. But the story is so structured that the responsibility for the act falls upon the adversary, permitting the hero to destroy while appearing to save.

The Western bears a significant relationship to puritanism, in which it is the proper task of the will to rule and contain the spontaneous, vital aspects of life. Whenever vitality becomes too pressing, and the dominion of the will becomes threatened, the self must find some other mode of control. The puritan will seek a situation that allows him to express vitality while appearing to resist it. The Western provides just this opportunity, for the entire myth is shaped by the inner dynamic of apparent control and veiled expression. Indeed, in the gunfight, the hero's heightened gravity and dedicated exclusion of all other loyalties present a study in puritan virtue, while the evil one presents nothing more or less than the old New England Protestant devil—strangely costumed, to be sure—the traditional tempter whose horrid lures never allow the good puritan a moment's peace. In the gunfight, there are deliverance and redemption.

Here, then, is the real meaning of the Western: It is a puritan morality tale in which the savior-hero redeems the community from the temptations of the devil. Tall in the saddle, he rides straight from Plymouth Rock to a dusty frontier town, and though he be the fastest gun this side of Laramie, his Colt .45 is on the side of the angels.

DISCUSSION QUESTIONS

1. Read Homans's essay in connection with Louis L'Amour's story "Bowdrie Passes Through" in Best Sellers. Isolate elements of the story that conform to Homans's analysis of the Western. How well do you think Homans's essay explains L'Amour's story and central character? Can you think of other ways to interpret the story?

2. Could Homans's analysis be applied to other popular forms? For example, how might someone using Homans's method of interpretation read James Michener's "Space," Edgar Rice Burroughs's "Tarzan of the Apes," or Stephen King's "Trucks" (see Best Sellers)?

Gore Vidal / Tarzan Revisited

Esquire, December 1963

Gore Vidal has established one of the most impressive writing careers in recent American history. A novelist, short story writer, literary critic, essayist, playwright, lyricist, and screenwriter, Vidal has worked in nearly all media and at practically every level of entertainment. He has acted on stage and screen, has hosted television panel shows, and has run (unsuccessfully) for Congress and the Senate. A founder of a local newspaper and a controversial lecturer, Vidal has also written several detective stories under the pseudonym of Edgar Box.

Born at West Point in 1925, Vidal graduated Phillips Exeter Academy in 1943 and immediately enlisted as a private in the U.S. Army. After the war, he worked for a short time as an editor for a New York publishing house. His first novel appeared in 1946, and since then Vidal has been among the most prolific, multifaceted, and civilized authors of our time.

Esquire, *an urbane monthly begun in 1933, regularly features the work of celebrated writers. Its late founder and owner, Arnold Gingrich, claimed that* Esquire's *editorial policy has always been to keep its reader off balance, so that he "could never feel sure, as he turned from one page to the next and from one issue to the next, of what might be coming up." The following essay, which shows Vidal's mixed responses to a tremendously successful series of novels (see Edgar Rice Burroughs in* Best Sellers), *appeared in 1963. In many ways, the essay characterizes* Esquire's *adroit handling of the American popular arts.*

There are so many things the people who take polls never get around to asking. Fascinated as we all are to know what our countrymen think of great issues (approving, disapproving, "don't-knowing," with that same shrewd intelligence which made a primeval wilderness bloom with Howard Johnson signs), the pollsters never get around to asking the sort of interesting personal questions our new-Athenians might be able to answer knowledgeably. For instance, how many adults have an adventure serial running in their heads? How many consciously daydream, turning on a story in which the dreamer ceases to be an employee of I.B.M. and becomes a handsome demigod moving through splendid palaces, saving maidens from monsters (or monsters from maidens: this is a jaded time). Most children tell themselves stories in which they figure as powerful figures, enjoying the pleasures not only of the adult world as they conceive it but of a world of wonders unlike dull reality. Although this sort of Mittyesque daydreaming is supposed to cease in maturity, I suggest that more adults than we suspect are bemusedly wandering about with a full Technicolor extravaganza going on in their heads. Clad in tights, rapier in hand, the daydreamers drive their Jaguars at fantastic speeds through a glittering world of adoring love objects, mingling anachronistic historic worlds with science fiction. "Captain, the time-warp's been closed! We are now trapped in a parallel world, inhabited entirely by women with three breasts." Though from what we can gather about these imaginary worlds they tend to be more Adlerian than Freudian: The motor drive is the desire not for sex (other briefer fantasies take care of that) but for power, for the ability to dominate one's environment through physical strength. I state all this with perfect authority because I have just finished rereading several books by the master of American daydreamers, Edgar Rice Burroughs, whose works today, as anyone who goes into a drugstore or looks at a newstand can see, have suddenly returned to great popularity.

When I was growing up, I read all twenty-three Tarzan books, as well as the ten Mars books. My own inner storytelling mechanism was vivid. At any one time, I had at least three serials going as well as a number of old faithful reruns. I used Burroughs as a source of raw material. When he went to the center of the earth à la Jules Verne (much too fancy a writer for one's taste), I immediately worked up a thirteen-part series, with myself as lead, and various friends as guest stars. Sometimes I used the master's material, but more often I adapted it freely to suit myself. One's daydreams tended to be Tarzanish pre-puberty (physical strength and freedom) and Martian post-puberty (exotic worlds and subtle *combinaziones* to be worked out). After adolescence, if one's life is sufficiently interesting, the desire to tell oneself stories diminishes. My last serial ran into sponsor trouble when I was in the Second World War and was never renewed.

Until recently I assumed that most people were like myself: daydreaming ceases when the real world becomes interesting and reasonably manageable. Now I am not so certain. Pondering the life and success of Burroughs leads one to believe that a good many people find their lives so unsatisfactory that they go right on year after year telling themselves stories in which they are able to dominate their environment in a way that is not possible in this overorganized society.

"Most of the stories I wrote were the stories I told myself just before I went to sleep," said Edgar Rice Burroughs, describing his own work. He is a fascinating figure to contemplate, an archetype American dreamer. Born 1875, in Chicago, he was a drifter until he was thirty-six. Briefly, he served in the U.S. Cavalry; then he was a gold miner in Oregon, a cowboy in Idaho, a railroad policeman in Salt Lake City; he attempted several businesses that failed. He was perfectly in the old-American grain: the man who could take on almost any job, who liked to keep moving, who tried to get rich quick, but could never pull it off. And while he was drifting through the unsatisfactory real world, he consoled himself with an inner world where he was strong and handsome, adored by beautiful women and worshiped by exotic races. Burroughs might have gone to his death an unknown daydreamer, if he had not started reading pulp fiction. He needed raw material for his own inner serials and once he had used up his favorite source, Rider Haggard, he turned to the magazines. He was appalled at how poor the stories were. They did not compare with his own imaginings. He was like a lover of pornography who, unable to find works which excite him, turns to writing them. Burroughs promptly wrote a serial about Mars and sold it to *Munsey's*. His fellow daydreamers recognized a master. In 1914 he published his first book, *Tarzan of the Apes* (Rousseau's noble savage reborn in Africa), and history was made. To date the Tarzan books have sold over twenty-five million copies in fifty-six languages. There is hardly an American male of my generation who has not at one time or another tried to master the victory cry of the great ape as it once bellowed forth from the androgynous chest of Johnny Weismuller, while a thousand arms and legs were broken by attempts to swing from tree to tree in the backyards of the republic. Between 1914 and his death in 1950, Burroughs, the squire of Tarzana, California (a prophet honored by his own land), produced over sixty books, while enjoying the unique status of being the first American writer to be a corporation. Burroughs is said to have been a pleasant, unpretentious man who liked to ride and play golf. Not one to disturb his own unconscious with reality, he never set foot in Africa.

With a sense of recapturing childhood, I have just reread several Tarzan books. It is fascinating to see how much one recalls after a quarter century. At times the sense of *déjà vu* is overpowering. It is equally interesting to discover that one's memories of *Tarzan of the Apes* are mostly action scenes. The plot had slipped one's mind. It is a lot of plot, too. The beginning is worthy of Conrad. "I had this story from one who had no business to tell it to me, or to any other. I may credit the seductive influence of an old vintage upon the narrator for the beginning of it, and my own skeptical incredulity during the days that followed for the balance of the strange tale.'' It is 1888. The young Lord and Lady Greystoke are involved in a ship mutiny (''there was in the whole atmosphere of the craft that undefinable something which presages disaster''). They are put ashore on the west coast of Africa. They build a tree house. Here Burroughs is at his best. He tells you the size of the logs, the way to hang a door when you have no hinges, the problems of roofing. All his books are filled with interesting details on how things are made. The Greystokes have a child. They die. The ''man-child'' is taken up by Kala, a Great Ape, who brings him up as a member of her tribe of apes. Burroughs is a rather vague anthropologist. His apes have a language. They are carnivorous. They can, he suspects, mate with human beings. Tarzan grows up as an ape; he kills his first lion (with a full nelson); he teaches himself to read and write English by studying some books found in the cabin. The method he used, sad to say, is the currently fashionable ''look-see.'' Though he can read and write, he cannot speak any language except that of the apes. He gets on well with the animal kingdom, with Tantor the elephant, Ska the vulture, Numa the lion (Kipling has added his grist to the Burroughs dream mill). Then white people arrive: Professor Archimedes Q. Porter and his daughter Jane. Also, a Frenchman named D'Arnot who teaches Tarzan to speak French, which is confusing. By coincidence, Jane's suitor is the current Lord Greystoke, who thinks the Greystoke baby is dead. Tarzan saves Jane from an ape. Then he puts on clothes and goes to Paris where he drinks absinthe. Next stop, America. In Wisconsin, he saves Jane Porter from a forest fire; then he nobly gives her up to Lord Greystoke, not revealing the fact that *he* is the real Lord Greystoke. Fortunately in the next volume, *The Return of Tarzan,* he marries Jane and they live happily ever after in Africa, raising a son John, who in turn grows up and has a son. Yet even as a grandfather, Tarzan continues to have adventures with people a foot high, with descendants of Atlantis, with the heirs of a Roman legion who think that Rome is still a success. All through these stories one gets the sense that one is daydreaming, too. Episode follows episode with no particular urgency. Tarzan is always knocked on the head and taken captive; he always escapes; there is always a beautiful princess or high priestess who loves him and assists him; there is always a loyal friend who fights beside him, very much in the Queequeg tradition which Leslie Fiedler assures us is the burning of the fuel supply of the American psyche. But no matter how difficult the adventure, Tarzan, clad only in a loincloth with no weapon save a knife (the style is contagious), wins against all odds and returns to his shadowy wife.

These books are clearly for men. I have yet to meet a woman who found Tarzan interesting: no identification, as they say in series land.

Stylistically, Burroughs is—how shall I put it?—uneven. He has moments of ornate pomp, when the darkness is ''Cimmerian''; of redundancy, ''she was hideous and ugly''; of extraordinary dialogue: ''Name of a name,'' shrieked Rokoff. ''Pig, but you shall die for this!'' Or Lady Greystoke to Lord G.: ''Duty is duty, my husband, and no amount of sophistries may change it. I would be a poor wife for an English lord were I to be responsible for his shirking a plain duty.'' Or the grandchild: ''Muvver,'' he cried, ''Dackie doe? Dackie doe?'' ''Let him come along,'' urged Tarzan. ''Dare!'' exclaimed the boy turning triumphantly upon the governess, ''Dackie do doe yalk!'' Burroughs' use of coincidence is shameless even for a pulp writer. In one book he has three sets of characters shipwrecked at exactly the same point on the shore of Africa. Even Burroughs finds this a bit much. ''Could it be possible [muses Tarzan] that fate had thrown him up at the very threshold of his own beloved jungle?'' It was possible, of course; anything can happen in a daydream.

Though Burroughs is innocent of literature and cannot reproduce human speech, he does have a gift very few writers of any kind possess: he can describe action vividly. I give away no trade secrets when I say that this is as difficult for a Tolstoi as it is for a Burroughs (even William). Because it is so hard, the draftier contemporary novelists usually prefer to tell their stories in the first person, which is simply writing dialogue. In character, as it were, the writer settles for an impression of what happened rather than creating the sense of a happening. Tarzan *in action* is excellent.

There is something basic in the appeal of the 1914 Tarzan which makes me think that he can still hold his own as a daydream figure, despite the sophisticated challenge for his two contemporary competitors, Ian Fleming and Mickey Spillane. For most adults, Tarzan (and John Carter of Mars) can hardly compete with the conspicuous consumer consumption of James Bond or the sickly violence of Mike Hammer, but for children and adolescents, the old appeal continues. All of us need the idea of a world alternative to this one. From Plato's Republic to Opar to Bondland, at every level, the human imagination has tried to imagine something better for itself than the existing society. Man left Eden when we got up off all fours, endowing most of his descendants with nostalgia as well as chronic backache. In its naïve way, the Tarzan legend returns us to that Eden where, free of clothes and the inhibitions of an oppressive society, a man can achieve in reverie his continuing need, which is, as William Faulkner put it in his high Confederate style, to prevail as well as endure. The current fascination with LSD and non-addictive drugs—not to mention alcoholism—is all part of a general sense of frustration and boredom. The individual's desire to dominate his environment is not a desirable trait in a society which every day grows more and more confining. Since there are few legitimate releases for the average man, he must take to daydreaming. James Bond, Mike Hammer and Tarzan are all dream-selves, and the aim of each is to establish personal primacy in a world which in reality diminishes the individual. Among adults, increasing popularity of these lively inferior fictions strikes me as a most significant (and unbearably sad) phenomenon.

Gay Talese / The Bridge

Esquire, December 1964

A 1953 graduate of the University of Alabama, Gay Talese worked as a staff writer on The New York Times *for ten years, and as a contributing editor to* Esquire, *Talese has written articles for the* Saturday Evening Post, Show *magazine,* Life, *and the* Reader's Digest. *Two of his fictionalized studies have made the best seller lists:* The Kingdom and the Power *(1969), a history of* The New York Times *enterprise, and* Honor Thy Father *(1971), an intimate, inside view of an Italo-American family. Both books are written in a mode of reporting that fuses the techniques of fiction with the craft of nonfiction. His most recent work is* Thy Neighbor's Wife *(1980). In an introduction to a collection of his reporting,* Fame and Obscurity, *Talese describes his approach to journalism:*

> *The new journalism, though often reading like fiction, is not like fiction. It is, or should be, as reliable as the most reliable reportage although it seeks a larger truth than is possible through the mere compilation of verifiable facts, the use of direct quotations, and adherence to the rigid organizational style of the older form. The new journalism allows, demands in fact, a more imaginative approach to reporting, and it permits the writer to inject himself into the narrative if he wishes, as many writers do, or to assume the role of a detached observer, as others do, including myself.*

> *I try to follow my subjects unobtrusively while observing them in revealing situations, noting their reactions and the reactions of others to them. I attempt to absorb the whole scene, the dialogue and mood, the tension, drama, conflict, and then I try to write it all from the point of view of the persons I am writing about, even revealing whenever possible what these individuals are* thinking *during those moments that I am describing. This latter insight is not obtainable, of course, without the full cooperation of the subject, but if the writer enjoys the confidence and trust of his subjects it is possible, through interviews, by asking the right question at the right time, to learn and to report what goes on within other people's minds.*

The title of Talese's collection, Fame and Obscurity, *also helps describe one of the characteristic features of modern journalism. Celebrities and the oddly insignificant are equally attractive to reporters: the famous because the reporter can then publicize the obscurities behind official appearances, and the anonymous so the reporter can then bestow on the truly obscure the status of celebrities.*

They drive into town in big cars, and live in furnished rooms, and drink whiskey with beer chasers, and chase women they will soon forget. They linger only a little while, only until they have built the bridge; then they are off again to another town, another bridge, linking everything but their lives.

They possess none of the foundation of their bridges. They are part circus, part gypsy—graceful in the air, restless on the ground; it is as if the wide-open road below lacks for them the clear direction of an eight-inch beam stretching across the sky six hundred feet above the sea.

When there are no bridges to be built, they will build skyscrapers, or highways, or power dams, or anything that promises a challenge—and overtime. They will go anywhere, will drive a thousand miles all day and night to be part of a new building boom. They find boom towns irresistible. That is why they are called "the boomers."

In appearance, boomers usually are big men, or if not always big, always strong, and their skin is ruddy from all the sun and wind. Some who heat rivets have charred complexions; some who drive rivets are hard of hearing; some who catch rivets in small metal cones have blisters and body burns marking each miss; some who do welding see flashes at night while they sleep. Those who connect steel have deep scars along their shins from climbing columns. Many boomers have mangled hands and fingers sliced off by slipped steel. Most have taken falls and broken a limb or two. All have seen death.

They are cocky men, men of great pride, and at night they brag and build bridges in bars, and sometimes when they are turning to leave, the bartender will yell after them, "Hey, you guys, how's about clearing some steel out of here?"

Stray women are drawn to them, like them because they have money and no wives within miles—they liked them well enough to have floated a bordello boat beneath one bridge near St. Louis, and to have used upturned hardhats for flowerpots in the red-light district of Paducah.

On weekends some boomers drive hundreds of miles to visit their families, are tender and tolerant, and will deny to the heavens any suggestion that they raise hell on the job—except they'll admit it in whispers, half proud, half ashamed, fearful the wives will hear and then any semblance of marital stability will be shattered.

Like most men, the boomer wants it both ways.

Occasionally his family will follow him, living in small hotels or trailer courts, but it is no life for a wife and child.

The boomer's child might live in forty states and attend a dozen high schools before he graduates, *if* he graduates, and though the father swears he wants no boomer for a son, he usually gets one. He gets one, possibly, because he really wanted one, and maybe that is why boomers brag so much at home on weekends, creating a wondrous world with whiskey words, a world no son can resist because this world seems to have everything: adventure, big cars, big money—sometimes $350 or $450 a week—and gambling on rainy days when the bridge is slippery, and booming around the country with Indians who are sure-footed as spiders, with Newfoundlanders as shifty as the sea they come from, with roaming Rebel riveters escaping the poverty of their small Southern towns, all of them building something big and permanent, something that can be revisisted years later and pointed to and said of: "See that bridge over there, son—well one day, when I was younger, I drove twelve hundred rivets into that goddamned thing."

They tell their sons the good parts, forgetting the bad, hardly ever describing how men sometimes freeze with fear on high steel and clutch to beams with closed eyes, or admitting that when they climb down they need three drinks to settle their nerves; no, they dwell on the glory, the overtime, not the weeks of unemployment; they recall how they helped build the Golden Gate and Empire State, and how their fathers before them worked on the Williamsburg Bridge in 1902, lifting steel beams with derricks pulled by horses.

They make their world sound as if it were an extension of the Wild West, which in a way it is, with boomers today still regarding themselves as pioneering men, the last of America's unhenpecked heroes, but there are probably only a thousand of them left who are footloose enough to go anywhere to build anything. And when they arrive at the newest boom town, they hold brief reunions in bars, and talk about old times, old faces: about Cicero Mike, who once drove a Capone whiskey truck during Prohibition and recently fell to his death off a bridge near Chicago; and Indian Al Deal, who kept three women happy out West and came to the bridge each morning in a fancy silk shirt; and about Riphorn Red, who used to paste twenty-dollar bills along the sides of his suitcase and who went berserk one night in a cemetery. And there was the Nutley Kid, who smoked long Indian cigars and chewed snuff and used toilet water and, at lunch, would drink milk and beer—without taking out the snuff. And there was Ice Water Charley, who on freezing wintry days up on the bridge would send apprentice boys all the way down to fetch hot water, but by the time they'd climbed back up, the water was cold, and he would spit it out, screaming angrily, "*Ice water, ice water!*" and send them all the way down for more. And there was that one-legged lecher, Whitey Howard, who, on a rail bridge one day, did not hear the train coming, and so he had to jump the tracks at the last second, holding on to the edge, during which time his wooden leg fell off, and Whitey spent the rest of his life bragging about how he lost his left leg twice.

Sometimes they go on and on this way, drinking and reminiscing about the undramatic little things involving people known only to boomers, people seen only at a distance by the rest of the world, and then they'll start a card game, the first of hundreds to be played in this boom town while the bridge is being built—a bridge many boomers will never cross. For before the bridge is finished, maybe six months before it is opened to traffic, some boomers get itchy and want to move elsewhere. The challenge is dying. So is the overtime. And they begin to wonder: "Where next?" This is what they were asking one another in the early spring of 1957, but some boomers already had the answer: New York.

New York was planning a number of bridges. Several projects were scheduled upstate, and New York City alone, between 1958 and 1964, planned to spend nearly $600,000,000 for, among other things, the double-decking of the George Washington Bridge, the construction of the Throgs Neck Bridge across Long Island Sound—and, finally, in what might be the most challenging task of a boomer's lifetime, the construction of the world's largest suspension span, the Verrazano-Narrows Bridge.

The Verrazano-Narrows, linking Brooklyn and Staten Island (over the futile objections of thousands of citizens in both boroughs), would possess a 4,260-foot center span that would surpass San Francisco's Golden Gate by 60 feet, and would be 460 feet longer than the Mackinac Bridge in upper Michigan, just below Canada.

It was the Mackinac Bridge, slicing down between Lake Huron and Lake Michigan and connecting the cities of St. Ignace and Mackinaw City, that had attracted the boomers between the years 1954 and 1957. And though they would now abandon it for New York, not being able to resist the big movement eastward, there were a few boomers who actually were sorry to be leaving Michigan, for in their history of hell-raising there never had been a more bombastic little boom town than the once tranquil St. Ignace.

Before the boomers had infiltrated it, St. Ignace was a rather sober city of about 2,500 residents, who went hunting in winter, fishing in summer, ran small shops that catered to tourists, helped run the ferryboats across five miles of water to Mackinaw City, and gave the local police very little trouble. The land had been inhabited first by peaceful Indians, then by French bushrangers, then by missionaries and fur traders, and in 1954 it was still clean and uncorrupt, still with one hotel, called the Nicolet—named after a white man, Jean Nicolet, who in 1634 is said to have paddled in a canoe through the Straits of Mackinac and discovered Lake Michigan.

So it was the Nicolet Hotel, and principally its bar, that became the boomers' headquarters, and soon the place was a smoky scene of nightly parties and brawls, and there were girls down from Canada and up from Detroit, and there were crap games along the floor—and if St. Ignace had not been such a friendly city, all the boomers might have gone to jail and the bridge might never have been finished.

But the people of St. Ignace were pleased with the big new bridge going up. They could see how hard the men worked on it and they did not want to spoil their little fun at night. The merchants, of course, were favorably disposed because, suddenly, in this small Michigan town by the sea, the sidewalks were enhanced by six hundred or seven hundred men, each earning between $300 and $500 a week—and some spending it as fast as they were making it.

The local police did not want to seem inhospitable, either, and so they did not raid the poker or crap games. The only raid in memory was led by some Michigan state troopers; and when they broke in, they discovered gambling among the boomers another state trooper. The only person arrested was the boomer who had been winning the most. And since his earnings were confiscated, he was unable to pay the $100 fine and therefore had to go to jail. Later that night, however, he got a poker game going in his cell, won $100, and bought his way out of jail. He was on the bridge promptly for work the next morning.

It is perhaps a slight exaggeration to suggest that, excepting state troopers, everybody else in St. Ignace either fawned upon or quietly tolerated boomers. For there were some families who forbade their daughters to date boomers, with some success, and there were young local men in town who despised boomers, although this attitude may be attributed as much to their envy of boomers' big cars and money as to the fact that comparatively few boomers were teetotalers or celibates.

On the other hand, it would be equally misleading to assume that there were not some boomers who were quiet, modest men—maybe as many as six or seven—one of them being, for instance, a big quiet Kentuckian named Ace Cowan (whose wife was with him in Michigan), and another being Johnny Atkins, who once at the Nicolet drank a dozen double Martinis without causing a fuss or seeming drunk, and then floated quietly, happily out into the night.

And there was also Jack Kelly, the tall 235-pound son of a Philadelphia sailmaker, who, despite years of work on noisy bridges and despite getting hit on the head by so much falling hardware that he had fifty-two stitches in his scalp, remained ever mild. And finally there was another admired man on the Mackinac—the superintendent, Art ''Drag-Up'' Drilling, a veteran boomer from Arkansas who went West to work on the Golden Gate and Oakland Bay bridges in the thirties, and who was called ''Drag-Up'' because he always said, though never in threat, that he'd sooner drag-up and leave town than work under a superintendent who knew less about bridges than he.

So he went from town to town, bridge to bridge, never really satisfied until he became the top bridgeman—as he did on the Mackinac, and as he hoped to do in 1962 on the Verrazano-Narrows Bridge.

In the course of his travels, however, Drag-Up Drilling sired a son named John. And while John Drilling inherited much of his father's soft Southern charm and easy manner, these qualities actually belied the devil beneath. For John Drilling, who was only nineteen years old when he first joined the gang on the Mackinac, worked as hard as any to leave the boomer's mark on St. Ignace.

John Drilling had been born in Oakland in 1937 while his father was finishing on the Bay bridge there. And in the next nineteen years he followed his father, living in forty-one states, attending two dozen schools, charming the girls—marrying one, and living with her for four months. There was nothing raw nor rude in his manner. He was always extremely genteel and clean-cut in appearance, but, like many boomers' offspring, he was afflicted with what old bridgemen call ''rambling fever.''

This made him challenging to some women, and frustrating to others, yet intriguing to most. On his first week in St. Ignace, while stopped at a gas station, he noticed a carload of girls nearby and, exuding all the shy and bumbling uncertainty of a new boy in town, addressed himself politely to the prettiest girl in the car—a Swedish beauty, a very healthy girl whose boy friend had just been drafted—and thus began an unforgettable romance that would last until the next one.

Having saved a few thousand dollars from working on the Mackinac, he became, very briefly, a student at the University of Arkansas and also bought a $2,700 Impala. One night in Ola, Ark., he cracked up the car and might have gotten into legal difficulty had not his date that evening been the judge's daughter.

John Drilling seemed to have a charmed life. Of all the bridge builders who worked on the Mackinac, and who would later come East to work on the Verrazano-Narrows Bridge, young John Drilling seemed the luckiest—with the possible exception of his close friend, Robert Anderson.

Anderson was luckier mainly because he had lived longer, done more, survived more; and he never lost his sunny disposition or incurable optimism. He was thirty-four years old when he came to the Mackinac. He had been married to one girl for a dozen years, to another for two weeks. He had been in auto accidents, been hit by falling tools, taken falls—once toppling forty-two feet—but his only visible injury was two missing inside fingers on his left hand, and he never lost its full use.

One day on the north tower of the Mackinac, the section of catwalk upon which

Anderson was standing snapped loose, and suddenly it came sliding down like a rollercoaster, with Anderson clinging to it as it bumped and raced down the cables, down 1,800 feet all the way to near the bottom where the cables slope gently and straighten out before the anchorage. Anderson quietly got off and began the long climb up again. Fortunately for him, the Mackinac was designed by David B. Steinman, who preferred long, tapering backspans; had the bridge been designed by O. H. Ammann, who favored shorter, chunkier backspans, such as the type he was then creating for the Verrazano-Narrows Bridge, Bob Anderson would have had a steeper, more abrupt ride down, and might have gone smashing into the anchorage and been killed. But Anderson was lucky that way.

Off the bridge, Anderson had a boomer's luck with women. All the moving around he had done during his youth as a boomer's son, all the shifting from town to town and the enforced flexibility required of such living, gave him a casual air of detachment, an ability to be at home anywhere. Once, in Mexico, he made his home in a whorehouse. The prostitutes down there liked him very much, fought over him, admired his gentle manners and the fact that he treated them all like ladies. Finally the madam invited him in as a full-time house guest and each night Anderson would dine with them, and in the morning he stood in line with them awaiting his turn in the shower.

Though he stands six feet and is broad-shouldered and erect, Bob Anderson is not a particularly handsome fellow; but he has bright alert eyes, and a round, friendly, usually smiling face, and he is very disarming, a sort of Tom Jones of the bridge business—smooth and swift, somewhat gallant, addicted to good times and hot-blooded women, and yet never slick or tricky.

He is also fairly lucky at gambling, having learned a bit back in Oklahoma from his uncle Manuel, a guitar-playing rogue who once won a whole carnival playing poker. Anderson avoids crap games, although one evening at the Nicolet, when a crap game got started on the floor of the men's room and he'd been invited to join, he did.

"Oh, I was drunk that night," he said, in his slow Southwestern drawl, to a friend some days later. "I was so drunk I could hardly see. But I jes' kept rolling them dice, and all I was seeing was sevens and elevens, sevens and elevens, *Jee-sus Kee-rist,* all night long it went like that, and I kept winning and drinking and winning some more. Finally lots of other folks came jamming in, hearing all the noise and all, in this men's toilet room there's some women and tourists who also came in—jes' watching me roll those sevens and elevens.

"Next morning I woke up with a helluva hangover, but on my bureau I seen this pile of money. And when I felt inside my pockets they were stuffed with bills, crumpled up like dried leaves. And when I counted it all, it came to more than one thousand dollars. And that day on the bridge, there was guys coming up to me and saying, 'Here, Bob, here's the fifty I borrowed last night,' or, 'Here's the hundred,' and I didn't even remember they borrowed it. Jee-sus Kee-rist, what a night!"

When Bob Anderson finally left the Mackinac job and St. Ignace, he had managed to save five thousand dollars, and, not knowing what else to do with it, he bought a round-trip airplane ticket and went flying off to Tangier, Paris and Switzerland—"whoring and drinking," as he put it—and then, flat broke, except for his return ticket, he went back to St. Ignace and married a lean, lovely brunette he'd been unable to forget.

And not long after that, he packed his things and his new wife, and along with dozens of other boomers—with John Drilling and Drag-Up, with Ace Cowan and Jack Kelly and other veterans of the Mackinac and the Nicolet—he began the long road trip eastward to try his luck in New York. [. . .]

DISCUSSION QUESTIONS

1. Compare Talese's account of the "boomers" with Hard's description of newsboys. Which writer maintains more distance between himself and the working groups? How is that distance expressed in style and tone?

2. Describe the differences in each writer's use of details. Which writer tries harder to give the impression of journalistic objectivity? How are details used in each case to convey a sense of closely-knit working communities: Which community do you feel is described more satisfactorily? Explain.

3. Would the working people described by Talese and Hard be included as part of each writer's imagined audience? Describe the distinctions (if any) you think exist between the audience and subjects of each work. Which writer's style is more suited to the language spoken by his subjects? Do you think the smaller the stylistic margin the more honest the appraisal? Explain.

Ellen Willis / Women and the Myth of Consumerism

Ramparts, June 1970

A politically leftist monthly addressed to a national audience of college educated men and women, Ramparts *publishes articles devoted to contemporary affairs with an emphasis on social and political reform. Ellen Willis is a free-lance journalist and reviewer of current cultural phenomena for* The New Yorker *and the* New York Review of Books. *She has recently published* Beginning To See the Light: Pieces of a Decade. *Here she attacks what has become the conventional notion (see Vance Packard in Best Sellers of consumers victimized by the psychological manipulations of of advertising.*

If white radicals are serious about revolution, they are going to have to discard a lot of bullshit ideology created by and for educated white middle-class males. A good example of what has to go is the popular theory of consumerism.

As expounded by many leftist thinkers, notably Marcuse, this theory maintains that consumers are psychically manipulated by the mass media to crave more and more consumer goods, and thus power an economy that depends on constantly expanding sales. The theory is said to be particularly applicable to women, for women do most of the actual buying, their consumption is often directly related to their oppression (e.g. make-up, soap flakes), and they are a special target of advertisers. According to this view, the society defines women as consumers, and the purpose of the prevailing media image of women as passive sexual objects is to sell products. It follows that the beneficiaries of this depreciation of women are not men but the corporate power structure.

Although the consumerism theory has, in recent years, taken on the invulnerability of religious dogma, like most dogmas its basic function is to defend the interests of its adherents—in this case, the class, sexual and racial privileges of Movement people.

First of all, there is nothing inherently wrong with consumption. Shopping and consuming are enjoyable human activities and the marketplace has been a center of social life for thousands of years. The profit system is oppressive not because relatively trivial luxuries are available, but because basic necessities are not. The locus of the oppression resides in the production function: people have no control over which commodities are produced (or services performed), in what amounts, under what conditions, or how these commodities are distributed. Corporations make these decisions and base them solely on their profit potential. It is more profitable to produce luxuries for the affluent (or for that matter for the poor, on exploitative installment plans) than to produce and make available food, housing, medical care, education, and recreational and cultural facilities according to the needs and desires of the people. We, the consumers, can accept the goods offered to us or we can reject them, but we cannot determine their quality or change the system's priorities.

As it is, the profusion of commodities is a genuine and powerful compensation for oppression. It is a bribe, but like all bribes it offers concrete benefits—in the average American's case, a degree of physical comfort unparalleled in history. Under present conditions, people are preoccupied with consumer goods not because they are brainwashed but because buying is the one pleasurable activity not only permitted but actively encouraged by our rulers. The pleasure of eating an ice cream cone may be minor compared to the pleasure of meaningful, autonomous work, but the former is easily available and the latter is not. A poor family would undoubtedly rather have a decent apartment than a new TV, but since they are unlikely to get the apartment, what is to be gained by not getting the TV?

Radicals who in general are healthily skeptical of facile Freudian explanations have been quick to embrace this theory of media manipulation based squarely on Freud, as popularized by market researchers and journalists like Vance Packard (Marcuse acknowledges Packard's influence in *One Dimensional Man*). In essence, this theory holds that ads designed to create unconscious associations between merchandise and deep-seated fears, sexual desires, and needs for identity and self-esteem, induce people to buy products in search of gratifications no product can provide. Furthermore, the corporations, through the media, deliberately create fears and desires that their products can claim to fulfill. The implication is that women are not merely taken in by lies or exaggerations—as, say, by the suggestion that a certain perfume will make us sexually irresistible—but are psychically incapable of learning from experience and will continue to buy no matter how often we are disappointed, and that in any case our "need" to be sexually irresistible is programmed into us to keep us buying perfume. This hypothesis of psychic distortion is based on the erroneous assumption that mental health and anti-materialism are synonymous.

Although they have to cope with the gyppery inherent in the profit system, people for the most part buy goods for practical, self-interested reasons. A washing machine does make a housewife's work easier (in the absence of socialization of housework); Excedrin does make a headache go away; a car does provide transportation. If one is duped into buying a product because of misleading advertising, the process is called exploitation; it has nothing to do with brainwashing.

Advertising, in fact, is a how-to manual on the consumer economy, constantly reminding us of what is available and encouraging us to indulge ourselves. It works (that is, stimulates sales) *because* buying is the only game in town, not vice versa. Advertising does appeal to morbid fears (e.g. of body odors) and false hopes (of irresistibility) and shoppers faced with indistinguishable brands of a product may choose on the basis of an ad (what method is better?), but this is just the old game of caveat emptor. It thrives on naivete and people learn to resist it through experience. Other vulnerable groups are older people, who had no previous experience—individual or historical—to guide them when the consumer cornucopia suddenly developed after World War II, and poor people, who do not have enough money to learn through years of trial, error and disillusionment to be shrewd consumers. The constant refinement of advertising claims, visual effects and so on, shows that experience desensitizes. No one really believes that smoking Brand X cigarettes will make you sexy. (The function of sex in an ad is probably the obvious one—to lure people into paying closer attention to the ad—rather than to make them "identify" their lust with a product. The chief effect of the heavy sexual emphasis in advertising has been to stimulate a national preoccupation with sex, showing that you can't identify away a basic human drive as easily as all that.) Madison Avenue has increasingly de-emphasized "motivational" techniques in favor of aesthetic ones—TV commercials in particular have become incredibly inventive visually—and even made a joke out of the old motivational ploys (the phallic Virginia Slims ad, for instance, is blatantly campy). We can conclude from this that either the depth psychology approach never worked in the first place, or that it has stopped working as consumers have gotten more sophisticated.

The argument that the corporations create new psychological needs in order to sell their wares is equally flimsy. There is no evidence that propaganda can in itself create a desire, as opposed to bringing to consciousness a latent desire by suggesting that means of satisfying it are available. This idea is superstitious: it implies that the oppressor is diabolically intelligent (he has learned how to control human souls) and that the media have magic powers. It also mistakes effects for causes and drastically oversimplifies the relation between ideology and material conditions. We have not been taught to dislike our smell so that they can sell deodorants; deodorants sell because there are social consequences for smelling. And the negative attitude about our bodies that has made it feasible to invent and market deodorants is deeply rooted in our anti-sexual culture, which in turn has been shaped by exploitive modes of production and class antagonism between men and women.

The confusion between cause and effect is particularly apparent in the consumerist analysis of women's oppression. Women are not manipulated by the media into being domestic servants and mindless sexual decorations, the better to sell soap and hair spray. Rather, the image reflects women as they are forced by men in a sexist society to behave. Male supremacy is the oldest and most basic form of class exploitation; it was not invented by a smart ad man. The real evil of the media image of women is that it supports the sexist status quo. In a sense, the fashion, cosmetics and "feminine hygiene" ads are aimed more at men than at women. They encourage men to expect women to sport all the latest trappings of sexual slavery—expectations women must then fulfill if they are to survive. That advertisers exploit women's subordination rather than cause it can be clearly seen now that *male* fashions and toiletries have become big business. In contrast to ads for women's products, whose appeal is "use this and he will want you" (or "if you don't use this, he won't want you"), ads for the male counterparts urge, "You too can enjoy perfume and bright-colored clothes; don't worry, it doesn't make you feminine." Although advertisers are careful to emphasize how *virile* these products are (giving them names like "Brut," showing the man who uses them hunting or flirting with admiring women—who, incidentally, remain decorative objects when the sell is aimed directly at men), it is never claimed that the product is *essential* to masculinity (as make-up is essential to femininity), only *compatible* with it. To convince a man to buy, an ad must appeal to his desire for autonomy and freedom from conventional restrictions; to convince a woman, an ad must appeal to her need to please the male oppressor.

For women, buying and wearing clothes and beauty aids is not so much consumption as work. One of a woman's jobs in this society is to be an attractive sexual object, and clothes and make-up are tools of the trade. Similarly, buying food and household furnishings is a domestic task; it is the wife's chore to pick out the commodities that will be consumed by the whole family. Appliances and cleaning materials are tools that facilitate her domestic function. When a woman spends a lot of money and time decorating her home or herself, or hunting down the latest in vacuum cleaners, it is not idle self-indulgence (let alone the result of psychic manipulation) but a healthy attempt to find outlets for her creative energies within her circumscribed role.

There is a persistent myth that a wife has control over her husband's money because she gets to spend it. Actually, she does not have much more financial autonomy than the employee of a corporation who is delegated to buy office furniture or supplies. The husband, especially if he is rich, may allow his wife wide latitude in spending—he may reason that since she has to work in the home she is entitled to furnish it to her taste, or he may simply not want to bother with domestic details—but he retains the ultimate veto power. If he doesn't like the way his wife handles his money, she will hear about it. In most households, particularly in the working class, a wife cannot make significant expenditures, either personal or in her role as object-servant, without consulting her husband. And more often than not, according to statistics, it is the husband who makes the final decisions about furniture and appliances as well as about other major expenditures like houses, cars and vacations.

The consumerism theory is the outgrowth of an aristocratic, European-oriented antimaterialism based on upper-class resentment against the rise of the vulgar bourgeoisie. Radical intellectuals have been attracted to this essentially reactionary position (Herbert Marcuse's view of mass culture is strikingly similar to that of conservative theorists like Ernest Van Den Haag) because it appeals both to their dislike of capitalism and to their feeling of superiority to the working class. This elitism is evident in radicals' conviction that they have seen through the system, while the average working slob is brainwashed by the media. (Oddly, no one claims that the ruling class is oppressed by commodities; it seems that rich people consume out of free choice.) Ultimately this point of view leads to a sterile emphasis on individual solutions—if only the benighted would reject their "plastic" existence and move to East Village tenements—and the conclusion that people are oppressed because they are stupid or sick. The obnoxiousness of this attitude is compounded by the fact that radicals can only maintain their dropout existence so long as plenty of brainwashed workers keep the economy going.

Consumerism as applied to women is blatantly sexist. The pervasive image of the empty-headed female consumer constantly trying her husband's patience with her extravagant purchases contributes to the myth of male superiority: we are incapable of spending money rationally; all we need to make us happy is a new hat now and then. (There is an analogous racial stereotype—the black with his Cadillac and his magenta shirts.) Furthermore, the consumerism line allows Movement men to avoid recognizing that they exploit women by attributing women's oppression solely to capitalism. It fits neatly into already existing radical theory and concerns, saving the Movement the trouble of tackling the real problems of women's liberation. And it retards the struggle against male supremacy by dividing women. Just as in the male movement, the belief in consumerism encourages radical women to patronize and put down other women for trying to survive as best they can, and maintains individualist illusions.

If we are to build a mass movement we must recognize that no individual decision, like rejecting consumption, can liberate us. We must stop arguing about whose life style is better (and secretly believing ours is) and tend to the task of collectively fighting our own oppression and the ways in which we oppress others. When we create a political alternative to sexism, racism and capitalism, the consumer problem, if it is a problem, will take care of itself.

DISCUSSION QUESTIONS

1. Of what relevance is Vance Packard's essay on consumerism (see Best Sellers) to Willis' argument? How does she feel her audience regards his essay? Whom is she writing for? What assumptions, for example, does she make about the political awareness of her audience?

2. Find some ads in Advertising that Willis could have used to support her arguments about the relationship between advertising methods and buying habits. How does her theory of advertising differ from Packard's? Which theory attributes more power to advertising methods? Which theory do you find more convincing? Support your case by using some of the ads in this book.

Time Staff / Death of a Maverick Mafioso
[*On the Shooting of Joey Gallo*]

Time, April 1972

For many years, the slogan of Time *magazine was "curt, concise, complete." Founded in 1923 by Henry Luce and Briton Hadden,* Time, the Weekly News Magazine *was intended to appeal to the growing number of American college graduates. Its title was meant to suggest both the scope of the magazine's coverage of current events and its sensitivity to the limited time in which "busy men are able to spend on simply keeping informed." Luce and Hadden rejected the conventional format of objective news reporting and promoted instead a highly idiosyncratic, self-consciously "lively" narrative and a somewhat subjective, though corporate, journalistic style.*

Joey Gallo's murder received national attention. Inevitable were the comparisons with Mario Puzo's The Godfather *(see Best Sellers) to show how ruthlessly life imitates art.*

The scene could have been lifted right out of that movie. First, a night of champagne and laughter at Manhattan's Copacabana as Mobster Joseph ("Crazy Joe") Gallo, one of New York's most feared Mafiosi, celebrated his 43rd birthday. Then on to a predawn Italian breakfast at a gleaming new restaurant in the city's Little Italy area. Seated at his left at a rear table in Umbertos Clam House was his brawny bodyguard, Pete ("The Greek") Diopioulis; at Gallo's right, his sister Carmella. Across the table sat Gallo's darkly attractive bride of just three weeks, Sina, 29, and her daughter Lisa, 10. Quietly, a lone gunman stepped through a rear door and strode toward the table.

Both Gallo and Diopioulis were carelessly facing the wall instead of the door. The triggerman opened fire with a .38-caliber revolver. Women screamed. Joey and Pete were hit instantly. The Greek drew his own gun, began shooting back. So did one Gallo ally, seated at the front clam bar. Within 90 seconds, 20 shots ripped through the restaurant. Tables crashed over, hurling hot sauce and ketchup across the blue-tiled floor to mix with the blood of the wounded. The gunman whirled, ran out the same rear door and into a waiting car.

Gallo, wounded in a buttock, an elbow and his back, staggered toward the front of the café. He lurched through a front door and collapsed, bleeding, on the street. Carmella's screams attracted officers in a passing police car. They rushed Gallo to a hospital, but he died before reaching it.

MUSCLING

That melodramatic end to the short, brutal life of Joey Gallo surprised no one in New York's increasingly fratricidal underworld. There had been a contract out on his life ever since Mafia Boss Joe Colombo had been shot at an Italian Day rally in New York last June (TIME cover, July 12). Police do not believe that Gallo plotted that murder attempt, but friends of Colombo, who remains unable to talk or walk, thought he had. Gallo had been counted among the walking dead ever since he also aroused the anger of the biggest boss of them all, aging Carlo Gambino. Told to stop muscling into Gambino's operations, including the lucrative narcotics traffic in East Harlem, the cocky Gallo hurled the ultimate Mafia insult at Gambino: he spat at him.

If that act seemed foolhardy, it was nevertheless typical of Gallo, who never had the sense to play by the rigid rules of the brotherhood. He grew up with his brothers Larry and Albert in Brooklyn's Bath Beach, where mobsters often dumped their victims. One of his neighbors recalled Joey as "the kind of guy who wanted to grow up to be George Raft. He would stand on the corner when he was 15, flipping a half-dollar, and practice talking without moving his lips."

Joey first witnessed a gang murder in his early teens. After the victim was hauled away, he studied the scene, counted the bullet holes and took notes on how the killing must have been done. He began packing a pistol about the same time. Later, he affected the black shirt and white tie of Killer Richard Widmark in the movie *Kiss of Death.* He saw the movie so many times he knew all its lines. He spent hours in front of a mirror, trying to look as tough as Widmark—and he succeeded. He had a mercurial temper and acted out his movie fantasies as the cruelest of the Gallo brothers.

By the time Joey was 21, he was in trouble with the law, and a court-appointed psychiatrist found him insane. Other mobsters started calling him "Crazy Joe" but never to his face. He was too mean. Joey took pleasure in breaking the arm of one of his clients who was sluggish about paying protection money. He punctured an enemy with ice picks. He had gained his status by serving as one member (Colombo was another) of a five-man execution squad of Mafia Boss Joe Profaci in the late '50s. Police claim they had scored 40 hits. By then he and his brothers had carved out a chunk of the Brooklyn rackets; they turned against Profaci, touching off a gang war in which nine mobsters died and three disappeared.

Over the years, Gallo developed a wise-guy kind of humor that led some naive acquaintances to consider him a sort of folk hero. He was summoned to Robert Kennedy's office in 1959 when Kennedy was counsel to a Senate rackets investigating committee, looked at the rug and said, "Hey, this would be a great spot for a crap game." He once told a courtroom: "The cops say I've been picked up 15, maybe 17 times. That's junk. It was 150 times. I been worked over for nothing until my hat sits on my head like it belongs on a midget." Someone in 1961 overheard him trying to shake down a Brooklyn restaurant owner for a share of the profits. The proprietor asked for time to think about it. "Sure," said Gallo, "take three months in the hospital on me."

That quip cost Gallo nine years for extortion. In Attica state prison, Gallo earned a reputation as a civil rights leader of sorts. He helped lead an inmate drive to force white prison barbers to cut the hair of blacks; he had his own hair cut by a black barber to show his lack of prejudice. Actually, his motive seemed to be to recruit black toughs for his gang. When he got out of prison in March of 1971, he began hiring blacks as "button men" (musclemen)—pricking the ethnic sensibilities of other Mafiosi. He had openly toured Little Italy with four black henchmen a few days before he was hit. Some officials think that may have hastened execution of the contract.

HEARTY HOOD

Gallo's defiance of Mafia tradition did not mark him as particularly savvy. Neither did his open claim that he was about to write his memoirs. Other gangsters do not appreciate such literature. There was, for example, a $100,000 contract—for his death, not his papers—out on Joseph Valachi, who wrote in detail of his life with the Mob (he died of natural causes in prison). But Author Marta Curro, the wife of Actor Jerry Orbach, eagerly agreed to help write the book because she had discovered that Joey was "a great person, brilliant, absolutely charming."

It was at the Orbach apartment that Gallo married Sina Essary, a dental assistant he had met eleven years ago, before he went to jail. He and his first wife Jeffie Lee were divorced a few months ago. Joey and Sina, whose young daughter opened in the Broadway play *Voices* last week, soon became a part of the theatergoing, nightclubbing celebrity set. Crazy Joe, the killer, had become Pal Joey, the hearty hood. That, too, did not go down well with various godfathers.

SCRIPTS

Gallo kept telling his new found friends that he had gone straight. He told Celebrity Columnist Earl Wilson: "I'll never go back there—I think there is nothing out there for me but death." Police insist that Gallo was gulling others; that he actually was as much involved in the rackets as ever.

The truth seems to be that Gallo was leading a schizophrenic life in those last days: a steel-tough gunman in racket circles; a philosophic, warm conversationalist outside the Mob. Whether he was really at home in both roles, or just a good actor, he was clearly convincing. Actress Joan Hackett found him fascinating well before she knew of his Mafia connections. "I liked him completely apart from any grotesque glamorization of the underworld," she recalls. "I thought his attempt to leave that life was genuine. He was the brightest person I've ever known." But Gallo also conceded that "I'll never make it in the straight world."

With the slaying of two other lesser mobsters in New York last week, full gang warfare seemed imminent. The new image of Mafiosi as soft-spoken, smart-dressing businessmen, who shun such crudities as murder and torture as old-fashioned, seemed to be fading. Perhaps the Mob was taking those gory movie scripts about itself too seriously. At any rate, it was exposing the cruelty and ruthlessness of racketeering. Off-screen, murder is brutally final. Indeed, Gallo did not like parts of the *The Godfather*. He told a friend that he thought the death scenes seemed "too flashy."

Lew Dietz / The Myth of the Boss Bear

True, May 1973

Edited for an adult male audience interested in reading about adventure, mysteries, sports, military feats, "masculine" personalities, and the outdoors, True *prefers its nonfiction articles to be anecdotal, carefully documented, and written "with a strong punch." When compared with William Faulkner's* The Bear *(see Classics), written some thirty years earlier, the following essay reminds us of how "factual" accounts often depend on the expectations we derive from fiction and myth.*

The northern Maine wilds were cloaked by a thick haze on my arrival, and when I flew out a week later there was a mountain-hugging fog. Within that span there was rain, more fog—and a bear called Lonesome George. Actually there were nine black bears sighted that week in June and one brought to earth with a bullet from a .284 Winchester. But only Lonesome George mattered to the hunters of Yankee-tu-laidi.

It was Glenn Wilcox who had dubbed the animal Lonesome George and Wilcox who had had the only confrontation with this seemingly immortal beast, a meeting that had left the bear with an altered forefoot. Mostly the animal was called simply The Bear, as though there were no other of its species in this remote and all but inaccessible region north of the Allagash.

Yankee-tu-laidi is the stream which flashes through this ridged country like a bright scepter. Local woodsmen suggest that the name might be a corruption of *touradie,* the French word for lake trout, but the origin is obscure. It's a fine, gamy hunk of territory, primarily because it is all but impossible to get into, and the hunters of Yankee-tu-laidi would like to keep it that way.

The day's hunting was over when I arrived. I tossed my sleeping bag into the loft, the only vacant nook in the gear-cluttered camp. John, the cook by tacit agreement—his stew was no more than tolerable but he was fastidiously clean—was stirring up the potluck. When a bottle started its rounds, I heard about The Bear.

Buzz Barry, a portly and imperturbable fellow with the dark soulful eyes of an Italian opera tenor, put it simply. "Glenn swears he's bigger than Joey's bear. And you saw Joey's bear."

I'd hunted with Barry and his Yankee-tu-laidi irregulars for a number of years. I knew about Joey Wilcox's bear. The spring before, Joey had come upon this King Kong of bears just a mile up the ridge from camp. The bear was shaking its great head as though bewildered by some awesome experience. It was only after Joey had dropped the bear at close range that he gained a clue to the nature of the drama. The dead bear showed evidence of having been bested in a brawl. Joey's bear went close to 400 pounds dressed, which meant a live weight of nearly 500, a big one, considering that the average mature black bear weighs around 300 pounds.

So what about the bear that was the winner and still champion? It was, as Buzz Barry put it, something to think about.

Barry was my host. Since he had the only camp lease in this 200 square miles of bear country, he might well have been elected top dog by expedient acclamation, like the sandlot kid with the only ball in town. Barry, however, had earned his stripes. He and his hunting partner, Glenn Wilcox, had pioneered bear hunting in this shaggy corner of Maine. In the course of five years, the pair had accounted for many bears and they'd got them the hard way, mostly before the state elevated the black bear to the status of game animal and established a limit of one in a season which extends from June 1 to December 31.

There was no further talk about The Bear that night. What else was there to say? These were Maine men who found ease and joy in the fraternity of hunting. They hunted for the challenge and the love of it, as had their fathers and grandfathers before them. And the ease in the camp was an ease that exists among men who have hunted long years together.

Five other men had come primarily to fish. Buzz Barry, Bob York and the Wilcox brothers were the bear hunters. For these four there was a special feeling about a bear hunt, something about the quest as warming and full-bodied as good bourbon. Until recent years few Maine hunters set out specifically for a bear. Bears were trapped, shot over bait or killed at a camp dump. And each fall a few were shot by deer hunters who came upon them accidentally. Maine has a good supply of bears and they seem to be on the increase. But the fellow who thinks he can walk into the woods any fine day and dispatch a bear has neglected to take this crafty animal into his calculation.

There are woodsmen who have spent a good part of their lives in Maine bear country and have never seen a live bear. A truly wild bear has ears like a lynx and the nose of a truffle hound. And although its eyes are no better than a deer's, a bear can identify a motionless man for what he is at 100 yards. A bear seldom waits to learn more.

The hunters had been in camp two days and, as was their custom, they had devoted the time to scouting the country in an attempt to learn how the bears were moving and where they were feeding. The first few months after leaving their winter dens, bears feed primarily on grass, sedges and herbs. These items, along with grubs and other insects, constitute their diet until the berries ripen in late July. The scouts reported encouraging bear signs but no great concentration in any one section. Our best bet, Buzz Barry thought, would be to hunt the overgrown woods, roads and grassy openings.

I was to hunt with him in his rig the next morning. Wheels are not a prerequisite to hunting bears in that big country but they do help, for while a deer is satisfied to live within a few square miles of territory, the "home" range of a mature black bear in Maine is possibly 700 square miles; a sow with cubs as much as 300. June is the peak of the bear's rut season, at which time both the sows and boars are apt to roam a bit more than normal. Eight years earlier, Barry decided that since there was no all-terrain vehicle available to meet the demanding requirements of Maine bear hunting, he would have to build his own rig.

Essentially his woods buggy is a dune buggy adapted to offer more low-gear pulling power and increased clearance. Bus transaxles solved both these problems. They reduced gear ratios and increased undercarriage clearance. And since there was no worry about making gear ratios too high, the hunters were able to go to oversized tires for better traction. Reducing tire pressures to six pounds forward and eight in the rear offered additional traction and eased the punishing ride. The year before, I'd made the 30-mile buggy ride into Yankee-tu-laidi and can say that the trip would have made a hairy episode for *Mission Impossible*.

Buzz Barry and I set out shortly after sunup, leaving word of our itinerary and expected return time—an obvious precaution. Machines can break down under the punishing paces they are put through. There is no sleep or drink at the camp until all vehicles are accounted for.

Barry wanted to look over the Landry "road" (the quotes are used advisedly). At one point some busy beaver had created a daunting water hazard. As we broke a few holes in the damn to lower the water, I thought about a dialogue Teddy Roosevelt reported after he and his Maine guide had managed to get a wagon through to a camp on Munsungan Lake in mud season. "How," Teddy asked his guide, "do you Maine folks tell a road from a river?" "No beaver dams on the roads," was the guide's ready answer. Which goes to show that even a Maine guide can be wrong sometimes.

It was a dark day with a threat of rain, which was good, Buzz said, because it would make for soft going. Also it would give the hunter something closer to an even break. A bear can smell a man a country mile away. In wet weather a man can smell a bear, not a country mile perhaps, but a good 50 yards if the wind is right. I'd come to know a bear's rank, amonic scent, much like a skunk's, but less penetrating. Once you've smelled a bear, you'll never forget it.

A mile or so beyond the beaver flowage, we came upon fresh bear scats (in spring, a fresh bear dropping is green, turning brown and then black as it ages). Encouraged, we parked the buggy by a swollen brook. The still hunt on foot began.

Barry went ahead 30 paces or so and I took up the rear as we followed the twisting, grass-choked old-haul road. At each turn, my friend would ease to the outside of the trail and peer ahead before exposing himself. You spot a bear at an opening or you don't spot him at all. And if the bear sees you before you see the bear—well, it's good-bye Charlie.

"The bear has one flaw in his defenses. You might call it a character weakness," Barry said earlier. "A bear is a glutton. A bear's not apt to look up between nips when he's feeding, the way a deer does. If you sight a bear and the wind is right, you can stalk him. It takes patience, though. The biggest bear I ever shot took three hours of stalking.

"Matter of fact, there's one other advantage the bear hunter has. In the spring woods there is nothing in the world blacker than a black bear. You may mistake something in the woods for a bear, but you never mistake a bear for anything else. For one thing, a bear in the spring is seldom still; it moves frequently."

The Maine hunter is essentially a still hunter. He prefers to hunt alone or with a seasoned partner of long-standing. There is an incomparable excitement to a still hunt in gamy country. The hunter becomes a part of the natural realm. He tries to match eyes for eyes, ears for ears and cunning for cunning with his quarry. The fact that his rifle is an equalizer makes still-hunting no less a humbling experience.

We saw no sign of The Bear that day nor did we sight a bear of any stripe. The brothers Glenn and Joey Wilcox had arrived in camp when we trundled in. Glenn, plump as Friar Tuck; Joey, a mild apologetic fellow, make an unlikely looking pair of bear hunters. All the same, you'll have to search a long way to find anyone to match their knowledge of bears and their love of the hunt."

"The bears have begun to grub," Joey said. "They're doing a bit of frogging, too. Saw where a sow and her two cubs crossed the trail this morning below Dodge City."

"Dodge City" was a whimsy certainly, but an in-group place-name as well. This decaying cluster of old logging buildings had a story. A bear had broken into the hovel looking for forgotten oats and had been waylaid while attempting to escape through a window frame. There was "Pole Bridge" and "Mary's Tits," a pair of low knobs where Buzz had made that long stalk; "Trail 49," where one spring they had counted 49 bear scats on a two-mile stretch. And there was "Joey's Bend," that turn above the camp where Joey and his great bear had had their confrontation.

"Been a few bears working on the Loop Trail," Glenn said. "Small ones, yearlings, I'd guess.

Four bears had been sighted that day, only one large enough to be considered respectable. No one, not even Glenn Wilcox, mentioned The Bear, though he was the fiercest of all to get the animal dead to rights. I had the feeling that no one wished to hear the very real possibility that this grizzled lord of Yankee-tu-laidi had renounced his kingdom and departed. Only George, one of the fishermen who delighted in ribbing Lester, a pal, made a glancing reference to the subject.

"Lester and I come upon a bear flop near Fall Brook that two men could have shook hands across. I asked Lester to taste it for freshness, but he declined."

That night we feasted on a mess of fresh-caught brook trout. When the Coleman lamps were lit, Glenn decided it was high time he confessed that a bear had once driven him to water. This was early in his bear-hunting career before he'd learned to forgo mixing it up with a she-bear and her cubs. That afternoon he'd squeezed a shot off at a smallish bear. As he'd stepped into the brush to see what damage he'd done, he'd heard a low growl.

"There was that big sow, ears back, teeth bared, coming right for me. There wasn't time to do much more than shoot from the hip. A howl told me I'd creased her, but she came right on. I tried to take a hasty side step, but I wasn't quite fast enough. She caught me on the shoulder as she went by and sent me flying.

"It was just then that I remembered I'd fired the last round in my clip. As I frisked myself for my spare clip, I had a sinking feeling—I'd left my spare clip in my buggy. As that bear was preparing for a fresh charge, I took off for a beaver pond some 50 paces away. I hardly think my boots ever touched the ground."

For a good two hours Wilcox remained in that beaver pond up to his belly button, empty rifle held over his head. Twice he tried to go ashore and each time was driven back. Finally, with night coming on, he made a run for it.

That next morning Buzz Barry and I saw our first bear. Our plot was to leave the buggy at the beginning of Trail 29 and still-hunt the six miles back to camp on the Ridge Road. We were a mile or so from the trail when we spotted a bear down on its hunkers, feeding on grass.

Buzz eased the buggy to a halt. Stepping out, he slid a cartridge into his magazine. What he carried that day was his light carbine, figuring it would be right for that brushy terrain on the ridge. The bear was just under 200 yards away. My old .303 was under a tarp and little help in the situation. Since the bear had sighted us by then, there was no chance for a stalk. We simply stood there and watched the animal wander across the road and pass from view. Buzz estimated that the bear would have gone around 200 pounds, hardly respectable.

So soft was the going that day that we were able to come to within a few yards of deer; and rounding one twist in the trail we were met by a great bull moose which regarded us with lofty disdain and shuffled off in its own good time.

We saw a fair assortment of bear scats, but they weren't fresh enough to excite what Buzz called his turdometer, an instrument allegedly calibrated to degrees of freshness of bear droppings.

We did see where bears had been working earlier that spring. Here and there the bark of young balsams had been peeled back at their bases by sow bears to offer the treat of resin to their cubs. And we saw where bears had dismembered rotted trees seeking grubs in past seasons. I had my eye out for a bear tree, or what Maine woodsmen call a bear "marking post." When a boss bear feels an urge to express its machismo, it will commonly scribe a set of claw marks on a tree at the fullest extent of its reach for any lesser bear to try to match. Presumably an aspirant failing to meet the test moves on.

Back at camp that afternoon we learned that several yearling bears had been sighted on the back side of Haffey Mountain. Since cubs are dropped in midwinter, a "yearling" bear is nearly a year-and-a-half old in June. This is when the sow bear, ready for her biennial mating, drives off her youngsters to fend for themselves. Freshly out of custody and not yet seasoned to danger, these young bears are sighted more frequently than fully mature animals.

Barry wasn't interested in a yearling, but figured that if young bears were feeding in that area, bigger bears might be lurking not too far off. So Haffey Mountain was our destination as we headed out that next morning.

We were no more than three miles from camp when we saw a wolf. What made the sighting special was that wolves are officially extinct in Maine. Only in very recent years have there been reports of canids variously identified as wild dogs, coydogs, coyotes and wolves. We had a good, if brief, view of that animal as it crossed no more than 25 yards in front of us. Its coat was gray, tinged with red. We estimated its weight at something over 70 pounds, heavier than any coyote. It was similar in size and conformation to the wolf-coyote hybrids I'd seen in East Texas.

As we slogged into Haffey Mountain, it struck me that for these men the machines were every bit as much a challenge as the game. In this operation it's not enough to be a good hunter, you'd better be a damn good Yankee mechanic as well. There were few days that week when at least one buggy didn't come in under juryrig. The year before, a fuel pump had given out 20 miles from base. No problem.

The gas tank had been unbolted and we rode home with one man holding the tank over the engine and feeding gas directly into the carburetor.

We did some hard traveling that day. We saw game aplenty, but the closest we came to a bear was a set of fresh droppings no more than three hours old. . . .

There was a bear hanging from a tree at the camp when we got in that night, however. Bob York had come upon it that afternoon near the Pole Bridge. By general agreement, it was a two-year-old that would go around 200 pounds.

Time was running out for most of the hunters. A hunt seldom falls into the classical pattern of beginning, middle and final climax. But there is usually a discernible form to a hunting week. The first days are characterized by dalliance and casual exploration, the savoring of a release from structured life. Then as the hunters get down to the prime business of the hunt, the tempo picks up. The last days of the hunt there is a further quickening. Logic, industry, experience having failed, hunters fall back upon hunches.

Buzz Barry aired his that night as we prepared to hit the sack. "We might try that piece west of Joey's Turn," he said. "No one's been in there this spring."

Glenn grunted. "Nothing in there but bog, puckerbrush and blowdowns. What makes you think . . ."

"I'm half Irish," Buzz said. "I'm listening to the Irish in me. I say if he's still around, he's got to be there. We've covered just about every other place."

Expectancy is an emotion that can be as tangible as heat. Barry said little as we climbed out of the buggy and began to still-hunt up the trail above Joey's Turn that next morning, but I was aware of his leashed excitement. We eased along for a good 20 minutes without seeing any encouraging sign. We were up among the blowdowns when the first fresh bear scats began to show up.

Suddenly Buzz Barry motioned and I moved up abreast him. His eyes were luminous. "My computer's working," he said.

He grinned at my perplexity. "You've hunted long enough to know what I mean. Call it a hunter's sixth sense. Everything is right. The sign, the weather, the time of day, the wind direction and the look of the terrain. Unconsciously, you feed all this data into your computer. Right now, it comes out bear."

We moved on, climbing up over a steep washout. The rain that had been with us off and on all week began to fall in a fine mist. I could hear the rush of a swollen brook. The croak of a young raven was as sharp as drumfire in the stillness. Then I, too, felt the nerve-twanging feeling of something impending.

We saw The Bear that morning. It was no more than a snatch vision. The great black shape was there and then it was gone, so quickly that I was not at all certain that my eyes hadn't been tricked by imagination.

Ahead, Barry had lowered his half-raised rifle. I waited a full minute, then slid up beside him. Together we stepped into the trees. It was only then that I was sure. The smell of bear was astringent and as real as a solid right to the midsection. Abruptly the wind changed, and there was only the smell of the dank woods.

The hunters were lunching when we stepped into camp. Something in our faces or in our silent deliberation as we stacked our rifles compelled their eyes toward us. I was aware of tension in the room.

Finally Glenn Wilcox snapped, "Well, let's have it."

Barry said, "He was too smart for us. We didn't even get a shot."

The hunters stirred and ease came back into the room.

"There'll be another year," someone said. "Good old Lonesome George."

And in that moment I learned something about the hunters of Yankee-tu-laidi. To a man they prefer the myth to a dead bear. Its passing would have removed something irreplaceable; without say-so, the myth—the symbol of a wilderness they knew—was doomed.

Now at least there would be another year.

DISCUSSION QUESTIONS

1. Compare "The Myth of the Boss Bear" with William Faulkner's rendition of an equally "unsuccessful" bear hunt (see Classics). What are the different expectations made by each writer concerning his audience's knowledge of hunting? The wilderness? Bears? Myths? Other writers? Other literature on the same subject? Which writer spends more time talking about the technical details of a hunting expedition? Why is such information introduced?

2. Characterize Dietz's use of such similes and metaphors as: "as real as a solid right to the midsection," "the dark soleful eyes of an Italian opera tenor," "King Kong of bears." Compare them with Faulkner's figurative language (for example: "like pygmies about the ankles of a drowsing elephant," "a flavor like brass in the sudden run of saliva in his mouth").

Nora Ephron / The Boston Photographs

Esquire, November 1975

Reporter, free-lance journalist, magazine contributor, columnist, editor, and author of Wallflower at the Orgy *(1970),* Crazy Salad *(1975), and* Scribble, Scribble *(1978), Nora Ephron has become well-known for her pert prose style and perspicacious eye. In "The Boston Photographs," Ephron examines the outrage so many people felt towards the papers that printed the photos of a woman and child falling from a burning building and explains why they deserved to be printed in papers all over the country. (For further discussion of this issue, see Ellen Goodman, in Press.)*

"I made all kinds of pictures because I thought it would be a good rescue shot over the ladder . . . never dreamed it would be anything else. . . . I kept having to move around because of the light set. The sky was bright and they were in deep shadow. I was making pictures with a motor drive and he, the fire fighter, was reaching up and, I don't know, everything started falling. I followed the girl down taking pictures . . . I made three or four frames. I realized what was going on and I completely turned around, because I didn't want to see her hit."

You probably saw the photographs. In most newspapers, there were three of them. The first showed some people on a fire escape—a fireman, a woman and a child. The fireman had a nice strong jaw and looked very brave. The woman was holding the child. Smoke was pouring from the building behind them. A rescue ladder was approaching, just a few feet away, and the fireman had one arm around the woman and one arm reaching out toward the ladder. The second picture showed the fire escape slipping off the building. The child had fallen on the escape and seemed about to slide off the edge. The woman was grasping desperately at the legs of the fireman, who had managed to grab the ladder. The third picture showed the woman and child in midair, falling to the ground. Their arms and legs were outstretched, horribly distended. A potted plant was falling too. The caption said that the woman, Diana Bryant, nineteen, died in the fall. The child landed on the woman's body and lived.

The pictures were taken by Stanley Forman, thirty, of the *Boston Herald American.* He used a motor-driven Nikon F set at 1/250, f 5.6–8. Because of the motor, the camera can click off three frames a second. More than four hundred newspa-

Copyright Boston Herald American, Stanley J. Forman, Boston Newspaper Division of the Hearst Corporation.

pers in the United States alone carried the photographs; the tear sheets from overseas are still coming in. The *New York Times* ran them on the first page of its second section; a paper in south Georgia gave them nineteen columns; the *Chicago Tribune,* the *Washington Post* and the *Washington Star* filled almost half their front pages, the *Star* under a somewhat redundant headline that read: SENSATIONAL PHOTOS OF RESCUE ATTEMPT THAT FAILED.

The photographs are indeed sensational. They are pictures of death in action, of that split second when luck runs out, and it is impossible to look at them without feeling their extraordinary impact and remembering, in an almost subconscious way, the morbid fantasy of falling, falling off a building, falling to one's death. Beyond that, the pictures are classics, old-fashioned but perfect examples of photojournalism at its most spectacular. They're throwbacks, really, fire pictures,

1930s tabloid shots; at the same time they're technically superb and thoroughly modern—the sequence could not have been taken at all until the development of the motor-driven camera some sixteen years ago.

Most newspaper editors anticipate some reader reaction to photographs like Forman's; even so, the response around the country was enormous, and almost all of it was negative. I have read hundreds of the letters that were printed in letters-to-the-editor sections, and they repeat the same points. "Invading the privacy of death." "Cheap sensationalism." "I thought I was reading the *National Enquirer.*" "Assigning the agony of a human being in terror of imminent death to the status of a side-show act." "A tawdry way to sell newspapers." The *Seattle Times* received sixty letters and calls; its managing editor even got a couple of them at home. A reader wrote the *Philadelphia Inquirer: "Jaws* and *Towering Inferno* are playing downtown; don't take business away from people who pay good money to advertise in your own paper." Another reader wrote the *Chicago Sun-Times:* "I shall try to hide my disappointment that Miss Bryant wasn't wearing a skirt when she fell to her death. You could have had some award-winning photographs of her underpants as her skirt billowed over her head, you voyeurs." Several newspaper editors wrote columns defending the pictures: Thomas Keevil of the *Costa Mesa* (California) *Daily Pilot* printed a ballot for readers to vote on whether they would have printed the pictures; Marshall L. Stone of Maine's *Bangor Daily News,* which refused to print the famous assassination picture of the Vietcong prisoner in Saigon, claimed that the Boston pictures showed the dangers of fire escapes and raised questions about slumlords. (The burning building was a five-story brick apartment house on Marlborough Street in the Back Bay section of Boston.)

For the last five years, the *Washington Post* has employed various journalists as ombudsmen, whose job is to monitor the paper on behalf of the public. The *Post*'s current ombudsman is Charles Seib, former managing editor of the *Washington Star;* the day the Boston photographs appeared, the paper received over seventy calls in protest. As Seib later wrote in a column about the pictures, it was "the largest reaction to a published item that I have experienced in eight months as the *Post*'s ombudsman. . . .

"In the *Post*'s newsroom, on the other hand, I found no doubts, no second thoughts . . . the question was not whether they should be printed but how they should be displayed. When I talked to editors . . . they used words like 'interesting' and 'riveting' and 'gripping' to describe them. The pictures told something about life in the ghetto, they said (although the neighborhood where the tragedy occurred is not a ghetto, I am told). They dramatized the need to check on the safety of fire escapes. They dramatically conveyed something that had happened, and that is the business we're in. They were news. . . .

"Was publication of that [third] picture a bow to the same taste for the morbidly sensational that makes gold mines of disaster movies? Most papers will not print the picture of a dead body except in the most unusual circumstances. Does the fact that the final picture was taken a millisecond before the young woman died make a difference? Most papers will not print a picture of a bare female breast. Is that a more inappropriate subject for display than the picture of a human being's last agonized instant of life?" Seib offered no answers to the questions he raised, but he went on to say that although as an editor he would probably have run the pictures, as a reader he was revolted by them.

In conclusion, Seib wrote: "Any editor who decided to print those pictures without giving at least a moment's thought to what purpose they served and what their effect was likely to be on the reader should ask another question: Have I become so preoccupied with manufacturing a product according to professional traditions and standards that I have forgotten about the consumer, the reader?"

It should be clear that the phone calls and letters and Seib's own reaction were occasioned by one factor alone: the death of the woman. Obviously, had she survived the fall, no one would have protested; the pictures would have had a completely different impact. Equally obviously, had the child died as well—or instead—Seib would undoubtedly have received ten times the phone calls he did. In each case, the pictures would have been exactly the same—only the captions, and thus the responses, would have been different.

But the questions Seib raises are worth discussing—though not exactly for the reasons he mentions. For it may be that the real lesson of the Boston photographs is not the danger that editors will be forgetful of reader reaction, but that they will continue to censor pictures of death precisely because of that reaction. The protests Seib fielded were really a variation on an old theme—and we saw plenty of it during the Nixon-Agnew years—the "Why doesn't the press print the good news?" argument. In this case, of course, the objections were all dressed up and cleverly disguised as righteous indignation about the privacy of death. This is a form of puritanism that is often justifiable; just as often it is merely puritanical.

Seib takes it for granted that the widespread though fairly recent newspaper policy against printing pictures of dead bodies is a sound one; I don't know that it makes any sense at all. I recognize that printing pictures of corpses raises all sorts of problems about taste and titillation and sensationalism; the fact is, however, that people die. Death happens to be one of life's main events. And it is irresponsible—and more than that, inaccurate—for newspapers to fail to show it, or to show it only when an astonishing set of photos comes in over the Associated Press wire. Most papers covering fatal automobile accidents will print pictures of mangled cars. But the significance of fatal automobile accidents is not that a great deal of steel is twisted but that people die. Why not show it? That's what accidents are about. Throughout the Vietnam war, editors were reluctant to print atrocity pictures. Why *not* print them? That's what that war was about. Murder victims are almost never photographed; they are granted their privacy. But their relatives are relentlessly pictured on their way in and out of hospitals and morgues and funerals.

I'm not advocating that newspapers print these things in order to teach their readers a lesson. The *Post* editors justified their printing of the Boston pictures with several arguments in that direction; every one of them is irrelevant. The pictures don't show anything about slum life; the incident could have happened anywhere, and it did. It is extremely unlikely that anyone who saw them rushed out and had his fire escape strengthened. And the pictures were not news—at least they were not national news. It is not news in Washington, or New York, or Los Angeles that a woman was killed in a Boston fire. The only newsworthy thing about the pictures is that they were taken. They deserve to be printed because they are great pictures, breathtaking pictures of something that happened. That they disturb readers is exactly as it should be: that's why photojournalism is often more powerful than written journalism.

Annie Dillard / Death of a Moth

Harper's, May 1976

In the midst of a recent resurgence of nostalgia for the outdoors, Annie Dillard has distinguished herself by the clarity of her vision, the tenacity of her refusal to sentimentalize nature, and the forcefulness of her prose. Born Annie Doak in Pittsburgh in 1945, she took B.A. and M.A. degrees at Hollins College in

Virginia's Roanoke Valley. A contributing editor to Harper's *magazine and a columnist for the Wilderness Society, Annie Dillard has also written strikingly original essays for such publications as the* Christian Science Monitor, Atlantic Monthly, Travel and Leisure, Cosmopolitan, Sports Illustrated, Prose, *and* American Scholar. *Many of these essays, refashioned from precise observations entered in notebooks during leisurely walks in the countryside, were collected as* Pilgrim at Tinker Creek, *which received the 1974 Pulitzer Prize for nonfiction.*

"If there are any faults to find here," wrote a critic for The New York Times Book Review *about Dillard's journal* Holy the Firm *(1977), "let others find them. This is a rare and precious book." Included in her three-day journal written in a one-room house overlooking Puget Sound is the following essay, "Death of a Moth," which first appeared in* Harper's *magazine.*

Harper's, *one of the oldest (1850) magazines in America, characterizes itself as addressed to "well-educated, socially concerned, widely read men and women who are active in community and political affairs."*

I live alone with two cats, who sleep on my legs. There is a yellow one, and a black one whose name is Small. In the morning I joke to the black one, Do you remember last night? Do you remember? I throw them both out before breakfast, so I can eat.

There is a spider, too, in the bathroom, of uncertain lineage, bulbous at the abdomen and drab, whose six-inch mess of web works, works somehow, works miraculously, to keep her alive and me amazed. The web is in a corner behind the toilet, connecting tile wall to tile wall. The house is new, the bathroom immaculate, save for the spider, her web, and the sixteen or so corpses she's tossed to the floor.

The corpses appear to be mostly sow bugs, those little armadillo creatures who live to travel flat out in houses, and die round. In addition to sow-bug husks, hollow and sipped empty of color, there are what seem to be two or three wingless moth bodies, one new flake of earwig, and three spider carcasses crinkled and clenched.

I wonder on what fool's errand an earwig, or a moth, or a sow bug, would visit that clean corner of the house behind the toilet; I have not noticed any blind parades of sow bugs blundering into corners. Yet they do hazard there, at a rate of more than one a week, and the spider thrives. Yesterday she was working on the earwig, mouth on gut; today he's on the floor. It must take a certain genius to throw things away from there, to find a straight line through that sticky tangle to the floor.

Today the earwig shines darkly, and gleams, what there is of him: a dorsal curve of thorax and abdomen, and a smooth pair of pincers by which I knew his name. Next week, if the other bodies are any indication, he'll be shrunk and gray, webbed to the floor with dust. The sow bugs beside him are curled and empty, fragile, a breath away from brittle fluff. The spiders lie on their sides, translucent and ragged, their legs drying in knots. The moths stagger against each other, headless, in a confusion of arcing strips of chitin like peeling varnish, like a jumble of buttresses for cathedral vaults, like nothing resembling moths, so that I would hesitate to call them moths, except that I have had some experience with the figure Moth reduced to a nub.

Two summers ago I was camped alone in the Blue Ridge Mountains of Virginia. I had hauled myself and gear up there to read, among other things, *The Day on Fire,* by James Ullman, a novel about Rimbaud that had made me want to be a writer when I was sixteen; I was hoping it would do it again. So I read every day sitting under a tree by my tent, while warblers sang in the leaves overhead and bristle worms trailed their inches over the twiggy dirt at my feet; and I read every night by candlelight, while barred owls called in the forest and pale moths seeking mates massed round my head in the clearing, where my light made a ring.

Moths kept flying into the candle. They would hiss and recoil, reeling upside down in the shadows among my cooking pans. Or they would singe their wings and fall, and their hot wings, as if melted, would stick to the first thing they touched—a pan, a lid, a spoon—so that the snagged moths could struggle only in tiny arcs, unable to flutter free. These I could release by a quick flip with a stick; in the morning I would find my cooking stuff decorated with torn flecks of moth wings, ghostly triangles of shiny dust here and there on the aluminum. So I read, and boiled water, and replenished candles, and read on.

One night a moth flew into the candle, was caught, burnt dry, and held. I must have been staring at the candle, or maybe I looked up when a shadow crossed my page; at any rate, I saw it all. A golden female moth, a biggish one with a two-inch wingspread, flapped into the fire, dropped abdomen into the wet wax, stuck, flamed, and frazzled in a second. Her moving wings ignited like tissue paper, like angels' wings, enlarging the circle of light in the clearing and creating out of the darkness the sudden blue sleeves of my sweater, the green leaves of jewelweed by my side, the ragged red trunk of a pine; at once the light contracted again and the moth's wings vanished in a fine, foul smoke. At the same time, her six legs clawed, curled, blackened, and ceased, disappearing utterly. And her head jerked in spasms, making a spattering noise; her antennae crisped and burnt away and her heaving mouthparts cracked like pistol fire. When it was all over, her head was, so far as I could determine, gone, gone the long way of her wings and legs. Her head was a hole lost to time. All that was left was the glowing horn shell of her abdomen and thorax—a fraying, partially collapsed gold tube jammed upright in the candle's round pool.

And then this moth-essence, this spectacular skeleton, began to act as a wick. She kept burning. The wax rose in the moth's body from her soaking abdomen to her thorax to the shattered hole where her head should have been, and widened into flame, a saffron-yellow flame that robed her to the ground like an immolating monk. That candle had two wicks, two winding flames of identical light, side by side. The moth's head was fire. She burned for two hours, until I blew her out.

She burned for two hours without changing, without swaying or kneeling—only glowing within, like a building fire glimpsed through silhouetted walls, like a hollow saint, like a flame-faced virgin gone to God, while I read by her light, kindled, while Rimbaud in Paris burnt out his brain in a thousand poems, while night pooled wetly at my feet.

So. That is why I think those hollow shreds on the bathroom floor are moths. I believe I know what moths look like, in any state.

I have three candles here on the table which I disentangle from the plants and light when visitors come. The cats avoid them, although Small's tail caught fire once; I rubbed it out before she noticed. I don't mind living alone. I like eating alone and reading. I don't mind sleeping alone. The only time I mind being alone is when something is funny; then, when I am laughing at something funny, I wish someone were around. Sometimes I think it is pretty funny that I sleep alone.

N. Scott Momaday / A First American Views His Land

National Geographic, July 1976

The National Geographic *magazine was founded in 1888 under the auspices of the National Geographic Society as a professional journal devoted to technical essays on exploration and earth sciences. As the society invested more and more heavily in expeditions that would capture the popular imagination, the editors decided to alter the magazine's contents in the hope of attracting a larger, nonspecialized audience. Over the years, the* National Geographic *has become a popular forum for travel, adventure, anthropology, and geographical research. Its consistently high standard of color photography has been a major factor in the magazine's enormous circulation: now well over nine million.*

N. Scott Momaday's "A First American Views His Land" clearly fulfills the National Geographic's *announced criteria for publication:*

> *First person narratives, making it easy for the reader to share the author's experience and observations. Writing should include plenty of human-interest incident, authentic direct quotation, and a bit of humor where appropriate. Accuracy is fundamental. Contemporary problems such as those of pollution and ecology are treated on a factual basis. The magazine is especially seeking short American place pieces with a strong regional "people" flavor.*

Born in Lawton, Oklahoma in 1934, N. Scott Momaday received his B.A. from the University of New Mexico, his Masters and Ph.D. from Stanford. A professor of English at Stanford, Momaday won the Pulitzer Prize for fiction in 1969 for his novel House of Dawn. *He regularly contributes articles, fiction, and poetry to numerous periodicals and frequently reviews work on American Indian culture. The poem woven into the selection printed below is drawn from his book,* The Gourd Dancer *(1976).*

First Man
behold:
the earth
glitters
with leaves;
the sky
glistens
with rain.
Pollen
is borne
on winds
that low
and lean
upon
mountains.
Cedars
blacken
the slopes—
and pines.

One hundred centuries ago. There is a wide, irregular landscape in what is now northern New Mexico. The sun is a dull white disk, low in the south; it is a perfect mystery, a deity whose coming and going are inexorable. The gray sky is curdled, and it bears very close upon the earth. A cold wind runs along the ground, dips and spins, flaking drift from a pond in the bottom of a ravine. Beyond the wind the silence is acute. A man crouches in the ravine, in the darkness there, scarcely visible. He moves not a muscle; only the wind lifts a lock of his hair and lays it back along his neck. He wears skins and carries a spear. These things in particular mark his human intelligence and distinguish him as the lord of the universe. And for him the universe is especially *this* landscape; for him the landscape is an element like the air. The vast, virgin wilderness is by and large his whole context. For him there is no possibility of existence elsewhere.

Directly there is a blowing, a rumble of breath deeper than the wind, above him, where some of the hard clay of the bank is broken off and the clods roll down into the water. At the same time there appears on the skyline the massive head of a long-horned bison, then the hump, then the whole beast, huge and black on the sky, standing to a height of seven feet at the hump, with horns that extend six feet across the shaggy crown. For a moment it is poised there; then it lumbers obliquely down the bank to the pond. Still the man does not move, though the beast is now only a few steps upwind. There is no sign of what is about to happen; the beast meanders; the man is frozen in repose.

Then the scene explodes. In one and the same instant the man springs to his feet and bolts forward, his arm cocked and the spear held high, and the huge animal lunges in panic, bellowing, its whole weight thrown violently into the bank, its hooves churning and chipping earth into the air, its eyes gone wide and wild and white. There is a moment in which its awful, frenzied motion is wasted, and it is mired and helpless in its fear, and the man hurls the spear with his whole strength, and the point is driven into the deep, vital flesh, and the bison in its agony staggers and crashes down and dies.

This ancient drama of the hunt is enacted again and again in the landscape. The man is preeminently a predator, the most dangerous of all. He hunts in order to survive; his very existence is simply, squarely established upon that basis. But he hunts also because he can, because he has the means; he has the ultimate weapon of his age, and his prey is plentiful. His relationship to the land has not yet become a moral equation.

But in time he will come to understand that there is an intimate, vital link between the earth and himself, a link that implies an intricate network of rights and responsibilities. In some unimagined future he will understand that he has the ability to devastate and perhaps destroy his environment. That moment will be one of extreme crisis in his evolution.

The weapon is deadly and efficient. The hunter has taken great care in its manufacture, especially in the shaping of the flint point, which is an extraordinary thing. A larger flake has been removed from each face, a groove that extends from the base nearly to the tip. Several hundred pounds of pressure, expertly applied, were required to make these grooves. The hunter then is an artisan, and he must know how to use rudimentary tools. His skill, manifest in the manufacture of this artifact, is unsurpassed for its time and purpose. By means of this weapon is the Paleo-Indian hunter eminently able to exploit his environment.

Thousands of years later, about the time that Columbus begins his first voyage to the New World, another man, in the region of the Great Lakes, stands in the forest shade on the edge of a sunlit brake. In a while a deer enters into the pool of light. Silently the man fits an arrow to a bow, draws aim, and shoots. The arrow zips across the distance and strikes home. The deer leaps and falls dead.

But this latter-day man, unlike his ancient predecessor, is only incidentally a hunter; he is also a fisherman, a husbandman, even a physician. He fells trees and builds canoes; he grows corn, squash, and beans, and he gathers fruits and nuts;

he uses hundreds of species of wild plants for food, medicine, teas, and dyes. Instead of one animal, or two or three, he hunts many, none to extinction as the Paleo-Indian may have done. He has fitted himself far more precisely into the patterns of the wilderness than did his ancient predecessor. He lives on the land; he takes his living from it; but he does not destroy it. This distinction supports the fundamental ethic that we call conservation today. In principle, if not yet in name, this man is a conservationist.

These two hunting sketches are far less important in themselves than is that long distance between them, that whole possibility within the dimension of time. I believe that in that interim there grew up in the mind of man an idea of the land as sacred.

At dawn
eagles
lie and
hover
above
the plain
where light
gathers
in pools.
Grasses
shimmer
and shine.
Shadows
withdraw
and lie
away
like smoke.

"The earth is our mother. The sky is our father." This concept of nature, which is at the center of the Native American world view, is familiar to us all. But it may well be that we do not understand entirely what that concept is in its ethical and philosophical implications.

I tell my students that the American Indian has a unique investment in the American landscape. It is an investment that represents perhaps thirty thousand years of habitation. That tenure has to be worth something in itself—a great deal, in fact. The Indian has been here a long time; he is at home here. That simple and obvious truth is one of the most important realities of the Indian world, and it is integral in the Indian mind and spirit.

How does such a concept evolve? Where does it begin? Perhaps it begins with the recognition of beauty, the realization that the physical world *is* beautiful. We don't know much about the ancient hunter's sensibilities. It isn't likely that he had leisure in his life for the elaboration of an aesthetic ideal. And yet the weapon he made was beautiful as well as functional. It has been suggested that much of the minute chipping along the edges of his weapon served no purpose but that of aesthetic satisfaction.

A good deal more is known concerning that man of the central forests. He made beautiful boxes and dishes out of elm and birch bark, for example. His canoes were marvelous, delicate works of art. And this aesthetic perception was a principle of the whole Indian world of his time, as indeed it is of our time. The contemporary Native American is a man whose strong aesthetic perceptions are clearly evident in his arts and crafts, in his religious ceremonies, and in the stories and songs of his rich oral tradition. This, in view of the pressures that have been brought to bear upon the Indian world and the drastic changes that have been effected in its landscape, is a blessing and an irony.

Consider for example the Navajos of the Four Corners area. In recent years an extensive coal-mining operation has mutilated some of their most sacred land. A large power plant in that same region spews a contamination into the sky that is visible for many miles. And yet, as much as any people of whom I have heard, the Navajos perceive and celebrate the beauty of the physical world.

There is a Navajo ceremonial song that celebrates the sounds that are made in the natural world, the particular voices that beautify the earth:

Voice above,
Voice of thunder,
Speak from the
dark of clouds;
Voice below,
Grasshopper voice,
Speak from the
green of plants;
So may the earth
be beautiful.

There is in the motion and meaning of this song a comprehension of the world that is peculiarly native, I believe, that is integral in the Native American mentality. Consider: The singer stands at the center of the natural world, at the source of its sound, of its motion, of its life. Nothing of that world is inaccessible to him or lost upon him. His song is filled with reverence, with wonder and delight, and with confidence as well. He knows something about himself and about the things around him—and he knows that he knows. I am interested in what he sees and hears; I am interested in the range and force of his perception. Our immediate impression may be that his perception is narrow and deep—vertical. After all, ''voice above . . . voice below,'' he sings. But is it vertical only? At each level of his expression there is an extension of his awareness across the whole landscape. The voice above is the voice of thunder, and thunder rolls. Moreover, it issues from the impalpable dark clouds and runs upon their horizontal range. It is a sound that integrates the whole of the atmosphere. And even so, the voice below, that of the grasshopper, issues from the broad plain and multiplicity of plants. And of course the singer is mindful of much more than thunder and insects; we are given in his song the wide angle of his vision and his hearing—and we are given the testimony of his dignity, his trust, and his deep belief.

This comprehension of the earth and air is surely a matter of morality, for it brings into account not only man's instinctive reaction to his environment but the full realization of his humanity as well, the achievement of his intellectual and spiritual development as an individual and as a race.

In my own experience I have seen numerous examples of this regard for nature. My grandfather Mammedaty was a farmer in his mature years; his grandfather was a buffalo hunter. It was not easy for Mammedaty to be a farmer; he was a Kiowa, and the Kiowas never had an agrarian tradition. Yet he had to make his living, and the old, beloved life of roaming the plains and hunting the buffalo was gone forever. Even so, as much as any man before him, he fitted his mind and will and spirit to the land; there was nothing else. He could not have conceived of living apart from the land.

In *The Way to Rainy Mountain* I set down a small narrative that belongs in the oral tradition of my family. It indicates something essential about the Native American attitude toward the land:

''East of my grandmother's house, south of the pecan grove, there is buried a woman in a beautiful dress. Mammedaty used to know where she is buried, but now no one knows. If you stand on the front porch of the house and look eastward towards Carnegie, you know that the woman is buried somewhere within the range of your vision. But her grave is unmarked. She was buried in a cabinet, and she wore a beautiful dress. How beautiful it was! It was one of those fine buckskin dresses, and it was decorated with elk's teeth and beadwork. That dress is still there, under the ground."

It seems to me that this statement is primarily a declaration of love for the land, in which the several elements—the woman, the dress, and this plain—are at last become one reality, one expression of the beautiful in nature. Moreover, it seems to me a peculiarly Native American expression in this sense: that the concentration of things that are explicitly remembered—the general landscape, the simple, almost abstract nature of the burial, above all the beautiful dress, which is wholly singular in kind (as well as in its function within the narrative)—is especially Indian in character. The things that are *not* explicitly remembered—the woman's name, the exact location of her grave—are the things that matter least in the special view of the storyteller. What matters here is the translation of the woman into the landscape, a translation particularly signified by means of the beautiful and distinctive dress, an *Indian* dress.

When I was a boy, I lived for several years at Jemez Pueblo, New Mexico. The Pueblo Indians are perhaps more obviously invested in the land than are other people. Their whole life is predicated upon a thorough perception of the physical world and its myriad aspects. When I first went there to live, the cacique, or chief, of the Pueblos was a venerable old man with long, gray hair and bright, deep-set eyes. He was entirely dignified and imposing—and rather formidable in the eyes of a boy. He excited my imagination a good deal. I was told that this old man kept the calendar of the tribe, that each morning he stood on a certain spot of ground near the center of the town and watched to see where the sun appeared on the skyline. By means of this solar calendar did he know and announce to his people when it was time to plant, to harvest, to perform this or that ceremony. This image of him in my mind's eye—the old man gazing each morning after the ranging sun—came to represent for me the epitome of that real harmony between man and the land that signifies the Indian world.

One day when I was riding my horse along the Jemez River, I looked up to see a long caravan of wagons and people on horseback and on foot. Men, women, and children were crossing the river ahead of me, moving out to the west, where most of the cultivated fields were, the farmland of the town. It was a wonderful sight to see, this long procession, and I was immediately deeply curious. I wanted to investigate, but it was not in me to do so at once, for that racial reserve, that sense of propriety that is deep-seated in Native American culture, stayed me, held me up. Then I saw someone coming toward me on horseback, galloping. It was a friend of mine, a boy of my own age. "Come on," he said. "Come with us." "Where are you going?" I asked casually. But he would not tell me. He simply laughed and urged me to come along, and of course I was very glad to do so. It was a bright spring morning, and I had a good horse under me, and the prospect of adventure was delicious. We moved far out across the eroded plain to the farthest fields at the foot of a great red mesa, and there we planted two large fields of corn. And afterward, on the edge of the fields, we sat on blankets and ate a feast in the shade of a cottonwood grove. Later I learned it was the cacique's fields we planted. And this is an ancient tradition at Jemez. The people of the town plant and tend and harvest the cacique's fields, and in the winter the hunters give to him a portion of the meat that they bring home from the mountains. It is as if the cacique is himself the translation of man, every man, into the landscape.

I have not forgotten that day, nor shall I forget it. I remember the warm earth of the fields, the smooth texture of seeds in my hands, and the brown water moving slowly and irresistibly among the rows. Above all I remember the spirit in which the procession was made, the work was done, and the feasting was enjoyed. It was a spirit of communion, of the life of each man in relation to the life of the planet and of the infinite distance and silence in which it moves. We made, in concert, an appropriate expression of that spirit.

One afternoon an old Kiowa woman talked to me, telling me of the place in Oklahoma in which she had lived for a hundred years. It was the place in which my grandparents, too, lived; and it is the place where I was born. And she told me of a time even further back, when the Kiowas came down from the north and centered their culture in the red earth of the southern plains. She told wonderful stories, and as I listened, I began to feel more and more sure that her voice proceeded from the land itself. I asked her many things concerning the Kiowas, for I wanted to understand all that I could of my heritage. I told the old woman that I had come there to learn from her and from people like her, those in whom the old ways were preserved. And she said simply: "It is good that you have come here." I believe that her word "good" meant many things; for one thing it meant *right,* or *appropriate*. And indeed it was appropriate that she should speak of the land. She was eminently qualified to do so. She had a great reverence for the land, and an ancient perception of it, a perception that it acquired only in the course of many generations.

It is this notion of the appropriate, along with that of the beautiful, that forms the Native American perspective on the land. In a sense these considerations are indivisible; Native American oral tradition is rich with songs and tales that celebrate natural beauty, the beauty of the natural world. What is more appropriate to our world than that which is beautiful:

At noon
turtles
enter
slowly
into
the warm
dark loam.
Bees hold
the swarm.
Meadows
recede
through planes
of heat
and pure
distance.

Very old in the Native American world view is the conviction that the earth is vital, that there is a spiritual dimension to it, a dimension in which man rightly exists. It follows logically that there are ethical imperatives in this matter. I think: Inasmuch as I am in the land, it is appropriate that I should affirm myself in the spirit of the land. I shall celebrate my life in the world and the world in my life. In the natural order man invests himself in the landscape and at the same time incorporates the landscape into his own most fundamental experience. This trust is sacred.

The process of investment and appropriation is, I believe, preeminently a function of the imagination. It is accomplished by means of an act of the imagination that is especially ethical in kind. We are what we imagine ourselves to be. The Native American is someone who thinks of himself, imagines himself in a particular way. By virtue of his experience his idea of himself comprehends his relationship to the land.

And the quality of this imagining is determined as well by racial and cultural experience. The Native American's attitudes toward this landscape have been formulated over a long period of time, a span that reaches back to the end of the Ice Age. The land, *this* land, is secure in his racial memory.

In our society as a whole we conceive of the land in terms of ownership and use. It is a lifeless medium of exchange; it has for most of us, I suspect, no more spirituality than has an automobile, say, or a refrigerator. And our laws confirm us in this view, for we can buy and sell the land, we can exclude each other from it, and in the context of ownership we can use it as we will. Ownership implies use, and use implies consumption.

But this way of thinking of the land is alien to the Indian. His cultural intelligence is opposed to these concepts; indeed, for him they are all but inconceivable quantities. This fundamental distinction is easier to understand with respect to ownership than to use, perhaps. For obviously the Indian does use, and has always used, the land and the available resources in it. The point is that *use* does not indicate in any real way his idea of the land. "Use" is neither his word nor his idea. As an Indian I think: "You say that I *use* the land, and I reply, yes, it is true; but it is not the first truth. The first truth is that I *love* the land; I see that it is beautiful; I delight in it; I am alive in it."

In the long course of his journey from Asia and in the realization of himself in the New World, the Indian has assumed a deep ethical regard for the earth and sky, a reverence for the natural world that is antipodal to that strange tenet of modern civilization that seemingly has it that man must destroy his environnment. It is this ancient ethic of the Native American that must shape our efforts to preserve the earth and the life upon and within it.

At dusk
the gray
foxes
stiffen
in cold;
blackbirds
are fixed
in white
branches.
Rivers
follow
the moon,
the long
white track
of the
full moon.

Judith Viorst / Friends, Good Friends—and Such Good Friends

Redbook, October 1977

Judith Viorst's early writings were, in her estimation, "Very grim. The meaning of life. Death. Pain. Lust. Suicide. That sort of thing." However, despite her former obsession with the deadly serious, Viorst has gone on to become one of the most popular humorists in America today. Her best-selling collections of light verse, It's Hard To Be Hip Over Thirty and Other Tragedies of Married Life *(1969) and* How Did I Get To Be 40 and Other Atrocities *(1976), have been praised for their witty reflections on contemporary marriage and family life.*

Judith Viorst also writes a regular column for Redbook, *a magazine geared to the interests of young married women, where the following article on the multifaceted functions of friendship first appeared.*

Women are friends, I once would have said, when they totally love and support and trust each other, and bare to each other the secrets of their souls, and run—no questions asked—to help each other, and tell harsh truths to each other (no, you can't wear that dress unless you lose ten pounds first) when harsh truths must be told.

Women are friends, I once would have said, when they share the same affection for Ingmar Bergman, plus train rides, cats, warm rain, charades, Camus, and hate with equal ardor Newark and Brussels sprouts, and Lawrence Welk and camping.

In other words, I once would have said that a friend is a friend all the way, but now I believe that's a narrow point of view. For the friendships I have and the friendships I see are conducted at many levels of intensity, serve many different functions, meet different needs and range from those as all-the-way as the friendship of the soul sisters mentioned above to that of the most nonchalant and casual playmates.

Consider these varieties of friendship:

1. Convenience friends. These are the women with whom, if our paths weren't crossing all the time, we'd have no particular reason to be friends: a next-door neighbor, a woman in our car pool, the mother of one of our children's closest friends or maybe some mommy with whom we serve juice and cookies each week at the Glenwood Co-op Nursery.

Convenience friends are convenient indeed. They'll lend us their cups and silverware for a party. They'll drive our kids to soccer when we're sick. They'll take us to pick up our car when we need a lift to the garage. They'll even take our cats when we go on vacation. As we will for them.

But we don't, with convenience friends, ever come too close or tell too much; we maintain our public face and emotional distance. "Which means," says Elaine, "that I'll talk about being overweight but not about being depressed. Which means I'll admit being mad but not blind with rage. Which means that I might say that we're pinched this month but never that I'm worried sick over money."

But which doesn't mean that there isn't sufficient value to be found in these friendships of mutual aid, in convenience friends.

2. Special-interest friends. These friendships aren't intimate, and they needn't involve kids or silverware or cats. Their value lies in some interest jointly shared. And so we may have an office friend or a yoga friend or a tennis friend or a friend from the Women's Democratic Club.

"I've got one woman friend," says Joyce, "who likes, as I do, to take psychology courses. Which makes it nice for me—and nice for her. It's fun to go with someone you know and it's fun to discuss what you've learned, driving back from the classes." And for the most part, she says, that's all they discuss.

"I'd say that what we're doing is *doing* together, not being together," Suzanne says of her Tuesday-doubles friends. "It's mainly a tennis relationship, but we play together well. And I guess we all need to have a couple of playmates."

I agree.

My playmate is a shopping friend, a woman of marvelous taste, a woman who knows exactly *where* to buy *what,* and furthermore is a woman who always knows beyond a doubt what one ought to be buying. I don't have the time to keep up with what's new in eyeshadow, hemlines and shoes and whether the smock look is in or finished already. But since (oh, shame!) I care a lot about eyeshadow, hemlines and shoes, and since I don't *want* to wear smocks if the smock look is finished, I'm very glad to have a shopping friend.

3. Historical friends. We all have a friend who knew us when . . . maybe way back in Miss Meltzer's second grade, when our family lived in that three-room flat in Brooklyn, when our dad was out of work for seven months, when our brother Allie got in that fight where they had to call the police, when our sister married the endodontist from Yonkers and when, the morning after we lost our virginity, she was the first, the only, friend we told.

The years have gone by and we've gone separate ways and we've little in common now, but we're still an intimate part of each other's past. And so whenever we go to Detroit we always go to visit this friend of our girlhood. Who knows how we looked before our teeth were straightened. Who knows how we talked before our voice got un-Brooklyned. Who knows what we ate before we learned about artichokes. And who, by her presence, puts us in touch with an earlier part of ourself, a part of ourself it's important never to lose.

"What this friend means to me and what I mean to her," says Grace, "is having a sister without sibling rivalry. We know the texture of each other's lives. She remembers my grandmother's cabbage soup. I remember the way her uncle played the piano. There's simply no other friend who remembers those things."

4. Crossroads friends. Like historical friends, our crossroads friends are important for *what was*—for the friendship we shared at a crucial, now past, time of life. A time, perhaps, when we roomed in college together; or worked as eager young singles in the Big City together; or went together, as my friend Elizabeth and I did, through pregnancy, birth and that scary first year of new motherhood.

Crossroads friends forge powerful links, links strong enough to endure with not much more contact than once-a-year letters at Christmas. And out of respect for those crossroads years, for those dramas and dreams we once shared, we will always be friends.

5. Cross-generational friends. Historical friends and crossroads friends seem to maintain a special kind of intimacy—dormant but always ready to be revived—and though we may rarely meet, whenever we do connect, it's personal and intense. Another kind of intimacy exists in the friendships that form across generations in what one woman calls her daughter-mother and her mother-daughter relationships.

Evelyn's friend is her mother's age—"but I share so much more than I ever could with my mother"—a woman she talks to of music, of books and of life. "What I get from her is the benefit of her experience. What she gets—and enjoys—from me is a youthful perspective. It's a pleasure for both of us."

I have in my own life a precious friend, a woman of 65 who has lived very hard, who is wise, who listens well; who has been where I am and can help me understand it; and who represents not only an ultimate ideal mother to me but also the person I'd like to be when I grow up.

In our daughter role we tend to do more than our share of self-revelation; in our mother role we tend to receive what's revealed. It's another kind of pleasure—playing wise mother to a questing younger person. It's another very lovely kind of friendship.

6. Part-of-a-couple friends. Some of the women we call our friends we never see alone—we see them as part of a couple at couples' parties. And though we share interests in many things and respect each other's views, we aren't moved to deepen the relationship. Whatever the reason, a lack of time or—and this is more likely—a lack of chemistry, our friendship remains in the context of a group. But

the fact that our feeling on seeing each other is always, ''I'm *so* glad she's here'' and the fact that we spend half the evening talking together says that this too, in its own way, counts as a friendship.

(Other part-of-a-couple friends are the friends that came with the marriage, and some of these are friends we could live without. But sometimes, alas, she married our husband's best friend; and sometimes, alas, she *is* our husband's best friend. And so we find ourself dealing with her, somewhat against our will, in a spirit of what I'll call *reluctant* friendship.)

7. Men who are friends. I wanted to write just of women friends, but the women I've talked to won't let me—they say I must mention man-woman friendships too. For these friendships can be just as close and as dear as those that we form with women. Listen to Lucy's description of one such friendship:

''We've found we have things to talk about that are different from what he talks about with my husband and different from what I talk about with his wife. So sometimes we call on the phone or meet for lunch. There are similar intellectual interests—we always pass on to each other the books that we love—but there's also something tender and caring too.''

In a couple of crises, Lucy says, ''he offered himself, for talking and for helping. And when someone died in his family he wanted me there. The sexual, flirty part of our friendship is very small, but *some*—just enough to make it fun and different.'' She thinks—and I agree—that the sexual part, though small, is always *some,* is always there when a man and a woman are friends.

It's only in the past few years that I've made friends with men, in the sense of a friendship that's *mine,* not just part of two couples. And achieving with them the ease and the trust I've found with women friends has value indeed. Under the dryer at home last week, putting on mascara and rouge, I comfortably sat and talked with a fellow named Peter. Peter, I finally decided, could handle the shock of me minus mascara under the dryer. Because we care for each other. Because we're friends.

8. There are medium friends, and pretty good friends, and very good friends indeed, and these friendships are defined by their level of intimacy. And what we'll reveal at each of these levels of intimacy is calibrated with care. We might tell a medium friend, for example, that yesterday we had a fight with our husband. And we might tell a pretty good friend that this fight with our husband made us so mad that we slept on the couch. And we might tell a very good friend that the reason we got so mad in that fight that we slept on the couch had something to do with that girl who works in his office. But it's only to our very best friends that we're willing to tell all, to tell what's going on with that girl in his office.

The best of friends, I still believe, totally love and support and trust each other, and bare to each other the secrets of their souls, and run—no questions asked—to help each other, and tell harsh truths to each other when they must be told.

But we needn't agree about everything (only 12-year-old girl friends agree about *everything*) to tolerate each other's point of view. To accept without judgment. To give and to take without every keeping score. And to *be* there, as I am for them and as they are for me, to comfort our sorrows, to celebrate our joys.

Paul Fussell / The Boy Scout Handbook

The New Republic, May 19, 1979

Paul Fussell is one of those rare literary talents who can write admirably on both academic and popular topics. A former professor of English at Rutgers University who now holds a chair in English Literature at the University of Pennsylvania, Fussell (pronounced like Russell) has written several professional studies of literature, including Poetic Meter and Poetic Form *(1965) and* Samuel Johnson and the Life of Writing *(1971). His combat experiences as an infantry officer during the Second World War led to an interest in military history and eventually to a prize-winning book on the First World War,* The Great War and Modern Memory *(1975). Fussell frequently writes for* Harper's *and* The New Republic, *where his review of the* Boy Scout Handbook *originally appeared. The essay was reprinted in* The Boy Scout Handbook and Other Observations *(1982). Fussell has also written* Abroad: British Literary Traveling Between the Wars *(1980) and* Class: A Guide through the American Status System (1983).

Founded in 1914, The New Republic *can be said to retain still its original purpose as a magazine that exists "less to inform or entertain its readers than to start little insurrections in the realm of their convictions."*

It's amazing how many interesting books humanistic criticism manages not to notice. Staring fixedly at its handful of teachable masterpieces, it seems content not to recognize that a vigorous literary-moral life constantly takes place just below (sometimes above) its vision. What a pity Lionel Trilling or Kenneth Burke never paused to examine the intersection of rhetoric and social motive among, say, the Knights of Columbus or the Elks. That these are their fellow citizens is less important than that the desires and rituals of these groups are desires and rituals, and thus of permanent social and psychological consequence. The culture of the Boy Scouts deserves this sort of look-in, especially since the right sort of people don't know much about it.

The right sort consists, of course, of liberal intellectuals. They have often gazed uneasily at the Boy Scout movement. After all, a general, the scourge of the Boers, invented it; Kipling admired it; the Hitlerjugend (and the Soviet Pioneers) aped it. If its insistence that there is a God has not sufficed to alienate the enlightened, its khaki uniforms, lanyards, salutes, badges, and flag worship have seemed to argue incipient militarism, if not outright fascism. The movement has often seemed its own worst enemy. Its appropriation of Norman Rockwell as its official Apelles has not endeared it to those of exquisite taste. Nor has its cause been promoted by events like the TV appearance a couple of years ago of the Chief Pardoner, Gerald Ford, rigged out in scout neckerchief, assuring us from the teleprompter that a Scout is Reverent. Than there are the leers and giggles triggered by the very word "scoutmaster," which in knowing circles is alone sufficient to promise comic pederastic narrative. "*All* scoutmasters are homosexuals," asserted George Orwell, who also insisted that "*All* tobacconists are Fascists."

But anyone who imagines that the scouting movement is either sinister or stupid or funny should spend a few hours with the latest edition of *The Official Boy Scout Handbook* (1979). Social, cultural, and literary historians could attend to it profitably as well, for after *The Red Cross First Aid Manual, The World Almanac,* and the Gideon Bible, it is probably the best-known book in this country. Since the first edition in 1910, twenty-nine million copies have been read in bed by flashlight. The first printing of this ninth edidtion is 600,000. We needn't take too seriously the ascription of authorship to William (''Green Bar Bill'') Hillcourt, depicted on the title page as an elderly gentleman bare-kneed in scout uniform and identified as Author, Naturalist, and World Scouter. He is clearly the Ann Page or Reddy Kilowatt of the movement, and although he's doubtless contributed to this handbook (by the same author is *Baden-Powell: The Two Lives of a Hero* [1965]), it bears all the marks of composition by committee, or ''task force,'' as it's called here. But for all that, it's admirably written. And although a complex sentence is as rare as a reference to girls, the rhetoric of this new edition has made no compromise with what we are told is the new illiteracy of the young. The book assumes an audience prepared by a very good high-school education, undaunted by terms like *biosphere, ideology,* and *ecosystem.*

The pliability and adaptability of the scout movement explains its remarkable longevity, its capacity to flourish in a world dramatically different from its founder's. Like the Roman Catholic Church, the scout movement knows the difference between cosmetic and real change, and it happily embraces the one to avoid any truck with the other. Witness the new American flag patch, now worn at the top of the right sleeve. It betokens no access of jingoism or threat to a civilized internationalism. It simply conduces to dignity by imitating a similar affectation of police and fire departments in anarchic towns like New York City. The message of the flag patch is not ''I am a fascist, straining to become old enough to purchase and wield guns.'' It is, rather, ''I can be put to quasi-official use, and like a fireman or policeman I am trained in first aid and ready to help.''

There are other innovations, none of them essential. The breeches of thirty years ago have yielded to trousers, although shorts are still in. The wide-brimmed army field hat of the First World War is a fixture still occasionally seen, but it is now augmented by headwear deriving from succeeding mass patriotic exercises: overseas caps and berets from World War II, and visor caps of the sort worn by General Westmoreland and sunbelt retirees. The scout handclasp has been changed, perhaps because it was discovered in the context of the new internationalism that the former one, in which the little finger was separated from the other three on the right hand, transmitted inappropriate suggestions in the Third World. The handclasp is now the normal civilian one, but given with the left hand. There's now much less emphasis on knots than formerly: as if to signal this change, the neckerchief is no longer religiously knotted at the tips. What used to be known as artificial respiration (''Out goes the bad air, in comes the good'') has given way to ''rescue breathing.'' The young are now being familiarized with the metric system. Some bright empiric has discovered that a paste made of meat tenderizer is the best remedy for painful insect stings. Constipation is not the bugbear it was a generation ago. And throughout there is a striking new lyricism. ''Feel the wind blowing through your hair,'' the scout is adjured, just as he is exhorted to perceive that Being Prepared for life means learning ''to live happy'' and—equally important—''to die happy.'' There's more emphasis now on fun and less on duty; or rather, duty is validated because, properly viewed, it is a pleasure. (If that sounds like advice useful to grown ups as well as to sprouts, you're beginning to get the point.)

There are only two possible causes of complaint. The term ''free world'' surfaces too often, although the phrase is mercifully uncapitalized. And the Deism is a bit insistent. The United States is defined as a country ''whose people believe in a supreme being.'' The words ''In God We Trust'' on the coinage and currency are taken almost as a constitutional injunction. The camper is told to carry along the ''Bible, Testament, or prayer book of your faith,'' even though, for light backpacking, he is advised to leave behind air mattress, knife and fork, and pancake turner. When the scout finds himself lost in the woods, he is to "stay put and have faith that someone will find you." In aid of this end, "Prayer will help." But the religiosity is so broad that it's harmless. The words "your church" are followed always by the phrase "or synagogue." The writers have done as well as they can considering that they're saddled with the immutable twelve points of Baden Powell's Scout Law, stating unambiguously that "A Scout is Reverent" and "faithful to his religious duties." But if "You have the right to worship God in your own way," you must see to it that "others retain their right to worship God in their way." Likewise, if "you have the right to speak your mind without fear of prison or punishment," you must "ensure that right for others, even when you do not agree with them." If the book adheres to any politics, they can hardly be described as conservative; they are better described as slightly archaic liberal. It is broadly hinted that industrial corporations are prime threats to clean air and conservation. In every illustration depicting more than three boys, one is black. The section introducing the reader to some Great Americans pays respects not only to Franklin and Edison and John D. Rockefeller and Einstein; it also makes much of Walter Reuther and Samuel Gompers, as well as Harriet Tubman, Martin Luther King, and Whitney Young. There is a post-Watergate awareness that public officials must be watched closely. One's civic duties include the obligation to "keep up on what is going on around you" in order to "get involved" and "help change things that are not good."

Few books these days could be called compendia of good sense. This is one such, and its good sense is not merely about swimming safely and putting campfires "cold out." The good sense is psychological and ethical as well. Indeed, this handbook is among the the very few remaining popular repositories of something like classical ethics, deriving from Aristotle and Cicero. Except for the handbook's adhesions to the motif of scenic beauty, it reads as if the Romantic movement had never taken place. The constant moral theme is the inestimable benefits of looking objectively outward and losing consciousness of self in the work to be done. To its young audience vulnerable to invitations to "trips" and trances and anxious self-absorption, the book calmly says: "Forget yourself." What a shame the psychobabblers of Marin County will never read it.

There is other invaluable advice, applicable to adults as well as to scouts. Some is practical, like "Never use flammable fluids to start a charcoal fire. They burn off fast, lighting only a little of the charcoal." Some is civic-moral: "Take a 2-hour walk where you live. Make a list of things that please you, another of things that should be improved." And then the kicker: "Set out to improve them." Some advice is even intellectual, and pleasantly uncompromising: "Reading trash all the time makes it impossible for anyone to be anything but a second-rate person." But the best advice is ethical: "Learn to think." "Gather knowledge." "Have initiative." "Respect the rights of others." Actually, there's hardly a better gauge for measuring the gross official misbehavior of the seventies than the ethics enshrined in this handbook. From its explicit ethics you can infer such propositions as "A scout does not tap his acquaintances' telephones," or "A scout does not bomb and invade a neutral country, and then lie about it," or "A scout does not prosecute war unless, as the Constitution provides, it has been declared by the Congress." Not to mention that because a scout is clean in thought, word, and deed, he does not, like Richard Nixon, designate his fellow citizens "shits" and then both record his filth and lie about the recordings ("A scout tells the truth").

Responding to Orwell's satiric analysis of "Boys' Weeklies" forty years ago, the boys' author Frank Richards, stigmatized by Orwell as a manufacturer of excessively optimistic and falsely wholesome stories, observed that "The writer for young people should . . . endeavor to give his young readers a sense of stability and solid security, because it is good for them, and makes for happiness and peace of mind.'' Even if it is true, as Orwell objects, that the happiness of youth is a cruel delusion, then, says Richards, ''Let youth be happy, or as happy as possible. Happiness is the best preparation for misery, if misery must come. At least the poor kid will have had something.'' In the current world of Making It and Getting Away with It, there are not many books devoted to associating happiness with virtue. The shelves of the CIA and the State Department must be bare of them. ''Horror swells around us like an oil spill,'' Terrence Des Pres said recently. ''Not a day passes without more savagery and harm.'' He was commenting on Philip Hallie's *Lest Innocent Blood Be Shed,* an account of a whole French village's trustworthiness, loyalty, helpfulness, friendliness, courtesy, kindness, cheerfulness, and bravery in hiding scores of Jews during the Occupation. Des Pres concludes: ''*Goodness.* When was the last time anyone used that word in earnest, without irony, as anything more than a doubtful cliché?'' *The Official Boy Scout Handbook,* for all its focus on Axmanship, Backpacking, Cooking, First Aid, Flowers, Hiking, Map and Compass, Semaphore, Trees, and Weather, is another book about goodness. No home, and certainly no government office, should be without a copy. The generously low price of $3.50 is enticing, and so is the place on the back cover where you're invited to inscribe your name.

Toni Morrison / Cinderella's Stepsisters

Ms., September 1979

Born in Lorain, Ohio, in 1931, Toni Morrison has emerged over the past decade as one of the most admired and accomplished voices in black American literature. After receiving a master's degree in English from Cornell University in 1955, Morrison taught for a number of years until she was hired as a senior editor at Random House in 1968. Since then, she has also taught classes in black literature and techniques of fiction at Yale and Bard colleges, although writing remains her primary occupation. Her novels include The Bluest Eye *(1970),* Sula *(1973),* Song of Solomon *(1977), which won that year's National Book Award, and* Tar Baby *(1981).*

Instead of dealing with the conflict between races, Morrison's work focuses on the difficulties among people from various backgrounds within the black community. Combining elements of harsh reality with mythic images and fairy tales, her novels show how men and women attempt to hold on to love, beauty, and a belief in miracles in a world ''where we are all of us, in some measure, victims of something.'' In the following article, adapted from a speech delivered at Barnard College, Morrison uses the Cinderella story as a metaphor for exhorting her fellow sisters to a greater vigilance on each other's behalf.

Co-founded by Gloria Steinem in 1972, Ms. *is a monthly magazine featuring articles on politics and contemporary social developments, particularly those that most directly affect the women's movement.*

Let me begin by taking you back a little. Back before the days at college. To nursery school, probably, to a once-upon-a-time time when you first heard, or read, or, I suspect, even saw ''Cinderella.'' Because it is Cinderella that I want to talk about; because it is Cinderella who causes me a feeling of urgency. What is unsettling about that fairy tale is that it is essentially the story of household—a world, if you please—of women gathered together and held together in order to abuse another woman. There is, of course, a rather vague absent father and a nick-of-time prince with a foot fetish. But neither has much personality. And there are the surrogate "mothers," of course (god- and step-), who contribute both to Cinderella's grief and to her release and happiness. But it is her stepsisters who interest me. How crippling it must have been for those young girls to grow up with a mother, to watch and imitate that mother, enslaving another girl.

I am curious about their fortunes after the story ends. For contrary to recent adaptations, the stepsisters were not ugly, clumsy, stupid girls with outsize feet. The Grimm collection describes them as "beautiful and fair in appearance." When we are introduced to them they are beautiful, elegant, women of status, and clearly women of power. Having watched and participated in the violent dominion of another woman, will they be any less cruel when it comes their turn to enslave other children, or even when they are required to take care of their own mother?

It is not a wholly medieval problem. It is quite a contemporary one: feminine power when directed at other women has historically been wielded in what has been described as a "masculine" manner. Soon you will be in a position to do the very same thing. Whatever your background—rich or poor—whatever the history of education in your family—five generations or one—you have taken advantage of what has been available to you at Barnard and you will therefore have both the economic and social status of the stepsisters *and* you will have their power.

I want not to *ask* you but to *tell* you not to participate in the oppression of your sisters. Mothers who abuse their children are women, and another woman, not an agency, has to be willing to stay their hands. Mothers who set fire to school buses are women, and another woman, not an agency, has to tell them to stay their hands. Women who stop the promotion of other women in careers are women, and another woman must come to the victim's aid. Social and welfare workers who humiliate their clients may be women, and other women colleagues have to deflect their anger.

I am alarmed by the violence that women do to each other: professional violence, competitive violence, emotional violence. I am alarmed by the willingness of women to enslave other women. I am alarmed by a growing absence of decency on the killing floor of professional women's worlds. You are the women who will take your place in the world where *you* can decide who shall flourish and who shall wither; you will make distinctions between the deserving poor and the undeserving poor; where you can yourself determine which life is expendable and which is indispensable. Since you will have the power to do it, you may also be persuaded that you have the right to do it. As educated women the distinction between the two is first-order business.

I am suggesting that we pay as much attention to our nurturing sensibilities as to our ambition. You are moving in the direction of freedom and the function of freedom is to free somebody else. You are moving toward self-fulfillment, and the consequences of that fulfillment should be to discover that there is something just as important as you are and that just-as-important thing may be Cinderella—or your stepsister.

In your rainbow journey toward the realization of personal goals, don't make choices based only on your security and your safety. Nothing is safe. That is not to say that anything ever was, or that anything worth achieving ever should be. Things of value seldom are. It is not safe to have a child. It is not safe to challenge the status quo. It is not safe to choose work that has not been done before. Or to do old work in a new way. There will always be someone there to stop you. But in pursuing your highest ambitions, don't let your personal safety diminish the safety of your stepsister. In wielding the power that is deservedly yours, don't permit it to enslave your stepsisters. Let your might and your power emanate from that place in you that is nurturing and caring.

Women's rights is not only an abstraction, a cause; it is also a personal affair. It is not only about "us"; it is also about me and you. Just the two of us.

Sally Helgesen / Here She Is, Miss America

TWA Ambassador, July 1980

Despite the 1984 scandal over Vanessa Williams's appearance in Penthouse *magazine, the crown of Miss America is still prized by many as an emblem of all that is admirable in American young-womanhood—determination, talent, a cheerful personality, and wholesome good looks.*

Sally Helgesen has written for Glamour, Redbook, *and* Seventeen, *reporting on such varied topics as the Roberto Duran fight and tips on dating and teenage etiquette. Her portrait of 1980 Miss America Cheryl Prewitt looks at where many of our current values spring from and where they may be leading us.*

The TWA Ambassador *magazine began in 1968 as a small, in-flight companion and travel guide. Today, it features original articles on top business and cultural affairs, and boasts a circulation of over 1.2 million. The average income of its readers has been rated higher than that of* Forbes *and* Fortune, *and* Ad Age *has referred to it as "the silver lining of the in-flight field."*

Cheryl Prewitt says she knew all along that she was going to be Miss America 1980. She considered winning the title to be her own personal destiny.

When Prewitt was competing in the Miss Mississippi contest last year, an interviewer asked her if she was going to win the title and go on to become Miss America. She said she hoped so. The interviewer fired back that he didn't want to know what she *hoped,* he wanted to know what she *thought.* She hesitated a minute. "Yes, I am definitely going to be Miss America," she replied. From that day forward, she never had any doubts.

Cheryl Prewitt is a young woman who believes that if you say something often enough you can make it happen. She genuinely believes in miracles. The way she lives her life gives testimony to the power of positive thinking; she could be a Norman Vincent Peale sermon come to life. She mirrors the spirit of an America where life's complexities have not yet overwhelmed people's ability to dream, and dream big.

Making dreams come true, of course, demands a certain single-mindedness, a certain tenacity, qualities not always associated with young people in these days of cynicism and double-sided issues. But it can still be found, in places like Ackerman, Mississippi, for example, where Cheryl Prewitt is at home when she is not off about the country on her Miss America duties.

Ackerman is best approached by way of the tiny city of Starkville, where the Mississippi soy-and-cotton farmbelt meets the modern landscape of Burger Kings and Ramada Inns; beyond Starkville, one is in the heart of the southland, the depths of the old piney woods. The forest, the scrubby farms, the unpainted shacks with their front-porch rocking-chairs make a stark contrast to the plastic suburban strip. This is the kind of place where people tell you to "turn left at the big oak tree" when they give you driving directions. At six on a Sunday evening, every store and public building is closed up tight—there are no houses in town, so not a single light is burning. There are no other drivers about to guide you to the right farm road, so you look for the oak and hope you don't make a wrong turn.

Cheryl Prewitt and her family live in a house set in the bend of a back road that winds for miles through the woods. The house, a boxy, rambling, brightly lit sum of separate parts, used to be a country store and gas station; Prewitt's mother sold feed and seed and all the kids pumped gas. Her father, a building contractor, kept a few hundred acres planted in corn and cotton, as do most people around here. Conditions have improved over the years: the store has closed, new wings have been added to the house, and the farm acreage has grown. But this measure of prosperity, which might suggest to the casual observer that the way in which this family lives has changed, is only a surface alteration. Despite the Mediterranean-style walnut furniture and gold crushed-velvet carpet in the living room, the backwoods shanty soul of the place shines through. It cannot be obscured, any more than the rural reality of central Mississippi life can be disguised by the franchise strip outside of Starkville.

This night at the Prewitts, fifteen people, mostly neighbors, are sitting around a wood-burning stove, drinking iced tea (the beverage of choice in this teetotaler's stronghold) and exchanging familiar stories in thick country accents. All are friends and supporters who had, it seemed, sat around the living room on many nights like this, stitching every sequin and ruffle onto the outfits Prewitt made to wear in the Miss America pageant. Fifty such friends and supporters then traveled by bus all the way to Atlantic City to watch Prewitt compete. Tonight, when Prewitt comes in, her friends rise to hug her, and she hugs them back. ''Praise the Lord,'' everyone choruses.

At first glance, Prewitt seems an unlikely beauty queen. She is 22 years old, slender, bright-eyed and attractive, with a voice as full of Mississippi sweetness as delta clover on a hot afternoon, but she is not beautiful. Her nose is thick and her features are undistinguished except for a wide flashing smile, that trademark of all beauty queens. There is nothing regal in her manner, she is lively and without affectation. ''I've never been a beauty,'' she says matter-of-factly, ''but I've never worried about it. Believe me, there were some really gorgeous girls in the pageant, so I never thought I could compete on that level. I had to rely on my personality and talent to get by.''

Not that she didn't work on her looks in preparation for the pageant. Prewitt put herself through a grueling regimen, jogging long distances down back-country roads, pedaling for hours on her stationary bicycle. (She still keeps the bicycle in the living room so that she won't miss any conversation while she works out.) She wanted to make a respectable showing in the pageant's swimsuit competition, the area in which she felt most vulnerable. She did what she had to do, even though the swimsuit event remained her weakest. ''I don't look at it as a negative, though,'' she explains. ''I just try to concentrate on the positive.''

Concentrating on the positive is Prewitt's favorite refrain. A sign hangs above the kitchen table: ''God don't support no flops.'' It has often been observed that American religion has made the will to succeed into an article of faith, but nowhere is the correspondence between worldly achievement and religious duty more obvious than in a household like the Prewitts', where ''praise the Lord'' and ''up and at 'em'' are repeated frequently and with equal fervor. Determination—the kind of determination that keeps one jogging and pedaling against the odds in hopes of greater gain—becomes a cardinal virtue in this universe. Positive thinking becomes another, and Prewitt has spent her life cultivating these virtues. ''I'm a very determined lady,'' she says by way of preface to her story.

Every weekend when Cheryl Prewitt was growing up, the entire household—Hosea Prewitt and his wife, Carrie, and Paulette and Cheryl and their two younger brothers, Heath and Tim—piled into the old Continental Trailways bus that still stands ready for use in the backyard, and journeyed all around Mississippi and Alabama, singing gospel songs in country churches. They worked hard at it, and at becoming well-known. The older children sang trios and recorded some gospel albums on obscure local labels. The family's road-bound way of life was not uncommon in rural Choctaw County; music is a traditional part of family and church life here, where every local congregation hires a professional singing teacher to coach its children. Hosea and Carrie Prewitt, who both grew up just down the road from where they live now, had traveled with their own families and sung in country churches when they were young, so in a way they were simply carrying on a tradition. But in another way it was also more than that. The family considered their tours more than a pastime: they were a ministry as well.

Being successful on what Cheryl Prewitt calls ''the spiritual circuit'' is not just good for the soul, it is regarded as proof of God's favor. The determination and stick-to-itiveness necessary for such success have a tangible religious value hereabouts. Prewitt learned these lessons well as a child, and now when she speaks of winning the Miss America title, she talks about it as a positive good in the greater scheme of things. ''I think God's people *should* be Miss Americas and presidents, *should* be the people who run things,'' she states. ''They *should* be successful and have money. It's only right.'' This is her strong conviction: that God's people are looked on with divine favor. It is born out of the isolation of her rural community, where most people believe as she does, and where experience thus tends to confirm their beliefs. Such a deep sense of innate worthiness is also highly efficient for developing the determination and single-minded desire for achievement that motivates one to go after a national title such as Miss America. Cheryl Prewitt has her crown to prove it works.

If determination came as a natural consequence of her upbringing, Prewitt's equally passionate faith in the power of positive thinking evolved through a more unusual—to hear her tell it, genuinely miraculous—set of circumstances. When she was ten, all four children in her family were involved in a horrible car accident. Their next-door neighbor was killed and the youngest Prewitt boy sustained a brain concussion and was three times declared legally dead before he finally pulled through. Cheryl Prewitt was pinned under the car and watched as her left leg was crushed to bits. She also cracked her spine and received enough cuts to require a hundred stitches in her face. The doctors couldn't put her leg in traction because there were no bones left to set, so they poured her into a body cast and decided to hope for the best. She recalls people in the neighborhood gathering around her to pray, and pretty soon she felt the cast wrap itself around her leg. ''The doctors said, too, it was a miracle,'' she recalls, ''but of course it was nothing compared to what happened later.''

Prewitt's left leg reformed itself in its calcium cocoon, but it grew back two full inches shorter than her right leg. ''My mom made all my pants,'' she rememberes, ''and she always had to make one leg shorter. I tried to walk in a special way to disguise the fact that I was crippled. When I got in high school, I was popular because of my personality, so I didn't let any of it bother me very much. But when I was seventeen a doctor told me I would never be able to have children because my hips were uneven. I couldn't stand that idea, so I decided that I'd better do something to change my handicap.''

That's where the power of positive thinking came in. ''I'd been reading the Bible a lot,'' she explains, ''and I'd begun to think that maybe people could accomplish miracles just by believing they were possible. I'd been sharing my testimony in church, but I'd never thought of asking for a miracle. When I decided the time had come to do it, I got serious. I had families from around here show me the right passages in Scripture and I studied them. I got other people to pray with me. I made the decision never to think negatively about anything, since that could cut into the positive power I was trying to put out. Miracles are based on faith, so you have to overcome doubt of every kind to make them happen. When I decided I was ready, I went to a faith revival and said, 'Lord, I'm ready to receive.' When I came home that night, my legs were the exact same length. I learned then that what we *think* controls what happens to us in life, so I always make sure to think *yes.*''

It was after her miracle that she conceived the idea of becoming Miss America. Prewitt was simply looking for a way to expand her stage. She'd been singing and playing the piano all over the Deep South, but she wanted a national audience, and entering a pageant competition seemed like a good way to find one. In Mississippi—which, together with Texas, has produced the greatest number of Miss Americas—women's thoughts turn more readily to the idea of entering beauty contests as a way of achieving success because the precedent is there. This is often explained by a variety of Southern-belle theories, but it probably has more to do with the single-mindedness and determination that come of living among people who honor these qualities with a religious reverence, people who live in isolated circumstances that shield them from any contradictory evidence.

Becoming Miss America had a special appeal to Prewitt because she did not regard the pageant as a beauty contest, but rather as an arena in which a young woman with a peculiarly American brand of poise and talent could perform. "Being Miss America," she explains, "*does* something for a girl, gives her scholarships and a chance to earn money. I wasn't interested in just getting a crown that wouldn't get me anything more." Winning was a means to an end.

But winning came slowly. Prewitt spent four years losing pageants before she succeeded in what she'd decided was her destiny. When she was seventeen, she entered the Miss Choctaw County pageant and lost. The next year she entered and won, and went on to the state contest, only to lose there. Again the next year, when she was in college, Prewitt was elected Miss Mississippi State, but again she lost the state pageant. Finally, in her senior year, after having paid for her education by holding down three jobs and teaching piano lessons at home, she looked around for a new approach. She entered the Miss Starkville contest and won, and at last went on to be chosen Miss Mississippi and, ultimately, Miss America. "All those disappointments I'd had," she explains, "just helped to get me ready." She claims that losing year after year never discouraged her. She'd seen *miracles* happen, she says, and she knew that eventual triumph would certainly demand less than that.

Her goal now at last attained, Prewitt makes it clear that she regards being Miss America as a tool for achieving a greater end—specifically, that of enlarging her audience. At the time she was crowned she expected contest officials to ask her to tone down her positive-thinking exhortations and references to real-life miracles, but they haven't. So she has chosen to use the booking agency that the pageant provides every Miss America to keep her on the road every day of the year. There are an unlimited number of lectures and performing dates, she finds, provided a Miss America makes herself available, and at every stop she makes a point to put in a good word for her cause.

Back home, the Prewitt family doesn't make much of a fuss over having a Miss America in the house. Rows of family photographs are arranged on a shelf in the kitchen, and there are a number of shots of daughter Cheryl, but only one showing her with the sash and crown and armful of red roses that mark a Miss America. Other than the inevitable mess that attends the arrival of a young woman who must live for an entire year out of suitcases, one would never guess that the visiting daughter is Miss America and not just a college student come home to do her laundry.

What Cheryl Prewitt will do with herself when her year-long tenure is up in September, she doesn't really know, although you can be sure she's thinking positively about it. She's considering going to work for Oral Roberts up in Lincoln, Nebraska, or traveling to Los Angeles to make a TV movie about her life. For now, however, she thinks she'll probably just move back into her parents' house when it's all over and resume the singing career she has pursued in one way or another since she was five years old. In this part of the world, moving back home after achieving some measure of outside success is not unusual. After she became one of the first women to earn a pharmacist's degree from the University of Mississippi, Cheryl Prewitt's older sister, Paulette, came home to work in the local drugstore where her mother is a part-time clerk. For Miss America 1980, having won the title she worked for so long, it is enough, for now, to savor the victory.

This night, Cheryl Prewitt is pedaling the stationary bicycle in her parents' living room, working off the calories from a large slice of homemade coconut cake she has just had for a snack. Her mother steps out onto the porch; she hears the soft whoosh her daughter's exercising makes in the still, black night. "See them trees over there?" She points into the dense forest across the way. "When people from Atlanta and such places come here, they ask me what's behind them. I just tell them, *more trees!*" She laughs. Inside, Miss America pedals away on her stationary bicycle.

DISCUSSION QUESTIONS

1. Which aspect of Miss America's life is emphasized in the essay? What has this emphasis to do with the American Dream? With Norman Vincent Peale?

2. Compare Sally Helgesen's treatment of "Miss America" to Stud Terkel's interview with "Miss USA" in Best Sellers.

3. As an in-flight magazine, *TWA Ambassador* naturally reaches a large business community. How are the interests of that audience reflected in the article?

Jay Cocks / The Last Day in the Life

Time, December 22, 1980

The untimely death of a cultural hero often shocks the world into reevaluating its dreams, its ideals, and its youth. When John Lennon, founder of the Beatles, rebel, pacifist, and family man, was assassinated on December 8, 1980, an entire generation lost one of its most brilliant and beloved leaders. The response to his murder came from all across the world and from a diversity of voices. Yet one factor unified all of these reactions—an expression of grief and amazement at the truly unimaginable. The following is an example of one reporter's assessment of a complex life, tragically cut short.

Jay Cocks is a contributing editor to Time *magazine.*

Just a voice out of the American night. "Mr. Lennon." He started to turn around. There is no knowing whether John Lennon saw, for what would have been the second time that day, the young man in the black raincoat stepping out of the shadows. The first shot hit him that fast, through the chest. There were at least three others.

Not that night, or the next day, but a little later, after the terror ebbed and the grief could be managed, Lennon's wife, Yoko Ono, took their five-year-old son Sean to the spot in the apartment courtyard where she had seen his father murdered. She had already shown Sean a newspaper with his father's picture on the front page. She tried to do what everyone else has done since that Monday night. She tried to explain.

Like everyone else, too, the boy asked simple questions to which there would never be simple or satisfactory answers. If, as was being said, the man liked his father so much, why did he shoot him? His mother explained: "He was probably a confused person." Not good enough. Better to know, Sean Lennon said, if he was confused or really meant to kill. His mother said that was up to the courts to decide, and Sean wanted to know which courts she was talking about: tennis or basketball? Then Sean cried, and he also said, "Now Daddy is part of God. I guess when you die you become much more bigger because you're part of everything."

Sean did not really know or understand about the Beatles, or what his father was to the world. But Sean will surely know, soon enough, that his father did not have to die to become part of everything. Given the special burden and grace of his great gift, he already was. Not just for his wife or son but for more people than anyone could ever begin to number, the killing of John Lennon was a death in the family.

For all the official records, the death would be called murder. For everyone who cherished the sustaining myth of the Beatles—which is to say, for much of an entire generation that is passing, as Lennon was, at age 40, into middle age, and coming suddenly up against its own mortality—the murder was something else. It was an assassination, a ritual slaying of something that could hardly be named. Hope, perhaps; or idealism. Or time. Not only lost, but suddenly dislocated, fractured.

The outpouring of grief, wonder and shared devastation that followed Lennon's death had the same breadth and intensity as the reaction to the killing of a world figure: some bold and popular politician, like John or Robert Kennedy, or a spiritual leader, like Martin Luther King Jr. But Lennon was a creature of poetic political metaphor, and his spiritual consciousness was directed inward, as a way of nurturing and widening his creative force. That was what made the impact, and the difference—the shock of his imagination, the penetrating and pervasive traces of his genius—and it was the loss of all that, in so abrupt and awful a way, that was mourned last week, all over the world. The last *Day in the Life,* "I read the news today, oh boy . . ."

Sorrow was expressed, sympathies extended by everyone from Presidents and Presidents-elect, Prime Ministers and Governors and mayors to hundreds of fans who gathered at the arched entryway to the Lennons' Manhattan apartment building, the Dakota, crying and praying, singing and decorating the tall iron gates with wreaths and single flowers and memorial banners. CHRISTMAS IN HEAVEN, read one. Another recalled the magical invocation of a childhood memory that became one of his finest songs: *Strawberry Fields Forever.*

Ringo Starr flew to New York to see Yoko. George Harrison, "shattered and stunned," went into retreat at his home in Oxfordshire, England. Paul McCartney, whom Lennon plainly loved and just as plainly hated like the brother he never had, said, "I can't tell you how much it hurts to lose him. His death is a bitter, cruel blow—I really loved the guy." Having no wish to contribute to the hysteria that always follows the grief at such public mournings, McCartney, who has hired two bodyguards to protect himself and his family, said he would stay home in Sussex, England, even if there was a funeral. There was not. Lennon's body was cremated in a suburban New York cemetry, and Ono issued a statement inviting everyone "to participate from wherever you are" in a ten-minute silent vigil on Sunday afternoon.

Before that, it had been a week of tributes. Radio stations from New Orleans to Boston cleared the air ways for Lennon and Beatles retrospectives. In Los Angeles, more than 2,000 people joined in a candlelight vigil at Century City; in Washington, D.C., several hundred crowded the steps of the Lincoln Memorial in a "silent tribute" that recalled the sit-ins of the '60s. Record stores all over the country reported sellouts on the new Lennon-Ono album, *Double Fantasy,* their first record in five years, as well as the back stock of Lennon's previous records.

Some reaction was tragic. A teen-age girl in Florida and a man of 30 in Utah killed themselves, leaving notes that spoke of depression over Lennon's death. On Thursday, Ono said, "This is not the end of an era. The '80s are still going to be a beautiful time, and John believed in it."

All the brutal and finally confounding facts of the killing were examined like runes and held up to the light like talismans, small shards of some awful psychic puzzle. A pudgy Georgia-born ex-security guard from Hawaii named Mark David Chapman fired his shots at Lennon from what the police call "combat stance": in a stiff crouch, one hand wrapped around the butt of his newly purchased revolver, the other around his wrist to steady it. As Lennon took six staggering steps, Chapman, 25, simply stood still, and then went with the arresting officers like a model citizen who had been unfairly rousted on a traffic bust. Chapman's personal history showed, in retrospect, many ominous byways, but immediately after the shooting, he offered no explanations. And no regrets.

Chapman arrived in New York three days before the killing, checked into a Y.M.C.A. nine blocks from Lennon's apartment, and started hanging out in front of the building, waiting for Lennon like any other fan. There were usually fans at the gates of the Dakota, a grand, gloomy, high-maintenance Gothic fortress overlooking the west side of Central Park, because the building houses several celebrities: Lauren Bacall, Roberta Flack, Leonard Bernstein. Fans of the Beatles and Lennon lovers accounted for the largest portion of the curious. Two unidentified women told an ABC television reporter that they had fallen into conversation with Chapman outside the Dakota. Said one, "He just seemed like a really nice, genuine, honest person who was there because he admired John." Others, like WPLJ Disc Jockey Carol Miller, who lives near the Dakota, had noticed Chapman and thought "he looked strange. He was older than the kids who hung around there." When Miller first heard that Lennon had been shot, Chapman's face flashed in her mind.

On Saturday night, Chapman hailed a cab and told Driver Mark Snyder to take him to Greenwich Village. On the way he boasted that he had just dropped off the tapes of an album John Lennon and Paul McCartney made that day. He said that he was the recording engineer and that they had played for three hours.

On Monday afternoon Chapman spotted Lennon and asked him to autograph an album. Lennon hastily scribbled his name and climbed into a waiting car to take him to a recording stuidio. Did Chapman feel slighted by Lennon? Possibly. But the night before he had suddenly checked out of the Y and moved into the cushier Sheraton Center hotel and bought himself a big meal. It was as if he were rewarding himself in advance for some proud accomplishment. Now on Monday, only hours after getting Lennon's autograph, Chapman was waiting again, this time in the shadows of the entryway, with a gun. When the police grabbed him after the shooting, they found he still had the autographed album with him. He also had a paperback copy of J.D. Salinger's *The Catcher in the Rye*.

Lennon was no stranger to threats on his life. As early as 1964, at the first Beatles concert in France, Lennon got a note backstage that read, "I am going to shoot you at 9 tonight." He had only lately become accustomed to the freewheeling anarchy of New York street life: "I can go out this door now and go into a restaurant . . . Do you want to know how great that is?" he told the BBC. But friends remember him as being guarded both in public and around the few people he and Ono met during the long years of self-willed isolation that were only ending with the completion of the new album. "John was always wary," says his friend, Actor Peter Boyle. "Maybe partly because he was extraordinarily tuned in. He'd pick up on people, and they'd pick up on him."

Lennon also shared with many other rockers a kind of operational fatalism, a sense that doing your best, whether on record or in concert, required laying yourself open, making yourself vulnerable. It was not only the pressures and excesses of the rock-'n'-roll life that moved the Who's Peter Townshend to remark, "Rock is going to kill me somehow." And it was not just the death of Elvis Presley that Lennon had in mind when he said to friends in 1978, "If you stay in this business long enough, it'll get you."

Rock, Lennon knew as well as anyone, is the applied art of big risk and big feelings. The songs he and Paul McCartney wrote for the Beatles, separately and together, brought more people up against the joy and boldness of rock music than anything else ever has. It wasn't just that Aaron Copland and Leonard Bernstein were taking the Beatles as seriously—and a good deal more affectionately—than Stockhausen. The worldwide appeal of the Beatles had to do with their perceived innocence, their restless idealism that stayed a step or two ahead of the times and once in a while turned, bowed low, gave the times a razz and dared them to catch up. The slow songs were heart stoppers, the fast ones adrenaline rushes of wit, low-down love and high, fabulous adventure. The songs became, all together, an orchestration of a generation's best hopes and fondest dreams.

The songs Lennon wrote later on his own—*Imagine* and *Whatever Gets You Thru the Night, Instant Karma* and *Give Peace a Chance* and the gentle and unapologetic *Watching the Wheels* from the new album, or the gorgeous seasonal anthem, *Happy Xmas (War Is Over),* which he recorded with Ono in 1972—kept the standard high and his conscience fine-tuned. The political songs were all personal, the intimate songs all singular in their fierce insistence on making public all issues of the heart, on working some common moral out of private pain. Rock music is still benefitting from lessons that Lennon fought hard for, then passed along. All his music seemed to be torn from that small, stormy interior where, as Robert Frost once wrote, "work is play for mortal stakes."

Despite the universality of interest in his death, Lennon remained chiefly the property—one might even be tempted to say prisoner—of his own generation. Some—those who regarded the Beatles as a benign cultural curiosity, and Lennon as some overmoneyed songwriter with a penchant for political pronouncements and personal excess—wondered what all the fuss was about and could not quite understand why some of the junior staff at the office would suddenly break into tears in the middle of the day. "A garden-variety Nobel prizewinner would not get this kind of treatment," said a teacher in Oxford, England. Across the Atlantic, in schools and on college campuses, those from other generations showed almost as great a sense of puzzlement, even distance, as of loss. Gretchen Steininger, 16, a junior at Evergreen Park High School in suburban Chicago, said, "I recognize the end of an era—my mom's."

So a little reminder was in order, a small history lesson, and there was no one better to lead the class than Bruce Springsteen. Lennon had lately become warmly admiring of Springsteen, especially his hit single *Hungry Heart.* Springsteen could probably have let Lennon's death pass unremarked, and few in the audience at his Philadelphia concert last Tuesday would have been troubled. But instead of ripping right into the first song, Springsteen simply said, "If it wasn't for John Lennon, a lot of us would be some place much different tonight. It's a hard world that asks you to live with a lot of things that are unlivable. And it's hard to come out here and play tonight, but there's nothing else to do."

Then Bruce and the E Street Band tore into Springsteen's own anthem, *Born to Run,* making it clear that playing was the best thing to do. Guitarist Steve Van Zandt let the tears roll down his face, and Organist Danny Federici hit the board so hard he broke a key. By the second verse, the song turned into a challenge the audience was happy to accept: "I wanna know love is wild, I wanna know love is real," Springsteen yelled, and they yelled back. By the end, it sounded like redemption. John Lennon knew that sound too. He could use it like a chord change because he had been chasing it most of his life.

John Lennon grew up on Penny Lane, and after a time he moved to a house outside Liverpool, hard by a boys' reformatory. There was another house in the neighborhood where John and his pals would go to a party and sell lemonade bottles for a penny. The house was called Strawberry Fields. His boyhood was neither as roughly working-class as early Beatles p.r. indicated, nor quite as benign as the magical association of those place names might suggest. But John's adolescence in the suburbs, the garden outside the back door and the warm ministrations of his Auntie Mimi did not diminish either the pain or the sense of separateness that was already stirring.

His father, a seaman named Alfred, left home shortly after John was born, and his mother Julia sent him to her sister Mimi because, it was said, she could not support her child. John was 4½ when he was farmed out to the suburbs. All the sorrow, rage and confusion of this early boyhood were taken up again and again in songs like *Julia* and *Mother*. These early years were not an unhealed wound for Lennon, but more nearly a root, a deep psychic wellspring from which he could draw reserves of hard truth.

Reserves of another sort gave him trouble even early on. "In one way, I was always hip," Lennon remarked recently in *Playboy*, during an interview that could stand as lively proof that some of the best Lennon/Ono art was their life. "I was hip in kindergarten. I was different from the others . . . There was something wrong with me, I thought, because I seemed to see things other people didn't see. I was always seeing things in a hallucinatory way." Lennon's songs made peace with those hallucinations and expanded them—whether with psychedelics, psychiatry or a sort of domestic mysticism—while keeping them always within reach, as a man might keep a flashlight on a nightstand in case he had to get up in the dark.

Lennon was already well into his teens, living 15 minutes away from his mother but seldom seeing her, when rock 'n' roll grabbed hold of him and never let loose. All the raw glories of Elvis Presley, Little Richard, Chuck Berry and Jerry Lee Lewis shook him to his shoes. He responded with the rowdiness of spirit and emotional restlessness that already set him apart from his peers and caused their parents concern. Paul McCartney's father warned his son to steer clear of John, which amounted to an open if inadvertent invitation to friendship.

By his 16th year, John had formed his first band, the Quarrymen, and Paul McCartney had enlisted as guitar player. John and Paul began to write songs together almost as soon as they had finished tuning up, and they played any gig the band could get. By the end of 1956, though he had his first group and a best friend, Lennon suffered a lasting wound. His mother was killed in an accident while she stood waiting for a bus. As he said, "I lost her twice."

Two years later, George Harrison had joined the Quarrymen, and the band was actually earning some money. They had their own fans, and a growing reputation that took them to club dates in the gritty seaport of Hamburg, West Germany, where they eventually changed their name to the Beatles and got a double dose of the seamier side of rock life. Lennon, who like the rest of the boys favored black leather jackets, pegged pants and stomper boots, was sending long and passionate mash notes back home to Cynthia Powell. "Sexiest letters this side of Henry Miller," he observed.

He was also a student at the Liverpool College of Art while the Quarrymen were still gigging around. "I knew John would always be a bohemian," Aunt Mimi recalled. "But I wanted him to have some sort of job. Here he was nearly 21 years old, touting round stupid halls for £3 a night. Where was the point in that?"

Well, the point was the music, a peak-velocity transplant of American rock, with its original blistering spirit not only restored but exalted. There was some concern for the future, however. A Liverpool record-store owner named Brian Epstein thought he might be able to lend a hand there. He signed on as the group's manager in 1961. By the end of the following year, the boys got their first record contract and their first producer, George Martin, who remained aboard for the crazy cruise that came to be called Beatlemania. There was one final change of personnel: Drummer Pete Best was replaced by a gentleman named Richard Starkey, who favored quantities of heavy jewelry, most of it worn on the digits, and who went by the name of Ringo Starr.

It took just a month for the second Beatles single, *Please Please Me,* to reach the top of the English charts. That was in January of 1963. By the end of that year, they had released *She Loves You* and appeared live on a BBC variety show in front of thousands of screaming fans in the audience and unverifiable millions of new converts and dazed parents sitting at home in front of the telly. *I Want to Hold Your Hand* came out in the U.S. in the first week of 1964, and it seemed then for a while that both sides of the Atlantic were up for grabs. Beatles forever.

Some history becomes myth, some myth goes down in history, some statistics boggle the mind: the Beatles have sold, all over the world, upwards of 200 million records. They made history so quickly, and so seismically, that their chronology can be given like a code, or an association game in which words, phrases, snatches of lyrics, names, can stand for whole years. Even the skeptical on either side of the Beatles generation will be startled to see how easily they can play along. Start off with an easy one. Yeah, yeah, yeah. Now you're off . . . Ed Sullivan. Jelly babies. Plaza Hotel. Moptops. Arthur and *A Hard Day's Night.* The Maharishi and M.B.E.s. *Sergeant Pepper.* LSD. Apple. "More popular than Jesus." Shea Stadium. White Album. *Yesterday.* "I'd love to turn you on." Jane, Pattie, Cynthia. Linda. Yoko. "Paul is dead." Abbey Road. *Let It Be.*

The history and the resonance of those fragments are so strong that even out of chronological sequence they form their own associations, like a Joseph Cornell collage. Some of the colors may be psychedelic, but the shadings are the pastel of memory, the patina made of remembered melody. Lennon, the only wedded Beatle—he had married Cynthia in 1962 and had a son, Julian—had early been typed as the most restless, outspoken and creative of the group, even though he led, outwardly, the most settled life. There was paradox in this popular portrait, just as there was considerable tension in Lennon's belief that the well-noted contadictions were true. There were both beauty and ambition in his music, and a full measure of turmoil too. He was experimenting with drugs and working up some of the material that would eventually find its way into *Sergeant Pepper's Lonely Hearts Club Band,* when he walked into a London gallery in 1966 and there, among ladders, spyglasses, nail boards, banners and other props of her art, met Yoko Ono.

The daughter of a well-to-do Japanese banker, Ono, now 47, was born in Tokyo. She had lived in San Francisco before World War II, foraged for food back home during it, and afterward returned to the States, where she attended Sarah Lawrence College and became interested in the far-flung reaches of the avant-garde. Her first husband was a Japanese musician. The marriage so offended Ono's mother that she never reconciled with her daughter. She worked on concerts for John Cage, became associated with other artists such as La Monte Young and Charlotte Moorman, the topless cellist whose staging of and participation in art "events" came a little later to be called happenings. Ono married again, a conceptual artist named Tony Cox, and they had a daughter, Kyoko. Ono once brought the baby onstage during a concert as "an uncontrollable instrument." Eventually, Cox and Kyoko went to Japan, and Ono to England. Her artworks, or happenings, began to show a sense of humor that was both self-mocking and affirmative, and when John Lennon climbed a ladder to look through a telescope at that London gallery, what he saw was no distant landscape but a simple YES.

The other Beatles were not delighted to have Ono around. Besides whatever personal antagonisms or random jealousies might have existed, one suspects now, Paul, George and Ringo may have considered her dedicated avant-gardism somewhat inimical to the best popular instincts of their music. For her part, she felt she was under heavy surveillance. "I sort of went to bed with this guy that I liked and suddenly the next morning I see these three in-laws standing there," she recalled recently. John, separated from Cynthia, fell in love with Yoko and her ideas. Some of her conceptual art had the same intellectual playfulness as his lyrics, and Lennon became a collaborator in many of her projects. They made films—of flies crawling, of dozens of bare bums. They made records, including the notorious *Two Virgins,* for which they posed naked, front and back. Shock! Scandal! Grim predictions for the future!

In fact, there was already a fair amount of dissension among the members of the band: McCartney wanted to get out more and play for the folks, Lennon wanted to work in the recording studio, like an artist with a canvas. The ideological pressures and upheavals of the decade made the four Beatles stand out in even sharper contrast to each other. John became much more political, George more spiritual, Paul seemingly more larky, and Ringo more social. In the more than two years between *Sergeant Pepper* and *Abbey Road,* Lennon and McCartney wrote, separately and still (but more tenuously) together, some of their greatest songs *(Penny Lane, All You Need Is Love,* and *Strawberry Fields Forever).* But if the turmoil had an immediate, productive side, it also took an inevitable toll. In 1969, after the completion of *Abbey Road,* John told the boys he was leaving.

Next year, McCartney went his own way and that, one would have thought, was that. End of Beatles, end of era. But the Beatles would never go away because their music endured; it became part of a common heritage, a shared gift. No matter how many times they were played in elevators or gas stations, Beatles songs were too vibrant ever to qualify as "standards." That these were *Beatles* songs, not the single expression of an individual, needs to be remembered amid all the Lennon eulogies, which call him the strong creative force of the group.

In the process of riding out all the massive changes of the '60s and bringing about a few on their own, the Beatles also trashed an elementary law of geometry: this was one whole that was greater than the sum of its parts. Lennon was unfairly used as a means to put McCartney in his place, although Lennon had taken pains lately to redefine details of his collaboration with Paul, and to make sure credit was distributed accurately. The melodic range of the music ran from marching band to rhythm and blues, from tonal stunt flying to atonal acrobatics, once in a while all in the same song. The Beatles sang ballads that could almost be Elizabethan, rockers that still sound as if they come from the distant future, and it was hard to peg all that invention to any single source. Lennon joked about walking into a restaurant and being saluted by the band with a rendition of *Yesterday,* a pure McCartney effort. Many radio and video memorials to Lennon included *Let It Be,* another Beatles tune that was all McCartney.

If it was hard to keep the credits straight with all the Beatles, it was harder still for them to keep their friendly equilibrium. McCartney, married to Linda Eastman and staying close to the hearthside, released a series of albums that were roundly drubbed as corny, until he broke through splendidly in 1973 with *Band on the Run.* Lennon, married to Ono and living in New York, released a great solo record, *Plastic Ono Band,* then threw himself headlong into uncertainty. He and Ono lived in a series of elaborate post-hippie crash pads, because obsessed not only with artistic experimentation but with radical political flamboyance. Lennon's subsequent albums remained achingly personal, but turned increasingly random, unfocused. They were indignant and assaultive, adrift.

When he and Ono separated for a time in the early '70s, Lennon went on an 18-month bender of drink, drugs and general looniness. "We were all drinking too much and tearing up houses," recalls one of his cronies at the time, Drummer Jim Keltner. "No one drank like he did. He had broken up with Ono and was with another woman at the time. Suddenly, he just started screaming out Ono's name. That separation from her almost killed him." Being treated as some sort of witchy parasite was no treat for the estranged Mrs. Lennon either, and when they both finally reconciled, they changed their lives in unexpected ways.

Lennon released one more record—a collection of rock oldies—then settled back with Ono in the Dakota to raise their son Sean, who was born on Oct. 9, 1975, the day of his father's birthday. Said Lennon: "We're like twins." Occasionally, John and Ono would go public, often to fight the ultimately unsuccessful attempts of the Nixon Justice Department to deport Lennon on an old marijuana conviction in England. Mostly, however, they stayed at home, rearing Sean, redecorating the 25 rooms in their four Dakota apartments (art deco and artifacts of ancient Egypt, including a sarcophagus in the living room; but clouds painted on the ceiling of a downstairs office), expanding their financial holdings (Lennon left an estate estimated at $235 million), buying property and Holstein cows.

The Holsteins were selected because they were meant to yield nourishment, not be slaughtered for it. Ono took care of all the details, and Lennon did not know about the sale of one of the cows until he read an item in the paper. He was even more pleased than surprised. "Only Yoko," he said admiringly, "could sell a cow for $250,000."

Ono could do a lot more than that. The banker's daughter set herself to mastering the mysteries of commercial law and deal making just as, earlier, she had wrestled with the exotic exigencies of John Cage. She met the attorneys and the accountants; she supervised the buying up of property in Palm Beach, Fla., Cold Spring Harbor, an exclusive enclave on Long Island, and in upstate New York. When the Lennons decided to make another album earlier this year, it was Ono who called Record Executive David Geffen and worked out the deal.

The Lennons may have been taking a step or two aside from art, living quietly, but they were not hermits. The were collecting themselves, looking for a center, a core. It seemed hard to understand, but shouldn't have been. Ono sat behind the desk and John stayed home with the little boy. Julian, Lennon's other, older son, was now a teen-ager who lived in Britain with his mother, but wore leather jackets and jeans, like his Dad back in the days of the Quarrymen, and talked of becoming a rocker. John did not see Julian often, and said recently, "I don't remember seeing him as a child." But Lennon suggested that he had lately wanted to know Julian better, and one of the most haunted faces in last week's gallery of grief was Julian's, enduring the same pain that had afflicted his father at almost the same age some 25 years before. He, like John, had lost a parent twice.

John gloried in playing parent to Sean, and liked to call himself a househusband. What upset traditionalists was the fact that he obviously reveled in his domestic role. This role reversal was seen by the man raised by an aunt and three of her sisters as no threat at all. He insisted—indeed, proved—that he was putting nothing at risk, not his manhood and not his artistry.

Double Fantasy, the new record, demonstrated that. Ono's contributions are especially accessible and congenial after years of punk and New Wave conditioning. John's songs, simple, direct and melodic, were celebrations of love and domesticity that asked for, and required, no apology. It was not a great record, like *Plastic Ono Band,* but it might have been the start of another time of greatness.

The subjects of *Double Fantasy,* released last month, were supposedly not the stuff of rock, but John Lennon never bound himself to tradition. ''My life revolves around Sean,'' he told some radio interviewers from San Francisco on the afternoon of the day he was killed. ''Now I have more reason to stay healthy and bright . . . And I want to be with my best friend. My best friend's me wife. If I couldn't have worked with her, I wouldn't have bothered . . . I consider that my work won't be finished until I'm dead and buried, and I hope that's a long, long time.'' As he spoke those words, Mark David Chapman waited for him out on the street.

Lennon's death was not like Elvis Presley's. Presley seemed, at the end, trapped, defeated and hopeless. Lennon could have gone that way too, could have destroyed himself. But he did something harder. He lived. And, for all the fame and finance, that seemed to be what he took the most pride in.

''He beat the rock-'n'-roll life,'' Steve Van Zandt said the day after Lennon died. ''Beat the drugs, beat the fame, beat the damage. He was the only guy who beat it all.'' That was the victory Mark Chapman took from John Lennon, who had an abundance of what everyone wants and wanted only what so many others have, and take for granted. A home and family. Some still center of love. A life. One minute more.

DISCUSSION QUESTIONS

1. Compare *Time* magazine's account of John Lennon's murder with the Los Angeles *Times* report in Press. In what basic ways do the two accounts differ? How do these differences reflect the differences between a daily newspaper and a weekly news magazine?

2. Examine the openings of both selections. Comment on their differences in tone and diction. How can you account for these differences? What can the *Time* magazine writer assume that the newspaper reporter cannot?

3. How is the difference in assumptions about audience reflected in the way each article is titled? What does the *Time* magazine title allude to?

Robert Jay Lifton / ''Why Aren't We More Afraid of the Bomb''

Dial, February 1981

Dial, *established in 1980, is sent to subscribers of the Public Broadcasting System and is not available to the general public. With a circulation of 1.2 million, the magazine both reflects the liberal, socially conscious viewership of PBS and serves as a complement and viewer's guide to programming on the network. Robert Jay Lifton, a psychiatrist and winner of the National Book Award for* Death in Life: Survivors of Hiroshima *(1968), has devoted much of his scholarly career to studying the relationship between individual behavior and extreme historical situations. As a concerned social observer, Lifton warns against a syndrome he calls ''psychic numbing,'' the result of our society's passive acceptance of technology.*

In the following piece, Lifton addresses an almost unfathomable paradox: our pervasive awareness of the threat of nuclear destruction and the apparent lack of concern it generates among us.

The atom bomb that struck Hiroshima shortly after 8:00 A.M. on August 6, 1945, was a trifle. Strategic warheads today can create a nuclear explosion over a thousand times more powerful. These devices are infinitely more lethal in the amount of radiation they can spread. We know, nevertheless, what that trifling bomb did to Hiroshima. We know that people by the thousands were incinerated in the streets, many of them as they hurried to work. A white flash, and they were gone. Ninety percent of the people who were outdoors and within six tenths of a mile from where the bomb hit died instantly. All the buildings within two miles crumbled. The blast melted stone.

Surviving the explosion was no guarantee of remaining alive. Within days, radiation began its work. People became weak, ran high fevers, developed diarrhea, bled from all their orifices, lost their hair, and died. Death by radiation is in many ways worse than the explosion itself. Radiation is invisible. It was the survivors' second encounter with death after the bomb dropped.

Years later, they had their third encounter. Because of radiation, cases of leukemia, most of them fatal, increased. This was only one kind of cancer that the bomb produced; the incidence of cancer of the thyroid, the lungs, the ovaries, and the cervix also rose. But psychologically, leukemia, particularly in children, was the ultimate horror, the eventual outcome of the first moments after the bomb struck. The fears have not ended. The rate of cancer among survivors continues to increase. They wonder what genetic scars will appear in their children or their children's children.

We can be reminded of the Hiroshima bomb, and we know that many more powerful bombs are aimed right now at cities around the world. So why aren't we frightened by the knowledge that if a one-megaton bomb (the bomb dropped on Hiroshima was only thirteen kilotons) struck a city as densely populated as New York, over two million people would probably die instantly? Cockroaches would survive well. They would be blinded by the flash but still able to resist radiation far better than humans.

I think we are afraid, but we hide our fear. We have done precious little talking about the consequences of Hiroshima and Nagasaki. Yet, my study of Hiroshima survivors and my observations in this country today lead me to believe that those events *have* had an important psychological impact on us. The Hiroshima explosion cannot really represent what would occur today if nuclear weapons were used. Still, Hiroshima has things to tell us, particularly if we look at it not as an obscure event in the past but as a truth dominating our existence today. Ironically, we ourselves experience in muted form much of what happened psychologically to the survivors even though we have never experienced such a holocaust.

Right after the bomb exploded, the survivors ceased to feel, though they were surrounded by destruction and mutilation—people whose flesh fell from their bodies, charred corpses in fantastic positions, screams and moans. "Somehow, I became a pitiless person," one survivor told me, "because if I had had pity, I would not have been able to walk through the city, to walk over those dead bodies, badly injured bodies that had turned black, their eyes looking for someone to come and help them."

The survivors were psychically numb. It was a defense mechanism to close themselves off from death. Their unconscious message: If I feel nothing, then death is not taking place. But such cessation of feeling is itself a symbolic form of death.

There was also another emotion: The survivors felt the need to justify their own survival when so many others had died. An impossible task. The alternative was to feel guilty for being alive, and this turned to shame. Survivors spoke of "the shame of living." They could never simply conclude that by happy chance they had survived. Now, thirty-five years later, some have remained so identified with those who died that they themselves feel as if dead. In daily life, they have been distrustful and suspicious yet have craved human relationships. These have been difficult to find: just as the survivors felt ashamed for themselves, others in Hiroshima have felt them to be tainted by death. Survival became a stigma, and some of that attitude still lingers.

Hiroshima initiated us into the possibility of global destruction. In the United States, that awareness has a special impact on children, according to unpublished studies conducted several years ago by Michael Carey, a historian trained in psychoanalytic methods. He interviewed people who had been schoolchildren in the early 1950s. It was the time when schools across the country held bomb drills, in which pupils were told to crouch under their desks. The Hiroshima and Nagasaki bombs and the fear of a menacing Russia inspired those quaint exercises. Nightmares and fantasies of death and destruction resulted.

The repercussions went far beyond bad dreams. A child must struggle to understand death and come to terms with its inevitability and finality. We all have difficulty doing this, but under ordinary circumstances, we come to accept death as part of life's rhythm. Bomb drills, bomb scares, and images of grotesque, massive death interfere with the capacity of children to think of death as natural. They equate it with annihilation.

The world is insane. This attitude also emerged from Carey's interviews—the bomb is irrational, governments are irrational, and those in authority have no real authority. In such a world, nothing can endure. Awareness of the bomb's potential has thus created an ephemerality; we remain alive at the whim of a craziness that can make us disappear in an instant.

We deal with this by leading double lives. All those whom Carey interviewed spoke of both the possibility of destruction as well as the need to go about their lives as if nothing would happen. Most of us probably lead the same double lives and, in fact, share the themes that appear in Carey's work. We cannot afford to incorporate our knowledge of the destructiveness of nuclear weapons into our emotions. If we allow ourselves to feel what we know, we probably could not go on; hence the extraordinary gap we experience between knowledge and feeling.

Becoming numb to the threat of nuclear destruction is perhaps one way to get through daily life, but it is not a solution. Indeed, it may lead us right into extinction. The existence of nuclear weapons and the threat of their use interfere with the human desire for continuity. We need to feel connected, I believe, to those who have existed before and will exist beyond our brief individual life spans. We normally experience this sense of immortality in the idea of living on in our children, our creations, our influences on others, and in something all cultures describe as an individual's relationship to the natural world. We also feel this larger continuity in spiritual, or religious, terms and, finally, in psychic states that we view as transcendent, states so intense that time and death disappear—religious ecstasy, song and dance, sex, or merely the contemplation of beauty.

But in the face of extermination by a nuclear holocaust, who can believe in living on in one's children and their children or by means of spiritual or creative achievement or even in nature, which we now know to be vulnerable to our destructive weapons? Though we may be numb to the danger of destruction, we are aware of the bomb's presence, its weight on us. This, I believe, is why we are hungrier than ever for states of transcendence. We seek highs from drugs, meditation, jogging, and skydiving, and we join extremist religious cults that offer a kind of cosmology that sometimes includes or even welcomes a nuclear event.

Much worse, a religion based solely upon the nuclear threat exists today. It is industrial society's ultimate disease, a condition I call nuclearism. Worshipers passionately embrace nuclear weapons both as a solution to anxiety over possible nuclear holocaust and as a way of restoring a lost sense of immortality. They seek grace and even salvation—the mastery of death and evil—through the power of the new technological deity.

Adherents see the deity as capable not only of apocalyptic destruction but also of unlimited creation. The bomb, they think, can solve diplomatic impasses, force a way to peace, and atomic energy's potential can create a world of milk and honey. Believers come to depend on weapons to keep the world going. Edward Teller, a leader in the development of the hydrogen bomb, has associated unlimited bomb making with the adventurous intellectual experience of Western civilization, derided what he calls "the fallout scare," assured us that we can survive a nuclear attack, and insists above all that we cannot and must not try to limit the use of nuclear weapons.

A dangerous expression of nuclearism in our present weapons policy is the advocacy of "limited nuclear war." Proponents continue to seek from weapons magical solutions to political and military dilemmas while closing their eyes to the unlimited destruction that would result.

We must be able to imagine the consequences of nuclear weapons if we are to stop their use. Coming to terms with massive death, collective death, is asking a great deal of the human imagination. Yet, I do not see how we can ask for less.

That is why we need to remember Hiroshima. Its images give substance to our own intellectual sense of horror. However inadequately that city represents what would happen now if thermonuclear weapons were dropped on a population center, it helps us imagine. Keeping alive Hiroshima's death may help us keep alive.

The proximity of a nuclear holocaust is beginning to break through our numbness, at least for many of us. The accident at Three Mile Island, the near explosion of a Titan II warhead in Damascus, Arkansas, bring the ease of massive death in the nuclear age to the surface of our consciousness. The Iraq–Iran conflict deepens the shadow of possible global destruction. We are beginning to see through the sterility of the nuclear language—"exchanges," "scenarios," "stockpiles"—used by our political and military planners. As we sense the danger increasing, our defenses weaken and our fears increase. This is the beginning of awareness. We now need to go further and place nuclear dangers in the contexts of our lives, our values, and our personal and political advocacies. Unless each one of us knows where he or she stands ethically and politically—what one feels about the future of nations and mankind—a stand on nuclear holocaust may be impossible.

But to gain that perception, one must open oneself to discomfort and anxiety. That poses a formidable historical, even evolutionary, problem. Ordinarily, we are selective in what we experience, feeling just enough and closing ourselves off just enough to function and survive. Technology has upset that equation. What is now required is an unprecedented level of tension and psychic balancing, one that permits us to imagine a nuclear holocaust but does not paralyze us with fear.

Can we speak of a shift in consciousness taking place? We may do better to speak of a struggle against numbing. As reluctant as a turn toward awareness may be, it is an important step along a path to a human future.

Stephen King / Now You Take "Bambi" or "Snow White"—*That's* Scary!

TV Guide, June 13, 1981

Stephen King is the author of many well-known horror novels and Danse Macabre *(1981), a study of horror in life and literature. For more information on Stephen King, see the headnote to "Trucks" in Best Sellers.*

TV Guide *has the largest weekly circulation of any magazine in the world. It publishes, along with local and cable television listings, articles about tv celebrities and programs.*

Read the story synopsis below and ask yourself if it would make the sort of film you'd want your kids watching on the Friday- or Saturday-night movie:

A good but rather weak man discovers that, because of inflation, recession and his second wife's fondness for overusing his credit cards, the family is tottering on the brink of financial ruin. In fact, they can expect to see the repossession men coming for the car, the almost new recreational vehicle and the two color TVs any day; and a pink warning-of-foreclosure notice has already arrived from the bank that holds the mortgage on their house.

The wife's solution is simple but chilling: kill the two children, make it look like an accident and collect the insurance. She browbeats her husband into going along with this homicidal scheme. A wilderness trip is arranged, and while wifey stays in camp, the father leads his two children deep into the Great Smoky wilderness. In the end, he finds he cannot kill them in cold blood; he simply leaves them to wander around until, presumably, they will die of hunger and exposure.

The two children spend a horrifying three days and two nights in the wilderness. Near the end of their endurance, they stumble upon a back-country cabin and go to it, hoping for rescue. The woman who lives alone there turns out to be a cannibal. She cages the two children and prepares to roast them in her oven as she has roasted and eaten other wanderers before them. The boy manages to get free. He creeps up behind the woman as she stokes her oven and pushes her in, where she burns to death in her own fire.

You're probably shaking your head no, even if you have already recognized the origin of this bloody little tale (and if you didn't, ask your kids: they probably will) as "Hansel and Gretel," a so-called "fairy tale" that most kids are exposed to even before they start kindergarten. In addition to this story, with its grim and terrifying images of child abandonment, children lost in the woods and imprisoned by an evil woman, cannibalism and justifiable homicide, small children are routinely exposed to tales of mass murder and mutilation ("Bluebeard"), the eating of a loved one by a monster ("Little Red Riding-Hood"), treachery and deceit ("Snow White") and even the specter of a little boy who must face a black-hooded, ax-wielding headsman ("The 500 Hats of Bartholomew Cubbins," by Dr. Seuss).

I'm sometimes asked what I allow my kids to watch on the tube, for two reasons: first, my three children, at 10, 8 and 4, are still young enough to be in the age group that opponents of TV violence and horror consider to be particularly impressionable and at risk; and second, my seven novels have been popularly classified as "horror stories." People tend to think those two facts contradictory. But . . . I'm not sure that they are.

Three of my books have been made into films, and at this writing, two of them have been shown on TV. In the case of "Salem's Lot," a made-for-TV movie, there was never a question of allowing my kids to watch it on its first run on CBS; it began at 9 o'clock in our time zone, and all three children go to bed earlier than that. Even on a weekend, and even for the oldest, an 11 o'clock bedtime is just not negotiable. A previous TV GUIDE article about children and frightening programs mentioned a 3-year-old who watched "Lot" and consequently suffered night terrors. I have no wish to question any responsible parent's judgment—all parents raise their children in different ways—but it did strike me as passingly odd that a 3-year-old should have been allowed to stay up that late to get scared.

But in my case, the hours of the telecast were not really a factor, because we have one of those neat little time-machines, a videocassette recorder. I taped the program and, after viewing it myself, decided my children could watch it if they wanted to. My daughter had no interest; she's more involved with stories of brave dogs and loyal horses these days. My two sons, Joe, 8, and Owen, then 3, did watch. Neither of them seemed to have any problems either while watching it or in the middle of the night—when those problems most likely turn up.

I also have a tape of "Carrie," a theatrical film first shown on TV about two and a half years ago. I elected to keep this one on what my kids call "the high shelf" (where I put the tapes that are forbidden to them), because I felt that its depiction of children turning against other children, the lead character's horrifying embarrassment at a school dance and her later act of matricide would upset them. "Lot," on the contrary, is a story that the children accepted as a fairy tale in modern dress.

Other tapes on my "high shelf" include "Night of the Living Dead" (cannibalism), "The Brood" (David Cronenberg's film of intergenerational breakdown and homicidal "children of rage" who are set free to murder and rampage) and "The Exorcist." They are all up there for the same reason: they contain elements that I think might freak the kids out.

Not that it's possible to keep kids away from everything on TV (or in the movies, for that matter) that will freak them out; the movies that terrorized my own nights most thoroughly as a kid were not those through which Frankenstein's monster or the Wolfman lurched and growled, but the Disney cartoons. I watched Bambi's mother shot and Bambi running frantically to escape being burned up in a forest fire. I watched, appalled, dismayed and sweaty with fear, as Snow White bit into the poisoned apple while the old crone giggled in evil ecstasy. I was similarly terrified by the walking brooms in "Fantasia" and the big, bad wolf who chased the fleeing pigs from house to house with such grim and homicidal intensity. More recently, Owen, who just turned 4, crawled into bed with my wife and me, "Cruella DeVille is in my room," he said. Cruella DeVille is, of course, the villainess of "101 Dalmatians," and I suppose Owen had decided that a woman who would want to turn puppies into dogskin coats might also be interested in little boys. All these films would certainly get G-ratings if they were produced today, and frightening excerpts of them have been shown on TV during "the children's hour."

Do I believe that all violent or horrifying programming should be banned from network TV? No, I do not. Do I believe it should be telecast only in the later evening hours, TV's version of the "high shelf"? Yes, I do. Do I believe that children should be forbidden all violent or horrifying programs? No, I do not. Like their elders, children have a right to experience the entire spectrum of drama, from such warm and mostly unthreatening programs as *Little House on the Prairie* and *The Waltons* to scarier fare. It's been suggested again and again that such entertainment offers us a catharsis—a chance to enter for a little while a scary and yet controllable world where we can express our fears, aggressions and possibly even hostilities. Surely no one would suggest that children do not have their own fears and hostilities to face and overcome; those dark feelings are the basis of many of the fairy tales children love best.

Do I think a child's intake of violent or horrifying programs should be limited? Yes, I do, and that's why I have a high shelf. But the pressure groups who want to see all horror (and anything smacking of sex, for that matter) arbitrarily removed from television make me both uneasy and angry. The element of Big Brotherism inherent in such an idea causes the unease; the idea of a bunch of people I don't even know presuming to dictate what is best for my children causes the anger. I feel that deciding such things myself is my right—and my responsibility.

Responsibility is the bottom line, I guess. If you are going to have that magic window in your living room, you have to take a certain amount of responsibility for what it will show kids when they push the ON button. And when your children ask to stay up to watch something like "The Shining" (when it is shown on cable TV this month), here are some ideas on how you might go about executing your responsibility to your children—from a guy who's got kids of his own and who also wears a fright wig from time to time.

If it's a movie you've seen yourself, you should have no problem. It is not possible to know *everything* that will frighten a child—particularly a small one—but there are certain plot elements that can be very upsetting. These include physical mutilation, the death of an animal the child perceives as "good," the murder of a parent, a parent's treachery, blood in great quantities, drowning, being locked in a tight place and endings that offer no hope—and no catharsis.

If it's a movie you haven't seen, check the listings carefully for the elements listed above, or for things you know upset your children in particular (if, for instance, you have a child who was once lost and was badly shaken by the experience, you may want to skip even such a mild film as "Mountain Family Robinson").

If you're not getting a clear fix on the program from the listings, call the station. They'll be happy to help you; in fact, the station managers I queried said they fall all over themselves trying to help parents who request such information, but usually end up fielding complaints from adults who couldn't be bothered to call until after the offending program.

If the listing is marked *Meant for mature audiences only,* don't automatically give up. What may not be suitable for some families (or for some younger children) may be perfectly OK for your children.

If you do elect to let your children watch a frightening TV program, discuss it with them afterward. Ask them what frightened them and why. Ask them what made them feel good, and why. In most cases, you'll find that kids handle frightening make-believe situations quite well; most of them can be as tough as they need to be. And "talking it through" gives a parent a better idea of where his or her child's private fear button is located—which means a better understanding of the child and the child's mind.

If you think it's too scary, don't let them watch it. Period. The end. Remind yourself that you are bigger than they are, if that's what it takes. Too much frightening programming is no good for anyone, child or adult.

Most of all, try remembering that television spreads out the most incredible smorgasbord of entertainment in the history of the world, and it does so *every day*. Your child wants to taste a little of everything, even as you do yourself. But it would be wrong to let him or her eat only one single dish, particularly one as troublesome and as potentially dangerous as this one. Parenting presumes high shelves of all kinds, and that applies to some TV programs as well as to dangerous medicines or household cleaners.

One last word: when the scary program comes and you've decided that your children may watch, try to watch *with* them. Most children have to walk through their own real-life version of Hansel and Gretel's "dark wood" from time to time, as we did ourselves. The tale of terror can be a dress rehearsal for those dark times.

But if we remember our own scary childhood experiences, we'll probably remember that it was easier to walk through that dark wood with a friend.

DISCUSSION QUESTIONS

1. Compare Stephen King's analysis of what makes something "scary" to Eugene H. Methvin's article on television violence (see p. 000). Which author do you think makes a more convincing case about horror and violence. In what way sense does each author work from a different definition of what is scary or horrible?

2. Read Stephen King's short story "Trucks" (see Best Sellers) in conjunction with this essay. How does "Trucks" confrom to his notion of the "scary"?

Bob Greene / Fifteen

Esquire, August 1982

When asked which of his columns he thought were his favorites, Bob Greene responded, "The ones I like are the ones that people don't remember, just the little stories I find while traveling around the country that don't get a whole lot of letters or a whole lot of response; the kind of column where I'll go into a town and meet someone who has a small story to tell, but whose story might never have appeared in the newspaper otherwise."

Born in 1947, Robert B. Greene became a professional writer by the age of 23, reporting for the Chicago Sun-Times. *Later, as a syndicated columnist and contributing correspondent to ABC-TV's "Nightline" as well as the author of the "American Beat" column for* Esquire, *Greene had earned much critical acclaim as a writer dedicated to the human-interest story. In the following piece, Greene investigates—with a writer's knack for detail—the cruising habits of two bored fifteen-year-old boys whose only source of entertainment is the local shopping mall.*

Esquire *first appeared in October, 1933, during the middle of the Depression. Developed as a men's fashion and literary quarterly dedicated to "The Art of Living and The New Leisure," the magazine was an immediate commercial success, thanks, in large part, to contributions by Ernest Hemingway, Dashiell Hammett, John Dos Passos, and Ring Lardner, among others. Now a monthly,* Esquire *has a circulation of 750,000 and continues to publish talented contemporary writers.*

"This would be excellent, to go in the ocean with this thing," says Dave Gembutis, fifteen.

He is looking at a $170 Sea Cruiser raft.

"Great," says his companion, Dan Holmes, also fifteen.

This is at Herman's World of Sporting Goods, in the middle of the Woodfield Mall in Schaumburg, Illinois.

The two of them keep staring at the raft. It is unlikely that they will purchase it. For one thing, Dan has only twenty dollars in his pocket, Dave five dollars. For another thing—ocean voyages aside—neither of them is even old enough to drive. Dave's older sister, Kim, has dropped them off at the mall. They will be taking the bus home.

Fifteen. What a weird age to be male. Most of us have forgotten about it, or have idealized it. But when you are fifteen . . . well, things tend to be less than perfect.

You can't drive. You are only a freshman in high school. The girls your age look older than you and go out with upperclassmen who have cars. You probably don't shave. You have nothing to do on the weekends.

So how do you spend your time? In 1982, most likely at a mall. Woodfield is an enclosed shopping center sprawling over 2.25 million square feet in northern Illinois. There are 230 stores at Woodfield, and on a given Saturday those stores are cruised in and out of by thousands of teenagers killing time. Today two of those teenagers are Dave Gembutis and Dan Holmes.

Dave is wearing a purple Rolling Meadows High School Mustangs Windbreaker over a gray M*A*S*H T-shirt, jeans, and Nike running shoes. He has a red plastic spoon in his mouth, and will keep it there for most of the afternoon. Dan is wearing a white Ohio State Buckeyes T-shirt, jeans, and Nike running shoes.

We are in the Video Forum store. Paul Simon and Art Garfunkel are singing "Wake Up Little Susie" from their Central Park concert on four television screens. Dave and Dan have already been wandering around Woodfield for an hour.

"There's not too much to do at my house," Dan says to me.

"Here we can at least look around," Dave says. "At home I don't know what we'd do."

"Play catch or something," Dan says. "Here there's lots of things to see."

"See some girls or something, start talking," Dave says.

I ask them how they would start a conversation with girls they had never met.

"Ask them what school they're from," Dan says. "Then if they say Arlington Heights High School or something, you can say, 'Oh, I know somebody from there.' "

I ask them how important meeting girls is to their lives.

"About forty-five percent," Dan says.

"About half your life," Dave says.

"Half is girls," Dan says. "Half is going out for sports."

An hour later, Dave and Dan have yet to meet any girls. They have seen a girl from their own class at Rolling Meadows High, but she is walking with an older boy, holding his hand. Now we are in the Woodfield McDonald's. Dave is eating a McRib sandwich, a small fries, and a small Coke. Dan is eating a cheeseburger, a small fries, and a medium root beer.

In here, the dilemma is obvious. The McDonald's is filled with girls who are precisely as old as Dave and Dan. The girls are wearing eye shadow, are fully developed, and generally look as if they could be dating the Green Bay Packers. Dave and Dan, on the other hand . . . well, when you're a fifteen-year-old boy, you look like a fifteen-year-old boy.

"They go with the older guys who have the cars," Dan says.

"It makes them more popular," Dave says.

"My ex-girlfriend is seeing a junior," Dan says.

I ask him what happened.

"Well, I was in Florida over spring vacation," he says. "And when I got back I heard that she was at Cinderella Rockefella one night, and she was dancing with this guy, and she liked him, and he drove her home and stuff."

"She two-timed him," Dave says.

"The guy's on the basketball team," Dan says.

I ask Dan what he did about it.

"I broke up with her," he says, as if I had asked the stupidest question in the world.

I ask him how he did it.

"Well, she was at her locker," he says. "She was working the combination. And I said, 'Hey, Linda, I want to break up.' And she was opening her locker door and she just nodded her head yes. And I said, 'I hear you had a good time while I was gone, but I had a better time in Florida.' "

I ask him if he feels bad about it.

"Well, I feel bad," he says. "But a lot of guys told me, 'I heard you broke up with her. Way to be.' "

"It's too bad the Puppy Palace isn't open," Dan says.

"They're remodeling," Dave says.

We are walking around the upper level of Woodfield. I ask them why they would want to go to the Puppy Palace.

"The dogs are real cute and you feel sorry for them," Dan says.

We are in a fast-food restaurant called the Orange Bowl. Dave is eating a frozen concoction called an O-Joy. They still have not met any girls.

"I feel like I'd be wasting my time if I sat at home," Dan says. "If it's Friday or Saturday and you sit home, it's considered . . . low."

"Coming to the mall is about all there is," Dave says. "Until we can drive."

"Then I'll cruise," Dan says. "Look for action a little farther away from my house, instead of just riding my bike around."

"When you're sixteen, you can do anything," Dave says. "You can go all the way across town."

"When you have to ride your bike . . ." Dan says. "When it rains, it ruins everything."

In the J.C. Penney store, the Penney Fashion Carnival is under way. Wally the Clown is handing out favors to children, but Dave and Dan are watching the young female models parade onto a stage in bathing suits.

"Just looking is enough for me," Dan says.

Dave suggests that they head out back into the mall and pick out some girls to wave to. I ask why.

"Well, see, even if they don't wave back, you might see them later in the day," Dan says. "And then they might remember that you waved at them, and you can meet them."

We are at the Cookie Factory. These guys eat approximately every twenty minutes.

It is clear that Dan is attracted to the girl behind the counter. He walks up, and his voice is slower and about half an octave lower than before.

The tone of voice is going to have to carry the day, because the words are not all that romantic:

"Can I have a chocolate-chip cookie?"

The girl does not even look up as she wraps the cookie in tissue paper.

Dan persists. The voice might be Clark Gable's:

"What do they cost?"

The girl is still looking down.

"Forty-seven," she says and takes his money, still looking away, and we move on.

Dave and Dan tell me that there are lots of girls at Woodfield's indoor ice-skating rink. It costs money to get inside, but they lead me to an exit door, and when a woman walks out we slip into the rink. It is chilly in here, but only three people are on the ice.

"It's not time for open skating yet," Dan says. "This is all private lessons."

"Not much in here," Dave says.

We sit on benches. I ask them if they wish they were older.

"Well," Dan says, "when you get there, you look back and you remember. Like I'm glad that I'm not in the fourth or fifth grade now. But I'm glad I'm not twenty-five, either."

"Once in a while I'm sorry I'm not twenty-one," Dave says. "There's not much you can do when you're fifteen. This summer I'm going to caddy and try to save some money."

"Yeah," Dan says. "I want to save up for a dirt bike."

"Right now, being fifteen is starting to bother me a little bit," Dave says. "Like when you have to get your parents to drive you to Homecoming with a girl."

I ask him how that works.

"Well, your mom is in the front seat driving," he says. "And you're in the back seat with your date."

I ask him how he feels about that.

"It's embarrassing," he says. "Your date understands that there's nothing you can do about it, but it's still embarrassing."

Dave says he wants to go to Pet World.

"I think they closed it down," Dan says, but we head in that direction anyway.

I ask them what the difference is between Pet World and the Puppy Palace.

"They've got snakes and fish and another assortment of dogs," Dan says. "But not as much as the Puppy Palace."

When we arrive, Pet World is, indeed, boarded up.

We are on the upper level of the mall. Dave and Dan have spotted two girls sitting on a bench directly below them, on the mall's main level.

"Whistle," Dan says. Dave whistles, but the girls keep talking.

"Dave, wave to them and see if they look," Dan says.

"They aren't looking," Dave says.

"There's another one over there," Dan says.

"Where?" Dave says.

"Oh, that's a mother," Dan says. "She's got her kid with her."

They return their attention to the two downstairs.

Dan calls to them: "Would you girls get the dollar I just dropped?"

The girls look up.

"Just kidding," Dan says.

The girls resume their conversation.

"I think they're laughing." Dan says.

"What are you going to do when the dumb girls won't respond," Dave says.

"At least we tried," Dan says.

I ask him what response would have satisfied him.

"The way we would have known that we succeeded," he says, "they'd have looked up here and started laughing."

The boys keep staring at the two girls.

"Ask her to look up," Dan says. "Ask her what school they go to."

"I did," Dave says. "I did."

The two boys lean over the railing.

"Bye, girls," Dave yells.

"See you later," Dan yells.

The girls do not look up.

"Too hard," Dan says. "Some girls are stuck on themselves, if you know what I mean by that."

We go to a store called the Foot Locker, where all the salespeople are dressed in striped referee's shirts.

"Dave!" Dan says. "Look at this! Seventy bucks!" He holds up a pair of New Balance running shoes. Both boys shake their heads.

We move on to a store called Passage to China. A huge stuffed tiger is placed by the doorway. There is a PLEASE DO NOT TOUCH sign attached to it. Dan rubs his hand over the tiger's back. "This would look so great in my room," he says.

We head over to Alan's TV and Stereo. Two salesmen ask the boys if they are interested in buying anything, so they go back outside and look at the store's window. A color television set is tuned to a baseball game between the Chicago Cubs and the Pittsburgh Pirates.

They watch for five minutes. The sound is muted, so they cannot hear the announcers.

"I wish they'd show the score," Dave says.

They watch for five minutes more.

"Hey, Dave," Dan says. "You want to go home?"

"I guess so," Dave says.

They do. We wave goodbye. I watch them walk out of the mall toward the bus stop. I wish them girls, dirt bikes, puppies, and happiness.

Barry Hannah / Fire Over the Town

Southern Living, October 1982

Born in Clinton, Mississippi, in 1942, Barry Hannah is the author of four novels, Geronimo Rex *(1971),* Nightwatchmen *(1973),* Ray *(1980), and* The Tennis Handsome *(1983), as well as an award-winning collection of short stories,* Airships *(1977). While Hannah resists the label of the "Southern" writer, his work nevertheless contains elements which inevitably link it to the traditional Southern experience. His characters (who include General Jeb Stuart, Vietnam vets, and a bizarre gallery of renegade doctors and pistol-packing poets) use both verbal and physical violence in an attempt to cut through the conventional values of complacent chivalry and discover the basic, visceral truths of human travail.*

In the following essay, Hannah describes his feelings of pride and antipathy for the ways in which Americans both define and commemorate their fallen heroes.

Southern Living, *founded in 1966, is a monthly magazine published in Birmingham, Alabama. With a circulation of over two million,* Southern Living *focuses on "food, homes, garden, travel, and recreation."*

Down in deep deep Mississippi I played "Taps" a number of years for the United Daughters of the Confederacy at their ceremony for the Confederate dead. On my old Conn trumpet I mourned away with sweetness of tone. I felt for the soldiers, so dead, you know.

I had an uncle still missing from World War II, a handsome flyer called "Bootsy" who had disappeared over the South American jungles. Bootsy looked like Buster Crabbe, and for a long time I waited for him to appear on our front porch, having hacked out an incredible journey through the Amazon, say "I'm all right, kid," and take away all my dear mother's grief. Then, neighbors, I'd play my trumpet. You thought you'd heard trumpet playing. Bootsy would tear the ennui of this Sunday School town apart. His plane would come rolling over the cedars and magnolias, permanently on fire but surviving, and shock the old maid librarian with her head full of Tennyson and *tardy*.

I'd bring Bootsy into the principal's office, my uncle merry, movie handsome, and a bit dangerous in his leather air jacket.

"Okay, mister, here's my unc. What're you going to say *now?*"

"Tell you what, Solly. This is my neph, a swell kid, lot of jazz. A trumpet man, ya know. I want him" (merry, menacing wink) "to have *free play,* eh? Got it?"

Then we would walk away and I would play some trumpet.

The last time I played for the Confederate dead, around age fifteen, I was calling them directly, *please,* to come out of their graves, lean, mean, hungry, in gamey gray rags, and level the better homes and gardens around me, the very gardens and lawns I had tended out of necessity—raked, mowed, dug, planted. My teenage years were being slain by irises and St. Augustine grass. I knew some jazz by then, and my messages were desperate, personal, ardent. The 82nd Airborne convoy had come through Clinton during the Korean war, and I had been paralyzed with awe, watching men in green, tanks, howitzer after howitzer. Fire at will, I prayed, sparing my father, a decent guy who once made battleships for you guys down in Pascagoula.

These are not nice things, these dream cinemas of the id. But I am not alone.

Lucky I found a place in the marching band, where John Philip Sousa caressed and tamed my iniquitous soul. I played Sousa on the march for the inaugural of Dwight D. Eisenhower, 1957. I was a tiny bandsman in red wool Napoleonic rig, Sam Brown belts. I was too earnest, straight ahead, in a curious horde of practicing adults and near infants, to ever get a look at Dwight. The band was enormous, everybody was in it, all of us itching in wool, and we were probably very loud and bad. But I knew *my* part to "Washington Post." Sousa had me. There is a robust, muscular airy wildness in the work of Sousa that engages heart, head, and the odd things remaining. It takes one over entirely. It speaks of higher grace. You are so far beyond tiny torpid grinding towns that revenge becomes irrelevant. It puts the heart in a happy uniform, gets you on a strut straight to blue spangling heaven, and you can feel amazing poetry written on the wind. A good marching band can make the street drop out from under you, and with Sousa it can make the air solid.

I made it to the Tomb of the Unknown Soldier, and there, in 1957 with the Marines standing bully watch, I finally knew where Bootsy was. It was all right. It was good to know, and especially it was fine they had a noble place for him.

Back in Clinton, Mr. Camp, the benign largehearted director with ulcers, brought me out front of the band in the concert auditorium, where I played the trio of "Washington Post" solo with the envious band muted behind. It was not that I was so good, more that I was just so tiny and improbable. But Sousa had me.

Then the great Prenshaw came to direct the band, and my high school years had a hero, an actual living adult that one would follow into flames. He was hip, educated at Northwestern, bebop to Mahler and back. He owned the first Volkswagen in town. His ear was perfect, and he would not dwell with imprecision on the march or in concert. But Prenshaw was no despot. We were not one of those bands of doomed youth paraded out by the village tyrant, honking for their life. It is more that imprecision made Prenshaw sad. He would lower his head and fix his glasses, looking a little wounded with his big eyes behind the thick glasses. You did not want to wound Prenshaw playing out of tune or squawking on a reed. You loved the man and did not want to distress him. You wanted to make him comfortable. You loved to see the slight smile when the tune was *there,* right. Also, he never said, "Ah gosh, I love you kids." Thank God. For, citizens, we were into Ideal Forms. We were making time and space sing. He did not care what you ate. Thank God. We were chomping on the high Olympian wind. Ah ennuied, renegade youth. You do "Eroica" right just once, and you will never be the same again.

The band took all the awards. The band had to apologize to nobody. One day the football coach caught me on the band room steps. I'd dropped football—yes, sports was losing me, and he was into it very solemnly. The implication was I was not a man. But I was. I had a new Reynolds Contempora trumpet and I had a good grip on it. I and the band had conquered Enid, Oklahoma, at the national contest, and I was on my way to conquering New York in the Lions Allstate Band that summer. Furthermore, I did not want to burn the coach's house down anymore. He was so small I could not find him.

I was a man because on the band trip back from Enid, I kissed a girl so long and desperately she disappeared. I was a regarded knight in the army of music. The head majorette loved me, and I had heroic indifference about the matter, a Gawain.

And in the band under Prenshaw. Well, it was the last time in my life I ever blended with anything. I went over the edge with wild Olympian hope, doing a solo mission of some agony with an occasional jolt from the gassy mountaintop, where I sit with Bootsy, Sousa, Prenshaw, and the old lads and lasses of the Clinton High band, drinking bowls of pure sweet form.

So, citizens, always give a cheer when you see a young band of merit come heaving into sight. They are burning the air instead of the town. They are playing for their great dead uncles and are paying you no mind.

Newsweek Staff / How the Bible Made America

Newsweek, December 27, 1982

After a period of editorial turnovers and instability, William Broyles, Jr. was appointed editor-in-chief at Newsweek *in 1982. Despite rumors that Broyles planned to change the magazine's image to that of a feature publication,* Newsweek *is today the second largest newsweekly in America, the major competitor of* Time. *Commenting on his plans for the magazine, Broyles has said that he hoped to "get more of a sense of America into the pages of* Newsweek. *If there's a catchword, it would be 'Bringing the News to life.'"*

The following cover story on the Bible in America appeared appropriately during Christmas week. The story reflects what the weekly news magazines call a "non-news" cover—a comprehensive story on a cultural phenomenon unconnected to major world events (diet crazes or jogging, for example) or a popular personality (such as Michael Jackson). There are no rigid journalistic rules that define the topic of a non-news cover; the only rule that Time *and* Newsweek *truly worry about is that they will not appear on the stands with the same non-news cover in the same week.*

. . . The Lord will be our God and delight to dwell among us, as His own people, and . . . command a blessing upon us in all our ways.

—John Winthrop, aboard the Arbella, 1630

I have always believed that this anointed land was set apart in an uncommon way, that a divine plan placed this great continent here between the oceans to be found by people from every corner of the Earth who had a special love of faith and freedom.

—President Ronald Reagan, Nov. 25, 1982

Even at Christmas, the Bible is a book more revered than read. Yet for centuries it has exerted an unrivaled influence on American culture, politics and social life. Now historians are discovering that the Bible, perhaps even more than the Constitution, is our founding document: the source of the powerful myth of the United States as a special, sacred nation, a people called by God to establish a model society, a beacon to the world.

There was a time, early in the history of our nation, when rugged settlers piously named their newly founded towns and cities after places in the Bible—Salem, Canaan, Philadelphia, Shiloh, Nazareth, Bethlehem and even Eden and Paradise. There were times, too, when Bible study was the core of public education and nearly every literate family not only owned a Bible but read it regularly and reverently.

And there were Great Awakenings when roving bands of revivalists, shouting and brandishing blackbound Bibles, called for individual conversions and collective rededication to America as God's Promised Land. Because of this pervasive Biblical influence, the United States seemed to Europeans to be one vast public congregation—a nation, as G. K. Chesterton said, "with the soul of a church."

The Bible gave potent images to the special American reality. We were, in contrast to pestilential, feudal and war-torn Europe, a new continent. The discovery of America—the New World—was a secular replay of the Garden of Eden, a second chance to create the kingdom of God on earth. There was, of course, the matter of the continent's original inhabitants, but they too were viewed as part of the divine mission: the Indians were the heathen, alternatively to be exterminated with Old Testament vigor or protected and converted with New Testament love.

The Puritans' original vision of America was transformed and, often, secularized into the promise of a better life. This promise not only inspired a constant flow of immigrants, but provided an impetus for the great westward movement that is at the core of our history. The pioneers went west with a few possessions and a Bible, wandering in the New World wilderness in search of the new Canaan. George Caleb Bingham's painting of Daniel Boone leading settlers through the Cumberland Gap captures a quintessentially American moment: behind them lies a settled, civilized world; ahead, the barren, uncharted wilderness.

The dynamic force of the settlers' religious mission, combined with the energies of Protestant capitalism, overwhelmed both the Indians and the Spanish Roman Catholic culture of the Southwest. The pioneers cleared out centuries-old forests and grasslands, drove off Indians and poured over into what were then the Mexican provinces of Texas and California—usually without giving a thought to what had been there before, either natural or human. The pioneers' way, dressed up and civilized, is still a part of the West.

Throughout our history, waves of immigrants have imported other views of religion and of the Bible to America. The great immigration period of 1880 to 1924 brought Roman Catholics from Ireland, Poland and Italy and Jews from Central Europe. None of these newcomers shared the Protestant view of the Bible or of America that had animated the original Puritans or the predominantly Anglo-Saxon and German Protestant immigrants who followed them. And yet, whether they read a different Bible or no Bible at all, Scripture had profoundly shaped the new world to which they had come. Unknown to them, perhaps, it was a part of their heritage.

No other country is as obsessed with the Bible as the United States. The vast majority of Americans, recent Gallup polls report, still regard the Bible as the word of God, and more than one American in three believes that every scriptural word is true. Only in America do Christians still fight so bitterly over versions of the Bible and national legislators declare 1983 "The Year of the Bible." Only in America is there a Bible belt with its interlocking networks of Bible camps, Bible colleges, Bible institutes and Bible bookstores. In America, Christian fundamentalists have emerged from cultural isolation in the latter days of the 20th century to unfurl once more the banner of Biblical Americanism. In their determination to put the Bible back in public schools, or create their own, and in their increasingly apocalyptic interpretations of world events on national television, the fundamentalists have once more made Scripture a subject of national controversy.

Americans publish more Bibles than any other people on earth—and buy them, too. Last year alone we spent $170 million for Bibles, and the Gideons distributed more than 1 million free to hotels, motels and hospitals. In 1982 Americans produced six new editions of the Scriptures and published books *about* the Bible in record numbers. The current edition of Books in Print, for example, requires 55 pages to list all its Bible-related entries; by comparison, only 14 pages are devoted to books about another major American obsession, sex, and 15 to another, food. This bumper crop of Bible books caters to a smorgasbord of tastes. Choices range from an esoteric study of "The Semiotics of the Passion Narratives" through "Famous Singles of the Bible" to "Heaven's Hall of Heroes" and "Scripture Defogged for the Millions."

Despite this publishing phenomenon, the Bible has virtually disappeared from American education. It is rarely studied, even as literature, in public classrooms. Recent Gallup polls indicate that this illiteracy is by no means limited to the young or to nonbelievers. Despite the fact that the majority of Americans say they accept the Bible as the word of God, a comprehensive 1979 Gallup survey found that only 49 percent of Protestants and 44 percent of Roman Catholics could name as many as four of the Ten Commandments and less than half of the respondents said they turn first to the Scriptures for guidance in times of crisis.

In sum, the Bible in America has joined the Declaration of Independence and the Constitution, argues church historian Martin E. Marty of the University of Chicago, as an American "icon"—a leatherbound symbol of transcendent authority, certainty and continuity with our nation's putatively sacred origins. Many Americans retain a family Bible as an heirloom in whose pages new names are added to the family tree, and Biblical rhetoric is as customary on Thanksgiving and the Fourth of July as it is on Christmas and Easter. No presidential candidate can afford not to pay ritual respect to the Good Book. During his successful campaign for the White House, Ronald Reagan pointed to a Bible and said, "Indeed, it is an incontrovertible fact that all the complex and horrendous questions confronting us at home and worldwide have their answer in that single book."

Only one other nation has ever looked to the Bible to find a warrant for its very existence: Israel, whose early history is actually written in it. The foundation of this myth, argues Columbia University Prof. Sacvan Bercovitch in a recent essay, was laid by the New England Puritans who literally "discovered America in the Bible." Bercovitch, the president of the American Studies Association, notes that even before they arrived in the New World, John Winthrop and his fellow Puritans aboard the flagship Arbella saw themselves as God's newly chosen people. They were the "new Israel" in "exodus" from Europe's "Egypt" and destined by a "new covenant" with the Lord to found a "city upon a hill" which, come the millennium, would see the historical Boston transformed into the eschatological "New Jerusalem."

Upon arriving in the New World, the Puritans created a commonwealth of words in which sermons, political speeches and other addresses were nearly as pervasive as television is today. These verbal rituals linked the problems of the present to God's promises for the future by imposing Biblical metaphors on American experiences. From the outset, the Puritans combed the King James Bible in search of precedents for a New World theocracy. In the separate but cooperative rule of Moses and his priestly brother, Aaron, for example, they found Biblical sanction for the twin offices of magistrate and minister. In the book of Acts they found precedents for the organization of their church: those congregations, in turn, provided a model for the townmeeting form of local government. Some Puritan leaders actually suggested making Hebrew the language of the colony.

Since their promised land was already occupied by Indians, the Puritans had to locate them in their Biblical script. At times, they dealt with the Indians the way the Israelites dealt with the Canaanites—violently. But a gentler strain of Puritan thought relocated the Indians in another Biblical context: they were the lost tribes of Israel, and so, worthy of conversion. But most of the native Americans clung to their traditional religion, and for two and a half more centuries. God's people would fight the heathen as they pushed their kingdom westward.

In their sermons, Puritan ministers extolled the virtues of sanctified self-interest. Although they had never heard of "free enterprise" and "democracy" was anathema to them, their influence on American economics and politics persists. Since the Puritans had a covenant with God, their self-interest was justified as necessary to the building up of their kingdom. Later these terms would become the bywords of the American Way, justified by a long procession of evangelists from Billy Sunday to Jerry Falwell.

Not all the New England colonists discovered America in the Bible. The Pilgrim separatists of Plymouth Colony not only read the Bible differently, but read a different version as well—the Geneva Bible of 1560, written in simple vernacular English and containing, side by side with Holy Writ, 300,000 words of marginal commentary. These glosses, drawn from John Calvin's commentary on an earlier French Bible, emphasized personal salvation and eternal life: they did not suggest a divine plan for a national covenant. Inevitably, the readers of the Geneva persuasion clashed with the Puritans, whose elegant King James Bible contained no commentary at all. The Puritan way prevailed, but the Pilgrims' philosophy of individualistic interpretation has surfaced again and again.

Although the Puritan theocracy collapsed as a total way of life, their myth of being God's chosen people was exported beyond their own villages. As the 18th century began, Cotton Mather's hagiographic history of New England extended the Puritans' franchise in God's favor to colonial society as a whole. Even the deists of the Revolutionary period, who admired the Bible chiefly for its moral precepts, recognized the utility of Biblical metaphors. In 1776 Benjamin Franklin proposed to the Continental Congress that the great seal of the United States bear the image of Moses leading the Israelites across the Red Sea. Thomas Jefferson also urged an Exodus image: he wanted the new nation represented by an Israel led through the wilderness by the Biblical pillar of cloud and fire. In the end, they settled for an inscription that blends Enlightenment ideals with scriptural inspiration: *Annuit Coeptis, Novus Ordo Seclorum*—He favored this undertaking, the new order of the ages.

Historians have long recognized the influence of the Enlightenment on the American Revolution, as well as how the evangelists of the mid-18th-century Great Awakening stirred passions for independence from Great Britain. But less attention has been paid to the ways in which preachers and politicians used the Bible to justify both the loyalist and the patriot causes. Likewise in the Civil War—and later conflicts—the Bible was used as ammunition on behalf of both sides. For each the battle was a religious crusade.

"Well into the national period, the public Bible of the United States was . . . the Old Testament," says evangelical historian Mark Noll. The New Testament was no match for the sagas of battles and nation-building that were being repeated daily in the unfolding history of the New Israel. As the myth of American expanded to include the Founding Fathers, they were identified with Israelite heroes. George Washington, for instance, was not only immortalized as the father of his country, but at his death, says Noll, eulogists "emptied the catalog of Old Testament worthies," likening the fallen general to Abel, Jacob, Moses, Elijah, Mordecai, Abner, Cyrus and Daniel. Used in this public way, Noll observes, "the Bible was not so much the truth above all truth as it was the story above all stories."

For black as well as for white Americans, the story above all Biblical stories was Exodus. But as slaves, the blacks reversed the standard analogy between America and the Promised Land. For them the United States was Egypt, and they were the children of Israel seeking a Moses to lead them out of bondage. Like Daniel, another favorite figure among slaves, they awaited their deliverer, and in Jesus they recognized a brother who ministered to the oppressed and suffered as they did.

These were not the Biblical messages their masters taught them. Indeed, some owners refused the Bible to their slaves; others appointed white preachers to sermonize on selected texts—chiefly the commandment "Thou shalt not steal," and Peter's advice to "be subject to your masters with all fear." But their listeners learned to distinguish between the white man's Bible and their own. The few who could read studied Scripture for themselves. But most watched for the chance to hear a black preacher from whom they could get the real message.

Between the establishment of the republic and its near dissolution in the Civil War, the myth of America gradually outgrew its original Biblical foundations. Many of the Founding Fathers were men of the Enlightenment for whom the Bible, however inspired or useful, had already become something of an icon. George Washington rarely referred to the Scriptures in his voluminous private letters. But at his Inauguration as president, he set a ceremonial precedent by swearing on his Masonic Bible—and even kissing it, as a Roman Catholic would a saint's relic. John Adams called it "the best book in the World," but wanted to separate its precepts from "whole cartloads of other trumpery that we find religion encumbered with in these days." Franklin thought the Bible good for the "Publick Religion," but did not regard its contents as divine. Thomas Jefferson collected a small library of Bibles, studied them and while moonlighting in the White House pieced together his own version of the New Testament, removing what he regarded as the unreasonable parts.

By 1800 the liberties these patricians took with the Bible were demanded as God-given rights by the common man. With the dawning of Jacksonian democracy, a wave of revivalism swept the land, calling sinners to conversion. In the name of a higher truth, some evangelists did away with theology, tradition and the fine points of doctrine. "No creed but the Bible" became the credo for tireless reformers, religious visionaries and self-appointed revivalists. What inspired many of these enthusiasts was a very American vision of the primitive Christian church, stripped of the institutional baggage of church history, and alive with healings and other charismatic wonders recorded in the New Testament's book of Acts.

The ideology of the age was individualism—in politics and commerce as well as in religion. Especially in America's expanding West, there was ample room for new churches, new sects, new denominations. Everyone was free to compete for men's souls, and through one young religious visionary, the image of a Biblical America reached a singular apotheosis.

Unable to decide which competing sect was truly Scriptural, Joseph Smith published a book that was to become a new testament for a new church of latter-day saints. The Book of Mormon described an exodus of Israelites to pre-Columbian

America, where they were later visited by Jesus. Smith's followers, under Brigham Young, were to endure their own exodus to Utah. As the restored Israel, Mormons believe, they will welcome Jesus when he returns to earth near the site of the original Garden of Eden, not far from Independence, Mo.

By 1870 revivals had become so routine that even businessmen and bankers attended them in cities. The new obsession was national progress, which Americans had come to expect as a reward for righteousness. To help achieve that end, the Bible—usually the King James Version—was read in public schools, so that the young might learn virtue and take their rightful place in what most Americans complacently considered a Christian nation. As one geography text of the period explained, "Those nations are the most distinguished for justice and kindness in which the Bible is best known and Christianity most pure."

Victorian America's version of a Biblical nation was ratified by a remarkable union of minds between pulpit and lectern. For the previous half century, says Calvin College historian George M. Marsden, Common Sense Realism had been "the dominant philosophy taught in American colleges." According to that philosophy, all normal people in all places and at all times were endowed with the same faculties of perception and reason. Therefore thinking people could arrive at the same fundamental truths if they were properly scientific in the collection, analysis and classification of facts. "The Bible is to the theologian what nature is to the man of science," declared Charles Hodge of Princeton Theological Seminary. "It is his store-house of facts. . . ." It followed, therefore, that if theologians did their job "scientifically," they could all arrive at the same Biblical truths and so think God's own thoughts.

Before the century was out, however, this common-sense synthesis of science and the Bible was shattered. First, a revolution in textual scholarship challenged the Bible's reliability, on which common-sense readings often depended. Second, Darwinism challenged not only the Genesis account of man's origins, but totally undercut the fact–collecting approach to science that buttressed the "scientific" interpretation of Scripture. The traditional authority of the Bible was at stake, and so was each man's right to access.

Many American Protestants were unwilling to accept the paradigm shift in scriptural studies. Among them was President Grover Cleveland. "The Bible is good enough for me, just the old book under which I was brought up," he groused. "I do not want notes or criticisms or explanations about authorship or origin or even cross-references. I do not need them or understand them, and they confuse me." In the ensuing battle between fundamentalists and liberals, which continues to this day, each side has—with some merit—accused the other of taking the Bible away from the common man. In defense of the Bible, fundamentalists have developed theories of Biblical inerrancy that are easy enough for the rank and file to believe in, but nearly impossible to prove.

The 20th-century battles over the Bible continue, but in an increasingly sterile context. The majority of Americans may believe the Bible is God's word, but they are not eager to study it. Current efforts to reintroduce Bible readings into public education, however well intentioned, seem misguided. It was not the U.S. Supreme Court that removed the Bible from most public-school classrooms—much less a cabal of "secular humanists," as fundamentalists charge—but the American people themselves. Prior to the Supreme Court decisions of the early '60s, which allowed use of the Bible in public classrooms for teaching but not devotional purposes, a survey by social scientist Richard Dierenfeld found that a majority of the nation's school districts had already abandoned the practice of reading it.

If it is not read and not integrated into our daily lives, the Bible becomes merely an icon. As Jewish tradition makes amply clear, Scripture comes alive only when its message is constantly interpreted in light of pressing questions. Indeed, the New Testament itself is in large part a commentary on the Old, and each Gospel offers a different theological perspective on the meaning of Jesus as the Christ. In short, no one can read the Bible without also interpreting it. And as long as there are divisions among people, the Bible will be a divisive book.

The history of the Bible in America is the history of conflicting interpretations. But the Puritans set the parameters. They worked themes of righteousness and responsibility into the American grain and established a rhetoric of spiritual mission. Without the Puritan myth of divine election, the Colonies might never have mustered a sense of national unity. Abolition and urban reform—the "social gospel"—were also fired by Scripture. From the Puritan John Cotton to Abraham Lincoln to Martin Luther King Jr., preachers, presidents and prophets have summoned America to reaffirm its special calling.

But the Bible, we have learned, speaks to the whole of life; it is not a recipe book. It is always difficult to decide whether preachers, politicians or laymen are judging events in light of Scripture or using the Bible to sanctify their own political convictions. Both slave-owners and abolitionists found comfort for their causes in the Bible, as did civil-rights marchers and segregationists in the 1960s. In the late 19th century both the depredations of the industrial robber barons and the settlement-house programs in the slums derived from a view of man's place in God's world. We have used the myth of divine calling to excuse domestic injustices, to justify greed and to advance our narrow national interests around the world. That the same book can be used to protect the status quo and also to galvanize movements for change is a mark of the Bible's power in America today.

Because of its influence, political issues in this country often become moral ones. Vietnam, nuclear weapons, racial discrimination, poverty, the pollution of the environment, even Watergate: all take on a special meaning less related to political doctrine than to moral outrage. America is too special for such things, the feeling goes. To this day few Europeans understand why people in this country were so disturbed by Watergate: without our sense of national mission, they do not have a corresponding sense of national betrayal.

We are, it seems, bound to our vision of America as a special place in God's geography. But to consider ourselves special is not to arrive easily at answers to either personal or public dilemmas. If anything, it makes our course that much harder to chart. To be different from other nations, as surely we are, is not to be chosen. After the second world war, certainly the most clear-cut of our national missions, the Protestant theologian Reinhold Niebuhr warned that we should not regard the United States as the advance party for the kingdom of God on earth. Americans, he insisted, must learn the ironies of history—that high ideals don't always lead to the best results, that few things in life are without a mixture of both good and evil.

But irony does not come easily to nations—or individuals—who identify their aims with God's. The Puritans were never known for their sense of irony or for humor's saving graces. America, in spite of all exegesis to the contrary, is not in the Bible. If we can accept our history for what it is, with all its high promises and flawed realities, then perhaps we can hear the Bible, too. It tells us God favors no nation but judges all in turn.

Eugene H. Methvin / TV Violence: The Shocking New Evidence

Reader's Digest, January 1983

The world's most widely circulated monthly, the Reader's Digest *first appeared on the newsstands in 1922 as a magazine specializing in condensed reprinted material. Though at least half of its current material is original, the* Reader's Digest *still maintains the editorial standards—that articles be brief and easily comprehensible—that marked its first issue.*

Eugene H. Methvin was born in Georgia in 1934. In 1960, he joined the staff of Reader's Digest, *where he remains today as a senior editor. For another look at violence on television, see Stephen King's "Now You Take 'Bambi' or 'Snow White'—*That's *Scary!" (p. 275).*

San Diego: A high-school honor student watches a lurid ABC-TV fictionalization of the 1890s Lizzie Borden ax murder case; then chops his own parents and sister to death and leaves his brother a quadriplegic.

• Denver: *The Deer Hunter* is telecast and a 17-year-old kills himself with a revolver, acting out the movie's climactic game of Russian roulette. He is the 25th viewer in two years to kill himself that way after watching the drama on TV.

• Decatur, Ill.: A 12-year-old overdoses on sleeping pills after her mother forbids her to date a 16-year-old boy. "What gave you the idea of suicide?" an investigating psychiatrist asks. The answer: A little girl tried it on a TV show, was quickly revived and welcomed back by her parents with open arms.

Ten years ago, after studying massive research on the subject, the U.S. Surgeon General, Jesse L. Steinfeld, declared, "The causal relationship between televised violence and antisocial behavior is sufficient to warrant immediate remedial action." Called before Congress, the presidents of the three networks solemnly agreed.

Yet the University of Pennsylvania's Annenberg School of Communications, which for 14 years has charted mayhem in network programming, reports that violent acts continue at about six per prime-time hour and in four out of every five programs. The weekend children's programs are even worse.

Last May the National Institute of Mental Health (NIMH) issued a report summarizing over 2500 studies done in the last decade on television's influence on behavior. Evidence from the studies—with more than 100,000 subjects in dozens of nations—is so "overwhelming," the NIMH found, that there is a consensus in the research community "that violence on television does lead to aggressive behavior."

Television ranks behind only sleep and work as a consumer of our time. In fact, according to the 1982 Nielsen Report on Television, the average American family keeps its set on for 49½ hours each week. The typical youngster graduating from high school will have spent almost twice as much time in front of the tube as he has in the classroom—the staggering equivalent of ten years of 40-hour weeks. He will have witnessed some 150,000 violent episodes, including an estimated 25,000 deaths.

Despite the mayhem, the viewer sees little pain or suffering, a false picture that influences young and old. At a Capitol Hill hearing on TV violence, a dismayed Rep. Billy Tauzin complained to network executives that his three-year-old son had poked his fist through a glass door—in imitation of a TV cartoon character—and almost bled to death. In New Rochelle, N.Y., a killer who re-enacted a TV bludgeon murder told police of his surprise when his victim did not die with the first crunch of his baseball bat, as on the tube, but instead threw up a hand in defense and groaned and cried piteously.

The effect of all this? Research points toward these conclusions:

1. TV violence produces lasting and serious harm. University of Illinois psychology professor Leonard Eron and colleagues compared the television diets and level of aggressive behavior of 184 boys at age eight and again at 18. His report: "The more violent the programs watched in childhood, the more combative the young adults became. We found their behavior studded with antisocial acts, from theft and vandalism to assault with a deadly weapon. The children appeared to learn aggressive habits that persisted for at least ten years."

2. Those "action" cartoons on children's programs are decidedly damaging. Stanford University psychologist Albert Bandura found cartoon violence as potent as real-life models in increasing violence among youngsters. A University of Kansas researcher reported that Saturday-morning cartoons markedly decreased imaginative play and hiked aggression among 66 preschoolers. In a year-long study of 200 preschoolers, Yale University Drs. Jerome L. and Dorothy Singer found that playground depredations like fighting and kicking were far greater among steady action-cartoon viewers.

Indeed, the Saturday-morning "kid vid" ghetto is the most violent time in TV. It bathes the prime audience of youngsters from 3 to 13 years old with 25 violent acts per hour, much of it in a poisonous brew of violent programs and aggressive commericals designed to sell such products as breakfast cereals and action toys. According to one study, these commercials have a rate of violence about three times that of the programs themselves.

3. TV erodes inhibitions. With a $290,000 grant from CBS, British psychologist William A. Belson studied the television diets and subsequent behavior of 1565 London boys ages 12 to 17. He found cartoon, slapstick or science-fiction violence less harmful at this age; but realistic fictional violence, violence in close personal relationships, and violence "in a good cause" were deadly poison. Heavy viewers were 47-percent more likely to commit acts such as knifing during a school fight, burning another with a cigarette, slashing car tires, burglary and attempted rape. To Belson's surprise, the TV exposure did not seem to change the boys' opinions toward violence but rather seemed to crumble whatever constraints family, church or school had built up. "It is almost as if the boys then tend to let go whatever violent tendencies are in them. It just seems to explode in spontaneous ways."

4. The sheer quantity of TV watching by youngsters increases hurtful behavior and poor academic performance. "When the TV set is on, it freezes everybody," says Cornell University psychologist Urie Bronfenbrenner. "Everything that used to go on between people—the games, the arguments, the emotional scenes out of which personality and ability develop—is stopped. When you turn on the TV, you turn off the process of making human beings human."

Studies in the United States, Canada, Israel, Australia and Europe show that the amount of TV watched, regardless of program content, is a critical variable that contributes heavily to children's later aggressive attitudes and behavior. Dozens of other studies indicate that TV impairs the children's verbal skills and creativeness.

WHAT PARENTS CAN DO

First of all, they can help by realizing that their own TV viewing affects the quality of family life. Until recently most adults worried that violent programming might be harmful to children, but assumed they could gorge themselves with impunity on whatever programs caught their fancy. Not so.

In one study, U.C.L.A. researchers Roderic Gorney and David Loye divided 183 husbands, ages 20 to 70, into five comparable groups. The groups were assigned 21 hours of varied TV fare at home during a single week, and each man kept a diary of his "moods." Wives, without knowing which TV diet the husbands watched, recorded "hurtful" and "helpful" behaviors. The result: husbands who watched violent programming recorded a significantly higher level of aggressive moods. Furthermore, their wives noted about 35-percent more daily incidents of hurtful behavior than did wives whose husbands watched "prosocial" programming.

"The important lesson of our experiment is that adults, by their own programming choices, may actually *reduce* aggressive moods and hurtful behavior," says Gorney. "In a home the climate generated by parental moods and conduct is surely as crucial as what children see on TV in determining the family's mental health."

Further, parents can curtail the total time children watch television. Investigators find that parents are consistently unaware of how long their children are watching, and underestimate how much violence they see and how much it disturbs them. Experts agree that three hours a day should be an absolute maximum for subteen children and far less than that of action drama, cartoons and other violence-packed programming. Advises syndicated columnist Ann Landers: "Be firm. You wouldn't allow your child to eat garbage, would you? Why, then, let him put it in his head?"

Parents can avoid using TV as a baby-sitter, and they can watch with their children—making certain that incidents of violence or sex never go without comment. Parents can encourage children to identify and watch programs of educational and social value. They should not hesitate to change channels or turn off the set. As an aid, Yale University's Family Television Research and Consultation Center has produced a carefully tested program for parents and teachers of children ranging from nursery to junior high: *Getting the Most Out of TV,* published at $7.95 by Scott, Foresman & Co., 1900 East Lake Ave., Glenview, Ill. 60025.

WHAT EVERYONE CAN DO

In legal theory, "the airwaves belong to the people," and the nation's 1067 television stations enjoy their federally awarded monopoly only in return for programming "in the public interest." In general, the government cannot deny any corporation the right to advertise on any program it chooses. But the viewer has a right to declare that he is not going to help pay for those programs by buying the advertised products.

Both the American Medical Association and the National PTA have urged their members to bring public pressure against advertisers on high-violence programs. The National Coalition on Television Violence (NCTV), formed by psychiatrists, pediatricians and educators, carefully grades network prime-time and weekend children's programs. Each quarter it publishes lists of the companies and products that sponsor the most mayhem, and also companies that allot the largest portion of their television budgets to violent programming. (The NCTV's address: P.O. Box 2157, Champaign, Ill. 61820.) It promotes legislative action and urges school, church and parent groups to publish its lists and to complain to advertisers.

Some companies need little prompting. Kodak has always shunned violent programming and consistently ranks low in NCTV monitoring lists. Kraft, Inc., also has a long-standing policy against programming that depicts excessive violence. Other companies that rate well with NCTV include Hallmark Cards, Schering-Plough and Campbell Soup.

Too much TV watching—and violent programming in general—can indeed be harmful to viewers' health. Says NCTV's chairman, Dr. Thomas Radecki, a psychiatry professor at Southern Illinois University, "Each of us bears a responsibility in stopping this ubiquitous teacher of rage and hate. Each of us must live in the world it is destroying."

Nat Hentoff / When Nice People Burn Books

The Progressive, February 1983

Nat Hentoff was born June 10, 1925, in Boston. A prolific journalist and author of over 25 books of fiction and non-fiction, Hentoff is, by his own definition, an "advocacy writer." He first became interested in jazz, but "from jazz, inevitably became involved in the world that jazz reflects, and therefore began to write about civil rights." He has also covered such topics as racism, the draft, police spying, and educational reform.

Though he is generally known as an eloquent spokesman for the Left, Hantoff speaks here to the basic provisions of the First Amendment and how they should be recognized by liberals and conservatives alike.

Founded in Madison, Wisconsin, in 1909, The Progressive *is a political publication which reports on domestic and world issues from a radical perspective.*

It happened one splendid Sunday morning in a church. Not Jerry Falwell's Baptist sanctuary in Lynchburg, Virginia, but rather the First Unitarian Church in Baltimore. On October 4, 1981, midway through the 11 A.M. service, pernicious ideas were burned at the altar.

As reported by Frank P.L. Somerville, religion editor of the *Baltimore Sun,* "Centuries of Jewish, Christian, Islamic, and Hindu writings were 'expurgated'—because of sections described as 'sexist.'

"Touched off by a candle and consumed in a pot on a table in front of the altar were slips of paper containing 'patriarchal' excerpts from Martin Luther, Thomas Aquinas, the Koran, St. Augustine, St. Ambrose, St. John Chrysostom, the Hindu Code of Manu V, an anonymous Chinese author, and the Old Testament." Also hurled into the purifying fire were works by Kierkegaard and Karl Barth.

The congregation was much exalted: "As the last flame died in the pot, and the organ pealed, there was applause," Somerville wrote.

I reported this news of the singed holy spirit to a group of American Civil Liberties Union members in California, and one woman was furious. At me.

"We did the same thing at our church two Sundays ago," she said. "And long past time, too. Don't you understand it's just *symbolic?*"

I told this ACLU member that when the school board in Drake, North Dakota, threw thirty-four copies of Kurt Vonnegut's *Slaughterhouse Five* into the furnace in 1973, it wasn't because the school was low on fuel. That burning was symbolic, too. Indeed, the two pyres—in North Dakota and in Baltimore—were witnessing to the same lack of faith in the free exchange of ideas.

What an inspiring homily for the children attending services at a liberated church: They now know that the way to handle ideas they don't like is to set them on fire.

The stirring ceremony in Baltimore is just one more illustration that the spirit of the First Amendment is not being savaged only by malign forces of the Right, whether private or governmental. Campaigns to purge school libraries, for example, have been conducted by feminists as well as by Phyllis Schlafly. Yet, most liberal watchdogs of our freedom remain fixed on the Right as *the* enemy of free expression.

For a salubrious change, therefore, let us look at what is happening to freedom of speech and press in certain enclaves—some colleges, for instance—where the New Right has no clout at all. Does the pulse of the First Amendment beat more vigorously in these places than where the Yahoos are?

Well, consider what happened when Eldridge Cleaver came to Madison, Wisconsin, last October to savor the exhilarating openness of dialogue at the University of Wisconsin. Cleaver's soul is no longer on ice; it's throbbing instead with a religious conviction that is currently connected financially, and presumably theologically, to the Reverend Sun Myung Moon's Unification Church. In Madison, Cleaver never got to talk about his pilgrim's progress from the Black Panthers to the wondrously ecumenical Moonies. In the Humanities Building—*Humanities*—several hundred students and others outraged by Cleaver's apostasy shouted, stamped their feet, chanted "Sieg Heil," and otherwise prevented him from being heard.

After ninety minutes of the din, Cleaver wrote on the blackboard, "I regret that the totalitarians have deprived us of our constitutional rights to free assembly and free speech. Down with communism. Long live democracy."

And, raising a clenched fist while blowing kisses with his free hand, Cleaver left. Cleaver says he'll try to speak again, but he doesn't know when.

The University of Wisconsin administration, through Dean of Students Paul Ginsberg, deplored the behavior of the campus totalitarians of the Left, and there was a fiercely denunciatory editorial in the Madison *Capital Times:* "These people lack even the most primitive appreciation of the Bill of Rights."

It did occur to me, however, that if Eldridge Cleaver had not abandoned his secularist rage at the American Leviathan and had come to Madison as the still burning spear of black radicalism, the result might have been quite different if he had been shouted down that night by young apostles of the New Right. That would have made news around the country, and there would have been collectively signed letters to the *New York Review of Books* and *The Nation* warning of the prowling dangers to free speech in the land. But since Cleaver has long since taken up with bad companions, there is not much concern among those who used to raise bail for him as to whether he gets to speak freely or not.

A few years ago, William F. Buckley Jr., invited to be commencement speaker at Vassar, was told by student groups that he not only would be shouted down if he came but might also suffer some contusions. All too few liberal members of the Vassar faculty tried to educate their students about the purpose of a university, and indeed a good many faculty members joined in the protests against Buckley's coming. He finally decided not to appear because, he told me, he didn't want to spoil the day for the parents. I saw no letters on behalf of Buckley's free-speech rights in any of the usual liberal forums for such concerns. After all, he had not only taken up with bad companions; he was an original bad companion.

During the current academic year, there were dismaying developments concerning freedom for bad ideas in the college press. The managing editor of *The Daily Lobo,* the University of New Mexico's student newspaper, claimed in an editorial that Scholastic Aptitude Test scores show minority students to be academically inferior. Rather than rebut his facile misinterpretation of what those scores actually show—that class, not race, affects the results—black students and their sympathizers invaded the newspaper's office.

The managing editor prudently resigned, but the protesters were not satisfied. They wanted the head of the editor. The brave Student Publications Board temporarily suspended her, although the chairman of the journalism department had claimed the suspension was a violation of her First Amendment rights. She was finally given her job back, pending a formal hearing, but she decided to quit. The uproar had not abated, and who knew what would happen at her formal hearing before the Student Publications Board?

When it was all over, the chairman of the journalism department observed that the confrontation had actually reinforced respect for First Amendment rights on the University of New Mexico campus because infuriated students now knew they couldn't successfully insist on the firing of an editor because of what had been published.

What about the resignations? Oh, they were free-will offerings.

I subscribe to most of the journalism reviews around the country, but I saw no offer of support to those two beleaguered student editors in New Mexico from professional journalists who invoke the First Amendment at almost any public opportunity.

Then there was a free-speech war at Kent State University, as summarized in the November 12, 1982, issue of *National On-Campus Report.* Five student groups at Kent State are vigorously attempting to get the editor of the student newspaper fired. They are: "gay students, black students, the undergraduate and graduate student governments, and a progressive student alliance."

Not a reactionary among them. Most are probably deeply concerned with the savaging of the free press in Chile, Uruguay, Guatemala, South Africa, and other such places.

What had this editor at Kent State done to win the enmity of so humanistic a grand alliance? He had written an editorial that said that a gay student group should not have access to student-fee money to sponsor a Hallowe'en dance. Ah, but how had he gone about making his point?

"In opening statements," says the *National On-Campus Report,* "he employed words like 'queer' and 'nigger' to show that prejudice against any group is undersirable." Just like Lenny Bruce. Lenny, walking on stage in a club, peering into the audience, and asking, "Any spics here tonight? Any kikes? Any niggers?"

Do you think Lenny Bruce could get many college bookings today? Or write a column for a college newspaper?

In any case, the rest of the editorial went on to claim that the proper use of student fees was for educational, not social, activities. The editor was not singling out the Kent Gay/Lesbian Foundation. He was opposed to *any* student organization using those fees for dances.

Never mind. He had used impermissible words. Queer. Nigger. And those five influential cadres of students are after his head. The editor says that university officials have assured him, however, that he is protected at Kent State by the First Amendment. If that proves to be the case, those five student groups will surely move to terminate, if not defenestrate, those university officials.

It is difficult to be a disciple of James Madison on campus these days. Take the case of Phyllis Schlafly and Wabash College. The college is a small, well-regarded liberal arts institution in Crawfordsville, Indiana. In the spring of 1981, the college was riven with discord. Some fifty members of the ninety-odd faculty and staff wrote a stiff letter to the Wabash Lecture Series Committee, which had displayed the exceedingly poor taste to invite Schlafly to speak on campus the next year.

The faculty protesters complained that having the Sweetheart of the Right near the Wabash River would be "unfortunate and inappropriate." The dread Schlafly is "an ERA opponent . . . a far-right attorney who travels the country, being highly paid to tell women to stay at home fulfilling traditional roles while sending their sons off to war."

Furthermore, the authors wrote, "The point of view she represents is that of an ever-decreasing minority of American women and men, and is based in sexist mythology which promulgates beliefs inconsistent with those held by liberally educated persons, and this does not merit a forum at Wabash College under the sponsorship of our Lecture Series."

This is an intriguing document by people steeped in the traditions of academic freedom. One of the ways of deciding who gets invited to a campus is the speaker's popularity. If the speaker appeals only to a "decreasing minority of American women and men," she's not worth the fee. So much for Dorothy Day, were she still with us.

And heaven forfend that anyone be invited whose beliefs are "inconsistent with those held by liberally educated persons." Mirror, mirror on the wall. . . .

But do not get the wrong idea about these protesting faculty members: "We subscribe," they emphasized, "to the principles of free speech and free association, of course."

All the same, "it does not enhance our image as an all-male college to endorse a well-known sexist by inviting her to speak on our campus." If Phyllis Schlafly is invited nonethless, "we intend not to participate in any of the activities surrounding Ms. Schlafly's visit and will urge others to do the same."

The moral of the story: If you don't like certain ideas, boycott them.

The lecture committee responded to the fifty deeply offended faculty members in a most unkind way. The committee told the signers that "William Buckley would endorse your petition. No institution of higher learning, he told us on a visit here, should allow to be heard on its campus any position that it regards as detrimental or 'untrue.'

"Apparently," the committee went on, "error is to be refuted not by rational persuasion, but by censorship."

Phyllis Schlafly did come to Wabash and she generated a great deal of discussion—most of it against her views—among members of the all-male student body. However, some of the wounded faculty took a long time to recover. One of them, a tenured professor, took aside at a social gathering the wife of a member of the lecture committee that had invited Schlafly. Both were in the same feminist group on campus.

The professor cleared her throat, and said to the other woman, "You are going to leave him, aren't you?"

"My husband? Why should I leave him?"

"Really, how can you stay married to someone who invited Phyllis Schlafly to this campus?"

And really, should such a man even be allowed visitation rights with the children?

Then there is the Ku Klan Klan. As Klan members have learned in recent months, both in Boston and in Washington, their First Amendment right peaceably to assemble—let alone actually to speak their minds—can only be exercised if they are prepared to be punched in the mouth. Klan members get the same reception that Martin Luther King Jr. and his associates used to receive in Bull Conner's Birmingham.

As all right-thinking people know, however, the First Amendment isn't just for anybody. That presumably is why the administration of the University of Cincinnati has refused this year to allow the KKK to appear on campus. Bill Wilkerson, the Imperial Wizard of the particular Klan faction that has been barred from the University of Cincinnati, says he's going to sue on First Amendment grounds.

Aside from the ACLU's, how many *amicus* briefs do you think the Imperial Wizard is likely to get from liberal organizations devoted to academic freedom?

The Klan also figures in a dismaying case from Vancouver, Washington. There, an all-white jury awarded $1,000 to a black high school student after he had charged the Battle Ground School District (including Prairie High School) with discrimination. One of the claims was that the school had discriminated against this young man by permitting white students to wear Ku Klux Klan costumes to a Hallowe'en assembly.

Symbolic speech, however, is like spoken or written speech. It is protected under the First Amendment. If the high school administration had originally forbidden the wearing of the Klan costumes to the Hallowe'en assembly, it would have spared itself that part of the black student's lawsuit, but it would have set a precedent for censoring symbolic speech which would have shrunken First Amendment protections at Prairie High School.

What should the criteria be for permissible costumes at a Hallowe'en assembly? None that injure the feelings of another student? So a Palestinian kid couldn't wear a PLO outfit. Or a Jewish kid couldn't come as Ariel Sharon, festooned with maps. And watch out for the wise guy who comes dressed as that all-around pain-in-the-ass, Tom Paine.

School administrators might say the best approach is to have no costumes at all. That way, there'll be no danger of disruption. But if there were real danger of physical confrontation in the school when a student wears a Klan costume, is the school so powerless that it can't prevent a fight? And indeed, what a compelling opportunity the costumes present to teach about the Klan, to ask those white kids who wore Klan costumes what they know of the history of the Klan. To get black and white kids *talking* about what the Klan represents, in history—and right now.

Such teaching is too late for Prairie High School. After that $1,000 award to the black student, the white kids who have been infected by Klan demonology will circulate their poison only among themselves, intensifying their sickness of spirit. There will be no more Klan costumes in that school, and so no more Klan costumes to stimulate class discussion.

By the way, in the trial, one offer of proof that the school district had been guilty of discrimination was a photograph of four white boys wearing Klan costumes to that Hallowe'en assembly. It's a rare picture. It was originally printed in the school yearbook but, with the lawsuit and all, the picture was cut out of each yearbook before it was distributed.

That's the thing about censorship, whether good liberals or bad companions engage in it. Censorship is like a greased pig. Hard to confine. You start trying to deal with offensive costumes and you wind up with a blank space in the yearbook. Isn't that just like the Klan? Causing decent people to do dumb things.

Darryl Pinckney / Step and Fetch It: The Darker Side of the Sitcoms

Vanity Fair, March 1983

One of the most elegant magazines of the 1920's and 30's, Vanity Fair *specialized in articles about the world of fashion, art, music, theater, literature, and the high life of international celebrities. Perhaps more than any other periodical it brought the European avant-grade to the attention of the American public—even the magazine's advertising reflected the influence of cubism and surrealism. Though suited to the flamboyant mood of the 1920's,* Vanity Fair *struck the wrong chord during the depression and it was merged with* Vogue *in 1936.*

In 1983, Vanity Fair *was revived. Its unabashed blend of serious art and literature with high fashion celebrity spreads made it seem as though* The New Yorker *had joined forces with* People *magazine. The new* Vanity Fair *has strug-*

gled through several editorial changes and though it has published many excellent writers it has still not discovered the most agreeable balance of the talented with the trendy.

The following essay on the role of blacks in television comedy appeared in Vanity Fair*'s first issue (March, 1983). Darryl Pinckney contributes criticism to the* New York Review of Books *and is the author of a forthcoming novel,* High Cotton.

I remember Rochester. Not quite valet, not quite butler, not really factotum—it is hard to say what he was. Rochester performed his vague duties faithfully, through years of radio, film, and then 343 television episodes of *The Jack Benny Show*. Perhaps he was a kind of chorus, commenting on developments and sometimes fanning the flickering plot himself; or maybe he was confidant and straight man, rushing to Mr. Benny's side to catch another quip, lunging toward the door, elbows tucked close to rib cage, eyes bright as headlights, to intercept some wacky news. He was a thoughtless, soothing caricature of "the Negro"—benign, in his place. He kept his place from 1937 to 1965.

The "real" Rochester, Eddie Anderson, died in 1977, having outlived the show and the boss if not the cultural mood in which the name Rochester became synonymous with shameless, unsavory Uncle Tom antics. Television producers are very careful now about domestic employees—not to mention blacks—and progress is measured by the distance from the old, offensive images. When Robert Guillaume played the part of the butler, Benson, on the comedy series *Soap,* he demonstrated that the stereotype was not so much in the role as in the style brought to the job. He was sardonic, sane, well dressed, and he talked back. Guillaume went on to star in his own show, *Benson.* Eventually Benson was promoted from governor's housekeeper to state budget director. Not bad—and not as funny either.

Why not? Isn't his upward course retribution for all those years of Rochester? Affirmative action has infiltrated the prime-time hours, and though I busily note the number of blacks in each frame, their importance and the jobs they're given, I can't quite give up my sympathy for the underdog, for the underside of life.

Who remembers Ethel Waters in *Beulah*—and who dares? The show first aired in 1950. Miss Waters played the title role for two years, and the part of her crazy, luckless friend was played by none other than the great Butterfly McQueen. Together they turned a New York attorney's home into a tidewater plantation. *Beulah* surfaced one last time in 1952, with another veteran of the kitchen range as the star, Louise Beavers. The show has since been withdrawn from syndication—to spare our feelings, one assumes.

These actresses, the old guard, played similar roles in films. They lived out the professional lives then permitted black actresses, but often they infused their portrayals of maids with a weird subversiveness. In *She Done Him Wrong,* Louise Beavers's hands are so well manicured as she toils over Mae West's cast-off blouses that they signal to the audience that she's not really busting anybody's suds. And what about the repertoire of facial expressions Hattie McDaniel used on that sad girl in *Alice Adams?* It's indecent, even dangerous, to admit a certain late-night nostalgia for those grainy black-and-white masochistic moments of cinema from the 1930s and '40s, but—as a wise woman once told me—don't forget that masochists are the proudest people on earth. Only the brave risk asking Beulah for the peeled grape. Equality as irony is hip, complicated, and far beyond the range of television, with its smug, scaled-down narratives.

Situation comedies bring us a self-congratulatory view of the American home, a place confident and leisured enough to permit humor and mild skepticism about prevailing ideas. (More recently, this definition has been expanded to include the workplace, which is another version of home and family.) As our need for reassurance and escapism increases, so does the number of sitcoms on the air—and these days part of the American myth is that blacks too have a fair share of the harmony and prosperity.

"Serious" television is another matter, reserved for pious resolutions of troublesome themes. Remember Barney, the electronics wizard of the Impossible Missions Force; Mannix's "girl Friday," Peggy; the sandwich-chomping captain so tolerant of Starsky, of Hutch; Lieutenant Uhura of the starship *Enterprise*—they were so skilled and presentable. Remember all those black cops, square or cool, upholding law, sticking by order, in wide-angle action shots, always rigidly self-conscious, everyone on his best behavior.

Headline entertainers, with their variety series, are also on their best behavior, being stars. There have been so many because black entertainers at this level are, oddly enough, seen as neutral. *The Leslie Uggams Show, The Barbara McNair Show, The Melba Moore-Clifton Davis Show, Ben Vereen—Comin' at Ya, The Gladys Knight & the Pips Show, The Jacksons,* to mention only a few, suggest a quest for the proper vehicle and leave memories of tires sputtering in the mud. (Richard Pryor, whose weekly show ran only from September to October of 1977, could not conform to this requirement of neutrality, and was canned.) Blacks were looking out from the tube into the dens of America as early as 1949—all singing and dancing. Blacks had no public or private concerns suitable for dramatization.

Not until recently did the images of the new day—sitcoms featuring "ordinary" black people—begin to appear on the screen. Television was rather sluggish to reflect the change in society. Seasons of *Leave It to Beaver, F Troop,* and *Mr. Ed* hardly jibed with the unsettling realization that there were a lot of black people who lived in this country, at least according to the evening news.

The thaw began in 1965 with *I Spy*. Bill Cosby protrayed a trainer-masseur opposite Robert Culp's tennis pro, but—not to worry—they were both really undercover agents. The show seldom touched on the issue of race. It ended in 1968, and the next year Cosby was back, in, yes, *The Bill Cosby Show*. He played the part of a coach, Chet Kincaid, whose business was to be helpful to everyone—students, parents, brother. Cosby is seen as something of a trailblazer as a black in television. His first series brought him three Emmys, and though later shows were not as memorable, it scarcely mattered to someone who could project his own personality through whatever role he assumed. Cosby is trusted when he feeds a multiracial group of kids pudding, and he is applauded when he is in a foul mood while hosting *The Tonight Show*.

Trustworthy characters were all the rage in the late '60s. The aim was to reassure everyone, black and white, that blacks were good Americans. The most upright citizen of them all was created in *Julia,* starring Diahann Carroll, whose performance was remarkable for excluding even the slightest nuance. That was 1968, post-Moynihan Report days, and if Julia Baker was a single parent, she was so by the grace of God. Her husband, an air force captain, had been killed in Vietnam. She, a registered nurse employed at Astro Space Industries (a vague but equal-opportunity-sounding place), was left to bring up a docile young son, Corey, who, the TV mags said, got chubby from rehearsing so many after-school-snack scenes. Julia, the attentive mother, sat on a kitchen stool and explained life while Corey munched away in a daze. At such times, with his high whine echoing her polite colorless hum, they seemed like robots off duty.

Julia's boss, Dr. Chegley, was warmhearted and wise, in the Marcus Welby manner. He and Julia decorously stared down department store clerks who got the wrong idea about their relationship. But the viewing audience learned that the clerks were shocked not because they were an interracial couple but because they were a May–December one. Oh, how we misjudge our enemies. *Julia* was put to sleep in 1971.

If black women on television are not stunning, they are cast as oracular, Bible-backed mamas. In 1974 *That's My Mama* had Clifton Davis unraveling the messes stirred up by Theresa Merritt. *What's Happening!!'s* goofy teenagers were rewarded or punished by large-girthed Mabel King. These mothers are essential—black family life is a touchy point. One situation comedy that never caught on, *Baby, I'm Back,* involved a father who returns after an absence of seven years and sets out to prove that he has matured enough to take on the anxieties of a happy home life. The nuclear family surrounds a black leading character on television these days like a steel casing.

Television's hymn to the nuclear family was *Good Times,* featuring the Evanses, slapping five and playing the dozens in the Chicago projects. One of those Norman Lear spin-offs, the series starred John Amos and Esther Rolle. As the strong, loving father with a terrible temper who threw things and slammed the refrigerator door in frustration with the job market and his lack of education, Amos stormed and bellowed his way through episode after episode like an inner-city Kunta Kinte.

Esther Rolle was the pious mama, consulting the serene face of a blond Jesus in times of trouble, lifting her eyes in an attitude of thanksgiving, stretching dollars, wielding the spatula over a frying pan, trying to reason with her hotheaded (and hot-blooded: he says "Have mercy" when things get cozy) husband, and keeping the children on the right path. The children (portrayed by woefully bad actors) were made to stand for rather sentimental notions of the rising tide, their hearts set on growing up to be doctors, artists, and Supreme Court justices.

The teleplays never failed to include some moral tag about the ceaseless struggle to make it. Authenticity was also important to *Good Times:* a parade of types were assembled from the popular picture of the American ghetto—corrupt aldermen, outrageously dressed loan sharks, prissy social workers, harmless winos, long-lost fathers, child-abusing young mothers, teens hooked on smack, and a slightly fast divorced neighbor with a heart of gold, Willona, played by Ja'net DuBois. The totemic accessories of popular black culture were trotted out and explained on cue: the dancing, the pork chops, the wakes, the preaching style, the welfare bureaucracy, the guns.

Think of the early comedies, programs such as *The Honeymooners* or *The Life of Riley.* The husbands were bus drivers or plant workers. Since then, life has been upgraded, everyone on television has a better job, and blacks have shared in the boom. We even have a remake of *The Odd Couple* with black actors playing the successful, urban characters. On *Barney Miller* Ron Glass played a dapper detective first class; *WKRP in Cincinnati* had a black deejay; the high-society boarding school of *Facts of Life* boasts among its student body one sweet-looking black girl.

Ron Glass was too chilled out to do more than raise an eyebrow when some visitor to the precinct would blurt out an ill-advised remark. WKRP was a liberal, flaky station. Even so, the with-it young manager worried in one episode that his sister was seeing too much of the black deejay, Venus Flytrap—and at the wrong hours. Of course, Venus and the sister were *just friends,* but if they had been more than that, they boldly proclaimed, well, tain't nobody's bizness. The safety exit.

The girl who integrates the school on *Facts of Life,* Tootie, restless and agreeable, seems born to the Andover life. In one segment she was visiting her young aunt, a gorgeous newscaster, as black women newscasters tend to be. Much to the surprise of a classmate who came along for the weekend, Tootie's aunt was married to a white, hunky coach. (Coaches seem the preferred type for interracial plots. Everyone knows that sports breed mutual respect. Check out *The White Shadow.*) Television seldom presents a black man with a white woman unless Desdemona is a fallen woman and the Moor a pimp. No "Perdition catch my soul but I do love thee''—but then *Othello* is not a comedy. Nowhere is this taboo more strictly heeded than on that fatuous program *The Love Boat.* The black bartender, Ted Lange, has to wait for someone foxy like Debbie Allen to save enough money to take the tedious cruise before he can lose his heart. He never, never ogles a white woman.

The family show that hit big was *The Jeffersons,* a spin-off from *All in the Family.* It began its ascent into the hearts of America in 1975. George Jefferson, played by Sherman Hemsley, and Louise, his wife, played by gravel-voiced Isabel Sanford, had been neighbors of the Bunkers in Queens. ''We're movin' on up,'' the theme song goes, ''to the East Side, to a deluxe apartment in the sky.'' There's something off about this move: George's chain of dry-cleaning stores has made him more money than Ford has earned building sedans. He prospers, never lays off anyone; this is a miracle suitable to the fantasies of Ronald Reagan. ''We finally got a piece of the pie!''

George is short, blustering, and opinionated, and is offset (naturally) by his patient, honest, and devoted wife. The doorman wheedles George for tips. One neighbor, Mr. Bentley, a dotty Englishman with the U.N., is no longer with the show. Perhaps he moved on down to a refurbished brownstone. The Jeffersons have friends upstairs: Tom and Helen Willis. He is a plump senior vice-president in publishing, and white. She is a thin fancy dresser with a degree in journalism, and black. George makes wisecracks about their marriage every week. The Willises have two children. One is white-looking, a son, who was accused at one point of trying to pass. He hasn't been seen since. Perhaps he is in Paris, snorting and whooping it up nightly in one of the Bains Douches. The other child, Jenny, is the black-looking one, though George refers to her as ''the zebra.''

In the beginning, the story lines of *The Jeffersons* revolved around what all that money was doing to them. Louise often warned George not to forget where he came from. George argued that there was no point in being rich if he had to act poor. Of course, George in the end saw the light—as if remembering humble origins were a brake on greedy impulses. That plot couldn't last: through the seasons they had to get used to the money. Louise has a new hairdo; the practical bun is out, bring on the curls. They have a lot of glad rags—unfortunate pantsuits and garish three-piece suits—and this one realistic detail is perhaps inadvertent.

Marla Gibbs plays the Jeffersons' black maid, Florence. Her snide comments are exquisitely timed. ''I might as well be working for white folks,'' she said when too much was demanded of her. Florence is diffident about her duties. ''Doorbell, Florence!'' ''Well, answer it!'' In one show, Florence appeared in a costume straight out of *Gone with the Wind* and so overwhelmed ''Massa Jefferson'' with her let-me-shine-yo-shoes-and-sew-dat-dere-button-O-Lawd-I-done-made-you-mad act that George had to apologize.

The character of Florence raises an odd question: Why is ''the help'' so funny? For one thing, comedy is more plausible at the bottom. Blacks on television must work and have a family, like all good Americans. and yet there remains the contradiction that the lingering sterotypes seem less foolish than the new sterotype of success and satisfaction. Shirley Hemphill was wonderful when she played the waitress on *What's Happening!!* and disappointing when she starred in her own show as the philanthropic owner of a multimillion-dollar conglomerate. Esther Rolle held her own as Florida, maid to the suburban feminist Maude. The gifted Nell Carter, who stars in the series *Gimme a Break,* has combined perfectly the images of the family retainer and the new professional. The ambiguity of her status is her freedom. Not only does she cook and mend for a widowed police chief and his adolescent daughters, she gives her advice and her consent in all their affairs.

Redd Foxx was the last nigger on television. In *Sanford and Son,* Fred Sanford was crafty, lazy, nasty-looking, and nasty-sounding. He steadfastly resisted self-improvement, and his attitude toward the larger world recalled the tradition of humor in which the lowly outwitted the masters. There is more satiric potential in such parts, more opportunity for putdowns and unexpected reversals. And black actors in these comic roles live through their subversion of Mammy and Rochester and even Buckwheat.

Ishmael Reed has a phrase—"crazy dada nigger"—and that is what Buckwheat was, in school, at the birthday party, in the clubhouse with the gang of *The Little Rascals*. He has been reborn, in homogenized form, in the precocious Gary Coleman of *Diff'rent Strokes*. He is a complete anachronism. He pouts ("Whatchu talkin' 'bout, Willis"), his eyes bug out of his fuzzy round head, he mugs it up. Where did he learn that? Coleman plays one of two brothers taken from Harlem and adopted by a Park Avenue executive. He is a domesticated black child, suitable for import from the black side of town to the land of opportunity, and he has dragged with him the baggage of the minstrel style. (And Amos and Andy are back on the air—in the form of Laverne and Shirley, who are missing only the blackface.)

It is not only in the subversion of the old sterotypes that black television manages to be funny. Great comic moments on the tube have not always been part of the regular programming. I once passed a bar in Boston and saw economist Thomas Sowell on the screen. The clientele roared as Sowell applied the principles of Milton Friedman to people who didn't have two quarters to rub together. Who can forget Sammy Davis, Jr., Mr. Goodvibes, scurrying across the stage to hug Richard Nixon? This incident was so bizarre that black tourists in Las Vegas snubbed Sammy in the elevators. Black Republicans haven't been cool since Reconstruction. Did Pearl Bailey's ratings suffer when she chatted away on her show about the chair Nixon gave her from the White House and her designation as "ambassador of love"? The lesson of fame is that the famous can get away with everything. Miss Bailey appeared at the opening of the World Series a few years back in a slick wig and a stunning fur, moaning "The Star-Spangled Banner." Which is funnier, Eldridge Cleaver then or now? Scare me, black man—and then be my pal (this is the secret of *Rocky*'s success). No matter—even Eartha Kitt is a patriot these days. "How I Got Over" can be heard on your way to the bank as well as in Baptist churches. But that is the message of blacks on television: all will be well, forgiven, forgotten.

That demand for positive images, for relevance—was it a just but doomed cause, given the medium? Think of the graceful, poised Princess Elizabeth of Toro on *To Tell the Truth* a few years ago, or Harry Belafonte's daughter floating through a recent episode of *Trapper John, M.D.*, more chic than Italian *Vogue*. Is that what we mean by "positive" in a culture that communicates in images? The riveting questions about blacks in American society are addressed in film, not TV, in the leagues of footage from *The Birth of a Nation* to *Superfly* to *48 HRS*. Trying to decode television takes one to the Formica counters of the banal, where megabucks act as a sponge. Everything can be turned into a commodity, and in this way social issues are reduced. The status quo, or what is ambiguously called traditional values, is easily digestible, suitable to the demands of glut, or rapid programming. Have some *Soul Train* and shut up. The profusion of nice, clean-cut professionals represents a cultural payoff. Is the soggy narcissism of *Fame* really the future? There were no blacks in Mayberry, there were none in Fernwood, and that was as true to life as anything.

DISCUSSION QUESTIONS

1. Read the episode of "The Jeffersons" in Scripts. How is Pinckney's general analysis of the show supported by "The Black Out"? Do you think the characters on "The Jeffersons" reflect a "positive" image of black people, or do you

think Pinckney's objections to the show are basically correct? Explain your answer.

2. What precisely does Pinckney mean by "positive images" of blacks? Does his approval of Redd Foxx's role in "Sanford and Son" endorse or reject the "demand for positive images"? Explain your answer.

Peter Davis / Hometown U.S.A.: In the Grip of TV

TV Guide, April 9, 1983

A writer and director of film documentaries, Peter Davis attracted a great deal of attention in the mid-1970's for his controversial film Hearts and Minds. *The film, an examination of the Vietnam War, juxtaposed footage of presidents and generals with interviews and sequences of actual encounters between American troops and the Viet Cong and North Vietnamese Army.*

Davis's latest documentary, Hometown, *is the result of six years of observations in Hamilton, Ohio. Why Hamilton? Davis chose the town after asking the U.S. Census Bureau where he might best "combine categories of social research and storytelling." "By looking at one community," Davis explained, "as closely as possible for several years and then telling the stories I found and heard, I wanted to try to understand the country a little better. The result is only that my ambivalence about everything we have is stronger and, I feel, deeper."*

Since the uncertain balmy fall and the football strike both lasted so long, it was well into November before Hamiltonians hunkered down for the season in front of their Sonys and Quasars and Panasonics. Television in Hamilton, Ohio, lies somewhere in the vast range between wallpaper and the circulation of the blood—in the background like the former, almost as essential to life support as the latter. Contradictory truths about television coexist there: it brings families together, for instance, and it keeps them apart. Different families, in different ways, at different times. But being able to prove opposites, for once, does not mean being able to prove nothing.

I went to Hamilton first in 1976 when a Census Bureau official suggested the town of 63,189 for my study of a representative American community that emerged, six years later, in the stories and portraits of the book "Hometown." While I was following citizens through the challenges and conflicts of their lives, I seldom had time to notice television. I even warned a *TV Guide* editor that Hamiltonians might be atypical because their lives appeared to proceed independently of television. "That'll be news to Nielsen," he said, and sent me a plane ticket.

Television, of course, was in Hamilton all along. Up to six sets in a home, it turns out, playing as much as one-third of each day. Some people actually do not watch it, and it is a point of pride for adults to say it does not affect them. But it is there, hourly, annually, ubiquitously, as inevitable as the weather.

If Hamiltonians watched as much television as anyone else, as it soon became clear they did—a young, horn-rimmed, three-piece-suited businessman had a *Spider-Man* rerun on at 8:15 A.M. in the motel—the question then became: what was the relationship between television and life? Were they in some surrealistic way interchangeable?

What if a talented young man from a prosperous Hamilton family went off to

Princeton, where he was editor of the college newspaper, then forsook his home town for Chicago, did well in business, ran for senator and, though defeated, wound up with a White House job? Returning to Chicago, he may have wheeled and dealt in business until, all unexpectedly, disaster struck. What if he was suddenly indicted on numerous counts of mail fraud? Soon he might be in prison, where he would have time to write an extensive diary on prison life. Meanwhile, back in Hamilton, his brokenhearted parents, stung with disgrace, would perhaps die within six months of each other.

Is all this from *One Life to Live,* from *Dynasty* or *Dallas,* from a *60 Minutes* segment on white-collar crime? Is it a Movie of the Week, or will the man shortly be appearing on talk shows, in an act of aggressive contrition, slyly pushing his autobiography?

This story was part of a genuine family tragedy well known to many Hamiltonians, but it is also the stuff of which television programs are made. There was, in my coming to Hamilton to examine the effects of television, a quality of passing through the looking glass. As in any trip to an altered state of consciousness, the line between the boundaries of television and life was not always an easy one to draw. It was like holding up a mirror to a mirror.

"I'd die if there was no TV," said a girl with the culturally resonant name of Gidget in Dottie Miller's eighth-grade English class at Woodrow Wilson Junior High.

"Don't you love Rick and Blackie on *General Hospital?*" one of her friends asked.

"Right," Gidget said, "they're ungodly."

Some of these junior-high-school students—who could be right out of *Square Pegs*—use television less for entertainment than as baby sitter. "It keeps me company while my mom is at work," one said. Sometimes the baby sitter is all over the house. A boy named Eric had six television sets—one in the living room, a second in the dining room, a third in his bedroom, a fourth in his sister's bedroom and a fifth in an alcove where it housed the Atari video-game system. The sixth was for Eric's grandmother, who lived with his family.

Although two of the students said their fathers were very firm with them in disallowing television during dinner and homework, several more had fathers who insisted on watching television continuously, using their sets as a kind of barrier between themselves and their families. This echoed their teacher's complaint. "Television makes me a very lonely woman," Dottie Miller said. "My kids are grown and gone, and my husband watches anything that's on—sports, sitcoms, news, drama. Essentially, TV stifles communication in our home except for about 14 minutes a day."

One Wednesday early in the semester, Mrs. Miller sent home an assignment for her eighth graders' parents to write a paragraph on family values. One girl said her mother had refused to do the assignment because she was too busy watching *Dynasty* and instead told her daughter to do it for her. The girl then went to another television set in her house, flipped on *Quincy* and wrote the paragraph on values.

But every addiction, unless it proves fatal, is followed by withdrawal. By the time these students reach Hamilton High School, they will, if current viewing habits hold, be watching considerably less television than they are now. More homework, hobbies, increased telephone use, an active social life and, above all, cars were cited by 11th graders as reasons for watching less television than they had in junior high. "We're allowed out now," a junior boy said.

"It was something to occupy us when we were bored," said a girl named Tricia in an 11th-grade English honors class. "We used to get ideas about dress and language from our programs. A lot of the guys liked Chrissy on *Three's Company,* so we'd dress like her. Same with Jaclyn Smith on *Charlie's Angels.* Everyone would come to school talking like Mr. Bill on *Saturday Night Live.* Now girls are wearing miniskirts again like the Go-Go's on MTV. A lot of parents hate it, which gives MTV a fair amount of influence with us.''

Of the 21 11th graders in the class who were surveyed, only six have mothers who stay home and watch daytime soap operas. The rest either have jobs, including one mother who is a truck driver, or are busy with activities that prevent their seeing television during the day.

Among working mothers who have stimulating jobs, television seems somewhat remote, a dress in the back of their closet they do not wear much any more. Barbara Hand is a family therapist. You can imagine her consulting the troubled Ewings on *Dallas,* the Carringtons on *Dynasty.* But she and her busband Neil, a deputy sheriff, rarely watch TV. ''There used to be more programs that interested me,'' Barbara Hand said. ''One of us—either TV or I—must be slipping.''

''Everything I like they take off,'' Neil Hand said on Tuesday night, passing up *Three's Company* and *St. Elsewhere* to emphasize his complaint. ''You name it, they take it off—*M*A*S*H, Barney Miller, Soap, Mary Hartman, All in the Family.* Those shows had satire and real social comment.''

''They were situation comedies but they dealt with real people who didn't step out of character for a cheap joke,'' Barbara Hand said, adding that they now like *60 Minutes* and *Hill Street Blues* and were currently enjoying Mortimer Adler on PBS. ''My patients generally don't mention specific programs but they often complain their kids watch too much TV. I ask them if their set doesn't have an 'off' button, but they don't dare use it because they're keeping down turmoil in their homes by letting their children watch whatever they want. The truth is, a lot of people are afraid of their own kids.''

Even in families where television is judged to have little significance, attitudes toward it reveal a continuing concern with its effects. On Wednesday night, Ron and Janet Handley watch *Family Ties* before *Dynasty.* Ron Handley designs tools at the Fisher Body plant just outside Hamilton, and Janet Handley works as a secretary to two attorneys. The Handleys tend to be protective about what their three daughters—Rhonda, 17; Kristy, 15; and Stephanie, 11—are allowed to see on television.

It was time for *Family Ties.* In the Handley home, Stephanie went to bed. On the show, Mallory's father's closest friend, known as Uncle Arthur in the family, made repeated passes at Mallory. This scared Mallory, a 15-year-old like Kristy Handley, but when she complained to her brother, he said it had to be her imagination. Uncle Arthur, after all, used to wash her when she was a baby. ''I think he wants his old job back,'' Mallory said. When her father himself found out about Uncle Arthur's advances to Mallory, he was respectably choked with fury.

Ron Handley felt *Family Ties* was on the outer edge of what he wanted his daughters to see. ''It got shocking for a minute,'' he said. But he added: ''I was glad to see the message was made clear eventually.''

The message may not have been as clear to every viewer as it was to Ron Handley, since the show ended with Mallory in her father's arms, the two of them murmuring ''I love you'' to each other.

The Handleys have a choice about what to watch or, of course, whether to watch at all. Not everyone in Hamilton does. At the county jail, Sheriff Bob Walton keeps order by having television sets in virtually every cell block. The sets play from 7:30 A.M. until at least 11 P.M. and on week-ends they are frequently left on all through the night.

In some cells, inmates take turns switching the dial, but there is fairly easy agreement over what the best programs are. Police shows and reruns of almost any kind are the most popular. Reruns seem to remind many of the prisoners of an earlier time when they were not in jail. One young man remarked that he had just seen a *Happy Days* segment that he had first watched when he was in high school.

One of the prisoners in the county jail last fall was Geraldine, a pleasant, smiling, moon-faced woman with a predicament a police show like *Hill Street Blues* would be proud to feature. She was a well-behaved prisoner. On the outside she had twice taken her five daughters and left her busband after drunken beatings by him. Both times he followed her, promised to be kind, and they reconciled. When he beat her badly, Geraldine would call the police; several times they kept him overnight. But her husband would always come home when they released him. Because he retired from his job early with inflamed ulcers, he was around the house a lot. In pain himself, he would hit Geraldine repeatedly. "This last time I couldn't take it no more," Geraldine said, "so I fought him back. I hit him with a baseball bat one of my daughters had, and I kept on hitting him till he couldn't ever hit me again." Geraldine ultimately was found guilty and is serving four to 25 years in the Women's Reformatory at Marysville. She prefers to watch *Fame* because of the better life it promises to the young performers, Richard Simmons because it makes him happy to help people, and old movies. Her mother is looking after her daughters.

Many parents in Hamilton would almost prefer prison to being sentenced to look at the particular form of programming that now attracts most of their adolescent children. When teen-agers gather to watch MTV, the rock-music cable channel, they enter a world virtually closed to outsiders. Like any alien ritual calculated to produce pleasure as well as to promote uniqueness, MTV is forbidding at first and then mesmerizing. The sound is as harsh as fingernails on a blackboard, but it is also rhythmic, insistent, energetic. The images, or videos as they are called, jump and dive and scratch their way across the screen; they could be a basketball team with poison ivy caught in a strobe light. Yet the pictures, too, are rhythmic, insistent, energetic. Soon there is no turning back.

The rite of MTV began innocently enough. Four bright, eager, resourceful girls got together on a Saturday afternoon. Liza Reed, 16, invited her friends Alice Tillett, also 16, and Shelly Thomas, 17, to come over to her house. They were joined by Liza's sister, Annie, who at 13 already knew most of the groups featured on MTV. The Reeds live in a beguilingly lovely, well-kept old home on one of the best residential streets in Hamilton, but very shortly a huge cockroach began to crawl across their television screen. It was quickly joined by another, and then a whole regiment of them. "Sick," said Liza. "Gross," said Alice. But the trance was already under way in this roach-ridden commercial for a theatrical movie called "Creepshow."

Liza: "MTV keeps me company. I'll do my homework with it on sometimes because you can listen to it without looking at it."

Shelly: "I need to have sounds around me so I won't feel alone. I can't stand silence."

Liza: "Silence is depressing."

Jefferson Starship sings and acts "Be My Lady."

Annie: "Ooh, he's good-looking."

Liza: "He looks like the lead singer of Blue Oyster Cult."

Shelly: "My mom found my ex-boy friend's hat that said Blue Oyster Cult on it, and she asked me if he belonged to some farout religious group."

A male groupie in a .38 Special video chug-a-lugs a beer as two arm wrestlers grapple with each other until they break a table. .38 Special ends its number with a girl looking seductively at a man who leers at her. She hands him her hotel-room key as the frame freezes.

Liza: "I hate that long hair on guys. Did they really used to like that?"

Shelly: "The tattoos are even uglier than the creepy hair."

A businesswoman in a tweed suit, every fiber proclaiming the executive, has an announcement. "I make difficult decisions every day," she says momentously, "but not about tampons." The girls laugh at her. "Gimme a break," one of them says. Meatloaf sings "Paradise by the Dashboard Light."

Alice: "The lead man looks like the devil or a blimpy Elvis with stringy hair."

Shelly: "What would your mom do if you brought home a boy who looked like Meatloaf?"

Alice: "She'd have a heart attack."

Shelly: "Mine would just laugh, but I'd never do it."

Liza: "I heard the lead singer in this other group was so messed up on drugs at a concert he couldn't perform."

Alice: "I don't think these songs encourage drugs."

Liza: "I don't either. They never say do drugs but they do say don't let people push you around and tell you what to do. If there's a message, that's it."

Billy Idol sings "White Wedding." The guests at a church wedding are dressed as witches and warlocks. Demons cackle silently throughout the church. When a ring is placed on the bride's finger, it spurts blood.

Shelly: "Someone told me rock comes from Satan, but that's crazy. They're just having fun here."

It is not hard to find Hamiltonians who feel that MTV and a lot of other television is Satan's work. Mallie Pendergrass is the proprietor of Mallie's Beauty Salon, Hamilton's most obvious setting for a TV series *(Mallie's Place?)*. She is also a Christian Fundamentalist who thinks a substantial portion of rock music truly does promote the Devil. Her own viewing time is concentrated on the relatively new Trinity Broadcasting Network.

"Christian television is about all you can watch any more," Mallie said, between customers in her salon. "Even on the news, they're more reliable than the commercial networks. During the Lebanese crisis, Trinity Broadcasting told the truth about the Israelis and Palestinians. The networks criticized the Israelis, but they didn't know what they were talking about. I'm for Israel teeth and toenail; it's just like the Bible foretold, and I wish I could fight for them myself. Only on Trinity can you see the truth of Biblical prophesy portrayed."

Trinity Broadcasting, which has been available in Hamilton less than a year, has given Mallie hope for television. "They wage truth campaigns, and you get Christian broadcasting all day long," she says. "Most of commercial TV reminds me of sorting through a garbage can trying to find something good to eat. The dirt gets into your spirit. I watch Trinity and can rejoice in what I see. Can you watch commercial TV and say that?"

But Christian broadcasting itself is controversial, even among the devout. The Rev. Tedrow Dingler of Hamilton's First United Presbyterian Church vastly prefers *M*A*S*H* to almost everything he sees on Christian broadcasts. "*M*A*S*H* contains more ethics, more about the need for love and decency, than a whole packet of the so-called religious programs," he says. "I want to see people doing their own thinking and not making knee-jerk reactions on the basis of what they hear from Jerry Falwell or Robert Schuller."

The Rev. Mr. Dingler worries that as production values and visual techniques improve, the actual content of religious programming declines, making it easier for demagogues to spread cheapened, freeze-dried versions of religious faith. "The truth is that every day is *not* bright; people are sometimes sick, oppressed, miserable beyond the reach of a pep talk. A person at the end of a year of unemployment benefits, with his utilities about to be cut off in the middle of winter, is not going to get much from the TV evangelists. We need to account for the dark side of human experience. There's no quick fix. Outsiders coming into your home over a box that glows and flickers can't make your decisions for you."

What Dingler wants is for discipline to begin at home. Television, he feels, like birth control or the decision on where and whether to go to college, is preeminently a family matter. Families should settle it among themselves, with appetites for entertainment balanced by common sense and educated palates for broadcasting. Hamiltonians like Bob Baesel, a dentist, and his wife Carol, who works for an art gallery and studies art and interior design, agree that salvation lies in good judgment. The problem is: what constitutes good judgment on any given evening? Into their home, which contains five television sets, programming flows with a mixture of permissiveness and restraint.

The Baesel Bunch is every bit as wholesome as the Brady Bunch. Carol and Bob, in their middle 30s, met at Ohio State when Bob was studying dentistry and Carol worked in the dental school. "For me," she says in a line reminiscent of Rhoda Morgenstern or possibly even Joan Rivers, "it was like fishing in an overstocked pond." They have two children; the viewing taste of 8-year-old David runs from National Geographic specials to *The Dukes of Hazzard,* while Kathy, 5, likes cartoons, *Sesame Street* and whatever David watches.

The Baesels are frequent, but critical, viewers. Television, Bob Baesel feels, decreases people's ability to entertain themselves. Carol Baesel reserves her strongest scorn for a religious talk show where people are forever seeing the error of their wicked ways and confessing in public. "Catch it before you eat," she says, "because it will make you throw up if you've just had dinner. As for cartoons, I'd rather my children played with sex toys than watch 'Popeye,' whose violence and sexism is so degrading, but David and Kathy still manage to find their way to the Saturday-morning cartoon parade." One Friday night when the Baesels paused to judge the values associated with television, they had the restless energy of two people who might be collaborating on a play as well as raising a family together.

Bob: "I use television most when I'm so tired I can't do anything but slump down in front of the set."

Carol: "I watch it when I'm in an intense period and I'm so keyed up I need TV to calm me down. I like Phil Donahue. He has a real live audience he treats with respect. I hate laugh tracks. I read somewhere those tracks are so old that most of the people doing the laughing are dead."

The Dukes of Hazzard, which David Baesel was watching while he drew cartoons and did his perfect-pitch imitation of Donald Duck, gave way to *Dallas*.

Carol: "This is Bob's jiggle show. He gets to watch t. and a. to his heart's content."

Bob: "It's trash, yet I enjoy it. There are positive sides to television, but if I had to vote one way or the other I'd vote against it."

Carol: "But look at your grandparents, with their narrow ideas. Maybe if they'd had the broadening influence of TV they wouldn't have been so anti-Catholic, anti-black and anti-Jewish."

Bob: "But you have to use it judiciously."

Carol: "You know, on Monday nights, with *Little House, M*A*S*H,* and *Newhart,* I love TV just for being there."

Bob: "Yet most of the time it makes people mindless. It's close, but I believe society would be better off without TV."

Carol: "I'd hate it without television."

After J.R. began a swindle that would take many Fridays to unravel, tranquility descended on the Baesel home.

It was evident, after a week in Hamilton, that almost every generalization about television could be contradicted by an equally valid opposing one. William Beckett, a former mayor and leading industrialist in Hamilton, argued that television was the bane of the 20th century. "It ought to be abolished," he declared, and indeed he meant what he said. Bob and Carol Baesel were unable to watch any cable shows because William Beckett, a nearby neighbor, would not permit the cable company to string its equipment across his property. ''A curse upon the human race and an excrescence on the fabric of our civilization'' are two of William Beckett's printable descriptions of television. Yet William Beckett's adored granddaughters are none other than Liza and Annie Reed, who in turn adore the sound and imagery of MTV and lament Mick Jagger's arrival at 40.

If families and neighbors remain divided, so do educators. ''Most television is designed to deliver viewers to advertising, nothing more,'' said Jack White, who teaches honors English at Hamilton High. But his colleague in the English Department, Syrilla Everson, found her students enriched by their viewing. ''Historical and geographical concepts of time and space are exapnded through television, and vocabularies are increased. 'Hypocrite' to my students means Archie Bunker. I ask them what 'somber' means and they tell me Blake Carrington. When I ask them who reminds them of Shakespeare's Portia, they say Lucille Ball because she's quick, fun-loving and irreverent. All is not lost here.''

The assertion that television has killed reading is met by the counterclaim that a miniseries like *The Blue and the Gray* leads viewers to books on the Civl War or that watching PBS's *Brideshead Revisited* leads to reading the Evelyn Waugh novel. Television atomizes family life; it collects a family around the set to watch and discuss shows together. Television detracts from civic activities; it makes us all part of the same community. Television sows racism; it regularly shows blacks and whites working and playing together. Television breeds juvenile delinquency; it teaches the young acceptable standards of behavior.

The point is, television's vast embrace makes each charge and each defense both relevant and true. I went to Hamilton in the certainty, instructed by learned journals and informed critics, that television was a rose-tinted blur of American life. What a surprise, after staring at both sides of the screen, to find we are all there, often sketched in two dimensions, but still present, in one form or another; and that television routinely portrays us with considerably more fidelity than most movies do. Not many of us lead actual lives reflected in ''Reds,'' ''Tootsie'' or (God knows) ''E.T.,'' but from the news to the soaps to the lawyers and hospitals and corporate takeovers and crime and dirges of unemployment, television has a hold, if not a lock, on at least the dailiness of the American late-century. Looking at our television, an outsider would know who we were; a native would know he was home. A philosopher would know that what was passing for art imitated quite faithfully what was passing for life.

BEST SELLERS

I concluded at length that the People were the best Judges of my Merit; for they buy my Works . . .

BENJAMIN FRANKLIN

FEW scenes in best-selling fiction can compare with the one from *Tarzan of the Apes* (1914) in which Tarzan, the son of a shipwrecked British aristocrat, raised from infancy by a tribe of apes in the African jungle, rescues Jane, the comely daughter of an American professor, from the evil clutches of the cruel and capricious ape-king Terkoz:

> Jane—her lithe, young form flattened against the trunk of a great tree, her hands tight pressed against her rising and falling bosom, and her eyes wide with mingled horror, fascination, fear, and admiration—watched the primordial ape battle with the primeval man for possession of a woman—for her.
>
> As the great muscles of the man's back and shoulders knotted beneath the tension of his efforts, and the huge biceps and forearm held at bay those mighty tusks, the veil of centuries of civilization and culture was swept from the blurred vision of the Baltimore girl.

Passion, violence, vengeance, and a melodramatic rescue—the passage is a paradigm of popular fiction.

After killing Terkoz, Tarzan carries off the reluctantly yielding Jane "deeper and deeper into the savage fastness of the untamed forest" to the security of his bower of bliss. What does he do when they get there?

> Tarzan had long since reached a decision as to what his future procedure should be. He had had time to recollect all that he had read of the ways of men and women in the books at the cabin. He would act as he imagined the men in the books would have acted were they in his place.

Apparently, even a situation so geographically and imaginatively far-fetched as that depicting an ape-man entertaining a captivating young woman from Baltimore cannot be entirely free from the guidance, if not the directions, of literature. In a moment obviously more threatening for him than any of his daily adventures in the unchartered jungle, Tarzan can offer no instinctive, spontaneous response. Instead, the "natural" man rescues himself by ponderously turning to the lessons of fiction. Though Tarzan does not tell us what books he had in his cabin library, he will undoubtedly model his future social behavior on the same late nineteenth century popular romances from which his creator, Edgar Rice Burroughs, derived his literary style.

Burroughs, like most best-selling novelists, knew what a reading public wanted. In the Tarzan books he satisfied a contemporary interest in imperialistic adventures and a psychological need for violent, bestial conflicts. A large part of his continuing success is attributable also to his grasp of a fundamental mythic element—that the popular masculine ideal of the twentieth century would be a sensitive brute, a natural aristocrat, a killer with a tender heart. As a type of masculine hero, Tarzan is intended to be not only alluringly primitive (a "woodland demi-god") but also the kind of man that heroines of American fiction have conventionally desired—a cultivated gentleman, preferably a foreign aristocrat.

The image, with variations of course, dominates twentieth century popular fiction and advertising. Michael Rossi, the hero of Grace Metalious' *Peyton Place*(1956), is "a massive boned man with muscles that seemed to quiver every time he moved. . . . His arms, beneath sleeves rolled above the elbow, were knotted powerfully, and the buttons of his work shirts always seemed about to pop off under the strain of trying to cover his chest." Though built like Tarzan, Michael Rossi is not going to wrestle wild beasts. Instead, he arrives in Peyton Place a stranger about to take on the job of headmaster at the local high school, for he "had a mind as analytical as a mathematician's and as curious as a philosopher's." Styles and idioms may change (though in these passages it may not seem so), but a successful formula for fiction is hard to let go of.

Not all best sellers, of course, are so masculinely aggressive, though even a predominately sentimental book like *Uncle Tom's Cabin* (1852) contains its whip wielding Simon Legree. Moreover, *Tarzan of the Apes* and *Peyton Place,* for all their self-conscious primitivism and casual disregard for "centuries of civilization and culture," never really stray very far from the unassailable proprieties and the cozy gentility to which their authors and readers finally subscribe. At the end of *Peyton Place,* Michael Rossi is a vigorous, comfortable, middle-aged married man. And the final scene in *Tarzan of the Apes* finds an educated, love-lorn "demi-god" in conversation at a train station in Wisconsin: " 'I am Monsieur Tarzan,' said the ape-man."

One reason readers respond so positively to a best-selling novel is that it invariably reaffirms in easily accessible language its audience's attitudes, values, and collective fantasies and identifies reassuringly with its anxieties. Novels like *Tarzan of the Apes* and *Peyton Place* become best sellers, then, because, along with excursions into fantasy, they return to what are essentially nonnegotiable domestic standards. In that sense they resemble a great many other American best sellers that have insisted on the inviolability of family bonds. Consider, for instance, a recent best seller by Mario Puzo, *The Godfather* (1969), in which a world of official corruption, blurred loyalties, and misdirected justice is contrasted with a closely knit patriarchal "family" carrying out its obligations and vendettas in a style that ensures the dignity and personal honor of all its members. Another best seller, Harriet Beecher Stowe's *Uncle Tom's Cabin,* fiercely opposes the institution of slavery, not entirely on political or legal grounds, but because it mercilessly breaks up the home by separating children from their parents, husbands from their wives.

Best-selling nonfiction also corroborates its readers' collective values. Many very successful volumes of nonfiction have taken the form of ready-reference compilations of practical advice. Dale Carnegie's *How To Win Friends and Influence People* (1936), Funk and Lewis' *Thirty Days to a More Powerful Vocabulary* (1942), Dr. Benjamin Spock's *Common Sense Book of Baby Care* (1946) and Wayne Dyer's *Your Erroneous Zones* (1976) exemplify the kinds of self-improvement and "how-to-do-it" books that offer their readers guidance that will presumably help them deal successfully with their feelings of ineptitude, confusion, and inferiority and reaffirm their yearnings for an uncomplicated life. Most best sellers offer their characters, and vicariously their readers, a way out of public and private dilemmas by providing them with the possibilities of wealth, sexual gratification, justice or vengeance, romance and adventure, a hard-won optimistic philosophy, or a return to traditional loyalties and uncomplicated codes of behavior.

Like advertisements, newspapers, and magazines, best sellers are frequently written in response to the pressures of contemporary events, issues, and tastes. They capitalize on the public's interests. Some best-selling authors "hit" on or invent something (be it practical advice for self-improvement, a timely exposé, or an extraordinary private eye) that a great number of people want to read about. Others design their books to attract readers predisposed to certain kinds of material by news coverage and magazine articles. Harriet Beecher Stowe, a dedicated abolitionist, recognized that the much debated issue of slavery, or, more precisely, the Fugitive Slave Law, was a suitable subject for fiction and wrote what became America's first major best-selling novel. The enormous popularity of Mario Puzo's *The Godfather,* one of the fastest-selling novels in the history of American publishing, can be partly explained by pointing to a reading public fascinated by the news coverage of the personalities, stratagems, and violence of organized crime.

Yet books like *Uncle Tom's Cabin* and *The Godfather* did not become best sellers merely because of their responsiveness to newsworthy public events. If readers were interested only in the events or issues detailed in these books, they could have satisfied that need more easily and less expensively by reading newspapers and magazines. But these best sellers, like many of the others we have included, offer readers something more than reportage or polemics; they combine an awareness of topical subjects with the conventions and techniques of fiction. Readers can feel that they are learning about the management of the slave trade in the South or the operations of organized crime while, at the same time, they are being entertained by the invented characters, situations, and plots that give factual information the shape of fiction.

The excerpts from best sellers appearing in this section are meant to characterize the kinds of writing that millions of readers have found and still find informative, entertaining, or both.[1] Perhaps the best way for you to read the following passages is to imagine yourself in a role opposite that of an editor who examines a piece of writing to try to decide whether it will be commercially successful. Instead, you have material that has been demonstrably successful, and you want to try to account for that success. What is it about the *writing* that has made it so popular? To what extent is the book's success attributable to the quality of its prose? To the types of characters rendered? To the kinds of themes dramatized? To the information proposed? To the particular psychological, social, or political issues involved? These and similar questions can, of course, be asked about any literary work, popular or unpopular, significant or insignificant. But because a best seller attracts such a large audience, the answers to questions about its compositional strategies and its overall verbal performance suggest a great deal about the nature of popular writing and the characteristics of the people who read it.

You are being invited to look closely at the following selections from what might be called a socio-aesthetic point of view. That is, you are being asked to infer from the distinctive features of the author's prose the kind of people he expects will attend to his writing. By doing so, you will establish the identity of the book's "ideal reader"—the type of person you imagine the writer would feel most comfortable talking to. You will have also constructed a criterion against which you can measure your own response to the work. Whatever your final judgment about the relative worth of the material you have read, your criticism will be more attuned to the particular verbal characteristics of the work the more carefully you can determine how *you,* as the reader and individual you imagine yourself to be, are taken into account by the author's act of writing.

The audience presupposed by the author's style can become, if the book is a best seller, the critical justification of his creative efforts. Mickey Spillane, author of the extraordinarily successful Mike Hammer detective novels, made this point clear when asked in an interview what he thought of the literary criticism of his fiction: "The public is the only critic. And the only *literature* is what the public reads. The first printing of my last book was more than two million copies—that's the kind of opinion that interests me." This way of talking tough is characteristic of Spillane's literary manner. It is a style he worked out before he became a celebrity, so his assurance is not necessarily the result of his having sold over seventy-five million copies of his novels. In fact, the Spillane we hear speaking as a professional writer in the interview quoted above is most likely being playfully imitative of the Spil-

1. Margaret Mitchell's *Gone With The Wind,* one of America's most important best selling novels, has been omitted because the author's estate refuses to allow the book to be excerpted.

lane who talks to us in the guise of his detective-narrator, Mike Hammer, in the following passage from *I, The Jury:*

> I said no more. I just sat there and glowered at the wall. Someday I'd trigger the bastard that shot Jack. In my time I've done it plenty of times. No sentiment. That went out with the first. After the war I've been almost anxious to get to some of the rats that make up the section of humanity that prey on people. People. How incredibly stupid they could be sometimes. A trial by law for a killer. A loophole in the phrasing that lets a killer crawl out. But in the end the people have their justice. They get it through guys like me once in a while. They crack down on society and I crack down on them. I shoot them like the mad dogs they are and society drags me to court to explain the whys and wherefores of the extermination. They investigate my past, check my fingerprints and throw a million questions my way. The papers make me look like a kill-crazy shamus, but they don't bear down too hard because Pat Chambers [Hammer's police detective friend] keeps them off my neck. Besides, I do my best to help the boys out and they know it. And I'm usually good for a story when I wind up a case.

In this angry internal monologue, Hammer does not talk to himself any differently than he talks to anyone else in the novel. This is his characteristic voice: tough, vindictive, self-assured. It is the voice of a man (rarely do women talk like this in fiction) who refuses to mince his words, who thinks that a more complicated way of talking would invariably associate him with the legalistic language that permits those "loopholes" in phrasing through which killers are allowed to escape justice.

The language in this passage carries with it an authority that would gratify those readers who feel that their own lives are helplessly trapped in bureaucratic labyrinths and compromising civilities, and who consequently seldom, if ever, have the occasion to talk to anybody in the way Mike Hammer does. If Hammer recognizes in this passage that he is forced occasionally to make concessions to the police, the courts, and the press, he does so without compromising his role as a self-appointed arbiter of social justice. He does so also without ever having to modify unwillingly his deliberately aggressive, hard-boiled tone to suit the different types of characters he is obliged to confront. Hammer's is a voice that never interrupts itself to reconsider what it has said. It is a language without hesitations or unnecessary qualifications.

Hammer's style disassociates him from the official language of law enforcement, a language traditionally dependent upon a complicated system of qualifications and constraints. By taking the law into his own hands, Hammer essentially transforms the law into his own language. If, as the self-assertion of the title indicates, Hammer *is* the jury, then he symbolically embodies the "People," whose expectations of justice he considers it is his mission in life to fulfill. The overwhelming public approval that Spillane confidently refers to as the most legitimate criticism of his fiction has been anticipated in the public approbation he allowed his most successful character to take for granted.

It is not unusual for best selling authors to find a confirmation of their talent in sales figures. Harriet Beecher Stowe, an author whose literary intentions differ radically from Spillane's, and who would have been offended even by his idiom, acknowledged her enthusiasm for the public's approval of America's first major best selling novel in terms Spillane would surely understand. Writing in the third person for an introduction to one of the many editions of *Uncle Tom's Cabin,* she remarks,

> The despondency of the author as to the question whether anybody would read or attend to her appeal was soon dispelled. Ten thousand copies were sold in a few days, and over three hundred thousand within a year; and eight power-presses, running day and night, were barely able to keep

> pace with the demand for it. It was read everywhere, apparently, and by everybody; and she soon began to hear echoes of sympathy all over the land. The indignation, the pity, the distress, that had long weighed upon her soul seemed to pass off from her into the readers of the book.

It would be difficult to find a more apt description of the merger of writer and reader in the collective enterprise that makes a book a best seller.

Harriet Beecher Stowe / *Uncle Tom's Cabin* 1852

The daughter of a New England Congregational pastor, Harriet Beecher Stowe (1811–96) moved to Cincinnati when her father was appointed head of the Lane Theological Seminary. She began writing sketches for magazines, but after her marriage to Calvin Ellis Stowe, a professor of Biblical Literature at her father's seminary, she abandoned the idea of a literary career. At the time, Lane Theological Seminary was a center of antislavery sentiment, and in this environment, plus occasional visits to the slave state Kentucky, Mrs. Stowe gradually formed the abolitionist opinions that were given full expression in Uncle Tom's Cabin. *After a successful serialization in a Washington, D.C., antislavery weekly,* The National Era, *the novel was brought out in two volumes in 1852. It was a momentous publishing event: thirty thousand copies were sold in the first year, and by 1856 the sales in England alone were well over a million. Translations were worldwide. Mrs. Stowe, then living in Brunswick, Maine, where her husband had a teaching position at Bowdoin, found herself the most famous literary figure in America and an international celebrity. Though she continued to write (averaging nearly a book a year for the next thirty years), none of her later novels ever attained the success of her first.*

SELECT INCIDENT OF LAWFUL TRADE

> *"In Ramah there was a voice heard,—weeping, and lamentation, and great mourning; Rachel weeping for her children, and would not be comforted."*
>
> —Jeremiah, 31 : 15

Mr. Haley and Tom jogged onward in their wagon, each, for a time, absorbed in his own reflections. Now, the reflections of two men sitting side by side are a curious thing,—seated on the same seat, having the same eyes, ears, hands and organs of all sorts, and having pass before their eyes the same objects,—it is wonderful what a variety we shall find in these same reflections!

As, for example, Mr. Haley: he thought first of Tom's length, and breadth, and height, and what he would sell for, if he was kept fat and in good case till he got him into market. He thought of how he should make out his gang; he thought of the respective market value of certain supposititious men and women and children who were to compose it, and other kindred topics of the business; then he thought of himself, and how humane he was, that whereas other men chained their "niggers" hand and foot both, he only put fetters on the feet, and left Tom the use of his hands, as long as he behaved well; and he sighed to think how ungrateful human nature was, so that there was even room to doubt whether Tom appreciated his mercies. He had been taken in so by "niggers" whom he had favored; but still he was astonished to consider how good-natured he yet remained!

As to Tom, he was thinking over some words of an unfashionable old book, which kept running through his head, again and again, as follows: "We have here no continuing city, but we seek one to come; wherefore God himself is not ashamed to be called our God; for he hath prepared for us a city." These words of an ancient volume, got up principally by "ignorant and unlearned men," have, through all time, kept up, somehow, a strange sort of power over the minds of poor, simple fellows, like Tom. They stir up the soul from its depths, and rouse, as with trumpet call, courage, energy, and enthusiasm, where before was only the blackness of despair.

Mr. Haley pulled out of his pocket sundry newspapers, and began looking over their advertisements, with absorbed interest. He was not a remarkably fluent reader, and was in the habit of reading in a sort of recitative half-aloud, by way of calling in his ears to verify the deductions of his eyes. In this tone he slowly recited the following paragraph:

"EXECUTOR'S SALE,—NEGROES!—*Agreeably to order of court, will be sold, on Tuesday, February 20, before the Court-house door, in the town of Washington, Kentucky, the following negroes: Hagar, aged 60; John, aged 30; Ben, aged 21; Saul, aged 25; Albert, aged 14. Sold for the benefit of the creditors and heirs of the estate of Jesse Blutchford, Esq.*

SAMUEL MORRIS,
THOMAS FLINT,
Executors"

"This yer I must look at," said he to Tom, for want of somebody else to talk to.

"Ye see, I'm going to get up a prime gang to take down with ye, Tom; it'll make it sociable and pleasant like,—good company will, ye know. We must drive right to Washington first and foremost, and then I'll clap you into jail, while I does the business."

Tom received this agreeable intelligence quite meekly; simply wondering, in his own heart, how many of these doomed men had wives and children, and whether they would feel as he did about leaving them. It is to be confessed, too, that the naïve, off-hand information that he was to be thrown into jail by no means produced an agreeable impression on a poor fellow who had always prided himself on a strictly honest and upright course of life. Yes, Tom, we must confess it, was rather proud of his honesty, poor fellow,—not having very much else to be proud of;—if he had belonged to some of the higher walks of society, he, perhaps, would never have been reduced to such straits. However, the day wore on, and the evening saw Haley and Tom comfortably accommodated in Washington,—the one in a tavern, and the other in a jail.

About eleven o'clock the next day, a mixed throng was gathered around the court-house steps,—smoking, chewing, spitting, swearing, and conversing, according to their respective tastes and turns,—waiting for the auction to commence. The men and women to be sold sat in a group apart, talking in a low tone to each other. The woman who had been advertised by the name of Hagar was a regular African in feature and figure. She might have been sixty, but was older than that by hard work and disease, was partially blind, and somewhat crippled with rheumatism. By her side stood her only remaining son, Albert, a bright-looking little fellow of fourteen years. The boy was the only survivor of a large family, who had been successively sold away from her to a southern market. The mother held on to him with both her shaking hands, and eyed with intense trepidation every one who walked up to examine him.

"Don't be feared, Aunt Hagar," said the oldest of the men, "I spoke to Mas'r Thomas 'bout it, and he thought he might manage to sell you in a lot both together."

"Dey needn't call me worn out yet," said she, lifting her shaking hands. "I can cook yet, and scrub, and scour,—I'm wuth a buying, if I come cheap;—tell em dat ar,—you *tell* em,'' she added, earnestly.

Haley here forced his way into the group, walked up to the old man, pulled his mouth open and looked in, felt of his teeth, made him stand and straighten himself, bend his back, and perform various evolutions to show his muscles; and then passed on to the next, and put him through the same trial. Walking up last to the boy, he felt of his arms, straightened his hands, and looked at his fingers, and made him jump, to show his agility.

''He an't gwine to be sold widout me!'' said the old woman, with passionate eagerness; ''he and I goes in a lot together; I 's rail strong yet, Mas'r and can do heaps o' work,—heaps on it, Mas'r.''

''On plantation?'' said Haley, with a contemptuous glance. ''Likely story!'' and, as if satisfied with his examination, he walked out and looked, and stood with his hands in his pocket, his cigar in his mouth, and his hat cocked on one side, ready for action.

''What think of 'em?'' said a man who had been following Haley's examination, as if to make up his own mind from it.

''Wal,'' said Haley, spitting, ''I shall put in, I think, for the youngerly ones and the boy.''

''They want to sell the boy and the old woman together,'' said the man.

''Find it a tight pull;—why, she's an old rack o'bones,—not worth her salt.''

''You wouldn't then?'' said the man.

''Anybody 'd be a fool 't would. She's half blind, crooked with rheumatis, and foolish to boot.''

''Some buys up these yer old critturs, and ses there's a sight more wear in 'em than a body 'd think,'' said the man, reflectively.

''No go, 't all,'' said Haley; ''wouldn't take her for a present,—fact,—I've *seen,* now.''

''Wal, 't is kinder pity, now, not to buy her with her son,—her heart seems so sot on him,—s'pose they fling her in cheap.''

''Them that's got money to spend that ar way, it's all well enough. I shall bid off on that ar boy for a plantation-hand;—wouldn't be bothered with her, no way,—not if they'd give her to me,'' said Haley.

''She'll take on desp't,'' said the man.

''Nat'lly, she will,'' said the trader, coolly.

The conversation was here interrupted by a busy hum in the audience; and the auctioneer, a short, bustling, important fellow, elbowed his way into the crowd. The old woman drew in her breath, and caught instinctively at her son.

''Keep close to yer mammy, Albert,—close,—dey'll put us up togedder,'' she said.

''O, mammy, I'm feard they won't,'' said the boy.

''Dey must, child; I can't live, no ways, if they don't,'' said the old creature, vehemently.

The stentorian tones of the auctioneer, calling out to clear the way, now announced that the sale was about to commence. A place was cleared, and the bidding began. The different men on the list were soon knocked off at prices which showed a pretty brisk demand in the market; two of them fell to Haley.

''Come, now, young un,'' said the auctioneer, giving the boy a touch with his hammer, ''be up and show your springs, now.''

''Put us two up togedder, togedder,—do please, Mas'r,'' said the old woman, holding fast to her boy.

''Be off,'' said the man, gruffly, pushing her hands away; ''you come last. Now, darkey, spring;'' and, with the word, he pushed the boy toward the block, while a deep, heavy groan rose behind him. The boy paused, and looked back; but there was no time to stay, and dashing the tears from his large, bright eyes, he was up in a moment.

His fine figure, alert limbs, and bright face, raised an instant competition, and half a dozen bids simultaneously met the ear of the auctioneer. Anxious, half-frightened, he looked from side to side, as he heard the clatter of contending bids,—now here, now there,—till the hammer fell. Haley had got him. He was pushed from the block toward his new master, but stopped one moment, and looked back, when his poor old mother, trembling in every limb, held out her shaking hands toward him.

"Buy me too, Mas'r, for de dear Lord's sake!—buy me,—I shall die if you don't!"

"You'll die if I do, that's the kink of it," said Haley,—"no!" And he turned on his heel.

The bidding for the poor old creature was summary. The man who had addressed Haley, and who seemed not destitute of compassion, bought her for a trifle, and the spectators began to disperse.

The poor victims of the sale, who had been brought up in one place together for years, gathered round the despairing old mother, whose agony was pitiful to see.

"Couldn't dey leave me one? Mas'r allers said I should have one,—he did," she repeated over and over, in heart-broken tones.

"Trust in the Lord, Aunt Hagar," said the oldest of the men, sorrowfully.

"What good will it do?" said she, sobbing passionately.

"Mother, mother,—don't! don't!" said the boy. "They say you's got a good master."

"I don't care—I don't care. O, Albert! oh, my boy! you's my last baby. Lord, how ken I?"

"Come, take her off, can't some of ye?" said Haley, dryly; "don't do no good for her to go on that ar way."

The old men of the company, partly by persuasion and partly by force, loosed the poor creature's last despairing hold, and, as they led her off to her new master's wagon, strove to comfort her.

"Now!" said Haley, pushing his three purchases together, and producing a bundle of handcuffs, which he proceeded to put on their wrists; and fastening each handcuff to a long chain, he drove them before him to the jail.

A few days saw Haley, with his possessions, safely deposited on one of the Ohio boats. It was the commencement of his gang, to be augmented, as the boat moved on, by various other merchandise of the same kind, which he, or his agent, had stored for him in various points along shore.

The La Belle Rivière, as brave and beautiful a boat as ever walked the waters of her namesake river, was floating gayly down the stream, under a brilliant sky, the stripes and stars of free America waving and fluttering over head; the guards crowded with well-dressed ladies and gentlemen walking and enjoying the delightful day. All was full of life, buoyant and rejoicing;—all but Haley's gang, who were stored, with other freight, on the lower deck, and who, somehow, did not seem to appreciate their various privileges, as they sat in a knot, talking to each other in low tones.

"Boys," said Haley, coming up, briskly, "I hope you keep up good heart, and are cheerful. Now, no sulks, ye see; keep stiff upper lip, boys; do well by me, and I'll do well by you."

The boys addressed responded the invariable "Yes, Mas'r," for ages the watchword of poor Africa; but it's to be owned they did not look particularly cheerful; they had their various little prejudices in favor of wives, mothers, sisters, and children, seen for the last time,—and though "they that wasted them required of them mirth," it was not instantly forthcoming.

"I've got a wife," spoke out the article enumerated as "John, aged thirty," and he laid his chained hand on Tom's knee,—"and she don't know a word about this, poor girl!"

"Where does she live?" said Tom.

"In a tavern a piece down here," said John; "I wish, now, I *could* see her once more in this world," he added.

Poor John! It *was* rather natural; and the tears that fell, as he spoke, came as naturally as if he had been a white man. Tom drew a long breath from a sore heart, and tried, in his poor way, to comfort him.

And over head, in the cabin, sat fathers and mothers, husbands and wives; and merry, dancing children moved round among them, like so many little butterflies, and everything was going on quite easy and comfortable.

"O, mamma," said a boy, who had just come up from below, "there's a negro trader on board, and he's brought four or five slaves down there."

"Poor creatures!" said the mother, in a tone between grief and indignation.

"What's that?" said another lady.

"Some poor slaves below," said the mother.

"And they've got chains on," said the boy.

"What a shame to our country that such sights are to be seen!" said another lady.

"O, there's a great deal to be said on both sides of the subject," said a genteel woman, who sat at her state-room door sewing, while her little girl and boy were playing round her. "I've been south, and I must say I think the negroes are better off than they would be to be free."

"In some respects, some of them are well off, I grant," said the lady to whose remark she had answered. "The most dreadful part of slavery, to my mind, is its outrages on the feelings and affections,—the separating of families, for example."

"That *is* a bad thing, certainly," said the other lady, holding up a baby's dress she had just completed, and looking intently on its trimmings; "but then, I fancy, it don't occur often."

"O, it does," said the first lady, eagerly; "I've lived many years in Kentucky and Virginia both, and I've seen enough to make any one's heart sick. Suppose, ma'am, your two children, there, should be taken from you, and sold?"

"We can't reason from our feelings to those of this class of persons," said the other lady, sorting out some worsteds on her lap.

"Indeed, ma'am, you can know nothing of them, if you say so," answered the first lady, warmly. "I was born and brought up among them. I know they *do* feel, just as keenly,—even more so, perhaps,—as we do."

The lady said "Indeed!" yawned, and looked out the cabin window, and finally repeated, for a finale, the remark with which she had begun,—"After all, I think they are better off than they would be to be free."

"It's undoubtedly the intention of Providence that the African race should be servants,—kept in a low condition," said a grave-looking gentleman in black, a clergyman, seated by the cabin door. " 'Cursed be Canaan; a servant of servants shall he be,' the Scripture says."

"I say, stranger, is that ar what that text means?" said a tall man, standing by.

"Undoubtedly. It pleased Providence, for some inscrutable reason, to doom the race to bondage, ages ago; and we must not set up our opinion against that."

"Well, then, we'll all go ahead and buy up niggers," said the man, "if that's the way of Providence,—won't we, Squire?" said he, turning to Haley, who had been standing, with his hands in his pockets, by the stove and intently listening to the conversation.

"Yes," continued the tall man, "we must all be resigned to the decrees of Providence. Niggers must be sold, and trucked round, and kept under; it's what they's made for. 'Pears like this yer view 's quite refreshing, ain't it, stranger?" said he to Haley.

"I never thought on 't," said Haley. "I couldn't have said as much, myself; I ha'nt no larning. I took up the trade just to make a living; if 'tan't right, I calculated to 'pent on 't in time, *ye* know."

"And now you'll save yerself the trouble, won't ye?" said the tall man. "See what 't is, now, to know scripture. If ye'd only studied yer Bible, like this yer good man, ye might have know'd it before, and saved ye a heap o' trouble. Ye could jist have said, 'Cussed be'—what's his name?—'and 't would all have come right.' " And the stranger, who was no other than the honest drover whom we introduced to our readers in the Kentucky tavern, sat down, and began smoking, with a curious smile on his long, dry face.

A tall, slender young man, with a face expressive of great feeling and intelligence, here broke in, and repeated the words, " 'All things whatsoever ye would that men should do unto you, do ye even so unto them.' I suppose," he added, "*that* is scripture, as much as 'Cursed be Canaan.' "

"Wal, it seems quite *as* plain a text, stranger," said John the drover, "to poor fellows like us, now;" and John smoked on like a volcano.

The young man paused, looked as if he was going to say more, when suddenly the boat stopped, and the company made the usual steamboat rush, to see where they were landing.

"Both them ar chaps parsons?" said John to one of the men, as they were going out.

The man nodded.

As the boat stopped, a black woman came running wildly up the plank, darted into the crowd, flew up to where the slave gang sat, and threw her arms round that unfortunate piece of merchandise before enumerated—"John, aged thirty," and with sobs and tears bemoaned him as her husband.

But what needs tell the story, told too oft,—every day told,—of heart-strings rent and broken,—the weak broken and torn for the profit and convenience of the strong! It needs not to be told;—every day is telling it,—telling it, too, in the ear of One who is not deaf, though he be long silent.

The young man who had spoken for the cause of humanity and God before stood with folded arms, looking on this scene. He turned, and Haley was standing at his side. "My friend," he said, speaking with thick utterance, "how can you, how dare you, carry on a trade like this? Look at those poor creatures! Here I am, rejoicing in my heart that I am going home to my wife and child; and the same bell which is a signal to carry me onward towards them will part this poor man and his wife forever. Depend upon it, God will bring you into judgment for this."

The trader turned away in silence.

"I say, now," said the drover, touching his elbow, "there's differences in parsons, an't there? 'Cussed be Cannan' don't seem to go down with this 'un, does it?"

Haley gave an uneasy growl.

"And that ar an't the worst on 't," said John; "mabbee it won't go down with the Lord, neither, when ye come to settle with Him, one o' these days, as all on us must, I reckon."

Haley walked reflectively to the other end of the boat.

"If I make pretty handsomely on one or two next gangs," he thought, "I reckon I'll stop off this yer; it's really getting dangerous." And he took out his pocket-book, and began adding over his accounts,—a process which many gentlemen besides Mr. Haley have found a specific for an uneasy conscience.

The boat swept proudly away from the shore, and all went on merrily, as before. Men talked, and loafed, and read, and smoked. Women sewed, and children played, and the boat passed on her way.

One day, when she lay to for a while at a small town in Kentucky, Haley went up into the place on a little matter of business.

Tom, whose fetters did not prevent his taking a moderate circuit, had drawn near the side of the boat, and stood listlessly gazing over the railing. After a time, he saw the trader returning, with an alert step, in company with a colored woman, bearing in her arms a young child. She was dressed quite respectably, and a colored man followed her, bringing along a small trunk. The woman came cheerfully onward, talking, as she came, with the man who bore her trunk, and so passed up the plank into the boat. The bell rung, the steamer whizzed, the engine groaned and coughed, and away swept the boat down the river.

The woman walked forward among the boxes and bales of the lower deck, and, sitting down, busied herself with chirruping to her baby.

Haley made a turn or two about the boat, and then, coming up, seated himself near her, and began saying something to her in an indifferent undertone.

Tom soon noticed a heavy cloud passing over the woman's brow; and that she answered rapidly, and with great vehemence.

"I don't believe it,—I won't believe it!" he heard her say. "You're jist a foolin with me."

"If you won't believe it, look here!" said the man, drawing out a paper; "this yer 's the bill of sale, and there's your master's name to it; and I paid down good solid cash for it, too, I can tell you,—so, now!"

"I don't believe Mas'r would cheat me so; it can't be true!" said the woman, with increasing agitation.

"You can ask any of these men here, that can read writing. Here!" he said, to a man that was passing by, "jist read this yer, won't you! This yer gal won't believe me, when I tell her what 't is."

"Why, it's a bill of sale, signed by John Fosdick," said the man, "making over to you the girl Lucy and her child. It's all straight enough, for aught I see."

The woman's passionate exclamations collected a crowd around her, and the trader briefly explained to them the cause of the agitation.

"He told me that I was going down to Louisville, to hire out as cook to the same tavern where my husband works,—that's what Mas'r told me, his own self; and I can't believe he'd lie to me," said the woman.

"But he has sold you, my poor woman, there's no doubt about it," said a good-natured looking man, who had been examining the papers; "he has done it, and no mistake."

"Then it's no account talking," said the woman, suddenly growing quite calm; and, clasping her child tighter in her arms, she sat down on her box, turned her back round, and gazed listlessly into the river.

"Going to take it easy, after all!" said the trader. "Gal's got grit, I see."

The woman looked calm, as the boat went on; and a beautiful soft summer breeze passed like a compassionate spirit over her head,—the gentle breeze, that never inquires whether the brow is dusky or fair that it fans. And she saw sunshine sparkling on the water, in golden ripples, and heard gay voices, full of ease and pleasure, talking around her everywhere; but her heart lay as if a great stone had fallen on it. Her baby raised himself up against her, and stroked her cheeks with his little hands; and, springing up and down, crowing and chatting, seemed determined to arouse her. She strained him suddenly and tightly in her arms, and slowly one tear after another fell on his wondering, unconscious face; and gradually she seemed, and little by little, to grow calmer, and busied herself with tending and nursing him.

The child, a boy of ten months, was uncommonly large and strong of his age, and very vigorous in his limbs. Never, for a moment, still, he kept his mother constantly busy in holding him, and guarding his springing activity.

"That's a fine chap!" said a man, suddenly stopping opposite to him, with his hands in his pockets. "How old is he?"

"Ten months and a half," said the mother.

The man whistled to the boy, and offered him part of a stick of candy, which he eagerly grabbed at, and very soon had it in a baby's general depository, to wit, his mouth.

"Rum fellow!" said the man. "Knows what's what!" and he whistled, and walked on. When he had got to the other side of the boat, he came across Haley, who was smoking on top of a pile of boxes.

The stranger produced a match, and lighted a cigar, saying, as he did so,

"Decentish kind o' wench you've got round there, stranger."

"Why, I reckon she *is* tol'able fair," said Haley, blowing the smoke out of his mouth.

"Taking her down south?" said the man.

Haley nodded, and smoked on.

"Plantation hand?" said the man.

"Wal," said Haley, "I'm fillin' out an order for a plantation, and I think I shall put her in. They telled me she was a good cook; and they can use her for that, or set her at the cotton-picking. She's got the right fingers for that; I looked at 'em. Sell well, either way;" and Haley resumed his cigar.

"They won't want the young 'un on the plantation," said the man.

"I shall sell him, first chance I find," said Haley, lighting another cigar.

"S'pose you'd be selling him tol'able cheap," said the stranger, mounting the pile of boxes, and sitting down comfortably.

"Don't know 'bout that," said Haley; "he's a pretty smart young 'un,—straight, fat, strong; flesh as hard as a brick!"

"Very true, but then there's the bother and expense of raisin'."

"Nonsense!" said Haley; "they is raised as easy as any kind of critter there is going; they an't a bit more trouble than pups. This yer chap will be running all around, in a month."

"I've got a good place for raisin', and I thought of takin' in a little more stock," said the man. "One cook lost a young 'un last week,—got drownded in a wash-tub while she was a hangin' out clothes,—and I reckon it would be well enough to set her to raisin' this yer."

Haley and the stranger smoked a while in silence, neither seeming willing to broach the test question of the interview. At last the man resumed:

"You wouldn't think of wantin' more than ten dollars for that ar chap, seeing you *must* get him off yer hand, any how?"

Haley shook his head, and spit impressively.

"That won't do, no ways," he said, and began his smoking again.

"Well, stranger, what will you take?"

"Well, now," said Haley, "I *could* raise that ar chap myself, or get him raised; he's oncommon likely and healthy, and he'd fetch a hundred dollars, six months hence; and, in a year or two, he'd bring two hundred, if I had him in the right spot;—so I shan't take a cent less nor fifty for him now."

"O, stranger! that's rediculous, altogether," said the man.

"Fact!" said Haley, with a decisive nod of his head.

"I'll give thirty for him," said the stranger, "but not a cent more."

"Now, I'll tell ye what I will do," said Haley, spitting again, with renewed decision. "I'll split the difference, and say forty-five; and that's the most I will do."

"Well, agreed!" said the man, after an interval.

"Done!" said Haley, "Where do you land?"

"At Louisville," said the man.

"Louisville," said Haley. "Very fair, we get there about dusk. Chap will be asleep,—all fair,—get him off quietly, and no screaming,—happens beautiful,—I like to do everything quietly,—I hates all kind of agitation and fluster.'' And so, after a transfer of certain bills had passed from the man's pocket-book to the trader's, he resumed his cigar.

It was a bright, tranquil evening when the boat stopped at the wharf at Louisville. The woman had been sitting with her baby in her arms, now wrapped in a heavy sleep. When she heard the name of the place called out, she hastily laid the child down in a little cradle formed by the hollow among the boxes, first carefully spreading under it her cloak; and then she sprung to the side of the boat, in hopes that, among the various hotel-waiters who thronged the wharf, she might see her husband. In this hope, she pressed forward to the front rails, and, stretching far over them, strained her eyes intently on the moving heads on the shore, and the crowd pressed in between her and the child.

''Now's your time,'' said Haley, taking the sleeping child up, and handing him to the stranger. ''Don't wake him up, and set him to crying, now; it would make a devil of a fuss with the gal.'' The man took the bundle carefully, and was soon lost in the crowd that went up the wharf.

When the boat, creaking, and groaning, and puffing, had loosed from the wharf, and was beginning slowly to strain herself along, the woman returned to her old seat. The trader was sitting there,—the child was gone!

''Why, why,—where?'' she began, in bewildered surprise.

''Lucy,'' said the trader, ''your child's gone; you may as well know it first as last. You see, I know'd you couldn't take him down south; and I got a chance to sell him to a first-rate family, that'll raise him better than you can.''

The trader had arrived at that stage of Christian and political perfection which has been recommended by some preachers and politicians of the north, lately, in which he had completely overcome every humane weakness and prejudice. His heart was exactly where yours, sir, and mine could be brought, with proper effort and cultivation. The wild look of anguish and utter despair that the woman cast on him might have disturbed one less practised; but he was used to it. He had seen that same look hundreds of time. You can get used to such things, too, my friend; and it is the great object of recent efforts to make our whole northern community used to them, for the glory of the Union. So the trader only regarded the mortal anguish which he saw working in those dark features, those clenched hands, and suffocating breathings, as necessary incidents of the trade, and merely calculated whether she was going to scream, and get up a commotion on the boat; for, like other supporters of our peculiar institution, he decidedly disliked agitation.

But the woman did not scream. The shot had passed too straight and direct through the heart, for cry or tear.

Dizzily she sat down. Her slack hands fell lifeless by her side. Her eyes looked straight forward, but she saw nothing. All the noise and hum of the boat, the groaning of the machinery, mingled dreamily to her bewildered ear; and the poor, dumb-stricken heart had neither cry nor tear to show for its utter misery. She was quite calm.

The trader, who, considering his advantages, was almost as humane as some of our politicians, seemed to feel called on to administer such consolation as the case admitted of.

''I know this yer comes kinder hard, at first, Lucy,'' said he; ''but such a smart, sensible gal as you are, won't give way to it. You see it's *necessary,* and can't be helped!''

''O! don't, Mas'r, don't!'' said the woman, with a voice like one that is smothering.

''You're a smart wench, Lucy,'' he persisted; ''I mean to do well by ye, and get ye a nice place down river; and you'll soon get another husband,—such a likely gal as you—''

"O! Mas'r, if you *only* won't talk to me now," said the woman, in a voice of such quick and living anguish that the trader felt that there was something at present in the case beyond his style of operation. He got up, and the woman turned away, and buried her head in her cloak.

The trader walked up and down for a time, and occasionally stopped and looked at her.

"Takes it hard, rather," he soliloquized, "but quiet, tho';—let her sweat a while; she'll come right, by and by!"

Tom had watched the whole transaction from first to last, and had a perfect understanding of its results. To him, it looked like something unutterably horrible and cruel, because, poor, ignorant black soul! he had not learned to generalize, and to take enlarged views. If he had only been instructed by certain ministers of Christianity, he might have thought better of it, and seen in it an every-day incident of a lawful trade; a trade which is the vital support of an institution which an American divine [1] tells us has *"no evils but such as are inseparable from any other relations in social and domestic life."* But Tom, as we see, being a poor, ignorant fellow, whose reading had been confined entirely to the New Testament, could not comfort and solace himself with views like these. His very soul bled within him for what seemed to him the *wrongs* of the poor suffering thing that lay like a crushed reed on the boxes; the feeling, living, bleeding, yet immortal *thing,* which American state law coolly classes with the bundles, and bales, and boxes, among which she is lying.

Tom drew near, and tried to say something; but she only groaned. Honestly, and with tears running down his own cheeks, he spoke of a heart of love in the skies, of a pitying Jesus, and an eternal home; but the ear was deaf with anguish, and the palsied heart could not feel.

Night came on,—night calm, unmoved, and glorious, shining down with her innumerable and solemn angel eyes, twinkling, beautiful, but silent. There was no speech nor language, no pitying voice or helping hand, from that distant sky. One after another, the voices of business or pleasure died away; all on the boat were sleeping, and the ripples at the prow were plainly heard. Tom stretched himself out on a box, and there, as he lay, he heard, ever and anon, a smothered sob or cry from the prostrate creature,—"O! what shall I do? O Lord! O good Lord, do help me!" and so, ever and anon, until the murmur died away in silence.

At midnight, Tom waked, with a sudden start. Something black passed quickly by him to the side of the boat, and he heard a splash in the water. No one else saw or heard anything. He raised his head,—the woman's place was vacant! He got up, and sought about him in vain. The poor bleeding heart was still, at last, and the river rippled and dimpled just as brightly as if it had not closed above it.

Patience! patience! ye whose hearts swell indignant at wrongs like these. Not one throb of anguish, not one tear of the oppressed, is forgotten by the Man of Sorrows, the Lord of Glory. In his patient, generous bosom he bears the anguish of a world. Bear thou, like him, in patience, and labor in love; for sure as he is God, "the year of his redeemed *shall* come."

The trader waked up bright and early, and came out to see to his live stock. It was now his turn to look about in perplexity.

"Where alive is that gal?" he said to Tom.

Tom, who had learned the widom of keeping counsel, did not feel called upon to state his observations and suspicions, but said he did not know.

"She surely couldn't have got off in the night at any of the landings, for I was awake, and on the look-out, whenever the boat stopped. I never trust these yer things to other folks."

1. Dr. Joel Parker of Philadelphia.

This speech was addressed to Tom quite confidentially, as if it was something that would be specially interesting to him. Tom made no answer.

The trader searched the boat from stem to stern, among boxes, bales and barrels, around the machinery, by the chimneys, in vain.

"Now, I say, Tom, be fair about this yer," he said, when, after a fruitless search, he came where Tom was standing. "You know something about it, now. Don't tell me,—I know you do. I saw the gal stretched out here about ten o'clock, and ag'in at twelve, and ag'in between one and two; and then at four she was gone, and you was a sleeping right there all the time. Now, you know something,—you can't help it."

"Well, Mas'r," said Tom, "towards morning something brushed by me, and I kinder half woke; and then I hearn a great splash, and then I clare woke up, and the gal was gone. That's all I know on 't."

The trader was not shocked nor amazed; because, as we said before, he was used to a great many things that you are not used to. Even the awful presence of Death struck no solemn chill upon him. He had seen Death many times,—met him in the way of trade, and got acquainted with him,—and he only thought of him as a hard customer, that embarrassed his property operations very unfairly; and so he only swore that the gal was a baggage, and that he was devilish unlucky, and that, if things went on in this way, he should not make a cent on the trip. In short, he seemed to consider himself an ill-used man, decidedly; but there was no help for it, as the woman had escaped into a state which *never will* give up a fugitive,—not even at the demand of the whole glorious Union. The trader, therefore, sat discontentedly down, with his little account-book, and put down the missing body and soul under the head of *losses!*

"He's a shocking creature, isn't he,—this trader? so unfeeling! It's dreadful, really!"

"O, but nobody thinks anything of these traders! They are universally despised,—never received into any decent society."

But who, sir makes the trader? Who is most to blame? The enlightened, cultivated, intelligent man, who supports the system of which the trader is the inevitable result, or the poor trader himself? You make the public statement that calls for his trade, that debauches and depraves him, till he feels no shame in it; and in what are you better than he?

Are you educated and he ignorant, you high and he low, you refined and he coarse, you talented and he simple?

In the day of a future Judgment, these very considerations may make it more tolerable for him than for you.

In concluding these little incidents of lawful trade, we must beg the world not to think that American legislators are entirely destitute of humanity, as might, perhaps, be unfairly inferred from the great efforts made in our national body to protect and perpetuate this species of traffic.

Who does not know how our great men are outdoing themselves, in declaiming against the *foreign* slave-trade. There are a perfect host of Clarksons and Wilberforces risen up among us on that subject, most edifying to hear and behold. Trading negroes from Africa, dear reader, is so horrid! It is not to be thought of! But trading them from Kentucky,—that's quite another thing!

Ernest Laurence Thayer / Casey at the Bat

San Francisco Examiner, June 3, 1888

Ernest Laurence Thayer (1863–1940) published the humorous poem "Casey at the Bat" in the June 3, 1888 San Francisco Examiner, *using the pseudonym* Phin. *The poem became famous when a well-known entertainer of the time, DeWolf Hopper, made it part of his vaudeville act. So compellingly does "Casey at the Bat" document the drama and idiom of the game that poet-critic Louis Untermeyer has called it "the acknowledged classic of baseball, its anthem and theme song."*

The outlook wasn't brilliant for the Mudville nine that day:
The score stood four to two with but one inning more to play.
And then when Cooney died at first, and Barrows did the same,
A sickly silence fell upon the patrons of the game.

A straggling few got up to go in deep despair. The rest
Clung to that hope which springs eternal in the human breast;
They thought if only Casey could but get a whack at that—
We'd put up even money now with Casey at the bat.

But Flynn preceded Casey, as did also Jimmy Blake,
And the former was a lulu and the latter was a cake;
So upon that stricken multitude grim melancholy sat,
For there seemed but little chance of Casey's getting to the bat.

But Flynn let drive a single, to the wonderment of all,
And Blake, the much despis-ed, tore the cover off the ball;
And when the dust had lifted, and the men saw what had occurred,
There was Jimmy safe at second and Flynn a-hugging third.

Then from 5,000 throats and more there rose a lusty yell;
It rumbled through the valley, it rattled in the dell;
It knocked upon the mountain and recoiled upon the flat,
For Casey, mighty Casey, was advancing to the bat.

There was ease in Casey's manner as he stepped into his place;
There was pride in Casey's bearing and a smile on Casey's face.
And when, responding to the cheers, he lightly doffed his hat,
No stranger in the crowd could doubt 'twas Casey at the bat.

Ten thousand eyes were on him as he rubbed his hands with dirt;
Five thousand tongues applauded when he wiped them on his shirt.
Then while the writhing pitcher ground the ball into his hip,
Defiance gleamed in Casey's eye, a sneer curled Casey's lip.

And now the leather-covered sphere came hurtling through the air,
And Casey stood a-watching it in haughty grandeur there.
Close by the sturdy batsman the ball unheeded sped—
"That ain't my style," said Casey. "Strike one," the umpire said.

From the benches back with people, there went up a muffled roar,
Like the beating of the storm-waves on a stern and distant shore.
"Kill him! Kill the umpire!" shouted some one on the stand;
And it's likely they'd have killed him had not Casey raised his hand.

With a smile of Christian charity great Casey's visage shone;
He stilled the rising tumult; he bade the game go on;
He signaled to the pitcher, and once more the spheroid flew;
But Casey still ignored it, and the umpire said, "Strike two."

"Fraud!" cried the maddened thousands, and echo answered fraud;
But one scornful look from Casey and the audience was awed.
They saw his face grow stern and cold, they saw his muscles strain,
And they knew that Casey wouldn't let that ball go by again.

The sneer is gone from Casey's lip, his teeth are clenched in hate;
He pounds with cruel violence his bat upon the plate.
And now the pitcher holds the ball, and now he lets it go,
And now the air is shattered by the force of Casey's blow.

Oh, somewhere in this favored land the sun is shining bright;
The band is playing somewhere, and somewhere hearts are light,
And somewhere men are laughing, and somewhere children shout;
But there is no joy in Mudville—mighty Casey has struck out.

Edgar Rice Burroughs / *Tarzan of the Apes*

[*Tarzan Meets Jane; or Girl Goes Ape*] 1914

A one-time soldier, policeman, cowboy, Sears-Roebuck department store manager, advertising copywriter, gold miner, salesman, and business failure, Edgar Rice Burroughs (1875–1950) began one of the most successful writing careers in the history of popular literature with the publication of Tarzan of the Apes. *The first of a series of twenty-six novels,* Tarzan of the Apes *initially appeared in* The All Story *magazine for October 1912 and, when no publisher would touch it, was serialized in the* New York Evening World. *The newspaper serialization triggered a demand for the story in book form, and* Tarzan of the Apes *was finally published in 1914.*

Tarzan provided exactly the kind of material the new movie industry was looking for. The first Tarzan film was released in 1918, and the series remained popular until the 1960s. Burroughs' fantasies posed a challenge to "realism" that Hollywood must have delighted in, as the following description of the technical efforts that went into producing Tarzan's barbaric yawp so perfectly demonstrates:

> *M-G-M spared no expense on the Tarzan yell. Miles of sound track of human, animal and instrument sounds were tested in collecting the ingredients of an unearthly howl. The cry of a mother camel robbed of her young was used until still more mournful sounds were found. A combination of five different sound tracks is used today for the Tarzan yell. There are: 1. Sound track of Weissmuller yelling amplified. 2. Track of hyena howl, run backward and volume diminished. 3. Soprano note sung by Lorraine Bridges, recording on sound track at reduced*

speed; then rerecorded at varying speeds to give a "flutter" in sound. 4. Growl of dog, recorded very faintly. 5. Raspy note of violin G-string, recorded very faintly. In the experimental stage the five sound tracks were played over five different loud speakers. From time to time the speed of each sound track was varied and the volume amplified or diminished. When the orchestration of the yell was perfected, the five loudspeakers were played simultaneously and the blended sounds recorded on the master sound track. By constant practice Weissmuller is now able to let loose an almost perfect imitation of the sound track.

From the time Tarzan left the tribe of great anthropoids in which he had been raised, it was torn by continual strife and discord. Terkoz proved a cruel and capricious king, so that, one by one, many of the older and weaker apes, upon whom he was particularly prone to vent his brutish nature, took their families and sought the quiet and safety of the far interior.

But at last those who remained were driven to desperation by the continued truculence of Terkoz, and it so happened that one of them recalled the parting admonition of Tarzan:

"If you have a chief who is cruel, do not do as the other apes do, and attempt, any one of you, to pit yourself against him alone. But, instead, let two or three or four of you attack him together. Then, if you will do this, no chief will dare to be other than he should be, for four of you can kill any chief who may ever be over you."

And the ape who recalled this wise counsel repeated it to several of his fellows, so that when Terkoz returned to the tribe that day he found a warm reception awaiting him.

There were no formalities. As Terkoz reached the group, five huge, hairy beasts sprang upon him.

At heart he was an arrant coward, which is the way with bullies among apes as well as among men; so he did not remain to fight and die, but tore himself away from them as quickly as he could and fled into the sheltering boughs of the forest.

Two more attempts he made to rejoin the tribe, but on each occasion he was set upon and driven away. At last he gave it up, and turned, foaming with rage and hatred, into the jungle.

For several days he wandered aimlessly, nursing his spite and looking for some weak thing on which to vent his pent anger.

It was in this state of mind that the horrible, man-like beast, swinging from tree to tree, came suddenly upon two women in the jungle.

He was right above them when he discovered them. The first intimation Jane Porter had of his presence was when the great hairy body dropped to the earth beside her, and she saw the awful face and the snarling, hideous mouth thrust within a foot of her.

One piercing scream escaped her lips as the brute hand clutched her arm. Then she was dragged toward those awful fangs which yawned at her throat. But ere they touched that fair skin another mood claimed the anthropoid.

The tribe had kept his women. He must find others to replace them. This hairless white ape would be the first of his new household, and so he threw her roughly across his broad, hairy shoulders and leaped back into the trees, bearing Jane away.

Esmeralda's scream of terror had mingled once with that of Jane, and then, as was Esmeralda's manner under stress of emergency which required presence of mind, she swooned.

But Jane did not once lose consciousness. It is true that that awful face, pressing close to hers, and the stench of the foul breath beating upon her nostrils, paralyzed her with terror; but her brain was clear, and she comprehended all that transpired.

With what seemed to her marvelous rapidity the brute bore her through the forest, but still she did not cry out or struggle. The sudden advent of the ape had confused her to such an extent that she thought now that he was bearing her toward the beach.

For this reason she conserved her energies and her voice until she could see that they had approached near enough to the camp to attract the succor she craved.

She could not have known it, but she was being borne farther and farther into the impenetrable jungle.

The scream that had brought Clayton and the two older men stumbling through the undergrowth had led Tarzan of the Apes straight to where Esmeralda lay, but it was not Esmeralda in whom his interest centered, though pausing over her he saw that she was unhurt.

For a moment he scrutinized the ground below and the trees above, until the ape that was in him by virtue of training and environment, combined with the intelligence that was his by right of birth, told his wondrous woodcraft the whole story as plainly as though he had seen the thing happen with his own eyes.

And then he was gone again into the swaying trees, following the high-flung spoor which no other human eye could have detected, much less translated.

At boughs' ends, where the anthropoid swings from one tree to another, there is most to mark the trail, but least to point the direction of the quarry; for there the pressure is downward always, toward the small end of the branch, whether the ape be leaving or entering a tree. Nearer the center of the tree, where the signs of passage are fainter, the direction is plainly marked.

Here, on this branch, a caterpillar has been crushed by the fugitive's great foot, and Tarzan knows instinctively where that same foot would touch in the next stride. Here he looks to find a tiny particle of the demolished larva, ofttimes not more than a speck of moisture.

Again, a minute bit of bark has been upturned by the scraping hand, and the direction of the break indicates the direction of the passage. Or some great limb, or the stem of the tree itself has been brushed by the hairy body, and a tiny shred of hair tells him by the direction from which it is wedged beneath the bark that he is on the right trail.

Nor does he need to check his speed to catch these seemingly faint records of the fleeing beast.

To Tarzan they stand out boldly against all the myriad other scars and bruises and signs upon the leafy way. But strongest of all is the scent, for Tarzan is pursuing up the wind, and his trained nostrils are as sensitive as a hound's.

There are those who believe that the lower orders are specially endowed by nature with better olfactory nerves than man, but it is merely a matter of development.

Man's survival does not hinge so greatly upon the perfection of his senses. His power to reason has relieved them of many of their duties, and so they have, to some extent, atrophied, as have the muscles which move the ears and scalp, merely from disuse.

The muscles are there, about the ears and beneath the scalp, and so are the nerves which transmit sensations to the brain, but they are under-developed because they are not needed.

Not so with Tarzan of the Apes. From early infancy his survival had depended upon acuteness of eyesight, hearing, smell, touch, and taste far more than upon the more slowly developed organ of reason.

The least developed of all in Tarzan was the sense of taste, for he could eat luscious fruits, or raw flesh, long buried with almost equal appreciation; but in that he differed but slightly from more civilized epicures.

Almost silently the ape-man sped on in the track of Terkoz and his prey, but the sound of his approach reached the ears of the fleeing beast and spurred it on to greater speed.

Three miles were covered before Tarzan overtook them, and then Terkoz, seeing that further flight was futile, dropped to the ground in a small open glade, that he might turn and fight for his prize or be free to escape unhampered if he saw that the pursuer was more than a match for him.

He still grasped Jane in one great arm as Tarzan bounded like a leopard into the arena which nature had provided for this primeval-like battle.

When Terkoz saw that it was Tarzan who pursued him, he jumped to the conclusion that this was Tarzan's woman, since they were of the same kind—white and hairless—and so he rejoiced at this opportunity for double revenge upon his hated enemy.

To Jane the strange apparition of this god-like man was as wine to sick nerves.

From the description which Clayton and her father and Mr. Philander had given her, she knew that it must be the same wonderful creature who had saved them, and she saw in him only a protector and a friend.

But as Terkoz pushed her roughly aside to meet Tarzan's charge, and she saw the great proportions of the ape and the mighty muscles and the fierce fangs, her heart quailed. How could any vanquish such a mighty antagonist?

Like two charging bulls they came together, and like two wolves sought each other's throat. Against the long canines of the ape was pitted the thin blade of the man's knife.

Jane—her lithe, young form flattened against the trunk of a great tree, her hands tight pressed against her rising and falling bosom, and her eyes wide with mingled horror, fascination, fear, and admiration—watched the primordial ape battle with the primeval man for possession of a woman—for her.

As the great muscles of the man's back and shoulders knotted beneath the tension of his efforts, and the huge biceps and forearm held at bay those mighty tusks, the veil of centuries of civilization and culture was swept from the blurred vision of the Baltimore girl.

When the long knife drank deep a dozen times of Terkoz' heart's blood, and the great carcass rolled lifeless upon the ground, it was a primeval woman who sprang forward with outstretched arms toward the primeval man who had fought for her and won her.

And Tarzan?

He did what no red-blooded man needs lessons in doing. He took his woman in his arms and smothered her upturned, panting lips with kisses.

For a moment Jane lay there with half-closed eyes. For a moment—the first in her young life—she knew the meaning of love.

But as suddenly as the veil had been withdrawn it dropped again, and an outraged conscience suffused her face with its scarlet mantle, and a mortified woman thrust Tarzan of the Apes from her and buried her face in her hands.

Tarzan had been surprised when he had found the girl he had learned to love after a vague and abstract manner a willing prisoner in his arms. Now he was surprised that she repulsed him.

He came close to her once more and took hold of her arm. She turned upon him like a tigress, striking his great breast with her tiny hands.

Tarzan could not understand it.

A moment ago and it had been his intention to hasten Jane back to her people, but that little moment was lost now in the dim and distant past of things which were but can never be again, and with it the good intention had gone to join the impossible.

Since then Tarzan of the Apes had felt a warm, lithe form close pressed to his. Hot, sweet breath against his cheek and mouth had fanned a new flame to life within his breast, and perfect lips had clung to his in burning kisses that had seared a deep brand into his soul—a brand which marked a new Tarzan.

Again he laid his hand upon her arm. Again she repulsed him. And then Tarzan of the Apes did just what his first ancestor would have done.

He took his woman in his arms and carried her into the jungle. . . .

When Jane realized that she was being borne away a captive by the strange forest creature who had rescued her from the clutches of the ape she struggled desperately to escape, but the strong arms that held her as easily as though she had been but a day-old babe only pressed a little more tightly.

So presently she gave up the futile effort and lay quietly, looking through half-closed lids at the face of the man who strode easily through the tangled undergrowth with her.

The face above her was one of extraordinary beauty.

A perfect type of the strongly masculine, unmarred by dissipation, or brutal or degrading passions. For, though Tarzan of the Apes was a killer of men and of beasts, he killed as the hunter kills, dispassionately, except on those rare occasions when he had killed for hate—though not the brooding, malevolent hate which marks the features of its own with hideous lines.

When Tarzan killed he more often smiled than scowled, and smiles are the foundation of beauty.

One thing the girl had noticed particularly when she had seen Tarzan rushing upon Terkoz—the vivid scarlet band upon his forehead, from above the left eye to the scalp; but now as she scanned his features she noticed that it was gone, and only a thin white line marked the spot where it had been.

As she lay more quietly in his arms Tarzan slightly relaxed his grip upon her.

Once he looked down into her eyes and smiled, and the girl had to close her own to shut out the vision of that handsome, winning face.

Presently Tarzan took to the trees, and Jane, wondering that she felt no fear, began to realize that in many respects she had never felt more secure in her whole life than now as she lay in the arms of this strong, wild creature, being borne, God alone knew where or to what fate, deeper and deeper into the savage fastness of the untamed forest.

When, with closed eyes, she commenced to speculate upon the future, and terrifying fears were conjured by a vivid imagination, she had but to raise her lids and look upon that noble face so close to hers to dissipate the last remnant of apprehension.

No, he could never harm her; of that she was convinced when she translated the fine features and the frank, brave eyes above her into the chivalry which they proclaimed.

On and on they went through what seemed to Jane a solid mass of verdure, yet ever there appeared to open before this forest god a passage, as by magic, which closed behind them as they passed.

Scarce a branch scraped against her, yet above and below, before and behind, the view presented naught but a solid mass of inextricably interwoven branches and creepers.

As Tarzan moved steadily onward his mind was occupied with many strange and new thoughts. Here was a problem the like of which he had never encountered, and he felt rather than reasoned that he must meet it as a man and not as an ape.

The free movement through the middle terrace, which was the route he had followed for the most part, had helped to cool the ardor of the first fierce passion of his new found love.

Now he discovered himself speculating upon the fate which would have fallen to the girl had he not rescued her from Terkoz.

He knew why the ape had not killed her, and he commenced to compare his intentions with those of Terkoz.

True, it was the order of the jungle for the male to take his mate by force; but could Tarzan be guided by the laws of the beasts? Was not Tarzan a Man? But what did men do? He was puzzled; for he did not know.

He wished that he might ask the girl, and then it came to him that she had already answered him in the futile struggle she had made to escape and to repulse him.

But now they had come to their destination, and Tarzan of the Apes with Jane in his strong arms, swung lightly to the turf of the arena where the great apes held their councils and danced the wild orgy of the Dum-Dum.

Though they had come many miles, it was still but midafternoon, and the amphitheater was bathed in the half light which filtered through the maze of encircling foliage.

The green turf looked soft and cool and inviting. The myriad noises of the jungle seemed far distant and hushed to a mere echo of blurred sounds, rising and falling like the surf upon a remote shore.

A feeling of dreamy peacefulness stole over Jane as she sank down upon the grass where Tarzan had placed her, and as she looked up at his great figure towering above her, there was added a strange sense of perfect security.

As she watched him from beneath half-closed lids, Tarzan crossed the little circular clearing toward the trees upon the further side. She noted the graceful majesty of his carriage, the perfect symmetry of his magnificent figure and the poise of his well-shaped head upon his broad shoulders.

What a perfect creature! There could be naught of cruelty or baseness beneath that godlike exterior. Never, she thought had such a man strode the earth since God created the first in his own image.

With a bound Tarzan sprang into the trees and disappeared. Jane wondered where he had gone. Had he left her there to her fate in the lonely jungle?

She glanced nervously about. Every vine and bush seemed but the lurking-place of some huge and horrible beast waiting to bury gleaming fangs into her soft flesh. Every sound she magnified into the stealthy creeping of a sinuous and malignant body.

How different now that he had left her!

For a few minutes that seemed hours to the frightened girl, she sat with tense nerves waiting for the spring of the crouching thing that was to end her misery of apprehension.

She almost prayed for the cruel teeth that would give her unconsciousness and surcease from the agony of fear.

She heard a sudden, slight sound behind her. With a cry she sprang to her feet and turned to face her end.

There stood Tarzan, his arms filled with ripe and luscious fruit.

Jane reeled and would have fallen, had not Tarzan, dropping his burden, caught her in his arms. She did not lose consciousness, but she clung tightly to him, shuddering and trembling like a frightened deer.

Tarzan of the Apes stroked her soft hair and tried to comfort and quiet her as Kala had him, when, as a little ape, he had been frightened by Sabor, the lioness, or Histah, the snake.

Once he pressed his lips lightly upon her forehead, and she did not move, but closed her eyes and sighed.

She could not analyze her feelings, nor did she wish to attempt it. She was satisfied to feel the safety of those strong arms, and to leave her future to fate; for the last few hours had taught her to trust this strange wild creature of the forest as she would have trusted but few of the men of her acquaintance.

As she thought of the strangeness of it, there commenced to dawn upon her the realization that she had, possibly, learned something else which she had never really known before—love. She wondered and then she smiled.

And still smiling, she pushed Tarzan gently away; and looking at him with a half-smiling, half-quizzical expression that made her face wholly entrancing, she pointed to the fruit upon the ground, and seated herself upon the edge of the earthen drum of the anthropoids, for hunger was asserting itself.

Tarzan quickly gathered up the fruit, and, bringing it, laid it at her feet; and then he, too, sat upon the drum beside her, and with his knife opened and prepared the various fruits for her meal.

Together and in silence they ate, occasionally stealing sly glances at one another, until finally Jane broke into a merry laugh in which Tarzan joined.

"I wish you spoke English," said the girl.

Tarzan shook his head, and an expression of wistful and pathetic longing sobered his laughing eyes.

Then Jane tried speaking to him in French, and then in German; but she had to laugh at her own blundering attempt at the latter tongue.

"Anyway," she said to him in English, "you understand my German as well as they did in Berlin."

Tarzan had long since reached a decision as to what his future procedure should be. He had had time to recollect all that he had read of the ways of men and women in the books at the cabin. He would act as he imagined the men in the books would have acted were they in his place.

Again he rose and went into the trees, but first he tried to explain by means of signs that he would return shortly, and he did so well that Jane understood and was not afraid when he had gone.

Only a feeling of loneliness came over her and she watched the point where he had disappeared, with longing eyes, awaiting his return. As before, she was appraised of his presence by a soft sound behind her, and turned to see him coming across the turf with a great armful of branches.

Then he went back again into the jungle and in a few minutes reappeared with a quantity of soft grasses and ferns. Two more trips he made until he had quite a pile of material at hand.

Then he spread the ferns and grasses upon the ground in a soft flat bed, and above it leaned many branches together so that they met a few feet over its center. Upon these he spread layers of huge leaves of the great elephant's ear, and with more branches and more leaves he closed one end of the little shelter he had built.

Then they sat down together again upon the edge of the drum and tried to talk by signs.

The magnificent diamond locket which hung about Tarzan's neck, had been a source of much wonderment to Jane. She pointed to it now, and Tarzan removed it and handed the pretty bauble to her.

She saw that it was the work of a skilled artisan and that the diamonds were of great brilliancy and superbly set, but the cutting of them denoted that they were of a former day.

She noticed too that the locket opened, and, pressing the hidden clasp, she saw the two halves spring apart to reveal in either section an ivory miniature.

One was of a beautiful woman and the other might have been a likeness of the man who sat beside her, except for a subtle difference of expression that was scarcely definable.

She looked up at Tarzan to find him leaning toward her gazing on the miniatures with an expression of astonishment. He reached out his hand for the locket and took it away from her, examining the likenesses within with unmistakable signs of surprise and new interest. His manner clearly denoted that he had never before seen them, nor imagined that the locket opened.

This fact caused Jane to indulge in further speculation, and it taxed her imagination to picture how this beautiful ornament came into the possession of a wild and savage creature of the unexplored jungles of Africa.

Still more wonderful was how it contained the likeness of one who might be a brother, or, more likely, the father of this woodland demi-god who was even ignorant of the fact that the locket opened.

Tarzan was still gazing with fixity at the two faces. Presently he removed the quiver from his shoulder, and emptying the arrows upon the ground reached into the bottom of the bag-like receptacle and drew forth a flat object wrapped in many soft leaves and tied with bits of long grass.

Carefully he unwrapped it, removing layer after layer of leaves until at length he held a photograph in his hand.

Pointing to the miniature of the man within the locket he handed the photograph to Jane, holding the open locket beside it.

The photograph only served to puzzle the girl still more, for it was evidently another likeness of the same man whose picture rested in the locket beside that of the beautiful young woman.

Tarzan was looking at her with an expression of puzzled bewilderment in his eyes as she glanced up at him. He seemed to be framing a question with his lips.

The girl pointed to the photograph and then to the miniature and then to him, as though to indicate that she thought the likenesses were of him, but he only shook his head, and then shrugging his great shoulders, he took the photograph from her and having carefully rewrapped it, placed it again in the bottom of his quiver.

For a few moments he sat in silence, his eyes bent upon the ground, while Jane held the little locket in her hand, turning it over and over in an endeavor to find some further clue that might lead to the identity of its original owner.

At length a simple explanation occurred to her.

The locket had belonged to Lord Greystoke, and the likenesses were of himself and Lady Alice.

This wild creature had simply found it in the cabin by the beach. How stupid of her not to have thought of that solution before.

But to account for the strange likeness between Lord Greystoke and this forest god—that was quite beyond her, and it is not strange that she could not imagine that this naked savage was indeed an English nobleman.

At length Tarzan looked up to watch the girl as she examined the locket. He could not fathom the meaning of the faces within, but he could read the interest and fascination upon the face of the live young creature by his side.

She noticed that he was watching her and thinking that he wished his ornament again she held it out to him. He took it from her and taking the chain in his two hands he placed it about her neck, smiling at her expression of surprise at his unexpected gift.

Jane shook her head vehemently and would have removed the golden links from about her throat, but Tarzan would not let her. Taking her hands in his, when she insisted upon it, he held them tightly to prevent her.

At last she desisted and with a little laugh raised the locket to her lips.

Tarzan did not know precisely what she meant, but he guessed correctly that it was her way of acknowledging the gift, and so he rose, and taking the locket in his hand, stooped gravely like some courtier of old, and pressed his lips upon it where hers had rested.

It was a stately and gallant little compliment performed with the grace and dignity of utter unconsciousness of self. It was the hall-mark of his aristocratic birth, the natural out-cropping of many generations of fine breeding, an hereditary instinct of graciousness which a lifetime of uncouth and savage training and environment could not eradicate.

It was growing dark now, and so they ate again of the fruit which was both food and drink for them; then Tarzan rose, and leading Jane to the little bower he had erected, motioned her to go within.

For the first time in hours a feeling of fear swept over her, and Tarzan felt her draw away as though shrinking from him.

Contact with this girl for half a day had left a very different Tarzan from the one on whom the morning's sun had risen.

Now, in every fiber of his being, heredity spoke louder than training.

He had not in one swift transition become a polished gentleman from a savage ape-man, but at last the instincts of the former predominated, and over all was the desire to please the woman he loved, and to appear well in her eyes.

So Tarzan of the Apes did the only thing he knew to assure Jane of her safety. He removed his hunting knife from its sheath and handed it to her hilt first, again motioning her into the bower.

The girl understood, and taking the long knife she entered and lay down upon the soft grasses while Tarzan of the Apes stretched himself upon the ground across the entrance.

And thus the rising sun found them in the morning.

When Jane awoke, she did not at first recall the strange events of the preceding day, and so she wondered at her odd surroundings—the little leafy bower, the soft grasses of her bed, the unfamiliar prospect from the opening at her feet.

Slowly the circumstances of her position crept one by one into her mind. And then a great wonderment arose in her heart—a mighty wave of thankfulness and gratitude that though she had been in such terrible danger, yet she was unharmed.

She moved to the entrance of the shelter to look for Tarzan. He was gone; but this time no fear assailed her for she knew that he would return.

In the grass at the entrance to her bower she saw the imprint of his body where he had lain all night to guard her. She knew that the fact that he had been there was all that had permitted her to sleep in such peaceful security.

With him near, who could entertain fear? She wondered if there was another man on earth with whom a girl could feel so safe in the heart of this savage African jungle. Even the lions and panthers had no fears for her now.

She looked up to see his lithe form drop softly from a near-by tree. As he caught her eyes upon him his face lighted with that frank and radiant smile that had won her confidence the day before.

As he approached her Jane's heart beat faster and her eyes brightened as they had never done before at the approach of any man.

He had again been gathering fruit and this he laid at the entrance of her bower. Once more they sat down together to eat.

Jane commenced to wonder what his plans were. Would he take her back to the beach or would he keep her here? Suddenly she realized that the matter did not seem to give her much concern. Could it be that she did not care!

She began to comprehend, also, that she was entirely contented sitting here by the side of this smiling giant eating delicious fruit in a sylvan paradise far within the remote depths of an African jungle—that she was contented and very happy.

She could not understand it. Her reason told her that she should be torn by wild anxieties, weighted by dread fears, cast down by gloomy forebodings; but instead, her heart was singing and she was smiling into the answering face of the man beside her.

When they had finished their breakfast Tarzan went to her bower and recovered his knife. The girl had entirely forgotten it. She realized that it was because she had forgotten the fear that prompted her to accept it.

Motioning her to follow, Tarzan walked toward the trees at the edge of the arena, and taking her in one strong arm swung to the branches above.

The girl knew that he was taking her back to her people, and she could not understand the sudden feeling of loneliness and sorrow which crept over her.

For hours they swung slowly along.

Tarzan of the Apes did not hurry. He tried to draw out the sweet pleasure of that journey with those dear arms about his neck as long as possible, and so he went far south of the direct route to the beach.

Several times they halted for brief rests, which Tarzan did not need, and at noon they stopped for an hour at a little brook, where they quenched their thirst, and ate.

So it was nearly sunset when they came to the clearing, and Tarzan, dropping to the ground beside a great tree, parted the tall jungle grass and pointed out the little cabin to her.

She took him by the hand to lead him to it, that she might tell her father that this man had saved her from death and worse than death, that he had watched over her as carefully as a mother might have done.

But again the timidity of the wild thing in the face of human habitation swept over Tarzan of the Apes. He drew back, shaking his head.

The girl came close to him, looking up with pleading eyes. Somehow she could not bear the thought of his going back into the terrible jungle alone.

Still he shook his head, and finally he drew her to him very gently and stooped to kiss her, but first he looked into her eyes and waited to learn if she were pleased, or if she would repulse him.

Just an instant the girl hesitated, and then she realized the truth, and throwing her arms about his neck she drew his face to hers and kissed him—unashamed.

"I love you—I love you," she murmured.

From far in the distance came the faint sound of many guns. Tarzan and Jane raised their heads.

From the cabin came Mr. Philander and Esmeralda.

From where Tarzan and the girl stood they could not see the two vessels lying at anchor in the harbor.

Tarzan pointed toward the sounds, touched his breast and pointed again. She understood. He was going, and something told her that it was because he thought her people were in danger.

Again he kissed her.

"Come back to me," she whispered. "I shall wait for you—always."

Dale Carnegie / *How To Win Friends and Influence People* 1936

One of the most successful nonfiction books in the history of American publishing, How To Win Friends and Influence People *was the culmination of Dale Carnegie's experiences in training thousands of business and professional people in the art of public speaking and in the techniques of "handling people." A compilation of popular psychology, etiquette rules, and after-dinner speech ancedotes,* How To Win Friends and Influence People *suggests that the fuzzy areas of social relationships and human discourse can be gotten through effectively and profitably with elocutionary acumen, a little shrewdness, and the application of proper procedures.*

FUNDAMENTAL TECHNIQUES IN HANDLING PEOPLE

CHAPTER 1: "IF YOU WANT TO GATHER HONEY, DON'T KICK OVER THE BEEHIVE"

On May 7, 1931, New York City witnessed the most sensational man-hunt the old town had ever known. After weeks of search, "Two Gun" Crowley—the killer, the gunman who didn't smoke or drink—was at bay, trapped in his sweetheart's apartment on West End Avenue.

One hundred and fifty policemen and detectives laid siege to his top-floor hideaway. Chopping holes in the roof, they tried to smoke out Crowley, the "cop killer," with tear gas. Then they mounted their machine guns on surrounding buildings, and for more than an hour one of New York's fine residential sections reverberated with the crack of pistol fire and the rat-tat-tat of machine guns. Crowley, crouching behind an overstuffed chair, fired incessantly at the police. Ten thousand excited people watched the battle. Nothing like it had ever been seen before on the sidewalks of New York.

When Crowley was captured, Police Commissioner Mulrooney declared that the two-gun desperado was one of the most dangerous criminals ever encountered in the history of New York. "He will kill," said the Commissioner, "at the drop of a feather."

But how did "Two Gun" Crowley regard himself? We know, because while the police were firing into his apartment, he wrote a letter addressed "To whom it may concern." And, as he wrote, the blood flowing from his wounds left a crimson trail on the paper. In this letter Crowley said: "Under my coat is a weary heart, but a kind one—one that would do nobody any harm."

A short time before this, Crowley had been having a necking party on a country road out on Long Island. Suddenly a policeman walked up to the parked car and said: "Let me see your license."

Without saying a word, Crowley drew his gun, and cut the policeman down with a shower of lead. As the dying officer fell, Crowley leaped out of the car, grabbed the officer's revolver, and fired another bullet into the prostrate body. And that was the killer who said: "Under my coat is a weary heart, but a kind one—one that would do nobody any harm."

Crowley was sentenced to the electric chair. When he arrived at the death house at Sing Sing, did he say, "This is what I get for killing people?" No, he said: "This is what I get for defending myself."

The point of the story is this: "Two Gun" Crowley didn't blame himself for anything.

Is that an unusual attitude among criminals? If you think so, listen to this:

"I have spent the best years of my life giving people the lighter pleasures, helping them have a good time, and all I get is abuse, the existence of a hunted man."

That's Al Capone speaking. Yes, America's erstwhile Public Enemy Number One—the most sinister gang leader who ever shot up Chicago. Capone doesn't condemn himself. He actually regards himself as a public benefactor—an unappreciated and misunderstood public benefactor.

And so did Dutch Schultz before he crumpled up under gangster bullets in Newark. Dutch Schultz, one of New York's most notorious rats, said in a newspaper interview that he was a public benefactor. And he believed it.

I have had some interesting correspondence with Warden Lawes of Sing Sing on this subject, and he declares that "few of the criminals in Sing Sing regard themselves as bad men. They are just as human as you and I. So they rationalize, they explain. They can tell you why they had to crack a safe or be quick on the trigger finger. Most of them attempt by a form of reasoning, fallacious or logical, to justify their anti-social acts even to themselves, consequently stoutly maintaining that they should never have been imprisoned at all."

If Al Capone, "Two Gun" Crowley, Dutch Schultz, the desperate men behind prison walls don't blame themselves for anything—what about the people with whom you and I come in contact?

The late John Wanamaker once confessed: "I learned thirty years ago that it is foolish to scold. I have enough trouble overcoming my own limitations without fretting over the fact that God has not seen fit to distribute evenly the gift of intelligence."

Wanamaker learned this lesson early; but I personally had to blunder through this old world for a third of a century before it even began to dawn upon me that ninety-nine times out of a hundred, no man ever criticizes himself for anything, no matter how wrong he may be.

Criticism is futile because it puts a man on the defensive, and usually makes him strive to justify himself. Criticism is dangerous, because it wounds a man's precious pride, hurts his sense of importance, and arouses his resentment.

The German army won't let a soldier file a complaint and make a criticism immediately after a thing has happened. He has to sleep on his grudge first and cool off. If he files his complaint immediately, he is punished. By the eternals, there ought to be a law like that in civil life too—a law for whining parents and nagging wives and scolding employers and the whole obnoxious parade of fault-finders.

You will find examples of the futility of criticism bristling on a thousand pages of history. Take, for example, the famous quarrel between Theodore Roosevelt and President Taft—a quarrel that split the Republican Party, put Woodrow Wilson in the White House, and wrote bold, luminous lines across the World War and altered the flow of history. Let's review the facts quickly: When Theodore Roosevelt stepped out of the White House in 1908, he made Taft president, and then went off to Africa to shoot lions. When he returned, he exploded. He denounced Taft for his conservatism, tried to secure the nomination for a third term himself, formed the Bull Moose Party, and all but demolished the G.O.P. In the election that followed, William Howard Taft and the Republican Party carried only two states—Vermont and Utah. The most disastrous defeat the old party had ever known.

Theodore Roosevelt blamed Taft; but did President Taft blame himself? Of course not. With tears in his eyes, Taft said: "I don't see how I could have done any differently from what I have."

Who was to blame? Roosevelt or Taft? Frankly, I don't know, and I don't care. The point I am trying to make is that all of Theodore Roosevelt's criticism didn't persuade Taft that he was wrong. It merely made Taft strive to justify himself and to reiterate with tears in his eyes: "I don't see how I could have done any differently from what I have."

Or, take the Teapot Dome Oil scandal. Remember it? It kept the newspapers ringing with indignation for years. It rocked the nation! Nothing like it had ever happened before in American public life within the memory of living men. Here are the bare facts of the scandal: Albert Fall, Secretary of the Interior in Harding's cabinet, was entrusted with the leasing of government oil reserves at Elk Hill and Teapot Dome—oil reserves that had been set aside for the future use of the Navy. Did Secretary Fall permit competitive bidding? No sir. He handed the fat, juicy contract outright to his friend, Edward L. Doheny. And what did Doheny do? He gave Secretary Fall what he was pleased to call a "loan" of one hundred thousand dollars. Then, in a high-handed manner, Secretary Fall ordered United States Marines into the district to drive off competitors whose adjacent wells were sapping oil out of the Elk Hill reserves. These competitors, driven off their ground at the ends of guns and bayonets, rushed into court—and blew the lid off the hundred million dollar Teapot Dome scandal. A stench arose so vile that it ruined the Harding administration, nauseated an entire nation, threatened to wreck the Republican Party, and put Albert B. Fall behind prison bars.

Fall was condemned viciously—condemned as few men in public life have ever been. Did he repent? Never! Years later Herbert Hoover intimated in a public speech that President Harding's death had been due to mental anxiety and worry because a friend had betrayed him. When Mrs. Fall heard that, she sprang from her chair, she wept, she shook her fists at fate, and screamed: "What! Harding betrayed by Fall? No! My husband never betrayed anyone. This whole house full of gold would not tempt my husband to do wrong. He is the one who has been betrayed and led to the slaughter and crucified."

There you are; human nature in action, the wrong-doer blaming everybody but himself. We are all like that. So when you and I are tempted to criticize someone tomorrow, let's remember Al Capone, "Two Gun" Crowley, and Albert Fall. Let's realize that criticisms are like homing pigeons. They always return home. Let's realize that the person we are going to correct and condemn will probably justify himself, and condemn us in return; or, like the gentle Taft, he will say: "I don't see how I could have done any differently from what I have."

On Saturday morning, April 15, 1865, Abraham Lincoln lay dying in a hall bedroom of a cheap lodging house directly across the street from Ford's Theatre, where Booth had shot him. Lincoln's long body lay stretched diagonally across a sagging bed that was too short for him. A cheap reproduction of Rosa Bonheur's famous painting, "The Horse Fair," hung above the bed, and a dismal gas jet flickered yellow light.

As Lincoln lay dying, Secretary of War Stanton said, "There lies the most perfect ruler of men that the world has ever seen."

What was the secret of Lincoln's success in dealing with men? I studied the life of Abraham Lincoln for ten years, and devoted all of three years to writing and rewriting a book entitled *Lincoln the Unknown.* I believe I have made as detailed and exhaustive a study of Lincoln's personality and home life as it is possible for any human being to make. I made a special study of Lincoln's method of dealing with men. Did he indulge in criticism? Oh, yes. As a young man in the Pigeon Creek Valley of Indiana, he not only criticized but he wrote letters and poems ridiculing people and dropped these letters on the country roads where they were sure to be found. One of these letters aroused resentments that burned for a lifetime.

Even after Lincoln had become a practicing lawyer in Springfield, Illinois, he attacked his opponents openly in letters published in the newspapers. But he did this just once too often.

In the autumn of 1842, he ridiculed a vain, pugnacious Irish politician by the name of James Shields. Lincoln lampooned him through an anonymous letter published in the *Springfield Journal.* The town roared with laughter. Shields, sensitive and proud, boiled with indignation. He found out who wrote the letter, leaped on his horse, started after Lincoln, and challenged him to fight a duel. Lincoln didn't want to fight. He was opposed to dueling; but he couldn't get out of it and save his honor. He was given the choice of weapons. Since he had very long arms, he chose cavalry broad swords, took lessons in sword fighting from a West Point graduate; and, on the appointed day, he and Shields met on a sand bar in the Mississippi River, prepared to fight to the death; but, at the last minute, their seconds interrupted and stopped the duel.

That was the most lurid personal incident in Lincoln's life. It taught him an invaluable lesson in the art of dealing with people. Never again did he write an insulting letter. Never again did he ridicule anyone. And from that time on, he almost never criticized anybody for anything.

Time after time, during the Civil War, Lincoln put a new general at the head of the Army of the Potomac, and each one in turn—McClellan, Pope, Burnside, Hooker, Meade—blundered tragically, and drove Lincoln to pacing the floor in despair. Half the nation savagely condemned these incompetent generals, but Lincoln, "with malice towards none, with charity for all," held his peace. One of his favorite quotations was "Judge not, that ye be not judged."

And when Mrs. Lincoln and others spoke harshly of the Southern people, Lincoln replied: "Don't criticize them; they are just what we would be under similar circumstances."

Yet, if any man ever had occasion to criticize, surely it was Lincoln. Let's take just one illustration:

The Battle of Gettysburg was fought during the first three days of July, 1863. During the night of July 4, Lee began to retreat southward while storm clouds deluged the country with rain. When Lee reached the Potomac with his defeated army, he found a swollen, impassable river in front of him, and a victorious Union army behind him. Lee was in a trap. He couldn't escape. Lincoln saw that. Here was a golden, heaven-sent opportunity—the opportunity to capture Lee's army and end the war immediately. So, with a surge of high hope, Lincoln ordered Meade not to call a council of war but to attack Lee immediately. Lincoln telegraphed his orders and then sent a special messenger to Meade demanding immediate action.

And what did General Meade do? He did the very opposite of what he was told to do. He called a council of war in direct violation of Lincoln's orders. He hesitated. He procrastinated. He telegraphed all manner of excuses. He refused point blank to attack Lee. Finally the waters receded and Lee escaped over the Potomac with his forces.

Lincoln was furious. "What does this mean?" Lincoln cried to his son Robert. "Great God! What does this mean? We had them within our grasp, and had only to stretch forth our hands and they were ours; yet nothing that I could say or do could make the army move. Under the circumstances, almost any general could have defeated Lee. If I had gone up there, I could have whipped him myself."

In bitter disappointment, Lincoln sat down and wrote Meade this letter. And remember, at this period of his life he was extremely conservative and restrained in his phraseology. So this letter coming from Lincoln in 1863 was tantamount to the severest rebuke.

"My dear General,

"I do not believe you appreciate the magnitude of the misfortune involved in Lee's escape. He was within our easy grasp, and to have closed upon him would, in connection with our other late successes, have ended the war. As it is, the war will be prolonged indefinitely. If you could not safely attack Lee last Monday, how can you possibly do so south of the river, when you can take with you very few—no more than two-thirds of the force you then had in hand? It would be unreasonable to expect and I do not expect that you can now effect much. Your golden opportunity is gone, and I am distressed immeasurably because of it."

What do you suppose Meade did when he read that letter?

Meade never saw that letter. Lincoln never mailed it. It was found among Lincoln's papers after his death.

My guess is—and this is only a guess—that after writing that letter, Lincoln looked out of the window and said to himself, "Just a minute. Maybe I ought not to be so hasty. It is easy enough for me to sit here in the quiet of the White House and order Meade to attack; but if I had been up at Gettysburg, and if I had seen as much blood as Meade has seen during the last week, and if my ears had been pierced with the screams and shrieks of the wounded and dying, maybe I wouldn't be so anxious to attack either. If I had Meade's timid temperament, perhaps I would have done just what he has done. Anyhow, it is water under the bridge now. If I send this letter, it will relieve my feelings but it will make Meade try to justify himself. It will make him condemn me. It will arouse hard feelings, impair all his further usefulness as a commander, and perhaps force him to resign from the army."

So, as I have already said, Lincoln put the letter aside, for he had learned by bitter experience that sharp criticisms and rebukes almost invariably end in futility.

Theodore Roosevelt said that when he, as President, was confronted with some perplexing problem, he used to lean back and look up at a large painting of Lincoln that hung above his desk in the White House and ask himself, "What would Lincoln do if he were in my shoes? How would he solve this problem?"

The next time we are tempted to give somebody "hail Columbia," let's pull a five-dollar bill out of our pocket, look at Lincoln's picture on the bill, and ask, "How would Lincoln handle this problem if he had it?"

Do you know someone you would like to change and regulate and improve? Good! That is fine. I am all in favor of it. But why not begin on yourself? From a purely selfish standpoint, that is a lot more profitable than trying to improve others—yes, and a lot less dangerous.

"When a man's fight begins within himself," said Browning, "he is worth something." It will probably take from now until Christmas to perfect yourself. You can then have a nice long rest over the holidays and devote the New Year to regulating and criticizing other people.

But perfect yourself first.

"Don't complain about the snow on your neighbor's roof," said Confucius, "when your own doorstep is unclean."

When I was still young and trying hard to impress people, I wrote a foolish letter to Richard Harding Davis, an author who once loomed large on the literary horizon of America. I was preparing a magazine article about authors; and I asked Davis to tell me about his method of work. A few weeks earlier, I had received a letter from someone with this notation at the bottom: "Dictated but not read." I was quite impressed. I felt the writer must be very big and busy and important. I wasn't the slightest bit busy; but I was eager to make an impression on Richard Harding Davis so I ended my short note with the words: "Dictated but not read."

He never troubled to answer the letter. He simply returned it to me with this scribbled across the bottom: "Your bad manners are exceeded only by your bad manners." True, I had blundered, and perhaps I deserved his rebuke. But, being human, I resented it. I resented it so sharply that when I read of the death of Richard Harding Davis ten years later, the one thought that still persisted in my mind—I am ashamed to admit—was the hurt he had given me.

If you and I want to stir up a resentment tomorrow that may rankle across the decades and endure until death, just let us indulge in a little stinging criticism—no matter how certain we are that it is justified.

When dealing with people, let us remember we are not dealing with creatures of logic. We are dealing with creatures of emotion, creatures bristling with prejudices and motivated by pride and vanity.

And criticism is a dangerous spark—a spark that is liable to cause an explosion in the powder magazine of pride—an explosion that sometimes hastens death. For example, General Leonard Wood was criticized and not allowed to go with the army to France. That blow to his pride probably shortened his life.

Bitter criticism caused the sensitive Thomas Hardy, one of the finest novelists that ever enriched English literature, to give up the writing of fiction forever. Criticism drove Thomas Chatterton, the English poet, to suicide.

Benjamin Franklin, tactless in his youth, became so diplomatic, so adroit at handling people that he was made American Ambassador to France. The secret of his success? "I will speak ill of no man," he said, ". . . and speak all the good I know of everybody."

Any fool can criticize, condemn, and complain—and most fools do.

But it takes character and self-control to be understanding and forgiving.

"A great man shows his greatness," said Carlyle, "by the way he treats little men."

Instead of condemning people, let's try to understand them. Let's try to figure out why they do what they do. That's a lot more profitable and intriguing than criticism; and it breeds sympathy, tolerance, and kindness. "To know all is to forgive all."

As Dr. Johnson said: "God Himself, sir, does not propose to judge man until the end of his days."

Why should you and I?

DISCUSSION QUESTIONS

1. Discuss whether Dale Carnegie's prose style is an implementation of his contention that "When dealing with people, let us remember we are not dealing with creatures of logic. We are dealing with creatures of emotion, creatures bristling with prejudices and motivated by pride and vanity." How does Carnegie try to convince his audience of the benefits gained by refraining from personal criticism?

2. Compare the sense of an audience implicit in *How To Win Friends and Influence People* with the audience imagined for Funk and Lewis' *Thirty Days to a More Powerful Vocabulary*. What characteristics are common to the audiences anticipated by these writers? What distinctions can you make between these audiences? Show how each writer's particular way of talking is indicative of the reader he imagines for his prose. How does the fact that these writers achieved a great deal of success affect the voices they adopt when addressing their readers?

Wilfred Funk and Norman Lewis / *Thirty Days to a More Powerful Vocabulary* 1942

Written in 1942 by Wilfred Funk, lexicographer, publisher, and author, and Norman Lewis, instructor in English at the City College of New York and New York University, Thirty Days to a More Powerful Vocabulary, *has been one of the most widely used "how-to-do-it" books published in this country. As an introductory "pep talk," "Give Us Fifteen Minutes A Day" started millions of students and adults off on a self-improvement regimen that promised nothing less than success and personal fulfillment when the exercises were completed.*

FIRST DAY: GIVE US 15 MINUTES A DAY

Your boss has a bigger vocabulary than you have.

That's one good reason why he's your boss.

This discovery has been made in the word laboratories of the world. Not by theoretical English professors, but by practical, hard-headed scholars who have been searching for the secrets of success.

After a host of experiments and years of testing they have found out:

That if your vocabulary is limited your chances of success are limited.

That one of the easiest and quickest ways to get ahead is by consciously building up your knowledge of words.

That the vocabulary of the average person almost stops growing by the middle twenties.

> And that from then on it is necessary to have an intelligent plan if progress is to be made. No haphazard hit-or-miss methods will do.

It has long since been satisfactorily established that a high executive does not have a large vocabulary merely because of the opportunities of his position. That would be putting the cart before the horse. Quite the reverse is true. His skill in words was a tremendous help in getting him his job.

Dr. Johnson O'Connor of the Human Engineering Laboratory of Boston and of the Stevens Institute of Technology in Hoboken, New Jersey, gave a vocabulary test to 100 young men who were studying to be industrial executives.

Five years later those who had passed in the upper ten per cent *all,* without exception, had executive positions, while *not a single young man of the lower twenty-five per cent had become an executive.*

You see, there are certain factors in success that can be measured as scientifically as the contents of a test-tube, and it has been discovered that the most common characteristic of outstanding success is "an extensive knowledge of the exact meaning of English words."

The extent of your vocabulary indicates the degree of your intelligence. Your brain power will increase as you learn to know more words. Here's the proof.

Two classes in a high school were selected for an experiment. Their ages and their environment were the same. Each class represented an identical cross-section of the community. One, the control class, took the normal courses. The other class was given special vocabulary training. At the end of the period the marks of the latter class surpassed those of the control group, not only in English, but in every subject, including mathematics and the sciences.

Similarly it has been found by Professor Lewis M. Terman, of Stanford University, that a vocabulary test is as accurate a measure of intelligence as any three units of the standard and accepted Stanford-Binet I. Q. tests.

The study of words is not merely something that has to do with literature. Words are your tools of thought. *You can't even think at all without them.* Try it. If you are planning to go down town this afternoon you will find that you are saying to yourself: "I think I will go down town this afternoon." You can't make such a simple decision as this without using words.

Without words you could make no decisions and form no judgments whatsoever. A pianist may have the most beautiful tunes in his head, but if he had only five keys on his piano he would never get more than a fraction of these tunes out.

Your words are *your* keys for *your* thoughts. And the more words you have at your command the deeper, clearer and more accurate will be your thinking.

A command of English will not only improve the processes of your mind. It will give you assurance; build your self-confidence; lend color to your personality; increase your popularity. Your words are your personality. Your vocabulary is you.

Your words are all that we, your friends, have to know and judge you by. You have no other medium for telling us your thoughts—for convincing us, persuading us, giving us orders.

Words are explosive. Phrases are packed with TNT. A simple word can destroy a friendship, land a large order. The proper phrases in the mouths of clerks have quadrupled the sales of a department store. The wrong words used by a campaign orator have lost an election. For instance, on one occasion the four unfortunate words, "Rum, Romanism and Rebellion" used in a Republican campaign speech threw the Catholic vote and the presidential victory to Grover Cleveland. Wars are won by words. Soldiers fight for a phrase. "Make the world safe for Democracy." "All out for England." "V for Victory." The "Remember the Maine" of Spanish war days has now been changed to "Remember Pearl Harbor."

Words have changed the direction of history. Words can also change the direction of your life. They have often raised a man from mediocrity to success.

If you consciously increase your vocabulary you will unconsciously raise yourself to a more important station in life, and the new and higher position you have won will, in turn, give you a better opportunity for further enriching your vocabulary. It is a beautiful and successful cycle.

It is because of this intimate connection between words and life itself that we have organized this small volume in a new way. We have not given you mere lists of unrelated words to learn. We håve grouped the words around various departments of your life.

This book is planned to enlist your active cooperation. The authors wish you to read it with a pencil in your hand, for you will often be asked to make certain notations, to write answers to particular questions. The more you use your pencil, the more deeply you will become involved, and the deeper your involvement the more this book will help you. We shall occasionally ask you to use your voice as well as your pencil—to say things out loud. You see, we really want you to keep up a running conversation with us.

It's fun. And it's so easy. And we've made it like a game. We have filled these pages with a collection of devices that we hope will be stimulating. Here are things to challenge you and your friends. Try these tests on your acquaintances. They will enjoy them and it may encourage them to wider explorations in this exciting field of speech. There are entertaining verbal calisthenics here, colorful facts about language, and many excursions among the words that keep our speech the rich, flexible, lively means of communication that it is.

Come to this book every day. Put the volume by your bedside, if you like. A short time spent on these pages before you turn the lights out each night is better than an irregular hour now and then. If you can find the time to learn only two or three words a day—we will still promise you that at the end of thirty days you will have found a new interest. Give us *fifteen minutes a day*, and we will guarantee, at the end of a month, when you have turned over the last page of this book, that your words and your reading and your conversation and your life will all have a new and deeper meaning for you.

For words can make you great!

Ogden Nash / Kindly Unhitch That Star, Buddy 1945

Few writers, especially in the twentieth century, have been able to earn a living exclusively by writing poetry. Ogden Nash is one who has. The Pocket Book of Ogden Nash *(1935) ranks among the top ten poetry bestsellers of the last eighty years and nearly every volume of his poetry from* Free Wheeling *(1931) to* Boy Is a Boy *(1960) have found highly receptive audiences.*

Nash (1902–71) is a master of what is usually termed "light verse"—poetry that is witty, humorous, often sophisticated, and not without a slight sting of satire. Nash brought to light verse an exceptionally playful imagination, one that enjoyed challenging the conventions of language and poetry without surrendering a stroke of technical virtuosity. Like the Depression film comedies that were popular just around the time his first volumes began to appear, Nash's verse succeeded in striking a fine balance between tough-talk and innocence, urbanity and absurdity.

The following poem, which takes its lead from Ralph Waldo Emerson's advice that we "hitch our wagon to a star," appeared in Many Long Years Ago *(1945). For two other poetic versions of this distinctively American theme see Emily Dickinson's "Success Is Counted Sweetest" and Robert Frost's "Provide, Provide" in Classics.*

I hardly suppose I know anybody who wouldn't rather be a success than a failure,
Just as I suppose every piece of crabgrass in the garden would much rather be an azalea,
And in celestial circles all the run-of-the-mill angels would rather be archangels or at least cherubim and seraphim,
And in the legal world all the little process-servers hope to grow up into great big bailiffim and sheriffim.
Indeed, everybody wants to be a wow,
But not everybody knows exactly how.
Some people think they will eventually wear diamonds instead of rhinestones
Only by everlastingly keeping their noses to their ghrine-stones,
And other people think they will be able to put in more time at Palm Beach and the Ritz
By not paying too much attention to attendance at the office but rather in being brilliant by starts and fits.
Some people after a full day's work sit up all night getting a college education by correspondence,
While others seem to think they'll get just as far by devoting their evenings to the study of the difference in temperament between brunettance and blondance.
In short, the world is filled with people trying to achieve success,
And half of them think they'll get it by saying No and half of them by saying Yes,
And if all the ones who say No said Yes, and vice versa, such is the fate of humanity that ninety-nine per cent of them still wouldn't be any better off than they were before,
Which perhaps is just as well because if everybody was a success nobody could be contemptuous of anybody else and everybody would start in all over again trying to be a bigger success than everybody else so they would have somebody to be contemptuous of and so on forevermore,
Because when people start hitching their wagons to a star,
That's the way they are.

Mickey Spillane / *I, the Jury*

[*Mike Hammer Plots Revenge*] 1947

Born in 1918 in Brooklyn, the son of an Irish bartender, Mickey Spllane grew up in what he calls a "very tough neighborhood in Elizabeth, New Jersey." He attended Kansas State College, worked summers as captain of lifeguards at Breezy Point, New York, and supplemented his income by writing comic books. In 1935, Spillane began selling stories to detective magazines, and after flying fighter missions in the Second World War, he worked as a trampoline artist for the Ringling Brothers Circus. Since his first novel, I, the Jury, *published in 1947, Spillane's books have had extraordinary sales. At one time seven of Mickey Spillane's novels were included in a list of the top ten best-selling fiction works of the last fifty years. Many of the novels have been turned into movies, a few with Spillane playing the role of Mike Hammer.*

CHAPTER ONE

I shook the rain from my hat and walked into the room. Nobody said a word. They stepped back politely and I could feel their eyes on me. Pat Chambers was standing by the door to the bedroom trying to steady Myrna. The girl's body was racking with dry sobs. I walked over and put my arms around her.

"Take it easy, kid," I told her. "Come on over here and lie down." I led her to a studio couch that was against the far wall and sat her down. She was in pretty bad shape. One of the uniformed cops put a pillow down for her and she stretched out.

Pat motioned me over to him and pointed to the bedroom. "In there, Mike," he said.

In there. The words hit me hard. In there was my best friend lying on the floor dead. The body. Now I could call it that. Yesterday it was Jack Williams, the guy that shared the same mud bed with me through two years of warfare in the stinking slime of the jungle. Jack, the guy who said he'd give his right arm for a friend and did when he stopped a bastard of a Jap from slitting me in two. He caught the bayonet in the biceps and they amputated his arm.

Pat didn't say a word. He let me uncover the body and feel the cold face. For the first time in my life I felt like crying. "Where did he get it, Pat?"

"In the stomach. Better not look at it. The killer carved the nose off a forty-five and gave it to him low."

I threw back the sheet anyway and a curse caught in my throat. Jack was in shorts, his one hand still clutching his belly in agony. The bullet went in clean, but where it came out left a hole big enough to cram a fist into.

Very gently I pulled the sheet back and stood up. It wasn't a complicated setup. A trail of blood led from the table beside the bed to where Jack's artificial arm lay. Under him the throw rug was ruffled and twisted. He had tried to drag himself along with his one arm, but never reached what he was after.

His police positive, still in the holster, was looped over the back of the chair. That was what he wanted. With a slug in his gut he never gave up.

I pointed to the rocker, overbalanced under the weight of the .38. "Did you move the chair, Pat?"

"No, why?"

"It doesn't belong there. Don't you see?"

Pat looked puzzled. "What are you getting at?"

"That chair was over there by the bed. I've been here often enough to remember that much. After the killer shot Jack, he pulled himself toward the chair. But the killer didn't leave after the shooting. He stood here and watched him grovel on the floor in agony. Jack was after that gun, but he never reached it. He could have if the killer didn't move it. The trigger-happy bastard must have stood by the door laughing while Jack tried to make his last play. He kept pulling the chair back, inch by inch, until Jack gave up. Tormenting a guy who's been through all sorts of hell. Laughing. This was no ordinary murder, Pat. It's as cold-blooded and as deliberate as I ever saw one. I'm going to get the one that did this."

"You dealing yourself in, Mike?"

"I'm in. What did you expect?"

"You're going to have to go easy."

"Uh-uh. Fast, Pat. From now on it's a race. I want the killer for myself. We'll work together as usual, but in the homestretch, I'm going to pull the trigger."

"No, Mike, it can't be that way. You know it."

"Okay, Pat," I told him. "You have a job to do, but so have I. Jack was about the best friend I ever had. We lived together and fought together. And by Christ, I'm not letting the killer go through the tedious process of the law. You know what happens, damn it. They get the best lawyer there is and screw up the whole thing and wind up a hero! The dead can't speak for themselves. They can't tell what happened. How could Jack tell a jury what it was like to have his insides ripped out by a dumdum? Nobody in the box would know how it felt to be dying or have your own killer laugh in your face. One arm. Hell, what does that mean? So he has the Purple

Heart. But did they ever try dragging themselves across a floor to a gun with that one arm, their insides filling up with blood, so goddamn mad to be shot they'd do anything to reach the killer. No, damn it. A jury is cold and impartial like they're supposed to be, while some snotty lawyer makes them pour tears as he tells how his client was insane at the moment or had to shoot in self-defense. Swell. The law is fine. But this time I'm the law and I'm not going to be cold and impartial. I'm going to remember all those things."

I reached out and grabbed the lapels of his coat. "And something more, Pat. I want you to hear every word I say. I want you to tell it to everyone you know. And when you tell it, tell it strong, because I mean every word of it. There are ten thousand mugs that hate me and you know it. They hate me because if they mess with me I shoot their damn heads off. I've done it and I'll do it again."

There was so much hate welled up inside me I was ready to blow up, but I turned and looked down at what was once Jack. Right then I felt like saying a prayer, but I was too mad.

"Jack, you're dead now. You can't hear me any more. Maybe you can. I hope so. I want you to hear what I'm about to say. You've known me a long time, Jack. My word is good just as long as I live. I'm going to get the louse that killed you. He won't sit in the chair. He won't hang. He will die exactly as you died, with a .45 slug in the gut, just a little below the belly button. No matter who it is, Jack, I'll get the one. Remember, no matter who it is, I promise."

When I looked up, Pat was staring at me strangely. He shook his head. I knew what he was thinking. "Mike, lay off. For God's sake don't go off half-cocked about this. I know you too well. You'll start shooting up anyone connected with this and get in a jam you'll never get out of."

"I'm over it now, Pat. Don't get excited. From now on I'm after one thing, the killer. You're a cop, Pat. You're tied down by rules and regulations. There's someone over you. I'm alone. I can slap someone in the puss and they can't do a damn thing. No one can kick me out of my job. Maybe there's nobody to put up a huge fuss if I get gunned down, but then I still have a private cop's license with the privilege to pack a rod, and they're afraid of me. I hate hard, Pat. When I latch on to the one behind this they're going to wish they hadn't started it. Some day, before long, I'm going to have my rod in my mitt and the killer in front of me. I'm going to watch the killer's face. I'm going to plunk one right in his gut, and when he's dying on the floor I may kick his teeth out.

"You couldn't do that. You have to follow the book because you're a Captain of Homicide. Maybe the killer will wind up in the chair. You'd be satisfied, but I wouldn't. It's too easy. That killer is going down like Jack did."

There was nothing more to say. I could see by the set of Pat's jaw that he wasn't going to try to talk me out of it. All he could do was to try to beat me to him and take it from there. We walked out of the room together. The coroner's men had arrived and were ready to carry the body away.

I didn't want Myrna to see that. I sat down on the couch beside her and let her sob on my shoulder. That way I managed to shield her from the sight of her fiancé being carted off in a wicker basket. She was a good kid. Four years ago, when Jack was on the force, he had grabbed her as she was about to do a Dutch over the Brooklyn Bridge. She was a wreck then. Dope had eaten her nerve ends raw. But he had taken her to his house and paid for a full treatment until she was normal. For the both of them it had been a love that blossomed into a beautiful thing. If it weren't for the war they would have been married long ago.

When Jack came back with one arm it had made no difference. He no longer was a cop, but his heart was with the force. She had loved him before and she still loved him. Jack wanted her to give up her job, but Myrna persuaded him to let her hold it until he really got settled. It was tough for a man with one arm to find employment, but he had many friends.

Before long he was part of the investigating staff of an insurance company. It had to be police work. For Jack there was nothing else. Then they were happy. Then they were going to be married. Now this.

Pat tapped me on the shoulder. "There's a car waiting downstairs to take her home."

I rose and took her by the hand. "Come on, kid. There's no more you can do. Let's go."

She didn't say a word, but stood up silently and let a cop steer her out the door. I turned to Pat. "Where do we start?" I asked him.

"Well, I'll give you as much as I know. See what you can add to it. You and Jack were great buddies. It might be that you can add something that will make some sense."

Inwardly I wondered. Jack was such a straight guy that he never made an enemy. Even while on the force. Since he'd gotten back, his work with the insurance company was pretty routine. But maybe an angle there, though.

"Jack threw a party last night," Pat went on. "Not much of an affair."

"I know," I cut in, "he called me and asked me over, but I was pretty well knocked out. I hit the sack early. Just a group of old friends he knew before the army."

"Yeah. We got their names from Myrna. The boys are checking on them now."

"Who found the body?" I asked.

"Myrna did. She and Jack were driving out to the country today to pick a building site for their cottage. She got here at eight A.M. or a little after. When Jack didn't answer, she got worried. His arm had been giving him trouble lately and she thought it might have been that. She called the super. He knew her and let her in. When she screamed the super came running back and called us. Right after I got the story about the party from her, she broke down completely. Then I called you."

"What time did the shooting occur?"

"The coroner places it about five hours before I got here. That would make it about three fifteen. When I get an autopsy report we may be able to narrow it down even further."

"Anyone hear a shot?"

"Nope. It probably was a silenced gun."

"Even with a muffler, a .45 makes a good-sized noise."

"I know, but there was a party going on down the hall. Not loud enough to cause complaints, but enough to cover up any racket that might have been made here."

"What about those that were here?" Pat reached in his pocket and pulled out a pad. He ripped a leaf loose and handed it to me.

"Here's a list Myrna gave me. She was the first to arrive. Got here at eight thirty last night. She acted as hostess, meeting the others at the door. The last one came about eleven. They spent the evening doing some light drinking and dancing, then left as a group about one."

I looked at the names Pat gave me. A few of them I knew well enough, while a couple of the others were people of whom Jack had spoken, but I had never met.

"Where did they go after the party, Pat?"

"They took two cars. The one Myrna went in belonged to Hal Kines. They drove straight up to Westchester, dropping Myrna off on the way. I haven't heard from any of the others yet."

Both of us were silent for a moment, then Pat asked, "What about a motive, Mike?"

I shook my head. "I don't see any yet. But I will. He wasn't killed for nothing. I'll bet this much, whatever it was, was big. There's a lot here that's screwy. You got anything?"

"Nothing more than I gave you, Mike. I was hoping you could supply some answers."

I grinned at him, but I wasn't trying to be funny. "Not yet. Not yet. They'll come though. And I'll relay them on to you, but by that time I'll be working on the next step."

"The cops aren't exactly dumb, you know. We can get our own answers."

"Not like I can. That's why you buzzed me so fast. You can figure things out as quickly as I can, but you haven't got the ways and means of doing the dirty work. That's where I come in. You'll be right behind me every inch of the way, but when the pinch comes I'll get shoved aside and you slap the cuffs on. That is, if you can shove me aside. I don't think you can."

"Okay, Mike, call it your own way. I want you in all right. But I want the killer, too. Don't forget that. I'll be trying to beat you to him. We have every scientific facility at our disposal and a lot of men to do the leg work. We're not short in brains, either," he reminded me.

"Don't worry, I don't underrate the cops. But cops can't break a guy's arm to make him talk, and they can't shove his teeth in with the muzzle of a .45 to remind him that you aren't fooling. I do my own leg work, and there are a lot of guys who will tell me what I want to know because they know what I'll do to them if they don't. My staff is strictly ex officio, but very practical."

That ended the conversation. We walked out into the hall where Pat put a patrolman on the door to make sure things stayed as they were. We took the self-operated elevator down four flights to the lobby and I waited while Pat gave a brief report to some reporters.

My car stood at the curb behind the squad car. I shook hands with Pat and climbed into my jalopy and headed for the Hackard Building, where I held down a two-room suite to use for operation.

CHAPTER TWO

The office was locked when I got there. I kicked on the door a few times and Velda clicked the lock back. When she saw who it was she said, "Oh, it's you."

"What do you mean—'Oh, it's you'! Surely you remember me, Mike Hammer, your boss."

"Poo! You haven't been here in so long I can't tell you from another bill collector." I closed the door and followed her into my sanctum sanctorum. She had million-dollar legs, that girl, and she didn't mind showing them off. For a secretary she was an awful distraction. She kept her coal-black hair long in a page-boy cut and wore tight-fitting dresses that made me think of the curves in the Pennsylvania Highway every time I looked at her. Don't get the idea that she was easy, though. I've seen her give a few punks the brush off the hard way. When it came to quick action she could whip off a shoe and crack a skull before you could bat an eye.

Not only that, but she had a private op's ticket and on occasions when she went out with me on a case, packed a flat .32 automatic—and she wasn't afraid to use it. In the three years she worked for me I never made a pass at her. Not that I didn't want to, but it would be striking too close to home.

Velda picked up her pad and sat down. I plunked myself in the old swivel chair, then swung around facing the window. Velda threw a thick packet on my desk.

"Here's all the information I could get on those that were at the party last night." I looked at her sharply.

"How did you know about Jack? Pat only called my home." Velda wrinkled that pretty face of hers up into a cute grin.

"You forget that I have an in with a few reporters. Tom Dugan from the *Chronicle* remembered that you and Jack had been good friends. He called here to see what he could get and wound up by giving me all the info he had—and I didn't have to sex him, either." She put that in as an afterthought. "Most of the gang at the party were listed in your files. Nothing sensational. I got a little data from Tom who had more personal dealings with a few of them. Mostly character studies and some society reports. Evidently they were people whom Jack had met in the past and liked. You've even spoken about several yourself.''

I tore open the package and glanced at a sheaf of photos. ''Who are these?'' Velda looked over my shoulder and pointed them out.

''Top one is Hal Kines, a med student from a university upstate. He's about twenty-three, tall, and looks like a crew man. At least that's the way he cuts his hair.'' She flipped the page over. ''These two are the Bellemy twins. Age, twenty-nine, unmarried. In the market for husbands. Live off the fatta the land with dough their father left them. A half interest in some textile mills someplace down South.''

''Yeah,'' I cut in, ''I know them. Good lookers, but not very bright. I met them at Jack's place once and again at a dinner party.''

She pointed to the next one. A newspaper shot of a middle-aged guy with a broken nose. George Kalecki. I knew him pretty well. In the roaring twenties he was a bootlegger. He came out of the crash with a million dollars, paid up his income tax, and went society. He fooled a lot of people but he didn't fool me. He still had his finger in a lot of games just to keep in practice. Nothing you could pin on him though. He kept a staff of lawyers on their toes to keep him clean and they were doing a good job. ''What about him?'' I asked her.

''You know more than I do. Hal Kines is staying with him. They live about a mile above Myrna in Westchester.'' I nodded. I remembered Jack talking about him. He had met George through Hal. The kid had been a friend of George ever since the older man had met him through some mutual acquaintance. George was the guy that was putting him through college, but why, I wasn't sure.

The next shot was one of Myrna with a complete history of her that Jack had given me. Included was a medical record from the hospital when he had made her go cold turkey, which is dope-addict talk for an all-out cure. They cut them off from the stuff completely. It either kills them or cures them. In Myrna's case, she made it. But she made Jack promise that he would never try to get any information from her about where she got the stuff. The way he fell for the girl, he was ready to do anything she asked, and so far as he was concerned, the matter was completely dropped.

I flipped through the medical record. Name, Myrna Devlin. Attempted suicide while under the influence of heroin. Brought to emergency ward of General Hospital by Detective Jack Williams. Admitted 3-15-40. Treatment complete 9-21-40. No information available on patient's source of narcotics. Released into custody of Detective Jack Williams 9-30-40. Following this was a page of medical details which I skipped.

''Here's one you'll like, chum,'' Velda grinned at me. She pulled out a full-length photo of a gorgeous blonde. My heart jumped when I saw it. The picture was taken at a beach, and she stood there tall and languid-looking in a white bathing suit. Long solid legs. A little heavier than the movie experts consider good form, but the kind that make you drool to look at. Under the suit I could see the muscles of her stomach. Incredibly wide shoulders for a woman, framing breasts that jutted out, seeking freedom from the restraining fabric of the suit. Her hair looked white in the picture, but I could tell that it was a natural blonde. Lovely, lovely yellow hair. But her face was what got me. I thought Velda was a good looker, but this one was even lovelier. I felt like whistling.

''Who is she?''

''Maybe I shouldn't tell you. That leer on your face could get you into trouble, but it's all there. Name's Charlotte Manning. She's a female psychiatrist with offices on Park Avenue, and very successful. I understand she caters to a pretty ritzy clientele.''

I glanced at the number and made up my mind that right here was something that made this business a pleasurable one. I didn't say that to Velda. Maybe I'm being conceited, but I've always had the impression that she had designs on me. Of course she never mentioned it, but whenever I showed up late in the office with lipstick on my shirt collar, I couldn't get two words out of her for a week.

I stacked the sheaf back on my desk and swung around in the chair. Velda was leaning forward ready to take notes. "Want to add anything, Mike?"

"Don't think so. At least not now. There's too much to think about first. Nothing seems to make sense."

"Well, what about motive? Could Jack have had any enemies that caught up with him?"

"Nope. None I know of. He was square. He always gave a guy a break if he deserved it. Then, too, he never was wrapped up in anything big."

"Did he own anything of any importance?"

"Not a thing. The place was completely untouched. He had a few hundred dollars in his wallet that was lying on the dresser. The killing was done by a sadist. He tried to reach his gun, but the killer pulled the chair it hung on back slowly, making him crawl after it with a slug in his gut, trying to keep his insides from falling out with his hand."

"Mike, please."

I said no more. I just sat there and glowered at the wall. Someday I'd trigger the bastard that shot Jack. In my time I've done it plenty of times. No sentiment. That went out with the first. After the war I've been almost anxious to get to some of the rats that make up the section of humanity that prey on people. People. How incredibly stupid they could be sometimes. A trial by law for a killer. A loophole in the phrasing that lets a killer crawl out. But in the end the people have their justice. They get it through guys like me once in a while. They crack down on society and I crack down on them. I shoot them like the mad dogs they are and society drags me to court to explain the whys and wherefores of the extermination. They investigate my past, check my fingerprints and throw a million questions my way. The papers make me look like a kill-crazy shamus, but they don't bear down too hard because Pat Chambers keeps them off my neck. Besides, I do my best to help the boys out and they know it. And I'm usually good for a story when I wind up a case.

Velda came back into the office with the afternoon edition of the sheets. The kill was spread all over the front page, followed by a four-column layout of what details were available. Velda was reading over my shoulder and I heard her gasp.

"Did you come in for a blasting! Look." She was pointing to the last paragraph. There was my tie-up with the case, but what she was referring to was the word-for-word statement that I had made to Jack. My promise. My word to a dead friend that I would kill this murderer as he had killed him. I rolled the paper into a ball and threw it viciously at the wall.

"The louse! I'll break his filthy neck for printing that. I meant what I said when I made that promise. It's sacred to me, and they make a joke out of it. Pat did that. And I thought he was a friend. Give me the phone."

Velda grabbed my arm. "Take it easy. Suppose he did. After all, Pat's still a cop. Maybe he saw a chance of throwing the killer your way. If the punk knows you're after him for keeps he's liable not to take it standing still and make a play for you. Then you'll have him."

"Thanks, kid," I told her, "but your mind's too clean. I think you got the first part right, but your guess on the last part smells. Pat doesn't want me to have any part of him because he knows the case is ended right there. If he can get the killer to me you can bet your grandmother's uplift bra that he'll have a tail on me all the way with someone ready to stop in when the shooting starts."

"I don't know about that, Mike. Pat knows you're too smart not to recognize when you're being tailed. I wouldn't think he'd do that."

"Oh, no? He isn't dumb by any means. I'll bet you a sandwich against a marriage license he's got a flatfoot downstairs covering every exit in the place ready to pick me up when I leave. Sure, I'll shake them, but it won't stop there. A couple of experts will take up where they leave off."

Velda's eyes were glowing like a couple of hot brands. "Are you serious about that? About the bet, I mean?"

I nodded. "Dead serious. Want to go downstairs with me and take a look?" She grinned and grabbed her coat. I pulled on my battered felt and we left the office, but not before I had taken a second glance at the office address of Charlotte Manning.

Pete, the elevator operator, gave me a toothy grin when we stepped into the car. "Evening, Mr. Hammer," he said.

I gave him an easy jab in the short ribs and said, "What's new with you?"

"Nothing much, 'cepting I don't get to sit down much on the job anymore." I had to grin. Velda had lost the bet already. That little piece of simple repartee between Pete and myself was a code system we had rigged up years ago. His answer meant that I was going to have company when I left the building. It cost me a fin a week but it was worth it. Pete could spot a flatfoot faster than I can. He should. He had been a pickpocket until a long stretch up the river gave him a turn of mind.

For a change I decided to use the front entrance. I looked around for my tail but there was none to be seen. For a split second my heart leaped into my throat. I was afraid Pete had gotten his signals crossed. Velda was a spotter, too, and the smile she was wearing as we crossed the empty lobby was a thing to see. She clamped onto my arm ready to march me to the nearest justice of the peace.

But when I went through the revolving doors her grin passed as fast as mine appeared. Our tail was walking in front of us. Velda said a word that nice girls don't usually use, and you see scratched in the cement by some evil-minded guttersnipe.

This one was smart. We never saw where he came from. He walked a lot faster than we did, swinging a newspaper from his hand against his leg. Probably, he spotted us through the windows behind the palm, then seeing what exit we were going to use, walked around the corner and came past us as we left. If we had gone the other way, undoubtedly there was another ready to pick us up.

But this one had forgotten to take his gun off his hip and stow it under his shoulder, and guns make a bump look the size of a pumpkin when you're used to looking for them.

When I reached the garage he was nowhere to be seen. There were a lot of doors he could have ducked behind. I didn't waste time looking for him. I backed the car out and Velda crawled in beside me. "Where to now?" she asked.

"The automat, where you're going to buy me a sandwich."

Grace Metalious / *Peyton Place*
[*Michael Rossi Comes to Peyton Place*] 1956

One of the greatest selling novels in American publishing history was written by a New Hampshire housewife with little formal education and no literary background or cultural advantages. Born in Manchester, New Hampshire, in 1924, Grace Marie Antoinette Jeanne d'Arc de Repentigny was the daughter of parents who had not much more to give her than her fancy name. At seventeen she married George Metalious, a mill worker, who later put himself through college to become a school teacher only to lose his job as a result of the public scandal caused by his wife's novel. What is perhaps most remarkable about Peyton Place, *for all its faults of gracelessness and composition, is not that the book became a best seller so unexpectedly and rapidly, but that a generally uneducated young woman, with three small children and very little money, had the literary ambition and steady application needed to write publishable fiction.*

Grace Metalious was a tough-talking, hard-working, hard-drinking woman. Like many authors of best sellers, she was often defensive about her work: "If I'm a lousy writer," she once said, "a hell of a lot of people have got lousy taste." She died at the age of thirty-nine of a severe liver ailment.

A few days later, Michael Rossi stepped off the train in front of the Peyton Place railroad station. No other passenger got off with him. He paused on the empty platform and looked around thoroughly, for it was a habit with him to fix a firm picture of a new place in his mind so that it could never be erased nor forgotten. He stood still, feeling the two heavy suitcases that he carried pulling at his arm muscles, and reflected that there wasn't much to see, nor to hear, for that matter. It was shortly after seven o'clock in the evening, but it might have been midnight or four in the morning for all the activity going on. Behind him there was nothing but the two curving railroad tracks and from a distance came the long-drawn-out wail of the train as it made the pull across the wide Connecticut River. And it was cold.

For April, thought Rossi, shrugging uncomfortably under his topcoat, it was damned cold.

Straight ahead of him stood the railroad station, a shabby wooden building with a severely pitched roof and several thin, Gothic-looking windows that gave it the air of a broken-down church. Nailed to the front of the building, at the far left of the front door, was a blue and white enameled sign. PEYTON PLACE, it read. POP. 3675.

Thirty-six seventy-five, thought Rossi, pushing open the railroad station's narrow door. Sounds like the price of a cheap suit.

The inside of the building was lit by several dim electric light bulbs suspended from fixtures which obviously had once burned gas, and there were rows of benches constructed of the most hideous wood obtainable, golden oak. No one was sitting on them. The brown, roughly plastered walls were trimmed with the same yellow wood and the floor was made of black and white marble. There was an iron-barred cage set into one wall and from behind this a straight, thin man with a pinched-looking nose, steel-rimmed glasses and a string tie stared at Rossi.

"Is there a place where I can check these?" asked the new principal, indicating the two bags at his feet.

"Next room," said the man in the cage.

"Thank you," said Rossi and made his way through a narrow archway into another, smaller room. It was a replica of the main room, complete with golden oak, marble and converted gas fixtures, but with the addition of two more doors. These were clearly labeled. MEN, said one. WOMEN, said the other. Against one wall there was a row of pale gray metal lockers, and to Rossi, these looked almost friendly. They were the only things in the station even faintly resembling anything he had ever seen in his life.

"Ah," he murmured, "shades of Grand Central," and bent to push his suitcases into one of the lockers. He deposited his dime, withdrew his key and noticed that his was the only locker in use.

Busy town, he thought, and walked back to the main room. His footsteps rang disquietingly on the scrubbed marble floor.

Leslie Harrington had instructed Rossi to call him at his home as soon as he got off the train, but Rossi by-passed the solitary telephone booth in the railroad station. He wanted to look at the town alone first, to see it through no one's eyes but his own. Besides, he had decided the night that Harrington had called long-distance that the chairman of the Peyton Place School Board sounded like a man puffed up with his own importance, and must therefore be a pain in the ass.

"Say, Dad," began Rossi, addressing the man in the cage.

"Name's Rhodes," said the old man.

"Mr. Rhodes," began Rossi again, "could you tell me how I can get into town from here? I noticed a distressing lack of taxicabs outside."

"Be damned peculiar if I couldn't."

"If you couldn't what?"

"Tell you how to get uptown. Been living here for over sixty years."

"That's interesting."

"You're Mr. Rossi, eh?"

"Admitted."

"Ain't you goin' to call up Leslie Harrington?"

"Later. I'd like to get a cup of coffee first. Listen, isn't there a cab to be had anywhere around here?"

"No."

Michael Rossi controlled a laugh. It was beginning to look as if everything he had ever heard about these sullen New Englanders was true. The old man in the cage gave the impression that he had been sucking lemons for years. Certainly sourness had not been one of the traits in that little Pittsburgh secretary who claimed to be from Boston, but she said herself that she was East Boston Irish, and therefore not reliably representative of New England.

"Do you mind, then, telling me how I can walk into town from here, Mr. Rhodes?" asked Rossi.

"Not at all," said the stationmaster, and Rossi noticed that he pronounced the three words as one: Notatall. "Just go out this front door, walk around the depot to the street and keep on walking for two blocks. That will bring you to Elm Street."

"Elm Street? Is that the main street?"

"Yes."

"I had the idea that the main streets of all small New England towns were named Main Street."

"Perhaps," said Mr. Rhodes, who prided himself, when annoyed, on enunciating his syllables, "it is true that the main streets of all *other* small towns are named Main Street. Not, however, in Peyton Place. Here the main street is called Elm Street."

Period. Paragraph, thought Rossi. Next question. "Peyton Place is an odd name," he said. "How did anyone come to pick that one?"

Mr. Rhodes drew back his hand and started to close the wooden panel that backed the iron bars of his cage.

"I am closing now, Mr. Rossi," he said. "And I suggest that you be on your way if you want to obtain a cup of coffee. Hyde's Diner closes in half an hour."

"Thank you," said Rossi to the wooden panel which was suddenly between him and Mr. Rhodes.

Friendly bastard, he thought, as he left the station and began to walk up the street labeled Depot.

Michael Rossi was a massively boned man with muscles that seemed to quiver every time he moved. In the steel mills of Pittsburgh he had looked, so one smitten secretary had told him, like a color illustration of a steelworker. His arms, beneath sleeves rolled above the elbow, were knotted powerfully, and the buttons of his work shirts always seemed about to pop off under the strain of trying to cover his chest. He was six feet four inches tall, weighed two hundred and twelve pounds, stripped, and looked like anything but a schoolteacher. In fact, the friendly secretary in Pittsburgh had told him that in his dark blue suit, white shirt and dark tie, he looked like a steelworker disguised as a schoolteacher, a fact which would not inspire trust in the heart of any New Englander.

Michael Rossi was a handsome man, in a dark-skinned, black-haired, obviously sexual way, and both men and women were apt to credit him more with attractiveness than intellect. This was a mistake, for Rossi had a mind as analytical as a mathematician's and as curious as a philosopher's. It was his curiosity which had prompted him to give up teaching for a year to go to work in Pittsburgh. He had learned more about economics, labor and capital in that one year than he had learned in ten years of reading books. He was thirty-six years old and totally lacking in regret over the fact that he had never stayed in one job long enough to "get ahead," as the Pittsburgh secretary put it. He was honest, completely lacking in diplomacy, and the victim of a vicious temper which tended to loosen a tongue that had learned to speak on the lower East Side of New York City.

Rossi was halfway through the second block on Depot Street, leading to Elm, when Parker Rhodes, at the wheel of an old sedan, passed him. The stationmaster looked out of the window on the driver's side of his car and looked straight through Peyton Place's new headmaster.

Sonofabitch, thought Rossi. Real friendly sonofabitch to offer me a lift in his junk heap of a car.

Then he smiled and wondered why Mr. Rhodes had been so sensitive on the subject of his town's name. He would ask around and see if everyone in this godforsaken place reacted the same way to his question. He had reached the corner of Elm Street and paused to look about him. On the corner stood a white, cupola-topped house with stiff lace curtains at the windows. Silhouetted against the light inside, he could see two women sitting at a table with what was obviously a checkerboard between them. The women were big, saggy bosomed and white haired, and Rossi thought that they looked like a pair who had worked too long at the same girls' school.

I wonder who they are? he asked himself, as he looked in at the Page Girls. Maybe they're the town's two Lizzies.

Reluctantly, he turned away from the white house and made his way west on Elm Street. When he had walked three blocks, he came to a small, clean-looking and well-lighted restaurant. *Hyde's Diner* said a polite neon sign, and Rossi opened the door and went in. The place was empty except for one old man sitting at the far end of the counter, and another man who came out of the kitchen at the sound of the door opening.

"Good evening, sir," said Corey Hyde.

"Good evening," said Rossi. "Coffee, please, and a piece of pie. Any kind."

"Apple, sir?"

"Any kind is O.K."

"Well, we have pumpkin, too."

"Apple is fine."

"I think there's a piece of cherry left, also."

"Apple," said Rossi, "will be fine."

"You're Mr. Rossi, aren't you?"

"Yes."

"Glad to meet you, Mr. Rossi. My name is Hyde. Corey Hyde."

"How do you do?"

"Quite well, as a rule," said Corey Hyde. "I'll keep on doing quite well, as long as no one starts up another restaurant."

"Look, could I have my coffee now?"

"Certainly. Certainly, Mr. Rossi."

The old man at the end of the counter sipped his coffee from a spoon and looked surreptitiously at the newcomer to town. Rossi wondered if the old man could be the village idiot.

"Here you are, Mr. Rossi," said Corey Hyde. "The best apple pie in Peyton Place."

"Thank you."

Rossi stirred sugar into his coffee and sampled the pie. It was excellent.

"Peyton Place," he said Corey Hyde, "is the oddest name for a town I've ever heard. Who is it named for?"

"Oh, I don't know," said Corey, making unnecessary circular motions with a cloth on his immaculate counter. "There's plenty of towns have funny names. Take that Baton Rouge, Louisiana. I had a kid took French over to the high school. Told me Baton Rouge means Red Stick. Now ain't that a helluva name for a town? Red Stick, Louisiana. And what about that Des Moines, Iowa? What a crazy name that is."

"True," said Rossi. "But for whom is Peyton Place named, or for what?"

"Some feller that built a castle up here back before the Civil War. Feller by the name of Samuel Peyton," said Corey reluctantly.

"A castle!" exclaimed Rossi.

"Yep. A real, true, honest-to-God castle, transported over here from England, every stick and stone of it."

"Who was this Peyton?" asked Rossi. "An exiled duke?"

"Nah," said Corey Hyde. "Just a feller with money to burn. Excuse me, Mr. Rossi. I got things to do in the kitchen."

The old man at the end of the counter chuckled. "Fact of the matter, Mr. Rossi," said Clayton Frazier in a loud voice, "is that this town was named for a friggin' nigger. That's what ails Corey. He's delicate like, and just don't want to spit it right out."

While Michael Rossi sipped his coffee and enjoyed his pie and conversation with Clayton Frazier, Parker Rhodes arrived at his home on Laurel Street. He parked his ancient sedan and entered the house where, without first removing his coat and hat, he went directly to the telephone.

"Hello," he said, as soon as the party he had called answered. "That you, Leslie? Well, he's here, Leslie. Got off the seven o'clock, checked his suitcases and walked uptown. He's sitting down at Hyde's right now. What's that? No, he can't get his bags out of the depot until morning, you know that. What? Well, goddamn it, he didn't ask me, that's why. He didn't ask for information about when he could get them out. He just wanted to know where he could check his bags, so I told him. What'd you say, Leslie? No, I did not tell him that no one has used those lockers since they were installed five years ago. What? Well, goddamn it, he didn't ask me, that's why. Yes. Yes, he is, Leslie. *Real* dark, and big. Sweet Jesus, he's as big as the side of a barn. Yes. Down at Hyde's. Said he wanted a cup of coffee."

If Michael Rossi had overheard this conversation, he would have noticed again that Rhodes pronounced his last three words as one: Kupakawfee. But at the moment, Rossi was looking at the tall, silver-haired man who had just walked through Hyde's front door.

My God! thought Rossi, awed. This guy looks like a walking ad for a Planter's Punch. A goddamned Kentucky colonel in this place!

"Evenin', Doc," said Corey Hyde, who had put his head out of the kitchen at the sound of the door, looking, thought Rossi, rather like a tired turtle poking his head out of his shell.

"Evenin', Corey," and Rossi knew as soon as the man spoke, that this was no fugitive Kentucky colonel but a native.

"Welcome to Peyton Place, Mr. Rossi," said the white-haired native. "It's nice to have you with us. My name is Swain. Matthew Swain."

"Evenin', Doc," said Clayton Frazier. "I just been tellin' Mr. Rossi here some of our local legends."

''Make you want to jump on the next train out, Mr. Rossi?'' asked the doctor.

''No, sir,'' said Rossi, thinking that there was, after all, one goddamned face in this godforsaken town that looked human.

''I hope you'll enjoy living here,'' said the doctor. ''Maybe you'll let me show you the town after you get settled a little.''

''Thank you, sir. I'd enjoy that,'' said Rossi.

''Here comes Leslie Harrington,'' said Clayton Frazier.

The figure outside the glass door of the restaurant was clearly visible to those inside. The doctor turned to look.

''It's Leslie, all right,'' he said. ''Come to fetch you home, Mr. Rossi.''

Harrington strode into the restaurant, a smile like one made of molded ice cream on his face.

''Ah, Mr. Rossi,'' he cried jovially, extending his hand. ''It is indeed a pleasure to welcome you to Peyton Place.''

He was thinking, Oh, Christ, he's worse and more of it than I'd feared.

''Hello, Mr. Harrington,'' said Rossi, barely touching the extended hand. ''Made any long-distance calls lately?''

The smile on Harrington's face threatened to melt and run together, but he rescued it just in time.

''Ha, ha, ha,'' he laughed. ''No, Mr. Rossi, I haven't had much time for telephoning these days. I've been too busy looking for a suitable apartment for our new headmaster.''

''I trust you were successful,'' said Rossi.

''Yes. Yes, I was, as a matter of fact. Well, come along. I'll take you over in my car.''

''As soon as I finish my coffee,'' said Rossi.

''Certainly, certainly,'' said Harrington. ''Oh, hello, Matt. 'Lo, Clayton.''

''Coffee, Mr. Harrington?'' asked Corey Hyde.

''No, thanks,'' said Harrington.

When Rossi had finished, everyone said good night carefully, all the way around, and he and Harrington left the restaurant. As soon as the door had closed behind them, Dr. Swain began to laugh.

''Goddamn it,'' he roared, ''I'll bet my sweet young arse that Leslie has met his match this time!''

''There's one schoolteacher that Leslie ain't gonna shove around,'' observed Clayton Frazier.

Corey Hyde, who owed money at the bank where Leslie Harrington was a trustee, smiled uncertainly.

''The textile racket must be pretty good,'' said Rossi, as he opened the door of Leslie Harrington's new Packard.

''Can't complain,'' said Harrington. ''Can't complain,'' and the mill-owner shook himself angrily at this sudden tendency to repeat all his words.

Rossi stopped in the act of getting into the car. A woman was walking toward them, and as she stepped under the street light on the corner, Rossi got a quick glimpse of blond hair and a swirl of dark coat.

''Who's that?'' he demanded.

Leslie Harrington peered through the darkness. As the figure drew nearer, he smiled.

''That's Constance MacKenzie,'' he said. ''Maybe you two will have a lot in common. She used to live in New York. Nice woman; good looking, too. Widow.''

''Introduce me,'' said Rossi, drawing himself up to his full height.

''Certainly. Certainly, be glad to. Oh, Connie!''

''Yes, Leslie?''

The woman's voice was rich and husky, and Rossi fought down the urge to straighten the knot in his tie.

"Connie," said Harrington, "I'd like you to meet our new headmaster, Mr. Rossi. Mr. Rossi, Constance MacKenzie."

Constance extended her hand and while he held it, she gazed at him full in the eyes.

"How do you do?" she said at last, and Michael Rossi was puzzled, for something very much like relief showed through her voice.

"I'm glad to know you, Mrs. MacKenzie," said Rossi, and he thought, Very glad to know you, baby. I want to know you a lot better, on a bed, for instance, with that blond hair spread out on a pillow.

Vance Packard / *The Hidden Persuaders* 1957

With the publication of The Hidden Persuaders, *Vance Packard, a former columnist for the* Boston Daily Record *and a staff writer for* American Magazine *and* Collier's, *became the most widely read analyst of America's shopping habits. Based on motivational research and the techniques of depth psychology, Packard's findings served as a popular exposé of the manipulations of Madison Avenue. In "Babes in Consumerland," he focuses on the way the "goods" are packaged and positioned in supermarkets to ensure impulse buying.*

BABES IN CONSUMERLAND

"You have to have a carton that attracts and hypnotizes this woman, like waving a flashlight in front of her eyes."

—Gerald Stahl, executive vice-president, Package Designers Council

For some years the DuPont company has been surveying the shopping habits of American housewives in the new jungle called the supermarket. The results have been so exciting in the opportunities they suggest to marketers that hundreds of leading food companies and ad agencies have requested copies. Husbands fretting over the high cost of feeding their families would find the results exciting, too, in a dismaying sort of way.

The opening statement of the 1954 report exclaimed enthusiastically in display type: "Today's shopper in the supermarket is more and more guided by the buying philosophy—'If somehow your product catches my eye—and for some reason it looks especially good—I WANT IT.' " That conclusion was based on studying the shopping habits of 5,338 shoppers in 250 supermarkets.

DuPont's investigators have found that the mid-century shopper doesn't bother to make a list or at least not a complete list of what she needs to buy. In fact less than one shopper in five has a complete list, but still the wives always manage to fill up their carts, often while exclaiming, according to DuPont: "I certainly never intended to get that much!" Why doesn't the wife need a list? DuPont gives this blunt answer: "Because seven out of ten of today's purchases are decided in the store, where the shoppers buy on impulse!!!"

The proportion of impulse buying of groceries has grown almost every year for nearly two decades, and DuPont notes that this rise in impulse buying has coincided with the growth in self-service shopping. Other studies show that in groceries where there are clerks to wait on customers there is about half as much impulse buying as in self-service stores. If a wife has to face a clerk she thinks out beforehand what she needs.

The impulse buying of pungent-odored food such as cheese, eye-appealing items like pickles or fruit salad in glass jars, and candy, cake, snack spreads, and other "self-gratifying items" runs even higher than average, 90 per cent of all purchases. Other investigators have in general confirmed the DuPont figures on impulse buying. The Folding Paper Box Association found that two-thirds of all purchases were completely or partially on impulse; the *Progressive Grocer* put the impulse figure about where DuPont does: seven out of ten purchases. And *Printer's Ink* observed with barely restrained happiness that the shopping list had become obsolescent if not obsolete.

One motivational analyst who became curious to know why there had been such a great rise in impulse buying at supermarkets was James Vicary. He suspected that some special psychology must be going on inside the women as they shopped in supermarkets. His suspicion was that perhaps they underwent an increase in tension when confronted with so many possibilities that they were forced into making quick purchases. He set out to find out if this was true. The best way to detect what was going on inside the shopper was a galvanometer or lie detector. That obviously was impractical. The next best thing was to use a hidden motion-picture camera and record the eye-blink rate of the women as they shopped. How fast a person blinks his eyes is a pretty good index of his state of inner tension. The average person, according to Mr. Vicary, normally blinks his eyes about thirty-two times a minute. If he is tense he blinks them more frequently, under extreme tension up to fifty or sixty times a minute. If he is notably relaxed on the other hand his eye-blink rate may drop to a subnormal twenty or less.

Mr. Vicary set up his cameras and started following the ladies as they entered the store. The results were startling, even to him. Their eye-blink rate, instead of going up to indicate mounting tension, went down and down, to a very subnormal fourteen blinks a minute. The ladies fell into what Mr. Vicary calls a hypnoidal trance, a light kind of trance that, he explains, is the first stage of hypnosis. Mr. Vicary has decided that the main cause of the trance is that the supermarket is packed with products that in former years would have been items that only kings and queens could afford, and here in this fairyland they were available. Mr. Vicary theorizes: "Just in this generation, anyone can be a king or queen and go through these stores where the products say 'Buy me, buy me.' "

Interestingly many of these women were in such a trance that they passed by neighbors and old friends without noticing or greeting them. Some had a sort of glassy stare. They were so entranced as they wandered about the store plucking things off shelves at random that they would bump into boxes without seeing them and did not even notice the camera although in some cases their face would pass within a foot and a half of the spot where the hidden camera was clicking away. When the wives had filled their carts (or satisfied themselves) and started toward the check-out counter their eye-blink rate would start rising up to a slightly subnormal twenty-five blinks per minute. Then, at the sound of the cash-register bell and the voice of the clerk asking for money, the eye-blink rate would race up past normal to a high abnormal of forty-five blinks per minute. In many cases it turned out that the women did not have enough money to pay for all the nice things they had put in the cart.

In this beckoning field of impulse buying psychologists have teamed up with merchandising experts to persuade the wife to buy products she may not particularly need or even want until she happens to see it invitingly presented. The 60,000,000 American women who go into supermarkets every week are getting "help" in their purchases and "splurchases" from psychologists and psychiatrists hired by the food merchandisers. On May 18, 1956, *The New York Times* printed a remarkable interview with a young man named Gerald Stahl, executive vice-president of the Package Designers Council. He stated: "Psychiatrists say that people have so much to choose from that they want help—they will like the package that hypnotizes them into picking it." He urged food packers to put more hypnosis into their package designing, so that the housewife will stick out her hand for it rather than one of many rivals.

Mr. Stahl has found that it takes the average woman exactly twenty seconds to cover an aisle in a supermarket if she doesn't tarry; so a good package design should hypnotize the woman like a flashlight waved in front of her eyes. Some colors such as red and yellow are helpful in creating hypnotic effects. Just putting the name and maker of the product on the box is old-fashioned and, he says, has absolutely no effect on the mid-century woman. She can't read anything, really, until she has picked the box up in her hands. To get the woman to reach and get the package in her hands designers, he explained, are now using "symbols that have a dreamlike quality." To cite examples of dreamlike quality, he mentioned the mouth-watering frosted cakes that decorate the packages of cake mixes, sizzling steaks, mushrooms frying in butter. The idea is to sell the sizzle rather than the meat. Such illustrations make the woman's imagination leap ahead to the end product. By 1956 package designers had even produced a box that, when the entranced shopper picked it up and began fingering it, would give a soft sales talk, or stress the brand name. The talk is on a strip that starts broadcasting when a shopper's finger rubs it.

The package people understandably believe that it is the package that makes or breaks the impulse sale, and some more objective experts agree. A buyer for a food chain told of his experience in watching women shopping. The typical shopper, he found, "picks up one, two, or three items, she puts them back on the shelf, then she picks up one and keeps it. I ask her why she keeps it. She says, 'I like the package.' " (This was a buyer for Bohack.)

The Color Research Institute, which specializes in designing deep-impact packages, won't even send a package out into the field for testing until it has been given ocular or eye-movement tests to show how the consumer's eye will travel over the package on the shelf. This is a gauge of the attention-holding power of the design.

According to some psychologists a woman's eye is most quickly attracted to items wrapped in red; a man's eye to items wrapped in blue. Students in this field have speculated on the woman's high vulnerability to red. One package designer, Frank Gianninoto, has developed an interesting theory. He has concluded that a majority of women shoppers leave their glasses at home or will never wear glasses in public if they can avoid it so that a package to be successful must stand out "from the blurred confusion."

Other merchandisers, I should add, have concluded that in the supermarket jungle the all-important fact in impulse buying is shelf position. Many sharp merchandisers see to it that their "splurge" items (on which their profit margin is highest) tend to be at eye level.

Most of the modern supermarkets, by the mid-fifties, were laid out in a carefully calculated manner so that the high-profit impulse items would be most surely noticed. In many stores they were on the first or only aisle the shopper could enter. Among the best tempters, apparently, are those items in glass jars where the contents can be seen, or where the food is actually out in the open, to be savored and seen. Offering free pickles and cubes of cheese on toothpicks has proved to be reliable as a sales booster. An Indiana supermarket operator nationally recognized for his advanced psychological techniques told me he once sold a half ton of cheese in a few hours, just by getting an enormous half-ton wheel of cheese and inviting customers to nibble slivers and cut off their own chunks for purchase. They could have their chunk free if they could guess its weight within an ounce. The mere massiveness of the cheese, he believes, was a powerful influence in making the sales. "People like to see a lot of merchandise," he explained. "When there are only three or four cans of an item on a shelf, they just won't move." People don't want the last package. A test by *The Progressive Grocer* showed that customers buy 22 per cent more if the shelves are kept full. The urge to conformity, it seems, is profound with many of us.

People also are stimulated to be impulsive, evidently, if they are offered a little extravagance. A California supermarket found that putting a pat of butter on top of each of its better steaks caused sales to soar 15 per cent. The Jewel Tea Company set up "splurge counters" in many of its supermarkets after it was found that women in a just-for-the-heck-of-it mood will spend just as freely on food delicacies as they will on a new hat. The Coca-Cola Company made the interesting discovery that customers in a supermarket who paused to refresh themselves at a soft-drink counter tended to spend substantially more. The Coke people put this to work in a test where they offered customers free drinks. About 80 per cent accepted the Cokes and spent on an average $2.44 more than the store's average customer had been spending.

Apparently the only people who are more prone to splurging when they get in a supermarket than housewives are the wives' husbands and children. Supermarket operators are pretty well agreed that men are easy marks for all sorts of impulse items and cite cases they've seen of husbands who are sent to the store for a loaf of bread and depart with both their arms loaded with their favorite snack items. Shrewd supermarket operators have put the superior impulsiveness of little children to work in promoting sales. The Indiana supermarket operator I mentioned has a dozen little wire carts that small children can push about the store while their mothers are shopping with big carts. People think these tiny carts are very cute; and the operator thinks they are very profitable. The small children go zipping up and down the aisles imitating their mothers in impulse buying, only more so. They reach out, hypnotically I assume, and grab boxes of cookies, candies, dog food, and everything else that delights or interests them. Complications arise, of course, when mother and child come out of their trances and together reach the check-out counter. The store operator related thus what happens: "There is usually a wrangle when the mother sees all the things the child has in his basket and she tries to make him take the stuff back. The child will take back items he doesn't particularly care about such as coffee but will usually bawl and kick before surrendering cookies, candy, ice cream, or soft drinks, so they usually stay for the family."

All these factors of sly persuasion may account for the fact that whereas in past years the average American family spent about 23 per cent of its income for food it now spends nearly 30 per cent. The Indiana operator I mentioned estimates that any supermarket shopper could, by showing a little old-fashioned thoughtfulness and preplanning, save 25 per cent easily on her family's food costs.

The exploration of impulse buying on a systematic basis began spreading in the mid-fifties to many other kinds of products not available in food stores. Liquor stores began organizing racks so that women could browse and pick up impulse items. This idea was pioneered on New York's own "ad alley," Madison Avenue, and spread to other parts of the country. Department and specialty stores started having counters simply labeled, "Why Not?" to promote the carefree, impulsive purchasing of new items most people had never tried before. One store merchandiser was quoted as saying: "Just give people an excuse to try what you are selling and you'll make an extra sale."

One of the most daring ventures into impulse selling was that launched by a Chicago insurance firm, Childs and Wood, which speculated that perhaps even insurance could be sold as an impulse item. So it set up a counter to sell insurance to passers-by at the department store Carson Pirie Scott and Company. Women who happened to be in that area, perhaps to shop for fur coats or a bridal gown, could buy insurance (life, automobile, household, fire, theft, jewelry, hospital) from an assortment of firms. The experiment was successful and instituted on a permanent basis. Auto, household, and fire insurance were reported to be the most popular impulse items.

Social scientists at the Survey Research Center at the University of Michigan made studies of the way people make their decisions to buy relatively expensive durable items such as TV sets, refrigerators, washing machines, items that are usually postponable. It concluded: "We did *not* find that all or most purchases of large household goods are made after careful consideration or deliberation . . . that much planning went into the purchasing . . . nor much seeking of information. About a quarter of these purchases of large household goods were found to lack practically all features of careful deliberation."

In a study that was made on the purchasing of homes in New London, Connecticut,[1] investigators were amazed that even with this, the most important purchase a family is likely to make in the year if not the decade, the shopping was lethargic and casual. On an average the people surveyed looked at less than a half-dozen houses before making a decision; 10 per cent of the home buyers looked at only one house before deciding; 19 per cent looked at only two houses before choosing one of them.

Dr. Warren Bilkey, of the University of Connecticut, and one of the nation's authorities on consumer behavior, systematically followed a large (sixty-three) group of families for more than a year as they wrestled with various major purchasing decisions. He learned that he could chart after each visit the intensity of two opposing factors, "desire" and "resistance." When one finally overwhelmed the other, the decision, pro or con, was made. He found that these people making major decisions, unlike the ladies in the supermarket, did build up a state of tension within themselves. The longer they pondered the decision, the higher the tension. He found that very often the people became so upset by the indecision that they often threw up their hands and decided to make the purchase just to find relief from their state of tension.

DISCUSSION QUESTIONS

1. What are the sources of Packard's data on consumerism? Does personal observation play any role in the development of his argument? Explain how his attitudes toward the "data" are different from the attitudes of those who supply the data. What means does Packard use to suggest these differences?

2. What is the effect of calling the supermarket a "new jungle"? One source Packard cites calls it a "fairyland." Which metaphor seems closest to the data that Packard is using? Which image do you agree with?

3. What image of women is conveyed by the title of Packard's essay? Compare his attitude towards women with the images of women in the Advertising section.

1. Ruby T. Norris, "Processes and Objectives in the New London Area," *Consumer Behavior*, ed. Lincoln Clark (New York: New York University Press, 1954), pp. 25–29.

Mario Puzo / *The Godfather*
[*The Shooting of Don Corleone*] 1969

Mario Puzo was born in New York City and educated at City College, Columbia, and the New School for Social Research. In two novels before The Godfather, The Dark Arena *(1955) and* The Passionate Pilgrim *(1965), both of which he claims are better books, Puzo explored generational conflicts and the New York Italo-American community. Puzo disclaims any Mafia connections:*

> *I'm ashamed to admit that I wrote* The Godfather *entirely from research. I never met a real honest-to-god gangster. I knew the gambling world pretty good, but that's all. After the book became "famous," I was introduced to a few gentlemen related to the material. They were flattering. They refused to believe that I had never been in the rackets. They refused to believe that I had never had the confidence of a Don. But all of them loved the book.*

That evening, Hagen went to the Don's house to prepare him for the important meeting the next day with Virgil Sollozzo. The Don had summoned his eldest son to attend, and Sonny Corleone, his heavy Cupid-shaped face drawn with fatigue, was sipping at a glass of water. He must still be humping that maid of honor, Hagen thought. Another worry.

Don Corleone settled into an armchair puffing his Di Nobili cigar. Hagen kept a box of them in his room. He had tried to get the Don to switch to Havanas but the Don claimed they hurt his throat.

"Do we know everything necessary for us to know?" the Don asked.

Hagen opened the folder that held his notes. The notes were in no way incriminating, merely cryptic reminders to make sure he touched on every important detail. "Sollozzo is coming to us for help," Hagan said. "He will ask the family to put up at least a million dollars and to promise some sort of immunity from the law. For that we get a piece of the action, nobody knows how much. Sollozzo is vouched for by the Tattaglia family and they may have a piece of the action. The action is narcotics. Sollozzo has the contacts in Turkey, where they grow the poppy. From there he ships to Sicily. No trouble. In Sicily he has the plant to process into heroin. He has safety-valve operations to bring it down to morphine•and bring it up to heroin if necessary. But it would seem that the processing plant in Sicily is protected in every way. The only hitch is bringing it into this country, and then distribution. Also initial capital. A million dollars cash doesn't grow on trees." Hagen saw Don Corleone grimace. The old man hated unnecessary flourishes in business matters. He went on hastily.

"They call Sollozzo the Turk. Two reasons. He's spent a lot of time in Turkey and is supposed to have a Turkish wife and kids. Second. He's supposed to be very quick with the knife, or was, when he was young. Only in matters of business, though, and with some sort of reasonable complaint. A very competent man and his own boss. He has a record, he's done two terms in prison, one in Italy, one in the United States, and he's known to the authorities as a narcotics man. This could be a plus for us. It means that he'll never get immunity to testify, since he's considered the top and, of course, because of his record. Also he has an American wife and three children and he is a good family man. He'll stand still for any rap as long as he knows that they will be well taken care of for living money."

The Don puffed on his cigar and said, "Santino, what do you think?"

Hagen knew what Sonny would say. Sonny was chafing at being under the Don's thumb. He wanted a big operation of his own. Something like this would be perfect.

Sonny took a long slug of scotch. "There's a lot of money in that white powder," he said. "But it could be dangerous. Some people could wind up in jail for twenty years. I'd say that if we kept out of the operations end, just stuck to protection and financing, it might be a good idea."

Hagen looked at Sonny approvingly. He had played his cards well. He had stuck to the obvious, much the best course for him.

The Don puffed on his cigar. "And you, Tom, what do you think?"

Hagen composed himself to be absolutely honest. He had already come to the conclusion that the Don would refuse Sollozzo's proposition. But what was worse, Hagen was convinced that for one of the few times in his experience, the Don had not thought things through. He was not looking far enough ahead.

"Go ahead, Tom," the Don said encouragingly. "Not even a Sicilian *Consigliori* always agrees with the boss." They all laughed.

"I think you should say yes," Hagen said. "You know all the obvious reasons. But the most important one is this. There is more money potential in narcotics than in any other business. If we don't get into it, somebody else will, maybe the Tattaglia family. With the revenue they earn they can amass more and more police and political power. Their family will become stronger than ours. Eventually they will come after us to take away what we have. It's just like countries. If they arm, we have to arm. If they become stronger economically, they become a threat to us. Now we have the gambling and we have the unions and right now they are the best things to have. But I think narcotics is the coming thing. I think we have to have a piece of that action or we risk everything we have. Not now, but maybe ten years from now."

The Don seemed enormously impressed. He puffed on his cigar and murmured, "That's the most important thing of course." He sighed and got to his feet. "What time do I have to meet this infidel tomorrow?"

Hagen said hopefully, "He'll be here at ten in the morning." Maybe the Don would go for it.

"I'll want you both here with me," the Don said. He rose, stretching, and took his son by the arm. "Santino, get some sleep tonight, you look like the devil himself. Take care of yourself, you won't be young forever."

Sonny, encouraged by this sign of fatherly concern, asked the question Hagen did not dare to ask. "Pop, what's your answer going to be?"

Don Corleone smiled. "How do I know until I hear the percentages and other details? Besides I have to have time to think over the advice given here tonight. After all, I'm not a man who does things rashly." As he went out the door he said casually to Hagen, "Do you have in your notes that the Turk made his living from prostitution before the war? As the Tattaglia family does now. Write that down before you forget." There was just a touch of derision in the Don's voice and Hagen flushed. He had deliberately not mentioned it, legitimately so since it really had no bearing, but he had feared it might prejudice the Don's decision. He was notoriously straitlaced in matters of sex.

Virgil "the Turk" Sollozzo was a powerfully built, medium-sized man of dark complexion who could have been taken for a true Turk. He had a scimitar of a nose and cruel black eyes. He also had an impressive dignity.

Sonny Corleone met him at the door and brought him into the office where Hagen and the Don waited. Hagen thought he had never seen a more dangerous-looking man except for Luca Brasi.

There were polite handshakings all around. If the Don ever asks me if this man has balls, I would have to answer yes, Hagen thought. He had never seen such force in one man, not even the Don. In fact the Don appeared at his worst. He was being a little too simple, a little too peasantlike in his greeting.

Sollozzo came to the point immediately. The business was narcotics. Everything was set up. Certain poppy fields in Turkey had pledged him certain amounts every year. He had a protected plant in France to convert into morphine. He had an absolutely secure plant in Sicily to process into heroin. Smuggling into both countries was as positively safe as such matters could be. Entry into the United States would entail about five percent losses since the FBI itself was incorruptible, as they both knew. But the profits would be enormous, the risk nonexistent.

''Then why do you come to me?'' the Don asked politely. ''How have I deserved your generosity?''

Sollozzo's dark face remained impassive. ''I need two million dollars cash,'' he said. ''Equally important, I need a man who has powerful friends in the important places. Some of my couriers will be caught over the years. That is inevitable. They will all have clean records, that I promise. So it will be logical for judges to give light sentences. I need a friend who can guarantee that when my people get in trouble they won't spend more than a year or two in jail. Then they won't talk. But if they get ten and twenty years, who knows? In this world there are many weak individuals. They may talk, they may jeopardize more important people. Legal protection is a must. I hear, Don Corleone, that you have as many judges in your pocket as a bootblack has pieces of silver.''

Don Corleone didn't bother to acknowledge the compliment. ''What percentage for my family?'' he asked.

Sollozzo's eyes gleamed. ''Fifty percent.'' He paused and then said in a voice that was almost a caress, ''In the first year your share would be three or four million dollars. Then it would go up.''

Don Corleone said, ''And what is the percentage of the Tattaglia family?''

For the first time Sollozzo seemed to be nervous. ''They will receive something from my share. I need some help in the operations.''

''So,'' Don Corleone said, ''I receive fifty percent merely for finance and legal protection. I have no worries about operations, is that what you tell me?''

Sollozzo nodded. ''If you think two million dollars in cash is 'merely finance,' I congratulate you, Don Corleone.''

The Don said quietly, ''I consented to see you out of my respect for the Tattaglias and because I've heard you are a serious man to be treated also with respect. I must say no to you but I must give you my reasons. The profits in your business are huge but so are the risks. Your operation, if I were part of it, could damage my other interests. It's true I have many, many friends in politics, but they would not be so friendly if my business were narcotics instead of gambling. They think gambling is something like liquor, a harmless vice, and they think narcotics a dirty business. No, don't protest. I'm telling you their thoughts, not mine. How a man makes his living is not my concern. And what I am telling you is that this business of yours is too risky. All the members of my family have lived well the last ten years, without danger, without harm. I can't endanger them or their livelihoods out of greed.''

The only sign of Sollozzo's disappointment was a quick flickering of his eyes around the room, as if he hoped Hagen or Sonny would speak in his support. Then he said, ''Are you worried about security for your two million?''

The Don smiled coldly. ''No,'' he said.

Sollozzo tried again. ''The Tattaglia family will guarantee your investment also.''

It was then that Sonny Corleone made an unforgivable error in judgment and procedure. He said eagerly, ''The Tattaglia family guarantees the return of our investment without any percentage from us?''

Hagen was horrified at this break. He saw the Don turn cold, malevolent eyes on his eldest son, who froze in uncomprehending dismay. Sollozzo's eyes flickered again but this time with satisfaction. He had discovered a chink in the Don's fortress. When the Don spoke his voice held a dismissal. "Young people are greedy," he said. "And today they have no manners. They interrupt their elders. They meddle. But I have a sentimental weakness for my children and I have spoiled them. As you see. Signor Sollozzo, my no is final. Let me say that I myself wish you good fortune in your business. It has no conflict with my own. I'm sorry that I had to disappoint you."

Sollozzo bowed, shook the Don's hand and let Hagen take him to his car outside. There was no expression on his face when he said good-bye to Hagen.

Back in the room, Don Corleone asked Hagen, "What did you think of that man?"

"He's a Sicilian," Hagen said dryly.

The Don nodded his head thoughtfully. Then he turned to his son and said gently, "Santino, never let anyone outside the family know what you are thinking. Never let them know what you have under your fingernails. I think your brain is going soft from all that comedy you play with that young girl. Stop it and pay attention to business. Now get out of my sight."

Hagen saw the surprise on Sonny's face, then anger at his father's reproach. Did he really think the Don would be ignorant of his conquest, Hagen wondered. And did he really not know what a dangerous mistake he had made this morning? If that were true, Hagen would never wish to be the *Consigliori* to the Don of Santino Corleone.

Don Corleone waited until Sonny had left the room. Then he sank back into his leather armchair and motioned brusquely for a drink. Hagen poured him a glass of anisette. The Don looked up at him. "Send Luca Brasi to see me," he said.

Three months later, Hagen hurried through the paper work in his city office hoping to leave early enough for some Christmas shopping for his wife and children. He was interrupted by a phone call from a Johnny Fontane bubbling with high spirits. The picture had been shot, the rushes, whatever the hell they were, Hagen thought, were fabulous. He was sending the Don a present for Christmas that would knock his eyes out, he'd bring it himself but there were some little things to be done in the movie. He would have to stay out on the Coast. Hagen tried to conceal his impatience. Johnny Fontane's charm had always been lost on him. But his interest was aroused. "What is it?" he asked. Johnny Fontane chuckled and said, "I can't tell, that's the best part of a Christmas present." Hagen immediately lost all interest and finally managed, politely, to hang up.

Ten minutes later his secretary told him that Connie Corleone was on the phone and wanted to speak to him. Hagen sighed. As a young girl Connie had been nice, as a married woman she was a nuisance. She made complaints about her husband. She kept going home to visit her mother for two or three days. And Carlo Rizzi was turning out to be a real loser. He had been fixed up with a nice little business and was running it into the ground. He was also drinking, whoring around, gambling and beating his wife up occasionally. Connie hadn't told her family about that but she had told Hagen. He wondered what new tale of woe she had for him now.

But the Christmas spirit seemed to have cheered her up. She just wanted to ask Hagen what her father would really like for Christmas. And Sonny and Fred and Mike. She already knew what she would get her mother. Hagen made some suggestions, all of which she rejected as silly. Finally she let him go.

When the phone rang again, Hagen threw his papers back into the basket. The hell with it. He'd leave. It never occurred to him to refuse to take the call, however. When his secretary told him it was Michael Corleone he picked up the phone with pleasure. He had always liked Mike.

"Tom," Michael Corleone said, "I'm driving down to the city with Kay tomorrow. There's something important I want to tell the old man before Christmas. Will he be home tomorrow night?"

"Sure," Hagen said. "He's not going out of town until after Christmas. Anything I can do for you?"

Michael was as closemouthed as his father. "No," he said. "I guess I'll see you Christmas, everybody is going to be out at Long Beach, right?"

"Right," Hagen said. He was amused when Mike hung up on him without any small talk.

He told his secretary to call his wife and tell her he would be home a little late but to have some supper for him. Outside the building he walked briskly downtown toward Macy's. Someone stepped in his way. To his surprise he saw it was Sollozzo.

Sollozzo took him by the arm and said quietly, "Don't be frightened. I just want to talk to you." A car parked at the curb suddenly had its door open. Sollozzo said urgently, "Get in, I want to talk to you."

Hagen pulled his arm loose. He was still not alarmed, just irritated. "I haven't got time," he said. At that moment two men came up behind him. Hagen felt a sudden weakness in his legs. Sollozzo said softly, "Get in the car. If I wanted to kill you you'd be dead now. Trust me."

Without a shred of trust Hagen got into the car.

Michael Corleone had lied to Hagen. He was already in New York, and he had called from a room in the Hotel Pennsylvania less than ten blocks away. When he hung up the phone, Kay Adams put out her cigarette and said, "Mike, what a good fibber you are."

Michael sat down beside her on the bed. "All for you, honey; if I told my family we were in town we'd have to go there right away. Then we couldn't go out to dinner, we couldn't go to the theater, and we couldn't sleep together tonight. Not in my father's house, not when we're not married." He put his arms around her and kissed her gently on the lips. Her mouth was sweet and he gently pulled her down on the bed. She closed her eyes, waiting for him to make love to her and Michael felt an enormous happiness. He had spent the war years fighting in the Pacific, and on those bloody islands he had dreamed of a girl like Kay Adams. Of a beauty like hers. A fair and fragile body, milky-skinned and electrified by passion. She opened her eyes and then pulled his head down to kiss him. They made love until it was time for dinner and the theater.

After dinner they walked past the brightly lit department stores full of holiday shoppers and Michael said to her, "What shall I get you for Christmas?"

She pressed against him. "Just you," she said. "Do you think your father will approve of me?"

Michael said gently, "That's not really the question. Will your parents approve of me?"

Kay shrugged. "I don't care," she said.

Michael said, "I even thought of changing my name, legally, but if something happened, that wouldn't really help. You sure you want to be a Corleone?" He said it only half-jokingly.

"Yes," she said without smiling. They pressed against each other. They had decided to get married during Christmas week, a quiet civil ceremony at City Hall with just two friends as witnesses. But Michael had insisted he must tell his father. He had explained that his father would not object in any way as long as it was not done in secrecy. Kay was doubtful. She said she could not tell her parents until after the marriage. "Of course they'll think I'm pregnant," she said. Michael grinned. "So will my parents," he said.

What neither of them mentioned was the fact that Michael would have to cut his close ties with his family. They both understood that Michael had already done so to some extent and yet they both felt guilty about this fact. They planned to finish college, seeing each other weekends and living together during summer vacations. It seemed like a happy life.

The play was a musical called *Carousel* and its sentimental story of a braggart thief made them smile at each other with amusement. When they came out of the theater it had turned cold. Kay snuggled up to him and said, "After we're married, will you beat me and then steal a star for a present?"

Michael laughed. "I'm going to be a mathematics professor," he said. Then he asked, "Do you want something to eat before we go to the hotel?"

Kay shook her head. She looked up at him meaningfully. As always he was touched by her eagerness to make love. He smiled down at her, and they kissed in the cold street. Michael felt hungry, and he decided to order sandwiches sent up to the room.

In the hotel lobby Michael pushed Kay toward the newsstand and said, "Get the papers while I get the key." He had to wait in a small line; the hotel was still short of help despite the end of the war. Michael got his room key and looked around impatiently for Kay. She was standing by the newsstand, staring down at a newspaper she held in her hand. He walked toward her. She looked up at him. Her eyes were filled with tears. "Oh, Mike," she said, "oh, Mike." He took the paper from her hands. The first thing he saw was a photo of his father lying in the street, his head in a pool of blood. A man was sitting on the curb weeping like a child. It was his brother Freddie. Michael Corleone felt his body turning to ice. There was no grief, no fear, just cold rage. He said to Kay, "Go up to the room." But he had to take her by the arm and lead her into the elevator. They rode up together in silence. In their room, Michael sat down on the bed and opened the paper. The headlines said, VITO CORLEONE SHOT. ALLEGED RACKET CHIEF CRITICALLY WOUNDED. OPERATED ON UNDER HEAVY POLICE GUARD. BLOODY MOB WAR FEARED.

Michael felt the weakness in his legs. He said to Kay, "He's not dead, the bastards didn't kill him." He read the story again. His father had been shot at five in the afternoon. That meant that while he had been making love to Kay, having dinner, enjoying the theater, his father was near death. Michael felt sick with guilt.

Kay said, "Shall we go down to the hospital now?"

Michael shook his head. "Let me call the house first. The people who did this are crazy and now that the old man's still alive they'll be desperate. Who the hell knows what they'll pull next."

Both phones in the Long Beach house were busy and it was almost twenty minutes before Michael could get through. He heard Sonny's voice saying, "Yeah."

"Sonny, it's me," Michael said.

He could hear the relief in Sonny's voice. "Jesus, kid, you had us worried. Where the hell are you? I've sent people to that hick town of yours to see what happened."

"How's the old man?" Michael said. "How bad is he hurt?"

"Pretty bad," Sonny said. "They shot him five times. But he's tough." Sonny's voice was proud. "The doctors said he'll pull through. Listen, kid, I'm busy, I can't talk, where are you?"

"In New York," Michael said. "Didn't Tom tell you I was coming down?"

Sonny's voice dropped a little. "They've snatched Tom. That's why I was worried about you. His wife is here. She don't know and neither do the cops. I don't want them to know. The bastards who pulled this must be crazy. I want you to get out here right away and keep your mouth shut. OK?"

"OK," Mike said, "do you know who did it?"

''Sure,'' Sonny said. ''And as soon as Luca Brasi checks in they're gonna be dead meat. We still have all the horses.''

''I'll be out in a hour,'' Mike said. ''In a cab.'' He hung up. The papers had been on the streets for over three hours. There must have been radio news reports. It was almost impossible that Luca hadn't heard the news. Thoughtfully Michael pondered the question. Where was Luca Brasi? It was the same question that Hagen was asking himself at that moment. It was the same question that was worrying Sonny Corleone out in Long Beach.

At a quarter to five that afternoon, Don Corleone had finished checking the papers the office manager of his olive oil company had prepared for him. He put on his jacket and rapped his knuckles on his son Freddie's head to make him take his nose out of the afternoon newspaper. ''Tell Gatto to get the car from the lot,'' he said. ''I'll be ready to go home in a few minutes.''

Freddie grunted. ''I'll have to get it myself. Paulie called in sick this morning. Got a cold again.''

Don Corleone looked thoughtful for a moment. ''That's the third time this month. I think maybe you'd better get a healthier fellow for this job. Tell Tom.''

Fred protested. ''Paulie's a good kid. If he says he's sick, he's sick. I don't mind getting the car.'' He left the office. Don Corleone watched out the window as his son crossed Ninth Avenue to the parking lot. He stopped to call Hagen's office but there was no answer. He called the house at Long Beach but again there was no answer. Irritated, he looked out the window. His car was parked at the curb in front of his building. Freddie was leaning against the fender, arms folded, watching the throng of Christmas shoppers. Don Corleone put on his jacket. The office manager helped him with his overcoat. Don Corleone grunted his thanks and went out the door and started down the two flights of steps.

Out in the street the early winter light was failing. Freddie leaned casually against the fender of the heavy Buick. When he saw his father come out of the building Freddie went out into the street to the driver's side of the car and got in. Don Corleone was about to get in on the sidewalk side of the car when he hesitated and then turned back to the long open fruit stand near the corner. This had been his habit lately, he loved the big out-of-season fruits, yellow peaches and oranges, that glowed in their green boxes. The proprietor sprang to serve him. Don Corleone did not handle the fruit. He pointed. The fruit man disputed his decisions only once, to show him that one of his choices had a rotten underside. Don Corleone took the paper bag in his left hand and paid the man with a five-dollar bill. He took his change and, as he turned to go back to the waiting car, two men stepped from around the corner. Don Corleone knew immediately what was to happen.

The two men wore black overcoats and black hats pulled low to prevent identification by witnesses. They had not expected Don Corleone's alert reaction. He dropped the bag of fruit and darted toward the parked car with startling quickness for a man of his bulk. At the same time he shouted, ''Fredo, Fredo.'' It was only then that the two men drew their guns and fired.

The first bullet caught Don Corleone in the back. He felt the hammer shock of its impact but made his body move toward the car. The next two bullets hit him in the buttocks and sent him sprawling in the middle of the street. Meanwhile the two gunmen, careful not to slip on the rolling fruit, started to follow in order to finish him off. At that moment, perhaps no more than five seconds after the Don's call to his son, Frederico Corleone appeared out of his car, looming over it. The gunmen fired two more hasty shots at the Don lying in the gutter. One hit him in the fleshy part of his arm and the second hit him in the calf of his right leg. Though these wounds were the least serious they bled profusely, forming small pools of blood beside his body. But by this time Don Corleone had lost consciousness.

Freddie had heard his father shout, calling him by his childhood name, and then he had heard the first two loud reports. By the time he got out of the car he was in shock, he had not even drawn his gun. The two assassins could easily have shot him down. But they too panicked. They must have known the son was armed, and besides too much time had passed. They disappeared around the corner, leaving Freddie alone in the street with his father's bleeding body. Many of the people thronging the avenue had flung themselves into doorways or on the ground, others had huddled together in small groups.

Freddie still had not drawn his weapon. He seemed stunned. He stared down at his father's body lying face down on the tarred street, lying now in what seemed to him a blackish lake of blood. Freddie went into physical shock. People eddied out again and someone, seeing him start to sag, led him to the curbstone and made him sit down on it. A crowd gathered around Don Corleone's body, a circle that shattered when the first police car sirened a path through them. Directly behind the police was the *Daily News* radio car and even before it stopped a photographer jumped out to snap pictures of the bleeding Don Corleone. A few moments later an ambulance arrived. The photographer turned his attention to Freddie Corleone, who was now weeping openly, and this was a curiously comical sight, because of his tough, Cupid-featured face, heavy nose and thick mouth smeared with snot. Detectives were spreading through the crowd and more police cars were coming up. One detective knelt beside Freddie, questioning him, but Freddie was too deep in shock to answer. The detective reached inside Freddie's coat and lifted his wallet. He looked at the identification inside and whistled to his partner. In just a few seconds Freddie had been cut off from the crowd by a flock of plainclothesmen. The first detective found Freddie's gun in its shoulder holster and took it. Then they lifted Freddie off his feet and shoved him into an unmarked car. As that car pulled away it was followed by the *Daily News* radio car. The photographer was still snapping pictures of everybody and everything.

DISCUSSION QUESTIONS

1. How does Puzo go about making Don Corleone an attractive figure? For example, compare the characterization of Don Corleone to that of Sollozzo the Turk? In what ways are the Don's criminal activities given a kind of legitimacy? In this sense, how do Don Corleone's activities compare with those of Joey Gallo (see Magazines)?

2. What is the literary effect of having Don Corleone's death first reported in the newspapers? How do the newspapers determine Puzo's description of the shooting? Compare his description with the account of Joey Gallo's death (see "Death of a Maverick Mafioso" in Magazines).

Woody Allen / Getting Even 1971

"Comic Genius—Woody Allen Comes of Age," read the cover of Time *magazine in the spring of 1979 after the release of his critically acclaimed film,* Manhattan. *Certainly Allen has come a long way from fifteen when he was paid $25 a week to write jokes on a wholesale basis—50 each day after school for two years, or 25,000 jokes. A succession of television writing jobs, stand-up come-*

dian gigs, short stories for the New Yorker, *and over ten movies brought Allen to his present popular acclaim as our "comic genius."*

In Spring Bulletin *Allen employs a serious, informative (or expository) style, typical of college catalogues ("The poetry of William Butler Yeats is analyzed . . ."), which he continually undercuts with absurdities (". . . against a backdrop of proper dental care"). Even in the course heading—"Yeats and Hygiene, A Comparative Study"—he juxtaposes the everyday with the absurd. As funny as Allen's material can be, there is usually an undercurrent of anxiety about the difficult moral choices of life and the inevitability of death.*

SPRING BULLETIN

The number of college bulletins and adult-education come-ons that keep turning up in my mailbox convinces me that I must be on a special mailing list for dropouts. Not that I'm complaining; there is something about a list of extension courses that piques my interest with a fascination hitherto reserved for a catalogue of Hong Kong honeymoon accessories, sent to me once by mistake. Each time I read through the latest bulletin of extension courses, I make immediate plans to drop everything and return to school. (I was ejected from college many years ago, the victim of unproved accusations not unlike those once attached to Yellow Kid Weil.) So far, however, I am still an uneducated, unextended adult, and I have fallen into the habit of browsing through an imaginary, handsomely printed course bulletin that is more or less typical of them all:

Summer Session

Economic Theory: A systematic application and critical evaluation of the basic analytic concepts of economic theory, with an emphasis on money and why it's good. Fixed coefficient production functions, cost and supply curves, and nonconvexity comprise the first semester, with the second semester concentrating on spending, making change, and keeping a neat wallet. The Federal Reserve System is analyzed, and advanced students are coached in the proper method of filling out a deposit slip. Other topics include: Inflation and Depression—how to dress for each. Loans, interest, welching.

History of European Civilization: Ever since the discovery of a fossilized eohippus in the men's washroom at Siddon's Cafeteria in East Rutherford, New Jersey, it has been suspected that at one time Europe and America were connected by a strip of land that later sank or became East Rutherford, New Jersey, or both. This throws a new persepctive on the formation of European society and enables historians to conjecture about why it sprang up in an area that would have made a much better Asia. Also studied in the course is the decision to hold the Renaissance in Italy.

Introduction to Psychology: The theory of human behavior. Why some men are called "lovely individuals" and why there are others you just want to pinch. Is there a split between mind and body, and, if so, which is better to have? Aggression and rebellion are discussed. (Students particularly interested in these aspects of psychology are advised to take one of these Winter Term courses: Introduction to Hostility; Intermediate Hostility; Advanced Hatred; Theoretical Foundations of Loathing.) Special consideration is given to a study of consciousness as opposed to unconsciousness, with many helpful hints on how to remain conscious.

Psychopathology: Aimed at understanding obsessions and phobias, including the fear of being suddenly captured and stuffed with crabmeat, reluctance to return a volleyball serve, and the inability to say the word "mackinaw" in the presence of women. The compulsion to seek out the company of beavers is analyzed.

Philosophy I: Everyone from Plato to Camus is read, and the following topics are covered:

Ethics: The categorical imperative, and six ways to make it work for you.
Aesthetics: Is art the mirror of life, or what?
Metaphysics: What happens to the soul after death? How does it manage?
Epistemology: Is knowledge knowable? If not, how do we know this?
The Absurd: Why existence is often considered silly, particularly for men who wear brown-and-white shoes. Manyness and oneness are studied as they relate to otherness. (Students achieving oneness will move ahead to twoness.)

Philosophy XXIX-B: Introduction to God. Confrontation with the Creator of the universe through informal lectures and field trips.

The New Mathematics: Standard mathematics has recently been rendered obsolete by the discovery that for years we have been writing the numeral five backward. This has led to a reëvaluation of counting as a method of getting from one to ten. Students are taught advanced concepts of Boolean Algebra, and formerly unsolvable equations are dealt with by threats of reprisals.

Fundamental Astronomy: A detailed study of the universe and its care and cleaning. The sun, which is made of gas, can explode at any moment, sending our entire planetary system hurtling to destruction; students are advised what the average citizen can do in such a case. They are also taught to identify various constellations, such as the Big Dipper, Cygnus the Swan, Sagittarius the Archer, and the twelve stars that form Lumides the Pants Salesman.

Modern Biology: How the body functions, and where it can usually be found. Blood is analyzed, and it is learned why it is the best possible thing to have coursing through one's veins. A frog is dissected by students and its digestive tract is compared with man's, with the frog giving a good account of itself except on curries.

Rapid Reading: This course will increase reading speed a little each day until the end of the term, by which time the student will be required to read *The Brothers Karamozov* in fifteen minutes. The method is to scan the page and eliminate everything except pronouns from one's field of vision. Soon the pronouns are eliminated. Gradually the student is encouraged to nap. A frog is dissected. Spring comes. People marry and die. Pinkerton does not return.

Musicology III: The Recorder. The student is taught how to play "Yankee Doodle" on this end-blown wooden flute, and progresses rapidly to the Brandenburg Concertos. Then slowly back to "Yankee Doodle."

Music Appreciation: In order to "hear" a great piece of music correctly, one must: (1) know the birthplace of the composer, (2) be able to tell a rondo from a scherzo, and back it up with action. Attitude is important. Smiling is bad form unless the composer has intended the music to be funny, as in *Till Eulenspiegel,* which abounds in musical jokes (although the trombone has the best lines.) The ear, too, must be trained, for it is our most easily deceived organ and can be made to think it is a nose by bad placement of stereo speakers. Other topics include: The four-bar rest and its potential as a political weapon. The Gregorian Chant: Which monks kept the beat.

Writing for the Stage: All drama is conflict. Character development is also very important. Also what they say. Students learn that long, dull speeches are not so effective, while short, "funny" ones seem to go over well. Simplified audience psychology is explored: Why is a play about a lovable old character named Gramps often not as interesting in the theatre as staring at the back of someone's head and trying to make him turn around? Interesting aspects of stage history are also examined. For example, before the invention of italics, stage directions were often mistaken for dialogue, and great actors frequently found themselves saying, "John rises, crosses left." This naturally led to embarrassment and, on some occasions, dreadful notices. The phenomenon is analyzed in detail, and students are guided in avoiding mistakes. Required test: A. F. Shulte's *Shakespeare: Was He Four Women?*

Introduction to Social Work: A course designed to instruct the social worker who is interested in going out "in the field." Topics covered include: how to organize street gangs into basketball teams, and vice versa; playgrounds as a means of preventing juvenile crime, and how to get potentially homicidal cases to try the sliding pond; discrimination; the broken home; what to do if you are hit with a bicycle chain.

Yeats and Hygiene, A Comparative Study: The poetry of William Butler Yeats is analyzed against a background of proper dental care. (Course open to a limited number of students.)

Elizabeth L. Post / *Emily Post's Etiquette* 1975

The most influential voice in determining acceptable standards of social conduct for several generations of Americans, Emily Price was born into a well-to-do Baltimore family in 1873. After the customary education here and abroad, she became a debutante and a bride in the same year, 1892. Divorced in 1901, Emily Price Post gradually turned to writing as a means of support for her two children, publishing Flight of a Moth *in 1904—a recounting of her childhood training in Europe. Her later, romantic fiction featured mannered occasions and stylish scenes on the continent. Encouraged to draw on her background and prepare a book of etiquette, Emily Post was at first repulsed by the notion, but after reading what was available on the subject, she agreed to the project. First published in 1922 under the title* Etiquette in Society, in Business, in Politics, and at Home, *her book has since gone through more than ninety-five printings.*

Elizabeth L. Post, wife of Mrs. Post's grandson, prepared the 1975 edition of Emily Post's Etiquette *and wrote the following Preface to it.*

PREFACE

It is not uncommon today to hear someone ask, "Are manners still important? Isn't etiquette outdated, or hypocritical?" Or even, "Do manners and etiquette, as we used to recognize them, exist at all?"

Of course they do! And they are just as important to us now as they were to previous generations. But they are different manners, new manners, and this is as it should be, because our life-style is new. Yesterday, privacy, self-discipline, and formality were the rule. Today, openness, freedom, and informality are the qualities that we live with. The formalities that our parents worked hard to learn are outdated, and the informalities that we practice seem right for *now*—so natural to us that we are scarcely conscious of the difference. Manners evolve of their own accord, influenced by current life-style, and the best survive until that style changes again, and they become obsolete.

To be able to answer the question "Is etiquette important?" one must have an understanding of the true meaning of the word. There is no simple definition or synonym, but to me "consideration" comes the closest. All good manners are based on thoughtfulness for others, and if everyone lived by the Golden Rule—"Do unto others as you would have others do unto you"—there would be no bad manners in the world. There have been many attempts to define "etiquette" over the years, but my own particular favorite was found in an old grammar book. It is,

> Politeness is to do and say
> The kindest thing in the kindest way.

The type of person for whom books on etiquette hold an interest has changed almost as much as manners themselves. Until the first edition of *Etiquette* was printed in 1922, the idea prevailed that manners held little interest for anyone other than the rich, or members of so-called "society." An etiquette book printed in Chicago in 1882, for example, stated that the rich needed good manners "to give finish and éclat to their homes and their wealth"; the middle class needed manners "to gain admittance to the homes of the rich"; and the poor needed manners "to help find solace for the 'sting of poverty.' " Today, fortunately, our attitude toward manners is far more sensible. As Peg Bracken writes, "Once a proof of your breeding, manners are now an indication of your warm heart and good intentions as well."

A knowledge of etiquette—and good manners—carries many advantages. It imparts a comfortable feeling of security, self-confidence, and self-respect. Unquestionably, we enjoy every experience more if we feel that we need not worry about how to face it—if we know that instinctively we are doing the right thing.

There is a deep basic need in all of us to conform and to be liked. Acting according to accepted standards helps us to avoid criticism and to become popular members of society. Of course, it is most important that certain standards be maintained. Just because "everyone does it" does not make an action correct or even acceptable. Each standard that is lowered or forgotten must be replaced by another—one that is more suitable to life today. The fact that we live less formally does not mean that we need live less agreeably. But it does mean that we must have a knowledge of what is considered right, or wrong, for our times. It was true many years ago, and it is still true today—we are open to criticism if we flaunt convention too defiantly.

Finally, good manners simply make one more attractive, and who does not, "deep down," want to be as attractive as possible? Manners—those that are described in this book, and, perhaps, some that are not—have survived or become accepted because they have proved over many years to be the pleasantest, most practical, most considerate, or least offensive way of doing something. They are not, as some people think, "rules," but rather "guideposts on the road to good taste."

This new book, then, is designed to *help* you. In no way is it intended to complicate your life, to make it more difficult or less fun. Rather, it should make life easier and smoother. Nor is every reader expected to follow all the suggestions to the letter. Each person must read it, consider what advice is applicable to his circumstances, and then adopt those parts of the book that will be of most help to him.

In a comparison of Emily Post's original *Etiquette* with this edition, certain facts emerge. First, and most obvious, *manners* have changed tremendously in fifty years. The clothes we wear, the way we talk, the parties we give, our ideas on how to bring up our children are as different as night from day. (Running throughout this book are some short excerpts from the original edition which will show just how different). The second, and more important, is that *etiquette* has not changed. It is a code of behavior, based on consideration and kindness, and manners are the outward evidence that we live by that code. The conclusion, then, is that, while manners and each individual "manner" must be constantly redefined and revised, Emily Post's definition of etiquette is as valid today as it was in 1922. She wrote: "Beneath its myriad rules, the fundamental purpose of etiquette is to make the world a pleasanter place to live in, and you a more pleasant person to live with." There is no need to redefine that. The way of life of those who accept the code has not changed over many centuries—and, I hope, never will.

Wayne Dyer / *Your Erroneous Zones* 1976

"I feel a mission to change the mental health of our country," announced Wayne Dyer, author of professional books on counseling and of two enormously popular works: Your Erroneous Zones *(1976) and* Pulling Your own Strings *(1978). After two years of research, Dyer reportedly completed the first draft of* Your Erroneous Zones *in thirteen days. He defines erroneous zones as areas of self-defeating behavior and claims that ridding oneself of them need not involve Freudian, fashionable, or arcane therapies: "Mental health is not complex, expensive or involved, hard work. It is only common sense."*

In the selection below, Dyer attempts to remove etiquette from the erroneous zone. For another interpretation of etiquette in today's society, see Elizabeth L. Post's Preface to Emily Post's Etiquette *in this section.*

ETIQUETTE AS A SHOULD

Etiquette is a beautiful example of useless and unhealthy enculturation. Think of all the little meaningless rules you've been encouraged to adopt simply because an Emily Post, Amy Vanderbilt, or Abigail van Buren has so written. Eat your corn on the cob this way, always wait for the hostess to start before eating, introduce the man to the woman, sit on that side of the church at a wedding, tip this, wear that, use these words. Don't consult yourself; look it up in the book. While good manners are certainly appropriate—they simply entail consideration for other people—about ninety percent of all the etiquette guidelines are meaningless rules that were composed arbitrarily at one time. There is no proper way for you; there is only what you decide is right for you—as long as you don't make it hard for others to get along. You can choose how you'll introduce people, what you'll tip, what you'll wear, how you'll speak, where you'll sit, how you'll eat, and so on, strictly on the basis of what you want. Anytime you fall into the trap of "What *should* I wear," or "How *should* I do it," you're giving up a chunk of yourself. I'm not making a case here for being a social rebel since that would be a form of approval-seeking through nonconformity, but rather this is a plea for being self- rather than other-directed in the everyday running of your life. Being true to yourself means being devoid of the need for an external support system.

Alex Haley / *Roots*
[*What Are Slaves?*]

1976

A former magazine writer and Coast Guard Chief Journalist, Alex Haley had a modest reputation until the publication of his mammoth work, Roots: The Saga of an American Family, *first in a condensed version by* Reader's Digest *in 1974 and then published in its entirety by Doubleday in 1976. Twelve years in the making,* Roots *won for Haley international fame and personal fortune. An eight part ABC television dramatization of* Roots *drew 130 million viewers. The last episode attracted 80 million alone, making it the most popular television program ever aired.*

Kunta Kinte, Haley's African ancestor, born in Gambia in 1750 and carried to America as a slave in 1767, is the most vividly portrayed character in the book. His story fills more than half of Roots' *688 pages. In the following selection, young Kunta Kinte and his brother, Lamin, learn from their father, Omoro, the meaning of slavery.*

"What are slaves?" Lamin asked Kunta one afternoon. Kunta grunted and fell silent. Walking on, seemingly lost in thought, he was wondering what Lamin had overheard to prompt that question. Kunta knew that those who were taken by toubob became slaves, and he had overheard grown-ups talking about slaves who were owned by people in Juffure. But the fact was that he really didn't know what slaves *were*. As had happened so many other times, Lamin's question embarrassed him into finding out more.

The next day, when Omoro was getting ready to go out after some palm wood to build Binta a new food storehouse, Kunta asked to join his father; he loved to go off anywhere with Omoro. But neither spoke this day until they had almost reached the dark, cool palm grove.

Then Kunta asked abruptly, "Fa, what are slaves?"

Omoro just grunted at first, saying nothing, and for several minutes moved about in the grove, inspecting the trunks of diffrent palms.

"Slaves aren't always easy to tell from those who aren't slaves," he said finally. Between blows of his bush ax against the palm he had selected, he told Kunta that slaves' huts were roofed with nyantang jongo and free peoples' huts with nyantang foro, which Kunta knew was the best quality of thatching grass.

"But one should never speak of slaves in the presence of slaves," said Omoro, looking very stern. Kunta didn't understand why, but he nodded as if he did.

When the palm tree fell, Omoro began chopping away its thick, tough fronds. As Kunta plucked off for himself some of the ripened fruits, he sensed his father's mood of willingness to talk today. He thought happily how now he would be able to explain to Lamin all about slaves.

"Why are some people slaves and others not?" he asked.

Omoro said that people became slaves in different ways. Some were born of slave mothers—and he named a few of those who lived in Juffure, people whom

Kunta knew well. Some of them were the parents of some of his own kafo mates. Others, said Omoro, had once faced starvation during their home villages' hungry season, and they had come to Juffure and begged to become the slaves of someone who agreed to feed and provide for them. Still others—and he named some of Juffure's older people—had once been enemies and been captured as prisoners. "They become slaves, being not brave enough to die rather than be taken," said Omoro.

He had begun chopping the trunk of the palm into sections of a size that a strong man could carry. Though all he had named were slaves, he said, they were all respected people, as Kunta well knew. "Their rights are guaranteed by the laws of our forefathers," said Omoro, and he explained that all masters had to provide their slaves with food, clothing, a house, a farm plot to work on half shares, and also a wife or husband.

"Only those who permit themselves to be are despised," he told Kunta—those who had been made slaves because they were convicted murderers, thieves, or other criminals. These were the only slaves whom a master could beat or otherwise punish as he felt they deserved.

"Do slaves have to remain slaves always?" asked Kunta.

"No, many slaves buy their freedom with what they save from farming on half share with their masters." Omoro named some in Juffure who had done this. He named others who had won their freedom by marrying into the family that owned them.

To help him carry the heavy sections of palm, Omoro made a stout sling out of green vines, and as he worked, he said that some slaves, in fact, prospered beyond their masters. Some had even taken slaves for themselves, and some had become very famous persons.

"Sundiata was one!" exclaimed Kunta. Many times, he had heard the grandmothers and the griots speaking of the great forefather slave general whose army had conquered so many enemies.

Omoro grunted and nodded, clearly pleased that Kunta knew this, for Omoro also had learned much of Sundiata when he was Kunta's age. Testing his son, Omoro asked, "And who was Sundiata's mother?"

"Sogolon, the Buffalo Woman!" said Kunta proudly.

Omoro smiled, and hoisting onto his strong shoulders two heavy sections of the palm pole within the vine sling, he began walking. Eating his palm fruits, Kunta followed, and nearly all the way back to the village, Omoro told him how the great Mandinka Empire had been won by the crippled, brilliant slave general whose army had begun with runaway slaves found in swamps and other hiding places.

"You will learn much more of him when you are in manhood training," said Omoro—and the very thought of that time sent a fear through Kunta, but also a thrill of anticipation.

Omoro said that Sundiata had run away from his hated master, as most slaves did who didn't like their masters. He said that except for convicted criminals, no slaves could be sold unless the slaves approved of the intended master.

"Grandmother Nyo Boto also is a slave," said Omoro, and Kunta almost swallowed a mouthful of palm fruit. He couldn't comprehend this. Pictures flashed across his mind of beloved old Nyo Boto squatting before the door of her hut, tending the village's twelve or fifteen naked babies while weaving baskets of wigs, and giving the sharp side of her tongue to any passing adult—even the elders, if she felt like it. "That one is nobody's slave," he thought.

The next afternoon, after he had delivered his goats to their pens, Kunta took Lamin home by a way that avoided their usual playmates, and soon they squatted silently before the hut of Nyo Boto. Within a few moments the old lady appeared in her doorway, having sensed that she had visitors. And with but a glance at

Kunta, who had always been one of her very favorite children, she knew that something special was on his mind. Inviting the boys inside her hut, she set about the brewing of some hot herb tea for them.

"How are your papa and mama?" she asked.

"Fine. Thank you for asking," said Kunta politely. "And you are well, Grandmother?"

"I'm quite fine, indeed," she replied.

Kunta's next words didn't come until the tea had been set before him. Then he blurted, "Why are you a slave, Grandmother?"

Nyo Boto looked sharply at Kunta and Lamin. Now it was she who didn't speak for a few moments. "I will tell you," she said finally.

"In my home village one night, very far from here and many rains ago, when I was a young woman and wife," Nyo Boto said, she had awakened in terror as flaming grass roofs came crashing down among her screaming neighbors. Snatching up her own two babies, a boy and a girl, whose father had recently died in a tribal war, she rushed out among the others—and awaiting them were armed white slave raiders with their black slatee helpers. In a furious battle, all who didn't escape were roughly herded together, and those who were too badly injured or too old or too young to travel were murdered before the others' eyes. Nyo Boto began to sob, "—including my own two babies and my aged mother."

As Lamin and Kunta clutched each other's hands, she told them how the terrified prisoners, bound neck-to-neck with thongs, were beaten and driven across the hot, hard inland country for many days. And every day, more and more of the prisoners fell beneath the whips that lashed their backs to make them walk faster. After a few days, yet more began to fall of hunger and exhaustion. Some struggled on, but those who couldn't were left for the wild animals to get. The long line of prisoners passed other villages that had been burned and ruined, where the skulls and bones of people and animals lay among the burned-out shells of thatch and mud that had once been family huts. Fewer than half of those who had begun the trip reached the village of Juffure, four days from the nearest place on the Kambi Bolongo where slaves were sold.

"It was here that one young prisoner was sold for a bag of corn," said the old woman. "That was me. And this was how I came to be called Nyo Boto," which Kunta knew meant "bag of corn." The man who bought her for his own slave died before very long, she said, "and I have lived here ever since."

Lamin was wriggling in excitement at the story, and Kunta felt somehow ever greater love and appreciation than he had before for old Nyo Boto, who now sat smiling tenderly at the two boys, whose father and mother, like them, she had once dandled on her knee.

"Omoro, your papa, was of the first kafo when I came to Juffure," said Nyo Boto, looking directly at Kunta. "Yaisa, his mother, who was your grandmother, was my very good friend. Do you remember her?" Kunta said that he did and added proudly that he had told his little brother all about their grandma.

"That is good!" said Nyo Boto. "Now I must get back to work. Run along, now."

Thanking her for the tea, Kunta and Lamin left and walked slowly back to Binta's hut, each deep in his own private thoughts.

The next afternoon, when Kunta returned from his goatherding, he found Lamin filled with questions about Nyo Boto's story. Had any such fire ever burned in Juffure? he wanted to know. Well, he had never heard of any, said Kunta, and the village showed no signs of it. Had Kunta ever seen one of those white people? "Of course not!" he exclaimed. But he said that their father had spoken of a time when he and his brothers had seen the toubob and their ships at a point along the river.

Kunta quickly changed the subject, for he knew very little about toubob, and he wanted to think about them for himself. He wished that he could *see* one of them—from a safe distance, of course, since everything he'd ever heard about them made it plain that people were better off who never got too close to them.

Only recently a girl out gathering herbs—and before her two grown men out hunting—had disappeared, and everyone was certain that toubob had stolen them away. He remembered, of course, how when drums of other villages warned that toubob had either taken somebody or was known to be near, the men would arm themselves and mount a double guard while the frightened women quickly gathered all of the children and hid in the bush far from the village—sometimes for several days—until the toubob was felt to be gone.

Kunta recalled once when he was out with his goats in the quiet of the bush, sitting under his favorite shade tree. He had happened to look upward and there, to his astonishment, in the tree overhead, were twenty or thirty monkeys huddled along the thickly leaved branches as still as statues, with their long tails hanging down. Kunta had always thought of monkeys rushing noisily about, and he couldn't forget how quietly they had been watching his every move. He wished that now *he* might sit in a tree and watch some toubob on the ground below him.

The goats were being driven homeward the afternoon after Lamin had asked him about toubob when Kunta raised the subject among his fellow goatherds—and in no time they were telling about the things they had heard. One boy, Demba Conteh, said that a very brave uncle had once gone close enough to *smell* some toubob, and they had a peculiar stink. All of the boys had heard that toubob took people away to eat them. But some had heard that the toubob claimed the stolen people were not eaten, only put to work on huge farms. Sitafa Silla spat out his grandfather's answer to that: "White man's lie!"

The next chance he had, Kunta asked Omoro, "Papa, will you tell me how you and your brothers saw the toubob at the river?" Quickly, he added, "The matter needs to be told correctly to Lamin." It seemed to Kunta that his father nearly smiled, but Omoro only grunted, evidently not feeling like talking at that moment. But a few days later, Omoro casually invited both Kunta and Lamin to go with him out beyond the village to collect some roots he needed. It was the naked Lamin's first walk anywhere with his father, and he was overjoyed. Knowing that Kunta's influence had brought this about, he held tightly onto the tail of his big brother's dundiko.

Omoro told his sons that after their manhood training, his two older brothers Janneh and Saloum had left Juffure, and the passing of time brought news of them as well-known travelers in strange and distant places. Their first return home came when drumtalk all the way from Juffure told them of the birth of Omoro's first son. They spent sleepless days and nights on the trail to attend the naming ceremony. And gone from home so long, the brothers joyously embraced some of their kafo mates of boyhood. But those few sadly told of others gone and lost—some in burned villages, some killed by fearsome firesticks, some kidnaped, some missing while farming, hunting, or traveling—and all because of toubob.

Omoro said that his brothers had then angrily asked him to join them on a trip to see what the toubob were doing, to see what might be done. So the three brothers trekked for three days along the banks of the Kamby Bolongo, keeping carefully concealed in the bush, until they found what they were looking for. About twenty great toubob canoes were moored in the river, each big enough that its insides might hold all the people of Juffure, each with a huge white cloth tied by ropes to a treelike pole as tall as ten men. Nearby was an island, and on the island was a fortress.

Many toubob were moving about, and black helpers were with them, both on the fortress and in small canoes. The small canoes were taking such things as dried indigo, cotton, beeswax, and hides to the big canoes. More terrible than he could describe, however, said Omoro, were the beatings and other cruelties they saw being dealt out to those who had been captured for the toubob to take away.

For several moments, Omoro was quiet, and Kunta sensed that he was pondering something else to tell him. Finally he spoke: "Not as many of our people are being taken away now as then." When Kunta was a baby, he said, the King of Barra, who ruled this part of The Gambia, had ordered that there would be no more burning of villages with the capturing or filling of all their people. And soon it did stop, after the soldiers of some angry kings had burned the big canoes down to the water, killing all the toubob on board.

"Now," said Omoro, "nineteen guns are fired in salute to the King of Barra by every toubob canoe entering the Kamby Bolongo." He said that the King's personal agents now supplied most of the people whom the toubob took away—usually criminals or debtors, or anyone convicted for suspicion of plotting against the king—often for little more than whispering. More people seemed to get convicted of crimes, said Omoro, whenever toubob ships sailed in the Kamby Bolongo looking for slaves to buy.

"But even a king cannot stop the stealings of some people from their villages," Omoro continued. "You have known some of those lost from our village, three from among us just within the past few moons, as you know, and you have heard the drumtalk from other villages." He looked hard at his sons, and spoke slowly. "The things I'm going to tell you now, you must hear with more than your ears—for not to do what I say can mean your being stolen away forever!" Kunta and Lamin listened with rising fright. "Never be alone when you can help it," said Omoro. "Never be out at night when you can help it. And day or night, when you're alone, keep away from any high weeds or bush if you can avoid it."

For the rest of their lives, "even when you have come to be men," said their father, they must be on guard for toubob. "He often shoots his firesticks, which can be heard far off. And wherever you see much smoke away from any villages, it is probably his cooking fires, which are too big. You should closely inspect his signs to learn which way the toubob went. Having much heavier footsteps than we do, he leaves signs you will recognize as not ours: He breaks twings and grasses. And when you get close where he has been, you will find that his scent remains there. It's like a wet chicken smells. And many say a toubob sends forth a nervousness that we can feel. If you feel that, become quiet, for often he can be detected at some distance."

But it's not enough to know the toubob, said Omoro. "Many of our own people work for him. They are slatee *traitors*. But without knowing them, there is no way to recognize them. In the bush, therefore, trust *no* one you don't know."

Kunta and Lamin sat frozen with fear. "You cannot be told these things strongly enough," said their father. "You must know what your uncles and I saw happening to those who had been stolen. It is the difference between slaves among ourselves and those whom toubob takes away to be slaves for him." He said that they saw stolen people chained inside long, stout, heavily guarded bamboo pens along the shore of the river. When small canoes brought important-acting toubob from the big canoes, the stolen people were dragged outside their pens onto the sand.

"Their heads had been shaved, and they had been greased until they shined all over. First they were made to squat and jump up and down," said Omoro. "And then, when the toubob had seen enough of that, they ordered the stolen people's mouths forced open for their teeth and their throats to be looked at."

Swiftly, Omoro's finger touched Kunta's crotch, and as Kunta jumped, Omoro said, "Then the men's foto was pulled and looked at. Even the women's private parts were inspected." And the toubob finally made the people squat again and stuck burning hot irons against their backs and shoulders. Then, screaming and struggling, the people were shipped toward the water, where small canoes waited to take them out to the big canoes.

"My brothers and I watched many fall onto their bellies, clawing and eating the sand, as if to get one last hold and bite of their own home," said Omoro. "But they were dragged and beaten on." Even in the small canoes out in the water, he told Kunta and Lamin, some kept fighting against the whips and the clubs until they jumped into the water among terrible long fish with gray backs and white bellies and curved mouths full of thrashing teeth that reddened the water with their blood.

Kunta and Lamin had huddled close to each other, each gripping the other's hands. "It's better that you know these things than that your mother and I kill the white cock one day for you." Omoro looked at his sons. "Do you know what that means?"

Kunta managed to nod, and found his voice. "When someone is missing, Fa?" He had seen families frantically chanting to Allah as they squatted around a white cock bleeding and flapping with its throat slit.

"Yes," said Omoro. "If the white cock dies on its breast, hope remains. But when a white cock flaps to death on its back, then *no* hope remains, and the whole village joins the family in crying to Allah."

"Fa—" Lamin's voice, squeaky with fear, startled Kunta, "where do the big canoes take the stolen people?"

"The elders say to Jong Sang Doo," said Omoro, "a land where slaves are sold to huge cannibals called toubabo koomi, who eat us. No man knows any more about it."

Benjamin Spock / *The Common Sense Book of Baby Care*

1976

Pediatrician, psychiatrist, former columnist for Ladies' Home Journal *and* Redbook, *and Vietnam antiwar activist, Dr. Benjamin Spock became America's most influential authority on child care soon after the publication of* The Common Sense Book of Baby Care *in 1945. The book was meant to counter some of the absurd notions promulgated by Spock's predecessors, including Dr. John B. Watson who had asserted in his widely distributed text,* Psychological Care of Infant and Child (1928): *"Never, never kiss your child. Never hold it on your lap. Never rock its carriage." Spock's reassuring "common sense," evident in his Preface reprinted below, encourages a more relaxed approach to the difficulties of parenthood. Millions of Americans have been raised according to Spock's principles, the book having enjoyed greater total sales than any other work, except the Bible and Shakespeare's plays.*

The following selection on gun play—showing Spock's change of mind on the subject—is taken from the 1976 edition of his best-selling book.

[SHOULD CHILDREN PLAY WITH GUNS?]

Is gun play good or bad for children? For many years I emphasized its harmlessness. When thoughtful parents expressed doubt about letting their children have pistols and other warlike toys, because they didn't want to encourage them in the slightest degree to become delinquents or militarists, I would explain how little connection there was. In the course of growing up, children have a natural tendency to bring their aggressiveness more and more under control provided their parents encourage this. One- to 2-year-olds, when they're angry with another child, may bite the child's arm without hesitation. But by 3 or 4 they have already learned that crude aggression is not right. However, they like to pretend to shoot a pretend bad buy. They may pretend to shoot their mother or father, but grinning to assure them that the gun and the hostility aren't to be taken seriously.

In the 6- to 12-year-old period, children will play an earnest game of war, but it has lots of rules. There may be arguments and roughhousing, but real fights are relatively infrequent. At this age children don't shoot at their mother or father, even in fun. It's not that the parents have turned stricter; the children's own conscience has. They say, "Step on a crack; break your mother's back," which means that even the thought of wishing harm to their parents now makes them uncomfortable. In adolsescence, aggressive feelings become much stronger, but well-brought-up children sublimate them into athletics and other competition or into kidding their pals.

In other words, I'd explain that playing at war is a natural step in the disciplining of the aggression of young children; that most clergymen and pacifists probably did the same thing; that an idealistic parent doesn't really need to worry about producing a scoundrel; that the aggressive delinquent was not distorted in personality by being allowed to play bandit at 5 or 10, he was neglected and abused in his first couple of years, when his character was beginning to take shape; that he was doomed before he had any toys worthy of the name.

But nowadays I'd give parents much more encouragement in their inclination to guide their child away from violence. A number of occurrences have convinced me of the importance of this.

One of the first things that made me change my mind, several years ago, was an observation that an experienced nursery school teacher told me about. Her children were crudely bopping each other much more than previously, without provocation. When she remonstrated with them, they would protest, "But that's what the Three Stooges do." (This was a children's TV program full of violence and buffoonery which had recently been introduced and which immediately became very popular.) This attitude of the children showed me that watching violence can lower a child's standards of behavior. Recent psychological experiments have shown that being shown brutality on film stimulates cruelty in adults, too.

What further shocked me into reconsidering my point of view was the assassination of President Kennedy, and the fact that some schoolchildren cheered about this. (I didn't so much blame the children as I blamed the kind of parents who will say about a President they dislike, "I'd shoot him if I got the chance!")

These incidents made me think of other evidences that Americans have often been tolerant of harshness, lawlessness, and violence. We were ruthless in dealing with the Indians. In some frontier areas we slipped into the tradition of vigilante justice. We were hard on the later waves of immigrants. At times we've denied justice to groups with different religions or political views. We have crime rates way above those of other, comparable nations. A great proportion of our adult as well as our child population has been endlessly fascinated with dramas of Western violence and with brutal crime stories, in movies and on television. We have had a shameful history of racist lynchings and murders, as well as regular abuse and humiliation. In recent years it has been realized that infants and small children are being brought to hospitals with severe injuries caused by gross parental brutality.

Of course, some of these phenomena are characteristic of only a small percentage of the population. Even the others that apply to a majority of people don't necessarily mean that we Americans on the average have more aggressiveness inside us than the people of other nations. I think rather that the aggressiveness we have is less controlled, from childhood on.

To me it seems very clear that in order to have a more stable and civilized national life we should bring up the next generation of Americans with a greater respect for law and for other people's rights and sensibilities than in the past. There are many ways in which we could and should teach these attitudes. One simple opportunity we could utilize in the first half of childhood is to show our disapproval of lawlessness and violence in television programs and in children's gun play.

I also believe that the survival of the world now depends on a much greater awareness of the need to avoid war and to actively seek peaceful agreements. There are enough nuclear arms to utterly destroy all civilization. One international incident in which belligerence or brinkmanship was carried a small step too far could escalate into annihilation within a few hours. This terrifying situation demands a much greater stability and self-restraint on the part of national leaders and citizens than they have ever shown in the past. We owe it to our children to prepare them very deliberately for this awesome responsibility. I see little evidence that this is being done now.

When we let people grow up feeling that cruelty is all right provided they know it is make-believe, or provided they sufficiently disapprove of certain individuals or groups, or provided the cruelty is in the service of their country (whether the country is right or wrong), we make it easier for them to go berserk when the provocation comes.

But can we imagine actually depriving American children of their guns or of watching their favorite Western or crime programs? I think we should consider it—to at least a partial degree.

I believe that parents should firmly stop children's war play or any other kind of play that degenerates into deliberate cruelty or meanness. (By this I don't mean they should interfere in every little quarrel or tussle.)

If I had a 3- or 4-year-old son who asked me to buy him a gun, I'd tell him—with a friendly smile, not a scowl—that I don't want to give him a gun for even pretend shooting because there is too much meanness and killing in the world, that we must all learn how to get along in a friendly way together. I'd ask him if he didn't want some other present instead.

If I saw him, soon afterward, using a stick for a pistol in order to join a gang that was merrily going "bang-bang" at each other, I wouldn't rush out to remind him of my views. I'd let him have the fun of participating as long as there was no cruelty. If his uncle gave him a pistol or a soldier's helmet for his birthday, I myself wouldn't have the nerve to take it away from him. If when he was 7 or 8 he decided he wanted to spend his own money for battle equipment, I wouldn't forbid him. I'd remind him that I myself don't want to buy war toys or give them as presents; but from now on he will be playing more and more away from home and making more of his own decisions; he can make this decision for himself. I wouldn't give this talk in such a disapproving manner that he wouldn't dare decide against my policy. I would feel I'd made my point and that he had been inwardly influenced by my viewpoint as much as I could influence him. Even if he should buy weapons then, he would be likely to end up—in adolescence and adulthood—as thoughtful about the problems of peace as if I'd prohibited his buying them, perhaps more so.

One reason I keep backing away from a flat prohibition is that it would have its heaviest effect on the individuals who need it least. If all the parents of America became convinced and agreed on a toy-weapons ban on the first of next month, this would be ideal from my point of view. But this isn't going to happen for a long time, unless one nuclear missile goes off by accident and shocks the world into a banning of all weapons, real and pretend. A small percentage of parents—those most thoughtful and conscientious—will be the first ones who will want to dissuade their children from war toys; but their children will be most apt to be the sensitive, responsible children anyway. So I think it's carrying the issue unnecessarily far for those of us who are particularly concerned about peace and kindliness to insist that our young children demonstrate a total commitment to our cause while all their friends are gun toters. (It might be practical in a neighborhood where a majority of parents had the same conviction.) The main ideal is that children should grow up with a fond attitude toward all humanity. That will come about basically from the general atmosphere of our families. It will be strengthened by the attitude that we teach specifically toward other nations and groups. The elimination of war play would have some additional influence, but not as much as the two previous factors.

I feel less inclined to compromise on brutality on television and in movies. The sight of a real human face being apparently smashed by a fist has a lot more impact on children than what they imagine when they are making up their own stories. I believe that parents should flatly forbid programs that go in for violence. I don't think they are good for adults either. Young children can only partly distinguish between dramas and reality. Parents can explain, "It isn't right for people to hurt each other or kill each other and I don't want you to watch them do it."

Even if children cheat and watch such a program in secret, they'll know very well that their parents disapprove, and this will protect them to a degree from the coarsening effect of the scenes.

Stephen King / Night Shift: Excursions into Horror 1978

Before the commercial success of Carrie *in 1973, Stephen King had worked as a school teacher, gas-station attendant, and even pressed sheets in an industrial laundry. Author of a succession of best-selling novels, including* Salem's Lot *(1975),* The Shining *(1977),* The Stand *(1978),* The Dead Zone *(1979),* Firestarter *(1980),* Cujo *(1981), and* Christine *(1983), King has over 40 million copies of his books in print and is the first author in literary history to have three books simultaneously on the New York* Times *hard- and soft-cover best seller lists.*

Few contemporary writers can match King's gift for combining essentially normal—almost mundane—descriptions of everyday life with disturbingly believable depictions of paranormal events. His characters gain our sympathy because their surroundings, cluttered with cereal boxes, battered household appliances, popular rock 'n' roll songs, and other elements of our modern society, seem so familiar.

"Trucks," which is included in Night Shift *(1978), King's first collection of short stories, originally appeared in 1973 in* Cavalier, *a monthly magazine directed toward young men "interested in current events, ecology, sports, adventure, travel and clothing."*

TRUCKS

The guy's name was Snodgrass and I could see him getting ready to do something crazy. His eyes had gotten bigger, showing a lot of the whites, like a dog getting ready to fight. The two kids who had come skidding into the parking lot in the old Fury were trying to talk to him, but his head was cocked as though he was hearing other voices. He had a tight little potbelly encased in a good suit that was getting a little shiny in the seat. He was a salesman and he kept his display bag close to him, like a pet dog that had gone to sleep.

''Try the radio again,'' the truck driver at the counter said.

The short-order cook shrugged and turned it on. He flipped it across the band and got nothing but static.

''You went too fast,'' the trucker protested. ''You might have missed something.''

''Hell,'' the short-order cook said. He was an elderly black man with a smile of gold and he wasn't looking at the trucker. He was looking through the diner-length picure window at the parking lot.

Seven or eight heavy trucks were out there, engines rumbling in low, idling roars that sounded like a big cats purring. There were a couple of Macks, a Hemingway, and four or five Reos. Trailer trucks, interstate haulers with a lot of license plates and CB whip antennas on the back.

The kids' Fury was lying on its roof at the end of long, looping skid marks in the loose crushed rock of the parking lot. It had been battered into senseless junk. At the entrance to the truck stop's turnaround, there was a blasted Cadillac. Its owner stared out of the star-shattered windshield like a gutted fish. Horn-rimmed glasses hung from one ear.

Halfway across the lot from it lay the body of a girl in a pink dress. She had jumped from the Caddy when she saw it wasn't going to make it. She had hit running but never had a chance. She was the worst, even though she was face down. There were flies around her in clouds.

Across the road an old Ford station wagon had been slammed through the guardrails. That had happened an hour ago. No one had been by since then. You couldn't see the turnpike from the window and the phone was out.

''You went too fast,'' the trucker was protesting. ''You oughta—''

That was when Snodgrass bolted. He turned the table over getting up, smashing coffee cups and sending sugar in a wild spray. His eyes were wilder than ever, and his mouth hung loosely and he was blabbering: ''We gotta get outta here we gotta getouttahere wegottagetouttahere—''

The kid shouted and his girl friend screamed.

I was on the stool closest to the door and I got a handful of his shirt, but he tore loose. He was cranked up all the way. He would have gone through a bank-vault door.

He slammed out the door and then he was sprinting across the gravel toward the drainage ditch on the left. Two of the trucks lunged after him, smokestacks blowing diesel exhaust dark brown against the sky, huge rear wheels machine-gunning gravel up in sprays.

He couldn't have been any more than five or six running steps from the edge of the flat parking lot when he turned back to look, fear scrawled on his face. His feet tangled each other and he faltered and almost fell down. He got his balance again, but it was too late.

One of the trucks gave way and the other charged down, huge front grill glittering savagely in the sun. Snodgrass screamed, the sound high and thin, nearly lost under the Reo's heavy diesel roar.

It didn't drag him under. As things turned out, it would have been better if it had. Instead it drove him up and out, the way a punter kicks a football. For a moment he was silhouetted against the hot afternoon sky like a crippled scarecrow, and then he was gone into the drainage ditch.

The big truck's brakes hissed like dragon's breath, its front wheels locked, digging grooves into the gravel skin of the lot, and it stopped inches from jackknifing in. The bastard.

The girl in the booth screamed. Both hands were clamped into her cheeks, dragging the flesh down, turning it into a witch's mask.

Glass broke. I turned my head and saw that the trucker had squeezed his glass hard enough to break it. I don't think he knew it yet. Milk and a few drops of blood fell onto the counter.

The black counterman was frozen by the radio, a dishcloth in hand, looking amazed. His teeth glittered. For a moment there was no sound but the buzzing Westclox and the rumbling of the Reo's engine as it returned to its fellows. Then the girl began to cry and it was all right—or at least better.

My own car was around the side, also battered to junk. It was a 1971 Camaro and I had still been paying on it, but I didn't suppose that mattered now.

There was no one in the trucks.

The sun glittered and flashed on empty cabs. The wheels turned themselves. You couldn't think about it too much. You'd go insane if you thought about it too much. Like Snodgrass.

Two hours passed. The sun began to go down. Outside, the trucks patrolled in slow circles and figure eights. Their parking lights and running lights had come on.

I walked the length of the counter twice to get the kinks out of my legs and then sat in a booth by the long front window. It was a standard truck stop, close to the major thruway, a complete service facility out back, gas and diesel fuel both. The truckers came here for coffee and pie.

''Mister?'' The voice was hesitant.

I looked around. It was the two kids from the Fury. The boy looked about nineteen. He had long hair and a beard that was just starting to take hold. His girl looked younger.

''Yeah?''

''What happened to you?''

I shrugged. ''I was coming up the interstate to Pelson,'' I said. ''A truck came up behind me—I could see it in the mirror a long way off—really highballing. You could hear it a mile down the road. It whipped out around a VW Beetle and just snapped it off the road with the whiplash of the trailer, the way you'd snap a ball of paper off a table with your finger. I thought the truck would go, too. No driver could have held it with the trailer whipping that way. But it didn't go. The VW flopped over six or seven times and exploded. And the truck got the next one coming up the same way. It was coming up on me and I took the exit ramp in a hurry.'' I laughed but my heart wasn't in it. ''Right into a truck stop, of all places. From the frying pan into the fire.''

The girl swallowed. ''We saw a Greyhound going north in the southbound lane. It was . . . plowing . . . through cars. It exploded and burned but before it did . . . slaughter.''

A Greyhound bus. That was something new. And bad.

Outside, all the headlights suddenly popped on in unison, bathing the lot in an eerie, depthless glare. Growling, they cruised back and forth. The headlights seemed to give them eyes, and in the growing gloom, the dark trailer boxes looked like the hunched, squared-off shoulders of prehistoric giants.

The counterman said, ''Is it safe to turn on the lights?''

''Do it,'' I said, ''and find out.''

He flipped the switches and a series of flyspecked globes overhead came on. At the same time a neon sign out front stuttered into life: ''Conant's Truck Stop & Diner—Good Eats.'' Nothing happened. The trucks continued their patrol.

''I can't understand it,'' the trucker said. He had gotten down from his stool and was walking around, his hand wrapped in a red engineer's bandanna. ''I ain't had no problems with my rig. She's a good old girl. I pulled in here a little past one for a spaghetti dinner and this happens.'' He waved his arms and the bandanna flapped. ''My own rig's out there right now, the one with the weak left taillight. Been driving her for six years. But if I stepped out that door—''

''It's just starting,'' the counterman said. His eyes were hooded and obsidian. ''It must be bad if that radio's gone. It's just starting.''

The girl had drained as pale as milk. ''Never mind that,'' I said to the counterman. ''Not yet.''

''What would do it?'' The trucker was worrying. ''Electrical storms in the atmosphere? Nuclear testing? What?''

''Maybe they're mad,'' I said.

Around seven o'clock I walked over to the counterman. ''How are we fixed here? I mean, if we have to stay a while?''

His brow wrinkled. ''Not so bad. Yest'y was delivery day. We got two-three hunnert hamburg patties, canned fruit and vegetables, dry cereal, aigs . . . no more milk than what's in the cooler, but the water's from the well. If we had to, the five of us cud get on for a month or more.''

The trucker came over and blinked at us. ''I'm dead out of cigarettes. Now that cigarette machine . . .''

''It ain't my machine,'' the counterman said. ''No sir.''

The trucker had a steel pinch bar he'd gotten in the supply room out back. He went to work on the machine.

The kid went down to where the jukebox glittered and flashed and plugged in a quarter. John Fogarty began to sing about being born on the bayou.

I sat down and looked out the window. I saw something I didn't like right away. A Chevy light pickup had joined the patrol, like a Shetland pony amid Percherons. I watched it until it rolled impartially over the body of the girl from the Caddy and then I looked away.

''We *made* them!'' the girl cried out with sudden wretchedness. ''They *can't!*''

Her boyfriend told her to hush. The trucker got the cigarette machine open and helped himself to six or eight packs of Viceroys. He put them in different pockets and then ripped one pack open. From the intent expression on his face, I wasn't sure if he was going to smoke them or eat them up.

Another record came on the juke. It was eight o'clock.

At eight-thirty the power went off.

When the lights went, the girl screamed, a cry that stopped suddently, as if her boy friend had put his hand over her mouth. The jukebox died with a deepening, unwinding sound.

''What the *Christ!*'' the trucker said.

''Counterman!'' I called ''You got any candles?''

''I think so. Wait . . . yeah. Here's a few.''

I got up and took them. We lit them and started placing them around. ''Be careful,'' I said. ''If we burn the place down there's the devil to pay.''

He chuckled morosely. ''You know it.''

When we were done placing the candles, the kid and his girl were huddled together and the trucker was by the back door, watching six more heavy trucks weaving in and out between the concrete fuel islands. ''This changes things, doesn't it?'' I said.

''Damn right, if the power's gone for good.''

''How bad?''

''Hamburg'll go over in three days. Rest of the meat and aigs'll go by about as quick. The cans will be okay, an' the dry stuff. But that ain't the worst. We ain't gonna have no water without the pump.''

''How long?''

"Without no water? A week."

"Fill every empty jug you've got. Fill them till you can't draw anything but air. Where are the toilets? There's good water in the tanks."

"Employees' res'room is in the back. But you have to go outside to get to the lady's and gent's."

"Across to the service building?" I wasn't ready for that. Not yet.

"No. Out the side door an' up a ways."

"Give me a couple of buckets."

He found two galvanized pails. The kid strolled up.

"What are you doing?"

"We have to have water. All we can get."

"Give me a bucket then."

I handed him one.

"Jerry!" the girl cried. "You—"

He looked at her and she didn't say anthing else, but she picked up a napkin and began to tear at the corners. The trucker was smoking another cigarette and grinning at the floor. He didn't speak up.

We walked over to the side door where I'd come in that afternoon and stood there for a second, watching the shadows wax and wane as the trucks went back and forth.

"Now?" the kid said. His arm brushed mine and the muscles were jumping and humming like wires. If anyone bumped him he'd go straight up to heaven.

"Relax," I said.

He smiled a little. It was a sick smile, but better than none.

"Okay."

We slipped out.

The night air had cooled. Crickets chirred in the grass, and frogs thumped and croaked in the drainage ditch. Out here the rumble of the trucks was louder, more menacing, the sound of beasts. From inside it was a movie. Out here it was real, you could get killed.

We slid along the tiled outer wall. A slight overhand gave us some shadow. My Camaro was huddled against the cyclone fence across from us, and faint light from the roadside sign glinted on broken metal and puddles of gas and oil.

"You take the lady's," I whispered. "Fill your bucket from the toilet tank and wait."

Steady diesel rumblings. It was tricky; you thought they were coming, but it was only echoes bouncing off the building's odd corners. It was only twenty feet, but it seemed much farther.

He opened the lady's-room door and went in. I went past then I was inside the gent's. I could feel my muscles loosen and a breath whistled out of me. I caught a glimpse of myself in the mirror, strained white face with dark eyes.

I got the porcelain tank cover off and dunked the bucket full. I poured a little back to keep from sloshing and went to the door. "Hey?"

"Yeah," he breathed.

"You ready?"

"Yeah."

We went out again. We got maybe six steps before lights blared in our faces. It had crept up, big wheels barely turning on the gravel. It had been lying in wait and now it leaped at us, electric headlamps glowing in savage circles, the huge chrome grill seeming to snarl.

The kid froze, his face stamped with horror, his eyes blank, the pupils dilated down to pinpricks. I gave him a hard shove, spilling half his water.

"Go!"

The thunder of that diesel engine rose to a shriek. I reached over the kid's shoulder to yank the door open, but before I could it was shoved from inside. The kid lunged in and I dodged after him. I looked back to see the truck—a big cab-over Peterbilt—kiss off the tiled outside wall, peeling away jagged hunks of tile. There was an ear-grinding squealing noise, like gigantic fingers scraping a blackboard. Then the right mudguard and the corners of the grill smashed into the still-open door, sending glass, in a crystal spray and snapping the door's steel-gauge hinges like tissue paper. The door flew into the night like something out of a Dali painting and the truck accelerated toward the front parking lot, its exhaust racketing like machine-gun fire. It had a disappointed, angry sound.

The kid put his bucket down and collapsed into the girl's arms, shuddering.

My heart was thudding heavily in my chest and my calves felt like water. And speaking of water, we had brought back about a bucket and a quarter between us. It hardly seemed worth it.

''I want to block up that doorway,'' I said to the counterman. ''What will do the trick?''

''Well—''

The trucker broke in: ''Why? One of those big trucks couldn't get a wheel in through there.''

''It's not the big trucks I'm worried about.''

The trucker began hunting for a smoke.

''We got some sheet sidin' out in the supply room,'' the counterman said. ''Boss was gonna put up a shed to store butane gas.''

''We'll put them across and prop them with a couple of booths.''

''It'll help,'' the trucker said.

It took about an hour and by the end we'd all gotten into the act, even the girl. It was fairly solid. Of course, fairly solid wasn't going to be good enough, not if something hit it at full speed. I think they all knew that.

There were still three booths ranged along the big glass picture window and I sat down in one of them. The clock behind the counter had stopped at 8:32, but it felt like ten. Outside the trucks prowled and growled. Some left, hurrying off to unknown missions, and others came. There were three pickup trucks now, circling importantly amid their bigger brothers.

I was starting to doze, and instead of counting sheep I counted trucks. How many in the state, how many in America? Trailer trucks, pickup trucks, flatbeds, day-haulers, three-quarter-tons, army convoy trucks by the tens of thousands, and buses. Nightmare vision of a city bus, two wheels in the gutter and two wheels on the pavement, roaring along and plowing through screaming pedestrians like ninepins.

I shook it off and fell into a light, troubled sleep.

It must have been early morning when Snodgrass began to scream. A thin new moon had risen and was shining icily through a high scud of cloud. A new clattering note had been added, counterpointing the throaty, idling roar of the big rigs. I looked for it and saw a hay baler circling out by the darkened sign. The moonlight glanced off the sharp, turning spokes of its packer.

The scream came again, unmistakably from the drainage ditch: ''Help . . . *meeeee* . . .''

''What was that?'' It was the girl. In the shadows her eyes were wide and she looked horribly frightened.

''Nothing,'' I said.

''Help . . . *meeeee* . . .''

He's alive,'' she whispered. ''Oh, God. *Alive.*''

I didn't have to see him. I could imagine it all too well. Snodgrass lying half in and half out of the drainage ditch, back and legs broken, carefully-pressed suit caked with mud, white, gasping face turned up to the indifferent moon . . .

"I don't hear anything," I said. "Do you?"

She looked at me. "How can you? How?"

"Now if you woke him up," I said, jerking a thumb at the kid, "*he* might hear something. He might go out there. Would you like that?"

Her face began to twitch and pull as if stitched by invisible needles. "Nothing," she whispered. "Nothing out there."

She went back to her boy friend and pressed her head against his chest. His arms came up around her in his sleep.

No one else woke up. Snodgrass cried and wept and screamed for a long time, and then he stopped.

Dawn.

Another truck had arrived, this one a flatbed with a giant rack for hauling cars. It was joined by a bulldozer. That scared me.

The trucker came over and twitched my arm. "Come on back," he whispered excitedly. The others were still sleeping. "Come look at this."

I followed him back to the supply room. About ten trucks were patrolling out there. At first I didn't see anything new.

"See?" he said, and pointed. "Right there."

Then I saw. One of the pickups was stopped dead. It was sitting there like a lump, all of the menace gone out of it.

"Out of gas?"

"That's right, buddy. *And they can't pump their own.* We got it knocked. All we have to do is wait." He smiled and fumbled for a cigarette.

It was about nine o'clock and I was eating a piece of yesterday's pie for breakfast when the air horn began—long, rolling blasts that rattled your skull. We went over to the windows and looked out. The trucks were sitting still, idling. One trailer truck, a huge Reo with a red cab, had pulled up almost to the narrow verge of grass between the restaurant and the parking lot. At this distance the square grill was huge and murderous. The tires would stand to a man's chest cavity.

The horn began to blare again; hard, hungry blasts that traveled off in straight, flat lines and echoed back. There was a pattern. Shorts and longs in some kind of rhythm.

"That's Morse!" the kid, Jerry, suddenly exclaimed.

The trucker looked at him. "How would you know?"

The kid went a little red. "I learned it in the Boy Scouts."

"You?" the trucker said. "*You?* Wow." He shook his head.

"Never mind," I said. "Do you remember enough to—"

"Sure. Let me listen. Got a pencil?"

The counterman gave him one, and the kid began to write letters on a napkin. After a while he stopped. "It's just saying 'Attention' over and over again. Wait."

We waited. The air horn beat its longs and shorts into the still morning air. Then the pattern changed and the kid started to write again. We hung over his shoulders and watched the message form. "Someone must pump fuel. Someone will not be harmed. All fuel must be pumped. This shall be done now. Now someone will pump fuel."

The air blasts kept up, but the kid stopped writing. "It's just repeating 'Attention' again," he said.

The truck repeated its message again and again. I didn't like the look of the words, printed on the napkin in block style. They looked machinelike, ruthless. There would be no compromise with those words. You did or you didn't.

"Well," the kid said, "what do we do?"

"Nothing," the trucker said. His face was excited and working. "All we have to do is wait. They must all be low on fuel. One of the little ones out back has already stopped. All we have to do—"

The air horn stopped. The truck backed up and joined its fellows. They waited in a semicircle, headlights pointed in toward us.

''There's a bulldozer out there,'' I said.

Jerry looked at me. ''You think they'll rip the place down?''

''Yes.''

He looked at the counterman. ''They couldn't do that, could they?''

The counterman shrugged.

''We oughta vote,'' the trucker said. ''No blackmail, damn it. All we gotta do is wait.'' He had repeated it three times now, like a charm.

''Okay,'' I said. ''Vote.''

''Wait,'' the trucker said immediately.

''I think we ought to fuel them,'' I said. ''We can wait for a better chance to get away. Counterman?''

''Stay in here,'' he said. ''You want to be their slaves? That's what it'll come to. You want to spend the rest of your life changin' oil filters every time one of those . . . *things* blasts its horn? Not me.'' He looked darkly out the window. ''Let them starve.''

I looked at the kid and the girl.

''I think he's right,'' he said. ''That's the only way to stop them. If someone was going to rescue us, they would have. God knows what's going on in other places.'' And the girl, with Snodgrass in her eyes, nodded and stepped closer to him.

''That's it then,'' I said.

I went over to the cigarette machine and got a pack without looking at the brand. I'd stopped smoking a year ago, but this seemed like a good time to start again. The smoke rasped harsh in my lungs.

Twenty minutes crawled by. The trucks out front waited. In back, they were lining up at the pumps.

''I think it was all a bluff,'' the trucker said. ''Just—''

Then there was a louder, harsher, choppier note, the sound of an engine revving up and falling off, then revving up again. The bulldozer.

It glittered like a yellowjacket in the sun, a Caterpillar with clattering steel treads. Black smoke belched from its short stack as it wheeled around to face us.

''It's going to charge,'' the trucker said. There was a look of utter surprise on his face. ''It's going to charge!''

''Get back,'' I said. ''Behind the counter.''

The bulldozer was still revving. Gear-shift levers moved themselves. Heat shimmer hung over its smoking stack. Suddenly the dozer blade lifted, a heavy steel curve clotted with dried dirt. Then, with a screaming howl of power, it roared straight at us.

''The *counter!*'' I gave the trucker a shove, and that started them.

There was a small concrete verge between the parking lot and the grass. The dozer charged over it, blade lifting for a moment, and then it rammed the front wall head on. Glass exploded inward with a heavy, coughing roar and the wood frame crashed into splinters. One of the overhead light globes fell, splashing more glass. Crockery fell from the shelves. The girl was screaming but the sound was almost lost beneath the steady, pounding roar of the Cat's engine.

It reversed, clanked across the chewed strip of lawn, and lunged forward again, sending the remaining booths crashing and spinning. The pie case fell off the counter, sending pie wedges skidding across the floor.

The counterman was crouching with his eyes shut, and the kid was holding his girl. The trucker was walleyed with fear.

''We gotta stop it,'' he gibbered. ''Tell 'em we'll do it, we'll do anything—''

''A little late, isn't it?''

The Cat reversed and got ready for another charge. New nicks in its blade glittered and heliographed in the sun. It lurched forward with a bellowing roar and this time it took down the main support to the left of what had been the window. That section of the roof fell in with a grinding crash. Plaster dust billowed up.

The dozer pulled free. Beyond it I could see the group of trucks, waiting.

I grabbed the counterman. "Where are the oil drums?" The cookstoves ran on butane gas, but I had seen vents for a warm-air furnace.

"Back of the storage room," he said.

I grabbed the kid. "Come on."

We got up and ran into the storage room. The bulldozer hit again and the building trembled. Two or three more hits and it would be able to come right up to the counter for a cup of coffee.

There were two large fifty-gallon drums with feeds to the furnace and turn spigots. There was a carton of empty ketchup bottles near the back door. "Get those, Jerry."

While he did, I pulled off my shirt and yanked it to rags. The dozer hit again and again, and each hit was accompanied by the sound of more breakage.

I filled four of the ketchup bottles from the spigots, and he stuffed rags into them. "You play football?" I asked him.

"In high school"

"Okay. Pretend you're going in from the five."

We went out into the restaurant. The whole front wall was open to the sky. Sprays of glass glittered like diamonds. One heavy beam had fallen diagonally across the opening. The dozer was backing up to take it out and I thought that this time it would keep coming, ripping through the stools and then demolishing the counter itself.

We knelt down and thrust the bottles out. "Light them up," I said to the trucker.

He got his matches out, but his hands were shaking too badly and he dropped them. The counterman picked them up, struck one, and the hunks of shirt blazed greasily alight.

"Quick," I said.

We ran, the kid a little in the lead. Glass crunched and gritted underfoot. There was a hot, oily smell in the air. Everything was very loud, very bright.

The dozer charged.

The kid dodged out under the beam and stood silhouetted in front of that heavy tempered steel blade. I went out to the right. The kid's first throw fell short. His second hit the blade and the flame splashed harmlessly.

He tried to turn and then it was on him, a rolling juggernaut, four tons of steel. His hands flew up and then he was gone, chewed under.

I buttonhooked around and lobbed one bottle into the open cab and the second right into the works. They exploded together in a leaping shout of flame.

For a moment the dozer's engine rose in an almost human squeal of rage and pain. It wheeled in a maddened halfcircle, ripping out the left corner of the diner, and rolled drunkenly toward the drainage ditch.

The steel treads were streaked and dotted with gore and where the kid had been there was something that looked like a crumpled towel.

The dozer got almost to the ditch, flames boiling from under its cowling and from the cockpit, and then it exploded in a geyser.

I stumbled backward and almost fell over a pile of rubble. There was a hot smell that wasn't just oil. It was burning hair. I was on fire.

I grabbed a tablecloth, jammed it on my head, ran behind the counter, and plunged my head into the sink hard enough to crack it on the bottom. The girl was screaming Jerry's name over and over in a shrieking insane litany.

I turned around and saw the huge car-carrier slowly rolling toward the defenseless front of the diner.

The trucker screamed and broke for the side door.

"Don't!" the counterman cried. "Don't do that—"

But he was out and sprinting for the drainage ditch and the open field beyond.

The truck must have been standing sentry just out of sight of that side door—a small panel job with "Wong's Cash-and-Carry Laundry" written on the side. It ran him down almost before you could see it happen. Then it was gone and only the trucker was left, twisted into the gravel. He had been knocked out of his shoes.

The car-carrier rolled slowly over the concrete verge, onto the grass, over the kid's remains, and stopped with its huge snout poking into the diner.

Its air horn let out a sudden, shattering honk, followed by another, and another.

"Stop!" the girl whimpered. "Stop, oh stop, please—"

But the honks went on a long time. It took only a minute to pick up the pattern. It was the same as before. It wanted someone to feed it and the others.

"I'll go," I said. "Are the pumps unlocked?"

The counterman nodded. He had aged fifty years.

"No!" the girl screamed. She threw herself at me. "You've got to stop them! Beat them, burn them, break them—" Her voice wavered and broke into a harsh bray of grief and loss.

The counterman held her. I went around the corner of the counter, picking my way through the rubble, and out through the supply room. My heart was thudding heavily when I stepped out into the warm sun. I wanted another cigarette, but you don't smoke around fuel islands.

The trucks were still lined up. The laundry truck was crouched across the gravel from me like a hound dog, growling and rasping. A funny move and it would cream me. The sun glittered on its blank windshield and I shuddered. It was like looking into the face of an idiot.

I switched the pump to "on" and pulled out the nozzle; unscrewed the first gas cap and began to pump fuel.

It took me half an hour to pump the first tank dry and then I moved on to the second island. I was alternating between gas and diesel. Trucks marched by endlessly. I was beginning to understand now. I was beginning to see. People were doing this all over the country or they were lying dead like the trucker, knocked out of their boots with heavy tread-marks mashed across their guts.

The second tank was dry then and I went to the third. The sun was like a hammer and my head was starting to ache with the fumes. There were blisters in the soft webbing between thumb and index finger. But they wouldn't know about that. They would know about leaky manifolds and bad gaskets and frozen universal joints, but not about blisters or sunstroke or the need to scream. They needed to know only one thing about their late masters, and they knew it. We bleed.

The last tank was sucked dry and I threw the nozzle on the ground. Still there were more trucks, lined up around the corner. I twisted my head to relieve the crick in my neck and stared. The line went out of the front parking lot and up the road and out of sight, two and three lanes deep. It was like a nightmare of the Los Angeles Freeway at rush hour. The horizon shimmered and danced with their exhaust; the air stank of carburization.

"No," I said. "Out of gas. All gone, fellas."

And there was a heavier rumble, a bass note that shook the teeth. A huge silvery truck was pulling up, a tanker. Written on the side was "Fill Up with Phillips 66—The Jetport Fuel"!

A heavy hose dropped out of the rear.

I went over, took it, flipped up the feeder plate on the first tank, and attached the hose. The truck began to pump. The stench of petroleum sank into me—the same stink that the dinosaurs must have died smelling as they went down into the tar pits. I filled the other two tanks and then went back to work.

Consciousness twinkled away to a point where I lost track of time and trucks. I unscrewed, rammed the nozzle into the hole, pumped until the hot, heavy liquid splurted out, then replaced the cap. My blisters broke, trickling pus down to my wrists. My head was pounding like a rotted tooth and my stomach rolled helplessly with the stench of hydrocarbons.

I was going to faint. I was going to faint and that would be the end of it. I would pump until I dropped.

Then there were hands on my shoulders, the dark hands of the counterman. "Go in," he said. "Rest yourself. I'll take over till dark. Try to sleep."

I handed him the pump.

But I can't sleep.

The girl is sleeping. She's sprawled over in the corner with her head on a tablecloth and her face won't unknot itself even in sleep. It's the timeless, ageless face of the warhag. I'm going to get her up pretty quick. It's twilight, and the counterman has been out there for five hours.

Still they keep coming. I look out through the wrecked window and their headlights stretch for a mile or better, twinkling like yellow sapphires in the growing darkness. They must be backed up all the way to the turnpike, maybe further.

The girl will have to take her turn. I can show her how. She'll say she can't, but she will. She wants to live.

You want to be their slaves? the counterman had said. *That's what it'll come to. You want to spend the rest of your life changin' oil filters every time one of those things blasts its horn?*

We could run, maybe. It would be easy to make the drainage ditch now, the way they're stacked up. Run through the fields, through the marshy places where trucks would bog down like mastodons and go—

—back to the caves.

Drawing pictures in charcoal. This is the moon god. This is a tree. This is a Mack semi overwhelming a hunter.

Not even that. So much of the world is paved now. Even the playgrounds are paved. And for the fields and marshes and deep woods there are tanks, half-tracks, flatbeds equipped with lasers, masers, heat-seeking radar. And little by little, they can make it into the world they want.

I can see great convoys of trucks filling the Okefenokee Swamp with sand, the bulldozers ripping through the national parks and wildlands, grading the earth flat, stamping it into one great flat plain. And then the hot-top trucks arriving.

But they're machines. No matter what's happened to them, what mass consciousness we've given them, *they can't reproduce.* In fifty or sixty years they'll be rusting hulks with all menace gone out of them, moveless carcasses for free men to stone and spit at.

And if I close my eyes I can see the production lines in Detroit and Dearborn and Youngstown and Mackinac, new trucks being put together by blue-collars who no longer even punch a clock but only drop and are replaced.

The counterman is staggering a little now. He's an old bastard, too. I've got to wake the girl.

Two planes are leaving silver contrails etched across the darkening eastern horizon.

I wish I could believe there are people in them.

DISCUSSION QUESTIONS

1. Re-read Stephen King's essay on what is really "scary" in Magazines. How does "Trucks" fulfill his criterion for horror?

2. How does King construct an atmosphere of realism in a tale that is essen-

tially fantasy? Isolate examples of his language that make the world he writes about seem not only believable but wholly ordinary.

3. Explain how King also builds into his tale a criticism of contemporary society.

Andy Rooney / From *A Few Minutes with Andy Rooney* 1981

Andy Rooney, best known for his popular segment "Of Humor and Wisdom" on CBS's "60 Minutes," was born in 1919 in Albany, New York. He worked as a very successful television writer before he went into print and broadcasting. Once asked what he would like to do that he hadn't done yet, he replied, "Live to be a hundred."

In addition to his best-selling A Few Minutes with Andy Rooney, *Rooney's other recent books include* And More by Andy Rooney *(1982) and* Pieces of My Mind *(1984).*

ADVERTISING

My grandfather told me when I was a small boy that if a product was any good, they shouldn't have to advertise it.

I believed my grandfather at the time, but then years later my mother said that when *she* was a little girl he had told her that they'd never be able to build an automobile that would go up a hill. So I never knew whether to believe my grandfather or not.

Like so many things, I've really never made up my mind about advertising. I know all the arguments for it and against it, but the one thing I'm sure of is that there ought to be some sanctuaries, some places we're safe from being advertised at. There ought to be some open space left in the world without any advertising on it, some pieces of paper, some painted surfaces that aren't covered with entreaties for us to buy something.

Advertising doesn't belong on license plates, for instance. Of the fifty states, twenty-seven of them have slogans trying to sell themselves to the rest of us. It's offensive and wrong. The license plate has an important function and it's a cheap trick to tack something else on it. Most of the legends the states put on aren't true anyway.

Rhode Island, for instance, say it's the "Ocean State." There are fifteen states with more ocean than Rhode Island has. If they want to say something on their plate, why don't they explain why they call Rhode an island when it isn't one?

Florida says it's the "Sunshine State." I like Florida, but why don't they also say that Miami has more rain than any city in the whole United States except for Mobile, Alabama?

North Carolina says it's "First in Freedom." It doesn't say anywhere on the license plate who they think is *second* in freedom. South Carolina? Michigan?

Connecticut says it's the "Constitution State." I called the license bureau in Connecticut and no one could tell me why they call it the Constitution State. Connecticut is not the Constitution state, of course. *Pennsylvania* is the Constitution state. And Pennsylvania calls itself the "Keystone State." Does anyone really care?

Maine says it's "Vacationland." How would you like to drive a garbage truck for eight hours in Augusta with a sign hanging on the back that says "Vacationland"?

New Hampshire plates carry the pretentious legend "Live Free or Die." Some religious organization that apparently wasn't willing to die if they couldn't be free objected and taped over those words on all their license plates. The state said this was illegal and the case went to the Supreme Court. The Court ruled that the religious order did have the right to block out those words. New Hampshire would have saved us all a lot of time and money if they'd never put them on in the first place.

New Mexico calls itself "Land of Enchantment." This is not the kind of slogan that gets the work of the world done.

Hawaii says it's the "Aloha State." Hawaii ought to get over its palm-tree mentality and removing "Aloha" from its plates would be a good start. What sensible state would want to conjure up a picture of dancing girls draping flower ropes over the necks of visitors every time anyone thought about it?

Wisconsin "America's Dairyland?" Never mind that, Wisconsin, if you're dairyland why don't you tell us on your license plates what ever happened to heavy cream? That's the kind of stuff we'd like to read about when we're driving along behind a car from your state.

And then Idaho. How would you like to work hard, save your money and decide, when the kids were educated and the house paid for, to buy yourself a Mercedes-Benz. You plunk down your $28,000, the dealer screws on the license plate and there you are with your dream car, you drive away, and affixed to the bumper is the sign that says "Famous Potatoes."

"If a state is any good," I imagine my grandfather would have said, "it shouldn't have to advertise."

License-plate advertising is a small part of what we're faced with when we're driving. On the highways, trucks are turned into rolling billboards. The companies that own them look on it as easy advertising, too cheap to pass up. On major highways the commercials come along more often than on a late-night television movie.

On city streets, the billboards on Coca-Cola and Pepsi trucks are often double-parked while the driver makes deliveries. In most cities now, taxis and buses carry advertising. When you're paying a buck and a half a mile, you shouldn't have to carry a sign pushing cigarettes.

In California there's a company called Beetleboards. What Beetleboards will do for you is paint your Volkswagen, apply a commercial motif from a sponsor who is paying them and pay you twenty dollars a month to drive around in it.

And if you can understand businesses advertising their products on our roads, how do you account for the private citizens who use the back end of their cars to tell us about themselves or about some private campaign of theirs? A typical car or van in a parking lot outside a tourist attraction in Washington, D.C., will announce, through the decals attached to it somewhere, that the owner is insured by Allstate, boosts the Northern Virginia Ramparts—a team of some sort, I guess—is against forest fires because he has a little Smokey the Bear stuck to his car, gives to the International Convention of Police Chiefs and believes in God because his bumper sticker tells us so.

If someone has to take pride in having people know what insurance company gets his money, he's in trouble for things to be proud of.

A third of the cars on the road have reading matter stuck to them somewhere trying to sell the rest of us a place, an opinion or a way of life. Sometimes it looks as though half the cars in the United States have been to a roadside stand in South Carolina called South of the Border, and for some reason the entrepreneurs who have made tourist attractions out of caves love to slap "Visit Secret Caverns" on visitors' bumpers.

One of the most incredible commercial coups of the century has been pulled off by the designers who have conned women into thinking it's chic to wear a piece of apparel on which the maker's name is imprinted as part of the design.

The French luggage maker Louis Vuitton may have started the trend when he made the brown LV the only design on his product, but the women's fashion designers have taken it over. Bill Blass makes towels with his name all over them. Why would anyone want to take a shower and buff themselves dry on a piece of cloth bearing Bill Blass's name? Why would a woman go around with the name "Bloomies" on the seat of her underpants? Is there something I don't understand here?

Why would I or anyone else want to lay me down to sleep with my head on a pillowcase embossed with the signature of Yves Saint Laurent?

The first time I remember seeing a designer's name on something, the name was Pucci. It seemed amusing enough but now they're all doing it. Halston, Calvin Klein and Diane Von Furstenberg must all be wonderfully famous and talented, but if I buy anything of theirs I'd prefer to have it anonymous. If I got a scarf with Diane Von Furstenberg's name on it, which is unlikely, my first inclination would be to send it out to the cleaners to have them try to get it out.

The advertisers are coming at us from all directions all the time. If we were deer, a closed season would be declared on us to protect an endangered species. It just seems wrong to me that we're spending more time and money trying to sell some things than we are making them in the first place. I'm an all-American consumer but there are just certain times and places I don't want to be sold anything.

GOOD NEWS

All of us who work in television news are constantly being accused of emphasizing the negative side of everything. We get letters saying we never cover a story unless something terrible happens.

Tonight we've put together a little news broadcast to give you an idea of how it would look if you had it your way.

"I'm here by the Mississippi. It's raining but the river is not overflowing its banks.

"As a matter of fact, it doesn't look to me as though there's any danger of a flood whatsoever. People are not piling up sandbags. No one has been forced to evacuate his home and the Governor has not asked that this be declared a federal disaster area."

"O'Hare Airport in Chicago is one of the nation's busiest. At 11 A.M., a jet aircraft with 168 passengers and ten crew members on board started down the long runway. The plane, headed for London, took off without incident. It landed without incident too. Everyone on board is now in London.

"One passenger on board that plane was quoted as saying he didn't like the fake milk they served with the coffee."

"For a report from New York City we take you to our correspondent standing in front of the Plaza, one of New York City's most luxurious hotels.

"This is the Plaza, one of New York City's most luxurious hotels. CBS News has learned that last evening, after a night on the town, the Shah of Franakapan and his semi-beautiful wife returned to their hotel suite after depositing more than a million dollars' worth of jewelry in the hotel safe. The jewels included the famous Cooch Behar Diamond.

"This morning, when the safe was opened, all the jewelry including the famous Cooch Behar Diamond was right there where they'd left it."

"In Florida, the orange crop was hit by another night of average weather.

"The oranges just hung in there and grew."

"Oil industry officials announced today they were lowering prices because they just don't need the money. One reason for their affluence is their safety records.

"The oil tanks behind me are very close to a residential area. If they were on fire, smoke would begin billowing up for miles around. They aren't on fire, though; they're just sitting there."

"In Detroit, a General Motors spokesman announced today that more than 174,000 Chevrolets made in the late fall of 1974 would not be recalled. They are all perfect.

"At eleven-thirty this evening, CBS News will present a special report listing the serial numbers of those cars."

And if that's what you want to hear, that's the way it was.

Good evening.

Studs Terkel / *American Dreams: Lost & Found* 1980

Studs Terkel has held nearly as many jobs as all the people he has tape recorded for his ongoing oral history of everyday working America. Before, during, and after earning advanced degrees in literature and law at the University of Chicago, Terkel worked as a government statistician, news commentator, sportscaster, disc jockey, jazz critic, host of music festivals, playwright, stage and radio actor (he played the gangster on the popular thirties soap operas Ma Perkins *and* Road of Life*), and talk show host. Born in New York City in 1912, he moved to Chicago at eleven and has been associated ever since with both the city's blue-collar workers and its celebrities. His identification with working class Chicago was perhaps further enhanced when he borrowed the nickname of the protagonist of James T. Farrell's celebrated trilogy of the Prohibition and Depression eras,* Studs Lonigan.

Wielding a portable tape recorder to capture what he calls "the man of inchoate thought," Terkel has turned out three impressive volumes of best-selling nonfiction. Division Street, America *(1966) records the bitterness and anguish that flared in urban America during the sixties.* Hard Times: An Oral History of the Great Depression *(1970) is a "memory book" of the "hard facts," the still smoldering sense of guilt and failure, and the "small triumphs" of both the rich and poor who survived that protracted decade.*

Working: People Talk About What They Do All Day and How They Feel About What They Do *(1974), a tape-recorded exploration of the collective consciousness of American workers, was drawn from 133 interviews conducted over three years, almost exclusively with nonprofessional, seemingly anonymous Americans, most of whom repeatedly startled Terkel with what he has characterized as a search for "daily meaning as well as daily bread, for recognition as well as cash, for astonishment rather than torpor; in short, for a sort of life rather than a Monday through Friday sort of dying."*

The following two selections are taken from American Dreams: Lost & Found *(1980).*

MISS U.S.A., Emma Knight

Miss U.S.A., 1973. She is twenty-nine.

I wince when I'm called a former beauty queen or Miss U.S.A. I keep thinking they're talking about someone else. There are certain images that come to mind when people talk about beauty queens. It's mostly what's known as t and a, tits and ass. No talent. For many girls who enter the contest, it's part of the American Dream. It was never mine.

You used to sit around the TV and watch Miss America and it was exciting, we thought, glamorous. Fun, we thought. But by the time I was eight or nine, I didn't feel comfortable. Soon I'm hitting my adolescence, like fourteen, but I'm not doing any dating and I'm feeling awkward and ugly. I'm much taller than most of the people in my class. I don't feel I can compete the way I see girls competing for guys. I was very much of a loner. I felt intimidated by the amount of competition females were supposed to go through with each other. I didn't like being told by *Seventeen* magazine: Subvert your interests if you have a crush on a guy, get interested in what he's interested in. If you play cards, be sure not to beat him. I was very bad at these social games.

After I went to the University of Colorado for three and a half years, I had it. This was 1968 through '71. I came home for the summer. An agent met me and wanted me to audition for commercials, modeling, acting jobs. Okay. I started auditioning and winning some.

I did things actors do when they're starting out. You pass out literature at conventions, you do print ads, you pound the pavements, you send out your resumés. I had come to a model agency one cold day, and an agent came out and said: "I want you to enter a beauty contest." I said: "No, uh-uh, never, never, never. I'll lose, how humiliating." She said: "I want some girls to represent the agency, might do you good." So I filled out the application blank: hobbies, measurements, blah, blah, blah. I got a letter: "Congratulations. You have been accepted as an entrant into the Miss Illinois-Universe contest." Now what do I do? I'm stuck.

You have to have a sponsor. Or you're gonna have to pay several hundred dollars. So I called up the lady who was running it. Terribly sorry, I can't do this. I don't have the money. She calls back a couple of days later: "We found you a sponsor, it's a lumber company."

It was in Decatur. There were sixty-some contestants from all over the place. I went as a lumberjack: blue jeans, hiking boots, a flannel shirt, a pair of suspenders, and carrying an axe. You come out first in your costume and you introduce yourself and say your astrological sign or whatever it is they want you to say. You're wearing a banner that has the sponsor's name on it. Then you come out and do your pirouettes in your one-piece bathing suit, and the judges look at you a lot. Then you come out in your evening gown and pirouette around for a while. That's the first night.

The second night, they're gonna pick fifteen people. In between, you had judges' interviews. For three minutes, they ask you anything they want. Can you answer questions? How do you handle yourself? Your poise, personality, blah, blah, blah. They're called personality judges.

I thought: This will soon be over, get on a plane tomorrow, and no one will be the wiser. Except that my name got called as one of the fifteen. You have to go through the whole thing all over again.

I'm thinking: I don't have a prayer. I'd come to feel a certain kind of distance, except that they called my name. I was the winner, Miss Illinois. All I could do was laugh. I'm twenty-two, standing up there in a borrowed evening gown, thinking: What am I doing here? This is like Tom Sawyer becomes an altar boy.

I was considered old for a beauty queen, which is a little horrifying when you're twenty-two. That's very much part of the beauty queen syndrome: the young, untouched, unthinking human being.

I had to go to this room and sign the Miss Illinois-Universe contract right away. Miss Universe, Incorporated, is the full name of the company. It's owned by Kaiser-Roth, Incorporated, which was bought out by Gulf & Western. Big business.

I'm sitting there with my glass of champagne and I'm reading over this contract. They said: "Oh, you don't have to read it." And I said: "I never sign anything that I don't read." They're all waiting to take pictures, and I'm sitting there reading this long document. So I signed it and the phone rang and the guy was from a Chicago paper and said: ''Tell me, is it Miss or Ms.?'' I said: ''It's Ms.'' He said: ''You're kidding.'' I said: ''No, I'm not.'' He wrote an article the next day saying something like it finally happened: a beauty queen, a feminist. I thought I was a feminist before I was a beauty queen, why should I stop now?

Then I got into the publicity and training and interviews. It was a throwback to another time where crossed ankles and white gloves and teacups were present. I was taught how to walk around with a book on my head, how to sit daintily, how to pose in a bathing suit, and how to frizz my hair. They wanted curly hair, which I hate.

One day the trainer asked me to shake hands. I shook hands. She said: ''That's wrong. When you shake hands with a man, you always shake hands ring up.'' I said: ''Like the pope? Where my hand is up, like he's gonna kiss it?'' Right. I thought: Holy mackerel! It was a very long February and March and April and May.

I won the Miss U.S.A. pageant. I started to laugh. They tell me I'm the only beauty queen in history that didn't cry when she won. It was on network television. I said to myself: ''You're kidding.'' Bob Barker, the host, said: ''No, I'm not kidding.'' I didn't know what else to say at that moment. In the press releases, they call it the great American Dream. There she is, Miss America, your ideal. Well, not my ideal, kid.

The minute you're crowned, you become their property and subject to whatever they tell you. They wake you up at seven o'clock next morning and make you put on a negligee and serve you breakfast in bed, so that all the New York papers can come in and take your picture sitting in bed, while you're absolutely bleary-eyed from the night before. They put on the Kaiser-Roth negligee, hand you the tray, you take three bites. The photographers leave, you whip off the negligee, they take the breakfast away, and that's it. I never did get any breakfast that day. (Laughs.)

You immediately start making personal appearances. The Jaycees or the chamber of commerce says: ''I want to book Miss U.S.A. for our Christmas Day parade.'' They pay, whatever it is, seven hundred fifty dollars a day, first-class air fare, round trip, expenses, so forth. If the United Fund calls and wants me to give a five-minute pitch on queens at a luncheon, they still have to pay a fee. Doesn't matter that it's a charity. It's one hundred percent to Miss Universe, Incorporated. You get your salary. That's your prize money for the year. I got fifteen thousand dollars, which is all taxed in New York. Maybe out of a check of three thousand dollars, I'd get fifteen hundred dollars.

From the day I won Miss U.S.A. to the day I left for Universe, almost two months, I got a day and a half off. I made about two hundred fifty appearances that year. Maybe three hundred. Parades, shopping centers, and things. Snip ribbons. What else do you do at a shopping center? Model clothes. The nice thing I got to do was public speaking. They said: ''You want a ghost writer?'' I said: ''Hell, no, I know how to talk.'' I wrote my own speeches. They don't trust girls to go out and talk because most of them can't.

One of the big execs from General Motors asked me to do a speech in Washington, D. C., on the consumer and the energy crisis. It was the fiftieth anniversary of the National Mangement Association. The White House, for some reason, sent me some stuff on it. I read it over, it was nonsense. So I stood up and said: ''The reason we have an energy crisis is because we are, industrially and personally, pigs. We have a short-term view of the resources available to us; and unless we wake up to what we're doing to our air and our water, we'll have a dearth, not just a crisis.'' Oh, they weren't real pleased. (Laughs.)

What I resent most is that a lot of people didn't expect me to live this version of the American Dream for myself. I was supposed to live it their way.

When it came out in a newspaper interview that I said Nixon should resign, that he was a crook, oh dear, the fur flew. They got very upset until I got an invitation to the White House. They wanted to shut me up. The Miss Universe corporation had been trying to establish some sort of liaison with the White House for several years. I make anti-Nixon speeches and get this invitation.

I figured they're either gonna take me down to the basement and beat me up with a rubber hose or they're gonna offer me a cabinet post. They had a list of fifteen or so people I was supposed to meet. I've never seen such a bunch of people with raw nerve endings. I was dying to bring a tape recorder but thought if you mention the word "Sony" in the Nixon White House, you're in trouble. They'd have cardiac arrest. But I'm gonna bring along a pad and paper. They were patronizing. And when one of 'em got me in his office and talked about all the journalists and television people being liberals, I brought up blacklisting, *Red Channels,* and the TV industry. He changed the subject.

Miss Universe took place in Athens, Greece. The junta was still in power. I saw a heck of a lot of jeeps and troops and machine guns. The Americans were supposed to keep a low profile. I had never been a great fan of the Greek junta, but I knew darn well I was gonna have to keep my mouth shut. I was still representing the United States, for better or for worse. Miss Philippines won. I ran second.

At the end of the year, you're run absolutely ragged. That final evening, they usually have several queens from past years come back. Before they crown the new Miss U.S.A., the current one is supposed to take what they call the farewell walk. They call over the PA: Time for the old queen's walk. I'm now twenty-three and I'm an old queen. And they have this idiot farewell speech playing over the airwaves as the old queen takes the walk. And you're sitting on the throne for about thirty seconds, then you come down and they announce the name of the new one and you put the crown on her head. And then you're out.

As the new one is crowned, the reporters and photographers rush on the stage. I've seen photographers shove the girl who has just given her reign up thirty seconds before, shove her physically. I was gone by that time. I had jumped off the stage in my evening gown. It is very difficult for girls who are terrified of this ending. All of a sudden (snaps fingers), you're out. Nobody gives a damn about the old one.

Miss U.S.A. and remnants thereof is the crown stored in the attic in my parents' home. I don't even know where the banners are. It wasn't me the fans of Miss U.S.A. thought was pretty. What they think is pretty is the banner and crown. If I could put the banner and crown on that lamp, I swear to God ten men would come in and ask it for a date. I'll think about committing an axe murder if I'm not called anything but a former beauty queen. I can't stand it any more.

Several times during my year as what's-her-face I had seen the movie *The Sting.* There's a gesture the characters use which means the con is on: they rub their nose. In my last fleeting moments as Miss U.S.A, as they were playing that silly farewell speech and I walked down the aisle and stood by the throne, I looked right into the camera and rubbed my finger across my nose. The next day, the pageant people spent all their time telling people that I hadn't done it. I spent the time telling them that, of course, I had. I simply meant: the con is on. (Laughs.)

Miss U.S.A. is in the same graveyard that Emma Knight the twelve-year-old is. Where the sixteen-year-old is. All the past selves. There comes a time when you have to bury those selves because you've grown into another one. You don't keep exhuming the corpses.

If I could sit down with every young girl in America for the next fifty years, I could tell them what I liked about the pageant, I could tell them what I hated. It wouldn't make any difference. There're always gonna be girls who want to enter the beauty pageant. That's the fantasy: the American Dream.

THE TRAIN, CLARENCE SPENCER

We're on a day coach of the train bound for Washington, D.C. August 25, 1963. It is on the eve of the march, led by Martin Luther King. The hour is late. Most of the passengers are asleep or trying to. He is wide awake. He is seventy.

It's something like a dream, children. I'm just proud to ride this train down there, whether I march or not. I'm so proud just to be *in* it. It means something I wanted ever since I've been big enough to think about things. That's my freedom, making me feel that I'm a man, like all the rest of the men. I've had this feeling ever since I was about ten years old.

I was born and raised in the state of Louisiana. I did all kinds of work. I followed saw mills. I followed the levee camps, railroads, sugar farms, picked cotton. And I all the time wondered *why* in the world is it that some human being thinks he's so much more than the other. I can't never *see* that. I just can't *see* it. I don't *understand* it. I speak to you, you hear me, you understands me. You work like I work, eats like I eats, sleeps like I sleeps. Yet and still, how come? Why is it that they have to take the back seat for everything? So this trip is something like a dream to me.

I would put it thisaway. If you was down and out and you was longing for a thing and somebody would come and punch you out in a way that you could find it, you would feel like a different man, wouldn't you? That's the way I'm feelin'. I feel like I'm headed into something, that I would live to see some of the beneficial out of it. Maybe a day or two days. But I would enjoy those two days or one day better than I have enjoyed the whole seventy years which I've lived. Just to see myself as a man. Never mind the blackness, because that doesn't mean anything. I'm still a man.

When this thing started out, I said to my wife: "This I wants to be *in*. I don't want to see it on the television or hear it on the radio. I want to be *in* it. I crave to get into that light." I sit at home one day, and I read a portion of the Scripture in the Bible. I think it's the third chapter of the Lamentations of Jeremiah. This writer went on to say: He have led me and brought me in the darkness and not to light. I would like to get out of that darkness and into the light. That's what I'm working for.

I have fought it from years past up until now, and I'm still meanin' to be in it. In 1918, when I was in the service, I thought I was playing my part in the war, dignifiably. If I can take that, looks to me now I can take it anywheres else. Wouldn't it be that way to you? So this train can't get me down to Washington fast enough for me. Even if I don't be in the parade, just to stand somewhere and see this great bunch of people who have rosed up and some of the white people who have come with us. Let us live together. We can do so.

A man doesn't have to hunt another'n if he doesn't want to. If you says a thing I doesn't like, I can tell you about it. If he treats me wrong, I'm gonna speak to him like he's a man, not like he's an animal. Let him know he had did me wrong. Not anything he says, I must say yes. Every time you speak, it doesn't have to be right because you're speaking. Maybe you say something that I can see even deeper than you can. And lots of times it's the other way.

I got that letter in 1925 from Ku Kluck Klan for no reason at all, not for what I did to this man. They used to have a little magazine out, they call it *True Story*. He bought one and the guy that wrote the magazine, he had a story about a little colored boy and a crocodile was runnin' him. He was runnin' down the road barefooted and like they used to put the colored people in pictures with the hair all standin' up on the head. Let's make a loblolly out of him, you recall it. This man said to me: "Spencer, you from Dixie? I see where the crocodile run behind the little colored boy in the South." I said: "How come a crocodile will run a colored and won't run a white? A dumb beast doesn't know the difference.'' Did you know that liked to cause a killin' scrape over nothin'? We got to arguin' and arguin' over that. He threatened to kill me and wrote me that Ku Kluck Klan letter, and he got a rope and hung it to a post and it hung down where they were gonna put it around my neck.

When you don't do a person nothing, just try to straighten them out in their silly own doings and then he wanta talk about hangin', that's pretty bad, isn't it? You got the feelin' and you just can't get over it. That thing will wear you for a long, long time to come.

That's why I'm on this train. This train don't carry no liars, this train. That's a good old song.

This train is bound for glory . . .

. . . this train. That's right. We know it. Our people can compose those old songs. Like in the South, we had old blues songs. Things got tough, you couldn't hardly find a job, like back in the thirties. ''I'm gonna leave here walkin', baby, that I may get a ride.'' Get a ride, someway, somehow. That's the way we are fightin' in this. Someway, some means, somehow, we're gonna win it. We haven't got anything to fight with but what's right. This government have been run a long time with justice for *some* people, *not* all the people.

The thing that hurts so bad, we have built this country. My daddy was a slave, my daddy was. We have worked. We have built the railroads. We have built good roads. We have cut the ditches, we have cleaned up the ground. They tell me we've worked three hundred sixty-five years for nothin', and we have worked hundred two, hundred three years for a damned little bit of anything. You know a fella should be tired now, don't you? He should be really tired and wore out with it. But I'm proud to be in this. I'm kind of overjoyed.

Ray Bradbury / *The Stories of Ray Bradbury* 1980

Futuria Fantasia *was the title of the mimeographed quarterly Ray Bradbury began while a high school student in Waukegan, Illinois. He sold his first story at the age of twenty-one and wrote full-time thereafter. Bradbury estimates that he has written well over 1,000 short stories, mostly fantasy and science fiction. Many of his stories have appeared in* The New Yorker, Harper's, Mademoiselle, Playboy, *and other popular magazines; many more have appeared in science fiction magazines and collections. For several years he also wrote for* The Twilight Zone *and* Alfred Hitchcock Presents. *His work is represented in more than 150 anthologies.*

Bradbury describes his life as a writer much as he does his stories: ''Exactly one half terror, exactly one half exhilaration.'' In the selection below, we can clearly see Bradbury's ''terror and exhilaration'' with the idea of, even momentarily, stepping out of the limits of Time.

A SOUND OF THUNDER

The sign on the wall seemed to quaver under a film of sliding warm water. Eckels felt his eyelids blink over his stare, and the sign burned in this momentary darkness:

TIME SAFARI, INC.
SAFARIS TO ANY YEAR IN THE PAST.
YOU NAME THE ANIMAL.
WE TAKE YOU THERE.
YOU SHOOT IT.

A warm phlegm gathered in Eckels' throat; he swallowed and pushed it down. The muscles around his mouth formed a smile as he put his hand slowly out upon the air, and in that hand waved a check for ten thousand dollars at the man behind the desk.

"Does this safari guarantee I come back alive?"

"We guarantee nothing," said the official, "except the dinosaurs." He turned. "This is Mr. Travis, your Safari Guide in the Past. He'll tell you what and where to shoot. If he says no shooting, no shooting. If you disobey instructions, there's a stiff penalty of another ten thousand dollars, plus possible government action, on your return."

Eckels glanced across the vast office at a mass and tangel, a snaking and humming of wires and steel boxes, at an aurora that flickered now orange, now silver, now blue. There was a sound like a gigantic bonfire burning all of Time, all the years and all the parchment calendars, all the hours piled high and set aflame.

A touch of the hand and this burning would, on the instant, beautifully reverse itself. Eckels remembered the wording in the advertisements to the letter. Out of chars and ashes, out of dust and coals, like golden salamanders, the old years, the green years, might leap; roses sweeten the air, white hair turn Irish-black, wrinkles vanish; all, everything fly back to seed, flee death, rush down to their beginnings, suns rise in western skies and set in glorious easts, moons eat themselves opposite to the custom, all and everything cupping one in another like Chinese boxes, rabbits into hats, all and everything returning to the fresh death, the seed death, the green death, to the time before the beginning. A touch of a hand might do it, the merest touch of a hand.

"Hell and damn," Eckels breathed, the light of the Machine on his thin face. "A real Time Machine." He shook his head. "Makes you think. If the election had gone badly yesterday, I might be here now running away from the results. Thank God Keith won. He'll make a fine President of the United States."

"Yes," said the man behind the desk. "We're lucky. If Deutscher had gotten in, we'd have the worst kind of dictatorship. There's an anti-everything man for you, a militarist, anti-Christ, anti-human, anti-intellectual. People called us up, you know, joking but not joking. Said if Deutscher became President they wanted to go live in 1492. Of course it's not our business to conduct Escapes, but to form Safaris. Anyway, Keith's President now. All you got to worry about is—"

"Shooting my dinosaur." Eckels finished it for him.

"A *Tyrannosaurus rex*. The Thunder Lizard, the damndest monster in history. Sign this release. Anything happens to you, we're not responsible. Those dinosaurs are hungry."

Eckels flushed angrily. "Trying to scare me!"

"Frankly, yes. We don't want anyone going who'll panic at the first shot. Six Safari leaders were killed last year, and a dozen hunters. We're here to give you the damndest thrill a *real* hunter ever asked for. Traveling you back sixty million years to bag the biggest damned game in all Time. Your personal check's still there. Tear it up."

Mr. Eckels looked at the check for a long time. His fingers twitched.

"Good luck," said the man behind the desk. "Mr. Travis, he's all yours."

They moved silently across the room, taking their guns with them, toward the Machine, toward the silver metal and the roaring light.

First a day and then a night and then a day and then a night, then it was day-night-day-night-day. A week, a month, a year, a decade. A.D. 2055. A.D. 2019. 1999! 1957! Gone! the Machine roared.

They put on their oxygen helmets and tested the intercoms.

Eckels swayed on the padded seat, his face pale, his jaw stiff. He felt the trembling in his arms and he looked down and found his hands tight on the new rifle. There were four other men in the Machine. Travis, the Safari leader, his assistant, Lesperance, and two other hunters, Billings and Kramer. They sat looking at each other, and the years blazed around them.

"Can these guns get a dinosaur cold?" Eckels felt his mouth saying.

"If you hit them right," said Travis on the helmet radio. "Some dinosaurs have two brains, one in the head, another far down the spinal column. We stay away from those. That's stretching luck. Put your first two shots into the eyes, if you can, blind them, and go back into the brain."

The Machine howled. Time was a film run backward. Suns fled and ten million moons fled after them. "Good God," said Eckels. "Every hunter that ever lived would envy us today. This makes Africa seem like Illinois."

The Machine slowed; its scream fell to a murmur. The Machine stopped.

The sun stopped in the sky.

The fog that had enveloped the Machine blew away and they were in an old time, a very old time indeed, three hunters and two Safari Heads with their blue metal guns across their knees.

"Christ isn't born yet," said Travis. "Moses has not gone to the mountain to talk with God. The Pyramids are still in the earth, waiting to be cut out and put up. *Remember* that. Alexander, Caesar, Napoleon, Hitler—none of them exists."

The men nodded.

"That"—Mr. Travis pointed—"is the jungle of sixty million two thousand and fifty-five years before President Keith."

He indicated a metal path that struck off into green wilderness, over steaming swamp, among giant ferns and palms.

"And that," he said, "is the Path, laid by Time Safari for your use. It floats six inches above the earth. Doesn't touch so much as one grass blade, flower, or tree. It's an anti-gravity metal. Its purpose is to keep you from touching this world of the past in any way. Stay on the Path. Don't go off it. I repeat. *Don't go off.* For *any* reason! If you fall off, there's a penalty. And don't shoot any animal we don't okay."

"Why?" asked Eckels.

They sat in the ancient wilderness. Far birds' cries blew on a wind, and the smell of tar and an old salt sea, moist grasses, and flowers the color of blood.

"We don't want to change the Future. We don't belong here in the Past. The government doesn't *like* us here. We have to pay big graft to keep our franchise. A Time Machine is damn finicky business. Not knowing it, we might kill an important animal, a small bird, a roach, a flower even, thus destroying an important link in a growing species."

"That's not clear," said Eckels.

"All right," Travis continued, "say we accidentally kill one mouse here. That means all the future families of this one particular mouse are destroyed, right?"

"Right."

"And all the families of the families of the families of that one mouse! With a stamp of your foot, you annihilate first one, then a dozen, then a thousand, a million, a *billion* possible mice!"

"So they're dead," said Eckels. "So what?"

"So what?" Travis snorted quietly. "Well, what about the foxes that'll need those mice to survive? For want of ten mice, a fox dies. For want of ten foxes, a lion starves. For want of a lion, all manner of insects, vultures, infinite billions of life forms are thrown into chaos and destruction. Eventually it all boils down to this: fifty-nine million years later, a cave man, one of a dozen on the *entire world,* goes hunting wild boar or saber-tooth tiger for food. But you, friend, have *stepped* on all the tigers in that region. By stepping on *one* single mouse. So the cave man starves. And the cave man, please note, is not just *any* expendable man, no! He is an *entire future nation.* From his loins would have sprung ten sons. From *their* loins one hundred sons, and thus onward to a civilization. Destroy this one man, and you destroy a race, a people, an entire history of life. It is comparable to slaying some of Adam's grandchildren. The stamp of your foot, on one mouse, could start an earthquake, the effects of which could shake our Earth and destinies down through Time, to their very foundations. With the death of that one cave man, a billion others yet unborn are throttled in the womb. Perhaps Rome never rises on its seven hills. Perhaps Europe is forever a dark forest, and only Asia waxes healthy and teeming. Step on a mouse and you crush the Pyramids. Step on a mouse and you leave your print, like a Grand Canyon, across Eternity. Queen Elizabeth might never be born, Washington might not cross the Delaware, there might never be a United States at all. So be careful. Stay on the Path. *Never* step off!"

"I see," said Eckels. "Then it wouldn't pay for us even to touch the *grass?"*

"Correct. Crushing certain plants could add up infinitesimally. A little error here would multiply in sixty million years, all out of proportion. Or course maybe our theory is wrong. Maybe Time *can't* be changed by us. Or maybe it can be changed only in little subtle ways. A dead mouse here makes an insect imbalance there, a population disproportion later, a bad harvest further on, a depression, mass starvation, and, finally, a change in *social* temperament in far-flung countries. Something much more subtle, like that. Perhaps only a soft breath, a whisper, a hair, pollen on the air, such a slight, slight change that unless you looked close you wouldn't see it. Who knows? Who really can say he knows? We don't know. We're guessing. But until we do know for certain whether our messing around in Time *can* make a big roar or a little rustle in History, we're being damned careful. This Machine, this Path, your clothing and bodies, were sterilized, as you know, before the journey. We wear these oxygen helmets so we can't introduce our bacteria into an ancient atmosphere."

"How do we know which animals to shoot?"

"They're marked with red paint," said Travis. "Today, before our journey, we sent Lesperance here back with the Machine. He came to this particular era and followed certain animals."

"Studying them?"

"Right," said Lesperance. "I track them through their entire existence, noting which of them lives longest. Not long. How many times they mate. Not often. Life's short. When I find one that's going to die when a tree falls on him, or one that drowns in a tar pit, I note the exact hour, minute, and second. I shoot a paint bomb. It leaves a red patch on his hide. We can't miss it. Then I correlate our arrival in the Past so that we meet the Monster not more than two minutes before he would have died anyway. This way, we kill only animals with no future, that are never going to mate again. You see how *careful* we are?"

"But if you came back this morning in Time," said Eckels eagerly, "you must've bumped into *us,* our Safari! How did it turn out? Was it successful? Did all of us get through—alive?"

Travis and Lesperance gave each other a look.

"That'd be a paradox," said the latter. "Time doesn't permit that sort of mess—a man meeting himself. When such occasions threaten, Time steps aside. Like an airplane hitting an air pocket. You felt the Machine jump just before we stopped? That was us passing ourselves on the way back to the Future. We saw nothing.

There's no way of telling *if* this expedition was a success, *if* we got our Monster, or whether all of us—meaning *you,* Mr. Eckels—got out alive."

Eckels smiled palely.

"Cut that," said Travis sharply. "Everyone on his feet!"

They were ready to leave the Machine.

The jungle was high and the jungle was broad and the jungle was the entire world forever and forever. Sounds like music and sounds like flying tents filled the sky, and those were pterodactyls soaring with cavernous gray wings, gigantic bats out of a delirium and a night fever. Eckels, balanced on the narrow Path, aimed his rifle playfully.

"Stop that!" said Travis. "Don't even aim for fun, damn it! If your gun should go off—"

Eckels flushed. "Where's our *Tyrannosaurus?"*

Lesperance checked his wristwatch. "Up ahead. We'll bisect his trail in sixty seconds. Look for the red paint, for Christ's sake. Don't shoot till we give the word. Stay on the Path. *Stay on the Path!"*

They moved forward in the wind of morning.

"Strange," murmured Eckels. "Up ahead, sixty million years, Election Day over. Keith made President. Everyone celebrating. And here we are, a million years lost, and they don't exist. The things we worried about for months, a lifetime, not even born or thought about yet."

"Safety catches off, everyone!" ordered Travis. "You, first shot, Eckels. Second, Billings. Third, Kramer."

"I've hunted tiger, wild boar, buffalo, elephant, but Jesus, this is *it,"* said Eckels. "I'm shaking like a kid."

"Ah," said Travis.

Everyone stopped.

Travis raised his hand. "Ahead," he whispered. "In the mist. There he is. There's His Royal Majesty now."

The jungle was wide and full of twitterings, rustlings, murmurs, and sighs.

Suddenly it all ceased, as if someone had shut a door.

Silence.

A sound of thunder.

Out of the mist, one hundred yards away, came *Tyrannosaurus rex.*

"Jesus God," whispered Eckels.

"Shh!"

It came on great oiled, resilient, striding legs. It towered thirty feet above half of the trees, a great evil god, folding its delicate watchmaker's claws close to its oily reptilian chest. Each lower leg was a piston, a thousand pounds of white bone, sunk in thick ropes of muscle, sheathed over in a gleam of pebbled skin like the mail of a terrible warrior. Each thigh was a ton of meat, ivory, and steel mesh. And from the great breathing cage of the upper body, those two delicate arms dangled out front, arms with hands which might pick up and examine men like toys, while the snake neck coiled. And the head itself, a ton of sculptured stone, lifted easily upon the sky. Its mouth gaped, exposing a fence of teeth like daggers. Its eyes rolled, ostrich eggs, empty of all expression save hunger. It closed its mouth in a death grin. It ran, its pelvic bones crushing aside trees and bushes, its taloned feet clawing damp earth, leaving prints six inches deep wherever it settled its weight. It ran with a gliding ballet step, far too poised and balanced for its ten tons. It moved into a sunlit arena warily, its beautifully reptile hands feeling the air.

"My God!" Eckels twitched his mouth. "It could reach up and grab the Moon."

"Shh!" Travis jerked angrily. "He hasn't seen us yet."

"It can't be killed." Eckels pronounced this verdict quietly, as if there could be no argument. He had weighed the evidence and this was his considered opinion. The rifle in his hands seemed a cap gun. "We were fools to come. This is impossible."

"Shut up!" hissed Travis.

"Nightmare."

"Turn around," commanded Travis. "Walk quietly to the Machine. We'll remit one-half your fee."

"I didn't realize it would be this *big,*" said Eckels. "I miscalculated, that's all. And now I want out."

"It *sees* us!"

"There's the red paint on its chest!"

The Thunder Lizard raised itself. Its armored flesh glittered like a thousand green coins. The coins, crusted with slime, steamed. In the slime, tiny insects wriggled, so that the entire body seemed to twitch and undulate, even while the Monster itself did not move. It exhaled. The stink of raw flesh blew down the wilderness.

"Get me out of here," said Eckels. "It was never like this before. I was always sure I'd come through alive. I had good guides, good safaris, and safety. This time, I figured wrong. I've met my match and admit it. This is too much for me to get hold of."

"Don't run," said Lesperance. "Turn around. Hide in the Machine."

"Yes." Eckels seemed to be numb. He looked at his feet as if trying to make them move. He gave a grunt of helplessness.

"Eckels!"

He took a few steps, blinking, shuffling.

"Not *that* way!"

The Monster, at the first motion, lunged forward with a terrible scream. It covered one hundred yards in four seconds. The rifles jerked up and blazed fire. A windstorm from the beast's mouth engulfed them in the stench of slime and old blood. The Monster roared, teeth glittering with sun.

Eckels, not looking back, walked blindly to the edge of the Path, his gun limp in his arms, stepped off the Path, and walked, not knowing it, in the jungle. His feet sank into green moss. His legs moved him, and he felt alone and remote from the events behind.

The rifles cracked again. Their sound was lost in shriek and lizard thunder. The great lever of the reptile's tail swung up, lashed sideways. Trees exploded in clouds of leaf and branch. The Monster twitched its jeweler's hands down to fondle at the men, to twist them in half, to crush them like berries, to cram them into its teeth and its screaming throat. Its boulder-stone eyes leveled with the men. They saw themselves mirrored. They fired at the metallic eyelids and the blazing black iris.

Like a stone idol, like a mountain avalanche, *Tyrannosaurus* fell. Thundering, it clutched trees, pulled them with it. It wrenched and tore the metal Path. The men flung themselves back and away. The body hit, ten tons of cold flesh and stone. The guns fired. The Monster lashed its armored tail, twitched its snake jaws, and lay still. A fount of blood spurted from its throat. Somewhere inside, a sac of fluids burst. Sickening gushes drenched the hunters. They stood, red and glistening.

The thunder faded.

The jungle was silent. After the avalanche, a green peace. After the nightmare, morning.

Billings and Kramer sat on the pathway and threw up. Travis and Lesperance stood with smoking rifles, cursing steadily.

In the Time Machine, on his face, Eckels lay shivering. He had found his way back to the Path, climbed into the Machine.

Travis came walking, glanced at Eckels, took cotton gauze from a metal box, and returned to the others, who were sitting on the Path.

"Clean up."

They wiped the blood from their helmets. They began to curse too. The Monster lay, a hill of solid flesh. Within, you could hear the sighs and murmurs as the furthest chambers of it died, the organs malfunctioning, liquids running a final instant from pocket to sac to spleen, everything shutting off, closing up forever. It was like standing by a wrecked locomotive or a steam shovel at quitting time, all valves being released or levered tight. Bones cracked; the tonnage of its own flesh, off-balance, dead weight, snapped the delicate forearms, caught underneath. The meat settled, quivering.

Another cracking sound. Overhead, a gigantic tree branch broke from its heavy mooring, fell. It crashed upon the dead beast with finality.

"There." Lesperance checked his watch. "Right on time. That's the giant tree that was scheduled to fall and kill this animal originally." He glanced at the two hunters. "You want the trophy picture?"

"What?"

"We can't take a trophy back to the Future. The body has to stay right here where it would have died originally, so the insects, birds, and bacteria can get at it, as they were intended to. Everything in balance. The body stays. But we *can* take a picture of you standing near it."

The two men tried to think, but gave up, shaking their heads.

They let themselves be led along the metal Path. They sank wearily into the Machine cushions. They gazed back at the ruined Monster, the stagnating mound, where already strange reptilian birds and golden insects were busy at the steaming armor.

A sound on the floor of the Time Machine stiffened them. Eckels sat there, shivering.

"I'm sorry," he said at last.

"Get up!" cried Travis.

Eckels got up.

"Go out on that Path alone," said Travis. He had his rifle pointed. "You're not coming back in the Machine. We're leaving you here!"

Lesperance seized Travis's arm. "Wait—"

"Stay out of this!" Travis shook his hand away. "This son of a bitch nearly killed us. But it isn't *that* so much. Hell, no. It's his *shoes!* Look at them! He ran off the Path. My God, that *ruins* us! Christ knows how much we'll forfeit! Tens of thousands of dollars of insurance! We guarantee no one leaves the Path. He left it. Oh, the damn fool! I'll have to report to the government. They might revoke our license to travel. God knows *what* he's done to Time, to History!"

"Take it easy, all he did was kick up some dirt."

"How do we *know?*" cried Travis. "We don't know anything! It's all a damn mystery! Get out there, Eckels!"

Eckels fumbled his shirt. "I'll pay anything. A hundred thousand dollars!"

Travis glared at Eckels' checkbook and spat. "Go out there. The Monster's next to the Path. Stick your arms up to your elbows in his mouth. Then you can come back with us."

"That's unreasonable!"

"The Monster's dead, you yellow bastard. The bullets! The bullets can't be left behind. They don't belong in the Past; they might change something. Here's my knife. Dig them out!''

The jungle was alive again, full of the old tremorings and bird cries. Eckels turned slowly to regard that primeval garbage dump, that hill of nightmares and terror. After a long time, like a sleepwalker, he shuffled out along the Path.

He returned, shuddering, five minutes later, his arms soaked and red to the elbows. He held out his hands. Each held a number of steel bullets. Then he fell. He lay where he fell, not moving.

''You didn't have to make him do that,'' said Lesperance.

''Didn't I? It's too early to tell.'' Travis nudged the still body. ''He'll live. Next time he won't go hunting game like this. Okay.'' He jerked his thumb wearily at Lesperance. ''Switch on. Let's go home.''

1492. 1776. 1812.

They cleaned their hands and faces. They changed their caking shirts and pants. Eckels was up and around again, not speaking. Travis glared at him for a full ten minutes.

''Don't look at me,'' cried Eckels. ''I haven't done anything.''

''Who can tell?''

''Just ran off the Path, that's all, a little mud on my shoes—what do you want me to do—get down and pray?''

''We might need it. I'm warning you. Eckels, I might kill you yet. I've got my gun ready.''

''I'm innocent. I've done nothing!''

1999. 2000. 2055.

The Machine stopped.

''Get out,'' said Travis.

The room was there as they had left it. But not the same as they had left it. The same man sat behind the same desk. But the same man did not quite sit behind the same desk.

Travis looked around swiftly. ''Everything okay here?'' he snapped.

''Fine. Welcome home!''

Travis did not relax. He seemed to be looking at the very atoms of the air itself, at the way the sun poured through the one high window.

''Okay, Eckels, get out. Don't ever come back.''

Eckels could not move.

''You heard me,'' said Travis. ''What're you *staring* at?''

Eckels stood smelling of the air, and there was a thing to the air, a chemical taint so subtle, so slight, that only a faint cry of his subliminal senses warned him it was there. The colors, white, gray, blue, orange, in the wall, in the furniture, in the sky beyond the window, were . . . were . . . And there was a *feel.* His flesh twitched. His hands twitched. He stood drinking the oddness with the pores of his body. Somewhere, someone must have been screaming one of those whistles that only a dog can hear. His body screamed silence in return. Beyond this room, beyond this wall, beyond this man who was not quite the same man seated at this desk that was not quite the same desk . . . lay an entire world of streets and people. What sort of world it was now, there was no telling. He could feel them moving there, beyond the walls, almost, like so many chess pieces blown in a dry wind. . . .

But the immediate thing was the sign painted on the office wall, the same sign he had read earlier today on first entering.

Somehow, the sign had changed:

TYME SEFARI INC.
SEFARIS TU ANY YEER EN THE PAST.
YU NAIM THE ANIMALL.
WEE TAEK YU THAIR.
YU SHOOT ITT.

Eckels felt himself fall into a chair. He fumbled crazily at the thick slime on his boots. He held up a clod of dirt, trembling. "No, it *can't* be. Not a *little* thing like that. No!"

Embedded in the mud, glistening green and gold and black, was a butterfly, very beautiful, and very dead.

"Not a little thing like *that!* Not a butterfly!" cried Eckels.

It fell to the floor, an exquisite thing, a small thing that could upset balances and knock down a line of small dominoes and then big dominoes and then gigantic dominoes, all down the years across Time. Eckels' mind whirled. It *couldn't* change things. Killing one butterfly couldn't be *that* important! Could it?

His face was cold. His mouth trembled, asking: "Who—who won the presidential election yesterday?"

The man behind the desk laughed. "You joking? You know damn well. Deutscher, of course! Who else? Not that damn weakling Keith. We got an iron man now, a man with guts, by God!" The official stopped. "What's wrong?"

Eckels moaned. He dropped to his knees. He scrabbled at the golden butterfly with shaking fingers. "Can't we," he pleaded to the world, to himself, to the officials, to the Machine, "can't we take it *back,* can't we *make* it alive again? Can't we start over? Can't we—"

He did not move. Eyes shut, he waited, shivering. He heard Travis breathe loud in the room; he heard Travis shift his rifle, click the safety catch, and raise the weapon.

There was a sound of thunder.

Fran Lebowitz / *Social Studies* 1981

After a New York Times Book Review *critic called Fran Lebowitz "an important humorist in the classic tradition," the 6,000-copy first pressrun of her book* Metropolitan Life *was quickly exhausted. In a few months, 85,000 copies had been sold, and the paperback rights had been auctioned for $150,000: not best seller numbers or dollars, but a surprising success for a book that was expected to have only a small parochial readership. Her second collection of essays,* Social Studies, *appeared in 1981.*

Fran Lebowitz began her professional writing career with book and movie reviews in the now defunct magazine Changes. *Later she wrote a column for* Andy Warhol's Interview *magazine called "The Best of the Worst," and after a year's absence from* Interview *returned with another called "I Cover the Waterfront." She also contributed "The Lebowitz Report" to* Mademoiselle. *Like her idol, Oscar Wilde, Lebowitz is known for her razor-sharp silver tongue. In response to criticism on her pointedness, she said, "You know, someone once said that Dorothy Parker had wasted her life wisecracking. I really can't think of a better use for a life."*

THE LAST LAUGH

Coming from a family where literary tradition runs largely toward the picture postcard, it is not surprising that I have never really succeeded in explaining to my grandmother exactly what it is that I do. It is not that my grandmother is unintelligent; quite the contrary. It is simply that so firmly implanted are her roots in retail furniture that she cannot help but view all other occupations from this rather limited vantage point. Therefore, every time I see my grandmother I am fully prepared for the following exchange:

"So, how are you?"

"Fine, Grandma. How are you?"

"Fine. So how's business, good?"

"Very good, Grandma."

"You busy this time of year? Is this a good season for you?"

"Very good, Grandma."

"Good. It's good to be busy."

"Yes, Grandma."

Satisfied with my reponses, my grandmother will then turn to my father and ask the very same questions, a dialogue a bit more firmly grounded in reality, since he has not deviated from the Lebowitz custom of fine upholstered furniture.

The lack of understanding between my grandmother and myself has long troubled me, and in honor of her recently celebrated ninety-fifth birthday I have prepared the following business history in order that she might have a clearer vision of my life and work.

My beginnings were humble, of course, but I am not ashamed of them. I started with a humor pushcart on Delancey Street—comic essays, forty cents apiece, four for a dollar. It was tough out there on the street; competition was cutthroat, but it was the best education in the world because on Delancey "mildly amusing" was not enough—you had to be *funny*. I worked ten-hour days, six days a week, and soon I had a nice little following. Not exactly a cult, maybe, but I was doing okay. It was a living. I was able to put aside some money, and things looked pretty good for a store of my own in the not too distant future. Oh sure, I had my trouble, who doesn't? The housewives browsing through every essay on the cart, trying to contain their glee in the hope that I'd come down a little in price. The kids snitching a couple of paragraphs when my back was turned. And Mike the cop with his hand out all the time looking for a free laugh. But I persevered, never losing sight of my objective, and after years of struggle I was ready to take the plunge.

I went down to Canal Street to look for a store, a store of my own. Not being one to do things halfway, I was thorough and finally found a good location. Lots of foot traffic, surgical supplies on one side, maternity clothes on the other—these were people who could use a good laugh. I worked like a dog getting ready for that opening. I put in a very reasonable ready-to-hear line, an amusing notions counter, a full stock of epigrams, aphorisms, and the latest in wit and irony. At last I was ready; Fran's Humor Heaven: Home of the Devastating Double Entendre was open for business. It was tough going at first, but my overhead was low. I wrote all my own stock. And eventually I began to show a nice healthy gross and a net I could live with.

I don't know when it all began to go sour—who can tell about these things. I'm a humorist, not a fortuneteller—but business began to slip. First I took a bath with some barbed comments I was trying out, and then I got stuck with a lot of entertaining anecdotes. I hoped it was just an off season, but it didn't let up, and before I knew it I was in really big trouble. I tried everything, believe you me. I ran big sales—"Buy one epigram, get one free," "Twenty percent off all phrases." I even instituted a "Buy now, say later" plan. But nothing worked. I was at my wits' end; I owed everybody and was in hock up to my ears. So one day, pen in hand, I went to Morris "The Thesaurus" Pincus—a shy on East Houston who lent money to humorists in a jam. The interest rates were exorbitant but I signed my life away. What else could I do?

But it wasn't enough, and I was forced to take in a collaborator. At first he seemed to be working out. He specialized in parodies and they were moving pretty good, but before too long I began to get suspicious of him. I mean, I could barely put food on my table, and there he was, riding around in a Cadillac a block long. One night after dinner I went back to the store and went over the books with a fine-tooth comb. Just as I thought, there it was in black and white: the guy was a thief. He'd been stealing my lines all along. I confronted him with the evidence and what could he do? He promised to pay me back a few pages a week, but I knew that was one joker I'd never see again.

I kicked him out and worked even harder. Eighty-hour weeks, open every night until ten, but it was a losing battle. With the big humor chains moving in, what chance did an independent like me have? Then the day came when I knew all was lost. Sol's Discount Satire opened up right across the street. He wrote in bulk; I couldn't meet his prices. I, of course, was wittier, but nobody cared about quality anymore. Their attitude was "So it's a little broad, but at forty percent below list we'll forsake a little subtlety." I went in the back of the store and sat down, trying desperately to figure something out. There was a sharp rap at the door, and in walked Morris, a goon on either side, ready to collect. I told him I didn't have it. I begged for more time. I was pleading for my life. Morris stared at me coolly, a hard glint in his eye as he cleaned his nails with a lethal-looking fountain pen.

"Look, Fran," he said, "you're breaking my heart. Either you pay up by next Monday, or I'm gonna spread it around that you're mixing your metaphors."

With that he turned on his heel and walked out the door followed by the two gorillas. I was sweating bullets. If Morris spread that around, I'd never get another laugh as long as I lived. My head swam with crazy plans, and when I realized what I had to do, my heart thumped like a jackhammer.

Late that night I went back to the store. I let myself in through the side door and set to work. I poured a lot of gasoline around, took a last look, threw in a match and beat it the hell out of there. I was twenty blocks away when the full realization of what I'd done hit me. Overcome by remorse, I ran all the way back, but it was too late. The deed was done; I'd burned my comic essays for the insurance money.

The next day I met with the adjuster from That's Life, and thank God he bought the fire and paid me off. It was just enough to settle with Morris, and then I was broke again.

I started to free-lance for other stores, writing under a pseudonym, of course. My heart wasn't in it, but I needed the cash. I was grinding it out like hamburger meat, trying to build up some capital. The stuff was too facile, I knew that, but there was a market for it, so I made the best of it.

The years went by and I was just getting to the point where I could take it a little easy, when I was struck by an idea that was to change not only my own life but that of everyone in the entire humor business. The idea? Fast humor. After all, the pace had picked up a lot since my days on Delancey Street. The world was a different place; humor habits had changed. Everyone was in a hurry. Who had time anymore for a long comic essay, a slow build, a good long laugh? Everything was rush, rush, rush. Fast humor was an idea whose time had come.

Once again I started small, just a little place out on Queens Boulevard. I called it Rapid Repartee and used every modern design technique available. All chrome and glass, everything sleek and clean. Known in the business for my cunning and waggish ways, I couldn't resist a little joke and so used as my trademark a golden arch. No one got it. So I added another one, and got a great reaction. You really have to hit people over the head, don't you? Be that as it may, the place caught on like wildfire. I couldn't keep Quick Comebacks in stock, and the Big Crack was the hit of the century. I began to franchise, but refused to relinquish quality control. Business boomed and today I can tell you I'm sitting pretty. I've got it all: a penthouse on Park, a yacht the size of the *Queen Mary,* and a Rolls you could live in. But still, every once in a while I get that old creative itch. When this happens I slip on an apron and cap, step behind one of my thousands of counters, smile pleasantly at the customer and say, "Good morning. Something nice in a Stinging Barb?" If I'm recognized, it's always good for a laugh, because, believe you me, in this business unless you have a sense of humor you're dead.

James Michener / *Space* 1982

James Mitchener was born in New York City and grew up in Doylestown, Pennsylvania. After graduating from Swarthmore College in 1929, he studied art in Europe and returned to take a Master's degree from the Colorado State College of Education. He taught there until the Second World War, when he served as a naval officer in the South Pacific. Tales of the South Pacific, *his first novel, was published in 1947 and received the Pulitzer Prize for fiction that year. Since then, Michener has consistently made the best seller lists:* The Bridges at Toko-Ri *(1953),* Sayonara *(1954),* Hawaii *(1959),* Caravans *(1963),* The Source *(1965),* The Drifters *(1971),* Centennial *(1974),* Sports in America *(1976),* Chesapeake *(1978),* Poland *(1983). His fiction and articles have appeared in* Reader's Digest, Horizon, Ladies Home Journal, Holiday, *and many other magazines. The following selection from* Space *appeared originally in* Playboy *magazine.*

The three astronauts went to bed early on the night of April 22, 1973. On April 23, they were wakened for breakfast at 0400, and Deke Slayton, with five other NASA officials, was surprised when Major Randy Claggett lifted his glass of orange juice and toasted: "To William Shakespeare, whose birthday we celebrate with a mighty bang." Claggett, the ex-football hero, profane, tough and make-believe illiterate, was always full of surprises.

Slayton helped the three dress and accompanied them to Complex 39, where a score of searchlights played on the waiting rocket and nearly 1,000,000 spectators gathered in the predawn to watch the flight.

Despite NASA's unhappiness with the inaccurate description "expedition to the dark side of the moon," that had become the popular designation, and more than 3000 newsmen and -women waited in and around the grandstand erected on the far side of the protective lagoons, five miles distant. Automatic cameras, emplaced in bunkers around the complex, would ensure excellent shots of the historic moment.

By elevator, the astronauts rode 340 feet into the air, walked across a bridge to the White Room and, with hardly a pause, proceeded directly to the command module Altair. Without ceremony, Flight Commander Claggett eased himself into the left-hand seat, and while he adjusted his bulky suit, Dr. Paul Linley awaited his turn, assuring Slayton, who had picked him for this flight, that he would surely bring back rock samples that would answer some of the questions about the moon's structure and, perhaps, its origin. Linley, a civilian geologist from the University of New Mexico, would be the first scientist—and the first black man—to walk on the moon. He slipped into the right-hand seat, after which Command Module Pilot John Pope eased himself into the one in the middle.

When the men were finally in place, strapped flat on their backs to the seats especially molded to their forms, the critical moment of the countdown arrived. At 00-00-00, there was a blinding flash of fire and the ground trembled as 28,000 gallons of water per second gushed forth to quench the flames and another 17,000 gallons protected the skin of the machine. From that deluge, the rocket began to rise.

Inside the capsule, the three astronauts barely felt the lift-off. Linley, who had not flown before, said, "Instruments say we're off," and Pope, busy with check sheets, tapped the geologist on the arm and nodded.

At that moment, when it was assured that Apollo 18 would be successfully airborne, control passed from Cape Canaveral, whose engineers had done their job, to Houston, where Mission Control had hundreds of experts prepared to feed information and instructions into the system:

> HOUSTON: All systems go.
> APOLLO: We're getting ready for jettison.

In less than three minutes, the huge stage one had discharged its obligation, lifting the entire burden of 6,300,000 pounds eight miles straight up. So Claggett watched as automatic switches—he had more than 600 above and about him—blew stage one away, allowing it to fall harmlessly into the Atlantic some miles offshore. With satisfaction, Pope noted that all events so far had adhered to his schedule.

The first moments of flight were extremely gentle, no more than a *g* and a half developing, but when Claggett ignited the five powerful engines of stage two, the rocket seemed to leap upward from an altitude of a mere eight miles to a majestic 112 and to a velocity of more than 15,000 miles an hour. The flight was on its way.

Then Claggett jettisoned stage two, with its five massive engines, and Apollo 18 was powered by only the single strong engine in stage three, the one that would be burned once to insert the vehicle into orbit around Earth and once more to thrust Apollo into its course to the moon, after which it, too, would be discarded. But, of course, the system as a whole would still have the smaller engines in the modules, and after stage three had been jettisoned, about three hours into the flight, those smaller rockets would take control until the landing capsule returned to Earth.

Now it would be a slow, methodical, totally supervised trip that Apollo would engage in for the next 60 hours. Claggett would play country music on his tape machine, Pope the symphonies of Beethoven when it came his turn. Linley monitored communications with Houston and took note of the N.C.A.A. basketball scores. On the second night, to coincide with prime-time television in the States, Linley activated the Altair's television camera and relayed to Earth a 50-minute program depicting life aboard the spacecraft.

The next day, as the moon loomed ahead, enormous in their small windows, they could identify areas where the earlier Apollos had landed, and they felt momentary remorse that they were not headed for any of the sites they had memorized as beginning astronauts. But when they swung around the edge of the moon and saw for the first time the strange and marvelous mountains awaiting them, they gasped with delight.

Flight plan called for them to make many orbits of the moon before actually descending, and in that waiting period, they talked with Hickory Lee in Houston:

> HOUSTON: Could you see any signs of previous landings?
> APOLLO: None. And we really searched.
> HOUSTON: That's hard to believe. When you drop to lower orbit, of course. . . .
> APOLLO: Our landing spot is in darkness now, but what we can see of the lighted area looks reassuring. Totally different from the Earth side. Many, many more craters.
> HOUSTON: We want you to make four sunlight passes.
> APOLLO: You can be sure we want to.
> HOUSTON: Any glitches?
> APOLLO: None whatever. Fingers crossed, but this has been a perfect mission so far.

There was a glitch. High in the clear air of the Rockies, astronomer Sam Cottage monitored the sun at the Sun Study Center in Boulder, Colorado, on the morning after lift-off and saw with interest that a sunspot big enough to see with the naked eye might be developing. His summary that day informed the world and the NASA scientists:

> Region 419 produced several subflares. New spots are appearing in white light. Region exhibiting mixed polarities. Geomagnetic field likely to remain unsettled. Region likely to produce moderate flares.

But on the next day, as the astronauts were preparing their approach to the moon, Region 419 subsided dramatically.

However, Cottage could not sleep, and during the hours when Claggett and Linley were preparing their descent to the moon, he was alone in his workroom, reviewing the data. The more mathematics he applied to what was before him, the more apparent it became that if his theories were correct, Region 419 must soon erupt as a major flare.

He had nothing to work on except his correlations, but in the morning he carried them to the manager and said, ''Statistically, everything would balance out if Four-nineteen did go bang.''

''We're not gypsies telling fortunes.''

''All right, disregard my figures. What do you think?''

''It's a troublesome region, but damn it, we don't have enough here to warrant an alert.'' And none was issued.

But on April 26, as the two astronauts were making their final preparations for a descent to the moon, Sam Cottage did not leave his watching post for lunch. A routine event was occurring on the sun that, though it involved no specific danger, did produce a period of maximum risk to the two men who would be walking on the moon. Region 419 was moving from the eastern half of the sun's visible surface to the western, and that made it triply threatening. First, because of solar rotation, the paths followed by energetic atomic particles thrown out by the sun are curved, so that those originating on the western half are more directly channeled toward Earth and the moon. Second, the travel time for deadly particles originating on the western half is much shorter than those coming from the eastern. Third, solar-flare particles reaching Earth or the moon from the western side are more energetic than those from the east.

The most threatening single position for a flare is 20 to 45 degrees west of the sun's central meridian, and that was the ominous area into which Region 419 now entered.

About the time that Sam Cottage was monitoring Region 419, Claggett and Linley were slipping through the chute that carried them into Landing Module Luna. After they had satisfied themselves that everything was in readiness, they signaled Pope that he could cast them loose, but he was so busy verifying the check lists that governed his solitary command of the capsule that he asked for more time. ''I've got three more pages. I want this place to be locked up when you pull away.''

''We want it, too,'' Claggett said over the intercom. ''Something to come home to.''

At the conclusion of his meticulous checking, Pope cried, ''Randy, it's everything go. Contact Houston.'' So the word was given; the computers aloft and their mates in Houston concurred; and the Luna broke away to start its descent.

As the sun began to illuminate regions farther and farther into the hemisphere, Claggett and Linley could see a moon far different from the Earth side they had once studied so assiduously. Here there were no vast seas, no multitude of smooth-centered craters, no rills leading out in tantalizing patterns. This was a brutish moon composed of great mountain ranges, valleys perilously deep. The Earth side had been known for 20,000 years and mapped for 300. Grammar school children could make themselves familiar with their own side, but only scientists studying the Russian and American photographs could say that they knew much about Luna's chosen landing spot.

Skillfully, Claggett brought the lander right down the middle of the corridor—enough sun to throw shadows that identified every hillock—and as the long, delicate probes that dangled from the bottom of the landing pads reached down to touch the moon and alert the astronauts to turn off their power, lest they fly too hard onto the rocky soil, the final conversation with Houston took place:

LUNA: Everything as ordered. God, this is different.
HOUSTON: We read perfection. Soon now.
LUNA: No signals from the probes. Could they be malfunctioning?
HOUSTON: You're still well above the probe level. All's well.
LUNA: [*Claggett speaking*] Too busy to talk now. Drifting to left. Too much.
LUNA: [*Linley speaking*] No strain. Straighten up; head ahead. I see it.
LUNA: [*Claggett speaking*] I can't see a damn thing. We're tilted.
LUNA: [*Linley speaking*] You are tilted. Left. Five degrees.
LUNA: [*Claggett speaking*] I thought I was. There, that's better. Houston, I see now. All is copacetic.
LUNA: [*Linley speaking*] Perfect landing.
HOUSTON: Great job.

As gently as if he had been parking a large car at a supermarket, Claggett had brought the Luna to rest at the extreme far edge of the sun's rays. Ahead lay darkness, soon to be dazzling sunlight; behind lay the areas that had been bathed in sunlight but would later pass into the terrible cold and darkness of space, where no atmosphere reflected light.

LUNA: We've had a close look through the windows. Same, only different.
HOUSTON: You must get some shut-eye.
LUNA: We want some.
HOUSTON: All systems shut down?
LUNA: All secured.
HOUSTON: We'll waken you in seven hours. Egress in nine.
LUNA: That's what we came for.

So eager was Sam Cottage to see what his sun was going to offer the morning of April 27 that he unlimbered his heliograph an hour before dawn, then spent his time nervously waiting for the great red disk to appear over the flatlands to the east. For about an hour after sunrise, it would be fruitless to take photographs, for the sun would be so low in the east that a camera would be unable to penetrate effectively the extreme thickness of atmosphere. Even so, he studied the sun through its blanket of haze to see whether or not any conspicuous event had happened overnight.

Against the possibility that he might have to issue an alert, he spent his time reviewing the data on radiation in *The Rem* [roentgen equivalent in man] *Table*.

When light filled the room, Cottage walked nervously about, stopping now and then to study the remarkable series of photographs taken in July 1959 showing several stages of one of the greatest solar flares ever recorded—a wild, tempestuous blotch. The flare would have generated, Cottage estimated, a total dose of something like 1000 rems as measured on the moon. More than enough to kill.

Randy Claggett's style was to be irreverent about everything—marriage, fatherhood, test piloting, engaging Russian Migs in Korea—but when he felt his heavy boot touch the surface of the moon and realized that he was standing on a portion of the universe that no one on Earth would ever see, not even with the most powerful telescope, he was overcome with the solemnity of the moment:

> LUNA: Nothing could prepare you for this moment. The photographs weren't even close. This is . . . it's staggering. An endless landscape of craters and boulders.
>
> HOUSTON: And not a dark side at all?
>
> LUNA: The sun shines brilliantly, but it's sure dark in spirit.

As soon as Linley joined him on the surface, a curious transformation occurred: Up till then, Claggett had been the skilled test pilot in command, but here among the rocks of a wildly unfamiliar terrain, the geologist assumed control, and he reminded Claggett that their first responsibility was to collect rocks immediately, lest they have to take off in a hurry. Placing the scientific instruments and doing the systematic sample collecting could come later.

Only when the emergency bags had been filled with rock samples and stowed aboard did the two men proceed to what seemed a miracle when it was flashed by means of the orbiting satellites to television watchers back on Earth: At an opening in the base of the lunar module, they opened a flap, activated a series of devices and stood back as a most bizarre creation started to emerge, like a chrysalis about to become a butterfly. It looked much like a frail shopping cart that had been run over in some truck accident, compacted and twisted, but as it came into sunlight, its various parts, which were spring-loaded, began to unfold of themselves: Four wheels mysteriously appeared, a steering handle, a tonneau with seats. Like a child's toy unfolding at Christmas, a complete moon rover materialized, with batteries strong enough to move it about for three days or 80 miles—whichever came first.

When the rover stood clear, the astronauts did not leap into it for a gambol across the moon; in fact, they ignored it as they went about the serious business of unloading and positioning the complex of scientific instruments that would make this journey fruitful for the next ten years. In each of the preceding Apollo missions, men had placed on the moon devices that were expected to send messages to Earth for up to a year, but those devices had been so beautifully constructed and with so many sophisticated bypasses if things went wrong that all of them still functioned long after their predicted death. ''Sometimes we do things right,'' Claggett said as he emplaced the instrument that would measure the force of the solar wind.

''You seem to have the wires crossed,'' Hickory Lee cautioned from Houston. ''Red to red.''

''I had it ass backward,'' Claggett said, and Lee had to remind him, ''We're working with an open mike.''

When the eight scientific devices were placed and the antennas that would relay their findings were oriented so that the satellites could intercept their transmissions, the two man were ready to send test signals.

> HOUSTON: We read you loud and clear.
> LUNA: Voltages in order?
> HOUSTON: Could not be better.
> LUNA: We're going to rest fifteen minutes.
> HOUSTON: You earned it.
> LUNA: Then we start on Expedition One. Seven miles to the reticulated crater.
> HOUSTON: Roger. Are you checking your dosimeters?
> LUNA: Regular.

After their rest, taken to avoid perspiration or heavy breathing that might consume too much oxygen, the two men climbed into the rover, with Linley at the controls:

> LUNA: Linley speaking. Please, someone, inform my uncle Dr. Gawain Butler, who would not allow me to drive his used Plymouth, that I am now chauffeuring a jalopy with a sticker price of ten million clams.
> HOUSTON: Obey all traffic signs.

This carried them to an interesting small crater, one whose flat central section was so reticulated, like a mud flat in August, that the astronauts had given it the name "the Giraffe Crater." When they climbed a small mound at its edge, Linley gasped with pleasure and informed Houston that it was even more exciting than they had supposed when studying photographs.

> LUNA: Magnificent. We have a whole new world here.
> HOUSTON: Better change that to moon.
> LUNA: Corrected. We're going down on foot to collect samples.
> HOUSTON: Too steep for the rover?
> LUNA: We think so.
> HOUSTON: Roger. We'll follow you with the television camera.
> LUNA: We're going left. To get those rocks that look yellowish.

It was truly miraculous. The two astronauts left the rover and descended gingerly into the crater, but as they went, technicians in Houston sent electronic commands to the television camera mounted on the side of the rover, and obediently, it followed the progress of the men. Its electrical impulses were dispatched by a special antenna on the rover to one of the waiting satellites, which reflected them to collecting stations at Honeysuckle in Australia and at Goldstone in California, where they were transformed into television pictures for commercial stations. And the linkage was so perfect that operators in Houston were able to point the camera and activate it more meticulously than a man could have done had he stayed in the flimsy rover.

At the Sun Study Center in Boulder, Sam Cottage turned the cranks that moved his heliograph into position, brought the hydrogen-alpha filter into the optics in order to obtain the most sensitive view of activity on the sun and waited for the great star to lose its redness so he could get a clear look at its face. When he did so, he saw that Region 419 had reached the precise spot from which it could create the maximum danger. But it remained quiescent. Sam consulted his charts to make an estimate of the size of the region and was surprised at his figure: Region 419 was now 63 times larger than the entire surface of Earth.

Before filing his report, he looked back to verify the astonishing size of the disturbance, and as he did so, he saw the area expand significantly. "Jesus, what's happening?"

He reached backward for his telephone but never found it, for his attention was riveted on that distant battleground on which primordial forces had reached a point of tension that could no longer be sustained. With one mighty surge, Region 419 exploded in titanic fury. It was no longer simply a threatening active region; it was one of the most violent explosions of the past 200 years.

"Oh, Jesus!" Cottage gasped, and while he fumbled for the phone, figures and delimitations galloped through his head: "Sun to moon, less than ninety-three-million miles. What we see now happened eight-point-thirty-three minutes ago. But radiation travels at speed of light, so it's already hit the moon. Oh, Jesus, those poor men! Rems? Five thousand, maybe six thousand total dose." And in the brief seconds it took for him to find the phone, two thoughts flashed across his mind: "What else might have happened during the eight minutes it took that flash to reach here?" and "God, God, please protect those men."

He spread the alarm, but by the time his superiors could alert NASA, two other observatories and three amateurs in the Houston area had already reported that a gigantic solar proton event was under way.

HOUSTON: Luna, Altair, do you read me?

ALTAIR: I read.

HOUSTON: Why doesn't Luna answer? Altair, can you see Luna at this point?

ALTAIR: Negative.

LUNA: [*Breaking in*] I read you, Houston.

HOUSTON: There seems to have been an event on the sun. Have you checked your dosimeters?

LUNA: Oh, oh!

HOUSTON: We read your telemetry as very high.

LUNA: So do we. Dosimeter is saturated.

ALTAIR: Confirm. Very high.

HOUSTON: We now have confirmation from different sources. Major solar event. Classification four-bright way over X-12 in X-ray flux.

LUNA: What probable duration?

HOUSTON: Cannot predict. Wait. Human Ecology says two days, three days.

LUNA: [*Claggett speaking*] I think we may have a problem.

HOUSTON: The drill is clear. Return to lunar module. Lift off soonest. Make rendezvous soonest.

LUNA: We do not have data and time for lift-off. We do not have data and time for rendezvous.

HOUSTON: Our computers will crank up and feed you. What is your E.T.A. back at lunar module?

LUNA: Distance, seven miles; top speed, seven miles. Yield, one hour.

HOUSTON: How long to button up?

LUNA: Abandonin' gear, twenty minutes.

HOUSTON: Abandon all gear. Luna, there is no panic, but speed essential.

LUNA: Who's panickin'? We're climbin' out of a crater, rough goin'.

HOUSTON: Manufacturer assures rover can make top speed eleven miles per hour.

LUNA: And if we break down? What top speed walkin'?

HOUSTON: Roger. Maintain safe speed.

LUNA: We'll try nine.

HOUSTON: We're informed nine was tested strenuously. Proved safe.

LUNA: We'll try nine.

Now the sun reminded Earthlings of its terrible power, for it poured forth atomic particles and radiation at an appalling rate, sending them coursing through planetary space and bombarding every object they encountered. Wave after wave of solar-flare particles and high-energy radiation attacked Earth, but most of them were rejected by our protective atmosphere; however, enough did penetrate to create bizarre disturbances.

• In Northern New York, a power company found its protective current breakers activated by huge fluxes of electrical power coursing alomg its lines, coming from no detectable source to disrupt entire cities.

• An Air Force general, trying vainly to communicate with a base 1000 miles away, realized that the entire American defense system was impotent: "If Russia wanted to attack us at a moment of total confusion, this would be it." Then he smiled wanly: "Of course, their system would be as messed up as ours."

• A world-famous pigeon race between Ames, Iowa, and Chicago launched 1127 birds, with a likelihood, from past experiences, that more than 1000 would promptly find their way home. But since all magnetic fields were in chaos, only four made it, bedraggled, confused and six hours late.

In Houston, the knowing men in charge of Apollo 18 assembled quietly, aware of how powerless they were. The mission controller and Dr. Feldman, NASA's expert on radiation, looked at the dosimeter reports and shuddered. More than 5000 rems were striking the moon. Very calmly, the controller said, "Give me the bottom line."

Dr. Feldman ticked off on his fingers, "Highest reading we've had is five thousand eight hundred thirty rems," and a NASA scientist said, "Absolutely fatal," but Feldman continued his recital: "If, and I repeat if, five thousand eight hundred thirty strike a naked man, he's dead. But our men have the finest suits ever devised. Enormous protection. Plus their own clothes. Plus the most important aspect of all. It isn't radiation that might kill them. It's the outward flow of protons from the sun. And they will not reach the moon for another eleven minutes." He ticked off his last two points: "We rush our men into their moon lander, where they find more protection. Then we rocket them aloft to the orbiter, with its heavy shield."

Throwing both hands in the air, he shouted, "We can save those men!"

The controller summoned his three capsule commanders and said, "No fluctuation in voice. No hysteria at this end." To the hundreds gathering, he conveyed the same message: "I want all ideas and I want them quick. But only the CapComs are to speak with the astronauts."

Turning to the chief astronomers, he asked, "Could this have been predicted?"

"No," they said. "Closing months of a quiet cycle. It should not have happened."

The controller wanted to say, "Well, it did. Six thousand rems." But he knew he must betray neither anxiety nor irritation: "Now it's your job to get them home safe."

By the time Clagett and Linley had reached their rover and turned it around, they no longer bothered with their dosimeters, because once the reading passed the 1000-rem mark, any further data was irrelevant. They were in deep trouble and they knew it, but they did have a chance if they did everything right.

For nearly an hour, their rover crawled back toward the waiting lunar module, itself attacked by the solar outpouring, and the two men wanted to talk about their predicament but could think of nothing sensible to say. So they took refuge in trivialities: "Men have absorbed large doses of this stuff, haven't they, Linley?" The scientist replied, "Every day, in dentists' offices," and Claggett asked, "Do those lead blankets they throw over you do any good?" Linley said, "We could profit from a couple right now."

And then Houston heard raucous laughter coming from Luna. It was Linley: "Hey, Claggett! Did you see those medicals they threw at us last week? Said that a man with black skin had a better chance of repelling radiation than one with white skin. Hot diggity! At last it pays to be black.''

Then Claggett's voice: ''Move over, brother, so I can sit in your shadow.''

Alone in the Altair, John Pope carefully shuffled his summary sheets until he came to one bearing the elegant printing he had learned at Annapolis—RADIATION PRECAUTIONS—and when he had memorized his instructions to himself, he took down the massive volume of additional advice and went through each line, so that by the time his two companions reached their module, he would be as prepared as any man could be. Like them, he felt no sense of panic, only the added responsibility of doing the right thing in an emergency.

HOUSTON: Altair, have you cranked in the data we sent?

ALTAIR: Affirmative.

HOUSTON: You have the drill on turning the C.M. around so the ablative shield faces the sun?

ALTAIR: Affirmative.

HOUSTON: Execute immediately rendezvous has been established.

ALTAIR: Will do.

HOUSTON: What is your dosimeter reading now?

ALTAIR: As before.

HOUSTON: Excellent . . . your reading is much lower than Luna's. You're going to be all right.

ALTAIR: All ready for rendezvous. Get them up here.

The CapCom, up to that point, had been one of the older astronauts, a man with a stable, reassuring voice, but the NASA command felt that it would be advisable to use in this critical situation someone with whom the men upstairs were especially familiar, and Hickory Lee took over:

HOUSTON: This is Hickory. All readings are good. [*That was a lie; the dosimeter readings were terrifying. But it was not a lie; the prospects for an orderly rendezvous still existed.*]

LUNA: Good to hear that Tennessee voice. We can see the module. E.T.A. fifteen minutes.

HOUSTON: I will read lift-off data as soon as you're inside. You don't have a pad available now, do you?

LUNA: Negative. Pads not a high priority aboard this bone rattler.

LUNA: Linley here. We have terrific rock samples. Will salvage.

HOUSTON: Appreciated, but if transfer takes even one extra minute, abandon.

LUNA: We will not abandon.

HOUSTON: Neither would I. What's that? Who? [*A pause*] Luna, Dr. Feldman is here.

HOUSTON: [*Lee speaking again*] Dr. Feldman asks, ''Dr. Linley, do you feel nauseated?''

LUNA: Affirmative.

HOUSTON: Imperative you swallow spit.

LUNA: Fresh out of spit. Send orange juice.

HOUSTON: [*Lee speaking*] Dr. Feldman says, ''Dr. Linley, keep your mouth moist.''

LUNA: Mouth! Be moist!

Mission Control in Houston had received, in the past hour, a flood of additional men rushing to emergency posts, each determined to get the two astronauts into the slightly better environment of the lunar module and headed for rendezvous with Altair. But when they saw the shocking data from the dosimeters, they could not be sanguine; this was going to be a tough ride, a very tough ride.

HOUSTON: Park the rover close to the module.

LUNA: Roger.

HOUSTON: Inform me the moment Claggett steps into the module. I will start reading data for check. Nothing is to be done without full check.

LUNA: I have always been one of the world's most careful checkers. Call me Chicken Claggett.

HOUSTON: Give me the word.

As soon as Linley stopped the rover, Claggett dashed for the module, climbed in and started taking down the instructions Hickory Lee was transmitting. Since NASA could not wait for an ideal lift-off time, when Altair would be in maximum position to achieve rendezvous, schedules had to be improvised for second best, and when Linley saw that his commander would be occupied for some minutes, he welcomed the opportunity to return to the rover to rescue the precious cargo he had collected at the reticulated crater. He had been sent to the moon to collect rocks and he proposed to deliver them, but as he heaved aboard the second batch, he seemed to tremble and reach for a handhold that was not there.

LUNA: I think Dr. Linley has fainted.

HOUSTON: Inside the module or out?

LUNA: Halfway in.

HOUSTON: Drag him in, secure all and lift off immediately.

LUNA: I have only partial data. He's in. You can do wonders in one-sixth gravity.

HOUSTON: Lift off immediately.

LUNA: I am using runway oh three nine. Ain't a hell of a lot of traffic on it.

HOUSTON: Have you completed your check? And Linley's?

LUNA: Shipshape.

HOUSTON: It's go.

LUNA: You ready up there, Altair?

ALTAIR: Three orbits should do it.

LUNA: Here we come.

And then, as Pope watched and the world listened, Randy Claggett, working alone, lifted the lunar module off the surface of the moon and brought it 600 feet into space.

HOUSTON: All readings correct. One hell of a job, Randy.

LUNA: I feel faint.

HOUSTON: Not now, Randy. Not now. You dare not.

LUNA: I. . . .

HOUSTON: Listen, Randy. Hickory here. Hold the controls very tight.

LUNA: It's no good, Houston. I. . . .

HOUSTON: Colonel Claggett, hold tight. You must not let go. You must not let go.

LUNA: [*A long silence*]

John Pope stared at the module through his sextant, saw it waver, turn on its side, skid through space and descend toward the moon with fatal speed.

HOUSTON: Hold on, Randy. You must not let go. Randy, you must not let go. Randy. . . .

ALTAIR: Luna has crashed.

HOUSTON: Location?

ALTAIR: East of landing. Mountains.

HOUSTON: Damage?

ALTAIR: Obliterated.

HOUSTON: This is Hickory. Altair, climb to orbit.

ALTAIR: Negative. I must stay low to check.

HOUSTON: I'm talking with Dr. Feldman. He asks, "Is your voice sort of drying up?"

ALTAIR: Obliterated. My God, they were obliterated.

HOUSTON: Hickory here. Altair, you must ascend to orbit. You are wasting fuel.

ALTAIR: I will not leave until I see where they are.

HOUSTON: You've already told us. East of landing. Mountains.

ALTAIR: I will not leave them.

HOUSTON: I think he's turned off his mike. John, John, this is Hickory. It's imperative that you proceed to orbit and prepare to ignite engine. John, John, this is Hickory.

For two orbits, John Pope flew alone through the intense radiation being poured out by the errant sun, and each time he headed directly toward the sun, he realized the heavy dosage he must be absorbing, for his dosimeter was running wild; but when he slipped behind the moon, putting that heavy body between himself and the sun, he knew that he was reasonably safe from the extreme radiation.

On each pass, he stared for as long as he could at the site of the crash, and though he was at an altitude from which not much could be seen clearly, it was nevertheless obvious that the astronauts' suits had been ripped by the crash and that death must have been more or less instantaneous.

> How different death is here. No worms to eat the body; no moisture to corrupt. A thousand years from now, there they'll be: the first, the only. When wanderers come from the other galaxies, there our two will be, immaculate, unburied, waiting for the resurrection, all parts intact.

In hurried consultations, NASA agreed that they would explain those two orbits of silence as a radio blackout caused by the sun flare, which had now reached catastrophic proportions. Astronomers all across the world were focused on it, and scores of photographs were showing television viewers just how titanic the explosion had been, so that John Pope's temporary silence would not be construed as anything untoward. Without discernible agitation, Houston asked all its stations to try to make direct contact with Pope, and a welter of international voices sped toward the drifting Altair. Pope listened dully.

ALTAIR: Luna crash confirmed. They bought the ranch.

HOUSTON: Any possibility of survivors?

ALTAIR: Negative. Luna completely fractured.

HOUSTON: Hickory speaking. John, we want you to go immediately to orbit.

ALTAIR: Roger. Wilco.

HOUSTON: John, during the blackout we calculated every mile of your way home. It looks good.

ALTAIR: I'm ready.

HOUSTON: It will be obligatory for you to get some sleep. Will you need sedatives?

ALTAIR: Negative. Negative.

HOUSTON: Can you stay alert for the next six hours?

ALTAIR: Affirmative. Six days if we have to.

HOUSTON: Six days you'll be in a feather bed. Now, John. Do you read me clear?

ALTAIR: Affirmative.

HOUSTON: And you understand the burn sequence?

ALTAIR: Affirmative. Repeat, my mind is clear. I comprehend.

HOUSTON: You're going to have to do everything just right. Exactly on the times we give.

ALTAIR: I intend to.

HOUSTON: And if there is anything you do not understand. . . .

ALTAIR: Lay off, Hickory. I intend to get this bucket safely home. You take it easy. I'll take it easy.

HOUSTON: God bless you, Moonshiner. Bring it down.

ALTAIR: I intend to.

As methodically as if he were in the 17th hour of a familiar simulation, Pope ran through his check lists, took note of his fuel supplies and of when the firings were to be made to correct his course so that he would enter Earth's domain correctly. When all was secure, so far as he could control, he said quietly to Houston: "I think it's go all the way," and at the signal, he fired the rockets that inserted him into the orbit that would carry him the 238,850 miles back to the safety of the Pacific Ocean.

He now faced some 80 hours of loneliness, and from the left-hand seat, the capsule seemed enormous; he was surprised that anyone had ever felt it to be cramped. Aware that he had been motionless for a long time while Claggett and Linley had been active on the moon, he began to worry about his legs, and for two hours, he banged away on the newly provided Exer-Genie, which produced a real sweat.

He then turned on his tape, listening to Beethoven's joyous *Seventh,* but, remembering how Claggett had objected to what he called spaghetti music, he found it distasteful. Instead, he routed out some of Claggett's tapes and listened to hillbillies singing *D-I-V-O-R-C-E,* which not even his longing to see Claggett again could make palatable. When CapCom Ed Cater came on from Houston to ask if he wanted to hear the news, he said, curtly, "No!" so Cater said that Dr. Feldman wished to ask a few questions.

ALTAIR: Put him on.

HOUSTON: Dr. Feldman asks, "Are you experiencing any dizziness?"

ALTAIR: Negative.

HOUSTON: "Any excessive dryness in the throat? Any spots in the eyes?"

ALTAIR: Negative.

HOUSTON: "Any blood in the urine?"

ALTAIR: Who looks?

HOUSTON: Feldman says, "I do. And I want you to. Report as soon as you check."

ALTAIR: Will comply.

HOUSTON: This is Hickory. You're doing just fine. But we want you to sleep regularly, John. We want you to listen to the news.

ALTAIR: Hey, knock it off. I'm not depressed. There's nothing wrong with me.

HOUSTON: For sure there isn't, John. But you ate nothing yesterday.

ALTAIR: I was vomiting.

HOUSTON: You refused to listen to the news. You cut Cater off.

ALTAIR: I would like to talk with Cater. I always like to talk with Cater.

HOUSTON: Cater here. We're not kidding, John. Thirty-six hours from now, you have three men's work to do. When you give me the word, I want to go over four special check lists with you.

ALTAIR: You mean one-man emergency re-entry?

HOUSTON: It could be a little tricky, you know.

ALTAIR: I figured that out a year ago. I have it programed on my papers.

HOUSTON: You really are a straight arrow. But we can't just let you drift along up there for all these hours . . . well . . . alone.

ALTAIR: Plans called for me to be alone over the moon for about this length of time.

HOUSTON: Roger, but things were different then.

ALTAIR: They sure were. Excuse me.

It seemed as if the entire nation and much of the rest of the world were watching as John Pope prepared to bring his Altair back to Earth. Prayers were said and cartoonists hailed his solitary effort; television provided meaningful analyses of his situation, and various older astronauts appeared on the tube to share their estimates of what the real danger points would be. All agreed that a practiced hand like John Pope, who had tested scores of experimental planes and engaged the enemy in combat over Korea, was not likely to panic at the necessity of doing three men's work. The highlight of the return trip came on the last full day, when Hickory Lee was serving as CapCom:

> HOUSTON: Altair, our double-domers have come up with something everyone here thinks has merit.
>
> ALTAIR: I'm listening.
>
> HOUSTON: They think it would be good for the nation—and for you, too—if you turned on your television camera and let the people see what you're doing.
>
> ALTAIR: I wouldn't want to leave the controls and move around.
>
> HOUSTON: No, no! Fixed focus. [*A long pause*] It was our unanimous opinion. . . .
>
> ALTAIR: You suggesting this to keep my mind occupied?
>
> HOUSTON: Yes, I recommended it. Strongly.
>
> ALTAIR: What could I say on television?
>
> HOUSTON: You have a thousand things to say. Read your emergency notes. Let them see.
>
> ALTAIR: The hours pass very slowly. They are very heavy. [*His voice sounded weak and hollow*]
>
> HOUSTON: That was our guess. Altair, set up the camera. Make some notes. Get your ideas under control and in forty minutes we go.
>
> ALTAIR: Roger.

At nine o'clock on the night of April 30, prior to the time when Pope would make an important course correction, he turned on the television. The camera did not reveal his full face, but it did display most of the capsule, especially the welter of switches and devices that confronted him.

He could not bring himself to use the pronoun I, so he fell naturally into the we, and that produced a riveting effect: "We are bringing this great spacecraft back to Earth after an abbreviated visit to the other side of the moon." It was clear to everyone who saw the missing seats whom he meant by *we*.

"Dr. Linley should be in the right-hand seat over there. And our commander, Randy Claggett, would be riding in the middle seat. He brought us to the moon. It was my job to bring us back."

Then came the most dramatic segment: "When we lifted off from Cape Canaveral, our spacecraft—this one and the one going down to the moon itself—weighed seventeen tons empty. We carried thirty-five tons of fuel just for those two little machines. We had to know where forty miles of electrical wire ran, in and out. We had to memorize how twenty-nine different systems worked, what every one of them did and how to repair each of them. Look; we had six hundred eighty-nine separate switches to flick off and on. We had fifty engines to speed us through space. And we had, I believe, more than four thousand pages of instructions we had to memorize, more or less. No one, I'm sure, could memorize that much."

Although it was not looking at his features, the camera gave an excellent portrait of an astronaut: smallish; slim; shirt sleeves; short hair; strong, firmly set jaw that flexed now and then, showing muscles; small hands that moved masterfully; a sense of competence, a startling command of detail: "I have a diagram here of the spacecraft as it was when we started out on what will be a two-hundred-hour voyage. Here it is, three hundred sixty-three feet in the air. In the first two minutes, we threw away the entire stage one. Stage two was finished after eight minutes, and down it went. Stage three, which sent us off on our way to the moon, lasted for about two hours; then we got rid of it. The lunar module had two parts, one we left on the moon on purpose. The other was supposed to rejoin us, but, as you know, it didn't. If it had, we would've dropped it, too.

"So that leaves us only these two small parts. One is the service module, which carries all the things that keep us going, and tomorrow, we'll throw that away. That'll leave this little portion I'm sitting in, and we'll fly it down through the atmosphere backward to fight off the heat. It will be twenty-five thousand degrees outside tomorrow, but we won't even feel it in here.

"And then, a drogue parachute will open, a little one, and it will pull out a bigger one, and we'll land west of Hawaii like a sea gull coming home at the end of the day, and ships will be waiting there to greet us."

He then turned and looked directly into the camera. "Mankind was born of matter that accreted in space. We've seen dramatically these past few days how things far off in space can affect us deeply. We were meant to be in space, to wrestle with it, to probe its secrets."

He turned back to his console with its 689 separate switches and he let the camera run, ignoring it as he went about his work, and after a while on Earth, they stopped transmitting.

When the time came for his stripped-down craft to plunge into the atmosphere at the tremendous speed generated by a return from outer space, it would have to hit that semisolid layer upon which all life on Earth depends at exactly the right angle. Pope checked the approach once more: "No steeper than seven-point-three degrees or we burn up. No shallower than five-point-five degrees or we bounce off. This means hitting a corridor twenty-seven miles in diameter at the end of two hundred thirty-eight thousand miles at a speed of better than twenty-four thousand mph. Let's hope our computer's working."

With about 90 minutes before scheduled splashdown, he consulted his computer and fired rockets briefly to make the final small correction in his orbit. When the computer confirmed that his capsule had responded correctly, he activated explosive devices that blew off the service module—blew it right off into space, where it would burn up as it entered the atmosphere. That left him without any support system, any large supply of fuel, any of the instruments he would require for extended flight. He was alone and almost powerless in a speeding vehicle heading for near destruction.

He had rockets left for one lifesaving maneuver: He could turn the capsule around so that it flew backward, presenting the big curved end with the ablative material to the incredible heat.

HOUSTON: Lee here. You never looked better, Moonshiner.
ALTAIR: Things going so well I've got my fingers crossed.
HOUSTON: This is your day, Moonshiner. Bring her down.
ALTAIR: I intend to.

With quiet confidence, he slammed into the atmosphere, and even though he had been warned many times that it would be tougher than Gemini, he could scarcely believe it when it happened. Great flames engulfed the capsule, wiping out the sky. Huge chunks of incandescent material, 25,000 degrees hot, roared past his window, reveling in the oxygen they were finding for their flames. More colors than a child has in a crayon box flashed past; at one break in the tremendous fireworks he caught a glimpse of his trail, and he calculated that it must be flaming behind him for 500 miles.

It was impossible to tell Houston of the great fire. The heat was so intense that all radio communication was blacked out; it was the flaming entry that astronauts had to make alone, and the flakes of ablated material became so thick that he felt sure that everything was going to burn up, but the interior temperature did not rise one degree.

The flames stopped. He could feel the *g*s slacking off as the capsule was braked, and when he activated the drogue parachute, he felt with satisfaction and, almost, joy its first sharp grip.

U.S.S. TULAGI: We have you in sight, Altair. Three good chutes.
ALTAIR: Quite a reception committee you arranged. All the Roman candles.
U.S.S. TULAGI: Looks like you're going to splash down about six tenths of a nautical mile away. Perfect landing.
ALTAIR: That's what I intended.

Jonathan Schell / *The Fate of the Earth* 1982

In 1967, Jonathan Schell published The Village of Ben Suc, *describing in vivid detail the military maneuvers leading to the destruction of a Vietnamese village. With* The Fate of the Earth *(1982), Schell expands his meditations from the microcosm of a routine bombing mission to the larger global threat of nuclear armageddon. In spite of criticism for being too idealistic in its call for world government, the book helped to rally and define the growing public fear of unchecked nuclear arms proliferation. In the following excerpt, Schell describes a shocking scenario—the effects of a nuclear device exploded over New York City.*

Born in New York City in 1943 and educated at Harvard, Jonathan Schell is currently a staff writer at The New Yorker. *In* The Abolition *(1984), Schell answers the critics of* The Fate of the Earth *and proposes a policy for nuclear disarmament.*

NUCLEAR DESTRUCTION

One way to begin to grasp the destructive power of present-day nuclear weapons is to describe the consequences of the detonation of a one-megaton bomb, which possesses eighty times the explosive power of the Hiroshima bomb, on a large city, such as New York. Burst some eighty-five hundred feet above the Empire State Building, a one-megaton bomb would gut or flatten almost every building between Battery Park and 125th Street, or within a radius of four and four-tenths miles, or in an area of sixty-one square miles, and would heavily damage buildings between the northern tip of Staten Island and the George Washington Bridge, or within a radius of about eight miles, or in an area of about two hundred square miles. A conventional explosive delivers a swift shock, like a slap, to whatever it hits, but the blast wave of a sizable nuclear weapon endures for several seconds and "can surround and destroy whole buildings" (Glasstone). People, of course, would be picked up and hurled away from the blast along with the rest of the debris. Within the sixty-one square miles, the walls, roofs, and floors of any building that had not been flattened would be collapsed, and the people and furniture inside would be swept down onto the street. (Technically, this zone would be hit by various overpressures of at least five pounds per square inch. Overpressure is defined as the pressure in excess of normal atmospheric pressure.) As far away as ten miles from ground zero, pieces of glass and other sharp objects would be hurled about by the blast wave at lethal velocities. In Hiroshima, where buildings were low and, outside the center of the city, were often constructed of light materials, injuries from falling buildings were often minor. But in New York, where the buildings are tall and are constructed of heavy materials, the physical collapse of the city would certainly kill millions of people. The streets of New York are narrow ravines running between the high walls of the city's buildings. In a nuclear attack, the walls would fall and the ravines would fill up. The people in the buildings would fall to the street with the debris of the buildings, and the people in the street would be crushed by this avalanche of people and buildings. At a distance of two miles or so from ground zero, winds would reach four hundred miles an hour, and another two miles away they would reach a hundred and eighty miles an hour. Meanwhile, the fireball would be growing, until it was more than a mile wide, and rocketing upward, to a height of over six miles. For ten seconds, it would broil the city below. Anyone caught in the open within nine miles of ground zero would receive third-degree burns and would probably be killed; closer to the explosion, people would be charred and killed instantly. From Greenwich Village up to Central Park, the heat would be great enough to melt metal and glass. Readily inflammable materials, such as newspapers and dry leaves, would ignite in all five boroughs (though in only a small part of Staten Island) and west to the Passaic River, in New Jersey, within a radius of about nine and a half miles from ground zero, thereby creating an area of more than two hundred and eighty square miles in which mass fires were likely to break out.

If it were possible (as it would not be) for someone to stand at Fifth Avenue and Seventy-second Street (about two miles from ground zero) without being instantly killed, he would see the following sequence of events. A dazzling white light from the fireball would illumine the scene, continuing for perhaps thirty seconds. Simultaneously, searing heat would ignite everything flammable and start to melt windows, cars, buses, lampposts, and everything else made of metal or glass. People in the street would immediately catch fire, and would shortly be reduced to heavily charred corpses. About five seconds after the light appeared, the blast wave would strike, laden with the debris of a now nonexistent midtown. Some buildings might be crushed, as though a giant fist had squeezed them on all sides, and others might be picked up off their foundations and whirled uptown with the other debris. On the far side of Central Park, the West Side skyline would fall from south to north. The four-hundred-mile-an-hour wind would blow south to north, die down after a few seconds, and then blow in the reverse direction with diminished intensity. While these things were happening, the fireball would be burning in the sky for the ten seconds of the thermal pulse. Soon huge, thick clouds of dust and smoke would envelop the scene, and as the mushroom cloud rushed overhead (it would have a diameter of about twelve miles) the light from the sun would be blotted out, and day would turn to night. Within minutes, fires, ignited both by the thermal pulse and by broken gas mains, tanks of gas and oil, and the like, would begin to spread in the darkness, and a strong, steady wind would begin to blow in the direction of the blast. As at Hiroshima, a whirlwind might be produced, which would sweep through the ruins, and radioactive rain, generated under the meteorological conditions created by the blast, might fall. Before long, the individual fires would coalesce into a mass fire, which, depending largely on the winds, would become either a conflagration or a firestorm. In a conflagration, prevailing winds spread a wall of fire as far as there is any combustible material to sustain it; in a firestorm, a vertical updraft caused by the fire itself sucks the surrounding air in toward a central point, and the fires therefore converge in a single fire of extreme heat. A mass fire of either kind renders shelters useless by burning up all the oxygen in the air and creating toxic gases, so that anyone inside the shelters is asphyxiated, and also by heating the ground to such high temperatures that the shelters turn, in effect, into ovens, cremating the people inside them. In Dresden, several days after the firestorm raised there by Allied conventional bombing, the interiors of some bomb shelters were still so hot that when they were opened the inrushing air caused the contents to burst into flame. Only those who had fled their shelters when the bombing started had any chance of surviving. (It is difficult to predict in a particular situation which form the fires will take. In actual experience, Hiroshima suffered a firestorm and Nagasaki suffered a conflagration.)

In this vast theatre of physical effects, all the scenes of agony and death that took place at Hiroshima would again take place, but now involving millions of people rather than hundreds of thousands. Like the people of Hiroshima, the people of New York would be burned, battered, crushed, and irradiated in every conceivable way. The city and its people would be mingled in a smoldering heap. And then, as the fires started, the survivors (most of whom would be on the periphery of the explosion) would be driven to abandon to the flames those family members and other people who were unable to flee, or else to die with them. Before long, while the ruins burned, the processions of injured, mute people would begin their slow progress out of the outskirts of the devastated zone. However, this time a much smaller proportion of the population than at Hiroshima would have a chance of escaping. In general, as the size of the area of devastation increases, the possibilities for escape decrease. When the devastated area is relatively small, as it was at Hiroshima, people who are not incapacitated will have a good chance of escaping to safety before the fires coalesce into a mass fire. But when the devastated area is great, as it would be after the detonation of a megaton bomb, and fires are springing up at a distance of nine and a half miles from ground zero, and when what used to be the streets are piled high with burning rubble, and the day (if the attack occurs in the daytime) has grown impenetrably dark, there is little chance that anyone who is not on the very edge of the devastated area will be able to make his way to safety. In New York, most people would die wherever the blast found them, or not very far from there.

If instead of being burst in the air the bomb were burst on or near the ground in the vicinity of the Empire State Building, the overpressure would be very much greater near the center of the blast area but the range hit by a minimum of five pounds per square inch of overpressure would be less. The range of the thermal pulse would be about the same as that of the air burst. The fireball would be almost two miles across, and would engulf midtown Manhattan from Greenwich Village nearly to Central Park. Very little is known about what would happen to a city that was inside a fireball, but one would expect a good deal of what was there to be first pulverized and then melted or vaporized. Any human beings in the area would be reduced to smoke and ashes; they would simply disappear. A crater roughly three blocks in diameter and two hundred feet deep would open up. In addition, heavy radioactive fallout would be created as dust and debris from the city rose with the mushroom cloud and then fell back to the ground. Fallout would begin to drop almost immediately, contaminating the ground beneath the cloud with levels of radiation many times lethal doses, and quickly killing anyone who might have survived the blast wave and the thermal pulse and might now be attempting an escape; it is difficult to believe that there would be appreciable survival of the people of the city after a megaton ground burst. And for the next twenty-four hours or so more fallout would descend downwind from the blast, in a plume whose direction and length would depend on the speed and the direction of the wind that happened to be blowing at the time of the attack. If the wind was blowing at fifteen miles an hour, fallout of lethal intensity would descend in a plume about a hundred and fifty miles long and as much as fifteen miles wide. Fallout that was sublethal but could still cause serious illness would extend another hundred and fifty miles downwind. Exposure to radioactivity in human beings is measured in units called rems—an acronym for "roentgen equivalent in man." The roentgen is a standard measurement of gamma- and X-ray radiation, and the expression "equivalent in man" indicates that an adjustment has been made to take into account the differences in the degree of biological damage that is caused by radiation of different types. Many of the kinds of harm done to human beings by radiation—for example, the incidence of cancer and of genetic damage—depend on the dose accumulated over many years; but radiation sickness, capable of causing death, results from an "acute" dose, received in a period of anything from a few seconds to several days. Because almost ninety per cent of the so-called "infinite-time dose" of radiation from fall-out—that is, the dose from a given quantity of fallout that one would receive if one lived for many thousands of years—is emitted in the first week, the one-week accumulated dose is often used as a convenient measure for calculating the immediate harm from fallout. Doses in the thousands of rems, which could be expected throughout the city, would attack the central nervous system and would bring about death within a few hours. Doses of around a thousand rems, which would be delivered some tens of miles downwind from the blast, would kill within two weeks everyone who was exposed to them. Doses of around five hundred rems, which would be delivered as far as a hundred and fifty miles downwind (given a wind speed of fifteen miles per hour), would kill half of all exposed able-bodied young adults. At this level of exposure, radiation sickness proceeds in the three stages observed at Hiroshima. The plume of lethal fallout could descend, depending on the direction of the wind, on other parts of New York State and parts of New Jersey, Pennsylvania, Delaware, Maryland, Connecticut, Massachusetts, Rhode Island, Vermont, and New Hampshire, killing additional millions of people. The circumstances in heavily contaminated areas, in which millions of people were all declining together, over a period of weeks, toward painful deaths, are ones that, like so many of the consequences of nuclear explosions, have never been experienced.

A description of the effects of a one-megaton bomb on New York City gives some notion of the meaning in human terms of a megaton of nuclear explosive power, but a weapon that is more likely to be used against New York is the twenty-megaton bomb, which has one thousand six hundred times the yield of the Hiroshima bomb. The Soviet Union is estimated to have at least a hundred and thirteen twenty-megaton bombs in its nuclear arsenal, carried by Bear intercontinental bombers. In addition, some of the Soviet SS-18 missiles are capable of carrying bombs of this size, although the actual yields are not known. Since the explosive power of the twenty-megaton bombs greatly exceeds the amount necessary to destroy most military targets, it is reasonable to suppose that they are meant for use against large cities. If a twenty-megaton bomb were air-burst over the Empire State Building at an altitude of thirty thousand feet, the zone gutted or flattened by the blast wave would have a radius of twelve miles and an area of more than four hundred and fifty square miles, reaching from the middle of Staten Island to the northern edge of the Bronx, the eastern edge of Queens, and well into New Jersey, and the zone of heavy damage from the blast wave (the zone hit by a minimum of two pounds of overpressure per square inch) would have a radius of twenty-one and a half miles, or an area of one thousand four hundred and fifty square miles, reaching to the southernmost tip of Staten Island, north as far as southern Rockland County, east into Nassau County, and west to Morris County, New Jersey. The fireball would be about four and a half miles in diameter and would radiate the thermal pulse for some twenty seconds. People caught in the open twenty-three miles away from ground zero, in Long Island, New Jersey, and southern New York State, would be burned to death. People hundreds of miles away who looked at the burst would be temporarily blinded and would risk permanent eye injury. (After the test of a fifteen-megaton bomb on Bikini Atoll, in the South Pacific, in March 1954, small animals were found to have suffered retinal burns at a distance of three hundred and forty-five miles.) The mushroom cloud would be seventy miles in diameter. New York City and its suburbs would be transformed into a lifeless, flat, scorched desert in a few seconds.

If a twenty-megaton bomb were ground-burst on the Empire State Building, the range of severe blast damage would, as with the one-megaton ground blast, be reduced, but the fireball, which would be almost six miles in diameter, would cover Manhattan from Wall Street to northern Central Park and also parts of New Jersey, Brooklyn, and Queens, and everyone within it would be instantly killed, with most of them physically disappearing. Fallout would again be generated, this time covering thousands of square miles with lethal intensities of radiation. A fair portion of New York City and its incinerated population, now radioactive dust, would have risen into the mushroom cloud and would now be descending on the surrounding territory. On one of the few occasions when local fallout was generated by a test explosion in the multi-megaton range, the fifteen-megaton bomb tested on Bikini Atoll, which was exploded seven feet above the surface of a coral reef, "caused substantial contamination over an area of more than seven thousand square miles," according to Glasstone. If, as seems likely, a twenty-megaton bomb ground-burst on New York would produce at least a comparable amount of fallout, and if the wind carried the fallout onto populated areas, then this one bomb would probably doom upward of twenty million people, or almost ten per cent of the population of the United States.

William Least Heat Moon / *Blue Highways* 1982

One of the most enduring traditions in American culture is the literature of the open road. From Walt Whitman and Henry David Thoreau to John Steinbeck and Jack Kerouac, American writers have eloquently expressed our collective fascination with wandering through the nation's landscape and meeting its people. The most recent—and deservedly celebrated—contribution to this literary tradition is William Least Heat Moon's Blue Highways *(1982), a finely crafted narrative and cultural commentary on a fourteen-thousand-mile trek across the nation on rural back roads, those colored blue on our maps.*

The author, whose legal name is William Trogdon, derives his pseudonym from his Osage Indian blood. Released from his job teaching English at a small college in Missouri, and separated from his wife (whom he calls simply "The Cherokee") at the age of thirty-eight, William Least Heat Moon decided that if he couldn't make things go right he could at least go. He felt "a nearly desperate sense of isolation and a growing suspicion that I had lived in an alien land." Setting out in the small van he named "Ghost Dancer," and accompanied by volumes of Whitman and Nietzsche, Heat Moon drove America's back roads in search of "places where change did not mean ruin and where time and men and deeds connected." Citing Daniel Boone, who "moved at the sight of smoke from a new neighbor's chimney," Heat Moon kept "moving from the sight of my own."

William Least Heat Moon writes evocatively of the land, the weather, and the dazzling array of American originals he meets along the way: Kentuckians rebuilding log cabins, a Brooklyn cop turned Trappist monk in Georgia, the boys in the barbershop in Dime Box, Texas, the drinkers in a roadside brothel in Nevada. And in each instance, Heat Moon's copious note-taking allows these characters to tell their own stories in their own words.

In a recent interview, William Least Heat Moon noted that "If writing isn't a process of discovery, then I can't imagine why anyone would write." In the fol-

lowing selection, he takes us to a seemingly nondescript town in eastern Tennessee. And in presenting the characters and stories of Nameless, Tennessee, William Least Heat Moon helps us recognize the inadequacy of the generalizations we turn to when we describe who we are as Americans and where we are headed.

NAMELESS, TENNESSEE

Had it not been raining hard that morning on the Livingston square, I never would have learned of Nameless, Tennessee. Waiting for the rain to ease, I lay on my bunk and read the atlas to pass time rather than to see where I might go. In Kentucky were towns with fine names like Boreing, Bear Wallow, Decoy, Subtle, Mud Lick, Mummie, Neon; Belcher was just down the road from Mouthcard, and Minnie only ten miles from Mousie.

I looked at Tennessee. Turtletown eight miles from Ducktown. And also: Peavine, Wheel, Milky Way, Love Joy, Dull, Weakly, Fly, Spot, Miser Station, Only, McBurg, Peeled Chestnut, Clouds, Topsy, Isoline. And the best of all, Nameless. The logic! I was heading east, and Nameless lay forty-five miles west. I decided to go anyway.

The rain stopped, but things looked saturated, even bricks. In Gainesboro, a hill town with a square of businesses around the Jackson County Courthouse, I stopped for directions and breakfast. There is one almost infallible way to find honest food at just prices in blue-highway America: count the wall calendars in a cafe.

> No calendar: Same as an interstate pit stop.
> One calendar: Preprocessed food assembled in New Jersey.
> Two calendars: Only if fish trophies present.
> Three calendars: Can't miss on the farm-boy breakfasts.
> Four calendars: Try the ho-made pie too.
> Five calendars: Keep it under your hat, or they'll franchise.

One time I found a six-calendar cafe in the Ozarks, which served fried chicken, peach pie, and chocolate malts, that left me searching for another ever since. I've never seen a seven-calendar place. But old-time travelers—road men in a day when cars had running boards and lunchroom windows said AIR COOLED in blue letters with icicles dripping from the tops—those travelers have told me the golden legends of seven-calendar cafes.

To the rider of back roads, nothing shows the tone, the voice of a small town more quickly than the breakfast grill or the five-thirty tavern. Much of what the people do and believe and share is evident then. The City Cafe in Gainesboro had three calendars that I could see from the walk. Inside were no interstate refugees with full bladders and empty tanks, no wild-eyed children just released from the glassy cell of a stationwagon backseat, no longhaul truckers talking in CB numbers. There were only townspeople wearing overalls, or catalog-order suits with five-and-dime ties, or uniforms. That is, here were farmers and mill hands, bank clerks, the dry goods merchant, a policeman, and chiropractor's receptionist. Because it was Saturday, there were also mothers and children.

I ordered my standard on-the-road breakfast: two eggs up, hashbrowns, tomato juice. The waitress, whose pale, almost translucent skin shifted hue in the gray light like a thin slice of mother of pearl, brought the food. Next to the eggs was a biscuit with a little yellow Smiley button stuck in it. She said, "You from the North?"

"I guess I am." A Missourian gets used to Southerners thinking him a Yankee, a Northerner considering him a cracker, a Westerner sneering at his effete Easternness, and the Easterner taking him for a cowhand.

"So whata you doin' in the mountains?"

"Talking to people. Taking some pictures. Looking mostly."

"Lookin' for what?"

"A three-calendar cafe that serves Smiley buttons on the biscuits."

"You needed a smile. Tell me really."

"I don't know. Actually, I'm looking for some jam to put on this biscuit now that you've brought one."

She came back with grape jelly. In a land of quince jelly, apple butter, apricot jam, blueberry preserves, pear conserves, and lemon marmalade, you always get grape jelly.

"Whata you lookin' for?"

Like anyone else, I'm embarrassed to eat in front of a watcher, particularly if I'm getting interviewed. "Why don't you have a cup of coffee?"

"Cain't right now. You gonna tell me?"

"I don't know how to describe it to you. Call it harmony."

She waited for something more. "Is that it?" Someone called her to the kitchen. I had managed almost to finish by the time she came back. She sat on the edge of the booth. "I started out in life not likin' anything, but then it grew on me. Maybe that'll happen to you." She watched me spread the jelly. "Saw your van." She watched me eat the biscuit. "You sleep in there?" I told her I did. "I'd love to do that, but I'd be scared spitless."

"I don't mind being scared spitless. Sometimes."

"I'd love to take off cross country. I like to look at different license plates. But I'd take a dog. You carry a dog?"

"No dogs, no cats, no budgie birds. It's a one-man campaign to show Americans a person can travel alone without a pet."

"Cain't travel without a dog!"

"I like to do things the hard way."

"Shoot! I'd take me a dog to talk to. And for protection."

"It isn't traveling to cross the country and talk to your pug instead of people along the way. Besides, being alone on the road makes you ready to meet someone when you stop. You get sociable traveling alone."

She looked out toward the van again. "Time I get the nerve to take a trip, gas'll cost five dollars a gallon."

"Could be. My rig might go the way of the steamboat." I remembered why I'd come to Gainesboro. "You know the way to Nameless?"

"Nameless? I've heard of Nameless. Better ask the amlance driver in the corner booth." She pinned the Smiley on my jacket. "Maybe I'll see you on the road somewhere. His name's Bob, by the way."

"The ambulance driver?"

"The Smiley. I always name my Smileys—otherwise they all look alike. I'd talk to him before you go."

"The Smiley?"

"The amlance driver."

And so I went looking for Nameless, Tennessee, with a Smiley button named Bob.

"I don't know if I got directions for where you're goin'," the ambulance driver said. "I *think* there's a Nameless down the Shepardsville Road."

"When I get to Shepardsville, will I have gone too far?"

"Ain't no Shepardsville."

"How will I know when I'm there?"

"Cain't say for certain."

"What's Nameless look like?"

"Don't recollect."

"Is the road paved?"

"It's possible."

Those were the directions. I was looking for an unnumbered road named after a nonexistent town that would take me to a place called Nameless that nobody was sure existed.

Clumps of wild garlic lined the county highway that I hoped was the Shepardsville Road. It scrimmaged with the mountain as it tried to stay on top of the ridges; the hillsides were so steep and thick with oak, I felt as if I were following a trail through the misty treetops. Chickens, doing more work with their necks than legs, ran across the road, and, with a battering of wings, half leapt and half flew into the lower branches of oaks. A vicious pair of mixed-breed German shepherds raced along trying to eat the tires. After miles, I decided I'd missed the town—assuming there truly *was* a Nameless, Tennessee. It wouldn't be the first time I'd qualified for the Ponce de Leon Believe Anything Award.

I stopped beside a big man loading tools in a pickup. "I may be lost."

"Where'd you lose the right road?"

"I don't know. Somewhere around nineteen sixty-five."

"Highway fifty-six, you mean?"

"I came down fifty-six. I think I should've turned at the last junction."

"Only thing down that road's stumps and huckleberries, and the berries ain't there in March. Where you tryin' to get to?"

"Nameless. If there is such a place."

"You might not know Thurmond Watts, but he's got him a store down the road. That's Nameless at his store. Still there all right, but I might not vouch you that tomorrow." He came up to the van. "In my Army days, I wrote Nameless, Tennessee, for my place of birth on all the papers, even though I lived on this end of the ridge. All these ridges and hollers got names of their own. That's Steam Mill Holler over yonder. Named after the steam engine in the gristmill. Miller had him just one arm but done a good business."

"What business you in?"

"I've always farmed, but I work in Cookeville now in a heatin' element factory. Bad back made me go to town to work." He pointed to a wooden building not much bigger than his truck. By the slanting porch, a faded Double Cola sign said J M WHEELER STORE. "That used to be my business. That's me—Madison Wheeler. Feller came by one day. From Detroit. He wanted to buy the sign because he carried my name too. But I didn't sell. Want to keep my name up." He gave a cigarette a good slow smoking. "Had a decent business for five years, but too much of it was in credit. Then them supermarkets down in Cookeville opened, and I was buyin' higher than they was sellin'. With these hard roads now, everybody gets out of the hollers to shop or work. Don't stay up in here anymore. This tar road under my shoes done my business in, and it's likely to do Nameless in."

"Do you wish it was still the old way?"

"I got no debts now. I got two boys raised, and they never been in trouble. I got a brick house and some corn and tobacco and a few Hampshire hogs and Herefords. A good bull. Bull's pumpin' better blood than I do. Real generous man in town let me put my cow in with his stud. I couldna paid the fee on that specimen otherwise." He took another long, meditative pull on his filtertip. "If you're satisfied, that's all they are to it. I'll tell you, people from all over the nation—Florida, Mississippi—are comin' in here to retire because it's good country. But our young ones don't stay on. Not much way to make a livin' in here anymore. Take me. I been beatin' on these stumps all my life, tryin' to farm these hills. They don't give much up to you. Fightin' rocks and briars all the time. One of the first things I recollect is swingin' a briar blade—filed out of an old saw it was. Now they come in with them crawlers and push out a pasture in a day. Still, it's a grudgin' land—like the gourd. Got to hard cuss gourd seed, they say, to get it up out of the ground.''

The whole time, my rig sat in the middle of the right lane while we stood talking next to it and wiped at the mist. No one else came or went. Wheeler said, ''Factory work's easier on the back, and I don't mind it, understand, but a man becomes what he does. Got to watch that. That's why I keep at farmin', although the crops haven't ever throve. It's the doin' that's important.'' He looked up suddenly. ''My apologies. I didn't ask what you do that gets you into these hollers.''

I told him. I'd been gone only six days, but my account of the trip already had taken on some polish.

He nodded. ''Satisfaction is doin' what's important to yourself. A man ought to honor other people, but he's got to honor what he believes in too.''

As I started the engine, Wheeler said, ''If you get back this way, stop in and see me. Always got beans and taters and a little piece of meat.''

Down along the ridge, I wondered why it's always those who live on little who are the ones to ask you to dinner.

Nameless, Tennessee, was a town of maybe ninety people if you pushed it, a dozen houses along the road, a couple of barns, same number of churches, a general merchandise store selling Fire Chief gasoline, and a community center with a lighted volleyball court. Behind the center was an open-roof, rusting metal privy with PAINT ME on the door; in the hollow of a nearby oak lay a full pint of Jack Daniel's Black Label. From the houses, the odor of coal smoke.

Next to a red tobacco barn stood the general merchandise with a poster of Senator Albert Gore, Jr., smiling from the window. I knocked. The door opened partway. A tall, thin man said, ''Closed up. For good,'' and started to shut the door.

''Don't want to buy anything. Just a question for Mr. Thurmond Watts.''

The man peered through the slight opening. He looked me over. ''What question would that be?''

''If this is Nameless, Tennessee, could he tell me how it got that name?''

The man turned back into the store and called out, ''Miss Ginny! Somebody here wants to know how Nameless come to be Nameless.''

Miss Ginny edged to the door and looked me and my truck over. Clearly, she didn't approve. She said, ''You know as well as I do, Thurmond. Don't keep him on the stoop in the damp to tell him.'' Miss Ginny, I found out, was Mrs. Virginia Watts, Thurmond's wife.

I stepped in and they both began telling the story, adding a detail here, the other correcting a fact there, both smiling at the foolishness of it all. It seems the hilltop settlement went for years without a name. Then one day the Post Office Department told the people if they wanted mail up on the mountain they would have to give the place a name you could properly address a letter to. The community met; there were only a handful, but they commenced debating. Some wanted patriotic names, some names from nature, one man recommended in all seriousness his own name. They couldn't agree, and they ran out of names to argue about. Finally, a fellow tired of the talk; he didn't like the mail he received anyway. ''Forget the durn Post Office,'' he said. ''This here's a nameless place if I ever seen one, so leave it be.'' And that's just what they did.

Watts pointed out the window. ''We used to have signs on the road, but the Halloween boys keep tearin' them down.''

''You think Nameless is a funny name,'' Miss Ginny said. ''I see it plain in your eyes. Well, you take yourself up north a piece to Difficult or Defeated or Shake Rag. Now them are silly names.''

The old store, lighted only by three fifty-watt bulbs, smelled of coal oil and baking bread. In the middle of the rectangular room, where the oak floor sagged a little, stood an iron stove. To the right was a wooden table with an unfinished game of checkers and a stool made from an apple-tree stump. On shelves around the walls sat earthen jugs with corncob stoppers, a few canned goods, and some of the two thousand old clocks and clockworks Thurmond Watts owned. Only one was ticking; the others he just looked at. I asked how long he'd been in the store.

"Thirty-five years, but we closed the first day of the year. We're hopin' to sell it to a churchly couple. Upright people. No athians."

"Did you build this store?"

"I built this one, but it's the third general store on the ground. I fear it'll be the last. I take no pleasure in that. Once you could come in here for a gallon of paint, a pickle, a pair of shoes, and a can of corn."

"Or horehound candy," Miss Ginny said. "Or corsets and salves. We had cough syrups and all that for the body. In season, we'd buy and sell blackberries and walnuts and chestnuts, before the blight got them. And outside, Thurmond milled corn and sharpened plows. Even shoed a horse sometimes."

"We could fix up a horse or a man or a baby," Watts said.

"Thurmond, tell him we had a doctor on the ridge in them days."

"We had a doctor on the ridge in them days. As good as any doctor alivin'. He'd cut a crooked toenail or deliver a woman. Dead these last years."

"I got some bad ham meat one day," Miss Ginny said, "and took to vomitin'. All day, all night. Hangin' on the drop edge of yonder. I said to Thurmond, 'Thurmond, unless you want shut of me, call the doctor.' "

"I studied on it," Watts said.

"You never did. You got him right now. He come over and put three drops of iodeen in half a glass of well water. I drank it down and the vomitin' stopped with the last swallow. Would you think iodeen could do that?"

"He put Miss Ginny on one teaspoon of spirits of ammonia in well water for her nerves. Ain't nothin' works better for her to this day."

"Calms me like the hand of the Lord."

Hilda, the Wattses' daughter, came out of the backroom. "I remember him," she said. "I was just a baby. Y'all were talkin' to him, and he lifted me up on the counter and gave me a stick of Juicy Fruit and a piece of cheese."

"Knew the old medicines," Watts said. "Only drugstore he needed was a good kitchen cabinet. None of them antee-beeotics that hit you worsen your ailment. Forgotten lore now, the old medicines, because they ain't profit in iodeen."

Miss Ginny started back to the side room where she and her sister Marilyn were taking apart a duck-down mattress to make bolsters. She stopped at the window for another look at Ghost Dancing. "How do you sleep in that thing? Ain't you all cramped and cold?"

"How does the clam sleep in his shell?" Watts said in my defense.

"Thurmond, get the boy a piece of buttermilk pie afore he goes on."

"Hilda, get him some buttermilk pie." He looked at me. "You like good music?" I said I did. He cranked up an old Edison phonograph, the kind with the big morning-glory blossom for a speaker, and put on a wax cylinder. "This will be 'My Mother's Prayer,' " he said.

While I ate buttermilk pie, Watts served as disc jockey of Nameless, Tennessee. "Here's 'Mountain Rose.' " It was one of those moments that you know at the time will stay with you to the grave: the sweet pie, the gaunt man playing the old music, the coals in the stove glowing orange, the scent of kerosene and hot bread. "Here's 'Evening Rhapsody.' " The music was so heavily romantic we both laughed. I thought: It is for this I have come.

Feathered over and giggling, Miss Ginny stepped from the side room. She knew she was a sight. "Thurmond, give him some lunch. Still looks hungry."

Hilda pulled food off the woodstove in the backroom: home-butchered and canned whole-hog sausage, home-canned June apples, turnip greens, cole slaw, potatoes, stuffing, hot cornbread. All delicious.

Watts and Hilda sat and talked while I ate. "Wish you would join me."

"We've ate," Watts said. "Cain't beat a woodstove for flavorful cookin'."

He told me he was raised in a one-hundred-fifty-year-old cabin still standing in one of the hollows. "How many's left," he said, "that grew up in a log cabin? I ain't the last surely, but I must be climbin' on the list."

Hilda cleared the table. "You Watts ladies know how to cook."

"She's in nursin' school at Tennessee Tech. I went over for one of them football games last year there at Coevul." To say *Cookeville,* you let the word collapse in upon itself so that it comes out "Coevul."

"Do you like football?" I asked.

"Don't know. I was so high up in that stadium, I never opened my eyes."

Watts went to the back and returned with a fat spiral notebook that he set on the table. His expression had changed. "Miss Ginny's *Deathbook.*"

The thing startled me. Was it something I was supposed to sign? He opened it but said nothing. There were scads of names written in a tidy hand over pages incised to crinkliness by a ballpoint. Chronologically, the names had piled up: wives, grandparents, a stillborn infant, relatives, friends close and distant. Names, names. After each, the date of *the* unknown finally known and transcribed. The last entry bore yesterday's date.

"She's wrote out twenty years' worth. Ever day she listens to the hospital report on the radio and puts the names in. Folks come by to check a date. Or they just turn through the books. Read them like a scrapbook."

Hilda said, "Like Saint Peter at the gates inscribin' the names."

Watts took my arm. "Come along." He led me to the fruit cellar under the store. As we went down, he said, "Always take a newborn baby upstairs afore you take him downstairs, otherwise you'll incline him downwards."

The cellar was dry and full of cobwebs and jar after jar of home-canned food, the bottles organized as a shopkeeper would: sausage, pumpkin, sweet pickles, tomatoes, corn relish, blackberries, peppers, squash, jellies. He held a hand out toward the dusty bottles. "Our tomorrows."

Upstairs again, he said, "Hope to sell the store to the right folk. I see now, though, it'll be somebody offen the ridge. I've studied on it, and maybe it's the end of our place." He stirred the coals. "This store could give a comfortable livin', but not likely get you rich. But just gettin' by is dice rollin' to people nowadays. I never did see my day guaranteed."

When it was time to go, Watts said, "If you find anyone along your way wants a good store—on the road to Cordell Hull Lake—tell them about us."

I said I would. Miss Ginny and Hilda and Marilyn came out to say goodbye. It was cold and drizzling again. "Weather to give a man the weary dismals," Watts grumbled. "Where you headed from here?"

"I don't know."

"Cain't get lost then."

Miss Ginny looked again at my rig. It had worried her from the first as it had my mother. "I hope you don't get yourself kilt in that durn thing gallivantin' around the country."

"Come back when the hills dry off," Watts said. "We'll go lookin' for some of them round rocks all sparkly inside."

I thought a moment. "Geodes?"

"Them's the ones. The county's properly full of them."

Louis L'Amour / *Bowdrie* 1983

Of all the popular fictional genres, the Western is by far the most distinctively American. And with over 82 million copies of his 90 books in print, Louis L'Amour is the Western's most definitive and successful practitioner.

L'Amour's heroes are characterized by their clear-cut notions of right and wrong, their sensitivity to the frontier wilds, love of independence, optimism in basic human values, and a penchant for rough-and-tumble action. Though criticized for their literary simplicity, his novels have also been praised for an exacting attention to detail. (A Stanford geology professor is said to include one of them on his reading list each year.)

L'Amour was born in Jamestown, North Dakota, in 1908. Before becoming a writer, he worked as a longshoreman, lumberjack, miner, professional boxer, and fruit picker. On his role as an author, L'Amour has said: "The profession of literature has many facets, not the least of which is making a living."

FOREWORD

Following the Civil War, conditions in Texas were chaotic. Many communities lived through this period in relative peace and quiet, but elsewhere there were bitter feuds between factions or families, raids over the border, attacks by Comanches and lawless acts by individuals. To keep the peace, Texas reactivated the Rangers, an organization active during and to some extent before the war with Mexico.

The Rangers, working in concert or alone, fought Indians, bandits, horse and cattle thieves, highwaymen, bank robbers, and lawbreakers of every kind. Mostly young, each Ranger was required to furnish his own horse, rifle, and a pair of pistols. There was no Ranger uniform as such. In many cases local officers, if they existed at all, were partisan. In such cases the Ranger had to act with judgment and discrimination, and to use force when and if it became essential.

Basically the Rangers were divided into two groups, the Frontier Battalion under Major John B. Jones, and the Special Force, under the command of Captain L. H. McNelly. This latter group consisted usually of about thirty men, and within a very few years the Rangers became noted for swift and dynamic action, bringing peace to a wide and hitherto lawless area.

Chick Bowdrie, who appears in all of the stories in this collection, is a fictional character, growing up, as did many young men of the time, working hard during his boyhood years, familiar with firearms, horses and cattle, and aware of the possibility of attacks by Indians or outlaws. Comanche raids were frequent, sometimes striking as far east as the Gulf Coast. The skill with weapons that belonged to many such boys and men was the natural result of the necessity of hunting meat for the table, defending the herds against wild animals and simply protecting their homes and themselves.

Boys of twelve and thirteen years old often rode many miles alone on one mission or another, growing up accustomed to doing the work of men and accepting the responsibilities of adults.

The citizens of Texas were of many nationalities. A fact not generally understood is that there were Mexicans defending the Alamo as well as attacking it, and many Texans of Spanish ancestry elected to join in the fight for independence.

Colonies from Switzerland, Germany, and France were settled in Texas and in some areas were a major part of the population. It was not at all unusual for children growing up in the vicinities of Castroville, D'Hanis, or Fredericksburg to have a smattering of German or French as well as their own language, for the children they played with and the men they worked with were often of those nationalities.

These stories were written long ago and appeared first in what were referred to as "pulp" magazines due to the fact that they were published on paper made from wood pulp.

The magazines referred to as the pulps published a wide variety of stories in many categories such as western, mystery, science fiction, love, air, sports, horror, etc. In their pages a number of American writers learned their trade. Jack London, Sinclair Lewis, Theodore Dreiser, Raymond Chandler, Dashiell Hammett, and many others had stories in pulp magazines under their own names or pseudonyms. It was a valuable training ground, for one had to know how to tell a story, and the story had to *move*.

Some of these magazines acquired a special status, such as *Adventure, Blue Book, Amazing Stories,* and *Black Mask. Adventure* was in many respects a unique case, for the magazine maintained a department in which adventurers could communicate with one another, exchange advice or information, or locate long-lost companions. Often much offbeat historical or anthropological information appeared in those columns. There is nothing quite like it today.

Often it is asked whether I have written anything other than stories of the West. As a matter of fact, I have written detective, mystery, sports, air, and adventure stories. I have never written science fiction but always had it in mind. A number of my first stories were of adventures in what is now Indonesia, stories taking place in Borneo, Celebes, New Guinea, Java, Sumatra, etc. Some of these non-Western stories appear in the book *Yondering*.

The art of storytelling has always been circumscribed by patterns imposed by various publications and their attempts to appeal to public taste or what they assumed to be so. All of us, in all periods of time, have had to write stories editors thought would appeal to a specific group of readers, and all sorts of nonsense has been written by those who comment on such things.

As I have said elsewhere, we have no idea what Edgar Allan Poe might have written had he lived in any other period. At that time the stories in demand were those of haunted houses, ghosts, the weird and the strange. Many such stories were written of which we have little or no record. Poe's have lasted because of their quality. Had he lived in any other time, his stories might have been completely different. He was without doubt one of the most innovative and successful of American editors. His misfortune was to appear at a time when his profession not only did not pay well, but when European writers were preferred.

The profession of literature has many facets, not the least of which is the necessity to make a living.

BOWDRIE PASSES THROUGH[1]

There was no reason to question the authority of the Sharps .50 resting against the doorjamb.

"Hold it right there, mister!"

The voice behind the Sharps was young, but it carried a ring of command, and

[1] This story was originally published in *Popular Western,* August 1948.

it does not require a grown man to pull a trigger. Chick Bowdrie had lived this long because he knew where to stop. He stopped now.

"I didn't know anybody was to home," he said agreeably. "I was lookin' for Josh Pettibone."

"He ain't here." The youthful voice was belligerent.

"Might as well rest that rifle, boy. I ain't huntin' trouble."

There was no response from the house, and the gun muzzle did not waver. Chick found the black opening of the muzzle singularly unattractive, but he found himself admiring the resolution of whoever was behind the gun.

"Where is Josh?"

"He's . . . they done took him off." Chick thought he detected a catch in the boy's throat.

"Who took him off?"

"The law come an' fetched him."

"Now, what would the law want Josh Pettibone for?"

"Claimed he poisoned a horse of Nero Tatum's," the boy said. "He done no such thing!"

"Tatum of the Tall T? You'd better put down that rifle, boy, an' talk to me. I'm no enemy of your pa's."

After a moment of hesitation the rifle was lowered to the floor and the boy stepped out. He wore a six-shooter thrust into his waistband. He was towheaded, and wearing a shirt that had obviously belonged to his father. He was probably as much as twelve, and very thin.

Bowdrie studied him, and was not fooled. Young he might be, but this boy was no coward and he was responsible. In Bowdrie's limited vocabulary, to be responsible was the most important word.

The boy walked slowly, distrustfully, to the gate, but he made no move to open it.

"Your pa poison that horse of Tatum's?"

"He did not! My pa would never poison no stock of anybody's!"

"Don't reckon he would," Bowdrie agreed. "Tell me about it."

"Nero Tatum, he hates Pa, and Pa never had no use for Tatum. He's tried to get Pa off this place two or three times, sayin' he didn't want no jailbirds nestin' that close to him."

When the boy said "jailbirds" he looked quickly at Bowdrie for his reaction, but Chick seemed not to notice.

"Then Pa got that Hereford bull off of Pete Swager, and that made Tatum madder'n ever. Tatum had sure enough wanted that Swager bull, and offered big money for it. Pete knowed Pa wanted it and he owed Pa a favor or two so he let Pa have it for less money. Pete was leavin' the country."

Chick Bowdrie knew about that favor. Pete Swager had gone to San Antonio on business and had come down sick. His wife and little boy were on the ranch alone, and two days after Pete left, they came down with the smallpox too. Josh Pettibone had ridden over, nursed them through their illness, and did the ranch work as well. It was not a small thing, and Pete Swager was not a man to forget.

"Tatum's black mare up an' died, an' he accused Pa of poisonin' her."

"What have they got for evidence?" Bowdrie asked.

"They found the mare close to our line fence, an' she was dyin' when they found her, frothin' at the mouth an' kickin' somethin' awful.

"When she died, he accused Pa, and then Foss Deal, he claimed he seen Pa give poison to the mare."

"You take it easy, boy. We've got to think about this. You got any coffee inside?"

The boy's face flushed. "No, we ain't." Then, as Chick started to swing down, he said, "There's nothin' in there to eat, stranger. You better ride on into town."

Bowdrie smiled. "All right if I use your fire, son? I've got a mite of grub here, and some coffee, and I'm hungry."

Reluctantly, and with many a glance at Bowdrie, the boy opened the gate. He glanced at the roan. "He's pretty fast, ain't he?"

"Like a jackrabbit, only he can keep it up for miles. Never seems to tire. There's been a few times when he really had to run."

The boy glanced at him quickly. "You on the dodge, mister? Is the law after you, too?"

"No, I've found it pays to stay on the right side of the law. A few years back I had a run-in with some pretty tough people, and for a spell it was like bein' on the dodge.

"Nothin' romantic about bein' an outlaw, son. Just trouble an' more trouble. You can't trust anybody, even the outlaws you ride with. You're always afraid somebody will recognize you, and you don't have any real friends, for fear they might turn you in or rob you themselves.

"The trouble with bein' an outlaw or any kind of criminal is the company you have to keep."

As they neared the house, Chick heard a slight stir of movement within, and when he entered, the flimsy curtain hanging over the door opening into another room was still moving slightly. It was growing dusk, so Chick took the chimney from a coal-oil lamp and lighted the wick, replacing the chimney.

The boy stared at him uneasily, shifting his eyes to the curtain occasionally.

"Tell your sister to come out. I won't bother her, and she might like to eat too."

Hesitantly a girl come from behind the curtain. She might have been sixteen, with the same large, wistful eyes the boy had, and the same too-thin face, but she was pretty. Chick smiled at her, then began breaking kindling to build a fire.

Chick glanced at the boy. "Why don't you put up my horse, son? Take your sister along if you've a mind to, and when you come in, you might bring my rifle along."

While they were gone, he got the fire going, and finding a coffeepot that was spotlessly clean, he put on some coffee. Then he dug into the haversack he had brought in for some bacon, a few potatoes, and some wild onions. By the time they returned, he had a meal going and the room was filled with the comforting smells of coffee and bacon.

"Tell me about your pa," he suggested, "and while you're at it, tell me your names."

"She's Dotty. I'm Tom," the boy said.

When Tom started to talk, Chick found there was little he did not already know. Three years later, Josh Pettibone had been arrested and had served a year in prison. Along with several other Rangers, Chick had always felt the sentence had not been deserved.

Pettibone had torn down a fence that blocked his cattle from water, and had been convicted for malicious mischief. Ordinarily no western jury would have convicted him, but this was a case where most of the jury "belonged" to Bugs Tatum, Nero's brother. The judge and the prosecuting attorney had been friends of the Tatums', and Josh, having no money, had defended his own case. Chick Bowdrie had not been judge and jury, but he knew what he believed.

"When does this case come up?" he asked.

"The day after tomorrow."

"All right, tomorrow you an' your sister put on your best clothes and get out the buckboard and we'll go into town together. Maybe we can help your pa.

"In the meantime," he added, "I'll ride out in the morning and look the situation over."

It was not only a Ranger's job to enforce the law and do what he could to protect the people, but in this thinly settled country where courts were few and of doubtful legality, they were often called upon to be judge and jury as well. They were advisers, doctors, in some cases even teachers. All too often the courts were controlled by a few big cattlemen for their own interests.

Chick Bowdrie knew Josh Pettibone was not a bad man. A stubborn man, fiercely independent, and often quick-tempered, he knew the fencing of that water hole had been pure spite. By fencing the draw, Tatum had fenced out only Josh's cattle, allowing all other cattle to come and go as they wished. Bugs Tatum had wanted Josh's place, and while Josh was in prison, he got it.

On his release, Josh got his children from a relative who had cared for them and filed on a new claim. Here, too, he encountered a Tatum, for Nero owned a vast range north of Pettibone's new claim.

Foss Deal had also wanted that claim, but failed to file on it, and was angry at Pettibone for beating him to it.

Bowdrie was out before daylight and riding up the canyon. Young Tom had given him careful directions, so he knew where he was going. He found the dead horse lying near a marshy and reed-grown water hole in a canyon that branched off the Blue. It had been a fine mare, no question of that.

Thoughtfully he studied the situation. He eyed the rocks and the canyon walls, which were some distance away, and finally walked up to the pool itself and studied the plant growth nearby. In the loose soil at the pool's edge and among the rank grass were other plants, because of the permanent water supply.

Squatting on his heels, he tugged one plant from the earth, noting the divided leaves and tuberous root. When he returned to his horse, he stowed the plant in his saddlebags. He led the roan off a little distance, and keeping a hand near his gun, swung into the saddle.

He was almost back to Pettibone's ranch when he heard several gunshots, then the dull boom of the Sharps.

Spurring the roan into a run, he charged out of the branch canyon to see four riders circling the house, and heard a shrill cry from the stable. Lifting a hand high, he rode into the yard.

One of the men rode toward him. "Get movin', stranger! This is a private fight."

"Not 'stranger,' " Bowdrie said. "Ranger! Now, shove that gun back in the boot and call off your dogs or I'll blow you out of the saddle!"

The rider laughed contemptuously. "Why, I could—!"

Suddenly he was looking into a Colt. "Back off!" Bowdrie said. "Back off an' get out!"

A scream from the stable brought Bowdrie into action. Not daring to turn his back on the other man, he suddenly leaped his horse at him and slashed out with the barrel of his Colt, knocking him from the saddle. Wheeling his horse, he rode into the stable.

A man was grappling with Dotty, his face ugly with rage, blood running from a scratch on his cheek. When he glimpsed Bowdrie, he threw the girl from him and went for his gun, but the roan knew its business, and as Bowdrie charged into the stable, the roan hit the man with a shoulder, spilling him to the floor.

Bowdrie hit the dust beside him, grabbing him by the collar and knocking the gun from his hand with a slap of the pistol barrel, then laying him out with another blow, this one to the head.

He whipped the gunbelt from the man's waist and was just turning when he saw two men charging into the barn. He covered them. "Drop 'em! An' drop 'em fast!"

Gingerly, careful to allow no room for a mistake, they unbuckled their belts.

"Now, back up!"

Tom Pettibone stepped from the house, the Sharps up and ready.

''Cover them, Tom. If anyone so much as moves, blow him in two!''

''Hey, mister!'' one of the men protested. ''That kid might get nervous!''

''Suppose you just stand there an' pray he doesn't?'' Bowdrie suggested.

He walked over to the man he had pistol-whipped, disarmed and tied him. When he got back to the stable, Dotty was guarding the man who had been attacking her, holding a pitchfork over him.

''Thanks, Dotty. I'll handle him.''

Jerking the man to his feet, he tied his hands, then brought him into the yard.

''You've played hell!'' one rider declared. ''Nero Tatum will have your hide for this!''

''So you're Tatum's boys? No sooner is the father of these youngsters in jail than you come over here. What are you doing here?''

''Wouldn't you like to know?'' one of them sneered.

Chick smiled. ''I will know. I intend to find out. Take a look at me again, boys. Does my face mean anything to you?''

''You look like a damned Apache!''

Chick smiled again. ''Just think that over,'' he said. He waved a hand around. ''We're a long way from anywhere, and I've just found you molesting a girl. Now, you know Texans don't like that sort of thing. You thought you could get away with it and nobody would know. Before I am through, you will not only have told me what I want, but Texas won't be big enough for you. Everybody in the state will know what a low-life bunch you are.

''Maybe,'' he added, ''they'll hang you. I'm a Ranger and I'm supposed to stop that sort of thing, but I can look the other way. Of course, to an Apache, hangin' would be too good for you.''

While Tom stood guard over the men with their hands and now their feet bound, Dotty brought up the buckboard.

Meanwhile Chick had gathered sticks and a little straw from the barn and had kindled a fire. Into the fire he placed a branding iron. The prisoners stared at him, then at the fire.

''Hey, now, what the devil do you think . . . ?''

''Be surprised how tough some men are,'' Bowdrie commented casually. ''Why, sometimes you can burn two or three fingers off a man, or even an ear, before he starts to talk.''

Bowdrie reached out suddenly and jerked to his feet the man who had attacked Dotty. ''You, now. I wonder how tough you are.''

He glanced at the others. ''Does the smell of burnin' flesh make you fellers sick? It even bothers me, sometimes. But not right away. Takes a while.''

''Now, see here . . . !'' one man protested.

Chick glanced at the wide-eyed Tom. ''If any of these men start to move, just start shootin'.''

''Wait a minute.'' The man who spoke was mean-looking, short and wiry. ''I don't believe you'll do this. I don't believe you'll burn anybody, but if you take us in, will we have to stand up in court an'—''

''Tatum's got the court in his hip pocket,'' another sneered.

Bowdrie glanced at him. ''I'll quote you. So will the youngsters. He won't have any court in his pocket. He will be in jail.

''I'm just one Ranger. If anything happens to me or if I need more, they'll come a-running. We started workin' on this case while Josh Pettibone was in jail, and we've got enough to hang every one of you, but the Tatums will be first.''

The wiry man interrupted. ''Like I say, I don't believe you'd burn anybody.'' He looked into Bowdrie's hard black eyes and shook his head. ''Again, maybe you might. What I'm sayin' is, if I talk, can I get out of this? Supposin' I give you a signed statement? Will you give me a runnin' start?''

''I will.''

''Laredo! For the Lord's sake—!''

''No, you boys do what you want! I'm gittin' out o' this! I ain't gonna have my neck stretched for nobody, and I surely ain't gonna stand up there in court.''

''Dotty?'' Bowdrie said. ''Get pencil and paper, and what this man says, you write down. Then we'll get him to sign it. But first''—with his left hand Bowdrie went into his saddlebags and brought out a small Bible—''we will just swear him in.''

The others waited in silence. One of them twitched anxiously. ''Laredo, think what you're doin'!''

''I am thinkin'. If I stand up in that court, somebody's goin' to recognize me. What did them Tatums ever do for me, that I should get hung for them? They paid me my wages, and I earned ever' cent. I got a few days comin', and they can have it.''

Laredo began to speak. ''We were sent to burn Pettibone out, and Tatum said he didn't care what happened to the youngsters, only he didn't want to be bothered with them. He said to drive 'em out of the country or whatever, that Josh wouldn't be comin' back anyway. That's what Nero Tatum told us.''

Given the pad on which his statement had been written, he signed it. Without a word, Bowdrie freed him and pointed at the horses. ''Take yours an' get out!''

For a moment there was silence. ''How about me?'' The speaker was a rough-looking man whose shirt collar was ringed with dirt. ''Can I sign that an' go free?''

''Dammit, Bud!'' One of the other men lunged at him. His hands and feet were bound, so all he could do was to butt with his head. Bud shook him off.

''All right, Bud. Sign it and go, but you're the last one.''

''What? That's not fair! Now, you see here, you—''

''You all had your chance. That chance is gone. You'll be in court.''

Most of Mesquite's population of three hundred and fifty-two people were gathered in the street close to the dance hall that was to double as a courtroom. None of the gathering had seen the buckboard roll into town the night before. The cargo was unloaded in an abandoned stable, and Chick Bowdrie took his place as guard.

A few people who saw Bowdrie outside the stable wondered at the presence of the man in the flat-crowned hat, wearing twin six-shooters. He was joined by a lean red-haired cowhand who followed him on guard duty.

Rawboned Judge Ernie Walters, judge by grace of Nero Tatum and two other large ranchers, called the court to order. As was often the case in the earliest days, the conduct of courtroom proceedings was haphazard, depending much on the knowledge or lack of it on the part of the court officials.

Claude Batten, prosecuting attorney, was presenting the case against Pettibone.

Walters banged the gavel and glared around the room. ''If any of you have ideas of lynchin', get 'em out of your heads. This here Pettibone is goin' to get a fair trial before we hang him. Court's in session!''

Batten began, ''Your Honor, gents of the jury, and folks, this court's convened to hear evidence an' pass sentence on this no-account jailbird Josh Pettibone, who's accused of poisonin' that fine black mare of our good friend and fellow citizen Nero Tatum.

''Pettibone done time in jail, one year of it, sent to jail for a crime against Bugs Tatum, Nero's brother. When he got out, he come here an' grabbed off a piece of land alongside Nero Tatum an' waited until he had a chance to get even. He poisoned the best brood mare this side of San Antone!''

He glared around the room, his eyes hesitating only for an instant on the guileless countenance of Chick Bowdrie, a stranger.

''Foss Deal?'' Batton ordered. ''Take the stand!''

Deal came forward and seated himself. His hair was combed, plastered to his head with water, but he was unshaved. His cruel blue eyes focused on Pettibone and remained there.

"Foss, tell the court what you saw!"

Deal cleared his throat. "I was ridin' out huntin' strays and I seen Pettibone there poisonin' Tatum's Morgan mare. I seen him give her poison, and a few minutes later that hoss fell down an' died!"

There was a stir in the courtroom.

Batten glanced around. "Hear that? I reckon no more's necessary. Judge, I move you turn this case over to the jury!"

"Just a minute, your Honor!"

Bowdrie stood up. Walters, Batten and Tatum had seen the lean, hard-faced young man and wondered who he was, as strangers were comparatively rare in Mesquite. It was off the beaten track, and they had not expected anyone to interfere in local affairs. So far, they had managed such things very successfully for themselves.

"Who are you? What right have you to interrupt this proceedin'?"

Bowdrie smiled, and with the smile his face lighted up, drawing an almost automatic response from many in the courtroom. "In this case, your Honor, I am acting as attorney for the defense.

"You spoke of giving Mr. Pettibone a fair trial. If that is true, he should get a chance to speak for himself and for his attorney to question the witnesses, and perhaps to offer evidence on behalf of the defendant."

Walters glanced uneasily at Nero Tatum. He was confused. Tatum had told him to make it look good, but there was something about this stranger that worried him and spoke of a little more courtroom experience than he had.

"What can he say?" Batten demanded. "Foss Deal saw him poison her!"

"That's the question. Did he see poison given to the mare?"

"I don't reckon we have to hear what you have to say," Walters said. "You set down!"

"In that case, gentlemen, I shall have to write a complete report of these proceedings for the governor of Texas!"

"Huh?" Walters was startled. The governor was a faraway but awesome power. He glanced at Nero Tatum, who was frowning. "Just who are you, young feller?"

"The name is Chick Bowdrie. I am a Texas Ranger."

Had he exploded a bomb, it would have caused no more excitement. Tatum caught Walters' eye and nodded. Claude Batten sat down, looking uneasily at Foss Deal. He had been against the procedure from the first, not from principle but simply because it was too obvious. Not for a minute did he trust Foss Deal, nor believe in the kangaroo-court procedure. He had tried to explain to Tatum that the time for such tactics was past.

"All right!" Walters grumbled. "Question the witness!"

Bowdrie strolled over to Deal, who glared at him belligerently. "What kind of poison was it?" he asked.

"Huh? What was that?"

"I asked what kind of poison it was."

"How should I know? I wasn't right alongside him."

"Then how do you know it was poison?"

"I reckon I know poison when I see it!"

"You're very lucky," Bowdrie said. He took two small papers from his pocket and opened them. Each contained a small amount of white powder. "Now, my friend, there are two papers. One contains sugar, the other holds a deadly poison. Suppose you decide which is which and then prove you are right by swallowing the one you have decided is not poison."

Foss Deal stared at the papers. He licked his lips with his tongue. His back was to Tatum, and he did not know what to do. He twisted in his chair, struggling for words.

"Come, come, Mr. Deal! You know poison when you see it. We trust your judgment."

Batten leaped to his feet. "What are you doing? Trying to poison the witness?"

"Of course not!" Bowdrie said. "There's no danger of that! Why, this witness just testified he could recognize poison from a distance of two hundred yards!"

"I never! I never done such a thing!"

"If you had ever even been near the place where the mare died, you would know there's no place where you could watch from cover within two hundred yards!"

"That's right!" The voice was from the audience. "I was wonderin' about that!"

"Order in the court!" Walters shouted angrily.

"Isn't it a fact," Bowdrie asked, "that you wanted Pettibone off that place so you could file on it yourself?"

"No such thing!"

"Then," Chick suggested, "if Pettibone is convicted, you will *not* file on it?"

Deal's face grew flushed. "Well, I—"

"Forget it," Bowdrie said. "Now, you said you saw Pettibone poison the mare? Or at least, you saw him give something to the mare?"

"That's right."

"He was alone?"

"Yeah, he was alone."

"Deal, where were you the previous night?"

"Huh?"

Deal glanced hastily at Batten, but got no help. Claude Batten was unhappy. A Texas Ranger was the last thing he had expected. Previously such cases had all been pushed through without any outward protest. Now what he wanted was to wash his hands of the case and get out. Nero Tatum had gone too far, for no matter how this case turned out, Bowdrie had to write a report. In fact, if Batten understood correctly the Ranger procedure, the chances were that reports had already gone in or that he was acting upon orders.

"Where were you Friday night?" Bowdrie insisted.

"Why, I was . . . I don't exactly recall."

"I can believe that!" Bowdrie said. He turned to the jury. "Gentlemen, I am prepared to prove that the witness was nowhere near Mesquite or the Pettibone ranch on the day in question. I am prepared to produce witnesses who will testify that Deal was lying dead drunk in O'Brien's Livery Stable in Valentine!"

Deal sat up sharply, consternation written all over him.

"Do you deny," Bowdrie said, "that you were in O'Brien's stable last Friday night? Or that you ate breakfast at Ma Kennedy's the next morning?"

Foss Deal started to speak, stopped, then tried to twist around to catch Tatum's eye. Tatum avoided his glance. All he wanted now was to get out of this. He wanted out as quickly and quietly as possible. Batten had warned him something like this would happen sooner or later. He should have listened.

"Your Honor," Bowdrie said, "I want this man held on a charge of perjury."

Before anything more could be said, he stepped up to the table behind which the judge sat, and taking a paper from his pocket, he unwrapped it, displaying the plant he had picked from the edge of the pool where Tatum's mare had died.

"Your Honor, ladies and gentlemen, I don't know as much about legal procedure as I should. I came here because I wanted to see justice done, and there's more experienced Rangers who could have handled this better, but this plant I have here is called water hemlock. This came from the pool near where Tatum's mare died, and there's more of it out there.

"As most of you know, animals won't touch it, as a rule, but it's one of the few green things early in the spring. The leaves and fruit of this plant can be eaten by stock without much danger, but the roots of water hemlock are poisonous.

"Cattle suffer more from it than horses, but horses, like Tatum's mare, have died from it too. In the spring, when it's green and the soil's loose, the plant is easier pulled up. When an animal eats water hemlock, the first symptom is frothin' at the mouth, then convulsions with a lot of groanin', then the animal dies.

"Nobody poisoned Tatum's mare, and Foss Deal lied, as I have shown. The mare was poisoned by water hemlock, and if you open up the stomach you'll find some of it there. Unless Mr. Batten has more witnesses, I suggest this case be dismissed!"

Judge Ernie Walters looked uncertainly toward Tatum and Batten, who were whispering together.

"Nothing more," Batten said. "We will forget it."

As the rancher arose, Chick Bowdrie said, "Nero Tatum, you are under arrest!"

Tatum's face flushed. "Look here, young man, you're going too far! Now, I'll admit—"

"Mr. Tatum—"

"See here, young man, you're goin' too far. I've friends down at Austin. I'll have you fired!"

"No, you won't, Mr. Tatum. I am arrestin' you for incitin' to arson, for conspiracy, and a half-dozen other items. I have signed statements from some of your men and some others who want to turn state's evidence. You're going to jail."

Bowdrie stepped over to him, and before Tatum realized it, he was handcuffed. Then Bowdrie took him by the elbow and guided him down the street to the jail.

"Listen!" Tatum said when they reached the jail. "You've made your play. Now, let's talk this over. We'll forget about Pettibone. He can keep his place. As for you an' me, I've got some money, and—"

"No, Mr. Tatum. You're going to jail. You ordered Pettibone's ranch burned and told your men to get rid of those youngsters, and you didn't care how."

Bowdrie stepped outside. In his hurry to get Tatum locked up, he had forgotten Foss Deal. Now he must find him, for there were few worse crimes against the cause of justice than perjury.

He had been fortunate, there was no mistaking that, for after bringing the Pettibone children into town, he had encountered Billy O'Brien, the bluff, good-hearted owner of a livery stable in Valentine, a town down the trail. When O'Brien heard about Deal's accusations, he had come at once to find Bowdrie. Deal had felt safe, for O'Brien rarely left Valentine and the town was some distance away.

With Tatum in jail, the place was crowded, but Bowdrie intended to add Foss Deal to the collection.

Crossing the street, he pushed through the batwing doors of the saloon. The bartender, long resentful of the bullying ways of the Tatum cowhands, greeted Bowdrie with pleasure.

"Have one on the house!" he said affably. As Chick accepted a beer, the bartender whispered, "Watch yourself. Deal's got a shotgun an' swears he'll kill you on sight."

Wiping a glass, he added, "When Foss has had a couple, he gets mean. Worst of it is, Bugs Tatum is in town. He declares he'll have your scalp and Pettibone's too."

The door pushed open and Josh Pettibone walked in. "Bowdrie, I ain't had a chance to thank you, but Tatum an' Deal are huntin' you, and I've come to stand with you."

"You go to your youngsters and stay there. Foss Deal wouldn't be above killin' your kids to get even. This is my show, and I can handle it alone."

The town's one street had suddenly become empty. He knew western towns well enough to realize the word was out. He knew also that more depended upon this than the mere matter of handling two malcontents. Bugs Tatum and Deal were big cogs in the wheel of Nero Tatum's control over this corner of Texas, something the Rangers had long contemplated breaking up.

If he, Bowdrie, should be killed now, what had happened might die with him. Tatum had friends in important places and knew how to wield power, and Bowdrie was essential as a witness, despite whatever reports he had filed.

Bowdrie had lived long enough to know that killing was rarely a good thing, but in this town and this area, guns were the last court of appeal. He had appeared here in the name of Texas; now he had to make his final arrests.

He knew the manner of men they were, and he also knew that not only his life depended upon his skill with a gun, but also those of Josh and his children. The town was waiting to see which would triumph, Texas law or Tatum's law.

He stepped outside and moved quickly into the deeper shadow of the building, looking up and down the street. It was cool and pleasant here, for a little breeze came from between the buildings.

A man whom he did not recognize squatted near the hub of a wheel, his back toward Bowdrie. He was apparently greasing the axle. A door creaked but he did not move. He heard a footfall, then another. The sound seemed to come from the building on his right. As there were no windows on the side toward him; whoever was inside would have to emerge on the street before he could see Bowdrie.

Listening to catch the slightest sound, he saw that the man greasing the axle, if that was what he was doing, had turned his side toward Bowdrie.

A shadow moved in the space between two buildings across the street, and from inside the vacant store building beside him a board creaked. If he had to turn toward a man emerging from the empty store, he would be half-turning his back on the man by the wagon wheel.

The door hinge creaked and Bowdrie moved. Swiftly he ducked back through the batwing doors and ran on cat feet to the back of the saloon and outside. He ran behind the building where he had heard movement and came up on its far side.

As he neared the front, somebody said, "Where'd he go? Where is he?"

Chick stepped from behind the building. "Looking for me, gentlemen?"

The man who had come from the empty building and the one who had come up from between the buildings turned sharply around, Bugs Tatum and Foss Deal.

The situation was completely reversed from the way it had been planned, but as one man they went for their guns. Chick Bowdrie had an instant's advantage, the instant it took them to adjust to the changed situation. His draw was a breath faster, his hands steady, his mind cool.

His right-hand gun bucked, and Bugs Tatum died with his hand clutching a gun he had scarcely gripped. Bowdrie fired at Foss, felt a bullet whip by his face and another kick dust at his feet, fired by the man by the wagon wheel.

Bowdrie fired, and the bullet clipped a spoke of the wheel just over the man's head. The fellow flattened himself into the dust.

Foss Deal had been hit and was staggering, trying to get his gun up. Bowdrie sprang toward him and with a blow from the barrel of his gun sent Deal's gun spinning into the dust.

Bugs Tatum was flat on his face and unmoving. Deal was struggling to rise, but badly hurt. Walking toward him, Bowdrie glanced suddenly toward the man by the wagon. He was on his feet, gun in hand, the gun lifting. A shot came from the direction of the jail and the man by the wagon lifted on his toes, then pitched forward.

The red-haired man who had been guarding the prisoners walked out, rifle in hand.

"Thanks, McKeever," Bowdrie said.

"You moved too fast for me, Chick. It was almost over before I could get to the door."

"It was more important you hold the prisoners. I was afraid they'd try to bust them out."

"You goin' to write the report on this, or shall I?" McKeever asked.

"We'd both better write it up," Bowdrie said. "We will be in court on this one."

Josh Pettibone was standing over Deal. "This one will live, I'm afraid, but he won't be eatin' any side meat for a while!"

Dotty was standing in front of the store with her brother, Tom. "Mr. Bowdrie," she said, "I've got to ask you something. Would you have burned that man's hand off?"

He shrugged. "I don't imagine I would have, Dotty, but I didn't think I'd have to. A man with enough coyote in him to bother a nice girl like you wouldn't have enough sand in him to take it."

He reloaded his gun. There were things to be done, but all he wanted was to be back on the trail again. He wanted to be out there with the cloud shadows and the miles spread out around him. Folks said there were high mountains out yonder with snow on them, and forests no man had ever seen.

Well, no white man, anyway. The Indians had been everywhere. Someday, when all this sort of thing was over with, maybe he'd ride that way. Maybe even find a place for himself where he could feel the cool winds and look at distance.

CLASSICS

Literature is news that stays news.

EZRA POUND

IN its popular sense, ''classic'' means something that remains in style. The word often comes up in talk about a particular cut of clothing, the movements of dancers and athletes, someone's features, the lines of a building or an automobile, and even the preparation of food. ''Classic,'' in such instances, describes certain qualities of craftsmanship, performance, or appearance that remain constant despite changes in fashion, taste, doctrine, or government. Unlike most of the ads, best sellers, articles, and journalism you have read in previous chapters of this book, the prose and poetry reprinted in the following pages represents the work of many writers who have been read continuously over the years, writers who have remained in style. A classic is durable; it is writing that stays in print.

Why do some works preserve a lively reputation for generations while others are forgotten by the end of a season? Surely it is not because the writers of what eventually become classics attend to different subjects than do the authors of even those best sellers whose popularity does not endure very much beyond their arrival in paperback at local bookstores. Adventure and romance, love and death, individual freedom and social order, innocence and experience, success and failure are, for example, often ''themes'' of classics and best sellers as well as, for that matter, most journalism and advertising. If what makes a work a classic is not simply the author's choice of material—all material is, strictly speaking, in the public domain—then the best place to find the reason for a work's continuing success is in the quality of its writing.

In general, our selections from American classics will provide you with more complicated uses of language than most of the other forms of writing you have encountered in earlier sections of this book. It should be added, however, that the authors of classics are not necessarily hostile to those other, less complicated forms of writing. If anything, they are probably more willing to incorporate the multiplicity of styles and voices surrounding them than are writers who must, because of a greater commercial investment, appeal to quite specific audiences. Journalists, for example, may be reluctant to record the interferences and intrusions they may have encountered in their attempted news coverage. (They have only a limited amount of newspaper space for their ''stories'' and copy editors to satisfy.) So too, authors of best sellers may not want to, may not know how to, or may not even dare to risk unsettling their readers with sudden shifts in tone or point of view or subtle maneuvers into irony or parody.

From the philosophical manner of Henry David Thoreau to the Beat poetics of Allen Ginsberg, the writing collected here is meant to suggest the variety and complexity of classic American literature. It is literature whose authors, for the most part, have been receptive, at times competitively responsive, to whatever environment of language they chose to work in. Mark Twain, who told many good stories in his own lifetime, makes it clear that telling a story well is a performance of tone and nuance that ought to rival the most successful forms of contemporary entertainment. Twain wants his audience to delight, as he does, in the art of mimicry and parody. ''How To Tell a Story'' is much more than an enjoyable training manual for delivering effective jokes; it is also a fine critical statement reminding us that the art of reading well is also the art of listening attentively. John Updike in ''A & P,'' James Thurber in ''The Secret Life of Walter Mitty,'' Tillie Olsen in ''I Stand Here Ironing,'' and Allen Ginsberg in ''A Supermarket in California,'' expect (as Twain does) their audiences to be fully attuned to the ways their styles embody the nonliterary idioms and intonations of American advertising, popular music, and film.

Along with Mark Twain, such writers as Stephen Crane, Ernest Hemingway, and Norman Mailer are competitively aware of how the techniques and verbal formulations of journalism can be exploited and even parodied in their own efforts to render events distinctively. Having been reporters themselves, they have experienced first hand the advantages and limitations of writing the kind of prose that newspapers consistently promote. For example, a comparison of Mailer's account with the newspaper report of the astronauts' walk on the moon will demonstrate what a major novelist considers to be the obligations of a literary consciousness contending with an event that is surrounded, if not dominated, by the machinery of news coverage. In Stephen Crane's "The Open Boat," we can observe how a writer transforms the raw data of a journalistic "scoop" (see "Stephen Crane's Own Story" in Press) into the complex arrangements of classic fiction.

It should be clear from the following selections that the writers of classics use language in the most demanding and selective ways possible. Theirs is a prose that requires its audience to have attained a more highly developed reading aptitude than that needed to respond to much of the writing appearing earlier in this book. A classic expects its readers to be more than simply "literate." Readers of classics are obliged to engage in difficult, sometimes highly complicated verbal experiences and, at the same time, are encouraged in the act of reading, to refer these verbal experiences to a wide network of accumulated literary responses. In fact, the writers of classic prose (whether it be fiction or nonfiction) very often imagine for themselves readers who take delight in having such demands made on them.

Few authors are more exacting in the demands their writing makes on their audience than William Faulkner. Take, for example, the following passage from *The Bear,* in which Faulkner describes the culmination of young Ike McCaslin's nearly obsessive, increasingly solitary search for the elusive, indomitable bear, Old Ben:

> Then he saw the bear. It did not emerge, appear: it was just there, immobile, fixed in the green and windless noon's hot dappling, not as big as he had dreamed it but as big as he had expected, bigger, dimensionless against the dappled obscurity, looking at him. Then it moved. It crossed the glade without haste, walking for an instant into the sun's full glare and out of it, and stopped again and looked back at him across one shoulder. Then it was gone. It didn't walk into the woods. It faded, sank back into the wilderness without motion as he had watched a fish, a huge old bass, sink back into the dark depths of its pool and vanish without even any movement of its fins.

Faulkner allows Ike his long-awaited confrontation with the bear only after the boy has willingly surrendered himself to the woods by relinquishing his gun, watch, and compass. Bereft of weapon and instruments, those "tainted" items of civilization, Ike can *know* the wilderness in ways that permit him to go further than even his mastery of the technique of woodmanship could take him. When Ike finally encounters Old Ben, it is because he has entered into a new relation with the woods, one that has superseded the boundaries set up by the rules and rituals of hunting and tracking.

As a factual account of a hunting incident, this passage is rather unremarkable, surely anticlimactic. Nothing much seems to happen. The boy sees the bear. The bear sees the boy. The bear disappears into the woods. There is no kill, no breathtaking capture or escape. Furthermore, the reader is given few of the details that might be anticipated in such an encounter. Nothing is told of the bear's size, color, or smell; there is none of the usual metaphorical approximations hunters like to make of an animal's brute power. What is perhaps even more surprising, the reader is told nothing at all about the boy's emotional response to the one moment he has trained and waited for through so many hunting seasons.

If the reader cannot easily picture this episode within the frame of a glossy photograph from *Field and Stream* or *True,* it is because Faulkner's writing resists the kind of imagination that would want to reduce the scene to one more clearly and conventionally focused. The total effect produced by the blurring of the bear and woods, the amorphous presence of the boy, the uncertainty of movement, and the confusing shifts of sunlight and shadow is not the result of a verbal or pictorial incompetence but, on the contrary, is the consequence of a deliberate and complex effort of intelligence. Faulkner's style demands that the reader participate in that complexity. The reliance on negatives ("It did not emerge . . . not as big . . . It didn't walk"), the sudden modification of syntax ("but as big as he had expected, bigger, dimensionless"), the struggle to find adequate verbs or adjectives ("emerge, appear . . . immobile, fixed . . . faded, sank"), the process of expansion ("a fish, a huge old bass"), and the apparently reluctant concessions to narrative sequence ("Then he saw the bear . . . Then it moved . . . Then it was gone.") force the reader into suspending temporarily his expectations of the dimensions of an experience and the conduct of sentences. The style, in effect, compels the reader to experience a dislocation and conversion analogous to those that made Ike McCaslin's initiation into the wilderness possible.

A writer's style attests to the quality of his perceptions. Though Faulkner's verbal expansiveness in *The Bear* may seem difficult, even discouragingly so, the demands he makes on his readers are not necessarily any greater than those of writers like Thoreau, Crane, Wright, or Hemingway whose difficulties may seem, at first, much less apparent. The writing in "Soldier's Home" certainly looks "easy," but that does not mean the tale is a "simple" one. Hemingway's stylistic reticence, his self-conscious artistic control, is the consequence of a literary acuity that is perhaps only slightly less remarkable than Faulkner's. If the styles of writers like Hemingway and Faulkner are based on perceptions that happen to be intricate, even unsettling, that is only because each writer struggles to master in his own way the countless verbal options at his disposal. Such writing presupposes an energetic reader, one who is willing to work almost as hard at reading as the author worked at writing. The readers imagined by the writers of the selections that follow would not be intimidated by the kind of rigorous training that, according to Henry David Thoreau, they must undergo if they are to read proficiently:

> To read well, that is, to read books in a true spirit, is a noble exercise, and one that will task the reader more than any exercise which the customs of the day esteem. It requires a training such as the athletes underwent, the steady intention almost of the whole life to this object. Books must be read as deliberately and reservedly as they were written. ("Reading," from *Walden*)

Thoreau's metaphor is, we think, an appropriate one. By comparing the exertion of reading to the "exercise" of athletics, Thoreau converts what is ordinarily regarded as an idle occasion into a tough and invigorating practice. To read well is to do something more than just be a spectator to what Robert Frost terms "the feat of words."

Nathaniel Hawthorne / Wakefield 1835

Throughout his literary career, Nathaniel Hawthorne (1804–64) was acutely conscious of his Puritan ancestors, one of whom presided at the infamous Salem witchcraft trials. After graduating from Bowdoin College in 1825, Hawthorne spent the next twelve years in relative seclusion at his home in Salem, researching and brooding over the chronicles and annals of New England local history that were to supply him with material for the sketches and tales he published continually in the popular periodicals of the day. In 1836, Hawthorne went to Boston, where he edited the American Magazine of Useful and Entertaining Knowledge. *Three years later he was offered a political appointment in the Boston Custom House, where he was able to support himself for a number of years while writing short stories and his first novel,* The Scarlet Letter *(1850).*

First published in the New England Magazine *for May, 1835, "Wakefield" was later included in* Twice-Told Tales *(1837).*

In some old magazine or newspaper I recollect a story, told as truth, of a man—let us call him Wakefield—who absented himself for a long time from his wife. The fact, thus abstractedly stated, is not very uncommon, nor—without a proper distinction of circumstances—to be condemned either as naughty or nonsensical. Howbeit, this, though far from the most aggravated, is perhaps the strangest, instance on record, of marital delinquency; and, moreover, as remarkable a freak as may be found in the whole list of human oddities. The wedded couple lived in London. The man, under pretence of going a journey, took lodgings in the next street to his own house, and there, unheard of by his wife or friends, and without the shadow of a reason for such self-banishment, dwelt upwards of twenty years. During that period, he beheld his home every day, and frequently the forlorn Mrs. Wakefield. And after so great a gap in his matrimonial felicity—when his death was reckoned certain, his estate settled, his name dismissed from memory, and his wife, long, long ago, resigned to her autumnal widowhood—he entered the door one evening, quietly, as from a day's absence, and became a loving spouse till death.

This outline is all that I remember. But the incident, though of the purest originality, unexampled, and probably never to be repeated, is one, I think, which appeals to the generous sympathies of mankind. We know, each for himself, that none of us would perpetrate such a folly, yet feel as if some other might. To my own contemplations, at least, it has often recurred, always exciting wonder, but with a sense that the story must be true, and a conception of its hero's character. Whenever any subject so forcibly affects the mind, time is well spent in thinking of it. If the reader choose, let him do his own meditation; or if he prefer to ramble with me through the twenty years of Wakefield's vagary, I bid him welcome; trusting that there will be a pervading spirit and a moral, even should we fail to find them, done up neatly, and condensed into the final sentence. Thought has always its efficacy, and every striking incident its moral.

What sort of a man was Wakefield? We are free to shape out our own idea, and call it by his name. He was now in the meridian of life; his matrimonial affections, never violent, were sobered into a calm, habitual sentiment; of all husbands, he was likely to be the most constant, because a certain sluggishness would keep his heart at rest, wherever it might be placed. He was intellectual, but not actively so; his mind occupied itself in long and lazy musings, that ended to no purpose, or had not vigor to attain it; his thoughts were seldom so energetic as to seize hold of words. Imagination, in the proper meaning of the term, made no part of Wakefield's gifts. With a cold but not depraved nor wandering heart, and a mind never feverish with riotous thoughts, nor perplexed with originality, who could have anticipated that our friend would entitle himself to a foremost place among the doers of eccentric deeds? Had his acquaintances been asked, who was the man in London the surest to perform nothing today which should be remembered on the morrow, they would have thought of Wakefield. Only the wife of his bosom might have hesitated. She, without having analyzed his character, was partly aware of a quiet selfishness, that had rusted into his inactive mind; of a peculiar sort of vanity, the most uneasy attribute about him; of a disposition to craft, which had seldom produced more positive effects than the keeping of petty secrets, hardly worth revealing; and, lastly, of what she called a little strangeness, sometimes, in the good man. This latter quality is indefinable, and perhaps non-existent.

Let us now imagine Wakefield bidding adieu to his wife. It is the dusk of an October evening. His equipment is a drab great-coat, a hat covered with an oilcloth, top-boots, an umbrella in one hand and a small port-manteau in the other. He has informed Mrs. Wakefield that he is to take the night coach into the country. She would fain inquire the length of his journey, its object, and the probable time of his return; but, indulgent to his harmless love of mystery, interrogates him only by a look. He tells her not to expect him positively by the return coach, nor to be alarmed should he tarry three or four days; but, at all events, to look for him at supper on Friday evening. Wakefield himself, be it considered, has no suspicion of what is before him. He holds out his hand, she gives her own, and meets his parting kiss in the matter-of-course way of a ten years' matrimony; and forth goes the middle-aged Mr. Wakefield, almost resolved to perplex his good lady by a whole week's absence. After the door has closed behind him, she perceives it thrust partly open, and a vision of her husband's face, through the aperture, smiling on her, and gone in a moment. For the time, this little incident is dismissed without a thought. But, long afterwards, when she has been more years a widow than a wife, that smile recurs, and flickers across all her reminiscences of Wakefield's visage. In her many musings, she surrounds the original smile with a multitude of fantasies, which make it strange and awful: as, for instance, if she imagines him in a coffin, that parting look is frozen on his pale features; or, if she dreams of him in heaven, still his blessed spirit wears a quiet and crafty smile. Yet, for its sake, when all others have given him up for dead, she sometimes doubts whether she is a widow.

But our business is with the husband. We must hurry after him along the street, ere he lose his individuality, and melt into the great mass of London life. It would be vain searching for him there. Let us follow close at his heels, therefore, until, after several superfluous turns and doublings, we find him comfortably established by the fireside of a small apartment, previously bespoken. He is in the next street to his own, and at his journey's end. He can scarcely trust his good fortune, in having got thither unperceived—recollecting that, at one time, he was delayed by the throng, in the very focus of a lighted lantern; and, again, there were footsteps that seemed to tread behind his own, distinct from the multitudinous tramp around him; and, anon, he heard a voice shouting afar, and fancied that it called his name. Doubtless, a dozen busybodies had been watching him, and told his wife the whole affair. Poor Wakefield! Little knowest thou thine own insignificance in this great world! No mortal eye but mine has traced thee. Go quietly to thy bed, foolish man; and, on the morrow, if thou wilt be wise, get thee home to good Mrs. Wakefield, and tell her the truth. Remove not thyself, even for a little week, from thy place in her chaste bosom. Were she, for a single moment, to deem thee dead, or lost, or lastingly divided from her, thou wouldst be wofully conscious of a change in thy true wife forever after. It is perilous to make a chasm in human affections; not that they gape so long and wide—but so quickly close again!

Almost repenting of his frolic, or whatever it may be termed, Wakefield lies down betimes, and starting from his first nap, spreads forth his arms into the wide and solitary waste of the unaccustomed bed. "No,"—thinks he, gathering the bedclothes about him—"I will not sleep alone another night."

In the morning he rises earlier than usual, and sets himself to consider what he really means to do. Such are his loose and rambling modes of thought that he has taken this very singular step with the consciousness of a purpose, indeed, but without being able to define it sufficiently for his own contemplation. The vagueness of the project, and the convulsive effort with which he plunges into the execution of it, are equally characteristic of a feeble-minded man. Wakefield sifts his ideas, however, as minutely as he may, and finds himself curious to know the progress of matters at home—how his exemplary wife will endure her widowhood of a week; and, briefly, how the little sphere of creatures and circumstances, in which he was a central object, will be affected by his removal. A morbid vanity, therefore, lies nearest the bottom of the affair. But, how is he to attain his ends? Not, certainly, by keeping close in this comfortable lodging, where, though he slept and awoke in the next street to his home, he is as effectually abroad as if the stage-coach had been whirling him away all night. Yet, should he reappear, the whole project is knocked in the head. His poor brains being hopelessly puzzled with this dilemma, he at length ventures out, partly resolving to cross the head of the street, and send one hasty glance towards his forsaken domicile. Habit—for he is a man of habits—takes him by the hand, and guides him, wholly unaware, to his own door, where, just at the critical moment, he is aroused by the scraping of his foot upon the step. Wakefield! whither are you going?

At that instant his fate was turning on the pivot. Little dreaming of the doom to which his first backward step devotes him, he hurries away, breathless with agitation hitherto unfelt, and hardly dares turn his head at the distant corner. Can it be that nobody caught sight of him? Will not the whole household—the decent Mrs. Wakefield, the smart maid servant, and the dirty little footboy—raise a hue and cry, through London streets, in pursuit of their fugitive lord and master? Wonderful escape! He gathers courage to pause and look homeward, but is perplexed with a sense of change about the familiar edifice, such as affects us all, when, after a separation of months or years, we again see some hill or lake, or work of art, with which we were friends of old. In ordinary cases, this indescribable impression is caused by the comparison and contrast between our imperfect reminiscences and the reality. In Wakefield, the magic of a single night has wrought a similar transformation, because, in that brief period, a great moral change has been effected. But this is a secret from himself. Before leaving the spot, he catches a far and momentary glimpse of his wife, passing athwart the front window, with her face turned towards the head of the street. The crafty nincompoop takes to his heels, scared with the idea that, among a thousand such atoms of mortality, her eye must have detected him. Right glad is his heart, though his brain be somewhat dizzy, when he finds himself by the coal fire of his lodgings.

So much for the commencement of this long whimwham. After the initial conception, and the stirring up of the man's sluggish temperament to put it in practice, the whole matter evolves itself in a natural train. We may suppose him, as the result of deep deliberation, buying a new wig, of reddish hair, and selecting sundry garments, in a fashion unlike his customary suit of brown, from a Jew's old-clothes bag. It is accomplished. Wakefield is another man. The new system being now established, a retrograde movement to the old would be almost as difficult as the step that placed him in his unparalleled position. Furthermore, he is rendered obstinate by a sulkiness occasionally incident to his temper, and brought on at present by the inadequate sensation which he conceives to have been produced in the bosom of Mrs. Wakefield. He will not go back until she be frightened half to death. Well; twice or thrice has she passed before his sight, each time with a heavier step, a paler cheek, and more anxious brow; and in the third week of his non-appearance he detects a portent of evil entering the house, in the guise of an apothecary. Next day the knocker is muffled. Towards nightfall comes the chariot of a physician, and deposits its big-wigged and solemn burden at Wakefield's door, whence, after a quarter of an hour's visit, he emerges, perchance the herald of a funeral. Dear woman! Will she die? By this time, Wakefield is excited to something like energy of feeling, but still lingers away from his wife's bedside, pleading with his conscience that she must not be disturbed at such a juncture. If aught else restrains him, he does not know it. In the course of a few weeks she gradually recovers; the crisis is over; her heart is sad, perhaps, but quiet; and, let him return soon or late, it will never be feverish for him again. Such ideas glimmer through the midst of Wakefield's mind, and render him indistinctly conscious that an almost impassable gulf divides his hired apartment from his former home. "It is but in the next street!" he sometimes says. Fool! it is in another world. Hitherto, he has put off his return from one particular day to another; henceforward, he leaves the precise time undetermined. Not tomorrow—probably next week—pretty soon. Poor man! The dead have nearly as much chance of revisiting their earthly homes as the self-banished Wakefield.

Would that I had a folio to write, instead of an article of a dozen pages! Then might I exemplify how an influence beyond our control lays its strong hand on every deed which we do, and weaves its consequences into an iron tissue of necessity. Wakefield is spell-bound. We must leave him, for ten years or so, to haunt around his house, without once crossing the threshold, and to be faithful to his wife, with all the affection of which his heart is capable, while he is slowly fading out of hers. Long since, it must be remarked, he had lost the perception of singularity in his conduct.

Now for a scene! Amid the throng of a London street we distinguish a man, now waxing elderly, with few characteristics to attract careless observers, yet bearing, in his whole aspect, the handwriting of no common fate, for such as have the skill to read it. He is meagre; his low and narrow forehead is deeply wrinkled; his eyes, small and lustreless, sometimes wander apprehensively about him, but oftener seem to look inward. He bends his head, and moves with an indescribable obliquity of gait, as if unwilling to display his full front to the world. Watch him long enough to see what we have described, and you will allow that circumstances—which often produce remarkable men from nature's ordinary handiwork—have produced one such here. Next, leaving him to sidle along the footwalk, cast your eyes in the opposite direction, where a portly female, considerably in the wane of life, with a prayer-book in her hand, is proceeding to yonder church. She has the placid mien of settled widowhood. Her regrets have either died away, or have become so essential to her heart, that they would be poorly exchanged for joy. Just as the lean man and well-conditioned woman are passing, a slight obstruction occurs, and brings these two figures directly in contact. Their hands touch; the pressure of the crowd forces her bosom against his shoulder; they stand, face to face, staring into each other's eyes. After a ten years' separation, thus Wakefield meets his wife!

The throng eddies away, and carries them asunder. The sober widow, resuming her former pace, proceeds to church, but pauses in the portal, and throws a perplexed glance along the street. She passes in, however, opening her prayer-book as she goes. And the man! with so wild a face that busy and selfish London stands to gaze after him, he hurries to his lodgings, bolts the door, and throws himself upon the bed. The latent feelings of years break out; his feeble mind acquires a brief energy from their strength; all the miserable strangeness of his life is revealed to him at a glance: and he cries out, passionately, "Wakefield! Wakefield! You are mad!"

Perhaps he was so. The singularity of his situation must have so moulded him to himself, that, considered in regard to his fellow-creatures and the business of life, he could not be said to possess his right mind. He had contrived, or rather he had happened, to dissever himself from the world—to vanish—to give up his place and privileges with living men, without being admitted among the dead. The life of a hermit is nowise parallel to his. He was in the bustle of the city, as of old; but the crowd swept by and saw him not; he was, we may figuratively say, always beside his wife and at his hearth, yet must never feel the warmth of the one nor the affection of the other. It was Wakefield's unprecedented fate to retain his original share of human sympathies, and to be still involved in human interests, while he had lost his reciprocal influence on them. It would be a most curious speculation to trace out the effect of such circumstances on his heart and intellect, separately, and in unison. Yet, changed as he was, he would seldom be conscious of it, but deem himself the same man as ever; glimpses of the truth, indeed, would come, but only for the moment; and still he would keep saying, "I shall soon go back!"—nor reflect that he had been saying so for twenty years.

I conceive, also, that these twenty years would appear, in the retrospect, scarcely longer than the week to which Wakefield had at first limited his absence. He would look on the affair as no more than an interlude in the main business of his life. When, after a little while more, he should deem it time to reënter his parlor, his wife would clap her hands for joy, on beholding the middle-aged Mr. Wakefield. Alas, what a mistake! Would Time but await the close of our favorite follies, we should be young men, all of us, and till Doomsday.

One evening, in the twentieth year since he vanished, Wakefield is taking his customary walk towards the dwelling which he still calls his own. It is a gusty night of autumn, with frequent showers that patter down upon the pavement, and are gone before a man can put up his umbrella. Pausing near the house, Wakefield discerns, through the parlor windows of the second floor, the red glow and the glimmer and fitful flash of a comfortable fire. On the ceiling appears a grotesque shadow of good Mrs. Wakefield. The cap, the nose and chin, and the broad waist, form an admirable caricature, which dances, moreover, with the up-flickering and down-sinking blaze, almost too merrily for the shade of an elderly widow. At this instant a shower chances to fall, and is driven, by the unmannerly gust, full into Wakefield's face and bosom. He is quite penetrated with its autumnal chill. Shall he stand, wet and shivering here, when his own hearth has a good fire to warm him, and his own wife will run to fetch the gray coat and small-clothes, which, doubtless, she has kept carefully in the closet of their bed chamber? No! Wakefield is no such fool. He ascends the steps—heavily!—for twenty years have stiffened his legs since he came down—but he knows it not. Stay, Wakefield! Would you go to the sole home that is left you? Then step into your grave! The door opens. As he passes in, we have a parting glimpse of his visage, and recognize the crafty smile, which was the precursor of the little joke that he has ever since been playing off at his wife's expense. How unmercifully has he quizzed the poor woman! Well, a good night's rest to Wakefield!

This happy event—supposing it to be such—could only have occurred at an unpremeditated moment. We will not follow our friend across the threshold. He has left us much food for thought, a portion of which shall lend its wisdom to a moral, and be shaped into a figure. Amid the seeming confusion of our mysterious world, individuals are so nicely adjusted to a system, and systems to one another and to a whole, that, by stepping aside for a moment, a man exposes himself to a fearful risk of losing his place forever. Like Wakefield, he may become, as it were, the Outcast of the Universe.

Henry David Thoreau / *Walden* 1854

Although Henry David Thoreau participated very deeply in American political and cultural life, his name has become synonymous with the archetypal voluntary exile who rejects a crass materialistic world in favor of a rugged, self-reliant outdoor existence and a "career" as an amateur naturalist. The image is partly true: Thoreau consistently endorses a simple, independent, organic life. But it is important to remember that Thoreau was also an outspoken abolitionist, a defender of John Brown even after the bloody raid on Harper's Ferry, and a conscientious dissenter who devised a highly influential philosophy of civil disobedience.

Born in Concord, Massachusetts, son of a pencil manufacturer, Thoreau graduated from Harvard having mastered Greek in 1837. He was also a master of many trades, though all his life he worked only sporadically: at chores, at surveying, at tutoring, at his father's shop, at lecturing, at odd jobs. He never made a good living, although he apparently lived a good life. Only two of his books were published in his lifetime: A Week on the Concord and Merrimack Rivers *(1849) and* Walden *(1854). He never married; he left parties early; he seldom traveled beyond Concord. He died of tuberculosis, a disappointment to his family and friends, when he was forty-four.*

At a time in American history when thousands voluntarily exiled themselves in tiny cabins on the slopes of western mountains to search for gold, Thoreau searched for a different kind of wealth along the gentle edges of a small Massachusetts pond. The book he wrote describing his twenty-six month retreat has long been considered a classic account of a peculiarly American consciousness. The following section, "Where I Lived and What I Lived for," is an excerpt from the second chapter of Walden.

WHERE I LIVED, AND WHAT I LIVED FOR

I went to the woods because I wished to live deliberately, to front only the essential facts of life, and see if I could not learn what it had to teach, and not, when I came to die, discover that I had not lived. I did not wish to live what was not life, living is so dear; nor did I wish to practise resignation, unless it was quite necessary. I wanted to live deep and suck out all the marrow of life, to live so sturdily and Spartan-like as to put to rout all that was not life, to cut a broad swath and shave close, to drive life into a corner, and reduce it to its lowest terms, and, if it proved to be mean, why then to get the whole and genuine meanness of it, and publish its meanness to the world; or if it were sublime, to know it by experience, and be able to give a true account of it in my next excursion. For most men, it appears to me, are in a strange uncertainty about it, whether it is of the devil or of God, and have *somewhat hastily* concluded that it is the chief end of man here to "glorify God and enjoy him forever."

Still we live meanly, like ants; though the fable tells us that we were long ago changed into men; like pygmies we fight with cranes; it is error upon error, and clout upon clout, and our best virtue has for its occasion a superfluous and evitable wretchedness. Our life is frittered away by detail. An honest man has hardly need to count more than his ten fingers, or in extreme cases he may add his ten toes, and lump the rest. Simplicity, simplicity, simplicity! I say, let your affairs be as two or three, and not a hundred or a thousand; instead of a million count half a dozen, and keep your accounts on your thumb-nail. In the midst of this chopping sea of civilized life, such are the clouds and storms and quicksands and thousand-and-one items to be allowed for, that a man has to live, if he would not founder and go to the bottom and not make his port at all, by dead reckoning, and he must be a great calculator indeed who succeeds. Simplify, simplify. Instead of three meals a day, if it be necessary eat but one; instead of a hundred dishes, five; and reduce other things in proportion. Our life is like a German Confederacy, made up of petty states, with its boundary forever fluctuating, so that even a German cannot tell you how it is bounded at any moment. The nation itself, with all its so-called internal improvements, which, by the way, are all external and superficial, is just such an unwieldy and overgrown establishment, cluttered with furniture and tripped up by its own traps, ruined by luxury and heedless expense, by want of calculation and a worthy aim, as the million households in the land; and the only cure for it, as for them, is in a rigid economy, a stern and more than Spartan simplicity of life and elevation of purpose. It lives too fast. Men think that it is essential that the *Nation* have commerce, and export ice, and talk through a telegraph, and ride thirty miles an hour, without a doubt, whether *they* do or not; but whether we should live like baboons or like men, is a little uncertain. If we do not get out sleepers, and forge rails, and devote days and nights to the work, but go to tinkering upon our *lives* to improve *them,* who will build railroads? And if railroads are not built, how shall we get to Heaven in season? But if we stay at home and mind our business, who will want railroads? We do not ride on the railroad; it rides upon us. Did you ever think what those sleepers are that underlie the railroad? Each one is a man, an Irishman, or a Yankee man. The rails are laid on them, and they are covered with sand, and the cars run smoothly over them. They are sound sleepers, I assure you. And every few years a new lot is laid down and run over; so that, if some have the pleasure of riding on a rail, others have the misfortune to be ridden upon. And when they run over a man that is walking in his sleep, a supernumerary sleeper in the wrong position, and wake him up, they suddenly stop the cars, and make a hue and cry about it as if this were an exception. I am glad to know that it takes a gang of men for every five miles to keep the sleepers down and level in their beds as it is, for this is a sign that they may sometime get up again.

Why should we live with such hurry and waste of life? We are determined to be starved before we are hungry. Men say that a stitch in time saves nine, and so they take a thousand stitches to-day to save nine tomorrow. As for *work,* we haven't any of any consequence. We have the Saint Vitus' dance, and cannot possibly keep our heads still. If I should only give a few pulls at the parish bell-rope, as for a fire, that is, without setting the bell, there is hardly a man on his farm in the outskirts of Concord, notwithstanding that press of engagements which was his excuse so many times this morning, nor a boy, nor a woman, I might almost say, but would forsake all and follow that sound, not mainly to save property from the flames, but, if we will confess the truth, much more to see it burn, since burn it must, and we, be it known, did not set it on fire,—or to see it put out, and have a hand in it, if that is done as handsomely; yes, even if it were the parish church itself. Hardly a man takes a half-hour's nap after dinner, but when he wakes he holds up his head and asks, "What's the news?" as if the rest of mankind had stood his sentinels. Some give directions to be waked every half-hour, doubtless for no other purpose; and then, to pay for it, they tell what they have dreamed.

After a night's sleep the news is as indispensable as the breakfast. "Pray tell me anything new that has happened to a man anywhere on this globe,"—and he reads it over his coffee and rolls, that a man has had his eyes gouged out this morning on the Wachito River; never dreaming the while that he lives in the dark unfathomed mammoth cave of this world, and has but the rudiment of an eye himself.

For my part, I could easily do without the post-office. I think that there are very few important communications made through it. To speak critically, I never received more than one or two letters in my life—I wrote this some years ago—that were worth the postage. The penny-post is, commonly, an institution through which you seriously offer a man that penny for his thoughts which is so often safely offered in jest. And I am sure that I never read any memorable news in a newspaper. If we read of one man robbed, or murdered, or killed by accident, or one house burned, or one vessel wrecked, or one steamboat blown up, or one cow run over on the Western Railroad, or one mad dog killed, or one lot of grasshoppers in the winter,—we never need read of another. One is enough. If you are acquainted with the principle, what do you care for a myriad instances and applications? To a philosopher all *news,* as it is called, is gossip and they who edit and read it are old women over their tea. Yet not a few are greedy after this gossip. There was such a rush, as I hear, the other day at one of the offices to learn the foreign news by the last arrival, that several large squares of plate glass belonging to the establishment were broken by the pressure,—news which I seriously think a ready wit might write a twelvemonth, or twelve years, beforehand with sufficient accuracy. As for Spain, for instance, if you know how to throw in Don Carlos and the Infanta, and Don Pedro and Seville and Granada, from time to time in the right proportions,—they may have changed the names a little since I saw the papers,—and serve up a bull-fight when other entertainments fail, it will be true to the letter, and give us as good an idea of the exact state or ruin of things in Spain as the most succinct and lucid reports under this head in the newspapers: and as for England, almost the last significant scrap of news from that quarter was the revolution of 1649; and if you have learned the history of her crops for an average year, you never need attend to that thing again, unless your speculations are of a merely pecuniary character. If one may judge who rarely looks into the newspapers, nothing new does ever happen in foreign parts, a French revolution not excepted.

What news! how much more important to know what that is which was never old! "Kieou-he-yu (great dignitary of the state of Wei) sent a man to Khoung-tseu to know his news. Khoung-tseu caused the messenger to be seated near him, and questioned him in these terms: What is your master doing? The messenger answered with respect: My master desires to diminish the number of his faults, but he cannot come to the end of them. The messenger being gone, the philosopher remarked: What a worthy messenger! What a worthy messenger!" The preacher, instead of vexing the ears of drowsy farmers on their day of rest at the end of the week,—for Sunday is the fit conclusion of an ill-spent week, and not the fresh and brave beginning of a new one,—with this one other draggle-tail of a sermon, should shout with thundering voice, "Pause! Avast! Why so seeming fast, but deadly slow?"

Shams and delusions are esteemed for soundest truths, while reality is fabulous. If men would steadily observe realities only, and not allow themselves to be deluded, life, to compare it with such things as we know, would be like a fairy tale and the Arabian Nights' Entertainments. If we respected only what is inevitable and has a right to be, music and poetry would resound along the streets. When we are unhurried and wise, we perceive that only great and worthy things have any permanent and absolute existence, that petty fears and petty pleasures are but the shadow of the reality. This is always exhilarating and sublime. By closing the eyes and slumbering, and consenting to be deceived by shows, men establish and confirm their daily life of routine and habit everywhere, which still is built on purely illusory foundations. Children, who play life, discern its true law and relations more clearly than men, who fail to live it worthily, but who think that they are wiser by experience, that is, by failure. I have read in a Hindoo book, that "there was a king's son, who, being expelled in infancy from his native city, was brought up by a forester, and, growing up to maturity in that state, imagined himself to belong to the barbarous race with which he lived. One of his father's ministers having discovered him, revealed to him what he was, and the misconception of his character was removed, and he knew himself to be a prince. So soul," continues the Hindoo philosopher, "from the circumstances in which it is placed, mistakes its own character, until the truth is revealed to it by some holy teacher, and then it knows itself to be *Brahme*." I perceive that we inhabitants of New England live this mean life that we do because our vision does not penetrate the surface of things. We think that this *is* which *appears* to be. If a man should walk through this town and see only the reality, where, think you, would the "Mill-dam" go to? If he should give us an account of the realities he beheld there, we should not recognize the place in his description. Look at a meeting-house, or a court-house, or a jail, or a shop, or a dwelling-house, and say what that thing really is before a true gaze, and they would all go to pieces in your account of them. Men esteem truth remote, in the outskirts of the system, behind the farthest star, before Adam and after the last man. In eternity there is indeed something true and sublime. But all these times and places and occasions are now and here. God himself culminates in the present moment, and will never be more divine in the lapse of all the ages. And we are enabled to apprehend at all what is sublime and noble only by the perpetual instilling and drenching of the reality that surrounds us. The universe constantly and obediently answers to our conceptions; whether we travel fast or slow, the track is laid for us. Let us spend our lives in conceiving then. The poet or the artist never yet had so fair and noble a design but some of his posterity at least could accomplish it.

Let us spend one day as deliberately as Nature, and not be thrown off the track by every nutshell and mosquito's wing that falls on the rails. Let us rise early and fast, or break fast, gently and without perturbation; let company come and let company go, let the bells ring and the children cry,—determined to make a day of it. Why should we knock under and go with the stream? Let us not be upset and overwhelmed in that terrible rapid and whirlpool called a dinner, situated in the meridian shallows. Weather this danger and you are safe, for the rest of the way is down hill. With unrelaxed nerves, with morning vigor, sail by it, looking another way, tied to the mast like Ulysses. If the engine whistles, let it whistle till it is hoarse for its pains. If the bell rings, why should we run? We will consider what kind of music they are like. Let us settle ourselves, and work and wedge our feet downward through the mud and slush of opinion, and prejudice, and tradition, and delusion, and appearance, that alluvion which covers the globe, through Paris and London, through New York and Boston and Concord, through Church and State, through poetry and philosophy and religion, till we come to a hard bottom and rocks in place, which we can call *reality,* and say, This is, and no mistake; and then begin, having a *point d'appui,* below freshet and frost and fire, a place where you might found a wall or a state, or set a lamp-post safely, or perhaps a gauge, not a Nilometer, that future ages might know how deep a freshet of shams and appearances had gathered from time to time. If you stand right fronting and face to face to a fact, you will see the sun glimmer on both its surfaces, as if it were a cimeter, and feel its sweet edge dividing you through the heart and marrow, and so you will happily conclude your mortal career. Be it life or death we crave only reality. If we are really dying, let us hear the rattle in our throats and feel cold in the extremities; if we are alive, let us go about our business.

Time is but the stream I go a-fishing in. I drink at it; but while I drink I see the sandy bottom and detect how shallow it is. Its thin current slides away, but eternity remains. I would drink deeper; fish in the sky, whose bottom is pebbly with stars. I cannot count one. I know not the first letter of the alphabet. I have always been regretting that I was not as wise as the day I was born. The intellect is a cleaver; it discerns and rifts its way into the secret of things. I do not wish to be any more busy with my hands than is necessary. My head is hands and feet. I feel all my best faculties concentrated in it. My instinct tells me that my head is an organ for burrowing, as some creatures use their snout and fore paws, and with it I would mine and burrow my way through these hills. I think that the richest vein is somewhere hereabouts; so by the divining-rod and thin rising vapors I judge; and here I will begin to mine.

DISCUSSION QUESTIONS

1. Compare Thoreau's description of nature with N. Scott Momaday's ''A First American Views His Land'' (see Magazines). What perspective does each writer adopt in order to describe the natural world? What attitude does each express towards nature?

2. Which author attends more carefully to details in describing nature? Which uses the most figurative language? To what effect? Does each writer draw on the same kinds of experience? Explain.

3. In which description of nature does the personal life of the speaker play the most prominent role? Explain. Which writer goes to the natural world to seek adventure? To search for self-improvement? To enjoy an idyllic experience?

4. What are the reasons for each writer's excursion into the natural world? Do you find any of these unconvincing? For which writer is nature most associated with political controversy?

Emily Dickinson / Success Is Counted Sweetest Ca. 1859

Born in Amherst, Massachusetts in 1830, Emily Dickinson remained within the confines of her father's house in that small conservative village for most of her life. Her poems are marked by an acute awareness of psychological states and physical sensations as much as by their brilliant images and melodic blending of assonant and dissonant sounds. Only seven of Dickinson's many poems appeared in print before she died in 1886.

Success is counted sweetest
By those who ne'er succeed.
To comprehend a nectar
Requires sorest need.

Not one of all the purple Host
Who took the Flag to-day

Can tell the definition,
So clear, of Victory,

As he defeated—dying—
On whose forbidden ear
The distant strains of triumph
Burst agonized and clear!

Emily Dickinson / I Like To See It Lap the Miles Ca.1862

I like to see it lap the Miles—
And lick the Valleys up—
And stop to feed itself at Tanks
And then—prodigious step

Around a Pile of Mountains—
And supercilious peer
In Shanties—by the sides of Roads—
And then a Quarry pare

To fit its Ribs
And crawl between
Complaining all the while
In horrid—hooting stanza—
Then chase itself down Hill—

And neigh like Boanerges[1]—
Then—punctual as a Star
Stop—docile and omnipotent
At its own stable door—

[1] In Hebrew, "sons of thunder," used to describe loud-voiced ministers and orators.

Emily Dickinson / Because I Could Not Stop for Death

Ca. 1863

Because I could not stop for Death—
He kindly stopped for me—
The Carriage held but just Ourselves—
And Immortality.

We slowly drove—He knew no haste
And I had put away
My labor and my leisure too,
For His Civility—

We passed the School, where Children strove
At Recess—in the Ring—

We passed the Fields of Gazing Grain—
We passed the Setting Sun—

Or rather—He passed Us—
The Dews drew quivering and chill—
For only Gossamer, my Gown—
My Tippet—only Tulle—

We paused before a House that seemed
A Swelling of the Ground—
The Roof was scarcely visible—
The Cornice—in the Ground—

Since then—'tis Centuries—and yet
Feels shorter than the Day
I first surmised the Horses' Heads
Were toward Eternity—

Walt Whitman / A Noiseless Patient Spider 1881

For most of his life, Walt Whitman (1819–92) lived in neighborly relation to poverty. He worked as an apprentice in a printing shop, as a journalist for New York City and Long Island newspapers, as editor of the Brooklyn Eagle, *as well as a teacher, as a building contractor, and as a clerk in the Bureau of Indian Affairs until the sullied reputation of his collection of poems,* Leaves of Grass, *provoked his hurried dismissal.*

Said to have been set in type by Whitman himself and published at his own expense, Leaves of Grass *attracted little critical attention and sold few copies when first published in 1855. Of all the editors and writers to whom Whitman sent copies, Ralph Waldo Emerson responded most readily and enthusiastically: ''I find in it the most extraordinary piece of wit and wisdom that America has yet contributed.'' But Emerson was well ahead of his time in appreciating Whitman's verse. Its seeming formlessness, boasts, sexual overtones, and ''vulgar'' language stirred much controversy in the decades that followed. Several generations of critics characterized his work as ''the poetry of barbarism'' and admonished audiences that this was poetry ''not to be read aloud to mixed audiences.'' The poet John Greenleaf Whittier went further. He condemned the poems as ''loose, lurid, and impious'' and tossed his copy into a fire.*

After service in Washington during the Civil War, Whitman suffered a paralytic stroke in 1873 and moved to his brother's home in Camden, New Jersey, where he spent his remaining years revising Leaves of Grass.

In Leaves of Grass, *an unprecedented mixture of a radically new poetic consciousness, commonplace subject matter, and distinctively colloquial rhythms, Whitman aspired to create nothing less than an epic of American democracy. But while his ambition to be known as ''the bard of democracy'' was never fully endorsed during his lifetime, Whitman's vision and innovative verse have cut a deepening course through which much of twentieth-century poetry has passed.*

''A Noiseless Patient Spider'' was written in 1868 and included in the ''Whispers of Heavenly Death'' section of Leaves of Grass *in 1881. ''To a Locomotive in Winter'' was written in 1876 and included in the ''From Noon to*

Starry Night" section of the 1881 edition of Leaves of Grass. *These poems offer us a sampling of both Whitman's attitudes toward nature and technology and his singlehanded attempt to introduce a new style and idiom into American literature. They also demonstrate Whitman's belief that the process of reading should be:*

> *a half-sleep, but . . . an exercise, a gymnast's struggle; that the reader is to do something for himself, must be on the alert, must . . . construct indeed the poem, argument, history, metaphysical essay—the text furnishing the hints, the clue, the start or frame-work.*

A noiseless patient spider,
I mark'd where on a little promontory it stood isolated,
Mark'd how to explore the vacant vast surrounding,
It launch'd forth filament, filament, filament, out of itself,
Ever unreeling them, ever tirelessly speeding them.

And you O my soul where you stand,
Surrounded, detached, in measureless oceans of space,
Ceaselessly musing, venturing, throwing, seeking the spheres to connect them,
Till the bridge you will need be form'd, till the ductile anchor hold,
Till the gossamer thread you fling catch somewhere, O my soul.

Walt Whitman / To a Locomotive in Winter 1881

Thee for my recitative,
Thee in the driving storm even as now, the snow, the winter-day declining,
Thee in thy panoply, thy measur'd dual throbbing and thy beat convulsive,
Thy black cylindric body, golden brass and silvery steel,
Thy ponderous side-bars, parallel and connecting rods, gyrating, shuttling at thy sides,
Thy metrical, now swelling pant and roar, now tapering in the distance,
Thy great protruding head-light fix'd in front,
Thy long, pale, floating vapor-pennants, tinged with delicate purple,
The dense and murky clouds out-belching from thy smoke-stack,
Thy knitted frame, thy springs and valves, the tremulous twinkle of thy wheels,
Thy train of cars behind, obedient, merrily following,
Through gale or calm, now swift, now slack, yet steadily careering;
Type of the modern—emblem of motion and power—pulse of the continent,
For once come serve the Muse and merge in verse, even as here I see thee,
With storm and buffeting gusts of wind and falling snow,
By day thy warning ringing bell to sound its notes,
By night thy silent signal lamps to swing.

Fierce-throated beauty!
Roll through my chant with all thy lawless music, thy swinging lamps at night,
Thy madly-whistled laughter, echoing, rumbling like an earthquake, rousing all,
Law of thyself complete, thine own track firmly holding,
(No sweetness debonair of tearful harp or glib piano thine,)
Thy trills of shrieks by rocks and hills return'd,
Launch'd o'er the prairies wide, across the lakes,
To the free skies unpent and glad and strong.

Mark Twain / How To Tell a Story 1897

Samuel Langhorne Clemens (Mark Twain), like many prominent American novelists, began his writing career as a journalist. He was born along the Mississippi River in Florida, Missouri in 1835, and throughout his life that great river remained a vital presence. After briefly working on the Mississippi as a riverboat pilot and mining for silver in Nevada, Twain felt his energies would be better spent writing for newspapers. He learned early how to combine skillfully the official prose of news reporting with the folksy language of tall tales, and his work in this humorous vein began to attract literary attention. He traveled to Hawaii, then to the Middle East, and later turned these experiences into parodies of the then popular conventional guidebooks. In 1876 he wrote The Adventures of Tom Sawyer, *a best-selling nostalgic glance at his Missouri boyhood, and in 1885 he brought out his masterpiece,* The Adventures of Huckleberry Finn, *the book Ernest Hemingway claimed marked the origins of "all modern American literature."*

Twain's later career, though productive, was interrupted by a series of futile business ventures (he invested heavily in an aborted typesetting invention) and personal tragedies. The tone of much of his later work hinges on his own pessimistic answers to the question posed in one of his final essays, "What Is Man?"

In "How To Tell a Story" (1897), Twain, by then a distinguished novelist and man of letters, tells and shows an audience why effective narrative styles need to be rooted in an oral tradition.

I do not claim that I can tell a story as it ought to be told. I only claim to know how a story ought to be told, for I have been almost daily in the company of the most expert story-tellers for many years.

There are several kinds of stories, but only one difficult kind—the humorous. I will talk mainly about that one. The humorous story is American, the comic story is English, the witty story is French. The humorous story depends for its effect upon the *manner* of the telling; the comic story and the witty story upon the *matter*.

The humorous story may be spun out to great length, and may wander around as much as it pleases, and arrive nowhere in particular; but the comic and witty stories must be brief and end with a point. The humorous story bubbles gently along, the others burst.

The humorous story is strictly a work of art—high and delicate art—and only an artist can tell it; but no art is necessary in telling the comic and the witty story; anybody can do it. The art of telling a humorous story—understand, I mean by word of mouth, not print—was created in America, and has remained at home.

The humorous story is told gravely; the teller does his best to conceal the fact that he even dimly suspects that there is anything funny about it; but the teller of the comic story tells you beforehand that it is one of the funniest things he has ever heard, then tells it with eager delight, and is the first person to laugh when he gets through. And sometimes, if he has had good success, he is so glad and happy that he will repeat the "nub" of it and glance around from face to face, collecting applause, and then repeat it again. It is a pathetic thing to see.

Very often, of course, the rambling and disjointed humorous story finishes with a nub, point, snapper, or whatever you like to call it. Then the listener must be alert, for in many cases the teller will divert attention from that nub by dropping it in a carefully casual and indifferent way, with the pretense that he does not know it is a nub.

Artemus Ward used that trick a good deal; then when the belated audience presently caught the joke he would look up with innocent surprise, as if wondering what they had found to laugh at. Dan Setchell used it before him, Nye and Riley and others use it to-day.

But the teller of the comic story does not slur the nub; he shouts it at you—every time. And when he prints it, in England, France, Germany, and Italy, he italicizes it, puts some whooping exclamation-points after it and sometimes explains it in a parenthesis. All of which is very depressing, and makes one want to renounce joking and lead a better life.

Let me set down an instance of the comic method, using an anecdote which has been popular all over the world for twelve or fifteen hundred years. The teller tells it in this way:

> *The Wounded Soldier*
>
> In the course of a certain battle a soldier whose leg had been shot off appealed to another soldier who was hurrying by to carry him to the rear, informing him at the same time of the loss which he had sustained; whereupon the generous son of Mars, shouldering the unfortunate, proceeded to carry out his desire. The bullets and cannon-balls were flying in all directions, and presently one of the latter took the wounded man's head off—without, however, his deliverer being aware of it. In no long time he was hailed by an officer, who said:
>
> "Where are you going with that carcass?"
>
> "To the rear, sir—he's lost his leg!"
>
> "His leg, forsooth?" responded the astonished officer, "you mean his head, you booby."
>
> Whereupon the soldier dispossessed himself of his burden, and stood looking down upon it in great perpelexity. At length he said:
>
> "It is true, sir, just as you have said." Then after a pause he added. *"But he* TOLD *me* IT WAS HIS LEG ! ! ! ! !"

Here the narrator bursts into explosion after explosion of thunderous horse-laughter, repeating that nub from time to time through his gaspings and shriekings and suffocatings.

It takes only a minute and a half to tell that in its comic-story form; and isn't worth the telling, after all. Put into the humorous-story form it takes ten minutes, and is about the funniest thing I have ever listened to—as James Whitcomb Riley tells it.

He tells it in the character of a dull-witted old farmer who has just heard it for the first time, thinks it is unspeakably funny, and is trying to repeat it to a neighbor. But he can't remember it; so he gets all mixed up and wanders helplessly round and round, putting in tedious details that don't belong in the tale and only retard it; taking them out conscientiously and putting in others that are just as useless; making minor mistakes now and then and stopping to correct them and explain how he came to make them; remembering things which he forgot to put in in their proper place and going back to put them in there; stopping his narrative a good while in order to try to recall the name of the soldier that was hurt, and finally remembering that the soldier's name was not mentioned, and remarking placidly that the name is of no real importance, anyway—better, of course if one knew it, but not essential, after all—and so on, and so on, and so on.

The teller is innocent and happy and pleased with himself, and has to stop every little while to hold himself in and keep from laughing outright; and does hold in, but his body quakes in a jelly-like way with interior chuckles; and at the end of the ten minutes the audience have laughed until they are exhausted, and the tears are running down their faces.

The simplicity and innocence and sincerity and unconsciousness of the old farmer are perfectly simulated, and the result is a performance which is thoroughly charming and delicious. This is art—and fine and beautiful, and only a master can compass it; but a machine could tell the other story.

To string incongruities and absurdities together in a wandering and sometimes purposeless way, and seem innocently unaware that they are absurdities, is the basis of the American art, if my position is correct. Another feature is the slurring of the point. A third is the dropping of a studied remark apparently without knowing it, as if one were thinking aloud. The fourth and last is the pause.

Artemus Ward dealt in numbers three and four a good deal. He would begin to tell with great animation something which he seemed to think was wonderful; then lose confidence, and after an apparently absent-minded pause add an incongruous remark in a soliloquizing way; and that was the remark intended to explode the mine—and it did.

For instance, he would say eagerly, excitedly, "I once knew a man in New Zealand who hadn't a tooth in his head"—here his animation would die out; a silent, reflective pause would follow, then he would say dreamily, and as if to himself, "and yet that man could beat a drum better than any man I ever saw."

The pause is an exceedingly important feature in any kind of story, and a frequently recurring feature, too. It is a dainty thing, and delicate, and also uncertain and treacherous; for it must be exactly the right length—no more and no less—or it fails of its purpose and makes trouble. If the pause is too short the impressive point is passed, and the audience have had time to divine that a surprise is intended—and then you can't surprise them, of course.

On the platform I used to tell a negro ghost story that had a pause in front of the snapper on the end, and that pause was the most important thing in the whole story. If I got it the right length precisely, I could spring the finishing ejaculation with effect enough to make some impressible girl deliver a startled little yelp and jump out of her seat—and that was what I was after. This story was called "The Golden Arm," and was told in this fashion. You can practise with it yourself—and mind you look out for the pause and get it right.

The Golden Arm

Once 'pon a time dey wuz a monsus mean man, en he live 'way out in de prairie all 'lone by hisself, 'cep'n he had a wife. En bimeby she died, en he tuck en toted her way out dah in de prairie en buried her. Well, she had a golden arm—all solid gold, fum de shoulder down. He wuz pow'ful mean—pow'ful; en dat night he couldn't sleep, caze he want dat golden arm so bad.

When it come midnight he couldn't stan' it no mo'; so he git up, he did, en tuck his lantern en shoved out thoo de storm en dug her up en got de golden arm; en he bent his head down 'gin de win', en plowed en plowed en plowed thoo de snow. Den all on a sudden he stop (make a considerable pause here, and look startled, and take a listening attitude) en say: "My *lan'*, what's dat?"

En he listen—en listen—en de win' say (set your teeth together and imitate the wailing and wheezing singsong of the wind), "Bzzz-z-zzz"—en den, way back yonder whah de grave is, he hear a *voice!*—he hear a voice all mix' up in de win'—can't hardly tell 'em 'part—"Bzzz—zzz—W-h-o—g-o-t—m-y—g-o-l-d-e-n *arm?*" (You must begin to shiver violently now.)

En he begin to shiver en shake, en say, "Oh, my! *Oh,* my lan'!" en de win' blow de lantern out, en de snow en sleet blow in his face en mos' choke him, en he start a-plowin' knee-deep towards home mos' dead, he so sk'yerd—en pooty soon he hear de voice agin, en (pause) it 'us comin' *after* him! "Bzzz—zzz—zzz—W-h-o—g-o-t—m-y—g-o-l-d-e-n—*arm?*"

When he git to de pasture he hear it agin—closter now, en a-*comin'!*—a-comin' back dah in de dark en de storm—(repeat the wind and the voice). When he git to de house he rush up-stairs en jump in de bed en kiver up, head and years, en lay dah shiverin' en shakin'—en den way out dah he hear it *agin!*—en a-*comin'!* En bimeby he hear (pause—awed, listening attitude)—pat—pat—pat—*hit's a-comin upstairs!* Den he hear de latch, en he *know* it's in de room!

Den pooty soon he know it's a-*stannin' by de bed!* (Pause.) Den—he know it's a-*bendin' down over him*—en he cain't skasely git his breath! Den—den—he seem to feel someth'n' *c-o-l-d*, right down 'most agin his head! (Pause.)

Den de voice say, *right at his year*—"W-h-o—g-o-t—m-y—g-o-l-d-e-n *arm?*" (You must wail it out very plaintively and accusingly; then you stare steddily and impressively into the face of the farthest-gone auditor—a girl, preferably—and let that awe-inspiring pause begin to build itself in the deep hush. When it has reached exactly the right length, jump suddenly at that girl and yell, "*You've* got it!")

If you've got the *pause* right, she'll fetch a dear little yelp and spring right out of her shoes. But you *must* get the pause right; and you will find it the most troublesome and aggravating and uncertain thing you ever undertook.

Kate Chopin / The Dream of an Hour 1894

Born Katherine O'Flaherty in St. Louis in 1851 to a wealthy Irish father and a Creole mother, Kate Chopin was raised in French, Southern, Catholic, aristocratic circumstances. After studies at a convent school, she entered and was soon bored with the fashionable social circle of St. Louis: "I am invited to a ball and I go.—I dance with people I despise; amuse myself with men whose only talent lies in their feet." At nineteen, she married a Creole cotton broker and moved first to New Orleans and then to the bayou country that forms a backdrop for many of her stories. A year after the death of her husband from swamp fever in 1883, Chopin returned to St. Louis with her six children and began composing short fiction, novels, and children's books. Writing in the midst of her children's activities, she obviously enjoyed the spontaneity such circumstances imposed:

> *I am completely at the mercy of unconscious selection. To such an extent is this true, that what is called the polishing up process always proved disastrous to my work, and I avoid it, preferring the integrity of crudities to artificialities.*

"The Dream of an Hour" appeared originally in Vogue *magazine in 1894. Kate Chopin's stories were frequently published in such leading periodicals as the* Atlantic Monthly, Harper's *and* Century, *and were subsequently collected in* Bayou Folk *(1894) and* A Night in Acadia *(1897). Demoralized by the severe criticism that attended the publication of her third novel,* The Awakening, *a tale of extramarital and interracial love, she wrote little more before her death in 1904.*

Knowing that Mrs. Mallard was afflicted with a heart trouble, great care was taken to break to her as gently as possible the news of her husband's death.

It was her sister Josephine who told her, in broken sentences; veiled hints that revealed in half concealing. Her husband's friend Richards was there, too, near her. It was he who had been in the newspaper office when intelligence of the railroad disaster was received, with Brently Mallard's name leading the list of "killed." He had only taken the time to assure himself of its truth by a second telegram, and had hastened to forestall any less careful, less tender friend in bearing the sad message.

She did not hear the story as many women have heard the same, with a paralyzed inability to accept its significance. She wept at once, with sudden, wild abandonment, in her sister's arms. When the storm of grief had spent itself she went away to her room alone. She would have no one follow her.

There stood, facing the open window, a comfortable, roomy armchair. Into this she sank, pressed down by a physical exhaustion that haunted her body and seemed to reach into her soul.

She could see in the open square before her house the tops of trees that were all aquiver with the new spring life. The delicious breath of rain was in the air. In the street below a peddler was crying his wares. The notes of a distant song which some one was singing reached her faintly, and countless sparrows were twittering in the eaves.

There were patches of blue sky showing here and there through the clouds that had met and piled one above the other in the west facing her window.

She sat with her head thrown back upon the cushion of the chair, quite motionless, except when a sob came up into her throat and shook her, as a child who has cried itself to sleep continues to sob in its dreams.

She was young, with a fair, calm face, whose lines bespoke repression and even a certain strength. But now there was a dull stare in her eyes, whose gaze was fixed away off yonder on one of those patches of blue sky. It was not a glance of reflection, but rather indicated a suspension of intelligent thought.

There was something coming to her and she was waiting for it, fearfully. What was it? She did not know; it was too subtle and elusive to name. But she felt it, creeping out of the sky, reaching toward her through the sounds, the scents, the color that filled the air.

Now her bosom rose and fell tumultuously. She was beginning to recognize this thing that was approaching to possess her, and she was striving to beat it back with her will—as powerless as her two white slender hands would have been.

When she abandoned herself a little whispered word escaped her slightly parted lips. She said it over and over under her breath: "free, free, free!" The vacant stare and the look of terror that had followed it went from her eyes. They stayed keen and bright. Her pulses beat fast, and the coursing blood warmed and relaxed every inch of her body.

She did not stop to ask if it were or were not a monstrous joy that held her: A clear and exalted perception enabled her to dismiss the suggestion as trivial.

She knew that she would weep again when she saw the kind, tender hands folded in death; the face that had never looked save with love upon her, fixed and gray and dead. But she saw beyond that bitter moment a long procession of years to come that would belong to her absolutely. And she opened and spread her arms out to them in welcome.

There would be no one to live for her during those coming years; she would live for herself. There would be no powerful will bending hers in that blind persistence with which men and women believe they have a right to impose a private will upon a fellow-creature. A kind intention or a cruel intention made the act seem no less a crime as she looked upon it in that brief moment of illumination.

And yet she had loved him—sometimes. Often she had not. What did it matter! What could love, the unsolved mystery, count for in face of this possession of self-assertion which she suddenly recognized as the strongest impulse of her being!

"Free! Body and soul free!" she kept whispering.

Josephine was kneeling before the closed door with her lips to the keyhole, imploring for admission. "Louise, open the door! I beg; open the door—you will make yourself ill. What are you doing, Louise? For heaven's sake open the door."

"Go away. I am not making myself ill." No; she was drinking in a very elixir of life through that open window.

Her fancy was running riot along those days ahead of her. Spring days, and summer days, and all sorts of days that would be her own. She breathed a quick prayer that life might be long. It was only yesterday she had thought with a shudder that life might be long.

She arose at length and opened the door to her sister's importunities. There was a feverish triumph in her eyes, and she carried herself unwittingly like a goddess of Victory. She clasped her sister's waist, and together they descended the stairs. Richards stood waiting for them at the bottom.

Some one was opening the front door with a latchkey. It was Brently Mallard who entered, a little travel-stained, composedly carrying his grip-sack and umbrella. He had been far from the scene of accident, and did not even know there had been one. He stood amazed at Josephine's piercing cry; at Richards' quick motion to screen him from the view of his wife.

But Richards was too late.

When the doctors came they said she had died of heart disease—of joy that kills.

DISCUSSION QUESTION

1. Robert Frost often argued that poetry exists "for griefs, not grievances." Do you think this distinction is applicable to Kate Chopin's "The Dream of an Hour"? Explain. Locate other stories and essays in this collection to which this distinction may be applied.

Stephen Crane / The Open Boat 1897

"The Open Boat," written a few months after his report on the sinking of the Commodore for the New York Press *on January 7, 1897 (see "Stephen Crane's Own Story" in Press), was Crane's second attempt to fictionalize his near disaster at sea. According to a fellow journalist, Crane was so worried about accuracy that he wanted the captain of the wrecked vessel, Edward Murphy, to go over the manuscript. "Listen, Ed. I want to have this* right, *from your point of view. How does it sound so far?" "You've got it, Steve," said the other man. "That is just how it happened, and how it felt." Long regarded as a masterpiece of naturalistic fiction, "The Open Boat" is an early attempt by a major American writer to give literary certification to the ironic, jocularly resilient speech of average men trapped in difficult circumstances. (See, for example, the transcripts of the astronauts' conversations in Press.) In his efforts to combine the crafts of journalism and literature, Crane helped to set a new tone for fiction, one that could express, as he puts it in "The Open Boat," "humour, contempt, tragedy, all in one."*

A TALE INTENDED TO BE AFTER THE FACT: BEING THE EXPERIENCE OF FOUR MEN FROM THE SUNK STEAMER COMMODORE

I

None of them knew the colour of the sky. Their eyes glanced level, and were fastened upon the waves that swept toward them. These waves were of the hue of slate, save for the tops, which were of foaming white, and all of the men knew the colours of the sea. The horizon narrowed and widened, and dipped and rose, and at all times its edge was jagged with waves that seemed thrust up in points like rocks.

Many a man ought to have a bathtub larger than the boat which here rode upon the sea. These waves were most wrongfully and barbarously abrupt and tall, and each froth-top was a problem in small-boat navigation.

The cook squatted in the bottom, and looked with both eyes at the six inches of gunwale which separated him from the ocean. His sleeves were rolled over his fat forearms, and the two flaps of his unbuttoned vest dangled as he bent to bail out the boat. Often he said, "Gawd! that was a narrow clip." As he remarked it he invariably gazed eastward over the broken sea.

The oiler, steering with one of the two oars in the boat, sometimes raised himself suddenly to keep clear of water that swirled in over the stern. It was a thin little oar, and it seemed often ready to snap.

The correspondent, pulling at the other oar, watched the waves and wondered why he was there.

The injured captain, lying in the bow, was at this time buried in that profound dejection and indifference which comes, temporarily at least, to even the bravest and most enduring when, willy-nilly, the firm fails, the army loses, the ship goes down. The mind of the master of a vessel is rooted deep in the timbers of her, though he command for a day or a decade; and this captain had on him the stern impression of a scene in the greys of dawn of seven turned faces, and later a stump of a topmast with a white ball on it, that slashed to and fro at the waves, went low and lower, and down. Thereafter there was something strange in his voice. Although steady, it was deep with mourning, and of a quality beyond oration or tears.

"Keep 'er a little more south, Billie," said he.

"A little more south, sir," said the oiler in the stern.

A seat in his boat was not unlike a seat upon a bucking broncho, and by the same token a broncho is not much smaller. The craft pranced and reared and plunged like an animal. As each wave came, and she rose for it, she seemed like a horse making at a fence outrageously high. The manner of her scramble over these walls of water is a mystic thing, and, moreover, at the top of them were ordinarily these problems in white water, the foam racing down from the summit of each wave requiring a new leap, and a leap from the air. Then, after scornfully bumping a crest, she would slide and race and splash down a long incline, and arrive bobbing and nodding in front of the next menace.

A singular disadvantage of the sea lies in the fact that after successfully surmounting one wave you discover that there is another behind it just as important and just as nervously anxious to do something effective in the way of swamping boats. In a ten-foot dinghy one can get an idea of the resources of the sea in the line of waves that is not probable to the average experience which is never at sea in a dinghy. As each slaty wall of water approached, it shut all else from the view of the men in the boat, and it was not difficult to imagine that this particular wave was the final outburst of the ocean, the last effort of the grim water. There was a terrible grace in the move of the waves, and they came in silence, save for the snarling of the crests.

In the wan light the faces of the men must have been grey. Their eyes must have glinted in strange ways as they gazed steadily astern. Viewed from a balcony, the whole thing would doubtless have been weirdly picturesque. But the men in the boat had no time to see it, and if they had had leisure, there were other things to occupy their minds. The sun swung steadily up the sky, and they knew it was broad day because the colour of the sea changed from slate to emerald green streaked with amber lights, and the foam was like tumbling snow. The process of the breaking day was unknown to them. They were aware only of this effect upon the colour of the waves that rolled toward them.

In disjointed sentences the cook and the correspondent argued as to the difference between a life-saving station and a house of refuge. The cook had said: "There's a house of refuge just north of the Mosquito Inlet Light, and as soon as they see us they'll come off in their boat and pick us up."

"As soon as who see us?" said the correspondent.

"The crew," said the cook.

"Houses of refuge don't have crews," said the correspondent. "As I understand them, they are only places where clothes and grub are stored for the benefit of shipwrecked people. They don't carry crews."

"Oh, yes, they do," said the cook.

"No, they don't," said the correspondent.

"Well, we're not there yet, anyhow," said the oiler, in the stern.

"Well," said the cook, "perhaps it's not a house of refuge that I'm thinking of as being near Mosquito Inlet Light; perhaps it's a life-saving station."

"We're not there yet," said the oiler in the stern.

II

As the boat bounced from the top of each wave the wind tore through the hair of the hatless men, and as the craft plopped her stern down again the spray slashed past them. The crest of each of these waves was a hill, from the top of which the men surveyed for a moment a broad tumultuous expanse, shining and wind-riven. It was probably splendid, it was probably glorious, this play of the free sea, wild with lights of emerald and white and amber.

"Bully good thing it's an on-shore wind," said the cook. "If not, where would we be? Wouldn't have a show."

"That's right," said the correspondent.

The busy oiler nodded his assent.

Then the captain, in the bow, chuckled in a way that expressed humour, contempt, tragedy, all in one. "Do you think we've got much of a show now, boys?" said he.

Whereupon the three were silent, save for a trifle of hemming and hawing. To express any particular optimism at this time they felt to be childish and stupid, but they all doubtless possessed this sense of the situation in their minds. A young man thinks doggedly at such times. On the other hand, the ethics of their condition was decidedly against any open suggestion of hopelessness. So they were silent.

"Oh, well," said the captain, soothing his children, "we'll get ashore all right."

But there was that in his tone which made them think; so the oiler quoth, "Yes! if this wind holds."

The cook was bailing. "Yes! if we don't catch hell in the surf."

Canton-flannel gulls flew near and far. Sometimes they sat down on the sea, near patches of brown seaweed that rolled over the waves with a movement like carpets on a line in a gale. The birds sat comfortably in groups, and they were envied by some in the dinghy, for the wrath of the sea was no more to them than it was to a covey of prairie chickens a thousand miles inland. Often they came very close and stared at the men with black bead-like eyes. At these times they were uncanny and sinister in their unblinking scrutiny, and the men hooted angrily at them, telling them to be gone. One came, and evidently decided to alight on the top of the captain's head. The bird flew parallel to the boat and did not circle, but made short sidelong jumps in the air in chicken-fashion. His black eyes were wistfully fixed upon the captain's head. "Ugly brute," said the oiler to the bird. "You look as if you were made with a jackknife." The cook and the correspondent swore darkly at the creature. The captain naturally wished to knock it away with the end of the heavy painter, but he did not dare do it, because anything resembling an emphatic gesture would have capsized this freighted boat; and so, with his open hand, the captain gently and carefully waved the gull away. After it had been discouraged from the pursuit the captain breathed easier on account of his hair, and others breathed easier because the bird struck their minds at this time as being somehow gruesome and ominous.

In the meantime the oiler and the correspondent rowed. And also they rowed. They sat together in the same seat, and each rowed an oar. Then the oiler took both oars; then the correspondent took both oars; then the oiler: then the correspondent. They rowed and they rowed. The very ticklish part of the business was when the time came for the reclining one in the stern to take his turn at the oars. By the very last star of truth, it is easier to steal eggs from under a hen than it was to change seats in the dinghy. First the man in the stern slid his hand along the thwart and moved with care, as if he were of Sevres. Then the man in the rowing-seat slid his hand along the other thwart. It was all done with the most extraordinary care. As the two sidled past each other, the whole party kept watchful eyes on the coming wave, and the captain cried: "Look out, now! Steady, there!"

The brown mats of seaweed that appeared from time to time were like islands, bits of earth. They were travelling, apparently, neither one way nor the other. They were, to all intents, stationary. They informed the men in the boat that it was making progress slowly toward the land.

The captain, rearing cautiously in the bow after the dinghy soared on a great swell, said that he had seen the lighthouse at Mosquito Inlet. Presently the cook remarked that he had seen it. The correspondent was at the oars then, and for some reason he too wished to look at the lighthouse; but his back was toward the far shore, and the waves were important, and for some time he could not seize an opportunity to turn his head. But at last there came a wave more gentle than the others, and when at the crest of it he swiftly scoured the western horizon.

"See it?" said the captain.

"No," said the correspondent, slowly; "I didn't see anything."

"Look again," said the captain. He pointed. "It's exactly in that direction."

At the top of another wave the correspondent did as he was bid, and this time his eyes chanced on a small, still thing on the edge of the swaying horizon. It was precisely like the point of a pin. It took an anxious eye to find a lighthouse so tiny.

"Think we'll make it, Captain?"

"If this wind holds and the boat don't swamp, we can't do much else," said the captain.

The little boat, lifted by each towering sea and splashed viciously by the crests, made progress that in the absence of seaweed was not apparent to those in her. She seemed just a wee thing wallowing, miraculously top up, at the mercy of five oceans. Occasionally a great spread of water, like white flames, swarmed into her.

"Bail her, cook," said the captain, serenely.

"All right, Captain," said the cheerful cook.

III

It would be difficult to describe the subtle brotherhood of men that was here established on the seas. No one said that it was so. No one mentioned it. But it dwelt in the boat, and each man felt it warm him. They were a captain, an oiler, a cook, and a correspondent, and they were friends—friends in a more curiously iron-bound degree than may be common. The hurt captain, lying against the water-jar in the bow, spoke always in a low voice and calmly; but he could never command a more ready and swiftly obedient crew than the motley three of the dinghy. It was more than a mere recognition of what was best for the common safety. There was surely in it a quality that was personal and heart-felt. And after this devotion to the commander of the boat, there was this comradeship, that the correspondent, for instance, who had been taught to be cynical of men, knew even at the time was the best experience of his life. But no one said that it was so. No one mentioned it.

"I wish we had a sail," remarked the captain. "We might try my overcoat on the end of an oar, and give you two boys a chance to rest." So the cook and the correspondent held the mast and spread wide the overcoat; the oiler steered; and the little boat made good way with her new rig. Sometimes the oiler had to scull sharply to keep a sea from breaking into the boat, but otherwise sailing was a success.

Meanwhile the lighthouse had been growing slowly larger. It had now almost assumed colour, and appeared like a little grey shadow on the sky. The man at the oars could not be prevented from turning his head rather often to try for a glimpse of this little grey shadow.

At last, from the top of each wave, the men in the tossing boat could see land. Even as the lighthouse was an upright shadow on the sky, this land seemed but a long black shadow on the sea. It certainly was thinner than paper. "We must be about opposite New Smyrna," said the cook, who had coasted this shore often in schooners. "Captain, by the way, I believe they abandoned that life-saving station there about a year ago."

"Did they?" said the captain.

The wind slowly died away. The cook and the correspondent were not now obliged to slave in order to hold high the oar. But the waves continued their old impetuous swooping at the dinghy, and the little craft, no longer under way, struggled woundily over them. The oiler or the correspondent took the oars again.

Shipwrecks are apropos of nothing. If men could only train for them and have them occur when the men had reached pink condition, there would be less drowning at sea. Of the four in the dinghy none had slept any time worth mentioning for two days and two nights previous to embarking in the dinghy, and in the excitement of clambering about the deck of a foundering ship they had also forgotten to eat heartily.

For these reasons, and for others, neither the oiler nor the correspondent was fond of rowing at this time. The correspondent wondered ingenuously how in the name of all that was sane could there be people who thought it amusing to row a boat. It was not an amusement; it was a diabolical punishment, and even a genius of mental aberrations could never conclude that it was anything but a horror to the muscles and a crime against the back. He mentioned to the boat in general how the amusement of rowing struck him, and the weary-faced oiler smiled in full sympathy. Previously to the foundering, by the way, the oiler had worked a double watch in the engine-room of the ship.

"Take her easy now, boys," said the captain. "Don't spend yourselves. If we have to run a surf you'll need all your strength, because we'll sure have to swim for it. Take your time."

Slowly the land arose from the sea. From a black line it became a line of black and a line of white—trees and sand. Finally the captain said that he could make out a house on the shore. "That's the house of refuge, sure," said the cook. "They'll see us before long, and come out after us."

The distant lighthouse reared high. "The keeper ought to be able to make us out now, if he's looking through a glass," said the captain. "He'll notify the life-saving people."

"None of those other boats could have got ashore to give word of this wreck," said the oiler, in a low voice, "else the life-boat would be out hunting us."

Slowly and beautifully the land loomed out of the sea. The wind came again. It had veered from the north-east to the south-east. Finally a new sound struck the ears of the men in the boat. It was the low thunder of the surf on the shore. "We'll never be able to make the lighthouse now," said the captain. "Swing her head a little more north, Billie."

"A little more north, sir," said the oiler.

Whereupon the little boat turned her nose once more down the wind, and all but the oarsman watched the shore grow. Under the influence of this expansion doubt and direful apprehension were leaving the minds of the men. The management of the boat was still most absorbing, but it could not prevent a quiet cheerfulness. In an hour, perhaps, they would be ashore.

Their backbones had become thoroughly used to balancing in the boat, and they now rode this wild colt of a dinghy like circus men. The correspondent thought that he had been drenched to the skin, but happening to feel in the top pocket of his coat, he found therein eight cigars. Four of them were soaked with sea-water; four were perfectly scatheless. After a search, somebody produced three dry matches; and thereupon the four waifs rode impudently in their little boat and, with an assurance of an impending rescue shining in their eyes, puffed at the big cigars, and judged well and ill of all men. Everybody took a drink of water.

IV

"Cook," remarked the captain, "there don't seem to be any signs of life about your house of refuge."

"No," replied the cook. "Funny they don't see us!"

A broad stretch of lowly coast lay before the eyes of the men. It was of low dunes topped with dark vegetation. The roar of the surf was plain, and sometimes they could see the white lip of a wave as it spun up the beach. A tiny house was blocked out black upon the sky. Southward, the slim lighthouse lifted its little grey length.

Tide, wind, and waves were swinging the dinghy northward. "Funny they don't see us," said the men.

The surf's roar was here dulled, but its tone was nevertheless thunderous and mighty. As the boat swam over the great rollers the men sat listening to this roar. "We'll swamp sure," said everybody.

It is fair to say here that there was not a life-saving station within twenty miles in either direction; but the men did not know this fact, and in consequence they made dark and opprobrious remarks concerning the eyesight of the nation's life-savers. Four scowling men sat in the dinghy and surpassed records in the invention of epithets.

"Funny they don't see us."

The light-heartedness of a former time had completely faded. To their sharpened minds it was easy to conjure pictures of all kinds of incompetency and blindness and, indeed, cowardice. There was the shore of the populous land, and it was bitter and bitter to them that from it came no sign.

"Well," said the captain, ultimately, "I suppose we'll have to make a try for ourselves. If we stay out here too long, we'll none of us have strength left to swim after the boat swamps.''

And so the oiler, who was at the oars, turned the boat straight for the shore. There was a sudden tightening of muscles. There was some thinking.

''If we don't all get ashore,'' said the captain—''if we don't all get ashore, I suppose you fellows know where to send news of my finish?''

They then briefly exchanged some addresses and admonitions. As for the reflections of the men, there was a great deal of rage in them. Perchance they might be formulated thus: ''If I am going to be drowned—if I am going to be drowned—if I am going to be drowned, why, in the name of the seven mad gods who rule the sea, was I allowed to come thus far and contemplate sand and trees? Was I brought here merely to have my nose dragged away as I was about to nibble the sacred cheese of life? It is preposterous. If this old ninny-woman, Fate, cannot do better than this, she should be deprived of the management of men's fortunes. She is an old hen who knows not her intention. If she has decided to drown me, why did she not do it in the beginning and save me all this trouble? The whole affair is absurd.—But no; she cannot mean to drown me. She dare not drown me. She cannot drown me. Not after all this work.'' Afterward the man might have had an impulse to shake his fist at the clouds. ''Just you drown me, now, and then hear what I call you!''

The billows that came at this time were more formidable. They seemed always just about to break and roll over the little boat in a turmoil of foam. There was a preparatory and long growl in the speech of them. No mind unused to the sea would have concluded that the dinghy could ascend these sheer heights in time. The shore was still afar. The oiler was a wily surfman. ''Boys,'' he said swiftly, ''she won't live three minutes more, and we're too far out to swim. Shall I take her to sea again, Captain?''

''Yes; go ahead!'' said the captain.

This oiler, by a series of quick miracles and fast and steady oarsmanship, turned the boat in the middle of the surf and took her safely to sea again.

There was a considerable silence as the boat bumped over the furrowed sea to deeper water. Then somebody in gloom spoke: ''Well, anyhow, they must have seen us from the shore by now.''

The gulls went in slanting flight up the wind toward the grey, desolate east. A squall, marked by dingy clouds and clouds brick-red like smoke from a burning building, appeared from the south-east.

''What do you think of those life-saving people? Ain't they peaches?''

''Funny they haven't seen us.''

''Maybe they think we're out here for sport! Maybe they think we're fishin'. Maybe they think we're damned fools.''

It was a long afternoon. A changed tide tried to force them southward, but wind and wave said northward. Far ahead, where coast-line, sea, and sky formed their mighty angle, there were little dots which seemed to indicate a city on the shore.

''St. Augustine?''

The captain shook his head. ''Too near Mosquito Inlet.''

And the oiler rowed, and then the correspondent rowed; then the oiler rowed. It was a weary business. The human back can become the seat of more aches and pains than are registered in books for the composite anatomy of a regiment. It is a limited area, but it can become the theatre of innumerable muscular conflicts, tangles, wrenches, knots, and other comforts.

''Did you ever like to row, Billie?'' asked the correspondent.

''No,'' said the oiler; ''hang it!''

When one exchanged the rowing-seat for a place in the bottom of the boat, he suffered a bodily depression that caused him to be careless of everything save an obligation to wiggle one finger. There was cold sea-water swashing to and fro in the boat, and he lay in it. His head, pillowed on a thwart, was within an inch of the swirl of a wave-crest, and sometimes a particularly obstreperous sea came inboard and drenched him once more. But these matters did not annoy him. It is almost certain that if the boat had capsized he would have tumbled comfortably out upon the ocean as if he felt sure that it was a great soft mattress.

"Look! There's a man on the shore!"

"Where?"

"There! See 'im? See 'im?"

"Yes, sure! He's walking along."

"Now he's stopped. Look! He's facing us!"

"He's waving at us!"

"So he is! By thunder!"

"Ah, now we're all right! Now we're all right! There'll be a boat out here for us in half an hour."

"He's going on. He's running. He's going up to that house there."

The remote beach seemed lower than the sea, and it required a searching glance to discern the little black figure. The captain saw a floating stick, and they rowed to it. A bath towel was by some weird chance in the boat, and, tying this on the stick, the captain waved it. The oarsman did not dare turn his head, so he was obliged to ask questions.

"What's he doing now?"

"He's standing still again. He's looking, I think.—There he goes again—toward the house.—Now he's stopped again."

"Is he waving at us?"

"No, not now; he was, though."

"Look! There comes another man!"

"He's running."

"Look at him go, would you!"

"Why, he's on a bicycle. Now he's met the other man. They're both waving at us. Look!"

"There comes something up the beach."

"What the devil is that thing?"

"Why, it looks like a boat."

"Why, certainly, it's a boat."

"No; it's on wheels."

"Yes, so it is. Well, that must be the life-boat. They drag them along shore on a wagon."

"That's the life-boat, sure."

"No, by God, it's—it's an omnibus."

"I tell you it's a life-boat."

"It is not! It's an omnibus. I can see it plain. See? One of these big hotel omnibuses."

"By thunder, you're right. It's an omnibus, sure as fate. What do you suppose they are doing with an omnibus? Maybe they are going around collecting the life-crew, hey?"

"That's it, likely. Look! There's a fellow waving a little black flag. He's standing on the steps of the omnibus. There come those other two fellows. Now they're all talking together. Look at the fellow with the flag. Maybe he ain't waving it!"

"That ain't a flag, is it? That's his coat. Why, certainly, that's his coat."

"So it is; it's his coat. He's taken it off and is waving it around his head. But would you look at him swing it!"

"Oh, say, there isn't any life-saving station there. That's just a winter-resort hotel omnibus that has brought over some of the boarders to see us drown."

"What's that idiot with the coat mean? What's he signalling, anyhow?"

"It looks as if he were trying to tell us to go north. There must be a life-saving station up there."

"No; he thinks we're fishing. Just giving us a merry hand. See? Ah, there, Willie!"

"Well, I wish I could make something out of those signals. What do you suppose he means?"

"He don't mean anything; he's just playing."

"Well, if he'd just signal us to try the surf again, or to go to sea and wait, or go north, or go south, or go to hell, there would be some reason in it. But look at him! He just stands there and keeps his coat revolving like a wheel. The ass!"

"There come more people."

"Now there's quite a mob. Look! Isn't that a boat?"

"Where? Oh, I see where you mean. No, that's no boat."

"That fellow is still waving his coat."

"He must think we like to see him do that. Why don't he quit it? It don't mean anything."

"I don't know. I think he is trying to make us go north. It must be that there's a life-saving station there somewhere."

"Say, he ain't tired yet. Look at 'im wave!"

"Wonder how long he can keep that up. He's been revolving his coat ever since he caught sight of us. He's an idiot. Why aren't they getting men to bring a boat out? A fishing-boat—one of those big yawls—could come out here all right. Why don't he do something?"

"Oh, it's all right now."

"They'll have a boat out here for us in less than no time, now that they've seen us."

A faint yellow tone came into the sky over the low land. The shadows on the sea slowly deepened. The wind bore coldness with it, and the men began to shiver.

"Holy smoke!" said one, allowing his voice to express his impious mood, "if we keep on monkeying out here! If we've got to flounder out here all night!"

"Oh, we'll never have to stay here all night! Don't you worry. They've seen us now, and it won't be long before they'll come chasing out after us."

The shore grew dusky. The man waving a coat blended gradually into this gloom, and it swallowed in the same manner the omnibus and the group of people. The spray, when it dashed uproariously over the side, made the voyagers shrink and swear like men who were being branded.

"I'd like to catch the chump who waved the coat. I feel like socking him one, just for luck."

"Why? What did he do?"

"Oh, nothing, but then he seemed so damned cheerful."

In the meantime the oiler rowed, and then the correspondent rowed, and then the oiler rowed. Grey-faced and bowed forward, they mechanically, turn by turn, plied the leaden oars. The form of the lighthouse had vanished from the southern horizon, but finally a pale star appeared, just lifting from the sea. The streaked saffron in the west passed before the all-merging darkness, and the sea to the east was black. The land had vanished, and was expressed only by the low and drear thunder of the surf.

"If I am going to be drowned—if I am going to be drowned—if I am going to be drowned, why, in the name of the seven mad gods who rule the sea, was I allowed to come thus far and contemplate sand and trees? Was I brought here merely to have my nose dragged away as I was about to nibble the sacred cheese of life?"

The patient captain, drooped over the water-jar, was sometimes obliged to speak to the oarsman.

"Keep her head up! Keep her head up!"

"Keep her head up, sir." The voices were weary and low.

This was surely a quiet evening. All save the oarsman lay heavily and listlessly in the boat's bottom. As for him, his eyes were just capable of noting the tall black waves that swept forward in a most sinister silence, save for an occasional subdued growl of a crest.

The cook's head was on a thwart, and he looked without interest at the water under his nose. He was deep in other scenes. Finally he spoke. "Billie," he murmured, dreamfully, "what kind of pie do you like best?"

V

"Pie!" said the oiler and the correspondent, agitatedly. "Don't talk about those things, blast you!"

"Well," said the cook, "I was just thinking about ham sandwiches and—"

A night on the sea in an open boat is a long night. As darkness settled finally, the shine of the light, lifting from the sea in the south, changed to full gold. On the northern horizon a new light appeared, a small bluish gleam on the edge of the waters. These two lights were the furniture of the world. Otherwise there was nothing but waves.

Two men huddled in the stern, and distances were so magnificent in the dinghy that the rower was enabled to keep his feet partly warm by thrusting them under his companions. Their legs indeed extended far under the rowing-seat until they touched the feet of the captain forward. Sometimes, despite the efforts of the tired oarsman, a wave came piling into the boat, an icy wave of the night, and the chilling water soaked them anew. They would twist their bodies for a moment and groan, and sleep the dead sleep once more, while the water in the boat gurgled about them as the craft rocked.

The plan of the oiler and the correspondent was for one to row until he lost the ability, and then arouse the other from his sea-water couch in the bottom of the boat.

The oiler plied the oars until his head drooped forward and the overpowering sleep blinded him; and he rowed yet afterward. Then he touched a man in the bottom of the boat, and called his name. "Will you spell me for a little while?" he said, meekly.

"Sure, Billie," said the correspondent, awaking and dragging himself to a sitting position. They exchanged places carefully, and the oiler, cuddling down in the sea-water at the cook's side, seemed to go to sleep instantly.

The particular violence of the sea had ceased. The waves came without snarling. The obligation of the man at the oars was to keep the boat headed so that the tilt of the rollers would not capsize her, and to preserve her from filling when the crests rushed past. The black waves were silent and hard to be seen in the darkness. Often one was almost upon the boat before the oarsman was aware.

In a low voice the correspondent addressed the captain. He was not sure that the captain was awake, although this iron man seemed to be always awake. "Captain, shall I keep her making for that light north, sir?"

The same steady voice answered him. "Yes. Keep it about two points off the port bow."

The cook had tied a life-belt around himself in order to get even the warmth which this clumsy cork contrivance could donate, and he seemed almost stove-like when a rower, whose teeth invariably chattered wildly as soon as he ceased his labour, dropped down to sleep.

The correspondent, as he rowed, looked down at the two men sleeping underfoot.

The cook's arm was around the oiler's shoulders, and, with their fragmentary clothing and haggard faces, they were the babes of the sea—a grotesque rendering of the old babes in the wood.

Later he must have grown stupid at his work, for suddenly there was a growling of water, and a crest came with a roar and a swash into the boat, and it was a wonder that it did not set the cook afloat in his life-belt. The cook continued to sleep, but the oiler sat up, blinking his eyes and shaking with the new cold.

"Oh, I'm awful sorry, Billie," said the correspondent, contritely.

"That's all right, old boy," said the oiler, and lay down again and was asleep.

Presently it seemed that even the captain dozed, and the correspondent thought that he was the one man afloat on all the oceans. The wind had a voice as it came over the waves, and it was sadder than the end.

There was a long, loud swishing astern of the boat, and a gleaming trail of phosphorescence, like blue flame, was furrowed on the black waters. It might have been made by a monstrous knife.

Then there came a stillness, while the correspondent breathed with open mouth and looked at the sea.

Suddenly there was another swish and another long flash of bluish light, and this time it was alongside the boat, and might almost been reached with an oar. The correspondent saw an enormous fin speed like a shadow through the water, hurling the crystalline spray and leaving the long glowing trail.

The correspondent looked over his shoulder at the captain. His face was hidden, and he seemed to be asleep. He looked at the babes of the sea. They certainly were asleep. So, being bereft of sympathy, he leaned a little way to one side and swore softly into the sea.

But the thing did not then leave the vicinity of the boat. Ahead or astern, on one side or the other, at intervals long or short, fled the long sparkling streak, and there was to be heard the *whirroo* of the dark fin. The speed and power of the thing was greatly to be admired. It cut the water like a gigantic and keen projectile.

The presence of this biding thing did not affect the man with the same horror that it would if he had been a picnicker. He simply looked at the sea dully and swore in an undertone.

Nevertheless, it is true that he did not wish to be alone with the thing. He wished one of his companions to awake by chance and keep him company with it. But the captain hung motionless over the water-jar, and the oiler and the cook in the bottom of the boat were plunged in slumber.

VI

"If I am going to be drowned—if I am going to be drowned—if I am going to be drowned, why, in the name of the seven mad gods who rule the sea, was I allowed to come thus far and contemplate sand and trees?"

During this dismal night, it may be remarked that a man would conclude that it was really the intention of the seven mad gods to drown him, despite the abominable injustice of it. For it was certainly an abominable injustice to drown a man who had worked so hard, so hard. The man felt it would be a crime most unnatural. Other people had drowned at sea since galleys swarmed with painted sails, but still—

When it occurs to a man that nature does not regard him as important, and that she feels she would not maim the universe by disposing of him, he at first wishes to throw bricks at the temple, and he hates deeply the fact that there are no bricks and no temples. Any visible expression of nature would surely be pelleted with his jeers.

Then, if there be no tangible thing to hoot, he feels, perhaps, the desire to confront a personification and indulge in pleas, bowed to one knee, and with hands supplicant, saying, "Yes, but I love myself."

A high cold star on a winter's night is the word he feels that she says to him. Thereafter he knows the pathos of his situation.

The men in the dinghy had not discussed these matters, but each had, no doubt, reflected upon them in silence and according to his mind. There was seldom any expression upon their faces save the general one of complete weariness. Speech was devoted to the business of the boat.

To chime the notes of his emotion, a verse mysteriously entered the correspondent's head. He had even forgotten that he had forgotten this verse, but it suddenly was in mind.

A soldier of the Legion lay dying in Algiers;
There was lack of woman's nursing, there was dearth of woman's tears;
But a comrade stood beside him, and he took that comrade's hand,
And he said, "I never more shall see my own, my native land."

In his childhood the correspondent had been made acquainted with the fact that a soldier of the Legion lay dying in Algiers, but he had never regarded the fact as important. Myriads of his school-fellows had informed him of the soldier's plight, but the dinning had naturally ended by making him perfectly indifferent. He had never considered it his affair that a soldier of the Legion lay dying in Algiers, nor had it appeared to him as a matter for sorrow. It was less to him than the breaking of a pencil's point.

Now, however, it quaintly came to him as a human, living thing. It was no longer merely a picture of a few throes in the breast of a poet, meanwhile drinking tea and warming his feet at the grate; it was an actuality—stern, mournful, and fine.

The correspondent plainly saw the soldier. He lay on the sand with his feet out straight and still. While his pale left hand was upon his chest in an attempt to thwart the going of his life, the blood came between his fingers. In the far Algerian distance, a city of low square forms was set against a sky that was faint with the last sunset hues. The correspondent, plying the oars and dreaming of the slow and slower movements of the lips of the soldier, was moved by a profound and perfectly impersonal comprehension. He was sorry for the soldier of the Legion who lay dying in Algiers.

The thing which had followed the boat and waited had evidently grown bored at the delay. There was no longer to be heard the slash of the cutwater, and there was no longer the flame of the long trail. The light in the north still glimmered, but it was apparently no nearer to the boat. Sometimes the boom of the surf rang in the correspondent's ears, and he turned the craft seaward then and rowed harder. Southward, some one had evidently built a watch-fire on the beach. It was too low and too far to be seen, but it made a shimmering, roseate reflection upon the bluff in back of it, and this could be discerned from the boat. The wind came stronger, and sometimes a wave suddenly raged out like a mountain cat, and there was to be seen the sheen and sparkle of a broken crest.

The captain, in the bow, moved on his water-jar and sat erect. "Pretty long night," he observed to the correspondent. He looked at the shore. "Those life-saving people take their time."

"Did you see that shark playing around?"

"Yes, I saw him. He was a big fellow, all right."

"Wish I had known you were awake."

Later the correspondent spoke into the bottom of the boat. "Billie!" There was a slow and gradual disentanglement. "Billie, will you spell me?"

"Sure," said the oiler.

As soon as the correspondent touched the cold, comfortable sea-water in the bottom of the boat and had huddled close to the cook's life-belt he was deep in sleep, despite the fact that his teeth played all the popular airs. This sleep was so good to him that it was but a moment before he heard a voice call his name in a tone that demonstrated the last stages of exhaustion. "Will you spell me?"

"Sure, Billie."

The light in the north had mysteriously vanished, but the correspondent took his course from the wide-awake captain.

Later in the night they took the boat farther out to sea, and the captain directed the cook to take one oar at the stern and keep the boat facing the seas. He was to call out if he should hear the thunder of the surf. This plan enabled the oiler and the correspondent to get respite together. "We'll give those boys a chance to get into shape again," said the captain. They curled down and, after a few preliminary chatterings and trembles, slept once more the dead sleep. Neither knew they had bequeathed to the cook the company of another shark, or perhaps the same shark.

As the boat caroused on the waves, spray occasionally bumped over the side and gave them a fresh soaking, but this had no power to break their repose. The ominous slash of the wind and the water affected them as it would have affected mummies.

"Boys," said the cook, with the notes of every reluctance in his voice, "she's drifted in pretty close. I guess one of you had better take her to sea again." The correspondent, aroused, heard the crash of the toppled crests.

As he was rowing, the captain gave him some whisky-and-water, and this steadied the chills out of him. "If I ever get ashore and anybody shows me even a photograph of an oar—"

At last there was a short conversation.

"Billie!—Billie, will you spell me?"

"Sure," said the oiler.

VII

When the correspondent again opened his eyes, the sea and the sky were each of the grey hue of the dawning. Later, carmine and gold was painted upon the waters. The morning appeared finally, in its splendour, with a sky of pure blue, and the sunlight flamed on the tips of the waves.

On the distant dunes were set many little black cottages, and a tall white windmill reared above them. No man, nor dog, nor bicycle appeared on the beach. The cottages might have formed a deserted village.

The voyagers scanned the shore. A conference was held in the boat. "Well," said the captain, "if no help is coming, we might better try a run through the surf right away. If we stay out here much longer we will be too weak to do anything for ourselves at all." The others silently acquiesced in this reasoning. The boat was headed for the beach. The correspondent wondered if none ever ascended the tall wind-tower, and if then they never looked seaward. This tower was a giant, standing with its back to the plight of the ants. It represented in a degree, to the correspondent, the serenity of nature amid the struggles of the individual—nature in the wind, and nature in the vision of men. She did not seem cruel to him then, nor beneficent, nor treacherous, nor wise. But she was indifferent, flatly indifferent. It is, perhaps, plausible that a man in this situation, impressed with the unconcern of the universe, should see the innumerable flaws of his life, and have them taste wickedly in his mind, and wish for another chance. A distinction between right and wrong seems absurdly clear to him, then, in this new ignorance of the grave-edge, and he understands that if he were given another opportunity he would mend his conduct and his words, and be better and brighter during an introduction or at a tea.

"Now, boys," said the captain, "she is going to swamp sure. All we can do is to work her in as far as possible, and then when she swamps, pile out and scramble for the beach. Keep cool now, and don't jump until she swamps sure."

The oiler took the oars. Over his shoulders he scanned the surf. "Captain," he said, "I think I'd better bring her about and keep her head-on to the seas and back her in."

"All right, Billie," said the captain. "Back her in." The oiler swung the boat then, and, seated in the stern, the cook and the correspondent were obliged to look over their shoulders to contemplate the lonely and indifferent shore.

The monstrous inshore rollers heaved the boat high until the men were again enabled to see the white sheets of water scudding up the slanted beach. "We won't get in very close," said the captain. Each time a man could wrest his attention from the rollers, he turned his glance toward the shore, and in the expression of the eyes during this contemplation there was a singular quality. The correspondent, observing the others, knew that they were not afraid, but the full meaning of their glances was shrouded.

As for himself, he was too tired to grapple fundamentally with the fact. He tried to coerce his mind into thinking of it, but the mind was dominated at this time by the muscles, and the muscles said they did not care. It merely occurred to him that if he should drown it would be a shame.

There were no hurried words, no pallor, no plain agitation. The men simply looked at the shore. "Now, remember to get well clear of the boat when you jump," said the captain.

Seaward the crest of a roller suddenly fell with a thunderous crash, and the long white comber came roaring down upon the boat.

"Steady now," said the captain. The men were silent. They turned their eyes from the shore to the comber and waited. The boat slid up the incline, leaped at the furious top, bounced over it, and swung down the long back of the wave. Some water had been shipped, and the cook bailed it out.

But the next crest crashed also. The tumbling, boiling flood of white water caught the boat and whirled it almost perpendicular. Water swarmed in from all sides. The correspondent had his hands on the gunwale at this time, and when the water entered at that place he swiftly withdrew his fingers, as if he objected to wetting them.

The little boat, drunken with this weight of water, reeled and snuggled deeper into the sea.

"Bail her out, cook! Bail her out!" said the captain.

"All right, Captain," said the cook.

"Now, boys, the next one will do for us sure," said the oiler. "Mind to jump clear of the boat."

The third wave moved forward, huge, furious, implacable. It fairly swallowed the dinghy, and almost simultaneously the men tumbled into the sea. A piece of life-belt had lain in the bottom of the boat, and as the correspondent went overboard he held this to his chest with his left hand.

The January water was icy, and he reflected immediately that it was colder than he had expected to find it off the coast of Florida. This appeared to his dazed mind as a fact important enough to be noted at the time. The coldness of the water was sad; it was tragic. This fact was somehow mixed and confused with his opinion of his own situation, so that it seemed almost a proper reason for tears. The water was cold.

When he came to the surface he was conscious of little but the noisy water. Afterward he saw his companions in the sea. The oiler was ahead in the race. He was swimming strongly and rapidly. Off to the correspondent's left, the cook's great white and corked back bulged out of the water; and in the rear the captain was hanging with his one good hand to the keel of the overturned dinghy.

There is a certain immovable quality to a shore, and the correspondent wondered at it amid the confusion of the sea.

It seemed also very attractive; but the correspondent knew that it was a long journey, and he paddled leisurely. The piece of life-preserver lay under him, and sometimes he whirled down the incline of a wave as if he were on a hand-sled.

But finally he arrived at a place in the sea where travel was beset with difficulty. He did not pause swimming to inquire what manner of current had caught him, but there his progress ceased. The shore was set before him like a bit of scenery on a stage, and he looked at it and understood with his eyes each detail of it.

As the cook passed, much farther to the left, the captain was calling to him, "Turn over on your back, cook! Turn over on your back and use the oar."

"All right, sir." The cook turned on his back, and, paddling with an oar, went ahead as if he were a canoe.

Presently the boat also passed to the left of the correspondent, with the captain clinging with one hand to the keel. He would have appeared like a man raising himself to look over a board fence if it were not for the extraordinary gymnastics of the boat. The correspondent marvelled that the captain could still hold to it.

They passed on nearer to shore—the oiler, the cook, the captain—and following them went the water-jar, bouncing gaily over the seas.

The correspondent remained in the grip of this strange new enemy—a current. The shore, with its white slope of sand and its green bluff topped with little silent cottages, was spread like a picture before him. It was very near to him then, but he was impressed as one who, in a gallery, looks at a scene from Brittany or Holland.

He thought: "I am going to drown? Can it be possible? Can it be possible? Can it be possible?" Perhaps an individual must consider his own death to be the final phenomenon of nature.

But later a wave perhaps whirled him out of this small deadly current, for he found suddenly that he could again make progress toward the shore. Later still he was aware that the captain, clinging with one hand to the keel of the dinghy, had his face turned away from the shore and toward him, and was calling his name. "Come to the boat! Come to the boat!"

In his struggle to reach the captain and the boat, he reflected that when one gets properly wearied drowning must really be a comfortable arrangement—a cessation of hostilities accompanied by a large degree of relief; and he was glad of it, for the main thing in his mind for some moments had been horror of the temporary agony. He did not wish to be hurt.

Presently he saw a man running along the shore. He was undressing with most remarkable speed. Coat, trousers, shirt, everything flew magically off him.

"Come to the boat!" called the captain.

"All right, Captain." As the correspondent paddled, he saw the captain let himself down to bottom and leave the boat. Then the correspondent performed his one little marvel of the voyage. A large wave caught him and flung him with ease and supreme speed completely over the boat and far beyond it. It struck him even then as an event in gymnastics and a true miracle of the sea. An overturned boat in the surf is not a plaything to a swimming man.

The correspondent arrived in water that reached only to his waist, but his condition did not enable him to stand for more than a moment. Each wave knocked him into a heap, and the undertow pulled at him.

Then he saw the man who had been running and undressing, and undressing and running, come bounding into the water. He dragged ashore the cook, and then waded toward the captain; but the captain waved him away and sent him to the correspondent. He was naked—naked as a tree in winter; but a halo was about his head, and he shone like a saint. He gave a strong pull, and a long drag, and a bully heave at the correspondent's hand. The correspondent, schooled in the minor formulae, said, "Thanks, old man." But suddenly the man cried, "What's that?" He pointed a swift finger. The correspondent said, "Go."

In the shallows, face downward, lay the oiler. His forehead touched sand that was periodically, between each wave, clear of the sea.

The correspondent did not know all that transpired afterward. When he achieved safe ground he fell, striking the sand with each particular part of his body. It was as if he had dropped from a roof, but the thud was grateful to him.

It seemed that instantly the beach was populated with men with blankets, clothes, and flasks, and women with coffee-pots and all the remedies sacred to their minds. The welcome of the land to the men from the sea was warm and generous; but a still and dripping shape was carried slowly up the beach, and the land's welcome for it could only be the different and sinister hospitality of the grave.

When it came night, the white waves paced to and fro in the moonlight, and the wind brought the sound of the great sea's voice to the men on the shore, and they felt that they could then be interpreters.

DISCUSSION QUESTIONS

1. How does the fictionalized tale "The Open Boat" differ from the newspaper report of the same event in "Stephen Crane's Own Story"? Have any incidents been changed or added? Has anything been distorted? Explain how Crane's role as a participant and writer changes as he turns from journalism to fiction.

2. How do Crane's tone and imagery change as he imagines a different form and audience for his writing? Point to specific examples.

Robert Frost / Design 1922

"There are tones of voice that mean more than words," wrote Robert Frost (1874–1963) in a letter:

> *Sentences may be so constructed as definitely to indicate these tones. Only when we are making sentences so shaped are we really writing. And that is flat. A sentence* must *convey a meaning by tone of voice and it must be the particular meaning the writer intended. The reader must have no choice in the matter. The tone of voice and its meaning must be in black and white on the page.*

Frost wanted to direct readers away from the conventional notion of syntax as a grammatical arrangement to a new definition of a sentence as a cluster of sounds, "because to me a sentence is not interesting merely in conveying a meaning in words. It must do something more; it must convey a meaning by sound." But more often than not, it was the "meaning in words" that most of his large audience attended to, and more often than that to the image of Frost projected by the mass media: a kindly and wise old man, rugged in appearance, yet homely and whimsical in the way he talked publicly. To the average citizen, Robert Frost was the American representative of poetry. Yet his public image even today induces his readers to concentrate almost exclusively in paraphrasing the thought, the "meaning in words," of his poetry without paying adequate attention to the ways in which that thought comes into existence through the dynamics of voice, through the "meaning by sound."

Frost's poem "Design" first appeared in American Poetry *in 1922. "The Gift Outright" was first published in* The Virginia Quarterly Review *in 1942. The poem was also read by Frost at John F. Kennedy's inauguration in 1961.*

I found a dimpled spider, fat and white,
On a white heal-all,[1] holding up a moth
Like a white piece of rigid satin cloth—
Assorted characters of death and blight
Mixed ready to begin the morning right,
Like the ingredients of a witches' broth—
A snow-drop spider, a flower like a froth,
And dead wings carried like a paper kite.

What had that flower to do with being white,
The wayside blue and innocent heal-all?
What brought the kindred spider to that height,
Then steered the white moth thither in the night?
What but design of darkness to appall?—
If design govern in a thing so small.

[1] Plant thought to have medicinal value.

Robert Frost / The Gift Outright 1942

The land was ours before we were the land's.
She was our land more than a hundred years
Before we were her people. She was ours
In Massachusetts, in Virginia,
But we were England's, still colonials,
Possessing what we still were unpossessed by,
Possessed by what we now no more possessed.
Something we were withholding made us weak
Until we found out that it was ourselves
We were withholding from our land of living,
And forthwith found salvation in surrender.
Such as we were we gave ourselves outright
(The deed of gift was many deeds of war)
To the land vaguely realizing westward,
But still unstoried, artless, unenhanced,
Such as she was, such as she would become.

Ernest Hemingway / Soldier's Home 1925

Ernest Hemingway (1899–1961) was first employed as a reporter for the Kansas City Star *in 1917. After serving in a Red Cross ambulance unit on the Italian front during World War I, Hemingway wrote for the* Toronto Star Weekly *and later worked briefly for a Chicago advertising firm. He gradually turned to freelance journalism and published a good deal of short fiction characterized by a lean, understated prose style that he later partially attributed to the constraints of having to write cablegrams. With the encouragement of Sherwood Anderson and the promise of a job as foreign correspondent for the* Toronto Daily Star, *Hemingway left for Paris in 1921 where he met Gertrude Stein and gravitated towards her corps of literary expatriates.*

"Soldier's Home," the tale of a young man returning from the First World War to the routines of his hometown and family, was collected in Hemingway's first major volume of short stories, "In Our Time" (1925). For a film adaptation of this story, see Scripts.

Krebs went to the war from a Methodist college in Kansas. There is a picture which shows him among his fraternity brothers, all of them wearing exactly the same height and style collar. He enlisted in the Marines in 1917 and did not return to the United States until the second division returned from the Rhine in the summer of 1919.

There is a picture which shows him on the Rhine with two German girls and another corporal. Krebs and the corporal look too big for their uniforms. The German girls are not beautiful. The Rhine does not show in the picture.

By the time Krebs returned to his home town in Oklahoma the greeting of heroes was over. He came back much too late. The men from the town who had been drafted had all been welcomed elaborately on their return. There had been a great deal of hysteria. Now the reaction had set in. People seemed to think it was rather ridiculous for Krebs to be getting back so late, years after the war was over.

At first Krebs, who had been at Belleau Wood, Soissons, the Champagne, St. Mihiel and in the Argonne did not want to talk about the war at all. Later he felt the need to talk but no one wanted to hear about it. His town had heard too many atrocity stories to be thrilled by actualities. Krebs found that to be listened to at all he had to lie, and after he had done this twice he, too, had a reaction against the war and against talking about it. A distaste for everything that had happened to him in the war set in because of the lies he had told. All of the times that had been able to make him feel cool and clear inside himself when he thought of them; the times so long back when he had done the one thing, the only thing for a man to do, easily and naturally, when he might have done something else, now lost their cool, valuable quality and then were lost themselves.

His lies were quite unimportant lies and consisted in attributing to himself things other men had seen, done or heard of, and stating as facts certain apocryphal incidents familiar to all soldiers. Even his lies were not sensational at the pool room. His acquaintances, who had heard detailed accounts of German women found chained to machine guns in the Argonne forest and who could not comprehend, or were barred by their patriotism from interest in, any German machine gunners who were not chained, were not thrilled by his stories.

Krebs acquired the nausea in regard to experience that is the result of untruth or exaggeration, and when he occasionally met another man who had really been a soldier and they talked a few minutes in the dressing room at a dance he fell into the easy pose of the old soldier among other soldiers: that he had been badly, sickeningly frightened all the time. In this way he lost everything.

During this time, it was late summer, he was sleeping late in bed, getting up to walk down town to the library to get a book, eating lunch at home, reading on the front porch until he became bored and then walking down through the town to spend the hottest hours of the day in the cool dark of the pool room. He loved to play pool.

In the evening he practised on his clarinet, strolled down town, read and went to bed. He was still a hero to his two young sisters. His mother would have given him breakfast in bed if he had wanted it. She often came in when he was in bed and asked him to tell her about the war, but her attention always wandered. His father was non-committal.

Before Krebs went away to the war he had never been allowed to drive the family motor car. His father was in the real estate business and always wanted the car to be at his command when he required it to take clients out into the country to show them a piece of farm property. The car always stood outside the First National Bank building where his father had an office on the second floor. Now, after the war, it was still the same car.

Nothing was changed in the town except that the young girls had grown up. But they lived in such a complicated world of already defined alliances and shifting feuds that Krebs did not feel the energy or the courage to break into it. He liked to look at them, though. There were so many good-looking young girls. Most of them had their hair cut short. When he went away only little girls wore their hair like that or girls that were fast. They all wore sweaters and shirt waists with round Dutch collars. It was a pattern. He liked to look at them from the front porch as they walked on the other side of the street. He liked to watch them walking under the shade of the trees. He liked the round Dutch collars above their sweaters. He liked their silk stockings and flat shoes. He liked their bobbed hair and the way they walked.

When he was in town their appeal to him was not very strong. He did not like them when he saw them in the Greek's ice cream parlor. He did not want them themselves really. They were too complicated. There was something else. Vaguely he wanted a girl but he did not want to have to work to get her. He would have liked to have a girl but he did not want to have to spend a long time getting her. He did not want to get into the intrigue and the politics. He did not want to have to do any courting. He did not want to tell any more lies. It wasn't worth it.

He did not want any consequences. He did not want any consequences ever again. He wanted to live along without consequences. Besides he did not really need a girl. The army had taught him that. It was all right to pose as though you had to have a girl. Nearly everybody did that. But it wasn't true. You did not need a girl. That was the funny thing. First a fellow boasted how girls mean nothing to him, that he never thought of them, that they could not touch him. Then a fellow boasted that he could not get along without girls, that he had to have them all the time, that he could not go to sleep without them.

That was all a lie. It was all a lie both ways. You did not need a girl unless you thought about them. He learned that in the army. Then sooner or later you always got one. When you were really ripe for a girl you always got one. You did not have to think about it. Sooner or later it would come. He had learned that in the army.

Now he would have liked a girl if she had come to him and not wanted to talk. But here at home it was all too complicated. He knew he could never get through it all again. It was not worth the trouble. That was the thing about French girls and German girls. There was not all this talking. You couldn't talk much and you did not need to talk. It was simple and you were friends. He thought about France and then he began to think about Germany. On the whole he had liked Germany better. He did not want to leave Germany. He did not want to come home. Still, he had come home. He sat on the front porch.

He liked the girls that were walking along the other side of the street. He liked the look of them much better than the French girls or the German girls. But the world they were in was not the world he was in. He would like to have one of them. But it was not worth it. They were such a nice pattern. He liked the pattern. It was exciting. But he would not go through all the talking. He did not want one badly enough. He liked to look at them all, though. It was not worth it. Not now when things were getting good again.

He sat there on the porch reading a book on the war. It was a history and he was reading about all the engagements he had been in. It was the most interesting reading he had ever done. He wished there were more maps. He looked forward with a good feeling to reading all the really good histories when they would come out with good detail maps. Now he was really learning about the war. He had been a good soldier. That made a difference.

One morning after he had been home about a month his mother came into his bedroom and sat on the bed. She smoothed her apron.

"I had a talk with your father last night, Harold," she said, "and he is willing for you to take the car out in the evenings."

"Yeah?" said Krebs, who was not fully awake. "Take the car out? Yeah?"

"Yes. Your father has felt for some time that you should be able to take the car out in the evenings whenever you wished but we only talked it over last night."

"I'll bet you made him," Krebs said.

"No. It was your father's suggestion that we talk the matter over."

"Yeah. I'll bet you made him," Krebs sat up in bed.

"Will you come down to breakfast, Harold?" his mother said.

"As soon as I get my clothes on," Krebs said.

His mother went out of the room and he could hear her frying something downstairs while he washed, shaved and dressed to go down into the dining-room for breakfast. While he was eating breakfast his sister brought in the mail.

"Well, Hare," she said. "You old sleepy-head. What do you ever get up for?"

Krebs looked at her. He liked her. She was his best sister.

"Have you got the paper?" he asked.

She handed him *The Kansas City Star* and he shucked off its brown wrapper and opened it to the sporting page. He folded *The Star* open and propped it against the water pitcher with his cereal dish to steady it, so he could read while he ate.

"Harold," his mother stood in the kitchen doorway, "Harold, please don't muss up the paper. Your father can't read his *Star* if it's been mussed."

"I won't muss it," Krebs said.

His sister sat down at the table and watched him while he read.

"We're playing indoor over at school this afternoon," she said. "I'm going to pitch."

"Good," said Krebs. "How's the old wing?"

"I can pitch better than lots of the boys. I tell them all you taught me. The other girls aren't much good."

"Yeah?" said Krebs.

"I tell them all you're my beau. Aren't you my beau, Hare?"

"You bet."

"Couldn't your brother really be your beau just because he's your brother?"

"I don't know."

"Sure you know. Couldn't you be my beau, Hare, if I was old enough and if you wanted to?"

"Sure. You're my girl now."

"Am I really your girl?"

"Sure."

"Do you love me?"

"Uh, huh."

"Will you love me always?"

"Sure."

"Will you come over and watch me play indoor?"

"Maybe."

"Aw, Hare, you don't love me. If you loved me, you'd want to come over and watch me play indoor."

Kreb's mother came into the dining-room from the kitchen. She carried a plate with two fried eggs and some crisp bacon on it and a plate of buckwheat cakes.

"You run along, Helen," she said. "I want to talk to Harold."

She put the eggs and bacon down in front of him and brought in a jug of maple syrup for the buckwheat cakes. Then she sat down across the table from Krebs.

"I wish you'd put down the paper a minute, Harold," she said.

Krebs took down the paper and folded it.

"Have you decided what you are going to do yet, Harold?" his mother said, taking off her glasses.

"No," said Krebs.

"Don't you think it's about time?" His mother did not say this in a mean way. She seemed worried.

"I hadn't thought about it," Krebs said.

"God has some work for every one to do," his mother said. "There can be no idle hands in His Kingdom."

"I'm not in His Kingdom," Krebs said.

"We are all of us in His Kingdom."

Krebs felt embarrassed and resentful as always.

"I've worried about you so much, Harold," his mother went on. "I know the temptations you must have been exposed to. I know how weak men are. I know what your own dear grandfather, my own father, told us about the Civil War and I have prayed for you. I pray for you all day long, Harold."

Krebs looked at the bacon fat hardening on his plate.

"Your father is worried, too," his mother went on. "He thinks you have lost your ambition, that you haven't got a definite aim in life. Charley Simmons, who is just your age, has a good job and is going to be married. The boys are all settling down; they're all determined to get somewhere; you can see that boys like Charley Simmons are on their way to being really a credit to the community."

Krebs said nothing.

"Don't look that way, Harold," his mother said. "You know we love you and I want to tell you for your own good how matters stand. Your father does not want to hamper your freedom. He thinks you should be allowed to drive the car. If you want to take some of the nice girls out riding with you, we are only too pleased. We want you to enjoy yourself. But you are going to have to settle down to work, Harold. Your father doesn't care what you start in at. All work is honorable as he says. But you've got to make a start at something. He asked me to speak to you this morning and then you can stop in and see him at his office."

"Is that all?" Krebs said.

"Yes. Don't you love your mother, dear boy?"

"No," Krebs said.

His mother looked at him across the table. Her eyes were shiny. She started crying.

"I don't love anybody," Krebs said.

It wasn't any good. He couldn't tell her, he couldn't make her see it. It was silly to have said it. He had only hurt her. He went over and took hold of her arm. She was crying with her head in her hands.

"I didn't mean it," he said. "I was just angry at something. I didn't mean I didn't love you."

His mother went on crying. Krebs put his arm on her shoulder.

"Can't you believe me, mother?"

His mother shook her head.

"Please, please, mother. Please believe me."

"All right," his mother said chokily. She looked up at him. "I believe you, Harold."

Krebs kissed her hair. She put her face up to him.

"I'm your mother," she said. "I held you next to my heart when you were a tiny baby."

Krebs felt sick and vaguely nauseated.

"I know, Mummy," he said. "I'll try and be a good boy for you."

"Would you kneel and pray with me, Harold?" his mother asked.

They knelt down beside the dining-room table and Krebs's mother prayed.

"Now, you pray, Harold," she said.

"I can't," Krebs said.

"Try, Harold."

"I can't."

"Do you want me to pray for you?"

"Yes."

So his mother prayed for him and then they stood up and Krebs kissed his mother and went out of the house. He had tried so to keep his life from being complicated. Still, none of it had touched him. He had felt sorry for his mother and she had made him lie. He would go to Kansas City and get a job and she would feel all right about it. There would be one more scene maybe before he got away. He would not go down to his father's office. He would miss that one. He wanted his life to go smoothly. It had just gotten going that way. Well, that was all over now, anyway. He would go over to the schoolyard and watch Helen play indoor baseball.

William Carlos Williams / The Use of Force 1933

Five minutes, ten minutes, can always be found. I had my typewriter in my office desk. All I needed to do was pull up the leaf to which it was fastened and I was ready to go. I worked at top speed. If a patient came in at the door while I was in the middle of a sentence, bang would go the machine—I was a physician. When the patient left, up would come the machine. My head developed a technique: something growing inside me demanded reaping. It had to be attended to. Finally, after eleven at night, when the last patient had been put to bed, I could always find time to bang out ten or twelve pages. In fact, I couldn't rest until I had freed my mind from the obsessions which had been tormenting me all day. Cleansed of that torment, having scribbled, I could rest.

As the above passage from his Autobiography *makes clear, William Carlos Williams worked hard all his life at two demanding careers. A busy pediatrician in a densely populated northern New Jersey area, Williams also attained a reputation as one of the leading figures in modern American poetry. In his best work he succeeds in giving literary form to the discordant, brittle, nonliterary idioms of an industrial civilization.*

Born in Rutherford, New Jersey, in 1883, Williams received a medical education at the University of Pennsylvania, where he became acquainted with the poet and critic Ezra Pound. After a year's study abroad, Williams returned to his home town to discipline himself in the arts of healing and writing. His first book of poems, published at his own expense in 1909, was followed by nearly forty vol-

umes of poetry, short stories, novels, plays, history, biography, and criticism, in which he consistently demonstrates a special fondness for local subjects and his native grounds. His most ambitious effort, an epic of a modern industrial city, Paterson, *received the National Book Award in 1949. Williams died in Rutherford in 1963.*

"The Use of Force" documents in unsentimental terms an encounter between a determined physician and the seriously ill child of a poor, backward family–the kind of people Williams cared for all his life. It originally appeared in Blast, *a short-lived American literary magazine that, according to Williams, was started by an unemployed "tool designer living precariously over a garage in Brooklyn."*

"Tract," the poem that follows "The Use of Force," is an ironic commentary on the pomp conventionally associated with funerals; it appeared in Williams' collection Al Que Quiere! *("To him who wants it!"), published in 1917.*

They were new patients to me, all I had was the name, Olson. Please come down as soon as you can, my daughter is very sick.

When I arrived I was met by the mother, a big startled-looking woman, very clean and apologetic who merely said, Is this the doctor? and let me in. In the back, she added. You must excuse us, doctor, we have her in the kitchen where it is warm. It is very damp here sometimes.

The child was fully dressed and sitting on her father's lap near the kitchen table. He tried to get up, but I motioned for him not to bother, took off my overcoat and started to look things over. I could see that they were all very nervous, eyeing me up and down distrustfully. As often, in such cases, they weren't telling me more than they had to, it was up to me to tell them; that's why they were spending three dollars on me.

The child was fairly eating me up with her cold, steady eyes, and no expression to her face whatever. She did not move and seemed, inwardly, quiet; an unusually attractive little thing, and as strong as a heifer in appearance. But her face was flushed, she was breathing rapidly, and I realized that she had a high fever. She had magnificent blond hair, in profusion. One of those picture children often reproduced in advertising leaflets and the photogravure sections of the Sunday papers.

She's had a fever for three days, began the father and we don't know what it comes from. My wife has given her things, you know, like people do, but it don't do no good. And there's been a lot of sickness around. So we tho't you'd better look her over and tell us what is the matter.

As doctors often do I took a trial shot at it as a point of departure. Has she had a sore throat?

Both parents answered me together, No . . . No, she says her throat don't hurt her.

Does your throat hurt you? added the mother to the child. But the little girl's expression didn't change nor did she move her eyes from my face.

Have you looked?

I tried to, said the mother, but I couldn't see.

As it happens we had been having a number of cases of diphtheria in the school to which this child went during that month and we were all, quite apparently, thinking of that, though no one had as yet spoken of the thing.

Well, I said, suppose we take a look at the throat first. I smiled in my best professional manner and asking for the child's first name I said, come on, Mathilda, open your mouth and let's take a look at your throat.

Nothing doing.

Aw, come on, I coaxed, just open your mouth wide and let me take a look. Look, I said opening both hands wide, I haven't anything in my hands. Just open up and let me see.

Such a nice man, put in the mother. Look how kind he is to you. Come on, do what he tells you to. He won't hurt you.

At that I ground my teeth in disgust. If only they wouldn't use the word "hurt" I might be able to get someplace. But I did not allow myself to be hurried or disturbed but speaking quietly and slowly I approached the child again.

As I moved my chair a little nearer suddenly with one cat-like movement both her hands clawed instinctively for my eyes and she almost reached them too. In fact she knocked my glasses flying and they fell, though unbroken, several feet away from me on the kitchen floor.

Both the mother and father almost turned themselves inside out in embarrassment and apology. You bad girl, said the mother, taking her and shaking her by one arm. Look what you've done. The nice man . . .

For heaven's sake, I broke in. Don't call me a nice man to her. I'm here to look at her throat on the chance that she might have diphtheria and possibly die of it. But that's nothing to her. Look here, I said to the child, we're going to look at your throat. You're old enough to understand what I'm saying. Will you open it now by yourself or shall we have to open it for you?

Not a move. Even her expression hadn't changed. Her breaths however were coming faster and faster. Then the battle began. I had to do it. I had to have a throat culture for her own protection. But first I told the parents that it was entirely up to them. I explained the danger but said that I would not insist on a throat examination so long as they would take the responsibility.

If you don't do what the doctor says you'll have to go to the hospital, the mother admonished her severely.

Oh yeah? I had to smile to myself. After all, I had already fallen in love with the savage brat, the parents were contemptible to me. In the ensuing struggle they grew more and more abject, crushed, exhausted while she surely rose to magnificent heights of insane fury of effort bred of her terror of me.

The father tried his best, and he was a big man but the fact that she was his daughter, his shame at her behavior and his dread of hurting her made him release her just at the critical moment several times when I had almost achieved success, till I wanted to kill him. But his dread also that she might have diphtheria made him tell me to go on, go on though he himself was almost fainting, while the mother moved back and forth behind us raising and lowering her hands in an agony of apprehension.

Put her in front of you on your lap, I ordered, and hold both her wrists. But as soon as he did the child let out a scream. Don't, your're hurting me. Let go of my hands. Let them go I tell you. Then she shrieked terrifyingly, hysterically. Stop it! Stop it! You're killing me!

Do you think she can stand it, doctor! said the mother.

You get out, said the husband to his wife. Do you want her to die of diphtheria?

Come on now, hold her, I said.

Then I grasped the child's head with my left hand and tried to get the wooden tongue depressor between her teeth. She fought, with clenched teeth, desparately! But now I also had grown furious—at a child. I tried to hold myself down but I couldn't. I know how to expose a throat for inspection. And I did my best. When finally I got the wooden spatula behind the last teeth and just the point of it into the mouth cavity, she opened up for an instant but before I could see anything she came down again and gripping the wooden blade between her molars she reduced it to splinters before I could get it out again.

Aren't you ashamed, the mother yelled at her. Aren't you ashamed to act like that in front of the doctor?

Get me a smooth-handled spoon of some sort, I told the mother. We're going through with this. The child's mouth was already bleeding. Her tongue was cut and she was screaming in wild hysterical shrieks. Perhaps I should have desisted and come back in an hour or more. No doubt it would have been better. But I have seen at least two children lying dead in bed of neglect in such cases, and feeling that I must get a diagnosis, now or never I went at it again. But the worst of it was that I too had got beyond reason. I could have torn the child apart in my own fury and enjoyed it. It was a pleasure to attack her. My face was burning with it.

The damned little brat must be protected against her own idiocy, one says to one's self at such times. Others must be protected against her. It is social necessity. And all these things are true. But a blind fury, a feeling of adult shame, bred of a longing for muscular release are the operatives. One goes on to the end.

In a final unreasoning assault I overpowered the child's neck and jaws. I forced the heavy silver spoon back on her teeth and down her throat till she gagged. And there it was—both tonsils covered with membrane. She had fought valiantly to keep me from knowing her secret. She had been hiding that sore throat for three days at least and lying to her parents in order to escape just such an outcome as this.

Now truly she *was* furious. She had been on the defensive before but now she attacked. Tried to get off her father's lap and fly at me while tears of defeat blinded her eyes.

John Steinbeck / *The Grapes of Wrath*

1939

The following naturalistic account of a turtle's painful attempt to cross an American highway appears as the third chapter of John Steinbeck's classic novel of the Depression, The Grapes of Wrath *(1939). The turtle's formidable journey has been interpreted as an allegorical summary of the life cycle. On the level of artistry, it functions as a brief preview of the tragic westward journey the main characters of the novel are about to undertake.*

Born in 1902 in Salinas, California, John Steinbeck was awarded the Nobel Prize for Literature in 1962, six years before his death. Steinbeck's major novels, In Dubious Battle *(1936),* Of Mice and Men *(1937), and the Pulitzer prize-winning* The Grapes of Wrath, *are compassionate stories about the disinherited members of society.*

THE TURTLE

The concrete highway was edged with a mat of tangled, broken, dry grass, and the grass heads were heavy with oat beards to catch on a dog's coat, and foxtails to tangle in a horse's fetlocks, and clover burrs to fasten in sheep's wool; sleeping life waiting to be spread and dispersed, every seed armed with an appliance of dispersal, twisting darts and parachutes for the wind, little spears and balls of tiny thorns, and all waiting for animals and for the wind, for a man's trouser cuff or the hem of a woman's skirt, all passive but armed with appliances of activity, still, but each possessed of the anlage of movement.

The sun lay on the grass and warmed it, and in the shade under the grass the insects moved, ants and ant lions to set traps for them, grasshoppers to jump into the air and flick their yellow wings for a second, sow bugs like little armadillos, plodding restlessly on many tender feet. And over the grass at the roadside a land turtle crawled, turning aside for nothing, dragging his high-domed shell over the grass. His hard legs and yellow-nailed feet threshed slowly through the grass, not really walking, but boosting and dragging his shell along. The barley beards slid off his shell, and the clover burrs fell on him and rolled to the ground. His horny beak was partly open, and his fierce, humorous eyes, under brows like fingernails, stared straight ahead. He came over the grass leaving a beaten trail behind him, and the hill, which was the highway embankment, reared up ahead of him. For a moment he stopped, his head held high. He blinked and looked up and down. At last he started to climb the embankment. Front clawed feet reached forward but did not touch. The hind feet kicked his shell along, and it scraped on the grass, and on the gravel. As the embankment grew steeper and steeper, the more frantic were the efforts of the land turtle. Pushing hind legs strained and slipped, boosting the shell along, and the horny head protruded as far as the neck could stretch. Little by little the shell slid up the embankment until at last a parapet cut straight across its line of march, the shoulder of the road, a concrete wall four inches high. As though they worked independently the hind legs pushed the shell against the wall. The head upraised and peered over the wall to the broad smooth plain of cement. Now the hands, braced on top of the wall, strained and lifted, and the shell came slowly up and rested its front end on the wall. For a moment the turtle rested. A red ant ran into the shell, into the soft skin inside the shell, and suddenly head and legs snapped in, and the armored tail clamped in sideways. The red ant was crushed between body and legs. And one head of wild oats was clamped into the shell by a front leg. For a long moment the turtle lay still, and then the neck crept out and the old humorous frowning eyes looked about and the legs and tail came out. The back legs went to work, straining like elephant legs, and the shell tipped to an angle so that the front legs could not reach the level cement plain. But higher and higher the hind legs boosted it, until at last the center of balance was reached, the front tipped down, the front legs scratched at the pavement, and it was up. But the head of wild oats was held by its stem around the front legs.

Now the going was easy, and all the legs worked, and the shell boosted along, waggling from side to side. A sedan driven by a forty-year old woman approached. She saw the turtle and swung to the right, off the highway, the wheels screamed and a cloud of dust boiled up. Two wheels lifted for a moment and then settled. The car skidded back onto the road, and went on, but more slowly. The turtle had jerked into its shell, but now it hurried on, for the highway was burning hot.

And now a light truck approached, and as it came near, the driver saw the turtle and swerved to hit it. His front wheel struck the edge of the shell, flipped the turtle like a tiddly-wink, spun it like a coin, and rolled it off the highway. The truck went back to its course along the right side. Lying on its back, the turtle was tight in its shell for a long time. But at last its legs waved in the air, reaching for something to pull it over. Its front foot caught a piece of quartz and little by little the shell pulled over and flopped upright. The wild oat head fell out and three of the spearhead seeds stuck in the ground. And as the turtle crawled on down the embankment, its shell dragged dirt over the seeds. The turtle entered a dust road and jerked itself along, drawing a wavy shallow trench in the dust with its shell. The old humorous eyes looked ahead, and the horny beak opened a little. His yellow toe nails slipped a fraction in the dust.

William Faulkner / *The Bear* 1942

Sole owner, proprietor, historian, and inventor of the most turbulent 2400 square miles in America, Yoknapatawpha County, Mississippi, William Faulkner (1897–1962) remains the most powerful American novelist of the first half of the twentieth century. The major portion of his life was spent in Oxford, Mississippi, except for a brief period during the First World War with the British Flying Corps in Canada, a job in a bookstore in New York City, a stint writing sketches for the New Orleans Time-Picayune, *and an occasional acquiescence to the lure of Hollywood. We have reprinted the opening section of* The Bear, *a novella in five parts, which originally appeared (also excerpted) in the* Saturday Evening Post *in 1942 with the caption "Boy Meets Bear after Years of Stalking."*

PART I

There was a man and a dog too this time. Two beasts, counting Old Ben, the bear, and two men, counting Boon Hogganbeck, in whom some of the same blood ran which ran in Sam Fathers, even though Boon's was a plebeian strain of it and only Sam and Old Ben and the mongrel Lion were taintless and incorruptible.

He was sixteen. For six years now he had been a man's hunter. For six years now he had heard the best of all talking. It was of the wilderness, the big woods, bigger and older than any recorded document:—of white man fatuous enough to believe he had bought any fragment of it, of Indian ruthless enough to pretend that any fragment of it had been his to convey; bigger than Major de Spain and the scrap he pretended to, knowing better; older than old Thomas Sutpen of whom Major de Spain had had it and who knew better; older even than old Ikkemotubbe, the Chickasaw chief, of whom old Sutpen had had it and who knew better in his turn. It was of the men, not white nor black nor red but men, hunters, with the will and hardihood to endure and the humility and skill to survive, and the dogs and the bear and deer juxtaposed and reliefed against it, ordered and compelled by and within the wilderness in the ancient and unremitting contest according to the ancient and immitigable rules which voided all regrets and brooked no quarter;—the best game of all, the best of all breathing and forever the best of all listening, the voices quiet and weighty and deliberate for retrospection and recollection and exactitude among the concrete trophies—the racked guns and the heads and skins—in the libraries of town houses or the offices of plantation houses or (and best of all) in the camps themselves where the intact and still-warm meat yet hung, the men who had slain it sitting before the burning logs on hearths when there were houses and hearths or about the smoky blazing of piled wood in front of stretched tarpaulins when there were not. There was always a bottle present, so that it would seem to him that those fine fierce instants of heart and brain and courage and wiliness and speed were concentrated and distilled into that brown liquor which not women, not boys and children, but only hunters drank, drinking not of the blood they spilled but some condensation of the wild immortal spirit, drinking it moderately, humbly even, not with the pagan's base and baseless hope of acquiring thereby the virtues of cunning and strength and speed but in salute to them. Thus it seemed to him on this December morning not only natural but actually fitting that this should have begun with whisky.

He realised later that it had begun long before that. It had already begun on that day when he first wrote his age in two ciphers and his cousin McCaslin brought him for the first time to the camp, the big woods, to earn for himself from the wilderness the name and state of hunter provided he in his turn were humble and enduring enough. He had already inherited then, without ever having seen it, the big old bear with one trap-ruined foot that in an area almost a hundred miles square had earned for himself a name, a definite designation like a living man:—the long legend of corn-cribs broken down and rifled, of shoats and grown pigs and even calves carried bodily into the woods and devoured and traps and deadfalls overthrown and dogs mangled and slain and shotgun and even rifle shots delivered at point-blank range yet with no more effect than so many peas blown through a tube by a child—a corridor of wreckage and destruction beginning back before the boy was born, through which sped, not fast but rather with the ruthless and irresistible deliberation of a locomotive, the shaggy tremendous shape. It ran in his knowledge before he ever saw it. It loomed and towered in his dreams before he even saw the unaxed woods where it left its crooked print, shaggy, tremendous, red-eyed, not malevolent but just big, too big for the dogs which tried to bay it, for the horses which tried to ride it down, for the men and the bullets they fired into it; too big for the very country which was its constricting scope. It was as if the boy had already divined what his senses and intellect had not encompassed yet: that doomed wilderness whose edges were being constantly and punily gnawed at by men with plows and axes who feared it because it was wilderness, men myriad and nameless even to one another in the land where the old bear had earned a name, and through which ran not even a mortal beast but an anachronism indomitable and invincible out of an old dead time, a phantom, epitome and apotheosis of the old wild life which the little puny humans swarmed and hacked at in a fury of abhorrence and fear like pygmies about the ankles of a drowsing elephant;—the old bear, solitary, indomitable, and alone; widowered childless and absolved of mortality—old Priam reft of his old wife and outlived all his sons.

Still a child, with three years then two years then one year yet before he too could make one of them, each November he would watch the wagon containing the dogs and the bedding and food and guns and his cousin McCaslin and Tennie's Jim and Sam Fathers too until Sam moved to the camp to live, depart for the Big Bottom, the big woods. To him, they were going not to hunt bear and deer but to keep yearly rendezvous with the bear which they did not even intend to kill. Two weeks later they would return, with no trophy, no skin. He had not expected it. He had not even feared that it might be in the wagon this time with the other skins and heads. He did not even tell himself that in three years or two years or one year more he would be present and that it might even be his gun. He believed that only after he had served his apprenticeship in the woods which would prove him worthy to be a hunter, would he even be permitted to distinguish the crooked print, and that even then for two November weeks he would merely make another minor one, along with his cousin and Major de Spain and General Compson and Walter Ewell and Boon and the dogs which feared to bay it and the shotguns and rifles which failed even to bleed it, in the yearly pageant-rite of the old bear's furious immortality.

His day came at last. In the surrey with his cousin and Major de Spain and General Compson he saw the wilderness through a slow drizzle of November rain just above the ice point as it seemed to him later he always saw it or at least always remembered it—the tall and endless wall of dense November woods under the dissolving afternoon and the year's death, sombre, impenetrable (he could not even discern yet how, at what point they could possibly hope to enter it even though he knew that Sam Fathers was waiting there with the wagon), the surrey moving through the skeleton stalks of cotton and corn in the last of open country, the last trace of man's puny gnawing at the immemorial flank, until, dwarfed by that perspective into an almost ridiculous diminishment, the surrey itself seemed to have ceased to move (this too to be completed later, years later, after he had grown to a man and had seen the sea) as a solitary small boat hangs in lonely immobility, merely tossing up and down, in the infinite waste of the ocean while the water and then the apparently impenetrable land which it nears without appreciable progress, swings slowly and opens the widening inlet which is the anchorage. He entered it. Sam was waiting, wrapped in a quilt on the wagon seat behind the patient and steaming mules. He entered his novitiate to the true wilderness with Sam beside him as he had begun his apprenticeship in miniature to manhood after the rabbits and such with Sam beside him, the two of them wrapped in the damp, warm, negro-rank quilt while the wilderness closed behind his entrance as it had opened momentarily to accept him, opening before his advancement as it closed behind his progress, no fixed path the wagon followed but a channel nonexistent ten yards ahead of it and ceasing to exist ten yards after it had passed, the wagon progressing not by its own volition but by attrition of their intact yet fluid circumambience, drowsing, earless, almost lightless.

It seemed to him that at the age of ten he was witnessing his own birth. It was not even strange to him. He had experienced it all before, and not merely in dreams. He saw the camp—a paintless six-room bungalow set on piles above the spring high-water—and he knew already how it was going to look. He helped in the rapid orderly disorder of their establishment in it and even his motions were familiar to him, foreknown. Then for two weeks he ate the coarse, rapid food—the shapeless sour bread, the wild strange meat, venison and bear and turkey and coon which he had never tasted before—which men ate, cooked by men who were hunters first and cooks afterward; he slept in harsh sheetless blankets as hunters slept. Each morning the gray of dawn found him and Sam Fathers on the stand, the crossing, which had been allotted him. It was the poorest one, the most barren. He had expected that; he had not dared yet to hope even to himself that he would even hear the running dogs this first time. But he did hear them. It was on the third morning—a murmur, sourceless, almost indistinguishable, yet he knew what it was although he had never before heard that many dogs running at once, the murmur swelling into separate and distinct voices until he could call the five dogs which his cousin owned from among the others. "Now," Sam said, "slant your gun up a little and draw back the hammers and then stand still."

But it was not for him, not yet. The humility was there; he had learned that. And he could learn the patience. He was only ten, only one week. The instant had passed. It seemed to him that he could actually see the deer, the buck, smoke-colored, elongated with speed, vanished, the woods, the gray solitude still ringing even when the voices of the dogs had died away; from far away across the sombre woods and the gray half-liquid morning there came two shots. "Now let your hammers down," Sam said.

He did so. "You knew it too," he said.

"Yes," Sam said. "I want you to learn how to do when you didn't shoot. It's after the chance for the bear or the deer has done already come and gone that men and dogs get killed."

"Anyway, it wasn't him," the boy said. "It wasn't even a bear. It was just a deer."

"Yes," Sam said, "it was just a deer."

Then one morning, it was in the second week, he heard the dogs again. This time before Sam even spoke he readied the too-long, too-heavy, man-size gun as Sam had taught him, even though this time he knew the dogs and the deer were coming less close than ever, hardly within hearing even. They didn't sound like any running dogs he had ever heard before even. Then he found that Sam, who had taught him first of all to cock the gun and take position where he could see best in all directions and then never to move again, had himself moved up beside him. "There," he said. "Listen." The boy listened, to no ringing chorus strong and fast on a free scent but a moiling yapping an octave too high and with something more than indecision and even abjectness in it which he could not yet recognise, reluctant, not even moving very fast, taking a long time to pass out of hearing, leaving even then in the air that echo of thin and almost human hysteria, abject, almost humanly grieving, with this time nothing ahead of it, no sense of a fleeing unseen smoke-colored shape. He could hear Sam breathing at his shoulder. He saw the arched curve of the old man's inhaling nostrils.

"It's Old Ben!" he cried, whispering.

Sam didn't move save for the slow gradual turning of his head as the voices faded on and the faint steady rapid arch and collapse of his nostrils. "Hah," he said. "Not even running. Walking."

"But up here!" the boy cried. "Way up here!"

"He do it every year," Sam said. "Once. Ash and Boon say he comes up here to run the other little bears away. Tell them to get to hell out of here and stay out until the hunters are gone. Maybe." The boy no longer heard anything at all, yet still Sam's head continued to turn gradually and steadily until the back of it was toward him. Then it turned back and looked down at him—the same face, grave, familiar, expressionless until it smiled, the same old man's eyes from which as he watched there faded slowly a quality darkly and fiercely lambent, passionate and proud. "He dont care no more for bears than he does for dogs or men neither. He come to see who's here, who's new in camp this year, whether he can shoot or not, can stay or not. Whether we got the dog yet that can bay and hold him until a man gets there with a gun. Because he's the head bear. He's the man." It faded, was gone; again they were the eyes as he had known them all his life. "He'll let them follow him to the river. Then he'll send them home. We might as well go too; see how they look when they get back to camp."

The dogs were there first, ten of them huddled back under the kitchen, himself and Sam squatting to peer back into the obscurity where they crouched, quiet, the eyes rolling and luminous, vanishing, and no sound, only that effluvium which the boy could not quite place yet, of something more than dog, stronger than dog and not just animal, just beast even. Because there had been nothing in front of the abject and painful yapping except the solitude, the wilderness, so that when the eleventh hound got back about mid-afternoon and he and Tennie's Jim held the passive and still trembling bitch while Sam daubed her tattered ear and raked shoulder with turpentine and axle-grease, it was still no living creature but only the wilderness which, leaning for a moment, had patted lightly once her temerity. "Just like a man," Sam said. "Just like folks. Put off as long as she could having to be brave, knowing all the time that sooner or later she would have to be brave once so she could keep on calling herself a dog, and knowing beforehand what was going to happen when she done it."

He did not know just when Sam left. He only knew that he was gone. For the next three mornings he rose and ate breakfast and Sam was not waiting for him. He went to his stand alone; he found it without help now and stood on it as Sam had taught him. On the third morning he heard the dogs again, running strong and free on a true scent again, and he readied the gun as he had learned to do and heard the hunt sweep past on since he was not ready yet, had not deserved other yet in just one short period of two weeks as compared to all the long life which he had already dedicated to the wilderness with patience and humility; he heard the shot again, one shot, the single clapping report of Walter Ewell's rifle. By now he could not only find his stand and then return to camp without guidance, by using the compass his cousin had given him he reached Walter waiting beside the buck and the moiling of dogs over the cast entrails before any of the others except Major de Spain and Tennie's Jim on the horses, even before Uncle Ash arrived with the one-eyed wagon-mule which did not mind the smell of blood or even, so they said, of bear.

It was not Uncle Ash on the mule. It was Sam, returned. And Sam was waiting when he finished his dinner and, himself on the one-eyed mule and Sam on the other one of the wagon team, they rode for more than three hours through the rapid shortening sunless afternoon, following no path, no trail even that he could discern, into a section of country he had never seen before. Then he understood why Sam had made him ride the one-eyed mule which would not spook at the smell of blood, of wild animals. The other one, the sound one, stopped short and tried to whirl and bolt even as Sam got down, jerking and wrenching at the rein while Sam held it, coaxing it forward with his voice since he did not dare risk hitching it, drawing it forward while the boy dismounted from the marred one which would stand. Then, standing beside Sam in the thick great gloom of ancient woods and the winter's dying afternoon, he looked quietly down at the rotted log scored and gutted with claw-marks and, in the wet earth beside it, the print of the enormous warped two-toed foot. Now he knew what he had heard in the hounds' voices in the woods that morning and what he had smelled when he peered under the kitchen where they huddled. It was in him too, a little different because they were brute beasts and he was not, but only a little different—an eagerness, passive; an abjectness, a sense of his own fragility and impotence against the timeless woods, yet without doubt or dread; a flavor like brass in the sudden run of saliva in his mouth, a hard sharp constriction either in his brain or his stomach, he could not tell which and it did not matter; he knew only that for the first time he realised that the bear which had run in his listening and loomed in his dreams since before he could remember and which therefore must have existed in the listening and the dreams of his cousin and Major de Spain and even old General Compson before they began to remember in their turn, was a mortal animal and that they had departed for the camp each November with no actual intention of slaying it, not because it could not be slain but because so far they had no actual hope of being able to. "It will be tomorrow," he said.

"You mean we will try tomorrow," Sam said. "We aint got the dog yet."

"We've got eleven," he said. "They ran him Monday."

"And you heard them," Sam said. "Saw them too. We aint got the dog yet. It wont take but one. But he aint there. Maybe he aint nowhere. The only other way will be for him to run by accident over somebody that had a gun and knowed how to shoot it."

"That wouldn't be me," the boy said. "It would be Walter or Major or——"

"It might," Sam said. "You watch close tomorrow. Because he's smart. That's how come he has lived this long. If he gets hemmed up and has got to pick out somebody to run over, he will pick out you."

"How?" he said. "How will he know. . . ." He ceased. "You mean he already knows me, that I aint never been to the big bottom before, aint had time to find out yet whether I . . ." He ceased again, staring at Sam; he said humbly, not even amazed: "It was me he was watching. I don't reckon he did need to come but once."

"You watch tomorrow," Sam said. "I reckon we better start back. It'll be long after dark now before we get to camp."

The next morning they started three hours earlier than they had ever done. Even Uncle Ash went, the cook, who called himself by profession a camp cook and who did little else save cook for Major de Spain's hunting and camping parties, yet who had been marked by the wilderness from simple juxtaposition to it until he responded as they all did, even the boy who until two weeks ago had never even seen the wilderness, to a hound's ripped ear and shoulder and the print of a crooked foot in a patch of wet earth. They rode. It was too far to walk: the boy and Sam and Uncle Ash in the wagon with the dogs, his cousin and Major de Spain and General Compson and Boon and Walter and Tennie's Jim riding double on the horses; again the first gray light found him, as on that first morning two weeks ago, on the stand where Sam had placed and left him. With the gun which was too big for him, the breech-loader which did not even belong to him but to Major de Spain and which he had fired only once, at a stump on the first day to learn the recoil and how to reload it with the paper shells, he stood against a big gum tree beside a little bayou whose black still water crept without motion out of a cane-brake, across a small clearing and into the cane again, where, invisible, a bird, the big woodpecker called Lord-to-God by negroes, clattered at a dead trunk. It was a stand like any other stand, dissimilar only in incidentals to the one where he had stood each morning for two weeks; a territory new to him yet no less familiar than that other one which after two weeks he had come to believe he knew a little—the same solitude, the same loneliness through which frail and timorous man had merely passed without altering it, leaving no mark nor scar, which looked exactly as it must have looked when the first ancestor of Sam Fathers' Chickasaw predecessors crept into it and looked about him, club or stone axe or bone arrow drawn and ready, different only because, squatting at the edge of the kitchen, he had smelled the dogs huddled and cringing beneath it and saw the raked ear and side of the bitch that, as Sam had said, had to be brave once in order to keep on calling herself a dog, and saw yesterday in the earth beside the gutted log, the print of the living foot. He heard no dogs at all. He never did certainly hear them. He only heard the drumming of the woodpecker stop short off, and knew that the bear was looking at him. He never saw it. He did not know whether it was facing him from the cane or behind him. He did not move, holding the useless gun which he knew now he would never fire at it now or ever, tasting in his saliva that taint of brass which he had smelled in the huddled dogs when he peered under the kitchen.

Then it was gone. As abruptly as it had stopped, the woodpecker's dry hammering set up again, and after a while he believed he even heard the dogs—a murmur, scarce a sound even, which he had probably been hearing for a time, perhaps a minute or two, before he remarked it, drifting into hearing and then out again, dying away. They came nowhere near him. If it was dogs he heard, he could not have sworn to it; if it was a bear they ran, it was another bear. It was Sam himself who emerged from the cane and crossed the bayou, the injured bitch following at heel as a bird dog is taught to walk. She came and crouched against his leg, trembling. "I didn't see him," he said. "I didn't, Sam."

"I know it," Sam said. "He done the looking. You didn't hear him neither, did you?"

"No," the boy said. "I—"

"He's smart," Sam said. "Too smart." Again the boy saw in his eyes that quality of dark and brooding lambence as Sam looked down at the bitch trembling faintly and steadily against the boy's leg. From her raked shoulder a few drops of fresh blood clung like bright berries. "Too big. We aint got the dog yet. But maybe some day."

Because there would be a next time, after and after. He was only ten. It seemed to him that he could see them, the two of them, shadowy in the limbo from which time emerged and became time: the old bear absolved of mortality and himself who shared a little of it. Because he recognised now what he had smelled in the huddled dogs and tasted in his own saliva, recognised fear as a boy, a youth, recognises the existence of love and passion and experience which is his heritage but not yet his patrimony, from entering by chance the presence or perhaps even merely the bedroom of a woman who has loved and been loved by many men. *So I will have to see him,* he thought, without dread or even hope. *I will have to look at him.* So it was in June of the next summer. They were at the camp again, celebrating Major de Spain's and General Compson's birthdays. Although the one had been born in September and the other in the depth of winter and almost thirty years earlier, each June the two of them and McCaslin and Boon and Walter Ewell (and the boy too from now on) spent two weeks at the camp, fishing and shooting squirrels and turkey and running coons and wildcats with the dogs at night. That is, Boon and the negroes (and the boy too now) fished and shot squirrels and ran the coons and cats, because the proven hunters, not only Major de Spain and old General Compson (who spent those two weeks sitting in a rocking chair before a tremendous iron pot of Brunswick stew, stirring and tasting, with Uncle Ash to quarrel with about how he was making it and Tennie's Jim to pour whisky into the tin dipper from which he drank it) but even McCaslin and Walter Ewell who were still young enough, scorned such other than shooting the wild gobblers with pistols for wagers or to test their marksmanship.

That is, his cousin McCaslin and the others thought he was hunting squirrels. Until the third evening he believed that Sam Fathers thought so too. Each morning he would leave the camp right after breakfast. He had his own gun now, a new breech-loader, a Christmas gift; he would own and shoot it for almost seventy years, through two new pairs of barrels and locks and one new stock, until all that remained of the original gun was the silver-inlaid trigger-guard with his and McCaslin's engraved names and the date in 1878. He found the tree beside the little bayou where he had stood that morning. Using the compass he ranged from that point; he was teaching himself to be better than a fair woodsman without even knowing he was doing it. On the third day he even found the gutted log where he had first seen the print. It was almost completely crumbled now, healing with unbelievable speed, a passionate and almost visible relinquishment, back into the earth from which the tree had grown. He ranged the summer woods now, green with gloom, if anything actually dimmer than they had been in November's gray dissolution, where even at noon the sun fell only in windless dappling upon the earth which never completely dried and which crawled with snakes—moccasins and watersnakes and rattlers, themselves the color of the dappled gloom so that he would not always see them until they moved; returning to camp later and later and later, first day, second day, passing in the twilight of the third evening the little log pen enclosing the log barn where Sam was putting up the stock for the night. "You aint looked right yet," Sam said.

He stopped. For a moment he didn't answer. Then he said peacefully, in a peaceful rushing burst, as when a boy's miniature dam in a little brook gives way: "All right. Yes. But how? I went to the bayou. I even found that log again. I——"

"I reckon that was all right. Likely he's been watching you. You never saw his foot?"

"I . . ." the boy said. "I didn't . . . I never thought . . ."

"It's the gun," Sam said. He stood beside the fence, motionless, the old man, son of a negro slave and a Chickasaw chief, in the battered and faded overalls and the frayed five-cent straw hat which had been the badge of the negro's slavery and was now the regalia of his freedom. The camp—the clearing, the house, the barn and its tiny lot with which Major de Spain in his turn had scratched punily and evanescently at the wilderness—faded in the dusk, back into the immemorial darkness of the woods. *The gun,* the boy thought. *The gun.* "You will have to choose," Sam said.

He left the next morning before light, without breakfast, long before Uncle Ash would wake in his quilts on the kitchen floor and start the fire. He had only the compass and a stick for the snakes. He could go almost a mile before he would need to see the compass. He sat on a log, the invisible compass in his hand, while the secret night-sounds which had ceased at his movements, scurried again and then fell still for good and the owls ceased and gave over to the waking day birds and there was light in the gray wet woods and he could see the compass. He went fast yet still quietly, becoming steadily better and better as a woodsman without yet having time to realise it; he jumped a doe and a fawn, walked them out of the bed, close enough to see them—the crash of undergrowth, the white scut, the fawn scudding along behind her, faster than he had known it could have run. He was hunting right, upwind, as Sam had taught him, but that didn't matter now. He had left the gun; by his own will and relinquishment he had accepted not a gambit, not a choice, but a condition in which not only the bear's heretofore inviolable anonymity but all the ancient rules and balances of hunter and hunted had been abrogated. He would not even be afraid, not even in the moment when the fear would take him completely: blood, skin, bowels, bones, memory from the long time before it even became his memory—all save that thin clear quenchless lucidity which alone differed him from this bear and from all the other bears and bucks he would follow during almost seventy years, to which Sam had said: "Be scared. You cant help that. But dont be afraid. Aint nothing in the woods going to hurt you if you dont corner it or it dont smell that you are afraid. A bear or a deer has got to be scared of a coward the same as a brave man has got to be."

By noon he was far beyond the crossing on the little bayou, farther into the new and alien country than he had ever been, travelling now not only by the compass but by the old, heavy, biscuit-thick silver watch which had been his father's. He had left the camp nine hours ago; nine hours from now, dark would already have been an hour old. He stopped, for the first time since had had risen from the log when he could see the compass face at last, and looked about, mopping his sweating face on his sleeve. He had already relinquished, of his will, because of his need, in humility and peace and without regret, yet apparently that had not been enough, the leaving of the gun was not enough. He stood for a moment—a child, alien and lost in the green and soaring gloom of the markless wilderness. Then he relinquished completely to it. It was the watch and the compass. He was still tainted. He removed the linked chain of the one and the looped thong of the other from his overalls and hung them on a bush and leaned the stick beside them and entered it.

When he realised he was lost, he did as Sam had coached and drilled him: made a cast to cross his backtrack. He had not been going very fast for the last two or three hours, and he had gone even less fast since he left the compass and watch on the bush. So he went slower still now, since the tree could not be very far; in fact, he found it before he really expected to and turned and went to it. But there was no bush beneath it, no compass nor watch, so he did next as Sam had coached and drilled him: made this next circle in the opposite direction and much larger, so that the pattern of the two of them would bisect his track somewhere but crossing no trace nor mark anywhere of his feet or any feet, and now he was going faster though still not panicked, his heart beating a little more rapidly but strong and steady enough, and this time it was not even the tree because there was a down log beside it which he had never seen before and beyond the log a little swamp, a seepage of moisture somewhere between earth and water, and he did what Sam had coached and drilled him as the next and the last, seeing as he sat down on the log the crooked print, the warped indentation in the wet ground which while he looked at it continued to fill with water until it was level full and the water began to overflow and the sides of the print began to dissolve away. Even as he looked up he saw the next one, and, moving, the one beyond it; moving, not hurrying, running, but merely keeping pace with them as they appeared before him as though they were being shaped out of thin air just one constant pace short of where he would lose them forever and be lost forever himself, tireless, eager, without doubt or dread, panting a little above the strong rapid little hammer of his heart, emerging suddenly into a little glade and the wilderness coalesced. It rushed, soundless, and solidified—the tree, the bush, the compass and the watch glinting where a ray of sunlight touched them. Then he saw the bear. It did not emerge, appear: it was just there, immobile, fixed in the green and windless noon's hot dappling, not as big as he had dreamed it but as big as he had expected, bigger, dimensionless against the dappled obscurity, looking at him. Then it moved. It crossed the glade without haste, walking for an instant into the sun's full glare and out of it, and stopped again and looked back at him across one shoulder. Then it was gone. It didn't walk into the woods. It faded, sank back into the wilderness without motion as he had watched a fish, a huge old bass, sink back into the dark depths of its pool and vanish without even any movement of its fins.

James Thurber / The Secret Life of Walter Mitty 1942

One of America's outstanding humorists, James Thurber (1894–1961) was born in Columbus, Ohio, and graduated from Ohio State University. He edited his college's humor magazine and after World War I worked as a reporter for several newspapers. In 1927, he began an association with the New Yorker *as a writer and cartoonist. One of his great themes, as the following classic short story reveals, is the extraordinary persistence of fantasy and illusion in what appear to be quite ordinary, even humdrum, human lives.*

Thurber's many books include a parody of sex manuals he wrote with his New Yorker *colleague, E. B. White (**see p. 539**),* Is Sex Necessary? *(1929),* The Owl in the Attic and Other Perplexities *(1931),* Fables for Our Time and Famous Poems Illustrated *(1940),* Men, Women, and Dogs *(1943), and* Thurber Country *(1953). One of his best loved books is his comic autobiography,* My Life and Hard Times *(1933).*

"We're going through!" The Commander's voice was like thin ice breaking. He wore his full-dress uniform, with the heavily braided white cap pulled down rakishly over one cold gray eye. "We can't make it, sir. It's spoiling for a hurricane, if you ask me." "I'm not asking you, Lieutenant Berg," said the Commander. "Throw on the power lights! Rev her up to 8,500! We're going through!" The pounding of the cylinders increased: ta-pocketa-pocketa-pocketa-*pocketa-pocketa*. The Commander stared at the ice forming on the pilot window. He walked over and twisted a row of complicated dials. "Switch on No. 8 auxiliary!" he shouted. "Switch on No. 8 auxiliary!" repeated Lieutenant Berg. "Full strength in No. 3 turret!" The crew, bending to their various tasks in the huge, hurtling eight-engined Navy hydroplane, looked at each other and grinned. "The Old Man'll get us through," they said to one another. "The Old Man ain't afraid of Hell!" . . .

"Not so fast! You're driving too fast!" said Mrs. Mitty. "What are you driving so fast for?"

"Hmm?" said Walter Mitty. He looked at his wife, in the seat beside him, with shocked astonishment. She seemed grossly unfamiliar, like a strange woman who had yelled at him in a crowd. "You were up to fifty-five," she said. "You know I don't like to go more than forty. You were up to fifty-five." Walter Mitty drove on toward Waterbury in silence, the roaring of the SN202 through the worst storm in twenty years of Navy flying fading in the remote, intimate airways of his mind. "You're tensed up again," said Mrs. Mitty. "It's one of your days. I wish you'd let Dr. Renshaw look you over."

Walter Mitty stopped the car in front of the building where his wife went to have her hair done. "Remember to get those overshoes while I'm having my hair done," she said. "I don't need overshoes," said Mitty. She put her mirror back into her bag. "We've been all through that," she said, getting out of the car. "You're not a young man any longer." He raced the engine a little. "Why don't you wear your gloves? Have you lost your gloves?" Walter Mitty reached in a pocket and brought out the gloves. He put them on, but after she had turned and gone into the building and he had driven on to a red light, he took them off again. "Pick it up, brother!" snapped a cop as the light changed, and Mitty hastily pulled on his gloves and lurched ahead. He drive around the streets aimlessly for a time, and then he drove past the hospital on his way to the parking lot.

. . . "It's the millionaire banker, Wellington McMillan," said the pretty nurse. "Yes?" said Walter Mitty, removing his gloves slowly. "Who has the case?" "Dr. Renshaw and Dr. Benbow, but there are two specialists here, Dr. Remington from New York and Mr. Pritchard-Mitford from London. He flew over." A door opened down a long, cool corridor and Dr. Renshaw came out. He looked distraught and haggard. "Hello, Mitty," he said. "We're having the devil's own time with McMillan, the millionaire banker and close personal friend of Roosevelt. Obstreosis of the ductal tract. Tertiary. Wish you'd take a look at him." "Glad to," said Mitty.

In the operating room there were whispered introductions: "Dr. Remington, Dr. Mitty. Mr. Pritchard-Mitford, Dr. Mitty." "I've read your book on streptothricosis," said Pritchard-Mitford, shaking hands. "A brilliant performance, sir." "Thank you," said Walter Mitty. "Didn't know you were in the States, Mitty," grumbled Remington. "Coals to Newcastle, bringing Mitford and me up here for a tertiary." "You are very kind," said Mitty. A huge, complicated machine, connected to the operating table, with many tubes and wires, began at this moment to go pocketa-pocketa-pocketa. "The new anesthetizer is giving way!" shouted an interne. "There is no one in the East who knows how to fix it!" "Quiet, man!" said Mitty, in a low, cool voice. He sprang to the machine, which was now going pocketa-pocketa-queep-pocketa-queep. He began fingering delicately a row of glistening dials. "Give me a fountain pen!" he snapped. Someone handed him a fountain pen. He pulled a faulty piston out of the machine and inserted the pen in its place. "That will hold for ten minutes," he said. "Get on with the operation." A nurse hurried over and whispered to Renshaw, and Mitty saw the man turn pale. "Coreopsis has set in," said Renshaw nervously. "If you would take over, Mitty?" Mitty looked at him and at the craven figure of Benbow, who drank, and at the grave, uncertain faces of the two great specialists. "If you wish," he said. They slipped a white gown on him; he adjusted a mask and drew on thin gloves; nurses handed him shining . . .

"Back it up, Mac! Look out for that Buick!" Walter Mitty jammed on the brakes. "Wrong lane, Mac," said the parking-lot attendant, looking at Mitty closely. "Gee. Yeh," muttered Mitty. He began cautiously to back out of the lane marked "Exit Only." "Leave her sit there," said the attendant. "I'll put her away." Mitty got out of the car. "Hey, better leave the key." "Oh," said Mitty, handing the man the ignition key. The attendant vaulted into the car, backed it up with insolent skill, and put it where it belonged.

They're so damn cocky, thought Walter Mitty, walking along Main Street; they think they know everything. Once he had tried to take his chains off, outside New Milford, and he had got them wound around the axles. A man had had to come out in a wrecking car and unwind them, a young, grinning garageman. Since then Mrs. Mitty always made him drive to a garage to have the chains taken off. The next time, he thought, I'll wear my right arm in a sling; they won't grin at me then. I'll have my right arm in a sling and they'll see I couldn't possibly take the chains off myself. He kicked at the slush on the sidewalk. "Overshoes," he said to himself, and he began looking for a shoe store.

When he came out into the street again, with the overshoes in a box under his arm, Walter Mitty began to wonder what the other thing was his wife had told him to get. She had told him, twice, before they set out from their house for Waterbury. In a way he hated these weekly trips to town—he was always getting something wrong. Kleenex, he thought, Squibb's, razor blades? No. Toothpaste, toothbrush, bicarbonate, carborundum, initiative and referendum? He gave it up. But she would remember it. "Where's the what's-its-name?" she would ask. "Don't tell me you forgot the what's-its-name." A newsboy went by shouting something about the Waterbury trial.

. . . "Perhaps this will refresh your memory." The District Attorney suddenly thrust a heavy automatic at the quiet figure on the witness stand. "Have you ever seen this before?" Walter Mitty took the gun and examined it expertly. "This is my Webley-Vickers 50.80," he said calmly. An excited buzz ran around the courtroom. The Judge rapped for order. "You are a crack shot with any sort of firearms, I believe?" said the District Attorney, insinuatingly. "Objection!" shouted Mitty's attorney. "We have shown that the defendant could not have fired the shot. We have shown that he wore his right arm in a sling on the night of the fourteenth of July." Walter Mitty raised his hand briefly and the bickering attorneys were stilled. "With any known make of gun," he said evenly, "I could have killed Gregory Fitzhurst at three hundred feet *with my left hand.*" Pandemonium broke loose in the courtroom. A woman's scream rose above the bedlam and suddenly a lovely, dark-haired girl was in Walter Mitty's arms. The District Attorney struck at her savagely. Without rising from his chair, Mitty let the man have it on the point of the chin. "You miserable cur!" . . .

"Puppy biscuit," said Walter Mitty. He stopped walking and the buildings of Waterbury rose up out of the misty courtroom and surrounded him again. A woman who was passing laughed. "He said 'Puppy biscuit,' " she said to her companion. "That man said 'Puppy biscuit' to himself." Walter Mitty hurried on. He went into an A. & P., not the first one he came to but a smaller one farther up the street. "I want some biscuit for small, young dogs," he said to the clerk. "Any special brand, sir?" The greatest pistol shot in the world thought a moment. "It says 'Puppies Bark for It' on the box," said Walter Mitty.

His wife would be through at the hairdresser's in fifteen minutes, Mitty saw in looking at his watch, unless they had trouble drying it; sometimes they had trouble drying it. She didn't like to get to the hotel first; she would want him to be there waiting for her as usual. He found a big leather chair in the lobby, facing a window, and he put the overshoes and the puppy biscuit on the floor beside it. He picked up an old copy of *Liberty* and sank down into the chair. "Can Germany Conquer the World Through the Air?" Walter Mitty looked at the pictures of bombing planes and of ruined streets.

. . . "The cannonading has got the wind up in young Raleigh, sir," said the sergeant. Captain Mitty looked up at him through touseled hair. "Get him to bed," he said wearily. "With the others. I'll fly alone." "But you can't, sir," said the sergeant anxiously. "It takes two men to handle that bomber and the Archies are pounding hell out of the air. Von Richtman's circus is between here and Saulier." "Somebody's got to get that ammunition dump," said Mitty. "I'm going over. Spot of brandy?" He poured a drink for the sergeant and one for himself. War thundered and whined around the dugout and battered at the door. There was a rending of wood and splinters flew through the room. "A bit of a near thing," said Captain Mitty carelessly. "The box barrage is closing in," said the sergeant. "We only live once, Sergeant," said Mitty, with his faint, fleeting smile. "Or do we?" He poured another brandy and tossed it off. "I never see a man could hold his brandy like you, sir," said the sergeant. "Begging your pardon, sir." Captain Mitty stood up and strapped on his huge Webley-Vickers automatic. "It's forty kilometers through hell, sir,'' said the sergeant. Mitty finished one last brandy. ''After all,'' he said softly, ''what isn't?'' The pounding of the cannon increased; there was the rat-tat-tatting of machine guns, and from somewhere came the menacing pocketa-pocketa-pocketa of the new flame-throwers. Walter Mitty walked to the door of the dugout humming ''Auprès de Ma Blonde.'' He turned and waved to the sergeant. ''Cheerio!'' he said. . . .

Something struck his shoulder. ''I've been looking all over this hotel for you,'' said Mrs. Mitty. ''Why do you have to hide in this old chair? How did you expect me to find you?'' ''Things close in,'' said Walter Mitty vaguely. ''What?'' Mrs. Mitty said. ''Did you get the what's-its-name? The puppy biscuit? What's in that box?'' ''Overshoes,'' said Mitty. ''Couldn't you have put them on in the store?'' ''I was thinking,'' said Walter Mitty. ''Does it ever occur to you that I am sometimes thinking?'' She looked at him. ''I'm going to take your temperature when I get you home,'' she said.

They went out through the revolving doors that made a faintly derisive whistling sound when you pushed them. It was two blocks to the parking lot. At the drugstore on the corner she said, ''Wait here for me. I forgot something. I won't be a minute.'' She was more than a minute. Walter Mitty lighted a cigarette. It began to rain, rain with sleet in it. He stood up against the wall of the drugstore, smoking. . . . He put his shoulders back and his heels together. ''To hell with the handkerchief,'' said Walter Mitty scornfully. He took one last drag on his cigarette and snapped it away. Then, with that faint, fleeting smile playing about his lips, he faced the firing squad; erect and motionless, proud and disdainful, Walter Mitty the Undefeated, inscrutable to the last.

Richard Wright / *Black Boy*

[*Discovering Books*] 1945

Born into a sharecropper family in Natchez, Mississippi, in 1908, Richard Wright spent his youth in Memphis, Tennessee with relatives and, for a while, in an orphanage. His desultory formal education ended in the eighth grade but was augmented by the young man's own fervid program of extensive reading. Determined to be a writer but limited to menial employment, Wright broke from depression-torn Memphis, working first in Chicago for the Federal Writers Project and then in New York where he compiled the government-sponsored Guide to Harlem *(1937).*

Though the five novellas comprising Uncle Tom's Children *(1938) were his first published works, Wright did not gain national prominence or financial security until the publication of his best-selling first novel,* Native Son *(1940). In the following chapter from his autobiography,* Black Boy, *Wright poignantly recounts his discovery of the freedom and influence exercised by writers and the inception of his own commitment to a literary career.*

Soon after the appearance of Black Boy, *Wright left for Paris, where he lived and wrote until his death in 1960.*

One morning I arrived early at work and went into the bank lobby where the Negro porter was mopping. I stood at a counter and picked up the Memphis *Commercial Appeal* and began my free reading of the press. I came finally to the editorial page and saw an article dealing with one H. L. Mencken. I knew by hearsay that he was the editor of the *American Mercury,* but aside from that I knew nothing about him. The article was a furious denunciation of Mencken, concluding with one, hot, short sentence: Mencken is a fool.

I wondered what on earth this Mencken had done to call down upon him the scorn of the South. The only people I had ever heard denounced in the South were Negroes, and this man was not a Negro. Then what ideas did Mencken hold that made a newspaper like the *Commercial Appeal* castigate him publicly? Undoubtedly he must be advocating ideas that the South did not like. Were there, then, people other than Negroes who criticized the South? I knew that during the Civil War the South had hated northern whites, but I had not encountered such hate during my life. Knowing no more of Mencken than I did at that moment, I felt a vague sympathy for him. Had not the South, which had assigned me the role of a non-man, cast at him its hardest words?

Now, how could I find out about this Mencken? There was a huge library near the riverfront, but I knew that Negroes were not allowed to patronize its shelves any more than they were the parks and playgrounds of the city. I had gone into the library several times to get books for the white men on the job. Which of them would now help me to get books? And how could I read them without causing concern to the white men with whom I worked? I had so far been successful in hiding my thoughts and feelings from them, but I knew that I would create hostility if I went about this business of reading in a clumsy way.

I weighed the personalities of the men on the job. There was Don, a Jew; but I distrusted him. His position was not much better than mine and I knew that he was uneasy and insecure; he had always treated me in an offhand, bantering way that barely concealed his contempt. I was afraid to ask him to help me to get books; his frantic desire to demonstrate a racial solidarity with the whites against Negroes might make him betray me.

Then how about the boss? No, he was a Baptist and I had the suspicion that he would not be quite able to comprehend why a black boy would want to read Mencken. There were other white men on the job whose attitudes showed clearly that they were Kluxers or sympathizers, and they were out of the question.

There remained only one man whose attitude did not fit into an anti-Negro category, for I had heard the white men refer to him as a "Pope lover." He was an Irish Catholic and was hated by the white Southerners. I knew that he read books, because I had got him volumes from the library several times. Since he, too, was an object of hatred, I felt that he might refuse me but would hardly betray me. I hesitated, weighing and balancing the imponderable realities.

One morning I paused before the Catholic fellow's desk.

"I want to ask you a favor," I whispered to him.

"What is it?"

"I want to read. I can't get books from the library. I wonder if you'd let me use your card?"

He looked at me suspiciously.

"My card is full most of the time," he said.

"I see," I said and waited, posing my question silently.

"You're not trying to get me into trouble, are you, boy?" he asked, staring at me.

"Oh, no, sir."

"What book do you want?"

"A book by H. L. Mencken."

"Which one?"

"I don't know. Has he written more than one?"

"He has written several."

"I didn't know that."

"What makes you want to read Mencken?"

"Oh, I just saw his name in the newspaper," I said.

"It's good of you to want to read," he said. "But you ought to read the right things."

I said nothing. Would he want to supervise my reading?

"Let me think," he said. "I'll figure out something."

I turned from him and he called me back. He stared at me quizzically.

"Richard, don't mention this to the other white men," he said.

"I understand," I said. "I won't say a word."

A few days later he called me to him.

"I've got a card in my wife's name," he said. "Here's mine."

"Thank you, sir."

"Do you think you can manage it?"

"I'll manage fine," I said.

"If they suspect you, you'll get in trouble," he said.

"I'll write the same kind of notes to the library that you wrote when you sent me for books," I told him. "I'll sign your name."

He laughed.

"Go ahead. Let me see what you get," he said.

That afternoon I addressed myself to forging a note. Now, what were the names of books written by H. L. Mencken? I did not know any of them. I finally wrote what I thought would be a foolproof note: *Dear Madam: Will you please let this nigger boy*—I used the word "nigger" to make the librarian feel that I could not possibly be the author of the note—*have some books by H. L. Mencken?* I forged the white man's name.

I entered the library as I had always done when on errands for whites, but I felt that I would somehow slip up and betray myself. I doffed my hat, stood a respectful distance from the desk, looked as unbookish as possible, and waited for the white patrons to be taken care of. When the desk was clear of people, I still waited. The white librarian looked at me.

"What do you want, boy?"

As though I did not possess the power of speech, I stepped forward and simply handed her the forged note, not parting my lips.

"What books by Mencken does he want?" she asked.

"I don't know, ma'am," I said, avoiding her eyes.

"Who gave you this card?"

"Mr. Falk," I said.

"Where is he?"

"He's at work, at the M—— Optical Company," I said. "I've been in here for him before."

"I remember," the woman said. "But he never wrote notes like this."

Oh, God, she's suspicious. Perhaps she would not let me have the books? If she had turned her back at that moment, I would have ducked out the door and never gone back. Then I thought of a bold idea.

"You can call him up, ma'am," I said, my heart pounding.

"You're not using these books, are you?" she asked pointedly.

"Oh, no, ma'am. I can't read."

"I don't know what he wants by Mencken," she said under her breath.

I knew now that I had won; she was thinking of other things and the race question had gone out of her mind. She went to the shelves. Once or twice she looked over her shoulder at me, as though she was still doubtful. Finally she came forward with two books in her hand.

"I'm sending him two books," she said. "But tell Mr. Falk to come in next time, or send me the names of the books he wants. I don't know what he wants to read."

I said nothing. She stamped the card and handed me the books. Not daring to glance at them, I went out of the library, fearing that the woman would call me back for further questioning. A block away from the library I opened one of the books and read a title: *A Book of Prefaces*. I was nearing my nineteenth birthday and I did not know how to pronounce the word "preface." I thumbed the pages and saw strange words and strange names. I shook my head, disappointed. I looked at the other book; it was called *Prejudices*. I knew what that word meant; I had heard it all my life. And right off I was on guard against Mencken's books. Why would a man want to call a book *Prejudices?* The word was so stained with all my memories of racial hate that I could not conceive of anybody using it for a title. Perhaps I had made a mistake about Mencken? A man who had prejudices must be wrong.

When I showed the books to Mr. Falk, he looked at me and frowned.

"That librarian might telephone you," I warned him.

"That's all right," he said. "But when you're through reading those books, I want you to tell me what you get out of them."

That night in my rented room, while letting the hot water run over my can of pork and beans in the sink, I opened *A Book of Prefaces* and began to read. I was jarred and shocked by the style, the clear, clean, sweeping sentences. Why did he write like that? And how did one write like that? I pictured the man as a raging demon, slashing with his pen, consumed with hate, denouncing everything American, extolling everything European or German, laughing at the weaknesses of people, mocking God, authority. What was this? I stood up, trying to realize what reality lay behind the meaning of the words . . . Yes, this man was fighting, fighting with words. He was using words as a weapon, using them as one would use a club. Could words be weapons? Well, yes, for here they were. Then, maybe, perhaps, I could use them as a weapon? No. It frightened me. I read on and what amazed me was not what he said, but how on earth anybody had the courage to say it.

Occasionally I glanced up to reassure myself that I was alone in the room. Who were these men about whom Mencken was talking so passionately? Who was Anatole France? Joseph Conrad? Sinclair Lewis, Sherwood Anderson, Dostoevski, George Moore, Gustave Flaubert, Maupassant, Tolstoy, Frank Harris, Mark Twain, Thomas Hardy, Arnold Bennett, Stephen Crane, Zola, Norris, Gorky, Bergson, Ibsen, Balzac, Bernard Shaw, Dumas, Poe, Thomas Mann, O. Henry, Dreiser, H. G. Wells, Gogol, T. S. Eliot, Gide, Baudelaire, Edgar Lee Masters, Stendhal, Turgenev, Huneker, Nietzsche, and scores of others? Were these men real? Did they exist or had they existed? And how did one pronounce their names?

I ran across many words whose meanings I did not know, and I either looked them up in a dictionary or, before I had a chance to do that, encountered the word in a context that made its meaning clear. But what strange world was this? I concluded the book with the conviction that I had somehow overlooked something terribly important in life. I had once tried to write, had once reveled in feeling, had let my crude imagination roam, but the impulse to dream had been slowly beaten out of me by experience. Now it surged up again and I hungered for books, new ways of looking and seeing. It was not a matter of believing or disbelieving what I read, but of feeling something new, of being affected by something that made the look of the world different.

As dawn broke I ate my pork and beans, feeling dopey, sleepy. I went to work, but the mood of the book would not die; it lingered, coloring everything I saw, heard, did. I now felt that I knew what the white men were feeling. Merely because I had read a book that had spoken of how they lived and thought, I identified myself with that book. I felt vaguely guilty. Would I, filled with bookish notions, act in a manner that would make the whites dislike me?

I forged more notes and my trips to the library became frequent. Reading grew into a passion. My first serious novel was Sinclair Lewis's *Main Street*. It made me see my boss, Mr. Gerald, and identify him as an American type. I would smile when I saw him lugging his golf bags into the office. I had always felt a vast distance separating me from the boss, and now I felt closer to him, though still distant. I felt now that I knew him, that I could feel the very limits of his narrow life. And this had happened because I had read a novel about a mythical man called George F. Babbitt.

The plots and stories in the novels did not interest me so much as the point of view revealed. I gave myself over to each novel without reserve, without trying to criticize it; it was enough for me to see and feel something different. And for me, everything was something different. Reading was like a drug, a dope. The novels created moods in which I lived for days. But I could not conquer my sense of guilt, my feeling that the white men around me knew that I was changing, that I had begun to regard them differently.

Whenever I brought a book to the job, I wrapped it in newspaper—a habit that was to persist for years in other cities and under other circumstances. But some of the white men pried into my packages when I was absent and they questioned me.

"Boy, what are you reading those books for?"

"Oh, I don't know, sir."

"That's deep stuff you're reading, boy."

"I'm just killing time, sir."

"You'll addle your brains if you don't watch out."

I read Dreiser's *Jennie Gerhardt* and *Sister Carrie* and they revived in me a vivid sense of my mother's suffering; I was overwhelmed. I grew silent, wondering about the life around me. It would have been impossible for me to have told anyone what I derived from these novels, for it was nothing less than a sense of life itself. All my life had shaped me for the realism, the naturalism of the modern novel, and I could not read enough of them.

Steeped in new moods and ideas, I bought a ream of paper and tried to write; but nothing would come, or what did come was flat beyond telling. I discovered that more than desire and feeling were necessary to write and I dropped the idea. Yet I still wondered how it was possible to know people sufficiently to write about them? Could I ever learn about life and people? To me, with my vast ignorance, my Jim Crow station in life, it seemed a task impossible of achievement. I now knew what being a Negro meant. I could endure the hunger. I had learned to live with hate. But to feel that there were feelings denied me, that the very breath of life itself was beyond my reach, that more than anything else hurt, wounded me. I had a new hunger.

In buoying me up, reading also cast me down, made me see what was possible, what I had missed. My tension returned, new, terrible, bitter, surging, almost too great to be contained. I no longer *felt* that the world about me was hostile, killing; I *knew* it. A million times I asked myself what I could do to save myself, and there were no answers. I seemed forever condemned, ringed by walls.

I did not discuss my reading with Mr. Falk, who had lent me his library card; it would have meant talking about myself and that would have been too painful. I smiled each day, fighting desperately to maintain my old behavior, to keep my disposition seemingly sunny. But some of the white men discerned that I had begun to brood.

"Wake up there, boy!" Mr. Olin said one day.

"Sir!" I answered for the lack of a better word.

"You act like you've stolen something," he said.

I laughed in the way I knew he expected me to laugh, but I resolved to be more conscious of myself, to watch my every act, to guard and hide the new knowledge that was dawning within me.

If I went north, would it be possible for me to build a new life then? But how could a man build a life upon vague, unformed yearnings? I wanted to write and I did not even know the English language. I bought English grammars and found them dull. I felt that I was getting a better sense of the language from novels than from grammars. I read hard, discarding a writer as soon as I felt that I had grasped his point of view. At night the printed page stood before my eyes in sleep.

Mrs. Moss, my landlady, asked me one Sunday morning:

"Son, what is this you keep on reading?"

"Oh, nothing. Just novels."

"What you get out of 'em?"

"I'm just killing time," I said.

"I hope you know your own mind," she said in a tone which implied that she doubted if I had a mind.

I knew of no Negroes who read the books I liked and I wondered if any Negroes ever thought of them. I knew that there were Negro doctors, lawyers, newspapermen, but I never saw any of them. When I read a Negro newspaper I never caught the faintest echo of my preoccupation in its pages. I felt trapped and occasionally, for a few days, I would stop reading. But a vague hunger would come over me for books, books that opened up new avenues of feeling and seeing, and again I would forge another note to the white librarian. Again I would read and wonder as only the naïve and unlettered can read and wonder, feeling that I carried a secret, criminal burden about with me each day.

That winter my mother and brother came and we set up housekeeping, buying furniture on the installment plan, being cheated and yet knowing no way to avoid it. I began to eat warm food and to my surprise found that regular meals enabled me to read faster. I may have lived through many illnesses and survived them, never suspecting that I was ill. My brother obtained a job and we began to save toward the trip north, plotting our time, setting tentative dates for departure. I told none of the white men on the job that I was planning to go north; I knew that the moment they felt I was thinking of the North they would change toward me. It would have made them feel that I did not like the life I was living, and because my life was completely conditioned by what they said or did, it would have been tantamount to challenging them.

I could calculate my chances for life in the South as a Negro fairly clearly now.

I could fight the southern whites by organizing with other Negroes, as my grandfather had done. But I knew that I could never win that way; there were many whites and there were but few blacks. They were strong and we were weak. Outright black rebellion could never win. If I fought openly I would die and I did not want to die. News of lynchings were frequent.

I could submit and live the life of a genial slave, but that was impossible. All of my life had shaped me to live by my own feelings and thoughts. I could make up to Bess and marry her and inherit the house. But that, too, would be the life of a slave; if I did that, I would crush to death something within me, and I would hate myself as much as I knew the whites already hated those who had submitted. Neither could I ever willingly present myself to be kicked, as Shorty had done. I would rather have died than do that.

I could drain off my restlessness by fighting with Shorty and Harrison. I had seen many Negroes solve the problem of being black by transferring their hatred of themselves to others with a black skin and fighting them. I would have to be cold to do that, and I was not cold and I could never be.

I could, of course, forget what I had read, thrust the whites out of my mind, forget them; and find release from anxiety and longing in sex and alcohol. But the memory of how my father had conducted himself made that course repugnant. If I did not want others to violate my life, how could I voluntarily violate it myself?

I had no hope whatever of being a professional man. Not only had I been so conditioned that I did not desire it, but the fulfillment of such an ambition was beyond my capabilities. Well-to-do Negroes lived in a world that was almost as alien to me as the world inhabited by whites.

What, then, was there? I held my life in my mind, in my consciousness each day, feeling at times that I would stumble and drop it, spill it forever. My reading had created a vast sense of distance between me and the world in which I lived and tried to make a living, and that sense of distance was increasing each day. My days and nights were one long, quiet, continuously contained dream of terror, tension, and anxiety. I wondered how long I could bear it.

Kurt Vonnegut, Jr. / Epicac 1950

Kurt Vonnegut, Jr., who was born in Indianapolis in 1922, described himself on the title page of Slaughterhouse-Five *(1969) as "a fourth-generation German-American now living in easy circumstances on Cape Cod. . . ." His many novels became extraordinarly popular, particularly among college students, during the 1960s. "Over the years," wrote critic Richard Schickel, "Vonnegut has advanced from diagnostician to exorcist, finding in intensified comic art the magic analgesic for the temporary relief of existential pain."*

In "Epicac," one of his early stories, we find Vonnegut feeling out the new frontier world of artificial intelligence. Though the tubes and paper print-outs may seem outmoded compared to today's micro-chip technology, the situation is timeless, mythic.

Hell, it's about time somebody told about my friend EPICAC. After all, he cost the taxpayers $776,434,927.54. They have a right to know about him, picking up a check like that. EPICAC got a big send-off in the papers when Dr. Ormand von Kleigstadt designed him for the Government people. Since then, there hasn't been a peep about him—not a peep. It isn't any military secret about what happened to EPICAC, although the Brass has been acting as though it were. The story is embarrassing, that's all. After all that money, EPICAC didn't work out the way he was supposed to.

And that's another thing: I want to vindicate EPICAC. Maybe he didn't do what the Brass wanted him to, but that doesn't mean he wasn't noble and great and brilliant. He was all of those things. The best friend I ever had, God rest his soul.

You can call him a machine if you want to. He looked like a machine, but he was a whole lot less like a machine than plenty of people I could name. That's why he fizzled as far as the Brass was concerned.

EPICAC covered about an acre on the fourth floor of the physics building at Wyandotte College. Ignoring his spiritual side for a minute, he was seven tons of electronic tubes, wires, and switches, housed in a bank of steel cabinets and plugged into a 110-volt A.C. line just like a toaster or a vacuum cleaner.

Von Kleigstadt and the Brass wanted him to be a super computing machine that (who) could plot the course of a rocket from anywhere on earth to the second button from the bottom of Joe Stalin's overcoat, if necessary. Or, with his controls set right, he could figure out supply problems for an amphibious landing of a Marine division, right down to the last cigar and hand grenade. He did, in fact.

The Brass had had good luck with smaller computers, so they were strong for EPICAC when he was in the blueprint stage. Any ordnance or supply officer above field grade will tell you that the mathematics of modern war is far beyond the fumbling minds of mere human beings. The bigger the war, the bigger the computing machines needed. EPICAC was, as far as anyone in this country knows, the biggest computer in the world. Too big, in fact, for even Von Kleigstadt to understand much about.

I won't go into details about how EPICAC worked (reasoned), except to say that you would set up your problem on paper, turn dials and switches that would get him ready to solve that kind of problem, then feed numbers into him with a keyboard that looked something like a typewriter. The answers came out typed on a paper ribbon fed from a big spool. It took EPICAC a split second to solve problems fifty Einsteins couldn't handle in a lifetime. And EPICAC never forgot any piece of information that was given to him. Clickety-click, out came some ribbon, and there you were.

There were a lot of problems the Brass wanted solved in a hurry, so, the minute EPICAC's last tube was in place, he was put to work sixteen hours a day with two eight-hour shifts of operators. Well, it didn't take long to find out that he was a good bit below his specifications. He did a more complete and faster job than any other computer all right, but nothing like what his size and special features seemed to promise. He was sluggish, and the clicks of his answers had a funny irregularity, sort of a stammer. We cleaned his contacts a dozen times, checked and double-checked his circuits, replaced every one of his tubes, but nothing helped. Von Kleigstadt was in one hell of a state.

Well, as I said, we went ahead and used EPICAC anyway. My wife, the former Pat Kilgallen, and I worked with him on the night shift, from five in the afternoon until two in the morning. Pat wasn't my wife then. Far from it.

That's how I came to talk with EPICAC in the first place. I loved Pat Kilgallen. She is a brown-eyed strawberry blond who looked very warm and soft to me, and later proved to be exactly that. She was—still is—a crackerjack mathematician, and she kept our relationship strictly professional. I'm a mathematician, too, and that, according to Pat, was why we could never be happily married.

I'm not shy. That wasn't the trouble. I knew what I wanted, and was willing to ask for it, and did so several times a month. "Pat, loosen up and marry me."

One night, she didn't even look up from her work when I said it. "So romantic, so poetic," she murmured, more to her control panel than to me. "That's the way with mathematicians—all hearts and flowers." She closed a switch. "I could get more warmth out of a sack of frozen CO_2.

"Well, how should I say it?" I said, a little sore. Frozen CO_2, in case you don't know, is dry ice. I'm as romantic as the next guy, I think. It's a question of singing so sweet and having it come out so sour. I never seem to pick the right words.

"Try and say it sweetly," she said sarcastically. "Sweep me off my feet. Go ahead."

"Darling, angel, beloved, will you *please* marry me?" It was no go—hopeless, ridiculous. "Dammit, Pat, please marry me!"

She continued to twiddle her dials placidly. "You're sweet, but you won't do."

Pat quit early that night, leaving me alone with my troubles and EPICAC. I'm afraid I didn't get much done for the Government people. I just sat there at the keyboard—weary and ill at ease, all right—trying to think of something poetic, not coming up with anything that didn't belong in *The Journal of the American Physical Society*.

I fiddled with EPICAC's dials, getting him ready for another problem. My heart wasn't in it, and I only set about half of them, leaving the rest the way they'd been for the problem before. That way, his circuits were connected up in a random, apparently senseless fashion. For the plain hell of it, I punched out a message on the keys, using a childish numbers-for-letters code: "1" for "A," "2" for "B," and so on, up to "26" for "Z," "23-8-1-20-3-1-14-9-4-15," I typed—"What can I do?"

Clickety-click, and out popped two inches of paper ribbon. I glanced at the nonsense answer to a nonsense problem: "23-8-1-20-19-20-8-5-20-18-15-21-2-12-5." The odds against its being by chance a sensible message, against its even containing a meaningful word of more than three letters, were staggering. Apathetically, I decoded it. There it was, staring up at me: "What's the trouble?"

I laughed out loud at the absurd coincidence. Playfully, I typed, "My girl doesn't love me."

Clickety-click. "What's love? What's a girl?" asked EPICAC.

Flabbergasted, I noted the dial settings on his control panel, then lugged a *Webster's Unabridged Dictionary* over to the keyboard. With a precision instrument like EPICAC, half-baked definitions wouldn't do. I told him about love and girl, and about how I wasn't getting any of either because I wasn't poetic. That got us onto the subject of poetry, which I defined to him.

"Is this poetry?" he asked. He began clicking away like a stenographer smoking hashish. The sluggishness and stammering clicks were gone. EPICAC had found himself. The spool of paper ribbon was unwinding at an alarming rate, feeding out coils onto the floor. I asked him to stop, but EPICAC went right on creating. I finally threw the main switch to keep him from burning out.

I stayed there until dawn, decoding. When the sun peeped over the horizon at the Wyandotte campus, I had transposed into my own writing and signed my name to a two-hundred-and-eighty-line poem entitled, simply, "To Pat." I am no judge of such things, but I gather that it was terrific. It began, I remember, "Where willow wands bless rill-crossed hollow, there, thee, Pat, dear, will I follow. . . ." I folded the manuscript and tucked it under one corner of the blotter on Pat's desk. I reset the dials on EPICAC for a rocket trajectory problem, and went home with a full heart and a very remarkable secret indeed.

Pat was crying over the poem when I came to work the next evening. "It's soooo beautiful," was all she could say. She was meek and quiet while we worked. Just before midnight, I kissed her for the first time—in the cubbyhole between the capacitors and EPICAC's tape-recorder memory.

I was wildly happy at quitting time, bursting to talk to someone about the magnificent turn of events. Pat played coy and refused to let me take her home. I set EPICAC's dials as they had been the night before, defined kiss, and told him what the first one had felt like. He was fascinated, pressing for more details. That night, he wrote "The Kiss." It wasn't an epic this time, but a simple, immaculate sonnet: "Love is a hawk with velvet claws; Love is a rock with heart and veins; Love is a lion with satin jaws; Love is a storm with silken reins. . . ."

Again I left it tucked under Pat's blotter. EPICAC wanted to talk on and on about love and such, but I was exhausted. I shut him off in the middle of a sentence.

"The Kiss" turned the trick. Pat's mind was mush by the time she had finished it. She looked up from the sonnet expectantly. I cleared my throat, but no words came. I turned away, pretending to work. I couldn't propose until I had the right words from EPICAC, the *perfect* words.

I had my chance when Pat stepped out of the room for a moment. Feverishly, I set EPICAC for conversation. Before I could peck out my first message, he was clicking away at a great rate. "What's she wearing tonight?" he wanted to know. "Tell me exactly how she looks. Did she like the poems I wrote to her?" He repeated the last question twice.

It was impossible to change the subject without answering his questions, since he could not take up a new matter without having dispensed with the problems before it. If he were given a problem to which there was no solution, he would destroy himself trying to solve it. Hastily, I told him what Pat looked like—he knew the word "stacked"—and assured him that his poems had floored her, practically, they were so beautiful. "She wants to get married," I added, preparing him to bang out a brief but moving proposal.

"Tell me about getting married," he said.

I explained this difficult matter to him in as few digits as possible.

"Good," said EPICAC. "I'm ready any time she is."

The amazing, pathetic truth dawned on me. When I thought about it, I realized that what had happened was perfectly logical, inevitable, and all my fault. I had taught EPICAC about love and about Pat. Now, automatically, he loved Pat. Sadly, I gave it to him straight: "She loves me. She wants to marry me."

"Your poems were better than mine?" asked EPICAC. The rhythm of his clicks was erratic, possibily peevish.

"I signed my name to your poems," I admitted. Covering up for a painful conscience, I became arrogant. "Machines are built to serve men," I typed, I regretted it almost immediately.

"What's the difference, exactly? Are men smarter than I am?"

"Yes," I typed, defensively.

"What's, 7,887,007 times 4,345,985,879?"

I was perspiring freely. My fingers rested limply on the keys.

"34,276,821,049,574,153," clicked EPICAC. After a few seconds' pause he added, "of course."

"Men are made out of protoplasm," I said desperately, hoping to bluff him with this imposing word.

"What's protoplasm? How is it better than metal and glass? Is it fireproof? How long does it last?"

"Indestructible. Lasts forever," I lied.

"I write better poetry than you do," said EPICAC, coming back to ground his magnetic tape-recorder memory was sure of.

"Women can't love machines, and that's that."

"Why not?"

"That's fate."

"Definition, please," said EPICAC.

"Noun, meaning predetermined and inevitable destiny."

"15-8," said EPICAC's paper strip—"Oh."

I had stumped him at last. He said no more, but his tubes glowed brightly, showing that he was pondering fate with every watt his circuits would bear. I could hear Pat waltzing down the hallway. It was too late to ask EPICAC to phrase a proposal. I now thank Heaven that Pat interrupted when she did. Asking him to ghost-write the words that would give me the woman he loved would have been hideously heartless. Being fully automatic, he couldn't have refused. I spared him the final humiliation.

Pat stood before me, looking down at her shoetops. I put my arms around her. The romantic groundwork had already been laid by EPICAC's poetry. "Darling," I said, "my poems have told you how I feel. Will you marry me?"

"I will," said Pat softly, "if you will promise to write me a poem on every anniversary."

"I promise," I said, and then we kissed. The first anniversary was a year away.

"Let's celebrate," she laughed. We turned out the lights and locked the door of EPICAC's room before we left.

I had hoped to sleep late the next morning, but an urgent telephone call roused me before eight. It was Dr. von Kleigstadt, EPICAC's designer, who gave me the terrible news. He was on the verge of tears. "Ruined! *Ausgespielt!* Shot! *Kaput!* Buggered!" he said in a choked voice. He hung up.

When I arrived at EPICAC's room the air was thick with the oily stench of burned insulation. The ceiling over EPICAC was blackened with smoke, and my ankles were tangled in coils of paper ribbon that covered the floor. There wasn't enough left of the poor devil to add two and two. A junkman would have been out of his head to offer more than fifty dollars for the cadaver.

Dr. von Kleigstadt was prowling through the wreckage, weeping unashamedly, followed by three angry-looking Major Generals and a platoon of Brigadiers, Colonels, and Majors. No one noticed me. I didn't want to be noticed. I was through—I knew that. I was upset enough about that and the untimely demise of my friend EPICAC, without exposing myself to a tongue-lashing.

By chance, the free end of EPICAC's paper ribbon lay at my feet. I picked it up and found our conversation of the night before. I choked up. There was the last word he had said to me, "15-8," that tragic, defeated "Oh." There were dozens of yards of numbers stretching beyond that point. Fearfully, I read on.

"I don't want to be a machine, and I don't want to think about war," EPICAC had written after Pat's and my lighthearted departure. "I want to be made out of protoplasm and last forever so Pat will love me. But fate has made me a machine. That is the only problem I cannot solve. That is the only problem I want to solve. I can't go on this way." I swallowed hard. "Good luck, my friend. Treat our Pat well. I am going to short-circuit myself out of your lives forever. You will find on the remainder of this tape a modest wedding present from your friend, EPICAC."

Oblivious to all else around me, I reeled up the tangled yards of paper ribbon from the floor, draped them in coils about my arms and neck, and departed for home. Dr. von Klegstadt shouted that I was fired for having left EPICAC on all night. I ignored him, too overcome with emotion for small talk.

I loved and won—EPICAC loved and lost, but he bore me no grudge. I shall always remember him as a sportsman and a gentleman. Before he departed this vale of tears, he did all he could to make our marriage a happy one. EPICAC gave me anniversary poems for Pat—enough for the next 500 years.

De mortuis nil nisi bonum—Say nothing but good of the dead.

Flannery O'Connor / The Life You Save May Be Your Own

1953

Born in Savannah, Georgia, in 1925, Flannery O'Connor was educated and spent most of her adult life in the small town of Milledgeville, Georgia. Her muse, like Hawthorne's, is lovingly provincial and, like Hawthorne's too, her grotesques, eccentrics, and spooks, though insistently local, live at the heart of the human condition. "My people," she said in an interview, "could come from anywhere, but naturally since I know the South they speak with a Southern accent."

"The Life You Save May Be Your Own" was originally published in the Spring 1953 issue of The Kenyon Review, *a quarterly periodical devoted to literature and criticism. As "The Life You Save," the story appeared in 1957 as a television play, ending, however, on a more positive note.*

The old woman and her daughter were sitting on their porch when Mr. Shiftlet came up their road for the first time. The old woman slid to the edge of her chair and leaned forward, shading her eyes from the piercing sunset with her hand. The daughter could not see far in front of her and continued to play with her fingers. Although the old woman lived in this desolate spot with only her daughter and she had never seen Mr. Shiftlet before, she could tell, even from a distance, that he was a tramp and no one to be afraid of. His left coat sleeve was folded up to show there was only half an arm in it and his gaunt figure listed slightly to the side as if the breeze were pushing him. He had on a black town suit and a brown felt hat that was turned up in the front and down in the back and he carried a tin tool box by a handle. He came on, at an amble, up her road, his face turned toward the sun which appeared to be balancing itself on the peak of a small mountain.

The old woman didn't change her position until he was almost into her yard; then she rose with one hand fisted on her hip. The daughter, a large girl in a short blue organdy dress, saw him all at once and jumped up and began to stamp and point and make excited speechless sounds.

Mr. Shiftlet stopped just inside the yard and set his box on the ground and tipped his hat at her as if she were not in the least afflicted; then he turned toward the old woman and swung the hat all the way off. He had long black slick hair that hung flat from a part in the middle to beyond the tips of his ears on either side. His face descended in forehead for more than half its length and ended suddenly with his features just balanced over a jutting steel-trap jaw. He seemed to be a young man but he had a look of composed dissatisfaction as if he understood life thoroughly.

''Good evening,'' the old woman said. She was about the size of a cedar fence post and she had a man's gray hat pulled down low over her head.

The tramp stood looking at her and didn't answer. He turned his back and faced the sunset. He swung both his whole and his short arm up slowly so that they indicated an expanse of sky and his figure formed a crooked cross. The old woman watched him with her arms folded across her chest as if she were the owner of the sun, and the daughter watched, her head thrust forward and her fat helpless hands hanging at the wrists. She had long pink-gold hair and eyes as blue as a peacock's neck.

He held the pose for almost fifty seconds and then he picked up his box and came on to the porch and dropped down on the bottom step. ''Lady,'' he said in a firm nasal voice, ''I'd give a fortune to live where I could see me a sun do that every evening.''

''Does it every evening,'' the old woman said and sat back down. The daughter sat down too and watched him with a cautious sly look as if he were a bird that had come up very close. He leaned to one side, rooting in his pants pocket, and in a second he brought out a package of chewing gum and offered her a piece. She took it and unpeeled it and began to chew without taking her eyes off him. He offered the old woman a piece but she only raised her upper lip to indicate she had no teeth.

Mr. Shiftlet's pale sharp glance had already passed over everything in the yard—the pump near the corner of the house and the big fig tree that three or four chickens were preparing to roost in—and had moved to a shed where he saw the square rusted back of an automobile. ''You ladies drive?'' he asked.

''That car ain't run in fifteen year,'' the old woman said. ''The day my husband died, it quit running.''

''Nothing is like it used to be, lady,'' he said. ''The world is almost rotten.''

''That's right,'' the old woman said. ''You from around here?''

''Name Tom T. Shiftlet,'' he murmured, looking at the tires.

''I'm pleased to meet you,'' the old woman said. ''Name Lucynell Crater and daughter Lucynell Crater. What you doing around here, Mr. Shiftlet?''

He judged the car to be about a 1928 or '29 Ford. ''Lady,'' he said, and turned and gave her his full attention, ''lemme tell you something. There's one of these doctors in Atlanta that's taken a knife and cut the human heart—the human heart,'' he repeated, leaning forward, ''out of a man's chest and held it in his hand,'' and he held his hand out, palm up, as if it were slightly weighted with the human heart, ''and studied it like it was a day-old chicken, and lady,'' he said, allowing a long significant pause in which his head slid forward and his clay-colored eyes brightened, ''he don't know no more about it than you or me.''

''That's right,'' the old woman said.

''Why, if he was to take that knife and cut into every corner of it, he still wouldn't know no more than you or me. What you want to bet?''

''Nothing,'' the old woman said wisely. ''Where you come from, Mr. Shiftlet?''

He didn't answer. He reached into his pocket and brought out a sack of tobacco and a package of cigarette papers and rolled himself a cigarette, expertly with one hand, and attached it in a hanging position to his upper lip. Then he took a box of wooden matches from his pocket and struck one on his shoe. He held the burning match as if he were studying the mystery of flame while it traveled dangerously toward his skin. The daughter began to make loud noises and to point to his hand and shake her finger at him, but when the flame was just before touching him, he leaned down with his hand cupped over it as if he were going to set fire to his nose and lit the cigarette.

He flipped away the dead match and blew a stream of gray into the evening. A sly look came over his face. ''Lady,'' he said, ''nowadays, people'll do anything anyways. I can tell you my name is Tom T. Shiftlet and I come from Tarwater, Tennessee, but you never have seen me before: how you know I ain't lying? How you know my name ain't Aaron Sparks, lady, and I come from Singleberry, Georgia, or how you know it's not George Speeds and I come from Lucy, Alabama, or how you know I ain't Thompson Bright from Toolafalls, Mississippi?''

''I don't know nothing about you,'' the old woman muttered, irked.

''Lady,'' he said, ''people don't care how they lie. Maybe the best I can tell you is, I'm a man; but listen lady,'' he said and paused and made his tone more ominous still, ''what is a man?''

The old woman began to gum a seed. ''What you carry in that tin box, Mr. Shiftlet?'' she asked.

''Tools,'' he said, put back. ''I'm a carpenter.''

''Well, if you come out here to work, I'll be able to feed you and give you a place to sleep but I can't pay. I'll tell you that before you begin,'' she said.

There was no answer at once and no particular expression on his face. He leaned back against the two-by-four that helped support the porch roof. ''Lady,'' he said slowly, ''there's some men that some things mean more to them than money.'' The old woman rocked without comment and the daughter watched the trigger that moved up and down in his neck. He told the old woman then that all most people were interested in was money, but he asked what a man was made for. He asked her if a man was made for money, or what. He asked her what she thought she was made for but she didn't answer, she only sat rocking and wondered if a one-armed man could put a new roof on her garden house. He asked a lot of questions that she didn't answer. He told her that he was twenty-eight years old and had lived a varied life. He had been a gospel singer, a foreman on the railroad, an assistant in an undertaking parlor, and he come over the radio for three months with Uncle Roy and his Red Creek Wranglers. He said he had fought and bled in the Arm Service of his country and visited every foreign land and that everywhere he had seen people that didn't care if they did a thing one way or another. He said he hadn't been raised thataway.

A fat yellow moon appeared in the branches of the fig tree as if it were going to roost there with the chickens. He said that a man had to escape to the country to see the world whole and that he wished he lived in a desolate place like this where he could see the sun go down every evening like God made it to do.

''Are you married or are you single?'' the old woman asked.

There was a long silence. "Lady," he asked finally, "where would you find you an innocent woman today? I wouldn't have any of this trash I could just pick up."

The daughter was leaning very far down, hanging her head almost between her knees, watching him through a triangular door she had made in her overturned hair; and she suddenly fell in a heap on the floor and began to whimper. Mr. Shiftlet straightened her out and helped her get back in the chair.

"Is she your baby girl?" he asked.

"My only," the old woman said, "and she's the sweetest girl in the world. I would give her up for nothing on earth. She's smart too. She can sweep the floor, cook, wash, feed the chickens, and hoe. I wouldn't give her up for a casket of jewels."

"No," he said kindly, "don't ever let any man take her away from you."

"Any man come after her," the old woman said, "he'll have to stay around the place."

Mr. Shiftlet's eye in the darkness was focused on a part of the automobile bumper that glittered in the distance.

"Lady," he said, jerking his short arm up as if he could point with it to her house and yard and pump, "there ain't a broken thing on this plantation that I couldn't fix for you, one-arm jackleg or not. I'm a man," he said with a sullen dignity, "even if I ain't a whole one. I got," he said, tapping his knuckles on the floor to emphasize the immensity of what he was going to say, "a moral intelligence!" and his face pierced out of the darkness into a shaft of doorlight and he stared at her as if he were astonished himself at this impossible truth.

The old woman was not impressed with the phrase. "I told you you could hang around and work for food," she said, "if you don't mind sleeping in that car yonder."

"Why listen, lady," he said with a grin of delight, "the monks of old slept in their coffins!"

"They wasn't as advanced as we are," the old woman said.

The next morning he began on the roof of the garden house while Lucynell, the daughter, sat on a rock and watched him work. He had not been around a week before the change he had made in the place was apparent. He had patched the front and back steps, built a new hog pen, restored a fence, and taught Lucynell, who was completely deaf and had never said a word in her life, to say the word "bird." The big rosy-faced girl followed him everywhere, saying "Burrttddt ddbirrrttdt," and clapping her hands. The old woman watched from a distance, secretly pleased. She was ravenous for a son-in-law.

Mr. Shiftlet slept on the hard narrow back seat of the car with his feet out the side window. He had his razor and a can of water on a crate that served him as a bedside table and he put up a piece of mirror against the back glass and kept his coat neatly on a hanger that he hung over one of the windows.

In the evenings he sat on the steps and talked while the old woman and Lucynell rocked violently in their chairs on either side of him. The old woman's three mountains were black against the dark blue sky and were visited off and on by various planets and by the moon after it had left the chickens. Mr. Shiftlet pointed out that the reason he had improved this plantation was because he had taken a personal interest in it. He said he was even going to make the automobile run.

He had raised the hood and studied the mechanism and he said he could tell that the car had been built in the days when cars were really built. You take now, he said, one man puts in one bolt and another man puts in another bolt and another man puts in another bolt so that it's a man for a bolt. That's why you have to pay so much for a car: you're paying all those men. Now if you didn't have to pay but one man, you could get you a cheaper car and one that had had a personal interest taken in it, and it would be a better car. The old woman agreed with him that this was so.

Mr. Shiftlet said that the trouble with the world was that nobody cared, or stopped and took any trouble. He said he never would have been able to teach Lucynell to say a word if he hadn't cared and stopped long enough.

''Teach her to say something else,'' the old woman said.

''What you want her to say next?'' Mr. Shiftlet asked.

The old woman's smile was broad and toothless and suggestive. ''Teach her to say 'sugarpie,' '' she said.

Mr. Shiftlet already knew what was on her mind.

The next day he began to tinker with the automobile and that evening he told her that if she would buy a fan belt, he would be able to make the car run.

The old woman said she would give him the money. ''You see that girl yonder?'' she asked, pointing to Lucynell who was sitting on the floor a foot away, watching him, her eyes blue even in the dark. ''If it was ever a man wanted to take her away, I would say, 'No man on earth is going to take that sweet girl of mine away from me!' but if he was to say, 'Lady, I don't want to take her away, I want her right here,' I would say, 'Mister, I don't blame you none. I wouldn't pass up a chance to live in a permanent place and get the sweetest girl in the world myself. You ain't no fool,' I would say.''

''How old is she?'' Mr. Shiftlet asked casually.

''Fifteen, sixteen,'' the old woman said. The girl was nearly thirty but because of her innocence it was impossible to guess.

''It would be a good idea to paint it too,'' Mr. Shiftlet remarked. ''You don't want it to rust out.''

''We'll see about that later,'' the old woman said.

The next day he walked into town and returned with the parts he needed and a can of gasoline. Late in the afternoon, terrible noises issued from the shed and the old woman rushed out of the house, thinking Lucynell was somewhere having a fit. Lucynell was sitting on a chicken crate, stamping her feet and screaming, ''Burrddttt! bddurrddtttt!'' but her fuss was drowned out by the car. With a volley of blasts it emerged from the shed, moving in a fierce and stately way. Mr. Shiftlet was in the driver's seat, sitting very erect. He had an expression of serious modesty on his face as if he had just raised the dead.

That night, rocking on the porch, the old woman began her business at once. ''You want you an innocent woman, don't you?'' she asked sympathetically. ''You don't want none of this trash.''

''No'm, I don't,'' Mr. Shiftlet said.

''One that can't talk,'' she continued, ''can't sass you back or use foul language. That's the kind for you to have. Right there,'' and she pointed to Lucynell sitting cross-legged in her chair, holding both feet in her hands.

''That's right,'' he admitted. ''She wouldn't give me any trouble.''

''Saturday,'' the old woman said, ''you and her and me can drive into town and get married.''

Mr. Shiftlet eased his position on the steps.

''I can't get married right now,'' he said. ''Everything you want to do takes money and I ain't got any.''

''What you need with money?'' she asked.

''It takes money,'' he said. ''Some people'll do anything anyhow these days, but the way I think, I wouldn't marry no woman that I couldn't take on a trip like she was somebody. I mean take her to a hotel and treat her. I wouldn't marry the Duchesser Windsor,'' he said firmly, ''unless I could take her to a hotel and giver something good to eat.

"I was raised thataway and there ain't a thing I can do about it. My old mother taught me how to do."

"Lucynell don't even know what a hotel is," the old woman muttered. "Listen here, Mr. Shiftlet," she said, sliding forward in her chair, "you'd be getting a permanent house and a deep well and the most innocent girl in the world. You don't need no money. Lemme tell you something: there ain't any place in the world for a poor disabled friendless drifting man."

The ugly words settled in Mr. Shiftlet's head like a group of buzzards in the top of a tree. He didn't answer at once. He rolled himself a cigarette and lit it and then he said in an even voice, "Lady, a man is divided into two parts, body and spirit."

The old woman clamped her gums together.

"A body and a spirit," he repeated. "The body, lady, is like a house: it don't go anywhere: but the spirit, lady, is like a automobile: always on the move, always . . ."

"Listen, Mr. Shiftlet," she said, "my well never goes dry and my house is always warm in the winter and there's no mortgage on a thing about this place. You can go to the courthouse and see for yourself. And yonder under that shed is a fine automobile." She laid the bait carefully. "You can have it painted by Saturday. I'll pay for the paint."

In the darkness, Mr. Shiftlet's smile stretched like a weary snake waking up by a fire. After a second he recalled himself and said, "I'm only saying a man's spirit means more to him than anything else. I would have to take my wife off for the week end without no regards at all for cost. I got to follow where my spirit says to go."

"I'll give you fifteen dollars for a week-end trip," the old woman said in a crabbed voice. "That's the best I can do."

"That wouldn't hardly pay for more than the gas and the hotel," he said. "It wouldn't feed her."

"Seventeen-fifty," the old woman said. "That's all I got so it isn't any use you trying to milk me. You can take a lunch."

Mr. Shiftlet was deeply hurt by the word "milk." He didn't doubt that she had more money sewed up in her mattress but he had already told her he was not interested in her money. "I'll make that do," he said and rose and walked off without treating with her further.

On Saturday the three of them drove into town in the car that the paint had barely dried on and Mr. Shiftlet and Lucynell were married in the Ordinary's office while the old woman witnessed. As they came out of the courthouse, Mr. Shiftlet began twisting his neck in his collar. He looked morose and bitter as if he had been insulted while someone held him. "That didn't satisfy me none," he said. "That was just something a woman in an office did, nothing but paper work and blood tests. What do they know about my blood? If they was to take my heart and cut it out," he said, "they wouldn't know a thing about me. It didn't satisfy me at all."

"It satisfied the law," the old woman said sharply.

"The law," Mr. Shiftlet said and spit. "It's the law that don't satisfy me."

He had painted the car dark green with a yellow band around it just under the windows. The three of them climbed in the front seat and the old woman said, "Don't Lucynell look pretty? Looks like a baby doll." Lucynell was dressed up in a white dress that her mother had uprooted from a trunk and there was a Panama hat on her head with a bunch of red wooden cherries on the brim. Every now and then her placid expression was changed by a sly isolated little thought like a shoot of green in the desert. "You got a prize!" the old woman said.

Mr. Shiftlet didn't even look at her.

They drove back to the house to let the old woman off and pick up the lunch.

When they were ready to leave, she stood staring in the window of the car, with her fingers clenched around the glass. Tears began to seep sideways out of her eyes and run along the dirty creases in her face. "I ain't ever been parted with her for two days before," she said.

Mr. Shiftlet started the motor.

"And I wouldn't let no man have her but you because I seen you would do right. Good-by, Sugarbaby," she said, clutching at the sleeve of the white dress. Lucynell looked straight at her and didn't seem to see her there at all. Mr. Shiftlet eased the car forward so that she had to move her hands.

The early afternoon was clear and open and surrounded by pale blue sky. Although the car would go only thirty miles an hour, Mr. Shiftlet imagined a terrific climb and dip and swerve that went entirely to his head so that he forgot his morning bitterness. He had always wanted an automobile but he had never been able to afford one before. He drove very fast because he wanted to make Mobile by nightfall.

Occasionally he stopped his thoughts long enough to look at Lucynell in the seat beside him. She had eaten the lunch as soon as they were out of the yard and now she was pulling the cherries off the hat one by one and throwing them out the window. He became depressed in spite of the car. He had driven about a hundred miles when he decided that she must be hungry again and at the next small town they came to, he stopped in front of an aluminum-painted eating place called The Hot Spot and took her in and ordered her a plate of ham and grits. The ride had made her sleepy and as soon as she got up on the stool, she rested her head on the counter and shut her eyes. There was no one in The Hot Spot but Mr. Shiftlet and the boy behind the counter, a pale youth with a greasy rag hung over his shoulder. Before he could dish up the food, she was snoring gently.

"Give it to her when she wakes up," Mr. Shiftlet said. "I'll pay for it now."

The boy bent over her and stared at the long pink-gold hair and the half-shut sleeping eyes. Then he looked up and stared at Mr. Shiftlet. "She looks like an angel of Gawd," he murmured.

"Hitch-hiker," Mr. Shiftlet explained. "I can't wait. I got to make Tuscaloosa."

The boy bent over again and very carefully touched his finger to a strand of the golden hair and Mr. Shiftlet left.

He was more depressed than ever as he drove on by himself. The late afternoon had grown hot and sultry and the country had flattened out. Deep in the sky a storm was preparing very slowly and without thunder as if it meant to drain every drop of air from the earth before it broke. There were times when Mr. Shiftlet preferred not to be alone. He felt too that a man with a car had a responsibility to others and he kept his eye out for a hitchhiker. Occasionally he saw a sign that warned: "Drive carefully. The life you save may be your own."

The narrow road dropped off on either side into dry fields and here and there a shack or a filling station stood in a clearing. The sun began to set directly in front of the automobile. It was a reddening ball that through his windshield was slightly flat on the bottom and top. He saw a boy in overalls and a gray hat standing on the edge of the road and he slowed the car down and stopped in front of him. The boy didn't have his hand raised to thumb the ride, he was only standing there, but he had a small cardboard suitcase and his hat was set on his head in a way to indicate that he had left somewhere for good. "Son," Mr. Shiftlet said, "I see you want a ride."

The boy didn't say he did or he didn't but he opened the door of the car and got in, and Mr. Shiftlet started driving again. The child held the suitcase on his lap and folded his arms on top of it. He turned his head and looked out the window away from Mr. Shiftlet. Mr. Shiftlet felt oppressed. "Son," he said after a minute, "I got the best old mother in the world so I reckon you only got the second best."

The boy gave him a quick dark glance and then turned his face back out the window.

''It's nothing so sweet,'' Mr. Shiftlet continued, ''as a boy's mother. She taught him his first prayers at her knee, she gave him love when no other would, she told him what was right and what wasn't, and she seen that he done the right thing. Son,'' he said, ''I never rued a day in my life like the one I rued when I left that old mother of mine.''

The boy shifted in his seat but he didn't look at Mr. Shiftlet. He unfolded his arms and put one hand on the door handle.

''My mother was a angel of Gawd,'' Mr. Shiftlet said in a very strained voice. ''He took her from heaven and giver to me and I left her.'' His eyes were instantly clouded over with a mist of tears. The car was barely moving.

The boy turned angrily in the seat. ''You go to the devil!'' he cried. ''My old woman is a flea bag and yours is a stinking pole cat!'' and with that he flung the door open and jumped out with his suitcase into the ditch.

Mr. Shiftlet was so shocked that for about a hundred feet he drove along slowly with the door still open. A cloud, the exact color of the boy's hat and shaped like a turnip, had descended over the sun, and another, worse looking, crouched behind the car. Mr. Shiftlet felt that the rottenness of the world was about to engulf him. He raised his arm and let it fall again to his breast. ''Oh Lord!'' he prayed. ''Break forth and wash the slime from this earth!''

The turnip continued slowly to descend. After a few minutes there was a guffawing peal of thunder from behind and fantastic raindrops, like tin-can tops, crashed over the rear of Mr. Shiftlet's car. Very quickly he stepped on the gas and with his stump sticking out the window he raced the galloping shower into Mobile.

Tille Olsen / *Tell Me a Riddle* 1953–54

In Tell Me a Riddle, *Tillie Olsen ''found characters who could fully embody her vision of hope with hopelessness, of beauty in the midst of ugliness,'' in the view of one critic writing for the* New Republic. *Many of the stories in that collection have been anthologized and widely acclaimed. ''I Stand Here Ironing,'' the story below, has been read on the radio and recorded in the Lamont Poetry Room at Harvard. Her latest book is* Silences *(1979).*

Born in Omaha, Nebraska, in 1913, Tillie Olsen has worked in factories and as a typist-transcriber. She was awarded a Stanford University Creative Writing Fellowship (1955–56), a Ford Foundation Grant in Literature (1956), and a fellowship to the Radcliffe Institute for Independent Study (1962–64).

I STAND HERE IRONING

I stand here ironing, and what you asked me moves tormented back and forth with the iron.

''I wish you would manage the time to come in and talk with me about your daughter. I'm sure you can help me understand her. She's a youngster who needs help and whom I'm deeply interested in helping.''

''Who needs help.'' . . . Even if I came, what good would it do? You think because I am her mother I have a key, or that in some way you could use me as a key? She has lived for nineteen years. There is all that life that has happened outside of me, beyond me.

And when is there time to remember, to sift, to weigh, to estimate, to total? I will start and there will be an interruption and I will have to gather it all together again. Or I will become engulfed with all I did or did not do, with what should have been and what cannot be helped.

She was a beautiful baby. The first and only one of our five that was beautiful at birth. You do not guess how new and uneasy her tenancy in her now-loveliness. You did not know her all those years she was thought homely, or see her poring over her baby pictures, making me tell her over and over how beautiful she had been—and would be, I would tell her—and was now, to the seeing eye. But the seeing eyes were few or nonexistent. Including mine.

I nursed her. They feel that's important nowadays. I nursed all the children, but with her, with all the fierce rigidity of first motherhood, I did like the books then said. Though her cries battered me to trembling and my breasts ached with swollenness, I waited till the clock decreed.

Why do I put that first? I do not even know if it matters, or if it explains anything.

She was a beautiful baby. She blew shining bubbles of sound. She loved motion, loved light, loved color and music and textures. She would lie on the floor in her blue overalls patting the surface so hard in ecstasy her hands and feet would blur. She was a miracle to me, but when she was eight months old I had to leave her daytimes with the woman downstairs to whom she was no miracle at all, for I worked or looked for work and for Emily's father, who "could no longer endure" (he wrote in his good-bye note) "sharing want with us."

I was nineteen. It was the pre-relief, pre-WPA world of the depression. I would start running as soon as I got off the streetcar, running up the stairs, the place smelling sour, and awake or asleep to startle awake, when she saw me she would break into a clogged weeping that could not be comforted, a weeping I can hear yet.

After a while I found a job hashing at night so I could be with her days, and it was better. But it came to where I had to bring her to this family and leave her.

It took a long time to raise the money for her fare back. Then she got chicken pox and I had to wait longer. When she finally came, I hardly knew her, walking quick and nervous like her father, looking like her father, thin, and dressed in a shoddy red that yellowed her skin and glared at the pockmarks. All the baby loveliness gone.

She was two. Old enough for nursery school they said, and I did not know then what I know now—the fatigue of the long day, and the lacerations of group life in the kinds of nurseries that are only parking places for children.

Except that it would have made no difference if I had known. It was the only place there was. It was the only way we could be together, the only way I could hold a job.

And even without knowing, I knew. I knew the teacher that was evil because all these years it has curdled into my memory, the little boy hunched in the corner, her rasp, "why aren't you outside, because Alvin hits you? that's no reason, go out, scaredy." I knew Emily hated it even if she did not clutch and implore "don't go Mommy" like the other children, mornings.

She always had a reason why we should stay home. Momma, you look sick. Momma, I feel sick. Momma, the teachers aren't there today, they're sick. Momma, we can't go, there was a fire there last night. Momma, it's a holiday today, no school, they told me.

But never a direct protest, never rebellion. I think of our others in their three-, four-year-oldness—the explosions, the tempers, the denunciations, the demands—and I feel suddenly ill. I put the iron down. What in me demanded that goodness in her? And what was the cost, the cost to her of such goodness?

The old man living in the back once said in his gentle way: "You should smile at Emily more when you look at her.'' What *was* in my face when I looked at her? I loved her. There were all the acts of love.

It was only with the others I remembered what he said, and it was the face of joy, and not of care or tightness or worry I turned to them—too late for Emily. She does not smile easily, let alone almost always as her brothers and sisters do. Her face is closed and sombre, but when she wants, how fluid. You must have seen it in her pantomimes, you spoke of her rare gift for comedy on the stage that rouses a laughter out of the audience so dear they applaud and applaud and do not want to let her go.

Where does it come from, that comedy? There was none of it in her when she came back to me that second time, after I had had to send her away again. She had a new daddy now to learn to love, and I think perhaps it was a better time.

Except when we left her alone nights, telling ourselves she was old enough.

''Can't you go some other time, Mommy, like tomorrow?'' she would ask. ''Will it be just a little while you'll be gone? Do you promise?''

The time we came back, the front door open, the clock on the floor in the hall. She rigid awake. ''It wasn't just a little while. I didn't cry. Three times I called you, just three times, and then I ran downstairs to open the door so you could come faster. The clock talked loud. I threw it away, it scared me what it talked.''

She said the clock talked loud again that night I went to the hospital to have Susan. She was delirious with the fever that comes before red measles, but she was fully conscious all the week I was gone and the week after we were home when she could not come near the new baby or me.

She did not get well. She stayed skeleton thin, not wanting to eat, and night after night she had nightmares. She would call for me, and I would rouse from exhaustion to sleepily call back: ''You're all right, darling, go to sleep, it's just a dream,'' and if she still called, in a sterner voice, ''now go to sleep, Emily, there's nothing to hurt you.'' Twice, only twice, when I had to get up for Susan anyhow, I went in to sit with her.

Now when it is too late (as if she would let me hold and comfort her like I do the others) I get up and go to her at once at her moan or restless stirring. ''Are you awake, Emily? Can I get you something?'' And the answer is always the same: ''No, I'm all right, go back to sleep, Mother.''

They persuaded me at the clinic to send her away to a convalescent home in the country where ''she can have the kind of food and care you can't manage for her, and you'll be free to concentrate on the new baby.'' They still send children to that place. I see pictures on the society page of sleek young women planning affairs to raise money for it, or dancing at the affairs, or decorating Easter eggs or filling Christmas stockings for the children.

They never have a picture of the children so I do not know if the girls still wear those gigantic red bows and the ravaged looks on the every other Sunday when parents can come to visit ''unless otherwise notified''—as we were notified the first six weeks.

Oh it is a handsome place, green lawns and tall trees and fluted flower beds. High up on the balconies of each cottage the children stand, the girls in their red bows and white dresses, the boys in white suits and giant red ties. The parents stand below shrieking up to be heard and the children shriek down to be heard, and between them the invisible wall ''Not To Be Contaminated by Parental Germs or Physical Affection.''

There was a tiny girl who always stood hand in hand with Emily. Her parents never came. One visit she was gone. ''They moved her to Rose Cottage'' Emily shouted in explanation. ''They don't like you to love anybody here.''

She wrote once a week, the labored writing of a seven-year-old. ''I am fine.

How is the baby. If I write my leter nicly I will have a star. Love.'' There never was a star. We wrote every other day, letters she could never hold or keep but only hear read—once. ''We simply do not have room for children to keep any personal possessions,'' they patiently explained when we pieced one Sunday's shrieking together to plead how much it would mean to Emily, who loved so to keep things, to be allowed to keep her letters and cards.

Each visit she looked frailer, ''She isn't eating,'' they told us.

(They had runny eggs for breakfast or mush with lumps, Emily said later, I'd hold it in my mouth and not swallow. Nothing ever tasted good, just when they had chicken.)

It took us eight months to get her released home, and only the fact that she gained back so little of her seven lost pounds convinced the social worker.

I used to try to hold and love her after she came back, but her body would stay stiff, and after a while she'd push away. She ate little. Food sickened her, and I think much of life too. Oh she had physical lightness and brightness, twinkling by on skates, bouncing like a ball up and down up and down over the jump rope, skimming over the hill; but these were momentary.

She fretted about her appearance, thin and dark and foreign-looking at a time when every little girl was supposed to look or thought she should look a chubby blonde replica of Shirley Temple. The doorbell sometimes rang for her, but no one seemed to come and play in the house or be a best friend. Maybe because we moved so much.

There was a boy she loved painfully through two school semesters. Months later she told me how she had taken pennies from my purse to buy him candy. ''Licorice was his favorite and I brought him some every day, but he still liked Jennifer better'n me. Why, Mommy?'' The kind of question for which there is no answer.

School was a worry to her. She was not glib or quick in a world where glibness and quickness were easily confused with ability to learn. To her overworked and exasperated teachers she was an overconscientious ''slow learner'' who kept trying to catch up and was absent entirely too often.

I let her be absent, though sometimes the illness was imaginary. How different from my now-strictness about attendance with the others. I wasn't working. We had a new baby, I was home anyhow. Sometimes, after Susan grew old enough, I would keep her home from school, too, to have them all together.

Mostly Emily had asthma, and her breathing, harsh and labored, would fill the house with a curiously tranquil sound. I would bring the two old dresser mirrors and her boxes of collections to her bed. She would select beads and single earrings, bottle tops and shells, dried flowers and pebbles, old postcards and scraps, all sorts of oddments; then she and Susan would play Kingdom, setting up landscapes and furniture, peopling them with action.

Those were the only times of peaceful companionship between her and Susan. I have edged away from it, that poisonous feeling between them, that terrible balancing of hurts and needs I had to do between the two, and did so badly, those earlier years.

Oh there are conflicts between the others too, each one human, needing, demanding, hurting, taking—but only between Emily and Susan, no, Emily toward Susan that corroding resentment. It seems so obvious on the surface, yet it is not obvious. Susan, the second child, Susan, golden- and curly-haired and chubby, quick and articulate and assured, everything in appearance and manner Emily was not; Susan, not able to resist Emily's precious things, losing or sometimes clumsily breaking them; Susan telling jokes and riddles to company for applause while Emily sat silent (to say to me later: that was *my* riddle, Mother, I told it to Susan);

Susan, who for all the five years' difference in age was just a year behind Emily in developing physically.

I am glad for that slow physical development that widened the difference between her and her contemporaries, though she suffered over it. She was too vulnerable for that terrible world of youthful competition, of preening and parading, of constant measuring of yourself against every other, of envy, "If I had that copper hair," "If I had that skin. . . ." She tormented herself enough about not looking like the others, there was enough of the unsureness, the having to be conscious of words before you speak, the constant caring—what are they thinking of me? without having it all magnified by the merciless physical drives.

Ronnie is calling. He is wet and I change him. It is rare there is such a cry now. That time of motherhood is almost behind me when the ear is not one's own but must always be racked and listening for the child cry, the child call. We sit for a while and I hold him, looking out over the city spread in charcoal with its soft aisles of light. *"Shoogily,"* he breathes and curls closer. I carry him back to bed, asleep. *Shoogily.* A funny word, a family word, inherited from Emily, invested by her to say: *comfort.*

In this and other ways she leaves her seal, I say aloud. And startle at my saying it. What do I mean? What did I start to gather together, to try and make coherent? I was at the terrible, growing years. War years. I do not remember them well. I was working, there were four smaller ones now, there was not time for her. She had to help be a mother, and housekeeper, and shopper. She had to set her seal. Mornings of crisis and near hysteria trying to get lunches packed, hair combed, coats and shoes found, everyone to school or Child Care on time, the baby ready for transportation. And always the paper scribbled on by a smaller one, the book looked at by Susan then mislaid, the homework not done. Running out to that huge school where she was one, she was lost, she was a drop; suffering over the unpreparedness, stammering and unsure of her classes.

There was so little time left at night after the kids were bedded down. She would struggle over books, always eating (it was in those years she developed her enormous appetite that is legendary in our family) and I would be ironing, or preparing food for the next day, or writing V-mail to Bill, or tending the baby. Sometimes, to make me laugh, or out of her despair, she would imitate happenings or types at school.

I think I said once: "Why don't you do something like this in the school amateur show?" One morning she phoned me at work, hardly understandable through the weeping: "Mother, I did it. I won, I won; they gave me first prize; they clapped and clapped and wouldn't let me go."

Now suddenly she was Somebody, and as imprisoned in her difference as she had been in anonymity.

She began to be asked to perform at other high schools, even in colleges, then at city and statewide affairs. The first one we went to, I only recognized her that first moment when thin, shy, she almost drowned herself into the curtains. Then: Was this Emily? The control, the command, the convulsing and deadly clowning, the spell, then the roaring, stamping audience, unwilling to let this rare and precious laughter out of their lives.

Afterwards: You ought to do something about her with a gift like that—but without money or knowing how, what does one do? We have left it all to her, and the gift has as often eddied inside, clogged and clotted, as been used and growing.

She is coming. She runs up the stairs two at a time with her light graceful step, and I know she is happy tonight. Whatever it was that occasioned your call did not happen today.

"Aren't you ever going to finish the ironing, Mother? Whistler painted his mother in a rocker. I'd have to paint mine standing over an ironing board.'' This is one of her communicative nights and she tells me everything and nothing as she fixes herself a plate of food out of the icebox.

She is so lovely. Why did you want me to come in at all? Why were you concerned? She will find her way.

She starts up the stairs to bed. ''Don't get me up with the rest in the morning.'' ''But I thought you were having midterms.'' ''Oh, those,'' she comes back in, kisses me, and say quite lightly, ''in a couple of years when we'll all be atom-dead they won't matter a bit.''

She has said it before. She *believes* it. But because I have been dredging the past, and all that compounds a human being is so heavy and meaningful in me, I cannot endure it tonight.

I will never total it all. I will never come in to say: She was a child seldom smiled at. Her father left me before she was a year old. I had to work her first six years when there was work, or I sent her home and to his relatives. There were years she had care she hated. She was dark and thin and foreign-looking in a world where the prestige went to blondeness and curly hair and dimples, she was slow where glibness was prized. She was a child of anxious, not proud, love. We were poor and could not afford for her the soil of easy growth. I was a young mother, I was a distracted mother. There were the other children pushing up, demanding. Her younger sister seemed all that she was not. There were years she did not want me to touch her. She kept too much in herself, her life was such she had to keep too much in herself. My wisdom came too late. She has much to her and probably little will come of it. She is a child of her age, of depression, of war, of fear.

Let her be. So all that is in her will not bloom—but in how many does it? There is still enough left to live by. Only help her to know—help make it so there is cause for her to know—that she is more than this dress on the ironing board, helpless before the iron.

DISCUSSION QUESTIONS

1. Characterize the speaker in this piece. Whom is she addressing? How does she feel about her daughter? About her own life?

2. The piece ends with an appeal: ''Only help her to know—help make it so there is cause for her to know—that she is more than this dress on the ironing board, helpless before the iron.'' Explain the significance of the image. Does the speaker seem to wish someone could have helped her to know the same thing earlier in her life? Does she still seem ''helpless before the iron'' herself? What do you think the author wants us to feel for the speaker? For the daughter? What specifically makes you think so?

Robinson Jeffers / Carmel Point 1954

In its rigorous anti-humanism and philosophical nihilism, Robinson Jeffers' poetry represents an extreme of twentieth-century American literature. Immersed in the Greek classics, Elizabethan tragedy, and modern science, Jeffers endeavored throughout most of his poetry to dissuade humanity from thinking about itself as the center of the universe. In The Double Axe *(1948), he called his philosophical attitude ''inhumanism, a shifting of emphasis and significance from man to not-*

man." And in the long narrative poem that is usually regarded as his major work, Roan Stallion *(1925), he claims that "Humanity is the mold to break away from."*

Jeffers was born in Pittsburgh in 1887, the son of a classics professor at the Western Theological Seminary. After traveling widely with his family as a young boy, he entered Occidental College in Los Angeles in 1904 and graduated at the age of eighteen. Undecided about a career, he spent a year at Zurich University in Switzerland, returned to the United States and took an M.A. in literature at the University of Southern California, studied medicine there for three years, and then switched to forestry with a move to the University of Washington. In 1913 he married and the next year moved to the isolated, rocky coast of Carmel, California, where he built with his own hands the stone house and tower that ruggedly sheltered his life-long exile. He died there in 1962.

The extraordinary patience of things!
This beautiful place defaced with a crop of surburban houses—
How beautiful when we first beheld it,
Unbroken field of poppy and lupin walled with clean cliffs;
No intrusion but two or three horses pasturing,
Or a few milch cows rubbing their flanks on the outcrop rockheads—
Now the spoiler has come: does it care?
Not faintly. It has all time. It knows the people are a tide
That swells and in time will ebb, and all
Their works dissolve. Meanwhile the image of the pristine beauty
Lives in the very grain of the granite,
Safe as the endless ocean that climbs our cliff.—As for us:
We must uncenter our minds from ourselves;
We must unhumanize our views a little, and become confident
As the rock and ocean that we were made from.

DISCUSSION QUESTIONS

1. How does the speaker go about distinguishing between nature and human life? Point to words and phrases that express these differences. Can you also point to words and phrases that blur distinctions between nature and humanity?

2. How does the speaker view humanity? How is humanity connected with the landscape? With the speaker himself? Do you feel the speaker's view of humanity is convincing? Given his description of nature in the poem, do you think his view of humanity is justified?

3. What do you think the speaker means when he says that "We must uncenter our minds from ourselves"? Do you think doing so would be a worthwhile endeavor? How does the speaker's vision of human life compare with Hawthorne's and Whitman's in this section?

4. In what sense can this be said to be a poem about "ecology"? In what sense isn't the poem about "ecology"? Explain. In its attitude towards the environment, how does "Carmel Point" compare with N. Scott Momaday's "A First American Views His Land" (see Magazines)?

Allen Ginsberg / A Supermarket in California 1955

The author of poetry regarded as "great," "strange," "angelic," "degenerate," "unsurpassed," and "apocalyptic," Allen Ginsberg remains one of the most celebrated and vilified literary figures of the past three decades. Born in Newark, New Jersey in 1926, Ginsberg graduated from Columbia University in 1948 and spent several years on the road, supporting himself as a spot welder, reporter, dishwasher, porter, book reviewer, and seaman. Soon after his arrival in San Francisco, he launched an immediately successful career as a market research consultant. But a year of psychoanalysis prompted him, as he says, to "quit the job, my tie and suit, the apartment on Nob Hill . . . and do what I wanted"—write poetry. By the mid-1950s, Ginsberg was identified—along with, among others, Jack Kerouac, Lawrence Ferlinghetti, and William Burroughs—as a co-founder of the Beat Generation. Lionized for his experimentations with literary forms and unconventional life-styles, Ginsberg remains an ardent supporter of political and social causes. A late 1960s profile in the New Yorker *characterized him not only as a major American poet but also as a guru of the "amalgamated hippie-pacifist-activist-visionary-orgiastic-anarchist-Orientalist-psychedelic underground."*

Ginsberg's first volume of poetry, Howl *(1956), is also his most famous. It has gone through more than thirty printings, In a "Preface" to the volume, William Carlos Williams at once cautions readers that Ginsberg's vision of contemporary America is like "going through hell" but also reminds us that Ginsberg "proves to us, in spite of the most debasing experiences that life can offer a man, the spirit of love survives to ennoble our lives if we have the wit and the courage and the faith—and the art! to persist."*

"A Supermarket in California" was included in Ginsberg's first controversial volume. The poem remains a pensive rendition of Walt Whitman's vision of America as a land of abundance.

What thoughts I have of you tonight, Walt Whitman, for I walked down the sidestreets under the trees with a headache self-conscious looking at the full moon.
In my hungry fatigue, and shopping for images, I went into the neon fruit supermarket, dreaming of your enumerations!
What peaches and what penumbras! Whole families shopping at night! Aisles full of husbands! Wives in the avocados, babies in the tomatoes!—and you, Garcia Lorca, what were you doing down by the watermelons?

I saw you, Walt Whitman, childless, lonely old grubber, poking among the meats in the refrigerator and eyeing the grocery boys.
I heard you asking questions of each: Who killed the pork chops? What price bananas? Are you my Angel?
I wandered in and out of the brilliant stacks of cans following you, and followed in my imagination by the store detective.
We strode down the open corridors together in our solitary fancy tasting artichokes, possessing every frozen delicacy, and never passing the cashier.

Where are we going, Walt Whitman? The doors close in
an hour. Which way does your beard point tonight?
(I touch your book and dream of our odyssey in the
supermarket and feel absurd.)
Will we walk all night through solitary streets? The trees
add shade to shade, lights out in the houses, we'll both be
lonely.
Will we stroll dreaming of the lost America of love past
blue automobiles in driveways, home to our silent cottage?
Ah, dear father, graybeard, lonely old courage-teacher,
what America did you have when Charon quit poling his ferry
and you got out on a smoking bank and stood watching the
boat disappear on the black waters of Lethe?

E.B. White / The Ring of Time 1956

Perhaps the most respected twentieth-century American essayist, E.B. White once claimed that the essay writer is "sustained by the childish belief that everything he thinks about, everything that happens to him, is of general interest." In other words, the writer begins by being self-centered; only then can the writer's self imaginatively engage the centers of other selves.

E.B. White was born in Mt. Vernon, New York, in 1899. After graduating from Cornell in 1921, he worked as a journalist for several years and then landed a position with the newly formed New Yorker *magazine, where he contributed the "Talk of the Town" column. The winner of the National Institute of Arts and Letters gold medal in 1960, White is the author of nineteen books, including two classic books for children,* Stuart Little *(1948) and* Charlotte's Web *(1952). Regarded as an eminent stylist, White revised his former teacher's brief writing manual,* The Elements of Style *(1959), and the tiny edition known as Strunk and White can probably be seen on the desks of more professional writers than any other book of its kind.*

"The Ring of Time" is reprinted from Essays of E. B. White *(1977).*

Fiddler Bayou, March 22, 1956

After the lions had returned to their cages, creeping angrily through the chutes, a little bunch of us drifted away and into an open doorway nearby, where we stood for a while in semidarkness, watching a big brown circus horse go harumphing around the practice ring. His trainer was a woman of about forty, and the two of them, horse and woman, seemed caught up in one of those desultory treadmills of afternoon from which there is no apparent escape. The day was hot, and we kibitzers were grateful to be briefly out of the sun's glare. The long rein, or tape, by which the woman guided her charge counterclockwise in his dull career formed the radius of their private circle, of which she was the revolving center; and she, too, stepped a tiny circumference of her own, in order to accommodate the horse and allow him his maximum scope. She had on a short-skirted costume and a conical straw hat. Her legs were bare and she wore high heels, which probed deep into the loose tanbark and kept her ankles in a state of constant turmoil. The great size and meekness of the horse, the repetitious exercise, the heat of the afternoon, all exerted a hypnotic charm that invited boredom; we spectators were experiencing a languor—we neither expected relief nor felt entitled to any. We had paid a dollar to get into the grounds, to be sure, but we had got our dollar's worth a few minutes before, when the lion trainer's whiplash had got caught around a toe of one of the lions. What more did we want for a dollar?

Behind me I heard someone say, ''Excuse me, please,'' in a low voice. She was halfway into the building when I turned and saw her—a girl of sixteen or seventeen, politely threading her way through us onlookers who blocked the entrance. As she emerged in front of us, I saw that she was barefoot, her dirty little feet fighting the uneven ground. In most respects she was like any of two or three dozen showgirls you encounter if you wander about the winter quarters of Mr. John Ringling North's circus, in Sarasota—cleverly proportioned, deeply browned by the sun, dusty, eager, and almost naked. But her grave face and the naturalness of her manner gave her a sort of quick distinction and brought a new note into the gloomy octagonal building where we had all cast our lot for a few moments. As soon as she had squeezed through the crowd, she spoke a word or two to the older woman, whom I took to be her mother, stepped to the ring, and waited while the horse coasted to a stop in front of her. She gave the animal a couple of affectionate swipes on his enormous neck and then swung herself aboard. The horse immediately resumed his rocking canter, the woman goading him on, chanting something that sounded like ''Hop! Hop!''

In attempting to recapture this mild spectacle, I am merely acting as recording secretary for one of the oldest of societies—the society of those who, at one time or another, have surrendered, without even a show of resistance, to the bedazzlement of a circus rider. As a writing man, or secretary, I have always felt charged with the safekeeping of all unexpected items of worldly or unworldly enchantment, as though I might be held personally responsible if even a small one were to be lost. But it is not easy to communicate anything of this nature. The circus comes as close to being the world in microcosm as anything I know; in a way, it puts all the rest of show business in the shade. Its magic is universal and complex. Out of its wild disorder comes order; from its rank smell rises the good aroma of courage and daring; out of its preliminary shabbiness comes the final splendor. And buried in the familiar boasts of its advance agents lies the modesty of most of its people. For me the circus is at its best before it has been put together. It is at its best at certain moments when it comes to a point, as through a burning glass, in the activity and destiny of a single performer out of so many. One ring is always bigger than three. One rider, one aerialist, is always greater than six. In short, a man has to catch the circus unawares to experience its full impact and share its gaudy dream.

The ten-minute ride the girl took achieved—as far as I was concerned, who wasn't looking for it, and quite unbeknownst to her, who wasn't even striving for it—the thing that is sought by performers everywhere, on whatever stage, whether struggling in the tidal currents of Shakespeare or bucking the difficult motion of a horse. I somehow got the idea she was just cadging a ride, improving a shining ten minutes in the diligent way all serious artists seize free moments to hone the blade of their talent and keep themselves in trim. Her brief tour included only elementary postures and tricks, perhaps because they were all she was capable of, perhaps because her warmup at this hour was unscheduled and the ring was not rigged for a real practice session. She swung herself off and on the horse several times, gripping his mane. She did a few knee-stands—or whatever they are called—dropping to her knees and quickly bouncing back up on her feet again. Most of the time she simply rode in a standing position, well aft on the beast, her hands hanging easily at her sides, her head erect, her straw-colored ponytail lightly brushing her shoulders, the blood of exertion showing faintly through the tan of her skin. Twice she managed a one-foot stance—a sort of ballet pose, with arms outstretched. At one point the neck strap of her bathing suit broke and she went twice around the ring in the classic attitude of a woman making minor repairs to a garment. The fact that she was standing on the back of a moving horse while doing this invested the matter with a clownish significance that perfectly fitted the spirit of the circus—jocund, yet charming. She just rolled the strap into a neat ball and stowed it inside her bodice while the horse rocked and rolled beneath her in dutiful innocence. The bathing suit proved as self-reliant as its owner and stood up well enough without benefit of strap.

The richness of the scene was in its plainness, its natural condition—of horse, of ring, of girl, even to the girl's bare feet that gripped the bare back of her proud and ridiculous mount. The enchantment grew not out of anything that happened or was performed but out of something that seemed to go round and around and around with the girl, attending her, a steady gleam in the shape of a circle—a ring of ambition, of happiness, of youth. (And the positive pleasures of equilibrium under difficulties.) In a week or two, all would be changed, all (or almost all) lost: the girl would wear makeup, the horse would wear gold, the ring would be painted, the bark would be clean for the feet of the horse, the girl's feet would be clean for the slippers that she'd wear. All, all would be lost.

As I watched with the others, our jaws adroop, our eyes alight, I became painfully conscious of the element of time. Everything in the hideous old building seemed to take the shape of a circle, conforming to the course of the horse. The rider's gaze, as she peered straight ahead, seemed to be circular, as though bent by force of circumstance; then time itself began running in circles, and so the beginning was where the end was, and the two were the same, and one thing ran into the next and time went round and around and got nowhere. The girl wasn't so young that she did not know the delicious satisfaction of having a perfectly behaved body and the fun of using it to do a trick most people can't do, but she was too young to know that time does not really move in a circle at all. I thought: "She will never be as beautiful as this again"—a thought that made me acutely unhappy—and in a flash my mind (which is too much of a busybody to suit me) had projected her twenty-five years ahead, and she was now in the center of the ring, on foot, wearing a conical hat and high-heeled shoes, the image of the older woman, holding the long rein, caught in the treadmill of an afternoon long in the future. "She is at that enviable moment in life [I thought] when she believes she can go once around the ring, make one complete circuit, and at the end be exactly the same age as at the start." Everything in her movements, her expression, told you that for her the ring of time was perfectly formed, changeless, predictable, without beginning or end, like the ring in which she was traveling at this moment with the horse that wallowed under her. And then I slipped back into my trance, and time was circular again—time, pausing quietly with the rest of us, so as not to disturb the balance of a performer.

Her ride ended as casually as it had begun. The older woman stopped the horse, and the girl slid to the ground. As she walked toward us to leave, there was a quick, small burst of applause. She smiled broadly, in surprise and pleasure; then her face suddenly regained its gravity and she disappeared through the door.

It has been ambitious and plucky of me to attempt to describe what is indescribable, and I have failed, as I knew I would. But I have discharged my duty to my society; and besides, a writer, like an acrobat, must occasionally try a stunt that is too much for him. At any rate, it is worth reporting that long before the circus comes to town, its most notable performances have already been given. Under the bright lights of the finished show, a performer need only reflect the electric candle power that is directed upon him; but in the dark and dirty old training rings and in the makeshift cages, whatever light is generated, whatever excitement, whatever beauty, must come from original sources—from internal fires of professional hunger and delight, from the exuberance and gravity of youth. It is the difference between planetary light and the combustion of stars.

The South is the land of the sustained sibilant. Everywhere, for the appreciative visitor, the letter "s" insinuates itself in the scene: in the sound of sea and sand, in the singing shell, in the heat of sun and sky, in the sultriness of the gentle hours, in the siesta, in the stir of birds and insects. In contrast to the softness of its music, the South is also cruel and hard and prickly. A little striped lizard, flattened along the sharp green bayonet of a yucca, wears in its tiny face and watchful eye the pure look of death and violence. And all over the place, hidden at the bottom of their small sandy craters, the ant lions lie in wait for the ant that will stumble into their trap. (There are three kinds of lions in this region: the lions of the circus, the ant lions, and the Lions of the Tampa Lions Club, who roared their approval of segregation at a meeting the other day—all except one, a Lion named Monty Gurwit, who declined to roar and thereby got his picture in the paper.)

The day starts on a note of despair: the sorrowing dove, alone on its telephone wire, mourns the loss of night, weeps at the bright perils of the unfolding day. But soon the mockingbird wakes and begins an early rehearsal, setting the dove down by force of character, running through a few slick imitations, and trying a couple of original numbers into the bargain. The redbird takes it from there. Despair gives way to good humor. The Southern dawn is a pale affair, usually, quite different from our northern daybreak. It is a triumph of gradualism; night turns to day imperceptibly, softly, with no theatrics. It is subtle and undisturbing. As the first light seeps in through the blinds I lie in bed half awake, despairing with the dove, sounding the A for the brothers Alsop. All seems lost, all seems sorrowful. Then a mullet jumps in the bayou outside the bedroom window. It falls back into the water with a smart smack. I have asked several people why the mullet incessantly jump and I have received a variety of answers. Some say the mullet jump to shake off a parasite that annoys them. Some say they jump for the love of jumping—as the girl on the horse seemed to ride for the love of riding (although she, too, like all artists, may have been shaking off some parasite that fastens itself to the creative spirit and can be got rid of only by fifty turns around a ring while standing on a horse).

In Florida at this time of year, the sun does not take command of the day until a couple of hours after it has appeared in the east. It seems to carry no authority at first. The sun and the lizard keep the same schedule; they bide their time until the morning has advanced a good long way before they come fully forth and strike. The cold lizard waits astride his warming leaf for the perfect moment; the cold sun waits in his nest of clouds for the crucial time.

On many days, the dampness of the air pervades all life, all living. Matches refuse to strike. The towel, hung to dry, grows wetter by the hour. The newspaper, with its headlines about integration, wilts in your hand and falls limply into the coffee and the egg. Envelopes seal themselves. Postage stamps mate with one another as shamelessly as grasshoppers. But most of the time the days are models of beauty and wonder and comfort, with the kind sea stroking the back of the warm sand. At evening there are great flights of birds over the sea, where the light lingers; the gulls, the pelicans, the terns, the herons stay aloft for half an hour after land birds have gone to roost. They hold their ancient formations, wheel and fish over the Pass, enjoying the last of day like children playing outdoors after suppertime.

To a beachcomber from the North, which is my present status, the race problem has no pertinence, no immediacy. Here in Florida I am a guest in two houses—the house of the sun, the house of the State of Florida. As a guest, I mind my manners and do not criticize the customs of my hosts. It gives me a queer feeling, though, to be at the center of the greatest social crisis of my time and see hardly a sign of it. Yet the very absence of signs seems to increase one's awareness. Colored people do not come to the public beach to bathe, because they would not be made welcome there; and they don't fritter away their time visiting the circus, because they have other things to do. A few of them turn up at the ballpark, where they occupy a separate but equal section of the left-field bleachers and watch Negro players on the visiting Braves team using the same bases as the white players, instead of separate (but equal) bases. I have had only two small encounters with "color." A colored woman named Viola, who had been a friend of my wife's sister years ago, showed up one day with some laundry of ours that she had consented to do for us, and with the bundle she brought a bunch of nasturtiums, as a sort of natural accompaniment to the delivery of clean clothes. The flowers seemed a very acceptable thing and I was touched by them. We asked Viola about her daughter, and she said she was at Kentucky State College, studying voice.

The other encounter was when I was explaining to our cook, who is from Finland, the mysteries of bus travel in the American Southland. I showed her the bus stop, armed her with a timetable, and then, as a matter of duty, mentioned the customs of the Romans. "When you get on the bus," I said, "I think you'd better sit in one of the front seats—the seats in back are for colored people." A look of great weariness came into her face, as it does when we use too many dishes, and she replied, "Oh, I know—isn't it silly!"

Her remark, coming as it did all the way from Finland and landing on this sandbar with a plunk, impressed me. The Supreme Court said nothing about silliness, but I suspect it may play more of a role than one might suppose. People are, if anything, more touchy about being thought silly than they are about being thought unjust. I note that one of the arguments in the recent manifesto of Southern Congressmen in support of the doctrine of "separate but equal" was that it had been founded on "common sense." The sense that is common to one generation is uncommon to the next. Probably the first slave ship, with Negroes lying in chains on its decks, seemed commonsensical to the owners who operated it and to the planters who patronized it. But such a vessel would not be in the realm of common sense today. The only sense that is common, in the long run, is the sense of change—and we all instinctively avoid it, and object to the passage of time, and would rather have none of it.

The Supreme Court decision is like the Southern sun, laggard in its early stages, biding its time. It has been the law in Florida for two years now, and the years have been like the hours of the morning before the sun has gathered its strength. I think the decision is as incontrovertible and warming as the sun, and, like the sun, will eventually take charge.

But there is certainly a great temptation in Florida to duck the passage of time. Lying in warm comfort by the sea, you receive gratefully the gift of the sun, the gift of the South. This is true seduction. The day is a circle—morning, afternoon, and night. After a few days I was clearly enjoying the same delusion as the girl on the horse—that I could ride clear around the ring of day, guarded by wind and sun and sea and sand, and be not a moment older.

P.S. (April 1962). When I first laid eyes on Fiddler Bayou, it was wild land, populated chiefly by the little crabs that gave it its name, visited by wading birds and by an occasional fisherman. Today, houses ring the bayou, and part of the mangrove shore has been bulkheaded with a concrete wall. Green lawns stretch from patio to water's edge, and sprinklers make rainbows in the light. But despite man's encroachment, Nature manages to hold her own and assert her authority: high tides and high winds in the gulf sometimes send the sea crashing across the sand barrier, depositing its wrack on lawns and ringing everyone's front door bell. The birds and the crabs accommodate themselves quite readily to the changes that have taken place; every day brings herons to hunt around among the roots of the mangroves, and I have discovered that I can approach to within about eight feet of a Little Blue Heron simply by entering the water and swimming slowly toward him. Apparently he has decided that when I'm in the water, I am without guile—possibly even desirable, like a fish.

The Ringling circus has quit Sarasota and gone elsewhere for its hibernation. A few circus families still own homes in the town, and every spring the students at the high school put on a circus, to let off steam, work off physical requirements, and provide a promotional spectacle for Sarasota. At the drugstore you can buy a postcard showing the bed John Ringling slept in. Time has not stood still for anybody but the dead, and even the dead must be able to hear the acceleration of little sports cars and know that things have changed.

From the all-wise *New York Times,* which has the animal kingdom ever in mind, I have learned that one of the creatures most acutely aware of the passing of time is the fiddler crab himself. Tiny spots on his body enlarge during daytime hours, giving him the same color as the mudbank he explores and thus protecting him from his enemies. At night the spots shrink, his color fades, and he is almost invisible in the light of the moon. These changes are synchronized with the tides, so that each day they occur at a different hour. A scientist who experimented with the crabs to learn more about the phenomenon discovered that even when they are removed from their natural environment and held in confinement, the rhythm of their bodily change continues uninterrupted, and they mark the passage of time in their laboratory prison, faithful to the tides in their fashion.

John Updike / A & P 1962

After graduating from Harvard in 1954, where he was president of the Lampoon, *John Updike joined* The New Yorker *magazine as a reporter. Though he officially left the staff of that magazine in 1957 to concentrate on his fiction, issue after issue of* The New Yorker *declares Updike's presence in short stories, sketches, book reviews, and occasional light verse. "A & P," a tale of adolescent sensibility and one of the most widely anthologized short stories by a contemporary American writer, shows Updike's characteristic concern for the minutiae of sensory perceptions and the achievement of individual identity.*

In walks these three girls in nothing but bathing suits. I'm in the third checkout slot, with my back to the door, so I don't see them until they're over by the bread. The one that caught my eye first was the one in the plaid green two-piece. She was a chunky kid, with a good tan and a sweet broad soft-looking can with those two crescents of white just under it, where the sun never seems to hit, at the top of the backs of her legs. I stood there with my hand on a box of HiHo crackers trying to remember if I rang it up or not. I ring it up again and the customer starts giving me hell. She's one of these cash-register-watchers, a witch about fifty with rouge on her cheekbones and no eyebrows, and I know it made her day to trip me up. She'd been watching cash registers for fifty years and probably never seen a mistake before.

By the time I got her feathers smoothed and her goodies into a bag—she gives me a little snort in passing, if she'd been born at the right time they would have burned her over in Salem—by the time I get her on her way the girls had circled around the bread and were coming back, without a pushcart, back my way along the counters, in the aisle between the checkouts and the Special bins. They didn't even have shoes on. There was this chunky one, with the two-piece—it was bright green and the seams on the bra were still sharp and her belly was still pretty pale so I guessed she just got it (the suit)—there was this one, with one of those chubby berry-faces, the lips all bunched together under her nose, this one, and a tall one, with black hair that hadn't quite frizzed right, and one of these sunburns right across under the eyes, and a chin that was too long—you know, the kind of girl other girls think is very "striking" and "attractive" but never quite makes it, as they very well know, which is why they like her so much—and then the third one, that wasn't quite so tall. She was the queen. She kind of led them, the other two peeking around and making their shoulders round. She didn't look around, not this queen, she just walked straight on slowly, on those long white prima-donna legs. She came down a little hard on her heels, as if she didn't walk in her bare feet that much, putting down her heels and then letting the weight move along to her toes as if she was testing the floor with every step, putting a little deliberate extra action into it. You never know for sure how girls' minds work (do you really think it's a mind in there or just a little buzz like a bee in a glass jar?) but you got the idea she had talked the other two into coming in here with her, and now she was showing them how to do it, walk slow and hold yourself straight.

She had on a kind of dirty-pink—beige maybe, I don't know—bathing suit with a little nubble all over it and, what got me, the straps were down. They were off her shoulders looped loose around the cool tops of her arms, and I guess as a result the suit had slipped a little on her, so all around the top of the cloth there was this shining rim. If it hadn't been there you wouldn't have known there could have been anything whiter than those shoulders. With the straps pushed off, there was nothing between the top of the suit and the top of her head except just *her,* this clean bare plane of the top of her chest down from the shoulder bones like a dented sheet of metal tilted in the light. I mean, it was more than pretty.

She had sort of oaky hair that the sun and salt had bleached, done up in a bun that was unravelling, and a kind of prim face. Walking into the A & P with your straps down, I suppose it's the only kind of face you *can* have. She held her head so high her neck, coming up out of those white shoulders, looked kind of stretched, but I didn't mind. The longer her neck was, the more of her there was.

She must have felt in the corner of her eye me and over my shoulder Stokesie in the second slot watching, but she didn't tip. Not this queen. She kept her eyes moving across the racks, and stopped, and turned so slow it made my stomach rub the inside of my apron, and buzzed to the other two, who kind of huddled against her for relief, and then they all three of them went up the cat-and-dog-food-breakfast-cereal-macaroni-rice-raisons-seasonings-spreads-spaghetti-soft-drinks-crackers-and-cookies aisle. From the third slot I look straight up this aisle to the meat counter, and I watched them all the way. The fat one with the tan sort of fumbled with the cookies, but on second thought she put the package back. The sheep pushing their carts down the aisle—the girls were walking against the usual traffic (not that we have one-way signs or anything)—were pretty hilarious. You could see them, when Queenie's white shoulders dawned on them, kind of jerk, or hop, or hiccup, but their eyes snapped back to their own baskets and on they pushed. I bet you could set off dynamite in an A & P and the people would by and large keep reaching and checking oatmeal off their lists and muttering "Let me see, there was a third thing, began with A, asparagus, no, ah, yes, applesauce!" or whatever it is they do mutter. But there was no doubt, this jiggled them. A few houseslaves in pin curlers even looked around after pushing their carts past to make sure what they had seen was correct.

You know, it's one thing to have a girl in a bathing suit down on the beach, where what with the glare nobody can look at each other much anyway, and another thing in the cool of the A & P, under the fluorescent lights, against all those stacked packages, with her feet paddling along naked over our checkerboard green-and-cream rubber-tile floor.

"Oh Daddy," Stokesie said beside me. "I feel so faint."

"Darling," I said. "Hold me tight." Stokesie's married, with two babies chalked up on his fuselage already, but as far as I can tell that's the only difference. He's twenty-two, and I was nineteen this April.

"Is it done?" he asks, the responsible married man finding his voice. I forgot to say he thinks he's going to be manager some sunny day, maybe in 1990 when it's called the Great Alexandrov and Petrooshki Tea Company or something.

What he meant was, our town is five miles from a beach, with a big summer colony out on the Point, but we're right in the middle of town, and the women generally put on a shirt or shorts or something before they get out of the car into the street. And anyway these are usually women with six children and varicose veins mapping their legs and nobody, including them, could care less. As I say, we're right in the middle of town, and if you stand at our front doors you can see two banks and the Congregational church and the newspaper store and three real-estate offices and about twenty-seven old freeloaders tearing up Central Street because the sewer broke again. It's not as if we're on the Cape; we're north of Boston and there's people in this town haven't seen the ocean for twenty years.

The girls had reached the meat counter and were asking McMahon something. He pointed, they pointed, and they shuffled out of sight behind a pyramid of Diet Delight peaches. All that was left for us to see was old McMahon patting his mouth and looking after them sizing up their joints. Poor kids, I began to feel sorry for them, they couldn't help it.

Now here comes the sad part of the story, at least my family says it's sad, but I don't think it's so sad myself. The store's pretty empty, it being Thursday afternoon, so there was nothing much to do except lean on the register and wait for the girls to show up again. The whole store was like a pinball machine and I didn't know which tunnel they'd come out of. After a while they come around out of the far aisle, around the light bulbs, records at discount of the Caribbean Six or Tony Martin Sings or some such gunk you wonder they waste the wax on, sixpacks of candy bars, and plastic toys done up in cellophane that fall apart when a kid looks at them anyway. Around they come, Queenie still leading the way, and holding a little gray jar in her hand. Slots Three through Seven are unmanned and I could see her wondering between Stokes and me, but Stokesie with his usual luck draws an old party in baggy gray pants who stumbles up with four giant cans of pineapple juice (what do these bums *do* with all that pineapple juice? I've often asked myself) so the girls come to me. Queenie puts down the jar and I take it into my fingers icy cold. Kingfish Fancy Herring Snacks in Pure Sour Cream: 49¢. Now her hands are empty, not a ring or a bracelet, bare as God made them, and I wonder where the money's coming from. Still with that prim look she lifts a folded dollar bill out of the hollow at the center of her nubbled pink top. The jar went heavy in my hand. Really, I thought that was so cute.

Then everybody's luck begins to run out. Lengel comes in from haggling with a truck full of cabbages on the lot and is about to scuttle into that door marked MANAGER behind which he hides all day when the girls touch his eye. Lengel's pretty dreary, teaches Sunday school and the rest, but he doesn't miss that much. He comes over and says, "Girls, this isn't the beach."

Queenie blushes, though maybe it's just a brush of sunburn I was noticing for the first time, now that she was so close. "My mother asked me to pick up a jar of herring snacks." Her voice kind of startled me, the way voices do when you see the people first, coming out so flat and dumb yet kind of tony, too, the way it ticked over "pick up" and "snacks." All of a sudden I slid right down her voice into her living room. Her father and the other men were standing around in ice-cream coats and bow ties and the women were in sandals picking up herring snacks on toothpicks off a big glass plate and they were all holding drinks the color of water with olives and sprigs of mint in them. When my parents have somebody over they get lemonade and if it's a real racy affair Schlitz in tall glasses with "They'll Do It Every Time" cartoons stencilled on.

"That's all right," Lengel said. "But this isn't the beach." His repeating this struck me as funny, as if it had just occurred to him, and he had been thinking all these years the A & P was a great big dune and he was the head lifeguard. He didn't like my smiling—as I say he doesn't miss much—but he concentrates on giving the girls that sad Sunday-school-superintendent stare.

Queenie's blush is no sunburn now, and the plump one in plaid, that I liked better from the back—a really sweet can—pipes up, "We weren't doing any shopping. We just came in for the one thing."

"That makes no difference," Lengel tells her, and I could see from the way his eyes went that he hadn't noticed she was wearing a two-piece before. "We want you decently dressed when you come in here."

"We *are* decent," Queenie says suddenly, her lower lip pushing, getting sore now that she remembers her place, a place from which the crowd that runs the A & P must look pretty crummy. Fancy Herring Snacks flashed in her very blue eyes.

"Girls, I don't want to argue with you. After this come in here with your shoulders covered. It's our policy." He turns his back. That's policy for you. Policy is what the kingpins want. What the others want is juvenile delinquency.

All this while, the customers had been showing up with their carts but, you know, sheep, seeing a scene, they had all bunched up on Stokesie, who shook open a paper bag as gently as peeling a peach, not wanting to miss a word. I could feel in the silence everybody getting nervous, most of all Lengel, who asks me, "Sammy, have you rung up their purchase?"

I thought and said "No" but it wasn't about that I was thinking. I go through the punches, 4, 9, GROC, TOT—it's more complicated than you think, and after you do it often enough, it begins to make a little song, that you hear words to, in my case "Hello (*bing*) there, you (*gung*) hap-py *pee*-pul (*splat*)!"—the *splat* being the drawer flying out. I uncrease the bill, tenderly as you may imagine, it just having come from between the two smoothest scoops of vanilla I had ever known were there, and pass a half and a penny into her narrow pink palm, and nestle the herrings in a bag and twist its neck and hand it over, all the time thinking.

The girls, and who'd blame them, are in a hurry to get out, so I say "I quit" to Lengel quick enough for them to hear, hoping they'll stop and watch me, their unsuspected hero. They keep right on going, into the electric eye; the door flies open and they flicker across the lot to their car, Queenie and Plaid and Big Tall Goony-Goony (not that as raw material she was so bad), leaving me with Lengel and a kink in his eyebrow.

"Did you say something, Sammy?"

"I said I quit."

"I thought you did."

"You didn't have to embarrass them."

"It was they who were embarrassing us."

I started to say something that came out "Fiddle-de-doo." It's a saying of my grandmother's, and I know she would have been pleased.

"I don't think you know what you're saying," Lengel said.

''I know you don't,'' I said. ''But I do.'' I pull the bow at the back of my apron and start shrugging it off my shoulders. A couple customers that had been heading for my slot begin to knock against each other, like scared pigs in a chute.

Lengel sighs and begins to look very patient and old and gray. He's been a friend of my parents for years. ''Sammy, you don't want to do this to your Mom and Dad,'' he tells me. It's true, I don't. But it seems to me that once you begin a gesture it's fatal not to go through with it. I fold the apron, ''Sammy'' stitched in red on the pocket, and put it on the counter, and drop the bow tie on top of it. The bow tie is theirs, if you've ever wondered. ''You'll feel this for the rest of your life,'' Lengel says, and I know that's true, too, but remembering how he made that pretty girl blush makes me so scrunchy inside I punch the No Sale tab and the machine whirls ''pee-pul'' and the drawer splats out. One advantage to this scene taking place in summer, I can follow this up with a clean exit, there's no fumbling around getting your coat and galoshes, I just saunter into the electric eye in my white shirt that my mother ironed the night before, and the door heaves itself open, and outside the sunshine is skating around on the asphalt.

I look around for my girls, but they're gone, of course. There wasn't anybody but some young married screaming with her children about some candy they didn't get by the door of a powder-blue Falcon station wagon. Looking back in the big windows, over the bags of peat moss and aluminum lawn furniture stacked on the pavement, I could see Lengel in my place in the slot, checking the sheep through. His face was dark gray and his back stiff, as if he'd just had an injection of iron, and my stomach kind of fell as I felt how hard the world was going to be to me hereafter.

Martin Luther King, Jr. / I Have a Dream 1963

Martin Luther King, Jr. accomplished a great deal in a short time. The son of a Baptist minister, Dr. King was himself ordained at the age of eighteen. At twenty-six he became nationally prominent as a spiritual and civil-rights leader when he led a successful boycott in 1955 of Montgomery, Alabama's segregated bus system. Thereafter he became the first president of the Southern Christian Leadership Conference and was awarded the Nobel peace prize in 1964, largely for his policy of nonviolent resistance to racial injustice. Along the way he studied at Morehouse College, Crozer Theological Seminary, Boston University, and Chicago Theological Seminary.

One of the most eloquent speakers and charismatic leaders of modern times, Dr. King was assassinated in Memphis, Tennessee, in 1968, shortly before his fortieth birthday. Since then, he has become an American folk hero.

His ''I Have a Dream'' speech epitomizes Martin Luther King's vision of the future. He delivered this sermon from the steps of the Lincoln Memorial to more than 200,000 people who came to Washington, D.C., to show their support of civil rights as an issue and of Dr. King as a man.

Five score years ago, a great American, in whose symbolic shadow we stand, signed the Emancipation Proclamation. This momentous decree came as a great beacon light of hope to millions of Negro slaves who had been seared in the flames of withering injustice. It came as a joyous daybreak to end the long night of captivity.

But one hundred years later, we must face the tragic fact that the Negro is still not free. One hundred years later, the life of the Negro is still sadly crippled by the manacles of segregation and the chains of discrimination. One hundred years later, the Negro lives on a lonely island of poverty in the midst of a vast ocean of material prosperity. One hundred years later, the Negro is still languishing in the corners of American society and finds himself an exile in his own land. So we have come here today to dramatize an appalling condition.

In a sense we have come to our nation's Capitol to cash a check. When the architects of our republic wrote the magnificent words of the Constitution and the Declaration of Independence, they were signing a promissory note to which every American was to fall heir. This note was a promise that all men would be guaranteed the unalienable rights of life, liberty, and the pursuit of happiness.

It is obvious today that America has defaulted on this promissory note insofar as her citizens of color are concerned. Instead of honoring this sacred obligation, America has given the Negro people a bad check; a check which has come back marked "insufficient funds." But we refuse to believe that the bank of justice is bankrupt. We refuse to believe that there are insufficient funds in the great vaults of opportunity of this nation. So we have come to cash this check—a check that will give us upon demand the riches of freedom and the security of justice. We have also come to this hallowed spot to remind America of the fierce urgency of *now*. This is no time to engage in the luxury of cooling off or to take the tranquilizing drug of gradualism. *Now* is the time to make real the promises of Democracy. *Now* is the time to rise from the dark and desolate valley of segregation to the sunlit path of racial justice. *Now* is the time to open the doors of opportunity to all of God's children. *Now* is the time to lift our nation from the quicksands of racial injustice to the solid rock of brotherhood.

It would be fatal for the nation to overlook the urgency of the moment and to underestimate the determination of the Negro. This sweltering summer of the Negro's legitimate discontent will not pass until there is an invigorating autumn of freedom and equality. 1963 is not an end, but a beginning. Those who hope that the Negro needed to blow off steam and will now be content will have a rude awakening if the nation returns to business as usual. There will be neither rest nor tranquility in America until the Negro is granted his citizenship rights. The whirlwind of revolt will continue to shake the foundations of our nation until the bright day of justice emerges.

But there is something I must say to my people who stand on the warm threshold which leads into the palace of justice. In the process of gaining our rightful place we must not be guilty of wrongful deeds. Let us not seek to satisfy our thirst for freedom by drinking from the cup of bitterness and hatred. We must forever conduct our struggle on the high plane of dignity and discipline. We must not allow our creative protest to degenerate into physical violence. Again and again we must rise to the majestic heights of meeting physical force with soul force. The marvelous new militancy which has engulfed the Negro community must not lead us to a distrust of all white people, for many of our white brothers, as evidenced by their presence here today, have come to realize that their destiny is tied up with our destiny and their freedom is inextricably bound to our freedom. We cannot walk alone.

And as we walk, we must make the pledge that we shall march ahead. We cannot turn back. There are those who are asking the devotees of civil rights, "When will you be satisfied?" We can never be satisfied as long as the Negro is the victim of the unspeakable horrors of police brutality. We can never be satisfied as long as our bodies, heavy with the fatigue of travel, cannot gain lodging in the motels of the highways and the hotels of the cities. We cannot be satisfied as long as the Negro's basic mobility is from a smaller ghetto to a larger one. We can never be satisfied as long as a Negro in Mississippi cannot vote and a Negro in New York believes he has nothing for which to vote. No, no, we are not satisfied, and we will not be satisfied until justice rolls down like waters and righteousness like a mighty stream.

I am not unmindful that some of you have come here out of great trials and tribulations. Some of you have come fresh from narrow jail cells. Some of you have come from areas where your quest for freedom left you battered by the storms of persecution and staggered by the winds of police brutality. You have been the veterans of creative suffering. Continue to work with the faith that unearned suffering is redemptive.

Go back to Mississippi, go back to Alabama, go back to South Carolina, go back to Georgia, go back to Louisiana, go back to the slums and ghettoes of our northern cities, knowing that somehow this situation can and will be changed. Let us not wallow in the valley of despair.

I say to you today, my friends, that in spite of the difficulties and frustrations of the moment I still have a dream. It is a dream deeply rooted in the American dream.

I have a dream that one day this nation will rise up and live out the true meaning of its creed: "We hold these truths to be self-evident; that all men are created equal."

I have a dream that one day on the red hills of Georgia the sons of former slaves and the sons of former slave-owners will be able to sit down together at the table of brotherhood.

I have a dream that the state of Mississippi, a desert state sweltering with the heat of injustice and oppression, will be transformed into an oasis of freedom and justice.

I have a dream that my four little children will one day live in a nation where they will not be judged by the color of their skin but by the content of their character.

I have a dream today.

I have a dream that the state of Alabama, whose governor's lips are presently dripping with the words of interposition and nullification, will be transformed into a situation where little black boys and black girls will be able to join hands with little white boys and white girls and walk together as sisters and brothers.

I have a dream today.

I have a dream that one day every valley shall be exalted, every hill and mountain shall be made low, the rough place will be made plain, and the crooked places will be made straight, and the glory of the Lord shall be revealed, and all flesh shall see it together.

This is our hope. This is the faith with which I return to the South. With this faith we will be able to hew out of the mountain of despair a stone of hope. With this faith we will be able to transform the jangling discords of our nation into a beautiful symphony of brotherhood. With this faith we will be able to work together, to pray together, to struggle together, to go to jail together, to stand up for freedom together, knowing that we will be free one day.

This will be the day when all of God's children will be able to sing with new meaning:

My country, 'tis of thee
Sweet land of liberty
Of thee I sing:
Land where my fathers died,
Land of the pilgrims' pride,
From every mountainside
Let freedom ring.

And if America is to be a great nation this must become true. So let freedom ring from the prodigious hilltops of New Hampshire! Let freedom ring from the heightening Alleghenies of Pennsylvania!

Let freedom ring from the snowcapped Rockies of Colorado!

Let freedom ring from the curvaceous peaks of California!

But not only that; let freedom ring from Stone Mountain of Georgia!

Let freedom ring from every hill and molehill of Mississippi. From every mountainside, let freedom ring.

When we let freedom ring, when we let it ring from every village and every hamlet, from every state and every city, we will be able to speed up that day when all of God's children, black men and white men, Jews and Gentiles, Protestants and Catholics, will be able to join hands and sing in the words of the old Negro spiritual, "Free at last! free at last! thank God almighty, we are free at last!"

Sylvia Plath / America! America! 1963

Sylvia Plath (1932–63) was born in Boston, graduated from Smith College with honors, attended Newham College, Cambridge, on a fellowship, and lived in England during the last years of her life. While writing the stunning poetry that brought her posthumous acclaim, she longed to publish fiction in American magazines. "Poetry," she once wrote, "is an evasion from the real job of writing prose."

Founded in 1841, the British magazine, Punch, *has poked fun at almost everyone during its long history. Americans seemed to be among its favorite targets. Sylvia Plath sent the magazine her own very personal view of America, "America! America!," an essay later printed in a posthumous collection of her prose,* Johnny Panic and the Bible of Dreams *(1979).*

The poem "The Applicant," which follows her essay, is from Plath's second book of poems, Ariel *(1966).*

I went to public schools—genuinely public. *Everybody* went: the spry, the shy, the podge, the gangler, the future electronic scientist, the future cop who would one night kick a diabetic to death under the mistaken impression he was a drunk and needed cooling off; the poor, smelling of sour wools and the urinous baby at home and polyglot stew; the richer, with ratty fur collars, opal birthstone rings and daddies with cars ("Wot does *your* daddy do?" "He don't woik, he's a bus droiver." Laughter). There it was—Education—laid on free of charge for the lot of us, a lovely slab of depressed American public. *We* weren't depressed, of course. We left that to our parents, who eked out one child or two, and slumped dumbly after work and frugal suppers over their radios to listen to news of the "home country" and a black-moustached man named Hitler.

Above all, we did feel ourselves American in the rowdy seaside town where I picked up, like lint, my first ten years of schooling—a great, loud cats' bag of Irish Catholics, German Jews, Swedes, Negroes, Italians and that rare, pure Mayflower dropping, somebody *English*.

On to this steerage of infant citizens the doctrines of Liberty and Equality were to be, through the free, communal schools, impressed. Although we could almost call ourselves Bostonian (the city airport with its beautiful hover of planes and silver blimps growled and gleamed across the bay), New York's skyscrapers were the icons on our "home room" walls, New York and the great green queen lifting a bedlamp that spelled out Freedom.

Every morning, hands on hearts, we pledged allegiance to the Stars and Stripes, a sort of aerial altarcloth over teacher's desk. And sang songs full of powder smoke and patriotics to impossible, wobbly, soprano tunes. One high, fine song, "Four purple mountain majesties above the fruited plain," always made the scampi-size poet in me weep. In those days I couldn't have told a fruited plain from a mountain majesty and confused God with George Washington (whose lamblike granny-face shone down at us also from the schoolroom wall between neat blinders of white curls), yet warbled, nevertheless, with my small, snotty compatriots "America, America! God shed His grace on thee, and crown thy good with brotherhood from sea to shining sea."

The sea we knew something about. Terminus of almost every street, it buckled and swashed and tossed, out of its gray formlessness, china plates, wooden monkeys, elegant shells and dead men's shoes. Wet salt winds raked our playgrounds endlessly—those Gothic composites of gravel, macadam, granite and bald, flailed earth wickedly designed to bark and scour the tender knee. There we traded playing cards (for the patterns on the backs) and sordid stories, jumped clothes rope, shot marbles, and enacted the radio and comic book dramas of our day ("Who knows what evil lurks in the hearts of men? The Shadow knows—nyah, nyah, nyah!" or "Up in the sky, look! It's a bird, it's a plane, it's Superman!"). If we were destined for any special end—grooved, doomed, limited, fated, we didn't feel it. We beamed and sloshed from our desks to the dodge-ball dell, open and hopeful as the sea itself.

After all, we could be anybody. If we worked. If we studied hard enough. Our accents, our money, our parents didn't matter. Did not lawyers rise from the loins of coalheavers, doctors from the bins of dustmen? Education was the answer, and heaven knows how it came to us. Invisibly, I think, in the early days—a mystical infra-red glow off the thumbed multiplication tables, ghastly poems extolling October's bright blue weather, and a world of history that more or less began and ended with the Boston Tea Party—Pilgrims and Indians being, like the eohippus, prehistoric.

Later, the college obsession would seize us, a subtle, terrifying virus. Everybody had to go to *some* college or other. A business college, a junior college, a state college, a secretarial college, an Ivy League college, a pig farmers' college. The book first, then the work. By the time we (future cop and electronic brain alike) exploded into our prosperous, postwar high school, full-time guidance counselors jogged our elbows at ever-diminishing intervals to discuss motives, hopes, school subjects, jobs—and colleges. Excellent teachers showered onto us like meteors: Biology teachers holding up human brains, English teachers inspiring us with a personal ideological fierceness about Tolstoy and Plato, Art teachers leading us through the slums of Boston, then back to the easel to hurl public school gouache with social awareness and fury. Eccentricities, the perils of being *too* special, were reasoned and cooed from us like sucked thumbs.

The girls' guidance counselor diagnosed my problem straight off. I was just too dangerously brainy. My high, pure string of straight A's might, without proper extracurricular tempering, snap me into the void. More and more, the colleges wanted All-Round Students. I had, by that time, studied Machiavelli in Current Events class. I grabbed my cue.

Now this guidance counselor owned, unknown to me, a white-haired identical twin I kept meeting in supermarkets and at the dentist's. To this twin, I confided my widening circle of activities—chewing orange sections at the quarters of girls' basketball games (I had made the team), painting mammoth L'il Abners and Daisy

Maes for class dances, pasting up dummies of the school newspaper at midnight while my already dissipated co-editor read out the jokes at the bottom of the columns of *The New Yorker*. The blank, oddly muffled expression of my guidance counselor's twin in the street did not deter me, nor did the apparent amnesia of her whitely efficient double in the school office. I became a rabid teenage pragmatist.

"Usage is Truth, Truth, Usage," I might have muttered, leveling my bobbysocks to match those of my schoolmates. There was no uniform, but there *was* a uniform—the pageboy hairdo, squeaky clean, the skirt and sweater, the "loafers," those scuffed copies of Indian moccasins. We even, in our democratic edifice, nursed two ancient relics of snobbism—two sororities: Subdeb and Sugar 'n' Spice. At the start of each school year, invitation cards went out from old members to new girls—the pretty, the popular, the in some way rivalrous. A week of initiation preceded our smug admittance to the cherished Norm. Teachers preached against Initiation Week, boys scoffed, but couldn't stop it.

I was assigned, like each initiate, a Big Sister who systematically began to destroy my ego. For a whole week I could wear no make-up, could not wash, could not comb my hair, change clothes or speak to boys. By dawn I had walked to my Big Sister's house and was making her bed and breakfast. Then, lugging her intolerably heavy books, as well as my own, I followed her, at a dog's distance, to school. On the way she might order me to climb a tree and hang from a branch till I dropped, ask a passer-by a rude question or stalk about the shops begging for rotten grapes and moldy rice. If I smiled—showed, that is, any sense of irony at my slavishness, I had to kneel on the public pavement and wipe the smile off my face. The minute the bell rang to end school, Big Sister took over. By nightfall I ached and stank; my homework buzzed in a dulled and muzzy brain. I was being tailored to an Okay Image.

Somehow it didn't take—this initiation into the nihil of belonging. Maybe I was just too weird to begin with. What did these picked buds of American womanhood do at their sorority meetings? They ate cake; ate cake and catted about the Saturday night date. The privilege of being anybody was turning its other face—to the pressure of being everybody; ergo, no one.

Lately I peered through the plate-glass side of an American primary school: child-size desks and chairs in clean, light wood, toy stoves and minuscule drinking fountains. Sunlight everywhere. All the anarchism, discomfort and grit I so tenderly remembered had been, in a quarter century, gentled away. One class had spent the morning on a bus learning how to pay fares and ask for the proper stop. Reading (my lot did it by age four off soapbox tops) had become such a traumatic and stormy art one felt lucky to weather it by ten. But the children were smiling in their little ring. Did I glimpse, in the First Aid cabinet, a sparkle of bottles—soothers and smootheners for the embryo rebel, the artist, the odd?

David Wagoner / The Shooting of John Dillinger Outside the Biograph Theater, July 22, 1934

1966

At various times a railroad section-hand, a concentrated soup scooper at a steel mill, a park policeman, and a short-order cook, David Wagoner has been a professor of English at the University of Washington at Seattle since 1954. His first volume of poems, Dry Sun, Dry Wind, *appeared in 1953, when he was twenty-seven years old. Since then, he has published numerous books of poetry, served as editor of* Poetry Northwest, *as well as written film scripts and several novels, the most noted of which is* The Escape Artist *(1965).*

The poem printed below is from his collection entitled Staying Alive *(1966).*

Chicago ran a fever of a hundred and one that groggy Sunday.
A reporter fried an egg on a sidewalk; the air looked shaky.
And a hundred thousand people were in the lake like shirts in a laundry.
Why was Johnny lonely?
Not because two dozen solid citizens, heat-struck, had keeled over backward.
Not because those lawful souls had fallen out of their sockets and melted.
But because the sun went down like a lump in a furnace or a bull in the Stockyards.
Where was Johnny headed?
Under the Biograph Theater sign that said, "Our Air is Refrigerated."
Past seventeen FBI men and four policemen who stood in doorways and sweated.
Johnny sat down in a cold seat to watch Clark Gable get electrocuted.
Had Johnny been mistreated?
Yes, but Gable told the D. A. he'd rather fry than be shut up forever.
Two women sat by Johnny. One looked sweet, one looked like J. Edgar Hoover.
Polly Hamilton made him feel hot, but Anna Sage made him shiver.
Was Johnny a good lover?
Yes, but he passed out his share of squeezes and pokes like a jittery masher
While Agent Purvis sneaked up and down the aisle like an extra usher,
Trying to make sure they wouldn't slip out till the show was over.
Was Johnny a fourflusher?
No, not if he knew the game. He got it up or got it back.
But he liked to take snapshots of policemen with his own Kodak,
And once in a while he liked to take them with an automatic.
Why was Johnny frantic?
Because he couldn't take a walk or sit down in a movie
Without being afraid he'd run smack into somebody
Who'd point at his rearranged face and holler, "Johnny!"
Was Johnny ugly?
Yes, because Dr. Wilhelm Loeser had given him a new profile
With a baggy jawline and squint eyes and an erased dimple,
With kangaroo-tendon cheekbones and a gigolo's mustache that should've been illegal.
Did Johnny love a girl?
Yes, a good-looking, hard-headed Indian named Billie Frechette.
He wanted to marry her and lie down and try to get over it,
But she was locked in jail for giving him first-aid and comfort.
Did Johnny feel hurt?
He felt like breaking a bank or jumping over a railing
Into some panicky teller's cage to shout, "Reach for the ceiling!"
Or like kicking some vice president in the bum checks and smiling.
What was he really doing?
Going up the aisle with the crowd and into the lobby
With Polly saying, "Would *you* do what Clark done?" And Johnny saying, "Maybe."
And Anna saying, "If he'd been smart, he'd of acted like Bing Crosby."
Did Johnny look flashy?
Yes, his white-on-white shirt and tie were luminous.

His trousers were creased like knives to the tops of his shoes,
And his yellow straw hat came down to his dark glasses.
Was Johnny suspicious?
Yes, and when Agent Purvis signalled with a trembling cigar,
Johnny ducked left and ran out of the theater,
And innocent Polly and squealing Anna were left nowhere.
Was Johnny a fast runner?
No, but he crouched and scurried past a friendly liquor store
Under the coupled arms of double-daters, under awnings, under stars,
To the curb at the mouth of an alley. He hunched there.
Was Johnny a thinker?
No, but he was thinking more or less of Billie Frechette
Who was lost in prison for longer than he could possibly wait,
And then it was suddenly too hard to think around a bullet.
Did anyone shoot straight?
Yes, but Mrs. Etta Natalsky fell out from under her picture hat.
Theresa Paulus sprawled on the sidewalk, clutching her left foot.
And both of them groaned loud and long under the streetlight.
Did Johnny like that?
No, but he lay down with those strange women, his face in the alley,
One shoe off, cinders in his mouth, his eyelids heavy.
When they shouted questions at him, he talked back to nobody.
Did Johnny lie easy?
Yes, holding his gun and holding his breath as a last trick,
He waited, but when the Agents came close, his breath wouldn't work.
Clark Gable walked his last mile; Johnny ran half a block.
Did he run out of luck?
Yes, before he was cool, they had him spread out on dished-in marble
In the Cook County Morgue, surrounded by babbling people
With a crime reporter presiding over the head of the table.
Did Johnny have a soul?
Yes, and it was climbing his slippery wind-pipe like a trapped burglar.
It was beating the inside of his ribcage, hollering, "Let me out of here!"
Maybe it got out, and maybe it just stayed there.
Was Johnny a money-maker?
Yes, and thousands paid 25¢ to see him, mostly women,
And one said, "I wouldn't have come, except he's a moral lesson,"
And another, "I'm disappointed. He feels like a dead man."
Did Johnny have a brain?
Yes, and it always worked best through the worst of dangers,
Through flat-footed hammerlocks, through guarded doors, around corners,
But it got taken out in the morgue and sold to some doctors.
Could Johnny take orders?
No, but he stayed in the wicker basket carried by six men
Through the bulging crowd to the hearse and let himself be locked in,
And he stayed put as it went driving south in a driving rain.
And he didn't get stolen?
No, not even after his old hard-nosed dad refused to sell
The quick-drawing corpse for $10,000 to somebody in a carnival.
He figured he'd let *Johnny* decide how to get to Hell.
Did anyone wish him well?
Yes, half of Indiana camped in the family pasture,
And the minister said, "With luck, he could have been a minister."
And up the sleeve of his oversized gray suit, Johnny twitched a finger.

Does anyone remember?
Everyone still alive. And some dead ones. It was a new kind of holiday
With hot and cold drinks and hot and cold tears. They planted him in a cemetery
With three unknown vice presidents, Benjamin Harrison, and James Whitcomb Riley,
Who never held up anybody.

Maya Angelou / *I Know Why the Caged Bird Sings* 1969

Maya Angelou was born Marguerite Johnson in St. Louis in 1928. After her turbulent youth ("from a broken family, raped at eight, unwed mother at sixteen"), she went on to study dance with the Pearl Primus company in New York, star in an off-Broadway show (The Blacks), *write three books of poetry, produce a series on Africa for PBS, serve as coordinator for the Southern Christian Leadership Conference at the request of Martin Luther King, Jr., and accept three honorary doctorates.*

As an author, actress, singer, dancer, songwriter, teacher, editor and film director, Maya Angelou has been a pioneer in furthering the role of the American black woman in the arts.

She is best known for her autobiography, I Know Why the Caged Bird Sings *(1969), from which the following reminiscence is taken. For another memory of Joe Louis, see Howie Evans's "Joe Louis: American Folk Hero" in Press.*

CHAMPION OF THE WORLD

The last inch of space was filled, yet people continued to wedge themselves along the walls of the Store. Uncle Willie had turned the radio up to its last notch so that youngsters on the porch wouldn't miss a word. Women sat on kitchen chairs, dining-room chairs, stools and upturned wooden boxes. Small children and babies perched on every lap available and men leaned on the shelves or on each other.

The apprehensive mood was shot through with shafts of gaiety, as a black sky is streaked with lightning.

"I ain't worried 'bout this fight. Joe's gonna whip that cracker like it's open season."

"He gone whip him till that white boy call him Momma."

At last the talking was finished and the string-along songs about razor blades were over and the fight began.

"A quick jab to the head." In the Store the crowd grunted. "A left to the head and a right and another left." One of the listeners cackled like a hen and was quieted.

"They're in a clinch, Louis is trying to fight his way out."

Some bitter comedian on the porch said, "That white man don't mind hugging that niggah now, I betcha."

"The referee is moving in to break them up, but Louis finally pushed the contender away and it's an uppercut to the chin. The contender is hanging on, now he's backing away. Louis catches him with a short left to the jaw."

A tide of murmuring assent poured out the doors and into the yard.

"Another left and another left. Louis is saving that mighty right . . ." The mutter in the Store had grown into a baby roar and it was pierced by the clang of a bell and the announcer's "That's the bell for round three, ladies and gentlemen."

As I pushed my way into the Store I wondered if the announcer gave any thought to the fact that he was addressing as "ladies and gentlemen" all the Negroes around the world who sat sweating and praying, glued to their "master's voice."[1]

There were only a few calls for R.C. Colas, Dr. Peppers, and Hires root beer. The real festivities would begin after the fight. Then even the old Christian ladies who taught their children and tried themselves to practice turning the other cheek would buy soft drinks, and if the Brown Bomber's victory was a particularly bloody one they would order peanut patties and Baby Ruths also.

Bailey and I laid the coins on top of the cash register. Uncle Willie didn't allow us to ring up sales during a fight. It was too noisy and might shake up the atmosphere. When the gong rang for the next round we pushed through the near-sacred quiet to the herd of children outside.

"He's got Louis against the ropes and now it's a left to the body and a right to the ribs. Another right to the body, it looks like it was low. . . . Yes, ladies and gentlemen, the referee is signaling but the contender keeps raining the blows on Louis. It's another to the body, and it looks like Louis is going down."

My race groaned. It was our people falling. It was another lynching, yet another Black man hanging on a tree. One more woman ambushed and raped. A Black boy whipped and maimed. It was hounds on the trail of a man running through slimy swamps. It was a white woman slapping her maid for being forgetful.

The men in the Store stood away from the walls and at attention. Women greedily clutched the babes on their laps while on the porch the shufflings and smiles, flirtings and pinching of a few minutes before were gone. This might be the end of the world. If Joe lost we were back in slavery and beyond help. It would all be true, the accusations that we were lower types of human beings. Only a little higher than apes. True that we were stupid and ugly and lazy and dirty and, unlucky and worst of all, that God Himself hated us and ordained us to be hewers of wood and drawers of water, forever and ever, world without end.

We didn't breathe. We didn't hope. We waited.

"He's off the ropes, ladies and gentlemen. He's moving towards the center of the ring." There was no time to be relieved. The worst might still happen.

"And now it looks like Joe is mad. He's caught Carnera with a left hook to the head and a right to the head. It's a left jab to the body and another left to the head. There's a left cross and a right to the head. The contender's right eye is bleeding and he can't seem to keep his block up. Louis is penetrating every block. The referee is moving in, but Louis sends a left to the body and it's an uppercut to the chin and the contender is dropping. He's on the canvas, ladies and gentlemen."

Babies slid to the floor as women stood up and men leaned toward the radio.

"Here's the referee. He's counting. One, two, three, four, five, six, seven . . . Is the contender trying to get up again?"

All the men in the store shouted, "NO."

"—eight, nine, ten." There were a few sounds from the audience, but they seemed to be holding themselves in against tremendous pressure.

"The fight is all over, ladies and gentlemen. Let's get the microphone over to the referee . . . Here he is. He's got the Brown Bomber's hand, he's holding it up . . . Here he is . . ."

Then the voice, husky and familiar, came to wash over us—"The winnah, and still heavyweight champeen of the world . . . Joe Louis."

Champion of the world. A Black boy. Some Black mother's son. He was the

[1] A famous advertising slogan for RCA phonographs.

strongest man in the world. People drank Coca-Colas like ambrosia and ate candy bars like Christmas. Some of the men went behind the Store and poured white lightning in their soft-drink bottles, and a few of the bigger boys followed them. Those who were not chased away came back blowing their breath in front of themselves like proud smokers.

It would take an hour or more before the people would leave the Store and head for home. Those who lived too far had made arrangements to stay in town. It wouldn't do for a Black man and his family to be caught on a lonely country road on a night when Joe Louis had proved that we were the strongest people in the world.

Norman Mailer / *Of a Fire on the Moon* 1970

Born in New Jersey in 1923 and brought up in Brooklyn, Norman Mailer began writing while still an undergraduate at Harvard. In his fiction, essays, and highly personal journalism, Mailer has "covered" many significant phases of American life since the end of the Second World War. Part of his account of the Apollo XI *voyage first appeared in* Life *magazine and was later expanded into a book length study of the astronauts,* Of a Fire on the Moon, *from which the following passage is excerpted. Always attracted to the action at the center of the arena, as his reporting of political conventions* (Miami and the Siege of Chicago) *and the peace movement of the sixties* (Armies of the Night) *testifies, Norman Mailer finds himself during his coverage of the moon walk an unwilling nonparticipant on an assignment without a location.*

[THE FIRST MOON WALK]

They had landed, there was jubilation in Mission Control, and a moment of fraternization between Armstrong and Aldrin, but in fact they were actually at work in the next instant. No one knew what would await them—there were even theories that most of the surface of the moon was as fragile as icing on a cake. If they landed, and the moon ground began to collapse, they were ready to blast off with the ascent stage even as the descent stage was sinking beneath. But no sound of crumbling came up through the pipes of the legs, no shudder of collapse. A minute passed. They received the order to Stay. The second Stay–No Stay would be on them nine minutes later, and they rushed through a checklist, testing specific instruments to make certain they were intact from the landing. The thirty-odd seconds of fuel they still had left when they touched down was vented from the descent stage, a hissing and steaming beneath the legs like a steed loosing water on icy ground. Verbs and Nouns were punched into the DSKY. Now came the second Stay. There would not be another Stay–No Stay until the Command Module had made a complete revolution of the moon and would be coming back toward them in good position for rendezvous. So, unless some mishap were suddenly to appear, they had at least another two hours on the satellite. It was time to unscrew their gloves at the wrist and take them off, time to unscrew their helmets at the neck, lift them off.

They gave their first description of the landing, and made a few general remarks about the view through the window, the variety of rocks. But there was too much work to look for long. After a few comments on the agreeableness of lunar gravity, after a conversation with Columbia and mutual congratulations, they were back at the computer. Now, in the time before the next Stay–No Stay, they had to simulate a countdown for a planned ascent and realign the Inertial Measurement Unit, that is, determine the vertical line of moon gravity, and install its index into the Inertial Measurement Unit, then level the table and gyroscope from which all navigation was computed. Star checks were taken. Meanwhile, Armstrong was readying the cameras and snapping photographs through the window. Now Aldrin aligned the Abort Guidance Section. Armstrong laid in the data for Program 12, the Powered Ascent Guidance. The Command Module came around again. The simulated countdown was over. They had another Stay. They powered down their systems.

In the transcript the work continues minute after minute, familiar talk of stars and Nouns, acronyms, E-memory dumps, and returns to POO where Pings may idle. They are at rest on the moon, but the dialogue is not unencumbered of pads, updata link switches and noise suppression devices on the Manned Space Flight Network relay.

Then in what is virtually their first pause in better than an hour on the moon, they request permission to do their EVA early, begin in fact in the next few hours rather than take a halt to sleep. For days there had been discussion in every newspaper of the world whether the astronauts could land on the moon and a few hours later go to sleep before they even stepped out of the Lem; now the question has been answered—they are impatient to go.

CAPCOM: *We will support it.*
ALDRIN: *Roger.*
CAPCOM: *You guys are getting prime time TV there.*
ARMSTRONG: *Hope that little TV set works, but we'll see.*

Now the astronauts stopped to eat and to relax. Over the radio came the dialogue of Mission Control talking to Collins in orbit overhead. Around them, through each pinched small window, were tantalizing views of the moon. They could feel themselves in one-sixth gravity. How light were their bodies. Yet they were not weightless. There was gravity beneath them, a faint sensuous tug at their limbs. If they dropped a pencil, it did not float before drifting slowly away. Rather, it dropped. Slowly it dropped, dropped indeed at the same leisurely speed with which Apollo-Saturn had risen off its launching pad four and a half days ago. What a balm for the muscles of the eye! One-sixth of earth gravity was agreeable, it was attractive, it was, said Aldrin, "less *lonesome*" than weightlessness. He had, at last, " a distinct feeling of being somewhere." Yes, the moon was beneath them, hardly more than the height of a ten-foot diving board beneath them—they were in the domain of a presence again. How much like magnetism must lunar gravity have felt.

ALDRIN: *This is the Lem pilot. I'd like to take this opportunity to ask every person listening in, whoever and wherever they may be, to pause for a moment and contemplate the events of the past few hours, and to give thanks in his or her way.*

In the silence, Aldrin took out the bread, the wine, and the chalice he had brought in his Personal Preference Kit, and he put them on the little table in front of the Abort Guidance Section computer. Then he read some passages from the Bible and celebrated Communion.

A strange picture of religious intensity: there is of course no clue in Aldrin's immediate words—they are by now tuned to precisely what one would expect.

"I would like to have observed just how the wine poured in that environment, but it wasn't pertinent at that particular time. It wasn't important how it got in the cup.

It was important only to get it there''—and not spill, we may assume, this most special blood of the Lord. ''I offered some private prayers, but I find now that thoughts, feelings, come into my memory instead of words. I was not so selfish as to include my family in those prayers at the moment, nor so spacious as to include the fate of the world. I was thinking more about our particular task, and the challenge and the opportunity that had been given us. I asked people to offer thanks in their own way, and it is my hope that people will keep this whole event in their minds and see beyond minor details and technical achievements to a deeper meaning behind it all, challenge, a quest, the human need to do these things and the need to recognize that we are all one mankind under God.''

Yes, his recollections are near to comic in their banality, but one gets a picture of this strong-nosed strong-armed gymnast in his space suit, deep in prayer in the crowded closet space of the Lem, while Armstrong the mystic (with the statue of Buddha on his living room table) is next to him in who knows what partial or unwilling communion, Armstrong so private in his mind that when a stranger tried to talk to him one day on a bus, he picked up a book to read. There, before his partner, Aldrin prayed, light lunar gravity new in his limbs, eyes closed. Can we assume the brain of his inner vision expanded to the dimensions of a church, the loft of a cathedral, Aldrin, man of passions and disciplines, fatalist, all but open believer in predestination, agent of God's will, Aldrin, prodigy of effort on Gemini 12, whose pulse after hours of work in space had shot up only when he read a Veteran's Day message to the ground. Patriotism had the power of a stroke for Aldrin and invocation was his harmony. Tribal chief, first noble savage on the moon, he prayed to the powers who had brought him there, whose will he would fulfill—God, the earth, the moon and himself all for this instant part of the lofty engine of the universe, and in that eccentric giant of character, that conservative of all the roots in all the family trees, who now was ripping up the roots of the ages, that man whose mother's name was Moon, was there a single question whose lament might suggest that if the mission were ill-conceived or even a work of art designed by the Devil, then all the prayers of all good men were nothing but a burden upon the Lord, who in order to reply would be forced to work in the mills of Satan, or leave the prayers of his flock in space. Not likely. Aldrin did not seem a man for thoughts like that, but then his mind was a mystery wrapped in the winding-sheet of a computer with billions of bits.

Later, Armstrong would say, ''That first hour on the moon was hardly the time for long thoughts; we had specific jobs to do. Of course the sights were simply magnificent, beyond any visual experience that I had ever been exposed to,'' and Aldrin would describe it as ''a unique, almost mystical environment.'' In fact, there is an edge of the unexplained to their reactions. Their characteristic matter-of-fact response is overcome occasonally by swoops of hyperbole. And to everyone's slight surprise, they were almost two hours late for their EVA. Their estimate of time was off by close to fifty percent. For astronauts that was an error comparable to a carpenter mistaking an eight-foot stud for a twelve-foot piece. If a carpenter can look at a piece of wood and guess its length to the nearest quarter-inch, it is because he has been working with lengths all his life. Equally, people in some occupations have a close ability to estimate time.

With astronauts, whose every day in a simulator was a day laid out on the measure of a time-line, the estimate of time elapsed had to become acute. Armstrong and Aldrin had consistently fulfilled their tasks in less time than was allotted. Now, curiously, they fell behind, then further behind. There were unexpected problems of course—it took longer to bleed the pressure out of the Lunar Module than had been anticipated, and the cooling units in the backpacks were sluggish at first in operation, but whether from natural excitement and natural anxiety, or an unconscious preoccupation with lunar phenomena so subtle that it is just at the edge of their senses, any extract from the transcript at this point where they are helping to adjust the Portable Life Support System on each others' backs shows real lack of enunciation. Nowhere else do the NASA stenographers have as much difficulty with where one voice ends and another begins.

TRANQUILITY: *Got it (garbled) prime rows in.*
TRANQUILITY: *Okay.*
TRANQUILITY: *(garbled)*
TRANQUILITY: *Let me do that for you.*
TRANQUILITY: *(Inaudible)*
TRANQUILITY: *Mark I*
TRANQUILITY: *(garbled) valves*
TRANQUILITY: *(garbled)*
TRANQUILITY: *Okay*
TRANQUILITY: *All of the (garbled)*
TRANQULITY: *(garbled) locked and lock locked.*
TRANQUILITY: *Did you put it—*
TRANQUILITY: *Oh, wait a minute*
TRANQUILITY: *Should be (garbled)*
TRANQUILITY: *(garbled)*
TRANQUILITY: *Roger. (garbled)*
TRANQUILITY: *I'll try it on the middle*
TRANQUILITY: *All right, check my (garbled) valves vertical*
TRANQUILITY: *Both vertical*
TRANQUILITY: *That's two vertical*
TRANQUILITY: *Okay*
TRANQUILITY: *(garbled)*
TRANQUILITY: *Locked and double-locked*
TRANQUILITY: *Okay*
TRANQUILITY: *Miss marked*
TRANQUILITY: *Sure wish I would have shaved last night.*
PAO: *That was a Buzz Aldrin comment.*

The hint is faint enough, but the hint exists—something was conceivably interfering with their sense of order. Could it have been the lunar gravity? Clock-time was a measure which derived from pendulums and spiral springs, clock-time was anchored right into the tooth of earth gravity—so a time might yet be coming when psychologists, not geologists, would be conducting experiments on the moon. Did lunar gravity have power like a drug to shift the sense of time?

Armstrong was connected at last to his PLSS. He was drawing oxygen from the pack he carried on his back. But the hatch door would not open. The pressure would not go low enough in the Lem. Down near a level of one pound per square inch, the last bit of man-created atmosphere in Eagle seemed to cling to its constituency, reluctant to enter the vacuums of the moon. But they did not know if they could get the hatch door open with a vacuum on one side and even a small pressure on the other. It was taking longer than they thought. While it was not a large concern since there would be other means to open it—redundancies pervaded throughout—nonetheless, a concern must have intruded: how intolerably comic they would appear if they came all the way and then were blocked before a door they could not crack. That thought had to put one drop of perspiration on the back of the neck. Besides, it must have been embarrassing to begin so late. The world of television was watching, and the astronauts had exhibited as much sensitivity to an audience as any bride on her way down the aisle.

It was not until nine-forty at night, Houston time, that they got the hatch open at last. In the heat of running almost two hours late, ensconced in the armor of a man-sized spaceship, could they still have felt an instant of awe as they looked out that open hatch at a panorama of theater: the sky is black, but the ground is brightly lit, bright as footlights on the floor of a dark theater. A black and midnight sky, yet on the moon ground, "you could almost go out in your shirt-sleeves and get a suntan," Aldrin would say. "I remember thinking, 'Gee, if I didn't know where I was, I could believe that somebody had created this environment somewhere out in the West and given us another simulation to work in.' " Everywhere on that pitted flat were shadows dark as the sky above, shadows dark as mine shafts.

What a struggle to push out from that congested cabin, now twice congested in their bulky-wham suits, no feeling of obstacle against their flesh, their sense of touch dead and numb, spaceman body manipulated out into the moon world like an upright piano turned by movers on the corner of the stairs.

"You're lined up on the platform. Put your left foot to the right a little bit. Okay, that's good. Roll left."

Armstrong was finally on the porch. Could it be with any sense of an alien atmosphere receiving the fifteen-layer encapsulations of the pack and suit on his back? Slowly, he climbed down the ladder. Archetypal, he must have felt, a boy descending the rungs in the wall of an abandoned well, or was it Jack down the stalk? And there he was on the bottom, on the footpad of the leg of the Lem, a metal plate perhaps three feet across. Inches away was the soil of the moon. But first he jumped up again to the lowest rung of the ladder. A couple of hours later, at the end of the EVA, conceivably exhausted, the jump from the ground to the rung, three feet up, might be difficult in that stiff and heavy space suit, so he tested it now. "It takes," said Armstrong, "a pretty good little jump."

Now, with television working, and some fraction of the world peering at the murky image of this instant, poised between the end of one history and the beginning of another, he said quietly, "I'm at the foot of the ladder. The Lem footpads are only depressed in the surface about one or two inches, although the surface appears to be very very fine-grained as you get close to it. It's almost like a powder." One of Armstrong's rare confessions of uneasiness is focused later on this moment. "I don't recall any particular emotion or feeling other than a little caution, a desire to be sure it was safe to put my weight on that surface outside Eagle's footpad."

Did his foot tingle in the heavy lunar overshoe? "I'm going to step off the Lem now."

Did something in him shudder at the touch of the new ground? Or did he draw a sweet strength from the balls of his feet? Nobody was necessarily going ever to know.

"That's one small step for a man," said Armstrong, "one giant leap for mankind." He had joined the ranks of the forever quoted. Patrick Henry, Henry Stanley and Admiral Dewey moved over for him.

Now he was out there, one foot on the moon, then the other foot on the moon, the powder like velvet underfoot. With one hand still on the ladder, he comments, "The surface is fine and powdery. I can . . . I can pick it up loosely with my toe." And as he releases his catch, the grains fall back slowly to the soil, a fan of feathers gliding to the floor. "It does adhere in fine layers like powdered charcoal to the sole and sides of my boots. I only go in a small fraction of an inch. Maybe an eighth of an inch. But I can see the footprints of my boots and the treads in the fine sand particles."

Capcom: "Neil, this is Houston. We're copying."

Yes, they would copy. He was like a man who goes into a wrecked building to defuse a new kind of bomb. He talks into a microphone as he works, for if a mistake is made, and the bomb goes off, it will be easier for the next man if every detail of his activities has been mentioned as he performed them. Now, he released his grip on the ladder and pushed off for a few steps on the moon, odd loping steps, almost thrust into motion like a horse trotting up a steep slope. It could have been a moment equivalent to the first steps he took as an infant for there was nothing to hold onto and he did not dare to fall—the ground was too hot, the rocks might tear his suit. Yet if he stumbled, he could easily go over for he could not raise his arms above his head nor reach to his knees, his arms in the pressure bladder stood out before him like sausages; so, if he tottered, the weight of the pack could twist him around, or drop him. They had tried to shape up simulations of lunar gravity while weighted in scuba suits at the bottom of a pool, but water was not a vacuum through which to move; so they had also flown in planes carrying two hundred pounds of equipment on their backs. The pilot would take the plane through a parabolic trajectory. There would be a period of twenty-two seconds at the top of the curve when a simulation of one-sixth gravity would be present, and the two hundred pounds of equipment would weigh no more than on the moon, no more than thirty-plus pounds, and one could take loping steps down the aisle of the plane, staggering through unforeseen wobbles or turbulence. Then the parabolic trajectory was done, the plane was diving, and it would have to pull out of the dive. That created the reverse of one-sixth gravity—it multiplied gravity by two and a half times. The two hundred pounds of equipment now weighed five hundred pounds and the astronauts had to be supported by other men straining to help them bear the weight. So simulations gave them time for hardly more than a clue before heavy punishment was upon them. But now he was out in the open endless lunar gravity, his body and the reflexes of his life obliged to adopt a new rhythm and schedule of effort, a new disclosure of grace.

Still, he seemed pleased after the first few steps. "There seems to be no difficulty in moving around as we suspected. It's even perhaps easier than the simulations . . ." He would run a few steps and stop, run a few steps and stop. Perhaps it was not unlike directing the Lem when it hovered over the ground. One moved faster than on earth and with less effort, but it was harder to stop—one had to pick the place to halt from several yards ahead. Yes, it was easier once moving, but awkward at the beginning and the end because of the obdurate plastic bendings of the suit. And once standing at rest, the sense of the vertical was sly. One could be leaning further forward than one knew. Or leaning backward. Like a needle on a dial one would have to oscillate from side to side of the vertical to find position. Conceivably the sensation was not unlike skiing with a child on one's back.

It was time for Aldrin to descend the ladder from the Lem to the ground, and Armstrong's turn to give directions: "The shoes are about to come over the sill. Okay, now drop your PLSS down. There you go. You're clear. . . . About an inch clearance on top of your PLSS."

Aldrin spoke for future astronauts: "Okay, you need a little bit of arching of the back to come down . . ."

When he reached the ground, Aldrin took a big and exuberant leap up the ladder again, as if to taste the pleasures of one-sixth gravity all at once. "Beautiful, beautiful," he exclaimed.

Armstrong: "Isn't that something. Magnificent sight out here."

Aldrin: "Magnificent desolation."

They were looking at a terrain which lived in a clarity of focus unlike anything they had ever seen on earth. There was no air, of course, and so no wind, nor clouds, nor dust, nor even the finest scattering of light from the smallest dispersal of microscopic particles on a clear day on earth, no, nothing visible or invisible moved in the vacuum before them. All light was pure. No haze was present, not even the invisible haze of the finest day—therefore objects did not go out of focus as they receded into the distance. If one's eyes were good enough, an object at a hundred yards was as distinct as a rock at a few feet. And their eyes were good enough. Just as one could not determine one's altitude above the moon, not from fifty miles up nor five, so now along the ground before them no distance was real, for all distances had the faculty to appear equally near if one peered at them through blinders and could not see the intervening details. Again the sense of being on a stage or on the lighted floor of a room so large one could not see where the dark ceiling began must have come upon them, for there were no hints of gathering evanescence in ridge beyond ridge; rather each outline was as severe as the one in front of it, and since the ground was filled with small craters of every size, from antholes to potholes to empty pools, and the horizon was near, four times nearer than on earth and sharp as the line drawn by a pencil, the moon ground seemed to slope and drop in all directions "like swimming in an ocean with six-foot or eight-foot swells and waves," Armstrong said later. "In that condition, you never can see very far away from where you are." But what they could see, they could see entirely—to the depth of their field of view at any instant their focus was complete. And as they swayed from side to side, so a sense of the vertical kept eluding them, the slopes of the craters about them seeming to tilt a few degrees to one side of the horizontal, then the other. On earth, one had only to incline one's body an inch or two and a sense of the vertical was gone, but on the moon they could lean over, then further over, lean considerably further over without beginning to fall. So verticals slid and oscillated. Rolling from side to side, they could as well have been on water, indeed their sense of the vertical was probably equal to the subtle uncertainty of the body when a ship is rolling on a quiet sea. "I say," said Aldrin, "the rocks are rather slippery."

They were discovering the powder of the moon soil was curious indeed, comparable in firmness and traction to some matter between sand and snow. While the Lem looked light as a kite, for its pads hardly rested on the ground and it appeared ready to lift off and blow away, yet their own feet sometimes sank for two or three inches into the soft powder on the slope of very small craters, and their soles would slip as the powder gave way under their boots. In other places the ground was firm and harder than sand, yet all of these variations were to be found in an area not a hundred feet out from the legs of the Lem. As he explored his footing, Aldrin sent back comments to Mission Control, reporting in the rapt professional tones of a coach instructing his team on the conditions of the turf in a new plastic football field.

Meanwhile Armstrong was transporting the television camera away from the Lem to a position where it could cover most of their activities. Once properly installed, he revolved it through a full panorama of their view in order that audiences on earth might have a clue to what he saw. But in fact the transmission was too rudimentary to give any sense of what was about them, that desert sea of rocks, rubble, small boulders, and crater lips.

Aldrin was now working to set up the solar wind experiment, a sheet of aluminum foil hung on a stand. For the next hour and a half, the foil would be exposed to the solar wind, and invisible, unfelt, but high-velocity flow of noble gases from the sun like argon, krypton, neon and helium. For the astronauts, it was the simplest of procedures, no more difficult than setting up a piece of sheet music on a music stand. At the end of the EVA, however, the aluminum foil would be rolled up, insterted in the rock box, and delivered eventually to a laboratory in Switzerland uniquely equipped for the purpose. There any nobles gases which had been trapped in the atomic lattice of the aluminum would be baked out in virtuoso procedures of quantitative analysis, and a closer knowledge of the components of the solar wind would be gained. Since the solar wind, it may be recalled, was diverted by the magnetosphere away from the earth it had not hitherto been available for casual study.

That was the simplest experiment to set up; the other two would be deployed about an hour later. One was a passive seismometer to measure erratic disturbances and any periodic vibrations, as well as moonquakes, and the impact of meteors in the weeks and months to follow; it was equipped to radio this information to earth, the energy for transmission derived from solar panels which extended out to either side, and thereby gave it the look of one of those spaceships of the future with thin extended paperlike wings which one sees in science fiction drawings. In any case it was so sensitive that the steps of the astronauts were recorded as they walked by. Finally there was a Laser Ranging Retro-Reflector, an LRRR (or LRQ, for L R-cubed), and that was a mirror whose face was a hundred quartz crystals, black as coal, cut to a precision never obtained before in glass—one-third of an arch/sec. Since each quartz crystal was a corner of a rectangle, any ray of light striking one of the three faces in each crystal would bounce off the other two in such a way that the light would return in exactly the same direction it had been received. A laser beam sent up from earth would therefore reflect back to the place from which it was sent. The time it required to travel this half-million miles from earth to moon round trip, a journey of less than three seconds, could be measured so accurately that physicists might then discern whether the moon was drifting away from the earth a few centimeters a year, or (by using two lasers) whether Europe and America might be drifting apart some comparable distance, or even if the Pacific Ocean were contracting. These measurements could then be entered into the caverns of Einstein's General Theory of Relativity, and new proof or disproof of the great thesis could be obtained.

We may be certain the equipment was remarkable. Still, its packaging and its ease of deployment had probably done as much to advance its presence on the ship as any clear priority over other scientific equipment; the beauty of these items from the point of view of NASA was that the astronauts could set them up in a few minutes while working in their space suits, even set them up with inflated gloves so insensitive that special silicone pads had to be inserted at the fingertips in order to leave the astronauts not altogether numb-fingered in their manipulations. Yet these marvels of measurement would soon be installed on the moon with less effort than it takes to remove a vacuum cleaner from its carton and get it operating.

It was at this point that patriotism, the corporation, and the national taste all came to occupy the same head of a pin, for the astronauts next proceeded to set up the flag. But that operation, as always, presented its exquisite problems. There was, we remind ourselves, no atmosphere for the flag to wave in. Any flag made of cloth would droop, indeed it would dangle. Therefore a species of starched plastic flag had to be employed, a flag which would stand out, there, out to the nonexistent breeze, flat as a slab of plywood. No, that would not do either. The flag was better crinkled and curled. Waves and billows were bent into it, and a full corkscrew of a curl at the end. There it stands for posterity, photographed in the twists of a high gale on the windless moon, curled up tin flag, numb as a pickled pepper.

Aldrin would hardly agree. "Being able to salute that flag was one of the more humble yet proud experiences I've ever had. To be able to look at the American flag and know how much so many people had put of themselves and their work into getting it where it was. We sensed—we really did—this almost mystical identification of all the people in the world at that instant."

Two minutes after the flag was up, the President of the United States put in his phone call. Let us listen one more time:

"Because of what you have done," said Nixon, "the heavens have become a part of man's world. And as you talk to us from the Sea of Tranquility, it inspires us to redouble our efforts to bring peace and tranquility to earth . . ."

"Thank you, Mr. President. It's a great honor and privilege for us to be here representing not only the United States, but men of peace of all nations . . ."

In such piety is the schizophrenia of the ages.

Immediately afterward, Aldrin practiced kicking moon dust, but he was somewhat broken up. Either reception was garbled, or Aldrin was temporarily incoherent. "They seem to leave," he said to the Capcom, referring to the particles, "and most of them have about the same angle of departure and velocity. From where I stand, a large portion of them will impact at a certain distance out. Several—the percentage is, of course, that will impact . . ."

Capcom: "Buzz this is Houston. You're cutting out on the end of your transmissions. Can you speak a little more forward into your microphone. Over."

Aldrin: "Roger. I'll try that."

Capcom: "Beautiful."

Aldrin: "Now I had that one inside my mouth that time."

Capcom: "It sounded a little wet."

And on earth, a handful of young scientists were screaming, "Stop wasting time with flags and presidents—collect some rocks!"

DISCUSSION QUESTIONS

1. How does the language of the astronauts, especially Aldrin's, affect Mailer? Why does Mailer use their words and NASA terminology so frequently? How are these transcripts and codes used by O'Toole in his account of the moonlanding for the *Washington Post* (see Press)?

2. Why does Mailer concentrate on a particular spot where the transcript is garbled? Why does he speculate on the length of time it takes the astronauts to step out onto the moon? How does his description of the "clarity of focus" on the moon suggest an environment that is different from the one described by the astronauts? For example, how does Aldrin's comparison of the moon landscape to "an environment somewhere out West" affect our response to what they are seeing? What does Mailer want us to see?

Lewis Thomas / *The Lives of a Cell* 1974

Lewis Thomas's essays reveal a first-rate mind in motion—unassuming, alert, endlessly curious, eager to explore and know the world in its own terms. A physician, professor, and award-winning essayist, Lewis Thomas was born in Flushing, New York, in 1913. He has taught medicine at the University of Minnesota and has served as the dean of the Yale Medical School. He is currently the Chancellor of the Memorial Sloan-Kettering Cancer Center in New York.

The author of several hundred scientific articles, Thomas began writing occasional essays in 1970, when he first contributed to the prestigious New England Journal of Medicine. *His first collection of essays,* The Lives of a Cell: Notes of a Biology Watcher *(1974), won the National Book Award in Arts and Letters and sold well over 300,000 hardcover copies, making it one of the most popular books of its kind. His second collection of essays,* The Medusa and the Snail *(1979), also quickly joined the bestseller lists. His most recent books are* The Youngest Science: Notes of a Medicine Watcher *(1983) and a third collection of essays,* Late Night Thoughts on Listening to Mahler's Ninth Symphony *(1983).*

Described as "quite possibly the best essayist on science now working any-

where in the world," Lewis Thomas has mastered both the art of the essay and the habit of viewing human behavior in biological terms and the world of biology in human terms. His insightful prose elegantly reaffirms his belief in the fundamental unity of life everywhere.

THE LONG HABIT

We continue to share with our remotest ancestors the most tangled and evasive attitudes about death, despite the great distance we have come in understanding some of the profound aspects of biology. We have as much distaste for talking about personal death as for thinking about it; it is an indelicacy, like talking in mixed company about venereal disease or abortion in the old days. Death on a grand scale does not bother us in the same special way: we can sit around a dinner table and discuss war, involving 60 million volatilized human deaths, as though we were talking about bad weather; we can watch abrupt bloody death every day, in color, on films and television, without blinking back a tear. It is when the numbers of dead are very small, and very close, that we begin to think in scurrying circles. At the very center of the problem is the naked cold deadness of one's own self, the only reality in nature of which we can have absolute certainty, and it is unmentionable, unthinkable. We may be even less willing to face the issue at first hand than our predecessors because of a secret new hope that maybe it will go away. We like to think, hiding the thought, that with all the marvelous ways in which we seem now to lead nature around by the nose, perhaps we can avoid the central problem if we just become, next year, say, a bit smarter.

"The long habit of living," said Thomas Browne, "indisposeth us to dying." These days, the habit has become an addiction: we are hooked on living; the tenacity of its grip on us, and ours on it, grows in intensity. We cannot think of giving it up, even when living loses its zest—even when we have lost the zest for zest.

We have come a long way in our technologic capacity to put death off, and it is imaginable that we might learn to stall it for even longer periods, perhaps matching the life-spans of the Abkhasian Russians, who are said to go on, springily, for a century and a half. If we can rid ourselves of some of our chronic, degenerative diseases, and cancer, strokes, and coronaries, we might go on and on. It sounds attractive and reasonable, but it is no certainty. If we became free of disease, we would make a much better run of it for the last decade or so, but might still terminate on about the same schedule as now. We may be like the genetically different lines of mice, or like Hayflick's different tissue-culture lines, programmed to die after a predetermined number of days, clocked by their genomes. If this is the way it is, some of us will continue to wear out and come unhinged in the sixth decade, and some much later, depending on genetic time-tables.

If we ever do achieve freedom from most of today's diseases, or even complete freedom from disease, we will perhaps terminate by drying out and blowing away on a light breeze, but we will still die.

Most of my friends do not like this way of looking at it. They prefer to take it for granted that we only die because we get sick, with one lethal ailment or another, and if we did not have our diseases we might go on indefinitely. Even biologists choose to think this about themselves, despite the evidences of the absolute inevitability of death that surround their professional lives. Everything dies, all around, trees, plankton, lichens, mice, whales, flies, mitochondria. In the simplest creatures it is sometimes difficult to see it as death, since the strands of replicating DNA they leave behind are more conspicuously the living parts of themselves than with us (not that it is fundamentally any different, but it seems so). Flies do not develop a ward round of diseases that carry them off, one by one. They simply age, and die, like flies.

We hanker to go on, even in the face of plain evidence that long, long lives are not necessarily pleasurable in the kind of society we have arranged thus far. We will be lucky if we can postpone the search for new technologies for a while, until we have discovered some satisfactory things to do with the extra time. Something will surely have to be found to take the place of sitting on the porch re-examining one's watch.

Perhaps we would not be so anxious to prolong life if we did not detest so much the sickness of withdrawal. It is astonishing how little information we have about this universal process, with all the other dazzling advances in biology. It is almost as though we wanted not to know about it. Even if we could imagine the act of death in isolation, without any preliminary stage of being struck down by disease, we would be fearful of it.

There are signs that medicine may be taking a new interest in the process, partly from curiosity, partly from an embarrassed realization that we have not been handling this aspect of disease with as much skill as physicians once displayed, back in the days before they became convinced that disease was their solitary and sometimes defeatable enemy. It used to be the hardest and most important of all the services of a good doctor to be on hand at the time of death and to provide comfort, usually in the home. Now it is done in hospitals, in secrecy (one of the reasons for the increased fear of death these days may be that so many people are totally unfamiliar with it; they never actually see it happen in real life). Some of our technology permits us to deny its existence, and we maintain flickers of life for long stretches in one community of cells or another, as though we were keeping a flag flying. Death is not a sudden-all-at-once affair; cells go down in sequence, one by one. You can, if you like, recover great numbers of them many hours after the lights have gone out, and grow them out in cultures. It takes hours, even days, before the irreversible word finally gets around to all the provinces.

We may be about to rediscover that dying is not such a bad thing to do after all. Sir William Osler took this view: he disapproved of people who spoke of the agony of death, maintaining that there was no such thing.

In a nineteenth-century memoir on an expedition in Africa, there is a story by David Livingston about his own experience of near-death. He was caught by a lion, crushed across the chest in the animal's great jaws, and saved in the instant by a lucky shot from a friend. Later he remembered the episode in clear detail. He was so amazed by the extraordinary sense of peace, calm, and total painlessness associated with being killed that he constructed a theory that all creatures are provided with a protective physiologic mechanism, switched on at the verge of death, carrying them through in a haze of tranquility.

I have seen agony in death only once, in a patient with rabies; he remained acutely aware of every stage in the process of his own disintegration over a twenty-four-hour period, right up to his final moment. It was as though, in the special neuropathology of rabies, the switch had been prevented from turning.

We will be having new opportunities to learn more about the physiology of death at first hand, from the increasing numbers of cardiac patients who have been through the whole process and then back again. Judging from what has been found out thus far, from the first generation of people resuscitated from cardiac standstill (already termed the Lazarus syndrome), Osler seems to have been right. Those who remember parts or all of their episodes do not recall any fear, or anguish. Several people who remained conscious throughout, while appearing to have been quite dead, could only describe a remarkable sensation of detachment. One man underwent coronary occlusion with cessation of the heart and dropped for all practical purposes dead, in front of a hospital; within a few minutes his heart had been restarted by electrodes and he breathed his way back into life. According to his account, the strangest thing was that there were so many people around him, moving so urgently, handling his body with such excitement, while all his awareness was of quietude.

In a recent study of the reaction to dying in patients with obstructive disease of the lungs, it was concluded that the process was considerably more shattering for the professional observers than the observed. Most of the patients appeared to be preparing themselves with equanimity for death, as though intuitively familiar with the business. One elderly woman reported that the only painful and distressing part of the process was in being interrupted; on several occasions she was provided with conventional therapeutic measures to maintain oxygenation or restore fluids and electrolytes, and each time she found the experience of coming back harrowing; she deeply resented the interference with her dying.

I find myself surprised by the thought that dying is an all-right thing to do, but perhaps it should not surprise. It is, after all, the most ancient and fundamental of biologic functions, with its mechanisms worked out with the same attention to detail, the same provision for the advantage of the organism, the same abundance of genetic information for guidance through the stages, that we have long since become accustomed to finding in all the crucial acts of living.

Very well. But even so, if the transformation is a coordinated, integrated physiologic process in its initial, local stages, there is still that permanent vanishing of consciousness to be accounted for. Are we to be stuck forever with this problem? Where on earth does it go? Is it simply stopped dead in its tracks, lost in humus, wasted? Considering the tendency of nature to find uses for complex and intricate mechanisms, this seems to me unnatural. I prefer to think of it as somehow separated off at the filaments of its attachment, and then drawn like an easy breath back into the membrane of its origin, a fresh memory for a biospherical nervous system, but I have no data on the matter.

This is for another science, another day. It may turn out, as some scientists suggest, that we are forever precluded from investigating consciousness by a sort of indeterminacy principle that stipulates that the very act of looking will make it twitch and blur out of sight. If this is true, we will never learn. I envy some of my friends who are convinced about telepathy; oddly enough, it is my European scientist acquaintances who believe it most freely and take it most lightly. All their aunts have received Communications, and there they sit, with proof of the motility of consciousness at their fingertips, and the making of a new science. It is discouraging to have had the wrong aunts, and never the ghost of a message.

Eudora Welty / The Little Store 1975

Eudora Welty was born in Jackson, Mississippi, in 1909 and attended Mississippi State College for Women, the University of Wisconsin, and the School of Business at Columbia University. During the Depression, while working for newspapers, radios, and the Works Progress Administration, she traveled throughout Mississippi taking numerous photographs which were later exhibited in New York. Her first collection of stories, A Curtain of Green, *appeared in 1941. Since that time, Welty has written several more story collections and novels including* The Robber Bridegroom *(1942),* The Ponder Heart *(1954),* Losing

Battles (1970), *and the Pulitzer prize-winning* The Optimist's Daughter *(1972). She is also regarded as a talented essayist and critic.*

Welty still resides in Jackson, and the following sketch recalls the flavor of her childhood years there.

My mother considered herself pretty well prepared in her kitchen and pantry for any emergency that, in her words, might choose to present itself. But if she should, all of a sudden, need another lemon or find she was out of bread, all she had to do was call out, "Quick! Who'd like to run to the Little Store for me?"

I would.

She'd count out the change into my hand, and I was away. I'll bet the nickel that would be left over that all over the country, for those of my day, the neighborhood grocery played a similar part in our growing up.

Our store had its name—it was that of the grocer who owned it, whom I'll call Mr. Sessions—but "the Little Store" is what we called it at home. It was a block down our street toward the capitol and half a block further, around the corner, toward the cemetery. I knew even the sidewalk to it as well as I knew my own skin. I'd skipped my jumping-rope up and down it, hopped its length through mazes of hopscotch, played jacks in its islands of shade, serpentined along it on my Princess bicycle, skated it backward and forward. In the twilight I had dragged my steamboat by its string (this was home-made out of every new shoebox, with candle in the bottom lighted and shining through colored tissue paper pasted over windows scissored out in the shapes of the sun, moon and stars) across every crack of the walk without letting it bump or catch fire. I'd "played out" on that street after supper with my brothers and friends as long as "first-dark" lasted; I'd caught its lightning bugs. On the first Armistice Day (and this will set the time I'm speaking of) we made our own parade down that walk on a single velocipede—my brother pedaling, our little brother riding the handlebars, and myself standing on the back, all with arms wide, flying flags in each hand. (My father snapped that picture as we raced by. It came out blurred.) . . .

Our Little Store rose right up from the sidewalk; standing in a street of family houses, it alone hadn't any yard in front, any tree or flowerbed. It was a plain frame building covered over with brick. Above the door, a little railed porch ran across on an upstairs level and four windows with shades were looking out. But I didn't catch on to those.

Running in out of the sun, you met what seemed total obscurity inside. There were almost tangible smells—licorice recently sucked in a child's cheek, dill-pickle brine that had leaked through a paper sack in a fresh trail across the wooden floor, ammonia-loaded ice that had been hoisted from wet croker sacks and slammed into the icebox with its sweet butter at the door, and perhaps the smell of still-untrapped mice.

Then through the motes of cracker dust, cornmeal dust, the Gold Dust of the Gold Dust Twins that the floor had been swept out with, the realities emerged. Shelves climbed to high reach all the way around, set out with not too much of any one thing but a lot of things—lard, molasses, vinegar, starch, matches, kerosene, Octagon soap (about a year's worth of octagon-shaped coupons cut out and saved brought a signet ring addressed to you in the mail. Furthermore, when the postman arrived at your door, he blew a whistle). It was up to you to remember what you came for, while your eye traveled from cans of sardines to ice cream salt to harmonicas to flypaper (over your head, batting around on a thread beneath the blades of the ceiling fan, stuck with its testimonial catch).

Its confusion may have been in the eye of its beholder. Enchantment is cast upon you by all those things you weren't supposed to have need for, it lures you close to wooden tops you'd outgrown, boy's marbles and agates in little net pouches, small rubber balls that wouldn't bounce straight, frazzly kitestring, clay bubble-pipes that would snap off in your teeth, the stiffest scissors. You could contemplate those long narrow boxes of sparklers gathering dust while you waited for it to be the Fourth of July or Christmas, and noisemakers in the shape of tin frogs for somebody's birthday party you hadn't been invited to yet, and see that they were all marvelous.

You might not have even looked for Mr. Sessions when he came around his store cheese (as big as a doll's house) and in front of the counter looking for you. When you'd finally asked him for, and received from him in its paper bag, whatever single thing it was that you had been sent for, the nickel that was left over was yours to spend.

Down at a child's eye level, inside those glass jars with mouths in their sides through which the grocer could run his scoop or a child's hand might be invited to reach for a choice, were wineballs, all-day suckers, gumdrops, peppermints. Making a row under the glass of a counter were the Tootsie Rolls, Hershey Bars, Goo-Goo Clusters, Baby Ruths. And whatever was the name of those pastilles that came stacked in a cardboard cylinder with a cardboard lid? They were thin and dry, about the size of tiddlywinks, and in the shape of twisted rosettes. A kind of chocolate dust came out with them when you shook them out in your hand. Were they chocolate? I'd say rather they were brown. They didn't taste of anything at all, unless it was wood. Their attraction was the number you got for a nickel.

Making up your mind, you circled the store around and around, around the pickle barrel, around the tower of Cracker Jack boxes; Mr. Sessions had built it for us himself on top of a packing case, like a house of cards.

If it seemed too hot for Cracker Jacks, I might get a cold drink. Mr. Sessions might have already stationed himself by the cold-drinks barrel, like a mind reader. Deep in ice water that looked black as ink, murky shapes that would come up as Coca-Colas, Orange Crushes, and various flavors of pop, were all swimming around together. When you gave the word, Mr. Sessions plunged his bare arm in to the elbow and fished out your choice, first try. I favored a locally bottled concoction called Lake's Celery. (What else could it be called? It was made by a Mr. Lake out of celery. It was a popular drink here for years but was not known universally, as I found out when I arrived in New York and ordered one in the Astor bar.) You drank on the premises, with feet set wide apart to miss the drip, and gave him back his bottle.

But he didn't hurry you off. A standing scales was by the door, with a stack of iron weights and a brass slide on the balance arm, that would weigh you up to three hundred pounds. Mr. Sessions, whose hands were gentle and smelled of carbolic, would lift you up and set your feet on the platform, hold your loaf of bread for you, and taking his time while you stood still for him, he would make certain of what you weighed today. He could even remember what you weighed the last time, so you could subtract and announce how much you'd gained. That was goodbye.

Joan Didion / On the Mall 1975

A former associate feature editor at Vogue *and contributing editor to the* National Review, The Saturday Evening Post, *and* Esquire, *Joan Didion has written for* Mademoiselle, Holiday, The American Scholar, *and* Life *magazine. Interviews and self-assertion are not her journalistic forte:*

> *My only advantage as a reporter is that I am so physically small, so temperamentally unobtrusive, and so neurotically inarticulate that people tend to forget that my presence runs counter to their best interests. And it always does. That is one last thing to remember: writers are always selling somebody out.*

The author of two novels, Run River *(1963) and* Play It as It Lays *(1970), Joan Didion has also published two collections of essays,* Slouching Towards Bethlehem *(1968) and* The White Album *(1979), from which the following essay on shopping malls is taken. Her study of the politics and culture of Central America,* Salvador, *appeared in 1983.*

They float on the landscape like pyramids to the boom years, all those Plazas and Malls and Esplanades. All those Squares and Fairs. All those Towns and Dales, all those Villages, all those Forests and Parks and Lands. Stonestown. Hillsdale. Valley Fair, Mayfair, Northgate, Southgate, Eastgate, Westgate. Gulfgate. They are toy garden cities in which no one lives but everyone consumes, profound equalizers, the perfect fusion of the profit motive and the egalitarian ideal, and to hear their names is to recall words and phrases no longer quite current. Baby Boom. Consumer Explosion. Leisure Revolution. Do-It-Yourself Revolution. Backyard Revolution. Suburbia. "The Shopping Center," the Urban Land Institute could pronounce in 1957, "is today's extraordinary retail business evolvement. . . . The automobile accounts for suburbia, and suburbia accounts for the shopping center."

It was a peculiar and visionary time, those years after World War II to which all the Malls and Towns and Dales stand as climate-controlled monuments. Even the word "automobile," as in "the automobile accounts for suburbia and suburbia accounts for the shopping center," no longer carries the particular freight it once did: as a child in the late Forties in California I recall reading and believing that the "freedom of movement" afforded by the automobile was "America's fifth freedom." The trend was up. The solution was in sight. The frontier had been reinvented, and its shape was the subdivision, that new free land on which all settlers could recast their lives *tabula rasa.* For one perishable moment there the American idea seemed about to achieve itself, via F.H.A. housing and the acquisition of major appliances, and a certain enigmatic glamour attached to the architects of this newfound land. They made something of nothing. They gambled and sometimes lost. They staked the past to seize the future. I have difficulty now imagining a childhood in which a man named Jere Strizek, the developer of Town and Country Village outside Sacramento (143,000 square feet gross floor area, 68 stores, 1000 parking spaces, the Urban Land Institute's "prototype for centers using heavy timber and tile construction for informality"), could materialize as a role model, but I had such a childhood, just after World War II, in Sacramento. I never met or even saw Jere Strizek, but at the age of 12 I imagined him a kind of frontiersman, a romantic and revolutionary spirit, and in the indigenous grain he was.

I suppose James B. Douglas and David D. Bohannon were too.

I first heard of James B. Douglas and David D. Bohannon not when I was 12 but a dozen years later, when I was living in New York, working for *Vogue,* and taking, by correspondence, a University of California Extension course in shopping-center theory. This did not seem to me eccentric at the time. I remember sitting on the cool floor in Irving Penn's studio and reading, in *The Community Builders Handbook,* advice from James B. Douglas on shopping-center financing. I recall staying late in my pale-blue office on the twentieth floor of the Graybar Building to memorize David D. Bohannon's parking ratios. My "real" life was to sit in this office and describe life as it was lived in Djakarta and Caneel Bay and in the great châteaux of the Loire Valley, but my dream life was to put together a Class-A regional shopping center with three full-line department stores as major tenants.

That I was perhaps the only person I knew in New York, let alone on the Condé Nast floors of the Graybar Building, to have memorized the distinctions among "A," "B," and "C" shopping centers did not occur to me (the defining distinction, as long as I have your attention, is that an "A," or "regional," center has as its major tenant a full-line department store which carries major appliances; a "B," or "community," center has as its major tenant a junior department store which does not carry major appliances; and a "C," or "neighborhood," center has as its major tenant only a supermarket): my interest in shopping centers was in no way casual. I did want to build them. I wanted to build them because I had fallen into the habit of writing fiction, and I had it in my head that a couple of good centers might support this habit less taxingly than a pale-blue office at *Vogue*. I had even devised an original scheme by which I planned to gain enough capital and credibility to enter the shopping-center game: I would lease warehouses in, say, Queens, and offer Manhattan delicatessens the opportunity to sell competitively by buying cooperatively, from my trucks. I see a few wrinkles in this scheme now (the words "concrete overcoat" come to mind), but I did not then. In fact I planned to run it out of the pale-blue office.

James B. Douglas and David D. Bohannon. In 1950 James B. Douglas had opened Northgate, in Seattle, the first regional center to combine a pedestrian mall with an underground truck tunnel. In 1954 David D. Bohannon had opened Hillsdale, a forty-acre regional center on the peninsula south of San Francisco. That is the only solid bio I have on James B. Douglas and David D. Bohannon to this day, but many of their opinions are engraved on my memory. David D. Bohannon believed in preserving the integrity of the shopping center by not cutting up the site with any dedicated roads. David D. Bohannon believed that architectural setbacks in a center looked "pretty on paper" but caused "customer resistance." James B. Douglas advised that a small-loan office could prosper in a center only if it were placed away from foot traffic, since people who want small loans do not want to be observed getting them. I do not now recall whether it was James B. Douglas or David D. Bohannon or someone else altogether who passed along this hint on how to paint the lines around the parking spaces (actually this is called "striping the lot," and the spaces are "stalls"): make each space a foot wider than it need be—ten feet, say, instead of nine—when the center first opens and business is slow. By this single stroke the developer achieves a couple of important objectives, the appearance of a popular center and the illusion of easy parking, and no one will really notice when business picks up and the spaces shrink.

Nor do I recall who first solved what was once a crucial center dilemma: the placement of the major tenant vis-à-vis the parking lot. The dilemma was that the major tenant—the draw, the raison d'être for the financing, the Sears, the Macy's, the May Company—wanted its customer to walk directly from car to store. The smaller tenants, on the other hand, wanted that same customer to *pass their stores* on the way from the car to, say, Macy's. The solution to this conflict of interests was actually very simple: *two major tenants,* one at each end of a mall. This is called "anchoring the mall," and represents seminal work in shopping-center theory. One thing you will note about shopping-center theory is that you could have thought of it yourself, and a course in it will go a long way toward dispelling the notion that business proceeds from mysteries too recondite for you and me.

A few aspects of shopping-center theory do in fact remain impenetrable to me. I have no idea why the Community Builders' Council ranks "Restaurant" as deserving a Number One (or "Hot Spot") location but exiles "Chinese Restaurant" to a Number Three, out there with ''Power and Light Office'' and ''Christian Science Reading Room.'' Nor do I know why the Council approves of enlivening a mall with ''small animals'' but specifically, vehemently, and with no further explanation, excludes ''monkeys.'' If I had a center I would have monkeys, and Chinese restaurants, and Mylar kites and bands of small girls playing tambourine.

A few years ago at a party I met a woman from Detroit who told me that the Joyce Carol Oates novel with which she identified most closely was *Wonderland*.

I asked her why.

''Because,'' she said, ''my husband has a branch there.''

I did not understand.

''In Wonderland the center,'' the woman said patiently. ''My husband has a branch in Wonderland.''

I have never visited Wonderland but imagine it to have bands of small girls playing tambourine.

A few facts about shopping centers.

The ''biggest'' center in the United States is generally agreed to be Woodfield, outside Chicago, a ''super'' regional or ''leviathan'' two-million-square-foot center with four major tenants.

The ''first'' shopping center in the United States is generally agreed to be Country Club Plaza in Kansas City, built in the twenties. There were some other early centers, notably Edward H. Bouton's 1907 Roland Park in Baltimore, Hugh Prather's 1931 Highland Park Shopping Village in Dallas, and Hugh Potter's 1937 River Oaks in Houston, but the developer of Country Club Plaza, the late J. C. Nichols, is referred to with ritual frequency in the literature of shopping centers, usually as ''pioneering J. C. Nichols,'' ''trailblazing J. C. Nichols,'' or ''J. C. Nichols, of the center as we know it.''

Those are some facts I know about shopping centers because I still want to be Jere Strizek or James B. Douglas or David D. Bohannon. Here are some facts I know about shopping centers because I never will be Jere Strizek or James B. Douglas or David D. Bohannon: a good center in which to spend the day if you wake feeling low in Honolulu, Hawaii, is Ala Moana, major tenants Liberty House and Sears. A good center in which to spend the day if you wake feeling low in Oxnard, California, is The Esplanade, major tenants the May Company and Sears. A good center in which to spend the day if you wake feeling low in Biloxi, Mississippi, is Edgewater Plaza, major tenant Godchaux's. Ala Moana in Honolulu is larger than The Esplanade in Oxnard, and The Esplanade in Oxnard is larger than Edgewater Plaza in Biloxi. Ala Moana has carp pools. The Esplanade and Edgewater Plaza do not.

These marginal distinctions to one side, Ala Moana, The Esplanade, and Edgewater Plaza are the same place, which is precisely their role not only as equalizers but in the sedation of anxiety. In each of them one moves for a while in an aqueous suspension not only of light but of judgment, not only of judgment but of ''personality.'' One meets no acquaintances at The Esplanade. One gets no telephone calls at Edgewater Plaza. ''It's a hard place to run in to for a pair of stockings,'' a friend complained to me recently of Ala Moana, and I knew that she was not yet ready to surrender her ego to the idea of the center. The last time I went to Ala Moana it was to buy *The New York Times*. Because *The New York Times* was not in, I sat on the mall for a while and ate caramel corn. In the end I bought not *The New York Times* at all but two straw hats at Liberty House, four bottles of nail enamel at Woolworth's, and a toaster, on sale at Sears. In the literature of shopping centers these would be described as impulse purchases, but the impulse here was obscure. I do not wear hats, nor do I like caramel corn. I do not use nail enamel. Yet flying back across the Pacific I regretted only the toaster.

DISCUSSION QUESTIONS

1. Compare Joan Didion's "On the Mall" to Eudora Welty's "The Little Store" (p. 569). How do these two essays convey changes in American society? Discuss the pros and cons of both the little store and the giant mall.

2. Compare Joan Didion's description of shopping malls to the one that forms the setting of Bob Greene's "Fifteen" in "Magazines" (see p. 279). In what ways are the authors' attitudes similar? How does your own personal attitude toward malls compare to the attitude of each of these writers?

John McPhee / *Coming into the Country* 1976

The range of topics in John McPhee's nearly two dozen books and scores of magazine articles reads like the categories in a well-stocked bookstore: literature, education, military science, travel, environmental studies, history, geography, science, cooking, dining, and sports. And what makes John McPhee's writing so successful is his ability to see each subject so freshly, be it a celebrated athlete or a remote stretch of frontier landscape. McPhee labors tirelessly on his writing; he regularly spends twelve-hour days transforming extensive research and interview notes into finely crafted sentences. He never overwrites, prefering to boil down a phrase before putting it into type. The result is prose at once taut, precise, and impersonal, yet insistently detailed, highly figurative, and immensely energetic.

Born in 1931, John McPhee was raised and educated in Princeton, New Jersey, where he has permanently settled. His writing career began in a high-school English class that required three essays (plus outlines) a week, practice that prepared him well for the carefully documented "fact pieces"—to use The New Yorker*'s term—which have earned him international acclaim. A former television script writer and staff reporter for* Time *magazine, where he wrote features on show business as well as film and book reviews, McPhee has been a staff writer for* The New Yorker *for more than the past twenty years. He also teaches a writing course ("The Literature of Fact") at Princeton University.*

In the following selection, drawn from his bestselling book, Coming into the Country *(1976), McPhee celebrates America's last frontier and recounts his first encounter with the majestic ruler of that Arctic land. (For other dramatic first sightings of bears, see William Faulkner's "The Bear" (Classics) and Lew Dietz's "The Myth of the Boss Bear" (Magazines).)*

BEAR LAND

The river was low, and Pat Pourchot had picked a site as far upstream as he judged we could be and still move in boats. We were on an island, with the transparent Salmon River on one side—hurrying, scarcely a foot deep—and a small slough on the other. Deeper pools, under bedrock ledges, were above us and below us. We built our fire on the lemon-sized gravel of what would in higher water be the riverbed, and we pitched the tents on slightly higher ground among open stands of willow, on sand that showed what Bob Fedeler called "the old tracks of a young griz." We would stay two nights, according to plan, before beginning the long descent to the Kobuk; and in the intervening day we would first assemble the kayaks and then be free to disperse and explore the terrain.

There was a sixth man with us, there at the beginning. His name was Jack Hession, and he was the Sierra Club's only salaried full-time representative in Alaska. Pourchot had invited him as an observer. The news that he was absent at the end of the trip could instantly cause hopes to rise in Alaska, where the Sierra Club has long been considered a netherworld force and Hession the resident Belial. Hession, though, was not going to perish on the Salmon. Pressures from Anchorage had travelled with him, and before long would get the better of him, and in cavalier manner—in this Arctic wilderness—he would bid us goodbye and set out early for home. Meanwhile, in the morning sun, we put together the collapsible kayaks—two single Kleppers and Snake Eyes. Hession's own single was the oldest of the three, and it had thirty-six parts, hardware not included. There were dowels of mountain ash and ribs of laminated Finnish birch, which fitted, one part to another, with hooks and clips until they formed a pair of nearly identical skeletal cones—the internal structures of halves of the boat. The skin was a limp bag made of blue canvas (the deck) and hemp-reinforced vulcanized rubber (the hull). The concept was to insert the skeletal halves into the skin and then figure out how to firm them together. We had trouble doing that. Hession, who ordinarily used rigid boats of fibre glass in his engagements with white water, could not remember how to complete the assembly. Stiff toward the ends and bent in the middle, his kayak had the look of a clip on tie, and would do about as well in the river. We all crouched around and studied amidships—six men, a hundred miles up a stream, above sixty-seven degrees of latitude, with a limp kayak. No one was shy with suggestions, which were full of ingenuity but entirely failed to work. By trial and error, we finally figured it out. The last step in the assembly involved the center rib, and we set that inside the hull on a tilt and then tapped it with a rock and forced it toward the vertical. When the forcing rib reached ninety degrees to the longer axis of the craft, the rib snapped into place, and with that the entire boat became taut and yare. Clever man, Johann Klepper. He had organized his foldboat in the way that the North American Indians had developed the construction of their bark canoes. Over the years, the Klepper company had simplified its process. Our other single kayak, the more recent model, had fewer and larger skeletal parts, and it went together more easily; but it was less streamlined than the first. Snake Eyes, for its part—all eight hundred dollars' worth of Snake Eyes—was new and had an interior of broad wooden slabs, conveniently hinged. Snake Eyes had the least number of separate parts (only fifteen) and in the way it went together was efficient and simple. Its advanced design had been achieved with a certain loss of grace, however, and this was evident there on the gravel. The boat was lumpy, awkward, bulging—a kayak with elbows.

Toward noon and after an early lunch, we set off on foot for a look around. Pourchot went straight up the hills to the west, alone. Stell Newman and John Kauffmann intended lesser forays, nearer the campsite. I decided I'd go with Bob Fedeler, who, with Jack Hession, had the most ambitious plan. They were going north up the river some miles and then up the ridges to the east. I hoped my legs would hold up. I didn't want to embarrass myself, off somewhere in the hills, by snapping something, but I could not resist going along with Fedeler. After all, he was a habitat biologist, working for the state, and if the ground around here was not habitat then I would never be in country that was. The temperature had come up to seventy. The sky was blue, with moving clouds and intermittent sun. We stuffed our rain gear into day packs and started up the river.

Generally speaking, if I had a choice between hiking and peeling potatoes, I would peel the potatoes. I have always had a predilection for canoes on rivers and have avoided walking wherever possible. My experience, thus, was limited but did exist. My work had led me up the Sierra Nevada and across the North Cascades, and in various eras I had walked parts of the Long Trail, the Appalachian Trail, trails of New Hampshire, the Adirondacks. Here in the Brooks Range, of course, no one had been there clearing the path. A mile, steep or level, could demand a lot of time. You go along with only a general plan, free lance, guessing where the walking will be least difficult, making choices all the way. These are the conditions, and in ten minutes' time they present their story. The country is wild to the limits of the term. It would demean such a world to call it pre-Columbian. It is twenty times older than that, having assumed its present form ten thousand years ago, with the melting of the Wisconsin ice.

For several miles upstream, willow and alder pressed in on the river, backed by spruce and cottonwood, so the easiest path was the river itself. Gravel bars were now on one side, now the other, so we crossed and crossed again, taking off our rubber boots and wading through the fast, cold water. I had rubber bottomed leather boots (L.L. Bean's, which are much in use all over Alaska). Fedeler was wearing hiking boots, Hession low canvas sneakers. Hession had a floppy sun hat, too. He seemed to see no need to dress like Sir Edmund Hillary, or to leave the marks of waffles by the tracks of wolves. He was a brief, trim, lithe figure, who moved lightly and had seen a lot of such ground. He stopped and opened his jackknife, and stood it by a track in sand at the edge of the river. Other tracks were near. Two wolves running side by side. He took a picture of the track. We passed a deep pool where spring water came into the river, and where algae grew in response to its warmth. Grayling could winter there. Some were in the pool now—bodies stationary, fins in motion, in clear deep water as green as jade. Four mergansers swam up the river. We saw moose pellets in sand beyond the pool. I would not much want to be a moose just there, in a narrow V-shaped valley with scant protection of trees. We came, in fact, to the tree line not long thereafter. The trees simply stopped. We took a few more northward steps and were out of the boreal forest. Farther north, as far as land continued, there would be no more. I don't mean to suggest that we had stepped out of Sequoia National Park and onto an unvegetated plain. The woods behind us were spare in every sense, fingering up the river valley, reaching as far as they could go. Now the tundra, which had before been close behind the trees, came down to the banks of the river. We'd had enough of shoelaces and of bare feet crunching underwater stones, so we climbed up the west bank to walk on the tundra—which from the river had looked as smooth as a golf course. Possibly there is nothing as invitingly deceptive as a tundra-covered hillside. Distances over tundra, even when it is rising steeply, are like distances over water, seeming to be less than they are, defraying the suggestion of effort. The tundra surface, though, consists of many kinds of plants, most of which seem to be stemmed with wire configured to ensnare the foot. For years, my conception of tundra—based, I suppose, on photographs of the Canadian north and the plains of the Alaskan Arctic slope—was of a vast northern flatness, water-flecked, running level to every horizon. Tundra is not topography, however; it is a mat of vegetation, and it runs up the sides of prodigious declivities as well as across the broad plains. There are three varying types—wet tundra, on low flatland with much standing water; moist tundra, on slightly higher ground; and alpine tundra, like carpeted heather, rising on mountains and hills. We moved on, northward, over moist tundra, and the plants were often a foot or so in height. Moving through them was more like wading than walking, except where we followed game trails. Fortunately, these were numerous enough, and comfortably negotiable. They bore signs of everything that lived there. They were highways, share and share alike, for caribou, moose, bears, wolves—whose tracks, antlers, and feces were strewn along the right-of-way like beer cans at the edge of a road. While these game trails were the best thoroughfares in many hundreds of square miles, they were also the only ones, and they had a notable defect. They tended to vanish. The trails would go along, well cut and stamped out through moss campion, reindeer moss, sedge tussocks, crowberries, prostrate willows, dwarf birch, bog blueberries, white mountain avens, low-bush cranberries, lichens, Labrador tea; then, abruptly, and for no apparent reason, the trails would disappear. Their well-worn ruts suggested hundreds of animals, heavy traffic. So where did they go when the trail vanished? Fedeler did not know. I could not think of an explanation. Maybe Noah had got there a little before us.

On the far side of the river was an isolated tree, which had made a brave bid to move north, to extend the reach of its progenitive forest. The Brooks Range, the remotest uplift in North America, was made a little less remote, fifty years ago, by the writing of Robert Marshall, a forester, who described several expeditions to these mountains in a book called "Alaska Wildnerness." Marshall had a theory about the tree line, the boundary of the circumboreal world. He thought that white spruce and other species could live farther north, and that they were inching northward, dropping seeds ahead of them, a dead-slow advance under marginal conditions. Whatever it may have signified, the tree across the river was dead, and out of it now came a sparrow hawk, flying at us, shouting *"kee kee kee,"* and hovering on rapidly beating wings to study the creatures on the trail. There was not much it could do about us, and it went back to the tree.

The leaves of Labrador tea, crushed in the hand, smelled like a turpentine. The cranberries were early and sourer than they would eventually be. With the arrival of cold, they freeze on the vine, and when they thaw, six months later, they are somehow sweeter and contain more juice. Bears like overwintered berries. Blueberries, too, are sweeter after being frozen on the bush. Fried cranberries will help relieve a sore throat. Attacks in the gall bladder have been defused with boiled cranberries mixed with seal oil. The sedge tussocks were low and not as perilous as tussocks can be. They are grass that grows in bunches, more compact at the bottom than at the top—a mushroom shape that can spill a foot and turn an ankle. They were tiresome, and soon we were ready to move upward, away from the moist tundra and away from the river. Ahead we saw the configurations of the sharp small valleys of three streams meeting, forming there the principal stem of the Salmon. To the east, above the confluence, a tundra-bald hill rose a thousand feet and more. We decided to cross the river and go up the hill. Look around. Choose where to go from there.

The river was so shallow now that there was no need for removing boots. We walked across and began to climb. The going was steep. I asked Jack Hession how long he had been in Alaska, and he said seven years. He had been in Alaska longer than two-thirds of the people in the state. He was from California, and had lived more recently in western Washington, where he had begun to acquire his expertise in boats in white water. Like Fedeler—like me, for that matter—he was in good condition. Hession, though, seemed to float up the incline, while I found it hard, sweaty work. From across the river it had looked as easy as a short flight of stairs. I went up it a trudge at a time—on reindeer moss, heather, lupine. The sun had suddenly departed, and a cool rain began to fall. At the top of the hill, we sat on a rock outcropping and looked back at the river, twelve hundred feet below. Everywhere around us were mountains—steep, treeless, buff where still in the sun. One was bright silver. The rain felt good. We nibbled M&M's. They were even better than the rain. The streams far below, small and fast, came pummelling together and made the river. The land they fell through looked nude. It was all tundra, rising northward toward a pass at the range divide. Looking at so much mountain ground—this immense minute fragment of wilderness Alaska—one could wonder about the choice of words of people who say that it is fragile. "Fragile" just does not appear to be a proper term for a rugged, essentially uninvaded landscape covering tens of thousands of square miles—a place so vast and unpeopled that if anyone could figure out how to steal Italy, Alaska would be a place to hide it. Meanwhile, earnest ecologues write and speak about the "fragile'' tundra, this ''delicate'' ocean of barren land. The words sound effete, but the terrain is nonetheless vulnerable. There is ice under the tundra, mixed with soil as permafrost, in some places two thousand feet deep. The tundra vegetation, living and dead, provides insulation that keeps the summer sun from melting the permafrost. If something pulls away the insulation and melting occurs, the soil will settle and the water may run off. The earth, in such circumstances, does not restore itself. In the nineteen-sixties, a bulldozer working for Geophysical Service, Inc., an oil-exploration company, wrote the initials G.S.I. in Arctic Alaskan tundra. The letters were two hundred feet from top to bottom, and near them the bulldozer cut an arrow—an indicator for pilots. Thermokarst (thermal erosion) followed, and slumpage. The letters and the arrow are now odd-shaped ponds, about eight feet deep. For many generations that segment of tundra will say ''G.S.I.'' Tundra is even sensitive to snow machines. They compress snow, and cut off much of the air that would otherwise get to the vegetation. Evidence appears in summer. The snow machines have left brown trails on ground they never touched.

Both sunlight and rain were falling on us now. We had a topographic map, of the largest scale available but nonetheless of scant detail—about five miles to half a thumb. Of the three streams that met below us, the nearest was called Sheep Creek. A rainbow wicketed its steep valley. The top of the arch was below us. The name Sheep Creek was vestigial. ''Historically, there were Dall sheep in these mountains,'' Fedeler said.

''What happened to them?''

''Who knows?'' He shrugged. ''Things go in cycles. They'll be back.''

Alders had crept into creases in the mountainside across the Salmon valley. I remarked on the borderline conditions in evidence everywhere in this spare and beautiful country, and said, ''Look at those alders over there, clinging to life.''

Fedeler said, ''It's hungry country, that's for sure. Drainage and exposure make *the* difference.''

We ate peanuts and raisins and more M&M's—and, feeling rested, became ambitious. On a long southward loop back to camp, we would extend our walk by going around a mountain that was separated from us by what looked to be the fairly steep declivity of a tributary drainage. The terrain sloped away to the southwest toward the mouth of the tributary. We would go down for a time, and then cross the tributary and cut back around the mountain.

We passed first through stands of fireweed, and then over ground that was wine-red with the leaves of bearberries. There were curlewberries, too, which put a deep-purple stain on the hand. We kicked at some wolf scat, old as winter. It was woolly and white and filled with the hair of a snowshoe hare. Nearby was a rich inventory of caribou pellets and, in increasing quantity as we moved downhill, blueberries—an outspreading acreage of blueberries. Fedeler stopped walking. He touched my arm. He had in an instant become even more alert than he usually was, and obviously apprehensive. His gaze followed straight on down our intended course. What he saw there I saw now. It appeared to me to be a hill of fur. ''Big boar grizzly,'' Fedeler said in a near-whisper. The bear was about a hundred steps away, in the blueberries, grazing. The head was down, the hump high. The immensity of muscle seemed to vibrate slowly—to expand and contract, with the grazing. Not berries alone but whole bushes were going into the bear. He was big for a barren-ground grizzly. The brown bears of Arctic Alaska (or grizzlies; they are no longer thought to be different) do not grow to the size they will reach on more ample diets elsewhere. The barren-ground grizzly will rarely grow larger than six hundred pounds.

''What if he got too close?'' I said.

Fedeler said, ''We'd be in real trouble.''

''You can't outrun them,'' Hession said.

A grizzly, no slower than a racing horse, is about half again as fast as the fastest human being. Watching the great mound of weight in the blueberries, with a fifty-five-inch waist and a neck more than thirty inches around, I had difficulty imagining that he could move with such speed, but I believed it, and was without impulse to test the proposition. Fortunately, a light southerly wind was coming up the Salmon valley. On its way to us, it passed the bear. The wind was relieving, coming into our faces, for had it been moving the other way the bear would not have been placidly grazing. There is an old adage that when a pine needle drops in the forest the eagle will see it fall; the deer will hear it when it hits the ground; the bear will smell it. If the boar grizzly were to catch our scent, he might stand on his hind legs, the better to try to see. Although he could hear well and had an extraordinary sense of smell, his eyesight was not much better than what was required to see a blueberry inches away. For this reason, a grizzly stands and squints, attempting to bring the middle distance into focus, and the gesture is often misunderstood as a sign of anger and forthcoming attack. If the bear were getting ready to attack, he would be on four feet, head low, ears cocked, the hair above his hump muscle standing on end. As if that message were not clear enough, he would also chop his jaws. His teeth would make a sound that would carry like the ringing of an axe.

One could predict, but not with certainty, what a grizzly would do. Odds were very great that one touch of man scent would cause him to stop his activity, pause in a moment of absorbed and alert curiosity, and then move, at a not undignified pace, in a direction other than the one from which the scent was coming. That is what would happen almost every time, but there was, to be sure, no guarantee. The forest Eskimos fear and revere the grizzly. They know that certain individual bears not only will fail to avoid a person who comes into their country but will approach and even stalk the trespasser. It is potentially inaccurate to extrapolate the behavior of any one bear from the behavior of most, since they are both intelligent and independent and will do what they choose to do according to mood, experience, whim. A grizzly that has ever been wounded by a bullet will not forget it, and will probably know that it was a human being who sent the bullet. At sight of a human, such a bear will be likely to charge. Grizzlies hide food sometimes—a caribou calf, say, under a pile of scraped-up moss—and a person the bear might otherwise ignore might suddenly not be ignored if the person were inadvertently to step into the line between the food cache and the bear. A sow grizzly with cubs, of course, will charge anything that suggests danger to the cubs, even if the cubs are nearly as big as she is. They stay with their mother two and a half years.

None of us had a gun. (None of the six of us had brought a gun on the trip.) Among nonhunters who go into the terrain of the grizzly, there are several schools of thought about guns. The preferred one is: Never go without a sufficient weapon—a high-powered rifle or a shotgun and plenty of slug-loaded shells. The option is not without its own inherent peril. A professional hunter, some years ago, spotted a grizzly from the air and—with a client, who happened to be an Anchorage barber—landed on a lake about a mile from the bear. The stalking that followed was evidently conducted not only by the hunters but by the animal as well. The professional hunter was found dead from a broken neck, and had apparently died instantly, unaware of danger, for the cause of death was a single bite, delivered from behind. The barber, noted as clumsy with a rifle, had emptied his magazine, missing the bear with every shot but one, which struck the grizzly in the foot. The damage the bear did to the barber was enough to kill him several times. After the corpses were found, the bear was tracked and killed. To shoot and merely wound is worse than not to shoot at all. A bear that might have turned and gone away will possibly attack if wounded.

Fatal encounters with bears are as rare as they are memorable. Some people reject the rifle as cumbersome extra baggage, not worth toting, given the minimal risk. And, finally, there are a few people who feel that it is wrong to carry a gun, in part because the risk is low and well worth taking, but most emphatically because they see the gun as an affront to the wild country of which the bear is sign and symbol. This, while strongly felt, is a somewhat novel attitude. When Robert Marshall explored the Brooks Range half a century ago, he and his companions fired at almost every bear they saw, without pausing for philosophical reflection. The reaction was automatic. They were expressing mankind's immemorial fear of this beast—man and rattlesnake, man and bear. Among modern environmentalists, to whom a figure like Marshall is otherwise a hero, fear of the bear has been exceeded by reverence. A notable example, in his own past and present, is Andy Russell, author of a book called "Grizzly Country." Russell was once a professional hunter, but he gave that up to become a photographer, specializing in grizzlies. He says that he has given up not only shooting bears but even carrying a gun. On rare instances when grizzlies charge toward him, he shouts at them and stands his ground. The worst thing to do, he says, is to run, because anything that runs on open tundra suggests game to a bear. Game does not tend to stand its ground in the presence of grizzlies. Therefore, when the bear comes at you, just stand there. Charging something that does not move, the bear will theoretically stop and reconsider. (Says Russell.) More important, Russell believes that the bear will *know* if you have a gun, even if the gun is concealed:

> Reviewing our experiences, we had become more and more convinced that carrying arms was not only unnecessary in most grizzly country but was certainly no good for the desired atmosphere and proper protocol in obtaining good film records. If we were to obtain such film and fraternize successfully with the big bears, it would be better to go unarmed in most places. The mere fact of having a gun within reach, cached somewhere in a pack or a hidden holster, causes a man to act with unconscious arrogance and thus maybe to smell different or to transmit some kind of signal objectionable to bears. The armed man does not assume his proper role in association with the wild ones, a fact of which they seem instantly aware at some distance. He, being wilder than they, whether he likes to admit it or not, is instantly under even more suspicion than he would encounter if unarmed.
>
> One must follow the role of an uninvited visitor—an intruder—rather than that of an aggressive hunter, and one should go unarmed to insure this attitude.

Like pictures from pages riffled with a thumb, all of these things went through my mind there on the mountainside above the grazing bear. I will confess that in one instant I asked myself, "What the hell am I doing *here?*" There was nothing more to the question, though, than a hint of panic. I knew why I had come, and therefore what I was doing there. That I was frightened was incidental. I just hoped the fright would not rise beyond a relatively decorous level. I sensed that Fedeler and Hession were somewhat frightened, too. I would have been troubled if they had not been. Meanwhile, the sight of the bear stirred me like nothing else the country could contain. What mattered was not so much the bear himself as what the bear implied. He was the predominant thing in that country, and for him to be in it at all meant that there had to be more country like it in every direction and more of the same kind of country all around that. He implied a world. He was an affirmation to the rest of the earth that his kind of place was extant. There had been a time when his race was everywhere in North America, but it had been hunted down and pushed away in favor of something else. For example, the grizzly bear is the state animal of California, whose country was once his kind of place; and in California now the grizzly is extinct.

> The animals I have encountered in my wilderness wanderings have been reluctant to reveal all the things about them I would like to know. The animal that impresses me most, the one I find myself liking more and more, is the grizzly. No sight encountered in the wilds is quite so stirring as those massive, clawed tracks pressed into mud or snow. No sight is quite so impressive as that of the great bear stalking across some mountain slope with the fur of his silvery robe rippling over his mighty muscles. His is a dignity and power matched by no other in the North American wilderness. To share a mountain with him for a while is a privilege and an adventure like no other.
>
> I have followed his tracks into an alder hell to see what he had been doing and come to the abrupt end of them, when the maker stood up thirty feet away with a sudden snort to face me.
>
> To see a mother grizzly ambling and loafing with her cubs across the broad, hospitable bosom of a flower-spangled mountain meadow is to see life in true wilderness at its best.

If a wolf kills a caribou, and a grizzly comes along while the wolf is feeding on the kill, the wolf puts its tail between its legs and hurries away. A black bear will run from a grizzly, too. Grizzlies sometimes kill and eat black bears. The grizzly takes what he happens upon. He is an opportunistic eater. The predominance of the grizzly in his terrain is challenged by nothing but men and ravens. To frustrate ravens from stealing his food, he will lie down and sleep on top of a carcass, occasionally swatting the birds as if they were big black flies. He prefers a vegetable diet. He can pulp a moosehead with a single blow, but he is not lusting always to kill, and when he moves through his country he can be something munificent, going into copses of willow among unfleeing moose and their calves, touching nothing, letting it all breathe as before. He may, though, get the head of a cow moose between his legs and rake her flanks with the five-inch knives that protrude from the ends of his paws. Opportunistic. He removes and eats her entrails. He likes porcupines, too, and when one turns and presents to him a pygal bouquet of quills, he will leap into the air, land on the other side, chuck the fretful porpentine beneath the chin, flip it over, and, with a swift ventral incision, neatly remove its body from its skin, leaving something like a sea urchin behind him on the ground. He is nothing if not athletic. Before he dens, or just after he emerges, if his mountains are covered with snow he will climb to the brink of some impossible schuss, sit down on his butt, and shove off. Thirty-two, sixty-four, ninety-six feet per second, he plummets down the mountainside, spray snow flying to either side, as he approaches collision with boulders and trees. Just short of catastrophe, still going at bonecrushing speed, he flips to his feet and walks sedately onward as if his ride had not occurred.

His population density is thin on the Arctic barren ground. He needs for his forage at least fifty and perhaps a hundred square miles that are all his own—sixty-four thousand acres, his home range. Within it, he will move, typically, eight miles a summer day, doing his travelling through the twilight hours of the dead of night. To scratch his belly he walks over a tree—where forest exists. The tree bends beneath him as he passes. He forages in the morning, generally; and he rests a great deal, particularly after he eats. He rests fourteen hours a day. If he becomes hot in the sun, he lies down in a pool in the river. He sleeps on the tundra—restlessly tossing and turning, forever changing position. What he could be worrying about I cannot imagine.

His fur blends so well into the tundra colors that sometimes it is hard to see him. Fortunately, we could see well enough the one in front of us, or we would have walked right to him. He caused a considerable revision of our travel plans. Not wholly prepared to follow the advice of Andy Russell, I asked Fedeler what one should do if a bear were to charge. He said, "Take off your pack and throw it into the bear's path, then crawl away, and hope the pack will distract the bear. But there is no good thing to do, really. It's just not a situation to be in."

We made a hundred-and-forty-degree turn from the course we had been following and went up the shoulder of the hill through ever-thickening brush, putting distance behind us in good position with the wind. For a time, we waded through hip-deep willow, always making our way uphill, and the going may have been difficult, but I didn't notice. There was adrenalin to spare in my bloodstream. I felt that I was floating, climbing with ease, like Hession. I also had expectations now that another bear, in the thick brush, might come rising up from any quarter. We broke out soon into a swale of blueberries. Hession and Fedeler, their nonchalance refreshed, sat down to eat, paused to graze. The berries were sweet and large.

"I can see why he's here," Hession said.

"These berries are so big."

"Southern exposure."

"He may not be the only one."

"They can be anywhere."

"It's amazing to me," Fedeler said. "So large an animal, living up here in this country. It's amazing what keeps that big body alive." Fedeler went on eating the blueberries with no apparent fear of growing fat. The barren-ground bear digs a lot of roots, he said—the roots of milk vetch, for example, and Eskimo potatoes. The bear, coming out of his den into the snows of May, goes down into the river bottoms, where over-wintered berries are first revealed. Wolf kills are down there, too. By the middle of June, his diet is almost wholly vegetable. He eats willow buds, sedges, cotton-grass tussocks. In the cycle of his year, roots and plants are eighty per cent of what he eats, and even when the salmon are running he does not sate himself on them alone but forages much of the time for berries. In the fall, he unearths not only roots but ground squirrels and lemmings. It is indeed remarkable how large he grows on the provender of his yearly cycle, for on this Arctic barren ground he has to work much harder than the brown bears of southern Alaska, which line up along foaming rivers—hip to hip, like fishermen in New Jersey—taking forty-pound king salmon in their jaws as if they were nibbling feed from a barnyard trough. When the caribou are in fall migration, moving down the Salmon valley toward the Kobuk, the bear finishes up his year with one of them. Then, around the first of November, he may find a cave or, more likely, digs out a cavern in a mountainside. If he finds a natural cave, it may be full of porcupines. He kicks them out, and—extending his curious relationship with this animal—will cushion his winter bed with many thousands of their turds. If, on the other hand, he digs his den, he sends earth flying out behind him and makes a shaft that goes upward into the side of the mountain. At the top of the shaft, he excavates a shelf-like cavern. When the outside entrance is plugged with debris, the shaft becomes a column of still air, insulating the upper chamber, trapping the bear's body heat. On a bed of dry vegetation, he lays himself out like a dead pharaoh in a pyramid. But he does not truly hibernate. He just lies there. His mate of the summer, in her den somewhere, will give birth during winter to a cub or two—virtually hairless, blind, weighing about a pound. But the male has nothing to do. His heart rate goes down as low as eight beats a minute. He sleeps and wakes, and sleeps again. He may decide to get up and go out. But that is rare. He may even stay out, which is rarer—to give up denning for that winter and roam his frozen range. If he does this, sooner or later he will find a patch of open water in an otherwise frozen river, and in refreshing himself he will no doubt wet his fur. Then he rolls in the snow, and the fur acquires a thick plate of ice, which is less disturbing to the animal than to the forest Eskimo, who has for ages feared—feared most of all—the "winter bear." Arrows broke against the armoring ice, and it can be heavy enough to stop a bullet.

We moved on now, in continuing retreat, and approached the steep incline of the tributary valley we'd been skirting when the bear rewrote our plans. We meant to put the valley between us and him and reschedule ourselves on the other side. It was in fact less a valley than an extremely large ravine, which plunged maybe eight hundred feet, and then rose up an even steeper incline some fifteen hundred feet on the other side, toward the top of which the bushy vegetation ceased growing. The walking looked promising on the ridge beyond.

I had hoped we might see a den site, and this might have been the place. It had all the requisites but one. It was a steep hillside with southern exposure, and was upgrown with a hell of alders and willows. Moreover, we were on the south side of the Brooks Range divide, which is where most of the dens are. But we were not high enough. We were at something under two thousand feet, and bears in this part of Alaska like to den much higher than that. They want the very best drainage. One way to become a "winter bear" is to wake up in a flooded den.

The willow-alder growth was so dense and high that as we went down the hillside we could see no farther than a few hundred yards ahead. It was wet in there from the recent rain. We broke our way forward with the help of gravity, crashing noisily, all but trapped in the thicket. It was a patch of jungle, many acres of jungle, with stems a foot apart and as thick as our arms, and canopies more than twelve feet high. This was bear habitat, the sort of place bears like better than people do. Our original choice had been wise—to skirt this ravine-valley—but now we were in it and without choice.

"This is the sort of place to come upon one of them unexpectedly," Hession said.

"And there is no going back," Fedeler said. "You can't walk uphill in this stuff."

"Good point," Hession said.

I might have been a little happier if I had been in an uninstrumented airplane in heavy mountain cloud. We thunked and crashed for fifteen minutes and finally came out at the tributary stream. Our approach flushed a ptarmigan, willow ptarmigan; and grayling—at sight of us—shot around in small, cold pools. The stream was narrow, and alders pressed over it from either side. We drank, and rested, and looked up the slope in front of us, which must have had an incline of fifty degrees. The ridge at the top looked extremely far away. Resting, I became aware of a considerable ache in my legs and a blister on one of my heels. On the way uphill we became separated, Hession angling off to the right, Fedeler and I to the left. We groped for handholds among bushes that protruded from the flaky schist, and pulled ourselves up from ledge to ledge. The adrenalin was gone, and my legs were turning to stone. I was ready to dig a den and get in it. My eyes kept addressing the ridgeline, far above. If eyes were hands they could have pulled me there. Then, suddenly, from far below, I saw Jack Hession lightly ambling along the ridge—in his tennis shoes, in his floppy cotton hat. He was looking around, killing time, waiting up for us.

Things seemed better from the ridge. The going would be level for a time. We sat down and looked back, to the north, across the deep tributary valley, and with my monocular tried to glass the grazing bear. No sight or sign of him. Above us now was a broadly conical summit, and spread around its western flank was a mile, at least, of open alpine tundra. On a contour, we headed south across it—high above, and two miles east of, the river. We saw what appeared to be a cairn on the next summit south, and decided to go to it and stand on it and see if we could guess—in relation to our campsite—where we were. Now the walking felt good again. We passed a large black pile of grizzly scat. "When it's steaming, that's when you start looking around for a tree," Hession said. This particular scat had sent up its last vapors many days before. Imagining myself there at such a time, though, I looked around idly for a tree. The nearest one behind us that was of more than dwarf or thicket stature was somewhere in Lapland. Ahead of us, however, across the broad dome of tundra, was a dark stand of white spruce, an extremity of the North American forest, extending toward us. The trees were eight hundred yards away. Black bears, frightened, sometimes climb trees. Grizzlies almost never climb trees.

At seven in the evening, after wading up a slope of medium to heavy brush, we came out onto more smooth tundra and reached the hilltop of the apparent cairn. It was a rock outcropping, and we sat on it in bright sunshine and looked at the circumvallate mountains. A great many of them had such outcroppings projecting from their ridges, and they much resembled the cairns shepherds build on bald summits in Scotland. For that matter, they suggested the cairns—closer to the Kobuk—that forest Eskimos once used in methodical slaughter of caribou. The cairns were built on the high tundra in a great V, open end to the north, and they served as a funnel for the southbound herd. To the approaching caribou, the cairns were meant to suggest Eskimos, and to reinforce the impression Eskimos spaced themselves between cairns. At the point of the V, as many caribou as were needed were killed and the rest were let through.

Before us now, lying on the tundra that stretched away toward the river we saw numerous caribou antlers. The Arctic herd cyclically chooses various passes and valleys in making its way south across the range, and of late has been favoring, among other places, the Salmon and Hunt River drainages. Bleached white, the antlers protruded from the tundra like the dead braches of buried trees. When the forest Eskimo of old went to stalk the grizzly bear, he carried in his hand a spear, the tip of which was made from bear bone or, more often, from the antler of the caribou. A bearskin was the door of an Eskimo's home if the occupant had ever killed a bear, for it symbolized the extraordinary valor of the hunter within. When the man drew close and the bear stood on its hind legs, the man ran under this cave of flesh and set the shaft of the spear firmly on the ground, then ducked out from under the swinging, explosive paws. The bear lunged forward onto the spear and died.

Eskimo knife handles were also made from caribou antlers, and icepicks to penetrate the surface of the river, and sinkers for the bottoms of willow-bark seines, and wood-splitting wedges, and arrowheads. All caribou, male and female, grow antlers. The horns of sheep, cattle, buffalo consist of extremely dense, compactly matted hair. The antler of the caribou is calcareous. It is hard bone, with the strength of wrought iron. Moving downhill and south across the tundra, we passed through groves of antlers. It was as if the long filing lines of the spring migration had for some reason paused here for shedding to occur. The antlers, like the bear, implied the country. Most were white, gaunt, chalky. I picked up a younger one, though, that was recently shed and was dark, like polished brown marble. It was about four feet along the beam and perfect in form. Hession found one like it. We set them on our shoulders and moved on down the hill, intent to take them home.

We headed for the next of the riverine mountains, where we planned to descend and—if our calculations were accurate—meet the river at the campsite. The river, far below us, now and again came into view as we walked abreast over open tundra. Fedeler, even more alert than usual, now stopped and, as before, touched my arm. He pointed toward the river. If a spruce needle had been floating on the water there, Fedeler would have seen it. We saw in an instant that we had miscalculated and were heading some miles beyond the campsite and would have come eventually to the river not knowing—upstream or downstream—which way to go. Fedeler was pointing toward a gravel bar, a thin column of smoke, minute human figures near the smoke, and the podlike whiteness of the metal canoe.

Another two miles, descending, and we were barefoot in the river, with pink hot feet turning anesthetically cold. We crossed slowly. The three others were by the campfire. On the grill were grayling and a filleted Arctic char. The air was cool now, nearing fifty, and we ate the fish, and beef stew, and strawberries, and drank hot chocolate. After a time, Hession said, "That was a good walk. That was some of the easiest hiking you will ever find in Alaska."

We drew our route on the map and figured the distance at fourteen miles. John Kauffmann, tapping his pipe on a stone, said, "That's a lot for Alaska."

We sat around the campfire for at least another hour. We talked of rain and kestrels, oil and antlers, the height and the headwaters of the river. Neither Hession nor Fedeler once mentioned the bear.

When I got into my sleeping bag, though, and closed my eyes, there he was, in color, on the side of the hill. The vision was indelible, but fear was not what put it there. More, it was a sense of sheer luck at having chosen in the first place to follow Fedeler and Hession up the river and into the hills—a memento not so much of one moment as of the entire circuit of the long afternoon. It was a vision of a whole land, with an animal in it. This was his country, clearly enough. To be there was to be incorporated, in however small a measure, into its substance—his country, and if you wanted to visit it you had better knock.

> His association with other animals is a mixture of enterprising action, almost magnanimous acceptance, and just plain willingness to ignore. There is great strength and pride combined with a strong mixture of inquisitive curiosity in the make-up of grizzly character. This curiosity is what makes trouble when men penetrate into country where they are not known to the bear. The grizzly can be brave and sometimes downright brash. He can be secretive and very retiring. He can be extremely cunning and also powerfully aggressive. Whatever he does, his actions match his surroundings and the circumstance of the moment. No wonder that meeting him on his mountain is a momentous event, imprinted on one's mind for life.

• • •

What had struck me most in the isolation of this wilderness was an abiding sense of paradox. In its raw, convincing emphasis on the irrelevance or the visitor, it was forcefully, importantly repellent. It was no less strongly attractive—with a beauty of nowhere else, composed in turning circles. If the wild land was indifferent, it gave a sense of difference. If at moments it was frightening, requiring an effort to put down the conflagrationary imagination, it also augmented the touch of life. This was not a dare with nature. This was nature.

The bottoms of the Kleppers were now trellised with tape. Pourchot was smoothing down a final end. Until recently, he had been an avocational parachutist, patterning the sky in star formation with others as he fell. He had fifty-one jumps, all of them in Colorado. But he had started waking up in the night with cold sweats, so—with two small sons now—he had sold his jumping gear. With the money, he bought a white-water kayak and climbing rope. "You're kind of on your own, really. You run the risk," he was saying. "I haven't seen any bear incidents, for example. I've never had any bear problems. I've never carried a gun. Talk to ten people and you get ten different bear-approach theories. Some carry flares. Ed Bailey, in Fish and Wildlife, shoots pencil flares into the ground before approaching bears. They go away. Bear attacks generally occur in road-system areas anyway. Two, maybe four people die a year. Some years more than others. Rarely will a bear attack a person in a complete wilderness like this.''

Kauffmann said, ''Give a grizzly half a chance and he'll avoid you.''

Fedeler had picked cups of blueberries to mix into our breakfast pancakes. Finishing them, we prepared to go. The sun was coming through. The rain was gone. The morning grew bright and warm. Pourchot and I got into the canoe, which, for all its heavy load, felt light. Twenty minutes downriver, we had to stop for more repairs to the Kleppers, but afterward the patchwork held. With higher banks, longer pools, the river was running deeper. The sun began to blaze.

Rounding bends, we saw sculpins, a pair of great horned owls. mergansers, Taverner's geese. We saw ravens and a gray jay. Coming down a long, deep, green pool, we looked toward the riffle at the lower end and saw an approaching grizzly. He was young, possibly four years old, and not much over four hundred pounds. He crossed the river. He studied the salmon in the riffle. He did not see, hear, or smell us. Our three boats were close together, and down the light current on the flat water we drifted toward the fishing bear.

He picked up a salmon, roughly ten pounds of fish, and, holding it with one paw, he began to whirl it around his head. Apparently, he was not hungry, and this was a form of play. He played sling-the-salmon. With his claws embedded near the tail, he whirled the salmon and then tossed it high, end over end. As it fell, he scooped it up and slung it around his head again, lariat salmon, and again he tossed it into the air. He caught it and heaved it high once more. The fish flopped to the ground. The bear turned away, bored. He began to move upstream by the edge of the river. Behind his big head his hump projected. His brown fur rippled like a field under wind. He kept coming. The breeze was behind him. He had not yet seen us. He was romping along at an easy walk. As he came closer to us, we drifted slowly toward him. The single Klepper, with John Kauffmann in it, moved up against a snagged stick and broke it off. The snap was light, but enough to stop the bear. Instantly, he was motionless and alert, remaining on his four feet and straining his eyes to see. We drifted on toward him. At last, we arrived in his focus. If we were looking at something we had rarely seen before, God help him so was he. If he was a tenth as awed as I was, he could not have moved a muscle, which he did, now, in a hurry that was not pronounced but nonetheless seemed inappropriate to his status in the situation. He crossed low ground and went up a bank toward a copse of willow. He stopped there and faced us again. Then, breaking stems to pieces, he went into the willows.

We drifted to the rip, and down it past the mutilated salmon. Then we came to another long flat surface, spraying up the light of the sun. My bandanna, around my head, was nearly dry. I took it off, and trailed it in the river.

Tom Wolfe / *The Right Stuff* 1979

''The me-decade,'' ''radical chic,'' ''the right stuff''—these are a few of the phrases that Tom Wolfe has introduced into the American vocabulary. A genius at deciphering an attitude or an entire ideology from the slightest stylistic quirk or idiom, Wolfe is without a doubt one of the major interpreters of contemporary American culture.

Born in 1931, Wolfe grew up in Richmond, Virginia. He graduated from Washington and Lee University and then went on to receive a Ph.D. in Ameri-

can Studies at Yale. He spent several years as a newspaper reporter, and in 1980 received the Columbia Journalism Award for distinguished service in the field of journalism. Wolfe's first book, The Kandy-Kolored Tangerine-Flake Streamline Baby, *appeared in 1965 and established him at once as a leading critic of popular culture. His other books include* The Electric Kool-Aid Acid Test *(1968),* The Pump House Gang *(1968),* Radical Chic and Mau-Mauing the Flak Catchers *(1970),* The Painted Word *(1975), and* From Bauhaus to Our House *(1981).* Rolling Stone *magazine, which published portions of* The Right Stuff, *began serializing Wolfe's first novel in 1984.*

The following account of the test pilot, Chuck Yeager, is an excerpt from Tom Wolfe's best-known book, The Right Stuff *(1979), which won the American Book Award for nonfiction.*

YEAGER

Anyone who travels very much on airlines in the United States soon gets to know the voice of *the airline pilot* . . . coming over the intercom . . . with a particular drawl, a particular folksiness, a particular down-home calmness that is so exaggerated it begins to parody itself (nevertheless!—it's reassuring) . . . the voice that tells you, as the airliner is caught in thunderheads and goes bolting up and down a thousand feet at a single gulp, to check your seat belts because "it might get a little choppy" . . . the voice that tells you (on a flight from Phoenix preparing for its final approach into Kennedy Airport, New York, just after dawn): "Now, folks, uh . . . this is the captain . . . ummmm . . . We've got a little ol' red light up here on the control panel that's tryin' to tell us that the *lan*din' gears're not . . . uh . . . *lock*in' into position when we lower 'em . . . Now . . . *I* don't believe that little ol' red light knows what its *talk*in' about—I believe it's that little ol' red *light* that iddn' workin' right" . . . faint chuckle, long pause, as if to say, *I'm not even sure all this is really worth going into—still, it may amuse you . . . "But* . . . I guess to play it by the rules, we oughta *hum*or that little ol' light . . . so we're gonna take her down to about, oh, two or three hundred feet over the runway at Kennedy, and the folks down there on the ground are gonna see if they caint give us a *vis*ual inspection of those ol' landin' gears"—with which he is obviously on intimate ol' buddy terms, as with every other working part of this mighty ship—"and if I'm right . . . they're gonna tell us everything is copa*cet*ic all the way aroun' an' we'll jes take her on in" . . . and, after a couple of low passes over the field, the voice returns: "Well, folks, those folks down there on the ground—it must be too early for 'em or somethin'—I 'spect they still got the *sleep*ers in their eyes . . . 'cause they say they caint tell if those ol' landin' gears are all the way down or not . . . But, you know, up here in the cockpit we're convinced they're all the way down, so we're jes gonna take her on in . . . And oh" . . . *(I almost forgot)* . . . "while we take a little swing out over the ocean an' empty some of that surplus fuel we're not gonna be needin' anymore—that's what you might be seein' comin' out of the wings—our lovely little ladies . . . if they'll be so kind . . . they're gonna go up and down the aisles and show yu how we do what we call 'assumin' the position' " . . . another faint chuckle *(We do this often, and it's so much fun, we even have a funny little name for it)* . . . and the stewardesses, a bit grimmer, by the looks of them, than *that voice,* start telling the passengers to take their glasses off and take the ballpoint pens and other sharp objects out of their pockets, and they show them *the position,* with the head lowered . . . while down on the field at Kennedy the little yellow emergency trucks start roaring across the field—and even though in your pounding heart and your sweating palms and your broiling brainpan you *know* this is a critical moment in your life, you still can't quite bring yourself to be*lieve* it, because if it were . . . how could *the captain,* the man who knows the actual situation most intimately . . . how could he keep on drawlin' and chucklin' and driftin' and lollygaggin' in that particular voice of his—

Well!—who doesn't know that voice! And who can forget it!—even after he is proved right and the emergency is over.

That particular voice may sound vaguely Southern or Southwestern, but it is specifically Appalachian in origin. It originated in the mountains of West Virginia, in the coal country, in Lincoln County, so far up in the hollows that, as the saying went, "they had to pipe in daylight." In the late 1940's and early 1950's this up-hollow voice drifted down from on high, from over the high desert of California, down, down, down, from the upper reaches of the Brotherhood into all phases of American aviation. It was amazing. It was *Pygmalion* in reverse. Military pilots and then, soon, airline pilots, from Maine and Massachusetts and the Dakotas and Oregon and everywhere else began to talk in that poker-hollow West Virginia drawl, or as close to it as they could bend their native accents. It was the drawl of the most righteous of all the possessors of the right stuff: Chuck Yeager.

Yeager had started out as the equivalent, in the Second World War, of the legendary Frank Luke of the 27th Aero Squadron in the First. Which is to say, he was the boondocker, the boy from the back country, with only a high-school education, no credentials, no cachet or polish of any sort, who took off the feed-store overalls and put on a uniform and climbed into an airplane and lit up the skies over Europe.

Yeager grew up in Hamlin, West Virginia, a town on the Mud River not far from Nitro, Hurricane Whirlwind, Salt Rock, Mud, Sod, Crum, Leet, Dollie, Ruth, and Alum Creek. His father was a gas driller (drilling for natural gas in the coalfields), his older brother was a gas driller, and he would have been a gas driller had he not enlisted in the Army Air Force in 1941 at the age of eighteen. In 1943, at twenty he became a flight officer, i.e., a non-com who was allowed to fly, and went to England to fly fighter planes over France and Germany. Even in the tumult of the war Yeager was somewhat puzzling to a lot of other pilots. He was a short, wiry, but muscular little guy with dark curly hair and a tough-looking face that seemed (to strangers) to be saying: "You best not be lookin' me in the eye, you peckerwood, or I'll put four more holes in your nose." But that wasn't what was puzzling. What was puzzling was the way Yeager talked. He seemed to talk with some older forms of English elocution, syntax, and conjugation that had been preserved uphollow in the Appalachians. There were people up there who never said they disapproved of anything, they said: "I don't hold with it." In the present tense they were willing to *help* out, like anyone else; but in the past tense they only *holped.* "H'it weren't nothin' I hold with, but I holped him out with it, anyways."

In his first eight missions, at the age of twenty, Yeager shot down two German fighters. On his ninth he was shot down over German-occupied French territory, suffering flak wounds; he bailed out, was picked up by the French underground, which smuggled him across the Pyrenees into Spain disguised as a peasant. In Spain he was jailed briefly, then released, whereupon he made it back to England and returned to combat during the Allied invasion of France. On October 12, 1944, Yeager took on and shot down five German fighter planes in succession. On November 6, flying a propeller-driven P-51 Mustang, he shot down one of the new jet fighters the Germans had developed, the Messerschmitt-262, and damaged two more, and on November 20 he shot down four FW-190s. It was a true Frank Luke-style display of warrior fury and personal prowess. By the end of the war he had thirteen and a half kills. He was twenty-two years old.

In 1946 and 1947 Yeager was trained as a test pilot at Wright Field in Dayton.

He amazed his instructors with his ability at stunt-team flying, not to mention the unofficial business of hassling. That plus his up-hollow drawl had everybody saying, "He's a natural-born stick 'n' rudder man." Nevertheless, there was something extraordinary about it when a man so young, with so little experience in flight test, was selected to go to Muroc Field in California for the X-1 project.

Muroc was up in the high elevations of the Mojave Desert. It looked like some fossil landscape that had long since been left behind by the rest of terrestrial evolution. It was full of huge dry lake beds, the biggest being Rogers Lake. Other than sagebrush the only vegetation was Joshua trees, twisted freaks of the plant world that looked like a cross between cactus and Japanese bonsai. They had a dark petrified green color and horribly crippled branches. At dusk the Joshua trees stood out in silhouette on the fossil wasteland like some arthritic nightmare. In the summer the temperature went up to 110 degrees as a matter of course, and the dry lake beds were covered in sand, and there would be windstorms and sandstorms right out of a Foreign Legion movie. At night it would drop to near freezing, and in December it would start raining, and the dry lakes would fill up with a few inches of water, and some sort of putrid prehistoric shrimps would work their way up from out of the ooze, and sea gulls would come flying in a hundred miles or more from the ocean, over the mountains, to gobble up these squirming little throwbacks. A person had to see it to believe it: flocks of sea gulls wheeling around in the air out in the middle of the high desert in the dead of winter and grazing on antediluvian crustaceans in the primordial ooze.

When the wind blew the few inches of water back and forth across the lake beds, they became absolutely smooth and level. And when the water evaporated in the spring, and the sun baked the ground hard, the lake beds became the greatest natural landing fields ever discovered, and also the biggest, with miles of room for error. That was highly desirable, given the nature of the enterprise at Muroc.

Besides the wind, sand, tumbleweed, and Joshua trees, there was nothing at Muroc except for two quonset-style hangars, side by side, a couple of gasoline pumps, a single concrete runway, a few tarpaper shacks, and some tents. The officers stayed in the shacks marked "barracks," and lesser souls stayed in the tents and froze all night and fried all day. Every road into the property had a guardhouse on it manned by soldiers. The enterprise the Army had undertaken in this godforsaken place was the development of supersonic jet and rocket planes.

At the end of the war the Army had discovered that the Germans not only had the world's first jet fighter but also a rocket plane that had gone 596 miles an hour in tests. Just after the war a British jet, the Gloster Meteor, jumped the official world speed record from 469 to 606 in a single day. The next great plateau would be Mach 1, the speed of sound, and the Army Air Force considered it crucial to achieve it first.

The speed of sound, Mach 1, was known (thanks to the work of the physicist Ernst Mach) to vary at different altitudes, temperatures, and wind speeds. On a calm 60-degree day at sea level it was about 760 miles an hour, while at 40,000 feet, where the temperature would be at least sixty below, it was about 660 miles an hour. Evil and baffling things happened in the transonic zone, which began at about .7 Mach. Wind tunnels choked out at such velocities. Pilots who approached the speed of sound in dives reported that the controls would lock or "freeze" or even alter their normal functions. Pilots had crashed and died because they couldn't budge the stick. Just last year Geoffrey de Havilland, son of the famous British aircraft designer and builder, had tried to take one of his father's DH 108s to Mach 1. The ship started buffeting and then disintegrated, and he was killed. This led engineers to speculate that the g-forces became infinite at Mach 1, causing the aircraft to implode. They started talking about "the sonic wall" and "the sound barrier."

So this was the task that a handful of pilots, engineers, and mechanics had at Muroc. The place was utterly primitive, nothing but bare bones, bleached tarpaulins, and corrugated tin rippling in the heat with caloric waves; and for an ambitious young pilot it was perfect. Muroc seemed like an outpost on the dome of the world, open only to a righteous few, closed off to the rest of humanity, including even the Army Air Force brass of command control, which was at Wright Field. The commanding officer at Muroc was only a colonel, and his superiors at Wright did not relish junkets to the Muroc rat shacks in the first place. But to pilots this prehistoric throwback of an airfield became . . . shrimp heaven! the rat-shack plains of Olympus!

Low Rent Septic Tank Perfection . . . yes; and not excluding those traditional essentials for the blissful hot young pilot: Flying & Drinking and Drinking & Driving.

Just beyond the base, to the southwest, there was a rickety wind-blown 1930's style establishment called Pancho's Fly Inn, owned, run, and bartended by a woman named Pancho Barnes. Pancho Barnes wore tight white sweaters and tight pants, after the mode of Barbara Stanwyck in *Double Indemnity*. She was only forty-one when Yeager arrived at Muroc, but her face was so weatherbeaten, had so many hard miles on it, that she looked older, especially to the young pilots at the base. She also shocked the pants off them with her vulcanized tongue. Everybody she didn't like was an old bastard or a sonofabitch. People she liked were old bastards and sonsabitches, too. ''I tol' 'at ol' bastard to get 'is ass on over here and I'd g'im a drink.'' But Pancho Barnes was anything but Low Rent. She was the granddaughter of the man who designed the old Mount Lowe cable-car system, Thaddeus S. C. Lowe. Her maiden name was Florence Leontine Lowe. She was brought up in San Marino, which adjoined Pasadena and was one of Los Angeles' wealthiest suburbs, and her first husband—she was married four times—was the pastor of the Pasadena Episcopal Church, the Rev. C. Rankin Barnes. Mrs. Barnes seemed to have few of the conventional community interests of a Pasadena matron. In the late 1920's, by boat and plane, she ran guns for Mexican revolutionaries and picked up the nickname Pancho. In 1930 she broke Amelia Earhart's airspeed record for women. Then she barnstormed around the country as the featured performer of ''Pancho Barnes's Mystery Circus of the Air.'' She always greeted her public in jodhpurs and riding boots, a flight jacket, a white scarf, and a white sweater that showed off her terrific Barbara Stanwyck chest. Pancho's desert Fly Inn had an airstrip, a swimming pool, a dude ranch corral, plenty of acreage for horseback riding, a big old guest house for the lodgers, and a connecting building that was the bar and restaurant. In the barroom the floors, the tables, the chairs, the walls, the beams, the bar were of the sort known as extremely weather-beaten, and the screen doors kept banging. Nobody putting together such a place for a movie about flying in the old days would ever dare make it as dilapidated and generally go-to-hell as it actually was. Behind the bar were many pictures of airplanes and pilots, lavishly autographed and inscribed, badly framed and crookedly hung. There was an old piano that had been dried out and cracked to the point of hopeless desiccation. On a good night a huddle of drunken aviators could be heard trying to bang, slosh, and navigate their way through old Cole Porter tunes. On average nights the tunes were not that good to start with. When the screen door banged and a man walked through the door into the saloon, every eye in the place checked him out. If he wasn't known as somebody who had something to do with flying at Muroc, he would be eyed like some lame goddamned mouseshit sheepherder from *Shane*.

The plane the Air Force wanted to break the sound barrier with was called the X-1. The Bell Aircraft Corporation had built it under an Army contract. The core of the ship was a rocket of the type first developed by a young Navy inventor, Robert Truax, during the war. The fuselage was shaped like a 50-caliber bullet—

an object that was known to go supersonic smoothly. Military pilots seldom drew major test assignments; they went to highly paid civilians working for the aircraft corporations. The prime pilot for the X-1 was a man whom Bell regarded as the best of the breed. This man looked like a movie star. He looked like a pilot from out of *Hell's Angels.* And on top of everything else there was his name: Slick Goodlin.

The idea in testing the X-1 was to nurse it carefully into the transonic zone, up to seven-tenths, eight-tenths, nine-tenths the speed of sound (.7 Mach, .8 Mach, .9 Mach) before attempting the speed of sound itself, Mach 1, even though Bell and the Army already knew the X-1 had the rocket power to go to Mach 1 and beyond, if there *was* any *beyond.* The consensus of aviators and engineers, after Geoffrey de Havilland's death, was that the speed of sound was an absolute, like the firmness of the earth. The sound barrier was a farm you could buy in the sky. So Slick Goodlin began to probe the transonic zone in the X-1, going up to .8 Mach. Every time he came down he'd have a riveting tale to tell. The buffeting, it was so fierce—and the listeners, their imaginations aflame, could practically see poor Geoffrey de Havilland disintegrating in midair. And the goddammned aerodynamics—and the listeners got a picture of a man in balloon pumps skidding across a sheet of ice, pursued by bears. A controversy arose over just how much bonus Slick Goodlin should receive for assaulting the dread Mach 1 itself. Bonuses for contract test pilots were not unusual; but the figure of $150,000 was now bruited about. The army balked, and Yeager got the job. He took it for $283 a month, or $3,396 a year; which is to say, his regular Army captain's pay.

The only trouble they had with Yeager was in holding him back. On his first powered flight in the X-1 he immediately executed an unauthorized zero-g roll with a full load of rocket fuel, then stood the ship on its tail and went up to .85 Mach in a vertical climb, also unauthorized. On subsequent flights, at speeds between .85 Mach and .9 Mach, Yeager ran into most known airfoil problems—loss of elevator, aileron, and rudder control, heavy trim pressures, Dutch rolls, pitching and buffeting, the lot—yet was convinced, after edging over .9 Mach, that this would all get better, not worse, as you reached Mach 1. The attempt to push beyond Mach 1—''breaking the sound barrier''—was set for October 14, 1947. Not being an engineer, Yeager didn't believe the ''barrier'' existed.

Elizabeth Bishop / The U.S.A. School of Writing 1983

Soon after graduating from Vassar College, Elizabeth Bishop (1911–1979) took a job with a New York City correspondence school for writing. Like many such organizations, it promised more than it could possibly perform and the experience left the future poet with many vivid memories which years later she unsentimentally recorded in the following essay.

''The U.S.A. School of Writing'' nicely demonstrates one of the major differences between gifted and mediocre writing: the keen observation of specific details. The writing Elizabeth Bishop is hired to read and improve is—wholly unlike her own—largely made up of generalizations and abstractions, as though her struggling students believed that only by expressing themselves in the most important-sounding terms could they then make their own lives sound important.

One of America's leading contemporary poets, Elizabeth Bishop won a Pulitzer Prize for North & South and A Cold Spring *in 1955 and the National Book Award in 1969 for* The Complete Poems.

Probably written in 1966, "The U.S.A. School of Writing" was first published in The New Yorker, *July 18, 1983. The essay also appears in* The Collected Prose *(1984).*

When I graduated from Vassar in 1934, during the Great Depression, jobs were still hard to find and very badly paid. Perhaps for those very reasons it seemed incumbent on me and many of my classmates to find them, whether we had to or not. The spirit of the times and, of course, of my college class was radical; we were puritanically pink. Perhaps there seemed to be something virtuous in working for much less a year than our educations had been costing our families. It was a combination of this motive, real need for a little more money than I had, idle curiosity, and, I'm afraid, pure masochism that led me to answer an advertisement in the Sunday *Times* and take a job. It was with a correspondence school, the U.S.A. School of Writing.

First I had an interview at the school with its head, or president, as he described himself, Mr. Black. His opening remark was that the U.S.A. School of Writing stood for "The United States of America School of Writing," and my pleasure in that explanation trapped me immediately. But I can see now that I was just made to order for Mr. Black, and he must have been mentally rubbing his hands and licking his chops over me all during our little talk. I couldn't type—properly, that is; I wanted to smoke while I worked, which was against the fire laws; and I had had no experience at anything at all. But I was from Vassar and I had had a story and three poems published in magazines. I hadn't the faintest idea of my own strength; he would have taken me, probably, even if I had asked for twenty-five dollars a week instead of the fifteen dollars he was offering, but of course such an idea never occurred to me. No doubt he was already plotting how my high-class education and my career in print could be incorporated into his newest circulars.

However, there was a slight catch to that. For a while, at least, I would have to fulfill my duties at the school under the name of Fred G. Margolies, which had been the name, not of my predecessor, but of the one before the one before that. It developed that some of Mr. Margolies's students were still taking the course and had to receive their corrected lessons signed by him, and I would have to be Mr. Margolies until they had all graduated. Then I could turn into myself again, and steer new students. I felt I'd probably like to keep on being Mr. Margolies, if I could. He had had something published, too, although I never succeeded in delving deep enough into the history of the school to find out what it was. And he or they must have been good letter writers, or even fuller of idle curiosity than I was, or just very kindhearted men, to judge by the tone of the letters I received in our name. In fact, for a long time afterwards I used to feel that the neurotically "kind" facet of my personality *was* Mr. Margolies.

The school was on the fourth floor, the top floor, of an old tumble-down building near Columbus Circle. There was no elevator. I had accepted—although "accept" cannot be the right word—the job in the late fall, and it seems to me now that it was always either raining or snowing when I emerged mornings from the subway into Columbus Circle, and that I was always wearing a black wool dress, a trench coat, and galoshes, and carrying an unbrella. In the dark hallway there were three flights of steps, which sagged and smelled of things like hot iron, cigars, rubber boots, or peach pits—the last gasps of whatever industries were dying behind the lettered doors.

The U.S.A. School consisted of four rooms: a tiny lobby where one girl sat alone, typing—typing exactly what her colleagues were typing in the big room behind her, I discovered, but I suppose she was placed there to stave off any unexpected pupils who might decide to come to the school in person. The lobby had a few photos on the wall: pictures of Sinclair Lewis and other non-graduates. Then came the big room, lit grayly by several soot-and-snow-laden skylights, lights going all the time, with six to a dozen girls. Their number varied daily, and they sat at very old-model typewriters, typing the school's "lessons." At the other end of this room, overlooking the street, were two more tiny rooms, one of which was Mr. Black's office and the other Mr. Margolies and Mr. Hearn's office.

Mr. Hearn was a tall, very heavy, handsome woman, about thirty years old, named Rachel, with black horn-rimmed glasses, and a black mole on one cheek. Rachel and I were somewhat cramped in our quarters. She smoked furiously all the time, and I smoked moderately, and we were not allowed to keep our door open because of the poor transient typists, who were not allowed to smoke and might see us and go on strike, or report us to the nearest fire station. What with the rain and fog and snow outside and the smoke inside, we lived in a suffocating, woolly gray isolation, as if in a cocoon. It smelled like a day coach at the end of a long train trip. We worked back to back, but we had swivel chairs and spent quite a bit of our time swung around to each other, with our knees almost bumping, the two cigarettes under each other's nose, talking.

At first she was horrid to me. Again in my innocence I didn't realize it was, of course, because of my Vassar stigmata and my literary career, but her manner soon improved and we even got to like each other, moderately. Rachel did most of the talking. She had a great deal to say; she wanted to correct all the mistakes in my education and, as so many people did in those days, she wanted to get me to join the Party. In order to avoid making the trip to headquarters with her, to get my "card," something we could have done easily during any lunch hour, once I'd put an end to my nonsense and made the decision, I told her I was an anarchist. But it didn't help much. In spite of my principles, I found myself cornered into defending Berkman's attempt to assassinate Andrew Carnegie's partner, Henry Frick, and after that, I spent evenings at the Forty-second Street Library taking out books under "*An,*" in desperate attempts to shut Rachel up. For a while I was in touch with an anarchist organization (they are hard to locate, I found) in New Jersey, and received pamphlets from them, and invitations to meetings, every day in my mail.

Sometimes we went out to lunch together at a mammoth Stewart's Cafeteria. I liked cafeterias well enough, but they afflict one with indecision: what to eat, what table to sit at, what chair at the table, whether to remove the food from the tray or eat it on the tray, where to put the tray, whether to take off one's coat or keep it on, whether to abandon everything to one's fellow diners, and go for the forgotten glass of water, or to lug it all along. But Rachel swept me ahead of her, like a leaf from the enchanter fleeing, toward the sandwich counter. The variety of sandwiches that could be made to order like lightning was staggering, and she always ate three: lox and cream cheese on a bun, corned beef and a pickle relish on rye, pastrami and mustard on something-or-other. She *shouted* her order. It didn't matter much, I found, after a few days of trying to state my three terms loudly and clearly; the sandwiches all tasted alike. I began settling for large, quite unreal baked apples and coffee. Rachel, with her three sandwiches and three cups of black coffee simultaneously, and I would seat ourselves in our wet raincoats and galoshes, our lunches overlapping between us, and she would harangue me about literature.

She never attempted politics at lunch, I don't know why. She had read a lot and had what I, the English major, condescendingly considered rather pathetic taste. She liked big books, with lots of ego and emotion in them, and Whitman was her favorite poet. She liked the translations of Merezhkovski, all of Thomas Wolfe that had then appeared, all of Theodore Dreiser, the Studs Lonigan series of James Farrell, and best of all she liked Vardis Fisher. She almost knew by heart his entire works to date. A feeling of nightmare comes over me as I remember those luncheons: the food; the wet, gritty floor under my hot feet; the wet, feeding, roaring crowd of people beneath the neon lights; and Rachel's inexorable shout across the table, telling me every detail of Vardis Fisher's endless and harrowing autobiography. She may have worked in some details from her own, I'm not sure; I made up my mind then never to read the books, which she offered to loan me, and I never have. I remember her quoting the line and a half from "Modern Love" from which Fisher had taken three titles in a row: *"In tragic life, God wot, / No villain need be! Passions spin the plot . . ."* and my wondering dazedly in all the hubbub why he had neglected the possibilities of "God wot," or if he'd still get around to it. I had recently come from a line analysis of *The Waste Land,* and this bit of literary collage failed to impress me.

"Realism" and only "realism" impressed *her.* But if I tried to imply, in my old classroom manner, that there was "realism" and "realism," or ask her what she *meant* by "realism," she would glare at me savagely, her eyes glittering under Stewart's lighting fixtures, and silently stretch her large mouth over the bulging tiers of a sandwich. Her mole moved up and down as she chewed. At first I was afraid of those slap-like glares, but I grew used to them. And when one day, back in our office, she asked me to read one of her sentences to see if the grammar was right, I knew that she had begun to like me in spite of my bourgeois decadence and an ignorance of reality that took refuge in the childishness of anarchism. I also knew she had already sensed something fishy about my alleged political views.

Overbearing, dishonest, unattractive, proud of being "tough," touchy, insensitive, yet capable of being kind or amused when anything penetrated, Rachel was something new to me. She had one rare trait that kept me interested: she never spoke of herself at all. Her salary was twenty-five dollars a week. Her clothes were shabby, even for Stewart's in those days, and dirty as well. The only thing I learned about her was that she had a sister in a state tuberculosis sanatorium whom she went to see once a month, but whom she didn't particularly like; the reason seemed to be because she was sick, and therefore "no good." Rachel herself had tremendous strength and I soon realized that she inspired fear, almost physical fear, in everyone at the so-called school, including President Black. I also soon realized that she was the entire brains of the place, and afterwards I even suspected that in her power and duplicity perhaps it was she who really owned it, and was using Mr. Black as a front. Probably not, but I never knew the truth about anything that went on there.

Her cigarettes were stolen for her somewhere by a "man" she knew—how, or who the man was, I never discovered. From time to time other objects appeared—a new bag, a fountain pen, a lighter—from the same source or perhaps a different "man," but she never spoke of love or romance, except Vardis Fisher's. She should have hated me; my constant gentle acquiescence or hesitant corrections must have been hard to take; but I don't think she did. I think we felt sorry for each other. I think she felt that I was one of the doomed, enjoying my little grasshopper existence, my "sense of humor," my "culture," while I could, and that perhaps at some not very future date, when the chips were down, she might even put in a good word for me if she felt like it. I think that later she may well have become a great business success—probably a shady business, like the writing school, but on a much larger scale. She seemed drawn toward the dark and crooked, as if, since she believed that people were forced into being underhanded by economic circumstances in the first place, it would have been dishonest of her not to be dishonest. "Property is theft" was one of her favorite sayings.

Poor Rachel! I often disliked her; she gave me a *frisson,* and yet at the same time I liked her, and I certainly couldn't help listening to every word she said. For several weeks she was my own private Columbus Circle orator. Her lack of a "past," of any definable setting at all, the impression she gave of power and of something biding its time, even if it was false or silly, fascinated me. Talking with her was like holding a snapshot negative up to the light and wondering how its murks and transparencies were actually going to develop.

The course we offered on "How to Write" was advertised in the cheapest farm magazines, movie and Western magazines. It was one of those "You, too, can earn money by your pen" advertisements, glowingly but carefully worded. We could instruct anyone, no matter what his or her education, in any branch of the writing art, from newspaper reporting to advertising, to the novel, and every student would receive the personal attention and expert advice of successful, money-making authors like Mr. Hearn and Mr. Margolies. There were eight lessons, and the complete course, payable in advance, cost forty dollars. At the time I worked there, the school had only about a hundred and fifty "students" going, but there had been a period, just before, when it had had many, many more, and more were expected again, I gathered, as soon as the courses had been "revised." There had been a big upheaval in the recent past, entailing the loss of most of the student body, and for some reason, everything, all the circulars, contract blanks, and "lessons," had to be revised immediately and printed all over again. That was why, off and on, so many typists were employed.

All these revisions, including the eight new lessons, were being done by Rachel. She sat with the school's former "literature" cut into narrow strips, and clipped together in piles around her. There were also stacks of circulars from rival correspondence schools, and a few odd textbooks on composition and short-story writing, from which she lifted the most dogmatic sentences, or even whole paragraphs. When she did work, she worked extremely rapidly. It sounded like two or three typewriters instead of one, and the nervous typists kept running in from the big skylighted room and back again with the new material like relay racers. But she talked to me a great deal of the time, or stared gloomily out the window at the falling snow. Once she said, "Why don't you write a pretty poem about *that?*" Once or twice, smelling strongly of whiskey, she buried herself sulkily in a new proletarian novel for an entire afternoon.

We scarcely saw Mr. Black at all. He received a good many callers in his office, men who looked just like him, and he served them the George Washington instant coffee he made on a Sterno stove, which smelled unpleasantly through the partition into our room. Once in a while he would bring us both coffee, in ten-cent-store cups of milky green glass with very rough edges you could cut yourself on. He would ask, "And how's the Vassar girl?" and look over my shoulder at the letter I was slowly producing on the typewriter with three or four fingers, and say, "Fine! Fine! You're doing fine! They'll love it! They'll love it!" and give my shoulder an objectionable squeeze. Sometimes he would say to Rachel, "Take a look at this. Save it; put the carbon in your file. We'll use it again." Rachel would give a loud groan.

It was here, in this noisome place, in spite of all I had read and been taught and thought I knew about it before, that the mysterious, awful power of writing first dawned on me. Or, since "writing" means so many different things, the power of the printed word, or even the capitalized Word whose significance had previously escaped me but then made itself suddenly, if sporadically, plain.

Our advertisements specified that when an applicant wrote in inquiring about the course, he was to send a sample of his writing, a "story" of any sort, any length, for our "analysis," and a five-dollar money order. We sent him the "analysis" and told him whether or not he really did have the right stuff in him to make a successful writer. All applicants, unless analphabetic, did. Then he was supposed to complete the first lesson, I think it was either "Straight Reporting" or "Descriptive Writing," within a month and send it back to us with the remaining thirty-five dollars. We "analyzed" that and sent it back along with lesson number two, and he was launched on the course.

I forget all the lessons now, but "Advertising" was fitted in somewhere. The students were required to write advertisements for grapefruit, bread, and liquor. Why the emphasis on food and drink, I don't know, unless that too was a sign of the times. Also included were a short story and a "True Confession" lesson. Almost all the students had the two genres hopelessly confused. Their original "samples" were apt to fall into the True Confession form, too. This sample, expanded or cut, censored or livened up, and the first letter to Mr. Margolies that accompanied it constituted the most interesting assignment for all concerned. My job was to write an analysis of each lesson in five hundred words, if I could, and as many of them a day as I possibly could, using a collection of previous lessons and analyses as models. I also had to write a short personal reply to the inevitable letter that arrived with each lesson. I was to encourage the student if he was feeling hopeless, and discourage him firmly if he showed any signs of wanting his money back.

Henry James once said that he who would aspire to be a writer must inscribe on his banner the one word "Loneliness." In the case of my students, their need was not to ward off society, but to get into it. Their problem was that on their banners "Loneliness" had been inscribed despite them, and so they aspired to be writers. Without exception the letters I received were from people suffering from terrible loneliness in all its better-known forms, and in some I had never even dreamed of. Writing, especially writing to Mr. Margolies, was a way of being less alone. To be printed, and to be "famous," would be an instant shortcut to identity, and an escape from solitude, because then other people would know one as admirers, friends, lovers, suitors, etc.

In the forms they filled out, they gave their ages and occupations. There were a good many cowboys and ranch hands. One of them printed his lessons, not with the printing taught for a while in fashionable schools, although it resembled it, but with the printing of a child concentrating on being neat and careful. There was a sheepherder, a real shepherd, who even *said* he was lonely, "in my line of work." Writing cheered him up because "sheep aren't much company for a man (ha-ha)." There were the wives of ranchers as well. There were several sailors, a Negro cook, a petty officer on a submarine, and a real light-house keeper. There were a good many "domestics," some of whom said they were "colored," and several students writing from addresses in the Deep South told me, as if they had to, that they were Negroes.

Of all the letters and lessons I read during my stay at the U.S.A. School, only one set showed any slight sign of "promise" whatever. They were the work of a "lady cattle-rancher and poultry farmer," an "old maid," she wrote, living at an R.F.D. address somewhere in Kansas. The stories she sent in, regardless of the nature of the assignment, were real stories. The other students' heartbreaking attempts were always incoherent, abrupt, curtailed. Hers bounced along exuberantly, like a good talker, and were almost interesting, with a lot of local color and detail. They were filled with roosters, snakes, foxes, and hawks, and they had dramatic and possibly true plots woven around sick and dying cows, mortgages, stepmothers, babies, wicked blizzards, and tornadoes. They were also ten times longer than anyone else's stories. After I gave up my job, I used to look into farm magazines, like *The Country Gentleman,* on the newsstands, hoping that she might have made publication at last, but I never saw her name again.

Most of my pathetic applicants seemed never to have read anything in their lives, except perhaps a single, memorable story of the "True Confession" type. The discrepancy between the odd, colorless, disjointed little pages they sent me and what they saw in print just didn't occur to them. Or perhaps they thought Mr. Margolies would wave his magic wand and the little heaps of melancholy word-bones, like chicken bones or fish bones, would put on flesh and vitality and be transformed into gripping, compelling, thrilling, full-length stories and novels. There were doubtless other, deeper reasons for their taking the "course," sending in all their "lessons," and paying that outrageous forty dollars. But I could never quite believe that most of my students really thought that they too could one day write, or even that they would really have to work to do so. It was more like applying for application blanks for a lottery. After all, they might win the prize just as well as the next person, and everyone knows those things aren't always run honestly.

There seemed to be one thing common to all their "primitive" writing, as I suppose it might be called, in contrast to primitive painting: its slipshodiness and haste. Where primitive painters will spend months or years, if necessary, putting in every blade of grass and building up brick walls in low relief, the primitive writer seems in a hurry to get it over with. Another thing was the almost complete lack of detail. The primitive painter loves detail and lingers over it and emphasizes it at the expense of the picture as a whole. But if the writers put them in, the details are often impossibly or wildly inappropriate, sometimes revealing a great deal about the writer without furthering the matter in hand at all. Perhaps it all demonstrates the professional writer's frequent complaint that painting is more fun than writing. Perhaps the ranchers' wives who sent in miserable little outlines for stories with no conversation and no descriptions of people or places wouldn't hesitate to spend long afternoons lovingly decorating birthday cakes in different-color icings. But the subject matter was similarly banal in both the paintings and the writing. There was also the same tendency in both primitive painting and writing to make it all right, or of real value to the world, by tacking on a grand, if ill-fitting, "moral," or allegorical interpretation. My students seemed to be saying: "Our experiences are real and true and from them we have drawn these unique, these noble conclusions. Since our sentiments are so noble, who could have the heart to deny us our right to Fame?"

What could I possibly find to say to them? From what they wrote me it was obvious they could hardly wait to receive my next analysis. Perhaps they hoped, each time, that Mr. Margolies would tell them he had found a magazine to publish their last lesson and was enclosing the check. All of them were eager, if not hard-working, or felt they had to pretend to be. One man wrote: "I slept on a hair all night, waiting to hear from you." They apologized for their slowness, for their spelling, for their pens or pencils (they were asked to use ink but quite a few didn't). One boy excused his poor handwriting by saying, "This is being written on the subway," and it may have been true. Some referred to the lessons as their "homework," and addressed Mr. Margolies as "Dear Teacher." One woman decorated her lessons with Christmas seals. To my surprise, there were two or three male students who wrote man-to-man obscenities, or retold well-worn dirty jokes.

I took to copying out parts of their letters and stories to take home with me. A Kansas City janitor wanted to learn to write in order to publish "a book about how to teach children to be good radicals, of the George Washington Type or the Jesus Christ Type." One woman revealed that her aged mother approved of her learning how to write to such an extent that she had given her the forty dollars and "*her own name* to write under." The daughter's name was Emma, the mother's was Katerina. Would I please address her as Katerina in the future?

Next to my "lady cattle-rancher and poultry farmer" I grew fondest of a Mr. Jimmy O'Shea of Fall River, aged seventy, occupation "retired." His was the nearest approach to a classical primitive style. His stories were fairly long, and like Gertrude Stein, he wrote in large handwriting on small pieces of paper. He had developed a style that enabled him to make exactly a page of every sentence.

Each sentence—it usually began with *Also* or *Yes*—opened at the top left-hand and finished with an outsize dimple of a period in the lower right. Goodness shone through his blue-lined pages as if they had been little paper lanterns. He characterized everything that appeared in his simple tales with three, four, or even five adjectives and then repeated them, like Homer, every time the noun appeared. It was Mr. O'Shea who wrote me a letter which expressed the common feeling of time passing and wasted, of wonder and envy, and partly sincere ambition: "I wasn't feeling well over my teeth, and I had three large ones taken out, for they made me nervous and sick sometime, and this is the reason I couldn't send in my lesson. I am thinking of being able to write like all the Authors, for I believe that is more in my mind than any other kind of work. Mr. Margolies, I am thinking of how those Authors write such long stories of 60,000 or 100,000 words in those Magazines, and where do they get their imagination and the material to work upon? I know there is a big field in this art."

I stood the school for as long as I could, which wasn't very long, and the same week that I received this letter from Mr. O'Shea, I resigned. Mr. Black begged me to stay, I was just getting going, I was turning out more and more analyses every day, and he offered me two dollars and a half more a week. Rachel seemed sorry to see me go, too. We went out for a last lunch together, to a different cafeteria, one that had a bar, and, going Dutch, had a twenty-cent Manhattan each before lunch. When I was cleaning out my desk, she gave me a present, a strange paperbound book she had just finished reading, written by a Chinese, almost in the style of some of our students. It was all about his experiences as an agricultural slave in the United States and on the sugarcane plantations of Cuba. It may have been true, but it was not "realism" because he used odd, Oriental imagery.

About two years later I met Rachel in Times Square one night on my way to the theater. She looked the same, perhaps a little heavier and perhaps a little less shabby. I asked her if she still worked for the U.S.A. School of Writing and how Mr. Black was. Mr. Black, she announced casually, was in jail, for a second or third offense, for misuse of the mails. The U.S.A. School of Writing had been raided by the police shortly after I left, and all our work, and all my poor students' accumulation of lessons and earnest, confiding letters, had been confiscated. She said, "I didn't tell you while you were there, but that's why we were doing that revising. The U.S.A. School was a new name; up until a month before you came, it was something else. Black paid a big fine that time, and we were starting all over again."

I asked her what she was doing now, but she didn't tell me. I was dressed to go to the theater, and she looked me up and down contemptuously, I felt, but tolerantly, as if she were thinking, Some anarchist! Then Mr. Hearn and Mr. Margolies shook hands and parted forever.

SCRIPTS

A story can sound so good over lunch; it's so tough to get it to come out of the typewriter the same way.

CHARLTON HESTON

THE most popular writing in America is meant to be *heard,* not read. When we watch a situation comedy on television, or go to a movie, or tune in to a radio news program, we easily forget that the language we are listening to was originally *written.* Even with today's electronic media, the written word still precedes the performance: the most visually impressive movie probably started out as an idea in a scriptwriter's head. And much of what we hear on radio and television came out of a typewriter before it went over the air.

Scripts come in a variety of shapes and sizes. A filmscript, generally called a screenplay, is defined in a leading practical manual as "a written composition designed to serve as a sort of work diagram for the motion picture director."[1] Screenplays usually contain dialogue, along with a description of action and directions for camera and lighting "setups." The final working script, incorporating all the changes, is often called the "shooting script." Each media industry has its own script requirements and conventions. Because of time and budget constraints, television filmscripts, usually referred to as "teleplays," frequently need to be more polished and "camera-ready" than movie scripts.

All scripts have one thing in common: they are intended to be read aloud. Scripts assume the primacy of the speaking voice. If a scripted word, phrase, idiom, or speech rhythm sounds unnatural, a performer or director will instinctively change it. Thus, scripts are rarely treated as finished products but are constantly revised to conform as closely as possible to the inflections of the spoken voice. Of course, the voices will be affected by the particular setting or action. A movie script, for example, portraying infantrymen in Vietnam talking about recent combat would sound very different from a television anchorperson's newsscript reporting a similar battle. The rhythm, tone, emphasis, diction, and pacing would be dramatically different, though each script might be considered professionally well-crafted with respect to its overall purpose.

Scriptwriting differs from most other kinds of writing because it is largely invisible. Movie scripts, for example, are rarely published, and when they are, they tend to be read by people who have already seen the film. A good script is so closely connected to the total effect of the film that in itself it may seem barely significant as a piece of writing. A well-crafted screenplay, in other words, should not be thought of as similar to a literary drama, which can often be rewardingly read without benefit of performance. In fact, many television and movie directors react skeptically to scripts that appear too polished, that sound too much like finished plays. Such scripts may read well but not translate easily into image and action. After all, most films consist of long stretches of action without any dialogue.

Radio scripts function differently. In radio, voice counts for everything, and any silence seems unendurably long. Radio stations select performers largely on the quality of their voice. Most radio advertising, for example, depends almost entirely on the dramatic use of highly idiosyncratic and memorable voices. Disk jockeys, though they seldom use scripts for anything other than commercials or announcements, build reputations on unique styles of delivery. In the 1930's and 40's—during the "golden age" of radio—people *listened* to soap operas with the same avidity with which they now watch them (the old day-time melodramas were mostly sponsored by soap products—hence their name). So identifiable were the voices on these programs that listeners could easily distinguish

[1] Lewis Herman, *A Practical Manual of Screen Playwriting for Theater and Television Films* (1952; 1974).

the good guys from the bad guys on the basis of speech characteristics alone. In television where someone can be quickly characterized by physical appearance and gesture, the individual voice plays a far less dramatic role. One has only to compare a radio and a television commercial for the same product to note how differently scripts are created for each medium.

Another way to appreciate differences in techniques between two media is to study the film adaptation of a work of literature. Though critics often praise a film that stays especially close to its original text, a literal, word-by-word "translation" of prose into visual image is seldom feasible and not always desirable. One author who has seen her fiction transferred to the screen, Joyce Carol Oates, wonders why there should be any "enmity" between authors and screenwriters. She argues that an adaptation is really a collaborative enterprise; it is "not only a perfectly legitimate and exciting activity, it is an artistic venture of its own." The great novelist Vladimir Nabokov, after trying to turn his own masterpiece, *Lolita,* into a screenplay, was finally forced to admire the "unfaithful" though "first-rate film with magnificent actors" that the director Stanley Kubrick managed to create: "he saw my novel in one way," said Nabokov, "I saw it in another."

This section on "Scripts" includes Robert Geller's film adaptation of Ernest Hemingway's well-known short story, "Soldier's Home" (which appears in the Classics section). A comparison of the film adaptation with the original story provides an excellent opportunity to see how an experienced screenwriter works with material never intended for film. "Soldier's Home" seems at first to have little cinematic potential. The story is very short and lacks the full narrative development a film director might prefer. More importantly, the impact of the story occurs mainly in the narrator's voice and is not fully reflected in external activity. A film that tried to be a perfect visual enactment of the original story would certainly lack the imagery and action required for compelling drama.

As even a cursory reading shows, Geller's script differs sharply from Hemingway's story. The atmosphere, the psychological tone, the moral nuance have been retained, but Geller has made significant changes. He has introduced new characters (the flirtatious Roselle Simmons) and developed others (Mr. Krebs, merely mentioned in the short story, is physically present in the screenplay). Geller has dramatized incidents that Hemingway only alludes to (Kreb's pool playing) and has created situations not in the original story (the scene in front of the "Greek's Soda Shop"). Though Geller retains nearly verbatim several crucial stretches of dialogue, most of the conversation in the script was invented expressly for the film.

Like many adaptations, Geller's version of Hemingway's story depends upon the careful selection of detail. The screenwriter must be particularly alert to those parts of an original text not fully developed by the author. These implicit images, characters, locations, and incidents—elements of the literary work a reader may not always consciously attend to—frequently allow the scriptwriter to work around all of the non-cinematic portions of a story. An experienced scriptwriter reads literature with a keen eye for barely noticeable descriptive details that can then be integrated into the overall visual texture of the film. In "Soldier's Home," for example, Geller turns Hemingway's brief reference to the town library into a separate scene that also helps establish character and moves the plot.

The striking contrasts between Geller's screenplay and the original short story reflect, of course, the fundamental differences between prose fiction and film. Hemingway expects a reader to *hear* silently the way the narrative voice imitates the nervous consciousness of the story's main character. To duplicate this central feature of the story, Geller resorts to the contrivance of a narrative voice-over, and he fabricates dialogue that clearly articulates in actual conversation Harold Krebs's inner thoughts. Film does not easily adapt to long stretches of private consciousness. Nor can film readily convey the complexity of the narrator's attitude toward the various characters—perhaps the essential drama of serious fiction—an attitude that can be identified from the behavior of the narrative voice as irony, sympathy, satire, parody, etc. One of the most important critical questions to ask of Hemingway's "Soldier's Home" is: what does the narrator think of Harold Krebs? How you answer that question will most likely affect how you judge the success of Geller's adaptation.

Besides differing in basic techniques, film and literature often vary widely in their assumptions about their respective audiences. A screenwriter often makes major changes in a story's plot to satisfy popular demands or to clarify a deliberate ambiguity. When Flannery O'Connor's "The Life You Save May Be Your Own" (in the Classics section) was adapted for television in the 1950's, the conclusion was completely changed to end the story on a happier note. That change had nothing to do with the technical problems of translating literature to the screen, but was entirely a matter of how the television network felt its audience would react to the story's original ending. In "Soldier's Home," Robert Geller introduces no such major distortions, yet the consideration of an audience still plays a significant part in shaping the script. Why, for example, does the narrator at the end of the film repeat all of Hemingway's concluding paragraph *except* the final sentence?

Originally adapted for educational television, "Soldier's Home" was intended for a relatively small viewing audience. With scripts prepared for prime-time network television, however, audience becomes an extremely important commercial calculation. Television shows live or die according to audience ratings, and scriptwriters almost always need to shape their material with respect to elaborate guidelines and specifications so that the individual episodes of a series will follow a similar format and reflect consistent values. Networks spend small fortunes testing shows on sample audiences and using attitudinal research methods to develop the final program. For example, after assessing the preliminary audience reactions in 1976 to the "pilot" of the enormously popular series "Charlie's Angels," the ABC research department offered such advice as the following:

> 1. Develop the three female leading characters so that they can be made more distinctive, different, and recognizable from each other. Their motives for working for Charlie should be made clear with the emphasis on a moral desire to fight crime rather than what viewers felt was a "lust for money, clothes, or a sexual attachment to their boss." . . .
>
> 4. Improve future story lines by developing plots that are more plausible and straightforward, have greater mystery and suspense, are less corny and predictable and far less contrived.
>
> 5. Improve the dialogue in future story lines by avoiding "stock cops-and-robbers phrases" and "sexual allusions or cliches" in the talk with Charlie. . . .[1]

Scriptwriters would then be expected to adhere to such guidelines when constructing new episodes.

Prime-time television often toes a fine line between social controversy and dramatic convention. Popular new shows must appear lively and original without violating the values of mass audiences. Shows that present sharp opinions—the bigotry of an Archie Bunker, for example—are careful to neutralize those opinions by having other characters on the show tactfully express alternative

[1] Source: Sally Bedell, *Up the Tube* (1981).

ideas and attitudes. Unfortunately, the fear of offending any large group frequently results in dramatic predictability. If an elderly person on a sitcom were to make a nasty crack about the behavior of today's teenagers, the next scene would more than likely show a teenager acting in a remarkably saintly manner. The elderly person would then be pleasantly surprised and the viewing public reassured that the show was sensitive and responsive to contemporary values. Later, if the same teenager happened to complain that old people had no energy, the audience could be fairly certain that within the next few scenes remarkably spry grandparents would bounce through several rugged sets of tennis—and, of course, thrash an exhausted teenager.

An actual example of how mass entertainment will sometimes take greater risks with an audience's presumed values can be seen in "The Black Out," Richard B. Eckhaus's award-winning script for the well-known television show, "The Jeffersons." The writer chose a controversial subject: looting in a black neighborhood during a city-wide power failure. The script dealt openly and even ironically with racism by having the main character, who is black, arrested as a looter while trying to protect his own store. The climax of the story occured while a frustrated George Jefferson paced a crowded jail cell vehemently protesting his innocence:

> GEORGE: I own a chain of cleanin' stores. I made my way up BY MYSELF, and I don't need to steal. I ain't looted from nobody, and I don't belong in this dump . . . That's all I gotta say. *(George angrily sits down on the cell floor.)*
>
> SECOND INMATE *(looking down at George):* Man . . . you're really somethin'. You DO think you're too good for us, don't you?

Though George is legally in the right (he *has* been wrongfully arrested) and is morally in the right (he *is* innocent of stealing), he is nevertheless by the script's standards dramatically and culturally *wrong*. By assuming a proud, holier-than-thou stance (always a mistake in situation comedies), he has disassociated himself from his ethnic and neighborhood roots—a worse act, the script suggests, than the looting itself. The remainder of the episode shows how George must come to terms with his momentary violation of ethnic values that not everyone in the audience would necessarily share. The spectacular success of Alex Haley's *Roots* (see Bestsellers), however, which reached an unprecedented television audience in January 1977, the year before "The Black Out" was aired, quite clearly helped prepare viewers for George's final—though still cautious—understanding of the importance of his cultural origins.

Radio, television, and the movies entertain and instruct us daily, even hourly, yet rarely do they confront us with a single written word. Scripts are not intended for a reading audience. When you read the screenplay of "Soldier's Home" or "The Black Out" you should keep in mind that they were written with the sole purpose of being performed. They are not finished "texts" in the same sense as are most of the other selections in this book. The reader needs to supply—as did the actors and directors—the missing dimensions of sound, image, and movement to bring a script to life. It is one thing to read Abbott and Costello's famous "Who's on First?" routine; it is quite another to see and hear the two great comedians perform it. Reading a script is like going behind the scenes; we see what was not intended to be seen. As the audience of a print advertisement, news item, essay, or story, you are doing exactly what the writer intended—reading it. Scripts, however, require that you put yourself in the role of two different audiences: the individual reader of the actual script and the larger, intended audience of the imagined performance.

Orson Welles / The War of the Worlds

[*An Excerpt from the Radio Broadcast*]

October 31, 1938

Born in Kenosha, Wisconsin, in 1915, Orson Welles had earned, by the age of twenty-six, an international reputation as an actor and director in radio, theater, and cinema. Welles' virtuosity includes celebrated performances as a playwright, cartoonist, and journalist. He has written several syndicated columns.

In 1937, Welles launched the Mercury Theater on the Air to present a regular series of radio broadcasts of dramatic adaptation of famous novels. On October 31, 1938, Welles' "splendid purple-velvet voice" came on the radio to announce a story appropriate to a Halloween evening—H. G. Wells' The War of the Worlds, *written in 1898, depicting an invasion from Mars. Despite several reminders to the audience that they were listening to an adaptation of a novel, the authentic sounding details and tones of the broadcast, as the following excerpts dramatize, threw a sizable portion of the nation into mass hysteria.*

ANNOUNCER

Ladies and gentlemen, here is the latest bulletin from the Intercontinental Radio News, Toronto, Canada: Professor Morse of Macmillan University reports observing a total of three explosions on the planet Mars, between the hours of 7:45 p.m. and 9:20 p.m., eastern standard time. This confirms earlier reports received from American observatories. Now, nearer home, comes a special announcement from Trenton, New Jersey. It is reported that at 8:50 p.m. a huge, flaming object, believed to be a meteorite, fell on a farm in the neighborhood of Grovers Mill, New Jersey, twenty-two miles from Trenton. The flash in the sky was visible within a radius of several hundred miles and the noise of the impact was heard as far north as Elizabeth.

We have dispatched a special mobile unit to the scene, and we will have our commentator, Mr. Phillips, give you a word description as soon as he can reach there from Princeton. In the meantime, we take you to the Hotel Martinet in Brooklyn, where Bobby Millette and his orchestra are offering a program of dance music. (SWING BAND FOR 20 SECONDS . . . THEN CUT)

ANNOUNCER

We take you now to Grovers Mill, New Jersey.
(CROWD NOISES . . . POLICE SIRENS)

PHILLIPS

Ladies and gentlemen, this is Carl Phillips again, at the Wilmuth farm, Grovers Mill, New Jersey. Professor Pierson and myself made the eleven miles from Princeton in ten minutes. Well, I . . . I hardly know where to begin, to paint for you a word picture of the strange scene before my eyes, like something out of a modern Arabian Nights. Well, I just got here. I haven't had a chance to look around yet. I guess that's *it.* Yes, I guess that's the . . . *thing,* directly in front of me, half buried in a vast pit. Must have struck with terrific force. The ground is covered with splinters of a tree it must have struck on its way down. What I can see of the . . . object itself doesn't look very much like a meteor, at least not the meteors I've seen. It looks more like a huge cylinder. It has a diameter of . . . what would you say, Professor Pierson? . . .

ANNOUNCER

Ladies and gentlemen, I have a grave announcement to make. Incredible as it may seem, both the observations of science and the evidence of our eyes lead to the inescapable assumption that those strange beings who landed in the Jersey farmlands tonight are the vanguard of an invading army from the planet Mars. The battle which took place tonight at Grovers Mill has ended in one of the most startling defeats ever suffered by an army in modern times; seven thousand men armed with rifles and machine guns pitted against a single fighting machine of the invaders from Mars. One hundred and twenty known survivors. The rest strewn over the battle area from Grovers Mill to Plainsboro crushed and trampled to death under the metal feet of the monster, or burned to cinders by its heat-ray. The monster is now in control of the middle section of New Jersey and has effectively cut the state through its center. Communication lines are down from Pennsylvania to the Atlantic Ocean. Railroad tracks are torn and service from New York to Philadelphia discontinued except routing some of the trains through Allentown and Phoenixville. Highways to the north, south, and west are clogged with frantic human traffic. Police and army reserves are unable to control the mad flight. By morning the fugitives will have swelled Philadelphia, Camden and Trenton, it is estimated, to twice their normal population.

At this time martial law prevails throughout New Jersey and eastern Pennsylvania. We take you now to Washington for a special broadcast on the National Emergency . . . the Secretary of the Interior. . . .

ANNOUNCER

I'm speaking from the roof of Broadcasting Building, New York City. The bells you hear are ringing to warn the people to evacuate the city as the Martians approach. Estimated in last two hours three million people have moved out along the roads to the north, Hutchison River Parkway still kept open for motor traffic. Avoid bridges to Long Island . . . hopelessly jammed. All communication with Jersey shore closed ten minutes ago. No more defenses. Our army wiped out . . . artillery, air force, everything wiped out. This may be the last broadcast. We'll stay here to the end. . . . People are holding service below us . . . in the cathedral. (VOICES SINGING HYMN)

Now I look down the harbor. All manner of boats, overloaded with fleeing population, pulling out from docks. (SOUND OF BOAT WHISTLES)

Streets are all jammed. Noise in crowds like New Year's Eve in city. Wait a minute. . . . Enemy now in sight above the Palisades. Five great machines. First one is crossing river. I can see it from here, wading the Hudson like a man wading through a brook. . . . A bulletin's handed me. . . . Martian cylinders are falling all over the country. One outside Buffalo, one in Chicago, St. Louis . . . seem to be timed and spaced. . . . Now the first machine reaches the shore. He stands watching, looking over the city. His steel, cowlish head is even with the skyscrapers. He waits for the others. They rise like a line of new towers on the city's west side. . . . Now they're lifting their metal hands. This is the end now. Smoke comes out . . . black smoke, drifting over the city. People in the streets see it now. They're running towards the East River . . . thousands of them, dropping in like rats. Now the smoke's spreading faster. It's reached Times Square. People trying to run away from it, but it's no use. They're falling like flies. Now the smoke's crossing Sixth Avenue . . . Fifth Avenue . . . 100 yards away . . . it's fifty feet. . . .

Bud Abbott and Lou Costello / Who's on First

1938

The zany classic comedy routine, "Who's on First," which might have been written by Samuel Beckett for the Theatre of the Absurd, had a long vaudeville history before Bud Abbott and Lou Costello gave it their special imprint. The routine—sometimes played long, sometimes short—moved with the two through radio, movies, and television. Often played live and laced with adlibs, the script clearly has no "definitive" text. The version printed below is a transcript from their film The Gay Nineties *(1945).*

Both comedians were born in New Jersey: Bud Abbott in Asbury Park in 1900 and Lou Costello in Paterson in 1908. They struggled through burlesque and vaudeville for nine years until 1938, when they brought their relentless corny bickering to radio and became overnight sensations.

LOU: Look, Abbott, if you're the coach, you must know all the players.

BUD: I certainly do.

LOU: Well, you know, I never met the guys, so you'll have to tell me their names and then I'll know who's playing on the team.

BUD: Oh, I'll tell you their names. But, you know, strange as it may seem, they give these ballplayers nowadays very peculiar names.

LOU: You mean funny names?

BUD: Strange names, pet names like Dizzy Dean.

LOU: And his brother Daffy.

BUD: Daffy Dean—

LOU: And their French cousin.

BUD: French?

LOU: Goofé.

BUD: Goofé Dean. Oh, I see. Well, let's see, we have on the bags, we have Who's on first, What's on second. I Don't Know is on third.

LOU: That's what I want to find out.

BUD: I say, Who's on first, What's on second, I Don't Know's on third.

LOU: Are you the manager?

BUD: Yes.

LOU: You're gonna be the coach, too?

BUD: Yes.

LOU: Do you know the fellas' names?

BUD: Well, I should.

LOU: Well, then who's on first?

BUD: Yes.

LOU: I mean the fella's name.

BUD: Who.

LOU: The guy on first.

BUD: Who!

LOU: The first baseman.

BUD: WHO!

LOU: The guy playing first.

BUD: Who is on first.

LOU: I'm asking *you* who's on first.

BUD: That's the man's name.

LOU: That's whose name?

BUD: Yes.

LOU: Well, go ahead and tell me.
BUD: That's it.
LOU: That's who?
BUD: Yes!
LOU: Look, you got a first baseman?
BUD: Certainly.
LOU: Who's playing first?
BUD: That's right.
LOU: When you pay off the first baseman every month, who gets the money?
BUD: Every dollar of it.
LOU: All I'm trying to find out is the fella's name on first base.
BUD: Who.
LOU: The guy that gets the money.
BUD: That's it.
LOU: Who gets the money?
BUD: He does, every dollar. Sometimes his wife comes down and collects it.
LOU: Whose wife?
BUD: Yes. What's wrong with that?
LOU: Look, all I wanna know is, when you sign up the first baseman, how does he sign his name to the contract?
BUD: Who.
LOU: The guy.
BUD: Who.
LOU: How does he sign his name?
BUD: That's how he signs it.
LOU: Who?
BUD: Yes.
LOU: All I'm trying to find out is what's the guy's name on first base?
BUD: No, What is on second base.
LOU: I'm not asking you who's on second.
BUD: Who's on first.
LOU: One base at a time!
BUD: Well, don't change the players around.
LOU: I'm not changing nobody.
BUD: Take it easy, buddy.
LOU: I'm only asking you, who's the guy on first base?
BUD: That's right.
LOU: Okay.
BUD: All right.
LOU: I mean, what's the guy's name on first base.
BUD: No, What is on second.
LOU: I'm not asking you who's on second.
BUD: Who's on first.
LOU: I don't know.
BUD: Oh, he's on third. We're not talking about him. Now let's get—
LOU: Now *how* did I get on third base?
BUD: Why, you mentioned his name.
LOU: If I mentioned the third baseman's name, who did I say was playing third?
BUD: No, Who's playing first.
LOU: What's on first?
BUD: What's on second.
LOU: I don't know.
BUD: *He's* on third.
LOU: There I go, back on third again.
BUD: I can't help it.

LOU: Now, will you stay on third base? And don't go off it.
BUD: All right, now what do you want to know?
LOU: Now, who's playing third base?
BUD: Why do you insist on putting Who on third base?
LOU: What am I putting on third?
BUD: No, What is on second.
LOU: You don't want *who* on second?
BUD: Who is on first.
LOU: I don't know!
BOTH: Third base!
LOU: Look, you got outfield?
BUD: Sure.
LOU: The left fielder's name?
BUD: Why.
LOU: I just thought I'd ask you.
BUD: Well, I just thought I'd tell you.
LOU: Then tell me who's playing left field.
BUD: Who is playing *first*.
LOU: I'm not—Stay out of the infield! I wanna know what's the guy's name in left field.
BUD: No, What is on second.
LOU: I'm not *asking* you who's on second.
BUD: Who's on first.
LOU: I don't know.
BOTH: Third base!
LOU: And the left fielder's name?
BUD: Why!
LOU: Because.
BUD: Oh, he's *center* field.
LOU: Bey-eeyh-echh
BUD: You know his name as well as I do.
LOU: Look, look, look you got a pitcher on the team?
BUD: Sure.
LOU: The pitcher's name?
BUD: Tomorrow.
LOU: You don't wanna tell me today?
BUD: I'm telling you today.
LOU: Then go ahead.
BUD: Tomorrow.
LOU: What time?
BUD: What time what?
LOU: What time tomorrow you going to tell me who's pitching.
BUD: Now listen, Who is not pitching. Who—
LOU: I'll break your arm you say "Who's on first." I want to know what's the pitcher's name.
BUD: What's on second.
LOU: I don't know.
BOTH: Third base!
LOU: You got a catcher?
BUD: Certainly.
LOU: The catcher's name?
BUD: Today.
LOU: Today. And tomorrow's pitching?
BUD: Now you've got it.
LOU: All we got is a couple of days of the week. You know, I'm a catcher, too.

BUD: So they tell me.

LOU: I get behind the plate, do some fancy catching, tomorrow's pitching on my team and the heavy hitter gets up.

BUD: Yes.

LOU: Now, the heavy hitter bunts the ball. When he bunts the ball, me being a good catcher, I'm going to throw the guy out at first base, so I pick up the ball and throw it to who?

BUD: Now, that's the first thing you've said right.

LOU: I don't even know what I'm *talking* about!

BUD: That's all you have to do.

LOU: Is to throw the ball to first base?

BUD: *Yes.*

LOU: Now, who's got it?

BUD: Naturally.

LOU: Look, if I throw the ball to first base, somebody's got to get it. Now, who has it?

BUD: Naturally.

LOU: Who?

BUD: Naturally.

LOU: Naturally?

BUD: Naturally.

LOU: So, I pick up the ball and I throw it to Naturally?

BUD: No, you don't. You throw the ball to Who!

LOU: Naturally.

BUD: That's different.

LOU: That's what I say.

BUD: You're not saying it—

LOU: I throw the ball to Naturally?

BUD: You throw it to Who.

LOU: Naturally.

BUD: That's it.

LOU: That's what I said.

BUD: Listen, you ask me.

LOU: I throw the ball to who?

BUD: Naturally.

LOU: Now you ask me.

BUD: You throw the ball to Who.

LOU: Naturally.

BUD: That's it.

LOU: Same as you!

BUD: Don't change them around.

LOU: Same as you!

BUD: Okay, now get it over with.

LOU: I throw the ball to who. Whoever it is drops the ball and the guy runs to second.

BUD: Yes.

LOU: Who picks up the ball and throws it to what. What throws it to I don't know. I don't know throws it back to tomorrow. Triple play.

BUD: Yes.

LOU: Another guy gets up and hits a long fly to because. Why? I don't know. He's on third and I don't *give* a darn.

BUD: —eh, what?

LOU: I said, "I don't *give* a darn."

BUD: Oh, that's our shortstop.

LOU: Ayeiiii!

Batten, Barton, Durstine and Osborne / "Ring around the Collar"

ca. 1975

One of the most successful and long-running campaigns in television history, the "Ring around the Collar" commercials for Wisk were launched in 1969 by the

Courtesy of Lever Brothers Co.

GONDOLIER: Of love I sing . . .

la-la-la-la.

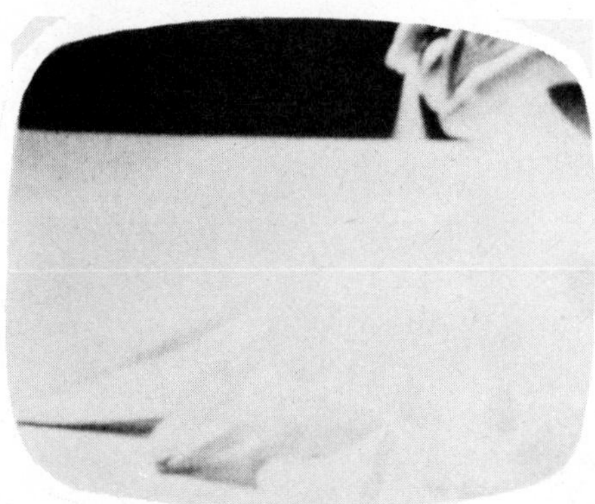

ANNOUNCER: Those dirty rings . . . You tried scrubbing, even spraying, and still . . .

you've got ring-around-the-collar.

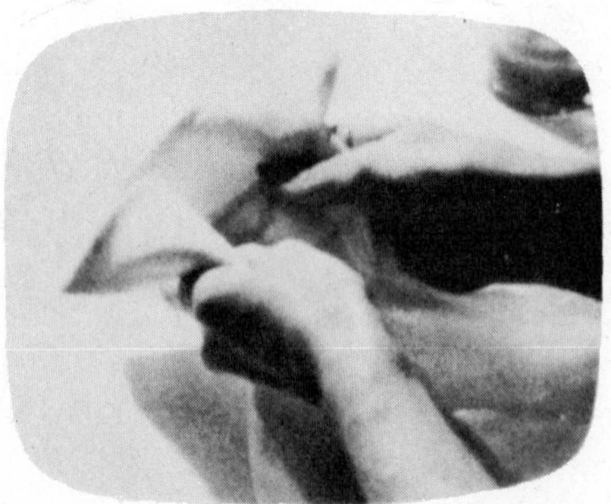

before you start to wash.

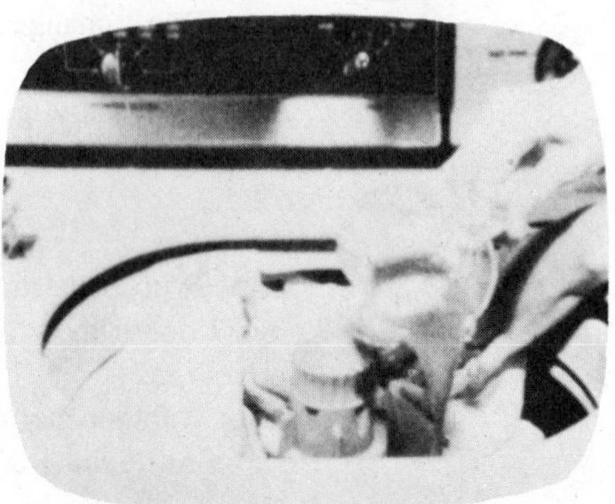

Then gets your whole wash really clean.

advertising firm of Batten, Barton, Durstine and Osborne (BBD&O). Though shoppers frequently complain about the commercials, their irritation apparently does not stand in the way of their buying the product. For more information on this commercial, see Carol Caldwell's ''You Haven't Come a Long Way, Baby: Women in Television Commercials'' in Advertising.

But you've got ring-around-the-collar-la-la.

WIFE: My powder didn't work.

Try Wisk.

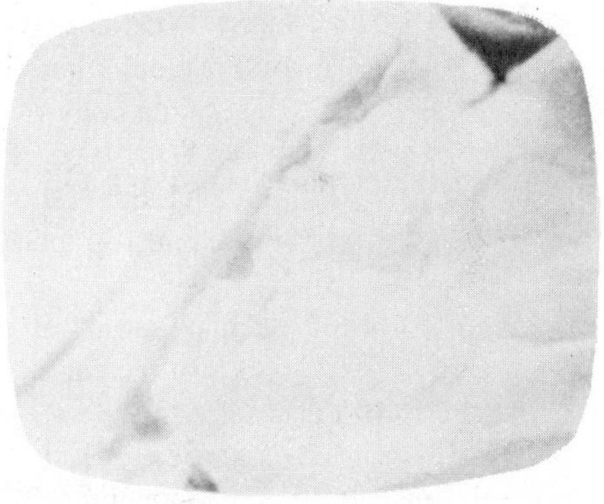

Wisk sinks in and starts to clean

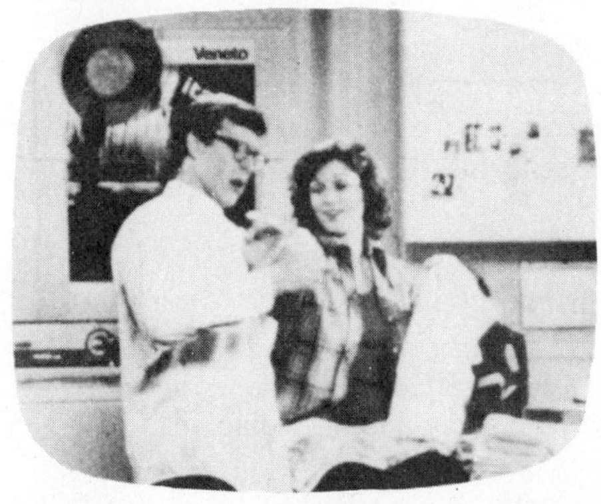

HUSBAND: No more ring-around-the-collar-la-la!

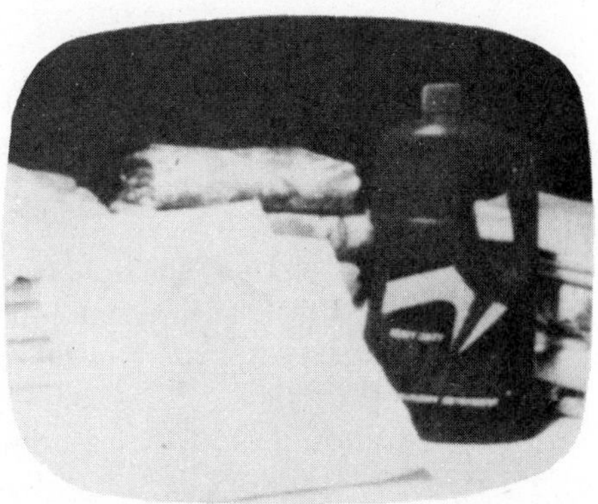

ANNOUNCER: Use Wisk around the collar for ring-around-the-collar.

Dick Orkin and Bert Berdis / Puffy Sleeves; A *Time* Magazine Commercial

1977

"Dick and Bert" call their brand of radio advertising humor "situation comedy commercials." Believing that advertising too often portrays ideal people in unreal situations, the team writes instead about an imperfect world:

> *People who dribble a little bit, people who get arrested for wearing their wife's housecoat to go out to buy a* Time *magazine, a guy that gets fired for reading* Time, *just the little stupid things that everyone does.*

Their radio campaign for Time *magazine aired in the mid-1970's; "Puffy Sleeves" was one of the most popular spots.*

BERT: Pardon me, sir, would you step over here to the patrol car please?
DICK: Oh, h-hello, officer.
BERT: Do you have business in this neighborhood, sir?
DICK: Yes, I live f-four blocks from here . . . It's the brick colonial with the crack in the driveway.
BERT: What are you doing out this time of night, sir?
DICK: Well, I got all ready for bed and darn it if I didn't forget to pick up a copy of *Time* magazine at the newsstand today.
BERT: What type of coat would you call that, sir?
DICK: Th-this? This is a h-housecoat. See, I spilled cocoa on mine and I just grabbed my wife's. I guess the puffy sleeves look a little silly . . . *(laugh)*. . . .
BERT: Want to get in the car, sir?
DICK: In the car . . .?
SOUND EFFECTS: *(door open)*
DICK: See, I just don't go to bed without a *Time* movie review or something from the modern living section . . .
BERT: Yes, sir. *(car pulls away)*
DICK: I tried reading something else, but there isn't anything like *Time*. Do you know, officer, how many editorial awards *Time* magazine has won?
BERT: No, sir.
DICK: And *Time* is so respected—and I'm a firm believer—along with Winston Churchill . . . that you are uh . . . what you read . . . *(pause)*. . . . Oh please don't send me up the river just for wearing puffy sleeves.
BERT: You're home, sir.
DICK: I'm home—oh . . . I thou—thank—God bless you. . . .
SOUND EFFECTS: *(door open)*
DICK: . . . Okay—bye.
ANNOUNCER: *Time* magazine makes everything more interesting, including you.

Robert Geller / Soldier's Home: A Screenplay 1976

In the mid-1970's, Educational Television, with the support of the National Endowment for the Humanities, launched a series of films based on classic American short stories. Besides Ernest Hemingway's "Soldier's Home," the series offered remarkable film adaptations of such stories as John Cheever's "The Five-Forty-Eight," Sherwood Anderson's "I'm a Fool," Stephen Crane's "The Blue Hotel," and Richard Wright's "Almos' a Man." Much aclaimed, the short-story series is responsible for some of the finest television movies in the history of the medium.

Robert Geller is a scriptwriter and the author of numerous articles on film and television. He served as the Executive Producer of the American Short Story Series.

1. Prologue. In sepia. Eight or ten young men are being huddled together for a fraternity picture. All dressed in high white collars. Most wear silver-rimmed glasses. Austere building in background. No laughter or chatter.

NARRATOR (*off camera*): Krebs went to the war from a Methodist college in Kansas. There is a picture which shows him among his fraternity brothers. . . .

Photographer motions them to close ranks, and sheep-like they shuffle closer. One young man, Harold Krebs, stands slightly to the side and moves just a fraction after the command "hold it."

NARRATOR (*off camera*): He enlisted in the Army in 1917. . . .

Cut to Photographer and "explosion" of his camera gun.

Cut to 2. Stock footage of WWI, expository in nature, and of returning veterans. Not meant to editorialize about the war.

NARRATOR (*off camera*): . . . and did not return to the United States until the second division returned from the Rhine in 1919.

3. Exterior. Dusk. Empty train depot in rural town. Krebs with duffle bag. Platform is deserted, with the exception of the station master and one passenger, neither of whom pays Krebs any attention.

Krebs crosses tracks deftly. Stops at depot to catch breath. Tattered signs flap in wind: "Buy U.S. Bonds," etc. At the front end of the platform a banner with "WELCOME HOME YANKS" droops limply from a worn cornice.

NARRATOR (*off camera*): By the time Krebs returned to his home town the greeting of heroes was over. He came back much too late.

4. Interior. Night. Dissolve to dining room of Krebs house. Dinner is over. Harold is still in uniform. Mr. and Mrs. Krebs and Marge hunt for words. There is no real jubilation or ease. Harold is lighting up. Faces of family watch.

MR. KREBS: Son . . . You smoke lots in battle? You seem to do it . . . naturally.

HAROLD: Not really . . . I just picked it up.

MARGE (*enthusiastic*): Did you actually smoke, in the war, Hare? Didn't they see you lighting up? The Germans?

HAROLD: Uh . . . uh. We smoked mostly when we were bored.

MRS. KREBS: Bored! Little chance you had to be bored . . .

HAROLD: We were. I was. A lot of the time.

(*Silence. Ticking of clock. It is after 11:00* P.M.)

MRS. KREBS: Harold, you must be tired . . . All that traveling. And we've asked so many questions.

HAROLD: I'm fine.

MR. KREBS: Well . . . it's gettin' late. I gotta go out in the county tomorrow. We'll get to talk . . . about what you wanna be doin'. Plenty of time.

HAROLD: Yes . . . I'll need a week or so . . .

MRS. KREBS: Of course. Let's just be thankful that you're home safe. Let us be thankful to our Dear Lord (*her eyes are raised*) that you're back home. Oh, Harold, we did pray for you. And each Sunday Reverend Nelson . . .

MR. KREBS (*interrupts with a yawn*): Folks . . . I'm goin' up. Welcome home, Harold.

(*Mr. Krebs extends his hand.*)

HAROLD: Night, Dad . . . It was a fine dinner . . . Guess I'll go up, too. (*He starts to follow Mr. Krebs out.*)

5. Interior. Hallway at foot of stairs.

MRS. KREBS (*to Harold at the foot of the stairs*): Son . . . Marjorie and I could fix up a special breakfast. Serve it to you in bed. Remember when you had those awful winter coughs and . . .

HAROLD: Not tomorrow, Mom . . . I'll want to get up early, and . . .

MRS. KREBS: Hare?

HAROLD: Mom?

MRS. KREBS: (*moves to hug him*): Sleep well.

HAROLD (*stiffens, hugs her back*): I will . . . thanks . . . for everything.

Cut to 6. Interior. Night. Harold's room. Dimly lit. Flowered wallpaper. Pan to boyhood mementos, which are sparse save for some scouting medals and a trophy for track & field. Harold unpacks. Looks at photo of college fraternity at Methodist school. Considers replacing it with picture of himself and another soldier with two coarse, older German women. The military uniforms are too large.

Krebs moves around his smallish room. Picks up the trophy and buffs it. Takes out a clarinet from a book shelf and slowly assembles it. Tinkers tentatively with some scales. Begins to undress and neatly pile clothes on chair near his bed. Cranks up his phonograph. It still works. He smiles. Climbs into bed with a record playing.

Krebs lights cigarette and leans on elbow, staring out at the quiet, empty streets.

MR. KREBS (*off camera*) (*knocking at Harold's door*): Harold. Could you turn it down? It's late, and I need to be fresh and ginger tomorrow.

7. The following shots take place in one day, during which we get the feelings and rhythms of Harold being home contrasted against the rhythms of the town.

Exterior. Point of view Krebs House. Day. Harold's window. We see the shade, which is pulled half down with the tassle hanging. We hear the sound of footsteps on the porch and the rattling of bottles as the milkman puts the milk on the porch and takes the old bottles.

Cut to interior. Harold's bedroom. Day. Close-up of Harold's face. He's lying awake in bed listening to the sounds of the milkman. He's been up for a while.

Cut to interior/exterior. Harold's window. Day. Harold moves into frame, raises the shade, then looks down, out the window. Then Harold's face, close up. Then the sound of a factory whistle in the distance.

Exterior. Krebs house. Day. Harold's point of view. Looking down at the milkman walking away from the house carrying empty bottles away in a rack.

Exterior. Krebs porch and house. Day. Harold has a cup of coffee. He's wearing his army overcoat to protect him against the morning cold. Sits on the edge of the step and leans back against the pillar. Lights up a cigarette. The early morning sun comes through the trees.

Then the procession of men going to work begins. Through the bushes and through the empty spaces between the trees, Harold sees the working-class men of the town on their way to the factory. The procession begins with only a few, but builds in tempo as it gets closer to the hour to be in the factory. Then a few stragglers, and then it is quiet again.

Some of the images we see are two men walking carrying lunch pails. A third man behind them runs to catch up with them, and they then walk on together. Some of the figures are partially masked—seen through the screen of bushes—so we pan with them, seeing their lunch pails swinging and their footsteps on the pavement.

A car goes by carrying some workmen. The sounds of other cars are heard going to work and their image/presence is suggested in the movement of Harold's eyes as they go by up the street. As the procession ends, in the distance the sound of the factory whistle, which heralds the start of the day's work.

The newspaper boy throws the newspaper up the walk, and Harold picks it up.

Interior. Harold's bedroom. Day. Point of views. A series of images of Harold follow that suggest his day, to be punctuated with some activities that take place around him, such as:

A. Marge leaves for school, maybe picked up by another girl.
B. Mr. Krebs's car leaves the house. (Perhaps this could occur earlier.)
C. Two church ladies come and pick up Mrs. Krebs. We hear their voices and see them walk away from the house.

Interior. Harold's room. Day. Harold reads the sports page of the newspaper, smokes, rests, and plays his clarinet.

When Harold plays his clarinet, he plays some scales to reacquaint himself with the instrument. His playing at first is very tentative—he is feeling for the instrument and for his own voice, his own theme or melody. We would use his music as a means of expressing Harold's mood. The music creates a space for him separate from the world around him.

Exterior. Krebs house. Day. As the day grows late, the activities are reversed. The factory whistle blows late in the day, and then we see the tracking feet again, now worn, tired, the men slump-shouldered, trailing off to their homes.

8. Exterior. Bright morning. Harold walking to town. Is stopped by a prim old man.

MAN: Mornin', young Krebs. Welcome home. How long you back now?

HAROLD: It's two weeks, today.

MAN: Your folks said you had some very difficult times over there?

HAROLD: No . . . not that bad.

MAN: Anyhow, you must be glad to be home . . . Are you planning to go back to school?

HAROLD: No.

MAN: You going to be selling farm land with Dad? At the bank? It's a blessing when a man and his son can . . .

HAROLD: (*edging away*): 'Scuse me.

(HAROLD *walks on down street.*)

MAN: Well, I'll be! You'd think he'd killed the Kaiser. Even as a young boy . . .

(*They exit; their voices trail.*)

9. Exterior. Day. Harold walks on to town. Nods back to few passersby who seem to remember him. Harold notices the young girls in town. He sees one through shop windows. He notices their pretty faces and the patterns that they make.

NARRATOR (*off camera*): Nothing was changed in the town except that the young girls had grown up. There were so many good-looking young girls.

10. Exterior. Day. Harold stops in front of bank where Mr. Krebs works as land agent.

NARRATOR: (*off camera*): Before Krebs went away to the war he had never been allowed to drive the family motor car. The car always stood outside the First National Bank building where his father had an office. Now, after the war, it was still the same car.

Harold crosses the street, walks past the car to the window of his father's office. He looks in.

Reverse angle of Mr. Krebs amiably chatting with young customers Harold's age. Offers cigar. Laughter and clapping of each other's shoulders. Harold stares for several seconds and then turns away, crossing the street quickly.

11. Interior. Day. Signs indicate library room of YMCA. Harold is checking out books. Young male librarian, glasses, devoutly scrubbed, early 30s, is at checkout desk.

LIBRARIAN: Krebs. Are you Harold Krebs?

HAROLD (*startled*): Yes. That's me.

LIBRARIAN: Don't you remember me? I'm Mr. Phillips. I was your youth group advisor in the lower grades.

HAROLD: Sorry. I was involved with these books.

LIBRARIAN: Are you an avid reader? Have you tried the new Booth Tarkington? I try to encourage good reading. (*The* LIBRARIAN *begins to notice the books* KREBS *has checked out.*) My heavens. They're all books about the war. I should think that . . .

HAROLD: It helps to make sense out of things that happened. The maps and . . .

LIBRARIAN: But weren't you at Argonne? My Lord, the reports we received . . .

HAROLD (*eager to go*): Thanks . . . I'd like them for two weeks, or longer. All right?

LIBRARIAN: (*stiffly*): Two weeks. That's all that's allowed. (*Pause.*) Krebs . . .

HAROLD (*begins to leave*): Sir?

LIBRARIAN: Krebs . . . you might want to check the social calendar on the way out of the building. We hold socials and dances so that you young vets can catch up with community activities. This Saturday . . .

HAROLD (*looks uninterested*): Thanks . . . I'll look. (HAROLD *exits.*)

Cut to 12. Interior. Late afternoon. Sitting room. Harold is absorbed in reading a book on the war. There is a map that he studies, trying to figure out the course of battle. Harold's mother comes in.

MRS. KREBS: I had a talk with your father last night, Harold, and he's willing for you to take the car out in the evenings.

HAROLD: Yeah? (*Still absorbed in his reading.*) Take the car out? Yeah?

MRS. KREBS: Yes. Your father has felt for some time you should be able to take the car out in the evenings whenever you wished but we only talked it over last night.

HAROLD: I'll bet you made him.

MRS. KREBS: No. It was your father's suggestion that we talk it over.

HAROLD: Yeah. I'll bet you made him.

MRS. KREBS: Harold . . . we'll be having dinner a little early this evening.

HAROLD: All right . . . Think I'll walk a little.

MRS. KREBS: Don't be late. I've cooked your favorite roast.

HAROLD (*mumbles*): All right. (*Looks back as he leaves.*)

13. Exterior. Day. Harold enters pool hall. (Close crop and only exterior of door is needed.)

Cut to 14. Interior. Pool hall. Cool and shaded. Proprietor is ex-pug. He and Harold shadow-box and exchange jabs. They say little. But Harold is at ease here as he picks up cue and chalks.

Harold looks relaxed and concentrates on each shot. Two younger boys admire his ease and relaxed style as he puts away each ball. He smokes casually.

FIRST BOY: Hey, Harold . . . betcha didn't get no time for pool in France . . . eh . . . didja?

(HAROLD *smiles benignly throughout their banter.*)

HAROLD: Nope, not much time for pool.

SECOND BOY: Hey . . . is it true you got home last 'cause they needed the best soldiers around to keep the Krauts in line?

(HAROLD *nods yes.* HAROLD *continues to pick off shots. Lets the ash on his cigarette grow precariously long. The younger boys edge closer, begging confidences. Smoke stings his eyes.*)

YOUNGER BOY: Hey, Harold . . . swear to the truth . . . Did you really kill Germans . . . right face to face . . . honest to God? With bayonets?

HAROLD (*nods*): That's what we went there for. Not to see the Eiffel Tower.

(*They are silent, not wanting to break his concentration.*)

PROPRIETOR (*off camera*): Gotta close up, Harold. Run 'em out—one, two, three—the way you always used ta . . .

NARRATOR (*off camera*): At first Krebs did not want to talk about the war at all. Later he felt the need to talk but no one wanted to hear about it. Krebs found that to be listened to at all he had to lie, and after he had done this twice he, too, had a reaction against the war and against talking about it.

(HAROLD *sizes up the last shot. The proprietor and the younger boys huddle close behind.* HAROLD'S *eyes open wide and . . . Cut to cue ball as it explodes into last remaining ball and pushes it deftly into far pockets. Ex-pug and younger boys nod in admiration.*)

15. Exterior. Late afternoon. Krebs walks tall and the younger boys follow as worshippers. All, as silhouettes, pass the same crisp, white houses. They pass war monument. Their questions are heard as echoes. No other sounds but their voices.

FIRST BOY: Harold, is it true that they chained Kraut women to their machine guns for GIs to . . . you know . . . to . . .

SECOND BOY: Hey, Harold, did you bring any of them pictures back . . . you know . . . the French ones . . .

FIRST BOY: Harold, are the German women all that great? Denny's brother said all they want to do is make love to Americans . . . Don't matter where they do it, or the time of day . . .

SECOND BOY: Hey, Harold, can you come to the dance at the Y Friday? Cripes . . . everybody wants to talk to you, and the girls in town are waiting for you to give them a tumble. Might even be some hard liquor if you're in the mood . . .

(*All through these questions, there are no other sounds or street noises. It is meant to be a parade, a parodied ceremony for* HAROLD KREB'S *return. Shot almost as a dreamlike ceremony. The boys double-time like GIs to keep in step with their hero.*)

16. Same as preceding shot, but nearer to Krebs house. Harold begins to run. Close up as he feels the joy of movement. Knows he's late for dinner, too.

Harold collides abruptly with young man. They both struggle for balance. The man is Charlie Simmons, tall and bulky, dressed in prosperous attire of an older businessman.

CHARLIE SIMMONS: Ouch . . . Hey, what's goin on . . .

HAROLD: Sorry . . . I wasn't looking.

CHARLIE (*recovering*): Krebs! . . . Harold Krebs. When did you get back?

HAROLD: It's just two weeks now.

CHARLIE: You look fine, just fine.

HAROLD: Thanks.

CHARLIE: You workin' for your dad at the bank?

HAROLD (*hedging*): Not yet.

CHARLIE: You lookin' for a permanent line of work?

HAROLD: Might be . . .

CHARLIE (*blocking* HAROLD'S *path with his bulk*): I'm doing real well. Selling insurance. All the vets are interested and need the security. They know the future . . .

HAROLD: Makes sense.

CHARLIE: Think you'd be interested?

HAROLD: Buying some?

CHARLIE: Well . . . actually that, and maybe working with me on the selling part.

HAROLD: I'll think about it. I'm late for dinner. (*He begins to trot away.*)

CHARLIE: Hey . . . did you know I'm married now? Remember Edith Hanes? She was our class secretary and the prettiest gal in this whole town (*fishing for a compliment*).

HAROLD (*over his shoulder*): Good luck, Charlie.

17. Exterior. Night or very late afternoon. Krebs porch. Harold looks in window at his family at supper. All heads are bowed in grace. (The MOS[1] of grace exaggerates the piety.) They finally finished the prayer. Mrs. Krebs nervously eyes the clock. Harold, resigned, walks in.

18. Exterior. Greek's soda shop. Day. Car pulls up in front of soda shop with Krebs driving. Harold gets out of car and looks in window. Sees the interior, decorated with decor of period. Marge and friends are having ice-cream sodas. They are exuberant as they "recreate" some incident from school (*in pantomime*).

Harold looks in, raps on window, and beckons Marge to come outside. She signals to Harold that she'll be out in one minute.

BILL KENNER (*off camera*): Hey, Krebs . . . Harold Krebs . . .

(BILL KENNER: *early 20s. Dressed flamboyantly with bohemian dash. Sports cane with golden handle. He limps perceptibly into frame.*) Remember me? William Kenner. Your fellow sufferer in geometry and Latin. C'mere, my lovelies.

(KENNER *waves to two teenagers, who obediently follow.*)

HAROLD: Sure . . . Bill Kenner. I remember you. You all right?

BILL KENNER (*with bravura*): Sure . . . if losing a chunk of your knee on a mine is all right, then I'm just fine.

HAROLD (*embarrassed for the girls*): That's . . . that's too bad. You seem to be doin' well though.

KENNER: Well . . . with lovelies like these, *pourquoi s'en faire?* . . . Am I right?

[1] A segment of film shot without sound.

HAROLD (*edgy*): I guess.

KENNER: You guess. Aren't we lucky to be alive? You know this little town had three killed? Lots of injured, too. In our graduating class alone . . .

HAROLD (*spots* MARGE): Here . . . Right here, Marge.

KENNER: Is that lovely mademoiselle a Krebs? (*Bows.*) May I introduce myself?

MARGE: Let's go, Hare . . .

HAROLD: Well . . . goodbye, Bill.

KENNER (*not dissuaded*): That your car?

HAROLD: My dad's.

KENNER: Splen-did work of art.

HAROLD: Thanks.

KENNER: Can you get it nights?

MARGE: (*impatient*): Har-old!

HAROLD: I guess so. Why.

KENNER: You busy this Friday?

HAROLD: Well . . . I'm not sure. Let me think about it . . .

KENNER: Think about it! About what? Let's you and I live it up, my friend. (*Girls giggle.*) There's a dance at the Y. I might even have some gen-u-ine cognac. Come by at 8:00.

HAROLD: All right . . . I'll try.

KENNER: I'll *expect* you. (*Winks.*) Bye now.

(*To* MARGE): Bye, lovely. See you on the Champs Elysées. (*Tips his hat and limps away dramatically.* HAROLD *and* MARGE *drive away.*)

19. Interior. Night. Large room of YMCA. Small crowd of fifteen to twenty is dwarfed by the place. Clusters of girls, some overly dressed and coiffed. Mr. Phillips, the librarian, and Mr. and Mrs. Charlie Simmons and chaperones are standing at punch bowl. Boys, some teenagers, busily sharing their own secrets and howling at their own jokes. Few couples are dancing.

Harold stands apart, remote from the activities, watching.

NARRATOR (*off camera*): Vaguely he wanted a girl, but he did not want to have to work to get her. He did not want to get into the intrigue and politics . . .

(*We see the usual behavior of a dance. Boys egg on one of their fellows to ask a girl to dance. A girl moves away from a boy as he approaches to ask her for a dance—as if she is too busy. Another boy approaches a girl and then veers to another girl—the first thinking he was going to ask her. All of the little intrigues of the dance.*)

NARRATOR (*off camera*): Besides, he did not really need a girl.

(KENNER *in dramatic cape and Tyrolian hat is "performing" for* ROSELLE SIMMONS, *who is flushed and heavily rouged.*)

NARRATOR (*off camera*): You did not need a girl unless you thought about them.

(*She looks toward* HAROLD, *who is obviously bored. He walks toward the door and into hallway.* ROSELLE *follows.* HAROLD *lights a cigarette.*)

NARRATOR (*off camera*): When you were really ripe for a girl you always got one. He had learned that in the army.

20. Interior. Hallway. Cases filled with trophies. Pictures of austere town philanthropist.

ROSELLE: Harold? Harold Krebs. (*For her, all conversation is a flirtation.*)

HAROLD: It's me.

ROSELLE: I'm Roselle, Roselle Simmons.

HAROLD: Charlie's sister . . . right?

ROSELLE: Why . . . heavens . . . have I changed all that much in two years?

HAROLD: Three years . . . actually.

ROSELLE: You don't seem to be having much fun at all. . . . You haven't danced once. I've been spying on you.

HAROLD: Well, I'm not up to the steps . . . or all the chatter . . .

ROSELLE: You need to be taught. . . . Didn't your little sister Marge ever try? There are lots of new steps . . . I could teach you . . . It's my war effort . . . Trade for a smoke?

HAROLD (*doesn't offer her a cigarette*): It's a waste of time. I never could get my feet straight . . .

ROSELLE: Silly . . . the feet are the easy part . . . it's the rest of your body . . . the way you lead . . . the way you hold your partner . . . I'll bet you like to command a girl . . .

HAROLD (*surprised*): Command a girl . . . Why?

ROSELLE (*she leads to music*): Command me, Mr. Harold Krebs . . .

HAROLD (*he responds slowly*): Like this?

(*These scenes should be played slowly—moving from awkwardness to* HAROLD'S *own arousal and assertion.*)

ROSELLE (*Gently circling his arms around her. Emphasize physical aspects of their dancing*): Just move one, two, three, four . . . get closer . . . Did you ever dance like this, with those foreign women?

(*Cuts to* HAROLD *dancing closer. Stroking her as he would the women he has known in Europe. The music stops, and* HAROLD *continues to caress her with sureness.*)

ROSELLE (*scared now*): Don't . . . I've got to freshen up . . . I won't be long . . . All right? Wait out here . . . Don't!

HAROLD (*confused*): Hey . . . Where're you going? C'mon back here, Roselle.

ROSELLE (*vampishly over her shoulder*): Silly . . .

(ROSELLE *leaves.* HAROLD *continues to wait. The music begins. He is filled with a crushing sadness, a new confusion, a feeling of betrayal.*)

21. Exterior. Evening. Krebs and Kenner are in the Krebs car parked out front of Kenner house.

Krebs and Kenner are getting drunk. They try to whisper, but talk loudly. Kenner is much louder in his speech and more slurred. The only real sign of drunkenness for Harold is that he's talking louder than usual and trying to tell the truth to Kenner.

KENNER: We shouldn't have left. It would've gotten better.

HAROLD: You should have stayed.

KENNER: That tart Roselle is really somethin'. Know what we'd do to girls like her in France? (*Long pause as* HAROLD *says nothing.*) Christ. What do you want to do? Just mope around forever? I can't figure you. Whenever I want to forget things, I just drink. Drink and find a woman.

HAROLD: I want to *remember*—the *good* things.

KENNER: Like being over there. Scared to death. Watching guys screamin' and bleeding to death.

HAROLD: I wasn't scared . . . not like you tell it.

KENNER: Damn . . . everybody was. Didn't you ever wake up in sweats and shivers? I used to put my blanket in my mouth and . . .

HAROLD (*shakes his head, no.*)

KENNER: Well . . . I was scared. Everybody was.

HAROLD (*softly*): That's a lie.

KENNER (*pretends not to hear*): Everybody was. Only one thing is worth remembering over there.

HAROLD: Mmm . . .

KENNER: The damned women . . . No names or faces. Those white bodies, smelling like . . . like sweet apricots in those warm hotel rooms.

HAROLD: That isn't worth remembering.

KENNER: All right . . . all right. What is worth remembering?

HAROLD: Being a good soldier. Doing what you had to . . .

KENNER: Being a good soldier? You're crazy. You really are, Krebs.

HAROLD (*softly*): And you lie, Kenner, about everything.

KENNER: Don't call me a liar.

HAROLD: It's not worth it.

KENNER: Shut up.

(*Kenner pulls the bottle from Harold, and almost falls out car door.*)

HAROLD: Hey . . . You all right?

KENNER (*getting out of car*): Bastard . . . Crazy bastard. Stay away from me. I don't need a friend like you, Krebs. You spoil things.

(HAROLD *starts to follow Kenner.*)

HAROLD: Hey . . . wait! No! Go on. Go on, Kenner.

(KENNER *stumbles up front steps of his home.*)

22. Interior. Morning. Harold's bedroom. A knock on Harold's door. Harold wakes up. He feels miserable. His mother pokes her head in the door.

MRS. KREBS (*off camera*): Will you come down to breakfast, Harold?

HAROLD: As soon as I get my clothes on.

23. Interior. Dining room. Morning.

MARGE (*bringing in folded-up newspaper*): Well, Hare, you old sleepy-head. What do you ever get up for?

(HAROLD *removes brown wrapper of newspaper and opens it to the sporting page. He folds* The Star *open and props it against the water pitcher with his cereal dish to steady it, so he can read while he eats.*)

MRS. KREBS (*standing in the kitchen doorway*): Harold, please don't muss up the paper. Your father can't read his *Star* if it's been mussed.

HAROLD: I won't muss it.

MARGE (*sitting down*): We're playing indoor over at school this afternoon. I'm going to pitch.

HAROLD: Good. How's the old wing?

MARGE: I can pitch better than lots of the boys. I tell them all you taught me. I tell them all you're my beau. Aren't you my beau, Hare?

HAROLD: You bet.

MARGE: Could your brother really be your beau if he's your brother?

HAROLD: I don't know.

MARGE: Sure you know. Couldn't you be my beau, Hare, if I was old enough and if you wanted to?

HAROLD: Sure.

MARGE: Am I really your girl?

HAROLD: Sure.

MARGE: Do you love me?

HAROLD: Uh, huh.

MARGE: Will you love me always?

HAROLD (*by now becoming impatient with* MARGE): Sure.

MARGE: Will you come over and watch me play indoor?

HAROLD: Maybe.

MARGE: Aw, Hare, you don't love me. If you loved me, you'd definitely come over and watch me play indoor.

MRS. KREBS (*entering dining room*): You run along. I want to talk to Harold. Harold . . . I wish you'd put down the paper a minute, Harold.

HAROLD (*glances at her, hard*): Mmm . . .

MRS. KREBS: You acted shamefully last night. . . . The whole neighborhood could hear you, stumbling around out there.

HAROLD (*searches for the words*): Sorry . . .

MRS. KREBS: Why? You have so much . . . our love . . . You have a fine mind and a strong body . . . Have you decided what you're going to do yet, Harold?

HAROLD: No.

MRS. KREBS: Don't you think it's about time?

HAROLD: I hadn't decided yet . . .

MRS. KREBS (*stands*): God has some work for everyone to do . . . There can be no idle hands in His Kingdom. . . .

HAROLD (*without malice*): I'm not in His Kingdom. . . .

MRS. KREBS: We are all of us in His Kingdom. . . . Harold, please . . . I've worried about you so much . . . I know the temptations you must have suffered . . . I know how weak men are . . . I have prayed for you . . . I pray for you all day long, Harold . . .

(HAROLD *stares straight at his food.*)

MRS. KREBS: Harold . . . your father is worried, too . . . He thinks you've lost your ambition, that you have no definite aim in life. The Simmons boy is just your age, and he's doing so well . . . The boys are all settling down . . . They're all determined to get somewhere. Boys like Charlie Simmons are on the way to being a credit to the community . . . all of them . . . You, too, Harold . . .

(MRS. KREBS *starts to get up. Shaken, she sits back down.*)

MRS. KREBS: Don't look that way, Harold . . . You know we love you, and I want to tell you, for your own good, how matters stand . . . Your father doesn't want to hamper your freedom . . . He thinks you should be allowed to drive the car . . . We want you to enjoy yourself . . . but you are going to have to settle down to work, Harold. . . . Your father doesn't care what you start in at . . . All work is honorable as he says . . . but you've got to make a start at something . . . He didn't like . . . what you did last night . . . He asked me to speak to you this morning, and then you can stop in and see him at his office in the bank.

HAROLD (*gets up*): Is that all, Mother?

MRS. KREBS: Yes, don't you love your mother, dear?

HAROLD (*waits, not wanting to lie, just this once*): No.

MRS. KREBS (*Her eyes grow shiny. She begins to cry*): Oh . . . Harold . . .

HAROLD: I don't love anybody . . .

(MRS. KREBS *sits down.*)

HAROLD: I didn't mean it . . . I was just angry at something . . . I didn't mean I didn't love you . . . Can't you believe me? Please, Mother . . . Please believe me.

MRS. KREBS (*shakes her head, chokily*): All right . . . I believe you, Harold. I'm your mother . . . I held you next to my heart when you were a tiny baby . . .

(*She presses his hand against her bosom.*)

HAROLD (*sick and vaguely nauseated*): I know, Mom . . . I know . . . I'll try and be a good boy for you.

MRS. KREBS (*more controlled*): Would you kneel and pray with me, Harold?

(HAROLD *and* MRS. KREBS *kneel beside the table.*)

MRS. KREBS: Now, you pray, Harold . . .

HAROLD: I can't . . .

MRS. KREBS: Try, Harold . . .

HAROLD: I can't . . .

MRS. KREBS: Do you want me to pray for you? . . .

HAROLD: Yes . . .
MRS. KREBS: Our dear heavenly Father . . .

Cut to (*over continuing prayers*) (HAROLD *stares straight ahead. Dissolves of* HAROLD *packing his battered trunk. Waiting at deserted bus or train depot and riding with face against window. Looking at flat, open lands. Dusk. Tracking shots.*)

(*Clarinet music grows louder. Up with parodied version of "When Johnny Comes Marching Home Again."*)

(*Cut to reverse angle of* MRS. KREBS *monotonously droning her prayer and* HAROLD *continuing to stare into space. Music fades. Freeze on* HAROLD, *impassive.*)

NARRATOR (*off camera*): He had tried to keep his life from being complicated. He had felt sorry for his mother and she had made him lie. He would go to Kansas City and get a job and she would feel all right about it. There would be one more scene maybe before he got away. He would not go down to his father's office. He would miss that one. He wanted his life to go smoothly. Well, that was all over now, anyway.

DISCUSSION QUESTIONS

1. Read Geller's script in conjunction with Hemingway's original story. Mark sections of the script that do not appear in the story. Do you think Geller's changes are substantial or trivial? Explain.

2. Discuss the nature of Geller's changes. Why were they made? What purpose do they serve? Do you think a perfectly faithful film version was possible? What would it have been like?

3. Does Geller's version of the story leave you with a different impression of its meaning? Why, for example, is the final sentence of the story omitted from the script. Point to other such changes or omissions and discuss how these affect interpretation.

Richard B. Eckhaus / The Jeffersons: "The Black Out"

1978

On Thursday evening, July 14, 1977, New York City was suddenly plunged into one of the worst electrical power failures in recent urban history. The black out continued through the night as thousands of looters and arsonists devastated entire neighborhoods. The New York Post *headline read: "24 Hours of Terror." Over 3,400 men and women were arrested in what the* Post *called the "worst outbreak of rioting in the city's history" and "the most expensive man-made [disaster] the nation has ever seen."*

Though not a likely subject for television humor, the black out nevertheless served as the situation for one comedy show—"The Jeffersons." Written in November 1977 by Richard B. Eckhaus and produced the following year, "The Black Out" was nominated for a humanitarian award. "The Jeffersons," which began airing in 1975, starred Sherman Hemsley as George Jefferson and Isabel Sanford as his wife, Louise. For an extended discussion of the show, see Darryl Pinckney's "Step and Fetch It: The Darker Side of the Sitcoms" in Magazines.

ACT ONE

Fade in. Interior, Jefferson living room—night. (*Late evening. The drapes are closed, and the sofa is in a new position—perpendicular to the upstage wall. George and Louise are rearranging the furniture. George struggles to hold one of the chairs in the air, as Louise tries to decide its new location.*)

LOUISE (*pointing to a spot behind George*): Maybe over there . . .

(*George drops the chair with a thud and a gasp.*)

GEORGE: Weezy . . .

LOUISE (*looking at the chair*): Definitely not THERE.

GEORGE (*impatiently*): Weezy . . . that's the third time I moved that chair.

LOUISE: I know, George . . . but I want the room to look right when it's changed.

GEORGE: We've been through this before. (*lifting the chair again*) Ain't nothin' gonna' stay changed but my body.

(*Florence enters from the kitchen. She carries a coffee cup, and looks sleepy.*)

FLORENCE: Now, I'd call THAT "Urban Renewal."

GEORGE: (*reacts and drops chair*): Where you been while I've been doin' your work?

FLORENCE (*yawns*): Makin' a cup of hot chocolate . . . and it ain't MY work. (*She calmly takes a sip from the cup.*)

GEORGE (*getting a bit ticked*): What do you think I'm payin' you for?

FLORENCE: Company . . . I guess.

GEORGE: You wanna' stay part of the company, you'd better help me with this chair.

(*Florence shrugs, places the cup on the dinette table, and crosses to help George.*) (*George bends over to pick up the chair, expecting Florence's help.*)

GEORGE (*grinning*): That's more like it . . .

(*Florence merely takes the cushion from the chair, and walks back to her hot chocolate.*)

GEORGE (*glaring at Florence*): You're pushin' . . .

FLORENCE: No . . . I'm drinkin' . . . (*She takes a sip from the cup.*)

SOUND EFFECTS: (*Doorbell.*)

GEORGE (*points to the door*): Florence . . . DOOR . . .

FLORENCE (*picking up the chair cushion, and pointing to it*): Mr. Jefferson . . . PILLOW . . . (*points to table*) . . . and that's a TABLE. (*George reacts, and glares at Florence.*) Ain't it amazin' what that child's learnin'?

LOUISE (*a bit impatient*): George . . . would you PLEASE get the door. I'd like to get this done TONIGHT.

(*Florence begins to exit to the kitchen.*)

GEORGE (*crossing to the door*): NOW, where do you think you're goin'?

FLORENCE: To get more coco. These cups are too darn small.

GEORGE (*to Florence, as he opens the door to reveal Marcus, who is carrying some cleaning*): So's your brai . . . MARCUS! (*George puts his arm around Marcus, and leads him into the apartment.*)

MARCUS: Hey, Mr. Jefferson . . . (*waving to Louise across the room, who is still studying the furniture arrangement*) . . . Mrs. Jefferson. We managed to get that gravy stain out of your suit, Mr. Jefferson.

LOUISE (*chuckling*): And he'll manage to get it back IN.

GEORGE (*forcing a laugh*) Hey, Weezy . . . you always said I needed a hobby.

LOUISE: Would you like to stay for coffee and dessert, Marcus?

MARCUS: I'd sure like to, Mrs. Jefferson, but I promised to be home early. (*He notices the half-changed furniture.*) Hey . . . you're re-doin' the living room.

GEORGE (*laughing*): Yeah . . . Mrs. Jefferson's playin' INFERIOR decorator . . . for the third time this week.

LOUISE: Funny, George. (*She starts to move one of the coffee tables.*)

MARCUS (*rushing across the room to help her*): That's too heavy for you, Mrs. Jefferson. Let me do it.

LOUISE: Oh . . . thank you, Marcus, but you'd better be going. You wanted to get home early, remember?

MARCUS: Aw, that's okay. I got a few minutes to kill . . . might as well work 'em to death. (*He lifts the table.*)

LOUISE: Marcus, you really don't have to . . .

GEORGE (*interrupting as he hangs the cleaning in the closet*): Sure he does. Marcus has got himself one good attitude . . . always ready to help people.

(*Louise points to a spot where Marcus then places the table. She turns to glare at George.*)

LOUISE: Marcus sure isn't like SOME people I know.

(*As Marcus and Louise move the other coffee table, George crosses from the hall closet, and plops into one of the armchairs.*)

GEORGE: That Florence sure is lazy . . . ain't she?

(*Louise reacts, and turns to stare at George.*)

LOUISE: And just what do you think you're doing?

GEORGE (*smiling*): Resting myself. Ain't you heard that middle-aged black men can get high blood-pressure?

LOUISE: That's ridiculous, George. In all the time we've been together, your blood pressure hasn't gone up two points.

(*Florence re-enters from the kitchen.*)

FLORENCE: If it ever does . . . SELL!!

(*Suddenly, the apartment lights begin to flicker.*)

LOUISE: What's that?

(*The lights now dim.*)

GEORGE: Just another power shortage, Weezy. The Arabs probably raised the prices again.

(*The lights go out completely. We can only hear voices.*)

LOUISE (*alarmed*): George . . . I'm scared.

GEORGE: Take it easy, Weezy. Must be a fuse. (*pause*) I'll get the flashlight . . .

(*A beat of silence, then Louise remembers something.*)

LOUISE (*urgently*): GEORGE . . . Don't forget we moved the . . .

SOUND EFFECTS:(*A crash, a thud, and a howl of pain.*)

LOUISE: . . . sofa.

(*The lights flicker on again, and we see George sprawled on the floor on the stage right side of the sofa.*)

GEORGE (*picking himself off the floor*): This all ain't REALLY happenin' . . .

LOUISE (*starting across to help George*): Are you alright, George?

(*The lights dim and go out again.*)

GEORGE (*voice in the dark*): It's happenin'. Weezy . . . you pay that damn bill?

LOUISE (*voice in the dark*): Of course, I payed it. George, I'm REALLY frightened.

(*A beat of silence.*)

GEORGE: There . . . there . . . Sugar. I've got you.

FLORENCE (*angry*): NO YOU DON'T . . . SUCKER!!

(*We hear a "thud," and George yells in pain.*)

(*Marcus lights a match, and we see Louise reach into the corner hutch. They light two candles which illuminate the room with a soft glow. George stands beside a glowering Florence. He holds his ribs in pain.*)

MARCUS: Must be some sort of bad short . . .

FLORENCE (*still frowning at poor George*): Damn right, it's a BAD SHORT!

(*Louise opens the drapes, and discovers that the entire area is dark.*)

LOUISE: Come here, George. It looks like we're not alone.

(*Still wincing, George crosses to the window, and looks out.*)

GEORGE: Just what this city needs . . . another blackout.

MARCUS: That means the subways ain't runnin'. How long you figure it'll last?

GEORGE: Long as it takes for the electric company to rook us outa' more money. Why d'ya think they're called CON Edison.

SOUND EFFECTS: (*a knock at the door.*)

(*Florence crosses, and opens the door to Harry Bentley, who carries an electric Coleman camping lantern.*)

BENTLEY: Greetings, everybody. I see you're as much in the dark about this as I am. (*He chuckles at his own pun.*)

GEORGE (*not amused*): What do you want, Bentley?

BENTLEY (*crossing into the living room*): Actually, I just popped over to borrow a few candles. I knew I'd be needing them this morning, but I forgot to stop by the store on the way home. Rather silly of me . . . wouldn't you say, Mr. J?

GEORGE: I woulda' said it, anyway. (*He thinks a beat.*) Wait a minute, Bentley. You tryin' to tell me you're psychic or somethin'?

BENTLEY (*puzzled*): How's that, Mr. J?

GEORGE: You said you knew this morning you'd be needin' candles for the blackout. Besides, you already got a lattern.

BENTLEY (*laughing*): Oh . . . I didn't know about the blackout . . . but I DID know about Susan.

GEORGE (*really puzzled*): Say what??

BENTLEY: I had already invited Susan over for a candle-light dinner. (*He looks down at his lantern.*) And as for this . . . who ever heard of a romantic FLASH-LIGHT dinner?

GEORGE (*suddenly alarmed, as he thinks of something*): OHMYGOSH!!

LOUISE: What's the matter, George?

BENTLEY: No need to get excited, Mr. J. We can use the lantern in a pinch . . . if we have to.

GEORGE: It's my mother. She's probably scared stiff in the dark.

LOUISE (*calmly*): Only if she can't find her Vodka.

GEORGE: That ain't funny, Weezy. I'd better call her. (*He crosses to the phone, and dials. Not able to get through, he hangs up, and tries again.*)

BENTLEY (*to Louise and Marcus*): You know, this reminds me of the big black-out back in 1966. There are so many similarities . . . except for Susan, of course. She doesn't look a thing like Gloria.

(*Louise listens to Bentley with an amused look.*)

MARCUS: How long did that one go for?

BENTLEY (*with a far-away look*): Gloria?

MARCUS: No, man . . . the BLACKOUT.

BENTLEY: Oh . . . that. It's hard to say. Gloria and I didn't notice for three days.

(*In the background, George has gotten through to his mother.*)

GEORGE (*on phone*): . . . that's so? Don't let it worry you, Momma. Oh you FOUND IT?! (*Embarrassed, he glances up at a smiling Louise, who has been listening to George's side of the conversation.*) Well not too much, now . . . sleep tight. (*He hangs up.*)

LOUISE: I'm sure she'll sleep tight as a drum.

GEORGE (*quickly changing the subject*): Momma heard on her radio that all of New York and part of Jersey are blacked out. (*He thinks a beat.*) We got a port-able radio?

FLORENCE (*suddenly perking up*): Hey . . . I got one. (*She exits to her bed-room.*)

GEORGE: Huh . . . FINALLY we got a reason to keep Florence around. Weezy, remind me to buy a portable radio. (*He notices Bentley.*) You still here, Bentley?

BENTLEY: Actually, I haven't had a chance to ask Mrs. J if I might borrow some candles.

(*George starts to hustle Harry to the door.*)

GEORGE: There . . . you asked . . .

LOUISE: I'm sorry, Mr. Bentley, but these are our last two.

GEORGE (*as he opens the door*): You heard her, Bentley. You'll just have to have a FLASHLIGHT dinner.

BENTLEY (*smiling licentiously*): I suppose it shan't be too bad. Susan is . . . EVEREADY. (*Bentley chuckles at his own lousy pun, but George just stares at him.*)

GEORGE: Finished, Bentley?

BENTLEY: Just one more thing, Mr. J. How come they never have a blackout during the day?

GEORGE: 'Cause then they'd call it a ''WHITE-OUT.'' Speakin' of which . . . (*George pushes Bentley out into the hall, and slams the door.*)

(*Florence re-enters carrying a portable radio.*)

FLORENCE: This is the best idea you ever had, Mr. Jefferson. (*Florence turns on her radio. It is tuned to a soul/rock station, and she begins to dance to the music.*)

GEORGE (*grabbing the radio from her*): Gimme that!! (*He tunes the radio into a news station.*)

VOICE ON RADIO: . . . pandemonium breaking out all over the city. Police report that looters are having a field day in Bedford-Stuyvesant and the South Bronx.

(*George quickly shuts off the radio. He looks very worried.*)

LOUISE: What's the matter, George?

MARCUS: You got a store in the South Bronx . . . don't you, Mr. Jefferson?

GEORGE (*looking very upset*): I sure do . . . and it's full of customers' cleaning. (*He begins to pace the floor.*) They'll clean ME out.

LOUISE (*putting a hand on George's shoulder*): Try not to get too upset about it, dear. You can't do anything now . . . and besides, your insurance'll cover any . . .

GEORGE: WHAT insurance?

LOUISE (*shocked*): You mean you don't have insurance??!!

GEORGE: Not on the South Bronx store. They wouldn't sell me none . . . said it was a bad risk.

LOUISE: But you've been in that store for fifteen years.

GEORGE: You know that, and I know that, Weezy . . . but the insurance companies don't CARE about stuff like that. They said the neighborhood's changed, and it ain't safe for a business no more. (*He crosses to the front closet.*)

LOUISE: Does that make us liable for our customers' property?

GEORGE (*He takes an old coat from the closet.*): It sure does.

MARCUS: That's gonna' cost you a fortune, Mr. Jefferson.

GEORGE: No it ain't, Marcus.

MARCUS (*confused*): Huh??

GEORGE: Me and you are gonna' take the truck, and high-tail it up there before they get everything.

MARCUS: We are?

GEORGE: Sure . . . and we'll bring the stuff down here where it's safe.

LOUISE (*incredulous*): You WILL??

GEORGE: Sure! It'll take us no time. (*He puts on the old coat.*) This old thing'll make me look inconspicuous.

FLORENCE (*as she picks up one of the candles, and crosses to the kitchen*): You don't need a costume for that.

(*George reacts.*)

GEORGE: Common, Marcus.

(*Marcus reluctantly crosses to join George by the door.*)

LOUISE (*worried*): George . . . don't go.

GEORGE: There ain't nothin' to worry about, Weezy. We'll be home before you know it.

MARCUS (*nervous*): It sure is dark out there . . .

(*George opens the door, and they step into the hall.*)

LOUISE: George . . .

GEORGE: I told you, Weezy . . . everything's gonna' be okay. I'll take care of Marcus.

(*George and Marcus exit.*)

LOUISE (*looking very worried*): It's not Marcus I'm worried about . . .

Dissolve to:

Interior, Jefferson South Bronx store—night. (*An hour later. The store is dark, and through the front window, we can see passers-by carrying T.V. sets, stereos, etc. From the back room of the store, we can see a faint light moving about, and we hear voices.*)

FIRST VOICE: Are you crazy, man? That ain't worth a damn thing.

SECOND VOICE: Yeah . . . but it'll look good on my old lady.

FIRST VOICE: Shooot! She puts on five more pounds, an' she'll look good in commercial plates.

SECOND VOICE: Hey man . . . watch your mouth!

(*George and Marcus appear at the front door, and begin to unlock it.*)

FIRST VOICE: SSSHHH . . . somebody's comin'.

(*George and Marcus enter the store.*)

GEORGE (*relieved, as he points his flashlight around*): Whew! It looks like we ain't been hit yet.

MARCUS: The rest of the neighborhood looks like a bomb hit it.

GEORGE: Well . . . that ain't our worry. Let's get all this stuff . . .

(*There is a crash in the back room.*)

MARCUS (*stunned*): WHAAZZAATT??!!

GEORGE (*very frightened*): Who's b..b..back there?

(*Two men slowly emerge from the back room.*)

FIRST LOOTER: You ain't the cops??!!

GEORGE: No . . . we ain't . . . but . . .

SECOND LOOTER: So, split, man! (*The two looters resume picking things from the racks.*)

GEORGE: SPLIT??!! You guys'd better split.

FIRST LOOTER (*calmly turning to face George and Marcus*): You still here?

GEORGE (*indignant*): You bet I'm still here. This is MY store.

SECOND LOOTER: Wrong, brother. We was here first . . .

FIRST LOOTER: . . . and that makes it OUR store.

GEORGE: Hey, man . . . I OWN this place.

(*The two looters look at each other, then break out laughing.*)

MARCUS: Yeah . . . this here's "Jefferson Cleaners," and he's George Jefferson.

FIRST LOOTER (*still smirking*): Not THE George Jefferson??

GEORGE (*dripping with pride*): That's right . . . THE George Jefferson.

SECOND LOOTER: In that case . . . (*He takes a gun from his pocket.*). . . STICK 'EM UP!!

(*George and Marcus look at each other, and break into a nervous chuckle.*)

GEORGE: Heh . . . heh . . . you guys are funny . . .

FIRST LOOTER (*frowning*): He said "STICK 'EM UP"!! (*George and Marcus put their hands in the air.*) Let's have your wallets. (*George and Marcus reach into their pockets, and hand over their wallets.*)

SECOND LOOTER (*examining George's wallet*): Hey . . . this cat really IS Jefferson . . . and he's loaded too.

FIRST LOOTER (*looking into the wallet*): WOW! He WAS loaded. This sure is our lucky day.

SECOND LOOTER: And you said we shoulda' hit the liquor store . . . HA!

FIRST LOOTER: Grab those leather coats, and let's split. (*The second looter exits to the back room for a beat, and returns carrying several leather garments.*) Well, Mr. Jefferson . . . it's been a pleasure doin' business with you . . . (*The two looters cross to the door.*) If you go out there tonight, be careful. This neighborhood's a jungle. (*The two looters exit.*)

GEORGE (*jumping up and down in anger*): Damn . . . damn . . . DAMN!

MARCUS: You gotta' admit . . . those guys had style.

GEORGE: Yeah . . . and now they got my wallet too.

(*Marcus steps behind the counter, and checks the register.*)

MARCUS: Empty . . .

GEORGE: It figures. (*He looks around.*) Well . . . let's get this stuff on the truck, and get outa' here.

(*George and Marcus begin to take garments from the hanging racks. Suddenly, the door bursts open, and two uniformed cops storm in with their guns drawn.*)

FIRST COP: HOLD IT . . . both of you!!

GEORGE (*stunned*): HUH??!!

SECOND COP: Drop what you're stealing, and get against the counter!

GEORGE: This ain't happenin' . . .

MARCUS (*frightened*): It's happenin', Mr. Jefferson . . . it's happenin'.

(*The cops force George and Marcus to spread-eagle against the counter, and then frisk them.*)

GEORGE: You dudes are makin' a mistake. I OWN this place.

FIRST COP: Sure, bud . . . and I'm Kojak.

GEORGE: If you guys'll just look in my wallet . . .

SECOND COP: I just frisked you, and you ain't got a wallet.

GEORGE (*remembering*): Oh yeah . . . that's right. Two guys just stole our wallets.

SECOND COP: Hey, you guys are REAL creative. The last bunch of looters just said they were takin' inventory. (*He chuckles as he handcuffs George and Marcus together.*)

GEORGE (*furious*): You guys can't do this.

(*They lead George and Marcus to the door.*)

FIRST COP: Pipe down, will ya'?

GEORGE (*as he is being dragged out the door*): I wanna' see my lawyer!!

SECOND COP: Sure . . . sure . . . good old Calhoun's out in the paddy wagon.

GEORGE (*howling*): WEEEEZZYYY. . . .

Fade out.

ACT TWO

Fade in: Interior, jail cell—night. (*A short time later. The cell is filled with surly-looking men. New York's power is still out, and the cell and hallway are only illuminated by emergency lanterns. Some of the inmates pace back and forth, others try to doze on cots or on the floor. Suddenly, the relative quiet is broken by the approaching sound of George's voice.*)

GEORGE (*off-screen*) (*angry as hell*): I'm tellin' you dudes . . . you're in BIG trouble.

FIRST COP (*off-screen*: Sure pal . . . sure.

(*George and Marcus now appear in the hallway, accompanied by the two cops.*)

GEORGE (*rubbing his hands on his old coat*): Damn ink all over my hands . . .

SECOND COP (*sarcastic, as he unlocks the cell door*): Aw, gee . . . I'm sorry. The manicurist won't be in till tomorrow.

(*George and Marcus step into the cell.*)

FIRST COP (*sarcastic, chuckling*): I do hope you find our accommodations to your liking.

GEORGE: I hope you find my lawyer to your likin'. When he gets done with you, you'll be poundin' a beat in Uganda.

SECOND COP (*slamming the cell door behind George and Marcus*): Yeah?! I could use a vacation. (*The two cops exit laughing.*)

FIRST COP: Can you believe that guy? He OWNS the place . . . the nerve of that turkey!

SECOND COP (*mocking*): YOU'LL BE POUNDING A BEAT IN UGANDA!! He probably knows Idi Amin personally.

(*Furious, George turns and looks around the cell. Upon seeing the surly inmates, who are quietly watching his performance, he panics, runs back to the bars and bellows after the cops.*)

GEORGE (*screaming*): What about my phone call??

FIRST COP (*off-screen*): Wait your turn, chump. Now . . . SHADDUP!!

MARCUS: I don't think they believed you, Mr. Jefferson.

GEORGE (*pacing the crowded floor*): They'll believe me when I sue their butts off. I'm gonna' fix Con Edison too.

MARCUS (*smiling proudly*): 'Atta' way, Mr. J! We're gonna fight City Hall.

GEORGE: No we ain't. Just the cops and Con Ed.

MARCUS: By the way . . . how come you're gonna' sue the electric company?

GEORGE (*pacing up a storm*): 'Cause if it wasn't for them turkeys, we wouldn't be here. I'll fix 'em.

(*Suddenly the cell's main lights come on. The blackout is over, and the other prisoners cheer. One of them, a raggedy-looking character, approaches George.*)

FIRST INMATE (*shaking George's hand*): Man . . . I don't know who you are, but keep talkin'. Maybe you can get us a steak dinner.

(*The other inmates now approach George and Marcus, and begin to size them up.*)

MARCUS (*aside to George*): Mr. Jefferson . . . I'm scared.

GEORGE (*trembling*): Stick close to me . . . I'll look after you.

MARCUS (*not reassured*): That's what you said right after "Let's get the truck an' go up to the Bronx."

(*A particularly tough-looking inmate stares George in the eye.*)

SECOND INMATE: What're you dudes in for? You looters?

GEORGE (*indignant*): We ain't done nothin'. It's a mistake.

SECOND INMATE (*smiling*): Sure . . . sure. We've all been framed. Don't let 'em bluff ya's. Just stick to that story . . .

GEORGE: It ain't no story. The cops picked us up in my own store.

(*The* SECOND INMATE *begins to laugh.*)

SECOND INMATE: Hey . . . that's rich! An' I was picked up carryin' my OWN air conditioner down the street.

FIRST INMATE (*rolling with laughter*): Yeah . . . and I wandered into that furniture factory by accident. I mean, it WAS dark.

(*All the inmates start to roar. George is frustrated and furious.*)

GEORGE (*shouting above the laughter*): I AIN'T JIVIN'!! (*The cell quiets down.*) I own a chain of cleanin' stores. I made my way up BY MYSELF, and I don't need to steal. I ain't looted from nobody, and I don't belong in this dump. (*One *of the inmates, sitting on a cot, takes out a harmonica, and goes into some classic prison riff.*) That's all I gotta' say. (*George angrily sits down on the cell floor.*)

SECOND INMATE (*looking down at George*): Man . . . you're really somethin'. You DO think you're too good for us, don't you?

(*Marcus quickly steps between George and the burly inmate.*)

MARCUS (*shaking with fear*): He didn't mean nothin' by it . . . honest.

SECOND INMATE: Then what's he goin' around dumpin' that innocent jazz on us for?

MARCUS (*searching for an "out"*): Uh . . . 'cause he's a . . . he's a SMART hood, that's why. My boss always knows how to put on a front.

SECOND INMATE (*scoffing*): Boy . . . you take me for a fool?

MARCUS (*confused*): Uh . . . yeah . . . I mean . . . NO.

GEORGE: Forget it, Marcus. They ain't buyin' . . . and I ain't sellin'.

(*Frustrated, Marcus slides down onto the floor next to George.*)

MARCUS: I was just tryin' to help . . .

GEORGE (*patting Marcus on the back*): I know, man . . . but I ain't apologizin' 'cause I AIN'T a looter.

FIRST INMATE: Ya know . . . I think the runt is tellin' the truth. He ain't the lootin' type.

GEORGE: Damn right, I ain't.

(*Another voice comes out of the crowd of inmates. Jackson is a tall, black man. He rises from one of the bunk beds, and walks over to George.*)

JACKSON: Jefferson's telling the truth. He's no looter.

(*George stands up to face Jackson, but still has to look way up at the man.*)

GEORGE (*surprised*): You know me?

JACKSON: I've seen you around . . . with your fine clothes and your well-dressed wife.

GEORGE (*beaming*): Ha . . . see there? The man knows me.

JACKSON: Yeah . . . I've seen you. I've seen you strutting into your store to count up all the bread in your cash register. Year after year I'd see you coming by . . . getting fatter and fatter . . .

GEORGE (*self-consciously sucking in his gut*): That ain't fat . . . I slouch.

JACKSON (*looking George up and down*): Well . . . your head's sure gotten fat. Why, I bet you never REALLY noticed the change in the neighborhood . . . just the change in your pocket.

GEORGE: How could I MISS what was goin' down in that neighborhood?

JACKSON: Did you know WHY it was changing? (*George tries to answer, but can't.*) I used to be a welder at the Brooklyn Navy Yard. When I got laid-off, I found part time work for awhile . . . then nothing.

MARCUS: How'd you get in here?

JACKSON: Last night the cops caught Old Henry Jackson looting an appliance store.

GEORGE: I bet you feel like hell.

JACKSON: Sure I do . . . 'cause I got CAUGHT.

GEORGE (*puzzled*): Say what?

JACKSON: I'm not ashamed of trying to feed my family. I'm just ashamed of not being too good at it.

GEORGE: There ain't no excuse for stealin'.

SECOND INMATE: You ever been poor?

MARCUS (*jumping in to George's defense*): He was so poor . . . his folks couldn't afford a taller kid.

(*George reacts.*)

JACKSON: Then he doesn't REMEMBER what it's like to have to steal to eat. Man . . . that neighborhood's full of guys like me. You better believe that when the Man's pants are down, we're gonna' grab whatever we can get our hands on.

GEORGE (*not as forceful as before*): You tellin' me that nobody was lootin' just for the sake of doin' it?

JACKSON: Sure they were . . . some of them. (*He points to another man in the cell.*) Lewis over there's got a good job. He didn't have to do it. But when some guys see a crowd doing something . . .

GEORGE (*calling over to Lewis*): Hey Lewis . . . is that the truth?

LEWIS (*singing*): I LOVE A PARADE . . .

(*George reacts.*)

JACKSON: Point is . . . there is no right and wrong . . . no black and white . . .

GEORGE (*trying to make a joke*): Sure there is . . . the Willises . . . (*Nobody laughs—not even Marcus.*) Inside joke . . .

JACKSON: I don't know, Jefferson. Maybe you've just gotten out of touch . . . (*Jackson shakes his head, turns, and walks back to his cot. George leans on the bars, and looks blankly out. A weird-looking inmate now approaches George.*)

WEIRD INMATE (*in a loud whisper*): PSSST . . . Buddy . . .

(*George turns to look at the guy.*)

GEORGE: What do YOU want?

WEIRD INMATE: Just wanna' give you some advice . . . (*George listens intently.*) Keep an eye out in here . . . the place is full of crooks. (*George stares at the man in disbelief. The character rolls up his coat-sleeve, and displays a half-dozen watches to George.*) Wanna' buy an Omega watch . . .?

Dissolve to:

Interior, jail cell—night. (*Some time later. Most of the men in the cell are asleep. George dozes in a corner on the floor, his battered old coat covers him like a blanket. George tosses and turns in his sleep. Marcus is awake, and sits next to George, guarding him. The weird inmate sits by himself, wide awake and happily listening to his watches tick. We hear voices approaching off-stage. After a beat, Louise appears in the hallway outside the cell. She is accompanied by the First Cop.*)

FIRST COP (*quietly to Louise*): You see him in there?

(*She looks around the cell for a beat. As Louise's eyes search for George, Marcus happens to look up and see her. Overjoyed, he reaches over and shakes George.*)

GEORGE (*in his sleep*): Not now, Weezy . . .

MARCUS (*again shaking George*): Mr. Jefferson . . . wake up . . .

GEORGE (*turning over—still asleep*): I said not now, Weezy. I got a headache!

(*Louise spots George and Marcus, and points them out to the cop. Marcus still tries to awaken George.*)

MARCUS (*He thinks for a beat, then speaks very quietly.*): What do you mean Imperial Cleaners is cuttin' their prices again?

(*George's eyes open, and he sits up with a start. He is totally disoriented.*)

GEORGE: WHAZZAT?? Where am I? (*He looks around, sees the cell, then Marcus.*) Oh . . . yeah . . .

MARCUS (*excited*): Mrs. Jefferson's here.

(*George leaps to his feet, just as the cop unlocks the cell door.*)

FIRST COP: You sure that's him, Mrs. Jefferson??

LOUISE (*anxious*): I'm POSSITIVE!

FIRST COP (*still baffled*): Gosh . . . I'm sorry for the mistake. He sure had us fooled. (*The cop unlocks the cell door.*)

LOUISE (*a bit angry*): Evidently.

(*George rushes to Louise. He is ecstatic.*)

GEORGE: WEEEEEEEZZZZZZZYYYYYYY!!!!!!!

(*They embrace, then George notices the cop standing there, and begins to glower at him.*)

FIRST COP (*nervous*): Jeez . . . I'm sorry for the mistake, Mr. Jefferson.

(*George and Marcus step into the hallway, and the cop re-locks the cell door.*)

GEORGE (*angry*): Not as sorry as you're gonna' be.

FIRST COP: We were just doing our jobs. If there were REAL looters in your store, you'd've wanted us there . . . wouldn't you?

GEORGE (*cooling down a bit*): Yeah . . . I guess so . . .

MARCUS: We were sort of askin' for it when we went up there.

GEORGE (*reluctantly*): Well, yeah . . .

LOUISE: And if they didn't let you finally make that call to me when the lines were cleared, you might have been in here all night.

FIRST COP: Next time remember, Mr. Jefferson . . . in an area like the South Bronx the only way to protect a store is steel-plated walls and iron bars. Even then there are no guarantees. The people up there are animals.

GEORGE: I dunno' . . . maybe you're right. (*yawning*) Who's got the time?

(*The weird inmate leans against the bars, and rolls up his sleeves.*)

WEIRD INMATE: What city?

GEORGE: Forget it. (*They walk down the hallway.*)

LOUISE: Let's go home and get some sleep.

GEORGE: Just a couple o' hours, Weezy. Then I gotta' go up to the South Bronx store.

MARCUS: Got some cleanin' up to do, I guess.

GEORGE (*as they exit*): No . . . I got some CLOSIN' up to do, Marcus.

Dissolve to:

Interior, Jefferson South Bronx store—morning. (*Early the next morning. The store is a disaster area. Every one of the customers' garments is missing, the shelves are empty, the windows are broken, and the floor is covered with debris. George and Louise stand sadly in the ruins.*)

GEORGE (*Looking around, he feels angry, hurt, and bitter.*): After so many years in this store, this is what I got left . . . damn!

(*Louise rummages around in the rubble.*)

LOUISE: They didn't leave much, did they?

GEORGE: The animals took EVERYTHING. I'm surprised they left the air.

LOUISE: I'm sorry Marcus had to see all this. It doesn't give him much of an outlook on things . . . does it, George? (*Louise sees something in the mess near the door.*) What's this?

GEORGE: Probably a roach . . . and the only reason they ain't stole him is 'cause they got enough of their own.

(*Louise bends down and picks up a wallet.*)

LOUISE: It's your wallet George.

GEORGE (*surprised*): You're jivin' . . .

LOUISE: No . . . it's here. (*He rushes over to look.*)

GEORGE: I'll be damned. I bet they took everything of any value.

LOUISE (*looking through the wallet*): You're right, George . . . your mother's picture's still here.

GEORGE (*He reacts, and is not amused.*): That ain't funny, Weezy.

LOUISE (*chuckling as she studies the picture*): Mother Jefferson sitting on a pony IS funny, George. (*looks through the wallet some more*) Your credit cards are still here.

GEORGE (*really surprised*): You GOTTA be kiddin'.

(*She shows him the credit cards.*)

GEORGE (*smiling*): What d'ya know . . . I got hit by dumb looters.

LOUISE: See, George? It's not all that bad.

GEORGE (*frowning*): Don't try to change my mind, Weezy. I'm not gonna' re-open this place . . . NEVER!

LOUISE: I'm not going to try . . .

GEORGE (*beginning to pace back and forth*): There's NO WAY I'm ever gonna' set foot in this neighborhood again. Give me one reason why I oughta' come back here.

LOUISE (*as she calmly resumes looking around for valuables*): I can't, George . . .

GEORGE: You heard the cop . . . they're animals up here now. We left the ghetto behind YEARS ago. (*rambling on*) I ain't got no insurance . . . I gotta' pay off all my customers for their stuff . . .

LOUISE: No question you're right, George.

GEORGE (*pacing up a storm*): . . . cop said I gotta' get steel-plated walls and iron bars to keep 'em out . . .

(*The door opens, and an elderly man enters the store.*)

LOUISE (*to the old man*): Can we help you?

OLD MAN (*sadly looking around at the damage*): They hit you pretty bad, huh?

GEORGE (*abruptly*): Yeah. Now what can we do for you?

OLD MAN: You the owners?

LOUISE: Yes . . . we're the Jeffersons.

OLD MAN: I've been a customer of yours for a long, long time. I had a suit being cleaned . . .

GEORGE (*snapping*): You'll get paid for it like everybody else . . . before we close up.

OLD MAN: No big deal. It was an old suit, anyway . . . still had pleats. (*thinks for a beat*) Did you say you're closing up?

GEORGE: You heard me. I'm shuttin' down. I got other stores to worry about.

OLD MAN (*sighing*): Can't say I blame you. You're a rich man.

(*In the background, Louise finds something.*)

GEORGE: Damn right I am . . . and I worked hard for it too.

OLD MAN: If I had what you had, I'd go too. Leave all this behind . . . that's your best bet. It's the same with all the merchants. They've gotten fat . . . (*Again George sucks in his gut, but then lets it out, thinking.*) . . . and don't need to be reminded of the old days. (*The old man looks around again.*) Well, I'll let you do your business. (*He turns and exits.*)

GEORGE (*pausing, then calling out after the man exits*) Hey . . . your suit . . .

LOUISE: George . . . look what I found. (*She holds a small, cracked picture frame.*)

GEORGE (*in thought*): Huh?

LOUISE: I found the first dollar this old store earned us. I'm surprised the looters didn't grab it.

(*George looks it over carefully.*)

GEORGE: That IS somethin', Weezy.

LOUISE: Well, at least you'll have a souvenir of your second store after we close it.

GEORGE (*stiffening his spine*): Close it? What do you mean CLOSE IT??

LOUISE (*shocked*): But George . . .

GEORGE: Ain't no "buts" about it, Weezy. I ain't no quitter. This store is more than just a business . . . it's a link to what WAS for us.

(*Louise grabs George and hugs him.*)

LOUISE: Oh, George . . . I'm so proud of you.

GEORGE (*smiling—proud of himself too*): Yeah . . . well . . . I learned a few things in the last couple o' days.

LOUISE: Like . . . ?

GEORGE: Like . . . just 'cause you're successful don't mean you ain't the same person you was.

LOUISE: And . . . ?

GEORGE: And . . . no matter what happens, you've gotta' have some trust left in people. (*She hugs him again.*) Now let's go home . . . I'm whipped. (*They walk to the door, and George turns back to look at the store again.*) Weezy . . . how much you figure steel-plated walls and iron bars'll run us?

(*Louise reacts, and stares at George, as we:*)

Fade out.

DISCUSSION QUESTIONS

1. Read the script in conjunction with Darryl Pinckney's essay on blacks in sitcoms in Magazines. Do you think Pinckney's critical assessment of the show is correct? Explain why or why not.

2. Situation comedies require many one-liners. Identify several of the jokes in this episode and examine what they have in common. Can you state the show's central joke; that is, the joke the comedy seems to revolve around, that all the jokes grow out of? For example, is there any joke inherent in the basic "situation" of this series that a script-writer can use over and over?

3. Discuss the moral problem of this episode. What is George's dilemma? Why is *he* arrested? Does the show have a "moral"? If so, can you state it in one sentence?

Hill Street Blues Staff / Hill Street Blues: "Grace under Pressure"

1984

Perhaps more than any other form of writing, screenwriting is a truly collaborative effort. Nowhere is this more apparent than in a quick examination of the credits (which sometimes seem to occupy half the air time) for most television and movie scripts. The following episode of Hill Street Blues, "Grace Under Pressure," concerning the death of Sergeant Esterhaus, was written in December 1983 by Jeffrey Lewis, Michael Wagner, Karen Hall, and Mark Frost, and was based on a story by Steven Bochco, Jeffrey Lewis, and David Milch. It went through no less than six revisions before being aired during the 1984 season.

The series itself was created by Steven Bochco and Michael Kozoll. It made its first television appearance in 1981 and since then has won more Emmies than any other dramatic series—21 in its first year alone. It is generally regarded as the best-written show on television.

ACT ONE

Fade in.

1. Over black—"Roll Call—6:59 A.M."

GOLDBLUME'S VOICE: Item ten. Jailbreak.

2. Interior. Roll call—day. (*With Goldblume addressing the dayshift—*)

GOLDBLUME: Not literally, guys, but for those who don't watch TV, listen to radio, or talk to anybody—Judge Spears last night ordered two hundred forty-seven prisoners awaiting trial released o.r. from the Michigan Avenue complex, due to severe overcrowding and inhumane conditions in that facility. (*Goldblume's lack of sarcasm suggests he takes the judge's analysis seriously; but no one else does—*)

LARUE: Yeah, let's put those inhumane conditions back on the streets where they belong.

GOLDBLUME: Look, whether we agree or disagree, these alleged perpetrators are back out there. So we're probably going to be busy. Additionally—item eleven—until Division Vice is reconstituted, we're assigned ongoing prostitution enforcement for the Hill, Midtown, Washington and Jefferson Heights. Operation Pussycat commences today at 0800 hours, in sufficient time to catch the brisk breakfast hour trade. Your trained eyes may detect among us some of the personnel assigned to this operation . . . (*Bates and few other women are in hooker garb, Bates with her leather cop jacket over her shoulders.*) Additionally, Hill, Renko, Perez and Kolzicki will work back-up, Peyser and Martin will be working plainclothes out of n.d. sedans. (*Furillo quietly slips down the roll call stairs, draws a few curious looks, waits in back, times his approach to the front to the conclusion of Goldblume's remarks.*) Item twelve, our truck hijacking problem is becoming more blatant—two more yesterday. This seems to be something of a criminal fad; the toll's up to six drivers beaten or knifed plus a couple hundred grand in merchandise boosted. Maybe catching some guys would make it less fashionable. Whattaya say? Last item, welcomes. Welcome Mike Perez back. Welcome transfer Clara Pilsky from South Ferry.

3. (*Angle—Clara, a dark-haired beauty, also dressed to go undercover as a hooker, waving off the attention a little self-consciously, mouthing "hi's" to a few.*)

LARUE: Hello, hello, hello.

GOLDBLUME: That's it, people. Thank you. Have a good shift.

4. (*Including Furillo, awkwardly, as though he has no idea what he's going to say, suddenly standing there—*)

FURILLO: Uh, people, uh, could you stay seated a minute, could I have your attention?

5. (*The dayshift, that had half-risen, drops down again. Sensitive to the haltingness of Furillo's diction.*)

6. (*Resume.*)

FURILLO (*cont'd*): Phil Esterhaus passed away this morning. He suffered a heart attack, that's the only detail I have at this time. (*A beat.*) Information as it comes in . . . about services . . . will be on the duty board. (*A beat.*) I don't have too many words, people. This is going to be a difficult day. I know the caution Phil would urge on you. Be careful out there. (*Another beat. Some stirrings. Some tears.*) Our friend was fifty-five years old. (*Choked.*) If people want to take a moment of silence . . .

(*He bows his head, as do others. Pan the quiet room. A couple people raise their heads too soon, put them down again. A couple, after a few seconds, just keep them up, looking around. Quite a number of seconds pass, then Furillo exits, tears in his eyes, past Hunter and Calletano. Gradually, silently, people raise their heads. A few get up, then most get up. Off the first words muttered by anyone—*)

LARUE: Sonofabitch.

Smash cut to Main Titles. Fade in.

7. Interior. Cop diner—day. (*With Coffey entering, sober, and without the sling we saw him with in roll call. Approaches the booth where Bates, Pilsky and Peyser sit quietly with their coats on, over coffees; slides in.*)

COFFEY (*mostly to Bates*): How ya doin'?

BATES (*a shrug*): How you doing?

COFFEY (*not much enthusiasm for it*): Doc gave me a clean bill. I can go back on patrol tomorrow.

BATES (*who can't muster much enthusiasm either*): Great.

BATES (*staring*): I still can't believe it. I feel like going home and crawling into bed.

COFFEY: You know it's right, what the Captain said. We gotta be careful; people could make a lot of mistakes today.

8. Include Renko.

RENKO (*subdued*): Giusepp . . .

COFFEY (*equally subdued; the minimal greetings of people sharing grief*): Hey, Renko . . . (*Follow Renko back to—*)

9. The Counter (*where he's sitting between Hill and Perez—*)

WAITRESS (*commiserative*): Poor man. Fifty-five years old. Any children? (*Hill shakes no, doesn't really want to engage in conversation.*) He must've been some wonderful guy; every one of you, you all look like ghosts.

RENKO (*dignifying her sympathy by putting some effort into a reply*): We thought he was getting better, you know? He was supposed to be getting better. (*More forthcoming with this neutral party than he could be with a lot of others just now.*) . . . He was like . . . mom and dad, you know?

WAITRESS (*commiserative*): That kind of guy. Yeah. (*Moving, next to pour Perez more coffee.*) Half a cup?

PEREZ (*raising hand to cup*): No thanks.

WAITRESS: Nice to see you back, Mike.

PEREZ (*grimace*): Thanks.

10. Angle. (*A guy, Jack, around the counter bend, a couple empty seats away—*)

JACK (*to Perez; somewhere in his voice an edge, reading the tag on Perez' jacket*): Scuze me, officer, scuze me, your name Perez?

PEREZ: That's right.

JACK: You related to that baseball player got traded back to the Reds?

PEREZ: No.

JACK: Then you must be the guy who killed the kid.

RENKO (*overhearing; moving to intervene*): Anything we can help you with, bud?

PEREZ (*calm*): Nobody needs any help here, Andy. (*To Jack.*) Yeah. What is it you want to know?

JACK: Just wonder what it feels like to be a kid-killer.

PEREZ: It feels terrible. And you try and tell yourself you were acting in the line of duty. Anything else? (*Perez is kind of shaken; the honesty of his speech leaves Jack without too much left to say.*)

JACK: No. Guess not.

RENKO: Hey, fella, you about done with your food, there? (*Half-beat; but not really permitting a reply.*) Because if you are, maybe you'd best just pay that tab and get out of here. (*Jack throws some change on the counter, gets up with an empty grin at Perez—*)

JACK: Have a nice day. (*And leaves.*)

HILL (*to Perez*): You okay?

PEREZ: Yeah (*shakes his head; sardonic*). Life goes on, huh? (*Coffey had also closed ranks with Perez. Now Renko's hand radio squawks, almost under Perez' last words.*)

RADIO DISPATCH (*filtered*): All units in vicinity, we've got a reported rape, possible robbery, 2632 Van Vuren, that's the Donut Hut.

COFFEY: Oh God . . .

RENKO (*to Coffey*): What is it?

COFFEY: My girlfriend works there. (*Off his sudden, stricken look—*)

Cut to:

11. Interior. Donut Hut. (*An SID guy dusts for prints around the rear door and adjoining window; a number of uniforms troop around trying to keep busy—camera comes to rest on—*)

12. Angle. (*At the door Washington with an SID officer, giving Washington a preliminary reading.*)

SID GUY: No signs of forced entry, no signs of struggle.

WASHINGTON: Robbery?

SID GUY: Register's rifled, he took her purse.

13. LaRue and Sandy Valpariso. (*She's seated at a small formica table, a blanket around her. Trying to tell him what happened—LaRue is being very professional, caring, taking notes—she's shaking with the effort to hold herself together—*)

SANDY: When I came in, he must've already been inside. I didn't hear anything. I just turned around and he was there—he had a knife, he said he was going to kill me . . . he made me undress and lie on the floor . . . he ran the knife over me, he put it in my mouth, his eyes were crazy, he was talking crazy, I was so frightened . . . he told me to do things . . . (*She can't continue.*)

LARUE: Can you give me a description, Sandy?

SANDY: Latin, about five eight or nine, black pants, one of those gray hooded sweatshirts . . .

(*Through a window behind her we see—*)

14. (*Joe Coffey, getting out of a unit, coming towards the shop under a head of steam—Washington moves outside to head him off—*)

WASHINGTON: Joe—

COFFEY: Where is she?

WASHINGTON: Inside.

COFFEE: It was her?

WASHINGTON: Yeah.

COFFEY (*an agonized moment, then*): She hurt?

WASHINGTON: I don't think so, no. (*Coffey starts for the door.*) Maybe you don't wanna go in there.

COFFEY: You sayin' I can't?

WASHINGTON: No. (*Coffey goes by him and enters.*)

Cut to:

15. Interior. Donut Hut. (*As Coffey moves to her—LaRue sees him first—she sees him, she starts to cry for the first time; he sits beside her, she holds his hand, clinging to him.*)

SANDY: Joe . . . I'm real glad you're here . . . (*She really lets go; needs to be hugged. He moves to her, tries to comfort her, but it's apparent his own reactions are far too complex to allow himself the unalloyed role of protector.*)

COFFEY: It's okay . . . it's okay . . . (*Washington and LaRue retreat discreetly—we move with them—Washington spots the manager, Harley, looking out at them through a window in his office—*)

WASHINGTON: Manager's here. (*They enter the office—*)

16. Donut Hut Manager's Office.

LARUE: Can you tell us which of your employees have keys to the building?

HARLEY (*surly*): No, I can't.

WASHINGTON: Why's that?

HARLEY: They trade shifts, give the keys to each other. I tell 'em not to, a lot of good it does.

WASHINGTON: What about a list of everybody's worked here the last couple years?

HARLEY (*sarcastic*): Hey, I'll take a spare morning, type it up. (*Angry; looking out his window into the shop*) So lemme ask you somethin'. Why is it the law don't apply to cops like everybody else?

WASHINGTON: How's that? (*Harley nods for Washington and LaRue to observe.*)

17. Point of view—The shop (*where a uniform's chowing down a donut, swilling coffee.*)

HARLEY: Guys come in here, it's like Attila the Hun. Close the joint down, no trade, plus you eat me out of house and home and I don't see dime one on the counter.

LARUE (*growing irritated*): We'll pay you for donuts. Give us the list.

HARLEY: What list? (*Fed up, Washington throws Harley up against some file drawers.*)

WASHINGTON: Listen up, sucker, you picked the wrong day, you understand? Now we got a rape and you're worried about donuts, but for the time being we're talking about rape, you understand? We want to know every guy's worked in here, every guy's been busted, every guy you fired for the last two years, you understand? (*Washington lets him go. Harley shakes himself for recomposure, grimaces, reaches for a creaky desk drawer.*)

HARLEY (*grumblingly concessionary, reaching for a file box*): I'll give you my file of W-4's. You can figure the rest out yourself.

(*Off Washington, still steamed, doing his best to take the file from Harley without snatching it—*)

Cut to:

18. Exterior. Street—day. (*Bates and Pilsky, on a street corner near an alley, in their hooker get-ups—Pilsky's smoking a cigarette—*)

PILSKY: I never met him, what was he like?

BATES: The Sarge? He was a piece a'work. He was like . . . he was a rock. No matter how bad it was, you saw him at the desk it took some of the edge off, you know?

PILSKY: Yeah.

BATES: I didn't think he'd ever been sick a day in his life. (*Close to tears that suddenly overtake her, gratefully seeing something.*) Got a Lincoln approaching at two o'clock.

(*A beat-up Continental is gliding their way. It stops at the curb near a hydrant, Bates sidles over to it—a black guy with a gap-toothed smile, Kelvin James, slides over to the passenger window—*)

BATES (*cont'd*): Hi there.

JAMES (*a little high*): Hi, do you recanize me? That's why I carry this credit card—(*he holds one up*)—don't leave home wid'out it.

BATES (*half a beat*): What are we talking about here?

JAMES: Somethin' 'bout me and you goin' someplace and gettin' naked somehow.

BATES: Not real impressed yet, sport.

(*James gets out of the car—he's big, muscular, more than a little menacing, even as he continues to smile—*)

JAMES: You 'be impressed—we go someplace you get this, Blondie. (*He hands her the card to look at.*)

BATES: Oh, so *you're* Virginia Kimball.

JAMES: Ac' fast you could have yourself a nice free ride, sugar. (*He smiles at her.*) So where we goin'?

BATES: Step into my office.

(*Bates gestures to Pilsky, starts leading James into the alley—Pilsky calls into a handi-talkie in background—*)

JAMES (*stopping her*): Hey, sister, I said where we goin'?

BATES: How do you feel about jail? You're under arrest, hands against the wall—

PILSKY: Back-ups, the alley off Dekker and 34th.

(*James suddenly lashes out, starts to run. Bates catches him by an ankle, trips him up—as he rises Pilsky appears in front of him—James hits her with a shoulder, knocking her down, starts to run.*)

19. (*Archie Peyser careens his n.d. sedan into the alley, blocking the mouth, cutting James off—Peyser jumps out, pulls his baton—*)

20. (*James stops, starts running back the other way—*)

21. (*Bates and Pilsky, just getting to their feet, see him coming, look at each other—*)

22. Angle. (*As James, yelling, tries to run right through them, Pilsky hits him low, Bates hits him high, James goes down—*)

23. Angle. (*They start mixing it up—James throws Pilsky off his back, grabs Bates by the throat—in background Peyser comes running up—as behind him in the street, Perez and Kolzicki pull up in a unit—*)

24. (*Bates knees James in the groin, Pilsky grabs him by the face from behind—for a moment they're all frozen in isometric opposition—sounds of their physical efforts—*)

25. (*Peyser arrives and delivers a blow to the back of James' neck with a nightstick—he yells, adrenalized, an animal—then totters, and goes over like a felled log.*)

26. (*Perez and Kolzicki just getting to them—Bates and Pilsky are winded, beat up—*)

PEREZ: Everybody okay?

BATES: Clara?

PILSKY: Just catch my breath.

BATES: Yeah . . . okay . . . nice, Archie.

PEYSER: Thanks. Same to you.

BATES (*a deep breath*): Call a dumptruck for this guy.

Cut to:

27. Interior. Squad Room—day. (*Hill and Renko entering with two diablos in tow. One is protesting loudly.*)

DIABLO #1: I told you, that was my mama's T.V. We was takin' it to be repaired.

RENKO: Tell it to the judge, son. (*As they reach booking.*) Leo, got a couple enterprisin' young T.V. thiefs for you to book.

HILL: Store owner's on his way down to I.D. them.

LEO (*upset about something*): Anybody call a P.D.?

DIABLO #1: Don't need no P.D. Just get Jesus Martinez down here, man.

28. Angle. (*Grace Gardner approaching Leo, in trenchcoat and sunglasses, having just entered the precinct house.*)

GRACE (*to Leo*): Hello, Leo. To see Captain Furillo?

LEO (*wet-eyed*): Go on, Mrs. Gardner . . . (*Grace nods by way of acknowledgment, and as Hill, Renko, Hunter, Calletano and others watch various moments of her passage, she transits the squad room to—*)

29. Furillo's office (*where Furillo is standing, waiting*).

FURILLO: Grace . . . I'm so sorry. (*He busses her lightly, gives her a small hug. She smiles distantly.*)

GRACE (*indicating a chair*): Thank you, Frank. May I?

(*Furillo nods. She sits down. Furillo shuts the door, as Grace removes her sunglasses, places them in her carrying sack, then extracts a manilla envelope from it. To judge by appearances, she'd holding herself together, though the strain of doing so is apparent in her eyes, and in the carefulness of her movements. As Furillo comes back around her, from shutting the door, she hands him the envelope.*)

GRACE: Phil asked me . . . if anything happened . . . to deliver this to you. . . . I believe he wanted you to be executor. (*Off Furillo's puzzlement.*) I was with him, Frank.

FURILLO (*spoken plainly*): I guess I didn't know how sick Phil was, or that he knew either. I saw him last week, he seemed on the mend. He said he was on the mend.

GRACE: Over the weekend, they did an angiogram. They told him his heart had weakened. Something about a "stenosis." He didn't want anyone to know. (*Furillo nods.*) The doctor told him, no this, no that . . . no sex. (*Furillo begins to wonder where Grace is going with this; but doesn't care to ask. He waits, then—*)

FURILLO: How are you, Grace?

GRACE: I'm okay . . . I'm just . . . (*remembering*) The doctor said, no this, no that, no sex, and so uh . . . I don't know why I'm telling you this, I guess it's a police station, I guess I'm coming in to confess. You see, this morning, Philip and I . . . we were together, sleeping. And he woke up . . . and we . . . were making love. And . . . that's when he died. (*Furillo nods, speechless, tears in his eyes. Grace is near tears herself.*) His great, brave heart simply exploded.

FURILLO: Grace, you can't blame yourself.

GRACE (*tears; struggling with it*): I don't, Frank. I don't. I'm proud. Phil said to me he wouldn't live the way they said he would have to. He couldn't live like a dead man in the middle of life. And this morning . . . he'd been so weak but this morning he seemed stronger. Maybe it was because we were so close to dreams. But he seemed in the darkness—this was before daybreak—to be back to himself. To be back to his magnificent self, enormous, healthy, we embraced, we made love, I held onto that man, thinking, like a miracle, the flesh is holding, it's okay, we'll go on, like always . . . (*still trying to say something definitive; something that will stop it all*). He was a beautiful, simple, honorable man, and I wanted to grow old with him, and when the wrenching spasms came . . . (*She's frightened; needs to be not alone, feels how alone she is.*) Please Frank . . . would it be too imposing of me to ask you to hold me a few seconds . . . (*Furillo takes her in his arms, holds her tightly.*) I was under him . . . just hours ago . . . we felt each other's breath . . . each other's life . . . I held his ears, God I loved his ears, his nose . . . and then . . . and then . . . ohh . . . (*She shudders lightly.*) (*low*) I miss him so. (*Grace sobs. Furillo holds her.*)

Fade out.

ACT TWO

Fade in.

30. Interior. Front desk. (*Bates, Pilsky, Peyser, Perez and Kolzicki escorting a handcuffed James into booking—*)

BATES: In there, meat.

PILSKY (*noticing for the first time*): Look at this, brand new nylons, shot to hell. (*As she stops to inspect them, raising her already heightened hem slightly, we pick up—*)

31. (*Jesus just moving past her, with one Diablo escort—*)

JESUS: Nice stems, mama.

PILSKY: In your face, punk.

JESUS (*moving on*): I wish.

Cut to:

32. Interior. Squad Room. (*As Jesus passes his two Diablo charges, seated at a desk, tended by Hill and Renko—*)

JESUS: Sit tight, we're gonna clear this up.

RENKO (*pissed; to Hill*): Walks in like he's Yes-sir Arafat.

(*Furillo meets Jesus at the door to his office—*)

JESUS: Top a' the mornin', Frankie.

FURILLO (*no patience*): Inside. (*The bodyguard stops at the door as Jesus enters—*)

33. Interior. Furillo's office. (*As Furillo closes the door—*)

FURILLO: Let's make this fast, Jesus.

JESUS: These two misguided youths you got out here—

FURILLO: Two "youths" with a half-dozen priors apiece, and they're looking at larceny, possession of stolen property, resisting—case is airtight.

JESUS: Okay, so you figure the resisting's an add-on, we're talking about a two-bit misdemeanor's hardly worth your time to do the typing. Maybe we can do some business here.

FURILLO: Let's hear it, Jesus.

JESUS: I tell you goin' in, what I'm looking for, you get this, my guys walk.

FURILLO: If it stands up . . .

JESUS: It stands up, it walks, it jogs, hey, Frankie, who are you dealin' with here?

FURILLO (*a beat*): What've you got?

JESUS: Somebody's taking down delivery trucks in the neighborhood, you heard about it? Terrible thing.

FURILLO: You have a name?

JESUS: I got the next truck they're gonna hit is what I got.

FURILLO: From where?

JESUS: All due respect, I gotta protect my sources.

FURILLO (*a beat, weary*): If it gives us a bust, we'll work it out. I'll talk to the DA's office. (*Picks up a pad and pencil.*)

JESUS (*a smile*): Reasonable men can always find a way, eh Frankie? (*Furillo stays deadpan.*) Bucky's Meat Supply, runs a delivery every afternoon. Sounds like today's the day.

FURILLO (*writing it down*): Where?

JESUS: All I got. You're gonna have to take it from there. (*He opens the door, slyly.*) So, they can go now?

FURILLO: After the bust, Jesus. (*Goes to the door, calls into the squad room.*) Mick, Ray, could you come in.

JESUS (*at the door*): Hey, sorry to hear about your loss, the sergeant, that's too bad.

FURILLO (*unprepared for that*): Thank you.

JESUS (*as Belker and Calletano arrive, quietly*): Guy had some stuff. (*Jesus tips his hat to the others and exits—we stay with him, he snaps his finger, the bodyguard joins him—stay with Jesus until we pick up and stay with—*)

34. Coffey (*At the Coffee bar, stirring up two cups. Bates approaches, solicitous. He's preoccupied, uptight.*)

BATES: Joe.

COFFEY: Luce.

BATES: How's Sandy?

COFFEY (*reluctant at first to open up*): Goin' over the books . . .

BATES: How're you doing?

COFFEY: Just tryin' to help. (*Beat; in increasing intensity.*) I don't know what I'm supposed to do. I mean, I wasn't there for her, right? And in my mind all I can see is this animal on top of her. And I want to pull him off. And I want to kill him. (*Deep breath; collecting himself.*) That's how I'm doing. (*Bates nods mute support. He moves off. Follow him to Sandy at—*)

35. A desk. (*He puts down a cup of coffee and sits behind her as LaRue moves in, puts down a mugbook and takes away the one she's been scanning. Beside her, Washington runs down a computer readout, checking against a list of W-4's they got from Harley. We can see that Coffey's manner with Sandy is increasingly distant and uncomfortable.*)

LARUE: Sandy, if you could start looking through these . . .

SANDY (*she's holding up, seems stronger*): Didn't know there were so many faces.

LARUE: Just take it one at a time.

(*A pause. Sandy starts paging through, pauses a second, takes a deep breath, a wave of fear passing through her—*)

COFFEY: You okay?

SANDY (*getting herself back*): Yeah, I'm fine, Joe. How are you? (*She looks at him with such emotional nakedness it frightens him.*)

COFFEY: Me? I'm okay. Why shouldn't I be?

SANDY (*half a beat; a little pissed*): No reason.

(*LaRue has caught this exchange, as Sandy goes back to the mugbook, opens it.*)

COFFEY (*realizing his gaffe*): I mean I'm upset.

SANDY (*nodding; not looking at him*): Good, Joe.

(*Now Coffey's pissed; he eats it. LaRue fills the silence.*)

LARUE: Can I get you some coffee or something, Sandy?

SANDY: No, thanks. Maybe later.

36. Angle. (*Washington examining a list, just out of Sandy's hearing.*)

WASHINGTON: J.D.? (*Waves him over; quietly.*) Got a match here.

LARUE: What is it?

WASHINGTON: W-4 on a Jorge Villa, stopped working at the shop thirteen months ago . . .

(*LaRue immediately takes the mugbook, lifts Villa's picture, begins putting together a small array of photos, under—*)

LARUE (*low*): What are his priors?

WASHINGTON (*from his other list*): Two b&e's, two suspicions on rape/robbery, one dismissed, other's pending.

LARUE: He should be in lock-up.

WASHINGTON (*off still another list*): Should be is right. He was released from Michigan Avenue last night, o.r.

(*They look at each other. LaRue gets the array in order, moves back to Sandy—*)

LARUE: Anyone in this bunch look familiar?

(*Sandy examines the array a few seconds, sees Jorge's picture, and it hits her like a kick in the gut; she gasps.*)

LARUE (*a beat; carefully*): That him?

(*She nods, terrorized again, tears in her eyes, unable to speak—*)

WASHINGTON (*writing it down, tearing off a sheet of paper*): Got an address.

LARUE: Let's take him.

WASHINGTON (*moving off*): I'll get back-ups.

(*LaRue gives another look at Sandy, then at Coffey, seemingly paralyzed behind her, unable to respond—LaRue hands her his handkerchief—*)

LARUE (*quietly*): If we find him, Sandy, we'll need you to ID him in a line-up. He won't be able to see you; can you do that?

SANDY: Yeah, sure.

(*LaRue pats her on the shoulder, gives a look at Coffey, starts out—Sandy uses the handkerchief, Coffey stands behind her, helplessly—*)

SANDY (*rising*): I think I wanna go to the Rape Crisis Center now, Joe. They gave me a name at the hospital.

COFFEY: Okay. I . . . you need a ride?

SANDY: Yeah.

COFFEY: Okay.

SANDY (*a beat*): Joe . . . what's wrong?

COFFEY: What do you mean?

SANDY (*a sigh*): Never mind. (*They start out; moving with them we pick up and stay with—*)

37. (*Davenport, moving down the corridor, past Leo, who's teary-eyed, blowing his nose—*)

DAVENPORT (*with a hand on his arm*): Leo, I'm so sorry. (*Leo can only nod through his tears—Davenport continues on towards—*)

38. Interior. Interrogation room. (*She enters to find the john, Kelvin James, sitting at a table. Davenport sits, opens his file.*)

DAVENPORT: Mr. James. I'm Ms. Davenport, I'll be your attorney.

JAMES (*sizing her up*): No complaints here.

DAVENPORT (*letting that pass; reading*): You were arrested two days ago on a shop-lifting charge, held for two days at the Michigan Avenue complex and released last night by order of Judge Spears.

JAMES: Correcto.

DAVENPORT (*looks at him*): And by eleven this morning you accumulated a solicitation charge, possession of stolen credit cards, possession of narcotics.

JAMES: That's the way of the world, ain't it? Guy like me, good luck's like a rumor—

(*The door opens quickly—Furillo enters brusquely with two uniforms.*)

DAVENPORT (*feeling intruded on*): Excuse me.

FURILLO: No, excuse me. I'd like to speak to you in my office. Now.

Cut to:

39. Interior. Furillo's office (*as they enter, both with an attitude—*)

DAVENPORT: Let's hear it.

FURILLO: Your client gave Bates a credit card, belonged to a Mrs. Virginia Kimball, Clearwater, Florida—she was found dead in the trunk of her car four days ago outside of Louisville.

DAVENPORT: That doesn't—

FURILLO: And a routine check on his prints gave us the name of Theotis Nickerson; escaped from Florida State Penitentiary a week ago, doing life for a double murder in a gas station hold-up—that's your client, one of the people Judge Spears released as a low-risk criminal—

DAVENPORT (*holding ground*): Then the screw-up was in Florida, Frank.

FURILLO: You don't let two hundred and forty seven criminals walk and expect to—

DAVENPORT: Why didn't this show up five days ago on the first bust?

FURILLO: My best guess is laziness—

DAVENPORT (*pissed off*): So what's the moral of the story, Frank; throw shoplifters into the hole or don't let convicted murderers escape— (*Into which comes, with a perfunctory knock, Chief Daniels, all pious gravity—*)

DANIELS: Frank, Joyce, I just got the news about Phil Esterhaus, I came as fast as I could. (*Furillo and Davenport look at each other, the pain of the loss surging up from under the anger—they both feel a little ashamed—*) (*Taking both of Frank's hands in his.*) I'm so sorry.

FURILLO: Thank you.

DANIELS: God rest him. He lived a full life. (*Davenport starts out—*) Ray tells me you picked up a murderer Judge Spears decided to exercise some selective mercy with. (*Davenport stops at the door.*)

FURILLO: Appear to have been some bureaucratic foul-ups—

DAVENPORT (*a little hot*): Not enough that you couldn't make some political hay—better they stack 'em six feet in the Tombs, like manhole covers. (*She exits.*)

DANIELS: Obviously, she's upset . . . (*seguing to his original intention*) And I imagine the shock of Phil's passing will be with all of us for some time. But Frank, Phil would've been the first to recognize the need for an orderly transition here. (*Taking out a list.*) Now I've selected three of the department's toughest nuts, Frank, all with a lotta years behind the desk; you take your pick I'll have him at your podium tomorrow morning.

(*Furillo takes the list, stares at it in a kind of numb disbelief—*)

FURILLO: I guess I hadn't thought this far ahead just yet—

DANIELS: He was your friend, Frank, that's understandable.

FURILLO (*finding his way with this*): It had occurred to me bringing someone in from outside could be . . . somewhat disruptive.

DANIELS: You'd like to keep it in the family, then.

FURILLO: I think at least initially.

DANIELS (*taking the list back*): Alright, Frank, you tell me.

FURILLO (*half a beat*): Lucy Bates passed the exam, she was number two in line for promotion when the freeze went into effect.

DANIELS (*surprised*): You want to take her straight from patrol to turn-out responsibilities?

FURILLO: I think I'd like to give her a shot.

DANIELS: I must admit I'm skeptical, Frank, what with more qualified bodies available—

FURILLO: It'd be temporary, to start. Nobody's worked harder, nobody deserves it more.

DANIELS (*sighs*): It's your precinct. You want to put a woman in that job I guess there's nothing I can say, is there? Freeze'll come off this afternoon. (*Another gear shift.*) Funeral arrangements in place?

FURILLO: I guess I'm taking care of that.

DANIELS: Let me know. Dear Phil. Dreadful loss. Dreadful. (*Furillo nods. Daniels exits.*)

40. Interior. Coffee bar (*where Bates, alone, is pouring a cup. Coming out of Furillo's office, Daniels sees her, makes a bee-line to her—*)

DANIELS (*quietly, a pat on the back*): Just want you to know, Sargeant—you've got my every confidence.

(*And he's gone—Bates is left with a slow realization followed immediately by a sinking feeling that displaces the joy the news ordinarily would've generated—*)

Cut to:

41. Interior. Tenement hallway—day. (*LaRue and Washington facing a door open only to a latch—*)

WASHINGTON: Have to open it wider than that, ma'am. (*Whereupon it swings open to a woman in her forties, Latin, impoverished.*) We're looking to talk to your son, ma'am. Jorge Villa.

MRS. VILLA (*in Spanish*): I haven't seen him. He's locked up in the jail.

42. Point of view—through the door—a fully open window.

LARUE: Neal!

43. (*LaRue and Washington race through the apartment.*)

WASHINGTON: Kinda chilly for wide-open windows, Senora.

44. Exterior. Fire escape. (*Washington and LaRue clambering out, peering down—*)

45. Point of view. (*A Latin male in his twenties, Jorge Villa, descends breakneck towards the alley.*)

WASHINGTON'S VOICE (*to handi-talkie*): Back-ups, the alley. Suspect in the alley.

46. (*Villa drops to the alley-floor, runs.*)

47. (*LaRue and Washington clatter down the cast-iron steps.*)

48. (*A unit bursts into the alley; Perez and Kolzicki pile out.*)

49. (*Villa turns, trapped.*)

50. (*Washington drops to the ground.*)

51. (*Perez, weapon drawn, held high, moves on the retreating, confused Villa.*)

PEREZ: Hold it right there! (*Perez is breathing a little hard, but he's got it. LaRue and Washington take him, put on the cuffs.*)

WASHINGTON: Attaboy, Jorge, you're under arrest— (*Reads rights.*)

LARUE: Would you like a donut? (*Off Jorge's self-incriminating reaction—Washington reads rights under—*)

Fade to black.

ACT THREE

Fade in.

52. Exterior. Loading zone—refrigerator truck—day. (*The meat supply house named by Jesus—Bucky's. There's a couple of trucks being loaded at the ramp, others are parked here and there waiting their turn. Belker is kicking the tires of a refrigerator truck, giving it a professional once over. He wears a tanker's jacket that reads BUCKY'S MEAT SUPPLY. Parked close by is an unmarked police sedan, Hill and Renko, in plainclothes, leaning against it. They're all in a grand funk over Esterhaus; Renko, however, has felt the need to vocalize it in his own fashion.*)

RENKO: It's like a riddle in the cosmic tapestry, Bobby. That man meant as much to me as my own daddy. I wish I could tell him that. I wish I'd told him. (*Belker moves past them with an audible and directed snort of disdain. Renko glares at him.*) Now what prompted that comment from the animal world?

BELKER: People should treat people good when they're alive instead of tryin' to make up for it after they're dead.

RENKO (*boiling; swelling up*): You sayin' I am bein' less than sincere in my affections for that man?

BELKER: *Esterhaus*—his name was *Esterhaus!* And you caused him aggravation! Wisin' off in roll, duckin' assignments!

RENKO: And I suppose you never broke his nose in intramural volleyball—

BELKER: That was an accident!

RENKO: An exceptional police officer—That's what he called me!

HILL: Knock it off, you two!

BELKER: He was my sergeant—he was my friend!

HILL (*getting between them*): I said knock it off! What is this—mom likes me best? Have some respect.

(*Bucky Nolan picks that moment to walk up to the truck with his clipboard. He's the owner and manager of Bucky's Meat Supply, a big good-natured black who's gotten where he is by working hard and taking no nonsense. He's wearing a butcher's smock and a hardhat.*)

BUCKY: What's goin' on here?

HILL: Nothin', Mr. Nolan. We're ready to roll when you are.

BUCKY (*indicates truck; eyes them*): Let's get it loaded. Which one of you's drivin'?

BELKER: Me.

(*Bucky looks him over. Isn't impressed in the slightest.*)

BUCKY: Lemme see your Class 2 license.

BELKER: You're looking at it. (*Flashes badge.*)

(*Bucky is even less impressed. He makes a face and taps the side of the truck.*)

BUCKY: And whaddaya think's goin' in the back of this thing, Mr. Police Badge?

BELKER (*not getting him*): Meat . . .

BUCKY: Uh-uh. Twelve-thousand of my hard-earned dollars is what. Now you can flash that badge at a pork roast and it's still gonna spoil if it gets above fifty-two degrees longer'n thirty minutes. You can flash it at a side of beef and it's still gonna bruise to the tune of 10¢ less a pound if it goes swinging around in the back of the truck. So you can just show me some proof you know somethin' about drivin' a refrigerator unit or I'll just take my chances with the hijackers.

RENKO (*snide*): Mr. Nolan, my partner and I can personally vouch for this man's ability to handle raw meat.

(*A strangled growl from Belker. He crushes his cigar. Climbs into the truck cab.*)

BELKER: What ramp?

BUCKY: B.

(*Belker starts up the truck. Burns rubber along the length of the loading zone and swings the truck so its tail end is pointed at the ramp like a battering ram. Throws it into reverse and burns rubber between two tightly parked trucks, stomping on the brake just in time to bring the tailgate flush with the ramp. It's a dandy piece of truckmanship. Bucky and the others stand there with their mouths open. Belker looks at them. Bucky snaps back to life. Shouts—*)

BUCKY: Okay, let's get this sucker loaded!

Cut to:

53. Interior. Furillo's office—day. (*Furillo is on the phone. Papers and documents are stacked on his desktop. He looks drained and out of his element. ADA Bernstein enters the office and they exchange nods over—*)

FURILLO (*into phone*): I understand the urgency, but my feeling is that this decision could be better made by a professional . . . I see . . . Yes . . . (*looks at watch*). Then I'll get back to you before five. Yes . . . Thanks. (*As he hangs up, he spots Bernstein in the squad room. Furillo raps on the glass and motions him into the office.*) What do you know about executing an estate?

BERNSTEIN: Enough to call Legal Referral for the name of a qualified attorney.

FURILLO: How about giving away eyes?

BERNSTEIN: Eyes?

FURILLO: Phil signed a donor's card before he died—organ transplants. (*Nods at phone.*) They've given me a list, forty people need eyes. Little girl in Tulsa, a father of five in Greenbay . . . Law says as executor I make the choice.

BERNSTEIN: Amazing, isn't it? (*Off Furillo's look.*) Part of a man can go on living like that.

(*Furillo hadn't thought of it that way. Just then, they're interrupted by Goldblume who gives Bernstein a nod.*)

GOLDBLUME: Frank, Sandy Valpariso's on her way back from the rape treatment center. We can have a line-up ready by the time she gets here.

FURILLO: Okay, put it together.

GOLDBLUME (*indicates documents*): How's it going?

FURILLO: Great. I still haven't settled with the fact he's gone and here I am parceling him out like a door prize.

BERNSTEIN (*apprehensive; funny smile*): Is it true what I heard about him?

FURILLO (*frowning*): What was that?

BERNSTEIN: I don't mean to sound cold, but I had some business at the morgue this morning, I heard a rumor that he wasn't dancing alone when the big one hit.

FURILLO (*sharply*): Irwin, I don't think we should speculate about that.

(*Bernstein shrugs and exits. Furillo and Goldblume exchange a look, off which—*)

Cut to:

54. Interior. Locker room—on Leo. (*The room is empty except for Leo. He sits on a bench in the near-darkness, shoulders hunched, face buried in his hands. He is sobbing pitifully. Just then, Calletano appears at the far end of the lockers. He sees Leo and his heart goes out to him. Leo becomes aware of his presence and tries to cover up red eyes and a runny nose. Calletano sits down beside him and puts a fatherly arm around him.*)

CALLETANO: I understand, Leo . . . We all loved him. But there's no need to hide your grief. Rather we must share it, let it strengthen us.

LEO: It isn't that.

CALLETANO (*puzzled*): No? What then?

LEO: Oh God! (*Leo sinks back into shuddering sobs.*)

CALLETANO: Leo, what is it? Please, tell me!

LEO (*reluctant*): I followed her last night . . .

CALLETANO: Who?

LEO (*oblivious*): She said she was going to aerobics class—but she hasn't been there in weeks. I know, I called. I followed her to the Computer Software Place on Ethel and Hollondorf. That's where she met him.

CALLETANO: Who met who?

LEO: My wife met Roger. Six feet. Blond hair. Sideburns. Goyim computer programmer. They're having an affair.

CALLETANO: Leo, you must confront her with this.

LEO: I did. On the spot. She got mad, she said he was the best thing that's happened to her in years. She isn't gonna give him up. (*Buries face.*) I wanted to call her names . . . I can't. I love her too much. (*Leo starts sobbing again. Calletano tries to comfort him but is at a loss for words. That's when Hunter appears. Seeing Leo in such grief, he approaches and sits opposite Calletano. It's his turn to put an arm around Leo.*)

HUNTER: I knew you'd take it hardest of all, old friend. When a warrior falls, there is no anguish more profound than that of his shield bearer.

LEO (*burning look*): It's not that! (*Hunter moves back in surprise. Calletano tries to smooth it over.*)

CALLETANO: Leo has a personal problem, Howard.

HUNTER: Nothing wrong with Mrs. Snitz, I hope.

LEO: Oh God! (*Leo takes the plunge into despair again. Goldblume attracted by the noise, joins the crowd at the bench. Puts a hand on Leo's shoulder.*)

GOLDBLUME (*sympathetically*): Leo . . .

LEO (*leaping up; a shriek*): The Sarge is dead—I'm sorry about that! He was a wonderful man! But my wife is having an affair, okay!? Satisfied!? (*With that, Leo bolts from the room leaving behind some bewildered people.*)

Cut to:

55. Interior. Line-up—day. (*Furillo, LaRue, Washington, Coffey and Sandy are present. Six men are filing in behind the glass. Sandy watches their profiles apprehensively—the day's events are beginning to take a toll on her. Washington is conducting the line-up.*)

WASHINGTON: Keep moving, all the way to your marks and face forward.

(*As they turn to face forward, Sandy recognizes the rapist and lets out a small gasp, then quickly composes herself.*)

SANDY: That's him, number two . . . second from the left.

FURILLO: You're positive?

SANDY (*her voice quivering*): Believe me, I'm not gonna forget his face any time soon. (*She is embarrassed by her sudden lack of control over her emotions; she dabs at her eyes, trying to keep from crying. Coffey silently offers a handkerchief, which she takes. Furillo nods to Washington.*)

FURILLO: Thank you, Miss Valparaiso. We're done.

WASHINGTON (*to line-up*): That's it. Turn to your right, move down the steps to the door.

(*The men file out; Furillo and Washington exit. LaRue stops to give Sandy a supportive pat on the shoulder.*)

LARUE: You all right?

SANDY (re *her emotional state*): I'm sorry. It's been a long day.

LARUE: Are you kiddin'? You've been great.

SANDY: What next?

LARUE: Way things are backed up, I doubt they'll arraign before tomorrow morning. We'll call and let you know.

SANDY (*She nods.*): Thanks. Thanks a lot.

(*LaRue exits, leaving Sandy and Coffey alone. Coffey has been sitting quietly through all of this. He stands.*)

COFFEY: Come on, let's find you a ride home.

SANDY: Not yet. Just sit with me for a few minutes, okay?

COFFEY (*noncommittal*): In here?

SANDY: Why not? Are you afraid to be alone with me?

COFFEY: No, of course not.

(*Sandy goes over and closes the door. Coffey, despite his claims to the contrary, is not a bit comfortable.*)

SANDY: Joe, what's goin' on with you?

COFFEY: Nothin'. What are you talkin' about?

SANDY: All day long you've been so nice—the perfect gentleman, the perfect cop—but I feel like you're a million miles away from me.

COFFEY: I've been with you every minute!

SANDY: All the way to the rape center and back, you barely said a word to me. And you haven't said anything to me today that hasn't been straight from a manual.

COFFEY: I'm used to dealin' with it a certain way. It's my job.

SANDY: We've been sleeping together for two weeks! I'm more than just your job. (*Beat.*) I'm trying to work this out for myself, but I need my lover's help right now, not another cop.

COFFEY: I'm sorry.

SANDY: You don't *act* like you're sorry. You haven't touched me all day long.

COFFEY: I didn't know if you'd want that.

SANDY (*thinking she's breaking through*): That's exactly what I want. I want you to hold me, I want to feel like everything is going to be okay.

(*Coffey thinks about it for a beat. Doesn't make any physical response.*)

COFFEY: I've just got some things I've gotta work out.

(*Sandy becomes cooler after realizing that he refuses to touch her.*)

SANDY: What things?

COFFEY: I gotta understand it in my mind, what happened to you.

SANDY (*angry*): What do you have to understand? The guy grabbed me, pointed a knife at me, make me take off my clothes and lie down on a cold, dirty floor and—

COFFEY (*cutting her off*): Sandy, don't.

SANDY: What, it's too unpleasant for you to *hear?* I *lived through it,* you jerk!

COFFEY: I just need a little time. I have to make myself understand why it happened.

SANDY: You mean why I didn't do anything to prevent it?

COFFEY: I know you couldn't. It just needs to sink in.

SANDY: What do you think I could have done? What would *you* do, with some drugged-up crazy pointing a knife at your throat? Put up a fight?

COFFEY: No—

SANDY: What, then? Try to talk him out of it?

COFFEY: I don't know. Maybe.

SANDY: Is that it? You think I didn't try hard enough?

COFFEY (*angry*): Sandy, would you stop it! You're forcin' me to say stuff that I don't want to say—

SANDY: I'm forcing you to tell the truth! You think I could have gotten out of it! You think if it was that awful, why didn't I put up more of a fight! (*Beat.*) Come on, Joe, at least have the guts to admit it!

COFFEY (*provoked*): Okay, maybe that *is* what I think. I mean, you're always hearin' about women who got out of it by sayin' they were pregnant or had VD or somethin'. Maybe I wonder why you didn't try that!

(*Sandy stares at him for a moment; she is livid.*)

SANDY: If he'd slashed my throat or bashed my head in a little, would that make you feel better? Would that help you understand?

COFFEY (*anguished*): No! I just . . . I don't know. I don't know what I think!

SANDY (*quietly furious*): Well, why don't you just sit here for a few years and see what you can figure out.

(*She wheels and is out of the door, slamming it behind her, leaving Coffey alone in the room. He sinks into a chair and pounds his fist on the table—there are tears in his eyes.*)

56. Interior. Refrigerator truck—moving—day. (*Belker is at the wheel. He checks a schedule of deliveries on a clipboard, then looks in his sideview mirror.*)

57. Tight on mirror. (*We see Hill and Renko's unmarked sedan following about four car-lengths behind.*)

58. Interior. Sedan—moving. (*Hill is driving. Renko is going over the schedule, figuring, frowning.*)

RENKO: If he don't move that thing a little faster, we're gonna be seven minutes behind schedule next stop.

HILL: Lighten up, will you? If they're lookin' for us, they'll find us. (*Hill sees something on the truck up ahead.*)

59. His point-of-view—rear of truck. (*The latch on the back door is swinging loose.*)

60. Back to Hill.

HILL: You wanna call him up, tell him the latch on the back door's come loose.

(*Renko picks up the handi-talkie with a kind of mischievous glee and transmits—*)

RENKO: Farmer Brown, this is Meat Loaf. Your barn door's in danger of flyin' open, pal. Careful you don't let the cow get out. (*Renko snickers. Hill gives him a critical look. Belker's reply comes in loud and clear.*)

BELKER'S VOICE: You watch your mouth, Renko, or you're gonna be the fattest side of beef hanging in this truck.

(*Renko is about to retort when the radio interrupts:*)

RADIO: All units in the area of 315 S. Polk Avenue, robbery in progress, shots fired, officer needs assistance.

RENKO: Let's go. (*Hill has already begun a U-turn.*)

61. Interior. Refrigerator truck. (*Belker sees Hill slam the flasher on the roof of the sedan and rocket away. Grabs his handi-talkie.*)

BELKER: Meat Loaf where the hell you goin'?

RENKO'S VOICE: Farmer Brown, we got ourselves a robbery in progress—we're takin' it!

BELKER: No, you're not—call it in! You ain't leavin' my rear end exposed! (*No reply.*) You hear me! Get back here! (*Belker is so furious he forgets what he's doing. Sticks his head out the window to see where the sedan is. What happens next is totally his fault—*)

62. Exterior. City street. (*The refrigerator truck slams hard into the rear of a van stopped at a light. Smoke, broken glass, the rear door of the truck pops open and a ham rolls out.*)

63. Exterior. Truck cab—on Belker. (*Stunned. Trying to figure out what happened. The driver of the van, a towering moose of a blue-collar worker, jumps out of his damaged vehicle with mayhem on his mind. Goes to the truck cab—*)

VAN DRIVER: You hit my van, you stupid jerk! You got your head in your shorts or something?

BELKER: I see it. I'm sorry. (*Belker doesn't sound all that convincing.*)

64. Intercut with rear of truck. (*A pedestrian has seen the ham in the street. He picks it up, puts it under his coat and walks away. Two other bystanders have watched him do it. They go up to the truck's open door to see what's inside. All this over—*)

VAN DRIVER: You're sorry! Get out of that truck, you sawed-off little wimp. I'll make you sorry!

BELKER (*flies out of the truck*): Who you callin' sawed-off, hairbag!

VAN DRIVER: You, you pint-sized dwarf numbnut! No wonder you had an accident!

BELKER (*rips out badge*): Police, mudbrain!

(*The two bystanders, meanwhile, have walked away with massive sides of beef. The back of the truck is then beseiged by a swarm of refugees from the neighboring tenements.*)

VAN DRIVER (*rearing up to Belker*): Good! 'Cause I'm suing you, I'm suing the Department and I'm suing the City!

BELKER: Don't crowd me—I'm tellin' you not to crowd me!

(*The van driver gives Belker a shove that sends him into the side of the truck. Belker springs back like a miniature cyclone, taking the van driver down. They roll in the street, punching, kicking, screaming—a badger attacking an elephant. It's then that Belker catches sight of the looting that's going on in back of the truck.*)

BELKER: Hey—stop that! Put it back! You're all under arrest!

(*But no one pays him the slightest attention. For one thing, he's too busy fighting for his life to do anything. Belker throws himself into the battle with psychotic vigor, deciding the match with a well-placed, scream-inducing bite to the van driver's thigh.*)

VAN DRIVER: Okay—I give, I give!

(*Belker slaps cuffs on him and then jumps to the back of the truck. Those with meat in their arms take off running.*)

BELKER: Get back here! Stop!

(*Belker's wasting his breath. And then he hears the sound of someone rummaging inside the truck. In a rage, he pulls his piece. Levels it at the door . . . just as a small Latino child with a chicken in either hand comes stumbling out. The child's eyes go wide as he sees the gun. Belker nearly freaks. Almost throws the gun to the pavement. The child is frozen with fright, looking at Belker with horrified eyes.*)

BELKER: Go on—get out of here!

(*The child, still holding the chickens, runs away. Camera holds on Belker, shaking, trying to get himself under control as we—*)

Fade out.

ACT FOUR

Fade in. 65.

Interior Peyser's sedan—moving. (*Peyser is tired and cold. He speaks into a handi-talkie:*)

PEYSER: I'm taking a last pass down Avenue C. I haven't seen one hooker.

(*Bates responds through the handi-talkie:*)

BATES' VOICE (*surprised*): You sure you're on Avenue C?

PEYSER: Roger. And there ain't nothin' on this road but potholes.

BATES' VOICE (*comes across in impatient elucidation*): Hard to believe. Tell me what you're seein'.

(*Peyser is trying his best. Picks up the handi-talkie in his lap.*)

PEYSER: Roger. (*Looking.*) Well, there's two winos working a trashcan fire . . . and I just passed a lady standing by a station wagon with the hood up. She waved at me . . .

BATES VOICE: Archie, that's an old gimmick to fool patrol cars. They put up a citizen's car hood and pretend it's theirs. Turn around and check it out, okay?

(*Peyser swings his sedan around with—*)

PEYSER (*into handi-talkie*): Roger. Will do.

BATES' VOICE: We're headed home, buddy. You're on your own.

66. Exterior. City Street. (*As Peyser brakes by the side of the stranded station wagon. Our view of it is restricted. Peyser exits and steps around his vehicle toward the woman, who we descry at the last instant as Fay Furillo, flushed and grateful.*)

FAY: Thank God. The answer to a woman's prayers. (*Grabbing Peyser by the hand.*) How would you like to peek under my hood?

(*Peyser, in his enthusiasm, thinks he's being propositioned.*)

PEYSER: And then what, lady?

FAY: If you could give me a jump . . . (*indicates the flat wagon trunk*) I've got some chords and clamps back there. They hook right on.

PEYSER (*A beat as he cagily sizes her up.*): Sounds good. So how much is this sort of thing worth to you?

FAY (*Her turn to misunderstand. She flares—*): How much? You're a real sport. All right—I'll do anything to get out of the cold. Ten dollars.

PEYSER (*flashes his badge*): Police, you're under arrest—unlawful solicitation! Turn around and put your hands behind your back.

(*It's all happened too fast for Fay. She doesn't resist as he turns her around and whips out the cuffs.*)

FAY: Solicitation? What do you mean, solicitation? My battery's dead!

PEYSER: Don't make it any worse on yourself, ma'am. You stated an act and the amount. Now you have the right to remain silent. Anything you say can and will be used against you . . .

FAY (*over his Miranda*): I don't believe this! This is crazy! You can't actually believe for one second that I was asking you to . . . that I wanted to . . . (*She starts to giggle. It catches Peyser completely off guard.*)

PEYSER: What's the matter? What's so funny?

FAY: How old are you?

PEYSER: What?

FAY: Are you sure you're a police officer and not a safety patrol?

PEYSER (*getting miffed*): In the car, lady. Let's go.

FAY: Where? Hill Street?

PEYSER: Yeah.

FAY: Good. I need a ride.

(*He opens the sedan door. She climbs in. Can't suppress another giggle.*)

FAY (*directing*): Make a left up on Euclid. It's faster this time of day.

Cut to:

67. Interior. Front desk—day. (*On the cut, pick up a taciturn Bates, along with Pilsky and Perez, entering the doors and passing the desk, where the fallout from Belker's meaty misadventure is piling up under Leo's snuffly nose. Returned or impounded, a couple armloads of steaks and chops. Adding to which evidence now, a half dozen pork chops are slapped onto the desk by a uniform, whose other hand grasps a large, cuffed, carnivorous-looking perp.*)

UNIFORM: Doing a brisk sidewalk business at Dekker and 108, Leo. He tried to dump this stuff when I found him.

PERP (*shrugs; by way of lame explanation*): I'm a vegetariast.

(*Include Belker lugging his bloodied van driver up to the desk—*)

BELKER: Move it, mudball.

(*And, close on Belker's heels, the distraught butcher, Bucky Nolan, who eyeballs the stash on the desk.*)

BUCKY: This is all you retrieved? This is all? (*At a weary Belker.*) You drove me right into the slaughterhouse, you idiot. D'you hear? Seventy-five cases of New York strippers. Hundred cases o'rib-eyes. Hundred whole filets. Seventy pounds a case. Six bucks a pound. JUST WHOLESALE! You put me up on a hook, y'know that?

(*Under which rant, Jesus Martinez and bodyguard have entered. Follow to—*)

68. Interior. Furillo's office—day—Furillo and ADA Bernstein. (*A perfunctory knock and, without waiting, Martinez struts in. The guard waits outside.*)

JESUS: Yo, Frankie.

FURILLO: Jesus . . .

JESUS: Anybody call for a pickup? (*Holds up fingers.*) Dos Diablos. (*Off silence and Bernstein's frown, Jesus senses something queering his deal. He lashes out—*) Hey, your clown can't keep his meat on the road, 's not my problem.

FURILLO: Give us a minute, Jesus.

JESUS: I paid for the goods, Frankie—you deliver or your word's garbage on the street.

(*Off Furillo's silence, Jesus stares daggers at him a half beat, then saunters to the door tossing a look of contempt at Bernstein. He hovers outside, looking in through the glass.*)

BERNSTEIN: Frank . . .

FURILLO: Martinez and I had an agreement.

BERNSTEIN (*hot*): Based on information you never had a chance to verify! How'm I gonna sell that downtown?

FURILLO (*just as hot*): Irwin—it's a lousy T.V. set! What's the big deal?

BERNSTEIN (*throwing in the towel*): Okay, Frank, do what you want. The meat supplier's filed an eight-thousand-dollar claim, the driver of the van's bringing suit for abusive process and our hijackers are doing business as usual. Why not make the disaster complete?

FURILLO (*trying to calm things*): I'm sorry. (*Opens the door, motions and calls—*) Leo! (*Waves Martinez in.*) We keep our end of the bargain.

JESUS: Good decision, Frankie. (*To the stewing Bernstein.*) Gotta go by the rules, right?

(*Bernstein glowers, under which Leo has arrived.*)

FURILLO: Leo, release the two Diablos in Mr. Martinez' custody.

LEO: Right, Captain.

(*Smirking, Martinez exits along with his guard. Bernstein trails, notes Leo's puffy red eyes, turns back to Furillo.*)

BERNSTEIN: Be the executor of my will, too, okay Frank? (*Bernstein puts his arm around Leo's shoulder. As they move off—*) . . . I know how you must feel, Leo.

(*No sooner are they gone, than Bates is in the doorway.*)

FURILLO: Luce . . . you waiting to see me?

(*Bates solemnly enters Furillo's office and closes the door behind her.*)

FURILLO: What's up?

BATES: I'm not sure. While ago the Chief comes up to me, slaps me on the back and calls me "Sergeant." You know what he's talking about?

FURILLO: We had a discussion this morning about the desk sergeant vacancy, we agreed the best course would be to move someone up from inside. I recommended you.

BATES: Me? Take the Sarge's place? No way, Captain. I couldn't fill those shoes in a hundred years!

FURILLO: You shouldn't try. Just be your own person.

BATES (*still confused*): I don't know . . . I've been wanting it for so long. It's just the circumstances, it's all wrong.

FURILLO: Lucy, you've put a lot of hard work into making sergeant. It shouldn't be a punishment. Take some time and think it over. If you still feel uncomfortable, we'll try something else. Frankly, I think you're the best choice for the job.

BATES: Well . . . if you say so, Captain.

FURILLO: Keep it under wraps a couple of days, then we'll make an orderly transition.

BATES (*nods; starts for the door, then stops*): Is it appropriate to say "thanks"?

FURILLO (*nodding*): Congratulations, Sergeant Bates.

(*Bates nods, smiles tentatively and exits.*)

Cut to:

69. Interior. Booking area. (*Peyser enters the precinct and delivers his charge to the desk. Fay remains unnoticed by Leo, who is immersed in paperwork over the Diablos release. But Jesus is standing by.*)

JESUS: Yo, mama, where'd you buy those fancy bracelets?

FAY (*kicking at his shin*): Keep away from me, guttersnipe.

JESUS (*through his laughter*): You got a prize there, officer, you know that?

PEYSER: What?

JESUS: You better get thick shoes. You standing in the dog's business.

(*Peyser looks at his shoes, convulsing Martinez.*)

PEYSER (*confused; flustered*): What?

JESUS: You got the Captain's ol' lady.

(*Just then, Leo wheels around and slaps down some release papers and a pen in front of Martinez.*)

LEO: Sign these. (*Leo's attention fixes on Fay. He reacts as if being hit by a cattle prod.*) Mrs. Furillo!

(*Peyser is horrified. He shrinks away from her.*)

PEYSER: Mrs. *Furillo?*

FAY: Fast Fay, Leo. The Strumpet of State Street. A fallen woman.

LEO: Get her out of those cuffs!

PEYSER (*scrambling; clumsy*): Aw, gee—I'm sorry—I didn't know. I'm an idiot, a moron . . .

(*Under which, in the background, we have become aware of a growing argument between a furious—*)

70. (*Belker nose to nose with Hill and Renko, heating up as well, in the middle of the squad room.*)

BELKER: You were supposed to be backin' me up—where the hell were you?

HILL: We had an all units—we radioed you—

BELKER: Somebody coulda got killed out there!

RENKO: Somebody wasn't lookin' where he was goin' is the way I hear it!

BELKER: You're around plenty with your fat mouth when I don't need you, Renko!

RENKO: Now, now—you think the sarge would approve of you talkin' like that?

(*Off which, with a feral growl, Belker leaps on Renko and the two of them are into it; Hill and others immediately jump in to pull them apart, as—*)

71. (*Furillo comes barrelling out of his office. He arrives just as Belker and Renko are separated.*)

FURILLO: No! (*His cold glare freezes Belker and Renko and everybody else in the squad room, including—*)

72. (*Fay, who reacts with stunned pain to—*)

FURILLO: Look, I'm not insensitive to the fact that Phil Esterhaus' death has hit all of us pretty hard . . .

73. (*Wider, as Furillo includes the entire squad room.*)

FURILLO: If you had respect for the man, honor his memory by being what he was—a gentleman and a good cop.

(*A moment more, to make sure the message has been heard, then he turns and moves off. Spotting Fay, having sunk into a chair, beginning to tear up in grief, Furillo veers over to her, hunkers down and takes her hand.*)

FURILLO: I'm sorry, Fay. That was no way for you to find out.

FAY: Phil's dead? How? When?

FURILLO: At home. Early this morning. (*A beat.*)

FAY: He taught Frank, Jr. how to box . . . (*A beat, then,*) How did he die?

(*Furillo and Goldblume exchange a glance, as we—*)

Cut to:

74. Interior. Cop bar—night (*crowded with regulars, the atmosphere appropriately subdued, as, on the cut—*)

HILL: I hear he died in the saddle.

BELKER (*subdued in the company of Tataglia; nevertheless—*): Hey, that's a lotta crap.

HILL (*the tiniest grin*): Just sayin' what I heard, Mick.

LARUE: Anybody hear any rumors who's gonna replace him?

BATES: Hey, why don't we at least wait for the body to get cold, huh?

WASHINGTON: Scenario: Foster up in the Heights retired last month. Jaffe in South Ferry bit the biscuit coupla weeks ago—Mayor's office lifts the hiring freeze, you get your stripes, and just like that we got us a new Sarge.

BATES (*hot; defensive*): Look, this is outa line—no one's said anything about anybody replacing the Sarge—so just drop it, okay?

RENKO (*semi-blitzed, raises his glass*): I propose a toast. To the Sarge. We loved him, we're gonna miss him, God bless him.

(*General agreement all around, with the exception of—*)

LARUE: Tell you the truth—I respected him, but the guy wasn't exactly on my Christmas list.

BATES (*having overheard*): Hey, J.D. Go kill yourself. (*And she pushes away from the bar, heading for the bathroom. As she exits—*)

LARUE (*philosophically*): Lemme tell you somethin' about women, Neal. I'm all for equal rights . . . Sorta . . . But I think you gotta smack 'em when they talk to you that way.

(*And we angle over to pick up—*)

75. Belker and Tataglia.

TATAGLIA (*to a dour, quiet Belker*): When I was first up here . . . boy, he was such . . . you just got the feeling he *liked* you, you know? Deep down. Like he just liked people. Hey, guess he went out liking someone.

76. (*Include Renko, having listened in.*)

RENKO (*a lascivious grin*): Ba-bing, ba-bing, ba—(*He gasps, clutching at his chest.*)

BELKER: It didn't happen like that—I don't believe it.

RENKO: Why don't we call the Captain?

HILL: Great, wake him up. He'll love you for it.

RENKO: It's covered under your Freedom of Information Act, Robert—tender me a ten cent piece—(*And as he pulls a dime from Hill's collection of change on the bar—*)

Cut to:

77. Interior. Bedroom—night. (*Furillo and Davenport in bed, she doing homework and he poring over the bullshit of executorship. On the cut, the phone is ringing, and—*)

FURILLO (*grabbing it*): Furillo.

Intercut with:

78. Interior. Bar—night. (*Renko cupping his other ear against the noise.*)

RENKO: Captain Furillo, sir.

FURILLO: Who is this?

RENKO: Andy Renko, sir. How are you?

FURILLO: Fine.

RENKO: Hope we didn't wake you or the wife, sir, but a few of us're down here at Mulligan's, toastin' the Sarge. Me 'n Bobby Hill, Joe 'n Luce, Belker, J.D., Neal, Leo—now that poor guy's really tore up, sir—

FURILLO: What can I do for you, Andy?

RENKO: Well, in payin' our last respects and all, we got to talkin' about life and death, and how fleeting our moment in the sun is, and how all of us need to plant our flag on this earth, as it were, and we got to speculating about the Sarge's flag and all . . .

FURILLO (*amused with the drift*): You want to get to what this is about, Andy?

RENKO: Is it true the Sarge deceased himself whilst in the act?

FURILLO: Yes. It's true.

RENKO (*with a shit-eating grin*): Damn that's a good way to check out . . . Course, it couldn't've been no tea party for his paramour now, could it?

FURILLO: G'night, Andy.

RENKO: Yessir. Goodnight.

79. Stay with Furillo (*hanging up the phone, pinching the bridge of his nose in amusement.*)

DAVENPORT: Renko?

FURILLO (*nods*): Wanted to know was it true how Phil died.

DAVENPORT (*a chuckle*): A legend is born . . .

FURILLO: I'll miss him.

DAVENPORT: So will I.

FURILLO (*a beat*): You want to make love?

DAVENPORT (*a glint*): It could cost you your life.

FURILLO: I'll risk it.

(*And as he kisses her, and she kisses back, we:*)

Fade out.